The Language
of Composition

READING | WRITING | RHETORIC

THIRD EDITION

The Language *of* Composition

READING | WRITING | RHETORIC

Renée H. Shea
Bowie State University, Maryland

Lawrence Scanlon
Brewster High School, New York

Robin Dissin Aufses
Lycée Français de New York

Megan Harowitz Pankiewicz
Rockville High School, Maryland

bedford, freeman & worth
high school publishers

Boston | New York

Senior Vice President of Content Strategy: Chuck Linsmeier
Senior Publisher for High School: Ann Heath
Executive Program Manager for High School Humanities: Nathan Odell
Developmental Editor: Caitlin Kaufman
Assistant Editor: Corrina Santos
Senior Content Project Manager: Peter Jacoby
Project Manager: Linda DeMasi, Lumina Datamatics, Inc.
Senior Workflow Project Manager: Jennifer Wetzel
Production Assistant: Brianna Lester
Media Editor: Kimberly Morté
Senior Media Producer: Allison Hart
Senior Marketing Manager: Lisa Erdely
Copy Editor: Kristin Ferraioli
Indexer: Nancy Crompton
Photo Researcher: Kerri Wilson, Lumina Datamatics, Inc.
Director of Rights and Permissions: Hilary Newman
Permissions Editor: Angela Boehler
Text Permissions Researcher: Elaine Kosta, Lumina Datamatics, Inc.
Permissions Manager: Kalina Ingham
Senior Art Director: Anna Palchik
Text Design: Jerilyn Bockorick
Cover Design: John Callahan
Composition: Lumina Datamatics, Inc.
Printing and Binding: LSC Communications, Inc.
Cover Photo: Will Yeung Photography/Konstantin Dimopoulos, *The Blue Trees*

Manufactured in the United States of America.

1 2 3 4 5 6 23 22 21 20 19 18

For information, write: BFW Publishers, One New York Plaza, Suite 4500,
New York, NY 10004   hsmarketing@bfwpub.com

ISBN 978-1-319-05614-8

Acknowledgments
Text acknowledgments and copyrights appear at the back of the book on pages 1241–46, which constitute an extension of the copyright page. Art acknowledgments and copyrights appear on the same page as the art selections they cover.

AP® is a trademark registered and/or owned by the College Board®, which was not involved in the production of, and does not endorse, this product.

To Michael Shea;

William and Mary Scanlon;

Arthur Aufses;

Oliver Pankiewicz

ABOUT THE AUTHORS

Renée H. Shea was professor of English and Modern Languages and director of freshman composition at Bowie State University in Maryland. A College Board® faculty consultant for more than thirty years in AP® Language and Literature, and Pre-AP® English, she has been a reader and question leader for both AP® English exams. Renée served as a member on three committees for the College Board®: the AP® Language and Composition Development Committee, the English Academic Advisory Committee, and the SAT Critical Reading Test Development Committee. She is co-author of *Literature & Composition*, *Conversations in American Literature*, *Advanced Language & Literature*, and *Foundations of Language & Literature*, as well as volumes on Amy Tan and Zora Neale Hurston for the NCTE High School Literature Series. Renée has also written about contemporary authors for publications such as *World Literature Today*, *Poets & Writers*, and *Kenyon Review*.

Lawrence Scanlon taught at Brewster High School for more than thirty years and now teaches at Iona College in New York. Over the past twenty years, he has been a reader and question leader for the AP® Language and Composition Exam. As a College Board® consultant in the United States and abroad, he has conducted AP® workshops in both language and literature and has served on the AP® English Language Test Development Committee. Larry is co-author of *Literature & Composition* and *Conversations in American Literature* and has published articles for the College Board® and elsewhere.

Robin Dissin Aufses is director of English Studies at Lycée Français de New York, where she teaches AP® English Language and Composition. Previous to this position, Aufses was the English department chair and a teacher at John F. Kennedy High School in Bellmore, New York, for ten years, and prior to that she taught English at Paul D. Schreiber High School in Port Washington, New York, for twenty years. She is co-author of *Literature & Composition* and *Conversations in American Literature* and has published articles for the College Board® on novelist Chang-Rae Lee and the novel *All the King's Men*.

Megan Harowitz Pankiewicz is a National Board Certified Teacher with over ten years of experience. She currently teaches at Rockville High School in Rockville, Maryland. Prior to this position, she taught at Winter Springs High School in Winter Springs, Florida. In addition to AP® English Language and Composition, she has taught all levels of high school English, creative writing, and journalism. She has served as a Department Chair and an AP® Coordinator, and she is a former President and Executive Director of the Florida Council of Teachers of English.

The Language *of* Composition, THIRD EDITION

"We designed *The Language of Composition* to be the first college-level textbook intended for the Advanced Placement English Language and Composition course. Its goal is to help high school students read, analyze, and write with the same level of skill and sophistication as they would in a first-year composition course in college. *The Language of Composition* offers a diverse collection of more than 200 college-level selections — including visual texts — that are both interesting and suitable for a high school audience; practical advice on rhetoric, argument, reading, and writing; and special attention to synthesis and visual analysis skills in keeping with the content of the AP® English Language and Composition course and exam.

The Language of Composition is the product of years of experience and collaboration. We met through workshops where we were learning how to incorporate the theory and practice of rhetoric into high school curricula. The conversation that began in these workshops extended to years of discussions about what worked with eleventh- and twelfth-graders and how to prepare students to succeed in or place outof first-year composition. The more we taught our students and worked with teachers, the more we came to appreciate the interrelationship among the three main components of this book: rhetoric, reading, and writing.

Sometimes we get lucky and life gives us second (and even third) chances, as it has with *The Language of Composition*. Because of the excitement of teachers and students who have been using the book and the insights they have so generously shared, we learned what was working well, what needed adjusting or expansion, and what updating would make it more engaging for today's students."

— Renée H. Shea, Lawrence Scanlon, Robin Dissin Aufses, and Megan Harowitz Pankiewicz

Welcome to *The Language of Composition*, Third Edition, a textbook designed specifically for the AP® English Language and Composition course. We offer this guided tour of the book to introduce you to its structure and features.

New to this Edition

NEW! Increased Emphasis on Writing for the AP® English Language Exam

Our opening four chapters provide the reading and the writing support your students need to succeed in the AP® English Language and Composition course and on the AP® Exam. Chapter 1 lays the groundwork for understanding rhetoric; Chapter 2 walks students through how to write an insightful rhetorical analysis essay, providing solid preparation for Free Response Question 2 on the AP® Language Exam; Chapter 3 offers instruction on how to write an effective argumentative essay; and Chapter 4 models how to write a synthesis essay that develops a position and supports it using multiple sources.

NEW! Full-Color Design, and Emphasis on Visual Analysis

Since visual texts and arguments play an increasingly significant role in how we interpret information, students need to be equipped with the critical-thinking skills to understand and analyze them. In this edition of *The Language of Composition*, we put greater emphasis on how visual arguments work. The opening chapters include Analyzing Visual Texts sections that take students step-by-step through visual rhetoric, and throughout the book we provide engaging full-color photos, fine art, posters, infographics, charts, and graphs. We believe that these images can help bring a text to life, foster creative analysis, and be a springboard to textual analysis for visually oriented students. And we know that visual analysis is part and parcel of most college composition courses. Never mere decoration, each image is accompanied by an analytical question connecting back to the text.

NEW! Chapter on Justice

The concept of justice has become increasingly vital in today's world. Our new chapter on justice addresses topics such as free speech, civil rights, and vengeance versus mercy — subjects that are both timeless and urgently current. With readings that span the ages, this chapter will capture your students' attention and spark dynamic class discussion.

NEW! Chapter on Money

In this edition, we have shifted the emphasis of the chapter on "The Economy" to "Money." Particularly relevant to our world, this chapter focuses on the role of money in everyday life and addresses both the personal and social issues attached to it.

MORE! Conversations

We have developed five entirely new Conversations on timely issues and thoroughly updated the remainder. Each Conversation features questions that help students transition from comparison to synthesis.

NEW!	Chapter 5:	The Future of High School
NEW!	Chapter 6:	The Value of Celebrity Activism
	Chapter 7:	Sustainable Eating
NEW!	Chapter 8:	Building Online Communities
	Chapter 9:	Paying College Athletes
NEW!	Chapter 10:	The Cost of College
	Chapter 11:	Redefining Masculinity
NEW!	Chapter 12:	The Limits of Free Speech

NEW! 130 New Pieces of Nonfiction

Selections new to this edition include high-interest contemporary essays by writers such as Chimamanda Ngozi Adichie, Ta-Nehisi Coates, Bob Dylan, Atul Gawande, Sebastian Junger, Nicholas Kristof, Carmen Maria Machado, Naomi Shihab Nye, Claudia Rankine, Rebecca Solnit, J. D. Vance, and Fareed Zakaria.

NEW! AP®-Style Exam Practice

This edition includes two sets of AP®-style multiple-choice questions at the end of each thematic chapter and a sample AP® Exam at the end of the book, giving all students the chance to grapple with both what is asked, and how it is asked. The multiple-choice questions at the end of each thematic chapter are also good opportunities for formative assessment, class discussion, group work, and other in-class activities.

NEW! Wraparound Teacher's Edition

Forget everything you think you know about Teacher's Editions! An invaluable tool, the new wraparound text — written by experienced AP® teachers — is like an ongoing workshop right in the margins of your book. With its planning tools, just-in-time teaching ideas, and more, this resource will leave you wondering how you ever lived without it.

Structure of *The Language of Composition*, Third Edition

Skill-Building Opening Chapters

1 Introducing Rhetoric: Using the "Available Means"
2 Close Reading: The Art and Craft of Rhetorical Analysis
3 Analyzing Arguments: From Reading to Writing
4 Synthesizing Sources: Entering the Conversation

◀ These introduce students to the principles and language of rhetoric and argument that are essential to AP® success. Each chapter uses brief and accessible texts to introduce key concepts. We then provide multiple opportunities for students to practice those skills. We believe students learn by doing; we also acknowledge that teachers need to scaffold and differentiate instruction in this challenging course. Each of the opening chapters ends with a culminating activity that allows students to demonstrate the reading and writing tasks required in AP® Language, providing another layer of scaffolding to help every student reach proficiency.

Thematic Readings Chapters

5   Education
6   Popular Culture
7   The Environment
8   Community
9   Sports
10 NEW! Money
11 Gender
12 NEW! Justice

◀ These chapters include readings, ranging from accessible to highly challenging, that exemplify excellent writing from the distant past to the present day. Each of these texts is accompanied by rigorous rhetoric and argument analysis questions and activities that are designed to help students sharpen and master the skills built in the opening chapters.

Appendices

A   Grammar as Rhetoric and Style
B   Argument Strategies
C   Practice AP® English Language and Composition Exam
D   MLA Guidelines for a List of Works Cited
    Glossary

◀ These brief reference guides provide resources for deepening students' understanding of how grammar serves rhetorical and stylistic purposes; exploring classic argument strategies; practicing additional AP® Exam skills; reinforcing documentation habits; and clarifying key terminology.

Inside the Opening Chapters (CHS. 1–4)

The four opening chapters introduce strategies and scaffolding that guide students through deep reading of difficult texts while fostering an understanding of key rhetorical strategies and argument analysis techniques. Many students today need more support than ever, and with that in mind, we designed these opening chapters to be practical, approachable, and activity oriented. Chapter 1 provides foundational instruction in key rhetorical concepts. Chapters 2, 3, and 4 are designed to introduce the skills needed for the three essay prompts on the AP® Exam. In the subsequent thematic chapters, these approaches to reading and writing are re-emphasized repeatedly through the close-reading questions that follow each text, and they are deepened through the Conversations and Suggestions for Writing at the end of each chapter.

Chapter 1—Introducing Rhetoric: Using the "Available Means"

Chapter 1 explores the basics of rhetoric, introducing key rhetorical concepts with explanations, examples, and scaffolded activities for student practice. Our instruction includes the rhetorical triangle, appeals, visual rhetoric, and more. This chapter provides the foundation for understanding and mastering the reading and writing skills vital to the AP® English Language course.

Chapter 2—Close Reading: The Art and Craft of Rhetorical Analysis

This chapter guides students through the close analysis of rhetorical strategies such as diction and syntax, with an emphasis on their effect. Our instruction also walks students through the process of writing the type of rhetorical analysis essay required by Free Response Question 2 of the AP® Exam.

Chapter 3—Analyzing Arguments: From Reading to Writing

Chapter 3 introduces the essential elements of argument — such as claims, evidence, fallacies, and arrangement — in an approachable and practical way. We take students through the process of constructing their own written arguments, both on a topic of their choice and in response to the kind of prompt that appears on Free Response Question 3 of the AP® Exam. With scaffolded activities and examples throughout, students move from exploring ideas to crafting an arguable claim to developing evidence and structuring the overall essay.

Chapter 4—Synthesizing Sources: Entering the Conversation

This chapter introduces students to the effective use of sources in developing an informed argument. We ask them first to analyze how skillful writers use sources, then we model the process of integrating sources to support their own viewpoints in the type of synthesis essay that appears on the AP® Exam.

Inside the Thematic Readings Chapters
(CHS. 5–12)

The thematic organization, focused by essential questions, encourages students to explore the complexities of a single issue and synthesize the different viewpoints represented. We chose the eight chapter themes — Education, Popular Culture, The Environment, Community, Sports, Money, Gender, and Justice — because students will find them interesting and relevant and teachers can easily supplement them with literary works or materials from current events. They are designed to foster classroom conversation, encourage students to ponder enduring questions, and promote connections not only between and among the texts themselves but also with the vibrant cultural conversations taking place in the world today.

The selections in *The Language of Composition*, Third Edition, range from the approachable to the challenging and everything in between, giving students of various skill levels points of entry and opportunities to join the conversation.

Thematic Chapter Overview Each thematic chapter includes the following key elements:

Central and Classic Essays Spark Discussion and Foster Critical Thinking

A Central Essay and a Classic Essay provide the foundation for each thematic chapter. The authors of these works explore enduring ideas and issues, articulate complex reasoning to build compelling arguments, and craft powerful rhetoric through their command of style. These works invite students to delve deeply into the chapter theme and lay the groundwork for analyzing the texts that appear in the rest of the chapter. The Classic Essays challenge students to read and write about nonfiction from an earlier time, written for an audience very different from today's, with syntax and diction that may be unfamiliar — yet the topics of these essays remain engaging. Such works as "A Modest Proposal" by Jonathan Swift, "Professions for Women" by Virginia Woolf, and "Corn-Pone Opinions" by Mark Twain expose students to the kinds of texts that often challenge students on the AP® English Language exam. Central Essays range from selections by twentieth-century writers and thinkers, such as Martin Luther King Jr., Rachel Carson, and George Orwell, to pieces written by celebrated contemporary luminaries, such as Barbara Ehrenreich, Fareed Zakaria, and Ta-Nehisi Coates.

Visual Text Sections Expand Rhetorical Analysis

VISUAL TEXTS

The Exam Room

CYRIL EDWARD POWER

Cyril Edward Power (1872–1951) was a prolific English artist, architect, and teacher primarily known for linocut, a printing process like woodcutting in which a design is cut into linoleum before being rolled with ink and impressed onto fabric or paper. He wrote *A History of English Mediaeval Architecture* (1912) before managing repairs for the Royal Flying Corps during World War I. After the war, Power engaged in a career of artistic printmaking, co-authoring many prints with the artist Sybil Andrews. Power also helped found and lectured frequently at The Grosvenor School of Modern Art in London. He was elected to the Royal Society of British Artists in 1930. Considered a Modernist work, *The Exam Room* is a linocut emblematic of Powers's style. It was made around 1934, the year it was exhibited alongside other linocuts in London's Redfern Gallery.

CHRISTIES IMAGES/Private Collection/Bridgeman Images

[1934]

◀ Knowing how important visuals have become as rhetorical texts in college study and in our society as a whole, we feature a Visual Texts section in every chapter. Among the included images are political cartoons, photographs, advertisements, tables or graphs, and paintings. We approach these visual texts as we do written ones — rhetorically — encouraging students to read them closely and ask questions about the ways artists and designers achieve their purposes.

Other Voices Offer Fresh Perspectives and Familiar Selections

The Central Essays and Classic Essays are followed by Other Voices, a collection of rich, rigorous nonfiction pieces that exemplify excellent writing. Whether a text is narrative, expository, or argumentative, we believe that students benefit from reading and analyzing exceptional rhetoric from contemporary and classic authors. This section includes readings that are important and relevant to students because we believe that provocative, often controversial topics promote active, critical reading. These texts span several centuries, drawing from writing both familiar and fresh, building on classics by authors such as Booker T. Washington, Abraham Lincoln, and Emmeline Pankhurst, but also offering a wealth of important contemporary voices, such as Carmen Maria Machado, Claudia Rankine, J. D. Vance, and Rebecca Solnit.

Conversations Develop and Reinforce Synthesis Skills

Because students' ability to synthesize multiple sources is a primary concern of college composition courses — as well as a skill that must be demonstrated on the AP® Exam — the Conversation section in each chapter provides source material and guiding questions to help students use the words and ideas of others to develop their own arguments. Making Connections questions help students compare and contrast the various arguments in the Conversations, a key intermediary step in moving from analysis toward synthesis. After they synthesize the written and visual sources provided, students are ready to develop their own voices and positions.

Comprehensive, In-Depth Questions — Targeted Practice for Key AP® Language Skills

The in-depth questions and writing prompts that follow each reading enable students to read with a writer's eye — that is, to see how they can use the techniques of professional and published writers in their own writing. Thus, we intend the questions that accompany the selections to link reading with writing. Always promoting active reading, the questions guide students from understanding what a text is about to how the content is presented and why — the rhetorical strategies.

For the Central and Classic Essays, the questions are more extensive and grouped into more discrete categories:

- **Questions for Discussion** probe content and connections and support students' careful reading to help them comprehend ideas, understand cultural and historical contexts, and make connections to compelling contemporary issues or influences.
- **Questions on Rhetoric and Style** address the *how* and *why* of a text by examining the choices the writer makes and the effect those choices have. On the micro level, these questions address such features as diction and syntax; on the macro level, they consider a text's patterns of organization; in both cases, students are analyzing rhetorical strategies. While Questions for Discussion are generally open-ended, Questions on Rhetoric and Style are close-reading inquiries requiring precise answers similar to analytical essay or multiple-choice responses.

- **Suggestions for Writing** guide students toward written responses that extend the Conversation from the reading and suggest ways that students might practice some of the strategies that the writer uses.

Other selections in the book are accompanied by **Exploring the Text** questions, which are approachable yet rigorous prompts for discussion, writing, and even group work to promote close reading and critical thinking. The questions take students from an understanding of the piece and its ideas to an investigation of how authors and artists shape meaning.

Conversations contain questions after each individual text, culminating in a set of **Making Connections** questions that move students from analysis to comparison and contrast — a key step on the path to synthesis — and **Entering the Conversation** questions, a set of synthesis and research prompts that give students an opportunity to bring multiple sources to bear in supporting an argument or illustrating an issue.

NEW! Additional Visual Texts—Images with a Purpose

While Troy Patterson does mention motorcycle gangs in his discussion of the history of the leather jacket, he does not bring up modern-day bikers such as the Hells Angels, which has 444 charters on five continents, according to its website. **To what extent do these modern bikers challenge the claims Patteson makes about the evolution of the leather jacket? Why do you think Patterson does not discuss them?**

Scott Olson/Getty Images

We believe that visual literacy is crucial to being able to understand and analyze our world, which is why the third edition of *The Language of Composition*, in addition to the Visual Text sections in each thematic chapter, includes visual texts that accompany nearly all of the readings in the book. These images are carefully chosen — each one has a clear, authentic pedagogical purpose. We made it our goal to carefully select images that inform the reading of a print text, suggest new ideas, or provide additional context.

more, you didn't even need a gang to enjoy the aura of a gangster, a fact attested by the many teenage rebels whose acquisition of a motorcycle jacket constituted the full extent of their rebellion. But for pseudogangs — that is, for rock bands and teen cliques devoted to them — the motorcycle jacket is an international uniform impervious to obsolescence. It is a garb for all tribes: goths in Kenya; rockabillies in Japan; you in your youth, wherever you wasted it.

Its signal plays on many frequencies, expanding its meanings when garbled. Writing about the Ramones,[2] the critic Tom Carson once sketched the dynamics of the masquerade: "Their leather jackets and strung-out, streetwise pose weren't so much an imitation of Brando in 'The Wild One' as a very self-conscious parody — they knew how phony it was for them to take on those tough-guy trappings, and that incongruousness was exactly what made the pose so funny and true." The Ramones' imitators did not necessarily get this, and instead, reading the self-parody as an uncomplicated statement of force, copied that. . . .

Over decades, women annexed this male program by degrees. Early colonists included the clients of designers who, riffing on the jacket,

explored leather's sculptural properties in the service of high fashion, and the followers of pop stars who, in simply sliding on the real McCoy, showed a knack for exploiting gender fluidity. An educated guess says that the motorcycle jacket began to be androgynized in earnest in the 1990s — an era, not coincidentally, when it seemed broadly unacceptable for an adult male to wear a motorcycle jacket unless he was actively playing a guitar solo. For a while there, the jacket looked like an affront to "authenticity" and stank, in its garish slick machismo, like a palmful of Drakkar Noir. But years of wear by women entailed a rearrangement of significations and made this jacket safe for men. And now, when a guy walks his dog while wearing black leather over a gray hoodie, it isn't risible. Now, when a guy whose line of work is in "the financial-technology space" turns up at a meeting in the guise of a tough, it sort of works for his disruptive personal brand. Recently, beneath the headline "Why Every Man Needs a Biker Jacket," a writer for *The Telegraph* confessed, "I fell in love with an inanimate object," which satisfies the definition of a fetish for both Freud and Marx, to the shame of no one in particular. We're all posers.

The modern woman in a motorcycle jacket tends to be a postmodern woman, her wardrobe a workshop for practicing pastiche, the jacket organizing other fragments of reference

[2] An American punk-rock band, prominent from the mid-1970s to the mid-1990s. — Eds.

338

XV

NEW! Practice AP® Multiple-Choice Questions Hone Close Reading and Rhetorical Analysis Skills

Practice AP® multiple-choice questions on passages from both the Central Essay and Classic Essay appear at the end of each chapter. These questions are designed to mirror the AP® Exam experience, providing students an invaluable opportunity to hone their close-reading and rhetorical analysis skills while they practice and study for the AP® Exam.

Suggestions for Writing — AP®-style Rhetorical Analysis, Argument, and Beyond

Suggestions for Writing at the end of each chapter guide students toward written responses that connect multiple pieces within the chapter or that connect to pieces beyond the chapter or even beyond the book. Expanding on the skills introduced in the opening chapters, these prompts give students the opportunity to practice the kind of writing required in the AP® English Language course and beyond. Each set includes — but is not limited to — essay prompts that simulate the rhetorical analysis, argument, and synthesis questions on the AP® Exam.

NEW! Seeing Connections Boxes Encourage Exploration and Inspire New Ideas

6 Popular Culture

seeing connections

Punk-rock singer Patti Smith accepted Bob Dylan's Nobel Prize on his behalf, singing his folk song, "A Hard Rain's A-Gonna Fall" (1962), with a full orchestral accompaniment. According to Amanda Petrusich, who wrote about the event for the *New Yorker* magazine, Dylan has said that particular song "was inspired, structurally, by seventeenth-century balladry: a question is posed, and answers stack up, though none are particularly comforting. It's the questioning, though — and, moreover, the accounting it inspires — that seems essential." Later in the article, Petrusich asserts that the way Dylan accepted the prize — "with a folk song (and this specific folk song) performed by a surrogate, a peer" — was an artistic statement in itself, "[communicating] something significant about how and what he considers his own work (musical, chiefly), and the fluid, unsteady nature of balladry itself — both the ways in which old songs are fairly reclaimed by new performers, and how their meanings change with time."

How does the idea of "questioning" and "accounting" figure into Bob Dylan's Nobel Banquet speech? To what extent do you agree with Petrusich's characterization of Dylan's attitude toward his work? Use evidence from his speech to support your response.

JESSICA GOW/Getty Images

360

◀ The Seeing Connections boxes in *The Language of Composition* give students the opportunity to explore how the ideas of a piece connect with images, films, and outside texts. These boxes are departures from the text that ask students to extend an understanding to the real world and make interesting connections that yield new insights.

Inside the Appendices (A–D)

NEW! Appendix A—Grammar as Rhetoric and Style

In this appendix, we use examples from the readings to reinforce students' understanding of grammar and to show how to use grammar and syntax to achieve a rhetorical purpose or stylistic effect. Each set of exercises focuses on one issue — such as coordination, parallel structures, or use of pronouns — and explores how what might seem a mechanical point can, in fact, be approached rhetorically. Thus, students can see, for instance, how and to what effect Martin Luther King Jr. uses parallel structure or how Gay Talese uses precise, active verbs.

NEW! Appendix B—Argument Strategies

This appendix walks students through the Toulmin model and Rogerian argument strategies with detailed instruction, accessible example texts, and scaffolded practice in reading and writing using these strategies.

NEW! Appendix C—Practice AP® English Language and Composition Exam

This appendix includes a full-length practice AP® English Language Exam that uses readings from throughout the book, giving all students a chance to encounter AP®-style items and grow accustomed to both what is asked, and how it is asked.

Appendix D—MLA Guidelines for a List of Works Cited

Our MLA Guidelines reinforce documentation habits.

World-Class Support for Teachers

NEW! Teacher's Edition

Written by teachers for teachers, the Teacher's Edition offers essential tools and tips from master teachers, including suggestions for building context, approaches for close reading, places to check for understanding, and teaching ideas designed to engage students and differentiate instruction. All of this support is placed as wraparound text in the margins of the book, so you always have it right where you need it.

NEW! Teacher's Resource Flash Drive

This handy flash drive contains the following additional teacher and student resources for *The Language of Composition*, Third Edition:

- **Suggested Responses** to all of the questions posed at the end of each text. These responses are not meant to be an "answer key" as much as they are a roadmap to help you see if your students are on the right track.

- **Instructional Strategies:** These tips on classroom strategies, such as fishbowl discussions, describe not only how to use the strategy in class, but how to use it *well* and for a clearly defined purpose.
- **Lesson Plans:** These in-depth lesson plans lay out day-by-day suggestions for teaching the texts that anchor each of the thematic chapters.
- **Vocabulary Exercises:** Challenging vocabulary for most pieces has been put into worksheets that ask students to work through both meaning and effect in context — perfect for pre-reading preparation or post-reading quizzing.
- **Key Passages:** These key passages are brief, rich excerpts from readings in *The Language of Composition*, double-spaced with wide margins ideal for annotation.
- **Grammar as Rhetoric and Style:** The grammar as rhetoric and style exercises from Appendix A have been made into assignable worksheets.
- **Answer Keys to Assessments in the Student Edition:** Answer keys for the multiple-choice question sets at the end of Chapters 5–12 in the student edition and the full-length practice AP® Exam appendix provide rationales for the correct answer.
- **Student Writing Workshops:** These assignable student writing workshops of in-progress papers by high school students and college freshman model the types of writing essential to success in the AP® English Language course. Accompanying questions are designed to encourage discussion, revision, and expansion.
- **Teacher-Facing Videos:** Featuring the authors of *The Language of Composition*, these videos provide invaluable support for creating a rigorous and engaging AP® English Language course and facilitating a dynamic classroom environment.
- **Student-Facing Videos:** Also available in the e-Book, these videos help students get the most out of the thematic chapter readings and prepare for the AP® Exam.

Test Bank for AP® English Language and Composition

With more than 1,000 simulated AP® multiple-choice questions and over sixty AP®-style exam prompts, this test bank provides truly comprehensive assessment support for *The Language of Composition,* Third Edition. In addition to multiple-choice question sets on the readings in this book, this resource also includes several question sets featuring cold readings. This test bank is integrated into the e-Book or available in ExamView format.

The ExamView Test Generator lets you quickly create paper, online, and LAN-based tests. You can create and format a test in minutes in a fully customizable platform that lets you enter your own questions, edit existing questions, set time limits, incorporate multimedia, and scramble both answer choice and question order to prevent cheating. Detailed results feed directly into a gradebook.

Your E-Book Solution

The Language of Composition, Third Edition's interactive e-Book offers the accessibility you want and the flexibility you need. The format features page fidelity that ensures the e-Book matches the print text and allows each user to download and read the e-Book on multiple devices. Use it on a PC or Mac, an iPad, or an Android tablet. All notes and assignments automatically sync to the device upon logging in. And our platform makes it supremely easy to communicate with your class, provide assignments, notes, and feedback, or give quizzes. Contact us for the latest digital options to support this text on your device of choice.

Teacher's Edition E-Book — The Ultimate Teacher's Resource

The Teacher's Edition of *The Language of Composition*, Third Edition, is also available in e-Book format, putting all of the teacher support materials right where you need them.

Acknowledgments

We want to extend our heartfelt appreciation to the team at Bedford, Freeman & Worth. We've enjoyed the support, guidance, and encouragement of many talented professionals, starting with the leadership of former president Joan Feinberg, former editorial director Nancy Perry, and former editor and marketing manager Dan McDonough — all committed to this project from the start, their encouragement brought it into existence. To our gifted editors Nathan Odell and Caitlin Kaufman, we would like to present academy awards for their exceptional judgment, appreciation for language, energy — and patience. Assigned to this project as our editors, they have become dear friends who every day remind us of the value of collaboration. Many thanks to senior marketing manager Lisa Erdely for her support, expertise, wise counsel, and enthusiasm. Also, our thanks to Corrina Santos, assistant editor, cheerful researcher, and invaluable resource.

We are fortunate to have had the assistance of some amazing teachers at key times in this project, especially with the development of the Teacher's Edition and Teacher's Resource Flash Drive. Our thanks to Kate Cordes, David Freeman, Mary-Grace DeNike Gannon, Greg Jones, Stephen Klinge, Mark Leidner, Dan O'Rourke, Kimberleigh Reifle, and Patricia Vandever.

We also want to thank our many dedicated and innovative colleagues in the Advanced Placement Program at the College Board, Educational Testing Service, and classrooms across the country for sharing their knowledge of their subject matter and their passion for preparing students for success in college. We want to single out Janet Heller, formerly director of the AP® Program in the Middle States Office of the College

Board, for giving us incredible opportunities to teach and learn. A remarkable teacher in her own right, Janet encouraged us by example and common classroom sense to seek better ways to motivate and move all students to do their best work, work that would make them as well as us proud.

We would like to thank our reviewers, whose expertise guided us at every turn: Jennifer Barbknecht, Allison Beers, Julie Bollich, Rebecca Cartee-Haring, Allison Casper, Chad Cooley, Kate Cordes, James Dam, Linda Davey, Dottie DePaolo, Amber Derbridge, Ryan Derenberger, Staci Devinson, Beth Dibler, Denise Hayden, Angie Hedges, Jasara Lee Hing Hines, Robert Hornbuckle, Paula Jay, Hope Keese, Mary Kirkpatrick, Sylvia Kranish, Shaylene Krupinski, Tonita Lang, Dianne Malueg, Jenny Massey, Daniel McKenna, Linda Mirro, Lisa Moore, Sherry Neaves, Jennifer O'Hare, Beth Priem, Emily Richardson, Susan Sanchez, Shital Shah, Nate Stearns, Paul Stevenson, Rebecca Swanigan, Gwendolyn Todd, Jennifer Troy, Patricia Vandever, Jason Webb, Peggy Winter, Eric Woodard, and Victoria Zavadsky.

We also want to thank our colleagues who model the high school–college partnerships that are fundamental to *The Language of Composition*: Kathleen L. Bell, Sandra Coker, Shirley Counsil, Robert DiYanni, Marilyn Elkins, George Gadda, Mary-Grace DeNike Gannon, Stephen Heller, David Jolliffe, Bernie Phelan, Mary-Jo Potts, Hephzibah Roskelly, Sylvia Sarrett, Ed Schmieder, and Norma Wilkerson. We offer a special remembrance to the late John Brassil, our brilliant colleague and remarkable teacher. The suggestions, advice, and insights of these talented individuals have made *The Language of Composition* a better book.

We thank our families for their unflagging support and encouragement through every stage of this project. A longer list of co-authors should include our children Meredith Barnes, Christopher Shea, Kate Aufses, Michael Aufses, Alison Scanlon, Lindsay Prezzano, Maura Liguori, Kaitlin Scanlon, Zoey Pankiewicz, and Owen Pankiewicz.

Finally, we are grateful to our students — the ones in our classrooms and the colleagues in our workshops — for teaching us well.

Renée H. Shea

Lawrence Scanlon

Robin Dissin Aufses

Megan Harowitz Pankiewicz

CONTENTS

3 ANALYZING ARGUMENTS: FROM READING TO WRITING 72

5 EDUCATION   176

To what extent do our schools serve the goals of a true education?

6 POPULAR CULTURE   298

To what extent does pop culture reflect our society's values?

7 THE ENVIRONMENT 394

What is our responsibility to the natural environment?

8 COMMUNITY 510

What is the relationship of the individual to the community?

9 SPORTS 646

How do the values of sports affect the way we see ourselves?

10 MONEY   756

What is the role of money in our everyday lives?

11 GENDER 868

What is the impact of the gender roles that society creates and enforces?

12 JUSTICE 978

To what extent do our laws and politics reflect the values of a just society?

CENTRAL ESSAY

CLASSIC ESSAY

OTHER VOICES

The Language
of Composition

READING | WRITING | RHETORIC

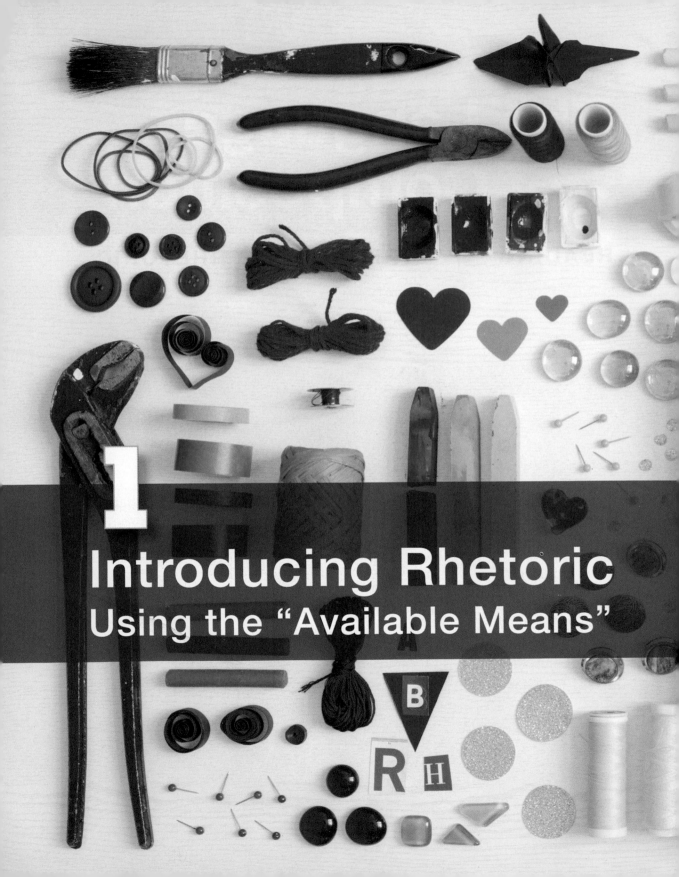

1

Introducing Rhetoric
Using the "Available Means"

To many people, the word *rhetoric* signals that trickery or deception is afoot. They assume that an advertiser is trying to manipulate a consumer, a politician wants to obscure a point, or a spin doctor is spinning. "Empty rhetoric!" is a common criticism — and at times, an indictment. Yet the ancient Greek philosopher Aristotle (384–322 B.C.E.) defined **rhetoric** as "the faculty of observing in any given case the available means of persuasion."

At its best, rhetoric is a thoughtful, reflective activity leading to effective communication, including the rational exchange of differing viewpoints. In our day, as in the time of Aristotle, those who understand and can use the available means to appeal to an **audience** of one or many find themselves in a position of strength. They have the tools to resolve conflicts without confrontation, to persuade readers or listeners to support their position, or to move others to take action.

Rhetoric is not just for Roman senators in togas. You might use rhetoric to convince a friend that Prince was the greatest musician of his generation, explain to readers of your blog why *Night of the Living Dead* is the most influential horror movie of all time, or persuade your parents that they should buy you the latest model of smartphone. Rhetoric is also not just about speeches. Every essay, political cartoon, photograph, and advertisement is designed to convince you of something. To simplify, we will call all of these things **texts** because they are cultural products that can be "read," meaning not just consumed and comprehended, but investigated. We need to be able to "read between the lines," regardless of whether we're reading a political ad, a political cartoon, or a political speech. The writer, speaker, or artist makes strategic decisions to appeal to an audience of a text. Even in documentary films, every decision — such as what lighting to use for an interview, what music to play, what to show and what to leave out — constitutes a rhetorical choice based on what the filmmaker thinks will be most persuasive.

And rhetoric is not just for English class. By approaching texts rhetorically in your other courses — whether you're analyzing an environmental issue, proposing a strategy to address an economic problem, or arguing the causes of a historical event — you can apply the critical literacy skills that you develop. But there's even a bigger picture: informed citizenship. That concept might sound distant and lofty, but democracy should not be taken for granted. Our nation's founders may have given us the basic tools for creating a democratic society, but a government by consent of the people will always need its people to be well-informed and to engage with others in civil discourse. Otherwise, how can we hope to elect a fair government and create a just society? As informed citizens and consumers who understand how rhetoric works, we can be wary of manipulation or deceit while still appreciating effective and civil communication.

Learning rhetoric will teach you to spot the tricks an advertiser is trying to play on you, to identify sources of misinformation and propaganda (including "fake news"), and to think critically. It's also important to go beyond critique to produce effective arguments of your own as you develop a public identity in various communities — whether you're at school, on social media, or out in the "real world." So, let's get started.

The Rhetorical Situation

Let's begin by looking at a speech that nearly everyone has read or heard: the farewell speech that baseball player Lou Gehrig gave at an Appreciation Day held in his honor on July 4, 1939. Gehrig had recently learned that he was suffering from amyotrophic lateral sclerosis (ALS), an incurable neurological disorder that has come to be known as Lou Gehrig's disease. Although Gehrig was a reluctant speaker, the fans' chant of "We want Lou!" brought him to the podium to deliver one of the most powerful and heartfelt speeches of all time.

Farewell Speech

LOU GEHRIG

Fans, for the past two weeks you have been reading about a bad break I got. Yet today I consider myself the luckiest man on the face of the earth. I have been in ballparks for seventeen years and have never received anything but kindness and encouragement from you fans.

Look at these grand men. Which of you wouldn't consider it the highlight of his career just to associate with them for even one day? Sure, I'm lucky. Who wouldn't consider it an honor to have known Jacob Ruppert? Also, the builder of baseball's greatest empire, Ed Barrow? To have spent six years with that wonderful little fellow, Miller Huggins? Then to have spent the next nine years with that outstanding leader, that smart student of psychology — the best manager in baseball today, Joe McCarthy? Sure, I'm lucky.

When the New York Giants, a team you would give your right arm to beat, and vice versa, sends you a gift — that's something! When everybody down to the groundskeepers and those boys in white coats remember you with trophies — that's something! When you have a wonderful mother-in-law who takes sides with you in squabbles against her own daughter — that's something! When you have a father and mother who work all their lives so that you can have an education and build your body — it's a blessing! When you have a wife who has been a tower of strength and shown more courage than you dreamed existed — that's the finest I know!

So I close in saying that I might have been given a bad break, but I have an awful lot to live for!

5

While in our time the word *rhetoric* may suggest deception, this speech reminds us that rhetoric can serve sincerity as well. No wonder one commentator wrote, "Lou Gehrig's speech almost rocked Yankee Stadium off its feet."

Occasion, Context, and Purpose

Why is this an effective speech? First of all, rhetoric is always situational. Every text is influenced by the historical, cultural, and social movements of its time. We call these broad influences **context**. Within that context, a text is also directly informed by the **occasion** — the specific circumstances, atmosphere, attitudes, and events surrounding the creation of the text. The occasion involves an opportune moment for decision or action — which gives rise to the text. Sometimes, the occasion is immediately apparent, such as in the case of an attack, an election, or a natural disaster. In other instances, the speaker must clarify, and even argue for, the occasion, to convince people of its urgency.

In the case of Gehrig's speech, the occasion is Lou Gehrig Appreciation Day. More specifically, his moment comes at home plate between games of a doubleheader. The context is first and foremost Gehrig's recent announcement of his illness and his subsequent retirement, but as is often the case, the context goes well beyond that. Gehrig, known as the "Iron Horse," held the record for consecutive games played (2,130) and was one of the greatest sluggers of all time. For such a durable and powerful athlete to fall victim to a disease that strips away strength and coordination seemed an especially cruel fate. Just a couple of weeks earlier, Gehrig was still playing ball; by the time he gave this speech, he was so weak that his manager had to help him walk out to the mound for the ceremony.

Purpose is the goal the speaker wants to achieve. One of Gehrig's chief purposes in delivering this speech is to thank his fans and teammates, but he also wants to demonstrate that he remains positive: he emphasizes his past luck and present optimism and downplays his illness. He makes a single reference to the diagnosis and does so in the strong, straightforward language of an athlete: he got a "bad break." There is no blame, no self-pity, no plea for sympathy. Throughout, he maintains his focus: to thank his fans and teammates for their support and get on with watching the ballgame. Gehrig responds as a true Yankee, not just the team but the can-do Yankee spirit of America, by acknowledging his illness and accepting his fate with dignity, honor, humility, and even a touch of humor.

ACTIVITY

Construct and analyze a rhetorical situation for writing a review of a particular movie, a new app, or a local restaurant. Be very specific in your analysis: What is your subject and its context? What is your purpose? Who is your audience? What is your relationship to the audience? Remember, you need not write a full review; just analyze the rhetorical situation.

The Rhetorical Triangle

Another important aspect of the rhetorical situation is the relationship among the speaker, audience, and subject. One way to conceptualize the relationship among these elements is through the **rhetorical triangle**. Some refer to it as the **Aristotelian**

triangle because Aristotle used a triangle to illustrate how these three elements are interrelated. How a speaker perceives the relationships among these elements will go a long way toward determining what he or she says and how he or she says it.

Let's use the rhetorical triangle to analyze Gehrig's speech.

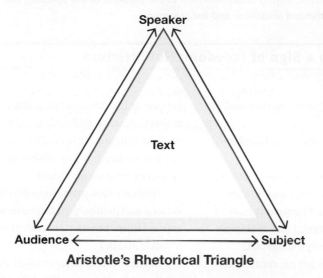

Aristotle's Rhetorical Triangle

The **speaker** is the person or group who creates a text. This might be a politician who delivers a speech, a commentator who writes an article, an artist who draws a political cartoon, or even a company that commissions an advertisement. Don't think of the speaker solely as a name, but consider a description of who the speaker is in the context of the text. The speaker of the speech we just read is not just Lou Gehrig, but baseball hero and ALS victim. Sometimes, there is a difference between who the speaker is in real life and the role the speaker plays when delivering the speech. This is called a **persona**. Persona comes from the Greek word for "mask"; it means the face or character that a speaker shows to his or her audience. Lou Gehrig is a famous baseball hero, but in his speech he presents himself as a common man who is modest and thankful for the opportunities he's had.

The **audience** is the listener, viewer, or reader of a text or performance, but it is important to note that there may be multiple audiences. Most of the time, there is a primary or intended audience, but there may also be secondary or even unintended audiences. Think, for instance, of someone giving a speech to a particular audience gathered in an auditorium — the primary and intended audience; if the speech, or part of it, ends up on social media, there is another larger audience that the speaker may or may not have anticipated. When making rhetorical decisions, speakers start by asking what values their intended audience holds, particularly whether the audience is hostile, friendly, or neutral, and how informed it is on the topic at hand. Sure, Gehrig's audience was his teammates and the fans in the stadium that day, but it was also the teams he played against, the fans listening on the radio, and posterity — us.

The **subject** is the topic. And the subject should not be confused with the purpose, which is the goal the speaker wants to achieve. Gehrig's subject is not only his illness, but also all the lucky breaks that preceded his diagnosis.

This essay is from the *Columbus Dispatch*, an Ohio newspaper with a weekly "First Person" forum that features articles by readers. At the time, the author was a high-school senior. Analyze the rhetorical situation, paying close attention to the persona of the speaker, the context, the subject, the intended audience, and the purpose.

For Teenager, Hijab a Sign of Freedom, Not Stricture

MINA SHAHINFAR

Why would you wear that? Aren't you hot under it? Are you bald?

Such questions are among those I field most every day.

Other people see my headscarf but cannot see why I make such a religious commitment.

As a Muslim-American, I frequently have to explain my hijab. I don't mind; I love that some people are curious about why I stand out.

But nothing could have left me more fasci-   5
nated, or utterly shocked, than this recent question: *Why does your religion denigrate women?*

I felt offended, disappointed, and heartbroken.

I'd met the girl in the lunch line during a summer program I was attending. She asked the question with the deepest sincerity. Evidently, to many other people, my religion cruelly symbolizes the oppression of women.

Eventually overcoming my bewilderment, I smiled, and responded: "Good question. But you've got it all wrong."

When outsiders look at the politics and culture of the Middle East, they inevitably see overwhelming male dominance. But culture and religion are not one and the same.

Yes, in some parts of the Islamic world,   10
unfortunately, women are victims — victims of compulsory hijab, domestic violence, rape, stoning and honor killings. These are remnants of a medieval world, of patriarchy and of misguided interpretation of the Quran.

Moreover, in the world today, excellent women are often defined by their relation to men. Many people can't comprehend the process of hijab as an expression of mutual respect, equality, and social harmony for both women and men. Hijab isn't merely a cloth around the head; it is an observance, a way of life, an expression of oneself.

Hijab for men primarily exists in dignified actions and manners. In the same way, women express hijab, but they also can choose to adopt a visible symbol.

My decision to observe hijab, the greatest gift I've ever given myself, confirms my status as a Muslim without altering my commitment to feminism.

For most of my life, I was the image of the typical American girl: long hair flowing, eyes sparkling, skirt perfectly fitting.

More recently, since I started high school,   15
I have made room for an addition to my morning routine: As I get dressed, I might go for my favorite Abercrombie skinny jeans and longsleeve T-shirt. But then I secure my hair with an elastic tie, carefully wrap my scarf along the rim of my face, drape it over my bun, and adjust any wrinkles along the edge.

What I reveal by the covering has a meaning entirely emblematic of my feminism. And I walk out the door consciously aware that I stand out.

By choosing hijab, I display who I am. But I choose to emphasize other aspects of myself that form my identity: my character, intellect, quirky personality, and illusory hopes and dreams — my inner-existence. By choosing hijab, I liberate myself from the shackles of the status quo, the same way a feminist counters social conformity. When others interact with me, they see and listen to my thoughts and ideas, rather than focus on my physical appearance.

My hijab reflects more of me than a million strands of hair ever could. I am anything but oppressed.

People shouldn't conceal their thoughts beneath their clothes to please society. Hijab was my solution. With it, I set myself free, all the while unapologetically defying gender norms. What could possibly be more feminist? *20*

ANALYZING VISUAL TEXTS

Recognizing Rhetoric

Understanding the rhetorical situation underlying a written text helps us read between the lines to fully grasp its message — and this is also true of all kinds of visual texts. Even artists create work within a specific context and use specific strategies to portray their subject matter in a particular light. As an example, let's look at the painting by the Mexican artist Frida Kahlo (1907–1954) entitled *Self-Portrait on the Borderline between Mexico and the United States*.

More than a self-portrait, this painting, completed in 1932, is a commentary on two societies — traditional Mexico and a heavily industrialized United States. In this case, the speaker is the artist, who stands at the center of the painting. The occasion is that Kahlo was traveling in the United States with her husband Diego Rivera, who was commissioned to paint murals for the Detroit Institute of the Arts. The subject is Kahlo's yearning for her homeland during her stay in what she referred to "Gringolandia."

If we examine the contrast Kahlo draws between Mexico and the United States, we begin to understand her purpose. Frida stands between a pre-Columbian temple that reminds us of Mexico's ancient, indigenous heritage, and a U.S. factory, which is depicted through smoke-belching chimney stacks labeled "Ford." In fact, the sun, moon, and lightning bolt on the Mexican side suggest the power of nature, while the smoke on the U.S. side portrays industrial waste and pollution. Along the bottom of the painting, there are native plants in bloom in Mexico, while in the United States, three alien-looking machines with black electric cords appear to be growing from the ground. The rich earth tones of plant life contrast sharply with the gray tones used to depict the mechanical environment of the factories.

So if Kahlo's purpose is to contrast a culture more attuned to natural forces with an industrialized and dehumanized one, who is her audience? This is not an easy question, but we might speculate that the central figure holding a Mexican flag is reminding her North American neighbors — and hosts — that theirs is not the only, nor necessarily the superior, society. We might even say that, to achieve her purpose, Kahlo idealizes her own more traditional, agrarian culture while she exaggerates the factories that dominate the U.S. landscape.

ACTIVITY

Covered Wagons Heading West, a painting by artist Newell Convers Wyeth (1882–1945) depicts American pioneers heading west during the mid-nineteenth century, possibly on the Oregon Trail. Analyze the rhetorical situation in this painting, making sure to pay close attention to the relationship between the artist, the context, the likely audience, and the purpose of the work.

Private Collection Peter Newark American Pictures/Bridgeman Images

Appeals to Ethos, Logos, and Pathos

Now that we've practiced analyzing the rhetorical situation, the next step is to use the tools of rhetoric to persuade an audience. Let's start with what Aristotle called **rhetorical appeals**. He identified three main appeals: ethos, logos, and pathos. These are important in that they provide a structure and a reminder that effective rhetoric takes into account all three, though rarely in equal measure.

Ethos

A speaker's **ethos** (Greek for "character") — expertise, knowledge, experience, sincerity, or a combination of these factors — gives the audience a reason for listening to this person on this subject. By effective ethos, we mean ways that the speaker demonstrates that he or she is trustworthy and credible. Think, for example, of a speech discouraging teenagers from drinking. Speakers might appeal to ethos by stressing that they are concerned parents, psychologists specializing in alcoholism or adolescent behavior, or recovering alcoholics themselves. Appeals to ethos often emphasize shared values between the speaker and the audience: when a parent speaks to other parents in the same community, there is a shared concern for their children's education or well-being. Lou Gehrig brings the ethos of being a legendary athlete to his speech, yet in it he establishes a different kind of ethos — that of a regular guy and a good sport who shares the audience's love of baseball and family. And like them, he has known good luck and bad breaks.

Automatic Ethos

In some instances, a speaker's reputation immediately establishes ethos. For example, the speaker may be a scholar in Russian history and economics as well as the nation's secretary of state. Or the speaker may be "the dog whisperer," a well-known animal behaviorist. In these instances, the speaker brings ethos to the text; but in other cases, a speaker establishes ethos through what he or she says in the text by sounding reasonable, acknowledging other opinions, or being thoughtful and well-informed.

Let's look at an example of how a speaker's title or status automatically brings ethos to the rhetorical situation. On September 3, 1939, King George VI gave a radio address to the British people declaring that the country was at war with Germany. The very fact that he is king gives him a certain degree of automatic ethos to speak on the subject of war, yet King George also emphasizes the shared values that unite everyone.

The King's Speech (September 3, 1939)

KING GEORGE VI

In this grave hour, perhaps the most fateful in history, I send to every household of my peoples, both at home and overseas, this message, spoken with the same depth of feeling for each one of you as if I were able to cross your threshold and speak to you myself.

For the second time in the lives of most of us, we are at war. Over and over again, we have tried to find a peaceful way out of the differences between ourselves and those who are now our enemies, but it has been in vain. We have been forced into a conflict, for we are called, with our allies, to meet the challenge of a principle which, if it were to prevail, would be fatal to any civilized order in the world.

It is a principle which permits a state in the selfish pursuit of power to disregard its treaties and its solemn pledges, which sanctions the use of force or threat of force against the sovereignty and independence of other states. Such a principle, stripped of all disguise, is surely the mere primitive doctrine that might is right, and if this principle were established throughout the world, the freedom of our own country and of the whole British Commonwealth of nations would be in danger. But far more than this, the peoples of the world would be kept in bondage of fear, and all hopes of settled peace and of the security

of justice and liberty among nations, would be ended.

This is the ultimate issue which confronts us. For the sake of all we ourselves hold dear, and of the world order and peace, it is unthinkable that we should refuse to meet the challenge.

It is to this high purpose that I now call my people at home and my people across the seas who will make our cause their own. I ask them to stand calm and firm and united in this time of trial. The task will be hard. There may be dark days ahead, and war can no longer be confined to the battlefield, but we can only do the right as we see the right, and reverently commit our cause to God. If one and all we keep resolutely faithful to it, ready for whatever service or sacrifice it may demand, then with God's help, we shall prevail.

May He bless and keep us all.

5

At the outset, King George expresses his commitment to his people, his subjects, knowing that he is asking them to make their own commitment and sacrifice. As their king, he is not expected to present himself as a common man, yet he establishes the ethos of a common experience. He tells them he speaks "with the same depth of feeling . . . as if I were able to cross your threshold and speak to you myself."

King George uses "we" in order to speak as one of the people. He acknowledges that "we are at war" for "the second time in the lives of most of us." He also uses the inclusive first person plural possessive as he identifies "our enemies," not Britain's enemies. This personalization and emphasis on the people themselves is followed by several sentences that are much more abstract in discussion of a "principle." At the end of that discussion, King George reinforces the nation's shared values: "For the sake of all we ourselves hold dear, and of the world order and peace, it is unthinkable that we should refuse to meet the challenge."

He then calls the citizenry to "this high purpose" and refers to them not as citizens or subjects but as "my people," a description that suggests a closeness rather than emphasizing the distance between a ruler and his subjects. The penultimate paragraph's references to "God" are another reminder of their shared beliefs: they worship the same god and "commit [their] cause" to him. King George brings ethos to his speech by virtue of his position, but when he assures his audience that "we shall prevail," rather than saying that England or Britain shall prevail, he is building ethos based on their common plight and common goals. They are all in this together, from king to commoner.

Building Ethos

So, what do you do if you're not a king? Writers and speakers often have to build their ethos by explaining their credentials or background to their readers, or by emphasizing shared values. You're more likely to listen to someone who is qualified to speak on a subject or who shares your interests and concerns. Following is the opening from *Hillbilly Elegy*, a 2016 memoir by J. D. Vance about the white working class in Appalachia. Note how Vance builds his ethos by acknowledging that he has no automatic ethos and anticipating concerns that his audience might have.

from Hillbilly Elegy

J. D. VANCE

My name is J. D. Vance, and I think I should start with a confession: I find the existence of the book you hold in your hands somewhat absurd. It says right there on the cover that it's a memoir, but I'm thirty-one years old, and I'll be the first to admit that I've accomplished nothing great in my life, certainly nothing that would justify a complete stranger paying money to read about it. The coolest thing I've done, at least on paper, is graduate from Yale Law School, something thirteen-year-old J. D. Vance would have considered ludicrous. But about two hundred people do the same thing every year, and trust me, you don't want to read about most of their lives. I am not a senator, a governor, or a former cabinet secretary. I haven't started a billion-dollar company or a world-changing nonprofit. I have a nice job, a happy marriage, a comfortable home, and two lively dogs.

So I didn't write this book because I've accomplished something extraordinary. I wrote this book because I've achieved something quite ordinary, which doesn't happen to most kids who grow up like me. You see, I grew up poor, in the Rust Belt, in an Ohio steel town that has been hemorrhaging jobs and hope for as long as I can remember. I have, to put it mildly, a complex relationship with my parents, one of whom has struggled with addiction for nearly my entire life. My grandparents, neither of whom graduated from high school, raised me, and few members of even my extended family attended college. The statistics tell you that kids like me face a grim future — that if they're lucky, they'll manage to avoid welfare; and if they're unlucky, they'll die of a heroin overdose, as happened to dozens in my small hometown just last year.

I was one of those kids with a grim future. I almost failed out of high school. I nearly gave in to the deep anger and resentment harbored by everyone around me. Today people look at me, at my job and my Ivy League credentials, and assume that I'm some sort of genius, that only a truly extraordinary person could have made it to where I am today. With all due respect to those people, I think that theory is a load of bullshit. Whatever talents I have, I almost squandered until a handful of loving people rescued me.

That is the real story of my life, and that is why I wrote this book.

Vance starts off by acknowledging that a memoir by someone who is just over 30 years old might seem presumptuous or downright ridiculous. He also freely admits that he hasn't done anything "extraordinary"; although graduating from Yale Law School is no small feat, he claims that this accomplishment should not compel people to spend money on his book or take time to read it. Vance further builds his ethos as a self-effacing, humble person when he thanks "a handful of loving people" who enabled his modest achievements. However, he also points out that what seems "ordinary" to most of his readers is hardly so to the community he's writing about — the community he was raised in and thus has credibility to speak of. When he describes a place "hemorrhaging jobs and hope," it is clearly a place he knows well, and his honesty about himself and his environment encourages readers to trust him. His attitude is likely to appeal to readers who believe in hard work and education, both qualities his life story reflects, though not at the expense of humility.

ACTIVITY

Imagine you must present your view on the same subject to two different audiences. For instance, you might be presenting your ideas on how to stop bullying to (1) the school board or a group of parents, and (2) a group of middle schoolers. Discuss how you would establish your ethos in each situation.

Logos

Speakers appeal to **logos**, or reason, by offering clear, rational ideas. Appealing to logos (Greek for "embodied thought") means thinking logically — having a clear main idea and using specific details, examples, facts, statistics, or expert testimony to back it up. Creating a logical argument often involves defining the terms of the argument and identifying connections such as causality. It can also require considerable research. Evidence from expert sources and authorities, facts, and quantitative data can be very persuasive if selected carefully and presented accurately. Sometimes, writers and speakers add charts and graphs as a way to present such information, but often they weave this information into their argument.

Although on first reading or hearing, Lou Gehrig's speech may seem largely emotional, it is actually based on irrefutable logic. He starts with the thesis that he is "the luckiest man on the face of the earth" and supports it with two points: (1) the love and kindness he's received in his seventeen years of playing baseball, and (2) a list of great people who have been his friends, family, and teammates in that time.

Conceding and Refuting

One way to appeal to logos is to acknowledge a **counterargument** — that is, to anticipate objections or opposing views. While you might worry that raising an opposing view could poke a hole in your argument, you'll be vulnerable if you ignore ideas that run counter to your own. In acknowledging a counterargument, you agree (concede) that an opposing argument may be true or reasonable, but then you deny (refute) the validity of all or part of the argument. This combination of **concession** and **refutation** actually strengthens your own argument; it appeals to logos by demonstrating that you understand a viewpoint other than your own, you've thought through other evidence, and you stand by your view.

In longer, more complex texts, the writer may address the counterargument in greater depth, but Lou Gehrig simply concedes what some of his listeners may think — that his bad break is a cause for discouragement or despair. Gehrig refutes this by saying that he has "an awful lot to live for!" Granted, he implies his concession rather than stating it outright; but in addressing it at all, he acknowledges a contrasting way of viewing his situation — that is, a counterargument.

Here is another example by Alice Waters, a famous chef, food activist, and author. Writing in the *Nation* magazine, she argues for acknowledgment of the full consequences of what she calls "our national diet."

---

from Slow Food Nation

ALICE WATERS

It's no wonder our national attention span is so short: We get hammered with the message that everything in our lives should be fast, cheap, and easy — especially food. So conditioned are we to believe that food should be almost free that even the rich, who pay a tinier fraction of their incomes for food than has ever been paid in human history, grumble at the price of an organic peach — a peach grown for flavor and picked, perfectly ripe, by a local farmer who is taking care of the land and paying his workers a fair wage. And yet, as the writer and farmer David Mas Masumoto recently pointed out, pound for pound, peaches that good still cost less than Twinkies. When we claim that eating well is an elitist preoccupation, we create a smokescreen that obscures the fundamental role our food decisions have in shaping the world. The reason that eating well in this country costs more than eating poorly is that we have a set of agricultural policies that subsidize fast food and make fresh, wholesome foods, which receive no government support, seem expensive. Organic foods seem elitist only because industrial food is artificially cheap, with its real costs being charged to the public purse, the public health, and the environment.

To develop a logical argument for better, healthier food for everyone, Waters refutes the counterargument that any food that is not "fast, cheap and easy" is "elitist." She does that by redefining terms such as "cheap," "[eating] well," "expensive," and "cost." She explains in a step-by-step fashion the "smokescreen" of price that many people use to argue that mass-produced fast food is the best alternative for all but the very wealthy. She points out that "[o]rganic foods *seem* elitist only because industrial food is *artificially* cheap" (emphasis added). Waters asks her readers to think more deeply about the relationships among availability, production, and distribution of food: she appeals to reason.

In the following excerpt from a 2016 *New York Times* editorial, "Mother Nature Is Brought to You by . . . ," Tim Wu, a professor at Columbia Law School, makes a case for the dangers inherent in allowing advertising in national parks. Discuss how Wu appeals to logos to make his case.

from Mother Nature Is Brought to You By . . .

TIM WU

This year, parks in several states including Idaho and Washington, and the National Park Service, will be blazing a new trail, figuratively at least, as they begin offering opportunities to advertisers within their borders.

King County in Washington, which manages 28,000 acres of parkland surrounding Seattle, offers a full branding menu: Naming rights or sponsorships may be had for park trails, benches and even trees. "Make our five million visitors your next customers," the county urges potential advertisers.

King County already partnered with Chipotle to hide 30 giant replica burritos on parkland bearing the logo of the agency and the restaurant chain. People who found the burritos won prizes from Chipotle.

In May, the National Park Service proposed allowing corporate branding as a matter of "donor recognition." As *The Washington Post* reported, under new rules set to go into effect at the end of the year, "an auditorium at Yosemite National Park named after Coke will now be permitted" and "visitors could tour Bryce Canyon in a bus wrapped in the Michelin Man."

The logic behind these efforts is, in its own way, unimpeachable. Many millions of people — that is, "green consumers" — visit parks every day, representing an unrealized marketing opportunity of great value. Yes, parks are meant to be natural, not commercial, but times are tough, or so say the backers of the new schemes.

The spread of advertising to natural settings is just a taste of what's coming. Over the

5

next decade, prepare for a new wave of efforts to reach some of the last remaining bastions of peace, quiet, and individual focus — like schools, libraries, churches, and even our homes.

Some of this reflects technological change, but the real reason is the business model of what I call the "attention merchants." Unlike ordinary businesses, which sell a product, attention merchants sell people to advertisers. They do so either by finding captive audiences (like at a park or school) or by giving stuff away to gather up consumer data for resale.

Once upon a time, this was a business model largely restricted to television and newspapers, where it remained within certain limits. Over the last decade, though, it has spread to nearly every new technology, and started penetrating spaces long thought inviolate.

In school districts in Minnesota and California, student lockers are sometimes covered by large, banner-style advertisements, so that the school hallways are what marketers call a fully immersive experience. Other schools have allowed advertising inside gymnasiums and on report cards and permission slips. The Associated Press reported this year that a high school near South Bend, Ind., "sold the naming rights to its football field to a bank for $400,000, its baseball field to an auto dealership, its softball field to a law firm, its tennis court to a philanthropic couple and its concession stands to a tire and auto-care company and a restaurant."

Even megachurches, with their large and loyal congregations, have come to see the upside of

10

applied myself thereto, which, I hope, I have accomplished with correctness and accuracy. A copy of which I have taken the liberty to direct to you, and which I humbly request you will favorably receive. And although you may have the opportunity of perusing it after its publication, yet I chose to send it to you in manuscript previous thereto, that thereby you might not only have an earlier inspection, but that you might also view it in my own handwriting.

And now, sir, I shall conclude and subscribe myself with the most profound respect.

Your most obedient, humble servant,   *15*

B. Banneker.

This brilliantly crafted letter reminds us why Aristotle claimed that of the three appeals, ethos is the most important. No matter how elegant the logical reasoning is or how eloquent the language of an argument might be, if the speaker lacks credibility with his or her audience, the rhetoric is unlikely to be persuasive. In 1791, an African American by definition lacked equal status with a white man in a position of political power. Banneker thus begins by acknowledging Jefferson's "distinguished and dignified station." He indulges in some flattery as he suggests Jefferson is more tolerant and open-minded than many of his colleagues: "less inflexible in sentiments . . . than many others." However, Banneker does not patronize Jefferson, nor does he pursue flattery at the expense of self-respect. Addressing Jefferson as "Sir" repeatedly throughout the letter, Banneker maintains a courteous but resolute tone, asserting his right to make his case to a man of enormous public stature.

Banneker also appeals to pathos as he characterizes the state of slavery — though he is careful to point out that he is a free man. At the outset, he characterizes his race as having "long labored under the abuse and censure of the world" because they "have long been considered rather as brutish than human." His strong language carries emotional weight. Banneker reminds Jefferson that he does not suffer under "that state of tyrannical thraldom, and inhuman captivity" of slavery, images that provoke a strong emotional response, yet he refers to the "groaning captivity and cruel oppression" of his brethren. That description is especially powerful in light of the fact that Jefferson himself owned slaves, though Banneker does not point that out directly.

Banneker dramatically appeals to reason when he draws a comparison between the fight for independence from "the arms and tyranny of the British crown" and slaves' fight for emancipation and civil rights. As evidence that Jefferson must recognize the similarities between the two situations, he cites Jefferson's own words from the Declaration of Independence: "'all men are created equal.'" This evidence also addresses the counterargument — that is, that black people are somehow inherently inferior to white people — when Banneker points out that "the Father of mankind" has bestowed "equal and impartial distribution of these rights and privileges." Ever conscious of his audience, Banneker softens his tone by refraining from telling Jefferson which course of action to take. Instead, he gently recommends that Jefferson "and all others . . . wean yourselves from those narrow prejudices."

Nowhere in the letter are the three appeals more intricately entwined than in Banneker's frequent allusions to Christianity. Early on, Banneker refers to one "universal Father" who guides both men. Later he calls upon those "who profess the obligations of Christianity, to extend their power and influence to the relief of every part of the human race." By invoking their shared Christian faith, Banneker establishes that they live by shared values, and he makes a strong emotional appeal by pointing out that they belong to the same religious community. These religious principles appeal to head as well as heart. Banneker rather boldly points out in paragraph 11 that it is "pitiable" for Jefferson to believe in the "benevolence of the Father of mankind, and of his equal and impartial distribution of the rights of mankind" at the same time his tolerance of slavery "counteract[s]" God's "mercies."

Did Banneker set out to methodically use one appeal after another in his letter? Likely not. But clearly he knew that starting with shared values often makes a case that is both logically sound and emotionally engaging.

ACTIVITY

Select one of the following rhetorical situations, and discuss how you would establish your ethos and appeal to logos and pathos. Explore whether and why emphasizing one of them would be more appropriate to the situation you have chosen.

1. You are trying to persuade your skeptical parents that a "gap year" — taking a year off between high school graduation and college — will be beneficial.

2. You have been asked to make a presentation to your school's principal and food service staff to propose healthier food choices in the cafeteria at a time when the overall school budget is constrained.

3. You are making the case for the purchase of a specific model and make of car that will best fit your family's needs, resources, and environmental concerns.

4. Your class intends to raise money for a gift to the school in its name; this gift may be a monetary contribution that goes toward a larger project or fund, a memorial or work of art, or something else that represents the group's interests. You are presenting your proposed choice to a meeting of interested students.

5. You are speaking to a local business to request significant financial support for an upgrade in computer equipment for student use at your school.

6. You are speaking to a local business to request financial backing to bring a particular author or public figure to speak at your school.

7. You are running for class president, and you must make a campaign speech the day before the election that explains your platform to the rest of the student body.

8. You are trying to persuade your school's principal to add a class on video games to the list of elective courses available to students.

9. You have been asked to give a presentation to next year's incoming freshman class on how to prepare to attend high school.

10. You are writing a cover letter as part of an application to a summer job or internship describing why you are the ideal candidate.

Identifying Rhetorical Appeals

Many visual texts are full-fledged arguments. Although they may not be written in paragraphs or have a traditional thesis, they are occasioned by specific circumstances, they have a purpose (whether it is to comment on a current event or simply to urge you to buy something), and they make a claim and support it with appeals to authority, emotion, and reason. Consider the following cartoon that Tom Toles created after the death of civil rights icon Rosa Parks in 2005. Parks was the woman who in 1955 refused to give up her seat on the bus in Montgomery, Alabama; that act came to symbolize the struggle for racial equality in the United States.

We can analyze this image rhetorically, just as we've been examining written texts. The occasion is the death of Rosa Parks, and the subject is her legacy. The speaker is an award-winning and respected political cartoonist, Tom Toles. The audience is made up of readers of the *Washington Post* and other newspapers — that is, it's a very broad audience. The speaker can assume that his audience shares his admiration and respect for Parks and that they view her passing as the loss of a public figure as well as a private woman. Finally, the context is a memorial for a well-loved civil rights activist, and Toles's purpose is to remember Parks as an ordinary citizen whose courage and determination brought extraordinary results.

Readers' familiarity with Toles as a nationally known political cartoonist — along with his obvious respect for his subject — establishes his ethos. The image in the cartoon appeals primarily to pathos. Toles shows Parks, who was a devout Christian, as she is about to enter heaven through the pearly gates; she is attended by an angel, probably Saint Peter, who is reading a ledger. Toles depicts Parks wearing a simple coat and carrying her pocketbook, as she did while sitting at the front of the bus many years earlier. By contrast, her features are somewhat detailed and realistic, making her stand out despite her modest posture and demeanor.

The commentary at the bottom right reads, "We've been holding it [the front row in heaven] open since 1955," a reminder that more than fifty years have elapsed since Parks resolutely sat where she pleased. The caption can be seen as an appeal to both pathos and logos. Its emotional appeal is its acknowledgement that, of course, heaven would have been waiting for this good woman. But Toles's mention of "the front row" appeals to logic as well, because Parks made her mark in history for refusing to sit at the back of the bus. Some readers might even interpret the caption as a criticism of how slow the country was both to integrate and to pay tribute to Parks herself — thus, the date reminds readers of what Toles portrays as the glacial speed of change long overdue.

ACTIVITY

The following political cartoon by artist Nate Beeler was published in 2013, following the leak of classified information about the National Security Administration's surveillance program's methods, which many viewed as ethically suspect. How does this political cartoon appeal to pathos, logos, and ethos?

Nate Beeler/Cagle Cartoons, Inc

Taking Rhetorical Risks

We've been analyzing examples of rhetoric that proved effective, though at the time some of these were written or spoken, the speaker might have been taking some risks. What exactly is the right strategy and how do we know it will resonate with our audience?

Most of the rhetoric we study in class models effective rhetoric. As you develop your skills of reading and writing rhetorically, you are preparing to join the ranks of such discussions by participating responsibly in controversial situations. After all, in a democracy, controversy is healthy — as long as the conversation remains civil. So, let's approach this question of rhetorical risks from the perspective of trying to understand the social interactions texts can perform between writers and their audience(s). As a reader and writer, you want to develop the skills to anticipate interpretive responses different from your own.

Let's turn to an essay, an op-ed piece that appeared in the *Washington Post* in 2011 after Japan was hit by a massive earthquake and tsunami that severely damaged nuclear reactors. Journalist Anne Applebaum uses this devastating situation to argue against further use of nuclear power. As you read the article, analyze it rhetorically and ask yourself if she is likely to achieve her purpose or if her strategies miss the mark.

If the Japanese Can't Build a Safe Reactor, Who Can?

ANNE APPLEBAUM

In the aftermath of a disaster, the strengths of any society become immediately visible. The cohesiveness, resilience, technological brilliance and extraordinary competence of the Japanese are on full display. One report from Rikuzentakata — a town of 25,000, annihilated by the tsunami that followed Friday's massive earthquake — describes volunteer firefighters working to clear rubble and search for survivors; troops and police efficiently directing traffic and supplies; survivors are not only "calm and pragmatic" but also coping "with politeness and sometimes amazingly good cheer."

Thanks to these strengths, Japan will eventually recover. But at least one Japanese nuclear power complex will not. As I write, three reactors at the Fukushima Daiichi nuclear power station appear to have lost their cooling capacity. Engineers are flooding the plant with seawater — effectively destroying it — and then letting off radioactive steam. There have been two explosions. The situation may worsen in the coming hours.

Yet Japan's nuclear power stations were designed with the same care and precision as everything else in the country. More to the point, as the only country in the world to have experienced true nuclear catastrophe, Japan had an incentive to build well, as well as the capability, laws and regulations to do so. Which leads to an unavoidable question: If the competent and technologically brilliant Japanese can't build a completely safe reactor, who can?

It can — and will — be argued that the Japanese situation is extraordinary. Few countries are as vulnerable to natural catastrophe as Japan, and the scale of this earthquake is unprecedented. But there are other kinds of extraordinary situations and unprecedented circumstances. In an attempt to counter the latest worst-possible scenarios, a Franco-German company began constructing a super-safe, "next-generation" nuclear reactor in Finland several years ago. The plant was designed to withstand the impact of an airplane — a post–Sept. 11 concern — and includes a chamber allegedly able to contain a core meltdown. But it was also meant to cost $4 billion and to be completed in 2009. Instead, after numerous setbacks, it is still unfinished — and may now cost $6 billion or more.

Ironically, the Finnish plant was meant to launch the renaissance of the nuclear power industry in Europe — an industry that has, of late, enjoyed a renaissance around the world, thanks almost entirely to fears of climate change. Nuclear plants emit no carbon. As a result, nuclear plants, after a long, post-Chernobyl lull, have became fashionable again. Some 62 nuclear reactors are under construction at the moment, a further 158 are being planned and 324 others have been proposed.

Increasingly, nuclear power is also promoted because it is safe. Which it is — except, of course, when it is not. Chances of a major disaster are tiny, one in a hundred million. But in the event of a statistically improbable major disaster, the damage

could include, say, the destruction of a city or the poisoning of a country. The cost of such a potential catastrophe is partly reflected in the price of plant construction, and it partly explains the cost overruns in Finland: Nobody can risk the tiniest flaw in the concrete or the most minimal reduction in the quality of the steel.

But as we are about to learn in Japan, the true costs of nuclear power are never reflected even in the very high price of plant construction. Inevitably, the enormous costs of nuclear waste disposal fall to taxpayers, not the nuclear industry. The costs of cleanup, even in the wake of a relatively small accident, are eventually borne by government, too. Health-care costs will also be paid by society at large, one way or another. If there is true nuclear catastrophe in Japan, the entire world will pay the price.

I hope that this will never, ever happen. I feel nothing but admiration for the Japanese nuclear engineers who have been battling catastrophe for several days. If anyone can prevent a disaster, the Japanese can do it. But I also hope that a near-miss prompts people around the world to think twice about the true "price" of nuclear energy, and that it stops the nuclear renaissance dead in its tracks.

5

Applebaum is taking some risks here by turning attention away from the immediate situation with human costs to another imminent problem — one with even higher stakes and potentially a more disastrous result. Of course, whether her argument misses the mark is a matter of debate. Does she use a worst-case scenario to make her case? Do her references to September 11 and World War II make nuclear power seem alarming, or do they just make Applebaum sound alarmist? Are her fears fully justified, or is this nothing but fear mongering? Consider that she does acknowledge that Japan's situation is unusual because the country is so "vulnerable to natural catastrophe" and the earthquake that struck was unusually strong. She cites facts and figures about the efforts in Finland to build a nuclear plant that is meant to be "super-safe" and withstand every imaginable contingency. She explains that other European nations are following the Finnish lead ("158 are being planned and 324 others have been proposed") because nuclear power, which does not emit carbon dioxide, is not thought to contribute to climate change. There is quite a bit to consider, even in this relatively brief piece.

Social media is notorious for mismatches between intention and result. Someone expresses a strong opinion on social media — to a wide and often unknown audience — and that text occasions unpleasant, angry, or uncivil responses. What advice for achieving effective rhetoric would you give to those who are communicating on social media? When are risks worth the potential consequences? Use examples (both effective and ineffective ones) from various social media to illustrate your advice.

Humorous and Satirical Rhetoric

Humor and satire can be effective appeals to pathos — as long as you understand your audience. Humor might work rhetorically by wrapping a challenge to our beliefs in something that makes us feel good — a joke — thus making us more receptive to that new idea. It can also work by exaggerating a concept in order to make us see its faults or vulnerabilities. Whether it's gentle, tongue-in-cheek teasing or bitter irony, humor may help a writer to make a point without, for instance, seeming to preach to the audience or take himself or herself too seriously.

But humor can be risky. If your aim is merely to poke fun as you share your thoughts on the world around you, how do you know ahead of time whether your audience will see it as hurtful mockery? This means that you need to know your audience very well to use humor effectively. If your audience thinks you have crossed over the line of playfulness and veered into disrespect, not only will you have failed to effectively communicate your argument, but you will have offended the very people you set out to win over.

Let's take a look at the following example about the "new Barbies" — that is, the newly-designed Barbie dolls that come in a variety of different sizes, shapes, and skin tones — you may wish to consider the following questions: What are the writer's main points? Where does she use humor to make them? Why is it effective?

Barbie Is Past Saving

ALEXANDRA PETRI

How do you fix a problem like Barbie?

She has been under fire for some time for being, in essence, a portable and inexpensive reminder of society's unrealistic beauty standards that we give little girls to carry around with them at all times. Which is nice, if that is what you are going for, but a bit disappointing if you are just trying to find a *toy*.

Now Mattel has hit on a solution: Give Barbie a plethora of bodies. Barbie now transcends the physical plastic plane. She is no longer limited to a single form. She has become multitudes, splitting her soul into a myriad of horcruxes with equally impeccable hair and tiny portable accessories. Now there's a Curvy Barbie, a Petite Barbie, and a Tall Barbie, all in a variety of skin tones and hair colors . . . so that all kids will get a doll in whom they can see themselves, kind of.

My parents were not Barbie parents and let me buy toys regardless of which gender-coded aisle they came from, so my idea of the ideal body type is Darth Vader. (Is this not correct?)

Now I see the modifications they are making to Barbie to bring her closer to

5

27

reality, giving her feet suitable for flats instead of NIGHTMARISHLY TINY FEET THAT SERVE NO PURPOSE, altering her shape and giving her a range of skin tones — but she is still hardly in hailing distance of reality. The body was the least of her problems.

The trouble with Barbie is that if you start taking away her unrealistic elements, she disappears altogether. Barbie is the kid in the Sideways Stories from Wayside School who turned out to be nothing but a dead rat beneath several layers of overcoat. Barbie is either the iconic, unattainable figure, blonde and waiflike, with huge eyes, or she is — what, exactly? Make her real, and she ceases to exist. She becomes a brand, a category heading, like American Girl, Monster High, Bratz.

Not that that would necessarily be awful.

Did Barbie ever look like us? (Taylor Swift, do not answer this one.) Barbie has never looked like me. We are both blonde if you look at us in the right lighting, but that is where the resemblance stops. Barbie, you see, is put-together. She has glossy hair and knows how to accessorize. I, on the other hand, still don't know what accessories are, other than things that a lot of people seem to use in committing murders.

Fixing her curves won't solve the fact that her hair, however tangled, is always impeccably glossy; that her outfits are color-coordinated and flawlessly accessorized; that even when she has spent the entire day fighting with a plastic dinosaur her makeup is still perfection. And she makes it look effortless!

The problem of seeing yourself in Barbie is not solved by resizing her. To fix that, she would **10**

need to arrive in a box that is just a big mess of laundry that she has not done, half of which has turned pink because she did not notice a lurking red sock in the white load until it was too late. Some of it should be dry-clean only, which means that she can wear it once to a nice event, spill red wine on it, and then it will sit in her closet reproaching her for months.

As far as shoes go, they should be neatly divided into two categories: Shoes she can walk in, and shoes that look good with the outfit she is wearing.

She should be equipped with Spanx.

Instead of a face of impeccable makeup, she should have a single tube of mascara, which she can use to poke herself in the eye with once before going out so that she resembles a temporarily blind raccoon.

But the most important thing for Barbie realism is that she should be constantly subjected to criticism of her appearance. She should go on TV to talk about being a marine biologist or an astronaut, and all the comments afterward should be about what her hair was doing and why on earth she picked *that* top.

Come to think of it, we have that part down. **15**

The one thing Barbie has absolutely nailed about the female appearance is that *something must always be the matter with it*. She was tiny and impossible and made of plastic for decades, and we still found fault with her. This change won't stop that. She is, as *Time* magazine points out, a body without a story, no matter what accessories you give her. And when that's your starting point, you're stuck.

The author approaches her subject matter with a light touch, poking fun both at Barbie's unattainable perfection as well as her own down-to-earth imperfections. The opening line, "How do you fix a problem like Barbie?" echoes the title of a song in the iconic musical *The Sound of Music* — "How Do You Solve a Problem Like Maria?" — which is sung by nuns whose main issue with the movie's main character, Maria, is that she's too happy-go-lucky to be one of them. So, from the start, this writer suggests that — in the grand scheme of things — Barbie's not really such a troubling problem. The description that follows contains many playful exaggerations, often sprinkled with pop culture references, such as "her soul [splitting] into a myriad of horcruxes with equally impeccable hair and tiny portable accessories." In this case, the *Harry Potter* reference implies that these new versions of Barbie are lacking in soul or substance; they merely pay lip service to the needs and interests of young children.

The writer goes on to characterize her younger self's perceptions of Barbie. For one, Barbie didn't have the "ideal body type" because she preferred Darth Vader from *Star Wars*. This comparison, already absurd on its own, also invokes the ubiquitous image of Darth Vader's floor-length black cape — a cape that conceals his body entirely. By calling attention to a fictional character whose body is unremarkable, Petri may be implying that Barbie's unrealistic body is not the root of the problem, and that changing her shape or size will not remedy what the toy lacks. Petri continues to draw on her own experiences as she shows how absurdly different a Barbie doll's appearance is from that of real women. She ends by making her serious point, that changing Barbie to reflect different body types and skin tones can't alter the basic problem: going to great and public lengths to correct Barbie's impossible perfection continues to send the message that "something must always be the matter" with "the female appearance." The humor works because so many readers, especially girls and women, will not only recognize the pop culture references Petri makes, but will also see how the author acknowledges the constant pressure to meet impossible beauty standards that our society places on women from early childhood. Barbie is a mere drop in a gigantic bucket of princess-themed toys, magazine ads, television shows, movies, diet books, and so on. It also helps that the author defuses some of her thornier points by poking fun at herself rather than solely at Barbie or at the audience.

Let's look at another humorous article that may have missed the mark. This short piece, from the *New Yorker*, alludes to a violent incident that took place on a United Airlines flight just one day before it was published. Dr. David Dao, a passenger who had paid for space on an overbooked flight, refused to give up his seat and was eventually dragged, unconscoius and bloody, off the plane by airport security. Video of the incident, taken by other passengers, went viral.

The Rules of United Airlines Fight or Flight Club

BROTI GUPTA

Welcome to the United Airlines Fight or Flight Club! We are happy to have some of you here, disappointed to have a few of you wearing leggings, and just straight-up incensed that one of you somehow sneaked in. We do not know who yet.

If this is your first time flying United, we'd like to welcome you onboard! If you are a frequent United flier, then you are either the pilot or a flight attendant. For the rest of you, we know how nerve-racking your first United flight must be, so please listen carefully to the following rules:

1. **You do not talk about Fight or Flight Club.**
   Members of our social-media team have taken a mental-health month, so just give them a break.

2. **Really, please, we're begging you: don't talk about Fight or Flight Club.** 5
   Maybe try talking about the weather? Or sports? Or Syria?

3. **No smoking at all times.**
   Smoking is not permitted on any United flight because cigarettes inhibit your body's ability to access enough oxygen to keep you in top fighting form for inflight physical altercations.

4. **Always keep your seat belt fastened when the seat-belt sign is on.**
When the seat-belt sign is on, the United Wrestling Ring is temporarily closed. To fasten your seat belt, please slide the metal end into the buckle and tighten using the strap. It will be harder to be yanked out of your seat if you have a belt tighly strapped on. And we at United enjoy a challenge.

5. **Please stow all electronic devices.**
We don't want a paper trail. Thank you.

6. **Make sure your oxygen mask is secure before assisting others with theirs.**
Should the cabin pressure drop, oxygen masks will drop down from above your seat, and we highly advise that you place an oxygen mask on yourself first. After that's done, we recommend that you try to steal other passengers' masks. As we already established: more oxygen equals better fighting.

7. **Familiarize yourself with your life vest.** 10
There is a life vest either under or near your seat. While our crew members are sparring with neighboring passengers, you can inflate the life vest and wrap it around your head for protection when it is your turn to throw some punches. It goes without saying: the more life vests you can accrue, the better.

8. **Please, enjoy the fight!**

While it's safe to assume that readers of the *New Yorker* are highly familiar with satire, which the magazine regularly publishes, we also have to keep in mind that the incident Broti Gupta satirizes here involved violence — sanctioned by the airline and carried out by airport staff — against a blameless and terrified passenger. Is *any* humor appropriate in these circumstances, especially so soon after the event? Gupta's "rules" very quickly turn in the direction of violence — the suggestion to talk about the war in Syria comes at the end of number two, and the first direct reference to passengers defending themselves from "in-flight altercations" comes with rule number three. A reference to United Airlines employees violently assaulting passengers is the focus of the next rule. However, two of the rules depict situations in which passengers turn on each other — which, given the fact that Gupta's central criticism is presumably of United Airlines's poor behavior toward passengers, may detract from the effectiveness of his central point. Do you believe Gupta's humor is effective in this case — that is, does he achieve his purpose? Does Gupta's writing shame United Airlines, or does it merely trivialize a serious and upsetting issue?

ACTIVITY

Following is a piece from the satirical news source, *The Onion*, entitled "Girl Moved To Tears By 'Of Mice And Men' Cliffs Notes." Here, the author pokes fun at students who grab the Cliffs Notes — which are a kind of study guide that outlines significant works of literature — as a substitute for reading the original work. As a student, do you find this hilarious? Sort of funny? Or does it verge on disrespectful? To what extent does this piece achieve its purpose?

Girl Moved To Tears By "Of Mice And Men" Cliffs Notes

THE ONION

In what she described as "the most emotional moment" of her academic life, University of Virginia sophomore communications major Grace Weaver sobbed openly upon concluding

Steinbeck's seminal work of American fiction *Of Mice And Men*'s Cliffs Notes early last week.

"This book has changed me in a way that only great literature summaries can," said Weaver, who was so shaken by the experience that she requested an extension on her English 229 essay. "The humanity displayed in the Character Flowchart really stirred something in me. And Lennie's childlike innocence was beautifully captured through the simple, ranch-hand slang words like 'mentally handicapped' and 'retarded.'"

Added Weaver: "I never wanted the synopsis to end."

Weaver, who formed an "instant connection" with Lennie's character-description paragraph, said she began to suspect the novel might end tragically after reading the fourth sentence which suggested the gentle giant's strength and fascination with soft things would "lead to his untimely demise."

"I was amazed at how attached to him I had 5 become just from the critical commentary," said Weaver, still clutching the yellow-and-black-striped study guide. "When I got to the last sentence — 'George shoots Lennie in the head,' — it seemed so abrupt. But I found out later that the 'ephemeral nature of life' is a major theme of the novel."

Weaver was assigned *Of Mice And Men* — a novel scholars have called "a masterpiece of austere prose" and "the most skillful example of American naturalism under 110 pages" — as part of her early twentieth-century fiction course, and purchased the Cliffs Notes from a cardboard rack at her local Barnes & Noble. John Whittier-Ferguson, her professor for the class, told reporters this was not the first time one of his students has expressed interest in the novel's plot summary.

"It's one of those universal American stories," said Ferguson after being informed of Weaver's choice to read the Cliffs Notes instead of the pocket-sized novel. "I look forward to skimming her essay on the importance of following your dreams and randomly assigning it a grade."

Though she completed the two-page brief synopsis in one sitting, Weaver said she felt strangely drawn into the plot overview and continued on, exploring the more fleshed-out chapter summaries.

"There's something to be said for putting in that extra time with a good story," Weaver said. "You just get more out of it. I'm also going to try to find that book about rabbits that George was always reading to Lennie, so that I can really understand that important allusion."

Within an hour of completing the Cliffs 10 Notes, Weaver was already telling friends and classmates that Steinbeck was her favorite author, as well as reciting select quotations from the "Important Quotations" section for their benefit.

"When I read those quotes, found out which characters they were attributed to, and inferred their context from the chapter outlines to piece together their significance, I was just blown away," said a teary-eyed Weaver. "And the way Steinbeck wove the theme of hands all the way through the section entitled 'Hands' — he definitely deserved to win the Nobel Prize."

Weaver's roommate, Giulia Crenshaw, has already borrowed the dog-eared, highlighted summary of the classic Depression-era saga, and is expecting to enjoy reading what Weaver described as "a really sad story about two brothers who love to farm."

"I loved this book so much, I'm going to read all of Steinbeck's Cliffs Notes," said Weaver. "But first I'm going to go the library to check out the original version *Of Mice And Men* starring John Malkovich and Gary Sinise."

Taking Rhetorical Risks

There's a reason that "a picture is worth a thousand words" is such a common saying. Because images can be so powerful, they are often used for shock value, to grab an audience's attention and elicit a reaction, regardless of whether that reaction is positive. Such images can be manipulative, even misleading — like "clickbait" headlines on the Internet, their aim is often to provoke a kneejerk response from viewers by engaging their emotions in an urgent, immediate way. For example, *Rolling Stone*, a biweekly news magazine with a large and diverse readership, featured the following cover in 2013.

This cover, which appeared just four months after the Boston Marathon bombings, features a selfie taken by the surviving terrorist behind the attacks, Dzhokhar Tsarnaev. The photograph is undeniably flattering: Tsarnaev looks disheveled in a stylish way, with long, curly hair that frames his face and falls into his eyes. His expression is open, his eyebrows are raised, and his mouth may even betray a hint of a smile. Tsarnaev, who was nineteen at the time, wears a t-shirt that might belong to any American teen. The lighting is soft, and what little background is visible matches the color of his shirt. Only the headline betrays the fact that he is a murderer, though the lede laments his apparent fall from grace: "How a Popular, Promising Student Was Failed by His Family, Fell into Radical Islam and Became a Monster."

The magazine's sales for this issue were double its usual circulation, but the choice to depict Tsarnaev in such a way drew many critics. Among them was Boston's mayor, Tom Menino, who asserted that the cover photo "reward[ed] a terrorist with celebrity treatment." Controversy roiled on both social media and in mainstream publications, where many agreed that it was outrageous, tasteless, and disrespectful to the victims and their loved ones. Writing for the *New Yorker* magazine, however, Ian Crouch took a different view, one based on the American value of free speech:

> [T]he vitriol and closed-mindedness of the Web response to the Rolling Stone cover, before anyone had the chance to read the article itself, is an example of two of the ugly public outcomes of terrorism: hostility toward free expression, and to the collection and examination of factual evidence; and a kind of culture-wide self-censorship encouraged by tragedy, in which certain responses are deemed correct and anything else is dismissed as tasteless or out of bounds.

Mark Joseph Stern took another tack in *Slate*, where he wrote that *Rolling Stone's* choice to "[depict] a terrorist as sweet and handsome rather than ugly and terrifying . . . has subverted our expectations and hinted at a larger truth. The cover presents a stark contrast with our usual image of terrorists."

In the wake of the controversy, the magazine also issued an official statement defending the cover:

> Our hearts go out to the victims of the Boston Marathon bombing, and our thoughts are always with them and their families. The cover story we are publishing this week falls within the traditions of journalism and Rolling Stone's long-standing commitment to serious and thoughtful coverage of the most important political and cultural issues of our day. . . . The fact that Dzhokhar Tsarnaev is young, and in the same age group as many of our readers, makes it all the more important for us to examine the complexities of this issue and gain a more complete understanding of how a tragedy like this happens.

Clearly, *Rolling Stone* took a huge rhetorical risk with this cover. Was that risk — in this case, portraying Dzhokhar Tsarnaev as an attractive young man rather than as a monster — an effective means to a worthwhile end? In other words, does the cover direct the audience's attention to the article and the issues it addresses, or does it distract from them? Does it prompt us to reflect on our own assumptions about terrorism? Or is this image simply too sympathetic to Tsarnaev to be anything but downright insensitive? Ultimately, the answers to these questions lie in the eyes of the beholder, but one thing is certain: this cover sparked a nationwide discussion.

ACTIVITY

Find a recent image — a magazine cover, a photograph, a political cartoon, an advertisement, or something else — that has generated controversy. What message do you believe this image conveys? What rhetorical risks does it take? To what extent do those risks pay off — that is, how effectively does this image achieve its purpose?

CULMINATING ACTIVITY

By this point, you've analyzed what we mean by the rhetorical situation, you've learned a number of key concepts and terms, and you've explored what distinguishes effective and ineffective rhetoric. It's time to put all of this information to work. Following is a letter to American author Mark Twain, written by Helen Keller in 1906. The two first met in 1895 and become fast friends; they remained so until Twain's death in 1910. This letter was important to both Keller and Twain — Keller included it in her 1920 book entitled *Out of the Dark: Essays, Letters and Addresses on Physical and Social Vision*, and Twain read it aloud at a meeting of the New York Association for the Blind on March 29, 1906.

Start by carefully considering the context and occasion of the letter, both as personal correspondence and as read aloud by Mark Twain to an audience. Then, discuss its purpose and how the interaction among speaker, audience, and subject affects the text. How does the letter appeal to ethos, pathos, and logos? Finally, how effective do you believe Keller's letter is, and why?

Letter to Mark Twain, 1906

HELEN KELLER

My Dear Mr. Clemens:

It is a great disappointment to me not to be with you and the other friends who have joined their strength to uplift the blind. The meeting in New York will be the greatest occasion in the movement which has so long engaged my heart, and I regret keenly not to be present and feel the inspiration of living contact with such an assembly of wit, wisdom, and philanthropy.

I should be happy if I could have spelled into my hand the words as they fall from your lips, and receive, even as it is uttered, the eloquence of our newest ambassador to the blind. We have not had such advocates before.

My disappointment is softened by the thought that never at any meeting was the right word so sure to be spoken. But superfluous as all other appeal must seem after you and Mr. Choate have spoken, nevertheless, as I am a woman, I cannot be silent, and I ask you to read this letter, knowing that it will be lifted to eloquence by your kindly voice.

To know what the blind man needs, you who can see must imagine what it would be not to see, and you can imagine it more vividly if you remember that before your journey's end you may have to go the dark way yourself. Try to realize what blindness means to those whose joyous activity is stricken to inaction.

It is to live long, long days — and life is made up of days. It is to live immured, baffled, impotent, all God's world shut out. It is to sit helpless, defrauded, while your spirit strains and tugs at its fetters and your shoulders ache for the burden they are denied, the rightful burden of labour.

The seeing man goes about his business confident and self-dependent. He does his share of the work of the world in mine, in quarry, in factory, in counting-room, asking of others no boon save the opportunity to do a man's part and to receive the labourer's guerdon.[1]

5

---

[1] A reward. —Eds.

In an instant accident blinds him. The day is blotted out. Night envelops all the visible world. The feet which once bore him to his task with firm and confident stride stumble and halt and fear the forward step. He is forced to a new habit of idleness, which like a canker consumes the mind and destroys its beautiful faculties.

Memory confronts him with his lighted past. Amid the tangible ruins of his life as it promised to be he gropes his pitiful way. You have met him on your busy thoroughfares, with faltering feet and outstretched hands, patiently dredging the universal dark, holding out for sale his petty wares, or his cap for your pennies; and this was a man with ambitions and capabilities.

It is because we know that these ambitions and capabilities can be fulfilled that we are working to improve the condition of the adult blind. You cannot bring back sight to the vacant eyes; but you can give a helping hand to the sightless along their dark pilgrimage.

You can teach them new skill. For work they once did with the aid of their eyes you can substitute work that they can do with their hands.

They ask only opportunity, and opportunity is the torch of darkness. They crave no charity, no pension, but the satisfaction that comes from lucrative toil, and this satisfaction is the right of every human being.

At your meeting New York will speak its word for the blind, and when New York speaks, the world listens. The true message of New York is not the commercial ticking of busy telegraphs, but the mightier utterances of such gatherings as yours.

Of late our periodicals have been filled with depressing revelations of great social evils. Querulous critics have pointed to every flaw in our civic structure. We have listened long enough to the pessimists.

You once told me you were a pessimist, Mr. Clemens; but great men are usually mistaken about themselves. You are an optimist. If you were not, you would not preside at the meeting. For it is an answer to pessimism. It proclaims that the heart and the wisdom of a great city are devoted to the good of mankind, that in this, the busiest city in the world, no cry of distress goes up but receives a compassionate and generous answer. Rejoice that the cause of the blind has been heard in New York, for the day after it shall be heard around the world.

10

35

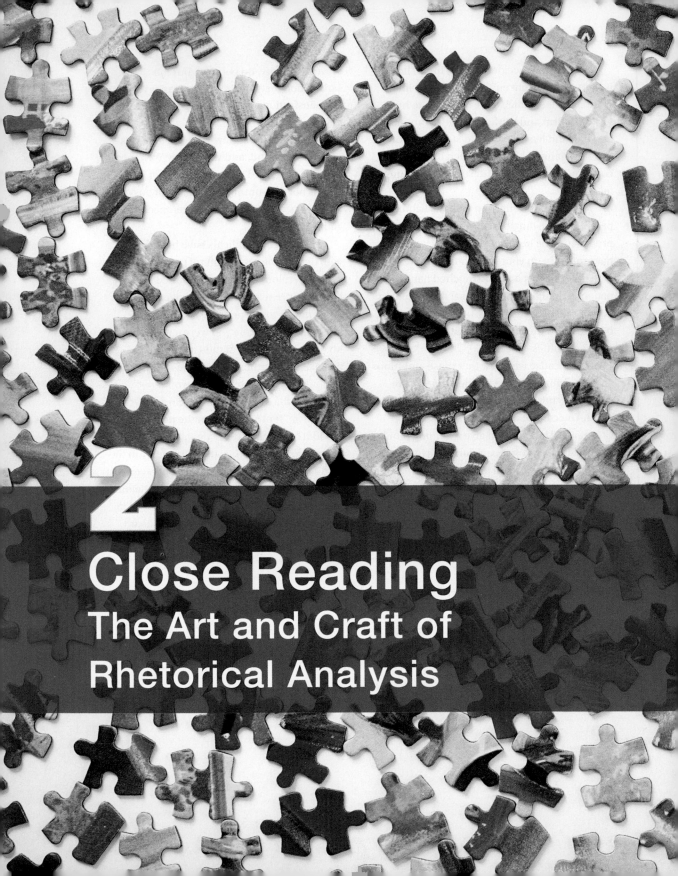

2
Close Reading
The Art and Craft of
Rhetorical Analysis

Have you ever wondered how your teachers can teach the same books year after year and not be bored by them? One reason is that the works we study in school have many layers of meaning, revealing something new each time we read them. That quality is what distinguishes them from literary potato chips — works that are satisfying, even delicious, but that offer little nutritional value. A mystery, romance, gossip blog, or sports rant may absorb us completely, but usually we do not read it a second time.

How do you find the "nutritional value" in the essays, speeches, stories, and poems you study in school? Your teacher may lead you through a work, putting it in context, focusing your attention on themes and techniques, asking for a response. Or you might do these things yourself through a process called close reading. When you read closely, you develop an understanding of a text that is based first on the words themselves and then on the larger ideas those words suggest. That is, you start with the small details, and as you think about them, you discover how they affect the text's larger meaning. When you *write* a rhetorical analysis, you start with the larger meaning you've discovered and use the small details — the language itself — to support your interpretation of a writer's choices.

Of course, as you read the speeches, essays, letters, editorials, and even blog posts in this book and in your class, you will find that many different factors dictate the stylistic and rhetorical choices a writer makes. Sometimes, it's the genre: a blog post will likely be less formal than, say, an acceptance speech; an editorial will be less personal than an exchange of letters between two friends. Often, it's the context or rhetorical situation — the relationship between the subject matter, the occasion, the audience, the speaker's purpose, and the speaker's persona. Nearly always, however, as you learned in Chapter 1, the choices writers make are related to the rhetorical strategies of the text: what words in what arrangement are most likely to create the desired effect in the audience? How will those choices help the writer achieve the purpose of the text?

Analyzing Rhetorical Strategies

As you've learned in Chapter 1, appeals to emotion, logic, and goodwill are considered rhetorical strategies. Writers make these appeals in their choice of language and structure. As with any skill, close reading becomes easier with practice, but it's important to remember that we use it unconsciously — and instantaneously — every day as we respond to people and situations. Just as we notice body language, gestures, facial expressions, and volume in our conversations, we can understand a text better by examining its sentence structure, diction, imagery, and figurative language. These elements make up the style of the written piece and help us to discover layers of meaning. Style contributes to the meaning, purpose, and effect of a text, whether it is written, oral, or visual.

A Model Analysis

Let's take a look at a very famous speech given in 1588 by Queen Elizabeth I to the English troops at Tilbury that were assembled in preparation for an attack by the Spanish Armada. Working with older pieces such as this one sometimes seems more difficult than working with texts from the twentieth or twenty-first century, yet you may find that you read the older ones more carefully and that their riches reveal themselves more quickly than you might expect. Often the biggest challenge is understanding the tone of the piece, but if you look carefully at the speaker's choices of words (also called **diction**) and how those words are arranged (called **syntax**), you will find plenty of clues.

It may help you to begin by picturing Queen Elizabeth as she might have been on that day in 1588. (Consider watching a reenactment of this speech; Helen Mirren's performance of it in the 2005 miniseries *Elizabeth I* is especially good and easy to find online.) Tradition has it that when Queen Elizabeth, who never married and was known as the Virgin Queen, gave this speech, she was dressed in armor and left her bodyguards in order to walk among her subjects. Her troops were vastly outnumbered by a Spanish Armada that was the most formidable naval force in the world, and it had been preparing to invade England for three years. England, in contrast, was in a precarious financial situation that made it impossible for its troops to go on the offensive; they had to wait for the attack. The English troops were bedraggled, underpaid, and hungry.

Speech to the Troops at Tilbury

QUEEN ELIZABETH I

My loving people,

We have been persuaded by some that are careful of our safety, to take heed how we commit our selves to armed multitudes, for fear of treachery; but I assure you I do not desire to live to distrust my faithful and loving people. Let tyrants fear, I have always so behaved myself that, under God, I have placed my chiefest strength and safeguard in the loyal hearts and good-will of my subjects; and therefore I am come amongst you, as you see, at this time, not for my recreation and disport, but being resolved, in the midst and heat of the battle, to live and die amongst you all; to lay down for my God, and for my kingdom, and my people, my honour and my blood, even in the dust.

I know I have the body but of a weak and feeble woman; but I have the heart and stomach of a king, and of a king of England too, and think foul scorn that Parma or Spain, or any prince of Europe, should dare to invade the borders of my realm; to which rather than any dishonour shall grow by me, I myself will take up arms, I myself will be your general, judge, and rewarder of every one of your virtues in the field.

I know already, for your forwardness you have deserved rewards and crowns; and We do assure you in the word of a prince, they shall be duly paid you. In the mean time, my lieutenant general shall be in my stead, than whom never prince commanded a more noble or worthy subject; not doubting but by your obedience to my general, by your concord in the camp, and your valour in the field, we shall shortly have a famous victory over those enemies of my God, of my kingdom, and of my people.

Using what you learned in Chapter 1, you can begin by identifying the passage's rhetorical situation. The speaker is the Queen of England, the last of the Tudor rulers, the daughter of Henry VIII and Anne Boleyn. Since she never married there was no king. She is exhorting her troops to face the battle with courage and determination on the eve of a confrontation in which England is the underdog. We can analyze the passage through the rhetorical triangle, considering the interaction of subject, audience, and speaker. The subject is Queen Elizabeth's support for her troops, and the audience is those soldiers gathered around to hear her. Of course, we can assume Elizabeth knew that her words would be communicated to the larger world as well.

You can also consider the ways the queen appealed to ethos, pathos, and logos. A popular queen, walking alone but with her loyal retinue nearby, her ethos as the monarch is established; nevertheless, she begins the speech humbly by stating her confidence in her subjects. She appeals to pathos in her characterization of herself as a "weak and feeble woman," although she reassures her listeners that on the inside she is as strong as a king. Less apparent is Elizabeth's appeal to logos; we could, however, consider her promise to repay her loyal troops with "rewards and crowns" to be a logical extension of her support for them.

ACTIVITY

Reread the speech, and think about the rhetorical strategies and style choices that help Queen Elizabeth convey her message. Think also about the persona she creates for herself and how that helps her achieve her purpose.

You probably noticed that Elizabeth begins by speaking of herself in the first person plural. This is a convention: the "royal we," meant to show that the ruling monarch embodies the entire nation. Even though it is conventional, you can see that it helps Elizabeth create a sense of common purpose. Interestingly, she quickly moves to the singular personal pronouns, "I" and "my," appropriate in a speech she is making on the same ground (literally) as her audience. She starts off by acknowledging those who might warn her against walking among her soldiers, those who urge her to "take heed how we commit our selves to armed multitudes." She asserts her independence and fortitude here, telling the troops that she considers them her "chiefest strength" and assures them that she is not that day among them for "recreation and disport." We can imagine that Elizabeth knew the power of image and even mythmaking; there in the flesh among her soldiers, her wish to "live and die amongst you all" would inspire confidence and courage. The sentence that begins the speech creates a sense of equity between Elizabeth and her troops. The second sentence builds up to the queen's dramatic commitment to die in the dust with her subjects.

The queen switches gears a bit in the third sentence (para. 2) with the speech's most famous phrase: "I know I have the body but of a weak and feeble woman; but I have the heart and stomach of a king, and of a king of England too. . . ." Here Elizabeth reinforces her image as the Virgin Queen. She never married, most likely for political reasons, and considered herself married to England. She reminds the assembled troops that she is the daughter of a king, however, and is, therefore, connected to the long line of royalty and the divine right of kings — the idea that royal power is bestowed by God. It is worth noting that only then, when she has characterized herself as a "weak and feeble woman," does she mention the enemies: Spain, Parma (Italy), and Europe in general. These references may serve a few purposes. They appeal to the gallantry of the troops who would feel obligated as gentlemen to defend their queen; they may also be a way to suggest that an attack by Spain is a Catholic threat to English Protestantism. In either case, Elizabeth reassures her troops that she is with them every step of the way and that their "virtues in the field" will be rewarded.

The final part of the speech reinforces the earlier call for national unity and a reassurance that Elizabeth has the interests of her people at heart. She reminds the troops of the rewards they will receive and reaffirms her support for her lieutenant general, who serves "in [her] stead." The last clause invokes the rule of three — "your obedience," "your concord," "your valour" — to predict a "famous victory over those enemies of my God, of my kingdom, and of my people." Although the Armada was defeated largely by bad weather and the light English boats that were able to ride out the storms, Elizabeth's troops were certainly strengthened by her glorious words of trust and confidence.

Let's discuss the tone of Elizabeth's speech, as this is a good way to begin thinking about how to write about what you've discovered in your rhetorical analysis. We often consider tone and mood together: **tone** is the speaker's attitude toward the subject as revealed by his or her choice of language, and **mood** is the feeling created by the work. As always, it's important to be able to support your description of tone and mood with evidence from the text. The speech at Tilbury begins with Elizabeth humbling herself to the soldiers: she drops the "royal we"; she puts her subjects before her own safety; she offers her life for her kingdom. In paragraph 2, Elizabeth makes a transition from humble (she has the body of a "weak and feeble woman") to defiant: she dares the Europeans to invade. Finally, she makes some practical concessions, promising her troops that they will be led by her most loyal lieutenant general and amply rewarded for their loyalty. We could describe the tone of her speech as humble yet inspiring and defiant.

ACTIVITY

The following op-ed piece by Henry Louis Gates Jr. was published by the *New York Times* in 2016. In it, he discusses the recent opening of the National Museum of African American History and Culture in Washington, D.C. Describe the tone of the editorial by using two adjectives or an adjective and an adverb; then explain why you chose those words, making specific reference to the text.

Restoring Black History

HENRY LOUIS GATES JR.

With the ringing of a bell and a speech from President Obama, the National Museum of African American History and Culture in Washington is to officially open its extraordinary collection to the public on Saturday. But the museum can claim another, equally important achievement: helping resolve the protracted debate about the contributions of black people to American history and, indeed, about whether they had a history worth preserving at all. Those questions were at the heart of the nation's original debate about whether, and how, black lives matter.

For years, the issue was whether black people were fit to be more than slaves. "Never yet could I find that a black had uttered a thought above the level of plain narration; never see even an elementary trait of painting or sculpture," Thomas Jefferson wrote. "I advance it, therefore, as a suspicion only, that the blacks, whether originally a distinct race, or made distinct by time and circumstances, are inferior to the whites in the endowments both of body and mind."

The connection between humanity and history was central to this debate, and in the estimation of some Enlightenment thinkers, blacks were without history and thus lacked humanity. The German philosopher Hegel argued that human beings are "human" in part because they have memory. History is written or collective memory. Written history is reliable, repeatable memory, and confers value. Without such texts, civilization cannot exist. "At this point we leave Africa," he pontificated, "not to mention it again. For it is no historical part of the world; it has no movement or development to exhibit."

Black people, of course, would fight back against these aspersions by writing histories about the African-American experience. In the 1880s, George Washington Williams, whom the historian John Hope Franklin called "the first serious historian of his race," published the "History of the Negro Race in America from 1619 to 1880"; he confessed that part of his motivation was "to call the attention to the absurd charge that the Negro does not belong to the human family."

About a decade later, W.E.B. Du Bois   5
became the first black person to earn a Ph.D. (in history) at Harvard, followed by Carter G. Woodson, a founder of Negro History Week, who wanted to make history by writing it. "If a race has no history," he wrote, "it stands in danger of being exterminated." Arthur A. Schomburg, the famous bibliophile, posited a solution: "The American Negro must remake his past in order to make his future." History "must restore what slavery took away."

This mandate to rewrite the status of the race by writing the history of its achievements was too broad to be contained only in books. Public history mattered, too. In 1915, Woodson and several of his friends established the Association for the Study of Negro Life and History, in part to popularize the study of black history. That same year, black leaders called for a memorial to honor black veterans. And a year later — exactly a century ago — Representative Leonidas C. Dyer, a Missouri Republican, introduced legislation to create a monument in their honor. After decades of resistance, that effort took a giant leap forward in 2003, when Congress passed bipartisan legislation to build the museum that was signed by President George W. Bush.

Some $540 million later, the first black president will open the museum's doors, admirably directed by another historian, Lonnie G. Bunch III. When he does, the long battle to prove Jefferson, Hegel and so many others wrong will have been won. We can only imagine the triumph that the pioneers of black history would feel had they lived to see this occasion.

More than a museum, the building on the National Mall is a refutation of two and a half centuries of the misuse of history to reinforce a social order in which black people were enslaved, then systematically repressed and denied their rights when freed. It also repudiates the long and dismal tradition of objectifying black people in museums. We cannot forget the parading of Saartjie Baartman, the so-called Hottentot Venus, at European freak shows in the 19th century, or the stuffed remains of an African man known only as the "Negro of Banyoles," on display for almost for a century in the Darder Museum of Natural History in Spain.

Other ironies, more present to us, abound: Remember the misguided rush eight years ago to declare the birth of a "post-racial" America in the aftermath of President Obama's first election? Now, at the end of his second term, that seems ages ago, given a recent poll showing that six out of 10 Americans think that race relations are worsening.

In contrast to the "post-racial" notion that history can or even should be waved away, the opening of the museum does something more vital. It reinscribes race at a symbolically central place in American culture, on the National Mall, where we celebrate our collective public histories, ensuring that a mountain of evidence about black contributions to America will be on permanent display. It does this on the same mall shared by those symbols of the founding

10

fathers' hypocritical slaveholding past, the Washington Monument and the Jefferson Memorial, which the new museum, brilliantly designed by David Adjaye, complements and also deconstructs.

"History," James Baldwin wrote, "is not merely something to be read. And it does not refer merely, or even principally, to the past. On the contrary, the great force of history comes from the fact that we carry it within us, are unconsciously controlled by it in many ways, and history is literally *present* in all that we do."

Talking with the Text

Effective close reading requires active reading, an exchange between the reader and the text that eventually reveals layers of meaning. The first step is to read and reread. That's a good start, but at some point you will have to talk back, ask questions, and make comments. In other words, have a conversation with the text. Let's look at some close reading techniques that will help you talk with the text.

Asking Questions

One of the simplest ways to talk with the text is to interrogate it — to ask questions. Remember that we're always trying to consider the choices writers make, so as you read, ask yourself why they chose the words or sentence patterns they did. You don't always need to know the answers to your questions; sometimes, just asking them will give you insights into a writer's choices.

Let's take a look at an excerpt from an essay titled "The Decline of Grammar," which appeared in the *Atlantic Monthly* in 1983. In it, linguist Geoffrey Nunberg explores the conflict between prescriptivists (those who believe there is a right and wrong when it comes to grammar rules) and descriptivists (those who believe that grammatical correctness is a matter of common usage).

from The Decline of Grammar

GEOFFREY NUNBERG

Is the English language — or to put it less apocalyptically, English prose writing — really in a bad way? How would one tell? The standard jeremiads of the Sunday supplements give only anecdotal evidence, and that of a curious sort; the examples of degradation that they present are drawn not from

current plays or novels, which are grammatically and syntactically *extra judicium*, but from advertisements, scholarly papers, and — most popular of all — memos from college deans. It is hard to believe that any of these texts will survive even until the next century, much less that late-twentieth-century

English will be judged by their example. Our picture of the English of previous centuries, after all, has been formed on the basis of a careful selection of the best that was said and thought back then; *their* hacks and bureaucrats are mercifully silent now. But while it is understandable that speakers of a language with a literary tradition would tend to be pessimistic about its course, there is no more hard evidence for a general linguistic degeneration than there is reason to believe that Aaron and Rose are inferior to Ruth and Gehrig.

Most of my fellow linguists, in fact, would say that it is absurd even to talk about a language changing for the better or the worse. When you have the historical picture before you, and can see how Indo-European gradually slipped into Germanic, Germanic into Anglo-Saxon, and Anglo-Saxon into the English of Chaucer, then Shakespeare, and then Henry James, the process of linguistic change seems as ineluctable and impersonal as continental drift. From this Olympian point of view, not even the Norman invasion had much of an effect on the structure of the language, and all the tirades of all the grammarians since the Renaissance sound like the prattlings of landscape gardeners who hope by frantic efforts to keep Alaska from bumping into Asia.

The long run will surely prove the linguists right: English will survive whatever "abuses" its current critics complain of. And by that I mean not just that people will go on using English and its descendants in their daily commerce but that they will continue to make art with it as well. Yet it is hard to take comfort in the scholars' sanguine detachment. We all know what Keynes said about the long run, and in the meantime does it really matter not at all how we choose to speak and write? It may be that my children will use *gift* and *impact* as verbs without the slightest compunction (just as I use *contact*, wondering that anyone ever bothered to object to it). But I can't overcome the feeling that it is wrong for me to use them in that way and that people of my generation who say "We decided to gift them with a desk set" are in some sense guilty of a moral lapse, whether because they are ignorant or because they are weak. In the face of that conviction, it really doesn't matter to me whether *to gift* will eventually prevail, carried on the historical tide. Our glory, Silone said, lies in not having to submit to history.

Linguistic manners are like any others. People have always found it worthwhile to reflect on how best to behave, for the sake of at least individual enlightenment and improvement. Since the eighteenth century, most of our great moralists have at one time or another turned their attention to the language, from Addison, Swift, and Johnson to Arnold, James, Shaw, Mencken, and Orwell. In their essays and in the great grammars and dictionaries, we find the most direct secular continuation of the homiletic tradition, reflecting the conviction that the mastery of polite prose is a moral accomplishment, to which we will be moved by appeals to our highest instincts.

Reread the excerpt, and see what you notice on a second reading. Jot down questions as you go, observing Nunberg's language choices.

Here are some questions about Nunberg's rhetorical choices that might come to mind, based on first and second impressions of the passage:

- In the first sentence, Nunberg alludes to a famous essay ("Politics and the English Language," p. 1033) by twentieth-century English writer George Orwell, who is perhaps best known for the dystopian novels *1984* and *Animal Farm*. What does the allusion suggest about Nunberg's intended audience?

- Why does Nunberg's essay begin with a question? Why does the question contain a separate phrase surrounded by em-dashes?

- What does the inclusion of the italicized Latin phrase *extra judicium* suggest about Nunberg's audience?

- What is the effect of the sports analogy at the end of the first paragraph?

- Why does Nunberg report from an "Olympian point of view"?

- What is the effect of the analogy about landscape gardeners at the end of the second paragraph? Why might Nunberg have chosen to end the first two paragraphs with this rhetorical strategy?

- Why does Nunberg allude to the British economist John Maynard Keynes and the Italian writer Ignazio Silone in paragraph 3?

- What is the purpose of the references to writers such as Addison, Arnold, James, and Orwell?

You may notice that these questions fall into the two categories we talked about in relation to Queen Elizabeth's speech: the choice of words (diction) and the way the words are arranged (syntax). When we talk about diction, we might look for interesting or powerful vocabulary, but we also consider figures of speech such as **metaphors**, **similes**, **personification**, and **hyperbole**. When we consider syntax, we want to notice interesting constructions such as **parallelism**, **juxtaposition**, and **antithesis**, along with sentence types such as **compound**, **complex**, **periodic**, **cumulative**, and **imperative**, among others. We also might look at the pacing of a piece of work: Does the writer reveal details quickly or slowly? How does he or she build suspense?

Here are some questions to ask when you analyze diction:

- What type of words draw your attention? Do they tend to be a particular part of speech, such as verbs, nouns, adjectives, or adverbs? Is the language general and abstract or specific and concrete?

- Is the language formal, informal, colloquial, or slang?

- Are some words nonliteral or figurative, creating figures of speech such as metaphors?

- Are there words with strong connotations? Words with a particular emotional punch?

When you analyze syntax, you might ask:

- What is the order of the parts of the sentence? Is it the conventional order (subject-verb-object), or is it inverted (object-subject-verb) or some other pattern that is out of the ordinary?

- What are the sentences like? Are they periodic (moving toward something important at the end) or cumulative (beginning with an important idea and then adding details)?

- Are many of the sentences simple? Complex? Compound? Are the sentences on the long side, or are they short?

- Does the writer ask questions?

- How does the writer connect words, phrases, and clauses?

These questions do not have simple yes or no answers. They lend themselves to discussion, but as you discuss them, be sure you can support your ideas with evidence from the text. Coming up with answers to questions like these will put you well on your way toward making an analysis of an author's style choices and how that style helps the author make his or her point.

ACTIVITY

The following excerpt from Geoffrey Nunberg's essay directly follows the paragraphs we have just discussed. Read it carefully and then generate two or three questions each about the rhetorical situation, diction, and syntax.

from The Decline of Grammar

GEOFFREY NUNBERG

Take *Modern English Usage*, by that good man H. W. Fowler, "a Christian in all but actual faith," as the *Dictionary of National Biography* called him. Despite a revision in 1965, it is out-of-date, yet it still has a coterie as devoted as the fans of Jane Austen or Max Beerbohm, who prize its diffident irony, its prose cadences, and, above all, the respect it shows for its readers' intelligence and principles. Here, for example, is Fowler on the insertion of quotation marks or an expression like "to use an expressive colloquialism" to mark off a slang word from which the writer wants to dissociate himself:

> Surprise a person of the class that is supposed to keep servants cleaning his own boots, & either he will go on with the job while he talks to you, as if it were the most natural thing in the world, or else he will explain that the bootboy or scullery-maid is ill & give you to understand that he is, despite appearances, superior to boot-cleaning. If he takes the second course, you conclude that he is not superior to it; if the first, that perhaps he is. So it is with the various apologies to which recourse is had by writers who wish to safeguard their dignity & yet be vivacious, to combine comfort with elegance, to touch pitch & not be defiled. . . . Some writers use a slang phrase because it suits them, & box the ears of people in general because it is slang; a refinement on the institution of whipping-boys, by which they not only have the boy, but do the whipping.

This passage would not be out of place in the company of Addison and Steele. It is apt, amusing, and above all instructive. It obviously has done little to stem the mania for quotation marks (WE ARE "CLOSED," I saw in the window of a shoe-repair shop the other day), but it did at least persuade me to remove the quotes from around the word *life-style* in a review I was writing, and I am a better person for it.

Annotating

Another close reading technique you can use is annotation. Annotating a text requires reading with a pencil in hand. If you are not allowed to write in your book, then write on sticky notes. As you read, circle words you don't know or write them on the sticky notes. Identify main ideas — thesis statements, topic sentences — and also words, phrases, or sentences that appeal to you, that seem important, or that you don't understand. Look for figures of speech such as metaphors, similes, and personification — as well as **imagery** and striking detail. If you don't know the technical term for something, just describe it. For example, if you come across an adjective-and-noun combination that seems contradictory, such as "meager abundance," and you don't know that the term for it is **oxymoron**, you might still note the juxtaposition of two words that have opposite meanings. Ask questions or comment on what you have read. In short, as you read, listen to the voice in your head, and write down what that voice is saying.

Let's try out this approach using a speech that social and political activist Florence Kelley delivered in 1905 to the National American Woman Suffrage Association in Philadelphia. Read the speech first, and see if you can come up with some ideas about Kelley's purpose. Then we will look closely at the choices she makes and the effects of those choices.

Speech on Child Labor

FLORENCE KELLEY

We have, in this country, two million children under the age of sixteen years who are earning their bread. They vary in age from six and seven years (in the cotton mills of Georgia) and eight, nine and ten years (in the coal-breakers of Pennsylvania), to fourteen, fifteen and sixteen years in more enlightened states. No other portion of the wage earning class increased so rapidly from decade to decade as the young girls from fourteen to twenty years. Men increase, women increase, youth increase, boys increase in the ranks of the breadwinners; but no contingent so doubles from census period to census period (both by percent and by count of heads), as does the contingent of girls between twelve and twenty years of age. They are in commerce, in offices, in manufacturing.

Tonight while we sleep, several thousand little girls will be working in textile mills, all the night through, in the deafening noise of the spindles and the looms spinning and weaving cotton and wool, silks and ribbons for us to buy.

In Alabama the law provides that a child under sixteen years of age shall not work in a cotton mill at night longer than eight hours, and Alabama does better in this respect than any other southern state. North and South Carolina and Georgia place no restriction upon the work of children at night; and while we sleep little white girls will be working tonight in the mills in those states, working eleven hours at night. In Georgia there is no restriction whatever! A girl of six or seven years, just tall enough to reach the bobbins, may work eleven hours by day or by night. And they will do so tonight, while we sleep. Nor is it only in the South that these things occur. Alabama does better than New Jersey. For Alabama limits the children's work at night to eight hours, while New Jersey permits it all night long. Last year New Jersey took a long backward step. A good law was repealed which had required women and [children] to stop work at six in the evening and at noon on Friday. Now, therefore, in New Jersey, boys and girls, after their fourteenth birthday, enjoy the pitiful privilege of working all night long.

In Pennsylvania, until last May it was lawful for children, thirteen years of age, to work twelve hours at night. A little girl, on her thirteenth birthday, could start away from her home at half past five in the afternoon, carrying her pail of midnight luncheon as happier people carry their midday luncheon, and could work in the mill from six at night until six in the morning, without violating any law of the Commonwealth.

If the mothers and the teachers in Georgia could vote, would the Georgia legislature have refused at every session for the last three years to stop the work in the mills of children under twelve years of age?

Would the New Jersey legislature have passed that shameful repeal bill enabling girls of fourteen years to work all night, if the mothers in New Jersey were enfranchised? Until the mothers in the great industrial states are enfranchised, we shall none of us be able to free our consciences from participation in this great evil. No one in this room tonight can feel free from such participation. [The children make our shoes in the shoe factories; they knit our stockings, our knitted underwear in the knitting factories. They spin and weave our cotton underwear in the cotton mills. Children braid straw for our hats, they spin and weave the silk and velvet wherewith we trim our hats.] They stamp buckles and metal ornaments of all kinds, as well as pins and hat-pins. Under the sweating system, tiny children make artificial flowers and neckwear for us to buy. They carry bundles of garments from the factories to the tenements, little beasts of burden, robbed of school life that they may work for us.

We do not wish this. We prefer to have our work done by men and women. But we are almost powerless. Not wholly powerless, however, are citizens who enjoy the right of petition. For myself, I shall use this power in every possible way until the right to the ballot is granted, and then I shall continue to use both. What can we do to free our consciences? There is one line of action by which we can do much. We can enlist the workingmen on behalf of our enfranchisement just in proportion as we strive with them to free the children. No labor organization in this country ever fails to respond to an appeal for help in the freeing of the children.

For the sake of the children, for the Republic in which these children will vote after we are dead, and for the sake of our cause, we should enlist the workingmen voters, with us, in this task of freeing the children from toil!

You probably observed that Kelley describes the plight of child workers in order to inspire her audience to take action to help them. She also has another underlying message— a thesis that she doesn't state until the seventh paragraph of the speech — which is that women must be able to vote to really be able to help. Her purpose is to abolish child labor, and the only way that can happen is if women — mothers — are enfranchised to vote. It may take you a few readings to see the effectiveness of Kelley's rhetorical strategies. Paying attention to the way she appeals to emotion and reason, as well as to the ways in which she establishes credibility, will help you analyze the choices she makes to achieve her purpose.

Following is an annotated version of Kelley's speech:

We have, in this country, two million children under the age of sixteen years who are earning their bread. They vary in age from six and seven years (in the cotton mills of Georgia) and eight, nine and ten years (in the coal-breakers of Pennsylvania), to fourteen, fifteen and sixteen years in more enlightened states. No other portion of the wage earning class increased so rapidly from decade to decade as the young girls from fourteen to twenty years. Men increase, women increase, youth increase, boys increase in the ranks of the breadwinners; but no contingent so doubles from census period to census period (both by percent and by count of heads), as does the contingent of girls between twelve and twenty years of age. They are in commerce, in offices, in manufacturing.

Tonight while we sleep, several thousand little girls will be working in textile mills, all the night through, in the deafening noise of the spindles and the looms spinning and weaving cotton and wool, silks and ribbons for us to buy.

In Alabama the law provides that a child under sixteen years of age shall not work in a cotton mill at night longer than eight hours, and Alabama does better in this respect than any other southern state. North and South Carolina and Georgia place no restriction upon the work of children at night; and while we sleep little white girls will be working tonight in the mills in those states, working eleven hours at night. In Georgia there is no restriction whatever! A girl of six or seven years, just tall enough to reach the bobbins, may work eleven hours by day or by night. And they will do so tonight, while we sleep. Nor is it only in the South that these

Starts right off with substantive data

An effective touch of irony—how enlightened are they, really?

Diction continues emotional appeal, especially effective as the noise and chaos take place "while we sleep." Could imply that it's morally wrong: it's being done by cover of night, and is thus purposely hidden from the waking world.

Strong appeal to pathos, involving audience through pronoun "we."

More identification with audience, acknowledging their complicity (and her own) in child labor. Strengthens her ethos as well.

"Alabama does better" is another touch of irony — working 8 hours instead of all 12 hours of a night is still horrendously inhumane.

Repetition of "while we sleep" further emphasizes appeal to pathos.

Another repetition of "while we sleep" — it's beginning to sound like a reproach. Maybe she's implying that most people are choosing to be unaware of these working conditions for children.

Kelley preempts possible objection from her audience with "Nor. . . ."

Kelley warns her
audience to stay
on guard. Progress
isn't something
you can just set
in motion and
walk away from.
It's not linear, and
the law can move
backwards.

things occur. Alabama does better than New Jersey. For Alabama
limits the children's work at night to eight hours, while New Jersey
permits it all night long. Last year New Jersey took a long
backward step. A good law was repealed which had required
women and [children] to stop work at six in the evening and at
noon on Friday. Now, therefore, in New Jersey, boys and girls,
after their fourteenth birthday, enjoy the pitiful privilege of
working all night long.

    In Pennsylvania, until last May it was lawful for children,
thirteen years of age, to work twelve hours at night. A little girl, on
her thirteenth birthday, could start away from her home at half
past five in the afternoon, carrying her pail of midnight luncheon
as happier people carry their midday luncheon, and could work
in the mill from six at night until six in the morning, without

Irony!— violating any law of the Commonwealth.

    If the mothers and the teachers in Georgia could vote, would
the Georgia legislature have refused at every session for the last
three years to stop the work in the mills of children under twelve
years of age?

Also effective
juxtaposition of
Georgia and New
Jersey, suggesting
that geographical
distinctions are
insignificant when
talking about
mothers and
children. Strong
appeal to pathos.

    Would the New Jersey legislature have passed that shameful
repeal bill enabling girls of fourteen years to work all night, if
the mothers in New Jersey were enfranchised? Until the mothers
in the great industrial states are enfranchised, we shall none of
us be able to free our consciences from participation in

Powerful phrase! this great evil. No one in this room tonight can feel free from
such participation. The children make our shoes in the shoe
factories; they knit our stockings, our knitted underwear in the
knitting factories. They spin and weave our cotton underwear
in the cotton mills. Children braid straw for our hats, they spin
and weave the silk and velvet wherewith we trim our hats.

More irony, and
a repetition that
Alabama's cruel
night labor law still
"does better" than
other states, North
or South.

More irony—
emphasized by
alliteration, too.

Powerful imagery
in this paragraph.

Effective
rhetorical question
introducing Kelly's
main idea and
thesis: if women
could vote, would
child labor exist?

Rhetorical question
from previous
paragraph leads
into this question,
emphasizing her
point.

Kelley's claim and
thesis statement—
no longer a
rhetorical question,
now plainly and
forcefully stated.

The audience is
again complicit
as children make
"our" goods.

The specifics of the goods are so vivid, and they are often merely ornamental.

They stamp buckles and metal ornaments of all kinds, as well as pins and hat-pins. Under the sweating system, tiny children make artificial flowers and neckwear for us to buy. They carry bundles of garments from the factories to the tenements,

Vivid imagery and jarring metaphor in "beasts of burden."

little beasts of burden, robbed of school life that they may work for us.

Parallel structure — "we" is repeated three times, emphasizing her point: we're all in this together.

We do not wish this. We prefer to have our work done by men and women. But we are almost powerless. Not wholly powerless, however, are citizens who enjoy the right of petition. For myself, I shall use this power in every possible way until the right to the ballot is granted, and then I shall continue to use both. What can we do to free our consciences? There is one line of action by which we can do much. We can enlist the workingmen on behalf

Call for action — these are concrete steps toward the vote for women.

of our enfranchisement just in proportion as we strive with them to free the children. No labor organization in this country ever fails to respond to an appeal for help in the freeing of the children.

For the sake of the children, for the Republic in which these children will vote after we are dead, and for the sake of our cause, we should enlist the workingmen voters, with us, in this task of freeing the children from toil!

Interesting qualifiers. "Almost" is then qualified by "not wholly," acknowledging that change will be tough to bring about, but not impossible.

She moves from "we" to "I" here, posing a challenge — if she can do it, so can the audience.

Ends on two notes of pathos: cooperation between men and women and continued references to the children.

Using a Graphic Organizer

Another way to organize your thoughts about a specific text is to use a graphic organizer. A graphic organizer lets you systematically look at short passages from a longer text. Your teacher may divide the text for you, or you may divide it yourself; you might use the paragraph divisions as natural breaking points, or you might consider smaller sections that seem interesting stylistically or rhetorically. Although a graphic organizer takes time to complete, it lets you gather a great deal of information that you can use as you prepare to write an essay. For example, it can help you identify patterns or a repetition of techniques.

The following graphic organizer asks you to take something the writer has said, restate it in your own words, identify some of the devices that the writer has used, and then analyze how the writer uses those devices to make his or her point. Note that you become increasingly analytical as you move from left to right. Below is an example of how you might complete a graphic organizer for some of the most powerful passages in Florence Kelley's speech.

Quotation	Paraphrase or Summarize	Rhetorical Strategy or Style Element	Effect or Function
We have, in this country, two million children under the age of sixteen years who are earning their bread. They vary in age from six and seven years (in the cotton mills of Georgia) and eight, nine and ten years (in the coal-breakers of Pennsylvania), to fourteen, fifteen and sixteen years in more enlightened states.	Throughout the United States, two million children, ages six through sixteen, work.	Pronoun "We"	"We" immediately establishes Kelley's connection with her audience.
		Many facts: numbers, ages, locations, job type	Substantive data appeals to both logic and ethos and shows Kelley knows the subject.
		"Enlightened" is possibly sarcastic	Hint of sarcasm signals Kelley's position on the child labor.
Tonight while we sleep, several thousand little girls will be working in textile mills, all the night through, in the deafening noise of the spindles and the looms spinning and weaving cotton and wool, silks and ribbons for us to buy.	The night work, done by thousands of young girls in a horrible, noisy setting, yields fabric and ribbons that women buy.	Pronoun "we" again	Kelley places responsibility on the audience in an emotional appeal. The audience can sleep while these young girls toil in unpleasant conditions.
		Vivid imagery, references to sound	
		Periodic sentence listing products	The list of these goods— soft and gentle fabrics— stands in stark contrast to the noise of the mills.
		Paragraph ends with "us"	Ending with "us" again emphasizes her audience's shared responsibility — she won't let them ignore it.
Last year New Jersey took a long backward step. A good law was repealed which had required women and [children] to stop work at six in the evening and at noon on Friday. Now, therefore, in New Jersey, boys and girls, after their fourteenth birthday, enjoy the pitiful privilege of working all night long.	There was a law that prevented some child labor, but it was overruled; so now, in New Jersey, kids work all night.	Very direct first sentence	Kelley sounds like she's scolding.
		"Pitiful privilege" oxymoron, alliteration	The sad and inhumane nature of "pitiful privilege," or legalized night work for children, is highlighted.

Quotation	Paraphrase or Summarize	Rhetorical Strategy or Style Element	Effect or Function
If the mothers and teachers in Georgia could vote, would the Georgia legislature have refused at every session for the last three years to stop the work in the mills of children under twelve years of age? Would the New Jersey legislature have passed that shameful bill enabling girls of fourteen years to work all night, if the mothers in New Jersey were enfranchised? Until the mothers in the great industrial states are enfranchised, we shall none of us be able to free our consciences from participation in this great evil.	Mothers and teachers could have changed the laws in Georgia and New Jersey if they had been able to vote. The only way to prevent this evil is for mothers to be able to vote.	Two rhetorical questions, citing two different geographical locations Kelley makes her thesis statement, asserting her central claim. No understating here: great evil	The rhetorical questions are attention getters and again put responsibility on the audience. The juxtaposition of two different locations suggests that differences are null and void. Kelley's powerful language makes a strong appeal to pathos in which the audience is complicit.
No one in this room tonight can feel free from such participation. The children make our shoes in the shoe factories; they knit our stockings, our knitted underwear in the knitting factories. They spin and weave our cotton underwear in the cotton mills. Children braid straw for our hats, they spin and weave the silk and velvet wherewith we trim our hats. They stamp buckles and metal ornaments of all kinds, as well as pins and hat-pins. Under the sweating system, tiny children make artificial flowers and neckwear for us to buy. They carry bundles of garments from the factories to the tenements, little beasts of burden, robbed of school life that they may work for us.	Children make things everyone uses every day. They miss out on an education in order to work in factories, live in squalor, and shuttle the product of their toil between the two. Not only are the children forced to make the goods, they must transport them as well.	Repetition of pronouns "our," "we," and "us" Vivid imagery describes all the details of the goods children make in factories Metaphor: children as "little beasts of burden"	Pronouns make the audience complicit as do the details of goods that are used by them. The level of detail in the description of the goods juxtaposes their frivolousness with the inhumane conditions in which children labor to create them. The message is clear: children are suffering for the sake of the audience's vanity. The language is both jarring and dehumanizing.

continued

Quotation	Paraphrase or Summarize	Rhetorical Strategy or Style Element	Effect or Function
We do not wish this. We prefer to have our work done by men and women. But we are almost powerless. Not wholly powerless, however, are citizens who enjoy the right of petition. For myself, I shall use this power in every possible way until the right to the ballot is granted, and then I shall continue to use both.	Most of us prefer to let grown men and women work, but we are almost powerless to change this. But we still have the right to petition. I will do this until women have the right to vote and then I'll vote to end child labor.	Qualifiers: *almost, not wholly, however*

Moves from "we" to "I" | If she can do it, so can the audience; they can fight for women's suffrage and move away from the "great evil."

She takes the responsibility for being a leader. |
| What can we do to free our consciences? There is one line of action by which we can do much. We can enlist the workingmen on behalf of our enfranchisement just in proportion as we strive with them to free the children. No labor organization in this country ever fails to respond to an appeal for help in the freeing of the children. | How can we be better people and help the children? Women can get men to help, both to get women the vote and to help end child labor. | Rhetorical question and answer | By providing an answer to her final question, Kelley drives home the practical and very concrete advice that getting men involved will help on two levels. |
| For the sake of the children, for the Republic in which these children will vote after we are dead, and for the sake of our cause, we should enlist the workingmen voters, with us, in this task of freeing the children from toil! | It's important for our children and the future of our country that male workers help us in changing the laws and securing the vote for women. | Periodic sentence ends with Kelley's most important message: child labor must be abolished, and giving women the vote is the best way to achieve that. | This builds momentum and galvanizes the audience in an appeal to pathos whose tone echoes the rising sense of urgency—men and women must unite for the future of the country. |

Breaking the text into small sections, looking at them closely, and writing down your ideas about them help you notice the rhetorical details in Kelley's speech. You will notice, for example, how she uses the pronouns "us," "our," and "we," or the vivid imagery she employs in her descriptions of child labor and the frivolous products it yields. You may also notice that Kelley poses many rhetorical questions to her audience, and her answers to them are practical solutions. Collecting these bits of information from the text and considering the impression they make prepare you to answer the following questions about Kelley's rhetoric and style.

- What effect is she striving for?
- How does she create that effect?
- How does the effect serve the purpose of her writing?

From Close Reading to Rhetorical Analysis

No matter what technique you choose, as you interact with the text you should keep in mind that you're not only identifying techniques and strategies, but also analyzing their effect — you're moving from close reading to analysis. As you read Kelley's speech, you probably got a feel for the choices she made to achieve her purpose. Her use of plural pronouns connects her to her audience, making them share the responsibility for child labor. There is a certain amount of repetition, which both drives home her message and may even echo the soul-deadening work the children do in mills and factories. Kelley uses data as well, with information about the numbers of children working in various states and the laws that allow that kind of work. This is irrefutable evidence that child labor is unfair and exploitative. Kelley creates images that are hard to ignore as she appeals to the emotions of her audience. And the images of the children working amid the noise as "beasts of burden" contrast sharply with the decorative goods they make and even the luxury of such fabrics as "cotton and wool, silks and ribbons." The tone is not quite scolding, but it is certainly direct. She doesn't mince words, and is clear that child labor is "a great evil" that can only be successfully fought by granting women suffrage. You might describe the tone as passionate and admonishing.

The passage's syntax also has a role. The speech is filled with rhetorical questions, several of which she answers, and all of which are attention-getters. Who doesn't want to pay attention when we're asked a question? A couple of periodic sentences end with the focus on "us," the audience who must take responsibility for changing the laws and ending child labor. The first begins "while we sleep" and ends with "us" enabling child labor with our consumer needs. The second, at the end of the speech, ends with freeing the "children from toil" but picks up speed with her suggestion for how to do that: uniting the workingmen with the women in order to secure the vote that will help change the laws.

So let's go back to those three key questions:

- What effect is Kelley striving for?
- How does she create that effect?
- How does the effect serve the purpose of her writing?

For the first question, we might say that she is calling for action. She hopes that by describing the plight of the child workers her audience will be moved to try to change the laws that allow child labor. She acknowledges that women's suffrage is integral to this task, for no mother would allow such terrible conditions for children. So her purpose is also to push her audience to demand the vote which they can use to abolish child labor. She also acknowledges the importance of the workingmen uniting with women to ensure social change for both women and children. Kelley creates the effect she is after by citing straightforward facts and figures alongside vivid images that bring to life the inhumane conditions under which children work. Through her use of plural pronouns and rhetorical questions, Kelley makes her audience feel complicit in the horrors of child labor — and also makes the case that it is everyone's responsibility to try and put a stop to its "great evil." Thus, even as she admonishes her audience, she also gives them the impression that they are empowered to make important social changes. It is difficult to imagine that these techniques didn't spur Kelley's audience on to work for the vote and change the laws.

ACTIVITY

Read the first speech Winston Churchill made to the House of Commons as Prime Minister of Britain in May 1940. Try one of the techniques you have learned for talking with the text. Then answer these questions: What effect is Churchill striving for? How does he create that effect? How does the effect serve the purpose of his speech? Try annotating or creating a graphic organizer to help you see the rhetorical strategies Churchill used to achieve his purpose.

Blood, Toil, Tears, and Sweat

WINSTON CHURCHILL

I beg to move,

That this House welcomes the formation of a Government representing the united and inflexible resolve of the nation to prosecute the war with Germany to a victorious conclusion.

On Friday evening last I received His Majesty's commission to form a new Administration. It is the evident wish and will of Parliament and the nation that this should be conceived on the broadest possible basis and that it should include all parties, both those who supported the late Government and also the parties of the Opposition. I have completed the most important part of this task. A War Cabinet has been formed of five Members, representing, with the Opposition Liberals, the unity of the nation. The three party Leaders have agreed to serve, either in the War Cabinet or in high executive office. The three Fighting Services have been filled. It was necessary that this should be done in one single day, on account of the extreme urgency and rigour of events. A number of other positions, key positions, were filled yesterday, and I am submitting a further list to His Majesty tonight. I hope to complete the appointment of the principal Ministers during tomorrow. The appointment of the other Ministers usually takes a little longer, but I trust that, when Parliament meets again, this part of my task will be completed, and that the Administration will be complete in all respects.

I considered it in the public interest to suggest that the House should be summoned to meet today. Mr. Speaker agreed, and took the necessary steps, in accordance with the powers conferred upon him by the Resolution of the House. At the end of the proceedings today, the Adjournment of the House will be proposed until Tuesday, 21st May, with, of course, provision for earlier meeting, if need be. The business to be considered during that week will be notified to Members at the earliest opportunity. I now invite the House, by the Motion which stands in my name, to record its approval of the steps taken and to declare its confidence in the new Government.

To form an Administration of this scale and complexity is a serious undertaking in itself, but it must be remembered that we are in the preliminary stage of one of the greatest battles in history, that we are in action at many other points in Norway and in Holland, that we have to be prepared in the Mediterranean, that the air battle is continuous and that many preparations, such as have been indicated by my hon. Friend below the Gangway, have to be made here at home. In this crisis I hope I may be pardoned if I do not address the House at any length today. I hope that any of my friends and colleagues, or former colleagues, who are affected by the political reconstruction, will make allowance, all allowance, for any lack of ceremony with which it has been necessary to act. I would say to the House, as I said to those who have joined this government: "I have nothing to offer but blood, toil, tears and sweat."

We have before us an ordeal of the most grievous kind. We have before us many, many long months of struggle and of suffering. You ask, what is our policy? I can say: It is to wage war, by sea, land and air, with all our might and with all the strength that God can give us; to wage war against a monstrous tyranny, never surpassed in the dark, lamentable catalogue of human crime. That is our policy. You ask, what is our aim? I can answer in one word: It is victory, victory at all costs, victory in spite of all terror, victory, however long and hard the road may be; for without victory, there is no survival. Let that be realised; no survival for the British Empire, no survival for all that the British Empire has stood for, no survival for the urge and impulse of the ages, that mankind will move forward towards its goal. But I take up my task with buoyancy and hope. I feel sure that our cause will not be suffered to fail among men. At this time I feel entitled to claim the aid of all, and I say, "come then, let us go forward together with our united strength."

5

Close Reading

Asking First-Impression Questions

Many of the tools of rhetorical analysis and close reading that we can apply to written texts are also useful for detecting how visual texts convey their messages. These tools work whether the visual texts are advertisements, photos, fine art, or political cartoons. Even conventional written texts have visual components: authors and publishers make decisions about fonts, spacing, and margins, and we make the same decisions when we write. Visual texts serve many different purposes and most have more than one. They can be informational — brochures, pamphlets, and PowerPoint presentations, for example — they can be persuasive — advertisements and political cartoons especially — and they can be inspirational, as with fine art such as photography, painting, or even graffiti. Like written texts, their purpose is very much connected to their audience. Let's take a look at this advertisement for the Dodge Durango and try to answer some first-impression questions.

- What is being said?
- Who is saying it?
- To whom is it being said?
- Why is it being said?
- How is it being said?

DODGE DURANGO. This is the most affordable SUV with a V-8. Dodge Durango. With nearly four tons of towing,* this baby carries around chunks of those wimpy wanna-bes in its tail pipe. For more info, call 800-4 A DODGE or visit dodge.com

GRAB LIFE BY THE HORNS

DODGE

IT'S A BIG FAT JUICY CHEESEBURGER IN A LAND OF TOFU.

*Depending on model and when properly equipped.

This magazine print advertisement is for the Dodge Durango, a sport utility vehicle (SUV). The ad is saying, "This is a great SUV." The ad was thought up and designed by both Dodge and the advertising company that created the ad. Dodge, like most car manufacturers, advertises widely in print and on television. It's likely that it appeared in publications targeted at a particular audience, which we might identify as potential car buyers. The reason for the ad is to convince a certain type of customer to buy a Dodge Durango.

We will talk more about how the ad says what it has to say and how it might achieve its purpose of selling Durangos to a particular target buyer.

Close Reading Visual Rhetoric

The rhetorical triangle also applies to visual texts, so we can ask what are the relationships among the text's subject (a powerful SUV), its audience (the potential SUV buyer), and the speaker (Dodge and the advertising agency it hired to create the ad)? In this case, the speaker — Dodge and the ad agency — are savvy about how to make the Durango appealing to its potential market and we see those elements in the ad: the beach, the cool Airstream, the humorous text, the Dodge logos, and more.

We can examine these relationships more closely by identifying the rhetorical strategies the text uses to appeal to its audience. In other words, how does this advertisement appeal to ethos, logos, and pathos? It banks on associations to Dodge cars and trucks — power, dependability, toughness — and, in this way, establishes its credibility or ethos. Its appeals to pathos play on preconceptions about food: a cheeseburger is real food, so tofu is somehow fake; cheeseburgers are what you want to eat, tofu is what you're supposed to eat; a big powerful truck is what you really want, a small fuel-efficient car is what you are supposed to have. As for logos, the Durango is affordable; it makes sense to own one. Why not enjoy life, drive an affordable SUV, and eat big, juicy cheeseburgers?

Let's look a little deeper. When we analyze a visual text, we still look at the words, both in terms of their meaning and in the way they are placed on the page. Look at the text on the top left part of the ad:

> **DODGE DURANGO.** This is the most affordable SUV with a V-8. Dodge Durango. With nearly four tons of towing, this baby carries around chunks of those wimpy wanna-bes in its tail pipe.

Note the aggressive tone. How is that aggressiveness created? It may be the repetition of "Dodge Durango" with its hard consonant sounds; it may be the prepositional phrase announcing that the vehicle can tow four tons. It's a "baby" that carries "chunks" of its competitors in its tailpipe. The use of the colloquialism "baby" contrasts nicely with the image of the car as a predator eating the competition. The owner of a Dodge Durango will be the kind of person whose car is his or her "baby" and who is the leader of the pack, not one "of those wimpy wanna-bes." The Dodge logo — a ram's head — and slogan "grab life by the horns" appear at the top right of the ad. Both the image and the words play with the connotations of horns: strength, masculinity, and noise. The imperative sentence is a call to action that can be paraphrased as "Don't be a wimp! Enjoy life now!" Finally, the text at the bottom of the ad has yet another message. The large white letters on the dark road are boldly designed, but the message is gentle and even funny. "[B]ig fat juicy cheeseburger" acknowledges our natural desire for pleasures that are not always healthy. But who can resist when the alternative is tofu? The antecedent of *it's* is, of course, the SUV, but the pronoun suggests an understanding, an insider's wink.

Analyzing Visual Rhetorical Strategies

Visual texts can be examined using the same close reading tools we use to analyze written texts, but images also use distinctly visual style elements to craft rhetoric and appeal to an audience. We study the visual aspects of an image the same way we do words: individually and in terms of **composition**, or arrangement on the page.

For instance, notice that though the Dodge logo and the text at the top are quite aggressive, the photo is less so. In fact, the photo shows a man and a woman in the car, pulling a vintage Airstream motor home, thus suggesting not only a family atmosphere but also good taste, as Airstreams are collectibles. Perhaps it's a pitch to the rising number of female car buyers, or the use of an SUV as a less stodgy replacement for a minivan. Though the front of the Dodge Durango is outsized (a reminder of the power under the hood), the ocean and sky in the **background** soften the aggressiveness of the looming SUV; it looks like a beautiful day for a cool couple with great taste to be out for a ride.

Looking at the visual elements even more closely, you might note the horizon **line**. Set as it is, between the sea and sky, it has the calming effect common to horizontal lines. In contrast, note the diagonal lines: the diving lines in the highway, the slant of the rooftops of the car and the Airstream. These diagonals have the effect of suggesting movement. This contrast adds to the advertisement's mixed messages. The color used in the image also has something to say. The calm blue water and sky are reflected in the hood of the Durango, tempering a bit the sense that it's a powerful macho machine. The gold reflected in the other side of the SUV shimmers, lending a magical touch to the couple's outing. Much of the ad is in high **focus**; it's easy to see the different elements. The exception is the couple inside the Durango. They are difficult to make out, lacking in detail, and even open to interpretation. The suggestion might be that there's not just one type of couple — or buyer — that would love the Dodge Durango.

You'll also notice the ad's use of **shape**. Neither the Durango nor the Airstream have sharp edges. Powerful as the SUV is, it has a gentle, almost organic, profile — again, a design element softens the aggressive qualities of the Dodge logo and the text to the right. Finally, take a look at the way the image's **framing** — what we see in the oblong box that frames the image and the vantage point of the viewer. The SUV is front and center, almost square in the middle of the shot. The water in the background wings away to the right; the Airstream to the left. The SUV is in the **foreground** — front and center. Plenty of room is given to the open highway ahead. Could it be telling us that adventures await?

So what is the advertisement's message? Or are there a few different messages? If you were to write an essay analyzing the "language" of the visual text, you might consider a thesis that argues for the ad's multiple messages. Here's one example:

> The Dodge Durango ad balances aggressiveness with humor: it appeals to men and women with its reminder that life is too short not to enjoy its guilty pleasures.

ACTIVITY

Use the following ad for Coach handbags, or find one on your own that appeals to you or provokes you, and analyze it as we have done with the Dodge Durango ad. Remember to ask yourself the following questions:

- What is being said?
- Who is saying it?
- To whom is it being said?
- Why is it being said?
- How is it being said?

From Analysis to Essay: Writing a Rhetorical Analysis Essay

We're going to look now at steps you can take toward writing a rhetorical analysis essay. Good writing comes from careful reading, so the first steps will always be to read, reread, ask questions, and either annotate or create a graphic organizer for the text you will be working with. The more we examine the rhetorical elements in a text and consider their effects, the deeper our understanding of an essay, a speech, or a visual text becomes. We have to reach that deeper understanding when we write about rhetoric or we will end up merely summarizing rather than analyzing the strategies a writer uses to achieve a particular purpose.

Following is an excerpt from a floor speech by Congresswoman Shirley Chisholm, the first she gave to the House of Representatives as a newly elected congresswoman in the spring of 1969. President Richard Nixon had also just been elected, in part because he had promised to end America's involvement in the Vietnam War, though that did not happen. Read Chisholm's words carefully, then read them again. Ask some questions, and either annotate the excerpt or make a graphic organizer. Pay close attention to the diction and syntax choices Chisholm makes and how they might help her achieve her purpose.

from People and Peace, Not Profits and War

SHIRLEY CHISHOLM

Mr. Speaker, on the same day President Nixon announced he had decided the United States will not be safe unless we start to build a defense system against missiles, the Head Start program in the District of Columbia was cut back for the lack of money.

As a teacher, and as a woman, I do not think I will ever understand what kind of values can be involved in spending $9 billion — and more, I am sure — on elaborate, unnecessary, and impractical weapons when several thousand disadvantaged children in the nation's capital get nothing.

When the new administration took office, I was one of the many Americans who hoped it would mean that our country would benefit from the fresh perspectives, the new ideas, the different priorities of a leader who had no part in the mistakes of the past. Mr. Nixon had said things like this: "If our cities are to be livable for the next generation, we can delay no longer in launching new approaches to the problems that beset them and to the tensions that tear them apart." And he said, "When you cut expenditures for education, what you are doing is shortchanging the American future."

But frankly, I have never cared too much what people say. What I am interested in is what they do. We have waited to see what the new administration is going to do. The pattern is now becoming clear. . . .

The new secretary of health, education, and welfare, Robert Finch, came to the Hill to tell the House Education and Labor Committee that he thinks we should spend more on education, particularly in city schools. But, he said, unfortunately we cannot "afford" to, until we have reached some kind of honorable solution to the Vietnam War. I was glad to read that the distinguished Member from Oregon [Mrs. Green] asked Mr. Finch this: "With the crisis we have in education, and the crisis in our cities, can we wait to settle the war? Shouldn't it be the other way around? Unless we can meet the crisis in education, we really can't afford the war."

Secretary of Defense Melvin Laird came to Capitol Hill, too. His mission was to sell the anti-ballistic missile insanity to the Senate. He was asked what the new administration is doing about the war. To hear him, one would have thought it was 1968, that the former secretary of state was defending the former policies, that nothing had ever happened, a president had never decided not to run because he knew the nation would reject him in despair over this tragic war we have blundered into. Mr. Laird talked to being prepared to spend at least two more years in Vietnam.

Two more years. Two more years of hunger for Americans, of death for our best young men, of children here at home suffering the lifelong handicap of not having a good education when they are young. Two more years of high taxes collected to feed the cancerous growth of a Defense Department budget that now consumes two-thirds of our federal income.

Two more years of too little being done to fight our greatest enemies — poverty, prejudice, and neglect — here in our own country. Two more years of fantastic waste in the Defense Department and of penny pinching on social programs. Our country cannot survive two more years, or four, of these kinds of policies. It must stop this year — now. . . .

We Americans have come to feel that it is our mission to make the world free. We believe that we are the good guys everywhere — in Vietnam, in Latin America, wherever we go. We believe that we are the good guys at home, too. When the Kerner Commission told white America what black America had always known, that prejudice and hatred built the nation's slums, maintain them, and profit by them, white America would not believe it. But it is true. Unless we start to fight and defeat the enemies of poverty and

5

racism in our own country and make our talk of equality and opportunity ring true, we are exposed as hypocrites in the eyes of the world when we talk about making other people free.

I am deeply disappointed at the clear evidence that the number-one priority of the new administration is to buy more and more weapons of war, to return to the era of the Cold War, to ignore the war we must fight here — the war that is not optional. There is only one way, I believe, to turn these policies around. The Congress can respond to the mandate that the American people have clearly expressed. They have said, "End this war. Stop the waste. Stop the killing. Do something for your own people first." We must find the money to "launch the new approaches," as Mr. Nixon said. We must force the administration to rethink its distorted, unreal scale of priorities. Our

children, our jobless men, our deprived, rejected, and starving fellow citizens must come first.

For this reason, I intend to vote "No" on every money bill that comes to the floor of this House *10* that provides any funds for the Department of Defense — any bill whatsoever — until the time comes when our values and priorities have been turned rightside up again, until the monstrous waste and the shocking profits in the defense budget have been eliminated and our country starts to use its strength, its tremendous resources, for people and peace, not for profits and war.

It was Calvin Coolidge, I believe, who made the comment that "the business of America is business." We are now spending $80 billion a year on defense. That is two-thirds of every tax dollar. At this time, gentlemen, the business of America is war, and it is time for a change.

Preparing to Write

Before beginning a deeper analysis of the message and rhetoric in Chisholm's speech, you may find it helpful to summarize it in a sentence, just to get the main idea on paper. We might sum up the excerpt from "People and Peace, Not Profits and War" as follows:

> Shirley Chisholm's speech urges the U.S. Congress to use the money it is spending on war to fix American cities instead.

This quick paraphrase certainly doesn't cover all the details of the speech or explain why Chisholm's words pack such a rhetorical punch, but it clarifies her purpose and the context of the speech, which is a good starting point.

Let's pause to consider the context, occasion, and purpose of the speech. The speaker, Shirley Chisholm, was an African American woman who began her career as a teacher and who was (at the time) only a couple months into her first term as a Congresswoman representing New York. President Richard Nixon had just been sworn into office, having campaigned on the promise to end America's involvement in the Vietnam War. When Chisholm gave this speech — her first ever on the floor of the House of Representatives — in March of 1969, Nixon had not yet announced plans to withdraw troops from Vietnam, despite how unpopular the war had become with the American public. Chisholm's purpose, as our paraphrase indicates, is to convince her fellow members of Congress to focus on alleviating American poverty instead of continuing to fund the Vietnam War.

ACTIVITY

Carefully reread Shirley Chisholm's speech and create a graphic organizer of your observations. What rhetorical strategies does the Congresswoman employ to convey her message? What is the effect of each of those strategies?

Developing a Thesis Statement

When it comes time to write a rhetorical analysis essay, the first thing to do is craft a **thesis statement**. Your thesis statement must make an argument about the choices the speaker makes and how they help her achieve her purpose. You may end up changing your thesis statement as you go, but having an idea of your argument will help you stay focused.

Let's say your teacher has assigned you the following prompt:

"People and Peace, Not Profits and War" was a speech delivered on the floor of the U.S. House of Representatives on March 26, 1969 by Congresswoman Shirley Chisholm (1924–2005). Read this excerpt from the speech carefully. Then write an essay in which you analyze the rhetorical strategies Chisholm uses to present her argument to her fellow members of Congress. Support your analysis with specific references to the text.

Remember, your thesis should reflect your analysis of the text and the ways in which its rhetoric achieves the speaker's purpose. You should avoid creating a thesis statement that is so broad that it is just a summary of the speech, such as the following:

In her speech "People and Peace, Not Profits and War," Congresswoman Shirley Chisholm attempts to convince her audience of her argument.

Not only does this thesis fail to mention the rhetorical strategies the writer plans to discuss, but it also fails to state the specifics of the argument. A strong thesis identifies both the speaker's purpose and the specific rhetorical strategies the speaker uses to achieve it. This helps create a good blueprint for the body of the essay, where you will analyze how those rhetorical choices contribute to the effectiveness of the speech.

You will also want to make sure that your thesis is not too narrow or just your personal opinion:

Shirley Chisholm's passionate speech to Congress appeals to pathos.

Although this thesis identifies a rhetorical strategy — appeals to pathos— it does not address Chisholm's purpose or the complexity of her argument speech. For example, it doesn't leave room for the writer to examine the ways in which Chisholm establishes credibility or the evidence that she provides to support her argument in the body of the essay. You could not discuss a thesis like this for long before running out of things to say. And, while this thesis expresses an opinion about the tone of the speech, the writer does not connect that opinion to Chisholm's purpose. A good thesis should be expressed clearly and should inform the reader of the scope of the argument you intend to make. It is the backbone of your essay, and everything in the essay will connect to it.

Working with the prompt above, let's consider first how Chisholm establishes credibility by appeals to ethos — and how that supports the strength of her argument. First, Chisholm is committing her speech to the Congressional Record, where it will reside publicly and for posterity. "Mr. Speaker" is the Speaker of the House of Representatives, the head of the body she is addressing. Although she is a junior member of Congress, as a woman and a former teacher she has expertise when it comes to talking about priorities in education and family life. Chisholm mentions several politicians in her speech by name: Richard Nixon, Robert Finch, and Melvin Laird, for example. Her understanding of their political platforms shows that she acknowledges the complexity of the issue, including the counterarguments. Chisholm, newly elected to her first term in office and an African American woman during an era in which feminists and civil rights activists were still struggling to achieve basic guarantees of equality in the eyes of the law, may have needed to establish more than the usual ethos, but her somewhat stiff and formal introduction pays off. Her audience will now be more willing to hear the logical arguments she presents and feel the full emotional impact of the details she weaves into her speech. Finally, of course, Chisholm publicly commits to her principles by announcing that she will vote "No" on every money bill that provides any funding for the Department of Defense "until the time comes when our values and priorities have been turned rightside up again" (para. 11). This forceful statement shows that she intends to stand by her values through concrete action, but also demonstrates her hope for a future in which her votes will not be statements of protest.

Chisholm's argument is guided by the connection she makes between defense spending and education: the announcement of a need for "a defense system against the missiles" happens the same time that "the Head Start program in the District of Columbia [is] cut back for the lack of money." She restates this pattern of cause and effect — money is being spent on "impractical weapons when several thousand disadvantaged children in the nation's capital get nothing" (para. 2) — several times during the speech. She even reminds her audience that President Nixon understood and publicly acknowledged this connection: "And he said, 'When you cut expenditures for education, what you are doing is shortchanging the American future'" (para. 3). The facts and statistics she refers to — "a Defense Department budget that now consumes two-thirds of our federal income" and "$80 billion a year on defense (para. 12)" — provide the evidence Chisholm needs to argue that our priorities must change: there's only so much money. She also includes Congresswoman Green's question to Robert Finch, who was Nixon's Secretary of Health, Education, and Welfare: "With the crisis we have in education, and the crisis in our cities, can we wait to settle the war? Shouldn't it be the other way around?" to further illustrate the poor logic that she argues is guiding policy on defense spending.

Some of Chisholm's most powerful language is reserved for her descriptions of the negative effects of war, both overseas and at home. She assumes her audience knows that she is talking about Lyndon Johnson's decision not to run for a second term because "he knew the nation would reject him in despair over this tragic war. . . ," suggesting that this is common knowledge to all Americans. And yet, Melvin Laird, secretary of defense, is telling the nation to expect at least "two more years in Vietnam" — the very issue that ended the previous president's political career. Chisholm takes those "two years" and, in the next two paragraphs, extends them by outlining what two years means in terms of suffering at home and abroad: young men dead in battle, children uneducated, high taxes, and continuing "poverty, prejudice, and neglect." She makes the issue sound like a disease that must be stopped in its tracks, using words like "handicap," "cancerous," and "consumes." These remind the audience of the very human toll of the policy of putting war and profits ahead of people and peace.

Remembering that it is always important to address a work's complexity, we might develop the following thesis statement in response to the original prompt:

In Shirley Chisholm's 1969 speech to Congress, the young congresswoman establishes her credibility, makes a clear connection between cause and effect, and focuses on the human costs of government policy to argue for the necessity of making people and peace America's first priority.

Organizing a Rhetorical Analysis Essay

Once you have an idea for a thesis statement — and, remember, this "working thesis" can change as you plan and write — you can begin to think about the way you will support it. Look back at the text and at your notes. Think about the ideas that inspired your thesis. Your essay might be organized around the elements of Chisolm's rhetorical strategies, with a paragraph each on how she establishes credibility, the logic of her argument, and its emotional impact, for example. Or you could approach it a different way: you might group your ideas according to the ways Chisholm uses cause and effect to show the consequences of policies she is against, with one paragraph on the causes and one or two paragraphs on the effects.

You've probably noticed that the thesis statement we've suggested is likely to lead to a five-paragraph essay. Perhaps you've been warned to stay away from this organization because it is formulaic or prescriptive. We agree: stay away from the formulaic or prescriptive. However, the five-paragraph essay may or may not fall into that category. There's no rule that says that every question or topic will fit neatly into an introduction, three body paragraphs, and a conclusion. Yet, if you happen to have three points to make, you'll end up with five paragraphs that could form a cogent and insightful essay.

Integrating Quotations

Rhetorical analysis, as you know, requires references to the text, and you should think of the language and rhetoric of a text as evidence to support your thesis. The key is to choose quotations carefully and integrate them as seamlessly as possible into your own writing, avoiding big chunks of quoted text. Just remember that your voice should prevail in a rhetorical analysis essay — that is, you must offer thoughtful commentary on what you quote. One way you might check to make sure that you're providing sufficient analysis of a work is to highlight all your quotations from the text. Here's an example of a paragraph that quotes from Shirley Chisholm's speech.

The idea of "American" values and beliefs is another theme that prevails throughout Chisholm's speech. First, she asks "what kind of values can be involved in spending $9 billion" "weapons when several thousand disadvantaged children in the nation's capital get nothing" (para. 2). The idea of "American" values returns when Chisholm states, "We Americans have come to feel that it is our mission to make the world free. We believe that we are the good guys everywhere." Chisholm talks of the "prejudice and hatred [that built] the nation's slums," pointing out that Americans are "exposed as hypocrites in the eyes of the world when we talk about making other people free." Finally, Chisholm quotes Calvin Coolidge, saying "'the business of America is business'. . . . At this time, gentlemen, the business of America is war, and it is time for a change." With the Vietnam War, the United States is at risk of losing its very identity.

Apart from the topic sentence, the paragraph mostly consists of quotations from the speech. There is little original commentary on the text, and as a result the reader has little insight into the essay writer's thoughts on how Chisholm appeals to her audience, and to what effect. Instead, this paragraph reads more like a list that catalogs the congresswoman's views on American values as expressed in her speech.

Compare that paragraph to the one that follows. While the structure and some of the quotations remain essentially the same, original commentary brings the writer's voice into the paragraph and moves it toward rhetorical analysis by discussing the ways that Chisholm's language choices craft effective rhetoric.

The idea of "American" values and beliefs is another theme that prevails throughout Chisholm's speech. The first mention of higher morals comes when Chisholm questions the administration's policy on financing war machines, asking "what kind of values can be involved in spending $9 billion" on "weapons when several thousand disadvantaged children in the nation's capital get nothing" (para. 2). In Chisholm's eyes, the American government is not upholding the "values" that Chisholm and others hold dear, which is to say education over war and mindless brutality. The idea of "American" values returns when Chisholm states, "We Americans have come to feel that it is our mission to make the world free. We believe that we are the good guys everywhere." The United States is a country built on the fundamental belief of liberty and equality for every one of its constituents, yet Chisholm talks of the "prejudice and hatred [that built] the nation's slums," pointing out that until those problems are solved, the United States is "exposed as hypocrites in the eyes of the world when we talk about making other people free." Finally, the idea of an "American way" comes back in the final paragraph, when Chisholm quotes Calvin Coolidge, saying "'the business of America is business'. . . . At this time, gentlemen, the business of America is war, and it is time for a change." With the Vietnam War, the United States is at risk of losing its very identity, and Chisholm calls for a rapid and important change to keep that from happening.

Documenting Sources

In a rhetorical analysis essay, you are likely only writing about one text, so you won't need a formal Works Cited page. Your teacher may ask you to use paragraph numbers to identify where your quotations can be found, but with a short speech or essay it may be unnecessary. If you do add paragraph numbers, they should go in parentheses after the quotation mark and before your punctuation, like this:

The idea of American values returns when Chisholm states, "We Americans have come to feel that it is our mission to make the world free. We believe that we are the good guys everywhere" (para. 9).

A Sample Rhetorical Analysis Essay

Below is a sample rhetorical analysis essay written by a high school student in response to the prompt we introduced on page 63. After reading the prompt and the essay carefully, respond to the questions that follow.

"People and Peace, Not Profits and War" was a speech delivered on the floor of the U.S. House of Representatives on March 26, 1969 by Congresswoman Shirley Chisholm (1924–2005). Read this excerpt from the speech carefully. Then write an essay in which you analyze the rhetorical strategies Chisholm uses to present her argument to her fellow members of Congress. Support your analysis with specific references to the text.

"People and Peace, Not Profits and War"

by Milutin Gjaja

When Shirley Chisholm took the floor in March 1969, the Vietnam War had been going on for close to 14 years, and the toll it took on the United States and the American people kept growing heavier. In this speech given in Washington D.C., Chisholm explored the consequences of a deadly war at home, emphasized the American values that the United States government should keep to, and entwined past, present, and future to show that, should nothing change, the lives of the American people and the country in general will only get worse.

One of the main rhetorical strategies that Chisholm uses is emphasis on the mindless war the United States is engaged in, and its consequences on U.S. soil. War is an ever-present theme in the speech from the very beginning of the speech, the title: "People and Peace, Not Profits and War." Right away, the Vietnam War is given a negative twist opposing it to the greater "people" and "peace." The first thing Chisholm criticizes about the war is its monetary cost, a gigantic nine billion plus dollars, a sum that feels heavy "when several thousand disadvantaged children in the nation's capital get nothing" (para. 2) because of the lack of funding of the Head Start program. But very quickly, Chisholm turns to the more important expense of the Vietnam War, the cost it has on the American people. This cost is first hinted at in paragraph five, when Chisholm quotes Mrs. Green, a fellow congresswoman, speaking about "'the crisis we have in education'" because of the war. But it is later, when Secretary of Defense Melvin Laird suggests that the war could continue for two more years, that Chisholm fully explores the consequences of further conflict: "Two more years of hunger for Americans, of death for our best young men, of children at home suffering the lifelong handicap of not having a good education"; "two more years of high taxes"; and "two more years of too little being done to fight . . . poverty, prejudice, and neglect" (para. 7). The impact of the war is not simply a financial one, or limited to one sector of everyday life; on the contrary, it touches all aspects of the American peoples' lives, from taxes to education to prejudice to death. As Chisholm explains, this is something that is deeply hurting the country, and until the change that the American people call for: "[The American people] have said, 'End this war. Stop the waste. Stop the killing. Do something for your own people first'" (para. 10) is realized, the country and its constituents will continue to suffer.

The idea of "American" values and beliefs is another theme that prevails throughout Chisholm's speech. The first mention of higher morals comes in the second paragraph, when Chisholm questions the administration's policy on financing war machines, asking "what kind of values can be involved in spending $9 billion" on "weapons when several thousand disadvantaged children in the nation's capital get nothing" (para. 2). In Chisholm's eyes, the American government is not upholding the "values" that Chisholm and others hold dear, which is to say education over war and mindless brutality. The idea of "American" values returns in paragraph nine, when Chisholm states, "We Americans have come to feel that it is our mission to make the world free. We believe that we are the good guys everywhere." The United States is a country built on the fundamental belief of liberty and equality for every one of its constituents, yet Chisholm talks of the "prejudice and hatred [that built] the nation's slums," pointing out that until those problems are solved, the United States is "exposed as hypocrites in the eyes of the world when we talk about making other people free." Finally, the idea of an "American way" comes back in the final paragraph, when Chisholm quotes Calvin Coolidge, saying "'the business of America is business'. . . . At this time, gentlemen, the business of America is war, and it is time for a change." With the Vietnam War, the United States is at risk of losing its very identity, and Chisholm calls for a rapid and important change to keep that from happening.

But perhaps the most powerful part of Chisholm's speech is how she entwines the past, present, and future of the country she serves. This theme is first taken up in the third paragraph, when Chisholm identifies herself as "one of the many Americans who hoped . . . that our country would benefit from the fresh perspectives, the new ideas . . . of a leader who had no part in the mistakes of the past." Right from the start, Chisholm paints a sharp contrast between a bleak past full of "mistakes" and a much more optimistic outlook, something the speaker quotes Mr. Nixon as calling "the American future" later in the paragraph. This theme of contrasting the past and present comes up again in paragraph six, when Chisholm criticizes Secretary of Defense Melvin Laird's views of the war, saying "[t]o hear him, one would have thought it was 1968." Once again, the past of the nation is given a negative connotation, but this time, this depressing past seems to be infecting the present and even the future, something demonstrated by the "two more years" repetition of the next paragraph: "two more years of hunger"; two more years "of death for our best young men"; and "[t]wo more years of high taxes." Chisholm continues with the problems of the present, denouncing the "prejudice and hatred [that built] the nation's slums" and affirming that the government must "fight and defeat the enemies of poverty and racism in our own country." What Chisholm is trying to demonstrate with all these observations is that the past, present, and future of the country are fundamentally intertwined; the mistakes of the past affect the present, and without fixing those mistakes, the future looks glum for the nation. To prevent this, a transformation must occur, something the author announces in her final line: "it is time for a change."

In this speech, Chisholm makes her point about the cost of the Vietnam War and its future consequences with passionate language and powerful rhetorical strategies. The procedures that Chisholm employs to prove her point are widely used by other writers and politicians, should it be the theme of time in Lincoln's Gettysburg Address, or the emphasis on American values in Martin Luther King Jr.'s "I Have a Dream" speech. But the wide use of these strategies only serves to prove their effectiveness, an effectiveness that Chisholm demonstrates in her "People and Peace, Not Profits and War."

QUESTIONS

1. Examine the relationship between the thesis and the topic sentences. Do you think the basic structure of the essay is effective or ineffective? Why?

2. How does the essay support its argument with evidence from the text? Cite evidence that you find especially effective and explain why.

3. The writer argues that Chisholm emphasizes the Vietnam War, shared American values, and the connection of past, present, and future. To

what extent do you think the rhetorical strategies Chisholm employs in her speech support this interpretation?

4. What is another argument you might make based on a rhetorical reading of the Chisholm speech? It does not have to contradict this writer's interpretation entirely, but rather offer another way to read the speech or a different conclusion than the one drawn in this sample essay.

CULMINATING ACTIVITY

Read this speech given by former Secretary of State Hillary Clinton when she conceded the 2016 presidential election to Donald Trump. First, try one of the pre-writing techniques you've learned for close reading to get your observations on paper. Then generate a thesis statement that makes an argument about the choices Clinton made and how they help her achieve her purpose. Finally, write an essay in which you analyze the rhetorical strategies Clinton uses to thank her supporters and encourage them to look to the future.

2016 Concession Speech

HILLARY CLINTON

Thank you. Thank you all very much. Thank you so much.

Very rowdy group. Thank you, my friends. Thank you. Thank you. Thank you so very much for being here. I love you all, too.

Last night I congratulated Donald Trump and offered to work with him on behalf of our country.

I hope that he will be a successful president for all Americans. This is not the outcome we wanted or we worked so hard for, and I'm sorry that we did not win this election for the values we share and the vision we hold for our country.

But I feel pride and gratitude for this wonderful campaign that we built together.

5

This vast, diverse, creative, unruly, energized campaign. You represent the best of America, and being your candidate has been one of the greatest honors of my life.

I know how disappointed you feel, because I feel it too. And so do tens of millions of Americans who invested their hopes and dreams in this effort. This is painful, and it will be for a long time. But I want you to remember this.

Our campaign was never about one person, or even one election. It was about the country we love and building an America that is hopeful, inclusive, and big-hearted. We have seen that our nation is more deeply divided than we thought. But I still believe in America, and I always will. And if you do, then we must accept this result and then look to the future. Donald Trump is going to be our president. We owe him an open mind and the chance to lead. Our constitutional democracy enshrines the peaceful transfer of power.

We don't just respect that. We cherish it. It also enshrines the rule of law; the principle we are all equal in rights and dignity; freedom of worship and expression. We respect and cherish these values, too, and we must defend them.

Let me add: Our constitutional democracy demands our participation, not just every four years, but all the time. So let's do all we can to keep advancing the causes and values we all hold dear. Making our economy work for everyone, not just those at the top, protecting our country and protecting our planet. And breaking down all the barriers that hold any American back from achieving their dreams.

We've spent a year and a half bringing together millions of people from every corner of our country to say with one voice that we believe that the American dream is *10*

big enough for everyone — for people of all races, and religions, for men and women, for immigrants, for LGBT people, and people with disabilities. For everyone.

So now, our responsibility as citizens is to keep doing our part to build that better, stronger, fairer America we seek. And I know you will.

I am so grateful to stand with all of you. I want to thank Tim Kaine and Anne Holton for being our partners on this journey.

It has been a joy getting to know them better, and it gives me great hope and comfort to know that Tim will remain on the front lines of our democracy representing Virginia in the Senate.

To Barack and Michelle Obama, our country owes you an enormous debt of gratitude.

We thank you for your graceful, determined *15* leadership that has meant so much to so many Americans and people across the world. And to Bill and Chelsea, Mark, Charlotte, Aidan, our brothers and our entire family, my love for you means more than I can ever express.

You crisscrossed this country on our behalf and lifted me up when I needed it most — even four-month-old Aidan, who traveled with his mom. I will always be grateful to the talented, dedicated men and women at our headquarters in Brooklyn and across our country.

You poured your hearts into this campaign. To some of you who are veterans, it was a campaign after you had done other campaigns. Some of you, it was your first campaign. I want each of you to know that you were the best campaign anybody could have ever expected or wanted.

And to the millions of volunteers, community leaders, activists and union organizers who knocked on doors, talked to their neighbors, posted on Facebook — even in secret private Facebook sites.

I want everybody coming out from behind that and make sure your voices are heard going forward.

To everyone who sent in contributions, 20 even as small as five dollars, and kept us going, thank you from all of us. And to the young people in particular, I hope you will hear this — I have, as Tim said, spent my entire life fighting for what I believe in.

I've had successes and I've had setbacks. Sometimes, really painful ones. Many of you are at the beginning of your professional, public, and political careers — you will have successes and setbacks too.

This loss hurts, but please never stop believing that fighting for what's right is worth it.

It is, it is worth it.

And so we need — we need you to keep up these fights now and for the rest of your lives. And to all the women, and especially the young women, who put their faith in this campaign and in me: I want you to know that nothing has made me prouder than to be your champion.

Now, I know we have still not shattered 25 that highest and hardest glass ceiling, but some day someone will — and hopefully sooner than we might think right now.

And to all of the little girls who are watching this, never doubt that you are valuable and powerful and deserving of every chance and opportunity in the world to pursue and achieve your own dreams.

Finally, I am so grateful for our country and for all it has given to me.

I count my blessings every single day that I am an American. And I still believe, as deeply as I ever have, that if we stand together and work together with respect for our differences, strengthen our convictions, and love for this nation, our best days are still ahead of us.

Because, you know, I believe we are stronger together and we will go forward together. And you should never, ever regret fighting for that. You know, scripture tells us, "Let us not grow weary of doing good, for in due season, we shall reap if we do not lose heart."

My friends, let us have faith in each other, 30 let us not grow weary and lose heart, for there are more seasons to come and there is more work to do.

I am incredibly honored and grateful to have had this chance to represent all of you in this consequential election.

May God bless you and may God bless the United States of America.

3

Analyzing Arguments
From Reading to Writing

Have you ever changed your mind about something? What caused you to re-examine a belief or idea? Most likely, you read or heard someone else's perspective that challenged you to think about an issue in a different way. It might have been a clear, thoughtful presentation of information, a personal story that tugged at your conscience, a startling statistic, or even a bit of humor or satire that presented a familiar issue in a new and enlightening way. It's less likely that you were bullied into reconsidering your opinion by a loud voice that belittled your ideas. By carefully and respectfully reading the viewpoints of others and considering a range of ideas on an issue, we develop a clearer understanding of our own beliefs — a necessary foundation to writing effective arguments. In this chapter, we're going to analyze elements of argument as a means of critical thinking and an essential step toward crafting your own argumentative essays.

What Is Argument?

Although we have been discussing argument in previous chapters, the focus has been primarily on rhetorical appeals and style. We'll continue examining those elements, but here we take a closer look at an argument's claim, evidence, and organization.

Let's start with some definitions. What is an argument? Is it a conflict? A contest between opposing forces to prove the other side wrong? A battle with words? Or is it, rather, a process of reasoned inquiry and rational discourse seeking common ground? If it is the latter, then we engage in argument whenever we explore ideas

rationally and think clearly about the world. Yet these days, argument is often no more than raised voices interrupting one another, exaggerated assertions without adequate support, and scanty evidence from sources that lack credibility. We might call this "crazed rhetoric," as political commentator Tom Toles does in this cartoon.

This cartoon appeared on January 16, 2011, a few days after Arizona congresswoman Gabrielle Giffords was the victim of a shooting; six people were killed and another thirteen injured. Many people saw this tragedy as stemming from vitriolic political discourse that included violent language. Toles argues that Uncle Sam, and thus the country, is in danger of being devoured by "crazed rhetoric." There may not be a "next trick" or a "taming" if the rhetorical lion continues to roar.

Is Toles's view exaggerated? Whether you answer yes or no to that question, it seems quite clear that partisanship and polarization often hold sway over dialogue and civility when people think of argument. In our discussions, however, we define **argument** as a persuasive discourse, a coherent and considered movement from a claim to a conclusion. The goal of this chapter is to avoid thinking of argument as a zero-sum game of winners and losers but, instead, to see it as a means of better understanding other people's ideas as well as your own.

In Chapter 1 we discussed concession and refutation as a way to acknowledge a counterargument, and we want to re-emphasize the usefulness of that approach. Viewing anyone who disagrees with you as an adversary makes it very likely that the conversation will escalate into an emotional clash, and treating opposing ideas disrespectfully rarely results in mutual understanding. Twentieth-century psychologist Carl Rogers stressed the importance of replacing confrontational argument tactics with ones that promote negotiation, compromise, and cooperation. **Rogerian arguments** are based on the assumption that having a full understanding of an opposing position is essential to responding to it persuasively and refuting it in a way that is accommodating rather than alienating or antagonizing. Ultimately, the goal of a Rogerian argument is not to destroy your opponents or dismantle their viewpoints but rather to reach a conclusion that is satisfying to all participants.

So what does a civil argument look like? Let's examine a short article that appeared in *Ode* magazine in 2009 entitled "Why Investing in Fast Food May Be a Good Thing." In this piece, Amy Domini, a financial advisor and leading voice for socially responsible investing, argues the counterintuitive position that investing in the fast-food industry can be an ethically responsible choice.

Why Investing in Fast Food May Be a Good Thing

AMY DOMINI

My friends and colleagues know I've been an advocate of the Slow Food movement for many years. Founded in Italy 20 years ago, Slow Food celebrates harvests from small-scale family farms, prepared slowly and lovingly with regard for the health and environment of diners. Slow Food seeks to preserve crop diversity, so the unique taste of "heirloom" apples, tomatoes and other foods don't perish from the Earth. I wish everyone would choose to eat this way. The

positive effects on the health of our bodies, our local economies and our planet would be incalculable. Why then do I find myself investing in fast-food companies?

The reason is social investing isn't about investing in perfect companies. (Perfect companies, it turns out, don't exist.) We seek to invest in companies that are moving in the right direction and listening to their critics. We offer a road map to bring those companies to the next level, step by step. No social standard causes us to reject restaurants, even fast-food ones, out of hand. Although we favor local, organic food, we recognize it isn't available in every community, and is often priced above the means of the average household. Many of us live more than 100 miles from a working farm.

Fast food is a way of life. In America, the average person eats it more than 150 times a year. In 2007, sales for the 400 largest U.S.-based fast-food chains totaled $277 billion, up 7 percent from 2006.

Fast food is a global phenomenon. Major chains and their local competitors open restaurants in nearly every country. For instance, in Greece, burgers and pizza are supplanting the traditional healthy Mediterranean diet of fish, olive oil and vegetables. Doctors are treating Greek children for diabetes, high cholesterol and high blood pressure — ailments rarely seen in the past.

The fast-food industry won't go away anytime soon. But in the meantime, it can be changed. And because it's so enormous, even seemingly modest changes can have a big impact. In 2006, New York City banned the use of trans-fats (a staple of fast food) in restaurants, and in 2008, California became the first state to do so. When McDonald's moved to non-trans-fats for making French fries, the health benefits were widespread. Another area of concern is fast-food packaging, which causes forest destruction and creates a lot of waste. In the U.S. alone, 1.8 million tons of packaging is generated each year. Fast-food containers make up about 20

percent of litter, and packaging for drinks and snacks adds another 20 percent.

A North Carolina — based organization called the Dogwood Alliance has launched an effort to make fast-food companies reduce waste and source paper responsibly. Through a campaign called No Free Refills, the group is pressing fast-food companies to reduce their impact on the forests of the southern U.S., the world's largest paper-producing region. They're pushing companies to:

- Reduce the overuse of packaging.
- Maximize use of 100 percent post-consumer recycled boxboard.
- Eliminate paper packaging from the most biologically important endangered forests.
- Eliminate paper packaging from suppliers that convert natural forests into industrial pine plantations.
- Encourage packaging suppliers to source fiber from responsibly managed forests certified by the Forest Stewardship Council.
- Recycle waste in restaurants to divert paper and other material from landfills.

Will the fast-food companies adopt all these measures overnight? No. But along with similar efforts worldwide, this movement signals that consumers and investors are becoming more conscious of steps they can take toward a better world — beginning with the way they eat.

While my heart will always be with Slow Food, I recognize the fast-food industry can improve and that some companies are ahead of others on that path.

Domini begins by reminding her readers of her ethos as "an advocate of the Slow Food movement for many years." By describing some of the goals and tenets of that movement, including the "positive effects" it can have, she establishes common ground before she discusses her position — one that the Slow Food advocates are not likely to embrace, at least not initially. In fact, instead of asserting her position in a strong declarative sentence, Domini asks a question that invites her audience to hear her explanation: "Why then do I find myself investing in fast-food companies?" She provides evidence that supports her choice to take that action: she uses statistics to show that slow food is not available in all communities, while fast food is an expanding industry. She uses the example of Greece to show that fast food is becoming a global phenomenon. By giving numerous examples of how fast-food companies are improving ingredients and reducing waste, she illustrates how working to change fast-food practices can have a significant impact on public health and the environment. After presenting her viewpoint, Domini ends by acknowledging that her "heart will always be with Slow Food"; but that fact should not preclude her supporting those in the fast-food industry who are making socially and environmentally responsible decisions.

ACTIVITY

Identify at least two points in Domini's article where she might have given way to accusation or blame or where she might have dismissed the Slow Food movement as being shortsighted or elitist. Discuss how, instead, she finds common ground and promotes dialogue with her audience through civil discourse.

Staking a Claim

Every argument has a **claim** — also called an assertion or proposition — that states the argument's main idea or position. A claim differs from a topic or a subject in that a claim has to be arguable. It can't just be a simple statement of fact; it has to state a position with which people might agree or disagree. Going from a simple topic to a claim means stating your informed opinion about a topic. In the essay you just read, the general topic is social investing — specifically, social investing in the fast-food industry. The arguable claim, however, is that investing in fast-food companies can be socially responsible. Notice that the topic may be a single word or a phrase, but the arguable claim has to be stated as a complete sentence.

It's important to note that neither a published author nor a student writer is likely to develop a strong claim without exploring a topic through reading about it, discussing it with others, brainstorming, taking notes, and rethinking. Only after looking into a topic thoroughly are you ready to develop a position on an issue. For example, let's use the topic of single-sex classrooms. You'll notice, first of all, that a simple statement of the topic does not indicate whether you support the notion or challenge it. Let's consider several directions to take with this topic.

- Many schools have single-sex classrooms.
- Single-sex classrooms have been around for years, especially in private schools.
- Single-sex classrooms are ineffective because they do not prepare students for the realities of the workplace.

The first statement may be true, but it is easily verified and not arguable; thus, it is simply a topic and not a claim. The second statement has more detail, but it's easy to verify whether it is true or not. Since it is not arguable, it's not a claim. The third statement is a claim because it is arguable. It argues that single-sex classrooms are ineffective and that preparation for the workplace is an important way to measure the effectiveness of an education. There are those who would disagree with both statements and those who would agree with both. Thus, it presents an arguable position and is a viable claim.

For each of the following statements, evaluate whether it is arguable or too easily verifiable to develop into an effective argument. Try revising the ones you consider too easily verifiable to make them into arguable claims.

1. Owners of SUVs should be required to pay an energy surcharge.
2. Charter schools are an alternative to public schools.
3. Ronald Reagan was the most charismatic president of the twentieth century.
4. Requiring students to wear uniforms improves school spirit.
5. The terms *global warming* and *climate change* describe different perspectives on this complex issue.
6. Students graduating from college today can expect to have more debt than any previous generation.
7. People who read novels are more likely to attend sports events and movies than those who do not.
8. Print newspapers will not survive another decade.
9. The competition among countries to become a site for the Olympic Games is fierce.
10. Plagiarism is a serious problem in today's schools.

Types of Claims

Typically, we speak of three types of claims: claims of fact, claims of value, and claims of policy. Each type can be used to guide entire arguments, which we would call arguments of fact, arguments of value, and arguments of policy. While it is helpful to separate the three for analysis, in practice it is not always that simple. Indeed, it's quite common for an argument to include more than one type of claim, as you will see in the following examples.

Claims of Fact

Claims of fact assert that something is true or not true. You can't argue whether Zimbabwe is in Africa or whether restaurants on Main Street serve more customers at breakfast than at lunch. These issues can be resolved and verified — in the first case, by checking a map, in the second, through observation or by checking sales figures. You can, however, argue that Zimbabwe has an unstable government or that restaurants on Main Street are more popular with older patrons than younger ones.

Those statements are arguable: What does "unstable" mean? What does "popular" mean? Who is "older" and who is "younger"?

Arguments of fact often pivot on what exactly is "factual." Facts become arguable when they are questioned, when they raise controversy, when they challenge people's beliefs. "It's a fact that the Social Security program will go bankrupt by 2025" is a claim that could be developed in an argument of fact. Very often, so-called facts are a matter of interpretation. At other times, new "facts" call into question older ones. The claim that cell phones increase the incidence of brain tumors, for instance, requires sifting through new "facts" from medical research and scrutinizing who is carrying out the research, who is supporting it financially, and so on. Whenever you are evaluating or writing an argument of fact, it's important to approach your subject with a healthy skepticism.

In "Why Investing in Fast Food May Be a Good Thing," Domini makes two claims of fact. The argument in paragraph 3 is guided by the claim of fact that "fast food is a way of life." Is it? She supports this claim with sales statistics and information on the growth of this industry. Paragraph 4 is guided by the claim of fact that "fast food is a global phenomenon." She supports this claim with an explanation of fast-food restaurants opening "in nearly every country" and a specific example discussing the changing diet in Greece.

Claims of Value

Perhaps the most common type of claim is a **claim of value**, which argues that something is good or bad, right or wrong, desirable or undesirable. Of course, just like any other claim, a claim of value must be arguable. Claims of value may be personal judgments based on taste, or they may be more objective evaluations based on external criteria. For instance, if you argue that Ryan Gosling is the best leading man in Hollywood, that's simply a matter of taste. The criteria for what is "best" and what defines a "leading man" are strictly personal. Another person could argue that while Gosling might be the best-looking actor in Hollywood, Dwayne "The Rock" Johnson — whose movies include critically panned blockbusters such as the *Fast and Furious* franchise — was the highest paid actor in 2016, and his movies tend to make more money. That is an evaluation based on external criteria — dollars and cents.

To develop an argument from a claim of value, you must establish specific criteria or standards and then show to what extent the subject meets your criteria. Amy Domini's argument is largely one of value as she supports her claim that investing in fast-food companies can be a positive thing. The very title of Domini's essay suggests a claim of value: "Why Investing in Fast Food May Be a Good Thing." She develops her argument by explaining the impact that such investing can have on what food choices are available, and what the impact of those choices is.

Entertainment reviews — of movies, television shows, concerts, books — are good examples of arguments developed from claims of value. Take a look at this 1977 review of the first *Star Wars* movie by movie critic Roger Ebert. He raved. Notice how he states his four-star claim — it's a great movie! — in several ways throughout the argument and sets up his criteria at each juncture.

Star Wars

ROGER EBERT

Every once in a while I have what I think of as an out-of-the-body experience at a movie. When the ESP people use a phrase like that, they're referring to the sensation of the mind actually leaving the body and spiriting itself off to China or Peoria or a galaxy far, far away. When I use the phrase, I simply mean that my imagination has forgotten it is actually present in a movie theater and thinks it's up there on the screen. In a curious sense, the events in the movie seem real, and I seem to be a part of them.

Ebert's first criterion is whether a film transports him.

Ebert's claim of value. Stated more formally, it might read: "Star Wars is so good that it will completely draw you in."

Star Wars works like that. My list of other out-of-the-body films is a short and odd one, ranging from the artistry of *Bonnie and Clyde* or *Cries and Whispers* to the slick commercialism of *Jaws* and the brutal strength of *Taxi Driver*. On whatever level (sometimes I'm not at all sure) they engage me so immediately and powerfully that I lose my detachment, my analytical reserve. The movie's happening, and it's happening to me.

What makes the *Star Wars* experience unique, though, is that it happens on such an innocent and often funny level. It's usually violence that draws me so deeply into a movie — violence ranging from the psychological torment of a Bergman character to the mindless crunch of a shark's jaws. Maybe movies that scare us find the most direct route to our imaginations. But there's hardly any violence at all in *Star Wars* (and even then it's presented as essentially bloodless swashbuckling). Instead, there's entertainment so direct and simple that all of the complications of the modern movie seem to vaporize.

Ebert asserts that Star Wars is not just different from the other films he has cited; it is "unique."

Ebert elaborates on why it is "unique" — pointing out that its power lies in directness and simplicity rather than violence and brutality.

Star Wars is a fairy tale, a fantasy, a legend, finding its roots in some of our most popular fictions. The golden robot, lion-faced space pilot, and insecure little computer on wheels must have been suggested by the Tin Man, the Cowardly Lion, and the Scarecrow in *The Wizard of Oz*. The journey from one end of the galaxy to another is out of countless thousands of space operas. The hardware is from *Flash Gordon* out of *2001: A Space Odyssey*, the chivalry is from Robin Hood, the heroes are from Westerns, and the villains are a cross between Nazis and sorcerers. *Star Wars* taps the pulp fantasies buried in our memories, and because it's done so brilliantly, it reactivates old thrills, fears, and exhilarations we thought we'd abandoned when we read our last copy of *Amazing Stories*.

Another criterion is the effectiveness of the storytelling. Here it is literally the stuff of legends, managing somehow to be both new and nostalgic.

Ebert addresses a counterargument. He knows that many people will praise the special effects in the film. He acknowledges that they are "good" — but that is not one of his chief criteria.

The movie works so well for several reasons, and they don't all have to do with the spectacular special effects. The effects are good, yes, but great effects have been used in such movies as *Silent Running* and *Logan's Run* without setting all-time box-office records. No, I think the key to *Star Wars* is more basic than that.

5

The movie relies on the strength of pure narrative, in the most basic storytelling form known to man, the Journey. All of the best tales we remember from our childhoods had to do with heroes setting out to travel down roads filled with danger, and hoping to find treasure or heroism at the journey's end. In *Star Wars*, George Lucas takes this simple and powerful framework into outer space, and that is an inspired thing to do, because we no longer have maps on Earth that warn, "Here there be dragons." We can't fall off the edge of the map, as Columbus could, and we can't hope to find new continents of prehistoric monsters or lost tribes ruled by immortal goddesses. Not on Earth, anyway, but anything is possible in space, and Lucas goes right ahead and shows us very nearly everything. We get involved quickly, because the characters in *Star Wars* are so strongly and simply drawn and have so many small foibles and large, futile hopes for us to identify with. And then Lucas does an interesting thing. As he sends his heroes off to cross the universe and do battle with the Forces of Darth Vader, the evil Empire, and the awesome Death Star, he gives us lots of special effects, yes — ships passing into hyperspace, alien planets, an infinity of stars — but we also get a wealth of strange living creatures, and Lucas correctly guesses that they'll be more interesting for us than all the intergalactic hardware.

The most fascinating single scene, for me, was the one set in the bizarre saloon on the planet Tatooine. As that incredible collection of extraterrestrial alcoholics and bug-eyed martini drinkers lined up at the bar, and as Lucas so slyly let them exhibit characteristics that were universally human, I found myself feeling a combination of admiration and delight. *Star Wars* had placed me in the presence of really magical movie invention: Here, all mixed together, were whimsy and fantasy, simple wonderment and quietly sophisticated storytelling.

When Stanley Kubrick was making *2001* in the late 1960s, he threw everything he had into the special effects depicting outer space, but he finally decided not to show any aliens at all — because they were impossible to visualize, he thought. But they weren't at all, as *Star Wars* demonstrates, and the movie's delight in the possibilities of alien life forms is at least as much fun as its conflicts between the space cruisers of the Empire and the Rebels.

And perhaps that helps to explain the movie's one weakness, which is that the final assault on the Death Star is allowed to go on too long. Maybe, having invested so much money and sweat in his special effects, Lucas couldn't bear to see them trimmed. But the magic of *Star Wars* is only dramatized by the special effects; the movie's heart is in its endearingly human (and non-human) people.

Ebert moves into his principal criterion: the value of the classic hero's journey that Star Wars embodies.

Another criterion: The movie is good because the characters are both familiar . . .

. . . and unfamiliar.

Ebert applies his criteria to one specific scene.

He reiterates his claim by emphasizing that it is not the technology of special effects but the humanity of the characters that makes the film great.

Ebert concedes that the film does have a flaw.

Find a review of a movie, a television show, a concert, an album or a song, or another form of popular culture. Identify the claim in the review. What criteria does the reviewer use to justify a thumbs-up or a thumbs-down?

Claims of Policy

Anytime you propose a change, you're making a **claim of policy**. It might be local: a group at your school proposes to raise money to contribute to a school in Haiti, or you want your parents to let you spend more time with friends on weeknights. Or, it might be a bigger issue, such as a proposal for transitioning to alternative energy sources, a change in copyright laws for digital music, a shift in foreign policy, or a change in legislation to allow former felons to vote.

An argument of policy generally begins with a definition of the problem (claim of fact), explains why it is a problem (claim of value), and then explains the change that needs to happen (claim of policy). Also, keep in mind that while an argument of policy usually calls for some direct action to take place, it may simply be a recommendation for a change in attitude or viewpoint.

Let's take a look at the opening paragraphs of an argument of policy. In this piece, published in 1999 in *Newsweek*, Anna Quindlen argues for a change in attitude toward the treatment of mental illness. Notice how she combines claims of fact and value to ground her claim of policy — that is, that attitudes toward mental illness must change so that treatment options become more available.

from The C Word in the Hallways

ANNA QUINDLEN

The saddest phrase I've read in a long time is this one: psychological autopsy. That's what the doctors call it when a kid kills himself and they go back over the plowed ground of his short life, and discover all the hidden markers that led to the rope, the blade, the gun.

Claim of value

There's a plague on all our houses, and since it doesn't announce itself with lumps or spots or protest marches, it has gone unremarked in the quiet suburbs and busy cities where it has been laying waste. The number of suicides and homicides committed by teenagers, most often young men, has exploded in the last three decades, until it has become commonplace to have black-bordered photographs in yearbooks and murder suspects with acne problems. And everyone searches for reasons, and scapegoats, and solutions, most often punitive. Yet one solution continues to elude us, and that is ending the ignorance about mental health, and moving it from the margins of care and into the mainstream where it belongs. As surely as any vaccine, this would save lives.

Claim of fact

Claim of policy

So many have already been lost. This month Kip Kinkel was sentenced to life in prison in Oregon for the murders of his parents and a shooting rampage at his high school that killed two students. A psychiatrist who specializes in the care of adolescents testified that Kinkel, now 17, had been hearing voices since he was 12. Sam Manzie is also 17. He is serving a 70-year sentence for luring an 11-year-old boy named Eddie Werner into his New Jersey home and strangling him with the cord of an alarm clock because his Sega Genesis was out of reach. Manzie had his first psychological evaluation in the first grade.

Quindlen calls for "ending the ignorance" about mental health and its care. As she develops her argument, she supports this claim of policy by considering both personal examples and general facts about mental health in America. To arrive at this claim of policy, however, she first makes a claim of value — "There's a plague on all our houses": that is, this is a problem deserving of our attention. She then offers a claim of fact that demonstrates the scope of the problem: teenage suicide and homicide in the last decades have "exploded." Granted, all three of these claims need to be explained with appropriate evidence, and Quindlen does that in subsequent paragraphs; but at the outset, she establishes claims of value and fact that lay the foundation for the claim of policy that is the main idea of her argument.

ACTIVITY

Read the following editorial, which appeared in the *New York Times* in 2004. Annotate it to identify claims of fact, value, and policy; then describe how these interact throughout the argument.

Felons and the Right to Vote

NEW YORK TIMES EDITORIAL BOARD

About 4.7 million Americans, more than 2 percent of the adult population, are barred from voting because of a felony conviction. Denying the vote to ex-offenders is anti-democratic, and undermines the nation's commitment to rehabilitating people who have paid their debt to society. Felon disenfranchisement laws also have a sizable racial impact: 13 percent of black men have had their votes taken away, seven times the national average. But even if it were acceptable as policy, denying felons the vote has been a disaster because of the chaotic and partisan way it has been carried out.

Thirty-five states prohibit at least some people from voting after they have been released from prison. The rules about which felonies are covered and when the right to vote is restored vary widely from state to state, and often defy logic. In four states, including New York, felons on parole cannot vote, but felons on probation can. In some states, felons must formally apply for restoration of their voting rights, which state officials can grant or deny on the most arbitrary of grounds.

Florida may have changed the outcome of the 2000 presidential election when Secretary of State Katherine Harris oversaw a purge of

83

suspected felons that removed an untold number of eligible voters from the rolls. This year, state officials are conducting a new purge that may be just as flawed. They have developed a list of 47,000 voters who may be felons, and have asked local officials to consider purging them. But the *Miami Herald* found that more than 2,100 of them may have been listed in error, because their voting rights were restored by the state's clemency process. Last week, the state acknowledged that 1,600 of those on the list should be allowed to vote.

Election officials are also far too secretive about felon voting issues, which should be a matter of public record. When Ms. Harris used inaccurate standards for purging voters, the public did not find out until it was too late. This year, the state tried to keep the 47,000 names on its list of possible felons secret, but fortunately a state court ruled this month that they should be open to scrutiny.

There is a stunning lack of information and transparency surrounding felon disenfranchisement across the country. The rules are often highly technical, and little effort is made to explain them to election officials or to the people affected. In New York, the Brennan Center for Justice at New York University Law School found that local elections offices often did not understand the law, and some demanded that felons produce documents that do not exist. 5

Too often, felon voting is seen as a partisan issue. In state legislatures, it is usually Democrats who try to restore voting rights, and Republicans who resist. Recently, Republicans and election officials in Missouri and South Dakota have raised questions about voter registration groups' employment of ex-felons, although they have every right to be involved in political activity. In Florida, the decision about whether a felon's right to vote will be restored lies with a panel made up of the governor and members of his cabinet. Some voting rights activists believe that Gov. Jeb Bush has moved slowly, and reinstated voting rights for few of the state's ex-felons, to help President Bush's re-election prospects.

The treatment of former felons in the electoral system cries out for reform. The cleanest and fairest approach would be simply to remove the prohibitions on felon voting. In his State of the Union address in January, President Bush announced a new national commitment to helping prisoners re-enter society. Denying them the right to vote belies this commitment.

Restoring the vote to felons is difficult, because it must be done state by state, and because ex-convicts do not have much of a political lobby. There have been legislative successes in recent years in some places, including Alabama and Nevada. But other states have been moving in the opposite direction. The best hope of reform may lie in the courts. The Atlanta-based United States Court of Appeals for the 11th Circuit and the San Francisco — based Court of Appeals for the Ninth Circuit have ruled recently that disenfranchising felons may violate equal protection or the Voting Rights Act.

Until the whole idea of permanently depriving felons of their right to vote is wiped away, the current rules should be applied more fairly. The quality of voting roll purges must be improved. Florida should discontinue its current felon purge until it can prove that the list it is using is accurate.

Mechanisms for restoring voting rights to felons must be improved. Even in states where felons have the right to vote, they are rarely notified of this when they exit prison. Released prisoners should be given that information during the discharge process, and helped with the paperwork. 10

The process for felons to regain their voting rights should be streamlined. In Nevada, early reports are that the restoration of felon voting rights has had minimal effect, because the paperwork requirements are too burdensome.

Ex-felons who apply to vote should have the same presumption of eligibility as other voters.

Voting rights should not be a political football. There should be bipartisan support for efforts to help ex-felons get their voting rights back, by legislators and by state and local election officials. American democracy is diminished when officeholders and political parties, for their own political gain, try to keep people from voting.

ANALYZING VISUAL TEXTS

Identifying Claims

We have just discussed three types of **claims** — also called assertions or propositions — that texts can make: claims of fact, claims of value, and claims of policy. Just as written texts do, images also make these types of claims. Remember, a claim differs from a subject in that it has to be debatable, and a strong claim derives from an informed and carefully considered opinion about the topic at hand. Consider the following public service announcement (PSA), created by an organization called Canadian Journalists for Free Expression (CJFE).

Let's consider the claims this PSA makes. It's hard to see a claim of fact here since we're looking at an assault weapon made up of camera and sound equipment — clearly an image generated by imagination rather than fact. The use of recording and film equipment to create a deadly weapon does, however, present a claim of value by establishing an overt connection between access to information and firepower. The text, overshadowed by the image, offers a verbal metaphor, "Information Is Ammunition," another claim of value rather than fact. There is a claim of policy as well: "Defend press freedom" by visiting the organization's website. The CJFE ad argues in favor of freedom of information by making a claim of value that connects information to power. Its claim of policy, asking the viewer to support their organization, calls the viewer to action.

ACTIVITY

The following image is one of several in a series of ads created by the World Wildlife Fund in 2007 to raise awareness about deforestation. What claims does this image make? Try to identify at least two.

15km² of rain forest disappears every minute

WWF

From Claim to Thesis

To develop a claim into a thesis statement, you have to be more specific about what you intend to argue. In her essay "The C Word in the Hallways," Anna Quindlen states her main idea explicitly:

> Yet one solution continues to elude us, and that is ending the ignorance about mental health, and moving it from the margins of care and into the mainstream where it belongs. As surely as any vaccine, this would save lives.

The "policy" that Quindlen advocates changing is removing the stigma from mental illness so it can be properly treated. Her second sentence emphasizes her thesis by drawing an analogy: just as vaccines save lives by preventing disease, a shift in policy toward mental illness would save lives by preventing violence.

Sometimes in professional essays the claim may be implicit, but in the formal essays that you will write for your classes, the claim is traditionally stated explicitly as a one-sentence thesis statement that appears in the introduction of your argument. To be effective, a thesis statement must preview the essay by encapsulating in clear, unambiguous language the main point or points the writer intends to make. Let's consider several different types of thesis statements: a closed thesis, an open thesis, and a thesis that includes the counterargument.

Closed Thesis Statements

A **closed thesis** is a statement of the main idea of the argument that also previews the major points the writer intends to make. It is "closed" because it limits the number of points the writer will make. For instance, here is a closed thesis on the appeal of the Harry Potter book series:

> The three-dimensional characters, exciting plots, and complex themes of the books in the Harry Potter series make them not only legendary children's books but enduring literary classics.

This thesis asserts that the series constitutes a "literary classic" and specifies three reasons — characters, plots, and themes — each of which would be discussed in the argument. A closed thesis often includes (or implies) the word *because*. This one might have been written as follows:

> The books in the Harry Potter series have become legendary children's books and enduring literary classics <u>because</u> of their three-dimensional characters, exciting plots, and complex themes.

Indeed, that statement might be a good working thesis.

A closed thesis is a reliable way to focus a short essay, particularly one written under time constraints. Explicitly stating the points you'll make can help you organize your thoughts when you are working against the clock, and it can be a way to address specific points that are required by the prompt or argument.

Open Thesis Statements

If, however, you are writing a longer essay with five, six, or even more main points, then an open thesis is probably more effective. An **open thesis** is one that does not list all the points the writer intends to cover in an essay. If you have six or seven points in an essay, for instance, stringing them all out in the thesis will be awkward; plus, while a reader can remember two or three main points, it's confusing to keep track of a whole string of points made way back in an opening paragraph. For instance, you might argue that the Harry Potter series is far from an enduring classic because you think its main characters are either all good or all bad rather than a bit of both, its minor characters devolve into caricatures, the plots are repetitive and formulaic, the magic does not follow a logical system of rules, and so on. Imagine trying to line all those ideas up in a sentence or two having any clarity and grace at all. By making the overall point without actually stating every subpoint, an open thesis can guide an essay without being cumbersome:

> The popularity of the Harry Potter series demonstrates that simplicity trumps complexity when it comes to the taste of readers, both young and old.

Counterargument Thesis Statements

A variant of the open and closed thesis is the **counterargument thesis**, in which a summary of a counterargument, usually qualified by *although* or *but,* precedes the writer's opinion. This type of thesis has the advantage of immediately addressing the counterargument. Doing so may make an argument seem both stronger and more reasonable. It may also create a seamless transition to a more thorough concession and refutation of the counterargument later in the argument. Using the Harry Potter example again, let's look at a counterargument thesis:

> Although the Harry Potter series may have some literary merit, its popularity has less to do with storytelling than with merchandising.

This thesis concedes a counterargument that the series "may have some literary merit" before refuting that claim by saying that the storytelling itself is less popular than the movies, toys, and other merchandise that the books inspired. The thesis promises some discussion of literary merit and a critique of its storytelling (concession and refutation) but will ultimately focus on the role of the merchandising machine in making Harry Potter a household name.

Note that the thesis that considers a counterargument can also lead to a position that is a modification or qualification rather than an absolute statement of support or rejection. If, for instance, you were asked to discuss whether the success of the Harry Potter series has resulted in a reading renaissance, this thesis would let you respond not with a firm "yes" or "no," but with a qualification of "in some respects." It would allow you to ease into a critique by first recognizing its strengths before leveling your criticism that the popularity was the result of media hype rather than quality and thus will not result in a reading renaissance.

Presenting Evidence

Once a writer has established a claim and developed a thesis statement, the next step is to support it with effective evidence. What evidence to present, how much is necessary, and how to present it are all rhetorical choices guided by an understanding of the audience. A person speaking to a group of scientists will more likely need facts and figures to persuade her audience, while one writing an essay for a local newspaper might want to use an anecdote to grab the audience's attention. Amy Domini, knowing that her audience — the generally affluent and liberal readers of *Ode* magazine — will include many who are hostile to fast food, presents evidence regarding the positive changes that fast-food companies are making, as well as numerical evidence showing that fast food is a growing phenomenon that could have either a positive or a negative impact on health and the environment. Keep audience in mind throughout this discussion of evidence, particularly in terms of whether your audience would be persuaded more by formal or informal sources.

Relevant, Accurate, and Sufficient Evidence

Regardless of the type of evidence a writer chooses to use, it should always be relevant, accurate, and sufficient. Relevant evidence is evidence that specifically applies to the argument being made. To argue that a particular car is superior from a dependability standpoint, bringing in evidence about its maintenance record would be relevant, but talking about its hand-tooled leather seats would not. Generally, good writers do not leave the relevance of a piece of evidence to the reader's imagination; they explicitly spell out what the relationship is between an example and the argument at hand.

Presenting accurate information means taking care to quote sources correctly without misrepresenting what the sources are saying or taking the information out of context. One way to ensure that you have accurate evidence is to get it from a credible source. Think carefully about the bias any source might have. Is it partisan or backed financially by a company or industry group? These concerns may be especially crucial when using sources from the Internet. Even statistical data can be inaccurate if it is from a source that has gathered the data in a way that fits its own agenda. Accuracy can also be a matter of the audience's perception. You should choose sources that they will find credible. If you want accurate dependability information about a car, some reliable sources might include a reputable mechanic, a magazine reviewer who has compared the car's performance to other similar cars, or simply someone who has owned the car for a long time.

Finally, you should include a sufficient amount of evidence to support your thesis. If you based your entire argument about the car's dependability on an interview with a single mechanic, that would not be persuasive. A mechanic only sees the cars that break down, so perhaps his viewpoint is overly negative.

Logical Fallacies

Before we turn to specific types of evidence, let's consider **logical fallacies**: potential vulnerabilities or weaknesses in an argument. Practically speaking, the logical breakdown in most weak arguments occurs in the use of evidence, since evidence is what we use to prove arguments. So a more practical definition of a fallacy might be a failure to make a logical connection between the claim and the evidence used to support that claim. Fallacies may be accidental, but they can also be used deliberately to manipulate or deceive.

Regardless of whether they are intentional or unintentional, logical fallacies work against the clear, civil discourse that should be at the heart of argument. By checking for logical fallacies in a published argument that you're analyzing, you can identify weak points; by checking for fallacies in your own writing, you can revise to strengthen your argument. It's more important that you notice these fallacies and be able to describe what you see than it is to be able to label them by their technical name. The concepts are more important than the terms.

Fallacies of Relevance

One characteristic of evidence we have just discussed is relevance. Fallacies that result from using evidence that's irrelevant to the claim fall under the general heading of red herrings. (The term derives from the dried fish that trainers used to distract dogs when teaching them to hunt foxes.) A **red herring** occurs when a speaker skips to a new and irrelevant topic in order to avoid the topic of discussion. If Politician X says, "We can debate these regulations until the cows come home, but what the American people want to know is, when are we going to end this partisan bickering?" she has effectively avoided providing evidence on the benefits or detriments of the regulations by trying to change the subject to that of partisanship.

One common type of red herring is an ***ad hominem* fallacy**. *Ad hominem* is Latin for "to the man"; the phrase refers to the diversionary tactic of switching the argument from the issue at hand to the character of the other speaker. If you argue that a park in your community should not be renovated because the person supporting it was arrested during a domestic dispute, then you are guilty of *ad hominem* — arguing against the person rather than addressing the issue. This fallacy is frequently misunderstood to mean that *any* instance of questioning someone's character is *ad hominem*. Not so. It is absolutely valid to call a person's character into question if it is *relevant* to the topic at hand. For example, if a court case hinges on the testimony of a single witness and that person happens to be a con artist, then his character is absolutely relevant in deciding whether he is a credible witness.

Analogy is the most vulnerable type of evidence because it is always susceptible to the charge that two things are not comparable, resulting in a **faulty analogy**. However, some analogies are more vulnerable than others, particularly those that focus on irrelevant or inconsequential similarities between two things. Whenever analogy is used, it's important to gauge whether the dissimilarities outweigh the similarities. Advertisements sometimes draw faulty analogies to appeal to pathos; for example, an ad for a very expensive watch might picture a well-known athlete or a ballet dancer and draw an analogy between the precision and artistry of (1) the person, and (2) the mechanism. When writers use analogy to add drama to a claim, it's important to question whether the similarities really fit and illuminate the point or simply add emotional appeal. For instance, to argue that "we put animals who are in irreversible pain out of their misery, so we should do the same for people" asks the reader to ignore significant and profound differences between animals and people. The analogy may at first glance appeal to emotions, but it is logically irrelevant.

Fallacies of Accuracy

Using evidence that is either intentionally or unintentionally inaccurate will result in a fallacy. The most common example of inaccurate evidence resulting in a fallacy is one called the straw man. A **straw man fallacy** occurs when a speaker chooses a deliberately poor or oversimplified example in order to ridicule and refute an opponent's viewpoint. For example, consider the following scenario. Politician X proposes that we put astronauts on Mars in the next four years. Politician Y ridicules this proposal by saying that his opponent is looking for "little green men in outer space." Politician Y is committing a straw man fallacy by inaccurately representing Politician X's proposal, which is about space exploration and scientific experimentation, not "little green men."

Another fallacy that results from using inaccurate evidence is the **either/or fallacy**, also called a **false dilemma**. In this fallacy, the speaker presents two extreme options as the only possible choices. For instance:

Either we agree to higher taxes, or our grandchildren will be mired in debt.

This statement offers only two ways to view the issue, and both are extreme and inaccurate.

Yet another fallacy of inaccuracy is **equivocation**, through which a writer or speaker intentionally misleads the audience by using a word with a double or ambiguous meaning. For example, in the statement, "We will bring our enemies to justice, or we will bring justice to them," the first instance of "justice" seems straightforward, while the second instance of "justice" suggests vengeance.

Fallacies of Insufficiency

Perhaps the most common of fallacies occurs when evidence is insufficient. We call this a **hasty generalization**, meaning that there is not enough evidence to support a particular conclusion. For instance: "Smoking isn't bad for you; my great aunt smoked a pack a day and lived to be 90." It could be that the story of the speaker's aunt is true, but this single anecdote does not provide enough evidence to discredit the results of years of medical research.

Another fallacy resulting from insufficient evidence is circular reasoning. **Circular reasoning** involves repeating the claim as a way to provide evidence, resulting in no evidence at all. For instance, a student who asserts, "You can't give me a C; I'm an A student" is guilty of circular reasoning; that is, the "evidence" that she should get an A is that she is an A student. The so-called evidence is insufficient because it is a mere repetition of the claim. You can frequently spot circular reasoning in advertising. For instance: "Buy this shampoo because it's the best shampoo!" or "Shop at this store because it's a shopper's paradise."

We will discuss other common logical fallacies as we examine specific types of evidence.

ACTIVITY

Read the following excerpt from the essay, "I Know Why the Caged Bird Cannot Read" by Francine Prose. Identify what you consider to be fallacies in her argument and discuss the effects those fallacies have on the soundness of her argument.

---

from I Know Why the Caged Bird Cannot Read

FRANCINE PROSE

First published in 1970, *I Know Why the Caged Bird Sings* is what we have since learned to recognize as a "survivor" memoir, a first-person narrative of victimization and recovery. Angelou transports us to her childhood in segregated Arkansas, where she was raised by her grandmother and was mostly content, despite the unpleasantness of her white neighbors, until, after a move to St. Louis, eight-year-old Maya was raped by her mother's boyfriend.

One can see why this memoir might appeal to the lazy or uninspired teacher, who can conduct the class as if the students were the studio audience for Angelou's guest appearance on *Oprah*. The author's frequently vented distrust of white society might rouse even the most sluggish or understandably disaffected ninth-graders to join a discussion of racism; her victory over poverty and abuse can be used to address what one fan, in a customer book review on Amazon.com, celebrated as "transcending that pain, drawing from it deeper levels of meaning about being truly human and truly alive." Many chapters end with sententious epigrams virtually begging to serve as texts for sophomoric rumination on such questions as: What does Angelou mean when she writes, "If growing up is painful for the Southern Black girl, being aware of her displacement is rust on the razor that threatens the throat"?

But much more terrifying than the prospect of Angelou's pieties being dissected for their deeper meaning is the notion of her language being used as a model of "poetic" prose style. Many

of the terrible mysteries that confront teachers of college freshman composition can be solved simply by looking at Angelou's writing. Who told students to combine a dozen mixed metaphors in one paragraph? Consider a typical passage from Angelou's opaque prose: "Weekdays revolved on a sameness wheel. They turned into themselves so steadily and inevitably that each seemed to be the original of yesterday's rough draft. Saturdays, however, always broke the mold and dared to be different.' Where do students learn to write stale, inaccurate similes? "The man's dead words fell like bricks around the auditorium and too many settled in my belly." Who seriously believes that murky, turgid, convoluted language of this sort constitutes good writing? "Youth and social approval allied themselves with me and we trammeled memories of slights and insults. The wind of our swift passage remodeled my features. Lost tears were pounded to mud and then to dust. Years of withdrawal were brushed aside and left behind, as hanging ropes of parasitic moss."

To hold up this book as a paradigm of memoir, of thought — of literature — is akin to inviting doctors convicted of malpractice to instruct our medical students. If we want to use Angelou's work to educate our kids, let's invite them to parse her language, sentence by sentence; ask them precisely what it means and ask why one would bother obscuring ideas that could be expressed so much more simply and felicitously.

Narrated affably enough by a nine-year-old girl named Scout, *To Kill a Mockingbird* is

5

the perennially beloved and treacly account of growing up in a small Southern town during the Depression. Its hero is Scout's father, the saintly Atticus Finch, a lawyer who represents everything we cherish about justice and democracy and the American Way, and who defends a black man falsely accused of rape by a poor white woman. The novel has a shadow hero, too, the descriptively named Boo Radley, a gooney recluse who becomes the occasion for yet another lesson in tolerance and compassion.

Such summary reduces the book, but not by all that much. To read the novel is, for most, an exercise in wish-fulfillment and self-congratulation, a chance to consider thorny issues of race and prejudice from a safe distance and with the comfortable certainty that the reader would *never* harbor the racist attitudes espoused by the lowlifes in the novel. We (the readers) are Scout, her childhood is our childhood, and Atticus Finch is our brave, infinitely patient American Daddy. And that creepy big guy living alone in the scary house turns out to have been watching over us with protective benevolent attention.

 # ANALYZING VISUAL TEXTS

Identifying Fallacies

As we've established, visual texts can use evidence and make claims just like their written counterparts; therefore, the arguments of visual texts are equally prone to logical fallacies. In fact, because a visual text can't develop its argument in an extended form and must rely heavily on pathos, it's even more likely that the connection between evidence and claim rests on tenuous assumptions or nebulous reasoning.

For example, let's examine this ad from PETA (People for the Ethical Treatment of Animals).

Our attention is first captured by the jarring image of a young boy smoking a cigar. We notice that the boy is wearing blue and leaning on his elbows over an open book, as though he has been reading. You may think he looks like a little man, and you'd be right. His pose, the color of his outfit, and the props in the image all evoke a sense of tough, serious masculinity — all of which are undermined and made absurd by the fact that this "man" is clearly a toddler. This comic imitation of an adult pose both grabs our attention and immediately primes our emotions for outrage and concern.

To the right of the smoking boy, we read the major premise of the advertisement in large, bold print: "You Wouldn't Let Your Child Smoke." — a statement with which everyone, PETA assumes, would agree. This assertion paves the way for the text below it, the minor premise that "Like smoking, eating meat increases the risk of heart disease and cancer." The conclusion the audience is meant to deduce — which is printed in small letters at the bottom right — is that everyone should "Go vegan!" Each component of the text is arranged to follow the natural downward path of the eye as the argument moves from premise to conclusion.

So what is PETA's reasoning here? Judging from the text of the ad, PETA equates smoking with eating meat because, according to them, both carry health risks. But is this a fair analogy or a faulty one? Smoking is unnecessary to physical survival, whereas people need to eat in order to stay alive. While there are no known benefits to smoking that may outweigh the risks, the same cannot be said of eating meat. Because the purpose of this ad is to make an impact quickly and emotionally, it doesn't bother to explain the analogy or prove that eating meat is a threat to your health; instead, PETA hopes the public will agree with the underlying assumption that we should avoid consuming any product that could lead to bodily disease. The lack of detail about the type or amount of meat needed to increase the risks of these diseases points to another fallacy: hasty generalization.

PETA's ad presents its argument by combining a picture with text, and it doesn't put forth any research or data to back up its claims. But what about images that visually represent quantitative data — such as graphs, charts, and tables? The automatic ethos we tend to attribute to such images stems from their use of numbers, which we usually perceive as unbiased and objective. But every visual containing quantitative data has a creator, and that creator chooses exactly how to display those numbers to an audience. In other words, data-driven visuals also make arguments — how the data in a graph or chart appears is an argument for the conclusion the author wants the audience to reach. For instance, a graph can appear to show a large disparity that is actually quite small by adjusting the scale of its axes, or an infographic can highlight one aspect of a study while downplaying — or neglecting to even mention — another. As good readers, we must think critically to evaluate whether these arguments are valid and accurate. Let's compare the effect of these two bar graphs:

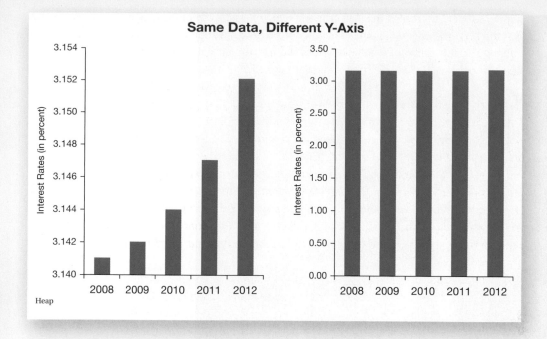

Heap

The interest rates on the graph on the right begin at 0.00 percent, as most readers would anticipate, and go up to 3.50 percent, meaning the *y*-axis shows a span of 3.50 percent. Alternately, the interest rates on the graph on the left begin at 3.140 percent and then go up to 3.154 percent, which means the *y*-axis only shows a span of 0.14 percent. Both graphs present the same information, yet a quick glance at the graph on the left would lead a reader to draw the conclusion that interest rates have increased steeply, while the graph on the right would lead one to conclude that interest rates have barely changed at all. As our world comes to rely more heavily on data, we need to be aware of the ways in which our readings of that data may be misled based on its visual presentation.

ACTIVITY

Identify the logical fallacies in the following images by completing the graphic organizer below.

Claim (implicit or explicit)	Evidence	Logical fallacy	What purpose does the fallacy serve?

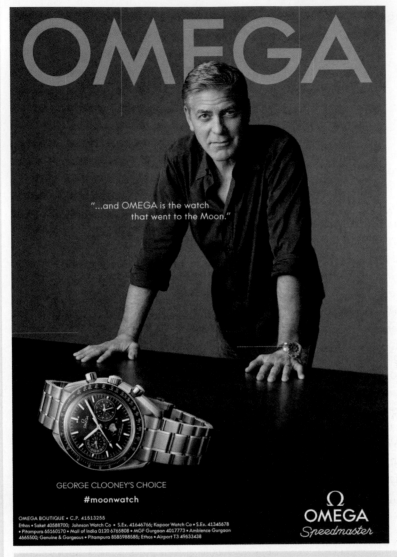

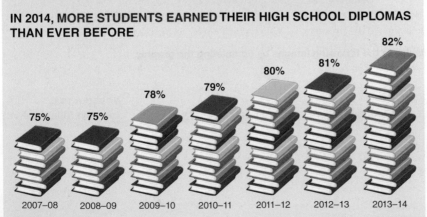

**IN 2014, MORE STUDENTS EARNED THEIR HIGH SCHOOL DIPLOMAS
THAN EVER BEFORE**

2007–08	2008–09	2009–10	2010–11	2011–12	2012–13	2013–14
75%	75%	78%	79%	80%	81%	82%

Data from U.S. Department of Education.

First-Hand Evidence

First-hand evidence is something you *know*, whether it's from personal experience, anecdotes you've heard from others, observations, or your general knowledge of events.

Personal Experience

The most common type of first-hand evidence is personal experience. Bringing in personal experience adds a human element and can be an effective way to appeal to pathos. For example, when writing about whether you do or do not support single-sex classrooms, you might describe your experience as a student, or you might use your observations about your school or classmates to inform your argument. Personal experience is a great way to make an abstract issue more human, and it is an especially effective technique for both introducing and concluding an argument. Personal experience can interest readers and draw them in, but they'll need more than just your perspective to be persuaded.

Personal experience works best if the writer can speak as an insider. For instance, you can speak knowledgeably about the issue of single-sex classrooms because you have inside knowledge about classrooms and how they work. In the following essay about the environmentalist movement, Jennifer Oladipo argues that minorities need to become more involved: "The terms *environmentalist* and *minority* conjure two distinct images in most people's minds — a false dichotomy that seriously threatens any chance of pulling the planet out of its current ecological tailspin." As a member of a minority group herself, she uses her personal experience as both an entrance into the essay and a source of evidence.

Why Can't Environmentalism Be Colorblind?

JENNIFER OLADIPO

In nearly two years of volunteering and working at an urban nature preserve, I have never seen another face like mine come through our doors. At least, I've not seen another black woman come for a morning hike or native-wildlife program. The few I do encounter are teachers and chaperones with school groups, or aides assisting people with disabilities. When I commute by bus to the preserve, located in the middle of Louisville, Kentucky, I disembark with blacks and other minorities. Yet none of them ever seems to make it to the trails.

I might have assumed they simply weren't interested, but then I saw that none of the center's newsletters were mailed to predominantly minority areas of town, nor did any press releases go to popular minority radio stations or newspapers. Not ever, as far as I could tell. Although the nature center seeks a stronger community presence and feels the same budget pinch as other small nonprofits, it has missed large swaths of the community with its message.

The terms *environmentalist* and *minority* conjure two distinct images in most people's minds — a false dichotomy that seriously threatens any chance of pulling the planet out of its current ecological tailspin. Some people think this country is on the precipice of a societal shift that will make environmental stewardship an integral part of our collective moral code. But that is not going to happen as long as we as a nation continue to think and act as if "green" automatically means "white."

Assumptions about who is amenable to conservation values cost the environmental movement numbers and dollars. Religion, capitalism, and even militarism learned ages ago to reach actively across the racial spectrum. In terms of winning over minorities, they have left environmentalism in the dust. Not until I joined an environmental-journalism organization was my mailbox flooded with information about serious environmental issues — even though I have been volunteering in organic gardens, hiking, and camping for years. I had received solicitations for credit cards and political parties, fast-food coupons, and a few Books of Mormon — but I had to seek out environmental groups.

Minorities make up one-third of the population, and we are growing as an economic and financial force as our numbers increase. We are a key to maintaining the energy that environmentalism has gained as a result of intense mainstream attention. That momentum will peter out without more people to act on the present sense of urgency. Imagine the power of 100 million Asians, African Americans, Latinos, and Native Americans invested in sustainable living, joining green organizations, voting for politicians and laws that protect the environment.

Nobody benefits from the perception that enjoying and caring for the environment is an exclusively white lifestyle. The truth is that brown, yellow, red, and black people like to go backpacking, too. Those of us with the means are buying organic, local, and hybrid. If environmentalism continues to appear mostly white and well-off, it will continue to be mostly white and well-off, even as racial and economic demographics change. The environmental movement will continue to overlook the nuances, found in diversity of experience, that reveal multiple facets of environmental problems — and their solutions.

Sooner or later, even global warming will be pushed off magazine covers, television screens, and the congressional floor. Before that time, we need to have in place something even more impressive: a racially diverse, numerically astounding mass of environmentalists ready to pick up the ball and run with it.

5

Oladipo writes most of her essay around her personal experience working in a Kentucky nature preserve, explaining why she chose the work and pointing out the lack of "another face like mine" in that setting. She describes her experiences of volunteering, of working at nature preserves and organic gardens, and also of joining an "environmental-journalism organization." Although she primarily draws on her own experiences in her essay, she also uses some statistics and a reasonable tone to make a persuasive case.

FALLACY ALERT   Hasty Generalization in First-Hand Evidence

As we described previously (p. 91), a hasty generalization is a fallacy in which there is not enough evidence to support a particular conclusion. When using personal experience as evidence, it's important to remember that while it might provide some ethos to speak on a topic and it may be an effective way to appeal to pathos, personal experience is rarely universal proof.

> **EXAMPLE:**   Pulling wisdom teeth is just another unnecessary and painful medical procedure. I still have all of mine, and they haven't given me any problems.

Anecdotes

First-hand evidence also includes anecdotes about other people that you've either observed or been told about. Like personal experience, anecdotes can be a useful way to appeal to pathos.

In the following excerpt from an op-ed piece, Fabiola Santiago argues against the policy that children born in the United States to immigrants, including those who are undocumented, must be treated as nonresidents when it comes to receiving state services. To make the case about the specific unfairness of imposing out-of-state tuition on Florida residents who fall into this category, Santiago uses an anecdote as part of her evidence.

from In College, These American Citizens Are Not Created Equal

FABIOLA SANTIAGO

"I lift my lamp beside the golden door!"
— Lady Liberty

On Saturday, the day after its 125th anniversary celebration, the Statue of Liberty will close its doors for a year-long, $27 million renovation of the monument's interior. One could only hope that the nation's soul will undergo some transformation as well. Emma Lazarus, the descendant of Sephardic Jews expelled from Spain who wrote in 1883 "The New Colossus," the moving sonnet at the base of the statue in New York harbor, would shed mournful tears at the lack of compassion for immigrants these days. She would weep at the ease with which words of disdain are spoken by some who lead and aspire to lead, and at the underhanded way in which ill-willed actions are taken against immigrants and their children. Lady Liberty's "golden door" is not only jammed, slammed shut, or slightly ajar depending on where you come from, but we've fallen so low on the scale of our founding values that in the United States of America of today not all U.S. citizens are created equal. There are states like Florida, Alabama, and Arizona where politicians and bureaucrats use the system to discriminate, to create classes of Americans, to disenfranchise some of the most deserving among us. The latest low blow was unveiled by a class-action lawsuit

and a bill filed in the Florida Legislature last week. Under rules established by the state's Department of Education and the university system's Board of Governors, students like Wendy Ruiz — born and raised in Miami — have to pay out-of-state tuition at rates that are more than three times what other Florida resident students pay for their education. Ruiz has lived in the state all her life. She has a Florida birth certificate, a Florida driver's license, and is registered to vote in Florida. But while other Miami Dade College students pay about $1,266 per term in tuition, she must pay $4,524 because the state considers her a dependent of nonresidents. Here's an institution that is supposed to defend education punishing a young American for the sins of her parents, who are undocumented immigrants. But we should all aspire to have neighbors like the Ruizes, who raised a daughter like Wendy, willing to work three part-time jobs to pay her tuition while maintaining a 3.7 grade-point average. "I know that I will be successful because I have never wanted something so bad in my life like I want this," Ruiz said of her education. Who knows what more Wendy Ruiz might accomplish, what more she could become if she were able to pay all of her attention to her education without the unfair financial burden of paying extravagantly unfair fees.

Santiago could have provided facts and figures about the legislative policy in question. Instead, she focuses on one person, Wendy Ruiz. Santiago points out that Ruiz "has lived in the state all her life. She has a Florida birth certificate, a Florida driver's license, and is registered to vote in Florida." Santiago then explains the difference in tuition for residents versus nonresidents, noting that Wendy is a model citizen "willing to work three part-time jobs to pay her tuition." She even quotes Wendy's comments about the premium she places on education. In this example, Santiago is not writing about herself, but she is telling an anecdote about another person that gives a human face to the argument. She appeals to pathos by describing the situation of Wendy Ruiz, being careful to point out that her situation typifies that of others who would suffer from a proposed policy.

Current Events

Current events are another type of evidence that is accessed first-hand through observation. Staying abreast of what is happening locally, nationally, and globally ensures a store of information that can be used as evidence in arguments. Remember that current events can be interpreted in many ways, so seek out multiple perspectives and be on the lookout for bias. Here is an example from a newspaper article by Fordham University professor Charles Camosy about the 2016 U.S. presidential election results. In this excerpt, he is writing in response to what he considers mistaken explanations in the media regarding Donald Trump's success with American voters.

---

from Trump Won Because College-Educated Americans Are Out of Touch

CHARLES CAMOSY

As the reality of President-elect Donald Trump settled in very early Wednesday morning, MSNBC's Chris Hayes summed up an explanation common to many on the left: The Republican nominee pulled ahead thanks to old-fashioned American racism.

But the attempt to make Trump's victory about racism appears to be at odds with what actually happened on Election Day. Consider the following facts.

Twenty-nine percent of Latinos voted for Trump, per exit polls. Remarkably, despite the near-ubiquitous narrative that Trump would have deep problems with this demographic given his comments and position on immigration, this was a higher percentage of those who voted for GOP nominee Mitt Romney in 2012. Meanwhile, African Americans did not turn out to vote against Trump. In fact, Trump received a higher percentage of African American votes than Romney did.

And while many white voters deeply disliked Trump, they disliked Democrat Hillary Clinton even more. Of those who had negative feelings about both Trump and Clinton, Trump got their votes by a margin of 2 to 1. Votes for Trump seemed to signal a rejection of the norms and values for which Clinton stood more than an outright embrace of Trump. He was viewed unfavorably, for instance, by 61 percent of Wisconsinites, but 1 in 5 in that group voted for him anyway.

The most important divide in this election was not between whites and non-whites. It was between those who are often referred to as "educated" voters and those who are described as "working class" voters.

The reality is that six in 10 Americans do not have a college degree, and they elected Donald Trump. College-educated people didn't just fail to see this coming — they have struggled to display even a rudimentary understanding of the worldviews of those who voted for Trump. This is an indictment of the monolithic, insulated political culture in the vast majority our colleges and universities.

As a college professor, I know that there are many ways in which college graduates simply know more about the world than those who do not have such degrees. This is especially true — with some exceptions, of course — when it comes to "hard facts" learned in science, history and sociology courses.

5

100

But I also know that that those with college degrees — again, with some significant exceptions — don't necessarily know philosophy or theology. And they have especially paltry knowledge about the foundational role that different philosophical or theological claims play in public thought compared with what is common to college campuses. In my experience, many professors and college students don't even realize that their views on political issues rely on a particular philosophical or theological stance.

Second-Hand Evidence

Second-hand evidence is evidence that is accessed through research, reading, and investigation. It includes factual and historical information, expert opinion, and quantitative data. Anytime you cite what someone else knows, not what you know, you are using second-hand evidence. Although citing second-hand evidence may occasionally appeal to pathos and certainly may establish a writer's ethos, the central appeal is to logos — reason and logic.

Historical Information

A common type of second-hand evidence is historical information — verifiable facts that a writer knows from research. This kind of evidence can provide background and context to current debates; it also can help establish the writer's ethos because it shows that he or she has taken the time and effort to research the matter and become informed. One possible pitfall is that historical events are complicated. You'll want to keep your description of the events brief, but be sure not to misrepresent the events. In the following paragraph from *Hate Speech: The History of an American Controversy* (1994), author Samuel Walker provides historical information to establish the "intolerance" of the 1920s era.

> The 1920s are remembered as a decade of intolerance. Bigotry was as much a symbol of the period as Prohibition, flappers, the stock market boom, and Calvin Coolidge. It was the only time when the Ku Klux Klan paraded en masse through the nation's capital. In 1921 Congress restricted immigration for the first time in American history, drastically reducing the influx of Catholics and Jews from southern and eastern Europe, and the nation's leading universities adopted admission quotas to restrict the number of Jewish students. The Sacco and Vanzetti case, in which two Italian American anarchists were executed for robbery and murder in a highly questionable prosecution, has always been one of the symbols of the anti-immigrant tenor of the period.

To support the claim that the 1920s was a period characterized by bigotry, Walker cites a series of historical examples: the Ku Klux Klan, immigration laws, restriction targeting certain ethnicities, and a high-profile court case.

Historical information is often used to develop a point of comparison or contrast to a more contemporary situation. In the following paragraph from Charles Krauthammer's op-ed "The 9/11 'Overreaction'? Nonsense," the political commentator does exactly that by comparing the War on Terror to previous military campaigns in U.S. history.

> True, in both [the Iraq and Afghanistan] wars there was much trial, error and tragic loss. In Afghanistan, too much emphasis on nation-building. In Iraq, the bloody middle years before we found our general and our strategy. But cannot the same be said of, for example, the Civil War, the terrible years before Lincoln found his general? Or the Pacific campaign of World War II, with its myriad miscalculations, its often questionable island-hopping, that cost infinitely more American lives?

Notice that Krauthammer's historical evidence is brief but detailed enough to both show his grasp of the history and explicitly lay out his comparison. Simply saying, "These wars are no different from the Civil War or World War II" would have been far too vague and thus ineffective.

FALLACY ALERT: *Post Hoc Ergo Propter Hoc*

The name of the *post hoc ergo propter hoc* fallacy is Latin for "after which therefore because of which." What that means is that it is incorrect to always claim that something is a cause just because it happened earlier. In other words, correlation does not imply causation.

> **EXAMPLE:**   We elected Johnson as president and look where it got us: hurricanes, floods, stock market crashes.

That's a simple example, but in reality causality is very tricky to prove because few things have only one cause. When using historical evidence, you should be especially aware of this fallacy. Check your facts. Consider the complexity of the situation. Proceed with caution.

Expert Opinion

Most everyone is an expert on something! And how often do we bolster our viewpoint by pointing out that so-and-so agrees with us? Expert opinion is a more formal variation on that common practice. An expert is someone who has published research on a topic or whose job or experience gives him or her specialized knowledge. Sometimes, you might cite the viewpoint of an individual who is an "expert" in a local matter but who is not widely recognized. If, for instance, you are writing about school policy, you might cite the opinion of a teacher or student government officer. The important point is to make certain that your expert is seen as credible by your audience so that his or her opinion will add weight to your argument.

Following is an excerpt from "Just a Little Princess" by Peggy Orenstein in which she critiques what she calls "the princess culture" that Disney promotes. In this paragraph, she is commenting on the phenomenon of "Supergirl." Note the use of an expert — and how that expert is identified — as evidence.

> The princess as superhero is not irrelevant. Some scholars I spoke with say that given its post-9/11 timing, princess mania is a response to a newly dangerous world. "Historically, princess worship has emerged during periods of uncertainty and profound social change," observes Miriam Forman-Brunell, a historian at the University of Missouri — Kansas City. Francis Hodgson Burnett's original *Little Princess* was published at a time of rapid

urbanization, immigration and poverty; Shirley Temple's film version was a hit during the Great Depression. "The original folk tales themselves," Forman-Brunell says, "spring from medieval and early modern European culture that faced all kinds of economic and demographic and social upheaval — famine, war, disease, terror of wolves. Girls play savior during times of economic crisis and instability." That's a heavy burden for little shoulders. Perhaps that's why the magic wand has become an essential part of the princess get-up. In the original stories — even the Disney versions of them — it's not the girl herself who's magic: it's the fairy godmother. Now if Forman-Brunell is right, we adults have become the cursed creatures whom girls have the thaumaturgic [miraculous] power to transform.

Orenstein is careful to present credentials (in this case, a university professor) and to either quote or paraphrase the relevant information as evidence. She quotes Forman-Brunell and then comments on this expert's viewpoint. Orenstein may have held the same opinion about fairy godmothers and their impact on girls' views of themselves, but the findings of a researcher add credibility to the argument.

FALLACY ALERT: Appeal to False Authority

Appeal to false authority occurs when someone who has no expertise to speak on an issue is cited as an authority. A TV star, for instance, is not a medical expert, even though pharmaceutical advertisements often use celebrity endorsements. When choosing whom to cite as an expert, be sure to verify the person's background and qualifications.

Quantitative Evidence

Quantitative evidence includes things that can be represented in numbers: statistics, surveys, polls, census information. This type of evidence can be persuasive in its appeal to logos. Amy Domini cites numerical evidence in her essay to support her contention that "[f]ast food is a way of life. In America, the average person eats it more than 150 times a year. In 2007, sales for the 400 largest U.S.-based fast-food chains totaled $277 billion, up 7 percent from 2006" (see p. 76).

Quantitative evidence need not be all percentages and dollar figures, however. In an article on American education entitled "When Will We Learn?," journalist Fareed Zakaria compares the education situation of the United States with that of other countries by citing quantitative information without a lot of numbers and figures.

U.S. schoolchildren spend less time in school than their peers abroad. They have shorter school days and a shorter school year. Children in South Korea will spend almost two years more in school than Americans by the end of high school. Is it really so strange that they score higher on tests?

If South Korea teaches the importance of hard work, Finland teaches another lesson. Finnish students score near the very top on international tests, yet they do not follow the Asian model of study, study and more study. Instead they start school a year later than in most countries, emphasize creative work and shun tests for most of the year. But Finland has great teachers, who are paid well and treated with the same professional respect that is accorded to doctors and lawyers. They are found and developed through an extremely competitive and rigorous process. All teachers are required to have master's degrees, and only 1 in 10 applicants is accepted to the country's teacher-training programs.

Zakaria includes quantitative data — two more years of school for South Korean students than their American counterparts, a highly competitive process for Finnish teacher-training programs that accept only one of every ten applicants — as part of his overall discussion. He could have cited dollar amounts as evidence of how well paid teachers are in Finland, but in the context of this column he makes the point and moves on; perhaps if he were writing for a more scholarly or skeptical audience, he would have thought it necessary to provide even more information.

FALLACY ALERT: Bandwagon Appeal

Bandwagon appeal (or *ad populum* fallacy) occurs when evidence boils down to "everybody's doing it, so it must be a good thing to do." Sometimes, statistics can be used to prove that "everybody's doing it" and thus give a bandwagon appeal the appearance of cold, hard fact.

   EXAMPLE: You should vote to elect Rachel Johnson—she has a strong lead in the polls!

Polling higher does not necessarily make Senator Johnson the "best" candidate, only the most popular.

ACTIVITY

Annotate the following essay by identifying the different types of first- and second-hand evidence presented to develop the argument. Analyze how each type of evidence appeals to ethos, logos, pathos, or a combination of those.

Do You Care More About a Dog Than a Refugee?

NICHOLAS KRISTOF

Last Thursday, our beloved family dog, Katie, died at the age of 12. She was a gentle giant who respectfully deferred even to any mite-size puppy with a prior claim to a bone. Katie might have won the Nobel Peace Prize if not for her weakness for squirrels.

I mourned Katie's passing on social media and received a torrent of touching condolences, easing my ache at the loss of a member of the family. Yet on the same day that Katie died, I published a column calling for greater international efforts to end Syria's suffering and civil war, which has claimed perhaps 470,000 lives so far. That column led to a different torrent of comments, many laced with a harsh indifference: Why should *we* help *them*?

These mingled on my Twitter feed: heartfelt sympathy for an American dog who expired of old age, and what felt to me like callousness toward millions of Syrian children facing starvation or bombing. If only, I thought, we valued kids in Aleppo as much as we did our terriers!

For five years the world has been largely paralyzed as President Bashar al-Assad has massacred his people, nurturing in turn the rise of ISIS and what the U.S. government calls genocide by ISIS. That's why I argued in my column a week ago that President Obama's passivity on Syria was his worst mistake, a shadow over his legacy.

The column sparked passionate disagreement *5* from readers, so let me engage your arguments.

"There is nothing in our constitution that says we are to be the savior of the world from all the crazies out there," a reader in St. Louis noted. "I cannot see any good in wasting a trillion dollars trying to put Humpty Dumpty together again. Bleeding hearts often cause more harm than good."

I agree that we can't solve all the world's problems, but it doesn't follow that we shouldn't try to solve any. Would it have been wrong during the Holocaust to try to bomb the gas chambers at Auschwitz? Was President Bill Clinton wrong to intervene in Kosovo to avert potential genocide there? For that matter, was President Obama wrong two years ago when he ordered airstrikes near Mount Sinjar on the Iraq-Syria border, apparently averting genocidal massacres of Yazidi there?

Agreed, we shouldn't dispatch ground forces to Syria or invest a trillion dollars. But why not, as many suggest, fire missiles from outside Syria to crater military runways and ground the Syrian Air Force?

A reader from Delaware commented, "I hear ya, Nicholas, but so far every Middle East venture has not turned out good for the world." Likewise, a reader in Minnesota argued, "Surely the George W. Bush experience taught us something."

Let me push back. I opposed the Iraq war, *10* but to me the public seems to have absorbed the wrong lesson — that military intervention never works, rather than the more complex lesson that it is a blunt and expensive tool with a very mixed record.

Yes, the Iraq war was a disaster, but the no-fly zone in northern Iraq after the first gulf war was a huge success. Vietnam was a monumental catastrophe, but the British intervention in Sierra Leone in 2000 was a spectacular success. Afghanistan remains a mess, but airstrikes helped end genocide in the Balkans. U.S. support for Saudi bombing in Yemen is counterproductive, but Bill Clinton has said that his worst foreign policy mistake was not halting the Rwandan genocide.

And even if we eschew the military toolbox, what excuse do we have for not trying harder to give Syrian refugee children an education in neighboring countries like Jordan and Lebanon? Depriving refugee kids of an education lays the groundwork for further tribalism, poverty, enmity and violence.

I grant that cratering runways or establishing a safe zone — even educating refugees — won't necessarily work as hoped, and Obama is right to be concerned about slippery slopes. Those concerns must be weighed against the lives of hundreds of thousands of children, particularly now that we have asserted that genocide is underway in Syria.

One reason past genocides have been allowed to unfold without outside interference is that there is never a perfect policy tool available to stop the killing. Another is that the victims don't seem "like us." They're Jews or blacks or, in this case, Syrians, so we tune out.

But, in fact, as even dogs know, a human is *15* a human.

I wonder what would happen if Aleppo were full of golden retrievers, if we could see barrel bombs maiming helpless, innocent puppies. Would we still harden our hearts and "otherize" the victims? Would we still say "it's an Arab problem; let the Arabs solve it"?

Yes, solutions in Syria are hard and uncertain. But I think even Katie in her gentle wisdom would have agreed that not only do all human lives have value, but also that a human's life is worth every bit as much as a golden retriever's.

Shaping Argument

The shape — that is, the organization or arrangement — of an argument reflects a host of factors, including audience and purpose, but it usually follows one of several patterns. We'll discuss classical oration, induction and deduction, Rogerian argument, and the Toulmin model as five common ways to structure an argument. Keep in mind that writers often modify these structures as needed. The essential point to remember is that the organization should fit the ideas, rather than forcing ideas to fit into a prescribed organizational pattern.

Classical Oration

Classical rhetoricians outlined a five-part structure for an oratory, or speech, that writers still use today, although perhaps not always consciously. We refer to this structure as the classical arrangement:

- The **introduction (*exordium*)** introduces the reader to the subject under discussion. In Latin, *exordium* means "beginning a web," which is an apt description for an introduction. Whether it is a single paragraph or several, the introduction draws the readers into the text by piquing their interest, challenging them, or otherwise getting their attention. Often the introduction is where the writer establishes ethos.
- The **narration (*narratio*)** provides factual information and background material on the subject at hand, thus beginning the developmental paragraphs, or establishes why the subject is a problem that needs addressing. Today, this is more commonly known as **exposition**. The level of detail a writer uses in this section depends largely on the audience's knowledge of the subject. Although classical rhetoric describes narration as appealing to logos, in actuality it often appeals to pathos because the writer attempts to evoke an emotional response about the importance of the issue being discussed.
- The **confirmation (*confirmatio*)**, usually the major part of the text, includes the development or the proof needed to make the writer's case — the nuts and bolts of the essay, containing the most specific and concrete detail in the text. The confirmation generally makes the strongest appeal to logos.
- The **refutation (*refutatio*)**, which addresses the counterargument, is in many ways a bridge between the writer's proof and conclusion. Although classical rhetoricians recommended placing this section at the end of the text as a way to anticipate objections to the proof given in the confirmation section, this is not a hard-and-fast rule. If opposing views are well known or valued by the audience, a writer will address them before presenting his or her own argument. The counterargument's appeal is largely to logos.
- The **conclusion (*peroratio*)** — whether it is one paragraph or several — brings the essay to a satisfying close. Here the writer usually appeals to pathos and reminds the reader of the ethos established earlier. Rather than simply repeating what has gone before, the conclusion brings all the writer's ideas together and answers the question, so what? Writers should remember the classical rhetoricians' advice that the last words and ideas of a text are those the audience is most likely to remember.

An example of this classical arrangement at work is the following piece written in 2006 by Sandra Day O'Connor, a former Supreme Court justice, and Roy Romer, then superintendent of the Los Angeles Unified School District.

Not by Math Alone

SANDRA DAY O'CONNOR AND ROY ROMER

Fierce global competition prompted President Bush to use the State of the Union address to call for better math and science education, where there's evidence that many schools are falling short.

We should be equally troubled by another shortcoming in American schools: Most young people today simply do not have an adequate understanding of how our government and political system work, and they are thus not well prepared to participate as citizens.

Introduction

This country has long exemplified democratic practice to the rest of the world. With the attention we are paying to advancing democracy abroad, we ought not neglect it at home.

Two-thirds of 12th-graders scored below "proficient" on the last national civics assessment in 1998, and only 9 percent could list two ways a democracy benefits from citizen participation. Yes, young people remain highly patriotic, and many volunteer in their communities. But most are largely disconnected from current events and issues.

A healthy democracy depends on the participation of citizens, and that participation is learned behavior; it doesn't just happen. As the 2003 report "The Civic Mission of Schools" noted: "Individuals do not automatically become free and responsible citizens, but must be educated for citizenship." That means civic learning — educating students for democracy — needs to be on par with other academic subjects.

5

Narration

This is not a new idea. Our first public schools saw education for citizenship as a core part of their mission. Eighty years ago, John Dewey said, "Democracy needs to be reborn in every generation and education is its midwife."

But in recent years, civic learning has been pushed aside. Until the 1960s, three courses in civics and government were common in American high schools, and two of them ("civics" and "problems of democracy") explored the role of citizens and encouraged students to discuss current issues. Today those courses are very rare.

Confirmation

What remains is a course on "American government" that usually spends little time on how people can — and why they should — participate. The effect of reduced civic learning on civic life is not theoretical. Research shows that the better people understand our history and system of government, the more likely they are to vote and participate in the civic life.

We need more and better classes to impart the knowledge of government, history, law and current events that students need to understand and participate in a democratic republic. And we also know that much effective civic learning takes place beyond the classroom — in extracurricular activity, service work that is connected to class work, and other ways students experience civic life.

Preserving our democracy should be reason enough to promote civic learning. But there are other benefits. Understanding society and how we relate to each other fosters the attitudes essential for success in college, work and communities; it enhances student learning in other subjects.

Economic and technological competitiveness is essential, and America's economy and technology have flourished because of the rule of law and the "assets" of a free and open society. Democracy has been good for business and for economic well-being. By the same token, failing to hone the civic tools of democracy will have economic consequences.

Bill Gates — a top business and technology leader — argues strongly that schools have to prepare students not only for college and career but for citizenship as well.

None of this is to diminish the importance of improving math and science education. This latest push, as well as the earlier emphasis on literacy, deserves support. It should also be the occasion for a broader commitment, and that means restoring education for democracy to its central place in school.

Refutation

We need more students proficient in math, science and engineering. We also need them to be prepared for their role as citizens. Only then can self-government work. Only then will we not only be more competitive but also remain the beacon of liberty in a tumultuous world.

Conclusion

10

Sandra Day O'Connor retired as an associate justice of the Supreme Court. Roy Romer, a former governor of Colorado, is superintendent of the Los Angeles Unified School District. They are co-chairs of the national advisory council of the Campaign for the Civic Mission of Schools.

Sandra Day O'Connor and Roy Romer follow the classical arrangement very closely. The opening two paragraphs are an introduction to the main idea the authors develop. In fact, the last sentence of paragraph 2 is their two-part claim, or thesis: "Most young people today simply do not have an adequate understanding of how our government and political system work, and they are thus not well prepared to participate as citizens." O'Connor's position as a former Supreme Court justice establishes her ethos as a reasonable person, an advocate for justice, and a concerned citizen. Romer's biographical note at the end of the article suggests similar qualities. The authors use the pronoun "we" in the article to refer not only to themselves but to all of "us" who are concerned about American society. The opening phrase, "Fierce global competition," connotes a sense of urgency, and the warning that we are not adequately preparing our young people to participate as citizens is sure to evoke an emotional response of concern, even alarm.

In paragraphs 3 to 6 — the narration — the authors provide background information, including facts that add urgency to their point. They cite statistics, quote from research reports, even call on the well-known educator John Dewey. They also include a definition of "civic learning," a key term in their argument. Their facts-and-figures appeal is largely to logos, though the language of "a healthy democracy" certainly engages the emotions.

Paragraphs 7 to 12 present the bulk of the argument — the confirmation — by offering reasons and examples to support the case that young people lack the knowledge necessary to be informed citizens. The authors link civic learning to other subjects as well as to economic development. They quote Bill Gates, co-founder of Microsoft, who has spoken about the economic importance of a well-informed citizenry.

In paragraph 13, O'Connor and Romer briefly address a major objection — the refutation — that we need to worry more about math and science education than about civic learning. While they concede the importance of math, science, and literacy, they point out that it is possible to increase civic education without undermining the gains made in those other subject areas.

The final paragraph — the conclusion — emphasizes the importance of a democracy to a well-versed citizenry, a point that stresses the shared values of the authors with their audience. The appeal to pathos is primarily through the vivid language, particularly the final sentence with its emotionally charged description "beacon of liberty," a view of their nation that most Americans hold dear.

Induction and Deduction

Induction and deduction are ways of reasoning, but they are often effective ways to structure an entire argument as well.

Induction

Induction (from the Latin *inducere*, "to lead into") means arranging an argument so that it leads from particulars to universals, using specific cases to draw a conclusion. For instance:

> Regular exercise promotes weight loss.
>
> Exercise lowers stress levels.
>
> Exercise improves mood and outlook.

GENERALIZATION: Exercise contributes to better health.

We use induction in our everyday lives. For example, if your family and friends have owned several cars made by Subaru that have held up well, then you are likely to conclude inductively that Subaru makes good cars. Yet induction is also used in more technical situations. Even the scientific method is founded on inductive reasoning. Scientists use experiments to determine the effects in certain cases, and from there they might infer a universal scientific principle. For instance, if bases neutralize acids in every experiment conducted, then it can reasonably be inferred that all bases neutralize acids. The process of induction involves collecting evidence and then drawing an inference based on that evidence in order to reach a conclusion.

When you write a full essay developed entirely by reasons, one after another supporting the main point, then your entire argument is inductive. For instance, suppose you are asked to take a position on whether the American Dream is alive and well today. As you examine the issue, you might think of examples from your own community that demonstrate that the Dream is not a reality for the average citizen; you might study current events and think about the way societal expectations have changed; you might use examples from fiction you have read, such as the novel *Salvage the Bones* by Jesmyn Ward or movies such as *Hell or High Water*, where economic pressures limit the characters' horizons. All of this evidence together supports the inference that the American Dream no longer exists for the average person. To write that argument, you would support your claim with a series of reasons explained through concrete examples: you would argue inductively.

Arguments developed inductively can never be said to be true or false, right or wrong. Instead, they can be considered strong or weak, so it's important to consider possible vulnerabilities — in particular, the exception to the rule. Let's consider an example from politics. An argument written in favor of a certain political candidate might be organized inductively around reasons that she is the best-qualified person for the job because of her views on military spending, financial aid for college students, and states' rights. However, the argument is vulnerable to an objection that her views on, for instance, the death penalty or environmental issues weaken her qualifications. Essentially, an argument structured inductively cannot lead to certainty, only probability.

Let's look at an excerpt from *Outliers* by Malcolm Gladwell for an example of how an argument can be structured largely by induction. Gladwell uses various types of evidence here to support his conclusion that "[w]hen it comes to math . . . Asians have a built-in advantage."

---

from **Outliers**

MALCOLM GLADWELL

Take a look at the following list of numbers: 4, 8, 5, 3, 9, 7, 6. Read them out loud. Now look away and spend twenty seconds memorizing that sequence before saying them out loud again.

If you speak English, you have about a 50 percent chance of remembering that sequence perfectly. If you're Chinese, though, you're almost certain to get it right every time. Why is that? Because as human beings we store digits in a memory loop that runs for about two seconds. We most easily memorize whatever we can say or read within that two-second span. And Chinese speakers get that list of numbers — 4, 8, 5, 3, 9, 7, 6 — right almost every time because, unlike English, their language allows them to fit all those seven numbers into two seconds.

That example comes from Stanislas Dehaene's book *The Number Sense*. As Dehaene explains:

> Chinese number words are remarkably brief. Most of them can be uttered in less than one-quarter of a second (for instance, 4 is "si" and 7 "qi"). Their English equivalents — "four," "seven," — are longer: pronouncing them takes about one-third of a second. The memory gap between English and Chinese apparently is entirely due to this difference in length. In languages as diverse as Welsh, Arabic, Chinese, English and Hebrew, there is a reproducible correlation between the time required to pronounce numbers in a given language and the memory span of its speakers. In this domain, the prize for efficacy goes to the Cantonese dialect of Chinese, whose brevity grants residents of Hong Kong a rocketing memory span of about 10 digits.

It turns out that there is also a big difference in how number-naming systems in Western and Asian languages are constructed. In English, we say fourteen, sixteen, seventeen, eighteen, and nineteen, so one might expect that we would also say oneteen, twoteen, threeteen, and fiveteen. But we don't. We use a different form: eleven, twelve, thirteen, and fifteen. Similarly, we have forty and sixty, which sound like the words they are related to (four and six). But we also say fifty and thirty and twenty, which sort of sound like five and three and two, but not really. And, for that matter, for numbers above twenty, we put the "decade" first and the unit number second (twenty-one, twenty-two), whereas for the teens, we do it the other way around (fourteen, seventeen, eighteen). The number system in English is highly irregular. Not so in China, Japan, and Korea. They have a logical counting system. Eleven is ten-one. Twelve is ten-two. Twenty-four is two-tens-four and so on.

That difference means that Asian children learn to count much faster than American children. Four-year-old Chinese children can count, on average, to forty. American children at that age can count only to fifteen, and most don't reach forty until they're five. By the age of five, in other words, American children are already a *year* behind their Asian counterparts in the most fundamental of math skills.

The regularity of their number system also means that Asian children can perform basic functions, such as addition, far more easily. Ask an English-speaking seven-year-old to add thirty-seven plus twenty-two in her head, and she has to convert the words to numbers (37 + 22). Only then can she do the math: 2 plus 7 is 9 and 30 and 20 is 50, which makes 59. Ask an Asian child to add three-tens-seven and two-tens-two, and then the necessary equation is right there, embedded in the sentence. No number translation is necessary: It's five-tens-nine.

"The Asian system is transparent," says Karen Fuson, a Northwestern University psychologist who has closely studied Asian-Western differences. "I think that it makes the whole attitude toward math different. Instead of being a rote learning thing, there's a pattern I can figure out. There is an expectation that I can do this. There is an expectation that it's sensible. For fractions, we say three-fifths. The Chinese is literally 'out of five parts, take three.' That's telling you conceptually what a fraction is. It's differentiating the denominator and the numerator."

The much-storied disenchantment with mathematics among Western children starts in the third and fourth grades, and Fuson argues that perhaps a part of that disenchantment is due to the fact that math doesn't seem to make sense; its linguistic structure is clumsy; its basic rules seem arbitrary and complicated.

Asian children, by contrast, don't feel nearly the same bafflement. They can hold more numbers in their heads and do calculations faster, and the way fractions are expressed in their languages corresponds exactly to the way a fraction actually

5

111

is — and maybe that makes them a little more likely to enjoy math, and maybe because they enjoy math a little more, they try a little harder and take more math classes and are more willing to do their homework, and on and on, in a kind of virtuous circle.

When it comes to math, in other words, Asians have a built-in advantage.

10

In each paragraph, Gladwell provides reasons backed by evidence. He begins in the opening two paragraphs by drawing in the reader with an anecdotal example that (he assumes) will demonstrate his point: if you speak English, you won't do as well as if you speak Chinese. In paragraph 3, he provides additional support by citing an expert who has written a book entitled *The Number Sense*. In the next two paragraphs, he discusses differences in the systems of Western and Asian languages that explain why Asian children learn certain basic skills that put them ahead of their Western counterparts at an early age. In paragraphs 6 and 7, he raises another issue — attitude toward problem solving — and provides evidence from an expert to explain the superiority of Asian students. By this point, Gladwell has provided enough specific information — from facts, experts, examples — to support an inference that is a generalization. In this case, he concludes that "[w]hen it comes to math. . . Asians have a built-in advantage." Gladwell's reasoning and the structure of his argument are inductive.

Deduction

When you argue using **deduction**, you reach a conclusion by starting with a general principle or universal truth (a major premise) and applying it to a specific case (a minor premise). Deductive reasoning is often structured as a **syllogism**, a logical structure that uses the major premise and minor premise to reach a necessary conclusion. Let's use the same example about exercise that we used to demonstrate induction, but now we'll develop a syllogism to argue deductively:

> **MAJOR PREMISE:**   Exercise contributes to better health.
>
> **MINOR PREMISE:**   Yoga is a type of exercise.
>
> **CONCLUSION:**   Yoga contributes to better health.

The strength of deductive logic is that if the first two premises are true, then the conclusion is logically valid. Keep in mind, though, that if either premise is false (or questionable in any way), then the conclusion is subject to challenge. Consider the following:

> **MAJOR PREMISE:**   Celebrities are role models for young people.
>
> **MINOR PREMISE:**   Kim Kardashian is a celebrity.
>
> **CONCLUSION:**   Kim Kardashian is a role model for young people.

As you can see in this example, the conclusion is logically valid — but is it true? You can challenge the conclusion by challenging the veracity of the major premise — that is, whether all celebrities are role models for young people.

Deduction is a good way to combat stereotypes that are based on faulty premises. Consider this one:

MAJOR PREMISE: Women are poor drivers.

MINOR PREMISE: Ellen is a woman.

CONCLUSION: Ellen is a poor driver.

Breaking this stereotype down into a syllogism clearly shows the faulty logic. Perhaps some women, just as some men, are poor drivers, but to say that women in general drive poorly is to stereotype by making a hasty generalization. Breaking an idea down into component parts like this helps expose the basic thinking, which then can yield a more nuanced argument. This example might be qualified, for instance, by saying that *some* women are poor drivers; thus, Ellen *might* be a poor driver.

Combining Induction and Deduction

While some essays are either completely inductive or completely deductive, it's more common for an essay to combine these methods depending on the situation. Induction — a series of examples — may be used to verify a major premise, then that premise can become the foundation for deductive reasoning. The Declaration of Independence is an example of deductive and inductive logic at work. Thomas Jefferson and the framers drafted this document to prove that the colonies were justified in their rebellion against King George III.

The Declaration of Independence

THOMAS JEFFERSON

In CONGRESS, July 4, 1776
The unanimous Declaration of the thirteen
united States of America

When in the Course of human events it becomes necessary for one people to dissolve the political bands which have connected them with another and to assume among the powers of the earth, the separate and equal station to which the Laws of Nature and of Nature's God entitle them, a decent respect to the opinions of mankind requires that they should declare the causes which impel them to the separation.

We hold these truths to be self-evident, that all men are created equal, that they are endowed by their Creator with certain unalienable Rights, that among these are Life, Liberty and the pursuit of Happiness. — That to secure these rights, Governments are instituted among Men, deriving their just powers from the consent of the governed, — That whenever any Form of Government becomes destructive of these ends, it is the Right of the People to alter or to abolish it, and to institute new Government, laying its foundation on such principles and organizing its powers in such form, as to them shall seem most likely to effect their Safety and Happiness. Prudence, indeed, will dictate that Governments long established should not be changed for light and transient causes; and accordingly all experience hath shewn that mankind are more disposed to suffer, while evils are sufferable than to right themselves by abolishing the forms to which they are accustomed. But when a long train of abuses and usurpations, pursuing invariably the same Object evinces a design to reduce them under absolute Despotism, it is their right, it is their duty, to throw off such Government, and to provide new Guards for their future security. — Such has been the patient sufferance of these Colonies; and such is now the necessity which constrains them to alter their former Systems of Government. The history of the present King of Great Britain is a history of repeated injuries and usurpations, all having in direct object the establishment of an absolute Tyranny over these States. To prove this, let Facts be submitted to a candid world.

He has refused his Assent to Laws, the most wholesome and necessary for the public good.

He has forbidden his Governors to pass Laws of immediate and pressing importance, unless suspended in their operation till his Assent should be obtained; and when so suspended, he has utterly neglected to attend to them.

He has refused to pass other Laws for the 5 accommodation of large districts of people, unless those people would relinquish the right of Representation in the Legislature, a right inestimable to them and formidable to tyrants only.

He has called together legislative bodies at places unusual, uncomfortable, and distant from the depository of their Public Records, for the sole purpose of fatiguing them into compliance with his measures.

He has dissolved Representative Houses repeatedly, for opposing with manly firmness his invasions on the rights of the people.

He has refused for a long time, after such dis-solutions, to cause others to be elected, whereby the Legislative Powers, incapable of Annihilation, have returned to the People at large for their exercise; the State remaining in the mean time exposed to all the dangers of invasion from with-out, and convulsions within.

He has endeavoured to prevent the popula-tion of these States; for that purpose obstructing the Laws for Naturalization of Foreigners; refusing to pass others to encourage their migra-tions hither, and raising the conditions of new Appropriations of Lands.

He has obstructed the Administration of 10 Justice by refusing his Assent to Laws for estab-lishing Judiciary Powers.

He has made Judges dependent on his Will alone for the tenure of their offices, and the amount and payment of their salaries.

He has erected a multitude of New Offices, and sent hither swarms of Officers to harass our people and eat out their substance.

He has kept among us, in times of peace, Standing Armies without the Consent of our legislatures.

He has affected to render the Military inde-pendent of and superior to the Civil Power.

He has combined with others to subject us 15 to a jurisdiction foreign to our constitution, and unacknowledged by our laws; giving his Assent to their Acts of pretended Legislation:

For quartering large bodies of armed troops among us:

For protecting them, by a mock Trial from punishment for any Murders which they should commit on the Inhabitants of these States:

For cutting off our Trade with all parts of the world:

For imposing Taxes on us without our Consent:

For depriving us in many cases, of the benefit 20 of Trial by Jury:

For transporting us beyond Seas to be tried for pretended offences:

For abolishing the free System of English Laws in a neighbouring Province, establishing therein an Arbitrary government, and enlarging its Boundaries so as to render it at once an exam-ple and fit instrument for introducing the same absolute rule into these Colonies:

For taking away our Charters, abolishing our most valuable Laws and altering fundamentally the Forms of our Governments:

For suspending our own Legislatures, and declaring themselves invested with power to legislate for us in all cases whatsoever.

He has abdicated Government here, by declaring us out of his Protection and waging War against us.

He has plundered our seas, ravaged our coasts, burnt our towns, and destroyed the lives of our people.

He is at this time transporting large Armies of foreign Mercenaries to compleat the works of death, desolation, and tyranny, already begun with circumstances of Cruelty & Perfidy scarcely paralleled in the most barbarous ages, and totally unworthy the Head of a civilized nation.

He has constrained our fellow Citizens taken Captive on the high Seas to bear Arms against their Country, to become the executioners of their friends and Brethren, or to fall themselves by their Hands.

He has excited domestic insurrections amongst us, and has endeavoured to bring on the inhabitants of our frontiers, the merciless Indian Savages whose known rule of warfare, is an undistinguished destruction of all ages, sexes and conditions.

In every stage of these Oppressions We have Petitioned for Redress in the most humble terms: Our repeated Petitions have been answered only by repeated injury. A Prince, whose character is thus marked by every act which may define a Tyrant, is unfit to be the ruler of a free people.

Nor have We been wanting in attentions to our British brethren. We have warned them from time to time of attempts by their legislature to extend an unwarrantable jurisdiction over us. We have reminded them of the circumstances of our emigration and settlement here. We have appealed to their native justice and magnanimity, and we have conjured them by the ties of our common kindred to disavow these usurpations, which would inevitably interrupt our connections and correspondence. They too have been deaf to the voice of justice and of consanguinity. We must, therefore, acquiesce in the necessity, which denounces our Separation, and hold them, as we hold the rest of mankind, Enemies in War, in Peace Friends.

We, therefore, the Representatives of the united States of America, in General Congress, Assembled, appealing to the Supreme Judge of the world for the rectitude of our intentions, do, in the Name, and by Authority of the good People of these Colonies, solemnly publish and declare, That these united Colonies are, and of Right ought to be Free and Independent States, that they are Absolved from all Allegiance to the British Crown, and that all political connection between them and the State of Great Britain, is and ought to be totally dissolved; and that as Free and Independent States, they have full Power to levy War, conclude Peace, contract Alliances, establish Commerce, and to do all other Acts and Things which Independent States may of right do. — And for the support of this Declaration, with a firm reliance on the protection of Divine Providence, we mutually pledge to each other our Lives, our Fortunes, and our sacred Honor.

The argument of the entire document can be distilled into this syllogism:

MAJOR PREMISE: Citizens have a right to rebel against a despot.

MINOR PREMISE: King George III is a despot.

CONCLUSION: Citizens have a right to rebel against King George III.

However, most of the text is inductive evidence — or "[f]acts . . . submitted to a candid world," as Jefferson called them. The document lists one example ("fact") after another of the king's behavior that support the generalization that he is a despot. For instance, "He has made Judges dependent on his Will alone," "He has affected to render the Military independent of and superior to the Civil Power," "He has plundered our seas," and "He has excited domestic insurrections amongst us." The evidence is overwhelming: the king is a despot; the colonists have every right to declare their independence.

Using Rogerian Argument

Another approach to argument is known as the **Rogerian** method, named for twentieth-century psychologist Carl Rogers, who stressed the importance of replacing confrontational argument tactics with ones that promote negotiation, compromise, and cooperation. Rogerian argumentation is particularly appropriate and useful for arguments on controversial subjects that for some are matters of belief — such as the death penalty, abortion, gun control, or the place of prayer or the teaching of evolution by natural selection in schools. Rogerian arguments are based on the assumption that having a full understanding of an opposing position is essential to responding to it persuasively and refuting it in a way that is accommodating rather than alienating. The key component of the Rogerian approach is finding common ground on which the speaker and an audience that holds opposing beliefs can both stand. The speaker must show that he or she has everyone's interest in mind, and thus be sympathetic to the audience's point of view. Ultimately, the goal is not necessarily to win the argument, but to reach a compromise through which both speaker and audience will feel that they have gained ground. For an example and analysis of a model Rogerian argument, see Appendix B (p. 1192).

Using the Toulmin Model

A useful way of both analyzing and structuring an argument is through the **Toulmin model**, an approach to argument created by British philosopher Stephen Toulmin in his book *The Uses of Argument* (1958). The Toulmin model is an effective tool in uncovering the assumptions that underlie arguments. Although at first this method — particularly its terminology — may seem complicated, it is actually very practical because it helps with analysis, structuring, qualifying a thesis, and understanding abstract arguments. Once mastered, it can be a very powerful tool.

The Toulmin model has six elements: claim, support (evidence), warrant (the assumption), backing, qualifier, and reservation. We have already discussed claims, which are arguable assertions. Toulmin defined a claim as "a conclusion whose merits we are seeking to establish." You have also already learned about support or evidence. A **warrant** expresses the **assumption** necessarily shared by the speaker and the audience. Similar to the minor premise of a syllogism, the assumption links the claim to the evidence; in other words, if the speaker and audience do not share the same assumption regarding the claim, all the evidence in the world won't be enough to sway them. **Backing** consists of further assurances or data without which the assumption lacks authority. The **qualifier**, when used (for example, *usually, probably, maybe, in most cases, most likely*), tempers the claim a bit, making it less absolute. The **reservation** explains the terms and conditions necessitated by the qualifier. In many cases, the argument will contain a **rebuttal** that gives voice to objections.

The following diagram illustrates the Toulmin model at work:

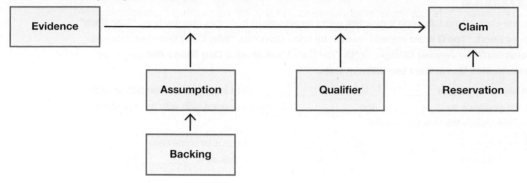

A Toulmin analysis will follow this form:

> Because (evidence as support), therefore (claim), since (assumption), on account of (backing), unless (reservation).

If there is a qualifier (such as *usually* or *maybe*), it will precede the claim. Here is a simple illustration:

> Because it is raining, therefore I should take my umbrella, since it will keep me dry.

You will immediately recognize the tacit assumption (that an umbrella will keep you dry) given explicit expression in the warrant. The backing would be "on account of the fact that the material is waterproof," and the reservation might be "unless there is a hole in it." In this case, the backing and reservation are so obvious that they don't need to be stated. The diagram below illustrates this argument — a simple one indeed, but one that demonstrates the process:

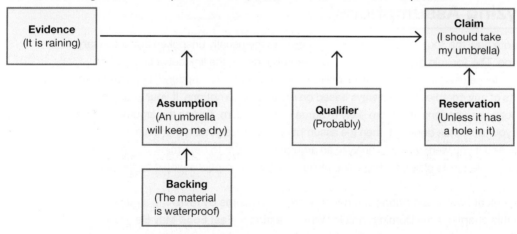

Fully expressed, this Toulmin argument would read:

> Because it is raining, therefore I should probably take my umbrella, since it will keep me dry on account of its waterproof material, unless, of course, there is a hole in it.

For an example analysis of an argument that applies the Toulmin model, see Appendix B (p. 1198).

ACTIVITY

Complete each of the following templates, using an argument from this chapter (e.g., "*Star Wars*" by Roger Ebert, "The C Word in the Hallways" by Anna Quindlen, "Why Can't Environmentalism Be Colorblind?" by Jennifer Oladipo, or "Do You Care More about a Dog Than a Refugee?" by Nicholas Kristof. Use at least two different texts.

1. In his/her argument _____ concludes _____ and supports the conclusion with such evidence as _____ and _____. To link this conclusion with the evidence, he/she makes the assumption that _____.

2. Although what _____ says about _____ may be true in some cases, his/her position fails to take _____ into account. A closer look at _____ reveals _____.

3. While the position advanced by X may seem reasonable, it assumes _____. If that were so, then _____. It might be more reasonable to consider _____.

4. One way to look at X would be to say _____; but if that were the case, then _____. Of course, another view might be _____. Yet another way to consider X might be _____.

5. Position X would be sound only if we chose to ignore _____. When we consider _____, then _____. In addition, _____.

6. Wouldn't it be wonderful if we could all agree about _____? The trouble is, _____. X says _____ and Y says _____. How can we come to a compromise that recognizes _____?

Analyzing Assumptions

You will note how the Toulmin model gives expression to the usually unspoken but necessary assumption. The Toulmin model shows us that assumptions are the link between a claim and the evidence used to support it. And, really, we should say "assumptions" here, because arguments of any complexity are always based on multiple assumptions. If your audience shares those assumptions, it is more likely to agree with the claim, finding the argument to be sound; if your audience does not, then the assumption becomes yet another claim requiring evidence. And if you were asked to analyze an argument in order to determine whether you support or challenge its claim, finding vulnerabilities in the assumptions would be the place to begin.

Let's look at how assumptions can become arguable claims by revisiting a piece from earlier in this chapter, Amy Domini's article "Why Investing in Fast Food May Be a Good Thing." We will see that by using the Toulmin method you could paraphrase her argument as follows:

> Because the fast-food industry continues to grow and is not going away, therefore even those of us who support Slow Food should invest in it, since investing has the power to persuade businesses to change.

The last part expresses one of the assumptions the audience must agree on in order for Domini's argument to be persuasive. Does investing have the power to persuade business to change?

Two examples from the education article by Zakaria will further illustrate the method. Paraphrased according to Toulmin, one of Zakaria's arguments would run as follows:

> Because South Korean children spend almost two years more in school than do Americans, therefore they outperform Americans on tests, since increased instructional time is responsible for increased test scores.

Do you agree with the assumption that increased instructional time is responsible for increased test scores? Alternatively, revealing another assumption, one might say:

> Because foreign students spend more time in school and achieve higher test scores, therefore they receive a better education, since quality of education and learning is indicated by test scores, on account of their accuracy in assessing learning.

Again, the assumption here might very well be debatable. Is learning indicated by test scores?

Sometimes, in the development of an argument, claims are presented implicitly early in the piece and more explicitly later. For an example, let's return to "The C Word in the Hallways" by Anna Quindlen. In the article, she makes several claims and supports them with credible evidence. Still, if you are to agree with her position, it is necessary to agree with the assumptions on which her arguments rest. Using the Toulmin model can help you to discover what they are, especially when the claim is implicit, as in the following:

> So many have already been lost. This month Kip Kinkel was sentenced to life in prison in Oregon for the murders of his parents and a shooting rampage at his high school that killed two students. A psychiatrist who specializes in the care of adolescents testified that Kinkel, now 17, had been hearing voices since he was 12. Sam Manzie is also 17. He is serving a 70-year sentence for luring an 11-year-old boy named Eddie Werner into his New Jersey home and strangling him with the cord of an alarm clock because his Sega Genesis was out of reach. Manzie had his first psychological evaluation in the first grade.

Using the Toulmin model, Quindlen's implicit argument here might be paraphrased as follows:

> Because Kinkel's and Manzie's mental illnesses were known for several years before they committed murder, therefore mental health care could have saved lives, since psychological intervention would have prevented them from committing these heinous acts.

As you finish the article, you come to realize that the entire argument rests on that assumption. Indeed, would psychological intervention have had that result? It certainly provokes discussion, which means that it is perhaps a point of vulnerability in Quindlen's argument.

ACTIVITY

For each of the following statements, identify the assumption that would link the claim to its support. Use the following format to discover the assumption: "Because (support), therefore (claim), since (assumption), on account of (backing), unless (reservation)." Decide whether each of the statements would require a qualifier.

1. Grades should be abolished because they add stress to the learning experience.

2. Until you buy me a diamond, I won't know that you love me!

3. Everyone should read novels because they make us more understanding of human foibles and frailties.

4. If we want to decrease gang violence, we should legalize drugs.

5. Don't get married if you believe that familiarity breeds contempt.

6. WiFi should be available to everyone without cost since the Internet has become a vital part of our lives.

7. You must obey her because she is your mother.

8. Because improving the educational system in this country is essential to competing with the other industrialized nations, we need to equip all classrooms with the latest computer technology.

ACTIVITY

In this chapter we have discussed four approaches to the analysis of argument: classical arrangement, induction and deduction, Rogerian argument, and the Toulmin model. Many arguments are more readily and effectively analyzed using one or two of these approaches; there are some, though, that contain elements of all four throughout. Read the following speech carefully, keeping Aristotle's rhetorical triangle in mind and identifying appeals to ethos, logos, and pathos. What elements of each of the four approaches to argument appear in this speech? Which one does Bloomberg make most use of in constructing his argument? How effective is his argument, overall? Explain.

Ground Zero Mosque Speech

MICHAEL BLOOMBERG

We have come here to Governors Island to stand where the earliest settlers first set foot in New Amsterdam, and where the seeds of religious tolerance were first planted. We've come here to see the inspiring symbol of liberty that, more than 250 years later, would greet millions of immigrants in the harbor, and we come here to state as strongly as ever — this is the freest City in the world. That's what makes New York special and different and strong.

Our doors are open to everyone — everyone with a dream and a willingness to work hard and play by the rules. New York City was built by immigrants, and it is sustained by immigrants — by people from more than a hundred different countries speaking more than two hundred different languages and professing every faith. And whether your parents were born here, or you came yesterday, you are a New Yorker.

We may not always agree with every one of our neighbors. That's life and it's part of living in such a diverse and dense city. But we also recognize that part of being a New Yorker is living with your neighbors in mutual respect and tolerance. It was exactly that spirit of openness and acceptance that was attacked on 9/11.

On that day, 3,000 people were killed because some murderous fanatics didn't want us to enjoy the freedom to profess our own faiths, to speak our own minds, to follow our own dreams and to live our own lives.

Of all our precious freedoms, the most important may be the freedom to worship as we wish. And it is a freedom that, even here in a city that is rooted in Dutch tolerance, was hard-won over many years. In the mid-1650s, the small Jewish community living in Lower Manhattan petitioned Dutch Governor Peter Stuyvesant for the right to build a synagogue — and they were turned down.

In 1657, when Stuyvesant also prohibited Quakers from holding meetings, a group of non-Quakers in Queens signed the Flushing Remonstrance, a petition in defense of the right of Quakers and others to freely practice their religion. It was perhaps the first formal, political petition for religious freedom in the American colonies — and the organizer was thrown in jail and then banished from New Amsterdam.

In the 1700s, even as religious freedom took hold in America, Catholics in New York were effectively prohibited from practicing their religion — and priests could be arrested. Largely as a result, the first Catholic parish in New York City was not established until the 1780s — St. Peter's on Barclay Street, which still stands just one block north of the World Trade Center site and one block south of the proposed mosque and community center.

This morning, the City's Landmark Preservation Commission unanimously voted not to extend landmark status to the building on Park Place where the mosque and community center are planned. The decision was based solely on the fact that there was little architectural significance to the building. But with or without landmark designation, there is nothing in the law that would prevent the owners from opening a mosque within the existing building. The simple fact is this building is private property, and the owners have a right to use the building as a house of worship.

The government has no right whatsoever to deny that right — and if it were tried, the courts would almost certainly strike it down as a violation of the U.S. Constitution. Whatever you may think of the proposed mosque and community center, lost in the heat of the debate has been a basic question — should government attempt to deny private citizens the right to build a house of worship on private property based on their particular religion? That may happen in other countries, but we should never allow it to happen here. This nation was founded on the principle that the government must never choose between religions or favor one over another.

The World Trade Center Site will forever hold a special place in our City, in our hearts. But we would be untrue to the best part of ourselves — and who we are as New Yorkers and Americans — if we said "no" to a mosque in Lower Manhattan.

Let us not forget that Muslims were among those murdered on 9/11 and that our Muslim neighbors grieved with us as New Yorkers and as Americans. We would betray our values — and play into our enemies' hands — if we were to treat Muslims differently than anyone else. In fact, to cave to popular sentiment would be to hand a victory to the terrorists — and we should not stand for that.

For that reason, I believe that this is an important test of the separation of church and state as we may see in our lifetime — as

121

important a test — and it is critically important that we get it right.

On September 11, 2001, thousands of first responders heroically rushed to the scene and saved tens of thousands of lives. More than 400 of those first responders did not make it out alive. In rushing into those burning buildings, not one of them asked "What God do you pray to?" "What beliefs do you hold?"

The attack was an act of war — and our first responders defended not only our City but also our country and our Constitution. We do not honor their lives by denying the very constitutional rights they died protecting. We honor their lives by defending those rights — and the freedoms that the terrorists attacked.

Of course, it is fair to ask the organizers of the mosque to show some special sensitivity to the situation — and in fact, their plan envisions reaching beyond their walls and building an interfaith community. By doing so, it is my hope that the mosque will help to bring our City even closer together and help repudiate the false and repugnant idea that the attacks of 9/11 were in any way consistent with Islam. Muslims are as much a part of our City and our country as the people of any faith and they are as welcome to worship in Lower Manhattan as any other group. In fact, they have been worshipping at the site for the better part of a year, as is their right.

The local community board in Lower Manhattan voted overwhelmingly to support the proposal and if it moves forward, I expect the community center and mosque will add to the life and vitality of the neighborhood and the entire City.

Political controversies come and go, but our values and our traditions endure — and there is no neighborhood in this City that is off limits to God's love and mercy, as the religious leaders here with us today can attest.

15

ANALYZING VISUAL TEXTS

Examining Arguments

As we've mentioned, visual texts make arguments, functioning rhetorically as they inform, enlighten, motivate, and persuade. A visual argument can be an advertisement, a political cartoon, a photograph, a bumper sticker, a T-shirt, a hat, a Web page, or even a piece of fine art. Yet the tools to analyze argument — identifying the claims; analyzing the way evidence is used; thinking critically about the artist's assumptions; examining how the piece is structured; considering appeals to ethos, pathos, and logos — are fairly similar for both visual and written arguments.

First-Impression Questions

You might start with the questions we asked above about subject, occasion, audience, purpose, and speaker, but let's expand those questions a bit to help guide our first impressions toward analysis:

- What is the subject? Does the visual text make a claim about the topic? Does it tell a story or suggest a narrative? If so, what is it?
- What emotions does the text evoke? What visual elements evoke those emotions? Are there any visual allusions that would conjure memories or emotions in viewers?
- What is the occasion? Where did the visual first appear?
- Who is the audience? Who might have seen the visual text when it first appeared? Who might be looking at it now? What cultural values might the viewer bring to the images?
- Who is the speaker? Does the speaker have political or organizational affiliations that are important to understanding the text?
- What is the purpose of the visual text? Does it have more than one purpose? What claim does the visual make about the issue(s) it addresses?

Library of Congress

You might not be able to answer all of these questions as you look at a visual text, but having some ideas about each will give you a head start in your analysis. Let's spend some time with *Migrant Mother*, a photograph taken in 1936 by Dorothea Lange (1895–1965). *Migrant Mother* has become iconic, a timeless symbol of the Great Depression, though Lange thought it "had a life of its own" and was a picture of a real person, not a symbol.

What is the subject? Does the visual text make a claim about the topic? Does the visual text tell a story or suggest a narrative? If so, what is it?

The subject of the photo is a mother holding a baby, flanked on both sides by her two daughters, who face away from the camera. The most obvious claim, then, is one about the experience of motherhood. The worn and dirty clothing and the mother's anxious look suggest a story of tough luck and hard times. The title and context of the image indicate that the subject is also the plight of migrant workers during the Great Depression.

123

What emotions does the visual text evoke? What visual elements evoke those emotions? Are there any visual allusions that would conjure memories or emotions in viewers?

The emotional tone is sadness, captured in the distracted and exhausted face of the mother — but there is also strength as she holds her baby tight and shields her daughters. Although the photo is in black and white, there is still a large range, from white through many grays to black. Since much of the photo is in shadow, the direct light on the mother's face brings her worn features into sharp focus. The darker shadows almost hide the children in the background. The photo may also evoke art you're familiar with: for instance, Renaissance paintings of the Madonna, which typically show Mary holding Jesus as angels look on from the background. In *Migrant Mother*, however, the two children are facing away from rather than smiling down on the baby.

What is the occasion? Where did the visual text first appear?

The photo, taken in 1936, was part of Dorothea Lange's work for the Federal Resettlement Administration. It first appeared in the *San Francisco News*, which reported that thousands of migrant workers were destitute. The federal government responded by sending 20,000 tons of food.

Who is the audience? Who might have seen the visual text when it first appeared? Who might be looking at it now? What cultural values might the viewer bring to the images?

The audience at the time the photo was published were readers of the *San Francisco News*, but the photo was also picked up by wire services and appeared in newspapers all over the country. Today, it is still considered one of the most potent images of the Great Depression and the plight of migrant workers.

Who is the speaker? Does the speaker have political or organizational affiliations that are important to understanding the visual text?

Dorothea Lange was born in 1895 and contracted polio as a child, which she believed made her more empathetic. During the Great Depression, she moved to Taos, New Mexico, and worked on several New Deal projects, which involved documenting the toll the Great Depression had taken on Americans.

What is the purpose of the visual text? Does it have more than one purpose?

We know that Dorothea Lange was a documentarian of the Great Depression. This photograph illustrates the terrible conditions of migrant workers in intimate detail, capturing an unguarded and vulnerable moment for a destitute family.

Examining Rhetoric in Visual Arguments

As we move on with our analysis of the argument made by *Migrant Mother*, let's consider how all of the aspects of the rhetorical triangle relate to each other: the speaker, in this case a photographer, is Dorothea Lange in her role as a documentarian of the Great Depression. The occasion is a crop failure that has exacerbated terrible conditions for migrant workers. The subject is a woman who looks older than her thirty-two years, one whose hard life shows in her worn and lined face, the dirty and ill-fitting clothes she and her children wear, and in her distracted and exhausted expression.

Let's also consider the appeals that *Migrant Mother* makes. It is a documentary photo that records a real event, and is certainly expressive in its appeal to emotion. While the focus in the photo is clear, there is little visible background; this makes it difficult to tell the time of day, even though the light seems natural. The foregrounding of the figures makes it seem like we can touch them and feel the roughness of their clothing. We see a range of values — from the mother's very dark hair to the light blanket wrapped around the baby — but the overall sense is one of grayness, and the sadness it evokes, beyond even the constraints of a black-and-white photo. The strong upward movement of the mother's arm provides a vertical line that anchors the photo, though it ends abruptly with her hand touching her chin. This movement is somewhat echoed in the line of the arm of the child on the right. We also see some repetition in the shape of the children's haircuts and in the angles formed by the bent arms of the mother and child. There is a sense of logic in these geometric shapes — hard angles suggest the hard lives of this young family. The photo seems shallow; it almost looks like the subjects are being forced outside. In fact, one of the reasons Lange visited this particular farm was that she had heard the workers were so poor they had to sell their tents to buy food. The composition of the photo ultimately reinforces Lange's credibility as a conscientious documentarian.

Connecting Visual Rhetoric to Argument

What can we make of our observation of the photo's rhetorical strategies? How does this particular connection between speaker, subject, and occasion form an argument? The tightness of the frame creates a sense of entrapment even as the shallowness of the picture field suggests the family's plight is pushing them out into the cold. The upward lines that end abruptly may remind us of the struggle for migrant farm workers who are destitute and at a dead end. We see the mother's vulnerability in her family's tattered clothes and in the claustrophobic lack of background — but we also see her strength in the way she gathers her children to her to comfort them, forming the loose outline of a triangle. You may have come across the idea of the triangle as representing stability, and Renaissance paintings of baby Jesus and his mother are similarly reassuring. Even if you didn't notice these allusions, the stability of the family unit resonates despite the poverty evident here.

So what argument does *Migrant Mother* make? There isn't a single correct answer, of course, but one interpretation, based on the photo's subject and its formal elements, is that Lange's iconic portrait of a mother and her children both humanizes the toll of the Great Depression and calls the viewer to action. In fact, some discussions of the photo note that the father is absent from the image and speculate that it is a call to him — perhaps in the form of government — to help rescue these workers from the destitution wrought by the Depression.

ACTIVITY

Look carefully at this *New Yorker* magazine cover from the summer of 2016. Try to answer some of the questions we've suggested in this section. What argument does this image make? How does the artist make that argument? How effective is the argument?

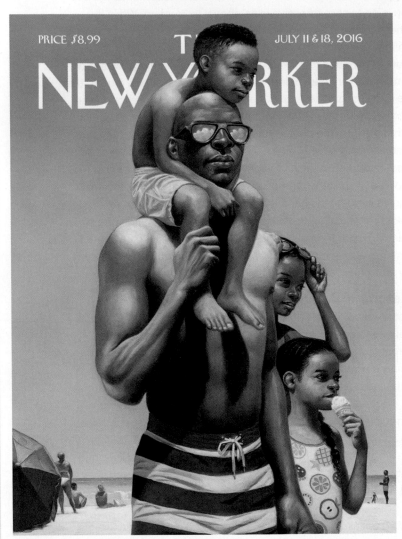

PRICE $8.99   THE NEW YORKER   JULY 11 & 18, 2016

Kadir Nelson/The New Yorker Collection © Conde Nast

From Reading to Writing: The Argumentative Essay

In this chapter, you've learned how to read an argument, analyze its components, and evaluate its strengths and flaws. You have also studied several methods of argument analysis, including classical arrangement, induction and deduction, Rogerian argument, and the Toulmin model. In addition to helping you understand how other people's arguments function, these methods can help you bring logic and clarity to your own writing.

Preparing to Write

The first step to developing an argument is to decide on an idea or issue worth arguing. If you aren't sure where to start, you may find it helpful to consider what interests you, what community issues you have a stake in, and what questions come to mind when you think about them. For instance, some questions immediately relevant to your life might include: Is the emphasis on sports in school appropriate? Should schools ban corporate sponsorship? Should there be parking privileges for seniors at your school? Should your school have a code of ethics? Is the SAT or the ACT an accurate measure of a student's potential? Should we lower the legal drinking age? Should we raise the minimum wage? Are we becoming addicted to our electronic devices? What is an appropriate penalty for plagiarism? Or, you might consider asking questions about even larger issues, such as global warming, religious freedom, immigration, or electronic surveillance.

In your English class, the arguments that you write will often be in response to prompts on assigned topics. You may be required to respond to the work of others, often by defending, challenging, or qualifying the author's particular viewpoint. You might also be asked to respond to an issue that outlines a problem in your local community, your state, your nation, or the world. For a homework assignment or a long-term project, you may have to research the topic. In that case, to help support your argument, you may refer to facts, statistics, and other quantitative data; to an authority, such as an expert testimony; or to historical details about the topic to place your argument in context. But you will often be asked to write an argumentative essay in a timed environment — whether in class or on an exam — which means you typically must use what you know and remember.

Let's say your teacher assigns you the following prompt:

The following passage, excerpted from an article that appeared in the Boston Globe *in March 2016, is about a Massachusetts high school that changed its start time from 7:35 a.m. to 8:45 a.m. Read the passage carefully and consider the pros and cons of an early or late start time. Then, write an essay that develops a position on the start time for your school or for high schools in general. Use evidence from your reading, observation, and experience to support your argument.*

> The lack of adequate shut-eye can have detrimental effects on the health and academic performance of teenagers, increasing their risks for early morning car crashes, suicidal tendencies, depression, binge drinking, drug overdoses, and bad grades, research has shown. Several studies in recent years have recommended starting high school at 8:30 a.m. or later, saying students should get between 8.5 and 9.5 hours of sleep per night — not the 6 hours that is often the case.
>
> Yet efforts in other districts to delay start times have often been stymied. Critics say the change creates conflicts with sports schedules and after-school programs, leaves students without enough time for afterschool jobs, and could interfere with bus schedules for elementary-school students who typically get out later in the afternoon.

Establishing a Position

Arguments often start with opinions. We all have them: gut feelings that often have more to do with our values than with reason and fact. The key to developing a successful argument is to remember that there is an important difference between having an opinion and establishing a position. Though a position you take on an issue can reflect your opinion, it must be supported by evidence.

The first step in establishing your position is taking a moment to determine just what you know about the topic at hand. What have your experiences and observations taught you? For instance, have you seen the ramifications of early (or later) school start times in your school, in your community, or in the media? What have you learned about the relationship between sleep and cognition in your classes or from your independent reading? All of these areas of knowledge and experience can serve as evidence to support the position you choose to take in your argumentative essay.

Considering Questions of Fact, Value, and Policy

Note as well that the prompt asks you to consider the pros and cons of an early or late start time. Obviously, for a teenager, a big pro might be sleeping in another hour before school; an obvious con would be staying in school an hour later — unless, of course, your last class of the day is English! At this point, you should ask yourself some questions about the facts. For example, do teenagers get enough sleep? How do you know whether they do or not? Why do high schools start earlier than most businesses? Think about your parents. What do they do for a living? What time do they start work?

Then you'll naturally progress to questions of value. What factors determine the start time for school? Are they fair? Do they relate to economics, convenience, learning and teaching, health, or to any other issues? What social and educational values does the start time of high schools reflect?

Finally, you should ask some questions of policy. Should we maintain the present school schedule or change it, and why? The answer to this question will form the core of your argument, and questions of policy are crucial to developing your position. What reasoning shaped the current policy — why *does* school start so early? Is it a leftover from an era when farming played a bigger role in many students' lives? Is it to accommodate after-school sports? Does the current start-time policy take into account what we now know about teenage health and brain development? As you use these questions to determine your position, you should also keep in mind the positions that others may hold, since you will want to address a counterargument in your essay.

Crafting a Thesis

Once you have considered these factors, it's time to construct your **thesis statement** — in other words, make a claim that states your position clearly.

Earlier in this chapter, we discussed how you might construct a closed thesis, an open thesis, and a counterargument thesis. Below are two examples of each type of thesis in response to the prompt on page 127:

CLOSED THESIS

Early start times for American high schools are necessary to accommodate extra-curricular activities and participation in sports during after-school hours and to ensure the safety of elementary students during early morning hours.

Because early start times have detrimental effects on the health and education of our adolescents, high schools should start no earlier than 8:30 a.m.

OPEN THESIS

Early start times for American high schools show that convenience and cost are more important concerns than the health and academic growth of our students.

Early start times for American high schools are economically viable and necessary to accommodate the busy lives of our students.

COUNTERARGUMENT THESIS

While the health and education of students must be the chief concerns of American school districts, economic realities and scheduling imperatives necessitate early start times for high schools.

Although school districts must consider economic constraints as well as scheduling difficulties in deciding school start times, the health and academic growth of our students must take precedence.

ACTIVITY

Develop a thesis statement that could focus an argument in response to each of the following prompts. Discuss why you think that the structure (open, closed, counterargument) you chose would be appropriate or effective.

1. Same-sex classrooms have gone in and out of favor in public education. Write an essay explaining why you would support or oppose same-sex classrooms for public schools in grades 10 through 12.

2. Write an essay supporting, challenging, or qualifying English author E. M. Forster's position in the following quotation: "I hate the idea of causes, and if I had to choose between betraying my country and betraying my friend, I hope I should have the guts to betray my country."

3. Today's world is full of conflicts and controversies. Choose a local or global issue, and write an essay that considers multiple viewpoints and proposes a solution or compromise.

4. Write an essay explaining why you agree or disagree with the following quotation: "Advertising degrades the people it appeals to; it deprives them of their will to choose."

5. Plagiarism is rampant in public high schools and colleges. In fact, some people argue that the definition of *plagiarism* has changed with the proliferation of the Internet, the ease of "cutting and pasting," and the practice of "sampling." Write an essay explaining what you believe the appropriate response of a teacher should be to a student who turns in a plagiarized essay or exam.

Organizing Your Argument

There are many ways to organize an argument, and which method you choose can depend on your topic, the amount of time you have to write, the resources you have access to as you develop your argument, or even personal preference. Among the methods for argument analysis that you have learned about in this chapter, we believe the classical arrangement (p. 106) is most useful for constructing an argumentative essay in a timed context. Let's explore how you might use the classical arrangement to develop a response to the prompt we have been discussing.

Introducing Your Argument

The introduction of an argumentative essay leads your audience into your subject. It should portray your subject as worthy of attention as well as establish that you are a credible speaker. Here is where you want to convince your readers that they should care about what you have to say. You will doubtless have noticed that many effective arguments begin with a rhetorical question that implies what the writer's thesis will be. For instance: Is our society overly materialistic? Should marijuana be legalized? Should assault weapons be restricted? Asking questions like these gets your audience thinking about the subject. Beginning with a "hook" — such as a quotation, an anecdote, a reference to a news item or authority, or an allusion to a historical event — is another tried and true way of capturing audience interest quickly. Your information should be accurate and your introduction brief; it should whet your audience's appetite and prompt them to continue reading or listening.

If you are having trouble crafting an introduction to your essay, you might ask yourself the following questions:

- Why is this topic important?
- What are the consequences of the various issues this topic raises?
- Why should my audience care?

Informing Your Audience

The closing of the introduction should lead smoothly into the next part of your argument: the narration, or exposition. This provides your audience with necessary context to grasp the problem or issue your essay will address. In writing this portion of your essay, it may be helpful to think of how courtroom proceedings are portrayed in TV and movies. Before lawyers introduce evidence and witnesses, they take a moment to lay out the facts of the case for the judge and jury. Keep this analogy in mind as you write this part of your argument. It's important to stick to simple facts, illustrative examples, and unbiased explanations.

Knowing your audience is crucial to writing a strong exposition. To make sure you are reaching your specific audience, you might ask yourself some questions:

- What is my audience likely to know — and feel— about my subject?
- Does my audience have a personal interest in the subject?
- What values does my audience likely hold?
- What are some of the pros and cons relating to the issue?

The more clearly you can answer these questions, the more effectively you will be able to establish a strong ethos, find some common moral ground with your readers, and make a personal connection with them.

Another way to consider audience is to frame your argument in emotional terms. Think back to arguments that you have read in which you felt you could identify with the ethos established by the voice of the writer, including the arguments made by the writers included in this chapter. Which of the readings appealed to you in ways that felt personal? What features of those arguments made the connection strong? Establishing this kind of deep connection with your audience will not only bolster your persuasive power, it will strengthen your grasp on your subject — by anticipating various reader viewpoints, you examine your own beliefs and automatically consider potential counterarguments.

Since your reader is typically your teacher, you should assume you are writing for an audience that will question not only your claims and your evidence but also the soundness of your reasoning. Your reader will evaluate the particular details and specific evidence that support your argument — that is, saying something is so does not make it so. Overly general, unsupported assertions are at the heart of many unsuccessful arguments, because they tend to be unconvincing; specific evidence that incorporates particular details, on the other hand, can be quite effective. The difference, for instance, between terms like *car* and *Subaru; classes* and *chemistry and U.S. History; books* and *Outliers* or *The Things They Carried; late,* and *four hours late to a noon lunch* is vast. Such differences in word choice clarify statements of fact and can even suggest distinct tones.

If, as is the case with our example prompt, you are responding to a written text, you may also want to include a brief summary of its main idea or position. The key is to keep it brief, avoiding bias and hyperbole as much as you can. If you're not sure whether this portion of your exposition is objective and neutral, check to make sure you have not included absolutes, such as *all, never, always, totally,* and the like. Such language will likely be dissuasive and damage your ethos right at the start.

Finally, your position — that is, your thesis — should be clear to your reader before you move from your exposition to the next section, the confirmation. There is no hard and fast rule as to where a thesis statement should appear, but for a timed response an excellent place is at the end of your opening paragraph or at the beginning of your second.

Supporting Your Argument

The next step in writing an argumentative essay that follows the classical model is to make your case by developing the confirmation, or proof that supports your position. If you are writing with a time limit, this part of your essay should make at least two claims that support your position. Be sure to back each claim with solid evidence. You should probably save your strongest, most compelling claim for last — making your first claim accessible and familiar to your audience develops your case incrementally. You're more likely to influence your audience using this strategy; the more a reader responds positively at first, the more likely it is that the reader will accept your argument as it unfolds.

As you develop your arguments, you should remember to consider what types of evidence you will use (see Presenting Evidence, pp. 89–105). If you aren't sure where to start, you might try thinking of what you have done — that is, your experiences that are relevant to your subject; what you have observed about your subject; and what you have learned about your subject. You can then draw your evidence from that experience, observation, and knowledge.

You may also find it helpful to decide on the logical approach you want to take at the outset — whether inductive or deductive. An inductive argument in response to our prompt might begin with a general statement about health and sleep deprivation, for instance, whereas a deductive approach might start with the sleepy student trying to concentrate in first period class.

Also remember that nearly all good arguments take other perspectives into consideration. In other words, they are **qualified arguments**, which acknowledge the limitations of their claims and positions. Qualifying your argument strengthens your ethos by showing you are open-minded and considerate of other views. It also gives heft to your appeal to logos in that it makes your position more reasoned, and also more reasonable.

Acknowledging and Refuting the Counterargument

As we have discussed earlier in the chapter, arguments in the classical model address the counterargument with a refutation. It is customary, and often highly effective, to do this following your confirmation. Placing your refutation here maintains the ethos that you established at the beginning of your essay and appeals to logos as it moves the reader from your proof to your conclusion. Even if you begin your essay with a counterargument thesis, it is still wise to include a refutation.

One useful strategy for choosing the counterargument you will address is to weigh the pros and cons surrounding the topic at hand. This will help you discover the counterargument you believe is the most reasonable objection to your own position. It's important to refute reasonable counterarguments rather than flimsy straw men; addressing such easily dismissed claims will ultimately damage your ethos, especially if your audience is perceptive.

Concluding Your Argument

Perhaps the most difficult part of an essay — especially in a timed environment — is the conclusion. How do you conclude without saying, "In conclusion . . ."? It may help to keep in mind that the most important function of a conclusion is to move the reader's attention from *what* your essay has argued to *so what*, or why your argument matters. In your introduction, you addressed why the reader should care about the subject; you can bring your essay full circle by returning to that idea. Why should the reader care about the position you have developed? You might appeal to pathos, reminding your audience that the issue has real-world consequences. Or, you might appeal to a value you share with your audience that bears on your subject and on your position, subtly emphasizing some common ground.

A Sample Argumentative Essay

Below is a sample argumentative essay written by a high school student in response to the prompt we introduced on page 125. After reading the prompt and the essay carefully, respond to the questions that follow.

The following passage, excerpted from an article that appeared in the Boston Globe *in March, 2016, is about a Massachusetts high school that changed its start time from 7:35 a.m. to 8:45 a.m. Read the passage carefully and consider the pros and cons of an early or late start time. Then, write an essay that develops a position on the start time for your school or for high schools in general. Use evidence from your reading, observation, and experience to support your argument.*

> The lack of adequate shut-eye can have detrimental effects on the health and academic performance of teenagers, increasing their risks for early morning car crashes, suicidal tendencies, depression, binge drinking, drug overdoses, and bad grades, research has shown. Several studies in recent years have recommended starting high school at 8:30 a.m. or later, saying students should get between 8.5 and 9.5 hours of sleep per night — not the 6 hours that is often the case.
>
> Yet efforts in other districts to delay start times have often been stymied. Critics say the change creates conflicts with sports schedules and afterschool programs, leaves students without enough time for afterschool jobs, and could interfere with bus schedules for elementary-school students who typically get out later in the afternoon.

"On Starting School Later"

by Leah Marchl

It's six thirty a.m. The alarm rings, it's time to get up. You've gotten a total of five hours of sleep, four hours less than the recommended amount. While in freshman year, this was due to watching Netflix into the early hours of the morning, you now go to bed at one in the morning because of a paper that's due first period. This is the sixth night in a row that you are sleep deprived, and you can just sense a panic attack coming. The increasingly higher demands and pressures on high schoolers are causing them to sleep less and less, which has disastrous consequences not only on their health, but on those around them. To address the growing concerns of the scientific community on teenage sleep deprivation, schools have adopted later start times. For example, some schools in Massachusetts have moved their start time from seven thirty-five a.m. to eight thirty a.m. Unfortunately, some are opposed to these changes because a mere one hour shift can have impacts on many aspects of a community's functioning. Considering the biology behind morning sleepiness and the consequences sleep deprivation can have on health, these later start times are perfectly logical. But the real change needed isn't a later start time, but a shift in the very nature of high school culture.

133

To understand why teenagers are so sleepy, we need to consider several factors. For one, the biology of a wacky inner clock. Studies have shown that the hormone that creates drowsiness in the teenaged brain only comes into effect around 11 p.m., several hours later than in prepubescent children or adults who have reached maturity. That means that by seven a.m., that hormone is still very much working on the brain, inducing drowsiness, while younger children are usually more alert by that time. Additionally, students, especially in their junior year, stay up until the early hours to complete assignments. Sure, some of it is due to lack of organization, but the simple fact is that the homework never ends. High schoolers also juggle multiple commitments to clubs, sports, and part-time jobs, which are all exhausting. All of this creates a day that is about fourteen to fifteen hours of activity, and I'm not accounting for the tiring periodic growth spurts and brain development that is characteristic of puberty. Despite all these factors that are entirely out of the hands of the affected students, adults continue to decry teenagers as weaklings that should just go to bed earlier.

Sleep deprivation, especially on a long-term basis, has terrible consequences. From poor academic performance to fatal car crashes, sleep deprivation is just bad for you. Multiple studies have found that it takes teenagers several classes to become fully alert. This means they are basically missing out on two to three hours of class work, which eventually leads to bad test scores. On the darker side, depression is also an effect of sleep deprivation. Teenagers are already susceptible to higher levels of anxiety that often go untreated. Mix that with sleep deprivation and nose-diving grades, the result is full-fledged depression that is discounted as attention-seeking, teenage whims. Lack of sleep is often compensated with overstimulation and overeating, making a perfectly healthy seventeen-year-old overweight and addicted to coffee, or worse, Adderall. Critics cite that a later start time creates "conflicts with sports schedules and after-school programs, leaves students without enough time for afterschool jobs, and could interfere with bus schedules for elementary-school students." These are all valid objections. But teenagers' health must take priority over sports in the educational checklist.

While earlier start times are finally addressing the problem of teenaged sleep deprivation, they barely scratch the surface. And as their critics have pointed out, they make things more complicated for a school district. The real source of the problem of depressed and exhausted students is the very culture of high school. Especially in junior year, things become less about learning and more about getting into the next best college. Students and their environment are hyperfocused on the marginal addition, just like cocaine-induced Wall Street bankers. We are encouraged to join one more club, become the captain of one more team, work one more hour, take one more course, intern one more time. All to prove to some admission officer making thirty grand a year that we are that one additional student they need. Even vacations and weekends are consecrated to school, leaving no time to focus on oneself and heal. I recently had surgery, and got a total of two days to rest. My doctor encouraged two weeks of off-time, but I was too afraid of falling behind. This frantic cyclical dance of competition and tears is extremely unhealthy, and I don't think that adding an extra hour of sleep will really change anything. There needs to be a shift in the mindset.

The recent efforts to start school later are a welcome breath of fresh air in the noise chamber of adults complaining about teenagers being crybabies who can't get their work in on time. But we are simply the product of a system they set up. So while this country's education experts as well as its students collectively reflect on how out of control the system has become, let students sleep one more hour for the sake of their health and sanity.

QUESTIONS

1. Identify the thesis of this essay. How adequately does it state a position that responds to the prompt?

2. How effectively does the writer establish her ethos? How effectively does the essay appeal to the audience?

3. To what extent has the writer fully responded to the prompt? Identify areas that show consideration of the pros and cons of an early or late start time.

4. What kinds of evidence does the writer use to support her claims? How adequately does that evidence do so? How effectively does the essay address the counterargument?

5. Can you think of any other evidence that would add to the cogency of the argument that this essay makes? Explain.

6. This essay was written as a timed, first draft response to the prompt. How might you edit and revise it to make it better?

CULMINATING ACTIVITY

Practicing what you have learned about argument in this chapter, write an argumentative essay in response to the following prompt:

Much attention has been given lately to the presence of cell phones in school. Many people — especially teachers — regard them as distractions that divert attention from learning and that they have no legitimate place in the classroom. Others, including an increasing number of teachers, claim that they have found ways to incorporate their use into classroom lessons to facilitate teaching and learning. Opponents of the first position suggest that those teachers are old-fashioned and should adapt themselves to the technologically driven world in which we live; opponents of the second group suggest that teachers are merely capitulating, giving in to corporate interests, administrative pressure, or student demands and even "addiction."

Consider carefully the effect of cell phones in the classroom. Are they distractions? Should they be banned? Should their use be restricted? Can they be used effectively for learning? Should they be permitted or encourages? Write an essay that develops a position on the use of cell phones in your school or in schools in general. Use evidence from your reading, observation, or experience to support your argument.

4

Synthesizing Sources
Entering the Conversation

Hiroshi Watanabe/Getty Images

We all draw on the ideas of others as we develop our own positions, regardless of the topic. Whether you are explaining your opinion about an issue specific to your community (such as whether to allow skateboarding in public parks), or you are developing a position on a national or global issue (such as whether to change immigration policies), you should know as much as possible about the topic. Rather than make a quick response that reflects an opinion based only on what you already know, you might research and read sources — that is, what others have written or researched. Then you can develop your own *informed* opinion, a measured response that considers multiple perspectives and possibilities. We call this process **synthesis**.

In his bestselling book *Consilience: The Unity of Knowledge* (1998), biologist and author E. O. Wilson asserted that those who are adept at synthesis will be the leading thinkers in our so-called information age. With an ability to take in a variety of information, evaluate it, and craft meaning from it to understand the modern world, the "synthesizers," as Wilson calls them, will be on the cutting edge: "We are drowning in information, while starving for wisdom. The world henceforth will be run by synthesizers, people able to put together the right information at the right time, think critically about it, and make important choices wisely."

What Is Synthesis?

The process of synthesis, though it may sound complicated, is actually part of everyday life. Anytime you take two or more ideas or concepts and combine them using your own ingenuity to create something new, you have synthesized those elements. For instance, if your favorite outfit is a leather motorcycle jacket over a floral dress, you might describe your fashion sense as a synthesis of classic and edgy. Any time you approach a concept with several possibilities or perspectives in mind, analyze each one, reflect on them, and arrive at a new way of seeing — or if not entirely new, then more informed — that's synthesis.

It may help to think of it this way: You show up at a party. There are a dozen different conversations going on. You approach one group of people who are having a heated debate. In order to understand what the specific topic of debate is, you'll need to listen for a while to figure out what they've already said, who is taking which perspective, and what it is that they're not saying. Then, by either expanding on what others are saying, challenging what they are saying, or filling in a gap in their understanding, you'll begin to enter this conversation and make your own contribution. And that's what synthesis is all about: entering the conversation that society is having about a topic. You enter the conversation by carefully reading and understanding the perspectives and ideas surrounding an issue, examining your own ideas on the matter, and then synthesizing these views into a more informed position than the one you began with.

However, your "position" need not present itself as a contest between competing viewpoints. Of course, developing a viewpoint of your own is important, but a critical part of this process involves consulting sources to gain a deeper appreciation of the complexity of the topic or issue in question. Whether your perspective takes the form of a conventional documented essay, a proposal, a multimedia presentation, or a speech, the range and quality of sources you consult will influence your audience's response.

When you're learning about a subject, look for reliable sources. Be aware of the **bias** that a source brings to the topic. Consider the speaker: What does he or she believe in? How might the speaker's position provide personal gain? Don't look for a pro-and-con debate that represents only polarized views; look for a range of viewpoints in dialogue with one another. This might sound like a lot to keep in mind, but don't worry; you work with sources all the time. For example, when you decide to buy a new smartphone, you gather information by exploring different sources. Maybe you consult *Consumer Reports* and other technology magazines that include charts and graphs, and you compare prices and technical specs and ask your friends for their opinions and experiences. You might also go to a computer store and talk with the experts, read reviews online, or use online forums as a quick source for many opinions. But what you might not find useful is to talk with your neighbor who's reluctant to give up his landline, nor would you get all of your information from a salesperson, who likely works on commission. The final result of your inquiries is a purchase, not an essay, but it requires you to synthesize a range of sources in order to make the argument to yourself that the phone you chose is the best fit for you.

Approaching Sources

Perhaps the most important trait you can bring to sources, whether they are texts already provided for you or ones you research yourself, is an open mind. While approaching your reading critically — always asking questions, looking for flaws in logic, assessing the evidence — is a valuable skill, exploring multiple sources that represent different, often opposing, views requires you to be willing to suspend judgment until you have examined each of those sources in turn. You may find yourself surprised by the merits of ways of seeing you had not previously considered.

Another way to think about this approach is the distinction that scholar Peter Elbow makes between "the doubting game" and "the believing game" in a 2009 article for the *Journal for The Assembly for Expanded Perspectives on Learning*. "The doubting game," according to Elbow, is the "disciplined practice of trying to be as skeptical and analytic as possible with every idea we encounter." He acknowledges that we honor this practice because it helps us to discover contradictions, poor reasoning, and other problems in ideas that may, on their surface, seem appealing. However, he argues, we may miss opportunities to fully understand an idea, especially one we disagree with, unless we engage in what he calls "the believing game," which he defines as "the disciplined practice of trying to be as welcoming as possible to every idea . . . not just listening to views different from our own and holding back from arguing with them, but actually trying to believe them." This practice not only allows us to find some virtue in ideas that at first seem to go against our own beliefs, but it can also help us recognize flaws in our own thinking. Elbow claims, "Our best hope for finding invisible flaws in what we can't see in our own thinking is to enter into different ideas or points of view — ideas that carry different assumptions." As you read the sources in the Conversations included in this chapter, try to play the "believing game" as often as you do the "doubting game."

ACTIVITY

Find an opinion piece — such as an editorial, a movie review, an op-ed column, or a blog — that represents an opinion different from your own. Respond to it by playing "the believing game" — that is, write a short paragraph in which you find a way to "believe" at least some part of your chosen piece. What did you learn by trying to "believe"? Did it affect your initial viewpoint on the subject of the piece?

Using Sources to Inform an Argument

As we discussed in Chapter 3, many different types of evidence can serve to support an argument. But it's important to remember that your sources should enhance, not replace, your argument. You may worry that the ideas of others are so persuasive that you have nothing new to say. Or you may think that the more sources you cite, the more impressed your reader (especially your teacher) will be. But as you develop your skills in writing synthesis essays, you will find that the sources inform your own ideas and demonstrate your understanding of opposing views. What *you* have to say is the main event; *your* position is central.

In the following example, Laura Hillenbrand, author of *Seabiscuit*, a Pulitzer Prize–winning book about a champion racehorse who beat the odds, maintains her own voice throughout, even when she uses the works of experts to help make a point. (She identifies the works in a section at the end of the book.) But whether she is quoting directly or paraphrasing, she never gets lost in the sources or allows them to overwhelm her ideas.

---

from Seabiscuit

LAURA HILLENBRAND

To pilot a racehorse is to ride a half-ton catapult. It is without question one of the most formidable feats in sport. The extraordinary athleticism of the jockey is unparalleled: A study of the elements of athleticism conducted by Los Angeles exercise physiologists and physicians found that of all major sports competitors, jockeys may be, pound for pound, the best overall athletes. They have to be. To begin with, there are the demands on balance, coordination, and reflex. A horse's body is a constantly shifting topography, with a bobbing head and neck and roiling muscle over the shoulders, back, and rump. On a running horse, a jockey does not sit in the saddle, he crouches over it, leaning all of his weight on his toes, which rest on the thin metal bases of stirrups dangling about a foot from the horse's topline. When a horse is in full stride, the only parts of the jockey that are in continuous contact with the animal are the insides of the feet and ankles — everything else is balanced in midair. In other words, jockeys squat on the pitching backs of their mounts, a task much like perching on the grille of a car while it speeds down a twisting, potholed freeway in traffic. The stance is, in the words of University of North Carolina researchers, "a situation of dynamic imbalance and ballistic opportunity." The center of balance is so narrow that if jockeys shift only slightly rearward, they will flip right off the back. If they tip more than a few inches forward, a fall is almost inevitable.

Jockey (video), Tel-Air Productions, 1980.
A. E. Waller et al., "Jockey Injuries in the United States," *Journal of the American Medical Association*, 2000; vol. 283, no. 10.

Rather than citing her sources within the text, Hillenbrand includes the information about the sources she cites at the end of her book. The first item is a videotape about the study by Los Angeles exercise physiologists and physicians; the second is an article in a medical journal. By including these sources, Hillenbrad acknowledges that she turned to authorities — sources — to deepen and supplement her own knowledge about the mechanics and physics of how a racehorse and a jockey move as one entity.

ACTIVITY

In the following passage from *A Level Playing Field: African American Athletes and the Republic of Sports*, Gerald L. Early discusses the complex character of Jackie Robinson, the first black athlete to play in major league baseball. What is the purpose of the sources Early chooses to include? How do they enhance or detract from his own voice? What is the purpose of each of the notes documenting the sources?

from A Level Playing Field

GERALD L. EARLY

But 1949 was also Robinson's year of liberation. According to Branch Rickey, known as the Mahatma by sportswriters, the Dodgers executive who signed Robinson and who pushed for integration: "For three years [that was the agreement] this boy was to turn the other cheek. He did, day after day, until he had no other to turn. They were both beat off. There were slight slip-ups on occasion in that first year in Montreal."[1]

Robinson had agreed to ignore all slights, insults, and abuses that he endured on the playing field during his first three years as a professional ballplayer in the white leagues. This generated, naturally, a certain public sympathy, as Robinson did, indeed, endure much abuse, and he did not have a natural or an easy camaraderie with most of his white teammates. He became almost a perfect Gandhi-like figure of sacrifice and forbearance, and he created the paradigm for how integration was to proceed in the United States in the 1950s and early 1960s — the Noble Negro who, through his nobility, a mystical product of his American heritage of suffering but enduring devotion to the foundational principles of American life, legitimates white institutions as he integrates them. As the *New York Times* put it in 1950, "The going wasn't easy. Jackie Robinson met open or covert hostility with the spirit of a gallant gentleman. He kept his temper, he kept his poise and he played good baseball. Now he has won his battle. No fan threatens to riot, no player threatens to go on strike when Jackie Robinson, or any one

[1]Branch Rickey, with Robert Riger, *The American Diamond: A Documentary of the Game of Baseball* (New York: Simon & Schuster, 1965), p. 46.

of several Negroes, takes the field."[2] This is the Robinson that is always remembered when his career is reexamined today. He is almost always sentimentalized.

But it must be remembered that Robinson played major league baseball with the Dodgers for ten years, only two of which were under this agreement. (The agreement also included the year in Montreal.) So for most of his career as a big league ballplayer, Robinson did not act

in any sort of self-sacrificing nonviolent way. He was a tough, almost chip-on-the-shoulder player, a particularly aggressive athlete who usually took umbrage at the least slight or unfairness he felt on the field. He understood that high-performance sports were about intimidation, and he was not about to be intimidated.[3]

---

[2]"Jackie Robinson's New Honor," *New York Times*, December 8, 1950.

[3]"In 1950, and the years to come, Jack battled with umpires over matters not simply of judgment but of ethics, in his growing belief that the umpires, all white, were abusing their power in order to put him in his place." See Rampersad, *Jackie Robinson*, p. 229; see also Jackie Robinson, "Now I Know Why They Boo Me!" *Look*, January 25, 1955, pp. 22–28.

Using Sources to Appeal to an Audience

If you were writing an in-class essay, would you take the time to put together a bibliography? Of course not. But you would prepare a bibliography for a formal research paper because that writing has a different purpose and the audience has different expectations. A writer must analyze the rhetorical situation in order to determine what is appropriate, even when it comes to sources and documentation. (See the rhetorical triangle, p. 7.)

Now let's consider a topic and examine how sources were used and identified for three different audiences. The following excerpts are from three pieces about indirect speech by the linguist and cognitive scientist Steven Pinker.

The first example, excerpted from an article in *Time* magazine, is written for a general audience of readers interested primarily in understanding the basics of Pinker's ideas.

from Words Don't Mean What They Mean

STEVEN PINKER

Why don't people just say what they mean? The reason is that conversational partners are not modems downloading information into each other's brains. People are very, very touchy about their relationships. Whenever you speak to someone, you are presuming the two of you have a certain degree of familiarity — which your words might alter. So every sentence has to do two things at once: convey a message and continue to negotiate that relationship.

The clearest example is ordinary politeness. When you are at a dinner party and want the salt, you don't blurt out, "Gimme

the salt." Rather, you use what linguists call a whimperative, as in "Do you think you could pass the salt?" or "If you could pass the salt, that would be awesome."

Taken literally, these sentences are inane. The second is an overstatement, and the answer to the first is obvious. Fortunately, the hearer assumes that the speaker is rational and listens between the lines. Yes, your point is to request the salt, but you're doing it in such a way that first takes care to establish what linguists call "felicity conditions," or the prerequisites to making a sensible request. The underlying rationale is that the hearer not be given a command but simply be asked or advised about one of the necessary conditions for passing the salt.

Your goal is to have your need satisfied without treating the listener as a flunky who can be bossed around at will.

Note that there are no formal sources cited. The technical terms that are introduced — *whimperative* and *felicity conditions* — are more playful than technical, and Pinker makes no attempt to cite the academic origin of these terms or the other ideas in this article. He does not go into the research that led to these conclusions. His goal in this brief article for the general reader is to inform and keep moving.

The audience for Pinker's book *The Stuff of Thought: Language as a Window into Human Nature* is interested in exploring his subject more deeply, and his use and citation of sources becomes correspondingly more extensive and formal.

---

from The Stuff of Thought

The double message conveyed with an implicature is nowhere put to greater use than in the commonest kind of indirect speech of all, politeness. Politeness in linguistics does not refer to social etiquette, like eating your peas without using your knife, but to the countless adjustments that speakers make to avoid the equally countless ways that their listeners might be put off. People are very, very touchy, and speakers go to great lengths not to step on their toes. In their magisterial work *Politeness: Some Universals in Language Use*, the anthropologists Penelope Brown and Stephen Levinson . . . extended Grice's theory by showing how people all over the world use politeness to lubricate their social interactions.[1]

Politeness Theory begins with Erving Goffman's observation that when people interact they constantly worry about maintaining a nebulous yet vital commodity called "face" (from the idiom "to save face").[2] Goffman defined face as a positive social value that a person claims for himself. Brown and Levinson divide it into positive face, the desire to be approved (specifically, that other people want for you what you want for yourself), and negative face, the desire to be unimpeded or autonomous. The terminology, though clumsy, points to a fundamental duality in social life, which has been discovered in many guises and goes by many names: solidarity and status, connection and autonomy, communion and agency, intimacy and power, communal sharing and authority ranking.[3]

---

[1]Brown & Levinson, 1987b. See also Brown, 1987; Brown & Gilman, 1972; Fraser, 1990; Green, 1996; Holtgraves, 2002.
[2]Goffman, 1967.
[3]Fiske, 1992; Fiske, 2004; Haslam, 2004; Holtgraves, 2002.

While this is not a scientific study, it is also not a brief and breezy article in a magazine with a very wide readership. The audience of a book of this sort has some interest in this topic — they have chosen to read a whole book on linguistics and cognition — and because of that, Pinker feels comfortable not just summarizing the latest thinking in the field, but introducing terminology common to research in linguistics and tracing the origins of concepts back to their academic origins. He also formally (and fully) cites his sources using extensive endnotes that appear at the back of the book.

Finally, take a look at this selection from a scholarly article by Pinker in the academic journal *Intercultural Pragmatics*.

from The Evolutionary Social Psychology of Off-Record Indirect Speech Acts

The double message conveyed with an implicature is nowhere put to greater use than in the commonest kind of indirect speech, politeness. In their seminal work *Politeness: Some Universals in Language Use*, Brown and Levinson (1987b) extended Grice's theory by showing how people in many (perhaps all) cultures use politeness to lubricate their social interactions.

Politeness Theory begins with Goffman's (1967) observation that when people interact they constantly worry about maintaining a commodity called "face" (from the idiom "to save face"). Goffman defined face as a positive social value that a person claims for himself. Brown and Levinson divide it into positive face, the desire to be approved (specifically, that other people want for you what you want for yourself), and negative face, the desire to be unimpeded or autonomous. The terminology points to a fundamental duality in social life which goes by many names: solidarity and status, connection and autonomy, communion and agency, intimacy and power, communal sharing and authority ranking (Fiske 1992, 2004; Haslam 2004; Holtgraves 2002). Later we will see how these wants come from two of the three major social relations in human life.

Brown and Levinson argue that Grice's Cooperative Principle applies to the maintenance of face as well as to the communication of data. Conversationalists work together, each trying to maintain his own face and the face of his partner. The challenge is that most kinds of speech pose at least some threat to the face of the hearer. The mere act of initiating a conversation imposes a demand on the hearer's time and attention. Issuing an imperative challenges her status and autonomy. Making a request puts her in the position where she might have to refuse, earning her a reputation as stingy or selfish. Telling something to someone implies that she was ignorant of the fact in the first place. And then there are criticisms, boasts, interruptions, outbursts, the telling of bad news, and the broaching of divisive topics, all of which can injure the hearer's face directly.

At the same time, people have to get on with the business of life, and in doing so they have to convey requests and news and complaints. The solution is to make amends with politeness: the speaker sugarcoats his utterances with niceties that reaffirm his concern for the hearer or that acknowledge her autonomy. Brown and Levinson call the stratagems positive and negative politeness, though better terms are sympathy and deference.

References

Brown, Penelope, and Stephen C. Levinson. 1987a. Introduction to the reissue: A review of recent work. In *Politeness: Some universals in language use*. New York: Cambridge University Press.

—. 1987b. *Politeness: Some universals in language usage*. New York: Cambridge University Press.

Fiske, Alan P. 1992. The four elementary forms of sociality: Framework for a unified theory of social relations. *Psychological Review*, 99: 689–723.

—. 2004. Four modes of constituting relationships: Consubstantial assimilation; space, magnitude, time, and force; Concrete procedures; Abstract symbolism. In N. Haslam (ed.), *Relational models theory: A contemporary overview*. Mahwah: Erlbaum Associates.

Goffman, Erving. 1959. *The presentation of self in everyday life*. New York: Doubleday.

—. 1967. On face-work: An analysis of ritual elements in social interaction. In *Interaction ritual: Essays on face-to-face behavior*. New York: Random House.

Grice, Herbert P. 1975. Logic and conversation. In P. Cole & J. L. Morgan (eds.), *Syntax & Semantics* Vol. 3: Speech acts. New York: Academic Press.

Haslam, Nick. (ed.). 2004. *Relational models theory: A contemporary overview*. Mahwah: Erlbaum Associates.

Holtgraves, Tom M. 2002. *Language as social action*. Mahwah: Erlbaum Associates.

Notice that, for this academic audience of researchers and scholars who bring a good deal of prior knowledge to the text, Pinker chooses other scholarly works as his sources and documents them thoroughly in a style that gives those sources more emphasis. Rather than just putting the citations at the back of the book, he embeds the source names throughout for direct reference and then includes a detailed Works Cited list at the end of the article. Many readers, likely familiar with these sources, will find Pinker's text more authoritative because he has included them.

As you can see, the type of evidence and the way it's documented depends on audience and situation. But what does all of this have to do with the writing you will be doing? The texts we have examined in this chapter were written by journalists, professors, and scholars; the sources they use and the ways they document them are appropriate for their audiences. In school, you have probably written essays for which you were required to use outside sources, sources that were assigned to you, or sources that were part of your classroom readings. Keep in mind that your goal in a synthesis essay is the same as that of professional writers: to use sources to support and illustrate your own ideas and to establish your credibility as a reasonable and informed writer. Whether your teacher wants you to make informal in-text citations or use formal in-text parenthetical documentation and an end-of-paper Works Cited list, as prescribed by the Modern Language Association (MLA), you must document sources to give credit where credit is due.

ACTIVITY

To set themselves apart, columnists and bloggers for print and online publications establish a viewpoint and style. The types of sources they use and the way they use them are part of that style. Using three columns or blogs by one writer, analyze the writer's audience by examining the types of sources he or she uses. You might consider a political blogger, a sportswriter, a movie or music reviewer, or a columnist in a local publication.

Conversation: Is Technology Making Us Dumber?

In this section, we will walk through the process of writing a synthesis essay: understanding the task, analyzing a series of readings, and writing an argument using them as sources.

Here is your prompt:

In today's world, we live and learn with technology that's more complex and changing at a faster pace than that of previous generations. Many see this new digital technology as a way to expand and distribute knowledge, even democratize the pursuit of knowledge by making information about everything under the sun accessible to anyone with an Internet connection. Others lament that the constant distractions accompanying such an onslaught of information have damaged our ability to think critically and independently. But, of course, there's a long tradition of critics bemoaning the harmful effects of technological change—whether it's the "horseless carriage" that is known, today, as the car, or the evolution of the telephone, from the first landlines to the latest smartphones.

After carefully reading the following sources, synthesize the information from at least three of them, incorporating it into a coherent, well-developed argument on whether you believe digital technology is having a positive or negative impact on human intelligence.

Before reading the sources included with this prompt, it might help to take a moment to think about how you will use them to complete the assignment. As we've discussed, sources can illustrate or support your own ideas. If, for example, you think that technology is having a negative impact on critical thinking skills or that social media encourages narcissism, then you can look to your sources to help you make that point. If you believe that digital devices are changing the way we experience the world for the better, the sources can help you think about that view as well. But it's important not to reject texts that disagree with your position or appear not to be directly relevant to it. In fact, you might use a text that presents an opinion in opposition to yours as a counterargument, and then concede and refute it. Most importantly, keep an open mind while you read the sources. so that your thesis shows you understand the complexity of the subject.

ACTIVITY

Before you read the sources, take five minutes to brainstorm your initial response to the prompt: Has technology had an overall negative or positive impact on human intelligence? Working with a partner or small group, share your responses. What ideas or issues were raised that you had not considered?

Sources

1. **Mark Bauerlein** / from *The Dumbest Generation*
2. **Alison Gopnik** / *Is "Screen Time" Dangerous for Children?*
3. **R. Smith Simpson** / from *Are We Getting Our Share of the Best?*
4. **Jacqueline Howard** / *This Is How the Internet Is Rewiring Your Brain*
5. **Nicholas Carr** / *The Illusion of Knowledge*
6. **Michael Agger** / from *Interview: Clive Thompson's* Smarter Than You Think
7. **Sherry Turkle** / from *Stop Googling. Let's Talk.*
8. ***Americans' Cell Phone Use During Social Activity*** (graph)

from **The Dumbest Generation**

MARK BAUERLEIN

The following excerpt is from *The Dumbest Generation: How the Digital Age Stupifies Young Americans and Jeopardizes Our Future*, a best-seller published in 2009 about the effects of digital media on young people. Mark Bauerlein (b. 1959) is a Professor of English at Emory University.

We have entered the Information Age, traveled the Information Superhighway, spawned a Knowledge Economy, undergone the Digital Revolution, converted manual workers into knowledge workers, and promoted a Creative Class, and we anticipate a Conceptual Age to be. However overhyped those grand social metaphors, they signify a rising premium on knowledge and communications, and everyone from *Wired* magazine to Al Gore to Thomas Friedman to the Task Force on the Future of American Innovation echoes the change. . . .

And yet, while teens and young adults have absorbed digital tools into their daily lives like no other age group, while they have grown up with more knowledge and information readily at hand, taken more classes, built their own Web sites, enjoyed more libraries, bookstores, and museums in their towns and cities . . . in sum, while the world has provided them extraordinary chances to gain knowledge and improve their reading/writing skills, not to mention offering financial incentives to do so, young Americans today are no more learned or skillful than their predecessors, no more knowledgeable, fluent, up-to-date, or inquisitive, except in the materials of youth culture. They don't know any more history or civics, economics or science, literature or current events. They read less on their own, both books and newspapers, and you would have to canvass a lot of college English instructors and employers before you found one who said that they compose better paragraphs. In fact, their technology skills fall well short of the common

claim, too, especially when they must apply them to research and workplace tasks. . . .

Teenagers and young adults mingle in a society of abundance, intellectual as well as material. American youth in the twenty-first century have benefited from a shower of money and goods, a bath of liberties and pleasing self-images, vibrant civic debates, political blogs, old books and masterpieces available online, traveling exhibitions . . . and on and on. Never have opportunities for education, learning, political action, and cultural activity been greater. All the ingredients for making an informed and intelligent citizen are in place.

But it hasn't happened. Yes, young Americans arc energetic, ambitious, enterprising, and good, but their talents and interests and money thrust them not into books and ideas and history and civics, but into a whole other realm and other consciousness. A different social life and a different mental life have formed among them. Technology has bred it, but the result doesn't tally with the fulsome descriptions of digital empowerment, global awareness, and virtual communities. Instead of opening young American minds to the stores of civilization and science and politics, technology has contracted their horizon to themselves, to the social scene around them. Young people have never been so intensely mindful of and present to one another, so enabled in adolescent contact. Teen images and songs, hot gossip and games, and youth-to-youth communications no longer limited by time or space wrap them up in a generational cocoon reaching all the way into their bedrooms. The autonomy has a cost: the more they attend to themselves, the less they remember the past and envision a future. They have all the advantages of modernity and democracy, but when the gifts of life lead to social joys, not intellectual labor, the minds of the young plateau at age 18. This is happening all around us.

The fonts of knowledge are everywhere, but the rising generation is camped in the desert, passing stories, pictures, tunes, and texts back and forth, living off the thrill of peer attention. Meanwhile, their intellects refuse the cultural and civic inheritance that has made us what we are up to now.

Before we get to Bauerlein's argument, let's look at the way he develops his ethos by acknowledging that millennials, who are his subject, have positive attributes. For one, they have "absorbed digital tools into their daily lives" and have access to many resources; they are "energetic, ambitious, enterprising, and good." Yet — and here's where he essentially says, *despite these advantages* — they have failed to demonstrate wider, more in-depth knowledge about history, current events, literature, and so forth than previous generations have. What millennials are experts in, he asserts, is their own "youth culture." He frames this as a problem with not only immediate educational consequences but long-term, potentially catastrophic effects: "The more they attend to themselves, the less they remember the past and envision a future." To what extent does this characterization ring true for teenagers today? Can you think of an example drawn from your own experience that refutes Bauerlein's stance in this excerpt? Can you think of an example that supports it?

ACTIVITY

Play "the believing game" with Bauerlein. Using your notations from your reading, explain to a partner what strengths you find in his perspective. Even if his ideas run counter to your opinion, commit to his position — and see where that approach leads you. You might begin by embracing the metaphor about being "camped in the desert" that Bauerlein uses at the end of the excerpt.

2 Is "Screen Time" Dangerous for Children?

ALISON GOPNIK

The following article appeared in the *New Yorker* magazine in 2016. Alison Gopnik (b. 1955) is a professor of psychology and affiliate professor of philosophy at the University of California, Berkeley.

I was in the garden with Augie, my four-year-old grandson, watching the bees in the lavender. "Bees make honey," I said, transmitting the wisdom of the ages in good grandmotherly fashion. After a pause, Augie replied, "How do they make the honey?" There is nothing like a child's question for exposing the limits of a grandmother's wisdom.

"Actually, Augie, I don't know," I said.

"But, Grandmom, you have your phone," he said. For Augie, a smartphone is as natural and unremarkable as the bees and the lavender, and holding one is almost synonymous with knowing.

I Googled "How do bees make honey?" There were dozens of videos explaining it. As we stood in the garden, shielding the screen against the sunlight, Augie and I learned that worker bees secrete an enzyme called invertase, which converts nectar into dextrose, then flap their wings to thicken the nectar into honey.

"It's kind of hard to see the bees," I said, squinting at the screen. 5

"Why don't we watch it on the big computer?" Augie said.

For the next hour, we sat inside, bee-surfing. Someone in Sweden had posted a speeded-up video of bees building a hive, months of construction compressed into two minutes. There was a whole subgenre of beekeeper selfie videos. Best of all was a BBC documentary about the "waggle dance," the remarkable communication system that allows bees to give one another directions to the places where they've found nectar.

My own childhood was dominated by a powerful device that used an optical interface to transport the user to an alternate reality. I spent most of my waking hours in its grip, oblivious of the world around me. The device was, of course, the book. Over time, reading hijacked my brain, as large areas once dedicated to processing the "real" world adapted to processing the printed word. As far as I can tell, this early immersion didn't hamper my development, but it did leave me with some illusions — my idea of romantic love surely came from novels.

English children's books, in particular, are full of tantalizing food descriptions. At some point in my childhood, I must have read about a honeycomb tea. Augie, enchanted, agreed to accompany me to the grocery store. We returned with a jar of honeycomb, only to find that it was an inedible, waxy mess.

Many parents worry that "screen time" will impair children's development, but recent research suggests that most of the common fears about children and screens are unfounded. (There 10 is one exception: looking at screens that emit blue light before bed really does disrupt sleep, in people of all ages.) The American Academy of Pediatrics used to recommend strict restrictions on screen exposure. Last year, the organization examined the relevant science more thoroughly, and, as a result, changed its recommendations. The new guidelines emphasize that what matters is content and context, what children watch and with whom. Each child, after all, will have some hundred thousand hours of conscious experience before turning sixteen. Those hours can be like the marvellous ones that Augie and I spent together bee-watching, or they can be violent or mindless — and that's true whether those hours are occupied by apps or TV or books or just by talk.

New tools have always led to panicky speculation. Socrates thought that reading and writing would have disastrous effects on memory; the novel, the telegraph, the telephone, and the television were all declared to be the End of Civilization as We Know It, particularly in the hands of the young. Part of the reason may be that adult brains require a lot of focus and effort to learn something new, while children's brains are designed to master new environments spontaneously. Innovative technologies always seem distracting and disturbing to the adults attempting to master them, and transparent and obvious — not really technology at all — to those, like Augie, who encounter them as children.

Like the bees, we live by the reports of others. Unlike the bees, we can invent new worlds, constructing them out of sonic vibrations, ink, or pixels. Sometimes those worlds deceive and confuse; at other times, they tell us something revelatory. When Augie's father got home, Augie rushed to meet him, his words tumbling out in excitement. "Daddy, Daddy, look," he said, reaching for the phone. "Do you know how bees make honey? I'll show you. . . ."

This article centering on the author's four-year-old grandson is anecdotal, yet it carries additional weight because of Gopnik's credentials as a psychologist. She tells a story that illustrates how naturally and cleverly little Augie suggests a smartphone as a way to "research" a question that puzzles both him and his grandmother. Gopnik uses this incident to reflect on the "panicky speculation" that new technologies (tools) have always initially incited, whether it was writing itself, the telephone, or television. Ultimately, she focuses on what it means to grow up in a world where digital devices are so common that they hardly seem to qualify as "technology." Since Gopnik usually writes for academic journals, often reporting her research, what do you think her purpose was for writing this rather light-hearted piece?

ACTIVITY

Write a letter to Alison Gopnik in the voice of Mark Bauerlein. Being careful to keep the tone respectful, explain specifically what aspects of her article you — as Bauerlein — disagree with, and why.

---

3 | from Are We Getting Our Share of the Best?

R. SMITH SIMPSON

The following excerpt, by R. Smith Simpson (1906–2010), is taken from a 1962 article in the U.S. government's *Foreign Service Journal*. The United States Foreign Service is an elite division of the State Department concerned with implementing American foreign policy.

My initial surprise was to find among the candidates an abysmal ignorance of so elementary a subject as the geography of the United States. Few could even place accurately the principal rivers: one with so descriptive a name as the Ohio was not infrequently identified as being "somewhere west of the Mississippi." Few could name the principal seaports, and, of course, any requirement demanding such detailed familiarity with this country as identifying the states comprising the "wheat belt" or the "corn belt" was completely beyond the average candidate's depth.

As to elementary economics and social data, most could only guess at the population, labor force, and gross national product of their country. Many did not know what constituted "gross national product." They had no clear idea as to the principal products of their country, nor as to its exports and imports. They could name a few of each, but had no notion of their relative importance and had given no thought to the role of imports in the American economy.

As with elementary geographic and economic aspects of the United States, so with historical, sociological, and cultural. Americans abroad are asked a great many questions about their country. How did the United States acquire the Panama Canal? What is its status now? Who started our war with Spain (or Mexico) and what came out of it? When did our labor movement start and where does it stand now? How does a Jimmy Hoffa get control of a powerful union? What were some of the reform movements in American history? What became of them?

A good half of our candidates could answer such questions with only the thinnest recital of facts; many could not discuss them at all. Some could not recall ever having heard of the Populist movement; few knew its connection with Woodrow Wilson's "New Freedom." Asked if he knew anything about the Progressive movement, one candidate replied, "Oh, yes, that was LaFollette's movement." To the question, "Where did LaFollette come from?" he could only reply vaguely, "Somewhere out West."

The first question that might occur to you after reading this source is a simple one: What does an excerpt from an article written in the 1960s have to do with this Conversation? You might find an answer in the excerpt's tone. Simpson, himself a Foreign Service Officer, uses almost derogatory language to describe candidates for the Foreign Service: according to him, they have "abysmal ignorance of so elementary a subject as . . . geography," and can demonstrate "only the thinnest recital of facts." In what ways are the author's complaints similar to those made by critics — such as Bauerlein — of the effects today's technology is having on younger generations?

4 This Is How the Internet Is Rewiring Your Brain

JACQUELINE HOWARD

Jacqueline Howard is a feature writer at CNN Health. An advocate for women in science, she was selected in 2014 to be part of the White House's "We the Geeks: Women Role Models" initiative and was featured in 2013 on the website Black Girl Nerds. The following article was published in the *Huffington Post* in 2016.

e email. We tweet. We facebook. We google. In this incredible age of technology, our computers sometimes seem to have taken control over our everyday lives — from how we buy groceries to how we find mates. How is all this screen time affecting our brains?

In his provocative 2010 book, *The Shallows: What The Internet Is Doing To Our Brain*, author Nicholas Carr wrote, "The Internet is an interruption system. It seizes our attention only to scramble it."

That doesn't sound good. Or, is it possible the online world simply helps us adapt to become better multi-taskers, all while we still maintain critical thinking skills? After all, the brain is plastic, meaning it changes based on our behavior and experiences.

So then when it comes to technology, what behavior are we practicing — and how does *that* affect our minds? Here are five freaky facts.

Fact #1: The Internet may give you an addict's brain. MRI research has shown that the brains of Internet users who have trouble controlling their craving to be constantly plugged-in exhibit changes similar to those seen in people addicted to drugs and alcohol. A 2011 study

showed that unplugging from technology for one day gave some users physical and mental withdrawal symptoms, *The Telegraph* reported.

"The majority of people we see with serious Internet addiction are gamers — people who spend long hours in roles in various games that cause them to disregard their obligations," Dr. Henrietta Bowden Jones, an Imperial College, London psychiatrist who runs a clinic for Internet addicts and problem gamblers, told *The Independent*.

Fact #2: You may feel more lonely and jealous. Social media may make it easier to connect with others, but recent research by German scientists suggests that constantly viewing images of others' vacation photos, personal achievements, etc, can trigger strong feelings of envy, even sadness. Researchers have even described the phenomenon as "Facebook depression."

"We were surprised by how many people have a negative experience from Facebook with envy leaving them feeling lonely, frustrated or angry," Hanna Krasnova, a researcher at Berlin's Humboldt University, told Reuters.

5

151

Fact #3: Internet use may heighten suicide risk in certain teens. After conducting a review of previous research on studies on teens' Internet use, researchers at the University of Oxford in England concluded that online time is linked to an increased risk of suicide and self-harm among vulnerable adolescents. Their paper was published online on Oct. 30 in the journal PLOS ONE.

"We are not saying that all young people who go on the Internet increase their risk of suicide or self-harm," one of the researchers, Dr. Paul Montgomery, professor of psycho-social intervention at the university, said in a written statement. "We are talking about vulnerable young people who are going online specifically to find out more about harming themselves or because they are considering suicide already. The question is whether the online content triggers a response so that they self-harm or take their own lives and we have found that there is a link."

Fact #4: Memory problems may be more likely. Even a rather typical session of social media browsing can lead to information overload and make it harder to file away information in your memory, according to Dr. Erik Fransén, professor of computer science at Sweden's KTH Royal Institute of Technology. A 2009 study from Stanford University suggests that the brains of people who are constantly bombarded with several streams of electronic information — from instant messaging to blogs — may find it difficult to pay attention and switch from one job to another efficiently.

"When they're in situations where there are multiple sources of information coming from the external world or emerging out of memory, they're not able to filter out what's not relevant to their current goal," Dr. Anthony Wagner, an associate professor of psychology at Stanford, said in a written statement. "That failure to filter means they're slowed down by that irrelevant information."

Fact #5: But it's not all bad — in moderation, the Internet can actually boost brain function. A 2008 study suggests that use of Internet search engines can stimulate neural activation patterns and potentially enhance brain function in older adults.

"The study results are encouraging, that emerging computerized technologies may have physiological effects and potential benefits for middle-aged and older adults," the study's principal investigator, Dr. Gary Small, professor of neuroscience and human behavior at UCLA, said in a written statement. "Internet searching engages complicated brain activity, which may help exercise and improve brain function."

In this short article, Howard discusses both positive and negative aspects of the Internet's effect on people, explaining each as a "freaky fact." While she explains several dangers, she ends with a potential benefit. As she discusses these "facts," how does she develop her ethos as a science and health writer?

ACTIVITY

Imagine a conversation between Jacqueline Howard and R. Smith Simpson. What questions would Howard be likely to ask Simpson in order to explore his viewpoint? What conclusions would Simpson be likely to draw from the "facts" Howard presents? What common ground might they find?

5 The Illusion of Knowledge

NICOLAS CARR

In 2008, Nicholas Carr (b. 1959) published an article in the *Atlantic* magazine entitled "Is Google Making Us Stupid?" He continued his exploration of the intellectual and cultural consequences of the Internet on our society in his book *The Shallows: What the Internet Is Doing to Our Brains* (2010). Carr continues to write on the impact of technology, often in his blog *Rough Type*, where the following post appeared in 2015.

The internet may be making us shallow, but it's making us think we're deep.

A newly published study, by three Yale psychologists, shows that searching the web gives people an "illusion of knowledge." They start to confuse what's online with what's in their head, which gives them an exaggerated sense of their own intelligence. The effect isn't limited to the particular subject areas that people explore on the web. It's more general than that. Doing searches on one topic inflates people's sense of how well they understand other, unrelated topics. As the researchers explain:

> One's self-assessed ability to answer questions increased after searching for explanations online in a previous, unrelated task, an effect that held even after controlling for time, content, and features of the search process. The effect derives from a true misattribution of the sources of knowledge, not a change in understanding of what counts as internal knowledge and is not driven by a "halo effect" or general overconfidence. We provide evidence that this effect occurs specifically because information online can so easily be accessed through search.

The researchers, Matthew Fisher, Marie Goddu, and Frank Keil, documented the effect, and its cause, through nine experiments. They divided test subjects into two groups. One group spent time searching the web, the other group stayed offline, and then both groups estimated, in a variety of ways, their understanding of various topics. The experiments consistently showed that searching the web gives people an exaggerated sense of their own knowledge.

To make sure that searchers' overconfidence in assessing their smarts stemmed from a misperception about the depth of knowledge in their own heads (rather than reflecting a confidence in their ability to Google the necessary information), the psychologists, in one of the experiments, had the test subjects make estimates of their brain activity:

> Instead of asking participants to rate how well they could answer questions about topics using a Likert scale ranging from 1 (very poorly) to 7 (very well), participants were shown a scale consisting of seven functional MRI (fMRI) images of varying levels of activation, as illustrated by colored regions of increasing size. Participants were told, "Scientists have shown that increased activity in certain brain regions corresponds with higher quality explanations." This dependent variable was designed to unambiguously emphasize one's brain as the location of personally held knowledge. Participants were then asked to select the image that would correspond with their brain activity when they answered the self-assessed knowledge questions.

The subjects who searched the net before the task rated their anticipated brain activity as being significantly stronger than did the control group who hadn't been looking up information online. 5

153

Similar misperceptions may be produced by consulting other external, or "transactive," sources of knowledge, the researchers note, but the illusion is probably much stronger with the web, given its unprecedented scope and accessibility:

> This illusion of knowledge might well be found for sources other than the Internet: for example, an expert librarian may experience a similar illusion when accessing a reference Rolodex. . . . While such effects may be possible, the rise of the Internet has surely broadened the scope of this effect. Before the Internet, there was no similarly massive, external knowledge database. People relied on less immediate and accessible inanimate stores of external knowledge, such as books — or, they relied on other minds in transactive memory systems. In contrast with other sources and cognitive tools for informational access, the Internet is nearly always accessible, can be searched efficiently, and provides immediate feedback. For these reasons, the Internet might become even more easily integrated with the human mind than other external sources of knowledge and perhaps even more so than human transactive memory partners, promoting much stronger illusions of knowledge.

This is just one study, but it comes on the heels of a series of other studies on how access to the web and search engines is influencing the way our minds construct, or don't construct, personal knowledge. A 2011 Columbia study found that the ready availability of online information reduces people's retention of facts: "when people expect to have future access to [online] information, they have lower rates of recall of the information itself and enhanced recall instead for where to access it," a phenomenon which indicates "that processes of human memory are adapting to the advent of new computing and communication technology." A 2014 Fairfield University study found that simply taking digital photographs of an experience will tend to reduce your memory of the experience. The University of Colorado's Adrian Ward has found evidence that the shift from "biological information storage" toward "digital information storage" may "have large-scale and long-term effects on the way people remember and process information." He says that the internet "may act as a 'supernormal stimulus,' hijacking preexisting cognitive tendencies and creating novel outcomes."

In "How Google Is Changing Your Brain," a 2013 *Scientific American* article written with the late Daniel Wegner, Ward reported on experiments revealing that

> using Google gives people the sense that the Internet has become part of their own cognitive tool set. A search result was recalled not as a date or name lifted from a Web page but as a product of what resided inside the study participants' own memories, allowing them to effectively take credit for knowing things that were a product of Google's search algorithms. The psychological impact of splitting our memories equally between the Internet and the brain's gray matter points to a lingering irony. The advent of the "information age" seems to have created a generation of people who feel they know more than ever before — when their reliance on the Internet means that they may know ever less about the world around them.

Ignorance is bliss, particularly when it's mistaken for knowledge.

In this blog post, Carr interprets research others have conducted, so he's doing his own synthesis of multiple sources. He cites studies from Yale University and the University of Colorado to support his thesis, which he states in his opening sentence. Using this research as evidence, he builds the case that the Internet makes us think we know far more than we do. He contends that this is a dangerous false impression — it's a risky business, he concludes, not to know what we don't know. Is Carr exhorting his readers to abandon the Internet as a research resource? Or is he warning them that relying solely on the Internet for information may limit not only the scope of our knowledge, but our ability to think critically?

6 from Interview: Clive Thompson's *Smarter Than You Think*

MICHAEL AGGER

Following is an excerpt from Michael Agger's interview with Clive Thompson in 2013, after the publication of Thompson's book *Smarter Than You Think: How Technology Is Changing Our Minds for the Better*. Thompson is a Canadian journalist who has written on technology for the *New York Times* and *Wired* magazine.

You've written a book about how technology is "changing our minds for the better." Have readers been agreeing or disagreeing with you?

I've had a lot of positive feedback to my discussion of "ambient awareness" — which is the deep, rich, intellectual, and social connections we develop with each other via short-form status updates. Most people have been trained — via a parade of gloomy opeds in their newspapers — to think of their online utterances as mere "narcissism"; that there could be no conceivable value in tweeting or using Instagram or using Facebook, apart from a sort of constant shilling of the self. So when I point out the interesting social science that underpins some of the pleasures and values of persistent connection to each other, I've found that people are really excited about that. It resonates.

What do you see as the social good of Twitter?

For many of the more avid users, it provides a lot of new, useful things to think about — serendipitous stories, insights from others. It's a sort of global watercooler, with all the good and bad that suggests. It's good because many folks feel like they're immersed in an interesting conversation that's going on — and even if they're just lurking, not actually talking (studies show the majority of folks using Twitter are listening but not contributing

that often), they get exposed to all sorts of material they'd never see otherwise. And bad, because, well, you can really get swept in and distracted from work that you're supposed to be doing. . . .

Nicholas Carr has written about how book-based learning taught us certain habits of mind, a more empathetic way of thinking that we are rapidly losing with screens and screen-reading. Do you agree? [5]

I quite agree with Carr that tools affect how we think — and considered as a tool, books have many absolutely fantastic and magical effects on the way we think. They encourage us to slow down, which is good; they synthesize large volumes of knowledge. But what Carr sells short are the enormous benefits that come from social thinking — and social thinking is where the Internet really shines.

There's an idea, popular with many text-based folks like — myself, and many journalists and academics — that reading books is thinking; that if you're not sitting for hours reading a tome, you're not, in some essential way, thinking. This is completely false. A huge amount of our everyday thinking — powerful, creative, and resonant stuff — is done socially: talking to other people, arguing with them, relying on them to recall information for us. This has been true for aeons in the offline world. But now we have new ways to think socially online — and to do so with likeminded folks around the world, which is still insanely mind-blowing. It never stops being lovely for me.

I was in a radio station the other day, and while I was waiting to go on the air I watched the staff work. There were six or seven of them, and they were all engaged in this incredibly complex activity that's behind the scenes of the show: they're talking about the next segment, writing down ideas, looking things up, organizing the next batch of things the host is going to talk about. This is what thinking looks like in the real world. A lot of it is incredibly, deeply social. And it has the effect of making the host put on this much smarter, richer show than he or she could do on their own.

When people get into discussions and arguments online, whether it's on Twitter or in a forum about their favorite TV show or even in a thread underneath an Instagram photo, this is the same thing transpiring. In the *Phaedrus*[1], Socrates worried that this dialogic nature of knowledge would die out with text, because text was inert: you asked it a question, and it couldn't answer back. What I love about the online world is that it's pitched neatly between those two poles. It's a lot of textual expression, but with the added dimension of it being text that we use to talk to each other, argue with each other, call each other names, compliment each other.

---

[1] Written by Plato around 370 B.C.E., the *Phaedrus* is a fictional conversation between Socrates, the ancient Greek philosopher, and Phaedrus, an ancient Greek aristocrat, about the art and practice of rhetoric.

From the context of the interview, it's clear that Thompson and Carr have been in dialog for some time in their explorations of and positions on technology. In this interview excerpt, Thompson makes the case for the "social thinking" that the Internet promotes while simultaneously establishing his ethos as being one of the "many text-based folks." He also asks us to consider how the Internet gives us "new ways to think socially" rather than dismissing such interactions as shallow. In fact, he cites the Greek philosopher Socrates in the same paragraph as he discusses television, Twitter, and Instagram. In what other ways does Thompson challenge the idea that communication via social media is an inherently narcissistic pursuit, as others — such as Bauerlein — argue?

ACTIVITY

Develop a Venn diagram using claims made by Carr, Thompson, and one other source in this Conversation. Given the commonalities you identify, what conclusions can you draw about the most important conversations we need to have about technology?

7 from Stop Googling. Let's Talk.

SHERRY TURKLE

The following is an excerpt from "Stop Googling. Let's Talk.," an op-ed essay that appeared in the *New York Times* in 2015. Currently a professor at Massachusetts Institute of Technology (MIT) and director of the university's Initiative on Technology and Self, psychologist Sherry Turkle (b. 1948) has written extensively on the interaction of humans and technology.

In solitude we find ourselves; we prepare ourselves to come to conversation with something to say that is authentic, ours. If we can't gather ourselves, we can't recognize other people for who they are. If we are not content to be alone, we turn others into the people we need them to be. If we don't know how to be alone, we'll only know how to be lonely.

A virtuous circle links conversation to the capacity for self-reflection. When we are secure in ourselves, we are able to really hear what other people have to say. At the same time, conversation with other people, both in intimate settings and in larger social groups, leads us to become better at inner dialogue.

But we have put this virtuous circle in peril. We turn time alone into a problem that needs to be solved with technology. Timothy D. Wilson, a psychologist at the University of Virginia, led a team that explored our capacity for solitude. People were asked to sit in a chair and think, without a device or a book. They were told that they would have from six to 15 minutes alone and that the only rules were that they had to stay seated and not fall asleep. In one experiment, many student subjects opted to give themselves mild electric shocks rather than sit alone with their thoughts.

People sometimes say to me that they can see how one might be disturbed when people turn to their phones when they are together. But surely there is no harm when people turn to their phones when they are by themselves? If anything, it's our new form of being together.

But this way of dividing things up misses the [5] essential connection between solitude and conversation. In solitude we learn to concentrate and imagine, to listen to ourselves. We need these skills to be fully present in conversation.

Every technology asks us to confront human values. This is a good thing, because it causes us to reaffirm what they are. If we are now ready to make face-to-face conversation a priority, it is easier to see what the next steps should be. We are not looking for simple solutions. We are looking for beginnings. Some of them may seem familiar by now, but they are no less challenging for that. Each addresses only a small piece of what silences us. Taken together, they can make a difference.

One start toward reclaiming conversation is to reclaim solitude. Some of the most crucial conversations you will ever have will be with yourself. Slow down sufficiently to make this possible. And make a practice of doing one thing at a time. Think of unitasking as the next big thing. In every domain of life, it will increase performance and decrease stress.

But doing one thing at a time is hard, because it means asserting ourselves over what technology makes easy and what feels productive in the short term. Multitasking comes with its own high, but when we chase after this feeling, we pursue an illusion. Conversation is a human way to practice unitasking. . . .

To reclaim conversation for yourself, your friendships and society, push back against viewing the world as one giant app. It works the other way, too: Conversation is the antidote to the algorithmic way of looking at life because it teaches you about fluidity, contingency and personality.

This is our moment to acknowledge the unin- [10] tended consequences of the technologies to which we are vulnerable, but also to respect the resilience that has always been ours. We have time to make corrections and remember who we are — creatures of history, of deep psychology, of complex relationships, of conversations, artless, risky and face to face.

In this excerpt, Turkle writes about the impact of digital technology on relationships and specifically considers the smartphone. She argues a sequence of causality: being comfortable in solitude (which she distinguishes from being lonely) is a prerequisite for being "fully present in conversation," which is in turn a necessary basis for developing complex human relationships. As part of her argument, Turkle makes a case for "unitasking," arguing that multitasking essentially yields only short-term results. To what extent do you agree with this chain of reasoning? To what extent might the other authors in this Conversation agree with Turkle?

ACTIVITY

Play the "yes, but" game with Turkle's argument. Identify three different statements she makes to which you can concede in some way but also refute in some way. You might set up each of your responses in one of the two following ways:

In this excerpt, Turkle asserts_____. While I can see that _____, Turkle fails to consider/understand/account for _____.

Yes, I agree with Turkle that _____ because _____.
But, that belief/assumption/claim neglects to take into account that _____.

8 Americans' Cell Phone Use During Social Activity

The following graph uses data from a Pew Research Center article on Americans' views on cell-phone etiquette in 2014. It shows the percentage of cell phone owners who used their phones to do a range of activities, listed on the x-axis, during their most recent social interaction.

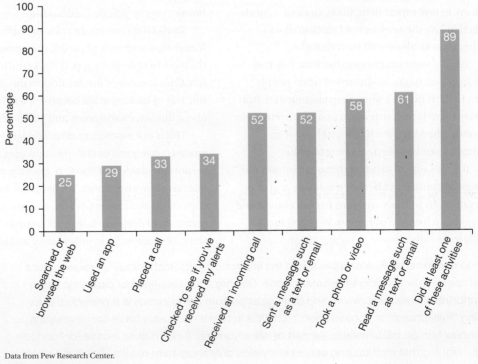

Data from Pew Research Center.

There is more than one way to interpret the message this graph conveys. On one hand, it's not surprising that people might take photos or receive incoming calls at a social gathering. People have done both of these things for decades — just not with a cell phone. On the other hand, smartphones now enable people to be connected to the Internet anywhere, anytime, and this constant access to social media may indeed distract from meaningful face-to-face contact. If 89 percent of people engage in an activity involving their phone while in a social setting, does that mean they're not paying attention — or that they are accustomed to multitasking? Is it possible that people are using their smartphones to enhance rather than escape in-person interactions?

ACTIVITY

Identify the key issues raised in this Conversation by completing the following chart. One issue is modeled for you. Try to come up with at least five other key issues that are addressed by some — but not necessarily all — of the sources. After you identify an issue, include a brief quotation that illustrates three authors' positions on it. Make sure you've used each source at least once in your completed chart.

Issue	Source	Source	Source
Depth of knowledge	Bauerlein rails that shallow is all there is — and young people don't even care: "technology has contracted their horizon."	Carr says we're "shallow" but the Internet "is making us think we're deep." According to a study he cites, people "start to confuse what's online with what's in their head, which gives them an exaggerated sense of their own intelligence.	Simpson, writing in 1962, suggests that the older generation has always seen the younger as problematic: "A good half of our candidates could answer such questions with only the thinnest recital of facts; many could not discuss them at all."

Writing a Synthesis Essay

Now that you have read the sources in this chapter's Conversation on the impact of technology, let's walk through the process of synthesizing the texts and then writing a synthesis essay. As you move from reading and analyzing the sources to integrating them into your own writing, you will engage in a process of selection. This is often a complex step in which, ideally, you explore the individual texts and start to see connections among them. Essential to this process is your willingness to understand each text on its own terms, even if you disagree with the ideas or position; in fact, texts that present perspectives different from those you initially hold are often the ones that become most important to the development of your argument. Remember Peter Elbow's "believing game": that is, be sure to think critically about each text — it's important to question and express skepticism — but also approach arguments you don't agree with by trying to "believe" the viewpoints they convey.

Identifying the Issues: Recognizing Complexity

The fact is, you can rarely change a reader's mind, at least not radically or immediately. Instead, what you want to aim for is a compelling argument that leaves the reader thinking, questioning, considering, and reconsidering. To do this, you have to acknowledge that the issue at hand is a complex one with no easy solutions and a variety of valid perspectives on the matter. You want to present a reasonable idea in a voice that is logical, sincere, and informed. To write a qualified argument using sources, you must anticipate objections to your position and recognize and respect the complexities of your topic, just as we discussed in Chapter 3. A reasonable voice recognizes that there are more than two sides to an issue — more than pro–con, which is the written equivalent of a shouting match.

Careful reading has already revealed some of the complexities surrounding the impacts of technology on human intelligence. Let's explore a few.

- Source 1, the excerpt from *The Dumbest Generation*, argues that a whole generation has squandered its potential to use technology to learn more about substantive intellectual issues and has instead used it to focus mainly on its own "youth culture." Instead of being empowered to participate in a larger world, millennials have chosen to create an echo chamber.
- Source 2, by a psychologist writing for the *New Yorker*, shifts the focus to very young children (in this case, a four-year-old) by pointing out that they are so accustomed to using digital devices that they are as familiar with them as older generations were with books. The article concludes by suggesting that the Internet, with its instant search results and vast breadth of knowledge, actually stimulates and rewards human curiosity.
- Source 3, taken from an article written in the 1960s, criticizes the younger generation for not being as informed as previous ones. The criticisms Simpson makes — although on different topics, such as geography — are very similar to those Source 1 and Source 5 make about digital technology's adverse effects on intelligence.
- Source 4, an article by a science editor, points out both benefits of and drawbacks to how we interact with people and spend our time on the Internet. She raises the possibility that the Internet may be changing how our brains work but is careful to note that the study of these effects is still ongoing.
- Source 5, a blog post by a well-known technology writer, argues that technology is changing the way we read and think for the worse. While Source 1 complains that digital technology's potential for accessing information goes unused by millennials, this source argues that it's used too much: we are exchanging deep engagement with a few texts for shallow acquaintance with many texts.
- Source 6, an interview with science and technology writer Clive Thompson, although not a direct response to Source 5, addresses that source's concern that new media has damaged our ability to learn about various subjects in-depth. Thompson emphasizes the complexity of the interactions people engage in with digital technology, including social media.

- Source 7, an op-ed for the *New York Times* written by a well-known psychologist, argues that constant interaction with digital devices such as the cell phone diminishes our capacity for true give-and-take conversation, which ultimately lessens our ability to build meaningful personal relationships.
- Source 8, a graph taken from a 2015 report on cell phone etiquette, shows that the vast majority of cell-phone owners used their phones during their most recent social activity. This graph could be taken as confirmation that, as Source 7 argues, distraction is a consequence of cell phone use.

Formulating Your Position

Before you formulate your position, it can be helpful to take stock of the issues. In analyzing the texts on the impact of technology on human intelligence, the following issues emerge:

- Is the easy access to information and instant gratification that digital technology affords creating an illusion that, when it comes to human knowledge, speed and volume are better?
- To what extent is digital technology changing the way we interact with one another? Are those changes positive or negative?
- Is a generation that has always experienced the world through digital technology upending traditional roles defined by age? To what extent have the skills that society values changed as a result? Has this undermined the concept of expert authority?
- Has the ubiquitous use of technology changed the way our brains work? Will it? Would that be good or bad?
- Are some technologies, particularly social media, better than others? More dangerous than others?
- To what extent has digital technology redefined basic concepts such as privacy, community, and public space in our society?
- Has digital technology deepened — or will it deepen — what we traditionally think of as generational divides? If so, is that inevitable?

These questions — and others you might have — illustrate the complexity of the issue and ensure that you do not develop an argument that is one-sided or polarized between yes and no. Instead, you are now prepared to write a documented essay that reflects the complexities surrounding the topic.

With these questions and issues in mind, you can begin to formulate a thesis, or claim, that captures your position on the topic. Consider the following working thesis statements:

- The traditional balance of power in our society is being reshaped by digital technology, since its most capable and creative users belong to a younger generation of digital natives.
- Although technological progress has changed the world in rapid and dramatic ways, the major benchmarks for personal and professional success all require skills that cannot be learned online.

- The alarm bells that ring predictions of doom about technology's effect on our ability to think critically and deeply about things that matter are less based in fact and instead more reflective of older generations' fear of change.
- Today's social media platforms may be old news in a flash, but their impact on the way we learn, interact with one another, and define ourselves will be revolutionary, enduring, and positive.
- While the Internet, including social media, may be alluring, it has led humanity to turn its back on critical thinking and expert knowledge for shallow and often partial understanding of complex issues.
- The immediate gratification offered by the Internet—especially social media—may seem problematic or even self-indulgent, but it has also been a great equalizing force in society; anyone can gain both new and previously difficult-to-access knowledge.

Although you might want to tailor one of these working thesis statements to use in your essay, each one suggests a clear focus while acknowledging the complexities of the issue.

ACTIVITY

Of the thesis statements above, select one you *disagree with*. Then, using the readings in the Conversation on the impact of technology, find three pieces of evidence supporting that thesis.

Framing Quotations

When writing with sources, it's important not to simply summarize or paraphrase the sources. You need to use the sources to strengthen your own argument. One easy way to make sure the sources are working for you is to include a sentence or two of explanation or commentary with each quotation. You might use a lead-in sentence or two, so your readers know what to look for, as is demonstrated below:

> The multiple distractions that digital technology makes so easily available are hard to resist since clicks and touches on phones and various screens yield instant gratification. Yet these are short-term satisfactions, as MIT professor Sherry Turkle points out: "Multitasking comes with its own high, but when we chase after this feeling, we pursue an illusion."

Alternatively, you might follow a quotation with a sentence or two of commentary to remind readers of your point and how the quotation reinforces it, as you see here:

> Clive Thompson, a well-regarded writer about technology, points out that the belief "that if you're not sitting for hours reading a tome, you're not, in some essential way, thinking" is "completely false." He claims that much of our thinking "is done socially: talking to other people, arguing with them, relying on them to recall information for us." This bias that only offline and alone can we concentrate, comprehend, and think critically is widespread among those who have not grown up with new media. When we read online,

not only are we actually "reading," but we are moving across the page (even a virtual one) at the same time we're following links that connect to and expand on ideas in the main text. In many instances, comments from other readers provide an opportunity to be part of a dialogue about the reading, thus deepening our understanding of it.

Here, the quotations from a source introduce the writer's ideas and provide a kind of foundation to amplify them rather than simply to support them, as we saw in the previous example. Of course, regardless of which strategy you use with quotations, be careful not to represent ideas or words as your own if they are not: give credit where it is due!

Integrating Quotations

When using multiple sources in your writing, it becomes even more important to incorporate the quotations in a way that is both clear and interesting. You want the transition from your own voice to others' words and ideas to be smooth and natural sounding. The most effective way to accomplish this is to integrate the quotations into your own sentences. This may be a bit challenging, but the benefit is seamless prose. When you integrate quotations in this way, the reader can follow your ideas and see the sources in the context of your argument. Be sure that the result is a grammatically correct and syntactically fluent sentence, like this one:

> Writing in 1962, R. Smith Simpson lamented the "abysmal ignorance" of candidates for the Foreign Service, a prestigious government agency that should expect the best and the brightest to apply; when it came to "so elementary a subject" as geography, he pointed out that "[f]ew could even place accurately the principal rivers," including ones named after an actual state, such as Ohio.

ACTIVITY

Below you will find a paragraph written using Mark Bauerlein as a source. Read the paragraph, and then rewrite it so that it makes more effective use of the source.

> Mark Bauerlein believes that the so-called Digital Revolution could jeopardize the "cultural and civic inheritance" that has made the United States a powerful democracy. He argues that teens and young adults "have grown up with more knowledge and information readily at hand, taken more classes, built their own Web sites, enjoyed more libraries, bookstores, and museums in their towns and cities," yet they are shallow thinkers who are more concerned about themselves than their society. They have a different social life and a different mental life as a result of their use of what he calls "digital tools." "Instead of opening young American minds to the stores of civilization and science and politics, technology has contracted their horizon to themselves, to the social scene around them." He is concerned that the consequences are more serious than just a generation of spoiled brats. He thinks this rising generation is camped in the desert of ignorance and instant gratification. "They have all the advantages of modernity and democracy, but when the gifts of life lead to social joys, not intellectual labor, the minds of the young plateau at age 18."

Citing Sources

Since you will be quoting from several works, you have to keep track of your sources for your reader. In timed situations, you'll probably include only the source number or the author's name in parentheses after the quotation or paraphrase, like this:

> One reason that digital technologies raise a red flag of concern among many adults is that young people, especially children, adapt to them quickly and easily, while adults find them not only more difficult to learn but generally "distracting and disturbing" (Gopnik).

You need to cite paraphrases as well, not just direct quotes. Anytime you are using someone else's ideas, you must give them credit. For example, you could alter the above sentence to read:

> One reason that digital technologies raise a red flag of concern among many adults is that young people, especially children, adapt to them quickly and easily, while adults find them not only more difficult to learn but experience them as bothersome distractions from their everyday lives (Gopnik).

Another, more elegant, option is to mention the author and title of the work in the sentence that includes the quotation:

> A psychologist and grandmother, Alison Gopnik uses herself and her four-year-old grandson to illustrate the ease with which young children learn to use new technologies, in contrast to adults like herself, who find them "distracting and disturbing."

If you are writing a more formal research paper, you will likely need to follow MLA documentation procedures, including a Works Cited page. Ask your teacher if you are unclear about what is required for an assignment. Guidelines for MLA documentation appear in the back of this book.

Occasionally, you'll encounter a source within a source. That is, an author you intend to quote has quoted another author. In that case, you enclose the entire quotation in double quotes and use single quotes to indicate what the author cites. Let's say, for instance, you want to quote from this portion of Nicholas Carr's blog post:

> Carr points out that perhaps the most dangerous part of researching on the Internet is that it gives people "an exaggerated sense of their own intelligence." He supports this assertion by referring to the results of a study by three Yale psychologists, which showed that "searching the web gives people an 'illusion of knowledge.'"

As you go through the readings and other texts in the following chapters, you will join conversations on a range of topics, reflecting on and integrating the ideas of others from different times and places into your own thinking and writing. Each chapter includes a Conversation in which you will practice this skill with a series of texts (including visuals) related to the chapter's theme. You should also be aware of the conversations going on around you all the time. How do people call on sources to reinforce their positions? And how do people enter an ongoing conversation and move it forward?

A Sample Synthesis Essay

Following is a brief synthesis essay about the influence of technology on human intelligence that incorporates the sources we've discussed. Note how the viewpoint expressed in the thesis statement remains central, with sources supplementing and supporting that view.

"Is Technology Making Us Dumber?"

By Noah Chapman

From crude stone tools, to the printing press, to the smartphone, humans have been creating new technologies since the beginning of our existence. We're constantly creating new technologies to improve our lives, but there have always been doubters predicting that the changes would bring destruction. However, these technologies are simply tools, and the result depends on how we use them. A hammer can be used to knock in a skull or to build a home—the hammer itself is neither good nor bad. New technologies, particularly the Internet, have the power to make us smarter if we use them to broaden our worldview and engage with complex materials, but moderate the time spent on them.

Technology will increase human intelligence only if we use it to expand our connection to the world. The Internet allows us to converse with almost anyone, on any topic, at any time; people on different sides of the world can discuss and learn together almost instantly. Appropriate use of social media exposes people to "a lot of new, useful things to think about—serendipitous stories, insights from others" (Agger). However good judgement is necessary for these interactions to be productive. Time spent on social media could result in users "contract[ing] their horizon to themselves, to the social scene around them" (Bauerlein). Instead of expanding our connection to the world, we've only expanded our connection to ourselves. There are some corners of the Internet that could do even worse damage, sites advocating white supremacy and forums radicalizing young teens. Internet interactions can lead to positive and enlightening discussion, or it can be limiting and damaging.

Because the Internet has changed how we research and find information, technology can either increase access to interesting and complex materials or restrict our intake to simplistic information bites. The Internet allows users to access, often for free, books, scholarly articles, and research at the click of a button. These materials help people learn things from sources they may not have been able to find in a physical library. However, tools like search engines and Ctrl+F also allow us to pass over some of the richness and nuance in these texts to get to the sound byte we want. Reading used to be a hunt for knowledge, not a search for a simple one-sentence summary. We have to choose to delve more deeply into the texts we read. But as Carr points out, Internet searches may give people "an 'illusion of knowledge'" rather than any deep understanding of complex issues. Because researching on the Internet can lead to "searchers' overconfidence in assessing their smarts," people are even less likely to attempt to deepen their knowledge. In fact, Carr reports that some studies show that when people research on the Internet, their retention of information decreases since they assume they can look up that same information again with speed and ease. Thus, using the tools technology provides to research can lead to limited and simplistic results or a plethora of rich and complex ideas.

One of the main challenges of technology is moderating our contact with it. Despite the many useful tools technology offers, overuse can lead to a number of problems. The first of which is changes in the brain itself: "MRI research has shown that the brains of Internet users who have trouble controlling their craving to be constantly plugged-in exhibit changes similar to those seen in people addicted to drugs and alcohol" (Howard). Addicts can even experience withdrawal symptoms when avoiding Internet use. However, Internet use does not always spell bad news for the brain "in moderation, the Internet can actually boost brain function" and "stimulate neural activity patterns" (Howard). Especially for older adults, technology use is a new skill, and learning it boosts intelligence. Even younger users develop new skills as software changes and develops, and with it the way it's used. Internet use is a balancing act, using it enough to boost brain function, but moderating use enough to avoid addiction.

Despite the fear and finger-pointing, it is not the technology itself that lowers human intelligence, but the choices we make when engaging with it. The vast resources made available by the Internet can serve to either widen our view of the world, or to support our existing narrow ideas. We can choose to lessen our cognitive abilities by searching for only surface level answers, or we can take the time to engage with the complexities of language. We can increase our brain function through use of technology or fry our brains when we spend too much time using it. It's by making these choices to use technology purposefully and appropriately that technology becomes a tool for good in our lives.

QUESTIONS

1. The essay opens with an analogy. How effectively does this engage the reader and lead into the writer's thesis?

2. In the second paragraph, the writer acknowledges a counterargument. How does this concession and refutation help develop her argument?

3. Identify one place where the writer's use of a source is particularly successful and one instance that could be improved. In each case, explain your response. What changes would you recommend

the writer make to use sources more effectively in her next draft?

4. What do you see as the greatest strength of this essay? Explain your response.

5. What is the best suggestion you can offer the writer to improve the effectiveness of her argument?

6. Imagine that, for the next draft of this essay, the writer must replace one of the sources. Which source should she replace, and why? What source would you recommend she use in its place?

CULMINATING CONVERSATION: MANDATORY COMMUNITY SERVICE

Many high schools have made community service — or service learning, as some call it — a graduation requirement. What qualifies as community service varies, from activities on school property to those involving the larger local community and even projects in other countries. Although some see community service as a way for young adults to focus their personal and academic development as well as learn civic responsibility, the concept of "required volunteerism" has encountered some opposition.

Read the following sources carefully, including the introductory material. Then, synthesize them into an essay that develops a position on whether high schools in general — or in your specific school or district — should make community service mandatory. Incorporate references to or quotations from a minimum of three of these sources in your argument.

Sources

1. **Barack Obama** / from *Commencement Address at Wesleyan University*
2. **Frank Bruni** / from *To Get to Harvard, Go to Haiti?*
3. **Lily Lou** / *The Downside of School Volunteer Requirements*
4. **Corporation for National and Community Service** / *Volunteering: A Pathway to Employment* (infographic)
5. *Detroit News* / *Volunteering Opens Teen's Eyes to Nursing*
6. **Eliza McGraw** / from *With a Homeless Center on Campus, Students Have an Unusual Chance to Serve*

1 from Commencement Address at Wesleyan University

BARACK OBAMA

The following excerpt is from the commencement address that President Barack Obama delivered at Wesleyan University in 2008. President Obama substituted for Senator Ted Kennedy, who was originally scheduled to speak but cancelled because of ill health.

I was born the year that Ted Kennedy's brother John called a generation of Americans to ask their country what they could do. And I came of age at a time when they did it. They were the Peace Corps volunteers who won a generation of goodwill toward America at a time when America's ideals were challenged. They were the teenagers and college students, not much older than you, who watched the Civil Rights Movement unfold on their television sets; who saw the dogs and the fire hoses and the footage of marchers beaten within an inch or their lives; who knew it was probably smarter and safer to stay at home, but still decided to take those Freedom Rides down south — who still decided to march. And because they did, they changed the world.

I bring this up because today, you are about to enter a world that makes it easy to get caught up in the notion that there are actually two different stories at work in our lives.

The first is the story of our everyday cares and concerns — the responsibilities we have to our jobs and our families — the bustle and busyness of what happens in our own life. And the second is the story of what happens in the life of our country — of what happens in the wider world. It's the story you see when you catch a glimpse of the day's headlines or turn on the news at night — a story of big challenges like war and recession; hunger and climate change; injustice and inequality. It's a story that can sometimes seem distant and separate from our own — a destiny to be shaped by forces beyond our control.

And yet, the history of this nation tells us this isn't so. It tells us that we are a people whose destiny has never been written for us, but by us — by generations of men and women, young and old, who have always believed that their story and the American story are not separate, but shared. And for more than two centuries, they have served this country in ways that have forever enriched both.

I say this to you as someone who couldn't 5 be standing here today if not for the service of others, and wouldn't be standing here today if not for the purpose that service gave my own life. . . .

Each of you will have the chance to make your own discovery in the years to come. And I say "chance" because you won't have to take it. There's no community service requirement in the real world; no one forcing you to care. You can take your diploma, walk off this stage, and chase only after the big house and the nice suits and all the other things that our money culture says you should by. You can choose to narrow your concerns and live your life in a way that tries to keep your story separate from America's.

But I hope you don't. Not because you have an obligation to those who are less fortunate, though you do have that obligation. Not because you have a debt to all those who helped you get here, though you do have that debt. It's because you have an obligation to yourself. Because our individual salvation depends on collective salvation. Because thinking only about yourself, fulfilling your immediate wants and needs, betrays a poverty of ambition. Because it's only when you hitch your wagon to something larger than yourself that you realize your true potential and discover the role you'll play in writing the next great chapter in America's story.

There are so many ways to serve and so much need at this defining moment in our history. You don't have to be a community organizer or do something crazy like run for President. Right here at Wesleyan, many of you have already volunteered at local schools, contributed to United Way, and even started a program that brings fresh produce to needy families in the area. One hundred and sixty-four graduates of this school have joined the Peace Corps since 2001, and I'm especially proud that two of you are about to leave for my father's homeland of Kenya to bring alternative sources of energy to impoverished areas.

I ask you to seek these opportunities when you leave here, because the future of this country — your future — depends on it. At a time when our security and moral standing depend on winning hearts and minds in the forgotten corners of this world, we need more of you to serve abroad. As President, I intend to grow the Foreign Service, double the Peace Corps over the next few years, and engage the young people of other nations in similar programs, so that we work side by side to take on the common challenges that confront all humanity.

---

2 from To Get to Harvard, Go to Haiti?

FRANK BRUNI

The following excerpt is from an op-ed essay that appeared in the *New York Times* in 2016.

This summer, as last, Dylan Hernandez, 17, noticed a theme on the social media accounts of fellow students at his private Catholic high school in Flint, Mich.

"An awfully large percentage of my friends — skewing towards the affluent — are taking 'mission trips' to Central America and Africa," he wrote to me in a recent email. He knows this from pictures they post on Snapchat and Instagram, typically showing one of them "with some poor brown child aged 2 to 6 on their knee," he explained. The captions tend to say something along the lines of, "This cutie made it so hard to leave."

But leave they do, after as little as a week of helping to repair some village's crumbling school or library, to return to their comfortable homes and quite possibly write a college-application essay about how transformed they are.

"It rubs me the wrong way," Hernandez told me, explaining that while many of his friends are well intentioned, some seem not to notice poverty until an exotic trip comes with it. He himself has done extensive, sustained volunteer work at the Flint Y.M.C.A., where, he said, the children he tutors and plays with would love it "if these same peers came around and merely talked to them."

"No passport or customs line required," he added.

Hernandez reached out to me because he was familiar with writing I had done about the college admissions process. What he described is something that has long bothered me and other critics of that process: the

169

persistent vogue among secondary-school students for so-called service that's sometimes about little more than a faraway adventure and a few lines or paragraphs on their applications to selective colleges.

It turns developing-world hardship into a prose-ready opportunity for growth, empathy into an extracurricular activity.

And it reflects a broader gaming of the admissions process that concerns me just as much, because of its potential to create strange habits and values in the students who go through it, telling them that success is a matter of superficial packaging and checking off the right boxes at the right time. That's true only in some cases, and hardly the recipe for a life well lived. . . .

But there's cynicism in the mix.

A college admissions counselor once told 10 me about a rich European client of his who called him in a panic, wanting to cancel her family's usual August vacation so that her son could go build roads in the developing world. She'd just read or heard somewhere that colleges would be impressed by that.

He asked her if she had a roadway or country in mind. She didn't.

Richard Weissbourd, a child psychologist and Harvard lecturer who has studied the admissions process in the interest of reforming it, recalled speaking with wealthy parents who had bought an orphanage in Botswana so their children could have a project to write and talk about. He later became aware of other parents who had bought an AIDS clinic in a similarly poor country for the same reason.

"It becomes contagious," he said. . . .

A college admissions officer told me that his favorite among recent essays by Trinity applicants came from someone "who spent the summer working at a coffee shop. He wrote about not realizing until he did this how invisible people in the service industry are. He wrote about how people looked right through him at the counter."

Helicopter parents, stand down! Pérez's 15 assessment doesn't mean that you should hustle your teenagers to the nearest Starbucks. It means that whatever they do, they should be able to engage in it fully and reflect on it meaningfully. And if that's service work, why not address all the need in your own backyard?

Many college-bound teenagers do, but not nearly enough, as Hernandez can attest. He feels awfully lonely at the Flint Y.M.C.A. and, in the context of that, wonders, "Why is it fashionable to spend $1,000-plus, 20 hours traveling, and 120 hours volunteering in Guatemala for a week?"

He wonders something else, too. "Aren't the children there sad, getting abandoned by a fresh crop of affluent American teens every few days?"

---

3 The Downside of School Volunteer Requirements

LILY LOU

The following op-ed appeared in 2015 on the website The Prospect, which states that it is "the largest student-run college access organization in the world" with a staff of college and high school students dedicated to helping other young people survive high school . . . and excel in college and beyond." Lily Lou is a student writing and living in Atlanta.

Many schools have begun requiring students to graduate with a certain amount of volunteer hours, including my own. Volunteering is a great way to help out your community, but there are also many other ways to become the Mother Teresa of your community without volunteering. Having service learning requirements for students promotes a point of view that volunteering is the only way to help your community, when in reality you could help the community through many other ways, such as participating in clubs, becoming an activist, performing random acts of kindness, becoming a mentor, researching, or even getting a job.

Not having volunteering requirements would not prevent anyone from volunteering, but it would encourage avid volunteers rather than generating a larger number of uninspired volunteers who glance at the clock every few minutes. Forcing community service on high school students only creates more volunteers who unexcitedly volunteer to fulfill volunteer requirements. Community service is about giving back to your community, but efforts to train volunteers and work with volunteers are futile if they are not dedicated to the cause. This wastes time both for the student and the volunteer organization. Requiring high school students to volunteer does not make them better people. "Schools should use other methods to inspire community and compassion," said Karen Zheng, a high school Junior from Northview High School. "Even though some kids might work at a homeless shelter for one hour each month, they might still pass by a homeless man on the street without doing anything."

In fact, according to Education Week, service learning requirements, such as the one in Maryland, actually reduce the amount of long term volunteering in communities.

Volunteering should be treated just like any other extracurricular, and students who participate in other extracurriculars such as clubs and sports will have a tougher time getting enough volunteer hours to graduate because of their other extracurricular involvements. Students already have a lot on their plate, and volunteering only adds more things to juggle. This balancing act only leads to more stress and less sleep (two-thirds of students already get less than seven hours of sleep). Volunteering is also biased against low income students who have to keep jobs to help their families earn money. Besides the time that could have been used earning money or helping out with family, transportation costs for volunteering make it harder for low income students to have a say in choosing their volunteer opportunities and they are forced to choose from a limited amount of opportunities near their schools or homes.

Volunteer requirements give students an idea that the more time students put into something, the more they are helping their communities. It gives students a mindset of quantity over quality. This leads students to seek out low-effort volunteer opportunities that offer more service learning hours rather than truly making an impact in their communities. Just like there are fluff clubs, there are fluff volunteer opportunities that credit more hours than actually performed. Similarly, many schools have deadlines for hours to be submitted, but some students miss those deadlines and do not receive credit for their service.

Requirements for volunteer hours also falsely elevate school rankings. Students racking up large numbers of school service hours is advantageous to the school systems and gives schools a better public image. Though extracurriculars play a small role in

5

influencing college rankings, some schools advertise their "commitment to service learning" through these required service hours.

Volunteering should not be a high school graduation requirement because volunteering isn't for everyone and there are plenty of other ways for students to find their passions and gain experience. It creates a culture that supports quantity over quality, and makes an insignificant impact on the community, even reducing long term volunteering.

4 Volunteering: A Pathway to Employment

CORPORATION FOR NATIONAL AND COMMUNITY SERVICE

The following infographic is part of a 2013 report by the Corporation for National and Community Service.

VOLUNTEERING: A PATHWAY TO EMPLOYMENT

The new report from the Corporation for National and Community Service provides the most compelling empirical evidence to date linking volunteering and employment in the United States.

Volunteers have higher odds of finding employment in today's job market.

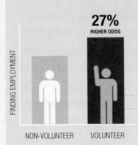

27%
HIGHER ODDS

FINDING EMPLOYMENT

NON-VOLUNTEER   VOLUNTEER

Volunteers have 27% higher odds of finding employment than non-volunteers.

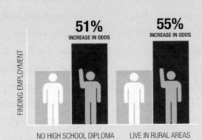

51%
INCREASE IN ODDS

55%
INCREASE IN ODDS

FINDING EMPLOYMENT

NO HIGH SCHOOL DIPLOMA   LIVE IN RURAL AREAS

The relationship between volunteering and employment was strongest for individuals without a high school diploma and those who live in rural areas.

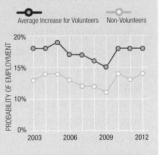

Average Increase for Volunteers   Non-Volunteers

PROBABILITY OF EMPLOYMENT

20%

15%

10%

0%

2003   2006   2009   2012

The relationship is stable across time and economic conditions.

Corporation for National and Community Service

5 Volunteering Opens Teen's Eyes to Nursing

The following human interest story appeared in the *Detroit News* in 2008.

If you asked 13-year-olds to make a list of their favorite after-school activities, visiting with the elderly probably wouldn't be a top choice. But it would be for John Prueter, son of Keith and Barbara Prueter of Essexville, who says he'd spend time with older generations every day if he could.

"All the older people are nice people," he said. "They like to see young people come visit in these homes." Prueter, a seventh-grader at Cramer Junior High School, spends much of his after-school time at the Alterra Sterling House, an assisted-living home in Hampton Township.

Prueter got into volunteering with the elderly almost two years ago when his great-grandmother, Mable Post, suffered a stroke. Always close to her, Prueter visited her regularly when she was in the hospital. After 100 days, she was transferred to Alterra, where she still lives. Now, instead of coming just to visit a relative, he comes to volunteer and visit with everyone. He is the youngest of Alterra's regular volunteers and one of the most frequent visitors.

Prueter spends his time there helping with activities such as cooking and gardening, playing games with residents and just chatting with them. He speaks to the residents on a level that makes them feel good, said Pam O'Laughlin, executive director for Alterra's Bay City campus. "He has a unique ability to communicate with these folks," she said. "He's not timid. They look forward to him coming." Prueter sometimes takes the residents small gifts, such as cake on a birthday, and often calls them when he cannot come in.

He's willing to help Alterra's staff with any activities, O'Laughlin said. For example, he helped residents make cheesecakes for Easter. He helps with gardening and crafts, and calls the bingo games each Sunday. He also helps with mail delivery, assists nurses and helps residents get ready for special trips or concerts.

Virginia Ball, an 85-year-old resident, says Prueter visits with her regularly when he stops in. He runs and answers her phone when he hears it ringing down the hall and helps out with other tasks. "He'll offer to fold laundry," she said. But if there is nothing to do to help, Prueter will just sit in her room and chat. "He seems to enjoy talking to older people," Ball said.

His service at Alterra earned him an outstanding youth volunteer award from Veterans of Foreign Wars Post 6950. Prueter wants to be in the marching band when he moves up to Garber High School. But he says he doesn't plan on letting practice get in the way of his visits to Alterra. Even after high school, Prueter hopes to continue working with the elderly by studying nursing. He says he became interested in the field because of his volunteer work.

His dream job, he says, is working where he volunteers now.

6 from With a Homeless Center on Campus, Students Have an Unusual Chance to Serve

ELIZA McGRAW

The following excerpt is from an article that appeared in the *Washington Post Magazine* in 2017.

Gonzaga College High School is on I Street NW, not far from Union Station. Just outside the campus, there are views of the U.S. Capitol and of people struggling with life on the street. "Gonzaga sits right in the middle of poverty and power," says senior Jirhe Love, who lives in the city, "and I mean, you can't avoid it. It's the real world."

At Gonzaga, dealing with the real world is built into the curriculum. The Father McKenna Center, a social service agency for men experiencing homelessness and poverty, is housed at the school. Students fulfilling the school's requirement to complete 40 hours of service during senior year can work there, serving lunch, giving computer tutorials and striking up friendships with clients. (Underclassmen can also serve in the center and participate in other programs, such as retreats and Campus Kitchen.)

"We're living in what seems like just a meaner world than we've ever been a part of," says Kristien Zenkov, a professor of education at George Mason who has written about social justice in education. He says that a culture of service like Gonzaga's "takes that on directly."

"Gonzaga attracts a unique kind of kid," says the school's president, the Rev. Stephen Planning. Prospective students, he notes, see the location of the school, the homeless shelter, the fact that many students walk several blocks to and from the Metro and get to know the homeless population by name. "And

there are some kids who find that exciting and thrilling and are drawn to that, and other kids might be a little intimidated by that, and they might choose something different."

"There is no other high school in the United 5 States that has a homeless shelter on its campus," says McKenna Center President Kim Cox. Watching the students interact with guests heartens her. "I know it is actually profound for me and the rest of our staff," she says. "There is hope for the future, seeing them engage at this level and at this depth. . . ."

Across the nation, only one state, Maryland, and the District have a service requirement for public school graduation. In other states, including Virginia, school districts, cities or counties can set their own standards, and some offer credit for service hours. In parochial, charter or private schools, such as Gonzaga, how — or if — service is part of school is an individual decision.

But Gonzaga — along with many other Jesuit schools — stands apart even from other schools that require service hours in the focus of its mandate. Students can't fulfill their obligation through activities such as carwashes, fundraising or work at animal shelters.

"Notably," the school's guidelines say, "the only acceptable service involves work that directly supports the poor, vulnerable, and marginalized. . . ."

The needs of the poor aren't only visible in the McKenna Center (and the school offers volunteer opportunities beyond it, such as spring break trips to live and work with immigrant laborers). Between classes students scurrying through the hallways pass stacks of diapers for a diaper drive; an image of Saint Bakhita, the patron saint of human-trafficking victims; and a model of a jail cell inspired by a recent guest speaker on mass incarceration. "It's very easy to be present to a culture of service if it's just everywhere you're looking," says Stephen Szolosi, the director of campus ministry. "You're hoping that people are being drawn in, saying, *Well, okay, what's going on in the real world around me? Where is there need? Where do I have resource to respond?*"

Love says that students have indeed been 10 captured by that culture of service. When students see homeless people by the Metro station, Love says, they don't "just, like, go around them as if they're not people. Many Gonzaga students have conversations with them. And there are actually many homeless people who have Gonzaga hoodies on." Love says that his service has informed his creative writing as well. He wrote a poem, called "Benning Road Flows," based on an encounter when he distributed food. "Imagine locking eyes / With one who looks through you," it begins.

◆ ◆ ◆

In teacher Katie Murphy's social justice classroom, signs read, "Let's Combat Terror With Love" and "We Stand With Immigrants." Sounds of buses, sirens and braking cars remind you that you're downtown. A group of seniors has gathered to talk about their experiences with service and with the class, through which they participate in projects that fulfill 20 hours of their obligation. It's a rare dress-down day for them, and they wear sweatshirts and sneakers as they eat pizza at desks pulled into a circle. They speak carefully, giving each other credit for introducing ideas: "like Jackson was saying," or "to go off what Patrick said."

"In classes like ethics and social justice you get all these stats thrown at you about homelessness or people who are without proper nutrition and all these numbers," says Thomas Pollack, who lives in Alexandria, "but it's hard to put a face to it. But once you start doing the service, that firsthand experience of helping give food to the homeless, or just talking to them, acknowledging they are there, you sort of put faces with those numbers, and you really humanize the issue instead of just thinking, *Oh,* man, *that number's bad.*"

"It's very easy to teach someone something. It's very difficult to teach someone to care about something," says Joseph Johnson, who lives in Arlington, Va. "This class has helped me care about those statistics a hell of a lot more."

The service requirement "doesn't just teach you the problems and the root causes," says Christian Tabash of Vienna, Va., who has had conversations with a regular guest at the McKenna Center. "It teaches you a sense of conviction. It makes you unsettled. As long as there's progress to be made, as long as there are people suffering . . . it stirs up, like, this hunger for justice."

5
Education

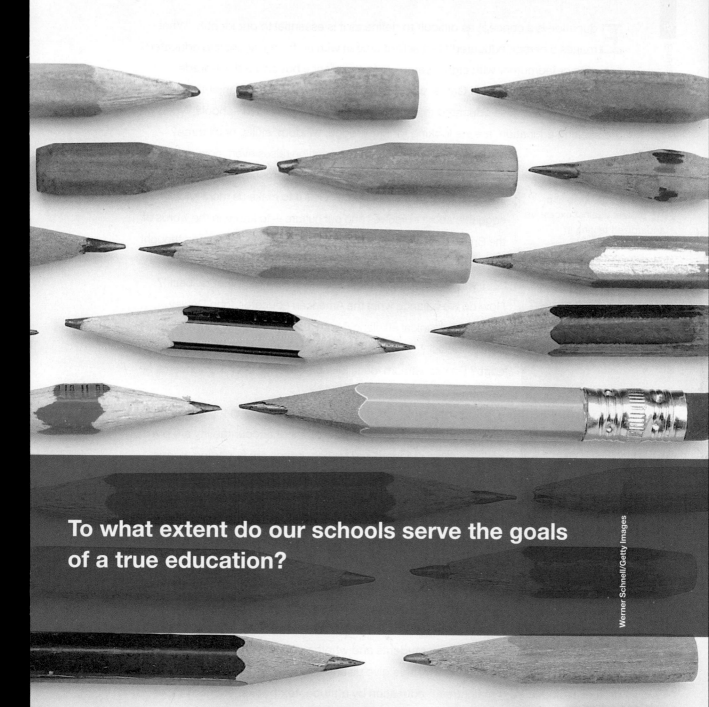

To what extent do our schools serve the goals of a true education?

Werner Schnell/Getty Images

Education is a concept as difficult to define as it is essential to our identity. What makes a person educated? Is a skilled artisan with no formal schooling educated? Is a wise grandmother with eighty years of life experience but only a third-grade education educated? Is Bill Gates, who dropped out of Harvard as a junior to found Microsoft, more or less educated than his classmates who stayed in school? When we are seeking education, are we looking for knowledge, wisdom, skills, or all three?

This photo of an eleven-year-old student was taken at a 2015 protest against excessive standardized testing in Colorado schools.
How does the message on this student's jacket frame the debate about standardized testing in American schools? How might proponents of such testing respond to this slogan?

David Zalubowski/AP Images

Describing the purpose of education raises even more questions. Is it to prepare citizens to participate in a democracy? Is it to teach practical skills for the workforce? Or is it to make us more knowledgeable about ourselves and our culture — to know, in the words of the British poet Matthew Arnold, "the best that is known and thought in the world"?

Even Arnold's focus begs several questions: What is "best"? How do we balance what the American educator John Dewey called "mechanical efficiency" with a deep understanding of "democratic ideals"? Should schools impart values as well as knowledge? Do mainstream ideas take precedence over the concerns of individual groups?

Such philosophical questions are often lost in the practical realities of schooling. While advocates of accountability are prescribing more standardized testing, critics are sounding alarms about its negative effects. We are far from agreement about the best ways to teach and learn, tasks made even more challenging by the demands of exponential technological changes. What information and skills do students need to compete in a global economy?

The selections in this chapter explore many of these issues. They explore the fundamental link between education and freedom and what a liberal education means in the twenty-first century. They ask how choices of required reading affect students and whether the humdrum routine of drill contributes to an education. The writers give us an insider's view of what it means to feel excluded from mainstream education by attitude, textbooks, economics, or choice. They discuss how schools in the United States compare with those in other countries. And they ask what the future of the American high school is. Together, they lead us to reflect on what education means and whether — and how — our schools embody that vision.

from In Defense of a Liberal Education

FAREED ZAKARIA

Fareed Zakaria (b. 1964) is an Indian American journalist who grew up in Mumbai and earned a BA from Yale University in 1986 and a PhD in Government from Harvard University in 1993. In 1992, at the age of 28, Zakaria became the managing editor of *Foreign Affairs*, an influential journal of international politics. He has since worked or written for *Newsweek, Time*, the *New York Times*, the *Wall Street Journal*, the *New Yorker*, the *New Republic*, and *Slate*. A best-selling author, he also hosts his own show on CNN, *Fareed Zakaria GPS* (Global Public Square), which focuses on international issues and foreign affairs, and writes a weekly column for the *Washington Post*. Zakaria's books include *From Wealth to Power: The Unusual Origins of America's World Role* (1998), *The American Encounter: The United States and the Making of the Modern World* (1998), which he co-edited, *The Future of Freedom* (2003), and *The Post-American World* (2008). The following excerpt appears in his most recent book, *In Defense of a Liberal Education* (2015).

Jason Andrew/Contour by Getty Images

If you want to live a good life these days, you know what you're supposed to do. Get into college but then drop out. Spend your days learning computer science and your nights coding. Start a technology company and take it public. That's the new American dream. If you're not quite that adventurous, you could major in electrical engineering.

What you are not supposed to do is study the liberal arts. Around the world, the idea of a broad-based "liberal" education is closely tied to the United States and its great universities and colleges. But in America itself, a liberal education is out of favor. In an age defined by technology and globalization, everyone is talking about skills-based learning. Politicians, business-people, and even many educators see it as the only way for the nation to stay competitive. They urge students to stop dreaming and start thinking practically about the skills they will need in the workplace. An open-ended exploration of knowledge is seen as a road to nowhere.

A classic liberal education has few defenders. Conservatives fume that it is too, well, liberal (though the term has no partisan meaning). Liberals worry it is too elitist. Students wonder what they would do with a degree in psychology. And parents fear that it will cost them their life savings.

This growing unease is apparent in the numbers. As college enrollment has grown[1] in recent decades, the percentage of students majoring in subjects like English and philosophy has declined sharply. In 1971, for example, 7.6 percent of all bachelor's degrees were awarded in English language and literature. By 2012, that number had fallen to 3.0 percent. During the same period, the percentage of business majors in the undergraduate population rose from 13.7 to 20.5.

Some believe this pattern makes sense — that 5 new entrants into higher education might simply prefer job training to the liberal arts. Perhaps. But in earlier periods of educational expansion,[2] this was not the case. In the 1950s and 1960s, for instance, students saw college as more than a glorified trade school. Newcomers, often from lower-middle-class backgrounds and immigrant families with little education, enthusiastically embraced the liberal arts. They saw it as a gateway to a career, and also as a way to assimilate into American culture. "I have to speak absolutely perfect English," says Philip Roth's character Alex Portnoy, the son of immigrants and hero of the novel *Portnoy's Complaint*.[3] Majors like English and history grew in popularity precisely during the decades of mass growth in American higher education.

The great danger facing American higher education is *not* that too many students are studying the liberal arts. Here are the data.[4] In the 2011–12 academic year, 52 percent of American undergraduates were enrolled in two-year or less-than-two-year colleges, and 48 percent were enrolled in four-year institutions. At two-year colleges, the most popular area of study was health professions and related sciences (23.3 percent). An additional 11.7 percent of students studied business, management, and marketing. At four-year colleges, the pattern was the same. Business led the list of majors, accounting for 18.9 percent of students, and health was

second, accounting for 13.4 percent. Another estimate[5] found that only a third of all bachelor's degree recipients study fields that could be classified as the liberal arts. And only about 1.8 percent of all undergraduates attend classic liberal arts colleges like Amherst, Swarthmore, and Pomona.

As you can see, we do not have an oversupply of students studying history, literature, philosophy, or physics and math for that matter. A majority is specializing in fields because they see them as directly related to the job market. It's true that more Americans need technical training, and all Americans need greater scientific literacy. But the drumbeat of talk about skills and jobs has not lured people into engineering and biology — not everyone has the aptitude for science — so much as it has made them nervously forsake the humanities and take courses in business and communications. Many of these students might well have been better off taking a richer, deeper set of courses in subjects they found fascinating — and supplementing it, as we all should, with some basic knowledge of computers and math. In any event, what is clear is that the gap in technical training is not being caused by the small percentage of students who choose four-year degrees in the liberal arts.

Jeff Parker/Cagle Cartoons Inc.

◀

The debate about the value of liberal arts courses — or any courses that are not directly related to a career — has generated satiric responses such as this cartoon lampooning Florida governor Rick Scott.

How does the artist portray Rick Scott's position on the issue? What is the cartoon's overall message about making this kind of connection between education and job prospects?

Usefulness of Major

Percentage of people in each field of study who say their current job is related to their major in college or graduate school

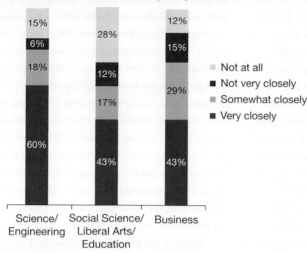

- Not at all
- Not very closely
- Somewhat closely
- Very closely

Science/Engineering — 15%, 6%, 18%, 60%

Social Science/Liberal Arts/Education — 28%, 12%, 17%, 43%

Business — 12%, 15%, 29%, 43%

Data from Pew Research Center.

What questions might Zakaria ask about the data shown in this graph? To what extent does the information in this graph undermine—or bolster—his argument?

Whatever the facts, the assaults continue and have moved from the realm of rhetoric to action. The governors[6] of Texas, Florida, North Carolina, and Wisconsin have announced that they do not intend to keep subsidizing the liberal arts at state-funded universities. "Is it a vital interest of the state to have more anthropologists?" Florida's Rick Scott* asked. "I don't think so." Wisconsin is planning to cut money from subjects that don't train students for a specific job right out of college. "How many PhDs in philosophy do I need to subsidize?" the radio show host William Bennett asked North Carolina's Patrick McCrory,* a sentiment with which McCrory enthusiastically agreed. (Ironically, Bennett himself has a PhD in philosophy, which appears to have trained him well for his multiple careers in government, media, nonprofits, and the private sector.)

It isn't only Republicans on the offensive.[7] Everyone's eager to promote the type of education that might lead directly to a job. In a speech in January 2014, President Barack Obama said, "I

promise you, folks can make a lot more, potentially, with skilled manufacturing or the trades than they might with an art history degree." He later apologized for what he described as a "glib" comment, but Obama has expressed similar sentiments during his presidency. His concern — that in today's world, college graduates need to focus on the tools that will get them good jobs — is shared by many liberals, as well as conservatives and independents. The irrelevance of a liberal education is an idea that has achieved that rare status in Washington: bipartisan agreement.

The attacks have an effect. There is today a loss of coherence and purpose surrounding the idea of a liberal education. Its proponents are defensive about its virtues, while its opponents are convinced that it is at best an expensive luxury, at worst actively counterproductive. Does it really make sense to study English in the age of apps?

In a sense, the question is un-American. For much of its history, America was distinctive in providing an education to all that was *not* skills based. In their comprehensive study of education,[8] the Harvard economists Claudia Goldin and Lawrence

10

*The governor of Florida in 2015, the year this book was first published. —Eds.

*The governor of North Carolina from 2013–2017. —Eds.

Katz note that, historically, Britain, France, and Germany tested children at a young age, educated only a few, and put them through a narrow program designed specifically to impart a set of skills thought to be key to their professions. "The American system," they write, "can be characterized as open, forgiving, lacking universal standards, and having an academic yet practical curriculum." America did not embrace the European model of specific training and apprenticeships because Americans moved constantly, to new cities, counties, and territories in search of new opportunities. They were not rooted in geographic locations with long-established trades and guilds that offered the only path forward. They were also part of an economy that was new and dynamic, so that technology kept changing the nature of work and with it the requirements for jobs. Few wanted to lock themselves into a single industry for life. Finally, Goldin and Katz argue, while a general education was more expensive than specialized training, the cost for the former was not paid by students or their parents. The United States was the first country to publicly fund mass, general education, first at the secondary-school level and then in college. Even now, higher education in America is a much broader and richer universe than anywhere else. Today a high school student can go to one of fourteen hundred institutions in the United States that offer a traditional bachelor's degree, and another fifteen hundred with a more limited course of study.[9] Goldin and Katz point out that on a per capita basis, Britain has only half as many undergraduate institutions and Germany just one-third. Those who seek to reorient U.S. higher education into something more focused and technical should keep in mind that they would be abandoning what has been historically distinctive, even unique, in the American approach to higher education.

And yet, I get it. I understand America's current obsession. I grew up in India in the 1960s and 1970s, when a skills-based education was seen as the only path to a good career. Indians in those days had an almost mystical faith in the power of technology. It had been embedded in the country's DNA since it gained independence in 1947. Jawaharlal Nehru,[10] India's first prime minister, was fervent in his faith in big engineering projects. He believed that India could move out of its economic backwardness only by embracing technology, and he did everything he could during his fourteen years in office to leave that stamp on the nation. A Fabian socialist, Nehru had watched with admiration as the Soviet Union jumpstarted its economy in just a few decades by following such a path. (Lenin once famously remarked, "Communism is Soviet power plus the electrification of the whole country.") Nehru described India's new hydroelectric dams as "temples of the new age."

I attended a private day school in Bombay (now Mumbai), the Cathedral and John Connon School. When founded by British missionaries in the Victorian era, the school had been imbued with a broad, humanistic approach to education. It still had some of that outlook when I was there, but the country's mood was feverishly practical. The 1970s was a tough decade everywhere economically, but especially in India. And though it was a private school, the tuition was low, and Cathedral catered to a broad cross section of the middle class. As a result, all my peers and their parents were anxious about job prospects. The assumption made by almost everyone at school was that engineering and medicine were the two best careers. The real question was, which one would you pursue?

At age sixteen, we had to choose one of three academic streams: science, commerce, or the humanities. We all took a set of board exams that year — a remnant of the British educational model — that helped determine our trajectory. In those days, the choices were obvious. The smart kids would go into science, the rich kids would do commerce, and the girls would take the humanities. (Obviously I'm exaggerating, but not by that much.) Without giving the topic much thought, I streamed into the sciences.

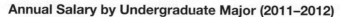

Based on data in this graph, what conclusions can you draw about how a liberal arts major can maximize his or her earning potential? How might Zakaria respond to it?

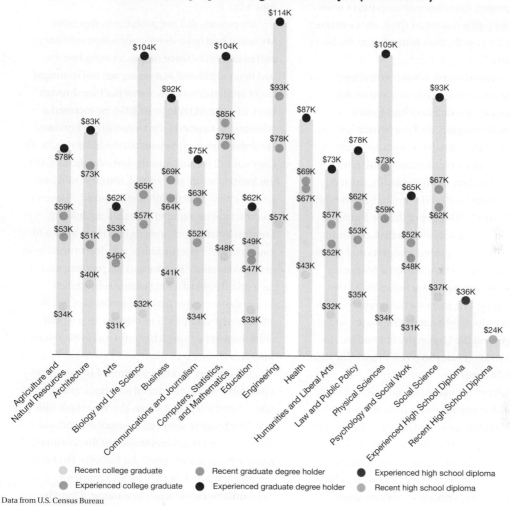

Annual Salary by Undergraduate Major (2011–2012)

○ Recent college graduate   ◐ Recent graduate degree holder   ● Experienced high school diploma
◐ Experienced college graduate   ● Experienced graduate degree holder   ○ Recent high school diploma

Data from U.S. Census Bureau

At the end of twelfth grade, we took another set of exams. These were the big ones. They determined our educational future, as we were reminded again and again. Grades in school, class participation, extracurricular projects, and teachers'

15 recommendations — all were deemed irrelevant compared to the exam scores. Almost all colleges admitted students based solely on these numbers. In fact, engineering colleges asked for scores in only three subjects: physics, chemistry, and mathematics. Similarly,

medical schools would ask for results in just physics, chemistry, and biology. No one cared what you got in English literature. The Indian Institutes of Technology (IITs) — the most prestigious engineering colleges in the country — narrowed the admissions criteria even further. They administered their own entrance test, choosing applicants entirely on the basis of its results.

The increased emphasis on technology and practicality in the 1970s was in part due to domestic factors: inflation had soared, the economy had slumped, and the private sector was crippled by nationalizations and regulations. Another big shift, however, took place far from India's borders. Until the 1970s, the top British universities offered scholarships to bright Indian students — a legacy of the raj. But as Britain went through its own hellish economic times that decade — placed under formal receivership in 1979 by the International Monetary Fund — money for foreign scholarships dried up. In an earlier era, some of the brightest graduates from India might have gone on to Oxford, Cambridge, and the University of London. Without outside money to pay for that education, they stayed home.

But culture follows power. As Britain's economic decline made its universities less attractive, colleges in the United States were rising in wealth and ambition. At my school, people started to notice that American universities had begun offering generous scholarships to foreign students. And we soon began to hear from early trailblazers about the distinctly American approach to learning. A friend from my neighborhood who had gone to Cornell came back in the summers bursting with enthusiasm about his time there. He told us of the incredible variety of courses that students could take no matter what their major. He also told tales of the richness of college life. I remember listening to him describe a film society at Cornell that held screenings and

discussions of classics by Ingmar Bergman and Federico Fellini. I had never heard of Bergman or Fellini, but I was amazed that watching movies was considered an integral part of higher education. Could college really be that much fun?

My parents did not push me to specialize. My father had been deeply interested in history and politics ever since he was a young boy. He had been orphaned at a young age but managed to get financial assistance that put him through high school and college. In 1944, he received a scholarship to attend the University of London. He arrived during the worst of the blitzkrieg,[*] with German V-2 rockets raining down on the city. On the long boat ride to England, the crew told him he was crazy. One member even asked, "Haven't you read the newspapers? People are leaving London by the thousands right now. Why would you go there?" But my father was determined to get an education. History was his passion, and he worked toward a PhD in that subject. But he needed a clearer path to a profession. So, in addition, he obtained a law degree that would allow him to become a barrister[*] upon his return to Bombay.

Though my mother was raised in better circumstances, she also faced a setback at a young age — her father died when she was eight. She briefly attended a college unusual for India at the time — a liberal arts school in the northern part of the country called the Isabella Thoburn College, founded in 1870 by an American Methodist missionary of that name. Though her education was cut short when she returned home to look after her widowed mother, my mother never forgot the place. She often fondly reminisced about its broad and engaging curriculum.

---

[*]A reference to Nazi Germany's bombing of London during World War II. The word means "lightning war" in German. —Eds.
[*]A lawyer. —Eds.

seeing connections

Following is an excerpt from *Not for Profit: Why Democracy Needs the Humanities*, a 2010 book by philosopher Emily Nussbaum.
Examine each of the points she makes about contemporary education. To what extent do they reflect Fareed Zakaria's stance on a liberal education?

from Not for Profit
Why Democracy Needs the Humanities

EMILY NUSSBAUM

If a nation wants to promote a humane, people-sensitive democracy dedicated to promoting opportunities for "life, liberty and the pursuit of the happiness" to each and every person, what abilities will it need to produce in its citizens? At least the following seem crucial:

- The ability to think well about political issues affecting the nation, to examine, reflect, argue, and debate, deferring to neither tradition nor authority
- The ability to recognize fellow citizens as people with equal rights, even though they may be different in race, religion, gender, and sexuality: to look at them with respect, as ends, not just as tools to be manipulated for one's own profit
- The ability to have concern for the lives of others, to grasp what policies of many types mean for the opportunities and experiences of one's fellow citizens, of many types, and for people outside one's own nation
- The ability to imagine well a variety of complex issues affecting the story of a human life as it unfolds: to think about childhood, adolescence, family relationships, illness, death, and much more in a way informed by an understanding of a wide range of human stories, not just by aggregate data
- The ability to judge political leaders critically, but with an informed and realistic sense of the possibilities available to them
- The ability to think about the good of the nation as a whole, not just that of one's own local group
- The ability to see one's own nation, in turn, as a part of a complicated world order in which issues of many kinds require intelligent transnational deliberation for their resolution

My parents' careers were varied and diverse. [20] My father started out as a lawyer before moving into politics and later founding a variety of colleges. He also created a small manufacturing company (to pay the bills) and always wrote books and essays. My mother began as a social worker and then became a journalist, working for newspapers and magazines. (She resigned from her last position in journalism last year, 2014, at the age of seventy-eight.) Neither of them insisted on early specialization. In retrospect, my parents must have worried about our future prospects — everyone else was worried. But to our good fortune, they did not project that particular anxiety on us.

My brother, Arshad, took the first big step. He was two years older than I and fantastically accomplished academically. (He was also a very good athlete, which made following in his footsteps challenging.) He had the kind of scores on his board exams that would have easily placed him in the top engineering programs in the

CENTRAL ESSAY   185

country. Or he could have taken the IIT exam, which he certainly would have aced. In fact, he decided not to do any of that and instead applied to American universities. A couple of his friends considered doing the same, but no one quite knew how the process worked. We learned, for example, that applicants had to take something called the Scholastic Aptitude Test, but we didn't know much about it. (Remember, this is 1980 in India. There was no Google. In fact, there was no color television.) We found a pamphlet about the test at the United States Information Service, the cultural branch of the U.S. embassy. It said that because the SAT was an aptitude test, there was no need to study for it. So, my brother didn't. On the day the test was scheduled, he walked into the makeshift exam center in Bombay, an almost empty room in one of the local colleges, and took the test.

It's difficult to convince people today how novel and risky an idea it was at the time to apply to schools in the United States. The system was still foreign and distant. People didn't really know what it meant to get into a good American university or how that would translate into a career in India. The Harvard alumni in Bombay in the 1970s were by no means a "Who's Who" of the influential and wealthy. Rather, they were an eclectic mix of people who either had spent time abroad (because their parents had foreign postings) or had some connection to America. A few friends of ours had ventured to the United States already, but because they hadn't yet graduated or looked for jobs, their experiences were of little guidance.

My brother had no idea if the admissions departments at American colleges would understand the Indian system or know how to interpret his report cards and recommendations. He also had no real Plan B. If he didn't take the slot offered by engineering schools, he wouldn't be able to get back in line the next year. In fact, things were so unclear to us that we didn't even realize American colleges required applications a full year in advance. As a result, he involuntarily took a gap year between school and college, waiting around to find out whether he got in anywhere.

As it happened, Arshad got in everywhere. He picked the top of the heap — accepting a scholarship offer from Harvard. While we were all thrilled and impressed, many friends remained apprehensive when told the news. It sounded prestigious to say you were going to attend Harvard, but would the education actually translate into a career?

My mother traveled to the United States to drop my brother off in the fall of 1982, an uneasy time in American history. The mood was still more 1970s malaise than 1980s boom. The country was in the midst of the worst recession since the Great Depression. Vietnam and Watergate had shattered the nation's confidence. The Soviet Union was seen as ascendant in our minds. Riots, protests, and urban violence had turned American cities into places of genuine danger. Our images of New York came from Charles Bronson[*] movies and news reports of crack and crime.

All of this was especially alarming to Indians. The country's traditional society had interpreted the 1960s and 1970s as a period of decay in American culture, as young people became morally lax, self-indulgent, permissive, and, perhaps most worrisome, rebellious. The idea that American youth had become disrespectful toward their elders was utterly unnerving to Indian parents. Most believed that any child who traveled to the United States would quickly cast aside family, faith, and tradition for sex, drugs, and rock and roll. If you sent your kids to America, you had to brace yourselves for the prospect that you might "lose" them.

In his first few weeks abroad, Arshad was, probably like all newcomers to Harvard, a bit nervous. My mother, on the other hand, returned

25

---

[*] An American film star best known for his roles in Westerns and crime dramas of the 1960s and 1970s. —Eds.

from her trip clear of any anxiety. She was enchanted with the United States, its college campuses, and the undergraduate experience. She turned her observations into an article for the *Times of India* titled "The Other America."[11] In it, she described how concerned she had been before the trip about permissiveness, drugs, and rebellion at American colleges. She then went on to explain how impressed she was after actually spending time on a campus to find that the place focused on education, hard work, and extracurricular activities. The students she met were bright, motivated, and, to her surprise, quite respectful. She met parents who were tearfully bidding their children good-bye, talking about their next visit, or planning a Thanksgiving reunion. "I feel I am in India," she wrote. "Could this be the heartless America where family ties have lost their hold?"

Indians had it all wrong about the United States, my mother continued. She tried to explain why they read so much bad news about the country. "America is an open society as no other. So they expose their 'failings' too as no other," she wrote. "[Americans] cheerfully join in the talk of their own decline. But the decline is relative to America's own previous strength. It remains the world's largest economy; it still disposes of

▼
_____

Colleges are often known by a motto that captures the institution's overall philosophy of education and the values it hopes to instill in matriculated students. This cartoon makes light of such mottos. **What would Zakaria likely say about whether those three "values" — tradition, competition, and tuition — prevail in colleges today? How well equipped would graduates of such institutions be to deal with civic responsibilities, the job market, and adult life in general?**

TRADITION · COMPETITION · TUITION

Michael Maslin/The New Yorker Collection/Conde Nast

the greatest military might the world has known; refugees from terror still continue to seek shelter in this land of immigrants. It spends millions of dollars in the hope that someone, somewhere may make a valuable contribution to knowledge. America remains the yardstick by which we judge America." As you can see, she was hooked.

In those years, it was fashionable in elite Indian circles to denounce the United States for its imperialism and hegemony. During the Cold War, the Indian government routinely sided with the Soviet Union. Indira Gandhi, the populist prime minister, would often blame India's troubles on the "foreign hand," a reference to the CIA. But my mother has always been stubbornly pro-American. When my father was alive, he would sometimes criticize America for its crimes and blunders, partly to needle my brother and me and partly because, as one who had struggled for India's independence, he had absorbed the worldview of his closest allies, who were all on the left. Yet my mother remained unmoved,

completely convinced that the United States was a land of amazing vitality and virtue. (I suspect it's what has helped her accept the fact that her sons chose the country as their home.)

Along with photographs and informa- 30
tion brochures from her trip, my mother also brought back Harvard's course book. For me, it was an astonishing document. Instead of a thin pamphlet containing a dry list of subjects, as one would find at Indian universities, it was a bulging volume overflowing with ideas. It listed hundreds of classes in all kinds of fields. And the course descriptions were written like advertisements — as if the teachers wanted you to join them on an intellectual adventure. I read through the book, amazed that students didn't have to choose a major in advance and that they could take poetry and physics and history and economics. From eight thousand miles away, with little knowledge and no experience, I was falling in love with the idea of a liberal education.

Notes

1. As college enrollment has grown: U.S. Department of Education, National Center for Education Statistics, *Digest of Education Statistics 2013*, Table 322.10. The *Digest,* published annually by the National Center for Education Statistics, is a highly accessible source for statistics on higher education. The data are updated throughout the year online at http://nces.ed.gov/programs/digest/.

2. In earlier periods of educational expansion: For more on the post-World War II expansion in higher education and the simultaneous rise in the humanities, see Louis Menand, "The Humanities Revolution," in *The Marketplace of Ideas: Reform and Resistance in the American University* (New York: W. W. Norton, 2010), 63–73; and William M. Chace, "The Decline of the English Department," *American Scholar*, Autumn 2009. The Humanities Indicators, a project of the American Academy of Arts and Sciences available online at www.humanitiesindicators.org, also tracks data on the twentieth-century rise and fall in the study of the humanities.

3. "I have to speak": Philip Roth, *Portnoy's Complaint* (New York: Vintage Books, 1994), 164.

4. Here are the data: National Center for Education Statistics, *Digest*, Table 311.60.

5. Another estimate: Measures of the liberal arts vary by source, depending largely on how academic fields are classified. Justin Pope, "Liberal Arts Colleges Forced to Evolve with Market," Associated Press, Dec. 30, 2012, estimates that between 100,000 and 300,000 of the country's approximately 17 million undergraduates attend a liberal arts college, that is, a residential college that exists independent of any larger university. The same article estimates that about one-third of bachelor's degrees in the United States are awarded in the liberal arts.

The *Digest* places the undergraduate population at 18 million as of 2012 (Table 303.60). It also divides degrees into six broad categories: humanities; social and behavioral sciences; natural sciences and mathematics; computer sciences and engineering; education; business; and other fields, a category that includes professional programs such as agriculture and law enforcement. If just the first three are classified as liberal, then about 40 percent of the 1.8 million bachelor's degrees conferred in 2011–12 were in the liberal arts (Table 318.20).

6. Governors: See Scott Jaschik, "Florida GOP vs. Social Science," *Inside Higher Ed*, Oct. 12, 2011 (Scott quote); Kevin Kiley, "A $10,000 Platform," *Inside Higher Ed*, Nov. 30, 2012; and Kiley, "Another Liberal Arts Critic," *Inside Higher Ed*, Jan. 30, 2013 (Bennett quote).

7. It isn't only Republicans: Scott Jaschik, "Apology from Obama," *Inside Higher Ed*, Feb. 19, 2014.

8. Their comprehensive study of education: Claudia Goldin and Lawrence Katz, *The Race between Education and Technology* (Cambridge: Harvard University Press, 2010), 28–29.

9. Today a high school student: Ibid., 254.

10. Jawaharlal Nehru: On Nehru's economic views, see Shashi Tharoor, *Nehru: The Invention of India* (New York: Arcade, 2003), 159–193; and Jawaharlal Nehru, "Temples of the New Age," July 8, 1954, available at http://www.nehruinternationalconference2014.com/nehru_speech4.aspx.

11. "The Other America": Fatma Zakaria, "The Other America," *Times of India*, Mar. 28, 1982.

[2015]

QUESTIONS FOR DISCUSSION

1. What does Fareed Zakaria mean by the "liberal education" he cites in his title? To what extent is it different from a "liberal arts education"?

2. According to Zakaria's analysis, why has a liberal education fallen out of favor in American colleges and universities? Specifically, what are two arguments against it that he cites?

3. A common criticism of liberal education is that it does not have the real-world applicability that courses in science, technology, engineering, and mathematics (STEM) have, and it does not teach students skills necessary for the jobs that are available in today's economy. How does Zakaria argue against this position? Cite specific passages to support your response.

4. Who are the principal targets of Zakaria's criticism — that is, who is most opposed to a liberal education, as he defines it? Is it educators? Parents? Students themselves? Politicians? The business community? The corporate world? Explain how you know.

5. If, as Zakaria writes, "The great danger facing American higher education is *not* that too many students are studying the liberal arts" (para. 6), then what is the danger? How effectively does Zakaria communicate this position?

6. When Zakaria makes the point that there is in our time "a loss of coherence and purpose surrounding the idea of a liberal education," he asks, "Does it really make sense to study English in the age of apps?" (para. 10). When he asserts, in the next paragraph, that the very question is "un-American," what do you think he means? What does he suggest is "un-American" about questioning the value of studying subjects such as literature, classics, or art history? Do you agree or disagree with his reasoning? Explain your response.

7. What does Zakaria mean when he refers to "the distinctly American approach to learning" (para. 17)? How is this different from what he has experienced in Indian schools, which often follow a British model of education?

8. Zakaria spends the last part of the essay describing his own experience, weaving in details about the education system in India and his own family. He ends by saying that he was "falling in love with the idea of a liberal education" (para. 30). Why was this idea so appealing to him?

QUESTIONS ON RHETORIC AND STYLE

1. Zakaria opens with a deliberately provocative paragraph about the "good life" and "the new American Dream." What was your response when you initially read this paragraph? Did it make you defensive? Or did you nod your head in agreement? Explain whether you think Zakaria risks alienating his audience with his use of rhetoric in this opening.

2. What rhetorical purpose does the mention of *Portnoy's Complaint*, a novel that centers on an immigrant family, serve? How does Zakaria use it to make a point?

3. Early in the essay, Zakaria uses statistical evidence — hard data — to make the case that the problem in education today is "*not that too many students are studying the liberal arts*" (para. 6). How do quantitative evidence and his analysis of politics in paragraphs 8 and 9 contribute to the development of his argument?

4. What is Zakaria's purpose in bringing in expert testimony in paragraph 11? To what extent does it serve as effective evidence for his argument?

5. Zakaria opens paragraph 12 with the short statement, "And yet, I get it." In what ways does this sentence signal a shift in the development of his argument? How effective a rhetorical strategy is it?

6. Zakaria devotes considerable space in this essay to quotations from his mother's writing about the United States for Indian publications in the 1980s (paras. 25–28). What is his purpose in doing this? How effective is this approach?

7. Reviews of *In Defense of a Liberal Education* were generally positive, including praise for Zakaria's easily readable style, which one reviewer termed, "breezy journalistic prose." What specific examples can you identify to support this characterization of Zakaria's writing? Overall, do you agree or disagree with this opinion of his writing style? Explain your response with specific details from the essay.

8. In this excerpt, which is the opening chapter in his book defending a liberal education, Zakaria makes his case largely through his personal experience. To what extent do you find this a compelling strategy? How successfully does he portray his experience in a broader context so that it does not seem to be exceptional?

SUGGESTIONS FOR WRITING

1. Zakaria argues that neglecting liberal education is short-sighted and, in fact, short changes both individuals and society at large by emphasizing job preparation and quantifiable skills at the expense of everything else. Write an argument explaining why you agree or disagree with his viewpoint.

2. How would you address the question, "Does it really make sense to study English in the age of apps?" (para. 10)? Write a brief argument stating your position, using both Zakaria's argument and your own experience as sources.

3. Gather information about one of the colleges you would like to attend. Judging from your sources, what is the school's attitude toward a liberal education, as Zakaria defines it? Cite specifics to support your assessment. To what extent has reviewing and evaluating these sources changed your perspective on the educational experience the college offers?

4. In 2017, the English Department of Harvard University accepted its first rap album as a senior thesis. Obasi Shaw, an African American student, submitted a ten-track album entitled *Liminal*

Minds, a wordplay on the title of the popular television show *Criminal Minds*. The album's structure is modeled on *Canterbury Tales*, Geoffrey Chaucer's fourteenth-century classic work, but it presents a multifaceted exploration of black identity in modern-day America, with each track giving the perspective of a different narrator. Write an argument explaining whether you think Harvard's decision to accept the album reflects a thriving liberal education or a lessening of rigorous academic standards. Is it an example of liberal education alive and well in the twenty-first century, or is it further proof that universities are not helping students develop the skills they need to enter a job market defined by technology and globalization?

5. In May 2017, Fareed Zakaria delivered the commencement address at Bucknell University. Continuing his quest to emphasize the importance of a liberal education in an increasingly polarized world, he pointed out that the word *liberal* does not refer to the current political notion of liberal and conservative but to its Latin root, meaning "pertaining to liberty." He continued:

There is, we all know, a kind of anti-intellectualism on the right these days — the denial of facts, of reason, of science. But there is also an anti-intellectualism on the left. An attitude of righteousness that says we are so pure, we are so morally superior, we cannot bear to hear an idea that we don't like or disagree with. There is no such idea. There is no idea that is beyond the pale. Everything should be within the arena, and should be worth contesting.

I talk about liberals because campuses are invariably more liberal than conservative. And it is a real problem to have this kind of silencing of conservative voices. . . . We want to celebrate every kind of diversity these days except intellectual diversity.

From what you have observed and read about college campuses and our society in general today, do you agree with Zakaria? Why or why not? Use specific examples to develop your viewpoint.

6. The table below was developed by the Association of American Colleges and Universities (AACU). Write an essay that provides an example of what each one of the characteristics of a liberal education in the twenty-first century might look like. As you develop examples (or cite ones you know of), you might also want to draw comparisons to the liberal education of the twentieth century.

7. Choose one of the following quotations and write an essay that develops a position in response to it. Use appropriate, specific evidence to illustrate and develop your position.

a. "If then the intellect is so excellent a portion of us, and its cultivation so excellent, it is not only beautiful, perfect, and admirable and noble in itself, but in a true and high sense it must be useful to the possessor and to all around him; not useful in any low, mechanical, mercantile sense, but as diffusing good, or as a blessing, or a gift, or power, or a treasure, first to the owner, then through him to the world. I say then, if a liberal education be good, it must necessarily be useful too."

— John Henry Newman (1801–1890),
The Idea of a University, Discourse VII, 1852

b. "Education can give you a skill, but a liberal education can give you dignity."

— Ellen Key (1849–1926),
Swedish writer and suffragist

c. "Science and everyday life cannot and should not be separated."

— Rosalind Franklin (1920–1958),
British chemist, ca. 1940

The Changing Nature of Liberal Education (See Question 6)

	Liberal Education in the Twentieth Century	Liberal Education in the Twenty-First Century
What	• intellectual and personal development • an option for the fortunate • viewed as non-vocational	• intellectual and personal development • a necessity for all students • essential for success in a global economy and for informed citizenship
How	• through studies in arts and sciences disciplines ("the major") and/or through general education in the initial years of college	• through studies that emphasize the essential learning outcomes across the entire educational continuum — from school through college — at progressively higher levels of achievement (recommended)
Where	• liberal arts colleges or colleges of arts and sciences in larger institutions	• all schools, community colleges, colleges, and universities, as well as across all fields of study (recommended)

d. "The only education that prepares us for change is a liberal education. In periods of change, narrow specialization condemns us to inflexibility — precisely what we do not need. We need the flexible intellectual tools to be problem solvers, to be able to continue learning over time."

— David Kearns,
former CEO of Xerox, 2002

e. "So what does business need from our educational system? One answer is that it needs more employees who excel in science and engineering. . . . But that is only the

beginning; one cannot live by equations alone. The need is increasing for workers with greater foreign language skills and an expanded knowledge of economics, history, and geography. And who wants a technology-driven economy if those who drive it are not grounded in such fields as ethics?"

— Norman Augustine, former chairman and
CEO of the Lockheed Martin Corporation, 2013

f. "Science literacy is the artery through which the solutions of tomorrow's problems flow."

— Neil deGrasse Tyson,
American astrophysicist, 2012

The Blessings of Liberty and Education

FREDERICK DOUGLASS

Frederick Douglass (1818–1895) was an African American writer, abolitionist, orator, and statesman. In 1838, he escaped from slavery in Maryland and soon became a national leader of the abolitionist movement in Massachusetts and New York, gaining fame for his brilliant oratory and persuasive antislavery writings. His widely read autobiographies include the bestselling *Narrative of the Life of Frederick Douglass, an American Slave* (1845), *My Bondage and My Freedom* (1855), and *Life and Times of Frederick Douglass* (1881). Throughout his life, Douglass was also an active campaigner for women's suffrage and argued for the equality of Native Americans and recent immigrants. As a preacher and statesman, he was known for his willingness to work across ideological divides to accomplish his ambitious political objectives. Douglass delivered the following address, entitled "The Blessings of Liberty and Education," at the 1894 dedication of the Manassas Industrial School for Colored Youth at Manassas, Virginia. The crowd that assembled to watch Douglass speak included many visitors from other Southern states and from Washington, D.C.

Library of Congress

Ladies, Gentlemen and Friends.

As I am a stranger among you and a sojourner, you will, I hope, allow me a word about myself, by way of introduction. I want to say something about the day upon which we are met. Coincidents are always more or less interesting, and here is one such of a somewhat striking character. This day has for me a special interest. It happens to be the anniversary of my escape from bondage. Fifty-six years ago to-day, it was my good fortune to cease to be a slave, a chattel personal, and to become a man. It was upon the 3d day of September, 1838, that I started upon my little life work in the world. It was a great day for me. With slavery behind me and all the great untried world before me, my heart throbbed with many anxious thoughts as to what the future might have in store for me. I will not attempt here any description of what were my emotions in this crisis. I leave to imagine the difference between what they were and what they are on this happy occasion. I then found myself in a strange land, unknown, friendless, and pursued as if I were a fugitive from justice. I was a stranger to every one I met in the streets of the great city of New York, for that city was the first place in which I felt at liberty to halt in my flight farther North, New York, at that day was by no means a city of refuge. On the contrary, it was a city in which slave-hunters and slave-catchers delighted to congregate. It was one of the best fields for that sport this side of Africa. The game once started was easily taken. If they had caught me, I should have been elsewhere to assist in founding an Industrial School for colored youth in Virginia. This is all I have to say on this point.

WASHINGTON, D. C.—FREDERICK DOUGLASS, THE NEW MARSHAL OF THE DISTRICT OF COLUMBIA.

WASHINGTON, D. C.—THE NEW ADMINISTRATION—COLORED CITIZENS PAYING THEIR RESPECTS TO MARSHAL FREDERICK DOUGLASS, IN HIS OFFICE AT THE CITY HALL.—SKETCHED BY OUR SPECIAL ARTIST.

Library of Congress

This illustration depicts Frederick Douglass in his office at city hall shortly after President Rutherford B. Hayes appointed him the U.S. Marshal of the District of Columbia in 1877.

What does this sketch suggest about the status Douglass enjoyed in the African American community? To what extent does it match the ethos he establishes at the outset of his dedication speech?

My first thought germain to the occasion, and which must have some interest for us all, very naturally relates to this noted place where we now happen to he assembled. Since the great and terrible battle with which its name is associated, and which has now passed into history as the birth of many battles,[1] no event has occurred here so important in its character and influence and so every way significant, as the event which we have this day met to inaugurate and celebrate. To found an educational institution for any people is worthy of note; but to found a school in which to instruct, improve and develop all that is noblest and best in the souls of a deeply wronged and long neglected people, is especially note worthy. This spot, once the scene of fratricidal war, and the witness of its innumerable and indescribal horrors, is, we hope to be hereafter the scene of brotherly kindness, charity and peace. We are to witness here a display of the best elements of advanced civilization and good citizenship. It is to be the place where the children of a once enslaved people may realize the blessings of liberty and education, and learn how to make for themselves and for all others the best of both worlds.

No spot on the soil of Virginia could have been more fitly chosen for planting this school, than this historic battle-field. It has not only the high advantage of forming an instructive contrast and illustrating the compensation possible to mankind, by patiently awaiting the quiet operation of time and events, but suggests the battle to be waged here against ignorance and vice. Thirty years ago, when Federal[2] and Confederate armies met here in deadly conflict over the question of the perpetual enslavement of the negro, who would or could have dreamed, that, in a single generation, such changes would have wrought in the minds of men that a school

---

[1] A reference to the First Battle of Bull Run, the first major land battle of the American Civil War, which took place in Manassas, Virginia, in 1861. —Eds.

[2] Union Army. —Eds.

seeing connections

Manassas, Virginia, was the site of two major Confederate victories during the Civil War: The First Battle of Bull Run (1861) and the Second Battle of Bull Run (1862). Read the following account of the consequences of the First Battle of Bull Run and look carefully at the photo, which shows Manassas Junction after the Second Battle of Bull Run.

How do the photograph and Rawley's account add dimension to your understanding of the rhetorical situation of Douglass's speech?

Library of Congress

from Turning Points of the Civil War

JAMES A. RAWLEY

At Bull Run the Union was given its baptism in blood and fire. The battle in its aftermath opened Northern eyes to the magnitude of the work of subduing a vast area in determined revolt. It prompted a reordering of Federal military affairs and it drove Northern opinion toward more extreme views on the Negro. It deepened the new President's sense of responsibility as Commander-in-chief. It caused the Union to turn toward a youthful commander — prematurely hailed after Philippi as a new Napoleon — who would play a leading role for the next three years. It presented the Confederacy with its first true military hero — Stonewall Jackson — and at the same time lulled the South into a false confidence. "Universal gratulation at our success inspired an overweening confidence," President Jefferson Davis later observed. And not the least result of the first battle of Bull Run was the fall of Union prestige in Europe.

would be founded here, for the mental, moral and industrial education of the children of this same people whose enslavement was sought even by the sword? Who would have imagined that Virginia would, after the agony of war and in a time so short, become so enlightened and so liberal as to be willing and even pleased to welcome here, upon her "sacred soil", a school of the children of her former slaves? Thirty years ago neither poet, priest nor prophet, could have foretold the vast and wonderful changes which have taken place in the opinions of the American people on this subject since the war. The North has changed, and the South has changed, and we have all changed, and all changed for the better. Otherwise, we should not be here to-day engaged in the business of establishing this institution.

The liberality on the part of the people of Virginia, a typical State of the South, which has encouraged and justified the founding the Industrial School, not only within her borders, but here on the very first great battle-field between the two great sections of our Union, is as much a cause of amazement, satisfaction and joy, as is the readiness with which the good people of the North have responded to the call for pecuniary aid and thus made this enterprise successful. Both circumstances are to-day causes of joy and congratulation. They show that the colored man need not despair; that he has friends in both sections of the Republic. In view of this school and the changes in public sentiment which it indicates, we may well exclaim with Milton, "Peace hath her victories no less renowned than war!"[3]

When first invited to speak a few words in celebration of the founding of this industrial school, I was disposed to decline the honor,

in favor of some of my younger and better educated brothers. But I am glad that I did not decline the honor. The duty devolved upon me, but which I then hesitated to assume, is, in every respect, an agreeable duty. I am glad that, at my time of life, the opportunity is afforded me to connect my name with a school so meritorious and which I can reasonably hope will be of so great and permanent service to a people so greatly needing it. It is in line with my relation to the negro. I have pleaded the cause of the oppressed against all comers, during more than fifty years of conflict. Were a period put to my career to-day, I could hardly wish for a time or place, or an occasion, better suited for a desired ending, than here and now. The founding of this and similar schools on the soil of Virginia — a State formerly the breeder, buyer and seller of slaves; a State so averse in the past to the education of colored people, as to make it a crime to teach a negro to read, — is one of the best fruits of the agitation of half a century, and a firm foundation of hope for the future.

The idea at the bottom of this Institution is rapidly gaining ground every where. Industrial education is, with me, however, no new idea. Nearly forty years ago I was its advocate, and at that time I held it to be the chief want of the free colored people of the North. I was then the editor and publisher of the North Star, a newspaper printed in Rochester, New York. I saw even then, that the free negro of the North, with every thing great expected of him, but with no means at hand to meet such expectations, could not hope to rise while he was excluded from all profitable employments. He was free by law, but was denied the chief advantages of freedom; he was indeed but nominally free; he was not compelled to call any man his master, and no one could call him slave, but he was still in fact a slave, a slave to society, and could only be a hewer of wood and a drawer of water. It was easier at that day to get a black boy into a lawyer's office to study law, or into a doctor's

5

---

[3] A famous line from "To the Lord General Cromwell," a 1652 sonnet by English poet John Milton (1608–1674). The poem praises Oliver Cromwell (1599–1658), an English statesman who was instrumental in overthrowing King Charles I in 1649 and who reigned as Lord Protector of the Commonwealth of England, Scotland, and Ireland, from 1653 until his death. —Eds.

office to study medicine, than it was to get him into a carpenter's shop to push a plane, or into a blacksmith's shop to hammer iron.

While I have no sympathy whatever with those who affect to despise labor, even the humblest forms of it, and hold that whatever is needful to be done it is honorable to do, it is, nevertheless, plain that no people, white or black, can, in my country, continue long respected who are confined exclusively to more menial service for which but little intelligence or skilled are required, and for which but the smallest wages are paid or received; especially if the laborer does not make an effort to rise above that condition. While the employment as waiters at hotels and on steamboats and railroads, is perfectly proper and entirely honorable, in the circumstances which now surround the colored people, no one variety of the American people can afford to be known only as waiters and domestic servants.

While I say this, I fully believe in the dignity of all needful labor. All honest effort to better human conditions is entitled to respect. I have met at Poland Springs, in the State of Maine, and at the White Mountains in New Hampshire, and at other places, as well as at the late World's Columbian Exposition at Chicago,[4] many young white ladies and gentleman, who were truly such, students and teachers in high schools and seminaries, gladly serving as waiters during their vacation, and doing so with no sense of being degraded in any degree, or embarrassed by such service. This would not have been the case with them, if society, by any law or custom, had decided that this service should be, for such persons, their only calling and vocation in life. Daniel Webster[5] used to say that New Hampshire was a good State to emigrate from. So I say of menial service — it is a good condition to separate from,

just as soon as one can find any other calling, which is more remunerative and more elevating in its tendency. It is not the labor that degrades, but the want of spirit to rise above it.

Exclusive service, or exclusive mastery, is not good for the moral or mental health of any class. Pride and insolence will certainly be developed in the one class, and weakness and servility in the other. The colored people, to be respected, must furnish their due proportion to each class. They must not be all masters, or all servants. They must command, as well as be commanded.

However much I may regret that it was my lot   10
to have been a slave, I shall never regret that I was once a common laborer; a servant, if you please so to term it. But I felt myself as much a man then, as I feel myself a man now; for I had an ambition above my calling, and I was determined then, as I have been ever since, to use every honorable means in my power to rise to a higher plane of service, just as soon and as fast as that should be possible.

My philosophy of work is, that a man is worked upon by that upon which he works. Some work requires more muscle than it does mind. The work which requires the most thought, skill and ingenuity, will receive the highest commendation, and will otherwise do most for the worker. Things which can be done simply with the exertion of muscle, and with little or no exertion of the intellect, will develop the muscle, but dwarf the mind.

Long ago it was asked, "How can he get wisdom, who holdeth the plow and whose talk is of oxen?"[6]

The school which we are about to establish here, is, If I understand its object, intended to teach the colored youth, who shall avail themselves of its privileges, the use of both mind and body. It is to educate the hand as well as the brain; to teach men to work as well as to think, and to think as well as to work. It is to teach them to join thought to work, and thus to get the very best result of thought and work. There is, in my opinion, no useful thing that

---

[4] An 1893 fair held in Chicago, Illinois, to celebrate the 400th anniversary of Christopher Columbus's landing in the New World. —Eds.

[5] Daniel Webster (1782–1852), a politician from New Hampshire, served in the House of Representatives and the Senate, and was Secretary of State under two different presidents. —Eds.

[6] A quotation from Ecclesiasticus 38:25, a book included in the Catholic and Eastern Orthodox New Testament but excluded from the Protestant canon. —Eds.

Library of Congress

Although this 1899 photograph is from Claflin University in Orangeburg, South Carolina, it depicts a classroom similar to those at the Manassas Industrial School.

What do the students' attire and body language suggest about the value placed on the skills they are learning and the self-identity the school strives to develop in them? How do those values relate to Frederick Douglass's main argument?

a man can do, that cannot be better done by an educated man than by an uneducated one.

In the old slave times, the colored people were expected to work without thinking. They were commanded to do as they were told. They were to be hands — only hands, not heads. Thought was the prerogative of the master. Obedience was the duty of the slave. I, in my ignorance, once told my master I thought a certain way of doing some work I had in hand was the best way to do it. He promptly demanded, "Who gave you the right to think?" I might have answered in the language of Robert Burns,

> "Were I designed yon lordling's slave,
> By Nature's law designed,
> Why was an independent thought
> E'er planted in my mind?"[7]

But I had not then read Robert Burns. Burns had high ideas of the dignity of simple manhood. In respect of the dignity of man we may well exclaim with the great Shakespeare concerning him: "What a piece of work is man! How noble in reason! How infinite in faculty! In apprehension how like a God! The beauty of the world, the paragon of animals!"[8] Yet, if man be benighted, this glowing description of his power and dignity is merely a "glittering generality," an empty tumult of words, without any support of facts.

In his natural condition, however, man is only potentially great. As a mere physical being, he does not take high rank, even among the beasts of the field. He is not so fleet as a horse or a hound or so strong as an ox or a mule. His true dignity is not to be sought in his arm, or in his legs, but in his head. Here is the seat and source of all that is of especially great or practical importance in him. There is fire in the flint and steel, but it is friction that causes it to flash, flame and burn, and give light where all else may be darkness. There is music in the violin, but the touch of the master is needed to fill the air and the soul with the concord of sweet sounds. There is power in the human mind, but education is needed for its development.

As man is the highest being on earth, it follows that the vocation of teacher is among the highest known to him. To properly teach is to educe man's potential and latent greatness, to discover and develop the noblest, highest and best that is in him. In view of this fact, no man whose business it is to teach should ever allow himself to feel that

15

---

[7] A quotation from "Man Was Made to Mourn. A Dirge" by Scottish poet Robert Burns (1759–1796). —Eds.

[8] From *Hamlet*, act 2, scene 2. —Eds.

his mission is mean, inferior, or circumscribed. In my estimation, neither politics nor religion present to us a calling higher than this primary business of unfolding and strengthening the powers of the human soul. It is a permanent vocation. Some know the value of education, by having it. I know its value by not having it. It is a want that begins with the beginning of human existence, and continues through all the journey of life. Of all the creatures that live and move and have their being on this green earth, man, at his birth, is the most helpless and most in need of instruction. He does not know even how to seek his food. His little life is menaced on every hand. The very elements conspire against him. The cattle upon a thousand hills, the wolves and bears in the forest, all come into the world better equipped for life than does man. From first to last, his existence depends upon instruction.

Yet this little helpless weakling, whose life can be put out as we put out the flame of a candle, with a breath, is the lord of creation. Though in his beginning, he is only potentially this lord, with education he is the commander of armies; the builder of cities; the tamer of wild beasts; the navigator of unknown seas; the discoverer of unknown islands, capes and continents, and the founder of great empires, and capable of limitless civilization.

But if man is without education, although with all his latent possibilities attaching to him, he is, as I have said, but a pitiable object; a giant in body, but a pigmy in intellect, and, at best, but half a man. Without education, he lives within the narrow, dark and grimy walls of ignorance. He is a poor prisoner without hope. The little light he gets comes to him as through dark corridors and grated windows. The sights and sounds which reach him, so significant and full of meaning to the well-trained mind, are to him of dim and shadowy and uncertain import. He sees, but does not perceive. He hears, but does not understand. The silent and majestic heavens, fretted with stars, so inspiring and uplifting, so sublime and glorious to the souls of other men, bear no message to him. They suggest to him no idea of the wonderful world in which he lives, or of the harmony of this great universe, and hence impart to him no happiness.

Education, on the other hand, means emancipation. It means light and liberty. It means the uplifting of the soul of man into the glorious light of truth, the light only by which man can be free. To deny education to any people is one of the greatest crimes against human nature. It is to deny them the means of freedom and the rightful   *20*

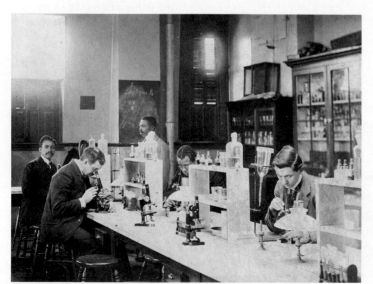

Library of Congress

Taken a few years after Douglass delivered his dedication speech, this photo depicts students in a bacteriology laboratory at Howard University in Washington, D.C. **In what ways does this scene embody the values that Douglass extolled in his speech?**

pursuit of happiness, and to defeat the very end of their being. They can neither honor themselves nor their creator. Than this, no greater wrong can be inflicted; and on the other hand, no greater benefit can be bestowed upon a long benighted people than giving to them, as we are here this day endeavoring to do, the means of useful education. It is aimed to make them both better and more useful in life and to furnish them with increased means of livelihood; to make of them more skilled workmen, more useful mechanics, and better workers in wood, leather, tin and iron.

It is sometimes said that we have done enough for the negro; that we have given him his liberty and we should now let him do for himself. This sounds well, but that is all. I do not undervalue freedom from chattel slavery. It was a great and glorious triumph of justice and humanity. It was the first of long years of labor, agitation and sacrifice. But let us look at this emancipation and see where it left the negro, and we shall see how far it falls short of the plainest demands of justice and of what we owe the negro.

To find an adequate measure of compensation for any wrong, we must first ascertain the nature and extent of the wrong itself. The mere act of enslaving the negro was not the only wrong done him, nor were the labors and stripes imposed upon him, though heavy and grievous to bear, the sum of his wrongs. They were, indeed, terrible enough; but deeper down and more terrible still were the mental and moral wrongs

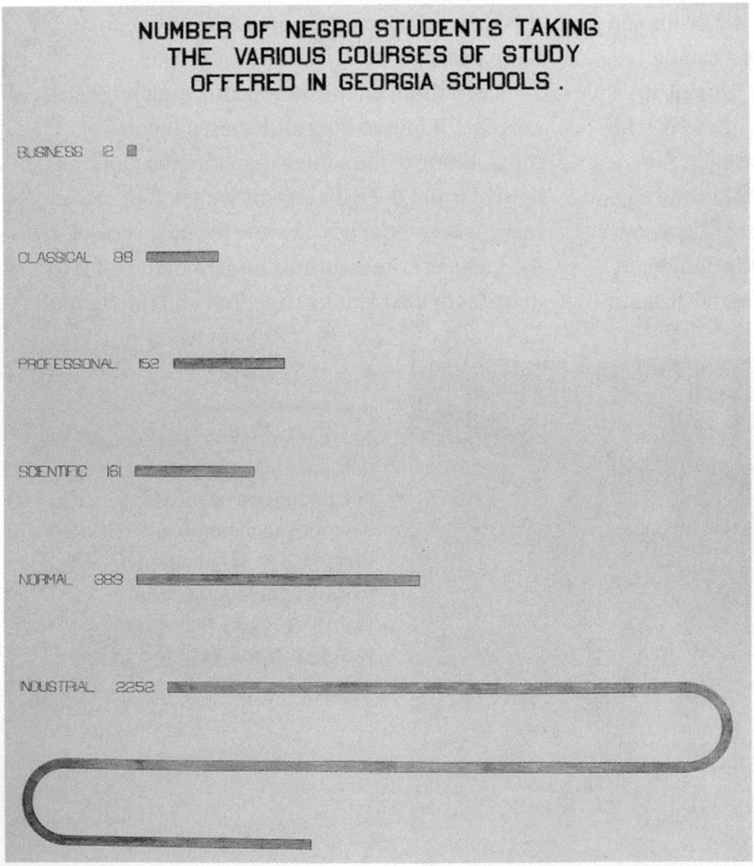

NUMBER OF NEGRO STUDENTS TAKING
THE VARIOUS COURSES OF STUDY
OFFERED IN GEORGIA SCHOOLS.

BUSINESS   2

CLASSICAL   98

PROFESSIONAL 152

SCIENTIFIC 161

NORMAL   883

INDUSTRIAL 2252

Library of Congress

This graph, created in 1899, shows the enrollment of African American students in various courses of study offered in Georgia public schools at the time.

How does this information add to your understanding of Douglass's beliefs about the value of education as expressed in his dedication speech?

which enter into his claim for a slight measure of compensation. For two hundred and forty years the light of letters was denied him, and the gates of knowledge were closed against him.

He was driven from time to eternity in the darkest ignorance. He was herded with the beasts of the field, was without marriage, without family, without schools and without any moral training, other than that which came by the slave driver's lash. People who live now and talk of doing too much for the negro, think nothing of these things, and those who know them seem to desire to forget them, especially when they are made the basis of a claim for a larger measure of justice to the negro. They forget that for these terrible wrongs there is no redress and no adequate compensation. The enslaved and battered millions have come, suffered, died and gone with all their moral and physical wounds into eternity. To them no recompense can be made. If the American people could put a school-house in every valley of the South and a church on every hill-top; supply with a teacher and preacher each respectively, and welcome the descendants of the former slaves to all the moral and intellectual benefits of the one and the other, without money and without price, such a sacrifice would not compensate their children for the terrible wrong done to their fathers and mothers by their enslavement and enforced degradation.

▼

_____

The sculpture on the left was installed outside the Frederick Douglass and Isaac Myers Maritime Park Museum in Baltimore, Maryland in 2015. On the right is a Washington, D. C. mural painted by G. Byron Peck in 1995. **What do each of these pieces of art — including their materials and size — suggest about the legacy of Frederick Douglass? What aspects of that legacy do you see reflected in this speech?**

Raymond Boyd/Getty Images

Library of Congress

I have another complaint. It is said that the colored people of the South have made but little progress since their emancipation. This complaint is not only groundless, but adds insult to injury. Under the whole heavens there never was a people liberated from bondage under conditions less favorable to the beginning of a new and free mode of life, than were the freedmen of the South. Criminals, guilty of heinous crimes against the State and society, are let go free on more generous conditions than were our slaves. The despotic government of Russia was more liberal and humane to its emancipated slaves than our Republic was to ours. Each head of a family of slaves in Russia was given three acres of land and necessary farming implements with which to begin life, but our slaves were turned loose without any thing — naked to the elements.

As one of the number of the enslaved, I am none the less disposed to observe and note with pleasure and gratitude every effort of our white friends and brothers to remedy the evils wrought by the long years of slavery and its concomitants. And in such wise I rejoice in the effort made here to-day.

I have a word now upon another subject, and what I have to say may be more useful than palatable. That subject is the talk now so generally prevailing about races and race lines. I have no hesitation in telling you that I think the colored people and their friends make a great mistake in saying so much of race and color. I know no such basis for the claims of justice. I know no such motive for efforts at self-improvement. In this race-way they put the emphasis in the wrong place. I do now and always have attached more importance to manhood than to mere kinship or identify with any variety of the human family. RACE, in the popular sense, is narrow; humanity is broad. The one is special; the other is universal. The one is transient; the other permanent. In the essential dignity of man as man, I find all necessary incentives and aspirations to a useful and noble life. Man is broad enough

25

and high enough as a platform for you and me and all of us. The colored people of the country should advance to the high position of the Constitution of the country. The Constitution makes no distinction on account of race and color, and they should make none.

We hear, since emancipation, much said by our modern colored leaders in commendation of race pride, race love, race effort, race superiority, race men, and the like. One man is praised for being a race man and another is condemned for not being a race man. In all this talk of race, the motive may be good, but the method is bad. It is an effort to cast out Satan by Beelzebub.[9] The evils which are now crushing the negro to earth have their root and sap, their force and mainspring, in this narrow spirit of race and color, and the negro has no more right to excuse and foster it than have men of any other race. I recognize and adopt no narrow basis for my thoughts, feelings, or modes of action. I would place myself, and I would place you, my young friends, upon grounds vastly higher and broader than any founded upon race or color. Neither law, learning, nor religion, is addressed to any man's color or race. Science, education, the Word of God, and all the virtues known among men, are recommended to us, not as races, but as men. We are not recommended to love or hate any particular variety of the human family more than any other. Not as Ethiopeans; not as Caucasians; not as Mongolians; not as Afro-Americans, or Anglo-Americans, are we addressed, but as men. God and nature speak to our manhood, and to our manhood alone. Here all ideas of duty and moral obligation are predicated. We are accountable only as men. In the language of Scripture, we are called upon to "quit ourselves like men."[10] To those who are everlastingly prating about race men, I have to say: Gentlemen, you reflect upon your best friends. It was not the race or the color

---

[9] Another name for Satan. —Eds.

[10] A quotation from 1 Samuel 4:9, a book included in the Old Testament of the Bible. —Eds.

of the negro that won for him the battle of liberty. That great battle was won, not because the victim of slavery was a negro, a mulatto, or an Afro-American, but because the victim of slavery was a man and a brother to all other men, a child of God, and could claim with all mankind a common Father, and therefore should be recognized as an accountable being, a subject of government, and entitled to justice, liberty and equality before the law, and every where else. Man saw that he had a right to liberty, to education, and to an equal chance with all other men in the common race of life and to the pursuit of happiness.

You know that, while slavery lasted, we could seldom get ourselves recognised in any form of law or language, as men. Our old masters were remarkably shy of recognising our manhood, even in words written or spoken. They called a man, with a head an white as mine, a boy. The old advertisements were carefully worded: "Run away, my boy Tom, Jim or Harry," never "my man."

Hence, at the risk of being deficient in the quality of love and loyalty to race and color, I confess that in my advocacy of the colored man's cause, whether in the name of education or freedom, I have had more to say of manhood and of what is comprehended in manhood and in womanhood, than of the mere accident of race and color; and, if this [is] disloyalty to race and color, I am guilty. I insist upon it that the lesson which colored people, not less than white people, ought now to learn, is, that there is no moral or intellectual quality in the color of a man's cuticle; that color, in itself, is neither good nor bad; that to be black or white is neither a proper source of pride or of shame. I go further, and declare that no man's devotion to the cause of justice, liberty and humanity, is to be weighed, measured and determined by his color or race. We should never forget that the ablest and most eloquent voices ever raised in behalf of the black man's cause, were the voices of white men. Not for the race; not for color, but for man and manhood alone, they labored, fought and died. Neither Phillips, nor Summer, nor Garrison, nor John Brown, nor

[Gerrit] Smith[11] were black men. They were white men, and yet no black men were ever truer to the black man's cause than were these and other men like them. They saw in the slave, manhood, brotherhood, womanhood outraged, neglected and degraded, and their own noble manhood, not their racehood, revolted at the offence. They placed the emphasis where it belonged; not on the mint, anise and cumin of race and color, but upon manhood and the weightier matters of the law.[12]

Thus compassed about by so great a cloud of witnesses, I can easily afford to be reproached and denounced for standing, in defence of this principle, against all comers. My position is, that it is better to regard ourselves as a part of the whole than as the whole of a part. It is better to be a member of the great human family, than a member of a particular variety of the human family. In regard to men as in regard to things, the whole is more than a part. Away then with the nonsense that a man must be black to be true to the rights of black men. I put my foot upon the effort to draw lines between the white and the black, or between blacks and so-called Afro-Americans, or to draw race lines any where in the domain of liberty. Whoever in for equal rights, for equal education, for equal opportunities for all men, of whatever race or color, — I hail him as a "countryman, clansman, kinsman, and brother beloved."

I must not further occupy your time, except to answer briefly the inquiry, "What of the night?" You young people have a right to ask me what the future has in store for you and the people with whom you are classed. I have been a watchman on your walls for more than fifty years, so long that you think I ought to know what the future will bring to pass and to discern for you the signs of the times. You want to know whether the hour is

30

---

[11] Wendell Phillips (1811–1884), Charles Sumner (1811–1874), William Lloyd Garrison (1805–1879), John Brown (1800–1859), and Gerrit Smith (1797–1874) were all prominent white American abolitionists. —Eds.

[12] This reference to Matthew 23:23 contrasts things of lesser value, such as herbs, with things of greater significance, such as justice, mercy, and faith. —Eds.

seeing connections

This 1948 photo shows a segregated classroom at the University of Oklahoma, where an African American student is seated at a single desk, apart from his white classmates.

Bettmann/Getty Images

What do you believe Frederick Douglass would have thought of this situation? Would he have seen it as progress for African Americans to be part of a university class-room, even if they were physically separated from other students? Cite specific examples from his speech to support your response.

one of hope or despair. I have no time to answer this solemn inquiry at length or as it deserves, and will content myself with giving you the assurance of my belief. I think the situation is serious, but it is not hopeless. On the contrary, there are many encouraging signs in the moral skies. I have seen many dark hours and yet have never despaired of the colored man's future. There is no time in our history that I would prefer to the present. Go back to the annexation of Texas,[13] the Fugitive Slave law times,[14] and the Border War in Kansas.[15] The existence of this Industrial School at Manassas is a triumphant rebuke to the cry of despair now

heard in some quarters. Nor does it stand alone. It is a type of such institution in nearly all the Southern States. Schools and colleges for colored youth are multiplying all over the land. Hampton, Tuskeegee, Cappahoosic, are brilliant examples. The light of education is shedding its beams more brightly and more effectively upon the colored people in the South, than it ever did in the cause of any other emancipated people in the world. These efforts cannot fail in the end to bear fruit.

But it is said that we are now being greatly persecuted. I know it. I admit it. I deplore it. I denounce it. Attempts are being made to set aside the amendments of the Constitution; to wrest from us the elective franchise; to exclude us from respectable railroad cars; to draw against us the color line in religious organizations; to exclude us from hotels and to make us a pro-scribe class. I know it all, and yet I see in it all

---

[13] Texas was annexed as an American state in 1845, leading to the Mexican-American War (1846–1848). —Eds.

[14] Laws requiring the governments in states and territories where slavery was abolished to aid in recapturing those slaves who had escaped from slaveholding states and territories. —Eds.

[15] A series of political confrontations between 1854 and 1861 over whether slavery would be allowed in the state of Kansas. —Eds.

◀ Taken around 1890, this photograph shows Douglass working in his library, where he wrote his third autobiography and many speeches, including this one. **What quotation from this dedication speech might you use as a caption for it? Explain what you think brings the image and your chosen caption together.**

Courtesy of the National Park Service, Frederick Douglass National Historic Site, Washington, DC, Photograph Frederick Douglass, FRDO 3886

a convincing evidence of our progress and the promise of a brighter future. The resistance that we now meet is the proof of our progress. We are not the only people who have been persecuted.

The resistance is not to the colored man as a slave, a servant or a menial, or as a person. It is aimed at the negro as a gentleman, as a successful man and a scholar. The negro in ignorance and in rags meets no resistance. He is rather liked than otherwise. He is thought to be in his place. It is only when he acquires education, property, popularity and influence; only when he attempts to rise above his ancient level, where he was numbered with the beasts of the field, and aspires to be a man and a man among men, that he invites repression. Even in the laws of the South excluding him from railroad cars and other places, care is taken to allow him to ride as a servant, a valet or a porter. He may make a bed, but must not sleep in it. He may handle bread, but must not eat it. It is not the negro, but the quality of the negro that disturbs popular prejudices. It is his character, not his personality, which makes him an offense or otherwise. In one

quality he is smiled upon as a very serviceable animal; in the other he is scorned as an upstart entirely out of his place, and is made to take a back seat. I am not much disturbed by this, for the same resistance in kind, though not in degree, has to be met by white men and white women who rise from lowly conditions. The successful and opulent esteem them as upstarts. A lady as elegant and splendid as Mrs. Potter Palmer of Chicago,[16] had to submit to the test. She was compelled to hear herself talked about as a "shoddy" upstart; the "wife of a tavern-keeper," and the like, during the Columbian Exposition. But the upstart of to-day is the elite of to-morrow.

A ship at anchor, with halliards[17] broken, sails mildewed, hull empty, her bottom covered with seaweed and barnacles, meets no resistance. She lies perfectly still; but when she spreads her canvas to the breeze, turns her prow to the open sea, and sets out on her voyage, the higher shall be her speed, the greater shall be her resistance. So it is

---

[16] A prominent American socialite and philanthropist during the late nineteenth and early twentieth centuries. —Eds.
[17] Lines used to lift a sail or flag on a ship. —Eds.

with the colored man. He meets with resistance now, because he is now, more than ever, fitting himself for a higher life. He is shedding the old rags of slavery and putting on the apparel of freedom.

In conclusion, my dear young friends, be not discouraged. Accept the inspiration to hope.

Imitate the example of the brave mariner, who, amid clouds and darkness, amid hail, rain and storm bolts, battles his way against all that the sea opposes to his progress. You will then reach the goal of your noble ambition in safety.

35

[1894]

QUESTIONS FOR DISCUSSION

1. What is the "striking character" of the day Frederick Douglass is delivering this speech? What impact does this have on the importance of the speech itself?

2. What is the significance of the physical setting of the school?

3. Douglass asserts that he believes "in the dignity of all needful labor" (para. 8), and he recalls that he "was once a common laborer" (para. 10). Yet he urges his student audience to aim for a higher station in life. For what purpose, then, does Douglass value education as a vocational enterprise?

4. What does Douglass mean by the statement, "My philosophy of work is, that a man is worked upon by that upon which he works" (para. 11)?

5. Throughout this speech, Douglass alludes to several social and political issues relevant to the specific situation at hand, at the same time that he reflects on broader, more philosophical ideas. What philosophical issues does he raise in the section beginning, "In his natural condition, however, man is only potentially great" (para. 16)? How does he relate that claim to the more specific context of the era in which he gave this speech?

6. How does Douglass respond to critics who would say that "we have done enough for the negro" (para. 21)? Include in your response his analysis of the link between compensation and "the nature and extent of the wrong itself" (para. 22).

7. How does Douglass respond to critics who claim that freed slaves of the South "have made but little progress since their emancipation" (para. 24)? Why would he even raise this criticism?

8. Douglass essentially acknowledges he may alienate his audience when he prefaces his advice against "saying so much of race and color" with the statement that "what I have to say may be more useful than palatable" (para. 26). What does he mean by this? Why do you think he raised a point with which his audience would likely disagree?

9. Why, ultimately, does Douglass affirm that he is hopeful about the future at that particular moment in history? What does he mean when he asserts, "The resistance that we now meet is the proof of our progress" (para. 32)?

10. What do you think is the most persuasive line of reasoning Douglass gives to support his belief that the freedom education grants people leads to more than economic empowerment?

QUESTIONS ON RHETORIC AND STYLE

1. Although Douglass was a widely known and celebrated figure by the time he delivered this speech, he goes to considerable length to establish his ethos in the first few paragraphs. What does he emphasize? Pay particular attention to paragraph 5.

2. Paragraph 3, which begins, "No spot on the soil of Virginia could have been more fitly chosen . . ." showcases Douglass's brilliant skill as an orator. How does he use rhetorical strategies such as

repetition, rhetorical questions, and imagery, among others, to achieve his purpose?

3. How does Douglass acknowledge both the financial and political support of "the good people of the North" (para. 4) throughout his speech?

4. What is the effect of Douglass's inclusion of quotes by literary figures, including poets John Milton, Robert Burns, and playwright William

Shakespeare? What kind of appeal is this, and how does it help him develop his argument?

5. To our contemporary ears, some of Douglass's rhetoric may seem almost hyperbolic, but it is important to consider that he delivered this speech within a rich, nineteenth-century tradition of uplift — that is, inspirational oratory. How does the figurative language in paragraphs 16–18 illustrate this tradition? How does he use these techniques to achieve his purpose?

6. One of the most difficult issues Douglass raises is his position that it is a mistake to frame social progress "in this narrow spirit of race and color" (para. 27). What is the logic of his argument on this point? Note how he develops the argument step-by-step through a series of if-then statements.

7. Identify at least two counterarguments that Douglass raises. How does he concede and refute in ways that strengthen his own argument?

8. While Douglass presents a strong logic-based argument, he develops it with lyrical appeals to pathos. Identify one paragraph that exemplifies this strategy and discuss how he engages his listeners' emotions.

9. How does Douglass weave his own experience into his speech? Consider in particular the impact of his persona as an elder community figure speaking to a youthful audience.

10. Douglass concludes his speech with an extended metaphor. What is this metaphor, and how does it help him achieve his overall purpose in this dedication speech?

SUGGESTIONS FOR WRITING

1. In paragraph 13, Douglass makes the following claim: "There is, in my opinion, no useful thing that a man can do, that cannot be better done by an educated man than by an uneducated one." Why do you think this statement would likely provoke controversy in the present day? In a well written essay, develop an argument that supports, challenges, or qualifies Douglass's claim.

2. One of the most famous lines in *The Autobiography of Frederick Douglass* is, "You have seen how a man was made a slave; you shall see how a slave was made a man." In what ways does this speech demonstrate what he means by this assertion, though in a different context? Cite specific passages to support your view.

3. Henry Louis Gates Jr., a prominent African American academic and current Director of the Hutchins Center for African and African American Research at Harvard University, has called Frederick Douglass "an electrifying speaker and a commanding writer." What evidence in this speech supports this characterization of Douglass?

4. To what extent does Douglass's argument about the connection between education and liberty hold true today? You need not limit your discussion to race or to the United States; you might expand it to other variables, such as culture and gender.

5. How might Frederick Douglass respond to the Black Lives Matter movement? Write an analysis of aspects of the movement that would appeal to him and of those that he might be more skeptical about. As part of your analysis, include images (e.g., photographs or political cartoons) as examples and evidence.

6. The Manassas Industrial School for Colored Youth evolved into part of the network of historically black colleges and universities that now includes Tuskegee University, Spelman College, and Howard University. Most of these institutions were established before 1964 with the intention of primarily serving the African American community, although they are open to all races. Today, there is some controversy about whether such institutions have outlived their purpose. After researching the subject, write an argument explaining your position.

7. In the Introduction to *Picturing Frederick Douglass* (2015), authors John Stauffer, Zoe Trodd, and Celeste-Marie Bernier explore Frederick Douglass's love of photography, a fairly new technology during his lifetime: "Like slave narratives . . . photographic images bore witness to African Americans' essential humanity, while also countering the racist caricatures that proliferated throughout the North." Discuss this statement by exploring photographs and illustrations of the late nineteenth century and by researching the history of photography itself through the present day.

from Education

RALPH WALDO EMERSON

Ralph Waldo Emerson (1803–1882), perhaps best known for his essay "Self-Reliance" (1841), was one of America's most influential thinkers and writers. After graduating from Harvard Divinity School, he followed nine generations of his family into the ministry but practiced for only a few years. In 1836, he and other like-minded intellectuals, including Henry David Thoreau, founded the Transcendental Club, and that same year he published his influential essay "Nature" (1836). Known as a great orator, Emerson made his living as a popular lecturer on a wide range of topics. From 1821 to 1826, he taught in city and country schools and later served on a number of school boards, including the Concord School Committee and the Board of Overseers of Harvard College. Emerson's essay "Education," from which the following excerpt is taken, was put together posthumously from his writings published in the *American Scholar* and from his commencement addresses.

I believe that our own experience instructs us that the secret of Education lies in respecting the pupil. It is not for you to choose what he shall know, what he shall do. It is chosen and fore-ordained, and he only holds the key to his own secret. By your tampering and thwarting and too much governing he may be hindered from his end and kept out of his own. Respect the child. Wait and see the new product of Nature. Nature loves analogies, but not repetitions. Respect the child. Be not too much his parent. Trespass not on his solitude.

But I hear the outcry which replies to this suggestion — Would you verily throw up the reins of public and private discipline; would you leave the young child to the mad career of his own passions and whimsies, and call this anarchy a respect for the child's nature? I answer — Respect the child, respect him to the end, but also respect yourself. Be the companion of his thought, the friend of his friendship, the lover of his virtue — but no kinsman of his sin. Let him find you so true to yourself that you are the irreconcilable hater of his vice and the imperturbable slighter of his trifling.

The two points in a boy's training are, to keep his *naturel* and train off all but that — to keep his *naturel*, but stop off his uproar, fooling, and horseplay — keep his nature and arm it with knowledge in the very direction to which it points. Here are the two capital facts, Genius and Drill. This first is the inspiration in the well-born healthy child, the new perception he has of nature. Somewhat he sees in forms or hears in music or apprehends in mathematics, or believes practicable in mechanics or possible in political society, which no one else sees or hears or believes. This is the perpetual romance of new life, the invasion of God into the old dead world, when he sends into quiet houses a young soul with a thought which is not met, looking for something which is not there, but which ought to be there: the thought is dim but it is sure, and he casts about restless for means and masters to verify it; he makes wild attempts to explain himself and invoke the aid and consent of the by-standers. Baffled for want of language and methods to convey his meaning, not yet clear to himself, he conceives that thought not in this house or town, yet in some other house or town is the wise master who can put him in possession of the rules and instruments to execute his will. Happy this child with a bias, with a thought which entrances him, leads him, now into deserts now into cities, the fool of an idea. Let him follow it in good and in evil report, in good or bad company; it will justify itself; it will lead him at last into the illustrious society of the lovers of truth.

In London, in a private company, I became acquainted with a gentleman, Sir Charles Fellowes, who, being at Xanthos, in the Aegean Sea, had seen a Turk point with his staff to some carved work on the corner of a stone almost buried in the soil. Fellowes scraped away the dirt, was struck with the beauty of the sculptured ornaments, and, looking about him, observed more blocks and fragments like this. He returned to the spot, procured laborers and uncovered many blocks. He went back to England, bought a Greek grammar and learned the language; he read history and studied ancient art to explain his stones; he interested Gibson the sculptor; he invoked the assistance of the English Government; he called in the succor of Sir Humphry Davy to analyze the pigments; of experts in coins, of scholars and connoisseurs; and at last in his third visit brought home to England such statues and marble reliefs and such careful plans that he was able to reconstruct, in the British Museum where it now stands, the perfect model of the Ionic trophy-monument, fifty years older than the Parthenon of Athens, and which had been destroyed by earthquakes, then by iconoclast Christians, then by savage Turks. But mark that in the task he had achieved an excellent education, and become associated with distinguished scholars whom he had interested in his pursuit; in short, had formed a college for himself; the enthusiast had found the master, the masters, whom he sought. Always

genius seeks genius, desires nothing so much as to be a pupil and to find those who can lend it aid to perfect itself.

Nor are the two elements, enthusiasm and drill, incompatible. Accuracy is essential to beauty. The very definition of the intellect is Aristotle's: "that by which we know terms or boundaries." Give a boy accurate perceptions. Teach him the difference between the similar and the same. Make him call things by their right names. Pardon in him no blunder. Then he will give you solid satisfaction as long as he lives. It is better to teach the child arithmetic and Latin grammar than rhetoric or moral philosophy, because they require exactitude of performance; it is made certain that the lesson is mastered, and that power of performance is worth more than the knowledge. He can learn anything which is important to him now that the power to learn is secured: as mechanics say, when one has learned the use of tools, it is easy to work at a new craft.

Letter by letter, syllable by syllable, the child learns to read, and in good time can convey to all the domestic circle the sense of Shakespeare. By many steps each just as short, the stammering boy and the hesitating collegian, in the school debates, in college clubs, in mock court, comes at last to full, secure, triumphant unfolding of his thought in the popular assembly, with a fullness of power that makes all the steps forgotten.

But this function of opening and feeding the human mind is not to be fulfilled by any mechanical or military method; is not to be trusted to any skill less large than Nature itself. You must not neglect the form, but you must secure the essentials. It is curious how perverse and intermeddling we are, and what vast pains and cost we incur to do wrong. Whilst we all know in our own experience and apply natural methods in our own business — in education our common sense fails us, and we are continually trying costly machinery against nature, in patent schools and academies and in great colleges and universities.

The natural method forever confutes our experiments, and we must still come back to it. The whole theory of the school is on the nurse's or mother's knee. The child is as hot to learn as the mother is to impart. There is mutual delight. The joy of our childhood in hearing beautiful stories from some skillful aunt who loves to tell them, must be repeated in youth. The boy wishes to learn to skate, to coast, to catch a fish in the brook, to hit a mark with a snowball or a stone; and a boy a little older is just as well pleased to teach him these sciences. Not less delightful is the mutual pleasure of teaching and learning the secret of algebra, or of chemistry, or of good reading and good recitation of poetry or of prose, or of chosen facts in history or in biography.

Nature provided for the communication of thought by planting with it in the receiving mind a fury to impart it. 'Tis so in every art, in every science. One burns to tell the new fact, the other burns to hear it. See how far a young doctor will ride or walk to witness a new surgical operation. I have seen a carriage-maker's shop emptied of all its workmen into the street, to scrutinize a new pattern from New York. So in literature, the young man who has taste for poetry, for fine images, for noble thoughts, is insatiable for this nourishment, and forgets all the world for the more learned friend — who finds equal joy in dealing out his treasures.

Happy the natural college thus self-instituted around every natural teacher; the young men of Athens around Socrates; of Alexander around Plotinus; of Paris around Abelard; of Germany around Fichte, or Niebuhr, or Goethe: in short the natural sphere of every leading mind. But the moment this is organized, difficulties begin. The college was to be the nurse and home of genius; but, though every young man is born with some determination in his nature, and is a potential genius;

10

is at last to be one; it is, in the most, obstructed and delayed, and, whatever they may hereafter be, their senses are now opened in advance of their minds. They are more sensual than intellectual. Appetite and indolence they have, but no enthusiasm. These come in numbers to the college: few geniuses: and the teaching comes to be arranged for these many, and not for those few. Hence the instruction seems to require skillful tutors, of accurate and systematic mind, rather than ardent and inventive masters. Besides, the youth of genius are eccentric, won't drill, are irritable, uncertain, explosive, solitary, not men of the world, not good for every-day association. You have to work for large classes instead of individuals; you must lower your flag and reef your sails to wait for the dull sailors; you grow departmental, routinary, military almost with your discipline and college police. But what doth such a school to form a great and heroic character? What abiding Hope can it inspire? What Reformer will it nurse? What poet will it breed to sing to the human race? What discoverer of Nature's laws will it prompt to enrich us by disclosing in the mind the statute which all matter must obey? What fiery soul will it send out to warm a nation with his charity? What tranquil mind will it have fortified to walk with meekness in private and obscure duties, to wait and to suffer? Is it not manifest that our academic institutions should have a wider scope; that they should not be timid and keep the ruts of the last generation, but that wise men thinking for themselves and heartily seeking the good of mankind, and counting the cost of innovation, should dare to arouse the young to a just and heroic life; that the moral nature should be addressed in the school-room, and children should be treated as the high-born candidates of truth and virtue?

[1878]

EXPLORING THE TEXT

1. In this excerpt, Ralph Waldo Emerson describes his view of an ideal education. What are its defining characteristics?

2. What does Emerson mean when he says, "Nature loves analogies, but not repetitions" (para. 1)?

3. Why is the relationship between "Genius and Drill" paradoxical, as Emerson explains in paragraph 3?

4. Paragraph 4 is taken up almost entirely by an extended example. What is Emerson's purpose in developing this long explanation?

5. Why does Emerson believe "[i]t is better to teach the child arithmetic and Latin grammar than rhetoric or moral philosophy" (para. 5)?

6. What exactly is the "natural method" to which Emerson refers in paragraph 8?

7. Why does Emerson criticize schools as bureaucratic institutions in paragraph 10?

8. Examine Emerson's appeals to pathos through highly emotional and evocative diction.

9. Emerson refers to educating "a boy" and "a man" and uses masculine pronouns when referring to students. As a reader, does this gender bias affect how receptive you are to Emerson's ideas? Are his ideas equally applicable to women? If you do not think so, then how would they need to be changed to be applicable to both men and women, boys and girls?

10. Explain why you agree or disagree with Emerson's assertion that "every young man [and woman] is born with some determination in his [or her] nature, and is a potential genius" (para. 10).

11. How does your own schooling measure up to the criteria presented in paragraph 10?

12. If you were responsible for the education of a child, which of Emerson's assertions about education would you choose as your guiding principle? Write an essay explaining why you would choose that principle over another of Emerson's beliefs.

A Talk to Teachers

JAMES BALDWIN

James Baldwin (1924–1987) was one of the most influential figures in American literature during the latter half of the twentieth century. His novels include *Go Tell It on the Mountain* (1953), *Giovanni's Room* (1956), *If Beale Street Could Talk* (1974), and *Just Above My Head* (1979). A sharp social critic of race relations and sexual identity, Baldwin wrote numerous essays that were collected in *Notes of a Native Son* (1955), *The Fire Next Time* (1963), and *The Devil Finds Work* (1976). He also wrote poetry and plays. By the late 1940s, Baldwin had moved to Europe. He lived in France and Turkey for most of the rest of his life, but he returned at times to the United States to lecture and participate in the civil rights movement. He delivered the following speech to a group of New York City schoolteachers in 1963, the height of the movement for equality for African Americans.

Let's begin by saying that we are living through a very dangerous time. Everyone in this room is in one way or another aware of that. We are in a revolutionary situation, no matter how unpopular that word has become in this country. The society in which we live is desperately menaced, not by [Nikita] Khrushchev,[1] but from within. So any citizen of this country who figures himself as responsible — and particularly those of you who deal with the minds and hearts of young people — must be prepared to "go for broke."

---

[1] Premier of the Soviet Union, 1958–1964. —Eds.

Or to put it another way, you must understand that in the attempt to correct so many generations of bad faith and cruelty, when it is operating not only in the classroom but in society, you will meet the most fantastic, the most brutal, and the most determined resistance. There is no point in pretending that this won't happen.

Since I am talking to schoolteachers and I am not a teacher myself, and in some ways am fairly easily intimidated, I beg you to let me leave that and go back to what I think to be the entire purpose of education in the first place. It would seem to me that when a child is born, if I'm the child's parent, it is my obligation and my high duty to civilize that child. Man is a social animal. He cannot exist without a society. A society, in turn, depends on certain things which everyone within that society takes for granted. Now, the crucial paradox which confronts us here is that the whole process of education occurs within a social framework and is designed to perpetuate the aims of society. Thus, for example, the boys and girls who were born during the era of the Third Reich,[2] when educated to the purposes of the Third Reich, became barbarians. The paradox of education is precisely this — that as one begins to become conscious one begins to examine the society in which he is being educated. The purpose of education, finally, is to create in a person the ability to look at the world for himself, to make his own decisions, to say to himself this is black or this is white, to decide for himself whether there is a God in heaven or not. To ask questions of the universe, and then learn to live with those questions, is the way he achieves his own identity. But no society is really anxious to have that kind of person around. What societies really, ideally, want is a citizenry which will simply obey the rules of society. If a society succeeds in this, that society is about to perish. The obligation of anyone who thinks of himself as responsible is to examine society and try to change it and to fight it — at no matter what

risk. This is the only hope society has. This is the only way societies change.

Now, if what I have tried to sketch has any validity, it becomes thoroughly clear, at least to me, that any Negro who is born in this country and undergoes the American educational system runs the risk of becoming schizophrenic. On the one hand he is born in the shadow of the stars and stripes and he is assured it represents a nation which has never lost a war. He pledges allegiance to that flag which guarantees "liberty and justice for all." He is part of a country in which anyone can become president, and so forth. But on the other hand he is also assured by his country and his countrymen that he has never contributed anything to civilization — that his past is nothing more than a record of humiliations gladly endured. He is assumed by the republic that he, his father, his mother, and his ancestors were happy, shiftless, watermelon-eating darkies who loved Mr. Charlie and Miss Ann,[3] that the value he has as a black man is proven by one thing only — his devotion to white people. If you think I am exaggerating, examine the myths which proliferate in this country about Negroes.

All this enters the child's consciousness much sooner than we as adults would like to think it does. As adults, we are easily fooled because we are so anxious to be fooled. But children are very different. Children, not yet aware that it is dangerous to look too deeply at anything, look at everything, look at each other, and draw their own conclusions. They don't have the vocabulary to express what they see, and we, their elders, know how to intimidate them very easily and very soon. But a black child, looking at the world around him, though he cannot know quite what to make of it, is aware that there is a reason why his mother works so hard, why his father is always on edge. He is aware that there is some reason why, if he sits down in the front of the bus, his father or mother slaps him and drags him to the back of the bus. He is aware that

---

[2] Nazi Germany under Adolph Hitler from 1933 until 1945. —Eds.

[3] Figurative characters invented by African slaves to represent male and female slave masters, respectively. —Eds.

seeing connections

These graphs show the correlation between race and school suspension in K-12 schools during the 2013–2014 school year.

Identify at least two assertions Baldwin makes that these graphs would support.

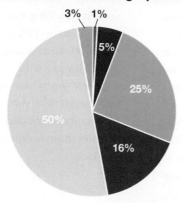

American Public School Demographics (2013–2014)

3% 1%
5%
25%
50%
16%

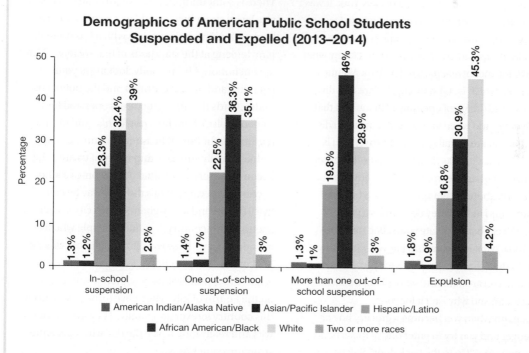

Demographics of American Public School Students Suspended and Expelled (2013–2014)

In-school suspension: 1.3%, 1.2%, 23.3%, 32.4%, 39%, 2.8%

One out-of-school suspension: 1.4%, 1.7%, 22.5%, 36.3%, 35.1%, 3%

More than one out-of-school suspension: 1.3%, 1%, 19.8%, 46%, 28.9%, 3%

Expulsion: 1.8%, 0.9%, 16.8%, 30.9%, 45.3%, 4.2%

Percentage

Legend: ■ American Indian/Alaska Native ■ Asian/Pacific Islander ■ Hispanic/Latino ■ African American/Black White ■ Two or more races

Data from U.S. Department of Education Office for Civil Rights.

there is some terrible weight on his parents' shoulders which menaces him. And it isn't long — in fact it begins when he is in school — before he discovers the shape of his oppression.

Let us say that the child is seven years old and I _5_ am his father, and I decide to take him to the zoo, or to Madison Square Garden, or to the U.N. Building, or to any of the tremendous monuments we find all over New York. We get into a bus and we go from where I live on 131st Street and Seventh Avenue downtown through the park and we get into New York City, which is not Harlem. Now, where the boy lives — even if it is a housing project — is in an undesirable neighborhood. If he lives in one of those housing projects of which everyone in New York is so proud, he has at the front door, if not closer, the pimps, the whores, the junkies — in a word, the danger of life in the ghetto. And the child knows this, though he doesn't know why.

I still remember my first sight of New York. It was really another city when I was born — where I was born. We looked down over the Park Avenue streetcar tracks. It was Park Avenue, but I didn't know what Park Avenue meant _downtown_. The Park Avenue I grew up on, which is still standing, is dark and dirty. No one would dream of opening a Tiffany's on that Park Avenue, and when you go downtown you discover that you are literally in the white world. It is rich — or at least it looks rich. It is clean — because they collect garbage downtown. There are doormen. People walk about as though they owned where they are — and indeed they do. And it's a great shock. It's very hard to relate yourself to this. You don't know what it means. You know — you know instinctively — that none of this is for you. You know this before you are told. And who is it for and who is paying for it? And why isn't it for you?

Later on when you become a grocery boy or messenger and you try to enter one of those buildings a man says, "Go to the back door." Still later, if you happen by some odd chance to have a friend in one of those buildings, the man says, "Where's your package?" Now this by no means is the core of the matter. What I'm trying to get at is that by this time

the Negro child has had, effectively, almost all the doors of opportunity slammed in his face, and there are very few things he can do about it. He can more or less accept it with an absolutely inarticulate and dangerous rage inside — all the more dangerous because it is never expressed. It is precisely those silent people whom white people see every day of their lives — I mean your porter and your maid, who never say anything more than "Yes, Sir" and "No, Ma'am." They will tell you it's raining if that is what you want to hear, and they will tell you the sun is shining if _that_ is what you want to hear. They really hate you — really hate you because in their eyes (and they're right) you stand between them and life. I want to come back to that in a moment. It is the most sinister of the facts, I think, which we now face.

◆ ◆ ◆

There is something else the Negro child can do, too. Every street boy — and I was a street boy, so I know — looking at the society which has produced him, looking at the standards of that society which are not honored by anybody, looking at your churches and the government and the politicians, understands that this structure is operated for someone else's benefit — not for his. And there's no reason in it for him. If he is really cunning, really ruthless, really strong — and many of us are — he becomes a kind of criminal. He becomes a kind of criminal because that's the only way he can live. Harlem and every ghetto in this city — every ghetto in this country — is full of people who live outside the law. They wouldn't dream of calling a policeman. They wouldn't, for a moment, listen to any of those professions of which we are so proud on the Fourth of July. They have turned away from this country forever and totally. They live by their wits and really long to see the day when the entire structure comes down.

The point of all this is that black men were brought here as a source of cheap labor. They were indispensable to the economy. In order to justify the fact that men were treated as though they were animals, the white republic had to brainwash itself into believing that they were, indeed, animals and *deserved* to be treated like animals. Therefore it is almost impossible for any Negro child to discover anything about his actual history. The reason is that this "animal," once he suspects his own worth, once he starts believing that he is a man, has begun to attack the entire power structure. This is why America has spent such a long time keeping the Negro in his place. What I am trying to suggest to you is that it was not an accident, it was not an act of God, it was not done by well-meaning people muddling into something which they didn't understand. It was a deliberate policy hammered into place in order to make money from black flesh. And now, in 1963, because we have never faced this fact, we are in intolerable trouble.

The Reconstruction, as I read the evidence, [10] was a bargain between the North and South to this effect: "We've liberated them from the land—and delivered them to the bosses." When we left Mississippi to come North we did not come to freedom. We came to the bottom of the labor market, and we are still there. Even the Depression of the 1930s failed to make a dent in Negroes' relationship to white workers in the labor unions. Even today, so brainwashed is this republic that people seriously ask in what they suppose to be good faith, "What does the Negro want?" I've heard a great many asinine questions in my life, but that is perhaps the most asinine and perhaps the most insulting. But the point here is that people who ask that question, thinking that they ask it in good faith, are really the victims of this conspiracy to make Negroes believe they are less than human.

In order for me to live, I decided very early that some mistake had been made somewhere. I was not a "nigger" even though you called me one. But if I was a "nigger" in your eyes, there was something about *you*—there was something *you* needed. I had to realize when I was very young that I was none of those things I was told I was. I was not, for example, happy. I never touched a watermelon for all kinds of reasons that had been invented by white people, and I knew enough about life by this time to understand that whatever you invent, whatever you project, is you! So where we are now is that a whole country of people believe I'm a "nigger," and I *don't*, and the battle's on! Because if I am not what I've been told I am, then it means that *you're* not what you thought *you* were *either*! And that is the crisis.

It is not really a "Negro revolution" that is upsetting the country. What is upsetting the country is a sense of its own identity. If, for example, one managed to change the curriculum in all the schools so that Negroes learned more about themselves and their real contributions to this culture, you would be liberating not only Negroes, you'd be liberating white people who know nothing about their own history. And the reason is that if you are compelled to lie about one aspect of anybody's history, you must lie about it all. If you have to lie about my real role here, if you have to pretend that I hoed all that cotton just because I loved you, then you have done something to yourself. You are mad.

Now let's go back a minute. I talked earlier about those silent people—the porter and the maid—who, as I said, don't look up at the sky if you ask them if it is raining, but look into your face. My ancestors and I were very well trained. We understood very early that this was not a Christian nation. It didn't matter what you said or how often you went to church. My father and my mother and my grandfather and my grandmother knew that Christians didn't act this way. It was as simple as that. And if that was so there was no point in dealing with white people in terms of their own moral professions, for they were not going to honor them. What one did was to turn away, smiling all the time, and tell white people what they wanted to hear. But people always accuse you of reckless talk when you say this.

All this means that there are in this country tremendous reservoirs of bitterness which have never been able to find an outlet, but may find an outlet soon. It means that well-meaning white liberals place themselves in great danger when they try to deal with Negroes as though they were missionaries. It means, in brief, that a great price is demanded to liberate all those silent people so that they can breathe for the first time and *tell* you what they think of you. And a price is demanded to liberate all those white children — some of them near forty — who have never grown up, and who never will grow up, because they have no sense of their identity.

◆ ◆ ◆

What passes for identity in America is a series of myths about one's heroic ancestors. It's astounding to me, for example, that so many people really appear to believe that the country was founded by a band of heroes who wanted to be free. That happens not to be true. What happened was that some people left Europe because they couldn't stay there any longer and had to go someplace else to make it. That's all. They were hungry, they were poor, they were convicts. Those who were making it in England, for example, did not get on the *Mayflower*. That's how the country was settled. Not

15

by Gary Cooper. Yet we have a whole race of people, a whole republic, who believe the myths to the point where even today they select political representatives, as far as I can tell, by how closely they resemble Gary Cooper. Now this is dangerously infantile, and it shows in every level of national life. When I was living in Europe, for example, one of the worst revelations to me was the way Americans walked around Europe buying this and buying that and insulting everybody — not even out of malice, just because they didn't know any better. Well, that is the way they have always treated me. They weren't cruel, they just didn't know you were alive. They didn't know you had any feelings.

What I am trying to suggest here is that in the doing of all this for 100 years or more, it is the American white man who has long since lost his grip on reality. In some peculiar way, having created this myth about Negroes, and the myth about his own history, he created myths about the world so that, for example, he was astounded that some people could prefer [Fidel] Castro, astounded that

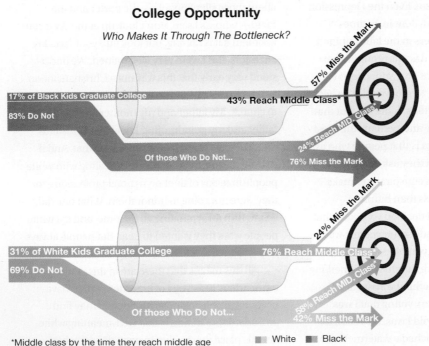

College Opportunity

Who Makes It Through The Bottleneck?

17% of Black Kids Graduate College

83% Do Not

57% Miss the Mark

43% Reach Middle Class*

24% Reach MID. Class*

Of those Who Do Not...

76% Miss the Mark

31% of White Kids Graduate College

69% Do Not

24% Miss the Mark

76% Reach Middle Class*

58% Reach MID. Class*

Of those Who Do Not...

42% Miss the Mark

*Middle class by the time they reach middle age

■ White ■ Black

With permission from the Brookings Institute.

> **What argument about the relationship between race and education does this infographic make? To what extent does it support — or challenge — Baldwin's assertion that "It is your responsibility to change society if you think of yourself as an educated person" (para. 19)?**

there are people in the world who don't go into hiding when they hear the word "Communism," astounded that Communism is one of the realities of the twentieth century which we will not overcome by pretending that it does not exist. The political level in this country now, on the part of people who should know better, is abysmal.

The Bible says somewhere that where there is no vision the people perish. I don't think anyone can doubt that in this country today we are menaced — intolerably menaced — by a lack of vision.

It is inconceivable that a sovereign people should continue, as we do so abjectly, to say, "I can't do anything about it. It's the government." The government is the creation of the people. It is responsible to the people. And the people are responsible for it. No American has the right to allow the present government to say, when Negro children are being bombed and hosed and shot and beaten all over the Deep South, that there is nothing we can do about it. There must have been a day in this country's life when the bombing of the children in Sunday School would have created a public uproar and endangered the life of a Governor [George] Wallace. It happened here and there was no public uproar.

I began by saying that one of the paradoxes of education was that precisely at the point when you begin to develop a conscience, you must find yourself at war with your society. It is your responsibility to change society if you think of yourself as an educated person. And on the basis of the evidence — the moral and political evidence — one is compelled to say that this is a backward society. Now if I were a teacher in this school, or any Negro school, and I was dealing with Negro children, who were in my care only a few hours of every day and would then return to their homes and to the streets, children who have an apprehension of their future which with every hour grows grimmer and darker, I would try to teach them — I would try to make them know — that those streets, those houses, those dangers, those agonies by which they are surrounded, are criminal. I would try to make each child know that these things are the result of a criminal conspiracy to destroy him. I would teach him that if he intends to get to be a man, he must at once decide that he is stronger than this conspiracy and that he must never make his peace with it. And that one of his weapons for refusing to make his peace with it and for destroying it depends on what he decides he is worth. I would teach him that there are currently very few standards in this country which are worth a man's respect. That it is up to him to begin to change these standards for the sake of the life and the health of the country. I would suggest to him that the popular culture — as represented, for example, on television and in comic books and in movies — is based on fantasies created by very ill people, and he must be aware that these are fantasies that have nothing to do with reality. I would teach him that the press he reads is not as free as it says it is — and that he can do something about that, too. I would try to make him know that just as American history is longer, larger, more various, more beautiful, and more terrible than anything anyone has ever said about it, so is the world larger, more daring, more beautiful and more terrible, but principally larger — and that it belongs to him. I would teach him that he doesn't have to be bound by the expediencies of any given administration, any given policy, any given morality; that he has the right and the necessity to examine everything. I would try to show him that one has not learned anything about Castro when one says, "He is a Communist." This is a way of his learning something about Castro, something about Cuba, something, in time, about the world. I would suggest to him that he is living, at the moment, in an enormous province. America is not the world and if America is going to become a nation, she must find a way — and this child must help her to find a way to use the tremendous potential and tremendous energy which this child represents. If this country does not find a way to use that energy, it will be destroyed by that energy.

[1963]

EXPLORING THE TEXT

1. What relationship does James Baldwin establish with his audience in the opening two paragraphs? How does he establish his ethos?

2. What is the "crucial paradox which confronts us here" (para. 2)?

3. Identify four appeals to pathos in paragraphs 3–5.

4. What is the effect of Baldwin's emphasizing his personal experience when he begins paragraph 6 with "I still remember my first sight of New York"?

5. Analyze Baldwin's use of pronouns in paragraphs 8 and 9. What is his purpose in alternating among first, second, and third person?

6. How would you describe Baldwin's perspective on history? What is the effect of using historical events to support his argument?

7. Why, in paragraph 11, does Baldwin use the term *nigger*? What effect would have been lost — or gained — had he used a less provocative term?

8. What does Baldwin mean when he writes, "What passes for identity in America is a series of myths about one's heroic ancestors" (para. 15)?

9. What is the effect of the short two-sentence paragraph 17?

10. Identify examples of parallelism and repetition in the long final paragraph. Discuss how Baldwin uses these strategies to achieve his purpose.

11. Where in this speech does Baldwin appeal to logos?

12. How would you describe Baldwin's overall tone? Cite specific passages to support your description.

Walking the Path between Worlds

LORI ARVISO ALVORD

The first Navajo woman surgeon, Lori Arviso Alvord (b. 1958) received her BA from Dartmouth College and her MD from Stanford University. At the start of her career, she served as a general surgeon in the Indian Health Service in her native New Mexico. She went on to serve as a dean of student affairs and a professor of surgery and psychiatry at Dartmouth Medical School, an associate dean at Central Michigan University College of Medicine, as the associate dean of student affairs and admissions at the University of Arizona College of Medicine, and she is currently an associate faculty member at the Center for American Indian Health at Johns Hopkins Bloomberg School of Public Health. Alvord has been honored with numerous awards, including the Governor's Award for Outstanding Women from the State of New Mexico (1992) and the Outstanding Women in Medicine Award from the University of Missouri–Kansas City School of Medicine (2001). Her autobiography, *The Scalpel and the Silver Bear* (1999), describes her efforts to combine Navajo healing practices with Western medicine. The following passage from that book focuses on her journey from the reservation to Dartmouth.

Today Navajo children are still standing on the playgrounds where I stood, facing the critical decision I would face after I graduated from high school: to leave the rez, or to stay and cleave to traditional ways. To let the desert live inside them, or to try to wash it away. They too hear the voice of the wind and the desert, smell the strong smells of our people, and feel the ways we came from. "*Decide*," the world whispers to them, "*you must choose.*"

I chose to leave and get an education, following the path of the books I loved so much. But leaving Dinetah was a frightening prospect. Navajo people believe we are safe within the four sacred mountains that bound the Navajo reservation — Mount Taylor, San Francisco Peak, Blanca Peak, and the La Plata Range. In our creation stories it is the place of our origins, of our emergence to the surface of the earth from other worlds below, the place where Changing Woman and First Man, Coyote, the Twins, and the monsters in our legends roamed. These mountains are central to everything in our lives. To leave this place is to invite imbalance, to break our precious link with the tribe, to leave the Walk of Beauty, and to court danger. It was a dangerous step, that into the unknown, unguarded world.

In our song called the Mountain Chant, each of the sacred mountains is honored. The words describe each mountain and its special qualities.

> The mountain to the east is Sisna'jin
> It is standing out.
> The strong White Bead is standing out
> A living mountain is standing out . . .
> The mountain to the south is Tsoodził
> It is standing out.
> The strong turquoise is standing out
> A living mountain is standing out . . .
> The mountain to the west is Dook'o'oosłííd.
> It is standing out.
> The strong white shell is standing out.
> A living mountain is standing out . . .
> The mountain to the north is Dibé Ntsaa.
> It is standing out.
> The strong jet is standing out.
> A living mountain is standing out . . .[1]

If I left, I would leave the enclosed and sacred world within the strong mountains, standing out.

I made good grades in high school, but I had received a very marginal education. I had a few good teachers, but teachers were difficult to recruit to our schools and they often didn't stay long. Funding was often inadequate. I spent many hours in classrooms where, I now see, very little was being taught. Nevertheless my parents always assumed, quite optimistically, that all their children would go to college. I don't remember any lectures from my father on the importance of higher education — just the quiet assurance that he and my mother and Grandmother all believed in us.

My college plans were modest; I assumed I would attend a nearby state school. But then I

5

happened to meet another Navajo student who was attending Princeton. I had heard of Princeton but had no idea where it was. I asked him how many Indians were there. He replied, "Five." I couldn't even imagine a place with only five Indians, since our town was 98 percent Indian. Then he mentioned Dartmouth, which had about fifty Indians on campus, and I felt a little better. *Ivy League* was a term I had heard, but I had no concept of its meaning. No one from my high school had ever attended an Ivy League college.

At my request, my high school counselor gave me the applications for all the Ivy League schools, but I only completed Dartmouth's because I knew there were fifty Indians there.

I waited anxiously, and one day the letter came. I was accepted, early decision. I was only sixteen years old. As I was only half Navajo in blood, I wondered if this meant it would be only half as dangerous to me to leave Dinetah, the place between the sacred mountains. Half of me belonged in Dinetah, but the other half of me belonged in that other world too, I figured. Still, in my heart I was all Navajo, and I instinctively felt afraid of the move. I had seen those who went away and came back: the Vietnam veterans, broken and lost, who aimlessly wandered the streets of Gallup, the others who came back but had forgotten Navajo ways.

My memories of my arrival in Hanover, New Hampshire, are mostly of the color green. Green cloaked the hillsides, crawled up the ivied walls, and was reflected in the river where the Dartmouth crew students sculled. For a girl who had never been far from Crownpoint, New Mexico, the green felt incredibly juicy, lush, beautiful, and threatening. Crownpoint had had vast acreage of sky and sand, but aside from the pastel scrub brush, mesquite, and chamiso, practically the only growing things there were the tiny stunted pines called piñon trees. Yet it is beautiful; you can see the edges and contours of red earth stretching all the way to the box-shaped faraway cliffs and the horizon. No horizon was in sight in Hanover, only trees. I felt claustrophobic.

---

[1] Aileen O'Bryan, *Navajo Indian Myths* (New York: Dover, 1994).

If the physical contrasts were striking, the cultural ones were even more so. Although I felt lucky to be there, I was in complete culture shock. I thought people talked too much, laughed too loud, asked too many personal questions, and had no respect for privacy. They seemed overly competitive and put a higher value on material wealth than I was used to. Navajos placed much more emphasis on a person's relations to family, clan, tribe, and the other inhabitants of the earth, both human and nonhuman, than on possessions. Everyone at home followed unwritten codes for behavior. We were taught to be humble and not to draw attention to ourselves, to favor cooperation over competition (so as not to make ourselves "look better" at another's expense or hurt someone's feelings), to value silence over words, to respect our elders, and to reserve our opinions until they were asked for.

Understanding the culture of Dartmouth was like taking a course in itself. I didn't know the meaning of fraternities or the class system (divided into the haves and the have-nots) which were so important there at first. Had the parents of my fellow students taught them survival skills through camping, tracking, and hunting? Did I have any interest in making four-story-high sculptures out of ice for Winter Carnival? Did they respect their elders, their parents? Did I know which fork to use at a formal dinner? What sort of ceremonies did their "tribes" practice? While they pondered such burning questions as the opening day of ski season, I was struggling just to stay warm during the frozen New Hampshire winter and not slip on the ice!

Indian reservations and pueblos could almost be seen as tiny Third World countries, lacking as they did electricity, indoor plumbing, and paved roads. When the Native American students arrived at Dartmouth, one of the first things we were told was that we could attend high tea at Sanborn Hall at four o'clock daily. I walked around the campus in awe, like a peasant visiting the castle of a great king.

The very stately, beautiful, and affluent campus could be intimidating and alienating. The college's unofficial mascot was the "Dartmouth Indian," a tomahawk-wielding red man whose presence was everywhere on the campus, in spite of the Native community's protests. He was like those TV Indians we had watched when we were little and thought so alien. Imagine young Native students seeing white students wearing loincloths and paint on their faces, jumping around with toy tomahawks. Like the rest of the Native community, I was shocked by this caricature.

I remember, distinctly, feeling alienated while walking around Dartmouth's campus that first year. By my sophomore year I understood what it meant to be invisible. People looked right through me — I moved around the campus as unseen as the air. Outside of my freshman roommate, Anne, I never made a close non-Indian friend. I wonder if other students of color felt the same way.

I was very homesick, wishing I didn't have to miss so many familiar events: the Navajo tribal fairs, the Zuni Shalako, the Laguna feast days, the Santa Fe Indian market, the Gallup ceremonial. Everyone at home was having a great time eating wonderful food — roasted corn from the Shiprock market, posole, red chile stew, venison jerky — and I was stuck in a library far away. I missed watching the Apache Devil Dancers and the Pueblo Buffalo Dancers. I missed the sight of Navajo traditional clothing, emblazoned with silver and turquoise, and the pink-and-purple-splashed sunsets of New Mexico. I missed that smell — that smell we had tried to wash away at our laundromat so long ago — the smell of wildness, the desert, and the Navajo world.

Sometimes I wondered: If I'd had a *kinaałdá* ceremony, could I have been stronger, more independent, better able to face this loneliness and alienation, less unassured. The *kinaałdá* is part of the Blessing Way set of ceremonies performed for girls when they reach puberty. Blessing Way tells the story of Changing Woman (a central Navajo deity), and the *kinaałdá* celebrates her coming into womanhood. The family and community gather around her, she is sung to, and her female relatives massage her from head to toe, giving her the power

10

15

and strength of womanhood. A large corn cake is baked underground in a corn husk–lined pit, and the girl sprinkles cornmeal over the top. Each day for four days, she runs for a mile toward the new sun, toward her new life. It gives a young woman strength and power, confidence and security, as she goes through menses for the first time. She takes that strength and those "good thoughts" with her into the world. I could have used that assurance. Because my family was less traditional, my sisters and I did not have *kinaaldá* ceremonies, although we attended those of our cousins. Nevertheless, since the Navajo culture is matriarchal, I think I was better prepared as a woman in a "man's world" than many white women I met.

A few things at Dartmouth, however, were comforting and did make me feel at home. For one thing, dogs roamed the campus freely. They didn't belong to anybody in particular but to everybody and were fed and cared for by the entire campus. Muttlike, wily, always after something to eat, they reminded me naturally of rez dogs. And everywhere I looked playful squirrels ran around, reminding me of the prairie dogs who run around their prairie dog cities on the mesas and sit up on their hind legs to watch the cars drive by.

Academically, due to my strong reading background, I held my own in classes like literature and social sciences, but I was totally unprepared for the physical and life sciences. After receiving the only D of my entire life in calculus, I retreated from the sciences altogether. The high school at Crownpoint had not prepared me adequately to compete with the Ivy Leaguers. Furthermore, I had an additional problem. As I mentioned earlier, Navajos are taught from the youngest age never to draw attention to ourselves. So Navajo children do not raise their hands in class. At a school like Dartmouth, the lack of participation was seen as a sign not of humility but lack of interest and a disengaged attitude. My Navajo humility was combined with a deep feeling of academic inferiority; it was hard to compete with students who had taken calculus and read Chaucer in high school. I sat in the back and tried not to reveal my ignorance.

This sense of being torn between worlds was reflected even in my studies: I chose a double major, psychology and sociology, modified with Native American studies. I received honors in my freshman seminar as well as in two Native American studies courses that stressed writing. As a result, I found myself thinking of teaching Native American studies as a career, and perhaps also becoming a writer.

In fact, I loved Dartmouth's Native American program. It had the tough job of recruiting students like us, who were very high risk. We frequently had had only marginal high school preparation; many were reluctant to come to school so far from home; and like skittish wild horses, some would turn tail and run home at the least provocation. We found great comfort in one another, for although we came from many different tribes, our experiences at Dartmouth were similar: We all felt disconnected from the mainstream student body. For the women, it was even worse. At the time I arrived on the scene, Dartmouth had only recently changed from an all-male to a coed student body, and many of the men resented the presence of women on campus. Referred to as cohogs instead of coeds, women were shunned for dates; instead girls were bused in from nearby women's colleges on weekends. Social life was dominated by the fraternities, and, if we went to their parties at all, we were often ignored.

For all these reasons, the few Native American [20] students at Dartmouth coalesced into a solid community who did almost everything together. Our group was made up of Paiutes, Sioux, Cherokees, Chippewas, Navajos, Pueblos, and many other tribes. We were friends, lovers, rivals, enemies. I have been a part of many other groups since then, but nothing compared in intensity to the experience of being a member of that Native American student group.

Though we often felt as though we didn't belong at Dartmouth, the ironic truth is that we did belong, or rather, we were entitled to be there. Eleazar Wheelock, the Connecticut minister who founded Dartmouth College in 1769, did so with funds that

Mead Art Museum, Amherst College, MA, USA/Bridgeman Images

This painting, completed in 1961 by James Wayne Yazzie, a self-taught Navajo artist, is entitled *Navajo Dance*.

How does it convey Alvord's assertion that a tribe "provides a feeling of inclusion in something larger, or having a set place in the universe where one always belongs" and "provides connectedness and a blueprint for how to live" (para. 23)?

came from King George II, who wished to establish a place to "educate the savages." The college flourished, but for literally hundreds of years its original founding purpose was not honored. "Educating savages" was not on the real agenda; it had simply been a way to get land and money. Before the 1960s fewer than twenty Native students graduated from Dartmouth. Then in the 1970s the Native American studies program was developed by college president John Kemeny and writer Michael Dorris, and Dartmouth began to take its mission in earnest.

We Indian students all knew why we were there. Without the vision of Kemeny and Dorris, we would never have had an opportunity to set foot on the grounds of such an institution, let alone actually enroll. We were there because of the generous scholarships the college had given us, and the money from our tribes.

Some years later, reflecting back on my college experiences, I realized something else. The outside, non-Indian world is tribeless, full of wandering singular souls, seeking connection through societies, clubs, and other groups. White people know what it is to be a family, but to be a tribe is something of an altogether different sort. It provides a feeling of inclusion in something larger, of having a set place in the universe where one always belongs. It provides connectedness and a blueprint for how to live.

At Dartmouth the fraternities and sororities seemed to be attempts to claim or create tribes. Their wild and crazy parties that often involved drugs and sex seemed to me to be unconscious re-creations of rituals and initiation ceremonies. But the fraternities emphasized exclusion as much as inclusion, and their rituals involved alcohol and hazing initiations. Although they developed from a natural urge for community, they lacked much that a real tribe has.

I began to honor and cherish my tribal membership, and in the years that followed I came to understand that such membership is central to mental health, to spiritual health, to physical health. A tribe is a community of people connected by blood or heart, by geography and tradition, who help one another and share a belief system. Community and tribe not only reduce the alienation people feel but in doing so stave off illness. In a sense they are a form of preventive medicine. Most Americans have lost their tribal identities, although at one time, most likely, everyone belonged to a tribe. One way to remedy this is to find and establish groups of people who can nurture and support one another. The Native American students at Dartmouth had become such a group.

Our new "tribe" had its ceremonies. Each year, in a primitive outdoor amphitheater called the Bema where concerts and plays were sometimes

25

put on, we held a campus powwow. Feathered fancy dancers and women in "jingle dresses" or in beaded and brightly colored fabric would spin and step to the drums of Plains Indians or to songs from an invited singer from a pueblo. The women would whirl, their shawls swirling and twisting into corkscrew shapes around them. They'd dance to two big hide-stretched drums, encircled by the men, who struck the drums rhythmically and sang. Their voices wove and resonated, rose and fell above the steady heartbeat of the drums. This ceremony was a chance for the Native and non-Native communities to come together as one. I felt then, briefly, that I belonged.

In the evening after the powwow the singing and drumming would continue at a party called a "49" — but here the ancient rhythms were mixed with modern English lyrics. The songs we sang could be romantic, funny, or political; they could be about reservation life and pickup trucks or the Bureau of Indian Affairs. They always sounded the same though, with a blend of voices rising around a drumbeat, and a melody that pulled out our memories of childhood songs.

Dartmouth was good for me. Singing with the other students melted some of my historical grief and anger into a larger powerful force, a force I would take with me into the world. I gained a new kind of family and tribe, with new songs that held us together. Once again, songs had the power to heal.

[1999]

EXPLORING THE TEXT

1. Lori Arviso Alvord writes that she "chose to leave [the reservation] and get an education" (para. 2). In what ways is this a more momentous decision for her than simply choosing which college to attend?

2. What culture shocks did Alvord experience as she moved from her home in New Mexico to college at Dartmouth? What was she most afraid of as she moved outside of her comfort zone?

3. Why do you think Alvord includes the Mountain Chant in this piece? What effect does it have on you as a reader? How would the tone of the essay be different without it?

4. What impact does the physical landscape in Hanover have on Alvord? Why does she describe the landscape of both Hanover and New Mexico in such vivid detail?

5. Which details of life on the reservation does Alvord recall in paragraph 15? Cite specific ones and explain their importance. Why is the kinaałdá ceremony especially significant?

6. Describe Alvord's tone in the two paragraphs on the history of Dartmouth and its Native American studies program (paras. 21–22). Cite specific language and examples to support your response.

7. Alvord observes, "White people know what it is to be a family, but to be a tribe is something of an altogether different sort" (para. 23). What does she

mean? In her view, is tribe necessarily exclusively determined by blood kinship?

8. What does Alvord mean in the concluding paragraph by "my historical grief and anger" (para. 28)? How does it "melt" into "a larger powerful force"? To what extent is her education responsible for this transformation?

9. Ultimately, what is Alvord's attitude toward Dartmouth and her choice to attend? Cite specific passages to support your response.

10. Once at Dartmouth, Alvord faces another significant choice: to assimilate into the dominant culture of that institution, to hold herself apart from it, or something in between. What does she choose and why?

11. What do you think Alvord believes is the most important part of the "education" she received at Dartmouth? Cite specific details from the essay in your response.

12. In what ways is Alvord's experience typical of first-generation college students? Research this topic by interviewing someone, perhaps in your own family, who was the first of their family to earn a college degree. If you will be the first generation in your family to go to college, how do the choices and concerns Alvord describes compare to your own?

I Know Why the Caged Bird Cannot Read
How American High School Students Learn to Loathe Literature

FRANCINE PROSE

Francine Prose (b. 1947) is a reporter, essayist, critic, editor, and author of more than twenty books, including poetry, fiction, and children's literature. Her novel *Blue Angel* (2000) was a finalist for the National Book Award, and her nonfiction works *The Lives of the Muses: Nine Women and the Artists They Inspired* (2002) and *Reading Like a Writer: A Guide for People Who Love Books and for Those Who Want to Write Them* (2006) were both national best-sellers. She has received numerous grants and awards, including Guggenheim and Fulbright fellowships. She is most recently the author of the satiric novel *Mister Monkey* (2016). Her book reviews have appeared in numerous magazines and periodicals, including the *New York Times Book Review* and *O*. The following essay, published in *Harper's* in September 1999, is a critique of the quality of required reading in American high schools.

Books discussed in this essay include:

I Know Why the Caged Bird Sings by Maya Angelou. Random House, 1969.
To Kill a Mockingbird by Harper Lee. Lippincott, 1960.
Teaching Values through Teaching Literature by Margaret Dodson. Eric/Edinfo Press, 1993.
Teaching the Novel by Becky Alano. Eric/Edinfo Press, 1989.
Teaching Literature by Women Authors by Carolyn Smith McGowen. Eric/Edinfo Press, 1993.

Like most parents who have, against all odds, preserved a lively and still evolving passion for good books, I find myself, each September, increasingly appalled by the dismal lists of texts that my sons are doomed to waste a school year reading. What I get as compensation is a measure of insight into why our society has come to admire Montel Williams and Ricki Lake so much more than Dante and Homer. Given the dreariness with which literature is taught in many American classrooms, it seems miraculous that any sentient teenager would view reading as a source of pleasure. Traditionally, the love of reading has been born and nurtured in high school English class — the last time many students will find themselves in a roomful of people who have all read the same text and are, in theory, prepared to discuss it. High school — even more than college — is where literary tastes and allegiances are formed: what we read in adolescence is imprinted on our brains as the dreary notions of childhood crystallize into hard data.

The intense loyalty adults harbor for books first encountered in youth is one probable reason for the otherwise baffling longevity of vintage mediocre novels, books that teachers may themselves have read in adolescence; it is also the most plausible explanation for the peculiar [1998] Modern Library list of the "100 Best Novels of the 20th Century," a roster dominated by robust survivors from the tenth-grade syllabus. *Darkness at Noon, Lord of the Flies, Brave New World*, and *The Studs Lonigan Trilogy* all speak, in various ways, to the vestigial teenage psyches of men of a certain age. The parallel list drawn up by students (younger, more of them female) in the Radcliffe Publishing Course reflects the equally romantic and tacky tastes (*Gone with the Wind, The Fountainhead*) of a later generation of adolescent girls.

Given the fact that these early encounters with literature leave such indelible impressions, it would seem doubly important to make sure

Cameron Harvey/The New Yorker Collection/Conde Nast

"Do you have any books on the white–male experience?"

This cartoon appeared in the *New Yorker* in 2015.
What point does the cartoonist make through humor? How might this cartoon be read as a response to Francine Prose's assertion that "much has been made of the lemminglike fervor with which our universities have rushed to sacrifice complexity for diversity" (para. 4)?

that high school students are actually reading literature. Yet every opportunity to instill adolescents with a lifelong affinity for narrative, for the ways in which the vision of an artist can percolate through an idiosyncratic use of language, and for the supple gymnastics of a mind that exercises the mind of the reader is being squandered on regimens of trash and semi-trash, taught for reasons that have nothing to do with how well a book is written. In fact, less and less attention is being paid to what has been written, let alone how; it's become a rarity for a teacher to suggest that a book might be a work of art composed of words and sentences, or that the choice of these words and sentences can inform and delight us. We hear that more books are being bought and sold than ever before, yet no one, as far as I know, is arguing that we are producing and becoming a nation of avid readers of serious literature.

Much has been made of the lemminglike fervor with which our universities have rushed to sacrifice complexity for diversity; for decades now, critics have decried our plummeting scholastic standards

and mourned the death of cultural literacy without having done one appreciable thing to raise the educational bar or revive our moribund culture. Meanwhile, scant notice has been paid, except by exasperated parents, to the missed opportunities and misinformation that form the true curriculum of so many high school English classes.

My own two sons, now twenty-one and seventeen, have read (in public and private schools) Shakespeare, Hawthorne, and Melville. But they've also slogged repeatedly through the manipulative melodramas of Alice Walker and Maya Angelou, through sentimental, middlebrow favorites (*To Kill a Mockingbird* and *A Separate Peace*), the weaker novels of John Steinbeck, the fantasies of Ray Bradbury. My older son spent the first several weeks of sophomore English discussing the class's summer assignment, *Ordinary People*, a weeper and former bestseller by Judith Guest about a "dysfunctional" family recovering from a teenage son's suicide attempt.

Neither has heard a teacher suggest that he read Kafka, though one might suppose

5

that teenagers might enjoy the transformative science-fiction aspects of *The Metamorphosis*, a story about a young man so alienated from *his* "dysfunctional" family that he turns — embarrassingly for them — into a giant beetle. No instructor has ever asked my sons to read Alice Munro, who writes so lucidly and beautifully about the hypersensitivity that makes adolescence a hell.

◆ ◆ ◆

In the hope of finding out that my children and my friends' children were exceptionally unfortunate, I recently collected eighty or so reading lists from high schools throughout the country. Because of how overworked teachers are, how hard to reach during the school day, as well as the odd, paranoid defensiveness that pervades so many schools, obtaining these documents seemed to require more time and dogged perseverance than obtaining one's FBI surveillance files — and what I came away with may not be a scientifically accurate survey. Such surveys have been done by the National Council of Teachers of English (published in the 1993 NCTE research report, *Literature in the Secondary Schools*), with results that both underline and fail to reflect what I found.

What emerges from these photocopied pages distributed in public, private, and Catholic schools as well as in military academies, in Manhattan and Denver, in rural Oregon and urban Missouri, is a numbing sameness, unaffected by geography, region, or community size. Nearly every list contains at least one of Shakespeare's plays. Indeed, in the NCTE report, Shakespeare (followed closely by John Steinbeck) tops the rosters of "Ten Most Frequently Required Authors of Book-Length Works, Grades 9–12."

Yet in other genres — fiction and memoir — the news is far more upsetting. On the lists sampled, Harper Lee's *To Kill a Mockingbird* and Maya Angelou's *I Know Why the Caged Bird Sings* are among the titles that appear most often, a grisly fact that in itself should inspire us to

examine the works that dominate our children's literary education.

First published in 1970, *I Know Why the Caged Bird Sings* is what we have since learned to recognize as a "survivor" memoir, a first-person narrative of victimization and recovery. Angelou transports us to her childhood in segregated Arkansas, where she was raised by her grandmother and was mostly content, despite the unpleasantness of her white neighbors, until, after a move to St. Louis, eight-year-old Maya was raped by her mother's boyfriend.

One can see why this memoir might appeal to the lazy or uninspired teacher, who can conduct the class as if the students were the studio audience for Angelou's guest appearance on *Oprah*. The author's frequently vented distrust of white society might rouse even the most sluggish or understandably disaffected ninth-graders to join a discussion of racism; her victory over poverty and abuse can be used to address what one fan, in a customer book review on Amazon.com, celebrated as "transcending that pain, drawing from it deeper levels of meaning about being truly human and truly alive." Many chapters end with sententious epigrams virtually begging to serve as texts for sophomoric rumination on such questions as: What does Angelou mean when she writes, "If growing up is painful for the Southern Black girl, being aware of her displacement is rust on the razor that threatens the throat"?

But much more terrifying than the prospect of Angelou's pieties being dissected for their deeper meaning is the notion of her language being used as a model of "poetic" prose style. Many of the terrible mysteries that confront teachers of college freshman composition can be solved simply by looking at Angelou's writing. Who told students to combine a dozen mixed metaphors in one paragraph? Consider a typical passage from Angelou's opaque prose: "Weekdays revolved on a sameness wheel. They turned into themselves so steadily and inevitably that each seemed to be the original of yesterday's rough draft. Saturdays, however, always broke the mold and dared to be different." Where do students learn to write stale, inaccurate similes? "The man's dead words fell like bricks around the auditorium and too many settled in my belly." Who seriously believes that murky, turgid, convoluted language of this sort constitutes good writing? "Youth and social approval allied themselves with me and we trammeled memories of slights and insults. The wind of our swift passage remodeled my features. Lost tears were pounded to mud and then to dust. Years of withdrawal were brushed aside and left behind, as hanging ropes of parasitic moss."

To hold up this book as a paradigm of memoir, of thought — of literature — is akin to inviting doctors convicted of malpractice to instruct our medical students. If we want to use Angelou's work to educate our kids, let's invite them to parse her language, sentence by sentence; ask them precisely what it means and ask why one would bother obscuring ideas that could be expressed so much more simply and felicitously.

Narrated affably enough by a nine-year-old girl named Scout, *To Kill a Mockingbird* is the perennially beloved and treacly account of growing up in a small Southern town during the Depression. Its hero is Scout's father, the saintly Atticus Finch, a lawyer who represents everything we cherish about justice and democracy and the American Way, and who defends a black man falsely accused of rape by a poor white woman. The novel has a shadow hero, too, the descriptively named Boo Radley, a gooney recluse who becomes the occasion for yet another lesson in tolerance and compassion.

Such summary reduces the book, but not by all that much. To read the novel is, for most, an exercise in wish-fulfillment and self-congratulation, a chance to consider thorny issues of race and prejudice from a safe distance and with the comfortable certainty that the reader would *never* harbor the racist attitudes espoused by the lowlifes in the novel. We (the readers) are

Scout, her childhood is our childhood, and Atticus Finch is our brave, infinitely patient American Daddy. And that creepy big guy living alone in the scary house turns out to have been watching over us with protective benevolent attention.

Maya Angelou and Harper Lee are not the only authors on the lists. The other most popular books are *The Great Gatsby*, *The Scarlet Letter*, *The Adventures of Huckleberry Finn*, and *The Catcher in the Rye*. John Steinbeck (*The Pearl*, *Of Mice and Men*, *The Red Pony*, *The Grapes of Wrath*) and Toni Morrison (*Song of Solomon*, *Sula*, *The Bluest Eye*, *Beloved*) are the writers — after Shakespeare — represented by the largest number of titles. Also widely studied are the novels of more dubious literary merit: John Knowles's *A Separate Peace*, William Golding's *Lord of the Flies*, Elie Wiesel's *Night*, and Ray Bradbury's *Fahrenheit 451*, *Dandelion Wine*, *The October Country*, and *Something Wicked This Way Comes*. Trailing behind these favorites, Orwell (*Nineteen Eighty-Four* and *Animal Farm*) is still being read, as are the Brontës (*Wuthering Heights* and *Jane Eyre*).

How astonishing then that students exposed to such a wide array of masterpieces and competent middlebrow entertainments are not mobbing their libraries and bookstores, demanding heady diets of serious or semi-serious fiction! And how puzzling that I should so often find myself teaching bright, eager college undergraduate and graduate students, would-be writers handicapped not merely by how little literature they have read but by their utter inability to read it; many are nearly incapable of doing the close line-by-line reading necessary to disclose the most basic information in a story by Henry James or a seemingly more straightforward one by Katherine Mansfield or Paul Bowles.

The explanation, it turns out, lies in how these books, even the best of them, are being presented in the classroom. My dogged search for

15

reading lists flushed out, in addition to the lists themselves, course descriptions, teaching guides, and anecdotes that reveal how English literature is being taught to high school students. Only rarely do teachers propose that writing might be worth reading closely. Instead, students are informed that literature is principally a vehicle for the soporific moral blather they suffer daily from their parents. The present vogue for teaching "values" through literature uses the novel as a springboard for the sort of discussion formerly conducted in civics or ethics classes — areas of study that, in theory, have been phased out of the curriculum but that, in fact, have been retained and cleverly substituted for what we used to call English. English — and everything about it that is inventive, imaginative, or pleasurable — is beside the point in classrooms, as is everything that constitutes style and that distinguishes writers, one from another, as precisely as fingerprints or DNA mapping.

The question is no longer what the writer has written but rather who the writer is — specifically, what ethnic group or gender identity an author represents. A motion passed by the San Francisco Board of Education in March 1998 mandates that "works of literature read in class in grades nine to eleven by each high school student must include works by writers of color which reflect the diversity of culture, race, and class of the students of the San Francisco Unified School District. . . . The writers who are known to be lesbian, gay, bisexual or transgender, shall be appropriately identified in the curriculum." Meanwhile, aesthetic beauty — felicitous or accurate language, images, rhythm, wit, the satisfaction of recognizing something in fiction that seems fresh and true — is simply too frivolous, suspect, and elitist even to mention.

Thus the fragile *To Kill a Mockingbird* is freighted with tons of sociopolitical ballast. A "Collaborative Program Planning Record of Learning Experience," which I obtained from the Internet, outlines the "overall goal" of teaching

the book ("To understand problems relating to discrimination and prejudice that exist in our present-day society. To understand and apply these principles to our own lives") and suggests topics for student discussion: "What type of people make up your community? Is there any group of people . . . a person (NO NAMES PLEASE) or type of person in your community that you feel uncomfortable around?"

A description of "The Family in Literature," an elective offered by the Princeton Day School — a course including works by Sophocles and Eugene O'Neill — begins: "Bruce Springsteen once tried to make us believe that 'No one can break the ties that bind / You can't for say-yay-yay-yay-yay-yay-yay-yake the ties that bind.' He has since divorced his wife and married his back-up singer. So what are these ties and just how strong are they, after all?" With its chilling echoes of New Age psychobabble, Margaret Dodson's *Teaching Values through Teaching Literature*, a sourcebook for high school English teachers, informs us that the point of Steinbeck's *Of Mice and Men* is "to show how progress has been made in the treatment of the mentally disadvantaged, and that more and better roles in society are being devised for them [and to] establish that mentally retarded people are human beings with the same needs and feelings that everyone else experiences."

An eighth-grader studying Elie Wiesel's overwrought *Night* in a class taught by a passionate gay-rights advocate came home with the following notes: "Many Jews killed during the Holocaust, but many *many* homosexuals murdered by Nazis. Pink triangle — Silence equals death."

It's cheering that so many lists include *The Adventures of Huckleberry Finn* — but not when we discover that this moving, funny novel is being taught not as a work of art but as a piece of damning evidence against that bigot, Mark Twain. A friend's daughter's English teacher informed a group of parents that the only reason to study *Huckleberry Finn* was to decide

20

seeing connections

These graphs show the percentage of children's books by and about people of color from 2002 through 2016.

To what extent does this data challenge the claims Prose makes in paragraph 19?

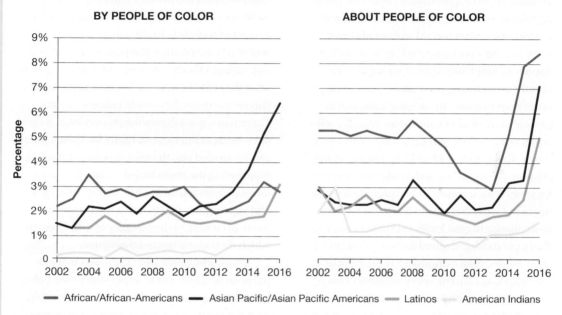

Children's Books By and About People of Color, 2002–2016

BY PEOPLE OF COLOR   ABOUT PEOPLE OF COLOR

— African/African-Americans   — Asian Pacific/Asian Pacific Americans   — Latinos   — American Indians

Data from Cooperative Children's Book Center, University of Wisconsin-Madison

whether it was a racist text. Instructors consulting *Teaching Values through Teaching Literature* will have resolved this debate long before they walk into the classroom to supervise "a close reading of *Huckleberry Finn* that will reveal the various ways in which Twain undercuts Jim's humanity: in the minstrel routines with Huck as the 'straight man'; in generalities about Blacks as unreliable, primitive and slow-witted. . . ."

Luckily for the teacher and students required to confront this fictional equivalent of a minstrel show, Mark Twain can be rehabilitated — that is to say, revised. In classes that sound like test

screenings used to position unreleased Hollywood films, focus groups in which viewers are invited to choose among variant endings, students are polled for possible alternatives to Huck's and Tom Sawyer's actions — should Tom have carried out his plan to "free" Jim? — and asked to speculate on what the fictional characters might have or should have done to become better people and atone for the sins of their creators.

In the most unintentionally hilarious of these lesson plans, a chapter entitled "*Ethan Frome*: An Avoidable Tragedy," Dodson warns teachers to expect resistance to their efforts to reform Wharton's

25

characters and thus improve her novel's outcome: "Students intensely dislike the mere suggestion that Ethan should have honored his commitment to Zeena and encouraged Mattie to date Dennie Eady, yet this would surely have demonstrated greater love than the suicide attempt."

Thus another puzzle confronting college and even graduate school instructors — Why do students so despise dead writers? — is partly explained by the adversarial stance that these sourcebooks adopt toward authors of classic texts. Teachers are counseled "to help students rise above Emerson's style of stating an idea bluntly, announcing reservations, and sometimes even negating the original idea" and to present "a method of contrasting the drab, utilitarian prose of *Nineteen Eighty-four* with a lyric poem 'To a Darkling Thrush,' by Thomas Hardy." Why not mention that such works have been read for years — for a reason! — and urge students to figure out what that reason is? Doesn't it seem less *valuable* to read Emily Dickinson's work as the brain-damaged mumblings of a demented agoraphobic than to approach the subject of Dickinson, as Richard Sewell suggests in his biography of her, on our knees? No one's suggesting that canonical writers should be immune to criticism. Dickens's anti-Semitism, Tolstoy's overly romantic ideas about the peasantry, Kipling's racism, are all problematic, and merit discussion. But to treat the geniuses of the past as naughty children, amenable to reeducation by the children of the present, evokes the educational theory of the Chinese Revolution.

No wonder students are rarely asked to consider what was actually written by these hopeless racists and sociopaths. Instead, they're told to write around the books, or, better yet, write their own books. Becky Alano's depressing *Teaching the Novel* advises readers of Sylvia Plath's *The Bell Jar* to construct a therapeutic evaluation of its suicidal heroine ("Do you think she is ready to go home? What is your prognosis for her future?")

and lists documents to be written as supplements to *Macbeth* (a script of the TV evening news announcing the murders; a psychiatrist's report on Lady Macbeth, or her suicide note to her husband; Macbeth's entry in *Who's Who*, or his obituary).

How should prospective readers of Anne Frank's *The Diary of a Young Girl* prepare? Carolyn Smith McGowen's *Teaching Literature by Women Authors* suggests: "Give each student a paper grocery bag. Explain that to avoid being sent to a concentration camp, many people went into hiding. Often they could take with them only what they could carry. . . . Ask your students to choose the items they would take into hiding. These items must fit into the grocery bag." A class attempting to interpret an Emily Dickinson poem can be divided into three groups, each group interpreting the poem based on one of Freud's levels of consciousness; thus the little ids, egos, and superegos can respond to the Dickinson poem according to the category of awareness to which their group has been assigned.

Those who might have supposed that one purpose of fiction was to deploy the powers of language to connect us, directly and intimately, with the hearts and souls of others, will be disappointed to learn that the whole point is to make us examine ourselves. According to Alano, *The Catcher in the Rye* will doubtless suggest an incident "in which you felt yourself to be an 'outsider' like Holden. Why did you feel outside? What finally changed your situation?" Stephen Crane's *The Red Badge of Courage* should make us compare our anxieties ("Describe an event that you anticipated with fear. . . . Was the actual event worth the dread?") with those of its Civil War hero. And what does *The Great Gatsby* lead us to consider? "Did you ever pursue a goal with single-minded devotion? . . . Would you have gained your end in any other way?" Are we to believe that the average eleventh-grader has had an experience comparable to that of

Jay Gatsby — or F. Scott Fitzgerald? And is it any wonder that teenagers should complete these exercises with little but contempt for the writer who so pointlessly complicated and obfuscated a personal true story that sixteen-year-olds could have told so much more interestingly themselves?

◆ ◆ ◆

I remember when it dawned on me that I might, someday, grow old. I was in the eleventh grade. Our marvelous and unusual English teacher had assigned us to read *King Lear* — that is, to read every line of *King Lear*. (As I recall, we were asked to circle every word or metaphor having to do with eyes and vision, a tedious process we grumbled about but that succeeded in focusing our attention.) Although I knew I would never ever resemble the decrepit adults around me, Shakespeare's genius, his poetry, his profound, encyclopedic understanding of personality, managed to persuade me that I could *be* that mythical king — an imaginative identification very different from whatever result I might have obtained by persuading myself that my own experience was the *same* as Lear's. I recall the hallucinatory sense of having left my warm bedroom, of finding myself — old, enraged, alone, despised — on that heath, in that dangerous storm. And I remember realizing, after the storm subsided, that language, that mere words on the page, had raised that howling tempest.

Lear is still the Shakespeare play I like best. I reread it periodically, increasingly moved now that age is no longer a theoretical possibility, and now that its portrayal of Lear's behavior so often seems like reportage. A friend whose elderly boss is ruining his company with irrational tests of fealty and refusals to cede power needs only six words to describe the situation at work: *King Lear*, Act One, Scene One.

Another high school favorite was the King James Version of the Book of Revelation. I don't think I'd ever heard of Armageddon, nor did I believe that when the seals of a book were opened horses would fly out. What delighted me was the language, the cadences and the rhythms, and the power of the images: the four horsemen, the beast, the woman clothed with the sun.

But rather than exposing students to works of literature that expand their capacities and vocabularies, sharpen their comprehension, and deepen the level at which they think and feel, we either offer them "easy" (Steinbeck, Knowles, Angelou, Lee) books that "anyone" can understand, or we serve up the tougher works predigested. We no longer believe that books were written one word at a time, and deserve to be read that way. We've forgotten the difference between a student who has never read a nineteenth-century novel and an idiot incapable of reading one. When my son was assigned *Wuthering Heights* in tenth-grade English, the complex sentences, archaisms, multiple narrators, and interwoven stories seemed, at first, like a foreign language. But soon enough, he caught on and reported being moved almost to tears by the cruelty of Heathcliff's treatment of Isabella.

In fact, it's not difficult to find fiction that combines clear, beautiful, accessible, idiosyncratic language with a narrative that conveys a complex worldview. But to use such literature might require teachers and school boards to make fresh choices, selections uncontaminated by trends, clichés, and received ideas. If educators continue to assume that teenagers are interested exclusively in books about teenagers, there *is* engaging, truthful fiction about childhood and adolescence, written in ways that remind us why someone might like to read. There is, for example, Charles Baxter's precise and evocative "Gryphon." And there are the carefully chosen details, the complex sentences, and the down-to-earth diction in Stuart Dybek's great Chicago story, "Hot Ice."

If English class is the only forum in which students can talk about racism and ethnic identity, why not teach Hilton Als's *The Women*, Flannery O'Connor's "Everything That Rises Must Converge," or any of the stories in James Alan McPherson's *Hue and Cry*, all of which eloquently and directly address the subtle, powerful ways in which race affects every tiny decision and gesture? Why not introduce our kids to the clarity and power of James Baldwin's great story "Sonny's Blues"?

My suspicion is that the reason such texts are not used as often as *I Know Why the Caged Bird Sings* is precisely the reason why they *should* be taught — that is, because they're complicated. Baldwin, Als, and McPherson reject obvious "lessons" and familiar arcs of abuse, self-realization, and recovery; they actively refute simplistic prescriptions about how to live.

Great novels can help us master the all-too-rare skill of tolerating — of being able to hold in mind — ambiguity and contradiction. Jay Gatsby has a shady past, but he's also sympathetic. Huck Finn is a liar, but we come to love him. A friend's student once wrote that Alice Munro's characters weren't people he'd choose to hang out with but that reading her work always made him feel "a little less petty and judgmental." Such benefits are denied to

seeing connections

In 2012, Dr. Natalie Phillips, an associate professor of English and the Director of the Digital Humanities & Literary Cognition Lab at Michigan State University, conducted a study on the benefits of close reading classic works of literature. Subjects were instructed to carefully read from books by nineteenth-century writer Jane Austen as an MRI measured their brain flow. "What took us by surprise," Phillips noted, "is how much the whole brain transformed in shifting from pleasure to close reading, and in regions far beyond those associated with attention and executive functions."

Look closely at this early data image from researchers at the Digital Humanities & Literary Cognition Lab, in which a participant demonstrates widespread activity across brain regions for close reading, visualized in horizontal slices from he top of the brain to its base. Regions in red represent areas of increased blood flow for all paragraphs of close reading, on average, compared to paragraphs of pleasure reading.

How might Prose use this scientific study to support her argument? How might a reader use it to challenge her argument?

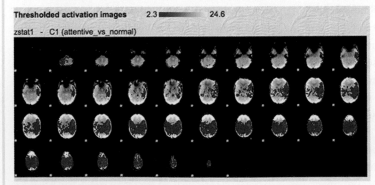

Thresholded activation images   2.3 ▬▬ 24.6

zstat1 - C1 (attentive_vs_normal)

Natalie Phillips

the young reader exposed only to books with banal, simple-minded moral equations as well as to the student encouraged to come up with reductive, wrong-headed readings of multilayered texts.

The narrator of *Caged Bird* is good, her rapist is bad; Scout and Atticus Finch are good, their bigoted neighbors are bad. But the characters in James Alan McPherson's "Gold Coast" are a good deal more lifelike. The cantankerous, bigoted, elderly white janitor and the young African American student, his temporary assistant, who puts up with the janitor's bullshit and is simultaneously cheered and saddened by the knowledge that he's headed for greater success than the janitor will ever achieve, both embody mixtures of admirable and more dubious qualities. In other words, they're more like humans. It's hard to imagine the lesson plans telling students exactly how to feel about these two complex plausible characters.

◆ ◆ ◆

No one's suggesting that every existing syllabus be shredded; many books on the current lists are great works of art. But why not *tell* the students that, instead of suggesting that Mark Twain be posthumously reprimanded? Why not point out how convincingly he captured the workings of Huck's mind, the inner voice of a kid trying desperately to sew a crazy quilt of self together from the ragged scraps around him? Why not celebrate the accuracy and vigor with which he translated the rhythms of American speech into written language?

In simplifying what a book is allowed to tell us — Twain's novel is wholly about racism and not at all about what it's like to *be* Huck Finn — teachers pretend to spark discussion but actually prevent it. They claim to relate the world of the book to the world of experience, but by concentrating on the student's own history they narrow the world of experience down to the personal and deny students *other* sorts of

experience — the experience of what's in the book, for starters. One reason we read writers from other times or cultures is to confront alternatives — of feeling and sensibility, of history and psyche, of information and ideas. To experience the heartbreaking matter-of-factness with which Anne Frank described her situation seems more useful than packing a paper bag with Game Boys, cigarettes, and CDs so that we can go into hiding and avoid being sent to the camps.

The pleasure of surrender to the world of a book is only one of the pleasures that this new way of reading — and teaching — denies. In blurring the line between reality and fiction (What happened to you that was exactly like what happened to Hester Prynne?), it reduces our respect for imagination, beauty, art, thought, and for the way that the human spirit expresses itself in words.

Writers have no choice but to believe that literature will survive, that it's worth some effort to preserve the most beautiful, meaningful lyrics or narratives, the record of who we were, and are. And if we want our children to begin an extended love affair with reading and with what great writing can do, we *want* them to get an early start — or any start, at all. Teaching students to value literary masterpieces is our best hope of awakening them to the infinite capacities and complexities of human experience, of helping them acknowledge and accept complexity and ambiguity, and of making them love and respect the language that allows us to smuggle out, and send one another, our urgent, eloquent dispatches from the prison of the self.

That may be what writers — and readers — desire. But if it's not occurring, perhaps that's because our culture wants it less urgently than we do. Education, after all, is a process intended to produce a product. So we have to ask ourselves: What sort of product is being produced by the current system? How does it change when certain factors are added to, or removed from, our literature curriculum? And is it really in the best

40

Christopher Weyant/The New Yorker Collection/Conde Nast

In paragraph 44, Prose states that "books are among the few remaining forms of entertainment not sustained by, and meant to further, the interests of advertising. Television, newspapers, and magazines are busily instilling us with new desires and previously unsuspected needs, while books sell only themselves." **To what extent does this cartoon support — or challenge — this claim?**

interests of our consumer economy to create a well-educated, smart, highly literate society of fervent readers? Doesn't our epidemic dumbing-down have undeniable advantages for those institutions (the media, the advertising industry, the government) whose interests are better served by a population not trained to read too closely or ask too many questions?

On the most obvious level, it's worth noting that books are among the few remaining forms of entertainment not sustained by, and meant to further, the interests of advertising. Television, newspapers, and magazines are busily instilling us with new desires and previously unsus-pected needs, while books sell only themselves. Moreover, the time we spend reading is time spent away from media that have a greater chance of alchemically transmuting attention into money.

But of course what's happening is more complex and subtle than that, more closely connected to how we conceive of the relation

between intellect and spirit. The new-model English-class graduate — the one who has been force-fed the gross oversimplifications proffered by these lesson plans and teaching manuals — values empathy and imagination less than the ability to make quick and irreversible judgments, to entertain and maintain simplistic immovable opinions about guilt and innocence, about the possibilities and limitations of human nature. Less comfortable with the gray areas than with sharply delineated black and white, he or she can work in groups and operate by consen-sus, and has a resultant, residual distrust for the eccentric, the idiosyncratic, the annoyingly . . . individual.

What I've described is a salable product, tailored to the needs of the economic and political moment. What results from these educational methods is a mode of think-₄₅ ing (or, more accurately, of *not* thinking) that equips our kids for the future: Future McDonald's employees. Future corporate

Danny Lawson – PA Images/Getty Images

This photograph captures the excitement of Harry Potter readers who are trying to break the Guinness World Record for the Largest Gathering of People Dressed as Harry. **Does evidence of such enthusiasm for the wildly popular series of books support or challenge Prose's main argument? Explain.**

board members. Future special prosecutors. Future makers of 100-best-books lists who fondly recall what they first read in high school — and who may not have read anything since. And so the roster of literary masterpieces we pass along to future generations will continue its downward shift, and those lightweight, mediocre high school favorites will continue to rise, unburdened by gravity, to the top of the list.

[1999]

EXPLORING THE TEXT

1. Francine Prose states, "Traditionally, the love of reading has been born and nurtured in high school English class" (para. 1). Do you think this is generally the case? Describe your experience on this subject.

2. Prose's opening paragraph includes such words as *appalled*, *dismal*, and *dreariness* — all with negative connotations. Why does she start out with such strong language? Does she risk putting off readers who do not share her views? Why or why not? What other examples of strongly emotional language do you find in the essay?

3. According to Prose, "To hold up [*I Know Why the Caged Bird Sings*] as a paradigm of memoir, of thought — of literature — is akin to inviting doctors convicted of malpractice to instruct our medical students" (para. 13). Do you agree with this analogy? Explain your answer. What other examples of figurative language can you find in this essay?

4. Toward the end of the essay (paras. 35, 39, and 43), Prose uses a series of rhetorical questions. What is her purpose in asking one rhetorical question after another?

5. What does Prose mean when she writes, "[B]y concentrating on the student's own history [teachers] narrow the world of experience down to the personal and deny students *other* sorts of experience — the experience of what's in the book, for starters" (para. 40)? Do you agree with Prose's statement? Why or why not?

6. What is Prose implying in the following statement about what she calls the "new-model English-class graduate": "But of course what's happening is more complex and subtle than [seeing books as unconnected to advertising], more closely

connected to how we conceive of the relation between intellect and spirit" (para. 45)?

7. According to Prose, why are American high school students learning to loathe literature? Cite at least four or five reasons.

8. What different roles, or personae, does Prose use to establish her ethos in this essay? How would you describe that ethos?

9. Prose makes several key assumptions about the role and impact of reading literary works in high school. What are they?

10. Does Prose propose a solution or recommendations to change this situation? If she does not offer a solution, is her argument weakened? Explain your answer.

11. Prose is highly critical of the quality of both *I Know Why the Caged Bird Sings* and *To Kill a Mockingbird*. If you have read either book, evaluate her criticism of one or both. Pay particular attention to the quotations she selects; is she setting up a straw man — that is, an argument that can be easily refuted?

12. Prose writes, "Great novels can help us master the all-too-rare skill of tolerating — of being able to hold in mind — ambiguity and contradiction" (para. 37). Select a novel you know well, and explain the "ambiguity and contradiction" at its heart.

13. This essay was written in 1999. Do you think Prose would or could make the same argument today? Why or why not?

Me Talk Pretty One Day

DAVID SEDARIS

David Sedaris (b. 1956) is a Grammy-nominated humorist, essayist, playwright, and frequent contributor to National Public Radio. Six of his essay collections have been best-sellers, including *Naked* (1997), *Holidays on Ice* (1997), *Me Talk Pretty One Day* (2000), *Dress Your Family in Corduroy and Denim* (2004), *When You Are Engulfed in Flames* (2008), and *Let's Explore Diabetes with Owls* (2013). He has also published a collection of humorous short stories, *Squirrel Seeks Chipmunk: A Modest Bestiary* (2010), and has been nominated for three Grammy Awards for Best Spoken Word and Best Comedy Album. Sedaris's writing frequently relies on autobiography, satire, and self-effacement to poke fun at the foolishness and foibles of the human condition.

At the age of forty-one, I am returning to school and have to think of myself as what my French textbook calls "a true debutant." After paying my tuition, I was issued a student ID, which allows me a discounted entry fee at movie theaters, puppet shows, and Festyland, a far-flung amusement park that advertises with billboards picturing a cartoon stegosaurus sitting in a canoe and eating what appears to be a ham sandwich.

I've moved to Paris with the hopes of learning the language. My school is an easy ten-minute walk from my apartment, and on the first day of class I arrived early, watching as the returning students greeted one another in the school lobby. Vacations were recounted, and questions were raised concerning mutual friends with names like Kang and Vlatnya. Regardless of their nationalities, everyone spoke in what sounded to me like excellent French. Some accents were better than others, but the students exhibited an ease and confidence I found intimidating. As an added discomfort, they were all young, attractive, and well dressed, causing me to feel not unlike Pa Kettle[1] trapped backstage after a fashion show.

The first day of class was nerve-racking because I knew I'd be expected to perform. That's the way they do it here — it's everybody into the language pool, sink or swim. The teacher marched in, deeply tanned from a recent vacation, and proceeded to rattle off a series of administrative announcements. I've spent quite a few summers in Normandy, and I took a month-long French class before leaving New York. I'm not completely in the dark, yet I understood only half of what this woman was saying.

"If you have not *meimslsxp* or *lgpdmurct* by this time, then you should not be in this room. Has everyone *apzkiubjxow*? Everyone? Good, we shall begin." She spread out her lesson plan and sighed, saying, "All right, then, who knows the alphabet?"

It was startling because (a) I hadn't been asked that question in a while and (b) I realized, while laughing, that I myself did *not* know the alphabet. They're the same letters, but in France they're pronounced differently. I know the shape of the alphabet but had no idea what it actually sounded like.

"Ahh." The teacher went to the board and sketched the letter *a*. "Do we have anyone in the room whose first name commences with an *ahh*?"

Two Polish Annas raised their hands, and the teacher instructed them to present themselves by stating their names, nationalities, occupations, and a brief list of things they liked and disliked in this world. The first Anna hailed from an industrial town outside of Warsaw and had front teeth the size of tombstones. She worked as a seamstress, enjoyed quiet times with friends, and hated the mosquito.

"Oh, really," the teacher said. "How very interesting. I thought that everyone loved the mosquito, but here, in front of all the world, you claim to detest him. How is it that we've been blessed with someone as unique and original as you? Tell us, please?"

The seamstress did not understand what was being said but knew that this was an occasion for shame. Her rabbity mouth huffed for breath, and she stared down at her lap as though the

appropriate comeback were stitched somewhere alongside the zipper of her slacks.

The second Anna learned from the first and claimed to love sunshine and detest lies. It sounded like a translation of one of those Playmate of the Month data sheets, the answers always written in the same loopy handwriting: "Turn-ons: Mom's famous five-alarm chili! Turnoffs: insecurity and guys who come on too strong!!!!"

The two Polish Annas surely had clear notions of what they loved and hated, but like the rest of us, they were limited in terms of vocabulary, and this made them appear less than sophisticated. The teacher forged on, and we learned that Carlos, the Argentine bandonion player, loved wine, music, and, in his words, "making sex with the womens of the world." Next came a beautiful young Yugoslav who identified herself as an optimist, saying that she loved everything that life had to offer.

The teacher licked her lips, revealing a hint of the saucebox we would later come to know. She crouched low for her attack, placed her hands on the young woman's desk, and leaned close, saying, "Oh yeah? And do you love your little war?"

While the optimist struggled to defend herself, I scrambled to think of an answer to what had obviously become a trick question. How often is one asked what he loves in this world? More to the point, how often is one asked and then publicly ridiculed for his answer? I recalled my mother, flushed with wine, pounding the tabletop late one night, saying, "Love? I love a good steak cooked rare. I love my cat, and I love . . ." My sisters and I leaned forward, waiting to hear our names. "Tums," our mother said. "I love Tums."

The teacher killed some time accusing the Yugoslavian girl of masterminding a program of genocide, and I jotted frantic notes in the margins of my pad. While I can honestly say that I love leafing through medical textbooks devoted to severe dermatological conditions, the hobby is beyond the reach of my French vocabulary, and acting it out would only have invited controversy.

---

[1] Ma and Pa Kettle were comic film characters from the 1940s to 1950s. They were caricatures of unsophisticated country folk. —Eds.

When called upon, I delivered an effortless list of things that I detest: blood sausage, intestinal pâtés, brain pudding. I'd learned these words the hard way. Having given it some thought, I then declared my love for IBM typewriters, the French word for *bruise*, and my electric floor waxer. It was a short list, but still I managed to mispronounce *IBM* and assign the wrong gender to both the floor waxer and the typewriter. The teacher's reaction led me to believe that these mistakes were capital crimes in the country of France.

"Were you always this *palicmkrexis*?" she asked. "Even a *fiuscrzsa ticiwelmun* knows that a typewriter is feminine."

I absorbed as much of her abuse as I could understand, thinking — but not saying — that I find it ridiculous to assign a gender to an inanimate object incapable of disrobing and making an occasional fool of itself. Why refer to Lady Crack Pipe or Good Sir Dishrag when these things could never live up to all that their sex implied?

The teacher proceeded to belittle everyone from German Eva, who hated laziness, to Japanese Yukari, who loved paintbrushes and soap. Italian, Thai, Dutch, Korean, and Chinese — we all left class foolishly believing that the worst was over. She'd shaken us up a little, but surely that was just an act designed to weed out the deadweight. We didn't know it then, but the coming months would teach us what is was like to spend time in the presence of a wild animal, something completely unpredictable. Her temperament was not based on a series of good and bad days, but, rather, good and bad moments. We soon learned to dodge chalk and protect our heads and stomachs whenever she approached us with a question. She hadn't yet punched anyone, but it seemed wise to protect ourselves against the inevitable.

Though we were forbidden to speak anything but French, the teacher would occasionally use us to practice any of her five fluent languages.

"I hate you," she said to me one afternoon. Her English was flawless. "I really, really hate you." Call me sensitive, but I couldn't help but take it personally.

After being singled out as a lazy *kfdtinvfm*, I took to spending four hours a night on my homework, putting in even more time whenever we were assigned an essay. I suppose I could have gotten by with less, but I was determined to create some sort of identity for myself: David the hard worker, David the cut-up. We'd have one of those "complete this sentence" exercises, and I'd fool with the thing for hours, invariably settling on something like "A quick run around the lake? I'd love to! Just give me a moment while I strap on my wooden leg." The teacher, through word and action, conveyed the message that if this was my idea of an identity, she wanted nothing to do with it.

My fear and discomfort crept beyond the borders of the classroom and accompanied me out onto the wide boulevards. Stopping for coffee, asking directions, depositing money in my bank account: these things were out of the question, as they involved having to speak. Before beginning school, there'd been no shutting me up, but now I was convinced that everything I sáid was wrong. When the phone rang, I ignored it. If someone asked me a question, I pretended to be deaf. I knew my fear was getting the best of me when I started wondering why they don't sell cuts of meat in vending machines.

My only comfort was the knowledge that I was not alone. Huddled in the hallways and making the most of our pathetic French, my fellow students and I engaged in the sort of conversation commonly overheard in refugee camps.

"Sometime me cry alone at night."

"That be common for I, also, but be more strong, you. Much work and someday you talk pretty. People start love you soon. Maybe tomorrow, okay."

Unlike the French class I had taken in New York, here there was no sense of competition. When the teacher poked a shy Korean in the eyelid with a freshly sharpened pencil, we took no comfort in the fact that, unlike Hyeyoon Cho, we all knew the irregular past tense of the verb *to*

How has this cartoonist captured the humor that Dave Sedaris uses in "Me Talk Pretty One Day"?

David Sipress/The New Yorker Collection/Conde Nast

defeat. In all fairness, the teacher hadn't meant to stab the girl, but neither did she spend much time apologizing, saying only, "Well, you should have been *vkkdyo* more *kdeynfulh.*"

Over time it became impossible to believe that any of us would ever improve. Fall arrived and it rained every day, meaning we would now be scolded for the water dripping from our coats and umbrellas. It was mid-October when the teacher singled me out, saying, "Every day spent with you is like having a cesarean section." And it struck me that, for the first time since arriving in France, I could understand every word that someone was saying.

Understanding doesn't mean that you can suddenly speak the language. Far from it. It's a small step, nothing more, yet its rewards are intoxicating and deceptive. The teacher continued her diatribe and I settled back, bathing in the subtle beauty of each new curse and insult.

"You exhaust me with your foolishness and reward my efforts with nothing but pain, do you understand me?"

The world opened up, and it was with great joy that I responded, "I know the thing that you speak exact now. Talk me more, you, plus, please, plus."

[2000]

EXPLORING THE TEXT

1. How does David Sedaris establish a humorous tone in the first two paragraphs? What details contribute to this tone?

2. How does Sedaris manage to make us laugh at the other students without seeming to mock or make fun of them? What effect does he achieve by including actual dialogue?

3. How does Sedaris characterize the teacher? Is she intentionally cruel, an effective teacher, an overly strict disciplinarian? Is she portrayed as a stereotype? Refer to specific details and passages from the essay to explain your response.

4. What does Sedaris mean when he writes that "understanding" another language is "a small step,

nothing more, yet its rewards are intoxicating and deceptive" (para. 28)?

5. Sedaris uses both understatement and hyperbole in this essay. Identify two examples of each and explain the effect.

6. Like most humorists, Sedaris makes a serious point through laughter and comedy. What is his point in this essay? Try stating it in one or two sentences.

7. Sedaris describes what for most of us would be a very unusual class — that is, a class in a foreign country with students from all over the world. Yet, for this essay to be funny, it must resonate with us

to some extent. What aspect of the experience of being a student does Sedaris count on as common ground between himself and his readers?

8. In *Laughter: An Essay on the Meaning of the Comic*, philosopher Henri Bergson writes, "Several have defined man as 'an animal which laughs.' They might equally as well have defined him as an animal which is laughed at; for if any other animal, or some lifeless object, produces the same effect, it is always because of some resemblance to man, or the stamp he gives it or the use he puts it to." Does "Me Talk Pretty One Day" more effectively present people as creatures who laugh or are laughed at?

Why Virtual Classes Can Be Better Than Real Ones

BARBARA OAKLEY

Barbara Oakley (b. 1955) is an educator, writer, and engineer. Originally from Lodi, California, Oakley enlisted in the U.S. Army after high school. The Army sent Oakley to the University of Washington where she completed a BA in Slavic languages and literature. Oakley then rose to the rank of Captain as Signal Officer in Germany. After the Army, she completed a BS in electrical engineering before spending a season as a radio operator at the South Pole Station in Antarctica. In 1998 she received her PhD in systems engineering at Oakland University, where she is now a professor. Oakley's writing and research covers STEM (Science, Technology, Engineering, and Mathematics) education and online learning. Some of her books include *Evil Genes: Why Rome Fell, Hitler Rose, Enron Failed, and My Sister Stole My Mother's Boyfriend* (2007); *A Mind for Numbers* (2014), which was a New York Times best-selling science book; and most recently, *Mindshift: Break Through Obstacles to Learning and Discover Your Hidden Potential* (2017). Oakley co-created and teaches "Learning How to Learn," an online course offered through Coursera that has attracted over 1.2 million students. The following essay was published in 2015 in *Nautilus*, a magazine dedicated to exploring the myriad ways in which science connects to everyday life.

I teach one of the world's most popular MOOCs (massive online open courses), "Learning How to Learn," with neuroscientist Terrence J. Sejnowski, the Francis Crick Professor at the Salk Institute for Biological Studies. The course draws on neuroscience, cognitive psychology, and education to explain how our brains absorb and process information, so we can all be better students. Since it launched on the website Coursera in August of 2014, nearly 1 million students from over 200 countries have enrolled

in our class. We've had cardiologists, engineers, lawyers, linguists, 12-year-olds, and war refugees in Sudan take the course. We get emails like this one that recently arrived: "I'll keep it short. I've recently completed your MOOC and it has already changed my life in ways you cannot imagine. I just turned 29, am in the middle of a career change to computer science, and I've never been more excited to learn."

It's a wonderful feeling to receive notes like this, as teachers around the world know. As gratifying as the note is personally, it also speaks for the impact of MOOCs. We all know about the importance of an education system, and how much society could gain if education, particularly for the disadvantaged, were improved. Online courses allow us to scale up those opportunities — a better education at lower cost. Already the numbers are impressive. More than 500 colleges and universities and 200 organizations and institutions offer MOOCs, with a total of 30 million users.

At the same time that "Learning How to Learn" has been one of the most satisfying experiences of my 20 years as a teacher — I am currently a professor of engineering at Oakland University in Michigan — I confess to feeling a little defensive. The success and tremendous educational potential for MOOCs has been dinged by some high-profile articles in the past couple of years. In an article called "Trapped in the Virtual Classroom" in the *New York Review of Books*, David Bromwich, the Sterling Professor of English at Yale University, claimed that the "MOOC movement cooperates with the tendency of mechanization" and "discourages more complex thinking about the content and aims of education." Some research papers have reported the dropout rate in MOOCs is above 90 percent. And Robert Zemsky, Chair of the Learning Alliance for Higher Education at the University of Pennsylvania Graduate School of Education, has written that MOOCs, facing diminishing prospects, "were neither pedagogically nor technically interesting."

I would venture to say most MOOC deniers have little experience with creating and teaching online courses. The reality is MOOCs can be artistically and technically fascinating and can have terrific pedagogical advantages. This is particularly true in the fraught area of STEM (Science, Technology, Engineering, Math), where difficult explanations often cry out for a student to replay a portion of a lecture, or simply to take a pause while comprehension works its way to consciousness. As for those dropout rates, Keith Devlin, a mathematician

at Stanford University, has pointed out that some widely cited papers on MOOC attrition have depended on traditional metrics of higher education that are "entirely misleading." People sign up for MOOCs for different reasons than they do for traditional college classes. "A great many never intend to complete the course," Devlin writes. They "come looking for an education. Pure and simple."

With the best MOOCs, students are getting an 5 education that does indeed encourage complex thinking about the goals of education. Online courses can hold students' attentions, at times better than teachers can. Creating "Learning How to Learn" provided an opportunity to do a "meta" on teaching and learning. Terry and I could use the online medium to help overcome some of the challenges that students experience when facing traditional methods of teaching, and give them insight into the learning process itself.

◆ ◆ ◆

Chilean recluse spiders are believed to be among the most dangerous recluse spiders. One bite can kill you. Those suckers are big — up to an inch and a half across. They're also very fast. Imagine you spot a Chilean recluse spider 20 feet in front of you on the floor. Look again — suddenly, it's two feet in front of you. *That* gets your attention, doesn't it?

We're beginning to tease out the neurocircuitry behind why motion — especially looming motion like that of a spider — attracts attention. When looming objects are detected, neurons send a cascade of information to the brain's amygdala, a processing center of emotions and motivation. Looming is a big deal, phylogenetically speaking — creatures as different as insects, reptiles, birds, and people respond to looming motion.[1]

Human brains have evolved with a flitting, fleeting ability to maintain focus on any one thing. Those who kept too fixed a gaze on the wildebeest they were stalking could end up being killed by the lions stalking them. So it shouldn't be a surprise to learn that humans may not have been meant to sit boxed up for prolonged periods, focused on a teacher in a classroom. No matter how much we might like or be interested in the material, a lecture is out of tune with how our brains work.

This is a problem for teaching. It sounds heretical to even ask whether teachers help us learn. Our intuition tells us they should. And in fact they do help us learn — the best teachers seem to get inside our heads to intuit just what we need to get that *ah ha!* of initial understanding. They can charm, bedevil, and inspire us to learn well, even when the mountaintop of mastery seems insurmountably high. Clear explanations, inspiration, humor, personal focus on individual pressure points of conceptual misunderstanding — they all help us want to keep moving forward in the sometimes difficult task of learning.

But counterintuitive research has shown that [10] teachers don't seem to help us learn very well. A 1985 paper, "The initial knowledge state of college physics students," by physics professors Ibrahim Abou Halloun and David Hestenes, revealed that when we put physics students in front of a traditional "talk-and-chalk" instructor, those students claw their understanding of physics forward by only a tiny amount — even when the teacher is an award-winner.[2]

The Halloun and Hestenes paper produced an upheaval in science education. How could it be that traditional methods did such a poor job of educating? As researchers grappled with the implications, they began to test out new and better methods for teaching. Seminal research by physicist Richard Hake and others revealed that interactive engagement in a classroom, including big classrooms with over 100 students, resulted in a marked improvement of knowledge gained in a semester, compared to more traditional "sage on the stage" approaches.[3] Maintaining students' attention can be improved, it seems, by allowing them to talk and work interactively with one another.

Many college classrooms have shifted to this approach. A meta-analysis by Scott Freeman and his colleagues in the *Proceedings of the National Academy of Sciences* revealed that "active" learning produces such an improvement in science, engineering, and math classrooms that it is almost pedagogical malpractice not to use it.[4] But learning can't all be interaction. Sometimes the more the interaction, the slower the progress. Usually, proponents of active learning (I'm one of them; I coauthored a 2004 paper on the subject) suggest that a good approach to teaching provides a balance of explanation time by the instructor coupled with "active" time, where students are able to grapple with the material themselves, often while interacting with teammates.[5]

The resolution to the paradox about the value of teachers lies, it seems, in the context of the researchers' studies. Private tutoring can naturally hold a student's attention by not only giving clear explanations, but by switching things up, asking questions, and taking short breaks as needed. In the traditional talk-and-chalk larger classrooms that Halloun and Hestenes were investigating, even the best teachers couldn't help but become boring as a lengthy college class among a herd of other students dragged on.

These findings point toward the flitting nature of our brains — driven much more than we might like to admit by elusive, unconscious factors. Our inability to maintain focus for lengthy periods of time, coupled with our need to try things out for ourselves and talk things out with others, reduces our ability to make the best use of teachers who teach in traditional sage-on-the-stage form.

With the advent of the Internet, an even newer [15] approach to teaching has been the "flipped" classroom. In this approach, professors are recorded on video so they can be viewed at home, helping to synthesize and bring key ideas to life. Class time is then taken up with answering questions and with collaborative interactions: solving problems, discussing issues and concepts in teams, and working out the misunderstandings that have arisen during the preliminary solitary study. These types of personal interactions are where the teacher, and other students, are both invaluable.

The development of the flipped class has led to MOOCs as the next important frontier in education.

◆ ◆ ◆

Perhaps my biggest asset to creating "Learning How to Learn" was that I had been a terrible student. I flunked my way through elementary, middle, and high school math and science. Remedial math didn't even hit my playbook until age 26, after I'd gotten out of the military. (Poor job prospects can be a great motivator for career change.) I couldn't learn well by listening to lectures — in class, virtually everything but the professor was a shiny object of glorious distraction for me. The only way I could ultimately be successful was to become a classroom stenographer — later studying the notes at my own pace and in my own way.

As I started to learn math as an adult, I was often terribly frustrated by the material — sometimes I felt that textbooks and professors ganged up to present matters in the most arcane

way possible. Whenever some professor with a near lifetime experience with Fourier and Laplace transforms would say something like, "Of course, it's intuitively obvious that . . . " I'd get a shiver, because I knew it wouldn't be intuitively obvious to *me*. I'm not a quick study — it would often take me a long time to see that what I was looking at was actually very simple.

Terry and I created "Learning How to Learn" to get students to grasp that simplicity themselves. We wanted to incorporate some of the advantages of face-to-face tutoring with recent lessons from video game makers and TV. From the fast pace of Grand Theft Auto to money flying in a dryer in *Breaking Bad*, motion is an important aspect of reaching deep into viewers' subconscious to get a lock on their attention.

In "Learning How to Learn," we make 20 assiduous use of motion. Using green screen, I can suddenly pop from one side of the screen to another. Or I can loom from full standing to a close up of my face. Or, as I laugh on the side of the screen, I can speed up the onscreen picture-in-picture video of my daughter ineptly backing the family car off the driveway and onto the lawn — a living example of what can happen when procedural fluency hasn't been acquired. It's all video trickery, of course, but it works to keep students' attentions.

Claudio Muoz/The Economist

◀

Does this cartoon support or challenge Oakley's claim that MOOCs are "the next important frontier in education" (para. 16)? Explain.

In fact, one of the tricks used by many of the past greats in science has been to imagine themselves transported into what they're trying understand. Einstein famously imagined himself chasing a beam of light to help him formulate theories of relativity. Nobel Prize winner Barbara McClintock imagined herself in the realm of the "jumping genes" she became famous for discovering. We can help our students to develop the same sort of intuition as these Nobel Prize winners by bringing objects to life in video in a way that's virtually impossible to do in a classroom. We can walk into the mitochondria of a cell, or the ionic interaction that sparks an aurora, or the spiraling epiphany of Euler's equation.

A technology often used in current "in person" classroom instruction is to have a PowerPoint slide on the screen while the instructor stands to the side. Mimicking this approach in video format, we often see a small talking head in the corner of the screen (which is basically, because of its limited range of motion, like a still image), while the main image — whether it's a piccolo or a Picasso — is enlarged and discussed on another part of the screen.

But this "two image" approach actually increases a learner's cognitive load. With two separate images on the screen, you've got to process two different things at once. However, green-screen technology can allow a professor to appear to walk around a digitally upsized Greek vase that's the same size as she. In a biology video, the professor can point to life-sized structures of the cell. In engineering, she can point to the counter flow aspects of a heat exchanger. This cinematic joining of professor and object-under-discussion into one image reduces cognitive load and focuses students' attention on important details — even when, in real life, those details are small. All this has a big effect in making it easier for students to grasp key ideas.

Metaphors and analogies are just as important to learning as reducing the cognitive load. A theory called "neural reuse" posits that we seem to often use the same neural circuits to understand a metaphor or analogy as we do to understand the underlying process itself.[6] When we use water flow as an analogy for electron flow, or the idea of a stalker who creeps ever closer to help us understand the concept of limits in calculus, we're calling into play the same neural circuits that underpin our ability to understand those abstract concepts. Science, engineering, and math professors can be a bit snooty about dumbing down their material through sometimes silly analogies. These types of pedagogical tools are extraordinarily valuable — they serve as intellectual on-ramps to get students on board with complex ideas more quickly by using pre-existing neural circuitry.

Good online courses make students feel professors are speaking directly to them. A teacher's direct focus on the camera translates as personal attention in the videos. Students develop a sense of familiarity; we are often seen as friendly private tutors. It makes us more approachable and "listen-to-able." It's not that we're replacing teachers in a classroom. It's that we serve as additional personalized resources, despite the fact that we're explaining at massive scales. And I should mention that every single video lecture I give in our MOOC is the *best* lecture on that topic I've ever given in my life.

Online classes make enhanced quizzing available. Testing, as it turns out, is one of the best ways we can learn.[7] Tests at key points in videos, and dozens of carefully created alternative quiz questions at the end of each module, can do a lot to improve students' understanding of the materials. Educators sometimes point to research from physics showing that students don't really learn from careful explanations — they learn from making mistakes. But physics, unlike most subjects, is rife with pre-existing misconceptions that induce students to skip past explanations because they think they already understand — a stuck-in-a-rut mindset known as "Einstellung."[8] Mistakes in the frequent low-stakes quiz questions available online can force students in physics — or any other subject — to revisit the explanation.

So online videos allow students to do what their brains are naturally geared for — first focusing,

25

then replaying the toughest parts of what they're trying to learn, then taking a little break. They can quiz themselves, or I can quiz them. They can stop the video and stare into the distance, thinking away until all of a sudden, it clicks. They can touch base on the discussion forums with a friend in Zimbabwe or Chile. Much of this is impossible to do in a conventional 2-hour class period. (Have you ever tried to follow 10 fully worked out examples of Bayes Theorem in a 2-hour class period?)

Not all MOOCs are fabulous. But with their increasing diversity and quality, what MOOCs offer students — those enrolled in colleges and those not — is choice. Students can sample a wealth of subjects and classes, and if they are not sparked, move on. And MOOCs alone aren't the answer to improved education. That will come from a variety of sources: MOOCs, resources developed by textbook companies, and teachers themselves. Online assets will not serve as a replacement for in-person instructors — rather, they'll serve as assets, providing high-quality personalized tutoring and great testing materials with rapid grading.

Terry and I made "Learning How to Learn" for less than $5,000, and largely in my basement. I had no previous film editing experience — in fact, I could barely click a camera shutter. Much of the moving imagery for the course was created using simple PowerPoint slides. So I would issue a challenge to MOOC critics. Make your own online course. Film the most interesting, most insightful lecture you've ever given in your life. If you don't think your lecture is good enough, reshoot it until you're

happy. Make your video available for millions of students around the world, not just the privileged few in your classes. Come up with questions for a quiz on the mistakes you most commonly see in your classes. You will learn more than you know about the outreach and capabilities of MOOCs. More importantly, you will exemplify a wonderful openness for learning to students everywhere.

References

1. Skarratt, P.A., Gellatly, A.R., Cole, G.G., Piling, M., & Hulleman, J. Looming motion primes the visuomotor system. *Journal of Experimental Psychology: Human Perception and Performance* **40**, 566–579 (2014).
2. Halloun, I.A. & Hestenese, D. The initial knowledge state of college physics students. *American Journal of Physics* **53**, 1043 (1985).
3. Hake, R.R. Interactive-engagement versus traditional methods: A six-thousand-student survey of mechanics test data for introductory physics courses. *American Journal of Physics* **66**, 64 (1998).
4. Freeman, S., *et al.* Active learning increases student performance in science, engineering, and mathematics. *Proceedings of the National Academy of Sciences* **111**, 8410–8415 (2014).
5. Oakley, B., Brent, R., Felder, R.M., & Elhajj, I. Turning student groups into effective teams. *Journal of Student Centered Learning* **2**, 9–34 (2004).
6. Anderson, M.L. Precis of after phrenology: Neural reuse and the interactive brain. *Behavioral and Brain Sciences* **16**, 1–22 (2015).
7. Keresztes, A., Kaiser, D., Kovacs, G., & Racsmany, M. Testing promotes long-term learning via stabilizing activation patterns in a large network of brain areas. *Cerebral Cortex* **24**, 3025–3035 (2014).
8. Bilalic, M., McLeod, P., & Gobet, F. Why good thoughts block better ones: The mechanism of the pernicious Einstellung (set) effect. *Cognition* **108**, 652–661 (2008).

[2015]

EXPLORING THE TEXT

1. What is the irony in the title of this article? Do you find it funny, powerful, caustic, confusing, attention-getting, a combination of these, or something else entirely? Explain your response.

2. Barbara Oakley is currently a professor of engineering who is co-teaching a massive online open course (MOOC), so part of her ethos is automatic: she's a credible academic. In what other ways does she establish her ethos with her readers? Does her use of informal language — e.g., "dinged" (para. 3), "[t]hose suckers are big" (para. 6); "flunked" (para. 17) — undermine her ethos

or add a dimension to it? Cite specific passages in your analysis, and pay close attention to the Reference list at the end of Oakley's essay.

3. What are two counterarguments that Oakley discusses? How effectively does she refute them? How does she use her refutation to build or qualify her own argument?

4. What evidence does Oakley provide to support her assertion that students in a good MOOC "are getting an education that does indeed encourage complex thinking about the goals of education" (para. 5)? You may wish to include a discussion of the "flipped" classroom in your response.

5. What does Oakley believe is "the paradox about the value of teachers" (para. 13)? How does this "paradox" relate to the argument she develops about MOOCs and online education in general?

6. More than halfway through her argument, Oakley brings in her personal experience of being "a terrible student" (para. 17). What effect does her narrative have on the argument? What different responses might her various audiences have, depending upon their own experiences?

7. In paragraph 8, Oakley refers to the brain's "flitting, fleeting ability to maintain focus," a concept she returns to throughout the essay. In what ways is this a key point in her argument? How is her

example of the Chilean recluse spider part of this reasoning? How does her championing of video instruction relate to this point?

8. How does Oakley support her assertion that metaphors and analogies are key strategies for effective learning? In your eyes, how successfully does she make the case that such strategies are more useful and/or accessible in an online environment than in a face-to-face classroom?

9. By the end of the essay, it seems clear that Oakley's intended audience — particularly other teachers and scientists — are skeptics of online learning. What assumptions does she make about their chief concerns? How effectively does she reassure them and invite them to try developing an online course or course component?

10. At the very end of the essay, Oakley brings up the issue of cost. Is this an effective placement, given her audience, or would it have been better to raise the topic earlier? Why or why not?

11. To what extent do you think that Oakley proves her thesis: "Online courses allow us to scale up those opportunities — a better education at lower cost" (para. 2)? To support your viewpoint, cite specifics from her argument, draw from your own experience if you've engaged in online learning (formally or informally), and conduct some independent research.

My Friend, the Former Muslim Extremist

NICHOLAS KRISTOF

Nicholas Kristof (b. 1959) is a Pulitzer Prize–winning American journalist best known for the opinion column he has written for the *New York Times* since 2001. Kristof grew up in Oregon and, after studying government at Harvard University, went on to study law at Oxford University as a Rhodes Scholar. In 1990, he and his wife Sheryl WuDunn earned a Pulitzer Prize for International Reporting for their coverage of the Tiananmen Square pro-democracy protests of 1989, and in 2006 Kristof won a Pulitzer for his coverage of genocide in Darfur. Kristof and Sheryl WuDunn have also co-authored several best-selling books, including *Thunder from the East: Portrait of a Rising Asia* (1999), *Half the Sky: Turning Oppression into Opportunity for Women Worldwide* (2009), and *A Path Appears: Transforming Lives, Creating Opportunity* (2014). The following op-ed column appeared in a 2016 issue of the *New York Times*.

WHENEVER a Muslim carries out a terror attack in the West, the question arises: *Why do they hate us?*

Provocative answers come from my friend Rafiullah Kakar, who has lived a more astonishing life than almost anyone I know. Rafi is a young

THE ONLY THING THAT WILL EVER STOP *THESE* BAD-GUYS-WITH-GUNS...

caglecartoons.com

TALIBAN

IS NOT A GUN.

MALALA YOUSAFZAI

Pat Bagley/Cagle Cartoons, Inc.

How might Nicholas Kristof use this cartoon of the Nobel Peace Prize Winner Malala to support one of the points he makes in his article?

Pakistani who used to hate the United States and support the Taliban. His brother joined the Taliban for a time, but now I worry that the Taliban might try to kill Rafi—ah, but I'm getting ahead of myself.

One of 13 children, Rafi is a Pashtun[1] who grew up in a mud home close to the Afghan border, in an area notorious for tribal feuds and violent clashes. His parents are illiterate farmers, and it looked as if Rafi's education would end in the fifth grade, when he was sent to a madrasa. His mom wanted him to become a hafiz, someone who has memorized the entire Quran.

"One reason people send kids to madrasa[2] is that a hafiz can get to paradise and take 10 other people along," Rafi notes, explaining a local belief about getting to heaven. "My mother wanted me to be a hafiz, so I could be her ticket to paradise."

Ultimately, Rafi's life was transformed because his eldest brother, Akhtar, pinched pennies and sent Rafi to the best public school in the family's home province, Balochistan. Rafi had an outstanding mind and rocketed to the top of his class. But he also fell under the spell of political Islam.

5

A charismatic Islamic studies teacher turned Rafi into a Taliban sympathizer who despised the West.

"I subscribed to conspiracy theories that 9/11 was done by the Americans themselves, that there were 4,000 Jews who were absent from work that day," Rafi recalls. "I thought the Taliban were freedom fighters."

I've often written about education as an antidote to extremism. But in Pakistan, it was high school that radicalized Rafi. "Education can be a problem," Rafi says dryly.

He's right. It's possible to be too glib about the impact of education: Osama bin Laden was an engineer. Ayman al-Zawahri, the current leader of Al Qaeda, is a trilingual surgeon. Rafi notes that Pakistani doctors or engineers are sometimes extremists because in that country's specialized education system they gain the confidence of a university degree without the critical thinking that (ideally) comes from an acquaintance with the liberal arts.

Donor countries should support education, Rafi says, but pay far more attention to the curriculum. I think he's right, and we should also put more pressure on countries like Saudi Arabia to stop financing extremist madrasas in poor countries in Africa and Asia.

[1] A member of a community from southern Afghanistan and northwestern Pakistan. —Eds.
[2] An Arabic term meaning "school." —Eds.

This photograph shows a boy at a Pakistani madrasa wearing an Osama bin Laden t-shirt. **How might Rafiullah Kakar respond to him if the two met?**

We should also invest in girls' education, for it changes entire societies. Educated women have fewer children, which reduces the youth bulge in a population — one of the factors that correlates most strongly to terrorism and war. And educating girls changes boys. Ones like Rafi.

When Rafi attended college in the city of Lahore, he encountered educated women for the first time. Previously, he had assumed that girls have second-rate minds, and that educated women have loose morals.

"I'd never interacted with a woman," he said. "Then in college there were these talented, outspoken women in class. It was a shock." It was part of an intellectual journey that led Rafi to become a passionate advocate for girls' education, including in his own family. His oldest sisters are illiterate, but his youngest sister is bound for college.

Rafi won a Fulbright scholarship to study at Augustana College in South Dakota, an experience that left him more understanding of the United States, though still exasperated at many American policies. After college he won a Rhodes scholarship, and last year he completed graduate studies at Oxford.

He's now in London, writing for Pakistani newspapers, and he plans to return to Pakistan to start a boarding school for poor children in Balochistan, and ultimately to enter politics — if the Taliban don't get him on a return trip to his village.

Today Rafi is a voice against the Taliban, against conspiracy theories and against blind anti-Americanism, in part because the United States did not take Donald Trump's advice to ban Muslims. Extremist American voices like Trump's, Rafi says, empower extremist voices throughout the Islamic world.

"It's people like Donald Trump who are put forward by the extremists back home," Rafi told me. "It pours cold water on us."

To fight Islamic terrorism, the West spends billions of dollars on drones, missiles and foreign bases. Yet we neglect education and the empowerment of women, which if done right can be even more transformative. The trade-offs are striking: For the cost of deploying one soldier for a year, we could start more than 20 schools.

Rafi teaches us that a book can be a more powerful force against extremism than a drone. But it has to be the right book!

[2016]

EXPLORING THE TEXT

1. Nicholas Kristof begins by asking a question — "Why do they hate us?" — referring to Muslim terrorists (para. 1). How effective is this opening strategy? To what extent does Kristof answer this question in this piece?

2. In the course of relaying Rafi's education to the audience, Kristof discusses both positive and negative results. What are they? What brought about a change in Rafi's attitude?

3. While he is telling Rafi's story, Kristof raises a number of larger issues. What are they? How does he relate these issues to Rafi's situation, and what effect does this have on his main argument?

4. Narrative — that is, storytelling — is Kristof's central rhetorical strategy in this column. What point is he making by telling us the story of Rafiullah Kakar? To what extent do you find Rafi's story compelling as evidence?

5. Readers of the *New York Times*, where this column was published, know Kristof as someone who often writes about international affairs and education. Does his reference to "my friend" Rafi (in both the title and the article itself) add to or undermine his ethos? Explain your response.

6. What does Kristof mean in his closing when he says that "Rafi teaches us that a book can be a more powerful force against extremism than a drone"? Why does he add "[b]ut it has to be the right book!" (para. 18) and how does that idea contribute to his central argument?

7. How does the language Kristof uses to describe Rafi emphasize his admiration of this young man? Cite specific examples to support your response.

8. Although this column received largely positive responses in social media, one thread of criticism that surfaced in its wake holds that Kristof oversimplifies the transformation from poverty to radicalism to educational success story. Do you think this is a fair criticism? Why or why not?

What Is Education For?

DANIELLE ALLEN

Danielle Allen (b. 1971) is an award-winning classicist and political scientist who studied classics as an undergraduate at Princeton and went on to earn doctorates from both the University of Cambridge and Harvard University. Allen is currently Director of the Edmond J. Safra Center for Ethics and professor of government and education at Harvard. She is the author of six books, including *The World of Prometheus: The Politics of Punishing in Democratic Athens* (2000), *Talking to Strangers: Anxieties of Citizenship Since* Brown v. the Board of Education (2004), and most recently, *Education and Equality* (2016). For her unique blend of classics and political science scholarship, Allen was named a MacArthur Foundation Fellow in 2001. In 2016, she became a James Bryant Conant University Professor, the highest faculty honor at Harvard. In the following article, published in the *Boston Review* in 2016, Allen discusses how the concept of citizenship relates to what she sees as the dominant paradigm, or worldview, on education policy in America.

In 2006, the highest court in New York affirmed that students in the state have a right to civic education. It was a decision thirteen years in the making, and it spoke to a fundamental question: What is an education for? Lawyers representing the Campaign for Fiscal Equity (CFE), which brought suit, argued that the purpose of education is to develop not only vocational capacities, but also civic agency. Students, in other words, are entitled to learn in public schools the "basic literacy, calculating, and verbal skills necessary to enable children to eventually function productively as civic participants capable of voting and serving on a jury."

The state, in the position of defendant, did not disagree with the need for civic education. But it argued that once students had completed eighth grade, the public schools had met their responsibility to enable children "to eventually function productively as civic participants." Not coincidentally, the state argued that this education level was adequate preparation for minimum-wage labor.

CFE disagreed, arguing that the standard should be set higher. "Capable" civic participation, Judge Leland DeGrasse finally ruled, includes, for instance, the ability to make sense of complex ballot propositions and follow argumentation about DNA evidence at trial. The court agreed that "meaningful civic participation" and prospects for "competitive employment," not simply minimum-wage employment, demanded a twelfth-grade level of verbal and math skills and similarly advanced competence in social studies and economics. The court ordered New York City to increase school funding with these goals in mind.

In part because of the Great Recession, the state and city failed to deliver, and a new lawsuit is underway. But the economic downturn cannot be blamed for the fact that citizenship remains effectively absent from discussions of education policy, not only in New York but also generally. The dominant policy paradigm attends almost exclusively to education's vocational purpose: the goal is to ensure that young people, and society generally, can compete in a global economy. This view is tightly connected to a technocratic economic policy that focuses on the dissemination of skills as a way to reduce inequality in a technology-dependent economy. The result has been massively increased investment in science, technology, engineering, and mathematics education — STEM — and correspondingly reduced outlays for the humanities.

Yet this is not the only possible response to contemporary inequalities. As economists such as Dani Rodrik have pointed out, gross economic inequalities do not result from an inexorable forward march of technology or globalization or from the nature of markets. They are products of policy choices, which are themselves the outcome of politics. "Inequality," as Joseph Stiglitz argues in *Rewriting the Rules of the American Economy* (2015), "has been a choice." Achieving an economy with more egalitarian outcomes will require different political choices and economic policies. It will require that we choose different rules to govern labor, housing, and financial markets.

Where does education enter the picture? At the most fundamental level.

When we think about education and equality, we tend to think first about distributive questions — for example, how to design a system that will offer the real possibility of equal educational attainment, if not achievement, to all students. The vocational approach imagines that this equal attainment will translate into a wider distribution of skills, which will reduce income inequality.

The civic conception of education suggests a very different way to understand the link between education and equality. This understanding begins with the recognition that fair economic outcomes are aided by a robust democratic process and, therefore, by genuine political equality. Thus an education focused not merely on technical skills, but also on what I call *participatory readiness*, provides a distinct and better way to promote equality through schooling.

Moreover, the aspiration to educate for civic participation and not merely work has important distributive implications. The participatory paradigm demands a higher educational standard than the vocational, and meeting that standard requires that more resources be allocated for schools.

It should not be necessary to argue for a vigorous public commitment to civic education in our society. The vast majority of state constitutions include a right to education tied either explicitly or through legislative history to a civic purpose. In addition, as scholar and litigator Michael Rebell writes, twenty-four state courts "have explicitly held that preparation for capable citizenship is a primary purpose of public education, and no state court has disputed this proposition."

And yet, the argument for civic education is now indispensable. To see why, we should begin by exploring more deeply how the vocational paradigm arose and why it can neither vindicate our rights nor overcome the challenge of inequality.

Equality and the Vocational Paradigm

The language of work and global competitiveness did not always dominate public conversations about education. Its recent ascendancy can be traced to 1957. The Soviet launch of Sputnik, the first satellite, provoked a sense that the United States was falling behind in a Cold War scientific contest. The response was the National Defense Education Act, signed into law in 1958, which increased funding for science and math education, as well as vocational training. The 1983 Reagan administration report *A Nation at Risk* deepened the country's anxiety: "If an unfriendly foreign power had attempted to impose on America the mediocre educational performance that exists today, we might well have viewed it as an act of war," reads one provocative sentence. Although its data were later debunked, *A Nation at Risk* is generally understood to have kicked off the era of school reform that currently shapes education discussion and policy. Tellingly, the commission that produced the report held hearings on "Science, Mathematics, and Technology Education" and "Education for a Productive Role in a Productive Society," but none concerning the humanities, social sciences, or civic education.

By 2007, when the National Academy of Sciences' *Rising above the Gathering Storm* again emphasized the need for significant

improvements in science and technology education, these disciplines had already been consolidated under the umbrella of STEM, a concept that has been employed with equal gusto by education reformers and politicians. "An educated, innovative, motivated workforce — human capital — is the most precious resource of any country in this new, flat world," the report asserts. "Yet there is widespread concern about our K-12 science and mathematics education system, the foundation of that human capital in today's global economy."

Consensus thus emerged in the 1980s around vocational education's essential role in global economic competitiveness. At the same time, economists drew closer connections between education and inequality. By the early 1990s, economists had identified technological change, which biased available jobs toward high-skilled workers, as the primary culprit. It was a short step from this diagnosis to the argument that education was the remedy. That was the lesson of Claudia Goldin and Larry Katz's important book on *The Race between Education and Technology* (2008). In *Capital in the Twenty-First Century* (2014), French economist Thomas Piketty writes, "Historical experience suggests that the principal mechanism for convergence [of incomes and wealth] at the international as well as the domestic level is the diffusion of knowledge. In other words, the poor catch up with the rich to the extent that they achieve the same level of technological know-how, skill, and education." Broad dissemination of skills is expected to drive down the wage premium on expertise and compress the income distribution. To the degree that Piketty's recommendations turn to educational policy, he focuses on access. When he considers curriculum, he is explicit only about vocational goals. Thus he argues that educational institutions should be made broadly accessible; elite institutions, which serve mainly privileged youth from the highest income brackets, should draw students from other backgrounds; schools should be run efficiently; and states should increase investment in "high-quality professional training."

Such arguments from economists — that [15] vocationalism generally and STEM in particular are the solutions both for inequality and for America's ostensibly precarious global economic standing — have been widely adopted at the highest levels of government. President Obama, in his 2013 State of the Union address, announced a competition to "redesign America's high schools." Rewards would go, he said, to schools that develop more classes "that focus on science, technology, engineering, and math — the skills today's employers are looking for to fill jobs right now and in the future." More recently, in his 2016 State of the Union address, the president announced a Computer Science for All initiative that would make students "job-ready on day one."

Today, these technologically oriented, vocational approaches to education and the problem of inequality leave almost no room for the civic alternative. It is not that civic education is incompatible with professional training, but policymakers, education specialists, and many parents — including low-income parents, whose children are most likely to see their civic education shortchanged — have narrowed their focus exclusively to the economic field. In the process, they have lost sight of the full range of inequalities from which our society suffers and which well-rounded education could alleviate.

Equality and the Participatory Paradigm

When we invoke the concept of equality in conversations about education, we generally don't bother to define it or to identify which concept of equality pertains. Is it political equality that concerns us? Social equality? Or economic equality only?

The technology-based analysis of inequality and the vocational paradigm focuses specifically on economic equality. Questions of political equality have no place in this picture. Indeed, the purely technocratic treatment of income and

wealth inequality as problems of technology to be solved through the dissemination of skills is blind precisely to politics.

This is shortsighted because economic inequality is an outgrowth of politics. "Today's world economy is the product of explicit decisions that governments had made in the past," Rodrik writes. "It was the choice of governments to loosen regulations on finance and aim for full cross-border capital mobility, just as it was a choice to maintain these policies largely intact, despite a massive global financial crisis." Or, as Daron Acemoğlu and Jim Robinson argue, "It is the institutions and the political equilibrium of a society that determine how technology evolves, how markets function, and how the gains from various different economic arrangements are distributed."

Piketty agrees that the wage premium [20] on skill can explain only part of growing U.S. income inequality: political forces shape distributive outcomes, and there are limits to how much the advantages of education can be moderated through the dissemination of technological skills. Income growth at the highest end, accruing to what he calls "supermanagers," reflects social acceptance of sky-high executive pay. In his argument, such social norms constitute and reinforce a political ideology endorsing "hypermeritocracy." Reining in income inequality therefore requires not only the dissemination of skill but also social and political change. If political choices determine the rules that shape distributive patterns, it makes sense to focus first on political, not economic, equality. And if we choose political equality as our orienting ideal — empowering all to participate capably in the life of a polity — a different view of education's purpose, content, and consequence comes into view.

In an important 2006 paper, "Why Does Democracy Need Education?" economists Edward L. Glaeser, Giacomo Ponzetto, and Andrei Shleifer argue that education is a causal force behind democracy. Specifically, they point to the relationship between education and participation, considering three hypotheses for why the former might be a source of the latter: through indoctrination, through the cultivation of skills that facilitate participation (reading and writing and "soft skills" of collaboration and interaction), and through the increased material benefits of participation. (On the last, the idea is that education increases income, and participation correlates to socioeconomic status.) The authors reject the first and third hypotheses in favor of the second. Education, they argue, fosters participation because it prepares people for democratic engagement. Reading, writing, and collaboration are, after all, the basic instruments of political action.

An education that prepares every student for civic and political engagement not only supports political equality but may also lead to increased economic fairness. As Acemoğlu and Robinson argue, the expansion of political participation drove egalitarian economic reforms in Britain in the nineteenth century and the United States in the early twentieth. We are currently seeing a resurgence of participation on both the right and left. These movements, dubbed populist by many commentators, are putting issues of distributive justice on the agenda once again.

This resurgence increases the stakes for participatory readiness. It also raises the question of how best to prepare students for their lives as civic agents. While the technological view of the link between education and equality reinforces a vocational approach to curriculum and pedagogy, a participatory view demands a renewed focus on the humanities and social sciences.

Participatory Readiness

So what exactly is participatory readiness, and how can education help people achieve it? To answer these questions, we first need to understand what students should be getting ready for: civic agency. While there is no single model of civic agency dominant in American culture, we can identify a handful at work.

Following philosopher Hannah Arendt,[1] I 25 take citizenship to be the activity of co-creating a way of life, of world-building. This co-creation can occur at many social levels: in a neighborhood or school; in a networked community or association; in a city, state, or nation; at a global scale. Because co-creation extends beyond legal categories of membership in political units, I prefer to speak of civic agency instead of citizenship.

Such civic agency involves three core tasks. First is disinterested deliberation around a public problem. Here the model derives from Athenian citizens gathered in the assembly, the town halls of colonial New Hampshire, and public representatives behaving reasonably in the halls of a legislature. Second is prophetic work intended to shift a society's values; in the public opinion and communications literature, this is now called "frame shifting." Think of the rhetorical power of nineteenth-century abolitionist Harriet Beecher Stowe, of Martin Luther King, Jr., or of Occupy Wall Street activists with their rallying cry of "we are the 99 percent." Finally, there is transparently interested "fair fighting," where a given public actor adopts a cause and pursues it passionately. One might think of early women's rights activists such as Elizabeth Cady Stanton, Susan B. Anthony, and Matilda Joslyn Gage.

The ideal civic agent carries out all three of these tasks — disinterested deliberation, prophetic frame shifting, and fair fighting — ethically and justly. Stanton is an example of this ideal at work. At the Seneca Falls Convention,[2] she was in

---

[1]A prominent twentieth-century political philosopher, Hannah Arendt (1906–1975) was born in Germany but fled after being imprisoned by the Gestapo in 1933. She eventually became a U.S. citizen. Her work primarily explores how democracy, totalitarianism, and authoritarianism function. —Eds.

[2]The first women's rights convention, which took place in Seneca Falls, New York in 1848. —Eds.

deliberative mode for the debate about the text of the Declaration of Sentiments.[3] However, before the convention's deliberations, when she drafted that text, she was in the prophetic mode, just as she was in her innumerable speeches. Finally, in campaigning for legal change, as in the adoption of the Woman's Property Bill[4] in New York and similar laws in other states, she was operating as an activist.

Yet if these three are the rudimentary components of civic agency, they do not in themselves determine the content of any given historical moment's conception of citizenship. There is no need for each of these functions to be combined in a single role or persona, nor is there any guarantee that all three will be carried out in each historical context. These tasks can also become separated from one another, generating distinguishable kinds of civic roles. This is the situation today, as roles have been divided among civically engaged individuals, activists or political entrepreneurs, and professional politicians.

The civically engaged individual focuses on the task of disinterested deliberation and actions that can be said to flow from it. Such citizens pursue what they perceive to be universal values, critical thinking, and bipartisan projects. Next comes the activist, who seeks to change hearts and minds by fighting fairly for particular outcomes, often making considerable sacrifices to do so. Finally, the professional politician, as currently conceived, focuses mainly on fighting, not necessarily fairly. In contemporary discourse, this role, in contrast to the other two, represents a degraded form of civic agency; for evidence one has only to look at Congress's all-time-low approval ratings.

In the current condition, we have lost sight of [30] the statesman, a professional politician capable of disinterested deliberation, just frame shifting, and fighting fair. And, even more importantly, we have lost sight of the ideal ordinary citizen, who is not a professional politician but who has nonetheless developed all of the competencies described above and who is proud to be involved in politics.

If we are to embrace an education for participatory readiness, we need to aim our pedagogic and curricular work not at any one of these three capacities but at what lies behind all of them: the idea of civic agency as the activity of co-creating a way of life. This view of politics supports all three models of citizenship because it nourishes future civic leaders, activists, and politicians. Such an education ought also to permit a reintegration of these roles.

The United States has a history of providing such an education: it is called the liberal arts. How, you may ask, can the seemingly antique liberal arts be of use in our mass democracies and globalized, multicultural world? Let us consider where we find ourselves and how we got here.

Science, technology, engineering, math, and medicine have done much to create the contemporary condition. Thanks to the industrial, aeronautical, biomedical, and digital revolutions, the world's population has grown from one to seven billion in little more than 200 years, a profound historical transformation. We surely need the STEM fields to navigate this new landscape. But if the STEM fields gave us the mass in "mass democracy," the humanities and social sciences gave us the democracy.

The Europeans and American colonists who designed systems of representative democracy capable of achieving continental scale — while employing genocidal techniques in the process — were broadly and deeply educated in history, geography, philosophy, literature, and art. The pithiest summary of the intellectual demands of democratic citizenship that I know appears

---

[3] A document modeled on the Declaration of Independence written primarily by Elizabeth Cady Stanton and signed in 1848 by one hundred attendees of the Seneca Falls Convention. —Eds.

[4] A collection of laws that allowed women to own property, work for an income, and participate in business matters independently of a husband. —Eds.

in the second sentence of the Declaration of Independence, especially the final clause:

> We hold these truths to be self-evident, that all men are created equal; that they are endowed by their Creator with certain unalienable Rights; that among these are Life, Liberty and the pursuit of Happiness — That to secure these Rights, Governments are instituted among Men, deriving their just Powers from the Consent of the Governed; *that whenever any Form of Government becomes destructive of these Ends, it is the Right of the People to alter or to abolish it, and to institute new Government, laying its Foundation on such Principles and organizing its Powers in such Form, as to them shall seem most likely to effect their Safety and Happiness.*

This final clause summarizes the central intellectual labor of the democratic citizen. Citizens must judge whether their governments meet their responsibility, spelled out earlier in the sentence, to secure rights. If a government fails in its core purposes, it is the job of the citizen to figure this out and decide how to change direction. This requires diagnosing social circumstances and making judgments about grounding principles for the political order and about possible alternatives to the formal organization of state power. Properly conducted, the citizen's intellectual labor should result in a probabilistic judgment answering this critical question: What combination of principle and organizational form is most likely to secure collective safety and happiness?

To make judgments about the course of human events and our government's role in them, we need history, anthropology, cultural studies, economics, political science, sociology, and psychology, not to mention math — especially the statistical reasoning necessary for probabilistic judgment — and science, as governmental policy naturally intersects with scientific questions. If we are to decide on the core principles that should orient our judgments about what will bring about safety

and happiness, surely we need philosophy, literature, and religion or its history. Then, since the democratic citizen does not make or execute judgments alone, we need the arts of conversation, eloquence, and prophetic speech. Preparing ourselves to exercise these arts takes us again to literature and to the visual arts, film, and music.

In other words, we need the liberal arts. They were called the free person's arts for a reason.

To say that we need all these disciplines in order to cultivate participatory readiness is not to say that we need precisely the versions of these disciplines that existed in the late eighteenth century. To the contrary, it is the job of today's scholars and teachers, learning from the successes and errors of our predecessors, to build the most powerful intellectual tools we can. Where their versions of the tools were compatible with preserving patriarchy, enslaving black Africans, and committing genocide against indigenous peoples, ours must not be. This revision of the liberal arts curriculum is controversial but necessary, for we want to retain the purposes and intellectual methods of the liberal arts, if not all of its content. We still need to cultivate capacities for social diagnosis, ethical reasoning, cause-and-effect analysis, and persuasive argumentation.

Given that the liberal arts are especially useful for training citizens, it should come as little surprise that attainment in the humanities and social sciences appears to correlate with increased engagement in politics. There is a statistically significant difference between the rates of political participation among humanities and STEM graduates. Data from the Department of Education reveal that, among 2008 college graduates, 92.8 percent of humanities majors have voted at least once since finishing school. Among STEM majors, that number is 83.5 percent. And, within ten years of graduation, 44.1 percent of 1993 humanities graduates had written to public officials, compared to 30.1 percent of STEM majors. As college graduates, the students are generally of

35

similar socioeconomic backgrounds, suggesting that other distinctions must account for the difference in political engagement.

Of course, the self-selection of students into the humanities and STEM majors may mean that these data reflect only underlying features of the students rather than the effects of teaching they receive. Yet the same pattern appears in a study by political scientist Sunshine Hillygus, which controls for students' preexisting levels of interest in politics.

Hillygus also finds that the differences in political engagement among college graduates are mirrored in K-12 education. High SAT verbal scores correlate with increased likelihood of political participation, while high SAT math scores correlate with decreased likelihood of participation. Again, since socioeconomic effects on SAT scores move both verbal and math scores in the same direction, this difference between how high verbal and high math scores affect the likelihood of participation must be telling us something about the relationship between attainment in specific subject domains and participatory readiness. Moreover, the SAT effect endures even when college-level curricular choices are controlled for. Just as Glaeser, Ponzetto, and Shleifer conclude, it is attainment

in the verbal domain that correlates with participatory readiness.

To identify a correlation is not, of course, to identify, let alone prove, causation. But those with more sophisticated verbal skills and with more skills at socio-political analysis are clearly more ready to participate in civic life. Another source of motivation may have engaged them in politics, leading them, once engaged, to seek out the verbal and analytical skills needed to thrive as civic participants. Or verbal competence and social analytical skills may make engagement easier in the first place. We don't have a study that considers levels of engagement before and after significant increases in these kinds of competence. Nonetheless, data suggest that the work of the humanities and social sciences on verbal empowerment and social analysis is intrinsically related to the development of participatory readiness. The riches of the liberal arts of course extend well beyond verbal empowerment and social analysis, but these core activities are themselves of immense value. Such equality as the world has managed to achieve — whether political or economic — can often be traced to the operations of these human capacities.

seeing connections

During the Great Depression, President Franklin Delano Roosevelt created the Works Progress Administration (WPA) in an effort to revive the economy. The WPA employed millions of Americans, who carried out everything from public works projects such as highway construction to artistic endeavors such as murals and music concerts. Look carefully at the WPA posters shown here.

How does each of them endorse the idea of "participatory readiness," especially as it relates to education? Why might such public forums be seen as particularly important during times of economic strife?

Library of Congress

Library of Congress

Library of Congress

Library of Congress

♦ ♦ ♦

Few among us pay adequate attention to the fact that almost all of our state constitutions guarantee a right to education. We pay even less attention to the fact that we have a right to civic education. Our state constitutions, in other words, are directed at the pursuit of equality. Through the acquisition of participatory readiness, a great diversity of citizens could tap into the power to challenge oligarchical social and political arrangements.

In the final analysis, the reliance on an exclusively vocational paradigm as the sole guide to education policy-making is a failure to meet the legal standard for securing a basic right. Precisely those parts of the K-12 curriculum most vulnerable during a recession — humanities, social studies, arts, and extracurricular activities such as debate and model UN — deserve rights-based legal protection. What is more, defending the right to civic education, and the kind of curriculum that delivers it, would benefit not only individual students but also society as a whole, advancing both political equality and distributive justice. This is an untapped source of advocacy around educational rights and on behalf of an egalitarian America.

[2016]

EXPLORING THE TEXT

1. Danielle Allen opens by summarizing the legal argument the Campaign for Fiscal Equity (CFE) makes: that "the purpose of education is to develop not only vocational capacities, but also civic agency" (para. 1). What does she mean by "civic agency"? To what extent do you agree with the CFE (and Allen) on this key point?

2. Allen argues that the "dominant policy paradigm" privileges job preparation "in a technology-dependent economy" (para. 4). How does she challenge the belief that this approach will help to level "contemporary inequalities" (para. 5)?

3. In paragraphs 7 and 8, Allen summarizes two different explanations of the link between education and equality. What are they? How is each related to what she calls "distributive implications" (para. 9)?

4. In the section entitled "Equality and the Vocational Paradigm," Allen provides a history, starting in the 1950s, of how concern for global competitiveness has influenced educational policy. How does this historical perspective contribute to the development of her argument?

5. In what ways does paragraph 16 ("Today, these technologically oriented, vocational approaches to education . . .") signal a shift in Allen's argument?

6. In paragraph 20, Allen discusses political, social, and economic inequality in relationship to education — and reaches the conclusion that we should shift the primary focus of education to political rather than economic equality. To what extent do you agree with her? Explain your response.

7. What does Allen mean by "participatory readiness," a phrase she introduces in paragraph 8 and uses throughout the essay? What distinction does she make between "civic agency" and "citizenship"? To what extent do you think your education thus far has fostered participatory readiness, according to Allen's definition?

8. In Allen's view, how does Elizabeth Cady Stanton embody the three core ideals of civic agency (disinterested deliberation, prophetic work, and fair fighting)? Can you think of another public figure, historic or contemporary, whose work also expresses these three ideals? Explain specifically how.

9. Allen argues that today's "professional politician . . . represents a degraded form of civic agency"; she says we have "lost sight of the statesman" (paras. 29–30). On what grounds does she support this claim? To what extent do you agree with her?

10. In the final part of her argument, Allen asserts the importance of "the seemingly antique liberal arts" in education (para. 32). In fact, she goes on to state that they are "the free person's arts" (para. 37). How does she support this position? What do you think is her strongest point? Her most vulnerable to criticism?

11. What is the correlation that Allen discusses between political engagement and education in the humanities and social sciences? How does she address potential counterarguments? Explain

why you find this analysis effective or ineffective evidence to support her argument about the importance of liberal arts.

12. Allen calls the final clause of the second sentence of the Declaration of Independence a summary of "the central intellectual labor of the democratic citizen" (para. 35). Why does she believe this to be the case? How persuasive is she is in tying this clause to her argument for a liberal arts education?

13. According to its website, the *Boston Review*, where this essay appeared, is a publication that is "a public space for robust discussion of ideas and culture. Independent and nonprofit, animated by hope and committed to equality, we believe in the power of collective reasoning and imagination to create a more just world." Keeping this in mind, what specific rhetorical strategies has Allen employed to reach her audience? Discuss at least three.

14. Allen's article provoked a number of responses, including challenges such as the following by Carleton College educational policy professor Jeffrey Aaron Snyder:

> In spite of its checkered track record, vocational education remains an integral part of schooling in the United States. The insistent call for more STEM education reflects a vocational training ideal, forecasting

that enhanced coursework in these fields will allow students to plug into the new digital economy after they graduate. While we have reason to be skeptical about tidy claims such as these, the human-capital approach to education is hard to resist in light of today's economic and political landscape. There are nearly 47 million Americans living in poverty, just under 15 percent of the population. There are, of course, stark racial disparities in play here as well, with the poverty rate for Latinos and African Americans higher than 20 percent. Recent polling shows Americans consider the economy the most important problem facing the country. . . . In an age of staggering economic inequality, how does Allen suggest we turn the public's attention to political equality?

How would you defend Allen's argument in light of such concerned criticism?

15. Allen cites philosopher Hannah Arendt's concept of citizenship as "the activity of co-creating a way of life," whether at the local level of neighborhood or school, a networked community, or a national or international level (para. 25). What is one way that you are trying to embody this view of citizenship at this point in your life? That is, how are you "co-creating a way of life, of world-building"?

Have We Lost Sight of the Promise of Public Schools?

NIKOLE HANNAH-JONES

Nikole Hannah-Jones (b. 1976) is an award-winning reporter known for her in-depth coverage of civil rights issues. Originally from Waterloo, Iowa, Hannah-Jones earned a BA in history and African American studies from Notre Dame in 1998 and an MA in journalism and mass communication from the University of North Carolina at Chapel Hill in 2003. After working for several news outlets across the country, she joined the *New York Times* in 2015. Hannah-Jones's coverage of race, inequality, and education, has earned her a National Magazine Award, a Peabody Award, and a Polk Award. The following article, published in the *New York Times Magazine* in 2017, was written in response to the confirmation of Betsy DeVos as secretary of education.

In the days leading up to and after Betsy DeVos's confirmation as secretary of education, a hashtag spread across Twitter: #publicschool-proud. Parents and teachers tweeted photos of

their kids studying, performing, eating lunch together. People of all races tweeted about how public schools changed them, saved them, helped them succeed. The hashtag and storytelling was a rebuttal to DeVos, who called traditional public schools a "dead end" and who bankrolled efforts to pass reforms in Michigan, her home state, that would funnel public funds in the form of vouchers into religious and privately operated schools and encouraged the proliferation of for-profit charter schools. The tweets railed against DeVos's labeling of public schools as an industry that needed to adopt the free-market principles of competition and choice. #Publicschoolproud was seen as an effort to show that public schools still mattered.

But the enthusiastic defense obscured a larger truth: We began moving away from the "public" in public education a long time ago. In fact, treating public schools like a business these days is largely a matter of fact in many places. Parents have pushed for school-choice policies that encourage shopping for public schools that they hope will give their children an advantage and for the expansion of charter schools that are run by private organizations with public funds. Large numbers of public schools have selective admissions policies that keep most kids out.

And parents pay top dollar to buy into neighborhoods zoned to "good" public schools that can be as exclusive as private ones. The glaring reality is, whether we are talking about schools or other institutions, it seems as if we have forgotten what "public" really means.

The word derives from the Latin word *publicus*, meaning "of the people." This concept — that the government belongs to the people and the government should provide for the good of the people — was foundational to the world's nascent democracies. Where once citizens paid taxes to the monarchy in the hope that it would serve the public too, in democracies they paid taxes directly for infrastructure and institutions that benefited society as a whole. The tax dollars of ancient Athenians and Romans built roads and aqueducts, but they also provided free meals to widows whose husbands died in war. "Public" stood not just for how something was financed — with the tax dollars of citizens — but for a communal ownership of institutions and for a society that privileged the common good over individual advancement.

Rob Tornoe/Cagle Cartoons, Inc.

How does this cartoon relate to Nikole Hannah-Jones's argument about the purpose of public schools? On what basis would she agree or disagree with the message this cartoon conveys?

Early on, it was this investment in public institutions that set America apart from other countries. Public hospitals ensured that even the indigent received good medical care — health problems for some could turn into epidemics for us all. Public parks gave access to the great outdoors not just to the wealthy who could retreat to their country estates but to the masses in the nation's cities. Every state invested in public universities. Public schools became widespread in the 1800s, not to provide an advantage for particular individuals but with the understanding that shuffling the wealthy and working class together (though not black Americans and other racial minorities) would create a common sense of citizenship and national identity, that it would tie together the fates of the haves and the have-nots and that doing so benefited the nation. A sense of the public good was a unifying force because it meant that the rich and the poor, the powerful and the meek, shared the spoils — as well as the burdens — of this messy democracy.

◆ ◆ ◆

Achieving this has never been an easy feat. The   5
tension between individual striving and the common good, between the beliefs that strong government protects and provides for its citizens and that big government leads to tyranny, has always existed in this country. As a result, support for public institutions and expansive government has ebbed and flowed. When Franklin Delano Roosevelt, in response to the Great Depression, ushered through the biggest expansion of federal programs in our nation's history, he did so because he thought that government regulation was necessary to empower common people against corporations and banks but also that government should provide certain protections for its citizens. Under the New Deal, we got Social Security and unemployment insurance. Federal housing projects — public housing — meant quality dwellings for the nation's working people.

Federal works projects employed millions of out-of-work Americans and brought infrastructure to communities that had not been able to pay for it on their own.

At the same time, the New Deal stoked the ire of a small-government, antiregulation minority, who began to push back, though it would take some decades before their views became mainstream. They promoted free-market principles, deregulation and the privatization of functions normally handled by the government and sought to define all things — like the benefits of education — strictly in terms of their economic value.

Nonetheless, Roosevelt's government expansion was widely supported, and Americans elected him to an unprecedented four terms as president. But the broad support of public programs and institutions hinged on a narrow definition of who that public was: white Americans. To get his New Deal passed, Roosevelt compromised with white Southerners in Congress, and much of the legislation either explicitly or implicitly discriminated against black citizens, denying them many of its benefits.

As the civil rights movement gained ground in the 1950s and 1960s, however, a series of court rulings and new laws ensured that black Americans now had the same legal rights to public schools, libraries, parks and swimming pools as white Americans. But as black Americans became part of the public, white Americans began to pull away. Instead of sharing their public pools with black residents — whose tax dollars had also paid for them — white Americans founded private clubs (often with public funds) or withdrew behind their fences where they dug their own pools. Public housing was once seen as a community good that drew presidents for photo ops. But after federal housing policies helped white Americans buy their own homes in the suburbs, black Americans, who could not get government-subsidized mortgages, languished in public housing, which became stigmatized. Where once public transportation showed a city's forward progress, white communities

seeing connections

Nikole Hannah-Jones refers to the Depression-era New Deal as she develops her argument. Public murals such as Maxine Albro's *California*, painted inside San Francisco's Coit Tower in 1934, were part of that program. Some details of that mural are shown below.

How does — or can — art created for public spaces contribute to the concept of "public good" that Hannah-Jones believes is essential to education in a democracy?

began to fight its expansion, fearing it would give unwanted people access to their enclaves.

And white Americans began to withdraw from public schools or move away from school districts with large numbers of black children once the courts started mandating desegregation. Some communities shuttered public schools altogether rather than allow black children to share publicly funded schools with white children. The very voucher movement that is at the heart of DeVos's educational ideas was born of white opposition to school desegregation as state and local governments offered white children vouchers to pay for private schools — known as segregation academies — that sprouted across the South after the Supreme Court struck down school segregation in 1954.

"What had been enjoyed as a public thing by   10
white citizens became a place of forced encounter with other people from whom they wanted to be separate," Bonnie Honig, a professor of political science and modern culture and media at Brown University and author of the forthcoming book *Public Things: Democracy in Disrepair*, told me. "The attractiveness of private schools and other forms of privatization are not just driven by economization but by the desire to control the community with which you interact."

◆ ◆ ◆

Even when they fail, the guiding values of public institutions, of the public good, are equality and justice. The guiding value of the free market is profit. The for-profit charters DeVos helped expand have not provided an appreciably better education for Detroit's children, yet they've continued to expand because they are profitable — or as Tom Watkins, Michigan's former education superintendent, said, "In a number of cases, people are making a boatload of money, and the kids aren't getting educated."

Democracy works only if those who have the money or the power to opt out of public things choose instead to opt in for the common good. It's called a social contract, and we've seen what happens in cities where the social contract is broken: White residents vote against tax hikes to fund schools where they don't send their children, parks go untended and libraries shutter because affluent people feel no obligation to help pay for things they don't need. "The existence of public things — to meet each other, to fight about, to pay for together, to enjoy, to complain about — this is absolutely indispensable to democratic life," Honig says.

If there is hope for a renewal of our belief in public institutions and a common good, it may reside in the public schools. Nine of 10 children attend one, a rate of participation that few, if any, other public bodies can claim, and schools, as segregated as many are, remain one of the few institutions where Americans of different classes and races mix. The vast multiracial, socioeconomically diverse defense of public schools that DeVos set off may show that we have not yet given up on the ideals of the public — and on ourselves.

[2017]

EXPLORING THE TEXT

1. Nikole Hannah-Jones opens her essay by discussing the 2017 hearings to approve Betsy DeVos as secretary of education, specifically reacting to DeVos's characterization of public schools as a "dead end" (para. 1). Was this an effective way to launch into her analysis of public education, its history, and its role in a democracy? Keep in mind the audience as you support your response.

2. How does Hannah-Jones support her claim that "treating public schools like a business these days is largely a matter of fact" (para. 2)?

3. When Hannah-Jones calls the United States "this messy democracy" (para. 4), is she being negative or positive? Is she setting herself up as a critic, a patriot, or a little of both?

4. Hannah-Jones supports her assertion that we have lost site of the "'public' in public education" (para. 2) with historical facts and analysis. In fact, she begins with ancient Greece and Rome, early democracies, and then moves to the United States. What is her reasoning in this section (paras. 3–10)? How effective do you believe her use of history as evidence is here? How does such evidence appeal to both logos and pathos?

5. Hannah-Jones shines a bright light on the role of race in changing the meaning of "public" schools in paragraphs 8–10. To what extent do you think she risks offending or alienating her audience with this brief interpretation? Or is this section key to achieving her purpose? Pay careful attention to her language and tone as you explain your viewpoint.

6. What does Hannah-Jones mean by the "social contract" (para. 12)? Why is this concept vital to her argument?

7. Hannah-Jones cites only one contemporary expert (Bonnie Honig) and a single statistic in her argument (in the final paragraph). To what extent were these choices an effective rhetorical strategy to develop her argument?

8. Ultimately, how does Hannah-Jones answer the question she poses in her title? Explain why you agree or disagree with her. Refer to specifics in the essay as well as your own experience and knowledge.

VISUAL TEXTS

The Exam Room

CYRIL EDWARD POWER

Cyril Edward Power (1872–1951) was a prolific English artist, architect, and teacher primarily known for linocut, a printing process like woodcutting in which a design is cut into linoleum before being rolled with ink and impressed onto fabric or paper. He wrote *A History of English Mediaeval Architecture* (1912) before managing repairs for the Royal Flying Corps during World War I. After the war, Power engaged in a career of artistic printmaking, co-authoring many prints with the artist Sybil Andrews. Power also helped found and lectured frequently at The Grosvenor School of Modern Art in London. He was elected to the Royal Society of British Artists in 1930. Considered a Modernist work, *The Exam Room* is a linocut emblematic of Powers's style. It was made around 1934, the year it was exhibited alongside other linocuts in London's Redfern Gallery.

CHRISTIES IMAGES/Private Collection/Bridgeman Images

[1934]

EXPLORING THE TEXT

1. In what ways does this image capture the tension and pressure of the experience of taking an exam? Pay attention to the lines (vertical and horizontal), the geometric shapes, and color.

2. In what ways do the eyes, the distorted clock, and the standing figure serve as symbols?

3. The style of this piece has been described as "hallucinatory realism." Is that an oxymoron — or does it capture the mood of the piece?

4. What argument is the artist making in this image? State his claim and then explain what visual rhetorical strategies he uses as evidence.

5. What music might you pair with this print? Working in groups, choose a piece of music, with or without lyrics, and discuss why you believe it comments on, reflects, or provides a counterpoint to the visual image.

6. Although the artist created this work in 1934, does it strike you as antiquated? To what extent is "the exam room" the same today — even if computer screens have entered the scene?

What I Learned
A Sentimental Education from Nursery School through Twelfth Grade

ROZ CHAST

Roz Chast (b. 1954) grew up in Brooklyn as the only child of a schoolteacher and an assistant principal, and received a BFA in painting from the Rhode Island School of Design. After she graduated, as she says on her website, she "reverted to type and began drawing cartoons once again." More than a thousand of her cartoons have been published in the *New Yorker* magazine since 1978. A collection of twenty-five years of her work was published in *Theories of Everything* (2006). Chast collaborated with comedian and novelist Steve Martin on the children's book *The Alphabet from A to Y with a Bonus Letter Z!* (2007), and has also written numerous children's books and cartoon collections, including *Too Busy Marco* (2010), *What I Hate: From A–Z* (2011), *Can't We Talk About Something More Pleasant?* (2014), and most recently, *Around the Clock* (2015). She has won many awards and received an Honorary Doctorate of Fine Arts from Pratt Institute and the Art Institute of Boston. Chast is known for her wry commentaries on the experiences of ordinary life, such as going to school, which the following cartoon depicts. She has written of her own experience: "I doodled all the time in school — that is what kept me from going completely out of my head."

WHAT I LEARNED:

© Roz Chast/The New Yorker Collection/www.cartoonbank.com

A Sentimental Education

...and boys played Cars and Trucks.

VROOM, VROOM!

BAM BAM BAM BAM!

RMMMM! RMMM! RMMM!

ACME

I liked the Art Corner.

Ooh! Is that a horsie?

No.

I learned that it was very unlikely that I'd become an Olympic anything.

GET THE BALL!

GET THE BALL!

GET THE BALL!

GET THE BALL!

GET THE BALL!

GET THE BALL!

GET THE BALL!

GET THE BALL!

Up through sixth grade, I learned lots of stuff: addition; spelling; all about explorers; how to do a chain stitch; subtraction; how to read and write; multiplication; fractions; how banks worked (a little); how to play punchball (theoretically); division; where crops came from; about planets; what was meant by "Current Events"; about George Washington and Johnny Appleseed; that a heart wasn't shaped like a heart at all; and lots, lots more.

E-I
R·E·C·I·E·V·E

DAILY TIMES

OUR FRIEND WHEAT

OUR FRIEND CORN

MID-BROOKLYN BANK FOR SAVINGS

PENSEYS PINKY

16)40687

THE STORY OF COLUMBUS
LEIF ERIKSSON
MAGELLAN'S TALE
WHO WAS VASCO da GAMA?

La, la, la.

APPLE SEEDS

371 × 86

AaBb   eFf

And, of course, I was learning more about being good.

- Do homework.
- Be neat.
- Be organized.
- Be quiet.
- Pay attention.
- **BE GOOD!!**

It wasn't until junior high that I really started to wonder about the whole setup.

Class, today we're going to memorize all the prepositions.

Oh, my GOD...

Why did we have to learn this? Who said?

...so the sine of a 36° angle is 0.5877853.

What is the Elgin-Marcy Treaty of 1854?

Can anyone tell me the atomic weight of...

FROM NURSERY SCHOOL THROUGH TWELFTH GRADE

[2006]

EXPLORING THE TEXT

1. Identify one part of this cartoon, a single frame or several, that you find to be an especially effective synergy of written and visual text. Why do you think the section you chose works so well?

2. On the second page, the middle frame is a large one with a whole list of what Roz Chast learned "Up through sixth grade." Is she suggesting that all these things are foolish or worthless? Explain your response.

3. The three-page cartoon presents a narrative, a story. Discuss the extent to which Chast uses the techniques of a fiction writer, such as plot, character, and setting.

4. Chast subtitles her cartoon "A Sentimental Education . . . ," which is a reference to a French novel of that title written by Gustave Flaubert in 1869. The American writer Henry James described *Sentimental Education* as far inferior to Flaubert's earlier and more successful novel *Madame Bovary*; in fact, he characterized the 1869 work as "elaborately and massively dreary." Why do you think Chast uses this reference to Flaubert's novel? Or do you think that she is not specifically alluding to Flaubert but, rather, to more generalized "sentimental" notions of education? Consider her audience as you respond to these questions.

5. What, ultimately, is Chast's critique? What is the relationship she sees among learning, K-12 school, and education?

The Future of High School

Each of the following texts presents a viewpoint on the American high school.

SOURCES

1   **Horace Mann** / from *Report of the Massachusetts Board of Education*
2   **Leon Botstein** / *Let Teenagers Try Adulthood*
3   ***Meditation in Schools across America*** (infographic)
4   **Nicholas Wyman** / *Why We Desperately Need to Bring Back Vocational Training in Schools*
5   **Amanda Ripley** / from *What America Can Learn from Smart Schools in Other Countries*
6   **Leslie Nguyen-Okwu** / *How High Schools Are Demolishing the Classroom*
7   **Brentin Mock** / from *We Will Pay High School Students to Go to School. And We Will Like It.*
8   **Amy Rolph** / *This High School Wants to Revolutionize Learning with Technology*

After you have read, studied, and synthesized these pieces, enter the Conversation through one of the suggested topics on p. 289.

from **Report of the Massachusetts Board of Education**

HORACE MANN

The following selection is taken from an official 1848 policy document by Horace Mann (1796–1859), who is known as the father of American public education.

Intellectual Education as a Means of Removing Poverty, and Securing Abundance

. . . According to the European theory, men are divided into classes, — some to toil and earn, others to seize and enjoy. According to the Massachusetts theory, all are to have an equal chance for earning, and equal security in the enjoyment of what they earn. The latter tends to equality of condition; the former, to the grossest inequalities. . . .

But is it not true that Massachusetts, in some respects, instead of adhering more and more closely to her own theory, is becoming emulous of the baneful examples of Europe? The distance between the two extremes of society is lengthening, instead of being abridged. With every generation,

fortunes increase on the one hand, and some new privation is added to poverty on the other. We are verging towards those extremes of opulence and of penury, each of which unhumanizes the human mind. A perpetual struggle for the bare necessaries of life, without the ability to obtain them, makes men wolfish. Avarice, on the other hand, sees, in all the victims of misery around it, not objects for pity and succor, but only crude materials to be worked up into more money.

I suppose it to be the universal sentiment of all those who mingle any ingredient of benevolence with their notions on political economy, that vast and overshadowing private fortunes are among the greatest dangers to which the happiness of the people in a republic can be subjected. Such fortunes would create a feudalism of a new kind, but one more oppressive and unrelenting than that of the middle ages. The feudal lords in England and on the Continent never held their retainers in a more abject condition of servitude than the great majority of foreign manufacturers and capitalists hold their operatives and laborers at the present day. The means employed are different; but the similarity in results is striking. What force did then, money does now. The villein[1] of the middle ages had no spot of earth on which he could live, unless one were granted to him by his lord. The operative or laborer of the present day has no employment, and therefore no bread, unless the capitalist will accept his services. The vassal had no shelter but such as his master provided for him. Not one in five thousand of English operatives or farm-laborers is able to build or own even a hovel; and therefore they must accept such shelter as capital offers them. The baron prescribed his own terms to his retainers: those terms were peremptory, and the serf must submit or perish. The British manufacturer or farmer prescribes the rate of wages he will give to his work-people; he reduces these wages under whatever pretext he pleases; and they, too, have no alternative but submission or starvation. In some respects, indeed, the condition of the modern dependent is more forlorn than that of the corresponding serf class in former times. Some attributes of the patriarchal relation did spring up between the lord and his lieges to soften the harsh relations subsisting between them. Hence came some oversight of the condition of children, some relief in sickness, some protection and support in the decrepitude of age. But only in instances comparatively few have kindly offices smoothed the rugged relation between British capital and British labor. The children of the work-people are abandoned to their fate; and notwithstanding the privations they suffer, and the dangers they threaten, no power in the realm has yet been able to secure them an education; and when the adult laborer is prostrated by sickness, or eventually worn out by toil and age, the poorhouse, which has all along been his destination, becomes his destiny. . . .

Now, surely nothing but universal education can counterwork this tendency to the domination of capital and servility of labor. If one class possesses all the wealth and the education, while the residue of society is ignorant and poor, it matters not by what name the relation between them may be called: the latter, in fact and in truth, will be the servile dependants and subjects of the former. But, if education be equally diffused, it will draw property after it by the strongest of all attractions, for such a thing never did happen, and never can happen, as that an intelligent and practical body of men should be permanently poor. Property and labor in different classes are essentially antagonistic; but property and labor in the same class are essentially fraternal. The people of Massachusetts have, in some degree, appreciated the truth, that the unexampled prosperity of the State — its comfort, its competence, its general intelligence and virtue — is attributable to the education, more or less perfect, which all its people have received: but are they sensible of a fact equally important; namely, that it is to this same education that two-thirds of the people are indebted for not being today the vassals of as severe a tyranny, in the form of capital, as the lower classes of Europe are bound to in the form of brute force?

Education, then, beyond all other devices of human origin, is the great equalizer of the conditions of men — the balance-wheel of the social machinery. I do not here mean that it so elevates the moral nature as to make men disdain and abhor the oppression of their fellow-men. This idea pertains to another of its

5

---

[1]In a feudal society, a serf who has the right to own property. —Eds.

attributes. But I mean that it gives each man the independence and the means by which he can resist the selfishness of other men. It does better than to disarm the poor of their hostility towards the rich: it prevents being poor. Agrarianism is the revenge of poverty against wealth. The wanton destruction of the property of others — the burning of hay-ricks and corn-ricks, the demolition of machinery because it supersedes hand-labor, the sprinkling of vitriol on rich dresses — is only agrarianism run mad. Education prevents both the revenge and the madness. On the other hand, a fellow-feeling for one's class or caste is the common instinct of hearts not wholly sunk in selfish regards for person or for family. The spread of education, by enlarging the cultivated class or caste, will open a wider area over which the social feelings will expand; and, if this education should be universal and complete, it would do more than all things else to obliterate factitious distinctions in society. . . .

For the creation of wealth, then, — for the existence of a wealthy people and a wealthy nation, — intelligence is the grand condition. The number of improvers will increase as the intellectual constituency, if I may call it, increases. In former times, and in most parts of the world even at the present day, not one man in a million has ever had such a development of mind as made it possible for him to become a contributor to art or science. Let this development precede, and contributions, numberless, and of inestimable value, will be sure to follow. That political economy, therefore, which busies itself about capital and labor, supply and demand, interest and rents, favorable and unfavorable balances of trade, but leaves out of account the element of a widespread mental development, is nought but stupendous folly. The greatest of all the arts in political economy is to change a consumer into a producer; and the next greatest is to increase the producer's producing power, — an end to be directly attained by increasing his intelligence. For mere delving, an ignorant man is but little better than a swine, whom he so much resembles in his appetites, and surpasses in his powers of mischief.

QUESTIONS

1. Why does Horace Mann begin with a description of the "feudal lords in England and on the Continent" (para. 3)?

2. What does Mann mean by the following statement: "Property and labor in different classes are essentially antagonistic; but property and labor in the same class are essentially fraternal" (para. 4)?

3. When Mann uses the term *intelligence*, does he mean innate ability or developed skill?

4. How does Mann draw the connection between democracy in a young nation and the educational opportunities for its citizenry?

5. Mann is writing about the foundations of American society and how education contributes to the country's sense of self. What are two issues that he raises in this context that are relevant to an assessment of high school as we know it today?

6. Identify one claim Mann makes and explain whether you believe it remains true today.

2 Let Teenagers Try Adulthood

LEON BOTSTEIN

The following opinion piece, published in the *New York Times* in 1999, was written by Leon Botstein, president of Bard College and author of *Jefferson's Children: Education and the Promise of American Culture* (1997).

The national outpouring after the Littleton [Columbine High School] shootings has forced us to confront something we have suspected for a long time: the American high school is obsolete and should be abolished. In the . . . month [after the shootings] high school students present and past [came] forward with stories about cliques and the artificial intensity of a world defined by insiders and outsiders, in which the insiders hold sway because of superficial definitions of good looks and attractiveness, popularity and sports prowess.

The team sports of high school dominate more than student culture. A community's loyalty to the high school system is often based on the extent to which varsity teams succeed. High school administrators and faculty members are often former coaches, and the coaches themselves are placed in a separate, untouchable category. The result is that the culture of the inside elite is not contested by the adults in the school. Individuality and dissent are discouraged.

But the rules of high school turn out not to be the rules of life. Often the high school outsider becomes the more successful and admired adult. The definitions of masculinity and femininity go through sufficient transformation to make the game of popularity in high school an embarrassment. No other group of adults young or old is confined to an age-segregated environment, much like a gang in which individuals of the same age group define each other's world. In no workplace, not even in colleges or universities, is there such a narrow segmentation by chronology.

Given the poor quality of recruitment and training for high school teachers, it is no wonder that the curriculum and the enterprise of learning hold so little sway over young people. When puberty meets education and learning in modern America, the victory of puberty masquerading as popular culture and the tyranny of peer groups based on ludicrous values meet little resistance.

By the time those who graduate from high school go on to college and realize what really is at stake in becoming an adult, too many opportunities have been lost and too much time has been wasted. Most thoughtful young people suffer the high school environment in silence and in their junior and senior years mark time waiting for college to begin. The Littleton killers, above and beyond the psychological demons that drove them to violence, felt trapped in the artificiality of the high school world and believed it to be real. They engineered their moment of undivided attention and importance in the absence of any confidence that life after high school could have a different meaning.

Adults should face the fact that they don't like adolescents and that they have used high school to isolate the pubescent and hormonally active adolescent away from both the picture-book idealized innocence of childhood and the more accountable world of adulthood. But the primary reason high school doesn't work anymore, if it ever did, is that young people mature substantially earlier in the late 20th century than they did when the high school was invented. For example, the age of first menstruation has dropped at least two years since the beginning of this century, and not surprisingly, the onset of sexual activity has dropped in proportion. An institution intended for children in transition now holds young adults back well beyond the developmental point for which high school was originally designed.

Furthermore, whatever constraints to the presumption of adulthood among young people may have existed decades ago have now fallen away. Information and images, as well as the real and virtual freedom of movement we associate with adulthood, are now accessible to every 15- and 16-year-old.

Secondary education must be rethought. Elementary school should begin at age 4 or 5 and end with the sixth grade. We should entirely abandon the concept of the middle school and junior high school. Beginning with the seventh grade, there should be four years of secondary education that we may call high school. Young people should graduate at 16 rather than 18.

They could then enter the real world, the world of work or national service, in which they would take a place of responsibility alongside older adults in mixed company. They could stay at home and attend junior college, or they could go away to college. For all the faults of college, at least the adults who dominate the world of colleges, the faculty, were selected precisely because they were exceptional and different, not because they were popular. Despite the often cavalier attitude toward teaching in college, at least physicists know their physics, mathematicians know and love their mathematics, and music is taught by musicians, not by graduates of education schools, where the disciplines are subordinated to the study of classroom management.

For those 16-year-olds who do not want to do 10 any of the above, we might construct new kinds of institutions, each dedicated to one activity, from science to dance, to which adolescents could devote their energies while working together with professionals in those fields.

At 16, young Americans are prepared to be taken seriously and to develop the motivations and interests that will serve them well in adult life. They need to enter a world where they are not in a lunchroom with only their peers, estranged from other age groups and cut off from the game of life as it is really played. There is nothing utopian about this idea; it is immensely practical and efficient, and its implementation is long overdue. We need to face biological and cultural facts and not prolong the life of a flawed institution that is out of date.

QUESTIONS

1. In his opening, Leon Botstein states, "[T]he American high school is obsolete and should be abolished" (para. 1). Why? What specific reasons does he provide?

2. Do you agree with Botstein that the Columbine High School violence is evidence that high school in general is antiquated? How persuasively does he prove this connection?

3. What does Botstein mean by "the rules of high school turn out not to be the rules of life" (para. 3)?

4. What is Botstein's proposed solution?

5. Where does Botstein address a counterargument? Does he refute (or concede) in sufficient detail to be persuasive?

6. Which parts of Botstein's reasoning do you find to be the strongest? The weakest? Explain.

7. Is this article, written in 1999, still relevant today? Has the situation in high schools as Botstein describes it remained pretty much the same?

3 Meditation in Schools across America

The following infographic was published in 2012 by Edutopia, a self-described "comprehensive website and online community that increases knowledge, sharing, and adoption of what works in K-12 education."

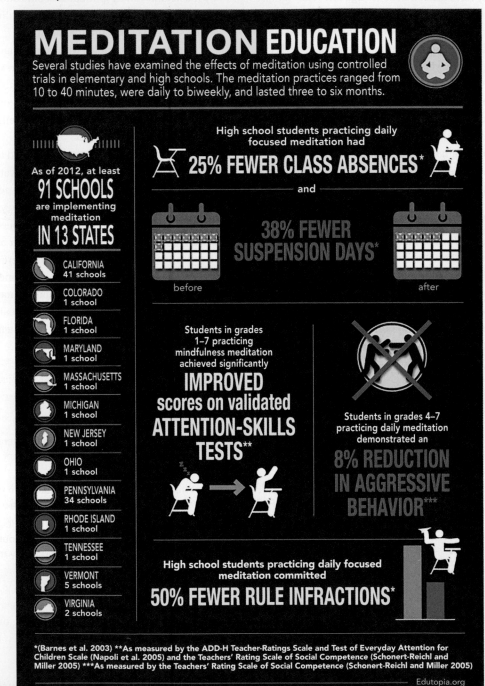

MEDITATION EDUCATION

Several studies have examined the effects of meditation using controlled trials in elementary and high schools. The meditation practices ranged from 10 to 40 minutes, were daily to biweekly, and lasted three to six months.

As of 2012, at least
91 SCHOOLS
are implementing meditation
IN 13 STATES

CALIFORNIA
41 schools

COLORADO
1 school

FLORIDA
1 school

MARYLAND
1 school

MASSACHUSETTS
1 school

MICHIGAN
1 school

NEW JERSEY
1 school

OHIO
1 school

PENNSYLVANIA
34 schools

RHODE ISLAND
1 school

TENNESSEE
1 school

VERMONT
5 schools

VIRGINIA
2 schools

High school students practicing daily focused meditation had
25% FEWER CLASS ABSENCES*
and
38% FEWER SUSPENSION DAYS*

before   after

Students in grades 1–7 practicing mindfulness meditation achieved significantly
IMPROVED scores on validated **ATTENTION-SKILLS TESTS****

Students in grades 4–7 practicing daily meditation demonstrated an
8% REDUCTION IN AGGRESSIVE BEHAVIOR***

High school students practicing daily focused meditation committed
50% FEWER RULE INFRACTIONS*

*(Barnes et al. 2003) **As measured by the ADD-H Teacher-Ratings Scale and Test of Everyday Attention for Children Scale (Napoli et al. 2005) and the Teachers' Rating Scale of Social Competence (Schonert-Reichl and Miller 2005) ***As measured by the Teachers' Rating Scale of Social Competence (Schonert-Reichl and Miller 2005)

Edutopia.org

This infographic was published in 2012 by Edutopia, a comprehensive web site and online community that increases knowledge, sharing, and adoption of what works in K-12 education.

QUESTIONS

1. What problems does this graphic suggest public schools need to address?

2. What additional information would you need to know about the studies the graphic is based on before you would endorse daily meditation as a part of high school curriculum?

3. Given the improvements that this infographic attributes to meditation, what can you conclude

are the skills and behaviors valued in high school? How does your conclusion affect your attitude toward meditation in school?

4. Have you ever practiced meditation? Based on this experience or what you know of meditation, how do you think your peers would respond to meditation as a requirement? As an extracurricular activity?

4 Why We Desperately Need to Bring Back Vocational Training in Schools

NICHOLAS WYMAN

Nicholas Wyman is the CEO of the Institute for Workplace Skills and Innovation, a global enterprise committed to skills and workforce development, and author of *Job U: How to Find Wealth and Success by Developing the Skills Companies Actually Need* (2015). Wyman published this article in *Forbes* magazine in 2015.

Throughout most of U.S. history, American high school students were routinely taught vocational and job-ready skills along with the three Rs: reading, writing and arithmetic. Indeed readers of a certain age are likely to have fond memories of huddling over wooden workbenches learning a craft such as woodwork or maybe metal work, or any one of the hands-on projects that characterized the once-ubiquitous shop class.

But in the 1950s, a different philosophy emerged: the theory that students should follow separate educational tracks according to ability. The idea was that the college-bound would take traditional academic courses (Latin, creative writing, science, math) and received no vocational training. Those students not headed for college would take basic academic courses, along with vocational training, or "shop."

Ability tracking did not sit well with educators or parents, who believed students were assigned to tracks not by aptitude, but by socio-economic status and race. The result being

that by the end of the 1950s, what was once a perfectly respectable, even mainstream educational path came to be viewed as a remedial track that restricted minority and working-class students.

The backlash against tracking, however, did not bring vocational education back to the academic core. Instead, the focus shifted to preparing all students for college, and college prep is still the center of the U.S. high school curriculum.

So what's the harm in prepping kids for college? Won't all students benefit from a high-level, four-year academic degree program? As it turns out, not really. For one thing, people have a huge and diverse range of different skills and learning styles. Not everyone is good at math, biology, history and other traditional subjects that characterize college-level work. Not everyone is fascinated by Greek mythology, or enamored with Victorian literature, or enraptured by classical music. Some students are mechanical; others are artistic. Some focus best in a lecture hall or classroom; still others learn best by doing, and would thrive in the studio, workshop or shop floor.

And not everyone goes to college. The latest figures from the U.S. Bureau of Labor Statistics (BLS) show that about 68% of high school students attend college. That means over 30% graduate with neither academic nor job skills.

But even the 68% aren't doing so well. Almost 40% of students who begin four-year college programs don't complete them, which translates into a whole lot of wasted time, wasted money, and burdensome student loan debt. Of those who do finish college, one-third or more will end up in jobs they could have had without a four-year degree. The BLS found that 37% of currently employed college grads are doing work for which only a high school degree is required.

It is true that earnings studies show college graduates earn more over a lifetime than high school graduates. However, these studies have some weaknesses. For example, over 53% of recent college graduates are unemployed or under-employed. And income for college graduates varies widely by major — philosophy graduates don't nearly earn what business studies graduates do. Finally, earnings studies compare college graduates to *all* high school graduates. But the subset of high school students who graduate with vocational training — those who go into well-paying, skilled jobs — the picture for non-college graduates looks much rosier.

Yet despite the growing evidence that four-year college programs serve fewer and fewer of our students, states continue to cut vocational programs. In 2013, for example, the Los Angeles Unified School District, with more than 600,000 students, made plans to cut almost all of its CTE programs by the end of the year. The justification, of course, is budgetary; these programs (which include auto body technology, aviation maintenance, audio production, real estate and photography) are expensive to operate. But in a situation where 70% of high school students do not go to college, nearly half of those who do go

fail to graduate, and over half of the graduates are unemployed or underemployed, is vocational education really expendable? Or is it the smartest investment we could make in our children, our businesses, and our country's economic future?

The U.S. economy has changed. The manufacturing sector is growing and modernizing, creating a wealth of challenging, well-paying, highly skilled jobs for those with the skills to do them. The demise of vocational education at the high school level has bred a skills shortage in manufacturing today, and with it a wealth of career opportunities for both under-employed college grads and high school students looking for direct pathways to interesting, lucrative careers. Many of the jobs in manufacturing are attainable through apprenticeships, on-the-job training, and vocational programs offered at community colleges. They don't require expensive, four-year degrees for which many students are not suited.

And contrary to what many parents believe, students who get job specific skills in high school and choose vocational careers often go on to get additional education. The modern workplace favors those with solid, transferable skills who are open to continued learning. Most young people today will have many jobs over the course of their lifetime, and a good number will have multiple careers that require new and more sophisticated skills.

Just a few decades ago, our public education system provided ample opportunities for young people to learn about careers in manufacturing and other vocational trades. Yet, today, high-schoolers hear barely a whisper about the many doors that the vocational education path can open. The "college-for-everyone" mentality has pushed awareness of other possible career paths to the margins. The cost to the individuals and the economy as a whole is high. If we want everyone's kid to succeed, we need to bring vocational education back to the core of high school learning.

QUESTIONS

1. According to Nicholas Wyman, why did vocational education fall out of favor in high schools?

2. On what grounds does Wyman argue that the current emphasis on college preparation is wrong-headed? Consider the reasons he gives and the data he uses as evidence in your response.

3. On what grounds does Wyman raise doubts about studies that show college graduates as having higher earnings over their lifetimes than high school graduates?

4. How does Wyman use the changing U.S. economy as further evidence that college is not the best choice for everyone?

5. Based on your own experience and the emphasis of your school, to what extent do you agree with Wyman's position?

---

5 from What America Can Learn from Smart Schools in Other Countries

AMANDA RIPLEY

Amanda Ripley is an investigative journalist and author of *The Smartest Kids in the World: And How They Got That Way* (2014). Her work has appeared in numerous publications including *Time*, the *New York Times*, the *Atlantic*, and the *Wall Street Journal*. The following excerpt is from an article published in the *New York Times* in 2016.

Every three years, half a million 15-year-olds in 69 countries take a two-hour test designed to gauge their ability to think. Unlike other exams, the PISA, as it is known, does not assess what teenagers have memorized. Instead, it asks them to solve problems they haven't seen before, to identify patterns that are not obvious and to make compelling written arguments. It tests the skills, in other words, that machines have not yet mastered.

The latest results, released Tuesday morning, reveal the United States to be treading water in the middle of the pool. In math, American teenagers performed slightly worse than they usually do on the PISA — below average for the developed world, which means they scored worse than nearly three dozen countries. They did about the same as always in science and reading, which is to say average for the developed world.

But that scoreboard is the least interesting part of the findings. More intriguing is what the PISA has revealed about which conditions seem to make smart countries smart. In that realm, the news was not all bad for American teenagers.

Like all tests, the PISA is imperfect, but it is unusually relevant to real life and provides increasingly nuanced insights into education for researchers like Andreas Schleicher, who oversees the test at the Organization for Economic Cooperation and Development. After each test, he and his team analyze the results, stripped of country names. They don't want to be biased by their pre-existing notions of what teenagers in Japan or Mexico can or cannot do.

◆ ◆ ◆

A year later, after their analysis is finished, team members gather in a small conference room at their Paris offices to guess which countries are which. It's a parlor game of the high-nerd variety — or, as Mr. Schleicher put it, "a stress test of the robustness of our analysis."

When the team started this game back in 2003, it could predict about 30 percent of the variation in scores using its statistical models, Mr. Schleicher said Now, the models can predict 85 percent of the variation.

So how do the researchers make their predictions? The process is not entirely intuitive. They can't, for example, assume that countries that spend the most will do the best (the world's biggest per-student spenders include the United States, Luxembourg and Norway, none of which are education superpowers).

Nor can they guess based on which countries have the least poverty or the fewest immigrants (places like Estonia, with significant child poverty, and Canada, with more immigrant students than the United States, now top the charts). All those factors matter, but they interact with other critical conditions to create brilliance — or not.

This year, when the PISA team made its guesses, it predicted the United States would show modest improvement. Eventually, it figured, the federal government's Ham-handed but consistent push to get states to prioritize their lowest-achieving students (under No Child Left Behind and other efforts) was likely to have some effect.

Team members expected Colombia to continue to improve, given policy makers' focus on enrolling more students at younger ages and raising standards for entering teaching. Singapore would probably crush every other country, raising the bar for what children are capable of doing.

"An easy guess, maybe," Mr. Schleicher said a bit sheepishly. "They are constantly looking outside for ways to improve, questioning the established wisdom. That's the classic thing that Singapore has always done."

Bad at Math

The United States is among the world's biggest per-student spenders on education, but its 15-year-olds still trail in math against peers in most developed countries.

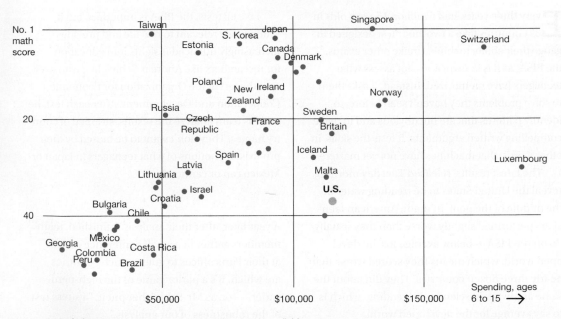

Math ranks include only countries for which spending data is available.

Source: OECD

◆ ◆ ◆

By contrast, the team did not expect good news out of France, where Mr. Schleicher lives and where his children are enrolled in school. "Most reforms have been on the surface, not reaching into the classroom," he said. "Nobody predicted France would be a star performer."

Finally, it was time for the results: The analysts looked at the country names to see how their predictions held up. It was, by statistician standards, a huge thrill. The United States had not raised its average scores, but on measures of equity, it had improved. One in every three disadvantaged American teenagers beat the odds in science, achieving results in the top quarter of students from similar backgrounds worldwide.

This is a major accomplishment, despite America's lackluster performance over all. In 2006, socioeconomic status had explained 17 percent of the variance in Americans' science scores; in 2015, it explained only 11 percent, which is slightly better than average for the developed world. No other country showed as much progress on this metric. (By contrast, socioeconomic background explained 20 percent of score differences in France—and only 8 percent in Estonia.) . . .

Here's what the models show: Generally speak- 15 ing, the smartest countries tend to be those that have acted to make teaching more prestigious and selective; directed more resources to their neediest children; enrolled most children in high-quality preschools; helped schools establish cultures of constant improvement; and applied rigorous, consistent standards across all classrooms.

Of all those lessons learned, the United States has employed only one at scale: A majority of states recently adopted more consistent and challenging learning goals, known as the Common Core State Standards, for reading and math. These standards were in place for only a year in many states, so Mr. Schleicher did not expect them to boost America's PISA scores just yet. (In addition, America's PISA sample included students living in states that have declined to adopt the new standards altogether.)

But Mr. Schleicher urges Americans to work on the other lessons learned—and to keep the faith in their new standards. "I'm confident the Common Core is going to have a long-term impact," he said. "Patience may be the biggest challenge." . . .

Some of the other reforms Americans have attempted nationwide in past years, including smaller class sizes and an upgrade of classroom technology, do not appear on the list of things that work. In fact, there is some evidence that both policies can have a negative impact on learning.

For now, the PISA reveals brutal truths about America's education system: Math, a subject that reliably predicts children's future earnings, continues to be the United States' weakest area at every income level. Nearly a third of American 15-year-olds are not meeting a baseline level of ability—the lowest level the O.E.C.D. believes children must reach in order to thrive as adults in the modern world.

And affluence is no guarantee of better results, 20 particularly in science and math: The latest PISA data (which includes private-school students) shows that America's most advantaged teenagers scored below their well-off peers in science in 20 other countries, including Canada and Britain.

The good news is that a handful of places, including Estonia, Canada, Denmark and Hong Kong, are proving that it is possible to do much better. These places now educate virtually all their children to higher levels of critical thinking in math, reading and science—*and* do so more equitably than Americans do. (Vietnam and various provinces in China are omitted here because many 15-year-olds are still not enrolled in school systems there, limiting the comparability of PISA results.)

As we drift toward a world in which more good jobs will require Americans to think critically—and to repeatedly prove their abilities before and after they are hired—it is hard to imagine a more pressing national problem. "Your president-elect has promised to make America great again," Mr. Schleicher said. But he warned, "He won't be able to do that without fixing education."

QUESTIONS

1. What is the bad news for American students, according to PISA results? What is the good news?

2. Based on PISA results, will upgrading technology in the classroom likely improve student performance in math, reading, or science?

3. According to the PISA test results, what are the characteristics of the countries with the highest performing students?

4. Why should America's poor performance in math signal an urgent need to take action to improve?

5. How would you describe Amanda Ripley's ethos in this article? Is she an objective observer? An engaged educator? A concerned citizen? Consider the extent to which she explains her own position on the education that today's high school students are receiving.

6. Based on what PISA tests have shown over the years in terms of the factors affecting students' performance, what measures should the United States be taking?

6 How High Schools Are Demolishing the Classroom

LESLIE NGUYEN-OKWU

Leslie Nguyen-Okwu is a recent graduate of Stanford University's international relations program, currently working as a journalist specializing in Southeast Asia. The following article appeared in 2017 in OZY, a daily global news website and digital magazine.

ool mist rises off the Mississippi and drifts across the deck of the classroom. Below, the murky waters of the Delta gush past in a torrent. In fact, little separates the gaggle of gossiping teenagers from the venomous snakes and oil-stained river beneath their feet. Not exactly Hogwarts Express, right?

New Harmony High in Louisiana isn't your typical little red schoolhouse. Instead, students live and learn on an armada of barges that floats along the gritty marshes and wetlands of the Bayou State. All the while, workshops on rising sea levels and coastal preservation allow students to confront the realities of climate change face-to-face. A winner of the XQ: Super School Project, New Harmony High's doors are set to open later this year, when students will learn in a living, breathing lab on the water and get hands-on experience in studying biology, river ecology and environmental justice, in addition to the usual reading, 'riting and 'rithmetic. "[The students] are out in the world, not in an ivory tower, not

clustered behind the fence," says Elliot Washor, one of the nontraditional education gurus behind New Harmony High. In fact, this high school isn't the only one venturing outside the four walls of the stuffy traditional classroom to teach the next generation of pupils.

- At The Mountain School in rural Vermont, students can go off-grid and spend a semester learning on an organic farm.

- Michigan's Grand Rapids Public Museum School is in a renovated, 80-year-old public museum.

- If you're stuck in an academic rut, you could always enroll in the Dongzhong Cave School in China.

- Stay in your pajamas while venturing through Fulton High School's forthcoming virtual reality campus.

- Avoid walls entirely and attend an "open classroom" with "squiggly" desk and a mountaintop for speeches, like the Telefonplan School in Stockholm.

- The Traveling School lets students learn and adventure in the Galapagos, Guatemala and Botswana.

These high schools probably don't look anything like your alma mater. But their atypical classrooms are designed to encourage out-of-school learning for those who don't work as well inside the mold of traditional education, says Christopher Hanks, the principal at the Grand Rapids Museum School. The 21st century has flooded schools with high-tech blackboards, virtual reality headsets and other fancy learning gizmos, yet the traditional four walls of most classrooms have mostly stayed put, thanks to an old-era approach to learning. During the Industrial Revolution, educators adopted a factory-model system that monolithically processed students in batches, funneling them in one door as raw material at age 5 and ejecting them out another as finished educational products 12 years later. Back then, isolated boxlike classrooms were designed for crowd control and stodgy lectures, and learning was thought to occur in only prescribed places.

Today, the same ol' shape, structure and style still persist inside most schools. However, a pioneering group of architects, designers and educators are calling for something decidedly different in the world's most avant-garde high schools. Research on classroom design has long touted the benefits of flexible learning spaces: Ever-changing surroundings keep students more engaged, spur creativity and motivation and, yes, improve grades. Couple that fact with another study from the University of Salford, in England, which found that the classroom environment can affect a child's academic progress over a year by as much as 25 percent — for better or worse. There's been a whole lot more attention paid to high school design as of late, says Kris Magnusson, the dean of education at Simon Fraser University in Vancouver, B.C.: "What that signals is we're moving away from a rigid, one-size-fits-all idea. . . . By broadening the repertoire of what we count as educational experiences and legitimizing the different ways in which students learn, we open the door to a whole new world."

So, just as architects are starting to build better hospitals to aid the dying and better parks to aid play and recreation, the same movement is taking place in schools to create spaces that are more conducive to learning, says Rosan Bosch, the intrepid designer behind the Telefonplan School in Sweden. "We have to accept that design impacts us," she says, "how we feel, how we react and how we function."

But not everyone works best in nontraditional environments, and for some students, unconventional settings could even serve as a distraction rather than as an aid to learning. Plus, it's not as though these ideas on better classroom design haven't been percolating for millennia — all of ancient Athens was a classroom to Socrates — but it's easier and cheaper to stick with the "old-school" model, Magnusson says. Most schools, he adds, are "designed to replicate themselves, not to imagine a different future." In the U.S., standardization is the bedrock of the current education system. So, how are we to evaluate the pedagogic benefits of a semester spent in an organic garden? "There's this massive inertia in effect" when it comes to today's massive, unwieldy educational systems, Magnusson claims. "It's difficult to get it to change course."

Still, who wouldn't have more fun learning on a river barge or in a spooky museum, a la Ben Stiller? Just like kids, the schools of the future will soon outgrow the classroom. Now, all we need is a flying, souped-up school bus to jet them there.

QUESTIONS

1. What is the philosophy of the schools described in this article?

2. What are the characteristics of the "factory-model" system of education that these innovative high schools are designed to challenge?

3. What potential problems or drawbacks can you imagine might occur if one of the new models discussed in this article were to fully supplant more traditional classroom education?

4. Leslie Nguyen-Okwu asks Kris Magnusson, an advocate of less traditional, more experiential models of education, how these unconventional approaches might be evaluated. He does not respond to the question directly except to say that change is difficult. Does this issue of assessing the impact of different classroom environments on student growth seem a significant problem? To what extent do you think colleges would be uneasy about such different approaches?

5. If given a choice, would you choose to attend a high school like one of those mentioned in the article or to stay in your current environment? Explain your response.

---

7 from We Will Pay High School Students to Go to School. And We Will Like It.

BRENTIN MOCK

Brentin Mock is a staff writer for CityLab, a website sponsored by the *Atlantic* magazine that focuses on ideas and issues facing urban environments.

When I read that my old high school in Harrisburg, Pennsylvania, suspended half of its student population for excessive absences — defined as roughly a week's worth of unexcused truancy over the last quarter — my first thought was, *Only half?*

School absence was a huge problem when I was a student there in the mid-90s. Not going to class was arguably a class of its own, and one that many of my peers mastered. (No comment on whether I was part of the problem.)

But to be clear, I'm not taking truancy lightly. It's a serious issue, then and now. I sympathize with Harrisburg High's new principal, Lisa Love, whose actions have made headlines internationally. The problems she's inherited go beyond attendance to poor test scores and low graduation rates; she can't deal with either of those problems when kids don't show up. She told the local press that she took the "radical" step of suspending over 500 students to send a message to parents and the community, and the district's

superintendent backed the mass suspension. "In order for us to get different results, we have to do something different," Superintendent Sybil Knight-Burney told PennLive.com.

The problem: Suspending kids who don't go to school isn't "different." That's what they did when I was there. At risk of stating the obvious here, suspension is no punishment for those who are already voluntarily suspending themselves. Suspension is better than criminalizing truancy, but it won't necessarily inspire kids to start coming to homeroom. For that kind of inspiration — and inspiration is truly what's needed here — educators will have to come up with something more creative, and competitive.

And here it is: We need to pay high school students to go to school. I don't mean some punk-ass weekly or monthly allowance, or a gift card for Dave & Busters. I'm talking about a deposit of somewhere in the ballpark of $50 to $100, every school day. That's not for making honor roll; it's just for making it to school in the morning and staying until the end of the day. Yes, compensated just for showing up. Think Universal Basic Income — but for kids.

This is my own unsolicited proposal. I promise my 8th grade son did not put me up to this (though he enthusiastically endorses it). But as crazy as it sounds, I'm pretty convinced this is the only solution to keeping as many kids as possible in school, ensuring timely graduation, and disrupting the school-to-prison pipeline. I see this solution as applicable exclusively for public high school students. And before you post your rebuttal — as I'm sure there are many — please hear out my five-point argument:

1: Paying kids gives them a financial incentive to pursue perfect attendance.

I know what you're going to say. "What they get out of going to school is an *education*! That should be motivation enough!"

Yeah, but it's not. Which is why we've been talking about this problem for decades and losing. Others will insist that paying kids to do what they should be doing will spoil their work ethic — except paying people to do what they should be doing is what already happens in the real world. It's called going to work.

Teenagers are the only people on the planet who we ask to go places they don't want to be, to do work they don't want to do, starting at an hour in which they are supposed to be asleep — and we not only require them to do it for free, but we require them to *like it*.

This is not preparing them for the real world. 10 This is more like preparing them for prison. That's the only other place in North America where people are held against their will to do unpaid work.

2: Paying kids will allow schools to compete with the *not-going-to school* market.

What's often overlooked in discussions about truancy is the fact that there is a very large market for not going to school. You can kick that story about how you went to school every day as a kid because it was an honor if you want. But you and I know the truth: You went to school every day because where else were you gonna go? Church? Mr. Adams's 5 & Dime store? That playground with two swings and a half-a-slide? You went to school every day because you had no choice.

Today's kids have *options*, especially when the parents are working two and three jobs and can't be home to regulate. For one, they can go to legit work — and seriously, for many low-income families that is the *only* choice. More uncomfortably, kids have the option to go to the corner and deal drugs, which is a much more lucrative prospect than math class. Most cities would happily pay now for schools to recapture these teens from the block so that they won't be caught up in the criminal justice system later.

Not to mention, there are the myriad entrepreneurial opportunities offered via the internet that did not exist in decades past, further incentivizing kids to pull a Zuckerburg and drop out early. A kid with a laptop can extract cash via YouTube, Snapchat, eBay, and all manner of sites and apps. Hell, you can make a gang of money just playing video games and talking about it, Pewdie Pie-style. Some innovative teenager might use his time off from school while suspended to make a mixtape online that will go viral and make him into a rap star. Oh, I forgot: Chance the Rapper already did that.

In other words: The *not-going-to-school* market is boomin', and schools are competing with it whether they acknowledge that market or not.

3: Salaried students will have a financial incentive to actually perform and behave well.

Just as it does in the adult working world, putting 15 kids on salary will fix a lot of behavior problems. Kids won't want to get suspended if it means their pay will get docked. Augmenting their base wages with daily performance bonuses — say, an extra $1 to $5 for achieving daily micro-goals like asking questions in class and doing extra assignments — could further entice kids to give classtime their all. (Those kinds of "secondary quest" rewards would also allow the classroom experience to more closely resemble more stimulating activities like videogames.)

4: Fewer parents will feel pressured to put their kids in a private or charter school.

It's paramount that the daily stipend be applied to public high schools exclusively. For one, these are the schools that usually take in kids from families at the bottom of the economic spectrum. With this kind of financial enticement, though, more families of all incomes would consider putting or keeping their kids in public schools, especially if the stipends produce the kind of academic and behavioral outcomes projected above.

And to be clear, I don't think a stipend should be available to children of families of all tax brackets. There should probably be a household income cap on families that are

able to participate in the program, with an opt-out clause for middle-class families (perhaps 80 percent of AMI) who don't need their kids to accept the stipend, but who might otherwise qualify for it. This way, we'll know that returning higher-income families — those who normally would flee to private/charters — are there for the educational outcomes, not for the checks.

5: Kids in K through 8 — especially middle school kids — will have something to look forward to.

We know that a lot of students coming up through the lower grades are anticipating high school more for reasons related to puberty than academics. But let's start seeding in their heads as early as third grade that they'll get paid once they hit the higher grades: By middle school they'll be developing study habits, learning how to stay organized, and getting all the goofball stuff out of their system. They understand that once 9th grade arrives, getting good grades and perfect attendance is serious business.

QUESTIONS

1. How does Brentin Mock define the problem that he believes offering financial incentives to attend high school classes will solve?

2. Why does Mock indicate that his proposal should be targeted at public school students, not those in charter or private schools?

3. Mock offers a five-point argument. Which of his reasons is most appealing to you and

why? Which do you find the least likely to be effective and why?

4. Mock writes in a lively, informal style and includes anecdotes from his own experience in school and as a parent. Does this approach enhance or detract from his argument? Why?

8   This High School Wants to Revolutionize Learning with Technology

AMY ROLPH

Amy Rolph, an independent journalist, wrote this article, published in *USA Today* in April 2017, about the Washington D.C. Leadership Academy, one of the award-winning schools from XQ, the Super School Project.

High school freshman Zoe Valladares has been the mayor of a major metropolis. She's chatted with former President Barack Obama. And she's been assigned a house within her school by a magical sorting hat, just like the lucky students of Hogwarts in a Harry Potter novel.

Each of these incredible experiences was powered by virtual reality and computer technology — cornerstones of learning at Washington Leadership Academy in Washington, D.C. Valladares is one of 110 freshmen at the new charter school, which admitted its inaugural class of 9th graders in 2016.

Along with her fellow classmates, Valladares uses virtual reality and computer science to supplement her studies — but she's not just a consumer of technology. She's also learning to write code and has ambitious plans for her life after high school. She wants a career in virtual reality, and to perhaps even found her own company.

She says virtual reality is the future, and she wants to be a part of it.

"It's going to take over the world someday," Valladares said.

Stacy Kane, one of Washington Leadership Academy's co-founders, explains that the school uses technology and online courses to meet students at their level, rather than teaching an entire grade the same content. "Our classes are really pushing boundaries in terms of their uses of technology," Kane said. "Our students can grow at their own paces."

And instead of taking the same sequence of classes available at most high schools, students assemble a unique blend of classes and projects based on their interests and goals.

The school's foundation in technology stretches far beyond virtual reality and computer science. Students also study what it means to participate in civic life as a digital citizen by creating blogs, coding complex websites and using social media tools. Leadership skills are another focus. Students are encouraged to practice crafting persuasive arguments and speaking in public.

Joseph Webb, Washington Leadership Academy's founding principal, explains that teachers encourage students to think like designers by examining problems from a user's perspective and subsequently hypothesizing possible solutions. Fittingly, Webb says this is the same approach educators should take to reimagining high school.

In 2016, Washington Leadership Academy was one of 10 schools to receive a $10 million grant from XQ: The Super School Project. XQ planned to award five grants, but doubled that number after 700 applications were submitted. The winners are all working to create high schools where students work to solve real-world problems in collaborative, flexible environments.

Sponsored by XQ Institute and backed by Laurene Powell Jobs' philanthropic organization Emerson Collective, XQ sought out innovative ideas from the education community. The project's mission statement reads: "We've gone from the Model T to the Tesla and from the switchboard to the smartphone. Yet high school has remained frozen in time."

In moving towards a more modern educational paradigm, XQ's Senior School Strategist Monica Martinez says faculty members must battle the biggest enemy of educational progress: Apathy.

"Using design thinking and the user experience when designing high school, rather than thinking about just what's been done in the past, is critical," she said. "There is so much apathy and so much boredom in high school."

"We are stuck with an irrelevant model, and students are dissatisfied, but what are we doing about it as a society?" said Martinez. "The high school is a cultural icon and everybody has experienced it and therefore do not question its usefulness for today's students and our future economic needs."

Washington Leadership Academy is already changing the face of education in Washington, D.C. The school's computer-science-for-all policy will triple the number of black students enrolled in AP computer science — and quadruple the number of girls.

The school is also one of just a handful of schools across the country making virtual reality a pillar of its curriculum. But co-founder Seth Andrew said he wants to see more schools adopt a similar approach to education. That's why Washington Leadership Academy makes its curriculum available to copy and revise on an open-source development platform.

"We're asking teachers and principals to steal it and make it their own," he said.

Andrew stresses that everything the school has built so far was funded with public dollars and is "100 percent sustainable," meaning it's feasible for other schools to do the same.

One goal of Andrew's is to develop a virtual reality chemistry lab that can reach students who might not have access to a real-world lab. There, he says, students could learn from the best teachers in a safe environment.

As for what the distant future holds in terms of educational development, the school's founders are intrigued to explore the use of holographic technology, which would allow educators from all over the world to virtually visit classrooms.   20

When imagining the next advances of education, Andrew is often reminded of something he heard Valladares say about virtual reality's endless possibilities for education. "She said, 'If virtual reality is infinite, that means education is infinite.'"

QUESTIONS

1. What characteristics does Washington Leadership Academy have that presents "a more modern educational paradigm" (para. 12)?

2. In what ways does the school's focus on technology stretch "far beyond virtual reality and computer science" (para. 8)?

3. How have the faculty of the Academy countered what they identify as the most significant problem of today's high schools: student apathy?

4. Would you like to attend Washington Leadership Academy? Why or why not?

MAKING CONNECTIONS

1. Based on his beliefs about the interconnection of democracy and education, why do you think that Horace Mann would or would not support the call for a new educational paradigm to replace the traditional high school, what some call the factory model?

2. In what ways does the fact that American students have a low-ranking achievement in math, as Amanda Ripley reports, challenge Leon Botstein's position? In what ways does it support his position?

3. How would Brentin Mock be likely to respond to the methods employed by the Washington Leadership Academy? Would he find the school's approach a promising way to address student truancy problems? Why or why not?

4. Based on his call to bring back vocational education, how would Nicholas Wyman respond to the PISA data that Amanda Ripley reports?

5. Given the conditions in other countries that promote student achievement, would the alternative classroom approaches that Leslie Nguyen-Okwu describes be likely to raise student test scores?

6. How do you think Nicholas Wyman would respond to Brentin Mock's proposal to pay students for attending school?

7. Which of the approaches represented in this Conversation do you think would be most open to making daily meditation a required part of high school curriculum? Cite specific evidence in the text to support your choice.

ENTERING THE CONVERSATION

As you respond to the following prompts, support your argument with references to at least three of the sources in this Conversation on the future of the American high school. For help using sources, see Chapter 4.

1. Write an essay explaining whether you agree with Leon Botstein's critique of the American high school (p. 274).

2. Using the texts in this Conversation on the American high school, as well as your own insights into high school, identify two serious problems with today's educational system, and propose recommendations for addressing them. Cite at least three sources from the Conversation in your response.

3. Statistical data show that nearly one in four students drops out of high school each year, making the United States fall below twenty other countries in graduation rates. The unemployment rate for recent dropouts is 50 percent because it's difficult to get even low-paying jobs without a high school diploma. Survey data show that most who do not graduate cite boring classes without relevance to real-world learning as their reason for dropping out. Write an argument explaining what measures you believe need to be taken to encourage teenagers to stay in school and graduate.

4. John Dewey (1859–1952), the father of experiential education, described the interaction of education and democracy as follows:

   > Democratic society is peculiarly dependent for its maintenance upon the use in forming a course of study of criteria which are broadly human. Democracy cannot flourish where the chief influences in selecting subject matter of instruction are utilitarian ends narrowly conceived for the masses, and, for the higher education of the few, the traditions of a specialized cultivated class. The notion that the "essentials" of elementary education are the three R's mechanically treated, is based upon ignorance of the essentials needed for realization of democratic ideals. . . . A curriculum which acknowledges the social responsibilities of education must present situations where problems are relevant to the problems of living together, and where observation and information are calculated to develop social insight and interest.
   >
   > — *Democracy and Education*, 1916

   Develop a position on the extent to which Dewey's vision for education, as he explains it in this excerpt, remains relevant to today's high schools. Draw on your experience and observation, and cite at least three of the readings from the Conversation to build your argument.

5. The mission statement of the XQ Initiative, the organization behind the Washington Leadership Academy, is as follows: "We've gone from the Model T to the Tesla and from the switchboard to the smartphone. Yet high school has remained frozen in time." Some might argue, however, that there are advantages to maintaining the more traditional model of high school, particularly during a time of such rapid change fostered by technological advances and globalization. What are the best qualities, values, and practices of a traditional high school? Write an argument explaining what is worth keeping even as schools adapt to new generations and changing times.

6. Suppose you had the freedom to design a high school that you want to attend. What would be the prevailing philosophy of the school? What would be three or four key characteristics of the school that implement this philosophy? Draw on at least three of the sources from the Conversation in your discussion.

7. How do popular movies depict life in high school? Choose one — maybe even an old movie — and explain what you'd think of high school based on the film. Possibilities include *10 Things I Hate about You* (1999); *The Breakfast Club* (1985); *Bring It On* (2000); *Clueless* (1995); *Cooley High* (1975); *Dead Poets Society* (1989); *Easy A* (2010); *Friday Night Lights* (2004); *Grease* (1978); *Mean Girls* (2004); *The Principal* (1987); *Rushmore* (1998); and *To Sir, with Love* (1967).

from In Defense of a Liberal Education

FAREED ZAKARIA

If you want to live a good life these days, you know what you're supposed to do. Get into college but then drop out. Spend your days learning computer science and your nights coding. Start a technology company and take it public. That's the new American dream. If you're not quite that adventurous, you could major in electrical engineering.

What you are not supposed to do is study the liberal arts. Around the world, the idea of a broad-based "liberal" education is closely tied to the United States and its great universities and colleges. But in America itself, a liberal education is out of favor. In an age defined by technology and globalization, everyone is talking about skills-based learning. Politicians, business-people, and even many educators see it as the only way for the nation to stay competitive. They urge students to stop dreaming and start thinking practically about the skills they will need in the workplace. An open-ended exploration of knowledge is seen as a road to nowhere.

A classic liberal education has few defenders. Conservatives fume that it is too, well, liberal (though the term has no partisan meaning). Liberals worry it is too elitist. Students wonder what they would do with a degree in psychology. And parents fear that it will cost them their life savings.

This growing unease is apparent in the numbers. As college enrollment has grown in recent decades, the percentage of students majoring in subjects like English and philosophy has declined sharply. In 1971, for example, 7.6 percent of all bachelor's degrees were awarded in English language and literature. By 2012, that number had fallen to 3.0 percent. During the same period, the percentage of business majors in the undergraduate population rose from 13.7 to 20.5.

Some believe this pattern makes sense — that new entrants into higher education might simply prefer job training to the liberal arts. Perhaps. But in earlier periods of educational expansion, this was not the case. In the 1950s and 1960s, for instance, students saw college as more than a glorified trade school. Newcomers, often from lower-middle-class backgrounds and immigrant families with little education, enthusiastically embraced the liberal arts. They saw it as a gateway to a career, and also as a way to assimilate into American culture. "I have to speak absolutely perfect English," says Philip Roth's character Alex Portnoy, the son of immigrants and hero of the novel Portnoy's Complaint. Majors like English and history grew in popularity precisely during the decades of mass growth in American higher education.

The great danger facing American higher education is not that too many students are studying the liberal arts. Here are the data. In the 2011–12 academic year, 52 percent of American undergraduates were enrolled in two-year or less-than-two-year colleges, and 48 percent were enrolled in four-year institutions. At two-year colleges, the most popular area of study was health professions and related sciences (23.3 percent). An additional 11.7 percent of students studied business, management, and marketing. At four-year colleges, the pattern was the same. Business led the list of majors, accounting for 18.9 percent of students, and health was second, accounting for 13.4 percent. Another estimate found that only a third of all bachelor's degree recipients study fields that could be classified as the liberal arts. And only about 1.8 percent of all undergraduates attend classic liberal arts colleges like Amherst, Swarthmore, and Pomona.

As you can see, we do not have an oversupply of students studying history, literature, philosophy, or physics and math for that matter. A majority is specializing in fields because they see them as directly related to the job market. It's true that more Americans need technical training, and all Americans need greater scientific literacy. But the drumbeat of talk about skills and jobs has not lured people into engineering and biology—not everyone has the aptitude for science—so much as it has made them nervously forsake the humanities and take courses in business and communications. Many of these students might well have been better off taking a richer, deeper set of courses in subjects they found fascinating—and supplementing it, as we all should, with some basic knowledge of computers and math. In any event, what is clear is that the gap in technical training is not being caused by the small percentage of students who choose four-year degrees in the liberal arts.

Whatever the facts, the assaults continue and have moved from the realm of rhetoric to action. The governors of Texas, Florida, North Carolina, and Wisconsin have announced that they do not intend to keep subsidizing the liberal arts at state-funded universities. "Is it a vital interest of the state to have more anthropologists?" Florida's Rick Scott asked. "I don't think so." Wisconsin is planning to cut money from subjects that don't train students for a specific job right out of college. "How many PhDs in philosophy do I need to subsidize?" the radio show host William

Bennett asked North Carolina's Patrick McCrory, a sentiment with which McCrory enthusiastically agreed. (Ironically, Bennett himself has a PhD in philosophy, which appears to have trained him well for his multiple careers in government, media, nonprofits, and the private sector.)

It isn't only Republicans on the offensive. Everyone's eager to promote the type of education that might lead directly to a job. In a speech in January 2014, President Barack Obama said, "I promise you, folks can make a lot more, potentially, with skilled manufacturing or the trades than they might with an art history degree." He later apologized for what he described as a "glib" comment, but Obama has expressed similar sentiments during his presidency. His concern—that in today's world, college graduates need to focus on the tools that will get them good jobs—is shared by many liberals, as well as conservatives and independents. The irrelevance of a liberal education is an idea that has achieved that rare status in Washington: bipartisan agreement.

The attacks have an effect. There is today a loss of coherence and purpose surrounding the idea of a liberal education. Its proponents are defensive about its virtues, while its opponents are convinced that it is at best an expensive luxury, at worst actively counterproductive. Does it really make sense to study English in the age of apps?

10

---

1. In context of the passage as a whole, the tone of paragraph 1 is best described as

   a. emphatic
   b. didactic
   c. lighthearted
   d. ironic
   e. optimistic

2. According to paragraph 1, "the new American dream" is based on

   a. hard work and persistence
   b. studies and social engagement
   c. entrepreneurship and monetary success

   d. academic ambition and individual commitment
   e. self-satisfaction and hedonistic pursuits

3. The primary function of paragraph 2 is

   a. to defend the idea of a liberal education against its detractors
   b. to explore the relevance of skills-based learning
   c. to suggest arguments a student might use when choosing a major
   d. to present the counter-arguments to studying technology-based subjects
   e. to summarize the views of the opponents of a liberal education

4. In context, the reference to "an open-ended exploration of knowledge" (para. 2) is best understood as

   a. a key tenet of a liberal education

   b. a central characteristic of a necessary tool in the technology fields

   c. an alternative pathway for those who drop out of college

   d. a primary quality of the traditional American dream

   e. a metaphor for the study of psychology

5. The primary function of paragraph 3 is

   a. to summarize arguments for a liberal education

   b. to list arguments against liberal education

   c. to identify the claims made by political supporters of liberal education

   d. to ridicule the interference of politicians in college education

   e. to lampoon opponents of liberal education

6. The primary purpose of the statistics in paragraphs 4 and 6 is

   a. to support the relevance of liberal education

   b. to demonstrate that participation in liberal education has declined

   c. to show that liberal arts major can still succeed in careers

   d. to undermine the arguments against liberal education

   e. to praise the growth of technology-based majors in America

7. The quotation from *Portnoy's Complaint* (para. 5) functions as

   a. criticism of the elitism of liberal arts colleges

   b. exemplification of the content covered in English and history departments

   c. evidence of the relevance of liberal education to first-generation college students

   d. satire of those who major in liberal arts subjects

   e. exaggeration of the rigors of a liberal education

8. In paragraph 7, which sentence functions as a concession?

   a. "A majority is specializing in fields because they see them as directly related to the job market."

   b. "It's true that more Americans need technical training, and all Americans need greater scientific literacy."

   c. "But the drumbeat of talk about skills and jobs has not lured people into engineering and biology — not everyone has the aptitude for science — so much as it has made them nervously forsake the humanities and take courses in business and communications."

   d. "Many of these students might well have been better off taking a richer, deeper set of courses in subjects they found fascinating — and supplementing it, as we all should, with some basic knowledge of computers and math."

   e. "In any event, what is clear is that the gap in technical training is not being caused by the small percentage of students who choose four-year degrees in the liberal arts."

9. Which of the following sentences most directly states the author's position?

   a. "The great danger facing American higher education is not that too many students are studying the liberal arts" (para. 6).

   b. "As you can see, we do not have an oversupply of students studying history, literature, philosophy, or physics and math for that matter" (para. 7).

   c. "Many of these students might well have been better off taking a richer, deeper set of courses in subjects they found fascinating — and supplementing it, as we all should, with some basic knowledge of computers and math" (para. 7).

   d. "Everyone's eager to promote the type of education that might lead directly to a job" (para. 9).

   e. "The irrelevance of a liberal education is an idea that has achieved that rare status in Washington: bipartisan agreement" (para. 9).

10. Over the course of the passage as a whole, the author's tone becomes increasingly

   a. ironic

   b. irrational

   c. personal

   d. bitter

   e. humorous

from The Blessings of Liberty and Education

FREDERICK DOUGLASS

In his natural condition, however, man is only potentially great. As a mere physical being, he does not take high rank, even among the beasts of the field. He is not so fleet as a horse or a hound, or so strong as an ox or a mule. His true dignity is not to be sought in his arm, or in his legs, but in his head. Here is the seat and source of all that is of especially great or practical importance in him. There is fire in the flint and steel, but it is friction that causes it to flash, flame and burn, and give light where all else may be darkness. There is music in the violin, but the touch of the master is needed to fill the air and the soul with the concord of sweet sounds. There is power in the human mind, but education is needed for its development.

As man is the highest being on earth, it follows that the vocation of teacher is among the highest known to him. To properly teach is to educe man's potential and latent greatness, to discover and develop the noblest, highest and best that is in him. In view of this fact, no man whose business it is to teach should ever allow himself to feel that his mission is mean, inferior, or circumscribed. In my estimation, neither politics nor religion present to us a calling higher than this primary business of unfolding and strengthening the powers of the human soul. It is a permanent vocation. Some know the value of education, by having it. I know its value by not having it. It is a want that begins with the beginning of human existence, and continues through all the journey of life. Of all the creatures that live and move and have their being on this green earth, man, at his birth, is the most helpless and the most in need of instruction. He does not know even how to seek his food. His little life is menaced on every hand. The very elements conspire against him. The cattle upon a thousand hills; the wolves and bears in the forest, all come into the world better equipped for life than does man. From first to last, his existence depends upon instruction.

Yet this little helpless weakling, whose life can be put out as we put out the flame of a candle, with a breath, is the lord of creation. Though in his beginning, he is only potentially this lord, with education he is the commander of armies; the builder of cities; the tamer of wild beasts; the navigator of unknown seas; the discoverer of unknown islands, capes and continents, and the founder of great empires, and capable of limitless civilization.

But if man is without education, although with all his latent possibilities attaching to him, he is, but a pitiable object; a giant in body, but a pigmy in intellect, and, at best, but half a man. Without education, he lives within the narrow, dark and grimy walls of ignorance. He is a poor prisoner without hope. The little light that he gets comes to him as through dark corridors and grated windows. The sights and sounds which reach him, so significant and full of meaning to the well-trained mind, are to him of dim and shadowy and uncertain importance. He sees, but does not perceive. He hears, but does not understand. The silent and majestic heavens, fretted with stars, so inspiring and uplifting, so sublime and glorious to the souls of other men, bear no message to him. They suggest to him no idea of the wonderful world in which he lives, or of the harmony of this great universe, and hence impart to him no happiness.

Education, on the other hand, means emancipation. It means light and liberty. It means the uplifting of the soul of man into the glorious light of truth, the light only by which men can be free. To deny education to any people is one of the greatest crimes against human nature. It is to

5

deny them the means of freedom and the rightful pursuit of happiness, and to defeat the very end of their being. They can neither honor themselves nor their Creator. Than this, no greater wrong can be inflicted; and, on the other hand, no greater benefit can be bestowed upon a long benighted people than giving to them, as we are here this day endeavoring to do, the means of useful education. It is aimed to make them both better and more useful in life and to furnish them with increased means of livelihood; to make of them more skilled workmen, more useful mechanics, and better workers in wood, leather, tin and iron.

1. In paragraph 1, the analogies of the flint and steel and the violin serve to

   a. define the specific benefits of education

   b. suggest the capabilities of the intellect as opposed to the body

   c. emphasize the need for education in forming a human

   d. contrast the practical with the aesthetic

   e. identify skills that distinguish humans from animals

2. The speaker's claim that "the vocation of teacher is among the highest known to him" is based on the reasoning that

   a. humans are the smartest creatures and teachers are the smartest humans

   b. humans have great capabilities, and teachers help students achieve them

   c. unlike politicians or religious leaders, teachers respond to a personal calling

   d. within American culture, teachers are universally admired

   e. teaching is a business that can be productive for both the teacher and the student

3. As used in paragraph 2, "to enduce" most nearly means:

   a. to catalyze

   b. to capture

   c. to realize

   d. to educate

   e. to recognize

4. Which of the following sentences from paragraph 2 signals the beginning of a rhetorical shift?

   a. "To properly teach it to enduce man's potential and latent greatness, to discover and develop the noblest, highest and best that is in him."

   b. "In view of this fact, no man whose business it is to teach should ever allow himself to feel that his mission is mean, inferior, or circumscribed."

   c. "It is a permanent vocation."

   d. "Some know the value of education, by having it."

   e. "It is a want that begins with the beginning of human existence, and continues through all the journey of life."

5. The speaker's use of the first person in paragraph 2 functions to do all of the following EXCEPT

   a. contrast his experience with others'

   b. enhance his ethos

   c. emphasize why he appreciates education

   d. criticize those who do not value teachers

   e. suggest that his experience has influenced his perspective

6. The list in paragraph 3 ("he is . . . limitless civilization") defines human achievement in terms of all of the following EXCEPT

   a. consensus-building

   b. leadership

   c. power over others

   d. risk-taking

   e. exploration

7. In paragraph 4, the speaker uses a central metaphor primarily to convey

   a. the role of teachers in unlocking the minds of students

   b. the experience students may have in authoritative schools

   c. the lack of opportunity afforded to the lower classes

   d. the value of books and libraries in the educational process

   e. the limitations of those who are not educated

8. In the context of paragraph 5, "benighted" primarily means

    a. rewarded
    b. darkened
    c. oppressed
    d. troubled
    e. irreligious

9. Which of the following is the primary emphasis of the final paragraph?

    a. the religious and social value of education
    b. the importance of teachers in the educational process

    c. the implications of education for the criminal justice system
    d. the benefits of education for manual laborers
    e. the intangible rewards received by educators

10. Taken as a whole, the tone of the speaker can best be described as

    a. frustrated and brash
    b. authoritative and reasonable
    c. fanciful and discursive
    d. defensive and combative
    e. pedantic and detached

EDUCATION

Now that you have examined a number of readings and other texts that focus on education, explore this topic yourself by synthesizing your own ideas and the readings. You might want to do more research or use readings from other classes as you write.

1. What do you believe are the two most important steps (or changes or actions) that the United States should take to improve K-12 education that will ensure the country's continued leadership on the world stage? Should we address economic inequities? Place a stronger emphasis on STEM? Return to a greater emphasis on liberal arts? Provide more job skills and training? Develop stronger character education? Express your viewpoint in a well-written essay, using at least three sources from this chapter in your response.

2. Many see standardized testing as the answer to improving public education in the United States. Thus, students face district- and state-mandated tests as well as national ones. What do you think? Write an essay discussing whether standardized testing is an effective way to improve instruction and performance. Be sure to research the topic, and broaden the scope of your essay beyond your own experience.

3. Homeschooling has become a popular alternative to public or private school for an increasing number of students in the United States. Research this trend by consulting print and electronic resources and, if possible, by interviewing someone involved with homeschooling. Would Ralph Waldo Emerson (p. 208) or Horace Mann (p. 271) support or oppose this method of education? Write an essay exploring both the benefits and the liabilities of homeschooling.

4. Many people believe that children should be required to attend at least one year of school prior to kindergarten. Write an essay explaining why tax dollars should or should not be used to pay for mandatory, government-funded preschool.

5. Write your own "Talk to Teachers," addressing either the teachers in your school or teachers in general. To start this assignment, replace the name *Khrushchev* with the word *terrorism* in the opening paragraph of James Baldwin's "A Talk to Teachers" (p. 211). How does this substitution set the stage for your more contemporary view?

6. Write a roundtable discussion among three or four of the authors in this chapter as they discuss *one* of the following quotations:

   a. The only real education comes from what goes counter to you.
   — André Gide

   b. I have never let my schooling interfere with my education.
   — Mark Twain

   c. Education is not filling a bucket but lighting a fire.
   — William Butler Yeats

   d. Rewards and punishments are the lowest form of education.
   — Chuang-Tzu

7. According to Francine Prose, "Education, after all, is a process intended to produce a product." Examine your school or another part of an educational system (for example, your school district, a Montessori class, a private religion-affiliated school). Describe specific parts of the educational process, and the "product" they strive to produce. Think of this as a cause-and-effect essay, with the process as the cause and the product as the effect.

8. Write a comparison/contrast of the high school classroom as you've experienced it in the United States with the high school experience in another country. If you've attended school in another country, you can use your own experience; if you know someone who has,

you might interview that person; or you can research the topic. Consider how the classroom, including the relationship of teacher and student, reflects the values of the larger society.

9. Congratulations class of 2045! What will high school be like for the next generation? Write an essay explaining what changes you anticipate for high schools in the not-too-distant future. Will the high school be pretty much the same as yours? Will students interact with teachers solely online? Or will future students face a backlash to a more traditional model? What books will students be reading? Will they be reading at all? Can you imagine yourself as one of the teachers?

10. Create your own version of Roz Chast's "What I Learned," presenting your thoughts on education as a cartoon with a narrative line. Feel free to develop your own illustration style, rather than emulating hers.

11. Write your own humorous account of a learning experience, either in a traditional classroom or in a different context. Use some of David Sedaris's rhetorical strategies, such as dialogue, a self-deprecating persona, or hyperbolic descriptions.

12. Suppose you are delivering the commencement address at your high school. What key characteristics do successful commencement addresses share? Consider watching and/or reading commencement speeches by people such as Donovan Livingston (Harvard University, 2016), Barack Obama (Wesleyan University, 2008), J. K. Rowling (Harvard University, 2008), and David Foster Wallace (Kenyon College, 2005). Then, write one that is tailored to your school and community.

6

Popular Culture

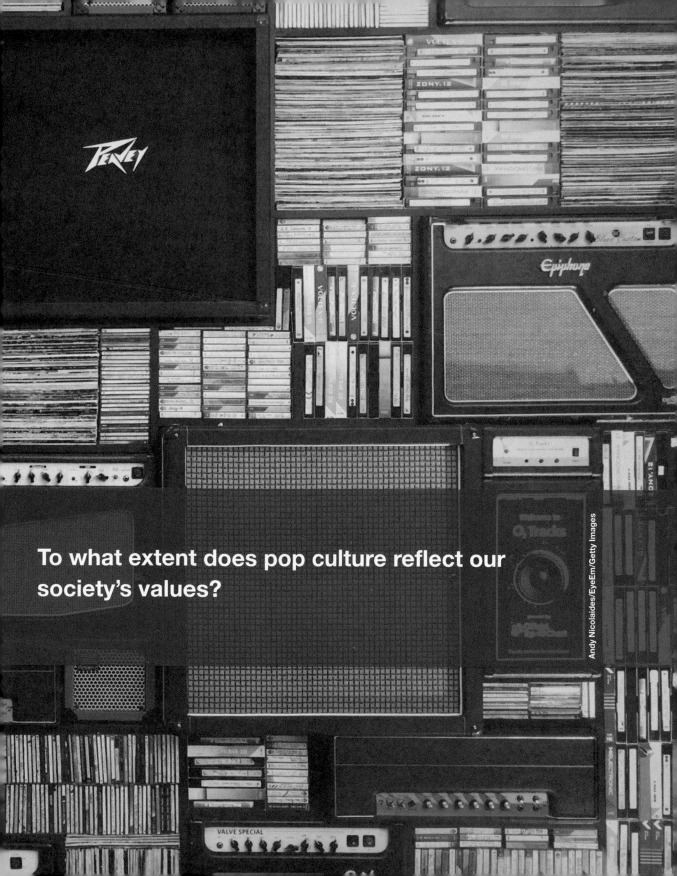

To what extent does pop culture reflect our society's values?

Popular culture is a term that once characterized mass-produced or lowbrow culture: pop music, potboilers and page-turners, movies, comics, advertising, radio, and television. Its audience was the masses. Opposite popular culture were highbrow forms of entertainment: opera, fine art, classical music, traditional theater, and literature. These were the realm of the wealthy and educated classes.

Today, the line between high and pop culture has blurred. Pop culture is often at the leading edge of what will become established culture. For example, the 1980s graffitist Jean-Michel Basquiat is now considered a leading figure in contemporary art.

Bettmann/Getty Images

When Marlon Brando won the 1973 Academy Award for Best Actor, he sent Native American activist Sacheen Littlefeather to refuse it on his behalf. At the awards ceremony, Littlefeather read part of a speech written by Brando that protested the mistreatment of Native Americans.
What does such a gesture suggest about the intersection of popular culture and activism? What role do you believe celebrities play in bringing about social change?

Popular culture moves through our world at warp speed. Rap music and mash-ups sample and remix current and past albums. Celebrity gossip in the morning is the talk-show host's monologue at night. Homemade videos are posted on the Internet, become cultural phenomena overnight, and are just as quickly forgotten. Albums and movies are exchanged on peer-to-peer networks months before they are officially released. What does this onslaught of entertainment and information mean?

These days, most people realize that pop culture asks many of the same questions that high culture does: Does it say something new? Does it tell us about ourselves? Popular culture also spawns new questions: What is pop? Should pop culture respect its roots? What is the relationship among pop culture, politics, and commerce? Do commercial interests control what is offered to the public, or does old-fashioned word of mouth still tell us what's hot and what's not?

The selections in this chapter are about media that you can access. Listen to the music, watch the films and TV shows, and look at the art. The connections made in this chapter prompt a conversation between the past and the present; enter that conversation, consider both, and imagine the future.

Hip Hop Planet

JAMES McBRIDE

American writer and musician James McBride (b. 1957) was born and raised in New York City. His father was an African American minister and his mother a Jewish immigrant from Poland who later converted to Christianity. His best-selling memoir, *The Color of Water* (1996), is about growing up in a large African American family and the influence of his Jewish mother, whose father was an orthodox rabbi. McBride is also a saxophonist and composer. His first novel, *Miracle at St. Anna* (2002), was made into a film by Spike Lee. His other novels include *Song Yet Sung* (2008) and *The Good Lord Bird* (2013). With Spike Lee, McBride also co-wrote the film *Red Hook Summer* (2012). Most recently, McBride wrote *Kill 'Em and Leave* (2016), a nonfiction exploration of the life and legacy of legendary funk and soul musician James Brown. McBride has written for the *Boston Globe, People* magazine, the *Washington Post*, and *Rolling Stone*. The essay that follows appeared in *National Geographic* in 2007.

JOEL SAGET/Getty Images

This is my nightmare: *My daughter comes home with a guy and says, "Dad, we're getting married." And he's a rapper, with a mouthful of gold teeth, a do-rag on his head, muscles popping out his arms, and a thug attitude. And then the nightmare gets deeper, because before you know it, I'm hearing the pitter-patter of little feet, their offspring, cascading through my living room, cascading through my life, drowning me with the sound of my own hypocrisy, because when I was young, I was a knucklehead, too, hearing my own music, my own sounds. And so I curse the day I saw his face, which is a reflection of my own, and I rue the day I heard his name, because I realize to my horror that rap — music seemingly without melody, sensibility, instruments, verse, or harmony, music with no beginning, end, or middle, music that doesn't even seem to be music — rules the world. It is no longer my world. It is his world. And I live in it. I live on a hip hop planet.*

High-Stepping

I remember when I first heard rap. I was standing in the kitchen at a party in Harlem. It was 1980. A friend of mine named Bill had just gone on the blink. He slapped a guy, a total stranger, in the face right in front of me. I can't remember why. Bill was a fellow student. He was short-circuiting. Problem was, the guy he slapped was a big guy, a dude wearing a do-rag who'd crashed the party with three friends, and, judging by the fury on their faces, there would be no Martin Luther King moments in our immediate future.

There were no white people in the room, though I confess I wished there had been, if only to hide the paleness of my own frightened face. We were black and Latino students about to graduate from Columbia University's journalism school, having learned the whos, whats, wheres, whens, and whys of American reporting. But the real storytellers of the American experience came from the world of the guy that Bill had just slapped. They lived less than a mile from us in the South Bronx. They had no journalism degrees. No money. No credibility. What they did have, however, was talent.

Earlier that night, somebody tossed a record on the turntable, which sent my fellow students stumbling onto the dance floor, howling with delight, and made me, a jazz lover, cringe. It sounded like a broken record. It was a version of an old hit record called "Good Times," the same four bars looped over and over. And on top of this loop, a kid spouted a rhyme about how he was the best disc jockey in the world. It was called "Rapper's Delight." I thought it was the most ridiculous thing I'd ever heard. More ridiculous than Bill slapping that stranger.

Bill survived that evening, but in many ways, **5** I did not. For the next 26 years, I high-stepped past that music the way you step over a crack in the sidewalk. I heard it pounding out of cars and alleyways from Paris to Abidjan, yet I never listened. It came rumbling out of boomboxes from Johannesburg to Osaka, yet I pretended not to hear. I must have strolled past the corner of St. James Place and Fulton Street in my native Brooklyn where a fat kid named Christopher Wallace, aka Biggie Smalls, stood amusing his friends with rhyme, a hundred times, yet I barely noticed. I high-stepped away from that music for 26 years because it was everything I thought it was, and more than I ever dreamed it would be, but mostly, because it held everything I wanted to leave behind.

In doing so, I missed the most important cultural event in my lifetime.

Not since the advent of swing jazz in the 1930s has an American music exploded across the world with such overwhelming force. Not since the Beatles invaded America and Elvis packed up his blue suede shoes has a music crashed against the world with such outrage. This defiant culture of song, graffiti, and dance, collectively known as hip hop, has ripped popular music from its moorings in every society it has permeated. In Brazil, rap rivals samba in popularity. In China, teens spray-paint graffiti on the Great Wall. In France it has been blamed, unfairly, for the worst civil unrest that country has seen in decades.

Its structure is unique, complex, and at times bewildering. Whatever music it eats becomes part of its vocabulary, and as the commercial world falls into place behind it to gobble up the powerful slop in its wake, it metamorphoses into the Next Big Thing. It is a music that defies definition, yet defines our collective societies in immeasurable ways. To many of my generation, despite all attempts to exploit it, belittle it, numb it, classify it, and analyze it, hip hop remains an enigma, a clarion call, a cry of "I am" from the youth of the world. We'd be wise, I suppose, to start paying attention.

Burning Man

Imagine a burning man. He is on fire. He runs into the room. You put out the flames. Then another burning man arrives. You put him out and go about your business. Then two, three, four, five, ten appear. You extinguish them all, send them to the hospital. Then imagine no one bothers to examine why the men caught fire in the first place. That is the story of hip hop.

It is a music dipped in the boiling caul- **10** dron of race and class, and for that reason it is clouded with mystics, snake oil salesmen, two-bit scholars, race-baiters, and sneaker salesmen, all professing to know the facts, to be "real," when the reality of race is like shifting sand, dependent on time, place, circumstance, and who's telling the history. Here's the real story: In the mid-1970s, New York City was nearly broke. The public school system cut funding for the arts drastically. Gone were the days when you could wander into the band room, rent a clarinet for a minimal fee, and march it home to squeal on it and drive your parents nuts.

The kids of the South Bronx and Harlem came up with something else. In the summer of 1973, at 1595 East 174th Street in the Bronx River Houses, a black teenager named Afrika Bambaataa stuck a speaker in his mother's first-floor living room window, ran a wire to the turntable in his bedroom, and set the housing project of 3,000 people alight with party music. At the same time, a Jamaican teenager named Kool DJ Herc was starting up the scene in the East Bronx, while a technical whiz named Grandmaster Flash was rising to prominence a couple of miles south. The Bronx became a music magnet for Puerto Ricans, Jamaicans, Dominicans, and black Americans from the surrounding areas. Fab 5 Freddy, Kurtis Blow, and Melle Mel were only a few of the pioneers. Grand Wizard Theodore, Kool DJ AJ, the Cold Crush Brothers, Spoony Gee, and the Rock Steady Crew of B-boys showed up to "battle" — dance, trade quips and rhymes, check out each other's records and equipment — not knowing as they strolled through the doors of the community center near Bambaataa's mother's apartment that they were writing musical history. Among them was an MC named Lovebug Starski, who was said to utter the phrase "hip hop" between breaks to keep time.

This is how it worked: One guy, the DJ, played records on two turntables. One guy — or girl — served as master of ceremonies, or MC. The DJs learned to move the record back and forth under the needle to create a "scratch," or to drop the needle on the record where the beat was the hottest, playing "the break" over and over to keep the folks dancing. The MCs "rapped" over the music to keep the party going. One MC sought to outchat the other. Dance styles were created — "locking" and "popping" and "breaking." Graffiti artists spread the word of the "I" because the music was all about identity: I am the best. I spread the most love in the Bronx, in Harlem, in Queens. The focus initially was not on the MCs, but on the dancers, or B-boys. Commercial radio ignored it. DJs sold

mix tapes out of the back of station wagons. "Rapper's Delight" by the Sugarhill Gang — the song I first heard at that face-slapping party in Harlem — broke the music onto radio in 1979.

That is the short history.

The long history is that spoken-word music made its way here on slave ships from West Africa centuries ago: Ethnomusicologists trace hip hop's roots to the dance, drum, and song of West African griots, or storytellers, its pairing of word and music the manifestation of the painful journey of slaves who survived the middle passage. The ring shouts, field hollers, and spirituals of early slaves drew on common elements of African music, such as call and response and improvisation. "Speech-song has been part of black culture for a long, long time," says Samuel A. Floyd, director of the Center for Black Music Research at Columbia College in Chicago. The "dozens," "toasts," and "signifying" of black Americans — verbal dueling, rhyming, self-deprecating tales, and stories of blacks outsmarting whites — were defensive, empowering strategies.

You can point to jazz musicians such as Oscar Brown, Jr., Edgar "Eddie" Jefferson, and Louis Armstrong, and blues greats such as John Lee Hooker, and easily find the foreshadowing of rap music in the verbal play of their work. Black performers such as poet Nikki Giovanni and Gil Scott-Heron, a pianist and vocalist who put spoken political lyrics to music (most famously in "The Revolution Will Not Be Televised"), elevated spoken word to a new level.

But the artist whose work arguably laid the groundwork for rap as we know it was Amiri Baraka, a beat poet out of Allen Ginsberg's Greenwich Village scene. In the late 1950s and '60s, Baraka performed with shrieks, howls, cries, stomps, verse floating ahead of or behind the rhythm, sometimes in staccato syncopation. It was performance art, delivered in a dashiki and Afro, in step with the anger of a bold and sometimes frightening nationalistic black

15

movement, and it inspired what might be considered the first rap group, the Last Poets.

I was 13 when I first heard the Last Poets in 1970. They scared me. To black America, they were like the relatives you hoped wouldn't show up at your barbecue because the boss was there — the old Aunt Clementine who would arrive, get drunk, and pull out her dentures. My parents refused to allow us to play their music in our house — so my siblings waited until my parents went to work and played it anyway. They were the first musical group I heard to use the N-word on a record, with songs like "N_____ Are Scared of Revolution." In a world where blacks were evolving from "Negroes" to "blacks," and the assassinations of civil rights leaders Malcolm X and Martin Luther King, Jr., still reverberated in the air like a shotgun blast, the Last Poets embodied black power. Their records consisted of percussion and spoken-word rhyme. They were wildly popular in my neighborhood. Their debut recording sold 400,000 records in three months, says Last Poet member Umar Bin Hassan. "No videos, no radio play, strictly word of mouth." The group's demise coincided with hip hop's birth in the 1970s.

It's unlikely that the Last Poets ever dreamed the revolution they sang of would take the form it has. "We were about the movement," Abiodun Oyewole, a founder of the group, says. "A lot of today's rappers have talent. But a lot of them are driving the car in the wrong direction."

The Crossover

Highways wrap around the city of Dayton, Ohio, like a ribbon bow-tied on a box of chocolates from the local Esther Price candy factory. They have six ladies at the plant who do just that: Tie ribbons around boxes all day. Henry Rosenkranz can tell you about it. "I love candy," says Henry, a slim white teenager in glasses and a hairnet, as he strolls the factory, bucket in hand. His full-time after-school job is mopping the floors.

Henry is a model American teenager — and the prototypical consumer at which the hip

20

Jack Mitchell/Getty Images

Examine this 1988 image of Chuck D and the members of the hip-hop group Public Enemy.

Identify some of the elements that draw on both the short and long history of hip hop as James McBride describes them. How does this photo relate to the Last Poets movement? Based on this image, would its founder, Abiodun Oyewole, think that Public Enemy was "driving the car in the wrong direction"? Would McBride?

hop industry is squarely aimed, which has his parents sitting up in their seats. The music that was once the purview of black America has gone white and gone commercial all at once. A sea of white faces now rises up to greet rap groups as they perform, many of them teenagers like Henry, a NASCAR fanatic and self-described redneck. "I live in Old North Dayton," he says. "It's a white, redneck area. But hip hop is so prominent with country people . . . if you put them behind a curtain and hear them talk, you won't know if they're black or white. There's a guy I work with, when Kanye West sings about a gold digger, he can relate because he's paying alimony and child support."

Obviously, it's not just working-class whites, but also affluent, suburban kids who identify with this music with African-American roots.

A white 16-year-old hollering rap lyrics at the top of his lungs from the driver's seat of his dad's late-model Lexus may not have the same rationale to howl at the moon as a working-class kid whose parents can't pay for college, yet his own anguish is as real to him as it gets. What attracts white kids to this music is the same thing that prompted outraged congressmen to decry jazz during the 1920s and Tipper Gore to campaign decades later against violent and sexually explicit lyrics: life on the other side of the tracks; its "cool" or illicit factor, which black Americans, like it or not, are always perceived to possess.

Hip hop has continually changed form, evolving from party music to social commentary with the 1982 release of Grandmaster Flash and the Furious Five's "The Message." Today,

▼

This photograph shows the opening song to *Hamilton* (2015), a hit Broadway musical about the life of founding father Alexander Hamilton. The score seamlessly blends rap, R&B, and pop, and the main cast is comprised entirely of people of color.
What does its popularity say about the mainstreaming of hip-hop and rap music?

Theo Wargo/Getty Images

alternative hip hop artists continue to produce socially conscious songs, but most commercial rappers spout violent lyrics that debase women and gays. Beginning with the so-called gangsta rap of the '90s, popularized by the still unsolved murders of rappers Biggie Smalls and Tupac Shakur, the genre has become dominated by rappers who brag about their lives of crime. 50 Cent, the hip hop star of the moment, trumpets his sexual exploits and boasts that he has been shot nine times.

"People call hip hop the MTV music now," scoffs Chuck D, of Public Enemy, known for its overtly political rap. "It's Big Brother controlling you. To slip something in there that's indigenous to the roots, that pays homage to the music that came before us, it's the Mount Everest of battles."

Most rap songs unabashedly function as walking advertisements for luxury cars, designer clothes, and liquor. Agenda Inc., a "pop culture brand strategy agency," listed Mercedes-Benz as the number one brand mentioned in *Billboard's* top 20 singles in 2005. Hip hop sells so much Hennessy cognac, listed at number six, that the French makers, deader

seeing connections

The following excerpt is from the 2017 revised edition of *Book of Rhymes: The Poetics of Hip Hop* by Adam Bradley.

What details of James McBride's argument support the claims Bradley makes here? What aspects of Bradley's argument might McBride disagree with, and why?

from Book of Rhymes
The Poetics of Hip Hop

ADAM BRADLEY

Rap is public art, and rappers are perhaps our greatest public poets, extending a tradition of lyricism that spans continents and stretches back thousands of years. Thanks to the engines of global commerce, rap is now the most widely disseminated poetry in the history of the world. Of course, not all rap is great poetry, but collectively it has revolutionized the way our culture relates to the spoken word. Rappers at their best make the familiar unfamiliar through rhythm, rhyme, and wordplay. They refresh the language by fashioning patterned and heightened variations of everyday speech. They expand our understanding of human experience by telling stories we might not otherwise hear. The best MCs — like Rakim, Jay Z, Tupac, and many others — deserve consideration alongside the giants of American poetry. We ignore them at our own expense. . . .

I believe that we are living in perhaps the most vital period that hip hop has ever seen. That's not to say that rap music has gotten better since what many consider its golden age, from the mid-1980s to the mid-1990s, only that rap's creative potential has never been more apparent. More people from more places are making more kinds of rap music than at any other time in history. There's something so durable about the structure of word rapped to a beat, something inclusive that resists any attempts to enforce some narrow orthodoxy or keep certain people out — be they from another borough or coast, another gender or sexual orientation, another race or life experience. Rap is free to all those willing to assume the heavy burden of mastering its craft, of learning how to rock the mic right.

than yesterday's beer a decade ago, are now rolling in suds. The company even sponsored a contest to win a visit to its plant in France with a famous rapper.

In many ways, the music represents an old dream. It's the pot of gold to millions of kids like Henry, who quietly agonizes over how his father slaves 14 hours a day at two tool-and-die machine jobs to make ends meet. Like teenagers across the world, he fantasizes about working in the hip hop business and making millions himself.

"My parents hate hip hop," Henry says, motoring his 1994 Dodge Shadow through traffic on the way home from work on a hot October afternoon. "But I can listen to Snoop Dogg and hear him call women whores, and I know he has a wife and children at home. It's just a fantasy. Everyone has the urge deep down to be a bad guy or a bad girl. Everyone likes to talk the talk, but not everyone will walk the walk."

Full Circle

You breathe in and breathe out a few times and you are there. Eight hours and a wake-up shake on the flight from New York, and you are on the tarmac in Dakar, Senegal. Welcome to Africa. The assignment: Find the roots of hip hop. The music goes full circle. The music comes home to Africa. That whole bit. Instead it was the old reporter's joke: You go out to cover a story and the story covers you. The stench of poverty in my nostrils was so strong it pulled me to earth like a hundred-pound ring in my nose. Dakar's Sandaga market is full of "local color" — unless you live there. It was packed and filthy, stalls full of new merchandise surrounded by shattered pieces of life everywhere, broken pipes, bicycle handlebars, fruit flies, soda bottles, beggars, dogs, cell phones. A teenage beggar, his body malformed by polio, crawled by on hands and feet, like a spider. He said, "Hey brother, help me." When I looked into his eyes, they were a bottomless ocean.

The Hotel Teranga is a fortress, packed behind a concrete wall where beggars gather at the front gate. The French tourists march past them, the women in high heels and stonewashed jeans. They sidle through downtown Dakar like royalty, haggling in the market, swimming in the hotel pool with their children, a scene that resembles Birmingham, Alabama, in the 1950s — the blacks serving, the whites partying. Five hundred yards (460 meters) away, Africans eat off the sidewalk and sell peanuts for a pittance. There is a restlessness, a deep sense of something gone wrong in the air.

The French can't smell it, even though they've had a mouthful back home. A good amount of the torching of Paris suburbs in October 2005 was courtesy of the children of immigrants from former French African colonies, exhausted from being bottled up in housing projects for generations with no job prospects. They telegraphed the punch in their music — France is the second largest hip hop market in the world — but the message was ignored. Around the globe, rap music has become a universal expression of outrage, its macho pose borrowed from commercial hip hop in the U.S.

In Dakar, where every kid is a microphone and turntable away from squalor, and American rapper Tupac Shakur's picture hangs in market stalls of folks who don't understand English, rap is king. There are hundreds of rap groups in Senegal today. French television crews troop in and out of Dakar's nightclubs filming the kora harp lute and tama talking drum with regularity. But beneath the drumming and the dance lessons and the jingling sound of tourist change, there is a quiet rage, a desperate fury among the Senegalese, some of whom seem to bear an intense dislike of their former colonial rulers.

"We know all about French history," says Abdou Ba, a Senegalese producer and musician. "We know about their kings, their castles, their

seeing connections

Shown here is an image taken from Sri Lankan rapper M.I.A.'s music video for her 2016 song, "Borders." The video makes extensive use of imagery that references the Syrian refugee crisis, and much of M.I.A.'s music and lyrics (including this song) stem from her own experience as a Sri Lankan refugee.

Look carefully at this image, and then answer the following questions.

1. To what extent might this scene from "Borders" be read as an "expression of outrage," as McBride calls rap music from "around the globe" (para. 29)?
2. What evidence do you see of what McBride calls a "macho pose borrowed from commercial hip hop in the U.S." (para. 29)?
3. What connections might McBride draw between rap songs like "Borders" and hip-hop's origins?

art, their music. We know everything about them. But they don't know much about us."

Assane N'Diaye, 19, loves hip hop music. Before he left his Senegalese village to work as a DJ in Dakar, he was a fisherman, just like his father, like his father's father before him. Tall, lean, with a muscular build and a handsome chocolate face, Assane became a popular DJ, but the equipment he used was borrowed, and when his friend took it back, success eluded him. He has returned home to Toubab Dialaw, about 25 miles (40 kilometers) south of Dakar, a

village marked by a huge boulder, perhaps 40 feet (12 meters) high, facing the Atlantic Ocean.

About a century and a half ago, a local ruler led a group of people fleeing slave traders to this place. He was told by a white trader to come here, to Toubab Dialaw. When he arrived, the slavers followed. A battle ensued. The ruler fought bravely but was killed. The villagers buried him by the sea and marked his grave with a small stone, and over the years it is said to have sprouted like a tree planted by God. It became a huge, arching boulder that stares out to sea, protecting the village behind it. When the fishermen went deep out to sea, the boulder was like a lighthouse that marked the way home. The Great Rock of Toubab Dialaw is said to hold a magic spirit, a spirit that Assane N'Diaye believes in.

In the shadow of the Great Rock, Assane has built a small restaurant, Chez Las, decorated with hundreds of seashells. It is where he lives his hip hop dream. At night, he and his brother and cousin stand by the Great Rock and face the sea. They meditate. They pray. Then they write rap lyrics that are worlds away from the bling-bling culture of today's commercial hip hoppers. They write about their lives as village fishermen, the scarcity of catch forcing them to fish in deeper and deeper waters, the hardship of fishing for 8, 10, 14 days at a time in an open pirogue in rainy season, the high fee they pay to rent the boat, and the paltry price their catches fetch on the market. They write about the humiliation of poverty, watching their town sprout up around them with rich Dakarians and richer French. And they write about the relatives who leave in the morning and never return, surrendered to the sea, sharks, and God.

The dream, of course, is to make a record. They have their own demo, their own logo, and their own name, Salam T. D. (for Toubab Dialaw). But rap music represents a deeper dream: a better life. "We want money to help our parents," Assane says over dinner. "We watch our mothers boil water to cook and have nothing to put in the pot."

He fingers his food lightly. "Rap doesn't belong to American culture," he says. "It belongs here. It has always existed here, because of our pain and our hardships and our suffering."

On this cool evening in a restaurant above their village, these young men, clad in baseball caps and T-shirts, appear no different from their African-American counterparts, with one exception. After a dinner of chicken and rice, Assane says something in Wolof to the others. Silently and without ceremony, they take every bit of the leftover dinner — the half-eaten bread, rice, pieces of chicken, the chicken bones — and dump them into a plastic bag to give to the children in the village. They silently rise from the table and proceed outside. The last I see of them, their regal figures are outlined in the dim light of the doorway, heading out to the darkened village, holding on to that bag as though it held money.

The City of Gods

Some call the Bronx River Houses the City of Gods, though if God has been by lately, he must've slipped out for a chicken sandwich. The 10 drab, red-brick buildings spread out across 14 acres (5.7 hectares), coming into view as you drive east across the East 174th Street Bridge. The Bronx is the hallowed holy ground of hip hop, the place where it all began. Visitors take tours through this neighborhood now, care of a handful of fortyish "old-timers," who 35 point out the high and low spots of hip hop's birthplace.

It is a telling metaphor for the state of America's racial landscape that you need a permit to hold a party in the same parks and playgrounds that produced the music that changed the world. The rap artists come and go, but the conditions that produced them linger. Forty percent of New York City's black males are jobless. One in three black males born in 2001 will end up in prison. The life expectancy of black men in the U.S. ranks below that of men in Sri Lanka and Colombia. It took a massive hurricane in New Orleans for the United States to wake up to its racial realities.

seeing connections

Contemporary artist Kerry James Marshall completed this painting, entitled *Past Times*, in 1997. Composed with acrylic paint on unstretched canvas and measuring nine and a half feet by thirteen feet, it is truly larger than life. The title can be read as a play on the idea of leisurely American pastimes and as a reference to both American history and the history of fine art — indeed, the image is an homage to Georges Seurat's *Sunday Afternoon on the Island of the Grand Jatte*, an iconic 1884 pointillist painting that shows a similar scene in a Parisian park. In the foreground of *Past Times*, bits of music emerge from the two boom boxes: The Temptations sing, "It was just my imagination running away with me," and Snoop Dogg raps his famous lyrics, "Got my mind on my money and my money on my mind."

What connections does this painting make between rap and African American experience? How does it address some of the same cultural issues and benchmarks that McBride focuses on in "Hip Hop Planet"?

© Kerry James Marshall. Courtesy of the artist and Jack Shainman Gallery, New York./Nathan Keay, © MCA Chicago

That is why, after 26 years, I have come to embrace this music I tried so hard to ignore. Hip hop culture is not mine. Yet I own it. Much of it I hate. Yet I love it, the good of it. To confess a love for a music that, at least in part, embraces violence is no easy matter, but then again our national anthem talks about bombs bursting in air, and I love that song, too. At its best, hip hop lays bare the empty moral cupboard that is our generation's legacy. This music that once made visible the inner culture of America's greatest social problem, its legacy of slavery, has taken

40 the dream deferred to a global scale. Today, 2 percent of the Earth's adult population owns more than 50 percent of its household wealth, and indigenous cultures are swallowed with the rapidity of a teenager gobbling a bag of potato chips. The music is calling. Over the years, the instruments change, but the message is the same. The drums are pounding out a warning. They are telling us something. Our children can hear it.

The question is: Can we?

[2007]

QUESTIONS FOR DISCUSSION

1. What do you consider James McBride's primary purpose in "Hip Hop Planet"? Do you think this is a personal essay or a cultural study? Explain your response.

2. "Hip Hop Planet" was included in the inaugural edition of *Best African American Essays* (2009). In her review of the collection on the *Kenyon Review's* website, Samantha Simpson notes that the collection "strains against the oversimplification of the African-American community's concerns. The collection does not only cull the voices concerned with the politics of race, but it also includes essays that deal with matters of the heart. That is, the collection is a far cry from the obligatory Black History Month lessons on important Black People." Do you consider McBride's essay to be about matters of the heart, or is it about the politics of race? Explain your answer.

3. McBride's lead (the opening paragraph of his essay) could be considered provocative, perhaps even confrontational. Having read the whole essay, go back and reread the lead. Is it an effective introduction to the essay, or could it be considered misleading? Explain.

4. David Brooks, writing in the *New York Times* in 2005 about riots in French housing projects, says,

"In a globalized age it's perhaps inevitable that the culture of resistance gets globalized, too. What we are seeing is what Mark Lilla of the University of Chicago calls a universal culture of the wretched of the earth. The images, modes and attitudes of hip hop and gangsta rap are so powerful they are having a hegemonic effect across the globe." How does that view of hip hop compare to McBride's? Do you think McBride would agree with Brooks? Explain why or why not.

5. In paragraph 23 McBride quotes Chuck D, of Public Enemy. What is your view of Chuck D's assertion? Are there ways in which rap music does pay "homage to the music that came before"? If so, what are they?

6. Read the description of the music composed by the would-be Senegalese rapper Assane N'Diaye (para. 34). Do you consider this to be a lesser form of rap or a truer form? Explain your answer.

7. In the next-to-last paragraph of McBride's essay, he justifies his acceptance of the violence that hip hop music embraces by saying that our national anthem is also about violence. What do you think of that comparison? In what ways does it help his argument? In what ways might it hinder it?

QUESTIONS ON RHETORIC AND STYLE

1. What rhetorical strategies does McBride use in his lead (the opening paragraph) to establish his persona and his credibility? Consider irony, hyperbole, metaphor, and colloquialisms.

2. Why do you think McBride calls the first section of his essay "High-Stepping"? In what ways does he play on the phrase? How do the rest of the essay's section names relate to their contents?

3. McBride transitions from the personal to the historical several times in "Hip Hop Planet." How does he achieve these transitions? What are some of the strategies he uses to make the transitions?

4. McBride names a dozen rappers in paragraph 11. What is the effect of mentioning all these names?

5. Find examples of figurative language in "Hip Hop Planet." How does McBride use them to connect to his audience and achieve his purpose?

6. How would you characterize Henry Rosenkranz, from Dayton, Ohio, whom we meet in the section

"The Crossover"? How does Rosenkranz help McBride establish his own credibility? What about Assane N'Diaye, the young Senegalese man whom we meet in "Full Circle"?

7. What is McBride's central argument? What are his secondary arguments? How does he bring them together?

8. How does McBride use cause and effect to provide the reasons for hip hop's development?

9. Look carefully at paragraph 12. How does McBride's style mirror the paragraph's subject matter?

10. McBride is a novelist as well as a memoirist and essayist. What techniques of fiction does he employ in "Hip Hop Planet"? What are their effects?

11. McBride ends the essay with a question. Why do you think he gives that question its own paragraph?

12. Who is the likely audience for this essay? How does McBride consider audience throughout his essay?

SUGGESTIONS FOR WRITING

1. McBride argues that hip hop music is a warning (para. 40). Write an essay in which you support, challenge, or qualify his assertion.

2. McBride quotes Abiodun Oyewole, a founder of what he considers the first rap group, the Last Poets (para. 18): "'A lot of today's rappers have talent. But a lot of them are driving the car in the wrong direction.'" Analyze Oyewole's statement, and write an essay in which you support, challenge, or qualify his assertion. Be sure to use examples of today's rappers who illustrate your argument.

3. Listen to the music and poetry of some of the old-school musicians and writers McBride cites, such as Louis Armstrong, Nikki Giovanni, and Amiri Baraka. Write an essay in which you examine their influence on specific hip hop musicians.

4. McBride suggests that the anger from the 2005 riots in the Paris suburbs found its way into hip

hop music, its "macho pose borrowed from commercial hip hop in the U.S." (para. 29). Judy Rosen, writing in the online magazine *Slate*, argues that "France, the nation that enshrines conversational grandiloquence as a civic virtue right up there with *fraternité*, would take to the most blabbermouthed genre in music history," suggesting that it has remade hip hop in its own fashion. Research rap music in countries such as France, Brazil, and England; then write an essay in which you examine the influence of American hip hop on the music of these countries as well as the influence of foreign musicians on American rap and hip hop.

5. Imagine and write a conversation between Henry Rosenkranz and Assane N'Diaye in which they discuss the sources, messages, and benefits of hip hop music.

Corn-Pone Opinions

MARK TWAIN

Mark Twain (1835–1910) is the pseudonym of Samuel Langhorne Clemens. Best known as a novelist — *The Adventures of Huckleberry Finn* (1884), *Tom Sawyer* (1876), and *A Connecticut Yankee in King Arthur's Court* (1889) are among Twain's most famous — Twain also worked as a typesetter, a riverboat pilot, a miner, a reporter, and an editor. His early writings reflect his pre–Civil War upbringing in their idyllic images as well as in their reminders of some of America's least acceptable social realities. Twain spent his life observing and reporting on his surroundings, and his work provides a glimpse into the mind-set of the late nineteenth century. "Corn-Pone Opinions," which was found in his papers after his death, was first published in 1923 in *Europe and Elsewhere*. In it, Twain comments — not always approvingly — on word of mouth as the spreader of popular opinion and culture.

Library of Congress

Fifty years ago, when I was a boy of fifteen and helping to inhabit a Missourian village on the banks of the Mississippi, I had a friend whose society was very dear to me because I was forbidden by my mother to partake of it. He was a gay and impudent and satirical and delightful young black man — a slave — who daily preached sermons from the top of his master's woodpile, with me for sole audience. He imitated the pulpit style of the several clergymen of the village, and did it well, and with fine passion and energy. To me he was a wonder. I believed he was the greatest orator in the United States and would some day be heard from. But it did not happen; in the distribution of rewards he was overlooked. It is the way, in this world.

He interrupted his preaching, now and then, to saw a stick of wood; but the sawing was a pretense — he did it with his mouth; exactly imitating the sound the bucksaw makes in shrieking its way through the wood. But it served its purpose; it kept his master from coming out to see how the work was getting along. I listened to the sermons from the open window of a lumber room at the back of the house. One of his texts was this:

"You tell me whar a man gits his corn pone, en I'll tell you what his 'pinions is."

I can never forget it. It was deeply impressed upon me. By my mother. Not upon my memory, but elsewhere. She had slipped in upon me while I was absorbed and not watching. The black philosopher's idea was that a man is not independent, and cannot afford views which might interfere with his bread and butter. If he would prosper, he must train with the majority; in matters of large moment, like politics and religion, he must think and feel with the bulk of his neighbors, or suffer damage in his social standing and in his business prosperities. He must restrict himself to corn-pone opinions — at least on the surface. He must get his opinions from other people; he must reason out none for himself; he must have no first-hand views.

GRAPHICA ARTIS/Private Collection/Bridgeman Images

Shown here is a World War I–era poster designed to encourage young British men to join the army. **What cultural values does the poster tap into to achieve its goal? What might Mark Twain have thought of this poster?**

I think Jerry was right, in the main, but I think he did not go far enough. 5

1. It was his idea that a man conforms to the majority view of his locality by calculation and intention. This happens, but I think it is not the rule.

2. It was his idea that there is such a thing as a first-hand opinion; an original opinion; an opinion which is coldly reasoned out in a man's head, by a searching analysis of the facts involved, with the heart unconsulted, and the jury room closed against outside influences. It may be that such an opinion has been born somewhere, at some time or other, but I suppose it got away before they could catch it and stuff it and put it in the museum.

I am persuaded that a coldly-thought-out and independent verdict upon a fashion in clothes, or manners, or literature, or politics, or religion, or any other matter that is projected into the field of our notice and interest, is a most rare thing — if it has indeed ever existed.

A new thing in costume appears — the flaring hoopskirt, for example — and the passers-by are shocked, and the irreverent laugh. Six months later everybody is reconciled; the fashion has established itself; it is admired, now, and no one laughs.

Public opinion resented it before, public opinion accepts it now, and is happy in it. Why? Was the resentment reasoned out? Was the acceptance reasoned out? No. The instinct that moves to conformity did the work. It is our nature to conform; it is a force which not many can successfully resist. What is its seat? The inborn requirement of self-approval. We all have to bow to that; there are no exceptions. Even the woman who refuses from first to last to wear the hoopskirt comes under that law and is its slave; she could not wear the skirt and have her own approval; and that she must have, she cannot help herself. But as a rule our self-approval has its source in but one place and not elsewhere — the approval of other people. A person of vast consequences can introduce any kind of novelty in dress and the general world will presently adopt it — moved to do it, in the first place, by the natural instinct to passively yield to that vague something recognized as authority, and in the second place by the human instinct to train with the multitude and have its approval. An empress introduced the hoopskirt, and we know the result. A nobody introduced the bloomer, and we know the result. If Eve should come again, in her ripe renown, and reintroduce her quaint styles — well, we know what would happen. And we should be cruelly embarrassed, along at first.

The hoopskirt runs its course and disappears. Nobody reasons about it. One woman abandons the fashion; her neighbor notices this and follows her lead; this influences the next woman; and so on and so on, and presently the skirt has vanished out of the world, no one knows how nor why, nor cares, for that matter. It will come again, by and by and in due course will go again.

Twenty-five years ago, in England, six or eight wine glasses stood grouped by each person's plate at a dinner party, and they were used, not left idle and empty; to-day there are but three or four in the group, and the average guest sparingly uses about two of them. We have not adopted this new fashion yet, but we shall do it presently. We shall not think it out; we shall merely conform, and let it go at that. We get our notions and habits and opinions from outside influences; we do not have to study them out.

Our table manners, and company manners and street manners change from time to time, but the changes are not reasoned out; we merely notice and 10

▼

How might Mark Twain have rewritten the thought bubble of this cartoon?

NEVER JUDGE A WORK UNTIL YOU KNOW WHO IT'S BY

CHRIS MADDEN

Chris Madden

conform. We are creatures of outside influences; as a rule we do not think, we only imitate. We cannot invent standards that will stick; what we mistake for standards are only fashions, and perishable. We may continue to admire them, but we drop the use of them. We notice this in literature. Shakespeare is a standard, and fifty years ago we used to write tragedies which we couldn't tell from — from somebody else's; but we don't do it any more, now. Our prose standard, three quarters of a century ago, was ornate and diffuse; some authority or other changed it in the direction of compactness and simplicity, and conformity followed, without argument. The historical novel starts up suddenly, and sweeps the land. Everybody writes one, and the nation is glad. We had historical novels before; but nobody read them, and the rest of us conformed — without reasoning it out. We are conforming in the other way, now, because it is another case of everybody.

The outside influences are always pouring in upon us, and we are always obeying their orders and accepting their verdicts. The Smiths like the new play; the Joneses go to see it, and they copy the Smith verdict. Morals, religions, politics, get their following from surrounding influences and atmospheres, almost entirely; not from study, not from thinking. A man must and will have his own approval first of all, in each and every moment and circumstance of his life — even if he must repent of a self-approved act the moment after its commission, in order to get his self-approval again: but, speaking in general terms, a man's self-approval in the large concerns of life has its source in the approval of the peoples about him, and not in a searching personal examination of the matter. Mohammedans are Mohammedans because they are born and reared among that sect, not because they have thought it out and can furnish sound reasons for being Mohammedans; we know why Catholics are Catholics; why Presbyterians are Presbyterians; why Baptists are Baptists; why Mormons are Mormons; why thieves are thieves; why monarchists are monarchists; why Republicans are

CLASSIC ESSAY 315

Republicans and Democrats, Democrats. We know it is a matter of association and sympathy, not reasoning and examination; that hardly a man in the world has an opinion upon morals, politics, or religion which he got otherwise than through his associations and sympathies. Broadly speaking, there are none but corn-pone opinions. And broadly speaking, corn-pone stands for self-approval. Self-approval is acquired mainly from the approval of other people. The result is conformity. Sometimes conformity has a sordid business interest — the bread-and-butter interest — but not in most cases, I think. I think that in the majority of cases it is unconscious and not calculated; that it's born of the human being's natural yearning to stand well with his fellows and have their inspiring approval and praise — a yearning which is commonly so strong and so insistent that it cannot be effectually resisted, and must have its way. A political emergency brings out the corn-pone opinion in fine force in its two chief varieties — the pocketbook variety, which has its origin in self-interest, and the bigger variety, the sentimental variety — the one which can't bear to be outside the pale; can't bear to be in disfavor; can't endure the averted face and the cold shoulder; wants to stand well with his friends, wants to be smiled upon, wants to be welcome, wants to hear the precious words, "He's on the right track!" Uttered, perhaps by an ass, but still an ass of high degree, an ass whose approval is gold and diamonds to a smaller ass, and confers glory and honor and happiness,

and membership in the herd. For these gauds many a man will dump his life-long principles into the street, and his conscience along with them. We have seen it happen. In some millions of instances.

Men think they think upon great political questions, and they do; but they think with their party, not independently; they read its literature, but not that of the other side; they arrive at convictions, but they are drawn from a partial view of the matter in hand and are of no particular value. They swarm with their party, they feel with their party, they are happy in their party's approval; and where the party leads they will follow, whether for right and honor, or through blood and dirt and a mush of mutilated morals.

In our late canvass half of the nation passionately believed that in silver lay salvation, the other half as passionately believed that that way lay destruction. Do you believe that a tenth part of the people, on either side, had any rational excuse for having an opinion about the matter at all? I studied that mighty question to the bottom — came out empty. Half of our people passionately believe in high tariff, the other half believe otherwise. Does this mean study and examination, or only feeling? The latter, I think. I have deeply studied that question, too — and didn't arrive. We all do no end of feeling, and we mistake it for thinking. And out of it we get an aggregation which we consider a boon. Its name is Public Opinion. It is held in reverence. It settles everything. Some think it the Voice of God.

[1923]

QUESTIONS FOR DISCUSSION

1. According to Mark Twain, "It is our nature to conform" (para. 7); he also says that we do so for self-approval. The two statements seem contradictory; how does Twain connect conformity and self-approval?

2. Twain makes a distinction between "standards" and "fashions" (para. 10). What is the difference? What examples does he provide for each?

How does the distinction apply to the twenty-first century?

3. Twain's essay is ultimately a denunciation of cultural chauvinism. What consequences does he suggest are the result of "corn-pone opinions"? Which are explicit? Which are implicit?

4. The last paragraph begins with a reference to a "late canvass" in which "half the nation

passionately believed" in one path and "the other half as passionately believed" in another. To what was Twain probably referring? Does he take sides? How does he distinguish between thinking and feeling?

5. In what two ways does a political emergency bring out corn-pone opinions? What does Twain mean by "an ass of high degree" (para. 11)?

QUESTIONS ON RHETORIC AND STYLE

1. What is Twain's purpose in "Corn-Pone Opinions"?

2. Trace Twain's use of the personal pronoun. What is the effect of changing from *I* to *we*?

3. Twain claims he got the idea of corn-pone opinions from a young slave with a talent for preaching. What does the anecdote add to his argument? Does it detract from it in any way? If so, how?

4. How does Twain expand Jerry's definition of corn-pone opinions? What is the effect of numbering the two items in which he begins to expand Jerry's definition (para. 5)?

5. Identify Twain's appeals to logos. Do the subjects of the appeals (hoopskirts, bloomers, wine glasses) strengthen the appeals or weaken them? Explain your response.

6. Explain the irony of Twain's qualification of Jerry's statement about calculation and intention in paragraph 5.

7. Why is paragraph 11 so long? Where, if anywhere, could Twain have broken it up? What is the effect of the series of subordinate clauses in the middle of the paragraph?

8. What is the effect of the parallelism in the two long sentences that make up paragraph 12?

9. What is the effect of capitalizing "Public Opinion" and "Voice of God" at the end of the essay (para. 13)?

10. How does a phrase such as "helping to inhabit" in the first paragraph contribute to the tone of the essay?

11. Find examples of understatement and hyperbole. Discuss their effects.

SUGGESTIONS FOR WRITING

1. Do you agree or disagree with Twain's assertion that "[i]t is our nature to conform" (para. 7)? Explain why.

2. Refute Twain's view of Public Opinion by defending word of mouth as the most reliable communicator of cultural innovation.

3. In paragraph 10, Twain contrasts prose styles that are "ornate and diffuse" with those that are characterized by "compactness and simplicity." Find examples of each, and write an essay comparing and contrasting the effects of the two prose styles.

4. Twain says he believed that the slave Jerry was "the greatest orator in the United States" (para. 1) but that "in the distribution of rewards he was overlooked." Write about how Jerry might have viewed his situation.

5. Write your own version of "Corn-Pone Opinions," giving examples from contemporary culture and politics. Do you end up making the same argument as Twain, or do you think Americans are more independent thinkers now? Explain why.

The Affluence of Despair

RAY BRADBURY

Ray Bradbury (1920–2012) was an American fantasy, science fiction, horror, and mystery writer and screenwriter. Bradbury was born in Waukegan, Illinois, and his family eventually settled in Los Angeles, California, when Bradbury was 14. After he was declared unfit for military service during World War II, he began his writing career. Over the course of his life, he wrote numerous books, including *Fahrenheit 451* (1953), a dystopian novel about the necessity of free speech. Bradbury's numerous awards and accolades include a star on the Hollywood Walk of Fame, a 2007 Pulitzer Citation, and a 2004 National Medal of the Arts. Bradbury's obituary in the *New York Times* calls him "the writer most responsible for bringing modern science fiction into the literary mainstream." He wrote the following op-ed for the *Wall Street Journal* in 1998.

How come? How come we're one of the greatest nations in the world . . . and yet, there is this feeling of Doom? How come, while our president walks wounded, we ourselves jog along nicely, but . . . under a dark cloud that says something awful is about to happen? How come, with 500,000 immigrants a year yammering to flood in . . . we enjoy what could be described as The Affluence of Despair?

America today: We wonder how we look at this hour, what we feel this minute, what we're imagining now. So we switch the television on. How do we look in the 80 million-lensed TV eye on America the beautiful? Did you catch

This graph, based on data published by Pew Research Center in 2016, shows how Americans prefer to get their news according to age group.

How could this data be used to support a counterargument to Bradbury's central thesis?

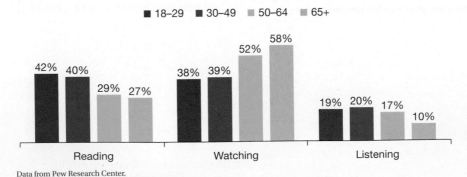

How Americans Prefer to Get Their News

■ 18–29 ■ 30–49 ▢ 50–64 ▢ 65+

	Reading	Watching	Listening
18–29	42%	38%	19%
30–49	40%	39%	20%
50–64	29%	52%	17%
65+	27%	58%	10%

Data from Pew Research Center.

J.C. Duffy/The New Yorker Collection/The Cartoon Bank

"Adding to the tragedy was the fact that no one caught it on tape for your amusement."

The novelist William Burroughs famously said that there is no such thing as an innocent bystander.
How does this cartoon comment on that idea? Which of Ray Bradbury's claims does this cartoon most closely reflect?

me last night confessing what I caught and what caught me?

Recall Starbuck's advice to mad Ahab?[1] "Do not fear me, old man. Beware of thyself, my captain." America should beware of itself. Today, we are everywhere loving to be watched. My God, look, I am on Channel Nine! We do not suffer from totalitarian lunatics, but from the astonishing proliferation of our images. We perform for ourselves, not Big Brother. We have fallen in love with mirrors. Flash a camera and your merest broccoli-headed citizen morphs into Travolta or Madonna.

And all of it on local TV news, in 15-second disaster updates. Breaking bones, breaking news, at 11. "Tell us, Mrs. Guiterrez, how's it feel with your son shotgunned minutes ago?"

We do not go to the theater, we are the theater. We have invaded the TV studios and run the country to mania on talking-head shows.

We display our brilliance on "Jeopardy," forgetting that its factoids are 90% useless once you kill the set. We don't ask who Napoleon was but where he was buried. Or why he invaded Russia, but when.

A friend of mine bragged he had bought a dish that could cup, cull, and catch 200 channels raining across a moron sky. Hell, I said, you've just got a bigger windmill to catch more of nothing: O.J. blood here, House of Usher AIDS there, the Killing Fields of America's high roads, each car a glorious pyre to mindless speed. And in every front yard a Mrs. Guiterrez being questioned but watching the TV mirror to see how she plays.

Those epileptic souls at football, baseball, hockey matches, who frenzy for the TV camera—how to end their pantomimes? We the judges and jurors trying, damning or freeing the guilty, weighing topics we're unqualified to answer—how to cork this motormouth?

The problem is not necessarily with our national full-coverage news, which can be only mildly depressing. It is with the assault of the

5

---

[1] In Herman Melville's iconic 1851 novel *Moby-Dick*, first mate Starbuck warns Captain Ahab to "beware of thyself." —Eds.

seeing connections

On Wednesday, December 2, 2015, a married coupled named Syed Rizwan Farook and Tashfeen Malik killed 14 people and injured 22 others in a mass shooting and attempted bombing of Inland Regional Center in San Bernardino, California. They were both killed by police in the ensuing chase and shootout. On the morning of Friday, December 4, Farook and Malik's landlord opened the couple's rented townhouse to news crews, who proceeded to go through their belongings on live television. National networks later came under fire for showing photographs and identifying documents of people who were not yet publicly identified as suspects.

While Bradbury warns against local news channels in "The Affluence of Despair," what might he have to say about the driving force behind the national networks' behavior in this case? How might he update his essay, which was first published in 1998, to account for the technological changes that have occurred since then?

local TV paparazzi, who machine-gun you with decapitations, sexual harassments, gangster executions in 15-second explosions for the full half-hour. No attack army could survive that fusillade. Bullets, real and psychological, wound and kill.

So we must stand alert, ward off a central core despair, target our Panic of the Week Syndrome, guard against the local TV séance. Every week, 52 weeks a year, they need a prime disaster focus to spin the garbage and glue the potato people to the tube.

Remember the Alar-poisoned apples that the dinner time newsbites claimed would destroy us, so they destroyed some part of the apple industry? Recall the poison cellar gas rising to asphyxiate your kids? Or those arsenic Peruvian grapes promising to strip our gears? Or the Three Mile Island[2] nuclear meltdown where nothing melted, no injuries, no deaths? Panic for two weeks, make it three. Ratings up. Morale down.

What to do? Leave a message on your local station's machine, describing their stupidity.

10

---

[2] A nuclear generating station in Pennsylvania, where a nuclear meltdown created panic among the general public in 1979. —Eds.

If you meet their news-readers, tell them that they are overpaid and underbrained. Ask them if it would be too much trouble to air 20-second newsbites instead of 15-second flashes. Think of the extra enrichment!

Stop saying that these TV hookers are high-class thinkers. Ask them to give back their fortunes and hand us real news. Instead of treating them as Cinderellas, tell them they are ugly sisters whose lips spew not diamonds and emeralds but spiders, frogs and toads: Each time they open their mouths, they spoil the ecology.

We must speak to these confessors of our dark souls and tell them that their awful truths in awesome repetition end with the Big Lie. We are not as bad as they say we are, but we feel this despair because they have somehow won us over.

The bottom line is that if you stare like stunned deer in mid-road, blinded by the lights that rush to run you down, you must expect that 1,000 such nights will convince you that the end of the world is at hand, that America is bestial, and that suicide, murder, rape, and AIDS are our lot.

We have condemned ourselves. Now we must save ourselves. No one else can. Shut off the set. Write your local TV news people. Tell them to go to hell. Go sit on the lawn with friends.

15

[1998]

EXPLORING THE TEXT

1. The essay begins with a fragment of a question that is repeated and expanded on in the second, third, and fourth sentences of that paragraph. Each of the sentences includes ellipses, pauses that slow the sentence down a bit. What is the effect of these ellipses, and how do they, along with the questions, set the tone for the essay? What ideas do they introduce?

2. Why do you think Ray Bradbury says we "enjoy" the affluence of despair (para. 1)?

3. What connection does Bradbury make between despair and affluence? What evidence does he offer in support of this viewpoint?

4. Paragraph 2 ends with two questions. How does Bradbury answer them in the essay?

5. What does Bradbury consider to be the worst aspect of late-night local news? Do you agree? Defend, challenge, or qualify his assertion in your response.

6. How does Bradbury characterize news anchors? How does that characterization contribute to the development of his argument? Does it ultimately strengthen or undermine Bradbury's main point? Explain your answer.

7. What does Bradbury means when he says "America should beware of itself" (para. 3)? What evidence does he offer elsewhere in the essay to support that assertion?

8. Who is Mrs. Guiterrez? What is her function in the essay?

9. How would you describe Bradbury's tone in "The Affluence of Despair"? To what extent is that tone a response to his audience and the subject matter? Explain whether you think this tone strengthens or undermines his argument.

10. In what ways does this essay appeal to ethos? How much "automatic ethos" does Bradbury bring to his argument? How much of his appeal comes from his voice?

11. What solutions does Bradbury offer for the affluence of despair? Are you convinced by them? Explain your answer. Could you apply any of these solutions to the effects of the Internet on our society?

12. To what extent do you find Bradbury's observations about local TV news relevant to the way we consume local and national news today? Does local news still have the impact that it had in 1998 when Bradbury wrote this essay?

High-School Confidential

Notes on Teen Movies

DAVID DENBY

David Denby (b. 1943), who lives in New York City, is a staff writer and film critic for the *New Yorker* and the former film critic for *New York*. His writing has also appeared in the *Atlantic*, the *New York Review of Books*, and the *New Republic*. His first book, *Great Books: My Adventures with Homer, Rousseau, Woolf, and Other Indestructible Writers of the Western World* (1996), was a finalist for the National Book Critics Circle Award. His other books include *American Sucker* (2004), *Snark: A Polemic in Seven Fits* (2009), *Do the Movies Have a Future?* (2012), and *Lit Up: One Reporter. Three Schools. Twenty-four Books That Can Change Lives* (2016). The essay that follows was originally published in the *New Yorker* in May 1999.

The most hated young woman in America is a blonde—well, sometimes a redhead or a brunette, but usually a blonde. She has big hair flipped into a swirl of gold at one side of her face or arrayed in a sultry mane, like the magnificent pile of a forties movie star. She's tall and slender, with a waist as supple as a willow, but she's dressed in awful, spangled taste: her outfits could have been put together by warring catalogues. And she has a mouth on her, a low, slatternly tongue that devastates other kids with such insults as "You're vapor, you're Spam!" and "Do I look like Mother Teresa? If I did, I probably wouldn't mind talking to the geek squad." She has two or three friends exactly like her, and together they dominate their realm— the American high school as it appears in recent teen movies. They are like wicked princesses, who enjoy the misery of their subjects. Her coronation, of course, is the senior prom, when she expects to be voted "most popular" by her class. But, though she may be popular, she is certainly not liked, so her power is something of a mystery. She is beautiful and rich, yet in the end she is preeminent because . . . she is preeminent, a position she works to maintain with Joan Crawford–like tenacity. Everyone is afraid of her; that's why she's popular.

She has a male counterpart. He's usually a football player, muscular but dumb, with a face like a beer mug and only two ways of speaking— in a conspiratorial whisper, to a friend; or in a drill sergeant's sudden bellow. If her weapon is the snub, his is the lame but infuriating prank— the can of Sprite emptied into a knapsack, or something sticky, creamy, or adhesive deposited in a locker. Sprawling and dull in class, he comes alive in the halls and in the cafeteria. He hurls people against lockers; he spits, pours, and sprays; he has a projectile relationship with food. As the crown prince, he claims the best-looking girl for himself, though in a perverse display of power he may invite an outsider or an awkward girl—a "dog"—to the prom, setting her up for some special humiliation. When we first see him, he is riding high, and virtually the entire school colludes in his tyranny. No authority figure—no teacher or administrator—dares correct him.

Thus the villains of the recent high-school movies. Not every American teen movie has these two characters, and not every social queen or jock shares all the attributes I've mentioned. (Occasionally, a handsome, dark-haired athlete can be converted to sweetness and light.) But as genre figures these two types are hugely familiar; that is, they are a common memory, a collective trauma, or at least a social and erotic fantasy. Such movies . . . as *Disturbing Behavior, She's All That, Ten Things I Hate about You,* and *Never Been Kissed* depend on them as stock figures. And

In what ways do these images from the films *Heathers* (1988) and *Mean Girls* (2004) and the television show *Riverdale* (2017) illustrate Denby's claim about who the real "enemy" is in teen movies? What do these images suggest about the durability of that claim?

◆ ◆ ◆

they may have been figures in the minds of the Littleton shooters, Eric Harris and Dylan Klebold, who imagined they were living in a school like the one in so many of these movies — a poisonous system of status, snobbery, and exclusion.

◆ ◆ ◆

Do genre films reflect reality? Or are they merely a set of conventions that refer to other films? Obviously, they wouldn't survive if they didn't provide emotional satisfaction to the people who make them and to the audiences who watch them. A half century ago, we didn't need to see ten Westerns a year in order to learn that the West got settled. We needed to see it settled ten times a year in order to provide ourselves with the emotional gratifications of righteous violence. By drawing his gun only when he was provoked, and in the service of the good, the classic Western hero transformed the gross tangibles of the expansionist drive (land, cattle, gold) into a principle of moral order. The gangster, by contrast, is a figure of chaos, a modern, urban person, and in the critic Robert Warshow's formulation he functions as a discordant element in an American society devoted to a compulsively "positive" outlook. When the gangster dies, he cleanses viewers of their own negative feelings.

High-school movies are also full of unease and odd, mixed-up emotions. They may be flimsy in conception; they may be shot in lollipop colors, garlanded with mediocre pop scores, and cast with goofy young actors trying to make an impression. Yet this most commercial and frivolous of genres harbors a grievance against the world. It's a very specific grievance, quite different from the restless anger of such fifties adolescent-rebellion movies as *The Wild One*, in which someone asks Marlon Brando's biker "What are you rebelling against?" and the biker replies "What have you got?" The fifties teen outlaw was against anything that adults considered sacred. But no movie teenager now revolts against adult authority, for the simple reason that adults have no authority. Teachers are rarely more than a minimal, exasperated presence, administrators get turned into a joke, and parents are either absent or distantly benevolent. It's a teen world bounded by school, mall, and car, with occasional moments set in the fast-food outlets where the kids work, or in the kids' upstairs bedrooms, with their pinups and rack stereo systems. The enemy is not authority; the enemy is other teens and the social system that they impose on one another.

The bad feeling in these movies may strike grownups as peculiar. After all, from a distance American kids appear to be having it easy these days. The teen audience is facing a healthy job market; at home, their parents are stuffing the den with computers and the garage with a bulky S.U.V. But most teens aren't thinking about the future job market. Lost in the eternal swoon of late adolescence, they're thinking about their identity, their friends, and their clothes. Adolescence is the present-tense moment in American life. Identity and status are fluid: abrupt, devastating reversals are always possible. (In a teen movie, a guy who swallows a bucket of cafeteria coleslaw can make himself a hero in an instant.) In these movies, accordingly, the senior prom is the equivalent of the shoot-out at the O.K. Corral; it's the moment when one's worth as a human being is settled at last. In the rather pedestrian new comedy *Never Been Kissed*, Drew Barrymore, as a twenty-five-year-old newspaper reporter, goes back to high school pretending to be a student, and immediately falls into her old, humiliating pattern of trying to impress the good-looking rich kids. Helplessly, she pushes for approval, and even gets herself chosen prom queen before finally coming to her senses. She finds it nearly impossible to let go.

❖ ❖ ❖

Genre films dramatize not what happens but how things feel — the emotional coloring of memory. They fix subjectivity into fable. At actual schools, there is no unitary system of status; there are many groups to be a part of, many places to excel (or fail to excel), many avenues of escape and self-definition. And often the movies, too, revel in the arcana of high-school cliques. In . . . *Disturbing Behavior*, a veteran student lays out the cafeteria ethnography for a newcomer: Motorheads, Blue Ribbons, Skaters, Micro-geeks ("drug of choice: Stephen Hawking's *A Brief History of Time* and a cup of jasmine tea on

Saturday night"). Subjectively, though, the social system in *Disturbing Behavior* (a high-school version of *The Stepford Wives*) and in the other movies still feels coercive and claustrophobic: humiliation is the most vivid emotion of youth, so in memory it becomes the norm.

The movies try to turn the tables. The kids who cannot be the beautiful ones, or make out with them, or avoid being insulted by them — these are the heroes of the teen movies, the third in the trio of character types. The female outsider is usually an intellectual or an artist. (She scribbles in a diary, she draws or paints.) Physically awkward, she walks like a seal crossing a beach, and is prone to drop her books and dither in terror when she stands before a handsome boy. Her clothes, which ignore mall fashion, scandalize the social queens. Like them, she has a tongue, but she's tart and grammatical, tending toward feminist pungency and precise diction. She may mask her sense of vulnerability with sarcasm or with Plathian rue (she's stuck in the bell jar), but even when she lashes out she can't hide her craving for acceptance.

The male outsider, her friend, is usually a mass of stuttering or giggling sexual gloom: he wears shapeless clothes; he has an undeveloped body, either stringy or shrimpy; he's sometimes a Jew (in these movies, still the generic outsider). He's also brilliant, but in a morose, preoccupied way that suggests masturbatory absorption in some arcane system of knowledge. In a few special cases, the outsider is not a loser but a disengaged hipster, either saintly or satanic. (Christian Slater has played this role a couple of times.) This outsider wears black and keeps his hair long, and he knows how to please women. He sees through everything, so he's ironic by temperament and genuinely indifferent to the opinion of others — a natural aristocrat, who transcends the school's contemptible status system. There are whimsical variations on the outsider figure, too. In the recent *Rushmore*, an obnoxious teen hero, Max Fischer

(Jason Schwartzman), runs the entire school: he can't pass his courses but he's a dynamo at extracurricular activities, with a knack for staging extraordinary events. He's a con man, a fund-raiser, an entrepreneur — in other words, a contemporary artist.

In fact, the entire genre, which combines self-pity and ultimate vindication, might be called "Portrait of the Filmmaker as a Young Nerd." Who can doubt where Hollywood's twitchy, nearsighted writers and directors ranked — or feared they ranked — on the high-school totem pole? They are still angry, though occasionally the target of their resentment goes beyond the jocks and cheerleaders of their youth. Consider this anomaly: the young actors and models on the covers of half the magazines published in this country, the shirtless men with chests like burnished shields, the girls smiling, glowing, tweezed, full-lipped, full-breasted (but not too full), and with skin so honeyed that it seems lacquered — these are the physical ideals embodied by the villains of the teen movies. The social queens and jocks, using their looks to dominate others, represent an American barbarism of beauty. Isn't it possible that the detestation of them in teen movies is a veiled strike at the entire abs-hair advertising culture, with its unobtainable glories of perfection? A critic of consumerism might even see a spark of revolt in these movies. But only a spark.

My guess is that these films arise from remembered hurts which then get recast in symbolic form. For instance, a surprising number of the outsider heroes have no mother. Mom has died or run off with another man; her child, only half loved, is ill equipped for the emotional pressures of school. The motherless child, of course, is a shrewd commercial ploy that makes a direct appeal to the members of the audience, many of whom may feel like outsiders, too, and unloved, or not loved enough, or victims of some prejudice or exclusion. But the motherless child also has powers, and will someday be a success, an artist,

10

a screenwriter. It's the wound and the bow all over again, in cargo pants.

As the female nerd attracts the attention of the handsomest boy in the senior class, the teen movie turns into a myth of social reversal — a Cinderella fantasy. Initially, his interest in her may be part of a stunt or a trick: he is leading her on, perhaps at the urging of his queenly girlfriend. But his gaze lights her up, and we see how attractive she really is. Will she fulfill the eternal specs? She wants her prince, and by degrees she wins him over, not just with her looks but with her superior nature, her essential goodness. In the male version of the Cinderella trip, a few years go by, and a pale little nerd (we see him at a reunion) has become rich. All that poking around with chemicals paid off. Max Fischer, of *Rushmore*, can't miss being richer than Warhol.

So the teen movie is wildly ambivalent. It may attack the consumerist ethos that produces winners and losers, but in the end it confirms what it is attacking. The girls need the seal of approval conferred by the converted jocks; the nerds need money and a girl. Perhaps it's no surprise that the outsiders can be validated only by the people who ostracized them. But let's not be too schematic: the outsider who joins the system also modifies it, opens it up to the creative power of social mobility, makes it bend and laugh, and perhaps this turn of events is not so different from the way things work in the real world, where merit and achievement stand a good chance of trumping appearance. The irony of the Littleton shootings is that Klebold and Harris, who were both proficient computer heads, seemed to have forgotten how the plot turns out. If they had held on for a few years they might have been working at a hip software company, or have started their own business, while the jocks who oppressed them would probably have wound up selling insurance or used cars. That's the one unquestionable social truth the teen movies reflect: geeks rule.

seeing connections

These graphs, from a 2016 study entitled "Gender and the Returns to Attractiveness," show the relationship researchers found between gender, attractiveness, and income. **What claim(s) does Denby make that could be challenged by this data? Does Denby make any claims that this data would appear to support? Explain.**

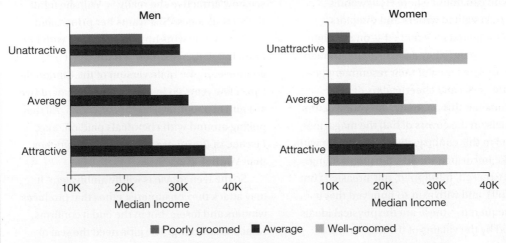

The Relationship between Attractiveness, Grooming Habits, and Income

Data from Wong, Jaclyn and Andrew Penner. "Gender and the returns to attractiveness." *Research in Social Stratification and Mobility,* vol. 44, June 2016, pp. 113–123.

◆ ◆ ◆

There is, of course, a menacing subgenre, in which the desire for revenge turns bloody. Thirty-one years ago, Lindsay Anderson's semi-surrealistic *If . . .* was set in an oppressive, class-ridden English boarding school, where a group of rebellious students drive the school population out into a courtyard and open fire on them with machine guns. In Brian De Palma's 1976 masterpiece *Carrie*, the pale, repressed heroine, played by Sissy Spacek, is courted at last by a handsome boy but gets violated — doused with pig's blood — just as she is named prom queen. Stunned but far from powerless, Carrie uses her telekinetic powers to set the room afire and burn down

the school. *Carrie* is the primal school movie, so wildly lurid and funny that it exploded the clichés of the genre before the genre was quite set: the heroine may be a wrathful avenger, but the movie, based on a Stephen King book, was clearly a grinning-gargoyle fantasy. So, at first, was *Heathers*, in which Christian Slater's satanic outsider turns out to be a true devil. He and his girlfriend (played by a very young Winona Ryder) begin gleefully knocking off the rich, nasty girls and the jocks, in ways so patently absurd that their revenge seems a mere wicked dream. I think it's unlikely that these movies had a direct effect on the actions of the Littleton shooters, but the two boys would surely have recognized the emotional world of *Heathers* and

Disturbing Behavior as their own. It's a place where feelings of victimization join fantasy, and you experience the social élites as so powerful that you must either become them or kill them.

But enough. It's possible to make teen movies that go beyond these fixed polarities — insider and outsider, blonde-bitch queen and hunch-shouldered nerd. In Amy Heckerling's 1995 comedy *Clueless*, the big blonde played by Alicia Silverstone is a Rodeo Drive clotheshorse who is nonetheless possessed of extraordinary virtue. Freely dispensing advice and help, she's almost ironically good — a designing goddess with a cell phone. The movie offers a sun-shiny satire of Beverly Hills affluence, which it sees as both absurdly swollen and generous in spirit. The most original of the teen comedies, *Clueless* casts away self-pity. So does *Romy and Michele's High School Reunion* (1997), in which two gabby, lovable friends, played by Mira Sorvino and Lisa Kudrow, review the banalities of their high-school

15

experience so knowingly that they might be criticizing the teen-movie genre itself. And easily the best American film of the year so far is Alexander Payne's *Election*, a high-school movie that inhabits a different aesthetic and moral world altogether from the rest of these pictures. *Election* shreds everyone's fantasies and illusions in a vision of high school that is bleak but supremely just. The movie's villain, an over-achieving girl (Reese Witherspoon) who runs for class president, turns out to be its covert heroine, or, at least, its most poignant character. A cross between Pat and Dick Nixon, she's a lower-middle-class striver who works like crazy and never wins anyone's love. Even when she's on top, she feels excluded. Her loneliness is produced not by malicious cliques but by her own implacable will, a condition of the spirit that may be as comical and tragic as it is mysterious. *Election* escapes all the clichés; it graduates into art.

[1999]

EXPLORING THE TEXT

1. What is David Denby's opinion of teen movies? Does he find anything redeeming in them? Do you agree that it is the "most commercial and frivolous of genres" (para. 5)? Explain your response.

2. Denby mentions three movies that "go beyond [the] fixed polarities" (para. 15): *Clueless*, *Romy and Michele's High School Reunion*, and *Election*. Do you agree? Do any recent teen movies transcend the genre? Explain.

3. What rhetorical strategies does Denby use in the first paragraph to create a picture of the female villain of teen movies? Consider such strategies as irony, hyperbole, metaphor, colloquialisms, and opposition. What are their effects?

4. Where do you detect changes in Denby's tone? How does Denby achieve these changes?

5. The essay makes several appeals to ethos. Denby is a well-known film critic. How does he use the expertise of others — implicitly and explicitly — to support his argument?

6. What is Denby's central argument? What are his secondary arguments? How does he bring them together?

7. In paragraph 13, Denby argues that the two teenage boys who killed classmates, teachers, and then themselves at Columbine High School did not learn the lesson of teen movies: "geeks rule." How does he support this argument?

8. Who is the likely audience for this essay? How does Denby consider audience in his essay?

The Price Is Right
What Advertising Does to TV

EMILY NUSSBAUM

Emily Nussbaum (b. 1966) is a Pulitzer Prize–winning TV critic for the *New Yorker*. She was educated at Oberlin College and New York University and has contributed to *Slate*, the *New York Times*, *New York* magazine, and has served as the editor-in-chief of *Nerve*. In 2014, Nussbaum was awarded a National Magazine Award for Columns and Commentary, and in 2016, she was awarded the Pulitzer Prize for Criticism. The essay that follows was originally published in the *New Yorker* in 2015.

Ever since the finale of "Mad Men," I've been meditating on its audacious last image. Don Draper, sitting cross-legged and purring "Ommmm," is achieving inner peace at an Esalen[1]-like retreat. He's as handsome as ever, in khakis and a crisp white shirt. A bell rings, and a grin widens across his face. Then, as if cutting to a sponsor, we move to the iconic Coke ad from 1971 — a green hillside covered with a racially diverse chorus of young people, trilling, in harmony, "I'd like to teach the world to sing." Don Draper, recently suicidal, has invented the world's greatest ad. He's *back*, baby.

The scene triggered a debate online. From one perspective, the image looked cynical: the viewer is tricked into thinking that Draper has achieved Nirvana, only to be slapped with the source of his smile. It's the grin of an adman who has figured out how to use enlightenment to peddle sugar water, co-opting the counter-culture as a brand. Yet, from another angle, the scene looked idealistic. Draper has indeed had a spiritual revelation, one that he's expressing in a beautiful way — through advertising, his great gift. The night the episode aired, it struck me as a dark joke. But, at a discussion a couple of days later, at the New York Public Library, Matthew Weiner, the show's creator, told the novelist A. M. Homes that viewers should see the hilltop ad as "very pure,"

the product of "an enlightened state." To regard it otherwise, he warned, was itself the symptom of a poisonous mind-set.

The question of how television fits together with advertising — and whether we should resist that relationship or embrace it — has haunted the medium since its origins. Advertising is TV's original sin. When people called TV shows garbage, which they did all the time, until recently, commercialism was at the heart of the complaint. Even great TV could never be good art, because it was tainted by definition. It was there to sell.

That was the argument made by George W. S. Trow in this magazine, in a feverish manifesto called "Within the Context of No Context." That essay, which ran in 1980, became a sensation, as coruscating denunciations of modernity so often do. In television, "the trivial is raised up to power," Trow wrote. "The powerful is lowered toward the trivial." Driven by "demography" — that is, by the corrupting force of money and ratings — television treats those who consume it like sales targets, encouraging them to view themselves that way. In one of several sections titled "Celebrities," he writes, "The most successful celebrities are products. Consider the real role in American life of Coca-Cola. Is any man as well-loved as this soft drink is?"

Much of Trow's essay, which runs to more than a hundred pages, makes little sense. It is written in the style of oracular poetry, full of elegant repetitions, elegant repetitions that induce

---

[1] A nonprofit retreat center located in California, founded in 1962 to support uncommon approaches to examining human mindfulness. —Eds.

5

seeing connections

Emily Nussbaum opens her essay with a discussion of the last scene of the series *Mad Men*. Don Draper, played by Jon Hamm, is seen meditating at a retreat in Big Sur. He utters the syllable "om" along with the rest of the group and smiles mysteriously. Just as the camera has finished zooming in on his face, the iconic 1971 Coca Cola commercial, "I'd Like to Buy the World a Coke," plays in its entirety. The commercial features a folk song and ends with the chorus, "It's the real thing."

The scene has been read many ways; how does Nussbaum use it to comment on the effects of advertising on television?

a hypnotic effect, elegant repetitions that suggest authority through their wonderful numbing rhythms, but which contain few facts. It's élitism in the guise of hipness. It is more nostalgic than "Mad Men" ever was for the era when Wasp men in hats ran New York. It's a screed against TV written at the medium's low point — after the energy of the sitcoms of the seventies had faded but before the innovations of the nineties — and it paints TV fans as brainwashed dummies.

And yet there's something in Trow's manifesto that I find myself craving these days: that rude resistance to being sold to, the insistence that there is, after all, such a thing as selling out. Those of us who love TV have won the war. The best scripted shows are regarded as significant art — debated, revered, denounced. TV show-runners are embraced as heroes and role models, even philosophers. At the same time, television's business model is in chaos, splintered and re-forming itself, struggling with its own history. Making television has always meant bending to the money — and TV history has taught us to be cool with any compromise. But sometimes we're knowing about things that we don't know much about at all.

◆ ◆ ◆

Once upon a time, TV made sense, economically and structurally: a few dominant network shows ran weekly, with ads breaking them up, like choruses between verses. Then came pay cable, the VCR, the DVD, the DVR, and the Internet. At this point, the model seems to morph every six months. Oceanic flat screens give way to palm-size iPhones. A cheap writer-dominated medium absorbs pricey Hollywood directors. You can steal TV; you can buy TV; you can get it free. Netflix, a distributor, becomes a producer. On Amazon, customers vote for which pilots will survive. Shows cancelled by NBC jump to Yahoo, which used to be a failing search engine. The two most ambitious and original début series this

summer came not from HBO or AMC but from a pair of lightweight cable networks whose slogans might as well be "Please underestimate us": Lifetime, with "Unreal," and USA Network, with "Mr. Robot." That there is a summer season at all is a new phenomenon. This fall, as the networks launch a bland slate of pilots, we know there are better options.

A couple of months ago, at a meeting of the Television Critics Association, the C.E.O. of FX, John Landgraf, delivered a speech about "peak TV," in which he lamented the exponential rise in production: three hundred and seventy-one scripted shows last year, more than four hundred expected this year — a bubble, Landgraf said, that would surely deflate. He got some pushback: Why now, when the door had cracked open to more than white-guy antiheroes, was it "too much" for viewers? But just as worrisome was the second part of Landgraf's speech, in which he wondered how the industry could fund so much TV. What was the model, now that the pie had been sliced into slivers? When Landgraf took his job, in 2005, ad buys made up more than fifty per cent of FX's revenue, he said. Now that figure was thirty-two per cent. When ratings drop, ad rates drop, too, and when people fast-forward producers look for new forms of access: through apps, through data mining, through deals that shape the shows we see, both visibly and invisibly. Some of this involves the ancient art of product integration, by which sponsors buy the right to be part of the story: these are the ads that can't be fast-forwarded.

This is both a new crisis and an old one. When television began, it was a live medium. Replicating radio, it was not merely supported by admen; it was run by them. In TV's early years, there were no showrunners: the person with ultimate authority was the product representative, the guy from Lysol or Lucky Strike. Beneath that man (always a man) was a network exec. A layer down were writers, who were fungible, nameless figures, with the exception of people like Paddy Chayefsky, machers[2] who often retreated when they grew frustrated by the industry's censorious limits. The result was that TV writers developed a complex mix of pride and shame, a sense that they were hired hands, not artists. It was a working-class model of creativity. The shows might be funny or beautiful, but their creators would never own them.

Advertisements shaped everything about early television programs, including their length and structure, with clear acts to provide logical inlets for ads to appear. Initially, there were rules governing how many ads could run: the industry standard was six minutes per hour. (Today, on network, it's about fourteen minutes.) But this didn't include the vast amounts of product integration that were folded into the scripts. (Product placement, which involves props, was a given.) Viewers take for granted that this is native to the medium, but it's unique to the U.S.; in the United Kingdom, such deals were prohibited until 2011. Even then, they were barred from the BBC, banned for alcohol and junk food, and required to be visibly declared — a "P" must appear onscreen.

In "Brought to You By: Postwar Television Advertising and the American Dream," Lawrence R. Samuel describes early shows like NBC's "Coke Time," in which Eddie Fisher sipped the soda. On an episode of "I Love Lucy" called "The Diet," Lucy and Desi smoked Philip Morris cigarettes. On "The Flintstones," the sponsor Alka-Seltzer ruled that no character get a stomach ache, and that there be no derogatory presentations of doctors, dentists, or druggists. On "My Little Margie," Philip Morris reps struck the phrase "I'm real cool!," lest it be associated with their competitors Kool cigarettes. If you were a big name — like Jack Benny, whom Samuel calls "the king of

integrated advertising" — "plugola" was par for the course. (Benny once mentioned Schwinn bikes, then looked directly into the camera and deadpanned, "Send three.") There were only a few exceptions, including Sid Caesar, who refused to tout brands on "Your Show of Shows."

Sponsors were a conservative force. They helped blacklist writers suspected of being Communists, and, for decades, banned plots about homosexuality and "miscegenation." In Jeff Kisseloff's oral history "The Box," from 1995, Bob Lewine, of ABC, describes pitching Sammy Davis, Jr., in an all-black variety show: Young & Rubicam execs walked out, so the idea was dropped. This tight leash affected even that era's version of prestige TV. In "Brought to You By," Samuel lists topics deemed off limits as "politics, sex, adultery, unemployment, poverty, successful criminality and alcohol" — now the basic food groups of cable. In one notorious incident, the American Gas Association sponsored CBS's anthology series "Playhouse 90." When an episode called "Portrait of a Murderer" ended, it created an unfortunate juxtaposition: after the killer was executed, the show cut to an ad with the slogan "Nothing but gas does so many jobs so well." Spooked, American Gas took a closer look at an upcoming project, George Roy Hill's "Judgment at Nuremberg." The company objected to any mention of the gas chambers — and though the writers resisted, the admen won.

This sponsor-down model held until the late fifties, around the time that the quiz-show scandals traumatized viewers: producers, in their quest to please ad reps, had cheated. Both economic pressures and the public mood contributed to increased creative control by networks, as the old one-sponsor model dissolved. But the precedent had been established: when people talked about TV,

10

---

[2] Yiddish: a mover and shaker. —Eds.

ratings and quality were existentially linked, the business and the art covered by critics as one thing. Or, as Trow put it, "What is loved is a hit. What is a hit is loved."

◆ ◆ ◆

Kenya Barris's original concept for the ABC series "Black-ish," last year's smartest network-sitcom début, was about a black writer in a TV writers' room. But then he made the lead role a copywriter at an ad agency, which allowed the network to cut a deal with Buick, so that the show's hero, Dre, is seen brainstorming ads for its car. In *Automotive News*, Buick's marketing manager, Molly Peck, said that the company worked closely with Barris. "We get the benefit of being part of the program, so people are actually watching it as opposed to advertising where viewers often don't watch it."

Product integration is a small slice of the advertising budget, but it can take on outsized symbolic importance, as the watermark of a sponsor's power to alter the story — and it is often impossible to tell whether the mention is paid or not. "The Mindy Project" celebrates Tinder. An episode of "Modern Family" takes place on iPods and iPhones. On the ABC Family drama "The Fosters," one of the main characters, a viceprincipal, talks eagerly about the tablets her school is buying. "Wow, it's so light!" she says, calling the product by its full name, the "Kindle Paperwhite e-reader," and listing its useful features. On last year's most charming début drama, the CW's "Jane the Virgin," characters make trips to Target, carry Target bags, and prominently display the logo.

Those are shows on channels that are explicitly commercialized. But similar deals ripple through cable television and the new streaming producers. FX cut a deal with MillerCoors, so that every character who drinks or discusses a beer is drinking its brands. (MillerCoors designs retro bottles for "The Americans.") According to *Ad Age*, Anheuser-Busch struck a deal with

"House of Cards," trading supplies of booze for onscreen appearances; purportedly, Samsung struck another, to be the show's "tech of choice." Unilever's Choco Taco paid for integration on Comedy Central's "Workaholics," aiming to be "the dessert for millennials." On NBC, Dan Harmon's avant-garde comedy, "Community," featured an anti-corporate plot about Subway paid for by Subway. When the show jumped to Yahoo, the episode "Advanced Safety Features" was about Honda. "It's not there were just a couple of guys driving the car; it was the whole episode about Honda," Tom Peyton, an assistant V.P. of marketing at Honda, told *Ad Week*. "You hold your breath as an advertiser, and I'm sure they did too — did you go too far and commercialize the whole thing and take it away from it? — but I think the opposite happened. . . . Huge positives."

Whether that bothers you or impresses you may depend on whether you laughed and whether you noticed. There's a common notion that there's good and bad integration. The "bad" stuff is bumptious — unfunny and in your face. "Good" integration is either invisible or ironic, and it's done by people we trust, like Stephen Colbert or Tina Fey. But it brings out my inner George Trow. To my mind, the cleverer the integration, the more harmful it is. It's a sedative designed to make viewers feel that there's nothing to be angry about, to admire the ad inside the story, to train us to shrug off every compromise as necessary and normal.

Self-mocking integration used to seem modern to me — the irony of a post-"Simpsons" generation — until I realized that it was actually nostalgic: Jack Benny did sketches in which he playfully "resisted" sponsors like Lucky Strike and Lipton tea. Alfred Hitchcock, on "Alfred Hitchcock Presents," made snide remarks about Bristol-Myers. The audience had no idea that those wisecracks were scripted by a copywriter who had submitted them to Bristol-Myers for approval.

15

A few weeks ago, Stephen Colbert began hosting CBS's "Late Show." In his first show, he pointed to a "cursed" amulet. He was under the amulet's control, Colbert moaned, and thus had been forced to "make certain" — he paused — "regrettable compromises." Then he did a bit in which he slavered over Sabra hummus and Rold Gold pretzels. Some critics described the act as satire, but that's a distinction without a difference. Colbert embraced "sponsortunities" when he was on Comedy Central, too, behind the mask of an ironic persona; it's likely one factor that made him a desirable replacement for Letterman, the worst salesman on late-night TV.

During this summer of industry chaos, [20] one TV show did make a pungent case against consumerism: "Mr. Robot," on USA Network. A dystopian thriller with Occupy-inflected politics, the series was refreshing, both for its melancholy beauty and for its unusually direct attack on corporate manipulation. "Mr. Robot" was the creation of a TV newcomer, Sam Esmail, who found himself in an odd position: his anti-branding show was itself rebranding an aggressively corporate network, known for its "blue sky" procedurals — a division of NBCUniversal, a subsidiary of Comcast.

"Mr. Robot" tells the story of Elliott Alderson, corporate cog by day, hacker by night, a mentally unstable junkie who is part of an Anonymous-like collective that conspires to delete global debt. In one scene, Elliott fantasizes about being conventional enough for a girlfriend: "I'll go see those stupid Marvel movies with her. I'll join a gym. I'll heart things on Instagram." He walks into his boss's office with a Starbucks vanilla latte, the most basic of beverages. This sort of straightforwardly hostile namecheck is generally taboo, both to avoid offending potential sponsors and to leave doors open for their competitors. Esmail says he fought to get real brands in the story, citing "Mad Men" as precedent, as his phone calls with the network's lawyers went from "weekly to daily."

Were any of these mentions paid for? Not in the first season — although Esmail says that he did pursue integrations with brands, some of which turned him down and some of which he turned down (including tech companies that demanded "awkward language" about their features). He's open to these deals in Season 2. "If the idea is to inspire an interesting debate over capitalism, I actually think (depending on how we use it) it can help provoke that conversation even more," he said. As long as such arrangements are "organic and not forced," they're fine with him — what's crucial is not the money but the verisimilitude that brands provide. Only one major conflict came up, Esmail said, in the finale, when Elliott's mysterious alter ego screams in the middle of Times Square, "I'm no less real than the fucking meat patty in your Big Mac." Esmail and USA agreed to bleep "Big Mac" — "to be sensitive to ad sales," Esmail told me — but they left it in for online airings. Esmail said he's confident that the network fought for him. "Maybe Comcast has a relationship with McDonald's?" he mused. (USA told me that the reason was "standards and practices.")

◆ ◆ ◆

"Are you asking me how I feel about product integration?" Matt Weiner said. "I'm for it." Everything on TV is an ad for something, he pointed out, down to Jon Hamm's beautifully pomaded hair — and he argued that a paid integration is far less harmful than other propaganda embedded in television, such as how cop shows celebrate the virtues of the state. We all have our sponsors. Michelangelo painted for the Pope! What's dangerous about modern TV isn't advertisers, Weiner told me; it's creatives not getting enough of a cut of the proceeds.

Weiner used to work in network television, in a more restrictive creative environment, until he got his break, on "The Sopranos." Stepping into HBO's subscription-only chamber meant being part of a prestige brand: no ads, that gorgeous hissing logo, critical bennies. The move to AMC, then a minor cable station, was a challenge. Weiner longed for the most elegant model, with one sponsor — the approach of "Playhouse 90." But getting ads took hustle, even in a show about them. Weiner's description of the experience of writing integrations is full of cognitive dissonance. On the one hand, he said, wistfully, he didn't realize at first that he could say no to integrations. Yet he was frustrated by the ones he couldn't get, like attaching Revlon to Peggy's "Basket of Kisses" plot about lipstick. Such deals were valuable — "money you don't leave on the floor" — but it was crucial that the audience not know about them, and that there be few.

The first integration on "Mad Men," for Jack Daniel's, was procured before Weiner got involved; writing it into the script made him feel "icky." (Draper wouldn't drink Jack Daniel's, Weiner told me.) Pond's cold cream was a more successful fit. But he tried to impose rules: the sponsor could see only the pages its brand was on; dialogue would mention competitors; and, most important, the company couldn't run ads the night its episode was on the air. Unilever cheated, Weiner claimed — and AMC allowed it. The company filmed ads mimicking the "Mad Men" aesthetic, making the tie with the show visible. If viewers knew that Pond's was integrated, they wouldn't lose themselves in the story, Weiner worried.

In the end, he says, he did only three — Heineken was the third (an integration procured after Michelob backed out). I naïvely remarked that Jaguar couldn't have paid: who would want to be the brand of sexual coercion? "You'd be surprised," he said. Jaguar didn't buy a plug, but the company loved the plot — and hired Christina Hendricks to flack the car, wearing a bright-red pantsuit.

Weiner had spent the Television Critics Association convention talking up "Mr. Robot" and he told me that he was "stunned" by

25

Esmail's show, which he called American TV's "first truly contemporary anti-corporate message." Then again, he said, "show business in general has been very good at co-opting the people that bite the hands that feed them." NBCUniversal was wise to buy into Esmail's radical themes, he said, because these are ideas that the audience is ready for — "even the Tea Party knows we don't want to give the country over to corporations."

Weiner made clear that Coke hadn't paid for any integration; he mentioned it a few times. Finally, I asked, Why not? "Mad Men" ended in a way that both Coke and viewers could admire. Why not take the money? Two reasons, he said. First, Coca-Cola could "get excited and start making demands." But, really, he didn't want to "disturb the purity of treating that ad as what it was." Weiner is proud that "Mad Men" had a lasting legacy, influencing how viewers saw television's potential, how they thought about money and power, creativity and the nature of work. He didn't want them to think that Coke had bought his finale.

◆ ◆ ◆

There is no art form that doesn't run a three-legged race with the sponsors that support its production, and the weaker an industry gets (journalism, this means you; music, too) the more ethical resistance flags. But readers would be grossed out to hear that Karl Ove Knausgaard[3] had accepted a bribe to put the Talking Heads into his childhood memories. They'd be angry if Stephen Sondheim[4] slipped a Dewar's jingle into "Company." That's not priggishness or élitism. It's a belief that art is powerful, that storytelling is real, that when we immerse ourselves in that way it's a vulnerable

---

[3] A contemporary Norwegian writer, known for writing a series of six autobiographical novels entitled *My Struggle*. —Eds.

[4] A widely celebrated contemporary composer and lyricist, known primarily for his work on several major Broadway musicals. —Eds.

act of trust. Why wouldn't this be true for television, too?

Viewers have little control over how any show [30] gets made; TV writers and directors have only a bit more — their roles mingle creativity and management in a way that's designed to create confusion. Even the experts lack expertise, these days. But I wonder if there's a way for us to be less comfortable as consumers, to imagine ourselves as the partners not of the advertisers but of the artists — to crave purity, naïve as that may sound. I miss "Mad Men," that nostalgic meditation on nostalgia. But embedded in its vision was the notion that television writing and copywriting are and should be mirrors, twins. Our comfort with being sold to may look like savvy, but it feels like innocence. There's something to be said for the emotions that Trow tapped into, disgust and outrage and betrayal — emotions that can be embarrassing but are useful when we're faced with something ugly.

Perhaps this makes me sound like a drunken twenty-two-year-old waving a battered copy of Naomi Klein's "No Logo."[5] But that's what happens when you love an art form. In my imagination, television would be capable of anything. It could offend anyone; it could violate any rule. For it to get there, we might have to expect of it what we expect of any art.

[2015]

---

[5] A 1999 nonfiction book by Canadian cultural critic Naomi Klein that explores the negative consequences of consumerism. —Eds.

EXPLORING THE TEXT

1. How does Emily Nussbaum establish credibility? Try to provide at least three different examples.

2. Nussbaum begins her essay with a description of the last scene of the series *Mad Men*, which she comes back to several times in the essay. As she notes, it's a scene that can be read several ways. How does she use it to develop her argument? Trace Nussbaum's use of the scene throughout the essay, noting the different ways she presents it as evidence.

3. What are some of the observations Nussbaum makes about the relationship between television and advertising? Find at least three examples that illustrate her observations of that relationship.

4. How would you describe the tone of *The Price Is Right*? How is that tone created?

5. How does Nussbaum use George W. S. Trow's "manifesto," "Within the Context of No Context," an essay she says "makes little sense," (para. 5) as both a counterargument and as evidence for her own argument?

6. Summarize the history of television advertising as Nussbaum portrays it. What are the most recent changes she mentions? What has changed since this essay's publication in 2015?

7. Identify at least two different types of evidence Nussbaum uses to develop her argument. How do they serve her purpose? How do they reflect the assumptions she makes about her audience?

8. What is Nussbaum's view of "product integration" (para. 8)? How does it relate to her central argument?

9. In paragraph 29 Nussbaum compares television to other arts, such as fiction and musical theater, noting that "art is powerful, that storytelling is real, that when we immerse ourselves in that way it's a vulnerable act of trust." She asks why this wouldn't be true for television. How does she answer this question? What is your answer to the question?

10. How does Nussbaum characterize the influence of advertising on early TV? Compare her views on the older model to her view of the modern practice of product integration. Which does she consider the lesser of two evils, and why?

How the Motorcycle Jacket Lost Its Cool and Found It Again

TROY PATTERSON

Troy Patterson is an American writer who was born in Virginia, educated at Princeton, and now lives in New York City. Patterson covers a range of topics for several outlets, including books for *National Public Radio*, TV for *Slate*, film for *Spin*, and luxury products for *Bloomberg*. He has contributed criticism to numerous other magazines, including the *New York Times Magazine*, the *New York Times Book Review*, *Men's Vogue*, *Wired*, and *Entertainment Weekly*. The following article, which explores the shifting cultural significance of the biker jacket, was originally published in the *New York Times* in 2015.

Out at dinner one recent night, I watched the couple at the next table drift into a moment of ultralight petting. She had on a black leather motorcycle jacket, and he was toying, not quite idly, with the zipper at the cuff of its tapered right sleeve. The chain of the zipper caught the candlelight, as did the supple surface of the leather, which seemed as soft as lambskin and poorly suited for riding (let alone very suddenly not riding) a bike down the blacktop. But her cuff could zip shut to seal out the wind, and he was playing with its pull. Zip, and then unzip; he was enchanted. I had seen motorcycle jackets look sharp, hard, camp, goonish, and corny, but this cuteness was new to me, and perhaps to the jacket, a garment that keeps compounding its power to activate imaginations.

The classic motorcycle jacket — double-breasted, distinguished by an asymmetric front zipper and ample lapels — was pioneered by Irving Schott in 1928. (People tend to abuse Schott's trademark, Perfecto, as a generic reference to any of the countless models inspired by its cut.) With its aerodynamic geometry and lavish romance of machines, the design exemplifies Art Deco values, a polished modernism no more likely to grow tiresome than the Chrysler Building. Leather seems to animate this industrial form with a primal spirit, as if

we had updated ancient beliefs associating animal hides and magical powers to suit our secular rituals.

On an autumn afternoon of what fashion blogs call "leather weather," I drifted south down Madison Avenue past boutiques where shopgirls who abbreviate motorcycle jacket to "moto" wore cropped motos on the job. At 68th Street, on a screen in the window at the luxury-sportswear store Belstaff, David Beckham wore a mandarin-collared racing jacket to preen through the night scape of a promotional film. At a sidewalk cafe near 62nd, two women lunched performatively, each reflecting the other's moto in her shades. At 61st Street, I stepped into Barneys, where motorcycle jackets priced up to $5,000 waited to seduce shoppers who were already wearing motorcycle jackets, the hardware of which coordinated with the buckles on their bootees, the chains on their purses, the gleams in their eyes.

I felt a need to put one on. What's *that* jacket? Margiela, a fashion house based in Paris, intended it as a replica of a 1950s Perfecto, according to a label sewn into a quilted red lining as rich as a juicy secret. Was I trying this on or was I auditioning for it? Zipped up and belted in, cased in black calfskin, studded with silvertone snap heads, I felt armored, cosseted, insulated against the world and its mundanity. In the mirror, Narcissus[1] was tingling. The thrust of the epaulets alone was good for a jolt of euphoria. The motorcycle jacket encourages a sense of confidence in its inhabitant. Foremost, it confirms the least suspicion that he has the brass to this pull off.

The motorcyclist of the popular imagination mutated from a genial daredevil into a diabolical marauder over the course of Independence Day weekend in 1947. Reviving a tradition of the 1930s, the town of Hollister, Calif., hosted a bike rally that got out of hand, swollen with men returned from the war and disturbing the peace. That the motorcycle club at the center of the action was called the Boozefighters indicates the flavor of the mayhem. Reporters covered the disorder as an epic of looting and pillage; a writer named Frank Rooney converted it into "Cyclists' Raid," a short story published in *Harper's Magazine*. Rooney's protagonist wore a brown windbreaker, but the film producer Stanley Kramer, adapting the story into "The Wild One," had a rather more vivid idea of how to outfit an antihero. Here was Marlon Brando, in a Schott Perfecto, prowling the frame, exaggerating an old standard of male beauty to arrive at a new ideal of neoclassical beefcake. The film debuted in 1953 — the year Elvis Presley made his earliest recordings and the first color TVs went on sale — and likewise announced the opening of a new era in imagery.

"The Wild One" has not aged well, but that scarcely matters. Brando's mumbles articulated a style of spite, and his poses in publicity stills shaped a creed of cool that does not age at all. Having hurtled into a Nowheresville of an Anytown, he is hypermasculine and stereotypically feminine at once as he leans on the bike, a brute with the grace of an odalisque on a divan,

5

Troy Patterson argues that Marlon Brando, in *The Wild One*, was "exaggerating an old standard of male beauty to arrive at a new ideal of neoclassical beefcake." **What elements of this image of Brando support his observation?**

Michael Ochs Archives/Getty Images

commanding adoration. Brando's jacket — until then most notable as the protective gear of aviators and highway patrolmen — became an institution on the strength of the way he wore it. Together they made a meme — a look swiftly mimicked, cloned, valorized, spoofed, appropriated by couturiers and silk-screened by Andy Warhol in a series of works that must constitute its sanctification. In "Four Marlons," Warhol printed one still in quadruplicate on a raw linen canvas evocative of gold. Here was a personality to build a cult around.

Just as actual 1930s gangsters aped the style of characters played by the actor George Raft, real-life delinquents turned to black leather. You didn't need a motorcycle to be in a "motorcycle gang," according to the moral-panicky logic of the day. What is

---

[1] A character in Greek mythology who saw his reflection in a pool, fell in love with his own beauty, and died there, unable to tear his eyes away. —Eds.

Scott Olson/Getty Images

While Troy Patterson does mention motorcycle gangs in his discussion of the history of the leather jacket, he does not bring up modern-day bikers such as the Hells Angels, which has 444 charters on five continents, according to its website. **To what extent do these modern bikers challenge the claims Patteson makes about the evolution of the leather jacket? Why do you think Patterson does not discuss them?**

more, you didn't even need a gang to enjoy the aura of a gangster, a fact attested by the many teenage rebels whose acquisition of a motorcycle jacket constituted the full extent of their rebellion. But for pseudogangs — that is, for rock bands and teen cliques devoted to them — the motorcycle jacket is an international uniform impervious to obsolescence. It is a garb for all tribes: goths in Kenya; rockabillies in Japan; you in your youth, wherever you wasted it.

Its signal plays on many frequencies, expanding its meanings when garbled. Writing about the Ramones,[2] the critic Tom Carson once sketched the dynamics of the masquerade: "Their leather jackets and strung-out, streetwise pose weren't so much an imitation of Brando in 'The Wild One' as a very self-conscious parody — they knew how phony it was for them to take on those tough-guy trappings, and that incongruousness was exactly what made the pose so funny and true." The Ramones' imitators did not necessarily get this, and instead, reading the self-parody as an uncomplicated statement of force, copied that. . . .

Over decades, women annexed this male program by degrees. Early colonists included the clients of designers who, riffing on the jacket,

explored leather's sculptural properties in the service of high fashion, and the followers of pop stars who, in simply sliding on the real McCoy, showed a knack for exploiting gender fluidity. An educated guess says that the motorcycle jacket began to be androgynized in earnest in the 1990s — an era, not coincidentally, when it seemed broadly unacceptable for an adult male to wear a motorcycle jacket unless he was actively playing a guitar solo. For a while there, the jacket looked like an affront to "authenticity" and stank, in its garish slick machismo, like a palmful of Drakkar Noir. But years of wear by women entailed a rearrangement of significations and made this jacket safe for men. And now, when a guy walks his dog while wearing black leather over a gray hoodie, it isn't risible. Now, when a guy whose line of work is in "the financial-technology space" turns up at a meeting in the guise of a tough, it sort of works for his disruptive personal brand. Recently, beneath the headline "Why Every Man Needs a Biker Jacket," a writer for *The Telegraph* confessed, "I fell in love with an inanimate object," which satisfies the definition of a fetish for both Freud and Marx, to the shame of no one in particular. We're all posers.

The modern woman in a motorcycle jacket tends to be a postmodern woman, her wardrobe a workshop for practicing pastiche, the jacket organizing other fragments of reference   *10*

[2]An American punk-rock band, prominent from the mid-1970s to the mid-1990s. —Eds.

to the surfaces of history. There is the gamin look of wearing the moto with a Breton-striped shirt and ballet flats, like Audrey Hepburn on a jaunt to Sturgis. Or — another of a thousand disguises — the streamlined b-girl thing, with skinny black jeans and sparkling Adidas Superstars, urban armor, completing the protective bubble of earbuds and sunglasses. What do we make of the recent development of draping a motorcycle jacket over their shoulders without deigning to fit the arms in the sleeves? It requires strict posture to wear a jacket in this way, and a lenient mood not to scorn the act as flagrant affectation.

The brooding bad attitude of the moto is meant to be worn lightly. Its aggression is a put-on easily shrugged off. The jacket tells you to embrace it as rock-idol clothing in a scheme where idolatry is of greater import than rock. It is a costume for the movie in which you imagine yourself to star.

[2015]

EXPLORING THE TEXT

1. Who do you think is the audience for this essay? Are they motorcycle jacket wearers? Explain why or why not.

2. Identify the thesis of "How the Motorcycle Jacket Lost Its Cool and Found It Again." How would you characterize the evidence Troy Patterson uses to support it? How effective is that evidence?

3. Look carefully at the combination of sensory details and figurative imagery in paragraph 2. What tone does this establish? What effect does this tone have on Patterson's credibility?

4. Describe Patterson's experience of shopping for and trying on a leather motorcycle jacket. How does he get in the mood? How does it make him feel? How does he use figurative language and specific diction choices to characterize his experience? What appeals do these details make, and how do they serve Patterson's overall argument?

5. What is Patterson's attitude toward the black leather jacket? How does he use it to comment on popular culture?

6. What does Patterson mean when he says that Marlon Brando, in *The Wild One,* was "exaggerating an old standard of male beauty to arrive at a new ideal of neoclassical beefcake" (para. 5)?

7. How does Patterson support his claim that "the motorcycle jacket is an international uniform impervious to obsolescence" (para. 7)? To what extent does the title of the essay undermine this claim? Do you agree? Explain your answer.

8. Patterson says that Brando in his leather jacket became a meme: "a look swiftly mimicked, cloned, valorized, spoofed, appropriated by couturiers and silk-screened by Andy Warhol in a series of works that must constitute its sanctification" (para. 6). What does he mean by this? Why does he consider being silk-screened by Andy Warhol (see *Myths*, page 365) an essential part of what makes that image a meme?

How to Listen to Music

HUA HSU

Hua Hsu (b. 1977) is currently an associate professor of English and director of the American Studies department at Vassar College and a board member of the Asian American Writers Workshop. His work has appeared in *Artforum,* the *Atlantic,* the *New Yorker, Slate,* and the *Wire.* Hsu's first book, *A Floating Chinaman: Fantasy and Failure across the Pacific* (2016), is a literary-critical examination of American perceptions of China between the two world wars. In the following article, originally published in the *New Yorker* in 2016, Hsu reviews a book by critic Ben Ratliff about the state of modern music.

There's a distinct possibility that I would never have been able to finish reading *Moby-Dick*, in my early twenties, had it not been for the Guns N' Roses song "November Rain." Released in 1991, when I was a teenager open to anything offered by MTV, "November Rain" was one of the many unusually long songs on the Los Angeles rock band's two-volume "Use Your Illusion." At the time, I was accustomed to songs that didn't outstay their welcome, maxing out, typically, at four or five minutes. Thanks in large part to a gloriously overblown video, I found all nine minutes of "November Rain" enthralling. I had no idea what the song's lyrics meant, or whether its drama really justified its lavish construction. But it was the first song I liked that could soundtrack my entire drive to school, or the time it took to run five laps. Perhaps it would have happened anyway, but "November Rain" ended up being the song that primed me for the pleasures of extravagantly long, immersive experiences. Before I could imagine making it through six-hundred-page novels,

endurance-test cinema, or hour-long jazz suites, I first loved a power ballad full of internal detours, false endings, and epic solos, and a music video highlighted by a man diving into a wedding cake.

Many of us first come to enjoy art in this way, not as a series of canons or genres to be mastered but as a web of deeply personal associations: affinities and phobias, echoes across time and space that resolve only in the most idiosyncratic spaces of your mind. This is the subject of *Every Song Ever*, the critic Ben Ratliff's meditation on listening to music "in an age of musical plenty." Ratliff has been a jazz and pop critic at the *New York Times* for nearly twenty years, and it's likely that the most radical changes that have come to music during this period have involved not style or taste but rather the way we consume it. Ratliff has championed esoteric sounds during his tenure at the *Times*, but this book, unlike his previous ones about jazz, concerns a common contemporary anxiety: how do we find our bearings at a time when there's simply too much out there?

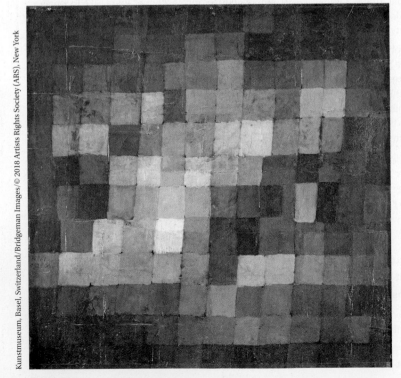

◀

In paragraph 2, Hua Hsu asserts that we enjoy both art and music by experiencing it as a "web of deeply personal associations: affinities and phobias, echoes across time and space that resolve only in the most idiosyncratic spaces of your mind."
How does this painting by artist Paul Klee, entitled *Ancient Harmony*, illustrate this claim?

What *Every Song Ever* offers isn't a set of critical edicts but the spectacle of an active mind processing a world in constant flux. The book is loosely inspired by the idea, popularized by Aaron Copland's classic *What to Listen for in Music*, that music can be appreciated according to standard metrics of rhythm and tone structure. "The old way of 'correct' listening," Ratliff explains, involved a kind of "preconditioning": "A certain language of rhythms and harmonies, signposts and cues, became consensual within a culture." But that past age of music

seeing connections

The painter Charles Burchfield (1893–1967) said, "An artist must paint, not what he sees in Nature, but what is there. To do so he must invent symbols, which, if properly used, make his work seem even more real than what is in front of him. He does not try to by-pass Nature; his work is superior to Nature's surface appearances, but not to its basic laws." In his work, Burchfield depicts sounds by using particular lines and shapes. Shown here is his painting *The Insect Chorus* (1917).

Munson-Williams-Proctor Arts Institute / Art Resource, NY

How does Burchfield circumvent the "standard metrics" of visual art — what Hsu calls "preconditioning" when he talks about listening to music — in this work to communicate sound? How might Hsu connect the experience of viewing this painting with Ben Ratliff's philosophy of how to listen to music?

appreciation, besides being no fun, presumed a kind of finitude — it presumed boundaries. Listening to music, then, was a devotional, often self-contained act. At the very least, that old idea assumed that we had the time or the desire to immerse ourselves repeatedly, distraction-free, in a single piece of music. This isn't the world most of us inhabit anymore. For the cost of a CD (or less), we have access to a near-endless supply of music, in a near-endless array of venues. Music appreciation in 2016 means curating your drive to work or your walk to class, playing a song a hundred times without ever stopping to scrutinize the lyrics.

It's quite possible that we have an even stronger attachment to music now that it is ubiquitous, woven into every moment of our lives, than we did then. But the age of the infinite playlist has also meant the proliferation of algorithms designed to give us exactly what makes us comfortable. It's a desire to resist these present-day forces of preconditioning that animates Ratliff's book. It is divided into twenty ways of processing a song, many of which — "loudness" and "density," for instance — are open and fairly intuitive. Songs across time and space cluster around these headings, leading Ratliff to insights about, for instance, the altered zones we encounter when we lose ourselves in "repetitive" music, or the ways in which "improvisation" tweaks our sense of the world as it is. There's a chapter on "virtuosity" that ranges from Sarah Vaughan and Art Tatum to YouTube videos of kids shredding on electric guitars. Another addresses really long songs — far longer than "November Rain" — and how they scramble our sense of what is comprehensible. "The point is a larger array of music than the eye can see on the shelf, than the ear can take in within one cycle of memory," Ratliff writes. "It doesn't reduce to a song or an album. It's a relationship." One of the book's most absorbing sections considers how performers use indifference, or a knowing suppression of their talents — that nudge-wink that happens when, for example, a rapper such

as Lil Wayne "melt[s] the ends off his own words." According to Ratliff, such moves provoke "a seemingly impossible thought: that the artist doesn't even need an audience, or that he has been put in front of it by random circumstances."

◆ ◆ ◆

The state of digital infinitude that we now largely take for granted has placed a special burden on music writing. It's been a while since I read a piece of music criticism to learn if a new album or artist was good or not. It's easy enough to drop the (now decidedly proverbial) needle and find out for myself. I'm far more interested in reading about how a critic hears: what they listen for, their desires and idiosyncrasies, the world that comes into focus for them when a record is playing. Some of Ratliff's most intriguing chapters muse on qualities that have come to seem normal and desirable, but for reasons that aren't clear. For example: is there a purpose for speed? Not in dance music, but as an approach to performance — in the manic solo of "Salt Peanuts," say, or the hard-core assault of D.R.I. For Ratliff, speed is a display, a relationship. "It doesn't inherently increase or enhance the feeling of the notes themselves, or the listener's physical pleasure," but it puts the listener in a place: "It represents a tacit contract between the player and the listener: we're in this together, and it might come to no good."

Another of his questions: what makes a song sad? Is it the "phantom quality" of knowing where the story of any song ends, after the session is over and everyone goes home? There are blue notes, of course, and there are the songs that become synonymous with the tragedy of their conception. But is heavy metal sad? Maybe, as Ratliff beautifully argues, the brooding aggression of metal obscures a deeper melancholy. "Punk is busking and journalism and dogma and accountability and unity and the humanities. Metal is virtuosity and philosophy and disposition and rumor and misanthropy and science." It's these occasional glimpses into Ratliff's own idiosyncratic responses to music that are the book's best moments. A chapter on "slowness"

5

This painting, entitled *Hot and Cool Jazz*, was completed in 2004 by contemporary artist Kaaria Mucherera. **What message does this painting convey about the idea of musical temperature? Based on Hsu's essay, what do you think Ratliff's take on this would be?**

KAARIA MUCHERERA (CONTEMPORARY ARTIST)/Private Collection/Bridgeman Images

begins with him messing around with a computer program that enables users to slow songs down to an ominous ooze. The chapter ranges from the late DJ Screw, famed for remixing hip-hop and R. & B. tracks to a death-defying crawl, to the sludgy "stoner doom" band Sleep. "Slowness in music invites reciprocity: it makes the listener want to fill the spaces with his own content, whether that be associations or movement or emotional response."

This insight may help to explain how the book itself works. "Sounds are running ahead of our vocabularies for describing them," Ratliff argues, and that sense of disorientation — "of not knowing what process makes what sounds" — has become an inherent part of listening to pop music. Maybe, in a few years, we will learn better strategies for apprehending all of it at once, making *Every*

Song Ever a quaint curio of a bygone era. But this seems to be Ratliff's point. The book meanders and muses, providing plenty of space for readers to wonder about their own fixations, to remain ambivalent about questions of genre or history and abide by their own deeply personal and far superior classification systems instead. It's best to think of *Every Song Ever* as a series of moods and provocations rather than a book to be read straight through. Each of the chapters seems to dissolve, to fade out, ending, every time, with a playlist, a fitting way to process the vertigo prompted by abundance. Which is to say: you don't have to process it all if you don't want to. You can just chase whatever you like, until you feel like chasing something else.

[2016]

EXPLORING THE TEXT

1. How would you describe Hua Hsu's opening strategy in the first two paragraphs? How effective are these paragraphs in capturing his audience's attention and establishing Hsu's authority as a reviewer of Ben Ratliff's book *Every Song Ever*?

2. What is Hsu's attitude toward Ratliff's book? How does he make the review of another writer's book a statement of his own views about how to listen to music?

3. At the end of paragraph 2 Hsu poses a question: "[H]ow do we find our bearings at a time when

there's simply too much out there?" How does he answer the question? How would you answer the question?

4. What do you think Hsu means by "digital infinitude" (para. 5)? What consequences does he believe that infinitude has?

5. What is the insight that Hsu argues "may help to explain how [Ratliff's] book itself works" (para. 7)?

6. Hsu's review contains several short quotations from Ratliff's book. How does he use these quotations to develop his argument? How effectively do these quotations support Hsu's central claim?

7. Hsu divides his short review into two discrete sections. What is the relationship between these sections? How do they function together to support Hsu's primary claim?

8. What assumptions does Hsu make about his audience? How are those reflected in the examples he gives as evidence, and how does Hsu use them to develop his argument? If possible, listen to some of the music he mentions. In light of your listening experience, how effective are his examples in supporting the claims he makes about how to listen to music?

9. Pick one of the artists Hsu mentions — maybe one you don't know — and try reviewing his or her music in the way Hsu suggests: describe what you listened for, how the work appealed to your desires and idiosyncrasies, and the world that came into focus for you as you listened. Do you agree that this is the best way to listen to music? Explain why or why not.

Have Superheroes Killed the Movie Star?

ANGELICA JADE BASTIÉN

Angelica Jade Bastién (b. 1989) is an American essayist, critic, and fiction writer based in Chicago. She is a contributing writer for *Vulture*, and her work has also appeared in the *Atlantic*, the *New York Times*, *New York* magazine, *Rolling Stone*, *Thrillist*, and the *Village Voice*. The following essay on the superhero film genre was originally published in a 2015 issue of the *Village Voice*.

Looking back at this dismal summer of superhero adaptations, I am reminded of something Chris Rock said during the 77th Academy Awards: "There are only four real stars, and the rest are just popular people." This was February 2005, mind you — a few months before Christopher Nolan's *Batman Begins* would hit theaters and three years before Marvel would kick-start its cinematic universe with *Iron Man*.

Stardom was already changing pretty dramatically thanks to reality television. But Rock's somewhat exaggerated statement is truer now than ever before. Yes, social media, YouTube vloggers, and reality TV have greatly altered who becomes a star and what it even means to be one. But movie stardom — once an integral part of the Hollywood ecosystem — has arguably taken its

biggest hit ever, thanks to the current dominance of onscreen superheroes.

Just take a look at the careers of actors like the various Marvel Chrises (they're interchangeable enough so choosing any will do). Each has achieved some level of popularity and even a somewhat dedicated fandom. But they have also been unable to translate the visibility their characters bring them into success elsewhere.

Watching one superhero film after another, it becomes undeniable that the actors aren't the stars — the characters and property are. Most ticket-buyers don't go to *Deadpool* because they're enamored of Ryan Reynolds's charm or see *Suicide Squad* because of Margot Robbie's skills. Perhaps that's why it's disorienting to see traditional, undeniable stars like Will Smith

In paragraph 4, Angelica Jade Bastién says, "Watching one superhero film after another, it becomes undeniable that the actors aren't the stars — the characters and property are. Pictured above are Michael Keaton, Christian Bale, and Ben Affleck, each playing Batman in a different reboot of the film.

To what extent do these images support — or challenge — Bastién's assertion?

Photofest

Photofest

Photofest

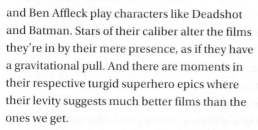

and Ben Affleck play characters like Deadshot and Batman. Stars of their caliber alter the films they're in by their mere presence, as if they have a gravitational pull. And there are moments in their respective turgid superhero epics where their levity suggests much better films than the ones we get.

With true movie stars, we bring baggage to every performance we watch — the emotions we attach to their early performances, their triumphs and their downfalls.

But superheroes and nostalgia-tinged reboots have replaced the alluring mythology of movie stars themselves. That isn't because we don't need stars.

If anything, Hollywood needs a new crop and to expand on what stardom means in the first place.

What Is a Star?

Bankability is often the easiest answer to the question of what makes a movie star. But box-office results aren't everything. Hollywood history is littered with actors whose films made bank but have little lasting cultural impact. Chris Pratt — now trading in the rugged American machismo that drew us to Harrison Ford — has found success leading *Jurassic World* and *Guardians of the Galaxy*. But it's hard to argue that he is successful on his own and not just replicating a bland approximation of actors before him. Is he truly bankable, or is he just choosing the properties that guarantee some level of financial success? Pratt is a good model of someone who is popular but has yet to become a true star, the kind who is either bankable in original films or in possession of a star image that alters the film around him.

So, what makes a movie star beyond box-office appeal? Looking at the careers of everyone from Bette Davis to Michelle Pfeiffer to Angelina Jolie, you can get a sense of the alchemy involved. A true star, in essence, is a potent mix of sex appeal, mystery, and relatability all spiced with the ability to surprise and a certain something extra that no one else has. This adds up to an identity that audiences come to recognize and seek out time and again.

When we go to a Brad Pitt film, we know we're getting a character actor in a leading man's body often wrestling with what his beauty means. When we see a Keanu Reeves film, we know we're getting an actor who asks us what it means for a man to be heroic in the first place, one who makes vulnerability central to his performance and who often interacts with the camera in ways that we expect of female sex symbols. Of course, there's always a level of trial and error with this. Even after figuring out who they are on-screen, the best stars often subvert, fight against, or deconstruct their own image.

Having this sort of crafted narrative is import- 10 ant; without it stars don't exist. That's the danger of new, hot actors joining comic franchises that lock them into absurd seven-picture deals: They don't have the ability or time to craft their own star image. The superhero characters they take on subsume their image. The moviegoing public has a hard time seeing these actors beyond the comic book and legacy franchise characters they play. These performers get stuck playing characters that all seem crafted from similar molds: the emotionally bruised white dude full of snappy comebacks. Or the badass, leather-clad heroine who has more of an interesting moral landscape than her peers

but still gets little to do. The stalwart all-American hero who is proud and true. If even stars as big as Will Smith now rarely bring the kind of box-office results that justify their huge paydays, do the studios really even need them? From the perspective of the executives, what is the point of a movie star beyond marketability?

Why Stars Matter

The studio system during Hollywood's golden age had one surefire commodity: the stars themselves. Whole genres were born out of the necessity to market these figures. Stars were under contract with the studios who groomed them, changed their names, created stories around them, and thrust them in front of the camera until they found a formula that they could package over and over again.

That may make movie stars seem, to today's audiences, unimportant. Many of the most popular stars from decades ago are unrecognizable to audiences today for a variety of reasons, including changing tastes. But when we look back on the stars with true legacies — the Cary Grants, the Paul Newmans, the Marilyn Monroes — it's clear they weren't ever just products of Hollywood's star system like their peers in the first place. They often had a clear hand in shaping their images, with actors such as Bette Davis notoriously reworking scripts, giving advice on direction, and making choices that directly affected the production of their films, even to the chagrin of directors and producers.

The great stars challenged the studios and America itself. Marlon Brando, Montgomery Clift, and River Phoenix helped us question what it means to be a man in this country. The stardom of Sidney Poitier gave white audiences a peek into the black experience and perhaps the ability to see the humanity of African-Americans. The activism of Harry Belafonte and Angelina Jolie brings attention to causes that many would like to forget. Stars can start trends in fashion, affect political conversations, and leave an important footprint on American culture. But most powerful is how they affect the medium itself.

Critics' conception of cinema's "canon" perhaps bends far too much toward directors. Great stars are often responsible for some of the more unforgettable images in film. And stars can be auteurs in their own right — playing with their images from film to film, always in conversation with the expectations of their audience. The rise of superhero films has taken some great actors off the table for years, skewing their ability to craft any sort of image outside the familiar heroes that they play.

What Has Been Lost

The rise of comic book movies is an integral part of the disappearance of an important kind of film: the mid-budget adult drama, where actresses like Sandra Bullock, Michelle Pfeiffer, and Meryl Streep cut their teeth. Going farther back, I can't help but think of the women's picture — a strange, somewhat feminist subgenre during the era of classic Hollywood that existed because the studio heads needed vehicles for their actresses. An actress can't become a star if she has no meaty leading roles, a truth that Hollywood seems to have forgotten. Mid-budget studio films are often where stars have been able to craft themselves. It's also where we most often see the consistent star and director collaborations. But now directors seem to jump directly from small independent films to gargantuan would-be blockbusters, and with so much money on the line, there's no room for experimentation or for directors to push themselves and their actors in bold directions.

Ultimately, I'm not worried about the white male actors — like the Marvel Chrises — when it comes to the changing and charged landscape of modern Hollywood. They will get chance after chance to prove their worth as stars even if they can barely inhabit the superhero roles they play, let alone figure out and craft their own public images. Just ask Jai Courtney. Or any of the interchangeable white, blond-ish, sharp-jawed men

that Hollywood can't get enough of despite audiences' difficulty in differentiating them.

Actors like Chris Hemsworth may never figure out what brand of stardom suits them, but their careers will be just fine. Although, with his turn in *Ghostbusters* and the more comic approach to Thor in the DVD-extra short film packaged with *Captain America: Civil War*, Hemsworth seems to be realizing what kind of star he truly is: someone a bit funnier and more subversive than the straight-up heartthrobs his physicality may lead us to expect of him. When it comes to the frustrating lack of mid-budget pictures — where true stardom finds its beginnings — the actors I'm worried about are the ones rarely given a chance to play superhero characters in the first place.

The ecstatic reaction to the casting of Marvel's upcoming *Black Panther*, a film with nary a light-skinned or white actor in sight, isn't just because of the character's history or the rarity of seeing black people headlining a major film where slavery isn't the thrust of the narrative. It's also a reaction to the dearth of black actors (especially dark-skinned black women) who become movie stars in the first place. And it's indicative of what a movie star can do for the culture and film itself. It's actors like Michael B. Jordan and Lupita Nyong'o who offer the most interesting opportunities for the evolution of movie stardom. But with no mid-budget pictures to give them the chance to create their own legacies — rather than adapt those of characters that have existed in comics for decades — will we see them get that opportunity? Will we see them collaborate with a writer/director over decades in a way that is both risky and rewarding? Will they be able to develop the intimacy with their audience that a great star turn can achieve if they're stuck vacillating between big-budget films that offer little to no narrative risks, very small independent films (if they're lucky), television, and the stage?

15

Tom Toro/The New Yorker Collection/The Cartoon Bank

"Fighting supervillians is a cinch—fighting misogyny is the real challenge."

How does this cartoon's message relate to Bastién's central argument in the final section of her essay?

To say that who becomes a star doesn't matter is to forget that Hollywood is a microcosm of America itself, and to forget how stardom has shaped the history of the medium. What is Alfred Hitchcock's greatest work without the way Cary Grant riffs on his own image in *North by Northwest* and *Notorious*? What is the arc of the antihero in cinema without Vivien Leigh's infuriating yet enchanting Scarlett O'Hara or the way Bette Davis wrestled with female anger? What is the history of the musical without the elegance of Fred Astaire or the bristling heat of Gene Kelly? Movie stars can make good films masterpieces, electrically charge a close-up, and alter our understanding of a film due to their image. They are often the reason certain genres like the women's picture exists in the first place. Film needs its movie stars. And television shouldn't be the only place they're allowed to breathe. Until Hollywood remembers this, the medium itself will continue to suffer.

[2016]

EXPLORING THE TEXT

1. Why do you believe Angelica Jade Bastién chose to quote comedian Chris Rock in the opening of her essay? Do you agree with Rock's observation that there are "only four real stars, and the rest are just popular people" (para. 1)?

2. What are some of the consequences Bastién predicts as a result of the dearth of true movie stars? How effectively does she support these claims?

3. What purpose do the "various Marvel Chrises" (para. 3) serve? How effectively does Bastién use them to develop her argument?

4. Why does Bastién consider movie stardom to have been an "integral part of the Hollywood ecosystem" (para. 2)? How does she define true movie stars? What does she think has taken their place?

5. How does Bastién use the genre of "mid-budget adult drama" as an example in her argument?

6. How does Bastién use questions throughout the essay? Trace several of her questions and analyze how they strengthen (or weaken) her argument.

7. Bastién divides her essay into three sections: "What Is a Star?," "Why Stars Matter," and "What Has Been Lost." What progression do you see in these sections? How do they relate to one another?

8. What are some of the ways that "Have Superheroes Killed the Movie Star?" appeals to logos? Look especially at places where Bastién finds cause-and-effect relationships.

9. Overall, how would you characterize Bastién's tone in this essay? Consider the role of humor in your response — is she sardonic, buoyant, bitter, playful, something else, or a combination?

Get Off the Treadmill
The Art of Living Well in the Age of Plenty

MARK GREIF

Mark Greif (b. 1975) is an author, educator, and cultural critic in New York City. An associate professor of liberal studies at the New School for Social Research and a professor of literary studies at the New School in New York, he co-founded and is a frequent contributor to *n+1*, a journal of literature, criticism, and politics. In 2016, he published a collection of essays entitled *Against Everything*, which was a finalist for the National Book Critics Circle Award in Criticism. His writing has appeared in the *New York Times*, the *Boston Globe*, *Harper's*, the *London Review of Books*, and the *Guardian*. The following essay was published by the *Guardian* in 2016.

Do you ever learn about health from the media? I do. Here are some things I've seen recently. "How to engineer maximum deliciousness, pack in nutrients, increase sustainability, and build crazy food mashups." But this is rather distant from my goal of eating when hungry. "More than 90% of us don't get enough potassium." But enough potassium for what? "Great Sleep Tonight: Pro Secrets, Revealed." I had not known anyone slept professionally.

◆ ◆ ◆

One would be more likely to blink at these follies if we were not so surrounded by nonstop fatuities in the imperative voice of advertising. "Tastes so pure you'll love it." Does anyone know what purity tastes like? "Discover how good your body was designed to feel." But who designed my body? "Stress less with the bestselling, multi-award-winning anti-stress drink." Surely caring about the best, most award-winning supplement beverage is a cause of stress?

Even the bag my fast-food hamburger arrives in won't shut up. It's covered with testimony to the franchise-corporation's caring, its love of me, its love of soil, tomatoes, our planet, friendship, farmers, heritage, my arteries and babies. Yet I can't even imagine who is caring — what human heart beats inside this paper trash. I think I am supposed to care about these things, and so the salesmen parrot what they suppose would be my aspirations.

Has any free people ever been so shouted at by caring fools and salesmen? Under the guise of useful knowledge, forces that frankly mean us no good, which range in mood between hysterical enthusiasm, indifference and careless exploitation, warn us with "health" advice that is variously incoherent, short-sighted (to be reversed or falsified five years later) and banal. You can tell people not to eat eggs, but a decade later you'll be telling people to eat eggs. It seems trivial, but it always costs something — in worry and stupefaction, and in hours of our lives.

You could say that this advice all comes in [5] bad faith. But the voices which approach us in good faith may be even more to blame.

Health, exercise, food, sex have become central preoccupations of our time. We preserve the living corpse in an optimal state, not so we may do something with it, but for the feeling of optimisation. More and more of life gets turned over to life maintenance at the very moment you'd think we'd be free to pursue something else.

I find it hard not to want to live longer. I also want to live without pain. This means I want health. But when I place myself at a point within the vast constellation of health knowledge and health behaviours, I can't help but detect some misunderstanding. The systems of health have little to do with my simple ambitions. There is something too much, or too many, in them; too arbitrary, or too controlling; too doom-laden, too managerial, too messianic.

We should spare a thought for the fate of what used to be called the "necessities of life." Necessity dictates what must be done for the body before anything can be done for the mind. For millennia, people have known what the necessities of life are. Food, shelter and clothes, made or won by labour. Sex and reproduction, tied to the labour of childbirth and work of child rearing. Sleep. (Alexander the Great said that sleep and sexual intercourse, more than anything else, reminded him that he was mortal). Movement, as has only come into focus since we began to sit for so much of our days. Touch, perhaps, as has become more obvious as the world became less tactile and rough, more screened and smoothed. Excretion.

But 3,000 years of civilisation have worked to make these necessities easy to come by. In the last three centuries, human progress has pacified necessity in the rich countries. Back-breaking labour has been reduced. Food is inexpensive and superabundant. Sexual desire has been decoupled from pregnancy. The dangers of infection, fever and accident have been diminished by medicine, and medical research seeks ways to head off more slow-growing diseases. For many, simply to be born in a rich nation is to have won the lottery for inexpensive access to the necessities of life; to be gloriously, unprecedentedly free from cares historically and in comparison to much of the globe. There is freedom to enjoy — and there are wealth and material freedom to spread to others. For progressive civilisation had always expected that meeting necessity in the west was a mere prerequisite to further, higher goals: justice, equality, democracy, and the extension of ease of access to the necessities of life to all.

But we have taken an unexpected detour on [10] the way to meeting those higher goals. Once progress had made it easy to acquire the necessities of life, other forces set about making those needs mentally complicated and hard. Into this category goes much of what passes for wisdom about health, exercise, food, and sex. Inexpensive things have become expensive, trivial matters require obsessive thought, universal biology is mazed with fashion and status-seeking, and free possessions are commoditised. If I feel sure of one thing, it is that this kind of "health" imperative is not moral. It is grooming — what monkeys do in picking nits out of their fur. We may find that grooming sits among the subordinate necessities of life. But surely the ceaseless grooming and optimisation of everyday life stands in the way of finding out how else we could spend our attention and our energy.

A decade ago I wrote an essay titled "Against Exercise." It came about from a trip to the gym to run on a treadmill. I was standing in the usual stance of mutual disregard, pretending not to notice my neighbours sweating through skintight pyjamas and making their angry — or, I suppose, fierce — faces. I tried not to look up when someone grunted or shouted, and kept my eyes politely on the calories ticking by on my readout, just as in a lift I'd keep my eyes on the floor numbers.

These graphs show data from the American Psychological Association's 2013 Stress in America survey.
What does this information suggest about American culture? How does it relate to Mark Greif's assertion that health and exercise "have become central preoccupations of our time" (para. 6)?

Americans' Views on Exercise

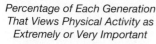

Percentage of Each Generation That Views Physical Activity as Extremely or Very Important

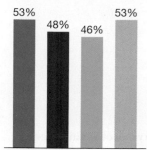

53% 48% 46% 53%

Percentage of Each Generation That Rates Itself as Doing an Excellent or Very Good Job at Physical Activity

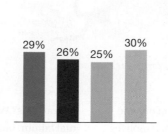

29% 26% 25% 30%

■ Millennials
■ Generation X
■ Baby Boomers
■ Silent Generation

Data from the American Psychological Association Stress in America™ survey (2013).

But then I breached convention and looked around, and was struck down by the sort of vision that must have come to William Blake,[1] a glance into heaven and hell, suddenly manifest in his garden in Felpham. There was a young man crucified on a lat pull-down. There was a young woman whose legs were madly turned by a spinning bike. No one looked happy: they either looked like executioners, grim as death, or victims. Certainly no one looked sociable — though this might be the space with the most people, together, supposedly at ease and enjoying leisure time, that they would enter all day. I turned from one unseeing face to the next, each chasing some number, and I said: "You are condemned. You are condemned. You are condemned." I, too, was condemned. I got down from the treadmill.

This, of course, had nothing to do with an intelligible argument. So when I got home, I began to try to figure out why we go to the gym. There

[1] An English Romantic poet who wrote primarily during the late eighteenth and early nineteenth centuries. —Eds.

are explicit rationales, and the precise words and phrases which recur in official injunctions to exercise. Then there are the quiet things people say in passing, about the pleasures and the ghastlinesses of it all. Modern exercise has a background in sport, even in the ancient gymnasia — but it is really quite different. It certainly seemed striking that, as advanced societies have done away with much industrial labour, and have automobilised transport, the new immaterial labourer spends his leisure mimicking the old repetitive gestures of the die press, or a stevedore's lifting of cargo, or a rural traveller's walk to a distant town, but turned into spectacle, sped-up, numbered, and producing muscles that serve no practical use but more of the same mimicry. And that this is so often experienced as obligation, rather than play. Then, I began to read and write about diet and food. Certainly we are in a golden intellectual age of political critiques of industrial food production. The pollution and cruelty of factory farms have come into public view. The dangers of pesticides and groundwater

Charlie Hankin/The New Yorker Collection/The Cartoon Bank

In what ways does this cartoon connect to Greif's characterization of exercise in the twenty-first century?

"As exercise, it's torture, but as torture it's not so bad."

contamination lie behind the progress of organic farming. But alongside the public-spirited motives for a return to heirloom products, artisanal production, and farm-to-table eating, there seems to be another push towards rarity, social distinction and hostility to the cheap mass provision of food as a fundamental civilised achievement.

Most ambiguous, to me, is the new figure of the foodie. Only in a culture cut off from agriculture and need can food become a hobby and grounds for individual identity. The old gourmet was a bit of a snob: he wed himself to France or Italy, learned to cook a single cuisine and became obsessed with importing, usually wine and cheese.

The foodie differs in having the whole globe at his fingertips. His cookbooks gravitate first to Europe (Provence; southern Italy), then quickly carry him to Turkey, Morocco, Vietnam, India. No single tradition exists for him to learn, no singular importers to patronise. Rather, an ocean of ingredients washes up on his shores. There is no food we can't access. There is no traditional food, moreover, that can't be further enchanted by our concentration, restriction, choice, and discrimination between better and worse specimens. Would you like some chipotle with your

lemongrass? We add the value of our intellectual labour, our "finishing" of the world's raw materials.

The foodie wades out and swims in possibility. And then, surprisingly, many a foodie will deliberately restrict his range. He sets rules or laws for himself that make the quest for food harder and the thinking more complex. Undiscovered foods only; "authentic" restaurants only, or kitsch diners or barbecue joints; organic food only; local or farmers' market food, raw food or slow food only. Foodieism is a natural hobby for first-world professionals, ostensibly showing an interest in the world, but referring back to domination and the perfection of the enriched, physical self.

◆ ◆ ◆

Having our food supply made simple, we devote ourselves to looking for ways to make it difficult. Another route is through dieting, ostensibly for health. Here, though, the weight-loss imperative, with its shadows of attractiveness and social distinction, and other fantasies of rarity, difficulty and expense, complicate the fairly mundane research consensus on improving health: eat moderately, move more. You can avoid bread,

15

eat only protein and fat, and lose weight—since too much weight is said to be a killer. But as you polish off your bacon, steak and cheese, nothing has falsified the old research that correlates animal fats with plaque-filled arteries, heart disease, stroke, and cancers.

You can rediscover your inner ape and revert to a "Paleolithic diet" with evolutionary justifications. But no 21st-century butcher can provide you the animals eaten by our Paleolithic ancestors. You will not eat it in the conditions of scarcity of our Paleolithic ancestors. None of the rest of your life, upbringing, habits or ingested substances resemble those of our Paleolithic ancestors. You might equally ground your fantasies of historical destiny in the fact that the entire history of human culture and civilisation has occurred in the Neolithic era—i.e., facilitated by the planting of grain and domestication of animals. *Star Trek* fans would seem to have a better grasp of the scientific method.

Then sex and sexuality began to interest me. We've had a remarkable sexual liberation —particularly since the 1960s. Major achievements have included the end of shame and illegality in sex outside of marriage, the feminist reorganisation of intercourse around the female orgasm as well as the male; the destigmatisation of homosexuality, and a new fluidity to the norms of gender identity. The underlying impetus in all these reforms was to remove social penalties for doing what people were doing anyway.

But competing with true liberation has been [20] sexual liberalisation—an effort to tell you that only expertise, exposure, advice and apparatus can let you enjoy, in the right way, what was already freely possessed by you. A true test of liberation, as distinct from liberalisation, is whether you have also been freed to be free from sex. To ignore it, or to be asexual, without consequent social opprobrium or imputation of deficiency. We ought to see social

How does this cartoon relate to Greif's claim that "we substitute life-preservation for living" (para. 22)? In what ways do the cartoonist and Greif each use humor to make their points?

Joe Dator/The New Yorker Collection/The Cartoon Bank

categories of asexuals, who are free to have no sex just as others are free to have endless spectacular sex, and not feel towards them either suspicion or pity. One of the cruel betrayals of sexual liberation is the illusion that a person can be free only if he holds sex as all-important and exposes it endlessly to others — providing it, proving it, enjoying it.

I think sometimes of a John Prine song: "We are living in the future, I'll tell you how I know / I read it in the paper, 15 years ago." We often speak about a coming age. In that near future, we'll enjoy heavenly ease and wellbeing, safety and leisure. How wonderful it will be! In fact, I think we ought to admit that many of us in the rich nations are already living in that future, and have been for some decades.

But our surprising response to our times has been the creation of new forms of pseudonecessity. We go to the gym to strain at imitations of hard labour, lifting nonexistent roofbeams, hoeing nonexistent fields. We pretend that our food — now safe, plentiful, cheap, delicious — matters so much to our bodies that we must perfect it, elaborating a new necessity of pollution and taboo for heritage grains and laborious artisanal manufacture. We refuse to recognise that an 80-year lifespan of activities and projects is functional immortality for the human animal. Or that dying is necessary, just to let new people come on to the earth. So we substitute life-preservation for living, spending invaluable portions of youth and middle age on trying to increase our odds for an extra one, two or five years at the very end.

Frankly, I suspect that an ethics of living in a rich nation at the dawn of the 21st century involves not caring so much about your health, your diet, your exercise and your thrills. The meaningful time is now. We should be prepared to enjoy our good luck, and drop dead after a sufficient length of time — but ask, along the way, what we actually wish to do with our time. A culture of health and futurity, right now, represents a terrified or intimidated flight from moral freedom — covering our eyes from the fact that we have no further urgent tasks of bodily improvement, and really need to choose between setting new social goals, or just grooming ourselves into eternity.

[2016]

EXPLORING THE TEXT

1. How does the series of questions in the essay's first two paragraphs introduce Mark Greif's argument? Are these questions meant to be answered? What other purpose might they serve?

2. How does Greif establish his ethos? Identify at least two places in the essay that help him accomplish this.

3. What are some of the primary consequences of what Greif sees as our obsession with food and exercise? What are the secondary ones? How effectively does he support these claims?

4. Why do you believe Greif mentions and summarizes his earlier essay, "Against Exercise"? What realization did he come to about why and how we exercise? How does this realization relate to the subject of this essay?

5. What exactly is Greif criticizing when he says, "there seems to be another push towards rarity, social distinction and hostility to the cheap mass provision of food as a fundamental civilised achievement" (para. 13)? To what extent do you agree with his criticism? Explain your response.

6. Trace the quest of the "foodie," as Greif describes it, in paragraphs 14–16. How does Greif use that journey as evidence in his argument?

7. Greif is particularly scathing in his debunking of the so-called "Paleolithic diet." How does he use humor as part of his criticism? How effective is this rhetorical strategy? Does he go too far? Explain your answer, and be sure to consider the likely audience for Greif's essay.

8. How would you characterize the tone Greif adopts in "Get Off the Treadmill"? How does this tone relate to the purpose of his essay? How well suited is this tone for the subject matter?

9. Do you think diet and exercise are aspects of popular culture? Explain why or why not.

The Ballad of Balloon Boy

JUSTIN PETERS

Justin Peters (b. 1981) is a correspondent for *Slate* magazine and former contributing editor at the *Columbia Journalism Review*. He has written for the *New York Times*, the *Washington Monthly*, and *Travel + Leisure*. Peters holds degrees from Cornell University and the Columbia University Graduate School of Journalism, and is author of *The Idealist: Aaron Swartz and the Rise of Free Culture on the Internet* (2016). In the following article, originally published on *Slate* in 2016, he critiques the penchant for theatricality in media journalism.

A t 2:42 p.m. on Oct. 15, 2009, CNN afternoon anchor Kyra Phillips interrupted a live broadcast of a town hall by President Obama to bring viewers a breaking story as alarming as it was irresistible. A large silver helium balloon had broken loose and was racing through the windy skies of Colorado — with a small boy trapped inside. By any journalistic criteria, a little boy trapped inside a runaway experimental balloon counts as a good story; by the reductive standards of cable news, which prize emotional simplicity and evocative imagery above all, the incident must have seemed like the greatest story of all time. Cable-news scientists in a hermetically sealed clean room could not have created a more perfect CNN segment. CNN vowed to stay with the story until Balloon Boy was brought safely home.

The homecoming would happen shortly, but the story itself was an epic, full of twists and turns. By the end of the day, we had learned that Balloon Boy had never been inside the balloon, that he had been home all along, hiding in an attic. By the end of the week, we had learned that his unscrupulous parents had probably staged the entire thing as a stunt to stoke interest in a possible reality show. Today, the Balloon Boy saga is remembered, if at all, as a weird artifact from a mildly simpler time, a moment when the media gatekeepers were briefly and harmlessly fooled by a particularly cunning specimen of indigenous American fame whore. We were tricked; we laughed it off; we learned nothing. It happens.

◆ ◆ ◆

But that summation sells Balloon Boy short. The Balloon Boy story crystallizes the problem of cable news in one historically stupid moment. Balloon Boy happened because CNN and its competitors couldn't help it from happening, because the production demands of a 24-hour news network left it vulnerable to the chicanery of an unscrupulous jerk. It deserves to be remembered as the moment when cable news emerged from its chrysalis and became the entity it was genetically destined to become: a fundamentally unjournalistic medium uniquely susceptible to the wheedlings of vain and manipulative grifters, condemned to follow shiny objects until the end of time. Sometimes those shiny objects are balloons. Sometimes they're loudmouths with dumb opinions. And sometimes they're presidential candidates.

The alleged boy in the silver balloon was 6-year-old Falcon Heene. His father, Richard Heene, an amateur scientist and storm chaser, kept a 20-foot-long experimental balloon — sorry, a "3-D low altitude vehicle" — tied up and inflated in the yard, as one does. Though his father had scolded him for playing in the contraption, Falcon nevertheless remained drawn to the balloon. This boy was a real Balloon Boy, you might say, and soon enough that was what we were *all* saying, because around noon on that fatefully dumb day, Falcon's older brother told his father that the younger child had climbed into the balloon and it had come unmoored. When he heard the news,

Heene made a curious choice for a distraught father: He called the local TV station.

No one seemed skeptical. A reporter's job can be a joy when the news comes to him. The story spread from local to national news faster than a sprinting llama; CNN and the other cable news networks carried the yarn for a breathless hour, teasing every possible bit of data and pathos out of the errant aircraft. What kind of balloon was it: hot air or helium? ("I mean, you think of Mylar balloons with helium, you think of birthday parties," said Phillips. "You don't think of some massive balloon taking your 6-year-old airborne.") How did the boy get inside the balloon? ("I do not know the details, I'm sorry," said a spokesperson for the Larimer County Sheriff's Department.) At 3 p.m., CNN's Rick Sanchez joined Phillips and ratcheted up the drama. "I want to grab through that screen, reach through that screen and grab that thing and bring it down to earth," he asserted. Minutes later, Phillips announced a terrible development: The sheriff's office feared the boy might have already fallen out of the balloon. "Boy, I will tell you, Kyra, that's heartbreaking news," said Sanchez. "Hopefully, it's wrong for some reason. Sometimes, in news, all we can do is hope that the information we get is wrong."

Finally, about an hour after CNN picked up the story, the balloon landed near Colorado Springs. "If you, uh, if you are predisposed to do so, and you want to say a little prayer . . . you might wanna do so now, because this 6-year-old boy is about 100 feet from the ground," said Sanchez. Rescue workers surrounded the craft — and discovered there was no Balloon Boy to be found in the Balloon Boy balloon.

What a twist! The interplay between Phillips and Sanchez at the moment of the reveal was priceless:

Sanchez: I'll tell you, this is one of those stories that really will tell itself shortly here. The picture . . .

Phillips: Rick, I don't know if anybody is in there.

Sanchez: . . . describe it for us.

Phillips: They would be going right in.

Sanchez: I'll tell you, it's, it's, you can only hope he's in there. But right now, I, I have not seen them go in, and, uh . . . I have not seen them go in and get the little boy out. It doesn't even look like they're making an effort to — I am confused.

Sanchez wasn't the only one. Had Balloon Boy really fallen out? Had he ever been in there at all? The Colorado Air National Guard sent a Blackhawk helicopter to scour the countryside for any sign of the child. "Right now, a search is underway for a 6-year-old boy who may or may not have climbed into a homemade helium balloon," announced Wolf Blitzer at the top of the 4 p.m. hour. Just over two hours later, we learned that Balloon Boy was hiding inside a box in the attic of the family garage. "I played with my toys and took a nap," he told reporters. And 300 million Americans muttered the immortal words of Uncle Frank in *Home Alone*: "Look what ya did, ya little jerk!"

But the true jerks in this situation, it turned out, were Balloon Boy's parents. The *New York Times* described Richard Heene as a "fame-seeking backyard scientist," which is the closest the *Times* will ever come to calling someone a jackass. Heene was a former stand-up comedian who co-hosted an online talk show called the *Psyience Detectives*; according to the YouTube clips I've found, the show's editorial priorities centered on determining whether the world would end in 2012. (It did not.) The Heenes had previously appeared on the reality show *Wife Swap*, on which they switched places with a family of psychics from Florida.

On the night of the Balloon Boy incident, Wolf Blitzer hosted the Heenes for an interview. In it, Blitzer accidentally broke some actual news: Asked

356

by his father why he had hidden in the garage attic and ignored searchers' cries, Falcon replied, "Um . . . you guys said . . . that, um . . . we did this for the show." ("Man . . ." said his father. "No . . . ?" said his mother.) It took about 30 minutes for Blitzer, God bless him, to follow up on that startling admission and ask Heene what his son had meant. Heene replied by repeatedly saying that he was "appalled" that Blitzer would ask that question. ("I was just grateful that he is just fine," Blitzer crumbled. "You have a beautiful family there.") This is what world-class liars do: They go big with their lies, and then bluster loudly when they're called out on them — even when the person calling them out is barely even calling them out!

But what *had* Falcon meant by "the show"? Three days later, the county sheriff announced that the Heenes had likely launched the hoax as a bid to stoke interest in a potential reality television program — ostensibly a revamped version of the *Psyience Detectives* in which Heene and his family would go around solving psyientific mysteries. In a sworn affidavit, Mayumi Heene admitted that the Balloon Boy stunt was a hoax. Both of the Heene parents were charged with crimes: Richard with attempting to influence a public servant, and Mayumi with false reporting to authorities. Each served a short stint in jail.

"Why continue the wall-to-wall coverage of a story that had turned into a non-story — on a political show — during a week when health care, financial reform, and Afghanistan are all at the tipping point?" asked Arianna Huffington in a column on her namesake website. The answer to that question is not novel or interesting — everyone, Arianna Huffington included, knows it. A credulous media that is enslaved to the production demands of our modern 17-second news cycle will pass along any dumb story without giving it much thought.

But the network wasn't wholly at fault, either. The balloon was in the air. The boy's family said he was in it. The boy was nowhere to be found at home. Who can blame CNN for going with it? It's hard to report accurately on a story when the prime mover of that story is blatantly lying to you. It's especially hard to report accurately when you carry the news as it happens, when you outsource the contextualization of the images you broadcast.

The media, especially cable news, seems essentially passive; they've been trained to wait for news to come to them. This assumed passivity conceals the media's own role in setting the news agenda, in elevating things from curiosities to actual news stories. After picking up the story toward the end of its 2 p.m. hour, CNN broadcast an entire workday's worth of Balloon Boy; the only host that day who *didn't* mention the Heenes was Lou Dobbs, who spent an hour on *Lou Dobbs Tonight* discussing much less

How does this image show the ways that cable news was developing the story of Balloon Boy as the day progressed? In what ways does it illustrate the points Justin Peters makes about the role media plays in focusing national attention on certain topics?

mediagenic topics like Wall Street bonuses and health care reform. "Yes, great story," said Blitzer after Falcon was found alive and it appeared the saga was over. "All right, there's other news. Remember the health insurance debate?" And then Lou Dobbs went to the health insurance debate, and CNN apparently found it boring, because the instant Dobbs' program ended the channel went directly back to Balloon Boy.

◆ ◆ ◆

The media always has a choice of which stories to carry, how to frame those stories, and how much credence to give their main actors. In the early hours of the Balloon Boy story, Phillips and Sanchez took care to emphasize how little they knew about the situation, which was good. But they also proceeded to bring in guests who knew even less about it than they did. Within minutes of cutting to the story, Phillips was interviewing a balloon expert named Craig Kennedy, who had no idea what was happening and who couldn't see any footage from wherever he was. "You're asking for a great deal of speculation without me being able to see anything that's going on," Kennedy said, and that is exactly what CNN and its competitors want their guests to do, and it then becomes the hosts' job to refrain from calling attention to their guests' limitations. It

15

works the same way with every afactual political commentator, every blustering politician, every in-the-dark aviation expert, every grinning ax-grinder who finds his way onto the air. And the more adept he is at confident speculation, the more airtime he receives.

Today, I use the term *Balloon Boy* as shorthand for a special species of jerk, a catchall term for unreliable narrators whose studied theatricality and sociopathic zeal for attention lets them successfully prey on our media's unceasing demand for new news. Unlike an actual boy in an actual balloon, America's Balloon Boys will never disappear into the clouds. Balloon Boys will always remain just off in the middle distance, hovering in the periphery of consciousness, waiting around for the right breeze to ride into the headlines. Balloon Boys are the future of jerks: people who will do anything to attract and maintain coverage, who recognize that, these days more so than ever, the public and the media will keep watching you if you commit to doing and saying the dumbest possible things with the straightest possible faces.

The Heenes did not land their reality television show, but otherwise they got what they wanted. News organizations write retrospectives about the story. Journalists sometimes ask, "Where are they now?" and I bet you care about the answer. So what are the Heenes up to now? It will not surprise

Gary Friedman/Getty Images

Pictured here is a young man dressed in a Balloon Boy costume at the 2009 West Hollywood Halloween Costume Carnaval. **Do you think this man would agree with Justin Peters about what made Balloon Boy such a fixture in the public imagination? Explain your answer.**

you to learn that they moved to Florida. It will also not surprise you to learn that Richard Heene now claims the hoax was not actually a hoax, which is exactly the sort of thing a hoaxster would say. It will *definitely* not surprise you to learn that they are big fans of Donald J. Trump, the ultimate Balloon Boy. The Heene boys are now in a heavy metal band called the Heene Boyz, and the front page of their website features a pro-Trump anthem with Falcon on lead vocals. "Say this for the Heenes . . . " began a recent article in the *Tampa Bay Times*, "they are persistent." Balloon Boys always are. The air is full of them now, and they're never going away.

[2016]

EXPLORING THE TEXT

1. What does the title "The Ballad of Balloon Boy" suggest to you? What hint might it give as to the contents of the essay? Having read the essay, how might the title be ironic?

2. Look carefully at the first paragraph, which seems to introduce the story of the boy trapped in a helium balloon floating in the Colorado skies. What other subject does Justin Peters introduce at the same time? What language in that paragraph reveals his attitude towards that subject?

3. Why does Peters think that the story of the Balloon Boy is more important than a "weird artifact from a mildly simpler time" (para. 2)?

4. How does Peters build suspense as he retells the saga of the Balloon Boy? What purpose does it serve in Peters's argument?

5. Peters cites several different sources in his essay. Characterize the sources he uses. Do they help him establish credibility? In what ways do they appeal to ethos? In what ways do they not?

6. Who were the "true jerks" in the situation (para. 9)? Why does Peters consider them jerks?

Who are the "special species of jerk" (para. 16), and what makes them special? Do you think Peters considers them dangerous? Explain.

7. What is Peters's thesis? Look carefully at paragraph 12 as you answer this question.

8. What do you think Peters means when he says, "It's especially hard to report accurately when you carry the news as it happens, when you outsource the contextualization of the images you broadcast" (para. 13)? Can you think of current situations where the contextualization of images used on the news are have been "outsourced"?

9. In paragraph 15, Peters states: "The media always has a choice of which stories to carry, how to frame those stories, and how much credence to give their main actors." What does he mean by this? Defend, challenge, or qualify his statement.

10. Do you care about where the Heenes are now? Based on what he writes in paragraph 17, why might Peters think his audience does?

Nobel Prize Banquet Speech

BOB DYLAN

Bob Dylan (b. 1941) is an American singer and songwriter. His numerous awards include eleven Grammys, a Golden Globe, an Academy Award, and induction into the Rock and Roll Hall of Fame. He was awarded the Nobel Prize in Literature in 2016. His early, iconic songs such as "The Times They Are a-Changin'" became anthems for the civil rights and antiwar movements of the 1960s. His songwriting is known for its lyricism, and his musical oeuvre is known for its wide range of political, social, philosophical, and literary influences. Dylan's music incorporates folk, blues, country, gospel, rock and roll, rockabilly, and jazz. His acceptance speech for the Nobel Prize was delivered in absentia to the Nobel Banquet by Azita Raji, the U.S. Ambassador to Sweden.

seeing connections

Punk-rock singer Patti Smith accepted Bob Dylan's Nobel Prize on his behalf, singing his folk song, "A Hard Rain's A-Gonna Fall" (1962), with a full orchestral accompaniment. According to Amanda Petrusich, who wrote about the event for the *New Yorker* magazine, Dylan has said that particular song "was inspired, structurally, by seventeenth-century balladry: a question is posed, and answers stack up, though none are particularly comforting. It's the questioning, though — and, moreover, the accounting it inspires — that seems essential." Later in the article, Petrusich asserts that the way Dylan accepted the prize — "with a folk song (and this specific folk song) performed by a surrogate, a peer" — was an artistic statement in itself, "[communicating] something significant about how and what he considers his own work (musical, chiefly), and the fluid, unsteady nature of balladry itself — both the ways in which old songs are fairly reclaimed by new performers, and how their meanings change with time."

How does the idea of "questioning" and "accounting" figure into Bob Dylan's Nobel Banquet speech? To what extent do you agree with Petrusich's characterization of Dylan's attitude toward his work? Use evidence from his speech to support your response.

JESSICA GOW/Getty Images

Good evening, everyone. I extend my warmest greetings to the members of the Swedish Academy and to all of the other distinguished guests in attendance tonight.

I'm sorry I can't be with you in person, but please know that I am most definitely with you in spirit and honored to be receiving such a prestigious prize. Being awarded the Nobel Prize for Literature is something I never could have imagined or seen coming. From an early age, I've been familiar with and reading and absorbing the works of those who were deemed worthy of such a distinction: Kipling, Shaw, Thomas Mann, Pearl Buck, Albert Camus, Hemingway. These giants of literature whose works are taught in the schoolroom, housed in libraries around the world and spoken of in reverent tones have always made a deep impression. That I now join the names on such a list is truly beyond words.

I don't know if these men and women ever thought of the Nobel honor for themselves, but I suppose that anyone writing a book, or a poem, or a play anywhere in the world might harbor that secret dream deep down inside. It's probably buried so deep that they don't even know it's there.

If someone had ever told me that I had the slightest chance of winning the Nobel Prize, I would have to think that I'd have about the same odds as standing on the moon. In fact, during the year I was born and for a few years after, there wasn't anyone in the *world* who was considered good enough to win this Nobel Prize. So, I recognize that I am in very rare company, to say the least.

I was out on the road when I received this surprising news, and it took me more than a few minutes to properly process it. I began to think about William Shakespeare, the great literary figure. I would reckon he thought of himself as a dramatist. The thought that he was writing literature couldn't have entered his head. His words were written for the stage. Meant to be spoken not read. When he was writing Hamlet,

5

I'm sure he was thinking about a lot of different things: "Who're the right actors for these roles?" "How should this be staged?" "Do I really want to set this in Denmark?" His creative vision and ambitions were no doubt at the forefront of his mind, but there were also more mundane matters to consider and deal with. "Is the financing in place?" "Are there enough good seats for my patrons?" "Where am I going to get a human skull?" I would bet that the farthest thing from Shakespeare's mind was the question "Is this *literature*?"

When I started writing songs as a teenager, and even as I started to achieve some renown for my abilities, my aspirations for these songs only went so far. I thought they could be heard in coffee houses or bars, maybe later in places like Carnegie Hall, the London Palladium. If I was really dreaming big, maybe I could imagine getting to make a record and then hearing my songs on the radio. That was really the big prize in my mind. Making records and hearing your songs on the radio meant that you were reaching a big audience and that you might get to keep doing what you had set out to do.

Well, I've been doing what I set out to do for a long time, now. I've made dozens of records and played thousands of concerts all around the world. But it's my songs that are at the vital center of almost everything I do. They seemed to have found a place in the lives of many people throughout many different cultures and I'm grateful for that.

But there's one thing I must say. As a performer I've played for 50,000 people and I've played for 50 people and I can tell you that it is harder to play for 50 people. 50,000 people have a singular persona, not so with 50. Each person has an individual, separate identity, a world unto themselves. They can perceive things more clearly. Your honesty and how it relates to the depth of your talent is tried. The fact that the Nobel committee is so small is not lost on me.

But, like Shakespeare, I too am often occupied with the pursuit of my creative endeavors and dealing with all aspects of life's mundane matters. "Who are the best musicians for these songs?" "Am I recording in the right studio?" "Is this song in the right key?" Some things never change, even in 400 years.

Not once have I ever had the time to ask myself, "Are my songs *literature*?" 10

So, I do thank the Swedish Academy, both for taking the time to consider that very question, and, ultimately, for providing such a wonderful answer.

My best wishes to you all,

Bob Dylan

[2017]

EXPLORING THE TEXT

1. How does Bob Dylan establish credibility in his Nobel Banquet Speech? Consider the fact that someone else is delivering it in his stead, and he is not in attendance.

2. How would you describe the tone of Dylan's speech? In what ways does he honor the occasion? In what ways does his distinctly American voice come through?

3. What central question does the speech pose? How does Dylan answer it?

4. In paragraph 4, Dylan alludes to the fact that the Nobel Prize in Literature was not awarded in 1940, 1941, 1942, or 1943 — the height of World War II, during which Sweden was able to maintain neutrality. Why might Dylan have mentioned that in his speech?

5. Why do you think Dylan used William Shakespeare as an example of a "great literary figure" who might not have asked if his work was literature? How does Dylan establish a connection to him?

6. In what ways does the speech appeal to logos?

7. What is the primary claim Dylan makes about audience? How does his speech reflect it?

8. Dylan's Nobel Prize win sparked an intense debate about whether he should have been given the award and whether his songs qualified as literature. How do you define literature? After listening to some of Dylan's music, do you believe it to be literature according to your definition? Do you think Dylan should have won the Nobel Prize? Explain your answer.

VISUAL TEXTS

Portrait of Mrs. Carl Meyer and Her Children

JOHN SINGER SARGENT

John Singer Sargent (1856–1925) was an American artist who was considered the leading portrait painter of his generation for his evocations of turn-of-the-century luxury. Born in Florence, Italy, to American expatriates, Sargent was well-traveled as a youth and went on to study at the École des Beaux-Arts in Paris. Eventually settling in London, Sargent went on to paint around 900 oil paintings, more than 2,000 watercolors, and countless sketches and charcoal drawings. During his lifetime, Sargent's work was highly prized for its detailed brushwork and ability to evoke the inner lives of his subjects. The subject of this painting is Mrs. Adele Meyer and her children. A philanthropist and social activist in her own right (she worked to establish minimum wage in England), Adele was the wife of a German-born and Jewish English financier.

EXPLORING THE TEXT

1. In this painting, it looks as if Mrs. Meyer is about to tumble out of her seat. A perspective (the view from which you see the subjects) with such extreme foreshortening was called a "worm's eye view" in John Singer Sargent's time. What do you make of the effect of the painting's perspective? Does it provide information about the subjects and their social position? About the painter? About the social norms of the era?

2. What clues does the painting offer about the dynamics of the Meyer family? Look at both the ways the subjects connect to each other as well as how Sargent utilizes color and contrast.

3. According to the *New York Times* review of a 2016 exhibit of the painting at New York's Jewish Museum, some of the initial reactions to the painting, which was generally very well received, were openly anti-Semitic: " 'Even Mr. Sargent's skill has not succeeded in making attractive these over-civilised European Orientals,' a critic for the *Spectator* wrote in 1897. And . . . another writer sniped, '$10,000 was not much for a multimillionaire Israelite to pay to secure social recognition for his family.' " What preconceptions might Sargent have expected his audience to have? Do you see any evidence of how this work addressed those preconceptions? Explain your answer.

4. In an 1897 review, the writer Henry James described Sargent's work — then on exhibit in London — as "a knockdown insolence of talent and truth of characterization, a wonderful rendering of life, of manners, of aspects, of types, of textures, of everything." What are some of the manners, aspects, types, and textures that you see here? What do those things tell us about the subjects of the painting? How can you tell there is "truth of characterization"?

CAROLINE SANDS/Private Collection/Bridgeman Images

[1896]

Myths

ANDY WARHOL

Andy Warhol (1928–1987) was an American artist who was as well-known for his persona as for his work. A leading figure in the pop art movement, Warhol is famous for his silkscreens and paintings of American manufactured products such as Campbell's Soup and Coca-Cola, as well as American celebrities such as Elizabeth Taylor and Marilyn Monroe. The ten figures in the painting below, from left to right, are Superman, Santa Claus, Howdy Doody, Greta Garbo, Mickey Mouse, Uncle Sam, Aunt Jemima, Dracula, the Wicked Witch of the West, and Warhol himself.

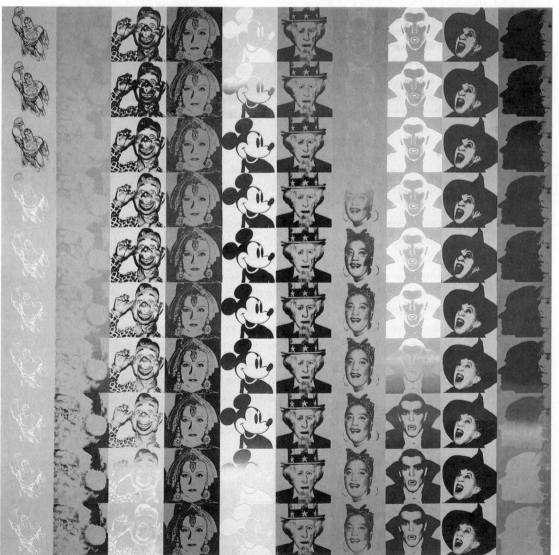

[1981]

EXPLORING THE TEXT

1. What do the strips of images remind you of? What might Andy Warhol have wanted the viewer to see in them?

2. The images in this piece were printed in black, in a process called silkscreening, onto a silver-painted canvas. The images are still shots from movies, and Warhol and his assistants printed them in an almost mechanical repetition. As they worked, however, they varied the pressure in squeezing the ink, sometimes allowing the screen to become clogged. Thus, no two images of the characters are exactly the same. What statement does Warhol make about these pop culture icons with the variations in clarity? What patterns do you see? Why might he have used a silver background?

3. The title of the work is *Myths*, a name Warhol gave to many of his works depicting celebrities and icons. What is he saying here about myths and mythmaking? Where do the myths come from? Who creates them?

4. Uncle Sam is nearly at the center of the work. What might Warhol be saying about that American icon? Consider the figures on either side of Uncle Sam: a cartoon character and an image that is considered a racial stereotype.

5. Look carefully at the image of Warhol at the far right. Characterize him through his image here and through his role as "speaker" in this work. Hint: he portrays himself doubly — in one perspective as "The Shadow," a popular radio crime fighter from the 1930s, and in another perspective looking straight out at the viewer.

6. Warhol is credited with saying, "Art is what you can get away with." Using this work and other Warhols with which you are familiar, support, challenge, or qualify that assertion.

from Formation

Directed by Melina Matsoukas, "Formation" is a Grammy-winning music video released simultaneously with the song "Formation," recorded by Beyoncé in 2016. The video stars Beyoncé herself and is notable for its references to New Orleans culture, Hurricane Katrina, African American culture, the empowerment of women of color, and of race relations in the United States in the wake of the controversies surrounding the 2014 death of Michael Brown in Ferguson, Missouri, and the 2012 death of Trayvon Martin in Sanford, Florida. The "Formation" video went viral upon release, inspiring many interpretations, much praise, and some criticism. The image that follows is emblematic of the historically and politically significant images collaged together throughout the video. As Jessica Bolanos explained in the *Huffington Post*, "The clothing worn in these scenes represent a time before and after slaves were freed. . . . White corsets, binding the women — during a time when slaves were technically 'free' but still being oppressed."

[2016]

EXPLORING THE TEXT

1. Looking carefully at this image from Beyoncé's "Formation" video, describe what you see. What are the women doing? How are they positioned? What are they wearing? What do the expressions on their faces convey? What do you notice in the background? Once you've made these observations, characterize the attitude of the women in the scene, taking their expressions, clothing, positions, and background into consideration.

2. The lyrics from this scene of the video are "Sometimes I go off (I go off), I go hard (I go hard), get what's mine (take what's mine), I'm a star (I'm a star) / 'Cause I slay (slay), I slay (hey), I slay (okay), I slay (okay) / Okay, okay, ladies now let's get in formation." These lyrics, with slight variations, are repeated in other scenes from the video, but what particular power do they have here? In other words, how does this image visually represent those lyrics? Consider such techniques as color, composition, and perspective.

3. Visual art can be analyzed through the rhetorical triangle (see Chapter 1). Consider the video, the artist, and the audience separately. What are the relationships among these three elements? What message do they convey?

4. The clothes worn by the women in this image are takes on antebellum fashion from the American South. What cultural statement might Beyoncé be making about the way the women are dressed? How does the women's clothing vary from the typical images of antebellum fashion? Why might these outfits — and other outfits Beyoncé dons in the video — be seen as controversial?

5. What similarities do you see in how the painting of the Meyer family (p. 364) and this still from the "Formation" music video address their respective audiences and mainstream cultures? In what ways might the message and rhetoric of each work be seen as parallel? In what ways do they differ?

6. A hallmark of twenty-first century art is the appropriation — quoting or borrowing — of other art. What has Beyoncé borrowed in this image? What is the relationship between the old and the new? How does the appropriation create a conversation between the artist and the viewer? Between the past and the present?

The Value of Celebrity Activism

The following eight texts comment directly or indirectly on celebrities' role in social change and their responsibility to society.

SOURCES

1 **C. Wright Mills** / from *The Power Elite*
2 **Dave Gilson** / *Dr. Clooney, I Presume?* (illustration)
3 **Brad Knickerbocker** / *West Memphis Three: Internet Campaign, Hollywood Drove Their Release*
4 **Andres Jimenez** / *Why Celebrity Activism Does More Harm Than Good*
5 **Jeffrey Kluger /** *Jim Carrey, Please Shut Up about Vaccines*
6 **Georgia Cole, Ben Radley, and Jean-Benoît Felisse** / *Who Really Benefits from Celebrity Activism?*
7 **Joshua Ostroff** / *Beyoncé and Why Celebrity Activists Matter*
8 **Jay Caspian Kang** / *Should Athletes Stick to Sports?*

After you have read, studied, and synthesized these pieces, enter the conversation by responding to one of the prompts on pages 384–85.

1 from **The Power Elite**

C. WRIGHT MILLS

C. Wright Mills (1916–1962) was an influential American sociologist. The following excerpt is from his 1956 book entitled *The Power Elite*, which examines the nature of celebrity and power.

All those who succeed in America — no matter what their circle of origin or their sphere of action — are likely to become involved in the world of the celebrity. This world, which is now the American forum of public honor, has not been build from below, as a slow and steady linking of local societies and metropolitan 400's. It has been created from above. Based upon nation-wide hierarchies of power and wealth, it is expressed by nation-wide means of mass communication. As these hierarchies and these media have come to overlay American society, new types of prestigeful men and women have come to compete with, to supplement, and even to displace the society lady and the man of pedigreed wealth.

With the incorporation of the economy, the ascendancy of the military establishment, and the centralization of the enlarged state, there have arisen the national elite, who, in occupying the command posts of the big hierarchies, have taken the spotlight of publicity and become subjects of the intensive build-up. At the same time, with the elaboration of the national means of mass communication, the professional celebrities of the entertainment world have come fully and continuously into the national view.

As personalities of national glamour, they are at the focal point of all the means of entertainment and publicity. Both the metropolitan 400 and the institutional elite must now compete with and borrow prestige from these professionals in the world of the celebrity.

But what are the celebrities? The celebrities are The Names that need no further identification. Those who know them so far exceed those of whom they know as to require no exact computation. Wherever the celebrities go, they are recognized, and moreover, recognized with some excitement and awe. Whatever they do has publicity value. More or less continuously, over a period of time, they are the material for the media communication and entertainment. And, when that time ends — as it must — and the celebrity still lives — as he may — from time to time it may be asked, "Remember him?" That is what celebrity means....

The professional celebrity, male and female, is the crowning result of the star system of a society that makes a fetish of competition. In America, this system is carried to the point where a man who can knock a small white ball into a series of holes in the ground with more efficiency and skill than anyone else thereby gains social access to the President of the United States. It is carried to the point where a chattering radio and television entertainer becomes the hunting chum of leading industrial executives, cabinet members, and the higher military. It does not seem to matter what the man is the very best at; so long as he has won out in competition over all others, he is celebrated. Then, a second feature of the star system begins to work: all the stars of any other sphere of endeavor or position are drawn toward the new star and he toward them. The success, the champion, accordingly, is one who mingles freely with other champions to populate the world of the celebrity.

This world is at once the pinnacle of the prestige system and a big-scale business. As a business, the networks of mass communication, publicity, and entertainment are not only the means whereby celebrities are celebrated; they also select and create celebrities for a profit. One type of celebrity, accordingly, is a professional at it, earning sizeable income not only from working in, but virtually living on, the mass media of communication and distraction.

The movie stars and the Broadway actress, the crooners and the TV clowns, are celebrities because of what they do on and to these media. They are celebrated because they are displayed as celebrities. If they are not thus celebrated, in due time — often very short — they lose their jobs. In them, the panic for status has become a professional craving: their very image of self is dependent upon publicity, and they need increasing doses of it. Often they seem to have celebrity and nothing else. Rather than being celebrated because they occupy positions of prestige, they occupy positions of prestige because they are celebrated. The basis of the celebration — in a strange and intricate way — is at once personal and synthetic: it is their Talent — which seems to mean their appearance value and their skill combined into what is known as A Personality. Their very importance makes them seem charming people, and they are celebrated all the time: they seem to live a sort of gay, high life, and others, by curiously watching them live it, celebrate them, as well as their celebrated way of life....

◆ ◆ ◆

In the meantime, the American celebrities include the trivial as well as the grim. Behind all The Names are the images displayed in tabloid and on movie screen, over radio and television — and sometimes not displayed but just imagined. For now all of the higher types are seen by those lower down as celebrities. In the world of the celebrities, seen through the magnifying glass of the mass media, men and women now form a kaleidoscope of highly distracting images:

In downtown New York, on a short street with a graveyard at one end and a river at the other, the rich are getting out of company limousines. On the flattened top of an Arkansas hill, the grandson of a

5

late mogul is creating a ranch with the enthusiasm of a schoolboy. Behind a mahogany table in the caucus room of the United States Senate, seven senators lean toward the television lenses. In Texas an oil man, it is said, is taking out two hundred thousand dollars a day. Somewhere in Maryland people in red coats are riding to hounds; in a Park Avenue apartment, a coal miner's daughter, having lived in the married state for twenty months, has just decided to accept a five-and-one-half million dollar settlement. At Kelly Field, the General walks carelessly between rows of painfully rigid men; on Fifty-Seventh Street, expensive women inspect the taut manikins. Between Las Vegas and Los Angeles, an American-born Countess is found dead in her railway compartment, lying full-length in a long mink coat alongside a quarter of a million dollars worth of jewelry. Seated in Boston, a board of directors orders three industrial plants moved, without employees, to Nashville. And in Washington, D.C., a sober politician, surrounded by high military aides and scientific advisers, orders a team of American airmen to fly toward Hiroshima.

In Switzerland are those who never know winter except as the chosen occasion for sport, on southern islands those who never sweat in the sun except at their February leisure. All over the world, like lords of creation, are those who, by travel, command the seasons and, by many houses, the very landscape they will see each morning or afternoon they are awakened. Here is the old whiskey and the new vice; the blonde girl with the moist mouth, always ready to go around the world; the silver Mercedes climbing the mountain bend, going where it wants to go for so long as it wants to stay. From Washington, D.C., and Dallas,

Texas, it is reported that 103 women have each paid $300 for a gold lipstick. On a yacht, with its crew of ten, somewhere off the Keys, a man of distinction lies on his bed and worries about the report from his New York office that the agents of the Bureau of Internal Revenue are busy again.

Here are the officials at the big desks with the four telephones, the ambassadors in the lounge-rooms, talking earnestly but somehow lightly. Here are the men who motor in from the airport with a secret service man beside the chauffeur, motorcycled outriders on either flank, and another tailing a block behind. Here are the people whose circumstances make them independent of the good will of others, never waiting for anyone but always waited upon. Here are the Very Important Persons who during the wars come and go, doubled up in the General's jeep. Here are those who have ascended to office, who have been elevated to distinguished employments. By the sound of their voices, it is evident that they have been trained, carefully yet casually, to be somebody. [10]

Here are the names and faces and voices that are always before you, in the newspapers and on the radio, in the newsreels and on the television screen; and also the names and faces you do not know about, not even from a distance, but who really run things, or so informed sources say, but you could never prove it. Here are the somebodies who are held to be worthy of notice: now they are news, later they will be history. Here are the men who own a firm of lawyers and four accountants. Here are the men who have the inside track. Here are all the expensive commodities, to which the rich seem appendages. Here is the money talking in its husky, silky voice of cash, power, celebrity.

QUESTIONS

1. What, according to C. Wright Mills, is a celebrity? How does he believe celebrities are created?

2. What does Mills mean when he asserts that we live in a "star system of a society that makes a fetish of competition" (para. 4)? According to him, what are some of the results?

3. Mills suggests that the world of the celebrity is the result of a prestige system but is also a "big-scale business" (para. 5). What does that business do?

Who participates in it? Who benefits from it? What pressures does it create?

4. What role does Mills believe money plays in the creation and placement of celebrities?

5. *The Power Elite,* from which this excerpt is taken, was published in 1956. What aspects of modern-day celebrity culture did Mills predict? Do you find this piece timely? Explain your answer.

2 Dr. Clooney, I Presume?
A Map of the Celebrity Recolonization of Africa

DAVE GILSON

The following illustration is taken from an interactive map detailing celebrity visits to Africa. First published on *Mother Jones's* website in 2010, it was prefaced with the following text.

Oversized shades have replaced pith helmets, but the new scramble for Africa has its share of adventurers, would-be saviors, and even turf battles. As Madonna's publicist explains, "She's focusing on Malawi. South Africa is Oprah's territory."

The map below takes a lighter look at the sometimes serious, sometimes silly business of celebrity altruism.

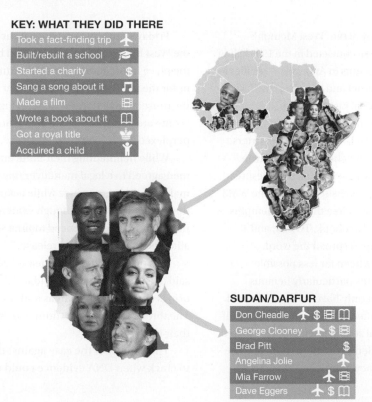

KEY: WHAT THEY DID THERE

Took a fact-finding trip	✈
Built/rebuilt a school	🎓
Started a charity	$
Sang a song about it	♫
Made a film	▦
Wrote a book about it	📖
Got a royal title	👑
Acquired a child	🧒

SUDAN/DARFUR

Don Cheadle	✈ $ ▦ 📖
George Clooney	✈ $ ▦
Brad Pitt	$
Angelina Jolie	✈
Mia Farrow	✈ ▦
Dave Eggers	✈ $ 📖

QUESTIONS

1. How would you characterize the tone of the map and its key to "celebrity recolonization"?

2. Why do you think the map is subtitled "An Interactive Map of the Celebrity Recolonization of Africa"?

3. What do the activities of each of the celebrities in the inset tell you about their interests and commitments?

4. "Dr. Clooney, I presume" is an allusion to "Dr. Livingstone, I presume," the greeting Henry

Morton Stanley gave to David Livingstone after finding him in Tanzania in 1871. Stanley, a British journalist, had been tasked with locating Livingstone, a medical missionary and antislavery crusader, who had not been seen or heard from since departing to explore the Nile River almost six years prior. Its humor and staying power are partly related to the fact that Livingstone was the only white man for hundreds of miles. Why might Dave Gilson have made George Clooney the subject of that famous quote?

---

3 West Memphis Three: Internet Campaign, Hollywood Drove Their Release

BRAD KNICKERBOCKER

The following article was published in the *Christian Science Monitor* in 2011 by longtime writer and editor Brad Knickerbocker.

The release Friday of the "West Memphis Three" — the men convicted in the 1993 killing of three young Cub Scouts in Arkansas — testifies to the power of the Internet and broadcast media in influencing the criminal justice system.

Questions about the prosecution of the case and conduct of the trial — raised by supporters of defendants Damien Echols, Jason Baldwin, and Jessie Misskelley Jr. — generated widespread interest through such websites as "Free the WM3 Support Fund" and its "Free the West Memphis Three Official Blog." Facebook, Twitter, and YouTube videos helped spread the word.

That would have been far less possible 18 years ago when this particularly heinous crime occurred. Not only have social media and websites aimed at affecting legal outcomes proliferated, but powerful search engines have created easy access to detailed case information and the assertions of advocacy groups.

Friday's outcome was not a clear victory for the West Memphis Three (so-called because of the place in Arkansas where the crime occurred) or for the families of the three 8-year old boys. As the prosecuting attorney, Scott Ellington, put it: "Some are happy, some are angry, and others are perplexed."

While maintaining their innocence, the three 5 men agreed to a legal maneuver that lets them maintain their innocence while acknowledging that prosecutors have enough evidence against them. They were sentenced to time served, allowing their immediate release.

"It's not perfect by any means," Mr. Echols said at a press conference Friday. "But it at least brings closure to some areas and some aspects." The three say they will continue to fight to prove their innocence.

The solidity of the case against them began to crack when DNA evidence could not be linked to the defendants while at the same time indicating the possible presence at the crime scene of one of the boy's stepfather. Questions also had been raised about the jury foreman discussing during jury deliberations a confession deemed inappropriate at trial. (That confession by Mr. Misskelley — reportedly elicited by police taking advantage of his low IQ — was quickly recanted.)

Last November, the Arkansas Supreme Court ordered a new hearing, asking a judge to consider allegations of juror misconduct and whether new DNA science could affect the conviction.

Over the years, much has been written about the case, and HBO is finishing up the third in a series of documentary films titled "Paradise Lost." The HBO series, along with books and websites, helped generate broad support from such celebrities as actor Johnny Depp, "Pearl Jam" front man Eddie Vedder, and country singer Natalie Maines of the "Dixie Chicks."

"This case is about the power of film and a main protagonist," says Nancy Snow, professor of communications at California State University in Fullerton. "Without the 'Paradise Lost' series, you simply would not have the same level of celebrity cheerleading for justice. The main wrongly accused character, Damien Echols [the one defendant who had received a death sentence], has himself become a celebrity author and poet."

Other observers say there's a lesson here for investigative writers and broadcasters.

"I think this is actually the media at their best, shining a light on a situation in which the machinery of government apparently failed to do its job," says Fordham University communications professor Paul Levinson, author of "New New Media." "It asks the question — 'What other failures of the criminal system are out there?' — and provides the impetus that journalists should get on those cases and investigate them more fully."

It's notable that Hollywood actors are spearheading the drive for social justice, including in the Memphis case, says Ben Agger, director of the Center for Theory at the University of Texas in Arlington.

"Many academics have become entrepreneurs oriented to getting grants that help public universities survive at an historical moment of massive disinvestment in higher education," he says. "Ironically, this leaves Hollywood as the site of critical thinking and moral activism. This is a version of Hollywood that clashes with a *People* magazine portrayal of Hollywood simply as a celebrity culture, where the Kardashian wedding is foregrounded as weekly tabloid fodder."

10

QUESTIONS

1. In this report, Brad Knickerbocker credits the "power of the Internet and broadcast media in influencing the criminal justice system" (para. 1) for the release of three men who were likely wrongly convicted of killing three young boys nearly twenty years prior. What relationship does Knickerbocker suggest exists between the media, the celebrities, and the West Memphis Three? What do you believe is Knickerbocker's attitude toward this relationship?

2. Knickerbocker notes that observers have said "there's a lesson here for investigative writers and broadcasters" (para. 11) in the story of the West Memphis Three. What is that lesson?

3. Knickerbocker asserts that it's "notable that Hollywood actors are spearheading the drive for social justice" (para. 13). How does he explain that irony?

4 Why Celebrity Activism Does More Harm Than Good

ANDRES JIMENEZ

The following article by Andres Jimenez, an international conflict analyst and activist, was published in 2013 on the website for Waging Nonviolence, an organization that describes itself as "a source for original news and analysis about struggles for justice and peace around the globe."

As I sat in the stands of Pece Stadium in the northern Uganda town of Gulu on a sunny Sunday morning, a couple of young men made their way close to where I was sitting. We struck up a conversation, and they said that it was a pity that I had not witnessed the event that had taken place not long before my arrival in town a few weeks earlier.

My new friends began to describe how there had been a massive gathering in the stadium for the screening of a video put together by a foreign NGO.[1] The video had profoundly upset a significant amount of those present that evening, and a riot broke out. I realized that, of course, they were talking about the launch of the first Kony 2012 video campaign by the U.S.–based organization Invisible Children. The video's portrayal of the over two-decade-long conflict had deeply angered many of those who had endured it firsthand. The crowd ended up having to be dispersed by police and tear gas.

As I listened to the men's account of how the crowd's anger turned to violence, I could hardly keep myself from thinking how emblematic and representative such an event was of countless celebrity-fueled, do-good awareness campaigns that I had already had the misfortune to witness over the years.

The tragedy behind these sorts of campaigns is that they are motivated by the belief that problems around the world remain unresolved due to the lack of international awareness of their existence or global commitment to resolve them.

If only enough people knew and cared about a certain conflict or problem, the assumption goes, then the combined energy and support could be harnessed in order to trigger an immediate flood of solutions. Any action taken toward this end is therefore righteous and will put us a step closer to fixing the problem; surely any little bit of help must be better than nothing.

It is this mindset that has motivated celebrities like the rock star Bono to take up the causes of debt cancelation, the increase in foreign aid and the promotion of the Millennium Development Goals. Actor George Clooney has taken great interest in Darfur; Madonna and Oprah Winfrey have embraced the fight for girls' education in Africa, while Angelina Jolie knocks at the doors of the major centers of power as a UNHCR[2] Goodwill Ambassador to promote support for humanitarian relief. Unfortunately, many of the policies and remedies promoted by this ever-growing influx of celebrity activists have been heavily criticized for being paternalistic, detached from reality and often dangerously counterproductive.

However, far from being deterred, celebrity activists find solace in the assurances of so-called experts, specialists and analysts who fill the ranks of leading international organizations, Washington think tanks and Ivy League universities. These people are the Nicholas Kristofs and the Jeffry Sachses of the world who often find their self-assurance and sense of certainty in their

5

---

[1]Non-governmental organization. —Eds.

[2]United Nations High Commissioner for Refugees, more commonly known as the UN Refugee Agency. —Eds.

Ivy League educations, in the power that their positions grant them or in the titles that they hold. Their almost complete confidence in their predictions and analyses, combined with the allure of celebrity, emboldens them to leap at the opportunity to promote what they consider to be the solutions for conflicts whose complexities they only superficially grasp.

Celebrity-led campaigns do often prove to be highly successful in generating broad public support. This is because they draw on the self-serving guilt trips that lead many people to believe that their privileged position has invested them with the burden and the responsibility to save those less fortunate from their plight. Celebrity activists provide us with a powerful outlet for our guilty consciences and our self-serving views of history. What better way to liberate ourselves from this burden than by taking up a global cause in a faraway land, and who better to show us the way to do it than our favorite celebrities?

My experience working with armed conflicts and humanitarian crises has shown me the disastrous effects that such views tend to have on the ground. Away from the fantasy world of easy-to-understand, black-and-white, single-story views of a conflict lays a world of complexity, depth and uncertainty. With the embrace of complexity we are able to discover that the way we seek to approach and work within a conflict must be incredibly flexible and diverse.

We need to distance ourselves from the powerful desire to follow simple solutions drafted by experts in conference rooms half a world away. We should begin, above all, by focusing on the creative energy already present among the local actors in a conflict in order to discover context-specific strategies that can help us to transform it.

Sadly, this approach does not fit well in a five-minute YouTube video or an inspirational TED Talk. Our fascination with pre-packaged solutions and our short attention spans are incompatible with appreciation for true complexity, humility and unpredictability. 10

If you feel invested in a cause, engage it with all your passion, but tread carefully. Ask yourself why you even care about this conflict in the first place? Whose voices are you listening to about it? Whose interests are they serving? What is already being tried by local actors on the ground? And, most importantly, why should you become involved?

If you do decide to take that leap, then start by listening rather than preaching, facilitating rather than commanding, cooperating rather than defeating, creating organically rather than planning mechanically, and seeking to unsettle the status quo rather than trying to control it in its entirety. Being told that you have an urgent responsibility to act in order to help solve a conflict that you hardly even knew existed in the first place is the first step down a slippery slope of continuous despair, wasted goodwill and neo-colonialism.

QUESTIONS

1. According to Andres Jimenez, what fuels "celebrity-fueled, do-good awareness campaigns" (para. 3)?

2. What is Jimenez's view of celebrities like Bono, George Clooney, Madonna, and Oprah Winfrey taking up causes such as debt cancelation, the increase in foreign aid, and others? What do people generally criticize about these efforts?

3. How, according to Jimenez, do celebrity activists generate broad support for their efforts? Why does Jimenez think the effects of those efforts are "disastrous . . . on the ground" (para. 8)? Does he see any upside? Explain your answer.

4. What does Jimenez consider to be the basic requirements for working with humanitarian or conflict crises? To what extent do you agree?

5 Jim Carrey, Please Shut Up about Vaccines

JEFFREY KLUGER

Jeffrey Kluger is a science writer and editor at large for *Time* magazine, which published the following column in 2015.

Say this for the anti-vax clown car: it never seems to run out of new punchinellos to climb inside. If it's not scientific fabulist Andrew Wakefield, he of the fraudulent study that got the whole vaccine-autism myth started, it's Jenny McCarthy, she of the supposedly vaccine-injured son whose autism was cured in part by — yes! — a gluten-free diet because, um, gluten is bad, very bad.

After McCarthy, there was *Saturday Night Live* alum Rob Schneider — because when you're looking for guidance on the wisdom of vaccines, who are you going to trust: the World Health Organization, the Centers for Disease Control and the National Institutes of Health, or the man who gave us Deuce Bigelow, Male Gigolo? I mean, hello, the movie was *huge*.

◆ ◆ ◆

Now, to this group of board-certified jesters add Jim Carrey — the ex-Mr. Jenny McCarthy — who rose on July 1 in all his orange-wigged, floppy-shoed, seltzer-down-the-pants fury to condemn California Governor Jerry Brown for the high crime of common sense, after Brown signed a law that requires virtually all kids in the state to be fully vaccinated as a pre-condition for attending public school. Carrey took — no surprise — to Twitter to air his peer-reviewed views.

"California Gov says yes to poisoning more children with mercury and aluminum in man-ditory [sic] vaccines. This corporate fascist must be stopped," said the erstwhile Ace Ventura, Pet Detective. That was followed by:

"They say mercury in fish is dangerous but [5] forcing all of our children to be injected with mercury in thimerosol [sic] is no risk. Make sense?" Which was followed by:

"I am not anti-vaccine. I am anti-thimerosal, anti-mercury. They have taken some of the mercury laden thimerosal out of vaccines. NOT ALL!"

And there was more too, but really, it doesn't matter. Never mind that Carrey does not understand the difference between ethylmercury and methylmercury or the fact that there is virtually no mercury of any kind left in vaccines. Never mind that he doesn't seem to know that to the extent that aluminum is in vaccines at all, it is there only as an adjuvant — or immune system stimulant — and is well-handled by the body, especially in the trace amounts that it's found in vaccines. And never mind too that if you're going for the ad hominem attack — a staple of anti-vaxxers — calling a man like Jerry Brown, better known as Governor Moonbeam, a "fascist" is a bit wide of the argumentative mark.

The anti-vax crowd has never been about reasoned argument or a cool-headed look at clinical science. They've been all about rage, all about echo-chamber misinformation. For every sensible action to boost vaccination rates, they have long been there, like a sort of perverse bit of Newtonian physics, with an equal and risible reaction.

Maybe that's the reason they roll out pratfall comics like Schneider and Carrey to plead their case — a bit of misdirection to hide the tragicomedy of their message behind the larger comedy of the messenger. Or maybe they're the best they've got.

That matters. A movement that begins with [10] a study conducted by a doctor so thoroughly discredited that he's not even allowed to practice medicine in his native United Kingdom anymore

(Wakefield) and takes flight thanks to the prat-tlings of a Playboy model and talk show guest (McCarthy) ought not to have a chance against the informed scientific opinion of virtually every medical group on Earth. That it does says something about the hucksters' ability to sell their nonsense and the human tendency to pay more attention to famous but wrong-headed people than to unglamorous but smart ones.

But that's finally changing. The anti-vax act has at last gotten old, and it's gotten tired and the cost — sick children, lost school days, outbreaks of diseases like measles, mumps and whooping cough — has gotten too high.

Like all fringe groups eventually do, the anti-vaxxers are now entering their rump-faction stage, dwindling to an angry, dense, immune-to-reason core. Soon enough, they'll be gone. The likes of Carrey — today's foghorn, tomorrow's footnote — will vanish with them. And America's children — not for nothing — will be better for it.

QUESTIONS

1. Jeffrey Kluger's views on vaccines are clear from the very first sentence of this piece. How does he establish credibility despite the strident tone and one-sided nature of the views he presents?

2. How does Kluger characterize the "anti-vax" crowd? What does he consider the "tragicomedy" (para. 9) of the anti-vaccine movement?

3. Why is Kluger optimistic that the "anti-vax act has at last gotten old" (para. 11)? Do you agree? Explain your answer.

6 Who Really Benefits from Celebrity Activism?

GEORGIA COLE, BEN RADLEY, AND JEAN-BENOÎT FALISSE

The following article, published in the *Guardian* in 2015, was written by researchers focused on African politics and economic development.

From George Clooney's Enough Project, rap-per Akon's newly launched Lighting Africa to the viral Kony 2012 campaign, there's no doubt celebrity activism has gone mainstream.

Mother Jones recently published an ironic map of the African countries celebrities have "claimed" through their charity work: Richard Branson, Oprah and Will Smith have South Africa, while Botswana is Kim Kardashian's.

But this kind of celebrity advocacy isn't new, either. At the turn of the 20th century, the prominent British journalist, author and politician Edmund Dene Morel and Anglo-Irish diplomat Roger Casement successfully challenged King Leopold of Belgium's violent and autocratic rule of the Congo Free State. They did so with the help of notable friends: writers Arthur Conan Doyle and Joseph Conrad, and chocolate magnate William Cadbury.

Between the 1930s and 1950s, suffragette Sylvia Pankhurst fought for a fascist-free, and later independent, Ethiopia, and a few decades later Bob Geldof and Band Aid raised £30m for the victims of the country's famine.

The latest generation of American celebrity activists has most commonly knocked at the doors of western governments, demanding changes in policy towards their chosen cause célèbre. But what are the consequences, and is this something we necessarily want to promote?

Just Causes vs Personal Brands

Should we question the motives of celebrities who hire expensive PR experts to "sell" their convictions? As Daniel Drezner writes in "When foreign policy goes glam," engaging in humanitarian causes clearly benefits the Clooneys, Jolies, and Damons of the world. It provides them with access to new outlets — political talk shows or international forums — and helps polish their personal brands.

Causes are to celebrities what corporate social responsibility is to business — every established name has to have at least one.

And while celebrities undoubtedly help bring serious issues to a larger audience — often encouraging pledges from governments, policy-makers and businesses — the problem lies in that they are much less effective at transforming all this into appropriate, tangible policies.

Academic Darrel West suggests that the fascination for celebrities raises the risk that "there will be more superficiality and less substance in our political process."

A stark example of this is provided in the new documentary, *We Will Win Peace,* which tracks the impact of Section 1502 of the US's Dodd-Frank Wall Street Reform and Consumer Protection Act.

Introduced in 2010 and championed by celebrities from Ben Affleck to Nicole Richie, the ruling required companies to disclose their use of conflict minerals originating in the Democratic Republic of the Congo or an adjoining country.

It was presented by the Enough Project as an essential precursor to preventing conflict and sexual violence in the DRC. But the new documentary, alongside other pieces of research, shows the very real and devastating effect of this simplified rendering of the facts.

With de facto international boycotts on minerals from the DRC, and a government ban on artisanal mining, tens of thousands of miners and businesses ended up unable to make a living. This pushed many individuals either towards the illicit mining industry or a rebel group, paradoxically exacerbating the very violence it set out to reduce.

So what went wrong? In an article for the World Peace Foundation, writer Alex de Waal says there are fundamental pillars of activism which should always be followed, most of all, the act of responding to and collaborating with local people, rather than imposing outside agendas.

The Dodd-Frank campaign should have involved asking local activists, populations and mining experts in the eastern DRC about mineral supply chains, he writes, to check whether they could be altered to improve the situation.

De Waal also argues that activism should speak to power, but also stand firmly against it, and should not presume that all change is possible from within.

A Simple, Catch All, Solution?

As recent research has shown, the problem with celebrity causes is that they tend to de-politicise activism. They too often obscure the complex dynamics of power and socioeconomic relations in favour of a simple, catch all, solution.

Celebrities speaking truth to power, rather than half-truths that may inadvertently serve the interests of power, may be a more promising way forward if celebrity advocacy is to lead to meaningful socioeconomic change.

The advocacy circuit for change in Africa lacks celebrity participation in bottom-up movements, as opposed to top-down campaigns.

Yet if the cycle of simplified celebrity messages leading to ineffective — even harmful — African policy is to be broken, genuine engagement with, and commitment to, the people they advocate on behalf of is critical.

QUESTIONS

1. Why do you think the Georgia Cole, Ben Radley, and Jean-Benoît Falisse discuss the history of celebrity involvement with social causes? How does this approach serve their main argument?

2. Who do the authors suggest benefits from celebrity involvement?

3. What are some of the negative consequences of celebrity involvement cited in this article? How convincing are these examples?

4. What do the authors consider to be the "fundamental pillars of activism" (para. 14)?

5. What do you think is the difference between "bottom-up movements" and "top-down campaigns" (para. 19)? What attitude do the authors take toward each?

7   Beyoncé and Why Celebrity Activists Matter

JOSHUA OSTROFF

The piece that follows was written by Joshua Ostroff, a senior editor at *HuffPost Canada*, in 2016 for *HuffPost*'s blog.

From the moment Beyoncé walked off the Super Bowl stage, halftime show sticking out of her back pocket after broadcasting black power imagery and black pride lyrics to an audience of 112 million people, the backlash began.

Actually, it took off on Twitter even beforehand with a #BoycottBeyonce hashtag response to the powerful imagery of her new music video, "Formation," released the day before the Super Bowl. It features a boy in a hoodie dancing in front of riot cops, "Stop shooting us!" graffiti and Beyonce atop a New Orleans cop car sinking in Katrina floodwaters.

But the halftime performance pushed it into overdrive. "I thought it was really outrageous that she used it as a platform to attack police officers," fumed former New York mayor Rudy Giuliani on Fox News. "You're talking to Middle America when you have the Super Bowl."

Congressman Peter King chimed in on Facebook that "Beyoncé may be a gifted entertainer but no one should really care what she thinks about any serious issue confronting our nation."

Even Toronto city councilor Jim Karygiannis 5 joined the attack, calling her performance "disturbing" and wondering if "perhaps Immigration Minister John McCallum should have her investigated first?" before she's allowed to tour here.

And on February 16 there is a planned anti-Beyonce protest in front of NFL headquarters:

"Are you offended as an American that Beyoncé pulled her race-baiting stunt at the Superbowl? Do you agree that it was a slap in the face to law enforcement? Come and let's stand together. Let's tell the NFL we don't want hate speech & racism at the Superbowl ever again!"

The goal here is to intimidate the pop star into silence because she holds power.

It's not the first time she's caused a stir on a big stage. Remember this [see photograph on p. 380]?

Now celebrity activists are an easy target. 10 Who doesn't like a good joke about Bono's latest Jesus Christ pose, cringe when they hear "Do

Michael Buckner/Getty Images

They Know It's Christmas?" or just generally gripe about our celeb-obsessed culture?

But here's the thing; celebrity activists matter. Being an artist does not mean that you cannot speak out about injustice, but critics push that agenda because having a following for your art does mean that people might actually listen when you do.

Sure, it doesn't compare to street-level activists like Black Lives Matter leader DeRay Mckesson, but it's a different job, it's about raising awareness, speaking truth to power and using cultural influence to point people toward a cause, movement or idea.

Consider the power of peak-era Public Enemy — which Chuck D has dubbed the group's "war years" — as they reached kids from the streets to suburbs with agit-raps about police brutality, 911 failing the black community, fighting the power and the establishment's "Fear of a Black Planet."

Or let's go further back to John Lennon, whose antiwar activism had him surveilled by the FBI and nearly deported. Professor Jon Weiner explained why to NPR:

> "The '72 election was going to be the first in which 18-year olds had the right to vote. Before that you had to be 21. Everybody knew that young people were the strongest anti-war constituency, so the question was, for Lennon, how could he use his power as a celebrity to get young people into the political process? And also, this is a time when kids are very alienated from, you know, mainstream politics. So to get Lennon out of the country, the strategic countermeasure is to deport Lennon so he won't be able to take this tour that would register young voters."

Further back we had Muhammad Ali going to jail because he refused to fight in Vietnam: "Why should they ask me to put on a uniform and go 10,000 miles from home and drop bombs and bullets on brown people in Vietnam while so-called Negro people in Louisville are treated like dogs and denied simple human rights? I ain't got no quarrel with them Viet Cong."

15

Back further still to the 1950s, Harry Belafonte used money from hits like the "Banana Boat Song" to help bankroll the civil rights movement and his fame to help bring people and media out to rallies and marches. He was blacklisted by McCarthy for his efforts. If there had been an old-timey Twitter no doubt #BoycottBelafonte would have been trending.

Belafonte also organized "We Are The World" back in 1985, the same year that Willie Nelson founded Farm Aid with Neil Young and John Mellencamp, which has since raised over $50 million to help farmers.

George Clooney and celeb friends Don Cheadle, Matt Damon and Brad Pitt founded Not on Our Watch, a human rights advocacy group "drawing upon the voices of cultural leaders to protect and assist the vulnerable, marginalized, and displaced."

Pitt's better half, Angelina Jolie, has long used her celebrity to draw attention to the plight of the dispossessed which led to her being named a Special Envoy for the United Nations High Commissioner for Refugees. Leonardo DiCaprio and Mark Ruffalo have also worked hard to raise awareness and money for environmental causes.

Rapper Killer Mike has helped boost Black [20] Lives Matter and Bernie Sanders, Canadian actress Ellen Page took on Ted Cruz over LGBTQ issues with a Vice camera crew in tow and "Harry Potter" star Emma Watson changed minds with her viral gender equality speech at the UN and "He for She" campaign.

Critics of celebrity activists feel these famous folks should "shut up and sing," as argued in the 2003 book by conservative radio host Laura Ingram, a title co-opted by the Dixie Chicks for a doc about that time they got death threats and banned from country radio for opposing the Iraq War.

These same critics, of course, seem to have no problem at all with billionaires or corporations using their financial influence to affect the political process.

But back to Beyoncé (who, by the way, has with her husband Jay Z been bailing BLM protesters out of jail and donated $1.5 million from their streaming service Tidal).

The reason why her video and halftime show are important, and why similar efforts by celebrity activists over the decades have mattered, is because they can leverage their fame to help sway public opinion, which is key to changing public policy. Sure, some celebs may be cynically building personal brands, but if they are educated and dedicated they can inspire people to look deeper, to do research, to get involved and affect change.

Or as Jessica Williams said in her spirited [25] "Daily Show" defense: "The point is Beyoncé is black and this is her message. It's what artists do."

Oh, and if that doesn't convince you, wouldn't you rather have the Kanye that blurted out "George Bush doesn't care about black people" back?

QUESTIONS

1. How does Joshua Ostroff consider his audience when he shares comments made by former New York mayor Rudolph Giuliani, Congressman Peter King, and Toronto city council mayor Jim Karygiannis about Beyoncé's performance at the Super Bowl?

2. Why does Ostroff suggest that celebrity activists are sometimes pushed into silence?

3. What are the historical examples Ostroff cites? How do they help him make his argument?

4. Why does Ostroff think celebrity activism matters? Do you find his argument convincing? Explain your response.

8 Should Athletes Stick to Sports?

JAY CASPIAN KANG

Jay Caspian Kang is a writer and correspondent on HBO's *VICE News Tonight*. The following article by Kang was published by the *New York Times Magazine* in 2017.

For the past few months, the sports media has been embroiled in a fight over "stick to sports." The phrase comes from a common online rebuke directed at sportswriters and pundits and players and coaches and anyone in the world of sports, really, who takes a political stance on anything that doesn't occur on a field or a court or in a locker room or front office. The dividing line is predictable: Many jocks and traditionalists argue for a separation of church and state; many young fans say that sports, just like everything else, *is* politics. But as the sports media critic Bryan Curtis has pointed out in *The Ringer*, the debate is mostly moot now: Trump's presidency, with its daily explosions, has made it impossible to cover pro sports, even in the simplest boxscore ways, without detouring onto the White House lawn. This comes, in part, from the way basic sports coverage works. Reporters ask questions before and after every game, and when the only thing anyone wants to talk about is Trump, some of those questions will be about the president.

In the past, a paradoxical yet symbiotic relationship generally characterized whatever relationship existed between sports and politics. The big American leagues, especially the N.F.L. and Major League Baseball, gave every indication of wanting to distance themselves from partisan frictions. They typically prefer to honor troops, fly fighter jets over stadiums and hold moments of silence to honor the victims of tragedies. When they tackle overtly political issues, it's through selective editing and legacy building. The settled politics of the past, where details can be kept few and the tone nostalgic, are fine.

We know, for example, that Jackie Robinson broke baseball's color line, stole home and wore 42 on his back. Muhammad Ali championed equality and said some funny stuff to Howard Cosell. Billie Jean King beat Bobby Riggs. Their lionization reassures us that the stands they took were good — and can now be consigned to bygone eras.

But the latest intrusion of political talk into sports — whether you deem it excessive or welcome — has had a drastic effect on coverage. It has brought with it a currency and immediacy that we haven't seen since the '60s and early '70s, when athletes like Jim Brown, Kareem Abdul-Jabbar and Curt Flood openly talked about civil rights. The day the White House declared its immigration and travel ban in January, the Milwaukee Bucks played the Toronto Raptors in Canada, and there was some concern that the Bucks' rookie center, Thon Maker, would not be let back into the United States after the game: Maker is a citizen of Australia, but his family emigrated there from Sudan. The day after the game, Alex Lasry, a Bucks executive and the son of one of the team's owners, tweeted: "I appreciate all the fans' concerns and prayers for Thon. And today a Sudanese refugee who fled oppression and is an incredible young man will make his second N.B.A. start. I'm incredibly excited and proud of him. He's a symbol of what makes America great and all immigrants believe about America."

Maker was directly affected by Trump's policies (though he reentered the United States without problem), and his teammates, fellow players and coaches in the N.B.A. publicized their support. This was not surprising, given the N.B.A.'s wealth of international players and its cosmopolitan fan base; in recent years, the league has encouraged its stars to speak out on matters important to them. More unexpected was the Super Bowl's inability to avoid the fray. During this year's primetime media day, usually a hollow parading of the players before the microphones and cameras, Tom Brady's continued refusal to talk about his presidential friend was big news. Brady had been ignoring these questions for almost a year and a half now, ever since reporters saw a red "Make America Great Again" hat in his locker, but he finally gave in. All he could muster was: "What's going on in the world? I haven't paid much attention. I'm just a positive person."

Brady's hamhanded elisions were hardly surprising — he, perhaps more than any athlete since Tiger Woods, has doggedly confronted us with his right to never publicly say anything interesting to anyone. But the fact that his act hasn't quite kept the inquisitors at bay suggests that the days of Woods, Derek Jeter and Michael Jordan just grinning through any edgy conversation are over, at least for now. Athletes, especially famous ones, are less likely to be left to stand alone as ciphers of sporting excellence. Their images will be shaded by their politics, even if these have to be assigned to them. And as players continue to be asked about their political beliefs by reporters — especially as the international players in basketball and baseball are prompted to talk about immigration — they have an opportunity to give voice to resistance. If they want a model, they should look toward the W.N.B.A., whose players have been exemplifying thoughtful political expression. Last summer, the W.N.B.A. fined several players for wearing black T-shirts in support of Black Lives Matter at pregame practices; following the next game after the fine was announced, some players refused to discuss basketball, instead using the postgame news conference to talk about police shootings. (The W.N.B.A. rescinded the fines soon after.) Last month, Breanna Stewart, the

league's reigning Rookie of the Year, attended the airport protest at LAX.

5   Stephen Curry, arguably the world's most popular basketball player, may be following the W.N.B.A. lead. After the chief executive of Under Armour recently referred to Trump as a "great asset" for the country, Curry, whose endorsement deal with the company runs through 2024, said, "There is no amount of money, there is no platform I wouldn't jump off, if it wasn't in line with who I am." Perhaps more than any other N.B.A. star lately, Curry has tended to project a charming blandness, but in putting his sponsorships and money at risk — however improbable the prospect of his losing any — he went further than most outspoken athletes.

In the week following the Super Bowl, at least six Patriots players — including Martellus Bennett and Devin McCourty, who earlier in the season raised fists in solidarity with Colin Kaepernick's national-anthem protest — said they would not make the traditional victory visit to the White House. (Brady went to Washington after his first three championships, when George W. Bush was president, but skipped the fourth trip during the Obama presidency.) "I was a black man yesterday, and I'm going to be a black man tomorrow," Bennett tweeted in response to the predictable storm his announcement kicked up from the "stick to sports" crowd. "My wife and daughter are women today and will be women tomorrow." The Patriots absent from the White House photo op will be the most conspicuous part of what usually is a goofy, perfunctory moment in the N.F.L.'s offseason, and reporters will reach out to them for comment, which will provide another occasion for criticism.

Those athletes who do speak out might find a curiously receptive ear in the White House. Let's remember that Trump, perhaps even more than his basketball-obsessed predecessor, is a sports fan. He owned a team in the United

States Football League (while almost single-handedly running the league into the ground); he hosted fights at his Atlantic City casinos; he tried to buy the Buffalo Bills; he brags about his friendship with Brady. Above all, he has shown a crippling sensitivity to the opinions of his fellow celebrities. Professional sports usually provides a poor, inaccurate reflection of politics, but sometimes elements of that imagery — the machismo, the posturing, the adoration of stars — align exactly. Jocks, if nothing else, know how to get the president's attention.

QUESTIONS

1. What does Jay Caspian Kang consider the dividing line between those who believe athletes and coaches should stick with sports and those who feel that "sports, just like everything else *is* politics" (para. 1)? Do you agree? Explain your answer.

2. According to Kang, what is the traditional "paradoxical yet symbiotic relationship" (para. 2) between sports and politics?

3. What does Kang believe caused the fairly recent changes in the relationship between sports and politics?

4. Kang suggests that the days of uncommitted "ciphers of sporting excellence" are over and that politics may have to be "assigned to them" (para. 5). What does he mean by that, and how might that happen?

5. What is your view of the relationship between sports celebrities and political causes?

MAKING CONNECTIONS

1. How does Jeffrey Kluger's reference to "pratfall comics like Schneider and Carrey" (para. 9) echo C. Wright Mills's discussion of why people listen to even the lightest celebrities?

2. What similarities do you see between Mills's take on celebrities' role in society and that expressed in "Who Really Benefits from Celebrity Activism"? Are there any differences? Explain.

3. Do you believe Andres Jimenez would approve of the efforts of celebrities who worked to free the West Memphis Three? Why or why not?

4. How might Joshua Ostroff respond to Kluger's assertion that there is a "human tendency to pay more attention to famous but wrong-headed people than to unglamorous but smart ones" (para. 10)?

5. Do you think Jay Caspian Kang would agree with Ostroff's views on celebrity activism? Do you think Ostroff's support for celebrity activism includes political commitment from athletes? Explain why or why not.

ENTERING THE CONVERSATION

As you respond to the following prompts, support your argument with references to at least three sources in this Conversation on the Value of Celebrity Activism. For help using sources, see Chapter 4.

1. Write an essay in which you take a stand on the value of celebrity in creating social change.

2. In the foreword to *Amusing Ourselves to Death*, media critic Neil Postman (1931–2003) suggests that the vision of Aldous Huxley's *Brave New World* (1932) turned out to be more terrifyingly true than the vision George Orwell created in *Nineteen Eighty-Four* (1949):

> What Orwell feared were those who would ban books. What Huxley feared was that there

would be no reason to ban a book, for there would be no one who wanted to read one. Orwell feared those who would deprive us of information. Huxley feared those who would give us so much that we would be reduced to passivity and egoism. Orwell feared that the truth would be concealed from us. Huxley feared the truth would be drowned in a sea of irrelevance. Orwell feared we would become a captive culture. Huxley feared we would become a trivial culture, preoccupied with some equivalent of the feelies, the orgy porgy, and the centrifugal bumblepuppy. As Huxley remarked in *Brave New World Revisited*, the civil libertarians and rationalists who are ever on the alert to oppose tyranny "failed to take into account man's almost infinite appetite for distractions." In *1984*, Huxley added, people are controlled by inflicting pain. In *Brave New World*, they are controlled by inflicting pleasure. In short, Orwell feared that what we hate will ruin us. Huxley feared that what we love will ruin us.

Write an essay explaining the extent to which you believe celebrity activism has proven (or undermined) Postman's argument. Refer to at least three sources.

3. In 2016, Chance the Rapper made a $1,000,000 donation to the Chicago Public Schools. He said, "It's not my job to propose any policy or be behind anything but the kids." Using at least three sources from this Conversation, write an essay in which you defend, challenge, or qualify Chance the Rapper's assertion, examining the responsibility of celebrities who work for social change. Should they propose policy? Should they know the issues thoroughly? Is money enough?

4. Using the arguments and evidence in this Conversation, answer the following question in an essay: Should celebrities use their influence and power to work for social change, or should they "just play ball"?

from **Hip Hop Planet**

JAMES MCBRIDE

You breathe in and breathe out a few times and you are there. Eight hours and a wake-up shake on the flight from New York, and you are on the tarmac in Dakar, Senegal. Welcome to Africa. The assignment: Find the roots of hip hop. The music goes full circle. The music comes home to Africa. That whole bit. Instead it was the old reporter's joke: You go out to cover a story and the story covers you. The stench of poverty in my nostrils was so strong it pulled me to earth like a hundred-pound ring in my nose. Dakar's Sandaga market is full of "local color" — unless you live there. It was packed and filthy, stalls full of new merchandise surrounded by shattered pieces of life everywhere, broken pipes, bicycle handlebars, fruit flies, soda bottles, beggars, dogs, cell phones. A teenage beggar, his body malformed by polio, crawled by on hands and feet, like a spider. He said, "Hey brother, help me." When I looked into his eyes, they were a bottomless ocean.

The Hotel Teranga is a fortress, packed behind a concrete wall where beggars gather at the front gate. The French tourists march past them, the women in high heels and stonewashed jeans. They sidle through downtown Dakar like royalty, haggling in the market, swimming in the hotel pool with their children, a scene that resembles Birmingham, Alabama, in the 1950s — the blacks serving, the whites partying. Five hundred yards (460 meters) away, Africans eat off the sidewalk and sell peanuts for a pittance. There is a restlessness, a deep sense of something gone wrong in the air.

The French can't smell it, even though they've had a mouthful back home. A good amount of the torching of Paris suburbs in October 2005 was courtesy of the children of immigrants from former French African colonies, exhausted from being bottled up in housing projects for generations with no job prospects. They telegraphed the punch in their music — France is the second largest hip hop market in the world — but the message was ignored. Around the globe, rap music has become a universal expression of outrage, its macho pose borrowed from commercial hip hop in the U.S.

In Dakar, where every kid is a microphone and turntable away from squalor, and American rapper Tupac Shakur's picture hangs in market stalls of folks who don't understand English, rap is king. There are hundreds of rap groups in Senegal today. French television crews troop in and out of Dakar's nightclubs filming the kora harp lute and tama talking drum with regularity. But beneath the drumming and the dance lessons and the jingling sound of tourist change, there is a quiet rage, a desperate fury among the Senegalese, some of whom seem to bear an intense dislike of their former colonial rulers.

"We know all about French history," says Abdou Ba, a Senegalese producer and musician. "We know about their kings, their castles, their art, their music. We know everything about them. But they don't know much about us."

Assane N'Diaye, 19, loves hip hop music. Before he left his Senegalese village to work as a DJ in Dakar, he was a fisherman, just like his father, like his father's father before him. Tall, lean, with a muscular build and a handsome chocolate face, Assane became a popular DJ, but the equipment he used was borrowed, and when his friend took it back, success eluded him. He has returned home to Toubab Dialaw, about 25 miles (40 kilometers) south of Dakar, a village marked by a huge boulder, perhaps 40 feet (12 meters) high, facing the Atlantic Ocean.

5

About a century and a half ago, a local ruler led a group of people fleeing slave traders to this place. He was told by a white trader to come here, to Toubab Dialaw. When he arrived, the slavers followed. A battle ensued. The ruler fought bravely but was killed. The villagers buried him by the sea and marked his grave with a small stone, and over the years it is said to have sprouted like a tree planted by God. It became a huge, arching boulder that stares out to sea, protecting the village behind it. When the fishermen went deep out to sea, the boulder was like a lighthouse that marked the way home. The Great Rock of Toubab Dialaw is said to hold a magic spirit, a spirit that Assane N'Diaye believes in.

In the shadow of the Great Rock, Assane has built a small restaurant, Chez Las, decorated with hundreds of seashells. It is where he lives his hip hop dream. At night, he and his brother and cousin stand by the Great Rock and face the sea. They meditate. They pray. Then they write rap lyrics that are worlds away from the bling-bling culture of today's commercial hip hoppers. They write about their lives as village fishermen, the scarcity of catch forcing them to fish in deeper and deeper waters, the hardship of fishing for 8, 10, 14 days at a time in an open pirogue in rainy season, the high fee they pay to rent the boat, and the paltry price their catches fetch on the market. They write about the humiliation of poverty, watching their town sprout up around them with rich Dakarians and richer French. And they write about the relatives who leave in the morning and never return, surrendered to the sea, sharks, and God.

The dream, of course, is to make a record. They have their own demo, their own logo, and their own name, Salam T. D. (for Toubab Dialaw). But rap music represents a deeper dream: a better life. "We want money to help our parents," Assane says over dinner. "We watch our mothers boil water to cook and have nothing to put in the pot."

He fingers his food lightly. "Rap doesn't belong to American culture," he says. "It belongs here. It has always existed here, because of our pain and our hardships and our suffering." *10*

---

1. The pattern of development in paragraph 1 can best be described as

  a. problem and solution

  b. cause and effect

  c. narration

  d. definition

  e. comparison and contrast

2. What is the purpose of paragraphs 2 and 3?

  I. to identify the historical context for the contemporary issue

  II. to introduce a counterargument to the main idea

  III. to qualify the author's thesis with a specific example

  a. I only

  b. I and II only

  c. III only

  d. I and III only

  e. I, II, and III

3. McBride uses all of the following in this passage EXCEPT

  a. figurative language

  b. analogy

  c. a sentence fragment

  d. expert testimony

  e. objective reporting

4. The quote in paragraph 10 serves primarily to

  a. defend McBride's position that hip hop is appreciated throughout the world

  b. criticize the negative impact of hip hop on cultures outside the United States

  c. support McBride's thesis of hip hop's African origins

  d. emphasize hip hop's ability to unite people from different countries

  e. illustrate the reason people in former French African colonies continue to market hip hop

5. In the sentence that begins "The villagers buried" in the middle of paragraph 7, which of the following has "sprouted like a tree planted by God"?

a. the supernatural spirit
b. hip hop music
c. the village border
d. the tomb marker
e. none of the above

6. The description of Assane's daily life in paragraph 8 contributes to the unity of the passage in which of the following ways?

a. as an example of the hardships that define hip hop
b. as an indication of the Great Rock's spirit at work in Assane's life
c. as a contrast to the experience of other Senegalese youth
d. as a parallel to the way American hip hop music is written

e. as a condemnation of Assane's foolish hopes

7. The final sentence of paragraph 4 is an example of which rhetorical device?

a. apostrophe
b. euphemism
c. humor
d. colloquialism
e. paradox

8. The style of this passage as a whole is most accurately characterized as

a. technical and ironic
b. descriptive and formal
c. personal and emotional
d. subjective and complex
e. none of the above

---

from **Corn-Pone Opinions**

MARK TWAIN

Fifty years ago, when I was a boy of fifteen and helping to inhabit a Missourian village on the banks of the Mississippi, I had a friend whose society was very dear to me because I was forbidden by my mother to partake of it. He was a gay and impudent and satirical and delightful young black man — a slave — who daily preached sermons from the top of his master's woodpile, with me for sole audience. He imitated the pulpit style of the several clergymen of the village, and did it well, and with fine passion and energy. To me he was a wonder. I believed he was the greatest orator in the United States and would some day be heard from. But it did not happen; in the distribution of rewards he was overlooked. It is the way, in this world.

He interrupted his preaching, now and then, to saw a stick of wood; but the sawing was

a pretense — he did it with his mouth; exactly imitating the sound the bucksaw makes in shrieking its way through the wood. But it served its purpose; it kept his master from coming out to see how the work was getting along. I listened to the sermons from the open window of a lumber room at the back of the house. One of his texts was this:

"You tell me whar a man gits his corn pone, en I'll tell you what his 'pinions is."

I can never forget it. It was deeply impressed upon me. By my mother. Not upon my memory, but elsewhere. She had slipped in upon me while I was absorbed and not watching. The black philosopher's idea was that a man is not independent, and cannot afford views which might interfere with his bread and butter. If he would prosper, he must train with the majority;

in matters of large moment, like politics and religion, he must think and feel with the bulk of his neighbors, or suffer damage in his social standing and in his business prosperities. He must restrict himself to corn-pone opinions — at least on the surface. He must get his opinions from other people; he must reason out none for himself; he must have no first-hand views.

I think Jerry was right, in the main, but I think he did not go far enough.

1. It was his idea that a man conforms to the majority view of his locality by calculation and intention. This happens, but I think it is not the rule.

2. It was his idea that there is such a thing as a first-hand opinion; an original opinion; an opinion which is coldly reasoned out in a man's head, by a searching analysis of the facts involved, with the heart unconsulted, and the jury room closed against outside influences. It may be that such an opinion has been born somewhere, at some time or other, but I suppose it got away before they could catch it and stuff it and put it in the museum.

I am persuaded that a coldly-thought-out and independent verdict upon a fashion in clothes, or manners, or literature, or politics, or religion, or any other matter that is projected into the field of our notice and interest, is a most rare thing — if it has indeed ever existed.

A new thing in costume appears — the flaring hoopskirt, for example — and the passers-by are shocked, and the irreverent laugh. Six months later everybody is reconciled; the fashion has established itself; it is admired, now, and no one laughs. Public opinion resented it before, public opinion accepts it now, and is happy in it. Why? Was the resentment reasoned out? Was the acceptance reasoned out? No. The instinct that moves to conformity did the work. It is our nature to conform; it is a force which not many can successfully resist. What is its seat? The inborn requirement of self-approval. We all have

to bow to that; there are no exceptions. Even the woman who refuses from first to last to wear the hoopskirt comes under that law and is its slave; she could not wear the skirt and have her own approval; and that she must have, she cannot help herself. But as a rule our self-approval has its source in but one place and not elsewhere — the approval of other people. A person of vast consequences can introduce any kind of novelty in dress and the general world will presently adopt it — moved to do it, in the first place, by the natural instinct to passively yield to that vague something recognized as authority, and in the second place by the human instinct to train with the multitude and have its approval. An empress introduced the hoopskirt, and we know the result. A nobody introduced the bloomer, and we know the result. If Eve should come again, in her ripe renown, and reintroduce her quaint styles — well, we know what would happen. And we should be cruelly embarrassed, along at first.

The hoopskirt runs its course and disappears. Nobody reasons about it. One woman abandons the fashion; her neighbor notices this and follows her lead; this influences the next woman; and so on and so on, and presently the skirt has vanished out of the world, no one knows how nor why, nor cares, for that matter. It will come again, by and by and in due course will go again. . . .

Men think they think upon great political questions, and they do; but they think with their party, not independently; they read its literature, but not that of the other side; they arrive at convictions, but they are drawn from a partial view of the matter in hand and are of no particular value. They swarm with their party, they feel with their party, they are happy in their party's approval; and where the party leads they will follow, whether for right and honor, or through blood and dirt and a mush of mutilated morals.

In our late canvass half of the nation passionately believed that in silver lay salvation, the other half as passionately believed that that way lay destruction. Do you believe that a tenth part of the people, on either side, had any ratio-nal excuse for having an opinion about the mat-ter at all? I studied that mighty question to the bottom — came out empty. Half of our people passionately believe in high tariff, the other half believe otherwise. Does this mean study and examination, or only feeling? The latter, I think.

I have deeply studied that question, too — and didn't arrive. We all do no end of feeling, and we mistake it for thinking. And out of it we get an aggregation which we consider a boon. Its name is Public Opinion. It is held in reverence. It settles everything. Some think it the Voice of God.

---

1. What is the primary rhetorical function of the writer's story about Jerry (paras. 1–4)?

   a. to create a humorous beginning in order to appeal to the reader's emotions

   b. to contrast the writer's childhood beliefs with the ideas he developed during adulthood

   c. to introduce the setting as a significant component of the writer's argument

   d. to establish the writer's veracity through the history of his interest in the subject

   e. to provide an example that will be further developed through later anecdotes

2. In paragraphs 1–3, the writer characterizes Jerry in which of the following ways?

   a. as a fascinating friend who was a productive worker

   b. as a philosopher who was influential in the writer's hometown

   c. as a role model who was appreciated by the writer's mother

   d. as a preacher who was encouraged to pursue his passion

   e. as a gifted speaker who illustrated his wiliness in his work efforts

3. What literary technique is exemplified in the following sentence from paragraph 3: "You tell me whar a man gits his corn pone, en I'll tell you what his 'pinions is"?

   a. dialect

   b. alliteration

   c. onomatopoeia

   d. allusion

   e. apostrophe

4. The term "corn-pone opinions" (para. 4) signifies which of the following?

   a. ideas that reflect a person's background and economic station in life

   b. ideas that are held because a person believes they will help him rise socially and economically

   c. ideas that are based on a geographical location, changing from one part of the country to another

   d. ideas that are based on a person's need for self-approval and group approval

   e. ideas that are so old-fashioned they should be put in a museum with other absurdities

5. The numbered items in paragraph 5 serve to

   a. enumerate Jerry's points and offer further explanation of his claims

   b. create a shift from personal anecdote to researched analysis of evidence

   c. undermine the author's reliable persona created within the first four paragraphs

   d. distinguish the writer's experience-based arguments from Jerry's theory-based arguments

   e. refute a counterargument suggested by the author's mother in paragraph 4

6. As the passage progresses, the speaker's focus shifts from

   a. a personal reflection establishing background to an assertion of an abstract point

   b. a childhood anecdote to adult observations of contemporary society

   c. a concrete example to hypothetical situations extending the original argument

d. a mocking characterization to scholarly assertions

e. an expert opinion to supportive evidence from outside sources

7. Paragraph 7 illustrates all of the following techniques EXCEPT

a. rhetorical question

b. parallelism

c. conditional statement

d. allusion

e. definition

8. The writer's reference to Eve at the end of paragraph 7 serves to

a. suggest that women are so conformist that they would adopt nakedness as a fashion

b. illustrate how women's concern with fashion goes back to the beginning of history

c. intimate the sacred nature of female accoutrements

d. offer an opposing example to the previous points about the empress and the "nobody"

e. emphasize that women's fashion choices will ultimately lead to their own downfall

9. All of the following statements contribute to the author's argument EXCEPT

a. "But it served its purpose; it kept his master from coming out to see how the work was getting along." (para. 2)

b. "Even the woman who refuses from first to last to wear the hoopskirt comes under that law and is its slave." (para. 7)

c. "[T]hey read its literature, but not that of the other side." (para. 9)

d. "Half of our people passionately believe in high tariff, the other half believe otherwise." (para. 10)

e. "Some think it the Voice of God." (para. 10)

10. The writer's attitude toward his subject can best be described as

a. sentimental appreciation

b. objective indifference

c. amused criticism

d. nostalgic condescension

e. guarded sarcasm

POPULAR CULTURE

Now that you have examined a number of readings and other texts that focus on popular culture, explore one dimension of the topic by synthesizing your own ideas and the texts. You might want to do more research or use readings from other classes as you prepare for the following projects.

1. Following Beyoncé's appearance at the 2016 Super Bowl and the release of her "Formation" video, which takes on police violence against minorities, as well as female empowerment, pundit Jessica Williams said in her spirited defense on *The Daily Show*, "The point is Beyoncé is black and this is her message. It's what artists do." Support, challenge, or qualify Williams's statement about the purpose of artists' messages.

2. Read this statement from "Celebrity Bodies" by Daniel Harris and write an essay in which you support, challenge, or qualify his assertion that we would be better off trying to be like the celebrities we admire.

   > Our fantasies engender a paralyzing awe that instills in us despair, a sense of hopelessness about maintaining our bodies, about achieving the buff perfections of stars spoon-fed by studio dieticians who force them to nibble on rice cakes and celery sticks and submit to grueling regimens of Pilates and kickboxing. In fact, we would almost certainly be healthier if we *did* imitate Hollywood, if we *did* work out and diet as compulsively as they do, if, like supermodel Dayle Haddon, we performed leg lifts while washing the dishes, side bends while standing in line at Starbucks, and thigh resistance exercises in the elevators of our four-star hotels.

3. In a paper entitled "Moral Pluck: Ethics in Popular Culture," Columbia Law School professor William H. Simon writes about the portrayal of lawyers in film and television. He notes:

   > While elite moralism is strongly authoritarian and categorical, popular culture exalts a quality that might be called Moral Pluck — a combination of resourcefulness and transgression in the service of basic but informal values.

   Consider the portrayals of professionals — in law, in medicine, in education — in popular culture. Do you agree with Simon that the ethics of popular culture are sometimes in conflict with traditional ethics? Write an essay defending your position on this question.

4. Each of the following statements addresses the subject of media. Select one that interests you, and write an essay that defends or challenges its assertion. To support your argument, refer to your own experience with media and to the selections in this chapter.

   a. The one function TV news performs very well is that when there is no news, we give it to you with the same emphasis as if there were.
      — David Brinkley, American TV network news anchor

   b. Whoever controls the media — the images — controls the culture.
      — Allen Ginsberg, poet

   c. If you want to use television to teach somebody something, you have first to teach somebody how to use television.
      — Umberto Eco, philosopher

   d. Visual chaos is not good for anyone. Billboard companies should not be allowed to sell what they don't own — our field of vision and our civic pride.
      — Meg Maguire, president, Scenic America

5. In his essay "High-School Confidential: Notes on Teen Movies" (p. 322), David Denby suggests that the teen movies from the turn of this century reflect the secret wishes — and geekiness — of their screenwriters and

directors. Watch a movie about teens from an earlier time — *Rebel without a Cause* (1955) or *Splendor in the Grass* (1961), for example — and discuss what the film said about the filmmakers of the era.

6. In "Corn-Pone Opinions," Mark Twain distinguishes between fashion and standards. Is it the same as the difference, discussed on page 313, between what was once considered popular culture and high culture? Write about what you see as the difference between fashion and standards.

7. "Hip Hop Planet" by James McBride (p. 301) refers to several different genres of popular music. Listen to an assortment of songs by the artists mentioned in his piece. Make a CD or create a playlist of the music, and write some liner notes in which you explain why you chose the songs and how you decided on the order in which they appear.

8. Using Ray Bradbury's "The Affluence of Despair" as a model, write an essay about the effect of the Internet on American society.

9. Consider a pairing in which one medium has been adapted into a new one — books and video games made into movies, or movies made into live theater, for example. Write about how the remake modified the original to suit the new medium and how the new medium honors the old.

10. Write a ballad about the Balloon Boy or about a viral story — true or not — that was quickly popularized online or in the news.

11. Write a review of a concert, album, movie, or graphic novel. Keep in mind that reviews are arguments either applauding artists, criticizing them, or both.

7 The Environment

What is our responsibility to the natural environment?

Throughout history we have tried to conquer the wilderness, tame the jungles, and master the elements, and we are still trying to conquer outer space. But are nature and humankind necessarily in conflict? We created civilization to protect us from the undesirable features of the outdoors and, to some degree, from harm. But now our experience of the natural world is so mediated that many of us know it only as it is presented on television or online. Has our relationship with nature changed so drastically that nature now exists *within* civilization, as contemporary naturalist Bill McKibben suggests? Do we now contain nature rather than being contained by it?

The Washington Post / Getty Images

▲

After the city of Flint, Michigan changed its water source to the Flint River in 2014, residents were exposed to high levels of lead in their drinking water. The Flint water crisis intensified as people were forced to use only bottled or filtered water, and President Obama declared a state of emergency in Flint on January 16, 2016. This photo, from a Flint city council meeting on February 3, 2016, was taken during a discussion about whether residents must pay their water bills.

How do you think most Americans view environmental issues? Who do you think is the intended audience for the message on the poster?

How does our perspective on Ralph Waldo Emerson's classic essay "Nature" change now that nature is threatened? Can we balance human progress and economic well-being with environmental protection?

In recent years, humankind's attitude toward the natural world has changed. Before Rachel Carson and others began to alert us to the dangers of pollution, most people simply didn't think about the environment. And looking back over the last half century, it is hard to imagine what may be in store for us over the next fifty years. Are we yet to see the consequences of what we have already done to alter the environment?

Once the environment becomes something we have to protect, our fundamental relationship with our world changes. We're still dwarfed by the awesome power of nature, but if we are creating conditions that may change nature itself, whether through pollution, development of open land, or global warming, then we need to consider our responsibility. Can we do enough right now to protect our world? Are we at risk of becoming an endangered species?

The selections in this chapter consider the environment from many perspectives. As you read, consider your responsibility to the natural world. What might we expect from it, and what might it expect from us?

from Silent Spring

RACHEL CARSON

Rachel Carson (1907–1964) was educated at Johns Hopkins University and conducted research at the Marine Biological Laboratory in Woods Hole, Massachusetts. She worked as a biologist for the U.S. Fish and Wildlife Service and served as chief editor of publications from 1947 to 1952. She wrote many books and articles about the sea, including *Under the Sea-Wind* (1941); *The Sea around Us* (1951), which won a National Book Award; and *The Edge of the Sea* (1955). Carson was among the first scientists to raise environmental issues for the general public, and her views and insights have greatly influenced the environmental movement. The readings that follow — "A Fable for Tomorrow" and "The Obligation to Endure" — are the first two chapters of *Silent Spring* (1962), a book that "changed the course of history," according to former vice president Al Gore. It led to John F. Kennedy's presidential commission on the environment, as well as to the worldwide ban on the agricultural use of the pesticide DDT.

Alfred Eisenstaedt/Getty Images

I. A Fable for Tomorrow

There was once a town in the heart of America where all life seemed to live in harmony with its surroundings. The town lay in the midst of a checkerboard of prosperous farms, with fields of grain and hillsides of orchards where, in spring, white clouds of bloom drifted above the green fields. In autumn, oak and maple and birch set up a blaze of color that flamed and flickered across a backdrop of pines. Then foxes barked in the hills and deer silently crossed the fields, half hidden in the mists of the fall mornings.

Along the roads, laurel, viburnum and alder, great ferns and wildflowers delighted the traveler's eye through much of the year. Even in winter the roadsides were places of beauty, where countless birds came to feed on the berries and on the seed heads of the dried weeds rising above the snow. The countryside was, in fact, famous for the abundance and variety of its bird life, and when the flood of migrants was pouring through in spring and fall people traveled from great distances to observe them. Others came to fish the streams, which flowed clear and cold out of the hills and contained shady pools where trout lay. So it had been from the days many years ago when the first settlers raised their houses, sank their wells, and built their barns.

Then a strange blight crept over the area and everything began to change. Some evil spell had settled on the community: mysterious maladies swept the flocks of chickens; the cattle and sheep sickened and died. Everywhere was a shadow of death. The farmers spoke of much illness among their families. In the town the doctors had become more and more puzzled by new kinds of sickness appearing among their patients. There had been several sudden and unexplained deaths, not only among adults but even among children, who would be stricken suddenly while at play and die within a few hours.

There was a strange stillness. The birds, for example — where had they gone? Many people spoke of them, puzzled and disturbed. The feeding stations in the backyards were deserted. The few birds seen anywhere were moribund; they trembled violently and could not fly. It was a spring without voices. On the mornings that had once throbbed with the dawn chorus of robins, catbirds, doves, jays, wrens, and scores of other bird voices there was now no sound; only silence lay over the fields and woods and marsh.

On the farms the hens brooded, but no chicks hatched. The farmers complained that they were unable to raise any pigs — the litters were small and the young survived only a few days. The apple trees were coming into bloom but no bees droned among the blossoms, so there was no pollination and there would be no fruit.

The roadsides, once so attractive, were now lined with browned and withered vegetation as though swept by fire. These, too, were silent, deserted by all living things. Even the streams were now lifeless. Anglers no longer visited them, for all the fish had died.

In the gutters under the eaves and between the shingles of the roofs, white granular powder still showed a few patches; some weeks before it had fallen like snow upon the roofs and the lawns, the fields and streams.

No witchcraft, no enemy action had silenced the rebirth of new life in this stricken world. The people had done it themselves.

◆ ◆ ◆

This town does not actually exist, but it might easily have a thousand counterparts in America or elsewhere in the world. I know of no community that has experienced all the misfortunes I describe. Yet every one of these disasters has actually happened somewhere, and many real communities have already suffered a substantial number of them. A grim specter has crept upon us almost unnoticed, and this imagined tragedy may easily become a stark reality we all shall know.

Shown below is *The Pelican* (2006, oil on wood), a painting by contemporary artist Alexis Rockman, who is known for his artwork reflecting environmental issues. Rockman exhibited this and nearly 50 other works as part of a 2010 exhibit entitled *A Fable for Tomorrow* at the Smithsonian American Art Museum in Washington, D.C. **What future "fable" is unfolding in this painting? In what way does it reflect the tone and message of Carson's opening paragraphs?**

© 2017 Alexis Rockman / Artists Rights Society (ARS), New York

What has already silenced the voices of spring in countless towns in America? This book is an attempt to explain.

II. The Obligation to Endure

The history of life on earth has been a history of interaction between living things and their surroundings. To a large extent, the physical form and the habits of the earth's vegetation and its animal life have been molded by the environment. Considering the whole span of earthly time, the opposite effect, in which life

This photograph, taken in 2012, shows a communications manager from the Environmental Protection Agency (EPA) with a sign that was posted at a former DDT processing plant and shipping terminal in Richmond, California. United Heckathorn, a pesticide processing company, dumped DDT into the Lauritzen Canal between the mid-1940s and 1966, and a cleanup effort initiated in 1990 had made no progress as of 2012.
How could this image be used to support Carson's argument?

Eric Risberg/AP Images

actually modifies its surroundings, has been relatively slight. Only within the moment of time represented by the present century has one species — man — acquired significant power to alter the nature of his world.

During the past quarter century this power has not only increased to one of disturbing magnitude but it has changed in character. The most alarming of all man's assaults upon the environment is the contamination of air, earth, rivers, and sea with dangerous and even lethal materials. This pollution is for the most part irrecoverable; the chain of evil it initiates not only in the world that must support life but in living tissues is for the most part irreversible. In this now universal contamination of the environment, chemicals are the sinister and little-recognized partners of radiation in changing the very nature of the world — the very nature of its life. Strontium 90, released through nuclear explosions into the air, comes to earth in rain or drifts down as fallout, lodges in soil, enters into the grass or corn or wheat grown there, and in time takes up its abode in the bones of a human being, there to remain until his death. Similarly, chemicals sprayed on croplands or forests or gardens lie long in soil, entering into living organisms, passing from one to another in a chain of poisoning and death. Or they pass mysteriously by underground streams

until they emerge and, through the alchemy of air and sunlight, combine into new forms that kill vegetation, sicken cattle, and work unknown harm on those who drink from once pure wells. As Albert Schweitzer[1] has said, "Man can hardly even recognize the devils of his own creation."

It took hundreds of millions of years to produce the life that now inhabits the earth — eons of time in which that developing and evolving and diversifying life reached a state of adjustment and balance with its surroundings. The environment, rigorously shaping and directing the life it supported, contained elements that were hostile as well as supporting. Certain rocks gave out dangerous radiation; even within the light of the sun, from which all life draws its energy, there were short-wave radiations with power to injure. Given time — time not in years but in millennia — life adjusts, and a balance has been reached. For time is the essential ingredient; but in the modern world there is no time.

The rapidity of change and the speed with which new situations are created follow the impetuous and heedless pace of man rather than

---

[1] Albert Schweitzer (1875–1965), a French philosopher, musician, and medical missionary, spent much of his life in Africa. He won the 1952 Nobel Peace Prize. —Eds.

the deliberate pace of nature. Radiation is no longer merely the background radiation of rocks, the bombardment of cosmic rays, the ultraviolet of the sun that have existed before there was any life on earth; radiation is now the unnatural creation of man's tampering with the atom. The chemicals to which life is asked to make its adjustment are no longer merely the calcium and silica and copper and all the rest of the minerals washed out of the rocks and carried in rivers to the sea; they are the synthetic creations of man's inventive mind, brewed in his laboratories, and having no counterparts in nature.

To adjust to these chemicals would require 15 time on the scale that is nature's; it would require not merely the years of a man's life but the life of generations. And even this, were it by some miracle possible, would be futile, for the new chemicals come from our laboratories in an endless stream; almost five hundred annually find their way into actual use in the United States alone. The figure is staggering and its implications are not easily grasped — 500 new chemicals to which the bodies of men and animals are required somehow to adapt each year, chemicals totally outside the limits of biologic experience.

Among them are many that are used in man's war against nature. Since the mid-1940s over 200 basic chemicals have been created for use in killing insects, weeds, rodents, and other organisms described in the modern vernacular as "pests"; and they are sold under several thousand different brand names.

These sprays, dusts, and aerosols are now applied almost universally to farms, gardens, forests, and homes — nonselective chemicals that have the power to kill every insect, the "good" and the "bad," to still the song of birds and the leaping of fish in the streams, to coat the leaves with a deadly film, and to linger on in soil — all this though the intended target may be only a few weeds or insects. Can anyone believe it is possible to lay down such a barrage of poisons on the surface of the earth without making it unfit for all

life? They should not be called "insecticides," but "biocides."

The whole process of spraying seems caught up in an endless spiral. Since DDT was released for civilian use, a process of escalation has been going on in which ever more toxic materials must be found. This has happened because insects, in a triumphant vindication of Darwin's principle of the survival of the fittest, have evolved super races immune to the particular insecticide used, hence a deadlier one has always to be

▼
_____

This photograph, taken in 1947 for *LIFE* magazine, shows a model being sprayed with DDT from an insecticidal fog applicator at Jones Beach, New York, to demonstrate that it will not contaminate food or drink. In this public test by the New York City Health Department, fogging machines blanketed a four-mile area.
What does this image imply about the American public's knowledge of — and attitude toward — DDT? How does it inform your understanding of how Carson addresses her audience?

George Silk/Getty Images

developed — and then a deadlier one than that. It has happened also because, for reasons to be described later, destructive insects often undergo a "flareback," or resurgence, after spraying, in numbers greater than before. Thus the chemical war is never won, and all life is caught in its violent crossfire.

Along with the possibility of the extinction of mankind by nuclear war, the central problem of our age has therefore become the contamination of man's total environment with such substances of incredible potential for harm — substances that accumulate in the tissues of plants and animals and even penetrate the germ cells to shatter or alter the very material of heredity upon which the shape of the future depends.

Some would-be architects of our future [20] look toward a time when it will be possible to alter the human germ plasm by design. But we may easily be doing so now by inadvertence, for many chemicals, like radiation, bring about gene mutations. It is ironic to think that man might determine his own future by something so seemingly trivial as the choice of an insect spray.

All this has been risked — for what? Future historians may well be amazed by our distorted sense of proportion. How could intelligent beings seek to control a few unwanted species by a method that contaminated the entire environment and brought the threat of disease and death even to their own kind? Yet this is precisely what we have done. We have done it, moreover, for reasons that collapse the moment we examine them. We are told that the enormous and expanding use of pesticides is necessary to maintain farm production. Yet is our real problem not one of *overproduction*? Our farms, despite measures to remove acreages from production and to pay farmers *not* to produce, have yielded such a staggering excess of crops that the American taxpayer in 1962 is paying out more than one billion dollars a year as the total carrying cost of the surplus-food storage program. And is the situation helped when one branch of the Agriculture Department tries to reduce production while another states, as it did in 1958, "It is believed generally that reduction of crop acreages under provisions of the Soil Bank will stimulate interest in use of chemicals to obtain maximum production on the land retained in crops."

All this is not to say there is no insect problem and no need of control. I am saying, rather, that control must be geared to realities, not to mythical situations, and that the methods employed must be such that they do not destroy us along with the insects.

◆ ◆ ◆

The problem whose attempted solution has brought such a train of disaster in its wake is an accompaniment of our modern way of life. Long before the age of man, insects inhabited the earth — a group of extraordinarily varied and adaptable beings. Over the course of time since man's advent, a small percentage of the more than half a million species of insects have come into conflict with human welfare in two principal ways: as competitors for the food supply and as carriers of human disease.

Disease-carrying insects become important where human beings are crowded together, especially under conditions where sanitation is poor, as in time of natural disaster or war or in situations of extreme poverty and deprivation. Then control of some sort becomes necessary. It is a sobering fact, however, as we shall presently see, that the method of massive chemical control has had only limited success, and also threatens to worsen the very conditions it is intended to curb.

Under primitive agricultural conditions the [25] farmer had few insect problems. These arose with the intensification of agriculture — the devotion of immense acreages to a single crop. Such a system set the stage for explosive increases in specific insect populations. Single-crop farming does not take advantage

seeing connections

Three long excerpts from *Silent Spring* were first published in the *New Yorker* magazine in June of 1962 and are currently available in the magazine's online archives, accompanied by these three illustrations by contemporary artist Emiliano Ponzi.

What argument does each of these images make? Which one most effectively conveys Rachel Carson's main points, and why?

Emiliano Ponzi/The New Yorker © Conde Nast

Emiliano Ponzi/The New Yorker © Conde Nast

Emiliano Ponzi/The New Yorker © Conde Nast

of the principles by which nature works; it is agriculture as an engineer might conceive it to be. Nature has introduced great variety into the landscape, but man has displayed a passion for simplifying it. Thus he undoes the built-in checks and balances by which nature holds the species within bounds. One important natural check is a limit on the amount of suitable habitat for each species. Obviously then, an insect that lives on wheat can build up its population to much higher levels on a farm devoted to wheat than on one in which wheat is intermingled with other crops to which the insect is not adapted.

The same thing happens in other situations. A generation or more ago, the towns of large areas of the United States lined their streets with the noble elm tree. Now the beauty they hopefully created is threatened with complete destruction as disease sweeps through the elms, carried by a beetle that would have only limited chance to build up large populations and to spread from tree to tree if the elms were only occasional trees in a richly diversified planting.

Another factor in the modern insect problem is one that must be viewed against a background of geologic and human history: the spreading of thousands of different kinds of organisms from their native homes to invade new territories. This worldwide migration has been studied and graphically described by the British ecologist Charles Elton in his recent book *The Ecology of Invasions*. During the Cretaceous Period, some hundred million years ago, flooding seas cut many land bridges between continents and living things found themselves confined in what Elton calls "colossal separate nature reserves." There, isolated from others of their kind, they developed many new species. When some of the land masses were joined again, about 15 million years ago, these species began to move out into new territories — a movement that is not only still in progress but is now receiving considerable assistance from man.

The importation of plants is the primary agent in the modern spread of species, for animals have almost invariably gone along with the plants, quarantine being a comparatively recent and not completely effective innovation. The United States Office of Plant Introduction alone has introduced almost 200,000 species and varieties of plants from all over the world. Nearly half of the 180 or so major insect enemies of plants in the United States are accidental imports from abroad, and most of them have come as hitchhikers on plants.

In new territory, out of reach of the restraining hand of the natural enemies that kept down its numbers in its native land, an invading plant or animal is able to become enormously abundant. Thus it is no accident that our most troublesome insects are introduced species.

These invasions, both the naturally occurring 30 and those dependent on human assistance, are likely to continue indefinitely. Quarantine and massive chemical campaigns are only extremely expensive ways of buying time. We are faced, according to Dr. Elton, "with a life-and-death need not just to find new technological means of suppressing this plant or that animal"; instead we need the basic knowledge of animal populations and their relations to their surroundings that will "promote an even balance and damp down the explosive power of outbreaks and new invasions."

Much of the necessary knowledge is now available but we do not use it. We train ecologists in our universities and even employ them in our governmental agencies but we seldom take their advice. We allow the chemical death rain to fall as though there were no alternative, whereas in fact there are many, and our ingenuity could soon discover many more if given opportunity.

Have we fallen into a mesmerized state that makes us accept as inevitable that which is inferior or detrimental, as though having lost the will or the vision to demand that which is good?

seeing connections

Fracking, a method of extracting natural gas and oil by injecting liquid into rock at high pressure, has been the subject of controversy, particularly in the last decade or so. Proponents believe that it has helped the American economy by making the country energy independent and that the process is environmentally safe if done correctly. Those who oppose fracking cite both environmental and public health risks.

Since 2005, fracking has been granted exemptions from some of the federal regulations contained in the Safe Drinking Water Act, the Clean Air Act, and the Clean Water Act. Federal right-to-know provisions also do not apply to fracking, which means that the chemicals used in the process do not have to be made public knowledge.

The excerpt below is taken from an essay entitled "The Fracking of Rachel Carson," by Sandra Steingraber. It was published by *Orion Magazine* in 2012. Read it carefully before answering the following questions.

How might Rachel Carson address fracking today? Write a letter to the Pennsylvania state legislature in her voice, using details from *Silent Spring* to construct an argument and convey Carson's position.

from The Fracking of Rachel Carson

SANDRA STEINGRABER

April 2012 was a silent spring in Pennsylvania. Funds for a statewide heath registry — which would track illnesses in residents who live near drilling and fracking operations — were quietly removed from the state budget. At the same time, a new state law, Act 13, went into effect, which allows a physician in Pennsylvania access to proprietary chemical information for purposes of treating a possibly exposed patient — but only if he or she signs a confidentiality agreement. Confounded, Pennsylvania doctors began asking questions. Does that mean no contacting the public health department? What about talking to

reporters or writing up case studies for the *New England Journal of Medicine*? Can a physician who signs the nondisclosure agreement (in order to treat a patient) and then issues an alert to the community at large (in order to fulfill an ethical obligation to prevent harm) be sued for breach of contract? The president of the Pennsylvania Medical Society registered her objections, to which Pennsylvania Speaker of the House Sam Smith furiously counter-objected. Denying that Act 13 constitutes a medical gag order, Smith's spokesman accused objecting doctors of yelling fire in a crowded theater.

Such thinking, in the words of the ecologist Paul Shepard, "idealizes life with only its head out of water, inches above the limits of toleration of the corruption of its own environment. . . . Why should we tolerate a diet of weak poisons, a home in insipid surroundings, a circle of acquaintances

who are not quite our enemies, the noise of motors with just enough relief to prevent insanity? Who would want to live in a world which is just not quite fatal?"

Yet such a world is pressed upon us. The crusade to create a chemically sterile, insect-free world seems to have engendered a fanatic zeal on the part of many specialists and most of the so-called control agencies. On every hand there is evidence that those engaged in spraying operations exercise a ruthless power. "The regulatory entomologists . . . function as prosecutor, judge and jury, tax assessor and collector and sheriff to enforce their own orders," said Connecticut entomologist Neely Turner. The most flagrant abuses go unchecked in both state and federal agencies.

It is not my contention that chemical insecticides must never be used. I do contend that we have put poisonous and biologically potent chemicals indiscriminately into the hands of persons largely or wholly ignorant of their potentials for harm. We have subjected enormous numbers of people to contact with these poisons, without their consent and often without their knowledge. If the Bill of Rights contains no guarantee that a citizen shall be secure against lethal poisons distributed either by private individuals or by public officials, it is surely only because our forefathers, despite their considerable wisdom and foresight, could conceive of no such problem.

I contend, furthermore, that we have allowed 35 these chemicals to be used with little or no

advance investigation of their effect on soil, water, wildlife, and man himself. Future generations are unlikely to condone our lack of prudent concern for the integrity of the natural world that supports all life.

There is still very limited awareness of the nature of the threat. This is an era of specialists, each of whom sees his own problem and is unaware of or intolerant of the larger frame into which it fits. It is also an era dominated by industry, in which the right to make a dollar at whatever cost is seldom challenged. When the public protests, confronted with some obvious evidence of damaging results of pesticide applications, it is fed little tranquilizing pills of half truth. We urgently need an end to these false assurances, to the sugar coating of unpalatable facts. It is the public that is being asked to assume the risks that the insect controllers calculate. The public must decide whether it wishes to continue on the present road, and it can do so only when in full possession of the facts. In the words of Jean Rostand,[2] "The obligation to endure gives us the right to know."

[1962]

_____
[2] Jean Rostand (1894–1977), a French biologist, science writer, and philosopher, spoke against nuclear proliferation. —Eds.

QUESTIONS FOR DISCUSSION

1. Why does Rachel Carson begin with "There was once a town . . . ," as though she were writing a fairy tale? Is this a fairy tale of sorts? How does Carson present the town in paragraphs 1 and 2?

2. Carson claims in paragraph 12 that "[t]he most alarming of . . . assaults upon the environment is the contamination of air, earth, rivers, and sea with dangerous and even lethal materials." Is contamination still the most alarming assault on the environment, or has another problem taken its place? Explain your response.

3. In paragraph 16, Carson claims that humankind is engaged in a "war against nature" and describes the targets of that war. Do you agree that targeting certain things for destruction (or at least control)

means we are at war with nature? Can we be at war with something that is not our intended target? Explain.

4. Carson says the products used to kill bugs should be called "biocides" instead of "insecticides" (para. 17). Why? What is the difference?

5. What has changed since Carson wrote *Silent Spring*? Has the natural environment improved? Has it declined? Since Carson's time, have we become more concerned with the effect we have on nature — or less concerned? Explain your response.

6. What does Jean Rostand mean by our "obligation to endure" (para. 36)? How is our "right to know" related to this obligation?

QUESTIONS ON RHETORIC AND STYLE

1. Why does Carson begin "A Fable for Tomorrow" with imagery rather than exposition? What is the effect?

2. How do Carson's tone, style, and purpose change in paragraphs 9 and 10? Why do they change? How does Carson's voice change from "A Fable for Tomorrow" to "The Obligation to Endure"? How does the difference serve the writer's rhetorical purpose?

3. Why does Carson call the insect problem a "train of disaster" (para. 23)? What is the effect of this metaphor?

4. How does Carson appeal to authority in paragraph 27? Where else in the selection does she appeal to authority? What is the effect of her use of statistics in paragraph 28?

5. What are the "agencies" to which Carson refers (para. 33)? Why are they reduced to "so-called control agencies"?

6. Why doesn't Carson mention her "contention" until she is nearly finished with the piece? Is her argument inductive or deductive? How do you know? Also, why does she tell the reader what her "contentions" *aren't* before stating what they *are*? What response from her readers might she anticipate at this point in their reading?

7. Carson says that the public "is fed little tranquilizing pills of half truth" when it contests the use of pesticides (para. 36). Why is this metaphor effective?

8. What do you think Carson's purpose was in ending the final paragraph (and the chapter) with someone else's words?

SUGGESTIONS FOR WRITING

1. In imitation of Rachel Carson, write an update of "A Fable for Tomorrow."

2. In paragraph 19, Carson says, "Along with the possibility of the extinction of mankind by nuclear war, the central problem of our age has therefore become the contamination of man's total environment." Write an essay in which you defend, challenge, or qualify the validity of this statement.

3. Carson writes in paragraph 35, "Future generations are unlikely to condone our lack of prudent concern for the integrity of the natural world that supports all life." As a member of one of the generations after Carson's, write a letter to her, to someone of her generation, or to a polluter of today. In the letter, identify and explain your response to Carson's statement.

4. Carson concludes with the words of French biologist and philosopher Jean Rostand: "The obligation to endure gives us the right to know."

Write an essay that defends or challenges Rostand's claim as it relates to our relationship to the natural world today.

5. Carson writes in paragraph 34, "If the Bill of Rights contains no guarantee that a citizen shall be secure against lethal poisons distributed either by private individuals or by public officials, it is surely only because our forefathers, despite their considerable wisdom and foresight, could conceive of no such problem." Imagine that the framers of the Constitution were here today, and write an essay explaining how they might use the Constitution to protect the environment.

6. Considering that *Silent Spring* was written fifty years ago, should we be optimistic or pessimistic in our attitude toward the preservation of the natural world? As you answer this question, consider what has changed since Carson's time in our approach toward the environment.

from **Nature**

RALPH WALDO EMERSON

Ralph Waldo Emerson (1803–1882), perhaps best known for his essay "Self-Reliance," was one of America's most influential thinkers and writers. After graduating from Harvard Divinity School, he followed nine generations of his family into the ministry but practiced for only a few years. Known as a great orator, Emerson made his living as a popular lecturer on a wide range of topics. From 1821 to 1826, he taught in city and country schools and later served on a number of school boards, including the Concord School Committee and the Board of Overseers of Harvard College. Central to Emerson's thought is recognizing the spiritual relationship between humans and the natural world. In 1836, he and other like-minded intellectuals, including Henry David Thoreau, founded the Transcendental Club, and that same year he published his influential essay "Nature," the first three chapters of which are included here.

Library of Congress

I. Nature

To go into solitude, a man needs to retire as much from his chamber as from society. I am not solitary whilst I read and write, though nobody is with me. But if a man would be alone, let him look at the stars. The rays that come from those heavenly worlds, will separate between him and what he touches. One might think the atmosphere was made transparent with this design, to give man, in the heavenly bodies, the perpetual presence of the sublime. Seen in the streets of cities, how great they are! If the stars should appear one night in a thousand years, how would men believe and adore; and preserve for many generations the remembrance of the city of God which had been shown! But every night come out these envoys of beauty, and light the universe with their admonishing smile.

The stars awaken a certain reverence, because though always present, they are inaccessible; but all natural objects make a kindred impression, when the mind is open to their influence. Nature never wears a mean appearance. Neither does the wisest man extort her secret, and lose his curiosity by finding out all her perfection. Nature never became a toy to a wise spirit. The flowers, the animals, the mountains, reflected the wisdom of his best hour, as much as they had delighted the simplicity of his childhood.

When we speak of nature in this manner, we have a distinct but most poetical sense in the mind. We mean the integrity of impression made by manifold natural objects. It is this which distinguishes the stick of timber of the wood-cutter, from the tree of the poet. The charming landscape which I saw this morning, is indubitably made up of some twenty or thirty farms. Miller owns this field, Locke that, and Manning the woodland beyond. But none of them owns the landscape. There is a property in the horizon which no man has but he whose eye can integrate all the parts, that is, the poet. This is the best part of these men's farms, yet to this their warranty-deeds give no title.

To speak truly, few adult persons can see nature. Most persons do not see the sun. At least they have a very superficial seeing. The sun illuminates only the eye of the man, but shines into the eye and the heart of the child. The lover of nature is he whose inward and outward senses are still truly adjusted to each other; who has retained the spirit of infancy even into the era of manhood. His intercourse with heaven and earth, becomes part of his daily food. In the presence of nature, a wild delight runs through the man, in spite of real sorrows. Nature says, — he is my creature, and maugre[1] all his impertinent griefs, he shall be glad with me. Not the sun or the summer alone, but every hour and season yields its tribute of delight; for every hour and change corresponds to and authorizes a different state of the mind, from breathless noon to grimmest midnight. Nature is a setting that fits equally well a comic or a mourning piece. In good health, the air is a cordial of incredible virtue. Crossing a bare common, in snow puddles, at twilight, under a clouded sky, without having in my thoughts any occurrence of special good fortune, I have enjoyed a perfect exhilaration. I am glad to the brink of fear. In the woods too, a man casts off his years, as the snake his slough, and at what period soever of life, is always a child. In the woods, is perpetual youth. Within these plantations of God, a decorum and sanctity reign, a perennial festival is dressed, and the guest sees not how he should tire of them in a thousand years. In the woods, we return to reason and faith. There I feel that nothing can befall me in life, — no disgrace, no calamity, (leaving me my eyes,) which nature cannot repair. Standing on the bare ground, — my head bathed by the blithe air, and uplifted into infinite space, — all mean egotism vanishes. I become a transparent eye-ball; I am nothing; I see all; the currents of the Universal Being circulate through me; I am part or particle of God. The name of the nearest friend sounds then foreign and accidental: to be

▼

Christopher Pearse Cranch, an American writer and artist, drew this sketch of Emerson as a walking eyeball shortly after *Nature* was first published. **To what extent is Cranch's take on Emerson's transformation into a "transparent eye-ball" (para. 4) meant to be read as humorous? What does this illustration suggest about Emerson's attitude toward the relationship between humans and the natural world?**

"Standing on the bare ground — my head bathed by the blithe air, & uplifted into infinite space, — all mean egotism va[nishes] I become a transparent Eyeball."
Nature. p.

From Christopher P. Cranch papers/Massachusetts Historical Society

brothers, to be acquaintances, — master or servant, is then a trifle and a disturbance. I am the lover of uncontained and immortal beauty. In the wilderness, I find something more dear and connate[2] than in streets or villages. In the tranquil landscape, and especially in the distant line of the horizon, man beholds somewhat as beautiful as his own nature.

---

[1] Despite. —Eds.

[2] Sympathetic. —Eds.

The greatest delight which the fields and woods minister, is the suggestion of an occult relation between man and the vegetable. I am not alone and unacknowledged. They nod to me, and I to them. The waving of the boughs in the storm, is new to me and old. It takes me by surprise, and yet is not unknown. Its effect is like that of a higher thought or a better emotion coming over me, when I deemed I was thinking justly or doing right.

Yet it is certain that the power to produce this delight, does not reside in nature, but in man, or in a harmony of both. It is necessary to use these pleasures with great temperance. For, nature is not always tricked in holiday attire, but the same scene which yesterday breathed perfume and glittered as for the frolic of the nymphs, is overspread with melancholy today. Nature always wears the colors of the spirit. To a man laboring under calamity, the heat of his own fire hath sadness in it. Then, there is a kind of contempt of the landscape felt by him who has just lost by death a dear friend. The sky is less grand as it shuts down over less worth in the population.

II. Commodity

Whoever considers the final cause of the world, will discern a multitude of uses that enter as parts into that result. They all admit of being thrown into one of the following classes; Commodity; Beauty; Language; and Discipline.

Under the general name of Commodity, I rank all those advantages which our senses owe to nature. This, of course, is a benefit which is temporary and mediate, not ultimate, like its service to the soul. Yet although low, it is perfect in its kind, and is the only use of nature which all men apprehend. The misery of man appears like childish petulance, when we explore the steady and prodigal provision that has been made for his support and delight on this green ball which floats him through the heavens. What angels invented these splendid ornaments, these rich conveniences, this ocean of air above, this ocean of water beneath, this firmament of earth between? this zodiac of lights, this tent of dropping clouds, this striped coat of climates, this fourfold year? Beasts, fire, water, stones, and corn serve him. The field is at once his floor, his workyard, his play-ground, his garden, and his bed.

> "More servants wait on man
> Than he 'll take notice of." — [3]

Nature, in its ministry to man, is not only the material, but is also the process and the result. All the parts incessantly work into each other's hands for the profit of man. The wind sows the seed; the sun evaporates the sea; the wind blows the vapor to the field; the ice, on the other side of the planet, condenses rain on this; the rain feeds the plant; the plant feeds the animal; and thus the endless circulations of the divine charity nourish man.

The useful arts are reproductions or new combinations by the wit of man, of the same natural benefactors. He no longer waits for favoring gales, but by means of steam, he realizes the fable of Æolus's bag,[4] and carries the two and thirty winds in the boiler of his boat. To diminish friction, he paves the road with iron bars, and, mounting a coach with a ship-load of men, animals, and merchandise behind him, he darts through the country, from town to town, like an eagle or a swallow through the air. By the aggregate of these aids, how is the face of the world changed, from the era of Noah to that of Napoleon! The private poor man hath cities, ships, canals, bridges, built for him. He goes to the post-office, and the human race run on his errands; to the book-shop, and the human race read and write of all that happens, for him; to the court-house, and nations repair his wrongs. He sets his house upon the road, and the human race

---

[3] The quotation is from *Man* by English poet George Herbert (1593–1633). —Eds.

[4] In Homer's *Odyssey*, Aeolus, the keeper of the winds, gave Odysseus an ox-hide bag containing all of the winds but the West wind, which he conjured up to send Odysseus safely home. While Odysseus was sleeping, his crew opened the bag and released the winds, causing a storm that sent their ship off course. —Eds.

go forth every morning, and shovel out the snow, and cut a path for him.

But there is no need of specifying particulars in this class of uses. The catalogue is endless, and the examples so obvious, that I shall leave them to the reader's reflection, with the general remark, that this mercenary benefit is one which has respect to a farther good. A man is fed, not that he may be fed, but that he may work.

III. Beauty

A nobler want of man is served by nature, namely, the love of Beauty.

The ancient Greeks called the world κόσμος,[5] beauty. Such is the constitution of all things, or such the plastic power of the human eye, that the primary forms, as the sky, the mountain, the tree, the animal, give us a delight *in and for themselves*; a pleasure arising from outline, color, motion, and grouping. This seems partly owing to the eye itself. The eye is the best of artists. By the mutual action of its structure and of the laws of light, perspective is produced, which integrates every mass of objects, of what character soever, into a well colored and shaded globe, so that where the particular objects are mean and unaffecting, the landscape which they compose, is round and symmetrical. And as the eye is the best composer, so light is the first of painters. There is no object so foul that intense light will not make beautiful. And the stimulus it affords to the sense, and a sort of infinitude which it hath, like space and time, make all matter gay. Even the corpse has its own beauty. But besides this general grace diffused over nature, almost all the individual forms are agreeable to the eye, as is proved by our endless imitations of some of them, as the acorn, the grape, the pine-cone, the wheat-ear, the egg, the wings and forms of most birds, the lion's claw, the serpent, the butterfly, sea-shells, flames, clouds, buds, leaves, and the forms of many trees, as the palm.

---

[5] *Cosmos*, Greek for "universe" or "order." Emerson is equating *order* with *beauty*. —Eds.

This cartoon, drawn by Edward Koren, was originally published in the *New Yorker* in 1979.
How does Koren poke fun at Emerson's ideas in this image?

Edward Koren/The New Yorker Collection/The Cartoon Bank

For better consideration, we may distribute the aspects of Beauty in a threefold manner.

1. First, the simple perception of natural forms is a delight. The influence of the forms and actions in nature, is so needful to man, that, in its lowest functions, it seems to lie on the confines of commodity and beauty. To the body and mind which have been cramped by noxious work or company, nature is medicinal and restores their tone. The tradesman, the attorney comes out of the din and craft of the street, and sees the sky and the woods, and is a man again. In their eternal calm, he finds himself. The health of the eye seems to demand a horizon. We are never tired, so long as we can see far enough.

But in other hours, Nature satisfies by its loveliness, and without any mixture of corporeal benefit. I see the spectacle of morning from the hill-top over against my house, from day-break to sun-rise, with emotions which an angel might share. The long slender bars of cloud float like fishes in the sea of crimson light. From the earth, as a shore, I look out into that silent sea. I seem to partake its rapid transformations: the active enchantment reaches my dust, and I dilate and conspire with the morning wind. How does Nature deify us with a few and cheap elements! Give me health and a day, and I will make the pomp of emperors ridiculous. The dawn is my Assyria; the sun-set and moon-rise my Paphos,[6] and unimaginable realms of faerie; broad noon shall be my England of the senses and the understanding; the night shall be my Germany of mystic philosophy and dreams.

Not less excellent, except for our less susceptibility in the afternoon, was the charm, last evening, of a January sunset. The western clouds divided and subdivided themselves into pink flakes modulated with tints of unspeakable softness; and the air had so much life and sweetness, that it was a pain to come within doors. What was it that nature would say? Was there no meaning in the live repose of the valley behind the mill, and which Homer or Shakespeare could not re-form for me in words? The leafless trees become spires of flame in the sunset, with the blue east for their back-ground, and the stars of the dead calices of flowers, and every withered stem and stubble rimed with frost, contribute something to the mute music.

The inhabitants of cities suppose that the country landscape is pleasant only half the year. I please myself with the graces of the winter scenery, and believe that we are as much touched by it as by the genial influences of summer. To the attentive eye, each moment of the year has its own beauty, and in the same field, it beholds, every hour, a picture which was never seen before, and which shall never be seen again. The heavens change every moment, and reflect their glory or gloom on the plains beneath. The state of the crop in the surrounding farms alters the expression of the earth from week to week. The succession of native plants in the pastures and roadsides, which makes the silent clock by which time tells the summer hours, will make even the divisions of the day sensible to a keen observer. The tribes of birds and insects, like the plants punctual to their time, follow each other, and the year has room for all. By water-courses, the variety is greater. In July, the blue pontederia or pickerel-weed blooms in large beds in the shallow parts of our pleasant river, and swarms with yellow butterflies in continual motion. Art cannot rival this pomp of purple and gold. Indeed the river is a perpetual gala, and boasts each month a new ornament.

But this beauty of Nature which is seen and felt as beauty, is the least part. The shows of day, the dewy morning, the rainbow, mountains, orchards in blossom, stars, moonlight, shadows in still water, and the like, if too eagerly hunted, become shows merely, and mock us with their unreality. Go out of the house to see the moon, and 't is mere tinsel; it will not please as when its light shines upon your necessary journey. The beauty that shimmers in the yellow afternoons of October, who ever could clutch it? Go forth to find it, and it is gone: 't is only a mirage as you look from the windows of diligence.

2. The presence of a higher, namely, of the spiritual element is essential to its perfection. The high and divine beauty which can be loved without effeminacy, is that which is found in combination with the human will. Beauty is the mark God sets upon virtue. Every natural action is graceful. Every heroic act is also decent, and causes the place and the bystanders to shine. We are taught by great actions that the universe is the property of every individual in it. Every rational creature has all nature for his dowry and estate.

20

---

[6] City in Cyprus. At its height, in the ninth century B.C.E., the Assyrian empire controlled much of the Middle East, including Cyprus. —Eds.

Brooklyn Museum of Art, New York, USA/Bridgeman Images

Shown here is *The Picnic*, an 1846 painting by Transcendentalist artist Thomas Cole.
What aspects of Emerson's central argument do you see reflected in this painting? What message about humans' relationship to nature does each convey?

It is his, if he will. He may divest himself of it; he may creep into a corner, and abdicate his kingdom, as most men do, but he is entitled to the world by his constitution. In proportion to the energy of his thought and will, he takes up the world into himself. "All those things for which men plough, build, or sail, obey virtue;" said Sallust.[7] "The winds and waves," said Gibbon,[8] "are always on the side of the ablest navigators." So are the sun and moon and all the stars of heaven. When a noble act is done — perchance in a scene of great natural beauty; when Leonidas and his three hundred martyrs consume one day in dying, and the sun and moon come each and look at them once in the steep defile of Thermopylæ;[9] when Arnold Winkelried,[10] in the high Alps, under the shadow of the avalanche, gathers in his side a sheaf of Austrian spears to break the line for his comrades, are not these heroes entitled to add the beauty of the scene to the beauty of the deed? When the bark of Columbus nears the shore of America; — before it, the beach lined with savages, fleeing out of all their huts of cane; the sea behind; and the purple mountains of the Indian Archipelago around, can we separate the man from the living picture? Does not the New World clothe his form with her palm-groves and savannahs as fit drapery? Ever does natural beauty steal in like air, and envelope great actions. When Sir Harry Vane[11] was dragged up the Tower-hill, sitting on a sled, to suffer death, as the champion of the English laws, one of the multitude cried out to him, "You never sate on so glorious a seat." Charles II, to intimidate the citizens of London, caused the patriot Lord Russel to be drawn in an open coach,[12] through the principal streets of the city, on his way to the scaffold. "But," his biographer says,

---

[7] Sallust (86–34 B.C.E.), Roman historian. —Eds.

[8] Edward Gibbon (1737–1794), English historian and author of *The History of the Decline and Fall of the Roman Empire.* —Eds.

[9] During the Battle of Thermopylae (480 B.C.E.), King Leonidas and three hundred Spartan soldiers held the front line against the huge Persian army. Though all were killed, they gave the remainder of the Greek army time to retreat to safety. —Eds.

[10] A legendary Swiss hero who sacrificed himself to secure the victory of the Old Swiss Confederacy in the Battle of Sempach. —Eds.

[11] Sir Harry Vane (1613-1662), an English politician and governor of the Massachusetts Bay Colony who was executed for high treason in 1662. —Eds.

[12] Before his execution for committing high treason, Lord Russell (1639–1683) was fastened to a wooden panel and drawn by horse throughout London. —Eds.

What aspects of Emerson's argument do you see reflected in this cartoon?

"the multitude imagined they saw liberty and virtue sitting by his side." In private places, among sordid objects, an act of truth or heroism seems at once to draw to itself the sky as its temple, the sun as its candle. Nature stretcheth out her arms to embrace man, only let his thoughts be of equal greatness. Willingly does she follow his steps with the rose and the violet, and bend her lines of grandeur and grace to the decoration of her darling child. Only let his thoughts be of equal scope, and the frame will suit the picture. A virtuous man is in unison with her works, and makes the central figure of the visible sphere. Homer, Pindar, Socrates, Phocion, associate themselves fitly in our memory with the geography and climate of Greece. The visible heavens and earth sympathize with Jesus. And in common life, whosoever has seen a person of powerful character and happy genius, will have remarked how easily he took all things along with him, — the persons, the opinions, and the day, and nature became ancillary to a man.

3. There is still another aspect under which the beauty of the world may be viewed, namely, as it becomes an object of the intellect. Beside the relation of things to virtue, they have a relation to thought. The intellect searches out the absolute order of things as they stand in the mind of God, and without the colors of affection.

The intellectual and the active powers seem to succeed each other, and the exclusive activity of the one, generates the exclusive activity of the other. There is something unfriendly in each to the other, but they are like the alternate periods of feeding and working in animals; each prepares and will be followed by the other. Therefore does beauty, which, in relation to actions, as we have seen, comes unsought, and comes because it is unsought, remain for the apprehension and pursuit of the intellect; and then again, in its turn, of the active power. Nothing divine dies. All good is eternally reproductive. The beauty of nature reforms itself in the mind, and not for barren contemplation, but for new creation.

All men are in some degree impressed by the face of the world; some men even to delight. This love of beauty is Taste. Others have the same love in such excess, that, not content with admiring, they seek to embody it in new forms. The creation of beauty is Art.

The production of a work of art throws a light upon the mystery of humanity. A work of art is an abstract or epitome of the world. It is the result or expression of nature, in miniature. For, although the works of nature are innumerable and all different, the result or the expression of them all is similar and single. Nature is a sea of

seeing connections

The following excerpt is from a review of "Nature" that appeared in *The Western Messenger*, a journal devoted to religion and literature, and was written by editor Samuel Osgood in 1837.

Based on this passage, how would you characterize Osgood's attitude toward Emerson's essay? How might you support — or challenge — his argument with details from this excerpt of *Nature*?

from Nature

SAMUEL OSGOOD

The many will call this book dreamy, and perhaps it is so. It may indeed naturally seem, that the author's mind is somewhat onesided, that he has not mingled enough with common humanity, to avoid running into eccentricity, that he has been so careful to keep his own individuality, that he has confounded his idiosyncrasies, with universal truth. All this may be. But it is not for the vulgar many to call such a man a dreamer. If he does dream, the many are more deluded dreamers. His dreams are visions of the eternal realities of the spiritual world: their's are of the fleeting phantoms of earth. Indeed the real visionary is not to be found, in the mystic's cell, or the philosopher's study, but in the haunts of busy life. The sensualist is a wretched visionary: he sees but a part, and that but a mean part of the reality of things, and sees all in a false light. The man of ambition is a dreamer. Those men, who pride themselves most on their practical turn of mind, are often far more visionary, than their more romantic neighbors, whom they are accustomed to deride. The [man] who makes himself an entire drudge to money getting, and boasts, that while other men are chasing shadows, such shadows, as beauty in nature and art, or truth in science or religion, he alone is grasping the substance; this man is constantly pursuing a phantom — he is chasing a joy, that never comes to him: from the toils of the present hour, he is ever looking forward to the future, and dreaming of some distant good, as the reward of his labors, and the enjoyment of his wealth. He dreams and toils, and heaps up his treasures, and forms visions of bliss, which are never realised; never finding the time, in which he may enjoy his wealth, he lives in a realm of illusion, until death, the stern teacher of reality, comes and touches him with his cold hand, and heaped treasures and fond visions at once disappear.

forms radically alike and even unique. A leaf, a sun-beam, a landscape, the ocean, make an analogous impression on the mind. What is common to them all, — that perfectness and harmony, is beauty. The standard of beauty is the entire circuit of natural forms, — the totality of nature; which the Italians expressed by defining beauty "il piu nell' uno."[13] Nothing is quite beautiful alone: nothing but is beautiful in the whole. A single object is only so far beautiful as it suggests this universal grace. The poet, the painter, the sculptor, the musician, the architect, seek each

[13] Italian, "the many in one." —Eds.

to concentrate this radiance of the world on one point, and each in his several work to satisfy the love of beauty which stimulates him to produce. Thus is Art, a nature passed through the alembic[14] of man. Thus in art, does nature work through the will of a man filled with the beauty of her first works.

The world thus exists to the soul to satisfy the desire of beauty. This element I call an

---

[14] A device that purifies or refines. —Eds.

ultimate end. No reason can be asked or given why the soul seeks beauty. Beauty, in its largest and profoundest sense, is one expression for the universe. God is the all-fair. Truth, and goodness, and beauty are but different faces of the same All. But beauty in nature is not ultimate. It is the herald of inward and eternal beauty, and is not alone a solid and satisfactory good. It must stand as a part, and not as yet the last or highest expression of the final cause of Nature.

[1836]

QUESTIONS FOR DISCUSSION

1. Explain Ralph Waldo Emerson's attitude toward nature in paragraphs 1 and 2.

2. In paragraph 4, Emerson writes, "I become a transparent eye-ball; I am nothing; I see all; the currents of the Universal Being circulate through me; I am part or particle of God." From those words, how would you describe Emerson's mental state here, and what has brought it about?

3. In paragraph 6, Emerson says, "Nature always wears the colors of the spirit." What does he mean? Do you agree? In paragraph 4, Emerson says, "Crossing a bare common, in snow puddles, at twilight, under a clouded sky . . . I have enjoyed a perfect exhilaration." Does this contradict his statement in paragraph 6? Explain how the relationship that Emerson describes between humans and nature works.

4. In paragraphs 7–9, what does Emerson suggest about the human condition?

5. In paragraph 10, what is Emerson's attitude toward the "useful arts" — what people now call technology? Would Emerson have the same attitude today? Why or why not?

6. In Part III of the selection, Emerson says that in regard to nature, loving its beauty is a nobler response than using it as a commodity. Do you agree or disagree? Explain why.

7. In paragraph 20, Emerson writes, "Nature stretcheth out her arms to embrace man, only let his thoughts be of equal greatness." What does he mean? What does this statement imply about the relationship between nature and humankind?

QUESTIONS ON RHETORIC AND STYLE

1. What is the effect of the comparisons (including figurative language) and distinctions that Emerson makes in paragraphs 1 and 2? In the conclusion to the first paragraph, Emerson says the stars give an "admonishing smile." What does he mean by this phrase? How does Emerson characterize nature? What is the purpose of this characterization?

2. Identify the juxtapositions in paragraph 4. What is their effect? Is there a relationship among

the juxtapositions that suggests a larger point? Explain.

3. In paragraph 8, Emerson speaks of "this green ball which floats him through the heavens." What is the effect of this metaphor? How does the repetition in the rest of the paragraph ("this ocean of air above, this ocean of water beneath, this . . . this . . .") contribute to this effect?

4. What three aspects of the beauty of nature does Emerson delineate in Part III? How does he use simile and metaphor to develop the first aspect? How do the rhetorical questions in paragraph 20 serve to develop the second aspect?

5. What is the relationship between paragraphs 18 and 19? What is the effect of the paradox that concludes paragraph 19?

6. In paragraph 21, what distinction does Emerson make between "barren contemplation" and "new creation"?

7. How does Emerson unite truth, goodness, and beauty in the final paragraph? Why is this a fitting conclusion for this section?

SUGGESTIONS FOR WRITING

1. Write an essay in which you support, challenge, or qualify Emerson's main idea in Part I.

2. In Part II, Emerson presents an optimistic view of the "useful arts." In the voice of a modern-day environmentalist such as Rachel Carson (p. 397), discuss whether his view holds true today.

3. Write a letter to Emerson describing an experience you have had with nature. Explain how it was similar to or different from the experience he describes in Part II.

4. Select a powerful, challenging, or thought-provoking statement from Emerson — such as

"The production of a work of art throws a light upon the mystery of humanity. A work of art is an abstract or epitome of the world" (para. 23). Write an essay that supports, qualifies, or refutes its assertion. Use evidence from your reading, as well as your own knowledge and experience, to defend your position.

5. Read the poem "Thanatopsis" by William Cullen Bryant, a contemporary of Emerson's, and write an essay comparing it with this excerpt from Emerson's essay "Nature."

OTHER VOICES

from The Land Ethic

ALDO LEOPOLD

Aldo Leopold (1887–1948) was born in Iowa. He attended the Sheffield Scientific School at Yale and subsequently enrolled in the Yale forestry school, the first graduate school of forestry in the United States. Graduating with a master's degree in 1909, he joined the U.S. Forest Service and stayed with that agency in various research and management positions until 1933, when he took a position at the University of Wisconsin. Throughout his life, Leopold was at the forefront of the conservation movement; many people acknowledge him as the father of wildlife conservation in America. He was also an internationally respected scientist who wrote over 350 articles, mostly on scientific and policy matters. In addition, he was an advisor on conservation to the United Nations. He died of a heart attack while fighting a fire on a neighbor's farm. Leopold is best known for his book *A Sand County Almanac* (1949), which includes the chapter excerpted here, "The Land Ethic."

When god-like Odysseus returned from the wars in Troy, he hanged all on one rope a dozen slave-girls of his household whom he suspected of misbehavior during his absence.

This hanging involved no question of propriety. The girls were property. The disposal of property was then, as now, a matter of expediency, not of right and wrong.

Concepts of right and wrong were not lacking from Odysseus' Greece: witness the fidelity of his wife through the long years before at last his black-prowed galleys clove the wine-dark seas for home. The ethical structure of that day covered wives, but had not yet been extended to human chattels. During the three thousand years which have since elapsed, ethical criteria have been extended to many fields of conduct, with corresponding shrinkages in those judged by expediency only.

The Ethical Sequence

This extension of ethics, so far studied only by philosophers, is actually a process in ecological evolution. Its sequences may be described in ecological as well as in philosophical terms.

An ethic, ecologically, is a limitation on freedom of action in the struggle for existence. An ethic, philosophically, is a differentiation of social from anti-social conduct. These are two definitions of one thing. The thing has its origin in the tendency of interdependent individuals or groups to evolve modes of co-operation. The ecologist calls these symbioses. Politics and economics are advanced symbioses in which the original free-for-all competition has been replaced, in part, by co-operative mechanisms with an ethical content.

The complexity of co-operative mechanisms has increased with population density, and with the efficiency of tools. It was simpler, for example, to define the anti-social uses of sticks and stones in the days of the mastodons than of bullets and billboards in the age of motors.

The first ethics dealt with the relation between individuals; the Mosaic Decalogue[1] is an example. Later accretions dealt with the

---
[1] The Ten Commandments found in the book of Exodus in the Bible. —Eds.

relation between the individual and society. The Golden Rule tries to integrate the individual to society; democracy to integrate social organization to the individual.

There is as yet no ethic dealing with man's relation to land and to the animals and plants which grow upon it. Land, like Odysseus' slave-girls, is still property. The land relation is still strictly economic, entailing privileges but not obligations.

The extension of ethics to this third element in human environment is, if I read the evidence correctly, an evolutionary possibility and an ecological necessity. It is the third step in a sequence. The first two have already been taken. Individual thinkers since the days of Ezekiel and Isaiah[2] have asserted that the despoliation of land is not only inexpedient but wrong. Society, however, has not yet affirmed their belief. I regard the present conservation movement as the embryo of such an affirmation.

An ethic may be regarded as a mode of guidance for meeting ecological situations so new or intricate, or involving such deferred reactions, that the path of social expediency is not discernible to the average individual. Animal instincts are modes of guidance for the individual in meeting such situations. Ethics are possibly a kind of community instinct in-the-making.

The Community Concept

All ethics so far evolved rest upon a single premise: that the individual is a member of a community of interdependent parts. His instincts prompt him to compete for his place in that community, but his ethics prompt him also to co-operate (perhaps in order that there may be a place to compete for).

The land ethic simply enlarges the boundaries of the community to include soils, waters, plants, and animals, or collectively: the land.

10

This sounds simple: do we not already sing our love for and obligation to the land of the free and the home of the brave? Yes, but just what and whom do we love? Certainly not the soil, which we are sending helter-skelter downriver. Certainly not the waters, which we assume have no function except to turn turbines, float barges, and carry off sewage. Certainly not the plants, of which we exterminate whole communities without batting an eye. Certainly not the animals, of which we have already extirpated many of the largest and most beautiful species. A land ethic of course cannot prevent the alteration, management, and use of these "resources," but it does affirm their right to continued existence, and, at least in spots, their continued existence in a natural state.

In short, a land ethic changes the role of *Homo sapiens* from conqueror of the land-community to plain member and citizen of it. It implies respect for his fellow-members, and also respect for the community as such.

In human history, we have learned (I hope) that the conqueror role is eventually self-defeating. Why? Because it is implicit in such a role that the conqueror knows, *ex cathedra*,[3] just what makes the community clock tick, and just what and who is valuable, and what and who is worthless, in community life. It always turns out that he knows neither, and this is why his conquests eventually defeat themselves.

In the biotic community, a parallel situation exists. Abraham[4] knew exactly what the land was for: it was to drip milk and honey into Abraham's mouth. At the present moment, the assurance with which we regard this assumption is inverse to the degree of our education.

15

---

[2] Judeo-Christian prophets and Biblical characters. —Eds.

[3] Latin for "from the chair," here meaning from the seat of authority, often a reference to infallible papal decrees. —Eds.

[4] A Judeo-Christian prophet and Biblical character; known as the founding father of the Covenant. —Eds.

The ordinary citizen today assumes that science knows what makes the community clock tick; the scientist is equally sure that he does not. He knows that the biotic mechanism is so complex that its workings may never be fully understood.

That man is, in fact, only a member of a biotic team is shown by an ecological interpretation of history. Many historical events, hitherto explained solely in terms of human enterprise, were actually biotic interactions between people and land. The characteristics of the land determined the facts quite as potently as the characteristics of the men who lived on it.

Consider, for example, the settlement of the Mississippi valley. In the years following the Revolution, three groups were contending for its control: the native Indian, the French and English traders, and the American settlers. Historians wonder what would have happened if the English at Detroit had thrown a little more weight into the Indian side of those tipsy scales which decided the outcome of the colonial migration into the cane-lands of Kentucky. It is time now to ponder the fact that the cane-lands, when subjected to the particular mixture of forces represented by the cow, plow, fire, and axe of the pioneer, became bluegrass. What if the plant succession inherent in this dark and bloody ground had, under the impact of these forces, given us some worthless sedge, shrub, or weed? Would Boone and Kenton[5] have held out? Would there have been any overflow into Ohio, Indiana, Illinois, and Missouri? Any Louisiana Purchase? Any transcontinental union of new states? Any Civil War?

Kentucky was one sentence in the drama of history. We are commonly told what the human actors in this drama tried to do, but we are seldom told that their success, or the lack of it, hung in large degree on the reaction of particular soils to the impact of the particular forces exerted

by their occupancy. In the case of Kentucky, we do not even know where the bluegrass came from — whether it is a native species, or a stowaway from Europe.

Contrast the cane-lands with what hindsight tells us about the Southwest, where the pioneers were equally brave, resourceful, and persevering. The impact of occupancy here brought no bluegrass, or other plant fitted to withstand the bumps and buffetings of hard use. This region, when grazed by livestock, reverted through a series of more and more worthless grasses, shrubs, and weeds to a condition of unstable equilibrium. Each recession of plant types bred erosion; each increment to erosion bred a further recession of plants. The result today is a progressive and mutual deterioration, not only of plants and soils, but of the animal community subsisting thereon. The early settlers did not expect this: on the ciénegas[6] of New Mexico some even cut ditches to hasten it. So subtle has been its progress that few residents of the region are aware of it. It is quite invisible to the tourist who finds this wrecked landscape colorful and charming (as indeed it is, but it bears scant resemblance to what it was in 1848).

This same landscape was "developed" once before, but with quite different results. The Pueblo Indians settled the Southwest in pre-Columbian times, but they happened *not* to be equipped with range livestock. Their civilization expired, but not because their land expired.

In India, regions devoid of any sod-forming grass have been settled, apparently without wrecking the land, by the simple expedient of carrying the grass to the cow, rather than vice versa. (Was this the result of some deep wisdom, or was it just good luck? I do not know.)

In short, the plant succession steered the course of history; the pioneer simply

20

[5] Daniel Boone (1734–1820) and Simon Kenton (1755–1836), famous American frontiersmen. —Eds.

[6] Spring-fed marshes. —Eds.

demonstrated, for good or ill, which successions inhered in the land. Is history taught in this spirit? It will be, once the concept of land as a community really penetrates our intellectual life.

The Ecological Conscience

Conservation is a state of harmony between men and land. Despite nearly a century of propaganda, conservation still proceeds at a snail's pace; progress still consists largely of letterhead pieties and convention oratory. On the back forty we still slip two steps backward for each forward stride.

The usual answer to this dilemma is "more 25 conservation education." No one will debate this, but is it certain that only the *volume* of education needs stepping up? Is something lacking in the *content* as well?

It is difficult to give a fair summary of its content in brief form, but, as I understand it, the content is substantially this: obey the law, vote right, join some organizations, and practice what conservation is profitable on your own land; the government will do the rest.

Is not this formula too easy to accomplish anything worth-while? It defines no right or wrong, assigns no obligation, calls for no sacrifice, implies no change in the current philosophy of values. In respect of land-use, it urges only enlightened self-interest. Just how far will such education take us? An example will perhaps yield a partial answer.

By 1930 it had become clear to all except the ecologically blind that southwestern Wisconsin's topsoil was slipping seaward. In 1933 the farmers were told that if they would adopt certain remedial practices for five years, the public would donate CCC labor to install them, plus the necessary machinery and materials. The offer was widely accepted, but the practices were widely forgotten when the five-year contract period was up. The farmers continued only those practices that yielded an immediate and visible economic gain for themselves.

This led to the idea that maybe farmers would learn more quickly if they themselves wrote the rules. Accordingly the Wisconsin Legislature in 1937 passed the Soil Conservation District Law. This said to farmers, in effect: *We, the public, will furnish you free technical service and loan you specialized machinery, if you will write your own rules for land-use. Each county may write its own rules, and these will have the force of law.* Nearly all the counties promptly organized to accept the proffered help, but after a decade of operation, *no county has yet written a single rule.* There has been visible progress in such practices as strip-cropping, pasture renovation, and soil liming, but none in fencing woodlots against grazing, and none in excluding plow and cow from steep slopes. The farmers, in short, have selected those remedial practices which were profitable anyhow, and ignored those which were profitable to the community, but not clearly profitable to themselves.

When one asks why no rules have been writ- 30 ten, one is told that the community is not yet ready to support them; education must precede rules. But the education actually in progress makes no mention of obligations to land over and above those dictated by self-interest. The net result is that we have more education but less soil, fewer healthy woods, and as many floods as in 1937.

The puzzling aspect of such situations is that the existence of obligations over and above self-interest is taken for granted in such rural community enterprises as the betterment of roads, schools, churches, and baseball teams. Their existence is not taken for granted, nor as yet seriously discussed, in bettering the behavior of the water that falls on the land, or in the preserving of the beauty or diversity of the farm landscape. Land-use ethics are still governed wholly by economic self-interest, just as social ethics were a century ago.

This poster was created by Stanley Thomas Clough (1905–1977) for the Federal Art Project, part of the Works Progress Administration, in 1938.

How does Leopold's concept of a land ethic relate to the appeal this poster makes?

PROTECT
YOUR PARKS

Library of Congress

To sum up: we asked the farmer to do what he conveniently could to save his soil, and he has done just that, and only that. The farmer who clears the woods off a 75 per cent slope, turns his cows into the clearing, and dumps its rainfall, rocks, and soil into the community creek, is still (if otherwise decent) a respected member of society. If he puts lime on his fields and plants his crops on contour, he is still entitled to all the privileges and emoluments of his Soil Conservation District. The District is a beautiful piece of social machinery, but it is coughing along on two cylinders because we have been too timid, and too anxious for quick success, to tell the farmer the true magnitude of his obligations. Obligations have no meaning without conscience, and the problem we face is the extension of social conscience from people to land.

No important change in ethics was ever accomplished without an internal change in our intellectual emphasis, loyalties, affections, and convictions. The proof that conservation has not yet touched these foundations of conduct lies in the fact that philosophy and religion have not yet heard of it. In our attempt to make conservation easy, we have made it trivial. . . .

Land Health and the A-B Cleavage

A land ethic, then, reflects the existence of an ecological conscience, and this in turn reflects a conviction of individual responsibility for the health of the land. Health is the capacity of the land for self-renewal. Conservation is our effort to understand and preserve this capacity.

Conservationists are notorious for their dissensions. Superficially these seem to add up to mere confusion, but a more careful scrutiny reveals a single plane of cleavage common to many specialized fields. In each field one group (A) regards the land as soil, and its function as commodity-production; another group (B) regards the land as a biota, and its function as something broader. How much broader is admittedly in a state of doubt and confusion.

In my own field, forestry, Group A is quite content to grow trees like cabbages, with cellulose as the basic forest commodity. It feels no inhibition against violence; its ideology is agronomic. Group B, on the other hand, sees forestry as fundamentally different from agronomy because it employs natural species, and manages a natural environment rather than creating an artificial one. Group B prefers natural reproduction on principle. It worries on biotic as well as economic grounds about the loss of species like chestnut, and the threatened loss of the white pines. It worries about a whole series of secondary forest functions: wildlife, recreation,

35

watersheds, wilderness areas. To my mind, Group B feels the stirrings of an ecological conscience.

In the wildlife field, a parallel cleavage exists. For Group A the basic commodities are sport and meat; the yardsticks of production are ciphers of take in pheasants and trout. Artificial propagation is acceptable as a permanent as well as a temporary recourse — if its unit costs permit. Group B, on the other hand, worries about a whole series of biotic side-issues. What is the cost in predators of producing a game crop? Should we have further recourse to exotics? How can management restore the shrinking species, like prairie grouse, already hopeless as shootable game? How can management restore the threatened rarities, like trumpeter swan and whooping crane? Can management principles be extended to wildflowers? Here again it is clear to me that we have the same A-B cleavage as in forestry.

In the larger field of agriculture I am less competent to speak, but there seem to be somewhat parallel cleavages. Scientific agriculture was actively developing before ecology was born, hence a slower penetration of ecological concepts might be expected. Moreover the farmer, by the very nature of his techniques, must modify the biota more radically than the forester or the wildlife manager. Nevertheless, there are many discontents in agriculture which seem to add up to a new vision of "biotic farming."

Perhaps the most important of these is the new evidence that poundage or tonnage is no measure of the food-value of farm crops; the products of fertile soil may be qualitatively as well as quantitatively superior. We can bolster poundage from depleted soils by pouring on imported fertility, but we are not necessarily bolstering food-value. The possible ultimate ramifications of this idea are so immense that I must leave their exposition to abler pens.

The discontent that labels itself "organic farming," while bearing some of the earmarks of a cult, is nevertheless biotic in its direction, particularly in its insistence on the importance of soil flora and fauna.

40

The ecological fundamentals of agriculture are just as poorly known to the public as in other fields of land-use. For example, few educated people realize that the marvelous advances in technique made during recent decades are improvements in the pump, rather than the well. Acre for acre, they have barely sufficed to offset the sinking level of fertility.

In all of these cleavages, we see repeated the same basic paradoxes: man the conqueror *versus* man the biotic citizen; science the sharpener of his sword *versus* science the searchlight on his universe; land the slave and servant *versus* land the collective organism. Robinson's injunction to Tristram[7] may well be applied, at this juncture, to *Homo sapiens* as a species in geological time:

> Whether you will or not
> You are a King, Tristram, for you are one
> Of the time-tested few that leave the world,
> When they are gone, not the same place it was.
> Mark what you leave.

The Outlook

It is inconceivable to me that an ethical relation to land can exist without love, respect, and admiration for land, and a high regard for its value. By value, I of course mean something far broader than mere economic value; I mean value in the philosophical sense.

Perhaps the most serious obstacle impeding the evolution of a land ethic is the fact that our educational and economic system is headed away from, rather than toward, an intense consciousness of land. Your true modern is separated from the land by many middlemen, and by innumerable physical gadgets. He has no vital relation to it; to him it is the space between cities on which crops grow. Turn him loose for a day on the land, and if the spot does not happen to be a golf links or a "scenic" area, he is bored stiff.

---

[7] A reference to Edwin Arlington Robinson's narrative poem "Tristram," which was written in 1927 and won a Pulitzer Prize. — Eds.

If crops could be raised by hydroponics instead of farming, it would suit him very well. Synthetic substitutes for wood, leather, wool, and other natural land products suit him better than the originals. In short, land is something he has "outgrown."

Almost equally serious as an obstacle to a land ethic is the attitude of the farmer for whom the land is still an adversary, or a taskmaster that keeps him in slavery. Theoretically, the mechanization of farming ought to cut the farmer's chains, but whether it really does is debatable.

One of the requisites for an ecological comprehension of land is an understanding of ecology, and this is by no means co-extensive with "education"; in fact, much higher education seems deliberately to avoid ecological concepts. An understanding of ecology does not necessarily originate in courses bearing ecological labels; it is quite as likely to be labeled geography, botany, agronomy, history, or economics. This is as it should be, but whatever the label, ecological training is scarce.

The case for a land ethic would appear hopeless but for the minority which is in obvious revolt against these "modern" trends.

45

The "key-log" which must be moved to release the evolutionary process for an ethic is simply this: quit thinking about decent land-use as solely an economic problem. Examine each question in terms of what is ethically and esthetically right, as well as what is economically expedient. A thing is right when it tends to preserve the integrity, stability, and beauty of the biotic community. It is wrong when it tends otherwise.

It of course goes without saying that economic feasibility limits the tether of what can or cannot be done for land. It always has and it always will. The fallacy the economic determinists have tied around our collective neck, and which we now need to cast off, is the belief that economics determines *all* land-use. This is simply not true. An innumerable host of actions and attitudes, comprising perhaps the bulk of all land relations, is determined by the land-users' tastes and predilections, rather than by his purse. The bulk of all land relations hinges on investments of time, forethought, skill, and faith rather than on investments of cash. As a land-user thinketh, so is he.

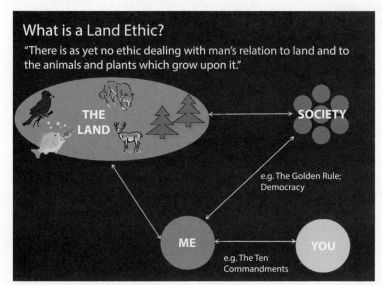

What is a Land Ethic?

"There is as yet no ethic dealing with man's relation to land and to the animals and plants which grow upon it."

THE LAND

SOCIETY

e.g. The Golden Rule; Democracy

ME

YOU

e.g. The Ten Commandments

Jen Kobylecky/The Aldo Leopold Foundation

This illustration is from the Aldo Leopold Foundation's website. **How does it interpret Leopold's concept of a land ethic? How does it relate to your understanding of a land ethic, based on your reading?**

I have purposely presented the land ethic *50* as a product of social evolution because nothing so important as an ethic is ever "written." Only the most superficial student of history supposes that Moses "wrote" the Decalogue; it evolved in the minds of a thinking community, and Moses wrote a tentative summary of it for a "seminar." I say tentative because evolution never stops.

The evolution of a land ethic is an intellectual as well as emotional process. Conservation is paved with good intentions which prove to be futile, or even dangerous, because they are devoid of critical understanding either of the land, or of economic land-use. I think it is a truism that as the ethical frontier advances from the individual to the community, its intellectual content increases.

The mechanism of operation is the same for any ethic: social approbation for right actions: social disapproval for wrong actions.

By and large, our present problem is one of attitudes and implements. We are remodeling the Alhambra[8] with a steam-shovel, and we are proud of our yardage. We shall hardly relinquish the shovel, which after all has many good points, but we are in need of gentler and more objective criteria for its successful use.

[1949]

---

[8] A famous Spanish palace. —Eds.

EXPLORING THE TEXT

1. What is the effect of the story about Odysseus that begins Aldo Leopold's essay?

2. How would you describe Leopold's tone at the beginning of section "The Ethical Sequence"?

3. What are the ecological and philosophical distinctions that Leopold makes regarding the land ethic? Think of two contemporary examples that illustrate how these are actually "two definitions of one thing" (para. 4).

4. Paragraph 15 ends: "At the present moment, the assurance with which we regard this assumption is inverse to the degree of our education." What is the assumption to which he refers? Who holds it? What is Leopold's attitude toward it? What can we infer from the allusion to Abraham that precedes this sentence?

5. How does Leopold use analogy, particularly in paragraph 31, as a rhetorical technique? Is the claim he develops in that paragraph still true today? Explain your response.

6. Identify the claim in paragraph 33. Do you agree with it? Explain.

7. In the section "Land Health and the A-B Cleavage," Leopold introduces two ways of looking at the land, which he labels A and B (para. 35). Which viewpoint is more prominent today?

8. How effective are Leopold's appeals to ethos in paragraphs 38 and 39? Do they make his argument more convincing? Explain.

9. Expressing a view widely held in 1949, Leopold writes of the "discontent that labels itself 'organic farming'" (para. 40). Do we still see organic farming as a discontent today? Explain.

10. At the beginning of the section "The Outlook," Leopold characterizes the "modern" (para. 44). Does that characterization hold true today? Explain your response.

11. How does Leopold's use of the "key-log" metaphor (para. 48) move his essay toward its conclusion?

12. Leopold wrote "The Land Ethic" over sixty years ago. To what extent do his ideas apply to our current environmental situation?

Natural Man

LEWIS THOMAS

Lewis Thomas (1913–1993) was educated at Harvard Medical School and worked as a medical researcher. He served as president and chancellor of Memorial Sloan-Kettering Cancer Center in New York and as professor of pathology and medicine at Cornell University. Thomas published many scientific articles and books, and in 1971 he began writing regularly for the *New England Journal of Medicine*. His columns were collected in 1974 to form the best-selling book *The Lives of a Cell*, which won the National Book Award and includes the essay presented here, "Natural Man." Thomas's other books include *The Medusa and the Snail* (1979) and *Late Night Thoughts on Listening to Mahler's Ninth Symphony* (1983). In honor of his stellar prose style as well as his engaging ideas, the Lewis Thomas Prize is awarded annually by the Rockefeller University to a scientist for artistic achievement. Thomas is widely known as one of the originators of the science-based personal essay.

The social scientists, especially the economists, are moving deeply into ecology and the environment these days, with disquieting results. It goes somehow against the grain to learn that cost-benefit analyses can be done neatly on lakes, meadows, nesting gannets, and even whole oceans. It is hard enough to confront the environmental options ahead, and the hard choices, but even harder when the price tags are so visible. Even the new jargon is disturbing: it hurts the spirit, somehow, to read the word "environments," when the plural means that there are so many alternatives there to be sorted through, as in a market, and voted on. Economists need cool heads and cold hearts for this sort of work, and they must write in icy, often skiddy, prose.

The degree to which we are all involved in the control of the earth's life is just beginning to dawn on most of us, and it means another revolution for human thought.

This will not come easily. We've just made our way through inconclusive revolutions on the same topic, trying to make up our minds how we feel about nature. As soon as we arrived at one kind of consensus, like an enormous committee, we found it was time to think it through all over, and now here we are, at it again.

The oldest, easiest to swallow idea was that the earth was man's personal property, a combination of garden, zoo, bank vault and energy source, placed at our disposal to be consumed, ornamented or pulled apart as we wished. The betterment of mankind was, as we understood it, the whole point of the thing. Mastery over nature, mystery and all, was a moral duty and social obligation.

In the last few years we were wrenched away from this way of looking at it, and arrived at something like general agreement that we had it wrong. We still argue the details, but it is conceded almost everywhere that we are not the masters of nature that we thought ourselves; we are as dependent as the leaves or midges or fish on the rest of life. We are part of the system. One way to put it is that the earth is a loosely formed, spherical organism, with all its working parts linked in symbiosis. We are, in this view, neither owners nor operators; at best, we might see ourselves as motile tissue[1] specialized for receiving information—perhaps, in the best of all possible worlds, functioning as a nervous system for the whole being.

There is, for some, too much dependency in this view, and they prefer to see us as a separate,

5

---

[1] Tissue cells that can move freely. —Eds.

How might the artist of this cartoon respond to Lewis Thomas's argument?

Lee Lorenz/The New Yorker Collection/The Cartoon Bank

qualitatively different, special species, unlike any other form of life, despite the sharing around of genes, enzymes and organelles. No matter, there is still the underlying idea that we cannot have a life of our own without concern for the ecosystem in which we live, whether in majesty or not. This idea has been strong enough to launch the new movements for the sustenance of wilderness, the protection of wild life, the turning off of insatiable technologies, the preservation of "whole earth."

But now, just when the new view seems to be taking hold, we may be in for another wrench, this time more dismaying and unsettling than anything we've come through. In a sense, we will be obliged to swing back again, still believing in the new way but constrained by the facts of life to live in the old. It may be too late, as things have turned out.

We are, in fact, the masters, like it or not.

It is a despairing prospect. Here we are, practically speaking 21st-century mankind, filled to exuberance with our new understanding of kinship to all the family of life, and here we are, still 19th-century man, walking bootshod over the open face of nature, subjugating and civilizing it. And we cannot stop this controlling, unless we vanish under the hill ourselves. If there were such a thing as a world mind, it should crack over this.

The truth is, we have become more deeply involved than we ever dreamed. The fact that we sit around as we do, worrying seriously about how best to preserve the life of the earth, is itself the sharpest measure of our involvement. It is not human arrogance that has taken us in this direction, but the most natural of natural events. We developed this way, we grew this way, we are this kind of species.

We have become, in a painful, unwished-for way, nature itself. We have grown into everywhere, spreading like a new growth over the entire surface, touching and affecting every other kind of life, incorporating ourselves. The earth risks being eutrophied by us. We are now the dominant feature of our own environment. Human beings, large terrestrial metazoans,[2] fired by energy from microbial symbionts[3] lodged in their cells, instructed by tapes of nucleic acid stretching back to the earliest live membranes, informed by neurons essentially the same as all the other neurons on earth, sharing structures with mastodons and lichens, living off the sun, are now in charge, running the place, for better or worse.

10

---

[2] Multicellular animals. —Eds.

[3] A microbial symbiont is an organism that shares a symbiotic relationship with another, usually larger, organism (its host). —Eds.

JIM WATSON/Getty Images

Shown here is a picture of an anti-global warming protester at the 2016 Republican National Convention. **How does Lewis Thomas's argument relate to the message this protester conveys?**

Or is it really this way? It could be, you know, just the other way round. Perhaps we are the invaded ones, the subjugated, used.

Certain animals in the sea live by becoming part animal, part plant. They engulf algae, which then establish themselves as complex plant tissues, essential for the life of the whole company. I suppose the giant clam, if he had more of a mind, would have moments of dismay on seeing what he has done to the plant world, incorporating so much of it, enslaving green cells, living off the photosynthesis. But the plant cells would take a different view of it, having captured the clam on the most satisfactory of terms, including the small lenses in his tissues that focus sunlight for their benefit; perhaps algae have bad moments about what they may collectively be doing to the world of clams.

With luck, our own situation might be similar, on a larger scale. This might turn out to be a special phase in the morphogenesis of the earth when it is necessary to have something like us, for a time anyway, to fetch and carry energy, look after new symbiotic arrangements, store up information for some future season, do a certain amount of ornamenting, maybe even carry seeds around the solar system. That kind of thing. Handyman for the earth.

I would much prefer this useful role, if I had any say, to the essentially unearthly creature we seem otherwise on the way to becoming. It would mean making some quite fundamental changes in our attitudes toward each other, if we were really to think of ourselves as indispensable elements of nature. We would surely become the environment to worry about the most. We would discover, in ourselves, the sources of wonderment and delight that we have discerned in all other manifestations of nature. Who knows, we might even acknowledge the fragility and vulnerability that always accompany high specialization in biology, and movements might start up for the protection of ourselves as a valuable, endangered species. We couldn't lose.

[1989]

15

EXPLORING THE TEXT

1. What is Lewis Thomas's complaint in the first paragraph? What does he find "disquieting"? Do you see evidence today of the trend that Thomas bemoans? Do you find it disquieting, or do you have a different perspective? Explain your response.

2. The first Earth Day celebration was on April 22, 1970, and it became international in 1990. Considering the increased environmental awareness we have experienced since the 1970s, have we achieved the "revolution for human thought" (para. 2) that Thomas mentions?

3. What is Thomas's attitude toward the preference he alludes to in paragraph 6?

4. Why does Thomas regard the recognition that we are masters as a "despairing prospect" (para. 9)?

5. How many times does Thomas use the pronoun "we"? What is its effect?

6. Do you agree with Thomas that "the earth risks being eutrophied" (para. 11)? Explain your response.

7. Note the appositive for human beings that Thomas uses in paragraph 11. How does such a characterization affect the reader? How does it affect Thomas's argument?

8. What rhetorical relationship does paragraph 13 have with paragraph 12?

9. What are the implications of the analogy Thomas develops in paragraph 13? How effectively does it serve his purpose? Explain your response.

The Clan of One-Breasted Women

TERRY TEMPEST WILLIAMS

Terry Tempest Williams (b. 1955) was raised in Salt Lake City, and studied at the University of Utah, where she became a professor of English. She has also been naturalist-in-residence at the Utah Museum of Natural History. Williams's work has appeared in the *New Yorker*, *Orion*, the *New York Times*, and the *Nation*. Her numerous awards include a Guggenheim Fellowship and a Lannan Literary Fellowship. Williams's writing is known for its lyricism, its open-ended approach to memoir, and its focus on environmental and social issues. Among her most well-known books are *An Unspoken Hunger: Stories from the Field* (1995), *Finding Beauty in a Broken World* (2008), *When Women Were Birds* (2012), *The Hour of Land: A Personal Topography of America's National Parks* (2016), and *Refuge: An Unnatural History of Family and Place* (1989). The following selection is taken from *Refuge*, and is based on her family's experience in Utah.

I belong to a Clan of One-breasted Women. My mother, my grandmothers, and six aunts have all had mastectomies. Seven are dead. The two who survive have just completed rounds of chemotherapy and radiation.

I've had my own problems: two biopsies for breast cancer and a small tumor between my ribs diagnosed as "a border-line malignancy."

This is my family history.

Most statistics tell us breast cancer is genetic, hereditary, with rising percentages attached to fatty diets, childlessness, or becoming pregnant after thirty. What they don't say is living in Utah may be the greatest hazard of all.

We are a Mormon family with roots in Utah since 1847. The word-of-wisdom, a religious doctrine of health, kept the women in my family aligned with good foods: no coffee, no tea, tobacco, or alcohol. For the most part, these women were finished having their babies by the time they were thirty. And only one faced breast cancer prior to 1960. Traditionally, as a group of people, Mormons have a low rate of cancer.

Is our family a cultural anomaly? The truth is we didn't think about it. Those who did, usually the men, simply said, "bad genes." The women's attitude was stoic. Cancer was part of life. On February 16, 1971, the eve before my mother's surgery, I accidently picked up the telephone and overheard her ask my grandmother what she could expect.

"Diane, it is one of the most spiritual experiences you will ever encounter."

I quietly put down the receiver.

Two days later, my father took my three brothers and me to the hospital to visit her. She met us in the lobby in a wheelchair. No bandages

This photograph was taken at a 1970 vigil outside of a nuclear weapons production facility run by the Atomic Energy Commission (AEC) and operated by Dow Chemical. The protesters were attempting to bring public attention to evidence that the AEC was knowingly endangering the public with radiation pollution. **What does this photo suggest about public knowledge and opinion of nuclear weapons production and testing?**

Dave Buresh/Getty Images

in natural gas lines for towns in southern Utah. He spoke of his love for the country: the sand-stoned landscape, bare-boned and beautiful. He had just finished hiking the Kolob trail in Zion National Park. We got caught up in reminiscing, recalling with fondness our walk up Angel's Landing on his fiftieth birthday and the years our family had vacationed there. This was a remembered landscape where we had been raised.

Over dessert, I shared a recurring dream of mine. I told my father that for years, as long as I could remember, I saw this flash of light in the night in the desert. That this image had so permeated my being, I could not venture south without seeing it again, on the horizon, illuminating buttes and mesas.

"You did see it," he said.

"Saw what?" I asked, a bit tentative.   *15*

"The bomb. The cloud. We were driving home from Riverside, California. You were sitting on your mother's lap. She was pregnant. In fact, I remember the date, September 7, 1957. We had just gotten out of the Service. We were driving north, past Las Vegas. It was an hour or so before dawn, when this explosion went off. We not only heard it, but felt it. I thought the oil tanker in front of us had blown up. We pulled over and suddenly, rising from the desert floor, we saw it, clearly, this golden-stemmed cloud, the mushroom. The sky seemed to vibrate with an eerie pink glow. Within a few minutes, a light ash was raining on the car."

I stared at my father. This was new information to me.

"I thought you knew that," my father said. "It was a common occurrence in the fifties."

It was at this moment I realized the deceit I had been living under. Children growing up in the American Southwest, drinking contaminated milk from contaminated cows, even from the contaminated breasts of their mother, my mother — members, years later, of the Clan of One-breasted Women.

were visible. I'll never forget her radiance, the way she held herself in a purple velour robe and how she gathered us around her.

"Children, I am fine. I want you to know I felt   *10* the arms of God around me."

We believed her. My father cried. Our mother, his wife, was thirty-eight years old.

Two years ago, after my mother's death from cancer, my father and I were having dinner together. He had just returned from St. George where his construction company was putting

• • •

It is a well-known story in the Desert West, "The Day We Bombed Utah," or perhaps, "The Years We Bombed Utah."[1] Above ground atomic testing in Nevada took place from January 27, 1951, through July 11, 1962. Not only were the winds blowing north, covering "low use segments of the population" with fallout and leaving sheep dead in their tracks, but the climate was right. The United States of the 1950s was red, white, and blue. The Korean War was raging. McCarthyism was rampant. Ike was it and the Cold War was hot. If you were against nuclear testing, you were for a Communist regime.

Much has been written about this "American nuclear tragedy." Public health was secondary to national security. The Atomic Energy Commissioner, Thomas Murray said, "Gentlemen, we must not let anything interfere with this series of tests, nothing."[2]

Again and again, the American public was told by its government, in spite of burns, blisters, and nausea, "It has been found that the tests may be conducted with adequate assurance of safety under conditions prevailing at the bombing reservations."[3] Assuaging public fears was simply a matter of public relations. "Your best action," an Atomic Energy Commission booklet read, "is not to be worried about fallout." A news release typical of the times stated, "We find no basis for concluding that harm to any individual has resulted from radioactive fallout."[4]

On August 30, 1979, during Jimmy Carter's presidency, a suit was filed entitled "Irene Allen vs. the United States of America." Mrs. Allen was the first to be alphabetically listed with

20

Shown here is an announcement of the Atomic Energy Commission's intent to test atomic weapons at the Las Vegas Bombing and Gunnery Range in 1951.
What do you notice about the tone and content of the announcement? How could it be used as evidence for Williams's claims?

WARNING

January 11, 1951

From this day forward the U. S. Atomic Energy Commission has been authorized to use part of the Las Vegas Bombing and Gunnery Range for test work necessary to the atomic weapons development program.

Test activities will include experimental nuclear detonations for the development of atomic bombs — so-called "A-Bombs" — carried out under controlled conditions.

Tests will be conducted on a routine basis for an indefinite period.

NO PUBLIC ANNOUNCEMENT OF THE TIME OF ANY TEST WILL BE MADE

Unauthorized persons who pass inside the limits of the Las Vegas Bombing and Gunnery Range may be subject to injury from or as a result of the AEC test activities.

Health and safety authorities have determined that no danger from or as a result of AEC test activities may be expected outside the limits of the Las Vegas Bombing and Gunnery Range. All necessary precautions, including radiological surveys and patrolling of the surrounding territory, will be undertaken to insure that safety conditions are maintained.

Full security restrictions of the Atomic Energy Act will apply to the work in this area.

RALPH P. JOHNSON, Project Manager
Las Vegas Project Office
U. S. Atomic Energy Commission

Nevada Test Site Guide January 11, 1951, a publication of the United States Atomic Energy Commission

twenty-four test cases, representative of nearly 1200 plaintiffs seeking compensation from the United States government for cancers caused from nuclear testing in Nevada.

Irene Allen lived in Hurricane, Utah. She was the mother of five children and had been widowed twice. Her first husband with their two oldest boys had watched the tests from the roof of the local high school. He died of leukemia in 1956. Her second husband died of pancreatic cancer in 1978.

---

[1] Fuller, John G., *The Day We Bombed Utah* (New York: New American Library, 1984).

[2] Szasz, Ferenc M., "Downwind from the Bomb," *Nevada Historical Society Quarterly*, Fall 1987, Vol. XXX, No. 3, p. 185.

[3] Fradkin, Philip L., *Fallout* (Tucson: University of Arizona Press, 1989), 98.

[4] Ibid., 109.

RJ Sangosti/Getty Images

Though Terry Tempest Williams first wrote "The Clan of One-Breasted Women" in 1991, this photograph was taken during a packed meeting about the results of a 2016 health survey taken by residents who lived downwind of the former Rocky Flats Nuclear Weapons Plant near Denver, Colorado.
How does this image add to your understanding of Williams's central argument?

In a town meeting conducted by Utah Senator Orrin Hatch, shortly before the suit was filed, Mrs. Allen said, "I am not blaming the government, I want you to know that, Senator Hatch. But I thought if my testimony could help in any way so this wouldn't happen again to any of the generations coming up after us . . . I am really happy to be here this day to bear testimony of this."[5]

God-fearing people. This is just one story in an anthology of thousands.

On May 10, 1984, Judge Bruce S. Jenkins handed down his opinion. Ten of the plaintiffs were awarded damages. It was the first time a federal court had determined that nuclear tests had been the cause of cancers. For the remaining fourteen test cases, the proof of causation was not sufficient. In spite of the split decision, it was considered a landmark ruling.[6] It was not to remain so for long.

In April, 1987, the 10th Circuit Court of Appeals overturned Judge Jenkins' ruling on the basis that the United States was protected from suit by the legal doctrine of sovereign immunity, the centuries-old idea from England in the days of absolute monarchs.[7]

25 In January, 1988, the Supreme Court refused to review the Appeals Court decision. To our court system, it does not matter whether the United States Government was irresponsible, whether it lied to its citizens or even that citizens died from the fallout of nuclear testing. What matters is that our government is immune. "The King can do no wrong."

◆ ◆ ◆

30 In Mormon culture, authority is respected, obedience is revered, and independent thinking is not. I was taught as a young girl not to "make waves" or "rock the boat."

"Just let it go — " my mother would say. "You know how you feel, that's what counts."

For many years, I did just that — listened, observed, and quietly formed my own opinions within a culture that rarely asked questions because they had all the answers. But one by one, I watched the women in my family die common, heroic deaths. We sat in waiting rooms hoping for good news, always receiving the bad. I cared for them, bathed their scarred bodies and kept their secrets. I watched beautiful women become bald as cytoxan, cisplatin and adriamycin were injected into their veins. I held their foreheads

[5] Town meeting held by Senator Orrin Hatch in St. George, Utah, April 17, 1979, transcript, 26–28.

[6] Fradkin, op. cit., 228.

[7] U.S. vs. Allen, 816 Federal Reporter, 2d/1417 (10th Circuit Court 1987), cert. denied, 108 S. Ct. 694 (1988).

seeing connections

Shown here are two caricatures of the atomic bomb, both drawn in 1945. How does each one characterize atomic power?

In what ways does Williams's essay support — or challenge — the viewpoints expressed here?

Photo 12/Getty Images

Photo 12/Getty Images

as they vomited green-black bile and I shot them with morphine when the pain became inhuman. In the end, I witnessed their last peaceful breaths, becoming a midwife to the rebirth of their souls. But the price of obedience became too high.

The fear and inability to question authority that ultimately killed rural communities in Utah during atmospheric testing of atomic weapons was the same fear I saw being held in my mother's body. Sheep. Dead sheep. The evidence is buried.

I cannot prove that my mother, Diane Dixon Tempest, or my grandmothers, Lettie Romney Dixon and Kathryn Blackett Tempest, along with my aunts contracted cancer from nuclear fallout in Utah. But I can't prove they didn't.

My father's memory was correct, the   35
September blast we drove through in 1957 was part of Operation Plumbbob, one of the most intensive series of bomb tests to be initiated. The flash of light in the night in the desert I had always thought was a dream developed

into a family nightmare. It took fourteen years, from 1957 to 1971, for cancer to show up in my mother — the same time, Howard L. Andrews, an authority on radioactive fallout at the National Institutes of Health, says radiation cancer requires to become evident.[8] The more I learn about what it means to be a "downwinder," the more questions I drown in.

What I do know, however, is that as a Mormon woman of the fifth generation of "Latter-Day-Saints," I must question everything, even if it means losing my faith, even if it means becoming a member of a border tribe among my own people. Tolerating blind obedience in the name of patriotism or religion ultimately takes our lives.

When the Atomic Energy Commission described the country north of the Nevada Test Site as "virtually uninhabited desert terrain," my family members were some of the "virtual uninhabitants."

———————
[8] Fradkin, op. cit., 116.

◆ ◆ ◆

One night, I dreamed women from all over the world were circling a blazing fire in the desert. They spoke of change, of how they hold the moon in their bellies and wax and wane with its phases. They mocked at the presumption of even-tempered beings and made promises that they would never fear the witch inside themselves. The women danced wildly as sparks broke away from the flames and entered the night sky as stars.

And they sang a song given to them by Shoshoni grandmothers:

> *Ah ne nah, nah*
> *nin nah nah —*
> *Ah ne nah, nah*
> *nin nah nah —*
> *Nyaga mutzi*
> *oh ne nay —*
> *Nyaga mutzi*
> *oh ne nay —* [9]

The women danced and drummed and sang ⁴⁰ for weeks, preparing themselves for what was to come. They would reclaim the desert for the sake of their children, for the sake of the land.

A few miles downwind from the fire circle, bombs were being tested. Rabbits felt the tremors. Their soft leather pads on paws and feet recognized the shaking sands while the roots of mesquite and sage were smoldering. Rocks were hot from the inside out and dust devils hummed unnaturally. And each time there was another nuclear test, ravens watched the desert heave. Stretch marks appeared. The land was losing its muscle.

The women couldn't bear it any longer. They were mothers. They had suffered labor pains but always under the promise of birth. The red hot pains beneath the desert promised death only as each bomb became a stillborn. A contract had been broken between human beings and the land. A new contract was being drawn by the women who understood the fate of the earth as their own.

Under the cover of darkness, ten women slipped under the barbed wire fence and entered the contaminated country. They were trespassing. They walked toward the town of Mercury in moonlight, taking their cues from coyote, kit fox, antelope squirrel, and quail. They moved quietly and deliberately through the maze of Joshua trees. When a hint of daylight appeared they rested, drinking tea and sharing their rations of food. The women closed their eyes. The time had come to protest with the heart, that to deny one's genealogy with the earth was to commit treason against one's soul.

At dawn, the women draped themselves in mylar, wrapping long streamers of silver plastic around their arms to blow in the breeze. They wore clear masks that became the faces of humanity. And when they arrived on the edge of Mercury, they carried all the butterflies of a summer day in their wombs. They paused to allow their courage to settle.

The town which forbids pregnant women ⁴⁵ and children to enter because of radiation risks to their health was asleep. The women moved through the streets as winged messengers, twirling around each other in slow motion, peeking inside homes and watching the easy sleep of men and women. They were astonished by such stillness and periodically would utter a shrill note or low cry just to verify life.

The residents finally awoke to what appeared as strange apparitions. Some simply stared. Others called authorities, and in time, the women were apprehended by wary soldiers dressed in desert fatigues. They were taken to a white, square building on the other edge of Mercury. When asked who they were and why they were there, the women replied, "We are mothers and we have come to reclaim the desert for our children."

---

[9] This song was sung by the Western Shoshone women as they crossed the line at the Nevada Test Site on March 18, 1988, as part of their "Reclaim the Land" action. The translation they gave was: "Consider the rabbits how gently they walk on the earth. Consider the rabbits how gently they walk on the earth. We remember them. We can walk gently also. We remember them. We can walk gently also."

The soldiers arrested them. As the ten women were blindfolded and handcuffed, they began singing:

> You can't forbid us everything
> You can't forbid us to think —
> You can't forbid our tears to flow
> And you can't stop the songs that we sing.

The women continued to sing louder and louder, until they heard the voices of their sisters moving across the mesa.

> Ah ne nah, nah
> nin nah nah —
> Ah ne nah, nah
> nin nah nah —
> Nyaga mutzi
> oh ne nay —
> Nyaga mutzi
> oh ne nay —

"Call for re-enforcement," one soldier said.

"We have," interrupted one woman. "We have — and you have no idea of our numbers."　　50

◆ ◆ ◆

On March 18, 1988, I crossed the line at the Nevada Test Site and was arrested with nine other Utahns for trespassing on military lands. They are still conducting nuclear tests in the desert. Ours was an act of civil disobedience. But as I walked toward the town of Mercury, it was more than a gesture of peace. It was a gesture on behalf of the Clan of One-breasted Women.

As one officer cinched the handcuffs around my wrists, another frisked my body. She found a pen and a pad of paper tucked inside my left boot.

"And these?" she asked sternly.

"Weapons," I replied.

Our eyes met. I smiled. She pulled the leg of　　55 my trousers back over my boot.

"Step forward, please," she said as she took my arm.

We were booked under an afternoon sun and bused to Tonapah, Nevada. It was a two-hour ride. This was familiar country to me. The Joshua trees standing their ground had been named by my ancestors who believed they looked like prophets

▼
Shown here is a sculpture of an atomic mushroom cloud constructed of chain links, located at Santa Monica Civic Center.

What do the message of this sculpture and "The Clan of One-Breasted Women" have in common?

Ken Hively/Getty Images

pointing west to the promised land. These were the same trees that bloomed each spring, flowers appearing like white flames in the Mojave. And I recalled a full moon in May when my mother and I had walked among them, flushing out mourning doves and owls.

The bus stopped short of town. We were released. The officials thought it was a cruel joke to leave us stranded in the desert with no way to get home. What they didn't realize is that we were home, soul-centered and strong, women who recognized the sweet smell of sage as fuel for our spirits.

[1991]

EXPLORING THE TEXT

1. The first section of the essay (paras. 1–19) begins and ends with a reference to the title. Why do you think Terry Tempest Williams frames this section this way? How does it affect the tone?

2. Williams claims that "[t]raditionally, as a group of people, Mormons have a low rate of cancer" (para. 5). What are some of the possible reasons for this?

3. Research the story that a group of women warriors called the Amazons each slashed off one breast to get better leverage when using bow and arrow. How effectively does Williams use the reference to this legend?

4. What is the effect of repeating the word *contaminated* three times in paragraph 19?

5. At paragraph 20, why does Williams interrupt the story of her own family's illness to begin to tell the story of Irene Allen and her family?

6. Williams says in paragraph 22, "Assuaging public fears was simply a matter of public relations" by the government. What does she mean? Is she

being ironic, or is she giving a matter-of-fact description of public policy at the time? Explain your response.

7. Why does Williams put a section break between paragraphs 29 and 30? Why is there no smooth transition from the Supreme Court case to Mormon culture?

8. How does footnote 9 differ from the others?

9. What is the effect of the footnotes Williams includes and of the reference to the National Institutes of Health in paragraph 35?

10. In paragraph 43, Williams writes, "The time had come to protest with the heart, that to deny one's genealogy with the earth was to commit treason against one's soul." What underlying assumption connects her support to this claim?

11. In paragraphs 43 and 58, how does Williams give the impression of a spiritual presence in nature?

12. What is the rhetorical effect of shifting among narration, exposition, and argument in this essay?

Nobel Prize Lecture

WANGARI MAATHAI

Wangari Muta Maathai (1940–2011) was a Nobel Peace Prize–winning activist and environmentalist who was also the first woman from central or eastern Africa to earn a PhD. Born in Kenya, she was educated there and at Mount St. Scholastica College in Atchison, Kansas, and at the University of Pittsburgh. Maathai founded the Green Belt Movement in 1977, which has planted tens of millions of trees on farms and at schools and churches in Kenya. Other African countries have since adopted the movement's methods. In 1991, when Maathai was arrested and imprisoned, the first of many times, for her revolutionary environmental activities, an Amnesty International letter-writing campaign helped free her. She went on to become one of the most effective environmental activists in the world, accepting a position as visiting fellow at Yale University in 2002 and receiving the Nobel Peace Prize in 2004. Maathai was later elected to parliament and served as deputy minister of the environment, natural resources, and wildlife in Kenya. Over the course of her life, Maathai wrote many books, including her memoir *Unbowed* (2006), *The Challenge for Africa* (2010), and *Replenishing the Earth* (2010). The following is Maathai's acceptance speech for the 2004 Nobel Peace Prize.

Your Majesties

Your Royal Highnesses

Honourable Members of the Norwegian Nobel
    Committee

Excellencies

Ladies and Gentlemen

I stand before you and the world humbled by this recognition and uplifted by the honour of being the 2004 Nobel Peace Laureate.

As the first African woman to receive this prize, I accept it on behalf of the people of Kenya and Africa, and indeed the world. I am especially mindful of women and the girl child. I hope it will encourage them to raise their voices and take more space for leadership. I know the honour also gives a deep sense of pride to our men, both old and young. As a mother, I appreciate the inspiration this brings to the youth and urge them to use it to pursue their dreams.

Although this prize comes to me, it acknowledges the work of countless individuals and groups across the globe. They work quietly and often without recognition to protect the environment, promote democracy, defend human rights and ensure equality between women and men. By so doing, they plant seeds of peace. I know they, too,

are proud today. To all who feel represented by this prize I say use it to advance your mission and meet the high expectations the world will place on us.

This honour is also for my family, friends, partners and supporters throughout the world. All of them helped shape the vision and sustain our work, which was often accomplished under hostile conditions. I am also grateful to the people of Kenya — who remained stubbornly hopeful that democracy could be realized and their environment managed sustainably. Because of this support, I am here today to accept this great honour.

I am immensely privileged to join my fellow African Peace laureates, Presidents Nelson Mandela and F. W. de Klerk, Archbishop Desmond Tutu, the late Chief Albert Luthuli, the late Anwar el-Sadat and the UN Secretary General, Kofi Annan.

I know that African people everywhere are encouraged by this news. My fellow Africans, as we embrace this recognition, let us use it to intensify our commitment to our people, to reduce conflicts and poverty and thereby improve their quality of life. Let us embrace democratic governance, protect human rights and

5

© Ionut Brigle/Greenpeace

This photograph was taken at a 2017 Greenpeace protest in Romania. **How do you interpret the meaning of this sign? How might you support the claim it makes with details from Maathai's speech?**

protect our environment. I am confident that we shall rise to the occasion. I have always believed that solutions to most of our problems must come from us.

In this year's prize, the Norwegian Nobel Committee has placed the critical issue of environment and its linkage to democracy and peace before the world. For their visionary action, I am profoundly grateful. Recognizing that sustainable development, democracy and peace are indivisible is an idea whose time has come. Our work over the past 30 years has always appreciated and engaged these linkages.

My inspiration partly comes from my childhood experiences and observations of Nature in rural Kenya. It has been influenced and nurtured by the formal education I was privileged to receive in Kenya, the United States and Germany. As I was growing up, I witnessed forests being cleared and replaced by commercial plantations, which destroyed local biodiversity and the capacity of the forests to conserve water.

Excellencies, ladies and gentlemen,

In 1977, when we started the Green Belt Movement, I was partly responding to needs identified by rural women, namely lack of firewood, clean drinking water, balanced diets, shelter and income.

Throughout Africa, women are the primary caretakers, holding significant responsibility for tilling the land and feeding their families. As a result, they are often the first to become aware of environmental damage as resources become scarce and incapable of sustaining their families.

The women we worked with recounted that unlike in the past, they were unable to meet their basic needs. This was due to the degradation of their immediate environment as well as the introduction of commercial farming, which replaced the growing of household food crops. But international trade controlled the price of the exports from these small-scale farmers and a reasonable and just income could not be guaranteed. I came to understand that when the environment is destroyed, plundered or mismanaged, we

undermine our quality of life and that of future generations.

Tree planting became a natural choice to address some of the initial basic needs identified by women. Also, tree planting is simple, attainable and guarantees quick, successful results within a reasonable amount of time. This sustains interest and commitment.

So, together, we have planted over 30 million trees that provide fuel, food, shelter, and income to support their children's education and household needs. The activity also creates employment and improves soils and watersheds. Through their involvement, women gain some degree of power over their lives, especially their social and economic position and relevance in the family. This work continues.

Initially, the work was difficult because historically our people have been persuaded to believe that because they are poor, they lack not only capital, but also knowledge and skills to address their challenges. Instead they are conditioned to believe that solutions to their problems must come from "outside." Further, women did not realize that meeting their needs depended on their environment being healthy and well managed. They were also unaware that a degraded environment leads to a scramble for scarce resources and may culminate in poverty and even conflict. They were also unaware of the injustices of international economic arrangements.

In order to assist communities to understand these linkages, we developed a citizen education program, during which people identify their problems, the causes and possible solutions. They then make connections between their own personal actions and the problems they witness in the environment and in society. They learn that our world is confronted with a litany of woes: corruption, violence against women and children, disruption and breakdown of families, and disintegration of cultures and communities. They also identify the abuse of drugs and chemical

Africans' Views on Urbanization and Sustainability

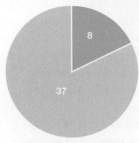

Are urbanization trends in your country ecologically sustainable?

Are urbanization trends in your country socially sustainable?

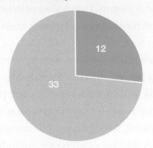

Are urbanization trends in your country economically sustainable?

■ Yes   ■ No

Data from the 2016 African Economic Outlook report.

These graphs use data from the 2016 African Economic Outlook report, which addresses sustainable cities and structural transformation. Economists from 45 African countries responded.
How could the data in these graphs be used to support Maathai's argument?

substances, especially among young people. There are also devastating diseases that are defying cures or occurring in epidemic proportions. Of particular concern are HIV/AIDS, malaria and diseases associated with malnutrition.

On the environment front, they are exposed to many human activities that are devastating to the environment and societies. These include widespread destruction of ecosystems, especially through deforestation, climatic instability, and contamination in the soils and waters that all contribute to excruciating poverty.

In the process, the participants discover that they must be part of the solutions. They realize their hidden potential and are empowered to overcome inertia and take action. They come to recognize that they are the primary custodians and beneficiaries of the environment that sustains them.

Entire communities also come to understand that while it is necessary to hold their governments accountable, it is equally important that in their own relationships with each other, they exemplify the leadership values they wish to see

in their own leaders, namely justice, integrity and trust.

Although initially the Green Belt Movement's 20 tree planting activities did not address issues of democracy and peace, it soon became clear that responsible governance of the environment was impossible without democratic space. Therefore, the tree became a symbol for the democratic struggle in Kenya. Citizens were mobilised to challenge widespread abuses of power, corruption and environmental mismanagement. In Nairobi's Uhuru Park, at Freedom Corner, and in many parts of the country, trees of peace were planted to demand the release of prisoners of conscience and a peaceful transition to democracy.

Through the Green Belt Movement, thousands of ordinary citizens were mobilized and empowered to take action and effect change. They learned to overcome fear and a sense of helplessness and moved to defend democratic rights.

In time, the tree also became a symbol for peace and conflict resolution, especially during ethnic conflicts in Kenya when the Green Belt Movement used peace trees to reconcile disputing communities. During the ongoing rewriting of the Kenyan constitution, similar trees of peace were planted in many parts of the country to promote a culture of peace. Using trees as a symbol of peace is in keeping with a widespread African tradition. For example, the elders of the Kikuyu carried a staff from the thigi tree that, when placed between two disputing sides, caused them to stop fighting and seek reconciliation. Many communities in Africa have these traditions.

Such practises are part of an extensive cultural heritage, which contributes both to the conservation of habitats and to cultures of peace. With the destruction of these cultures and the introduction of new values, local biodiversity is no longer valued or protected, and as a result, it is quickly degraded and disappears. For this reason, the Green Belt Movement explores the concept of cultural biodiversity, especially with respect to indigenous seeds and medicinal plants.

As we progressively understood the causes of environmental degradation, we saw the need for good governance. Indeed, the state of any county's environment is a reflection of the kind of governance in place, and without good governance there can be no peace. Many countries, which have poor governance systems, are also likely to have conflicts and poor laws protecting the environment.

In 2002, the courage, resilience, patience and commitment of members of the Green Belt Movement, other civil society organizations, and the Kenyan public culminated in the peaceful transition to a democratic government and laid the foundation for a more stable society.

Excellencies, friends, ladies and gentlemen,

It is 30 years since we started this work. Activities that devastate the environment and societies continue unabated. Today we are faced with a challenge that calls for a shift in our thinking, so that humanity stops threatening its life-support system. We are called to assist the Earth to heal her wounds and in the process heal our own — indeed, to embrace the whole creation in all its diversity, beauty and wonder. This will happen if we see the need to revive our sense of belonging to a larger family of life, with which we have shared our evolutionary process.

In the course of history, there comes a time when humanity is called to shift to a new level of consciousness, to reach a higher moral ground. A time when we have to shed our fear and give hope to each other.

That time is now.

25

SIMON MAINA/Getty Images

This 1999 photograph, taken in Nairobi, depicts a confrontation between Wangari Maathai and security hired to keep her and other Green Belt Movement protesters from planting trees in a section of the Karura Forest that had been allocated to private developers. After being injured by the security guards, Maathai was hospitalized with a head wound. **How does the photographer portray Maathai here? How does this portrayal inform your understanding of the tone and content of her Nobel speech?**

The Norwegian Nobel Committee has ³⁰ challenged the world to broaden the understanding of peace: there can be no peace without equitable development; and there can be no development without sustainable management of the environment in a democratic and peaceful space. This shift is an idea whose time has come.

I call on leaders, especially from Africa, to expand democratic space and build fair and just societies that allow the creativity and energy of their citizens to flourish. Those of us who have been privileged to receive education, skills, and experiences and even power must be role models for the next generation of leadership. In this regard, I would also like to appeal for the freedom of my fellow laureate Aung San Suu Kyi[1] so that she can continue her work for peace and democracy for the people of Burma and the world at large.

Culture plays a central role in the political, economic and social life of communities. Indeed, culture may be the missing link in the development of Africa. Culture is dynamic and evolves over time, consciously discarding retrogressive traditions, like female genital mutilation (FGM), and embracing aspects that are good and useful.

Africans, especially, should rediscover positive aspects of their culture. In accepting them, they would give themselves a sense of belonging, identity and self-confidence.

Ladies and Gentlemen,

There is also need to galvanize civil society ³⁵ and grassroots movements to catalyse change. I call upon governments to recognize the role of these social movements in building a critical mass of responsible citizens, who help maintain checks and balances in society. On their part,

civil society should embrace not only their rights but also their responsibilities.

Further, industry and global institutions must appreciate that ensuring economic justice, equity and ecological integrity are of greater value than profits at any cost. The extreme global inequities and prevailing consumption patterns continue at the expense of the environment and peaceful co-existence. The choice is ours.

I would like to call on young people to commit themselves to activities that contribute toward achieving their long-term dreams. They have the energy and creativity to shape a sustainable future. To the young people I say, you are a gift to your communities and indeed the world. You are our hope and our future.

The holistic approach to development, as exemplified by the Green Belt Movement, could be embraced and replicated in more parts of Africa and beyond. It is for this reason that I have established the Wangari Maathai Foundation to ensure the continuation and expansion of these activities. Although a lot has been achieved, much remains to be done.

Excellencies, ladies and gentlemen,

As I conclude I reflect on my childhood experi- ⁴⁰ ence when I would visit a stream next to our home to fetch water for my mother. I would drink water straight from the stream. Playing among the arrowroot leaves I tried in vain to pick up the strands of frogs' eggs, believing they were beads. But every time I put my little fingers under them they would break. Later, I saw thousands of tadpoles: black, energetic and wriggling through the clear water against the background of the brown earth. This is the world I inherited from my parents.

Today, over 50 years later, the stream has dried up, women walk long distances for water, which is not always clean, and children will never know what they have lost. The challenge is to restore the home of the tadpoles and give back to our children a world of beauty and wonder.

Thank you very much.

[2004]

---

[1] A Burmese author and politician who was imprisoned under house arrest from 1989 to 2010. She is now the Foreign Minister and State Counsellor of Myanmar. At the time Matthaai made this speech, and for several years after, Suu Kyi was a civil rights icon. However, her denial of the ethnic cleansing of the Rohingya people in recent years has drawn significant criticism, and some believe her Nobel Peace Prize should be revoked. —Eds.

EXPLORING THE TEXT

1. Wangari Muta Maathai addresses her audience several times, at the beginning of her speech and again in paragraphs 9, 26, 34, and 39. What is the purpose of this repetition? Does each address serve a unique purpose, or are the purposes all the same? Do you think the occasion affected Maathai's decision to use multiple addresses? Explain.

2. In accepting the Nobel Peace Prize, Maathai discusses democracy and the natural environment more than she discusses peace. Explain why you do or do not agree that they are inextricably linked to peace, as she says.

3. In paragraph 12, Maathai says, "I came to understand that when the environment is destroyed, plundered or mismanaged, we undermine our quality of life and that of future generations." What is the underlying assumption that connects her claim and support in this statement?

4. Based on paragraph 15, what were the main impediments to the work of the Green Belt Movement? What is the relationship between paragraphs 15 and 16?

5. In paragraph 16, Maathai discusses the importance of education. To what extent do you agree with her views?

6. What is the rhetorical effect of recognizing, as Maathai does throughout, the power of the Nobel Peace Prize?

7. Maathai says, "[t]hat time is now" (para. 29), when discussing the need for a shift in our consciousness regarding our relationship with the natural world. Do you agree with her sense of urgency? Why or why not?

8. How does Maathai use examples from her youth, including the one about tadpoles (para. 40), to appeal to ethos?

9. How does the context of this speech — the occasion of the Nobel Peace Prize and Maathai's status as a "first" — influence its content and tone?

A Moral Atmosphere

BILL McKIBBEN

Author of a dozen books about the environment, Bill McKibben (b. 1960) grew up in Massachusetts and attended Harvard University, where he was president of the *Harvard Crimson* newspaper. After college he joined the *New Yorker*, where he was a staff writer until 1987. His first book, *The End of Nature*, was published in 1989 after being serialized in the *New Yorker*. It is regarded as the first book about climate change for a general audience and has been printed in more than twenty languages. Among McKibben's other books are *Long Distance: Testing the Limits of Body and Spirit in a Year of Living Strenuously* (2000), *Enough* (2003), *Wandering Home* (2005), *Eaarth: Making a Life on a Tough New Planet* (2010), and *Oil and Honey: The Education of an Unlikely Activist* (2013). *Time* magazine has called McKibben "the planet's best green journalist," and the *Boston Globe* has said that he is "probably the country's most important environmentalist." McKibben is currently the Schumann Distinguished Scholar in Environmental Studies at Middlebury College in Vermont. The article included here was published in *Orion* in 2013.

The list of reasons for not acting on climate change is long and ever-shifting. First it was "there's no problem"; then it was "the problem's so large there's no hope." There's "China burns stuff too," and "it would hurt the economy," and, of course, "it would hurt the economy." The

Benjamin Schwartz/The New Yorker Collection/The Cartoon Bank

How can this cartoon be
read as a comment on the
arguments against McKibben's
environmentalist activism tour?

*"I recognize that climate change is a complex subject with
multiple causes, but this really isn't helping."*

excuses are getting tired, though. Post Sandy[1] (which hurt the economy to the tune of $100 billion) and the drought ($150 billion), 74 percent of Americans have decided they're very concerned about climate change and want something to happen.

But still, there's one reason that never goes away, one evergreen excuse not to act: "you're a hypocrite." I've heard it ten thousand times myself — how can you complain about climate change and drive a car/have a house/turn on a light/raise a child? This past fall, as I headed across the country on a bus tour to push for divestment from fossil fuels, local newspapers covered each stop. I could predict, with great confidence, what the first online comment from a reader following each account would be: "Do these morons not know that their bus takes gasoline?" In fact, our bus took biodiesel — as we headed down the East Coast, one job was watching the web app that showed the nearest

station pumping the good stuff. But it didn't matter, because the next comment would be: "Don't these morons know that the plastic fittings on their bus, and the tires, and the seats are all made from fossil fuels?"

Actually, I do know — even a moron like me. I'm fully aware that we're embedded in the world that fossil fuel has made, that from the moment I wake up, almost every action I take somehow burns coal and gas and oil. I've done my best, at my house, to curtail it: we've got solar electricity, and solar hot water, and my new car runs on electricity — I can plug it into the roof and thus into the sun. But I try not to confuse myself into thinking that's helping all that much: it took energy to make the car, and to make everything else that streams into my life. I'm still using far more than any responsible share of the world's vital stuff.

And, in a sense, that's the point. If those of us who are trying really hard are still fully enmeshed in the fossil fuel system, it makes it even clearer that what needs to change are not individuals but precisely that system. We simply can't move fast enough, one by one, to make any

---

[1] A Category 3 hurricane that damaged twenty-four states on the East Coast of America in October 2012; known as the second-costliest hurricane in American history. —Eds.

Leo Cullum/The New Yorker Collection/The Cartoon Bank

How does this cartoon illustrate the cause of the "psychic tension" (para. 6) McKibben describes?

"It saves energy and makes me feel holier."

real difference in how the atmosphere comes out. Here's the math, obviously imprecise: maybe 10 percent of the population cares enough to make strenuous efforts to change — maybe 15 percent. If they all do all they can, in their homes and offices and so forth, then, well . . . nothing much shifts. The trajectory of our climate horror stays about the same.

But if 10 percent of people, once they've changed the light bulbs, work all-out to change the system? That's enough. That's more than enough. It would be enough to match the power of the fossil fuel industry, enough to convince our legislators to put a price on carbon. At which point none of us would be required to be saints. We could all be morons, as long as we paid attention to, say, the price of gas and the balance in our checking accounts. Which even dummies like me can manage.

I think more and more people are coming to realize this essential truth. Ten years ago,

5

half the people calling out hypocrites like me were doing it from the left, demanding that we do better. I hear much less of that now, mostly, I think, because everyone who's pursued those changes in good faith has come to realize both their importance and their limitations. Now I hear it mostly from people who have no intention of changing but are starting to feel some psychic tension. They feel a little guilty, and so they dump their guilt on Al Gore because he has two houses. Or they find even lamer targets.

For instance, as college presidents begin to feel the heat about divestment, I've heard from several who say, privately, "I'd be more inclined to listen to kids if they didn't show up at college with cars." Which in one sense is fair enough. But in another sense it's avoidance at its most extreme. Young people are asking college presidents to stand up to oil companies. (And the ones doing the loudest asking are often the most painfully idealistic, not to mention the hardest on themselves.) If as a college president you *do* stand up to oil companies, then you stand some chance of changing the outcome of the debate, of weakening the industry that has poured billions into climate denial and lobbying against science. The action you're demanding of your students — less driving — can't rationally be expected to change the outcome. The action they're demanding of you has at least some chance. That makes you immoral, not them.

Yes, they should definitely take the train to school instead of drive. But unless you're the president of Hogwarts, there's a pretty good chance there's no train that goes there. Your students, in other words, by advocating divestment, have gotten way closer to the heart of the problem than you have. They've taken the lessons they've learned in physics class and political science and sociology and economics and put them to good use. And you — because it would be uncomfortable to act, because you don't want to get crosswise with the board of trustees — have summoned a basically bogus response. If you're a college president making the argument that you won't act until your

students stop driving cars, then clearly you've failed morally, but you've also failed intellectually. Even if you just built an energy-efficient fine arts center, and installed a bike path, and dedicated an acre of land to a college garden, you've failed. Even if you drive a Prius, you've failed.

Maybe especially if you drive a Prius. Because there's a certain sense in which Prius-driving can become an out, an excuse for inaction, the twenty-first-century equivalent of "I have a lot of black friends." It's nice to walk/drive the talk; it's much smarter than driving a semi-military vehicle to get your groceries. But it's become utterly clear that doing the right thing in your personal life, or even on your campus, isn't going to get the job done in time; and it may be providing you with sufficient psychic comfort that you don't feel the need to do the hard things it will take to get the job done. It's in our role as citizens — of campuses, of nations, of the planet — that we're going to have to solve this problem. We each have our jobs, and none of them is easy.

[2013]

EXPLORING THE TEXT

1. In paragraph 1, why does Bill McKibben cite "it would hurt the economy" twice as a reason for not acting on climate change? How does this repetition help McKibben introduce his argument, and what effect does it have on the reader?

2. Consider the title of this essay. What are the connotations of the words in the title? What does this title imply about McKibben's attitude toward the subject of the essay? What is the nature of the appeal suggested by the title?

3. In paragraph 2, McKibben — adopting the voice of would-be critics — asks, "[H]ow can you complain about climate change and drive a car/have a house/turn on a light/raise a child?," "Do these morons not know that their bus takes gasoline?," and "Don't these morons know that the plastic fittings on their bus, and the tires, and the seats are all made from fossil fuels?" How convincing are these questions as criticism of McKibben's

position? What is McKibben's purpose in including them? Do they ultimately strengthen his argument? Explain why or why not.

4. In three paragraphs McKibben uses the word "moron" four times and also "dummies." How does such language affect his credibility as an author? To what extent does it undermine the strength of his argument? What does it suggest about McKibben's view of his audience's position on climate change?

5. Why does McKibben acknowledge his own complicity in contributing to climate change? How effective is this acknowledgement in building his argument?

6. How can we move from changing "individuals" to the "system," as McKibben suggests we need to? What are some specific things that we can do?

7. What is the "essential truth" that McKibben mentions in paragraph 6? Do you agree with his statement? Why or why not?

8. How would you characterize McKibben's attitude toward college presidents in paragraph 7? What purpose does the perspective shift in that paragraph serve?

9. What does McKibben mean when he says, "That makes you immoral, not them" (para. 7)? How effectively does he support that claim? Do you agree with the position McKibben takes here? Why or why not?

10. Where, according to McKibben, does responsibility for the environment lie?

11. In paragraph 9, McKibben writes, "But it's become utterly clear that doing the right thing in your personal life, or even on your campus, isn't going to get the job done in time. . . ." How effective is such a statement in developing his argument? What might be its effect on the reader? Is it persuasive? Dissuasive? Explain.

12. Is McKibben's view on society's role in protecting the environment essentially an optimistic or a pessimistic one? Explain your response.

From Billions to None

BARRY YEOMAN

Barry Yeoman is an award-winning freelance journalist living in Durham, North Carolina. His writing has appeared in numerous publications, including the *New York Times*, *Mother Jones*, *Rolling Stone*, and *Discover*. He has also earned a National Magazine Award and a Batten Medal for public-service journalism. The following article, originally published in 2014 in *Audubon*, was included in the anthology *The Best American Science and Nature Writing* (2015).

Men still live who, in their youth, remember pigeons; trees still live who, in their youth, were shaken by a living wind. But a few decades hence only the oldest oaks will remember, and at long last only the hills will know.

— Aldo Leopold, "On a Monument to the Pigeon," 1947

In May 1850 a 20-year-old Potawatomi tribal leader named Simon Pokagon was camping at the headwaters of Michigan's Manistee River during trapping season when a far-off gurgling sound startled him. It seemed as if "an army of horses laden with sleigh bells was advancing through the deep forests towards me," he later wrote. "As I listened more intently, I concluded that instead of the tramping of horses it was distant thunder; and yet the morning was clear, calm, and beautiful." The mysterious sound came "nearer and nearer," until Pokagon deduced its source: "While I gazed in wonder and astonishment, I beheld moving toward me in an unbroken front millions of pigeons, the first I had seen that season."

These were passenger pigeons, *Ectopistes migratorius,* at the time the most abundant bird in North America and possibly the world. Throughout the 19th century, witnesses had described similar sightings of pigeon migrations: how they took hours to pass over a single spot, darkening the firmament and rendering normal conversation inaudible. Pokagon remembered how sometimes a traveling flock, arriving at a deep valley, would "pour its living mass" hundreds of feet into a downward plunge. "I have stood by the grandest waterfall of America," he wrote, yet never have my astonishment, wonder, and admiration been so stirred as when I have witnessed these birds drop from their course like meteors from heaven."

Pokagon recorded these memories in 1895, more than four decades after his Manistee River observation. By then he was in the final years of his life. Passenger pigeons too were in their final years. In 1871 their great communal nesting sites had covered 850 square miles of Wisconsin's sandy oak barrens — 136 million breeding adults, naturalist A. W. Schorger later estimated. After that the population plummeted until, by the mid-1890s, wild flock sizes numbered in the dozens rather than the hundreds of millions (or even billions). Then they disappeared altogether, except for three captive breeding flocks spread across the Midwest. About September 1, 1914, the last known passenger pigeon, a female named Martha, died at the Cincinnati Zoo. She was roughly 29 years old, with a palsy that made her tremble. Not once in her life had she laid a fertile egg.

This year marks the 100th anniversary of the passenger pigeon's extinction. In the intervening years researchers have agreed that the bird was hunted out of existence, victimized by the fallacy that no amount of exploitation could endanger a creature so abundant. Between now and the end of the year, bird groups and museums will commemorate the centenary in a series of conferences, lectures, and exhibits. Most prominent among them is Project Passenger Pigeon, a wide-ranging effort by a group of scientists, artists, museum curators, and other bird lovers. While their focus is on public education, an unrelated organization called Revive & Restore is attempting something far more ambitious and controversial: using genetics to bring the bird hack.

Project Passenger Pigeon's leaders hope that by sharing the pigeon's story, they can impress upon adults and children alike our critical role in environmental conservation. "It's surprising to me how many educated people I talk to who are completely unaware that the passenger pigeon even existed," says ecologist David Blockstein, senior scientist at the National Council for Science and the Environment. "Using the centenary is a way to contemplate questions like 'How was it possible that

5

Seppo Leinonen

What does this artist imply will happen if scientists are able to successfully resurrect extinct species?

446

this extinction happened?' and `What does it say about contemporary issues like climate change?'"

◆ ◆ ◆

They were evolutionary geniuses. Traveling in fast, gargantuan flocks throughout the eastern and midwestern United states and Canada — the males slate-blue with copper undersides and hints of purple, the females more muted — passenger pigeons would search out bumper crops of acorns and beechnuts. These they would devour, using their sheer numbers to ward off enemies, a strategy known as "predator satiation." They would also outcompete other nut lovers — not only wild animals but also domestic pigs that had been set loose by farmers to forage.

In forest and city alike, an arriving flock was a spectacle — "a feathered tempest," in the words of conservationist Aldo Leopold. One 1855 account from Columbus, Ohio, described a "growing cloud" that blotted out the sun as it advanced toward the city. "Children screamed and ran for home," it said. "Women gathered their long skirts and hurried for the shelter of stores. Horses bolted. A few people mumbled frightened words about the approach of the millennium, and several dropped on their knees and prayed." When the flock had passed over, two hours later, "the town looked ghostly in the now-bright sunlight that illuminated a world plated with pigeon ejecta."

Nesting birds took over whole forests, forming what John James Audubon in 1831 called "solid masses as large as hogsheads." Observers reported trees crammed with dozens of nests apiece, collectively weighing so much that branches would snap off and trunks would topple. In 1871 some hunters coming upon the morning exodus of adult males were so overwhelmed by the sound and spectacle that some of them dropped their guns. "Imagine a thousand threshing machines running under full headway, accompanied by as many steamboats groaning off steam, with an equal quota of R.R. trains passing through covered bridges — imagine

these massed into a single flock, and you possibly have a faint conception of the terrific roar," the *Commonwealth,* a newspaper in Fond du Lac, Wisconsin, reported of that encounter.

The birds weren't just noisy. They were tasty too, and. their arrival guaranteed an abundance of free protein. "You think about this especially with the spring flocks," says Blockstein, the ecologist. "The people on the frontiers have survived the winter. They've been eating whatever food they've been able to preserve from the year before. Then, all of a sudden, here's all this fresh meat flying by you. It must have been a time for great rejoicing: the pigeons are here!" (Not everyone shouted with joy. The birds also devoured crops, frustrating farmers and prompting Baron de Lahontan, a French soldier who explored North America during the 17th century, to write that "the Bishop has been forc'd to excommunicate 'em oftner than once, upon the account of the Damage they do to the Product of the Earth.")

The flocks were so thick that hunting was easy — even waving a pole at the low-flying birds would kill some. Still, harvesting for subsistence didn't threaten the species' survival. But after the Civil War came two technological developments that set in motion the pigeon's extinction: the national expansions of the telegraph and the railroad. They enabled a commercial pigeon industry to blossom, fueled by professional sportsmen who could learn quickly about new nestings and follow the flocks around the continent. "Hardly a train arrives that does not bring hunters or trappers," reported Wisconsin's *Kilbourn City Mirror* in 1871. "Hotels are full, coopers are busy making barrels, and men, women, and children are active in packing the birds or filling the barrels. They are shipped to all places on the railroad, and to Milwaukee, Chicago, St. Louis, Cincinnati, Philadelphia, New York, and Boston."

The professionals and amateurs together outflocked their quarry with brute force. They shot the pigeons and trapped them with nets, torched their roosts, and asphyxiated them with

10

447

burning sulfur. They attacked the birds with rakes, pitchforks, and potatoes. They poisoned them with whiskey-soaked corn. Learning of some of these methods, Potawatomi leader Pokagon despaired. "These outlaws to all moral sense would touch a lighted match to the bark of the tree at the base, when with a flash — more like an explosion — the blast would reach every limb of the tree," he wrote of an 1880 massacre, describing how the scorched adults would flee and the squabs would "burst open upon hitting the ground." Witnessing this, Pokagon wondered what type of divine punishment might be "awaiting our white neighbors who have so wantonly butchered and driven from our forests these wild pigeons, the most beautiful flowers of the animal creation of North America."

Ultimately the pigeons' survival strategy — flying in huge predator-proof flocks — proved their undoing. "If you're unfortunate enough to be a species that concentrates in time and space, you make yourself very, very vulnerable," says Stanley Temple, a professor emeritus of conservation at the University of Wisconsin.

Passenger pigeons might have even survived the commercial slaughter if hunters weren't also disrupting their nesting grounds — killing some adults, driving away others, and harvesting the squabs. "It was the double whammy," says Temple. "It was the demographic nightmare of overkill and impaired reproduction. If you're killing a species far faster than they can reproduce, the end is a mathematical certainty." The last known hunting victim was "Buttons," a female, which was shot in Pike County, Ohio, in 1900 and mounted by the sheriff's wife (who used two buttons in lieu of glass eyes). Almost seven decades later a man named Press Clay Southworth took responsibility for shooting Buttons, not knowing her species, when he was a boy.

Even as the pigeons' numbers crashed, "there was virtually no effort to save them," says Joel Greenberg, a research associate with Chicago's Peggy Notebaert Nature Museum and the Field Museum. "People just slaughtered them more intensely. They killed them until the very end."

◆ ◆ ◆

Contemporary environmentalism arrived too late to prevent the passenger pigeon's demise. But the two phenomena share a historical connection. "The extinction was part of the motivation for the birth of modern twentieth-century conservation," says Temple. In 1900, even before Martha's death in the Cincinnati Zoo, Republican congressman John F. Lacey of Iowa introduced the nation's first wildlife protection law, which banned the interstate shipping of unlawfully killed game. "The wild pigeon, formerly in flocks of millions, has entirely disappeared from the face of the earth," Lacey said on the House floor. "We have given an awful exhibition of slaughter and destruction, which may serve as a warning to all mankind. Let us now give an example of wise conservation of what remains of the gifts of nature." That year Congress Passed the Lacey Act, followed by the tougher Weeks-McLean Act in 1913 and, five years later, the Migratory Bird Treaty Act, which protected not just birds but also their eggs, nests, and feathers.

The passenger pigeon story continued to resonate throughout the century. In the 1960s populations of the dickcissel, a sparrow-like neotropical migrant, began crashing, and some ornithologists predicted its extinction by 2000. It took decades to uncover the reason: During winters the entire world population of the grass-lands bird converged into fewer than a dozen huge flocks, which settled into the *llanos* of Venezuela. There rice farmers who considered the dickcissels a pest illegally crop-dusted their roosts with pesticides. "They were literally capable, in a matter of minutes, of wiping out double-digit percentages of the world's population," says Temple, who studied the bird. "The accounts are very reminiscent of the passenger pigeon." As conservationists negotiated with rice growers during the 1990s — using research that showed the dickcissel was not an economic threat — they also invoked the passenger pigeon extinction to rally their colleagues in North America and Europe. The efforts paid off: the bird's population has stabilized, albeit at a lower level.

Today the pigeon inspires artists and scientists alike. Sculptor Todd McGrain, creative director of the Lost Bird Project, has crafted enormous bronze memorials of five extinct birds; his passenger pigeon sits at the Grange Insurance Audubon Center in Columbus, Ohio. The Lost Bird Project has also designed an origami pigeon and says thousands have been folded — a symbolic recreation of the historic flocks.

The most controversial effort inspired by the extinction is a plan to bring the passenger pigeon back to life. In 2012 Long Now Foundation president Stewart Brand (a futurist best known for creating the *Whole Earth Catalog*) and genetics entrepreneur Ryan Phelan cofounded Revive & Restore, a project that plans to use the tools of molecular biology to resurrect extinct animals. The project's "flagship" species is the passenger pigeon, which Brand learned about from his mother when he was growing up in Illinois. Revive & Restore hopes to start with the band-tailed pigeon, a close relative, and "change its genome

This chart shows what scientists critical of de-extinction have termed the "re-extinction vortex." **How does this image articulate an argument against de-extinction? How, based on details from "From Billions to None," might Yeoman respond to it?**

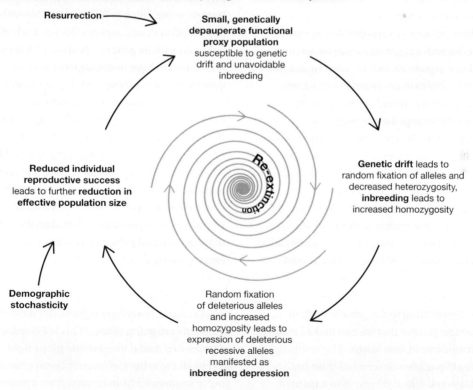

Republished with the permission of John Wiley & Sons, Inc., Steeves, T. E., Johnson, J. A. and Hale, M. L. (2017), Maximising evolutionary potential in functional proxies for extinct species: a conservation genetic perspective on de-extinction. Funct Ecol, 31: 1032–1040. doi:10.1111/1365-2435.12843, Figure 1. Permission conveyed through Copyright Clearance Center, Inc.

seeing connections

Journalist M. R. O'Connor wrote *Resurrection Science: Conservation, De-extinction, and the Precarious Future of Wild Things* in 2015. In the introduction to her book, O'Connor touched on the subject of de-extinction.

Identify at least three claims O'Connor makes or refers to in this excerpt. Then, choose one claim to defend, challenge, or qualify, drawing on Yeoman's essay as well as your own knowledge or outside research to support your position.

from Resurrection Science
Conservation, De-extinction, and the Precarious Future of Wild Things

M. R. O'CONNOR

The technology of "resurrection science" is real and upon us. Scientists have not only successfully cloned endangered animals such as the European mouflon and the African wildcat, they are also working to bring back animals that are already extinct. . . .

These attempts to repopulate the modern landscape with extinct fauna rest on an intriguing ethical argument: that humans have a moral responsibility to make amends for overexploitation by our ancient and recent ancestors.

Take the case of the passenger pigeon, whose potential de-extinction has become symbolic of both our incredible faith in science to solve our ecological problems as well as a metaphysical predicament. Is a bird born of human ingenuity in the laboratory the same as a bird born of natural selection in the wild? Or is it a case of what sociologists call bio-objectification, defined as the process by which life is made

an object by humans? In 1982, Robert Elliot penned a paper called "Faking Nature" that rebuked the idea that an ecosystem disturbed or damaged by humans could be restored to its original state or has equal value to wilderness. Nature, wrote Elliot, is "not replaceable without depreciation in one aspect of its value which has to do with its genesis, its history." It seems that today we have to decide whether that genesis in the wild is something we value.

Some scientists see de-extinction as irrelevant to the real grunt work of fighting for the survival of species. "For people who are doing this work, the passenger pigeon stuff is just an offensive conversation," one biologist told me. "It's publicity for newspaper articles." There is real concern that the very idea that de-extinction is possible will weaken the will of the public and policy makers to protect endangered species or habitat.

into the closest thing to the genetic code of the passenger pigeon that we can make," says research consultant Ben Novak. The resulting creature will not have descended from the original species. "[But] if I give it to a team of scientists who have no idea that it was bioengineered, and I say, 'Classify this,' if it looks and

behaves like a passenger pigeon, the natural historians are going to say, 'This is *Ectopistes migratorius.*' And if the genome plops right next to all the other passenger pigeon genomes you've sequenced from history, then a geneticist will have to say, 'This is a passenger pigeon. It's not a band-tailed pigeon.'"

Revive & Restore plans to breed the birds in captivity before returning them to the wild in the 2030s. Novak says the initial research indicates that North American forests could support a reintroduced population. He hopes animal brought back from extinction — not just birds but eventually also big creatures like woolly mammoths — will draw the public to zoos in droves, generating revenues that can be used to protect wildlife. "De-extinction [can] get the public interested in conservation in a way that the last forty years of doom and gloom has beaten out of them," he says.

Other experts aren't so sanguine. They question whether the hybrid animal could really be called a passenger pigeon. They doubt the birds could survive without the enormous flocks of the 19th century. And they question Novak's belief that the forests could safely absorb the reintroduction. "The ecosystem has moved on," says Temple. "If you put the organism back in, it could be disruptive to a new dynamic equilibrium. It's not altogether clear that putting one of these extinct species from the distant past back into an ecosystem today would be much more than introducing an exotic species. It would have repercussions that we're probably not fully capable of predicting."

◆ ◆ ◆

Blockstein says he wanted to use the 100th anniversary as a "teachable moment." Which eventually led him to Greenberg, the Chicago researcher, who had been thinking independently about 2014's potential. The two men reached out to others until more than 150 institutions were on board for a year-long commemoration: museums, universities, conservation groups (including Audubon state offices and local chapters), libraries, arts organizations, government agencies, and nature and history centers.

Project Passenger Pigeon has since evolved to be a multimedia circus of sorts. Greenberg has published *A Feathered River Across the Sky*, a book-length account of the pigeon's glory days and demise. Filmmaker David Mrazek plans to release a documentary called *From Billions to None.* At least four conferences will address the pigeon's extinction, as will several exhibits. "We're trying to take advantage of every possible mechanism to put the story in front of audiences that may not necessarily be birdwatchers, may not necessarily even be conservationists," says Temple.

The commemoration goes beyond honoring one species. Telling the pigeon's story can serve as a jumping-off point for exploring the many ways humans influence, and often jeopardize, their own environment. Today an estimated 13 percent of birds are threatened, according to the International Union for Conservation of Nature. So are 25 percent of mammals and 41 percent of amphibians, in large part because of human activity. Hydropower and road construction imperil China's giant pandas. The northern bald ibis, once abundant in the Middle East, has been driven almost to extinction by hunting, habitat loss, and the difficulties of doing conservation work in war-torn Syria. Hunting and the destruction of wetlands for agriculture drove the population of North America's tallest bird, the whooping crane, into the teens before stringent protections along the birds' migratory route and wintering grounds helped the wild flock build back to a few hundred. Little brown bats are dying off in the United States and Canada from a fungus that might have been imported from Europe by travelers. Of some 300 species of freshwater mussels in North America, fully 70 percent are extinct, imperiled, or vulnerable, thanks to the impacts of water pollution from logging, dams, farm runoff, and shoreline development. Rising sea temperatures have disrupted the symbiotic relationship between corals and plant-like zooxanthellae, leading to a deadly phenomenon called coral bleaching. One third of the world's reef-building coral species are now threatened.

seeing connections

Shown here are cartoons created by artist Tania Arbic. They illustrate the following questions from a 2014 poll on de-extinction created by the Canadian Museum of Nature:

Left: It is possible that some resurrected species may contain valuable pharmaceutical properties that could be processed into life-saving drugs. Would it be acceptable to breed formerly extinct animals to harvest them for drugs that would benefit humans? Who would own the resurrected animals?

Right: There would be considerable interest in seeing formerly extinct animals in the flesh. Undoubtedly zoos would be created for public viewing of these animals. Is it proper to have animals in zoos for which there are no wild populations? What if the funds raised from these zoos were used to support protection of endangered animals? Would seeing resurrected animals permit people to think about extinction as being reversible? Would conservation ecology suffer as a result?

Based on your reading of Yeoman's article, how would you answer the questions posed by the museum? Why do you think Yeoman does not address these issues in his essay?

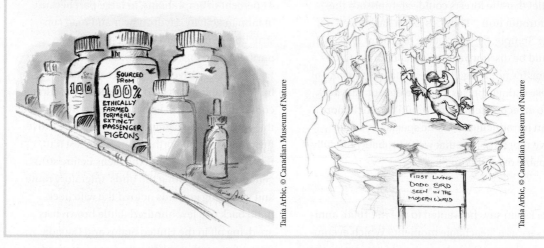

Tania Arbic, © Canadian Museum of Nature

Tania Arbic, © Canadian Museum of Nature

If public disinterest helped exterminate the passenger pigeon, then one modern-day parallel might be public skepticism about climate change. In an October poll by the Pew Research Center for the People and the Press, only 44 percent of Americans agreed there was solid evidence that the earth is warming because of human activity, as scientists now overwhelmingly believe. Twenty-six percent didn't think there was significant proof of global warming at all. In another Pew poll, conducted last spring,

40 percent of Americans considered climate change a major national threat, compared with 65 percent of Latin Americans and slimmer majorities in Europe, Africa, and the Asia-Pacific region.

This denial of both the threat and our own responsibility sounds eerily familiar to those who study 19th-century attitudes toward wildlife. "Certainly if you read some of the writings of the time," says Blockstein, "there were very few people who put stock in the idea that humanity

25

could have any impact on the passenger pigeons." (Audubon himself dismissed those who believed that "such dreadful havoc" as hunting would "soon put an end to the species.") Today attitudes toward climate change sound similar, continues Blockstein. "It's the same kind of argument: 'The world is so big and the atmosphere is so big; how could we possibly have an impact on the global climate?'"

Even the political rhetoric of those who don't want to address climate change aggressively has 19th-century echoes. "The industry that paid people to kill these birds said, 'If you restrict the killing, people will lose their jobs,'" notes Greenberg — "the very same things you hear today."

Project Passenger Pigeon might not change the minds of hardcore climate skeptics. For the rest of us, though, it could serve as a call to take responsibility for how our personal and collective actions affect wildlife and climate. Maybe a close look at the history of human folly will keep us from repeating it.

[2015]

EXPLORING THE TEXT

1. Why does Barry Yeoman begin his essay with Simon Pokagon's account of seeing a flock of passenger pigeons? How effectively does it prepare the reader for the rest of his essay and for the argument that he develops?

2. Yeoman reports the names of two passenger pigeons: "Martha," the last one to have lived, and "Buttons," the last one to have been shot. How does including these particular details contribute to the effectiveness of the essay as a whole?

3. What is the relationship between the two questions posed in paragraph 5? To what extent does Yeoman answer them in this essay?

4. Why do you think Yeoman returns to another account by Simon Pokagon in paragraph 11? How does this help him develop his argument?

5. If flocks of passenger pigeons were indeed as overwhelming and destructive as they are described, why do so many scientists mourn their loss? Why would they want to restore them to life?

6. Reread paragraph 14, replacing the word "pigeons" in the first sentence with an animal that is currently critically endangered, such as the black rhino or the orangutan. How does this change affect your reaction to the claim made in this paragraph?

7. How would you characterize the picture that Yeoman paints in paragraph 23? What rhetorical strategies does he employ to create it?

8. What is Yeoman's thesis? How would you summarize his position in a sentence?

9. What is the nature of the controversy over "Revive & Restore"? What is Yeoman's attitude toward it? Do you think it might be a good idea to bring back extinct animals such as the passenger pigeon, the Tasmanian tiger, and even the wooly mammoth, as scientists are considering? Why or why not?

10. Why do you think it is that "the passenger pigeon story continued to resonate throughout the century" (para. 16)? What issue — or issues — does Yeoman suggest the passenger pigeon has become emblematic of? Why has the passenger pigeon become more such an important symbol? Explain.

11. Why do you think there is such a discrepancy between what science tells us and what people believe, as the Pew Research Center indicates? Explain the parallel that Yeoman begins to develop in paragraph 24. How compelling is it?

12. Yeoman divides his essay into several sections. How would you characterize the progression of these sections?

13. How would you describe the tone of Yeoman's essay? Why might it be particularly well suited to both his subject matter and his audience?

14. In paragraph 10 Yeoman discusses "two technological developments that set in motion the pigeon's extinction." Can you think of two contemporary technological developments that might have a similar effect on the environment today? Why do you believe they will have this effect? To what extent do you believe Yeoman would agree with your argument? Explain your response.

Why Science Is So Hard to Believe

JOEL ACHENBACH

Joel Achenbach (b. 1960) is a journalist covering science and politics for the *Washington Post*. He has also written several books, including *It Looks Like a President Only Smaller* (2001), *Captured by Aliens: The Search for Life and Truth in a Very Large Universe* (1999), *The Grand Idea: George Washington's Potomac and the Race to the West* (2005), and *A Hole at the Bottom of the Sea: The Race to Kill the BP Oil Gusher* (2011). Achenbach has also contributed to *Slate, National Geographic*, and National Public Radio's *Morning Edition*. His writing style has been praised for its versatility and humor in explaining complex subjects. The following op-ed was published in the *Washington Post* in 2015.

There's a scene in Stanley Kubrick's comic masterpiece "Dr. Strangelove" in which Jack D. Ripper, an American general who's gone rogue and ordered a nuclear attack on the Soviet Union, unspools his paranoid worldview — and the explanation for why he drinks "only distilled water, or rainwater, and only pure grain alcohol" — to Lionel Mandrake, a dizzy-with-anxiety group captain in the Royal Air Force.

Ripper:	"Have you ever heard of a thing called fluoridation? Fluoridation of water?"
Mandrake:	"Ah, yes, I have heard of that, Jack. Yes, yes."
Ripper:	"Well, do you know what it is?"
Mandrake:	"No. No, I don't know what it is, no."
Ripper:	"Do you realize that fluoridation is the most monstrously conceived and dangerous communist plot we have ever had to face?"

The movie came out in 1964, by which time the health benefits of fluoridation had been thoroughly established and anti-fluoridation conspiracy theories could be the stuff of comedy. Yet half a century later, fluoridation continues to incite fear and paranoia. In 2013, citizens in Portland, Ore., one of only a few major American cities that don't fluoridate, blocked a plan by local officials to do so. Opponents didn't like the idea of the government adding "chemicals" to their water. They claimed that fluoride could be harmful to human health.

Actually fluoride is a natural mineral that, in the weak concentrations used in public drinking-water systems, hardens tooth enamel and prevents tooth decay — a cheap and safe way to improve dental health for everyone, rich or poor, conscientious brushers or not. That's the scientific and medical consensus.

To which some people in Portland, echoing anti-fluoridation activists around the world, reply: We don't believe you.

We live in an age when all manner of scientific knowledge — from the safety of fluoride and vaccines to the reality of climate change — faces organized and often furious opposition. Empowered by their own sources of information and their own interpretations of research, doubters have declared war on the consensus of experts. There are so many of these controversies these days, you'd think a diabolical agency had put something in the water to make people argumentative.

Science doubt has become a pop-culture meme. In the recent movie "Interstellar," set in a futuristic, downtrodden America where NASA

5

has been forced into hiding, school textbooks say the Apollo moon landings were faked.

In a sense this is not surprising. Our lives are permeated by science and technology as never before. For many of us this new world is wondrous, comfortable and rich in rewards — but also more complicated and sometimes unnerving. We now face risks we can't easily analyze.

We're asked to accept, for example, that it's safe to eat food containing genetically modified organisms (GMOs) because, the experts point out, there's no evidence that it isn't and no reason to believe that altering genes precisely in a lab is more dangerous than altering them wholesale through traditional breeding. But to some people, the very idea of transferring genes between species conjures up mad scientists running amok — and so, two centuries after Mary Shelley wrote "Frankenstein," they talk about Frankenfood.

The world crackles with real and imaginary hazards, and distinguishing the former from the latter isn't easy. Should we be afraid that the Ebola virus, which is spread only by direct contact with bodily fluids, will mutate into an airborne super-plague? The scientific consensus says that's extremely unlikely: No virus has ever been observed to completely change its mode of transmission in humans, and there's zero evidence that the latest strain of Ebola is any different. But Google "airborne Ebola" and you'll enter a dystopia where this virus has almost supernatural powers, including the power to kill us all.

In this bewildering world we have to decide what to believe and how to act on that. In principle, that's what science is for. "Science is not a body of facts," says geophysicist Marcia McNutt, who once headed the U.S. Geological Survey and is now editor of *Science*, the prestigious journal. "Science is a method for deciding whether what we choose to believe has a basis in the laws of nature or not."

The scientific method leads us to truths that are less than self-evident, often mind-blowing and sometimes hard to swallow. In the early 17th century, when Galileo claimed that the Earth spins on its axis and orbits the sun, he wasn't just rejecting church doctrine. He was asking people to believe something that defied common sense — because

10

Paul Noth/The New Yorker Collection/The Cartoon Bank

"First we need some hard evidence that the climate is actually changing."

How does this cartoon use humor to illustrate Achenbach's main point?

seeing connections

These graphs use data from a 2016 Pew study on Americans' views on vaccination.
What details from Achenbach's article could be used to explain these results?

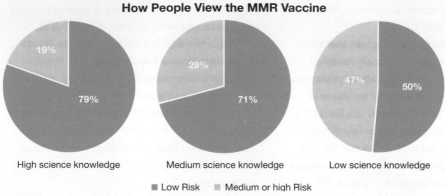

How People View the MMR Vaccine

19%
79%
High science knowledge

29%
71%
Medium science knowledge

47%
50%
Low science knowledge

■ Low Risk   ■ Medium or high Risk

Data from Pew Research Center.

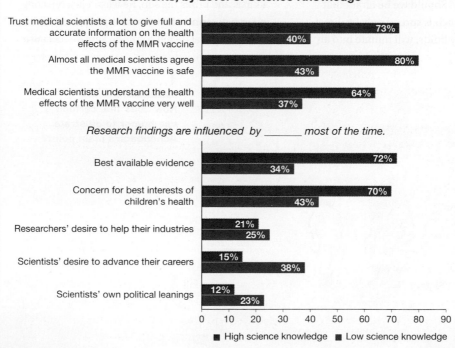

Percentage of People Who Agree with the Following Statements, by Level of Science Knowledge

Trust medical scientists a lot to give full and accurate information on the health effects of the MMR vaccine
73%
40%

Almost all medical scientists agree the MMR vaccine is safe
80%
43%

Medical scientists understand the health effects of the MMR vaccine very well
64%
37%

Research findings are influenced by _____ most of the time.

Best available evidence
72%
34%

Concern for best interests of children's health
70%
43%

Researchers' desire to help their industries
21%
25%

Scientists' desire to advance their careers
15%
38%

Scientists' own political leanings
12%
23%

0 10 20 30 40 50 60 70 80 90

■ High science knowledge   ■ Low science knowledge

Data from Pew Research Center.

it sure looks like the sun's going around the Earth, and you can't feel the Earth spinning. Galileo was put on trial and forced to recant. Two centuries later, Charles Darwin escaped that fate. But his idea that all life on Earth evolved from a primordial ancestor and that we humans are distant cousins of apes, whales and even deep-sea mollusks is still a big ask for a lot of people.

Even when we intellectually accept these precepts of science, we subconsciously cling to our intuitions—what researchers call our naive beliefs. A study by Andrew Shtulman of Occidental College showed that even students with an advanced science education had a hitch in their mental gait when asked to affirm or deny that humans are descended from sea animals and that the Earth goes around the sun. Both truths are counterintuitive. The students, even those who correctly marked "true," were slower to answer those questions than questions about whether humans are descended from tree-dwelling creatures (also true but easier to grasp) and whether the moon goes around the Earth (also true but intuitive).

Shtulman's research indicates that as we become scientifically literate, we repress our naive beliefs but never eliminate them entirely. They nest in our brains, chirping at us as we try to make sense of the world.

Most of us do that by relying on personal experience and anecdotes, on stories rather than statistics. We might get a prostate-specific antigen test, even though it's no longer generally recommended, because it caught a close friend's cancer—and we pay less attention to statistical evidence, painstakingly compiled through multiple studies, showing that the test rarely saves lives but triggers many unnecessary surgeries. Or we hear about a cluster of cancer cases in a town with a hazardous-waste dump, and we assume that pollution caused the cancers. Of course, just because two things happened together doesn't mean one caused the other, and just because events are clustered doesn't mean they're not random. Yet we have trouble digesting randomness; our brains crave pattern and meaning.

Even for scientists, the scientific method is a hard discipline. They, too, are vulnerable to confirmation bias — the tendency to look for and see only evidence that confirms what they already believe. But unlike the rest of us, they submit their ideas to formal peer review before publishing them. Once the results are published, if they're important enough, other scientists will try to reproduce them — and, being congenitally skeptical and competitive, will be very happy to announce that they don't hold up. Scientific results are always provisional, susceptible to being overturned by some future experiment or observation. Scientists rarely proclaim an absolute truth or an absolute certainty. Uncertainty is inevitable at the frontiers of knowledge.

That provisional quality of science is another thing a lot of people have trouble with. To some climate-change skeptics, for example, the fact that a few scientists in the 1970s were worried (quite reasonably, it seemed at the time) about the possibility of a coming ice age is enough to discredit what is now the consensus of the world's scientists: The planet's surface temperature has risen by about 1.5 degrees Fahrenheit in the past 130 years, and human actions, including the burning of fossil fuels, are extremely likely to have been the dominant cause since the mid-20th century.

It's clear that organizations funded in part by the fossil-fuel industry have deliberately tried to undermine the public's understanding of the scientific consensus by promoting a few skeptics. The news media gives abundant attention to such mavericks, naysayers, professional controversialists and table thumpers. The media would also have you believe that science is full of shocking discoveries made by lone geniuses. Not so. The (boring) truth is that science usually advances incrementally, through the steady accretion of data and insights gathered by many people over many years. So it has with the consensus on climate change. That's not about to go poof with the next thermometer reading.

15

But industry PR, however misleading, isn't enough to explain why so many people reject the scientific consensus on global warming.

The "science communication problem," as it's blandly called by the scientists who study it, has yielded abundant new research into how people decide what to believe — and why they so often don't accept the expert consensus. It's not that they can't grasp it, according to Dan Kahan of Yale University. In one study he asked 1,540 Americans, a representative sample, to rate the threat of climate change on a scale of zero to 10. Then he correlated that with the subjects' science literacy. He found that higher literacy was associated with stronger views — at both ends of the spectrum. Science literacy promoted polarization on climate, not consensus. According to Kahan, that's because people tend to use scientific knowledge to reinforce their worldviews.

Americans fall into two basic camps, Kahan says. Those with a more "egalitarian" and "communitarian" mind-set are generally suspicious of industry and apt to think it's up to something dangerous that calls for government regulation; they're likely to see the risks of climate change. In contrast, people with a "hierarchical" and "individualistic" mind-set respect leaders of industry and don't like government interfering in their affairs; they're apt to reject warnings about climate change, because they know what accepting them could lead to — some kind of tax or regulation to limit emissions.

In the United States, climate change has become a litmus test that identifies you as belonging to one or the other of these two antagonistic tribes. When we argue about it, Kahan says, we're actually arguing about who we are, what our crowd is. We're thinking: People like us believe this. People like that do not believe this.

Science appeals to our rational brain, but our beliefs are motivated largely by emotion, and the biggest motivation is remaining tight with our peers. "We're all in high school. We've never left high school," says Marcia McNutt.

"People still have a need to fit in, and that need to fit in is so strong that local values and local opinions are always trumping science. And they will continue to trump science, especially when there is no clear downside to ignoring science."

Meanwhile the Internet makes it easier than ever for science doubters to find their own information and experts. Gone are the days when a small number of powerful institutions — elite universities, encyclopedias and major news organizations — served as gatekeepers of scientific information. The Internet has democratized it, which is a good thing. But along with cable TV, the Web has also made it possible to live in a "filter bubble" that lets in only the information with which you already agree.

How to penetrate the bubble? How to convert science skeptics? Throwing more facts at them doesn't help. Liz Neeley, who helps train scientists to be better communicators at an organization called Compass, says people need to hear from believers they can trust, who share their fundamental values. She has personal experience with this. Her father is a climate-change skeptic and gets most of his information on the issue from conservative media. In exasperation she finally confronted him: "Do you believe them or me?" She told him she believes the scientists who research climate change and knows many of them personally. "If you think I'm wrong," she said, "then you're telling me that you don't trust me." Her father's stance on the issue softened. But it wasn't the facts that did it.

If you're a rationalist, there's something a little dispiriting about all this. In Kahan's descriptions of how we decide what to believe, what we decide sometimes sounds almost incidental. Those of us in the science-communication business are as tribal as anyone else, he told me. We believe in scientific ideas not because we have truly evaluated all the evidence but because we feel an affinity for the scientific community. When I mentioned to Kahan that I fully accept evolution, he said: "Believing in evolution is just a description about you. It's not an account of how you reason."

seeing connections

These graphs represent the findings of a 2017 study published in *Political Psychology*, an academic journal. The study found that both Democrats and Republicans with the highest levels of "science intelligence" also held the most deeply entrenched views on polarizing topics such as global warming. However, people who scored high on the "science curiosity" scale, regardless of political affiliation, were not as polarized. **How does this data relate to Achenbach's argument? To what extent does it challenge Achenbach's claim that "science tells us the truth rather than what we'd like the truth to be" (para. 30)?**

"How much <u>risk</u> do you believe XXX poses to human health, safety, or prosperity?"

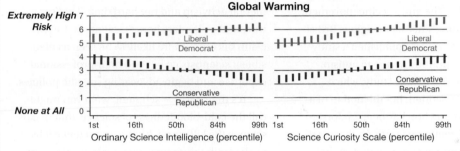

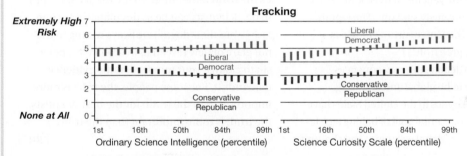

There is "solid evidence" of recent global warming due "mostly" to "human activity such as burning fossil fuels."

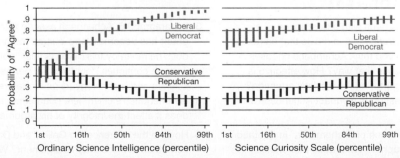

Maybe — except that evolution is real. Biology is incomprehensible without it. There aren't really two sides to all these issues. Climate change is happening. Vaccines save lives. Being right does matter — and the science tribe has a long track record of getting things right in the end. Modern society is built on things it got right.

Doubting science also has consequences, as seen in recent weeks with the measles outbreak that began in California. The people who believe that vaccines cause autism — often well educated and affluent, by the way — are undermining "herd immunity" to such diseases as whooping cough and measles. The anti-vaccine movement has been going strong since a prestigious British medical journal, the *Lancet*, published a study in 1998 linking a common vaccine to autism. The journal later retracted the study, which was thoroughly discredited. But the notion of a vaccine-autism connection has been endorsed by celebrities and reinforced through the usual Internet filters. (Anti-vaccine activist and actress Jenny McCarthy famously said on "The Oprah Winfrey Show," "The University of Google is where I got my degree from.")

In the climate debate, the consequences of doubt are likely to be global and enduring. Climate-change skeptics in the United States have achieved their fundamental goal of halting legislative action to combat global warming. They haven't had to win the debate on the merits; they've merely had to fog the room enough to keep laws governing greenhouse gas emissions from being enacted.

Some environmental activists want scientists to emerge from their ivory towers and get more involved in the policy battles. Any scientist going that route needs to do so carefully, says Liz Neeley. "That line between science communication and advocacy is very hard to step back from," she says. In the debate over climate change, the central allegation of the skeptics is that the science saying it's real and a serious threat is politically tinged, driven by environmental activism and not hard data. That's not true, and it slanders honest scientists. But the claim becomes more likely to be seen as plausible if scientists go beyond their professional expertise and begin advocating specific policies.

It's their very detachment, what you might   *30* call the cold-bloodedness of science, that makes science the killer app. It's the way science tells us the truth rather than what we'd like the truth to be. Scientists can be as dogmatic as anyone else — but their dogma is always wilting in the hot glare of new research. In science it's not a sin to change your mind when the evidence demands it. For some people, the tribe is more important than the truth; for the best scientists, the truth is more important than the tribe.

[2015]

EXPLORING THE TEXT

1. Joel Achenbach opens with a description of a scene from *Dr. Strangelove*, a movie that came out in 1964. Why do you think Achenbach chooses to begin his essay in that way? How effective is this strategy in capturing the reader's attention? How, in your eyes, does it impact Achenbach's credibility?

2. Why does Achenbach put "chemicals" in quotation marks in paragraph 2? What does that choice suggest about his tone and meaning?

3. In paragraph 6, Achenbach asserts that "Science doubt has become a pop-culture meme." What does he mean by this? Why is this, "not surprising," if, as he continues, "our lives are permeated by science and technology as never before" (para. 7)? Is Achenbach's claim here counterintuitive? How does it affect the integrity of his argument? Explain.

4. How do the references to Galileo and Darwin contribute to Achenbach's argument? What do such examples suggest about his intended audience?

5. According to Achenbach, what is the nature of the relationship between knowledge and intuition? What role does he suggest "naive beliefs" play in our attempt to "make sense of the world" (paras. 12–13)?

6. In paragraph 17, Achenbach claims that "news media gives abundant attention to such mavericks, naysayers, professional controversialists and table thumpers," though he names none in particular. Whom do you think he is writing about? How well does the rest of the essay support this claim? Does the attitude he expresses in those descriptions enhance or detract from his argument?

7. In paragraph 22, Achenbach quotes Marcia McNutt, geophysicist and President of the National Academy of Sciences, who says, "We're all in high school. We never left high school." What does she mean by this? How does Achenbach use her statement to develop his argument?

8. Discussing the relationship between the media and scientific information, Achenbach states: "The Internet has democratized it, which is a good thing" (para. 23). How well supported is this claim? Do you agree that the Internet has democratized science? To what extent might it be harmful to the achievement of scientific goals? Explain. In your answer, consider what Achenbach says about Google.

9. What strategies does Achenbach use to appeal to authority? Cite specific places in the essay where this occurs. How effective are these appeals?

10. Achenbach begins paragraph 26 with "Maybe — ...." What does that word suggest about the author's attitude toward Kahan's position? Be specific.

11. What problem does Achenbach address in paragraph 29? What purpose does acknowledging this problem serve?

12. Achenbach writes that "science tells us the truth rather than what we'd like to be the truth to be" (para. 30). What does this statement suggest about the relationship between the citizen and the environment? Is this his main argument? How do you know?

13. Why do you think actual science news has such a small place among the overall news as reported by the media? Do you think the American public would want more and more accurate science news? Why or why not?

Save the Galapagos with GMO Rats. What Could Go Wrong?

SARAH ZHANG

Sarah Zhang is an American health and science journalist currently serving as a staff writer for the *Atlantic*. Before becoming a journalist, Zhang studied neurobiology at Harvard University. Zhang's writing has appeared in *Mother Jones, Nautilus, Nature, Wired*, and many other publications. The following article, originally published in *Wired* in 2016, considers the use of genetic manipulation to fight invasive species.

The Galapagos Islands are famous for exotic birds, tortoises, and iguanas, but recently the archipelago had become overrun with more prosaic animals: rats and mice. Rodents that came on old sailing ships. Rodents that stowed away on modern cruises. Wherever they came from, rodents that eat the eggs and chicks and hatchlings of the animals that so dazzled Charles Darwin.

The same story plays out on islands all over the world. So Island Conservation, a nonprofit that rids islands of invasive species, has come up with a daring plan: genetically engineer the rodents so that they all turn into males, shrinking the population one lonely pest at a time.

This plan is far from going into effect, but it gets a serious airing in a report out today from the National Academy of Sciences, a prestigious group that often makes recommendations on controversial areas of research. The make-all-rodents-boys idea is one of seven case studies for the use of "gene drives" — engineered pieces of DNA that spread more quickly through a wild population than any normal gene would. You might say gene drives are a way to cheat evolution. Gene drives could also be dangerous and unpredictable; once a manmade DNA sequence gets into a wild population, it's hard to get back out again. The National Academy's report lays out guidelines for scientists to responsibly study this method of genetically altering wild plants and animals.

Gene drives have gotten a lot of attention as a way to prevent mosquitoes from spreading

disease: Scientists have engineered mosquitoes with gene drives that kill the parasite behind malaria, and they're working on gene drives that either eradicate the mosquitoes that spread dengue, chikungunya, and Zika or make them resistant to the viruses. The recent rise of Crispr gene-editing technology has made it easier than ever for scientists to construct gene drives.

But using gene drives not to benefit humans but to restore natural habitats — like tropical islands beset with invasive rats — forces you to answer a very basic question: What is natural? What does it mean to engineer animals to restore nature? Environmentalists have long decried genetically modified organisms, but will they embrace them for conservation? 5

A New Natural

Kent Redford, former director of the Wildlife Conservation Society Institute, has questioned the working definition of "natural," and in 2013

> ◀
> **What point does this cartoon make about genetic engineering? Does Sarah Zhang make the same point? Explain.**

Sam Gross/The New Yorker Collection/The Cartoon Bank

"Genetic engineering got us into this mess, and genetic engineering will get us out of it."

he wrote about the lack of dialogue between synthetic biologists and conservationists. The reaction among conservationists he says, was "a range of anger and disgust to enthusiasm and excitement." Since then Redford, along with Ryan Phelan, executive director of Revive and Restore — an organization that promotes synthetic biology for the "genetic rescue" of endangered and extinct species — have held meetings to get the two groups talking about specific problems, like invasive rodents on islands.

No matter how you feel about genetic modification, the current approach to killing island invasives might make you understand the "enthusiasm" for gene drives. It is not pretty. Recently, on the British island of South Georgia, pilots spread 200 tons of bait one helicopter load at a time, blanketing the island in a rat poison called brodifacoum. Brodifacoum keeps blood from clotting, so the rodents die of internal bleeding — as can birds and other mammals at high enough doses. But gene drives? "We could do it in the most humane way possible by having them just turn to an all-male popula-tion and live out their natural lives," says Heath Packard, communications director for Island Conservation.

Islands are also well suited for gene drive solutions because the ocean is a natural barrier against their spread. And invasive rodents are a critical problem: As Darwin discovered, islands are hotbeds of biodiversity, and 40 percent of the critically endangered species in the world live on islands. Plus rats and mice are an easy genetic target because scientists have long tinkered with their genetics in the lab. The downside, of course, are unintended consequences. Ecology is com-plicated, and nobody has put a gene out in the wild before.

Island Conservation's scientists were investigating gene drives as a possible "game-changing" eradication technology even before

Crispr became hot. Their research partners at Texas A&M University and North Carolina State University are studying a naturally-occurring gene drive in mice that doesn't even require Crispr technology. Island Conservation has also partnered with the US Department of Agriculture and Australia's national Commonwealth Scientific and Industrial Research Organisation so when the time comes, it gets regulatory approval for field tests in the future. That's all years away, says Packard, though the group is now planning to fundraise for the gene drive research.

The National Academy report considers   10
other conservation scenarios for gene drives: killing off mosquitoes that spread avian malaria in Hawaii and controlling invasive knapweeds in US forests. But reading the report, you get a sense that the scientists realize they are out of their depth. "Questions about how to define 'nature' and how to understand the value attached to nature raise a number of difficult philosophical and social problems," says the report. "They are left here as open questions, and are part of a growing and heated debate among environmentalists about the values that underpin environmentalism." Consider this: Gene drives may be "unnatural," but how natural is dropping tons of rat poison out of the sky?

In any case, if scientists can construct such a gene drive, if conservationists can get permission to release mice carrying them, and if everything goes as planned, then islands like the Galapagos stand to benefit. A huge rat poisoning campaign from 2007 to 2014 rid the Galapagos of most of its pests, but with so much boat traffic there, rodents could make their way to the islands again. Where Darwin first made the observations that led him to understand the laws of evolution, scientists could use the technology that will try to cheat the game.

[2016]

EXPLORING THE TEXT

1. Zhang's title refers to "GMO Rats." What are GMOs, and why are they so controversial? Why have environmentalists "long decried" them, as Zhang declares (para. 5)?

2. Zhang titles the second part of her article "A New Natural." What are some of the implications suggested by that phrase? What is the effect of dividing such a short article in this way? How does it help develop her argument?

3. What are some of the pros and cons of "gene drives" that Zhang discusses?

4. In paragraph 8, Zhang writes that "[t]he downside, of course, are unintended

consequences." What might some of those consequences be? What is the effect of leaving the reader to dream these up instead of naming some she believes will result?

5. What is the effect of the rhetorical question with which Zhang concludes paragraph 10?

6. What is Zhang's position regarding GMOs and "gene drives"? In which paragraph does she make it most clear? Explain.

7. How would you characterize the tone of the title of this article? Does this tone accurately reflect the author's attitude toward her subject? Why or why not?

A Biologist's Manifesto for Preserving Life on Earth

E. O. WILSON

Edward O. Wilson (b. 1929) is an American biologist, researcher, naturalist, and author. As a boy growing up around Washington, D.C., and Mobile, Alabama, Wilson found companionship in nature and was determined early on to become an entomologist. Wilson received his PhD from Harvard University and is recognized as the world's leading authority on ants — he discovered their use of pheromones for communication. In 1975, Wilson published his first major book, *Sociobiology*. In *On Human Nature*, for which he won the Pulitzer Prize in 1979, Wilson examined the scientific arguments surrounding the role of biology in the evolution of human culture. Officially retired from teaching at Harvard in 1996, he continues to hold the posts of Professor Emeritus and Honorary Curator in Entomology. Wilson's most recent books are *The Creation: An Appeal to Save Life on Earth* (2006); *Anthill: a Novel* (2010); *The Social Conquest of Earth* (2012); and, most recently, *Half-Earth: Our Planet's Fight for Life* (2016). The following selection was published in 2016 in *Sierra*, the magazine of the Sierra Club.

1

We are playing a global endgame. Humanity's grasp on the planet is not strong; it is growing weaker. Freshwater is growing short; the atmosphere and the seas are increasingly polluted as a result of what has transpired on the land. The climate is changing in ways unfavorable to life, except for microbes, jellyfish, and fungi. For many species, these changes are already fatal.

Because the problems created by humanity are global and progressive, because the prospect of a

point of no return is fast approaching, the problems can't be solved piecemeal. There is just so much water left for fracking,[1] so much rainforest cover available for soybeans and oil palms, so much room left in the atmosphere to store excess carbon. The impact on the rest of the biosphere is everywhere negative, the environment becoming unstable and less pleasant, our long-term future less certain.

---

[1] A method of extracting natural gas and oil by injecting liquid into rock at high pressure. —Eds.

Only by committing half of the planet's surface to nature can we hope to save the immensity of life-forms that compose it. Unless humanity learns a great deal more about global biodiversity and moves quickly to protect it, we will soon lose most of the species composing life on Earth. The Half-Earth proposal offers a first, emergency solution commensurate with the magnitude of the problem: By setting aside half the planet in reserve, we can save the living part of the environment and achieve the stabilization required for our own survival.

Why one-half? Why not one-quarter or one-third? Because large plots, whether they already stand or can be created from corridors connecting smaller plots, harbor many more ecosystems and the species composing them at a sustainable level. As reserves grow in size, the diversity of life surviving within them also grows. As reserves are reduced in area, the diversity within them declines to a mathematically predictable degree swiftly — often immediately and, for a large fraction, forever.

A biogeographic scan of Earth's principal habitats shows that a full representation of its ecosystems and the vast majority of its species can be saved within half the planet's surface. At one-half and above, life on Earth enters the safe zone. Within that half, more than 80 percent of the species would be stabilized.

There is a second, psychological argument for protecting half of Earth. Half-Earth is a goal — and people understand and appreciate goals. They need a victory, not just news that progress is being made. It is human nature to yearn for finality, something achieved by which their anxieties and fears are put to rest. We stay afraid if the enemy is still at the gate, if bankruptcy is still possible, if more cancer tests may yet prove positive. It is our nature to choose large goals that, while difficult, are potentially game changing and universal in benefit. To strive against odds on behalf of all of life would be humanity at its most noble.

2

Extinction events are not especially rare in geological time. They have occurred in randomly varying magnitude throughout the history of life. Those that are truly apocalyptic, however, have occurred at only about 100-million-year intervals. There have been five such peaks of destruction of which we have record, the latest being Chicxulub, the mega-asteroid that wiped out the dinosaurs. Earth required roughly 10 million years to recover from each mass extinction. The peak of destruction that humanity has initiated is often called the Sixth Extinction.

5

Rick Friedman/Getty Images

This photograph of E. O. Wilson was taken in his office at Harvard University in 2012. **What does this image suggest about the ethos Wilson brings to the topic of this essay? How does it portray Wilson, and where do you see those qualities represented in his writing?**

Many authors have suggested that Earth is already different enough to recognize the end of the Holocene and the beginning of a new geological epoch. The favored name, coined by the biologist Eugene F. Stoermer in the early 1980s and popularized by the atmospheric chemist Paul Crutzen in 2000, is the Anthropocene, the Epoch of Man.

The logic for distinguishing the Anthropocene is sound. It can be clarified by the following thought experiment. Suppose that in the far-distant future geologists were to dig through Earth's crusted deposits to the strata spanning the past thousand years of our time. They would encounter sharply defined layers of chemically altered soil. They would recognize signatures of rapid climate changes. They would uncover abundant fossil remains of domesticated plants and animals that had replaced most of Earth's prehuman fauna and flora. They would excavate fragments of machines, and a veritable museum of deadly weapons.

3

Biodiversity as a whole forms a shield protecting each of the species that together compose it, ourselves included. What will happen if, in addition to the species already extinguished by human activity, say, 10 percent of those remaining are taken away? Or 50 percent? Or 90 percent? As more species vanish or drop to near extinction, the rate of extinction of the survivors accelerates. In some cases the effect is felt almost immediately. When a century ago the American chestnut, once a dominant tree over much of eastern North America, was reduced to near extinction by an Asian fungal blight, seven moth species whose caterpillars depended on its vegetation vanished. As extinction mounts, biodiversity reaches a tipping point at which the ecosystem collapses. Scientists have only begun to study under what conditions this catastrophe is most likely to occur.

Human beings are not exempt from the iron law of species interdependency. We were not inserted as ready-made invasives into an Edenic world. Nor were we intended by providence to rule that world. The biosphere does not belong to us; we belong to it. The organisms that surround us in such beautiful profusion are the product of 3.8 billion years of evolution by natural selection. We are one of its present-day products, having arrived as a fortunate species of old-world primate. And it happened only a geological eye-blink ago. Our physiology and our minds are adapted for life in the biosphere, which we have only begun to understand. We are now able to protect the rest of life, but instead we remain recklessly prone to destroy and replace a large part of it.

4

Earth remains a little-known planet. Scientists and the public are reasonably familiar with the vertebrates (fishes, amphibians, reptiles, birds, mammals), mostly because of their large size and immediate visible impact on human life. The best known of the vertebrates are the mammals, with about 5,500 species known and, according to experts, a few dozen remaining to be discovered. Birds have 10,000 recognized species, with an average of two or three new species turning up each year. Reptiles are reasonably well known, with slightly more than 9,000 species recognized and 1,000 estimated to await discovery. Fishes have 34,000 known species and as many as 10,000 awaiting discovery. Amphibians (frogs, salamanders, wormlike caecilians), among the most vulnerable to destruction, are less well known than the other land vertebrates: a bit over 6,600 species discovered out of a surprising 16,000 believed to exist. Flowering plants come in with about 270,000 species known and as many as 94,000 awaiting discovery.

For most of the rest of the living world, the picture is radically different. When expert estimates for invertebrates (such as the insects, crustaceans, and earthworms) are added to estimates for algae, fungi, mosses, and gymnosperms as well as for bacteria and other microorganisms, the total added up and then projected has varied wildly, from 5 million to more than 100 million species.

If the current rate of basic descriptions and analyses continues, we will not complete the global census of biodiversity — what is left of it — until well into the 23rd century. Further, if Earth's fauna and flora is not more expertly mapped and protected, and soon, the amount of biodiversity will be vastly diminished by the end of the present century. Humanity is losing the race between the scientific study of global biodiversity and the obliteration of countless still-unknown species.

5

From 1898 to 2006, 57 kinds of freshwater fish *15* declined to extinction in North America. The causes included the damming of rivers and streams, the draining of ponds and lakes, the filling in of springheads, and pollution, all due to human activity. Here, to bring them at least a whisper closer to their former existence, is a partial list of their common

names: Maravillas red shiner, plateau chub, thicktail chub, phantom shiner, Clear Lake splittail, deepwater cisco, Snake River sucker, least silverside, Ash Meadows poolfish, whiteline topminnow, Potosi pupfish, La Palma pupfish, graceful priapelta, Utah Lake sculpin, Maryland darter.

There is a deeper meaning and long-term importance of extinction. When these and other species disappear at our hands, we throw away part of Earth's history. We erase twigs and eventually whole branches of life's family tree. Because each species is unique, we close the book on scientific knowledge that is important to an unknown degree but is now forever lost.

The biology of extinction is not a pleasant subject. The vanishing remnants of Earth's biodiversity test the reach and quality of human morality. Species brought low by our hand now deserve our constant attention and care.

6

How fast are we driving species to extinction? For years paleontologists and biodiversity experts

Doug Chayka/Sierra Club

This illustration appeared with Wilson's original article in Sierra Club magazine. **How does it portray humans' impact on the environment? How effectively does it convey Wilson's message?**

have believed that, before the coming of humanity about 200,000 years ago, the rate of origin of new species per extinction of existing species was roughly one species per million species per year. As a consequence of human activity, it is believed that the current rate of extinction overall is between 100 and 1,000 times higher than it was originally.

This grim assessment leads to a very important question: How well is conservation working? How much have the efforts of global conservation movements achieved in slowing and halting the devastation of Earth's biodiversity?

Despite heroic efforts, the fact is that due to *20* habitat loss, the rate of extinction is rising in most parts of the world. The preeminent sites of biodiversity loss are the tropical forests and coral reefs. The most vulnerable habitats of all, with the highest extinction rate per unit area, are rivers, streams, and lakes in both tropical and temperate regions.

Biologists recognize that across the 3.8-billion-year history of life, over 99 percent of all species that lived are extinct. This being the case, what, we are often asked, is so bad about extinction?

The answer, of course, is that many of the species over the eons didn't die at all — they turned into two or more daughter species. Species are like amoebas; they multiply by splitting, not by making embryos. The most successful are the progenitors of the most species through time, just as the most successful humans are those whose lineages expand the most and persist the longest. We, like all other species, are the product of a highly successful and potentially important line that goes back all the way to the birth of humanity and beyond that for billions of years, to the time when life began. The same is true of the creatures still around us. They are champions, each and all. Thus far.

7

The surviving wildlands of the world are not art museums. They are not gardens to be arranged and tended for our delectation. They are not recreation centers or reservoirs of natural resources or sanatoriums or undeveloped sites of business opportunities — of any kind. The wildlands and the bulk of Earth's biodiversity protected within them are another world from the one humanity is throwing together pell-mell. What do we receive from them? The stabilization of the global environment they provide and their very existence are gifts to us. We are their stewards, not their owners.

Each ecosystem — be it a pond, meadow, coral reef, or something else out of thousands

This cartoon by Eldon Dedini was published in the *New Yorker* in 1983. **What does it imply about humanity's effect on the natural world? What does it suggest about human nature? How might Wilson respond to the position this cartoon humorously expresses?**

"But can they save themselves?"

that can be found around the world — is a web of specialized organisms braided and woven together. The species, each a freely interbreeding population of individuals, interact with a set of the other species in the ecosystem either strongly or weakly or not at all. Given that in most ecosystems even the identities of most of the species are unknown, how are biologists to define the many processes of their interactions? How can we predict changes in the ecosystem if some resident species vanish while other, previously absent species invade? At best we have partial data, working off hints, tweaking everything with guesses.

What does knowledge of how nature works tell us about conservation and the Anthropocene? This much is clear: To save biodiversity, it is necessary to obey the precautionary principle in the treatment of Earth's natural ecosystems, and to do so strictly. Hold fast until we, scientists and the public alike, know much more about them. Proceed carefully — study, discuss, plan. Give the rest of Earth's life a chance. Avoid nostrums and careless talk about quick fixes, especially those that threaten to harm the natural world beyond return.

8

Today every nation-state in the world has a protected-area system of some kind. All together the reserves number about 161,000 on land and 6,500 over marine waters. According to the World Database on Protected Areas — a joint project of the United Nations Environment Programme and the International Union for Conservation of Nature — they occupied by 2015 a little less than 15 percent of Earth's land area and 2.8 percent of Earth's ocean area. The coverage is increasing gradually. This trend is encouraging. To have reached the existing level is a tribute to those who have participated in the global conservation effort. But is the level enough to halt the acceleration of species extinction? It is in fact nowhere close to enough.

The declining world of biodiversity cannot be saved by the piecemeal operations in current use. It will certainly be mostly lost if conservation continues to be treated as a luxury item in national budgets. The extinction rate our behavior is imposing, and seems destined to continue imposing, on the rest of life is more correctly viewed as the equivalent of a Chicxulub-size asteroid strike played out over several human generations.

The only hope for the species still living is a human effort commensurate with the magnitude of the problem. The ongoing mass extinction of species, and with it the extinction of genes and ecosystems, ranks with pandemics, world war, and climate change as among the deadliest

25

Barcroft Media/Getty Images

In this photograph, taken at a London protest in 2017, indigenous leaders from Latin America, Indonesia, and Africa take part in a "Guardians of the Forest" demonstration. Protesters called for recognition of indigenous rights to ancestral territory as a solution to climate change. **How do protests like this one fit into Wilson's vision for setting aside half the earth? Why do you think Wilson does not discuss indigenous rights in his "manifesto"?**

threats that humanity has imposed on itself. To those who feel content to let the Anthropocene evolve toward whatever destiny it mindlessly drifts to, I say, please take time to reconsider. To those who are steering the growth of nature reserves worldwide, let me make an earnest request: Don't stop. Just aim a lot higher.

Populations of species that were dangerously small will have space to grow. Rare and local species previously doomed by development will escape their fate. The unknown species will no longer remain silent and thereby be put at highest risk. People will have closer access to a world that is complex and beautiful beyond our present imagining. We will have more time to put our own house in order for future generations. Living Earth, all of it, can continue to breathe.

[2016]

EXPLORING THE TEXT

1. What is a "manifesto"? What connotations does the word carry? What tone does it establish for E. O. Wilson's title? To what extent does calling his essay a manifesto enhance or undermine his authority? Is there anything else about the title that might affect the reader's view of Wilson's ethos? Explain.

2. How would you characterize Wilson's opening strategy in the first two paragraphs? What is the effect of beginning the essay in this way?

3. In paragraph 3, Wilson offers two reasons for "committing half of the planet's surface to nature." What are they? Which do you find more compelling? Why?

4. Why does Wilson organize his essay into numbered sections? How does that arrangement serve his rhetorical purpose? How do these sections build on and relate to each other?

5. In part 2 Wilson states: "The logic for distinguishing the Anthropocene is sound" (para. 9). What leads him to this conclusion? How convincing do you find his argument to be here?

6. Why does Wilson say, at the beginning of part 4, that "Earth remains a little-known planet" (para. 12)? How does this claim relate to his overall argument?

7. In part 7, what does Wilson mean when he says, "The surviving wildlands of the world are not art museums" (para. 23)? Wilson continues to list other things that he believes do not describe the wildlands. How does beginning the section with these descriptions serve Wilson's rhetorical purpose? If he had begun that section with a list of things that *do* define the wildlands, how would this have affected his argument?

8. In part 3 Wilson states: "The biosphere does not belong to us; we belong to it" (para. 11). In part 7 he reiterates this point, this time in reference to wildlands: "We are their stewards, not their owners" (para. 23). What point is he trying to make with each of these statements? How do they inform the logic of his main argument?

9. What does E. O. Wilson find encouraging regarding humankind's approach to conserving the environment? Explain.

10. Wilson states, in part 1 and again in the final section, that his proposed solution is "commensurate with the magnitude of the problem" (paras. 4 and 28). What rhetorical purpose does repeating this exact phrase achieve?

11. What does Wilson say are the four "deadliest threats that humanity has imposed on itself" (para. 28)? What effect does Wilson achieve by placing his subject in the company of other widely recognized threats to humanity? Is his belief that these threats are "self-imposed" likely to alienate his audience? Why or why not? How did you react as a reader to such a claim?

12. How would you compare the tone and content of Wilson's final paragraph with that of his first two? What is the effect of beginning and ending this way?

13. How effectively does Wilson communicate the urgency of his message? Be sure to cite specific rhetorical strategies he uses in this essay in your response.

14. How likely is it that Wilson's argument will have a strong effect on American environmental policy? Explain why you hold this view.

Our Climate Future Is Actually Our Climate Present

JON MOOALLEM

Jon Mooallem is an American journalist and author. He is a contributing writer for the *New York Times Magazine*, where he often covers the relationship between humans and other animals. His book *Wild Ones* (2013), which analyzes Americans' cultural relationship to observing animals and conserving endangered species, was chosen as a best book of 2013 by the *New York Times Book Review*, the *New Yorker*, National Public Radio's *Science Friday*, and *Gizmodo*. Mooallem also contributes to the public radio program *This American Life* and has been a guest on *Fresh Air*, *Radiolab*, and *The Colbert Report*. The following article appeared in the *New York Times Magazine* in 2017.

A few years ago, a locally famous blogger in San Francisco, known as Burrito Justice, created an exquisitely disorienting map, with help from a cartographer named Brian Stokle, and started selling copies of it online. The map imagined the city in the year 2072, after 60 years of rapid sea-level rise totaling 200 feet. At present, San Francisco is a roughly square-shaped, peninsular city. But on the map, it is severed clean from the mainland and shaved into a long, fat smudge. The shape of the land resembles a sea bird diving underwater for prey, with odd bays chewing into the coastlines and, farther out, a sprawl of bulging and wispy islands that used to be hills. If you lived in San Francisco, it was a map of where you already were and, simultaneously, where you worried you might be heading. "The San Francisco Archipelago," Burrito Justice called it — a formerly coherent city in shards.

The map wasn't science; it didn't even pretend to be. I want to be very clear about that, because I worry it's reckless to inject any more false facts into a conversation about climate change. Projecting the effect of sea-level rise on a specific location typically involves recondite computer models and calculations; Burrito Justice was just a fascinated hobbyist, futzing around on his laptop in his backyard. His entire premise was unscientific; for now, it is unthinkable that seas will rise so high so quickly. Even as most credible scientific estimates keep increasing

and the poles melt faster than imagined, those estimates currently reach only between six and eight feet by the year 2100. That's still potentially cataclysmic: Water would push into numerous cities, like Shanghai, London and New York, and displace hundreds of millions of people. And yes, there are some fringe, perfect-storm thought experiments out there that can get you close to 200 feet by the end of the century. But in truth, Burrito Justice settled on that number only because that's how high he needed to jack up the world's oceans if he wanted to wash out a particular road near his house. He has a friendly rivalry with another blogger, who lives in an adjacent neighborhood known for being a cloistered hamlet, and Burrito Justice thought it would be funny to see it literally become an island. So again: The map wasn't science. It didn't pretend to be. The point, initially, was just to needle this other guy named Todd.

Still, the San Francisco Archipelago has always stuck with me, because, almost in spite of itself, it managed to convey something peculiar and destabilizing about our climatological future. Burrito Justice hadn't just redrawn the geography of a place; he'd also carried a sense of that place forward in time. And by transposing some of the grit and silly shibboleths[1] of contemporary city

---

[1] A word or saying used by adherents of a party, sect, or belief and usually regarded by others as empty of real meaning. —Eds.

life onto that alternate landscape, the map (and the little blog posts he wrote to accompany it) prodded you to entertain the possibility that this ruined future might not feel like an emergency to those living it, that life in that archipelago might have all the richness, realness and inanity of ours.

There were, most obviously, the breezy, optimistic names given to every new feature of the redrawn city, as though its ever-peppy real estate agents had gone on rebranding neighborhoods as the landscape drowned. Climate change, in this scenario, had more in common with gentrification than with a natural disaster: a ceaseless upheaval of familiar spaces that left old-timers shaking their heads, then kept accelerating. Instead of Telegraph Hill rising north of Market Street downtown, Telegraph Island now offered a tranquil view of Market Shoals. Dolores Park was gone. But Cape Dolores jutted toward it, overlooking the submerged Mission District — now Mission Gulf. The former San Francisco Zoo, out at Ocean Beach, was labeled San Francisco Aquarium.

Life went on, in other words — albeit in some bleak and greatly diminished capacity. Taco boats replaced taco trucks, the public-transit agency's "sea bus" system exaggerated its on-time performance statistics and the city government was offering to extend the notorious tax break it offered Twitter in 2011 if the tech company relocated to "disadvantaged Nob Island." The only people who remembered us, or validated our earlier reality, came off as loopy, Nimby activists aiming to obstruct development on one of the new coasts. "Old San Francisco is still alive in our hearts and minds," a statement from the Submerged Historic San Francisco Preservation Association insists, "even if only the tops of the buildings can be seen!"

The map was a joke. But the longer I looked at it, the less funny and more upsetting it got. I pictured the first apartment my wife and I rented in San Francisco, how I'd parked the car out front while, just home from the hospital, she carried our first baby up the stairs. Then I pictured that all under water, and a man pushing off in his kayak for a paddle far overhead.

◆ ◆ ◆

The future we've been warned about is beginning to saturate the present. We tend to imagine climate change as a destroyer. But it also traffics in disruption, disarray: increasingly frequent and more powerful storms and droughts; heightened flooding; expanded ranges of pests turning forests into fuel for wildfires; stretches of inhospitable heat. So many facets of our existence — agriculture, transportation, cities and the architecture they spawned — were designed to suit specific environments. Now they are being slowly transplanted into different, more volatile ones, without ever actually moving.

We're accustomed to hearing about the tragically straightforward cases of island nations that will simply disappear: countries like Tuvalu and Kiribati that face the possibility of having to broker the wholesale resettlement of their people in other countries. Yet there must also be, in any corner of the planet, and for each human living on it, a threshold at which a familiar place becomes an unfamiliar one: an altered atmosphere, inundated by differentness and weirdness, in which, on some level, we'll live on, in exile. The Australian philosopher Glenn Albrecht describes this feeling as "solastalgia": "a form of homesickness one gets when one is still at `home.´"

Some communities will face new problems and varieties of weather; in others, existing ones will intensify. Already-vulnerable societies — the poor, the poorly governed — may be stressed to grim breaking points. Consider the mass starvation in South Sudan, Nigeria, Yemen and Somalia, where a total of nearly a million and a half children are predicted to die this year — and that climate change is projected to worsen the kind of droughts that caused it. Consider, too, a 2015 Department of Defense report, which framed climate change as a geopolitical "threat multiplier" that will "threaten domestic stability in a number of countries," and cited a study showing how a five-year drought in Syria contributed to the outbreak of the current conflict there. Nonetheless, denial is coming back in fashion among the most powerful. We have a president who dismisses climate change as a hoax, and a budget director who belittles government programs to study and adapt to our new reality as a "waste of your money."

Still, we insulate ourselves from the disorientation and alarm in other, more pernicious ways, too. We seem able to normalize catastrophes as we absorb them, a phenomenon that points to what Peter Kahn, a professor of psychology at the University of Washington, calls "environmental generational amnesia." Each generation, Kahn argues, can recognize only the ecological changes its members witness during their lifetimes. When we spoke recently, Kahn pointed to the living conditions in megacities like Kolkata, or in the highly polluted, impoverished areas affected by Houston's oil refineries, where he conducted his initial research in the early '90s. In Houston, Kahn found that two-thirds of the children he interviewed understood that air and water pollution were environmental issues. But only one-third believed *their* neighborhood was polluted. "People are born into this life," Kahn told me, "and they think it's normal."

A University of British Columbia fisheries scientist, Daniel Pauly, hit upon essentially the same idea around the same time, recognizing that as populations of large fish collapsed, humanity had gone on obliviously fishing slightly smaller species. One result, Pauly wrote, was a "creeping disappearance" of overall fish stocks behind ever-changing and "inappropriate reference points." He called this impaired vision "shifting baseline syndrome."

There are, however, many subtler shifts in our awareness that can't be as precisely demarcated. Scenarios that might sound dystopian or satirical as broad-strokes future projections unassumingly materialize as reality. Last year, melting permafrost in Siberia released a strain of anthrax, which had been sealed in a frozen reindeer carcass, sickening 100 people and killing one child. In July 2015, during the hottest month ever recorded on earth (until the following year), and the hottest day ever recorded in England (until the following summer), the *Guardian* newspaper had to shut down its live-blogging of the heat wave when the servers overheated. And low-lying cities around the world are experiencing increased "clear-sky flooding," in which streets or entire neighborhoods are washed out temporarily by high tides and storm surges. Parts of Washington now experience flooding 30 days a year, a figure that has roughly quadrupled since 1960. In Wilmington, N.C., the number is 90 days. But scientists and city planners have conjured a term of art that defuses that astonishing reality: "nuisance flooding," they call it.

Kahn calls our environmental generational amnesia "one of the central psychological problems of our lifetime," because it obscures the magnitude of so many concrete problems. You can wind up not looking away, exactly, but zoomed in too tightly to see things for what they are. Still, the tide is always rising in the background, swallowing something. And the longer you live, the more anxiously trapped you may feel between the losses already sustained and the ones you see coming.

Such shifting baselines muddle the idea of adaptation to climate change, too. Adaptation, Kahn notes, can mean anything from the human eye's adjusting to a darker environment within a few milliseconds to wolves' changing into dogs over thousands of years. It doesn't always mean progress, he told me; "it's possible to adapt and diminish the quality of human life." Adapting to avoid or cope with the suffering wrought by climate change might gradually create *other* suffering. And because of environmental generational amnesia, we might never fully recognize its extent. Think of how Shel Silverstein's *Giving Tree*, nimbly accommodating each of the boy's needs, eventually winds up a stump.

On the most fundamental level, Kahn argues, 15 we are already adapting to climate change through a kind of tacit acquiescence, the way people in a city like Beijing accept that simply breathing the air outside can make them sick. "People are aware — they're coughing and wheezing," he told me, "but they're not staging political revolutions." Neither are we. And, Kahn went on, we risk imprisoning ourselves, through gradual adaptation, into a condition of "unfulfilled flourishing." A wolf becomes a dog, genetically; it *wants* to fetch tennis balls and sleep at the foot of your bed. But imagine a dog that isn't yet a dog, that still wants to be a wolf.

Sure, I told him, but at some point it would all be too much. Potentially, Kahn said. But assumptions about the future, no matter how self-evident they may feel, don't automatically come true. "The amazing thing is that none of this seems to work the way we think it should. When I was growing up in the Bay Area in the 1970s, the traffic was really bad. And I said, If it just gets a little bit worse, you're going to have a major upheaval in consciousness. And every five years it got worse." He went silent for a second, then continued, "I'm just thinking about how many five-year periods I've lived through."

◆ ◆ ◆

One more thing about Burrito Justice and the origins of his archipelago map: Shortly after moving to San Francisco in the early 2000s, he happened upon a map of the city from 1853. Like other cities — New York, Boston, Seattle — San Francisco expanded its natural coastline with thousands of acres of "made land," filling in mud flats and harbors with phenomenal amounts

of debris and sand. But much of this happened after 1853; on the map Burrito Justice was looking at, San Francisco was smaller — physically smaller. And he was struck by how much its former shape might resemble its future one. It wouldn't take much water for climate change to unmake the made land. The city would revert to its previous version, as though leveled by some cosmic control-Z.[2]

As Burrito Justice described this to me on the phone one recent afternoon, I thought of a woman in San Francisco named Pamela Buttery, whom I'd heard about on National Public Radio in January. Buttery owned a condo in the Millennium Tower, a waterfront skyscraper downtown. But the tower had started sinking at an irregular angle, even before its completion in 2010; by now, it has tilted six inches and sunk a foot into the hodgepodge Victorian landfill on which it was constructed. Buttery lived on the 57th floor. "I've moved on into a depression about it," she said. Though she used to unwind by putting golf balls, the reporter noted that even this didn't "give her the same joy it once did. No matter which way she hits them, they all end up in the same corner." And I realized that if someone in 1853 had tried to anticipate the texture and oddities of future life in his artificially expanding city, and imagined a woman who can't satisfactorily putt golf balls on the 57th floor because her luxury condo is sinking into old garbage — well, I probably would have bought a copy of that guy's map, too.

The future is always somebody else's present — it will very likely feel as authentic, and only as horrific, as our moment does to us. But the present is also somebody else's future: We are already standing on someone else's ludicrous map. Except none of us are in on the joke, and I'm guessing that it won't feel funny any time soon.

[2017]

---

[2] Computer keyboard shortcut for "undo." —Eds.

EXPLORING THE TEXT

1. Jon Mooallem, speaking about a map created to show San Francisco in 2072, states that it "wasn't science; it didn't even pretend to be" (para. 2) and that it "was a joke" (para. 6). Why does the map appeal to him? Does using a map by a blogger who calls himself Burrito Justice ultimately undermine Mooallem's credibility or successfully draw the reader into his argument? Explain your response.

2. What does Mooallem mean when he says that "[t]he future we've been warned about is beginning to saturate the present" (para. 7)? What are some examples of this that you can think of?

3. Find at least one rhetorical strategy that Mooallem uses in paragraph 9. How effectively does he use this strategy? How does it contribute to his overall argument?

4. What are the main points raised by Peter Kahn and Daniel Pauly? How does Mooallem leverage their ideas to make his argument?

5. In paragraph 12, Mooallem presents three recent events that demonstrate how "[s]cenarios that might sound dystopian or satirical as broad-strokes future predictions unassumingly materialize as reality." Which of them best fits Mooallem's characterization? Of the three, which do you find most compelling? Explain why.

6. Discussing Kahn's ideas, Mooallem develops an analogy with Shel Silverstein's *The Giving Tree*, one with air pollution in Beijing, and another based on the evolution of wolf to dog. How do these analogies help advance Mooallem's argument? Which one is most effective, and why?

7. In paragraph 6, Mooallem quotes Kahn speaking of the traffic problem he has had to deal with. What are some implications of Kahn's point? Can you think of an example of your own that also illustrates Kahn's point?

8. How would you paraphrase the message of Mooallem's final paragraph? What are its implications for the future of the environment? What does it suggest Mooallem believes is humanity's degree of responsibility for it?

VISUAL TEXTS

A Short History of America

ROBERT CRUMB

Robert Crumb (b. 1943) was one of the originators of "underground" comics in the 1960s. The comic strip included here first appeared in *CoEvolution Quarterly* in 1979.

Robert Crumb, A Short History of America (cartoon panels depicting country turning into city)

[1979]

EXPLORING THE TEXT

1. How would you paraphrase the narrative sequence depicted in the twelve frames?

2. Imagine that you are living in the time that one of the frames presents. In a letter to someone living in an earlier frame, write about the progress the country has made. Or, write a warning to future generations who might occupy later frames.

3. What can you infer about Robert Crumb's attitude toward the progress depicted in the cartoon? Do you agree with his perspective? Why or why not?

4. Write an answer to the question posed — "*WHAT NEXT?!!*" — at the end of the final frame. Then create your own visual that supports your response. You can create your visual in one of three ways: draw the next frame or sequence of frames, take photos that depict the next frame or sequence, or find images online or in magazines that do so.

Let's Go

ROYAL DUTCH/SHELL

The following advertisement for the major oil company Royal Dutch/Shell has appeared in several national magazines.

LET'S GO FURTHER ON ONE LITRE OF FUEL.

We must learn to use energy more efficiently. For over 25 years, the Shell Eco-marathon has supported teams worldwide who explore ways to maximise fuel economy. The current record holder is capable of travelling 3,771km on the equivalent of one litre of fuel. This spirit epitomises our relationship with car manufacturers, finding ways to make cars more efficient. And is typical of our ambition to help build a better energy future. www.shell.com/letsgo

LET'S GO.

EXPLORING THE TEXT

1. Based on your reading of this ad, how would you define Shell's position on fuel efficiency and energy conservation?

2. What is the relationship between the graphic and the text in this ad? Explain how each complements the other.

3. The text begins with the inclusive "we." Notice also the repetition of "Let's go" (i.e., let *us* go) in the caption and the text. How does such a hortatory approach influence the effectiveness of the ad?

4. Shell makes much of its living selling gasoline. If we convert kilometers to miles and litres to gallons,

the car featured could get as much as 8,700 miles per gallon. Why would such a company extol the efficiency of such a vehicle? What is the rhetorical effect of such an advertisement?

5. What is the primary appeal of the ad? To ethos, logos, or pathos? Explain.

6. Considering its claims, assumptions, and evidence, how would you analyze this ad according to the Toulmin model that you learned about in Chapter 3?

7. After reading and thinking about the ad, how do you feel about the Shell oil company? How do you feel about the issues raised by the ad?

CONVERSATION

Sustainable Eating

The following texts each present a viewpoint on the issue of eating in an environmentally sustainable way.

SOURCES

1   **Michael Pollan** / from *Unhappy Meals*
2   **James McWilliams** / *The Locavore Myth*
3   **Nicolette Hahn Niman** / *The Carnivore's Dilemma*
4   **Jonathan Safran Foer** / *Let Them Eat Dog: A Modest Proposal for Tossing Fido in the Oven*
5   **Will Allen** / *A Good Food Manifesto for America*
6   **Aliza Eliazarov** / from *Waste Not* (photo essay)
7   **Emily Anthes** / from *Could Insects Be the Wonder Food of the Future?*
8   **Bahar Gholipour** / *Lab-Grown Meat May Save a Lot More Than Farm Animals' Lives*

After you have read, studied, and synthesized these pieces, enter the Conversation by responding to one of the writing prompts on pages 501–2.

 ## from **Unhappy Meals**

MICHAEL POLLAN

The following selection is comprised of a "few (flagrantly unscientific) rules of thumb" author Michael Pollan has developed for eating well. They appear at the end of an article titled "Unhappy Meals," which first appeared in the *New York Times* magazine in 2007.

1. Eat food. Though in our current state of confusion, this is much easier said than done. So try this: Don't eat anything your great-great-grandmother wouldn't recognize as food. (Sorry, but at this point Moms are as confused as the rest of us, which is why we have to go back a couple of generations, to a time before the advent of modern food products.) There are a great many foodlike items in the supermarket your ancestors wouldn't recognize as food (Go-Gurt? Breakfast-cereal bars? Nondairy creamer?); stay away from these.

2. Avoid even those food products that come bearing health claims. They're apt to be heavily processed, and the claims are often dubious at best. Don't forget that margarine, one of the first industrial foods to claim that it was more healthful than the traditional food it replaced, turned out to give people heart attacks. When Kellogg's can boast about its Healthy Heart Strawberry Vanilla cereal bars, health claims have become hopelessly compromised. (The American Heart Association charges food makers for their endorsement.) Don't take the silence of the yams as a sign that they have nothing valuable to say about health.

3. Especially avoid food products containing ingredients that are a) unfamiliar, b) unpronounceable c) more than five in number — or

that contain high-fructose corn syrup. None of these characteristics are necessarily harmful in and of themselves, but all of them are reliable markers for foods that have been highly processed.

4. Get out of the supermarket whenever possible. You won't find any high-fructose corn syrup at the farmer's market; you also won't find food harvested long ago and far away. What you will find are fresh whole foods picked at the peak of nutritional quality. Precisely the kind of food your great-great-grandmother would have recognized as food.

5. Pay more, eat less. The American food system has for a century devoted its energies and policies to increasing quantity and reducing price, not to improving quality. There's no escaping the fact that better food — measured by taste or nutritional quality (which often correspond) — costs more, because it has been grown or raised less intensively and with more care. Not everyone can afford to eat well in America, which is shameful, but most of us can: Americans spend, on average, less than 10 percent of their income on food, down from 24 percent in 1947, and less than the citizens of any other nation. And those of us who can afford to eat well should. Paying more for food well grown in good soils — whether certified organic or not — will contribute not only to your health (by reducing exposure to pesticides) but also to the health of others who might not themselves be able to afford that sort of food: the people who grow it and the people who live downstream, and downwind, of the farms where it is grown.

"Eat less" is the most unwelcome advice of all, but in fact the scientific case for eating a lot less than we currently do is compelling. "Calorie restriction" has repeatedly been shown to slow aging in animals, and many researchers (including Walter Willett, the Harvard epidemiologist) believe it offers the single strongest link between diet and cancer

prevention. Food abundance is a problem, but culture has helped here, too, by promoting the idea of moderation. Once one of the longest-lived people on earth, the Okinawans practiced a principle they called "Hara Hachi Bu": eat until you are 80 percent full. To make the "eat less" message a bit more palatable, consider that quality may have a bearing on quantity: I don't know about you, but the better the quality of the food I eat, the less of it I need to feel satisfied. All tomatoes are not created equal.

6. Eat mostly plants, especially leaves. Scientists may disagree on what's so good about plants — the antioxidants? Fiber? Omega-3s? — but they do agree that they're probably really good for you and certainly can't hurt. Also, by eating a plant-based diet, you'll be consuming far fewer calories, since plant foods (except seeds) are typically less "energy dense" than the other things you might eat. Vegetarians are healthier than carnivores, but near vegetarians ("flexitarians") are as healthy as vegetarians. Thomas Jefferson was on to something when he advised treating meat more as a flavoring than a food.

7. Eat more like the French. Or the Japanese. Or the Italians. Or the Greeks. Confounding factors aside, people who eat according to the rules of a traditional food culture are generally healthier than we are. Any traditional diet will do: if it weren't a healthy diet, the people who follow it wouldn't still be around. True, food cultures are embedded in societies and economies and ecologies, and some of them travel better than others: Inuit not so well as Italian. In borrowing from a food culture, pay attention to how a culture eats, as well as to what it eats. In the case of the French paradox, it may not be the dietary nutrients that keep the French healthy (lots of saturated fat and alcohol?!) so much as the dietary habits: small portions, no seconds or snacking, communal meals — and the serious pleasure

taken in eating. (Worrying about diet can't possibly be good for you.) Let culture be your guide, not science.

8. Cook. And if you can, plant a garden. To take part in the intricate and endlessly interesting processes of providing for our sustenance is the surest way to escape the culture of fast food and the values implicit in it: that food should be cheap and easy; that food is fuel and not communion. The culture of the kitchen, as embodied in those enduring traditions we call cuisines, contains more wisdom about diet and health than you are apt to find in any nutrition journal or journalism. Plus, the food you grow yourself contributes to your health long before you sit down to eat it. So you might want to think about putting down this article now and picking up a spatula or hoe.

9. Eat like an omnivore. Try to add new species, not just new foods, to your diet. The greater the diversity of species you eat, the more likely you are to cover all your nutritional bases. That of course is an argument from nutritionism, but there is a better one, one that takes a broader view of "health." Biodiversity in the diet means less monoculture in the fields. What does that have to do with your health? Everything. The vast monocultures that now feed us require tremendous amounts of chemical fertilizers and pesticides to keep from collapsing. Diversifying those fields will mean fewer chemicals, healthier soils, healthier plants and animals and, in turn, healthier people. It's all connected, which is another way of saying that your health isn't bordered by your body and that what's good for the soil is probably good for you, too.

10

QUESTIONS

1. Michael Pollan opens with a deceptively simple assertion: "Eat food." How could those two words serve as a summary of the entire piece?

2. Why is Pollan suspicious of "health claims" (para. 2) made about food?

3. Pick out a few packages, boxes, packages, or cans from your pantry or refrigerator and read the list of ingredients. How much of it qualifies as "food," by Pollan's standards?

4. In paragraph 5, Pollan states: "Americans spend, on average, less than 10 percent of their income on food, down from 24 percent in 1947." Are you surprised by those statistics? What does this data suggest about our economy? About American values? What is Pollen's purpose in including that information?

5. What are some of the collateral effects — both positive and negative — of the "American food system" (para. 5)?

6. How does Pollan use humor in his list? Identify two examples and explain how the humor contributes to his overall argument.

7. Pollan addresses science — sometimes directly, sometimes indirectly — in "rules of thumb" 2, 5, 6, 7, and 9. What do these rules reveal about Pollan's attitude toward science?

8. How do the "rules," particularly number 8, reveal Pollan's values? To what extent do you share those values?

9. What inferences can you make about Pollen's intended audience? Consider various characteristics such as socioeconomic status, educational attainment, and core values. To what extent does his argument take into account those who have no choice but to use a local supermarket?

10. How would you rank the "rules" in order of ease? Would your ranking change for practicality or likelihood of being followed? Explain why or why not.

2   The Locavore Myth

JAMES McWILLIAMS

The following article challenging the locavore movement appeared in 2009 in *Forbes*, a business magazine. McWilliams is a professor of history at Texas State University.

Buy local, shrink the distance food travels, save the planet. The locavore movement has captured a lot of fans. To their credit, they are highlighting the problems with industrialized food. But a lot of them are making a big mistake. By focusing on transportation, they overlook other energy-hogging factors in food production.

Take lamb. A 2006 academic study (funded by the New Zealand government) discovered that it made more environmental sense for a Londoner to buy lamb shipped from New Zealand than to buy lamb raised in the U.K. This finding is counterintuitive — if you're only counting food miles. But New Zealand lamb is raised on pastures with a small carbon footprint, whereas most English lamb is produced under intensive factory-like conditions with a big carbon footprint. This disparity overwhelms domestic lamb's advantage in transportation energy.

New Zealand lamb is not exceptional. Take a close look at water usage, fertilizer types, processing methods and packaging techniques and you discover that factors other than shipping far outweigh the energy it takes to transport food. One analysis, by Rich Pirog of the Leopold Center for Sustainable Agriculture, showed that transportation accounts for only 11% of food's carbon footprint. A fourth of the energy required to produce food is expended in the consumer's kitchen. Still more energy is consumed per meal in a restaurant, since restaurants throw away most of their leftovers.

Locavores argue that buying local food supports an area's farmers and, in turn, strengthens the community. Fair enough. Left unacknowledged, however, is the fact that it also hurts farmers in other parts of the world. The U.K. buys most of its green beans from Kenya. While it's true that the beans almost always arrive in airplanes — the form of transportation that consumes the most energy — it's also true that a campaign to shame English consumers with small airplane stickers affixed to flown-in produce threatens the livelihood of 1.5 million sub-Saharan farmers.

Another chink in the locavores' armor involves the way food miles are calculated. To choose a locally grown apple over an apple trucked in from across the country might seem easy. But this decision ignores economies of scale. To take an extreme example, a shipper sending a truck with 2,000 apples over 2,000 miles would consume the same amount of fuel per apple as a local farmer who takes a pickup 50 miles to sell 50 apples at his stall at the green market. The critical measure here is not food miles but apples per gallon.

The one big problem with thinking beyond food miles is that it's hard to get the information you need. Ethically concerned consumers know very little about processing practices, water availability, packaging waste and fertilizer application. This is an opportunity for watchdog groups. They should make life-cycle carbon counts available to shoppers.

Until our food system becomes more transparent, there is one thing you can do to shrink the carbon footprint of your dinner: Take the meat off your plate. No matter how you slice it, it takes more energy to bring meat, as opposed to plants, to the table. It takes 6 pounds of grain to make a pound of chicken and 10 to 16 pounds to make a pound of beef. That difference translates into big differences in inputs. It requires 2,400 liters of water to make a burger and only 13 liters to grow a tomato. A majority of the water in the American West goes toward the production of pigs, chickens and cattle.

The average American eats 273 pounds of meat a year. Give up red meat once a week and you'll save as much energy as if the only food miles in your diet were the distance to the nearest truck farmer.

If you want to make a statement, ride your bike to the farmer's market. If you want to reduce greenhouse gases, become a vegetarian.

QUESTIONS

1. According to James McWilliams, locavores point to what serious problems? What are some of the unexpected disadvantages of the locavore movement?

2. Do you find McWilliams's use of lamb as an example to be convincing? Why or why not?

3. In paragraph 4, McWilliams writes, "Fair enough." What is the rhetorical effect of this sentence fragment? How does it contribute to his argument?

4. McWilliams writes, "To take an extreme example, a shipper sending a truck with 2,000 apples over 2,000 miles would consume the same amount of fuel per apple as a local farmer who takes a pickup 50 miles to sell 50 apples at his stall at the green market"

   (para. 5). Do you find the example of the local farmer to be realistic? Is McWilliams's "extreme example" perhaps too extreme? Is it a "straw man"? How does it affect the persuasiveness of his argument? Explain your response.

5. Go back and read the title of the article. Which features of the locavore movement does McWilliams regard as "myth"? Which does he regard as real?

6. In paragraph 7, McWilliams shifts his attention to the topic of meat. Do you think this shift in focus is effective, or is it an unnecessary tangent? What is the rhetorical effect of the final sentence? Explain.

---

3   The Carnivore's Dilemma

NICOLETTE HAHN NIMAN

In the following selection, published in the *New York Times* in 2009, Nicolette Hahn Niman, who is a lawyer and rancher, argues the case for eating meat.

Is eating a hamburger the global warming equivalent of driving a Hummer? This week an article in the *Times* of London carried a headline that blared: "Give Up Meat to Save the Planet." Former Vice President Al Gore, who has made climate change his signature issue, has even been assailed for omnivorous eating by animal rights activists.

It's true that food production is an important contributor to climate change. And the claim that meat (especially beef) is closely linked to global warming has received some credible backing, including by the United Nations and University of Chicago. Both institutions have issued reports that have been widely summarized as condemning meat-eating.

But that's an overly simplistic conclusion to draw from the research. To a rancher like me, who raises cattle, goats and turkeys the traditional way (on grass), the studies show only that the prevailing methods of producing meat — that is, crowding animals together in factory farms, storing their waste in giant lagoons and cutting down forests to grow crops to feed them — cause substantial greenhouse gases. It could be, in fact, that a conscientious meat eater may have a more environmentally friendly diet than your average vegetarian.

So what is the real story of meat's connection to global warming? Answering the question requires examining the individual greenhouse gases involved: carbon dioxide, methane and nitrous oxides.

Carbon dioxide makes up the majority of agriculture-related greenhouse emissions. In American farming, most carbon dioxide emissions come from fuel burned to operate vehicles and equipment. World agricultural carbon emissions, on the other hand, result primarily from the clearing of woods for crop growing and livestock grazing. During the 1990s, tropical deforestation in Brazil, India, Indonesia, Sudan and other developing countries caused 15 percent to 35 percent of annual global fossil fuel emissions.

Much Brazilian deforestation is connected to soybean cultivation. As much as 70 percent of areas newly cleared for agriculture in Mato Grosso State in Brazil is being used to grow soybeans. Over half of Brazil's soy harvest is controlled by a handful of international agribusiness companies, which ship it all over the world for animal feed and food products, causing emissions in the process.

Meat and dairy eaters need not be part of this. Many smaller, traditional farms and ranches in the United States have scant connection to carbon dioxide emissions because they keep their animals outdoors on pasture and make little use of machinery. Moreover, those farmers generally use less soy than industrial operations do, and those who do often grow their own, so there are no emissions from long-distance transport and zero chance their farms contributed to deforestation in the developing world.

In contrast to traditional farms, industrial livestock and poultry facilities keep animals in buildings with mechanized systems for feeding, lighting, sewage flushing, ventilation, heating and cooling, all of which generate emissions. These factory farms are also soy guzzlers and acquire much of

their feed overseas. You can reduce your contribution to carbon dioxide emissions by avoiding industrially produced meat and dairy products.

Unfortunately for vegetarians who rely on it for protein, avoiding soy from deforested croplands may be more difficult: as the Organic Consumers Association notes, Brazilian soy is common (and unlabeled) in tofu and soymilk sold in American supermarkets.

Methane is agriculture's second-largest greenhouse gas. Wetland rice fields alone account for as much as 29 percent of the world's human-generated methane. In animal farming, much of the methane comes from lagoons of liquefied manure at industrial facilities, which are as nauseating as they sound.

This isn't a problem at traditional farms. "Before the 1970s, methane emissions from manure were minimal because the majority of livestock farms in the U.S. were small operations where animals deposited manure in pastures and corrals," the Environmental Protection Agency says. The E.P.A. found that with the rapid rise of factory farms, liquefied manure systems became the norm and methane emissions skyrocketed. You can reduce your methane emissions by seeking out meat from animals raised outdoors on traditional farms.

◆ ◆ ◆

Critics of meat-eating often point out that cattle are prime culprits in methane production. Fortunately, the cause of these methane emissions is understood, and their production can be reduced.

Much of the problem arises when livestock eat poor quality forages, throwing their digestive systems out of balance. Livestock nutrition experts have demonstrated that by making minor improvements in animal diets (like providing nutrient-laden salt licks) they can cut enteric methane by half. Other practices, like adding certain proteins to ruminant diets, can reduce methane production per unit of milk or meat by a factor of six, according to research at Australia's

University of New England. Enteric methane emissions can also be substantially reduced when cattle are regularly rotated onto fresh pastures, researchers at University of Louisiana have confirmed.

Finally, livestock farming plays a role in nitrous oxide emissions, which make up around 5 percent of this country's total greenhouse gases. More than three-quarters of farming's nitrous oxide emissions result from man-made fertilizers. Thus, you can reduce nitrous oxide emissions by buying meat and dairy products from animals that were not fed fertilized crops — in other words, from animals raised on grass or raised organically.

In contrast to factory farming, well-managed, non-industrialized animal farming minimizes greenhouse gases and can even benefit the environment. For example, properly timed cattle grazing can increase vegetation by as much as 45 percent, North Dakota State University researchers have found. And grazing by large herbivores (including cattle) is essential for well-functioning prairie ecosystems, research at Kansas State University has determined.

Additionally, several recent studies show that pasture and grassland areas used for livestock reduce global warming by acting as carbon sinks. Converting croplands to pasture, which reduces erosion, effectively sequesters significant amounts of carbon. One analysis published in the journal *Global Change Biology* showed a 19 percent increase in soil carbon after land changed from cropland to pasture. What's more, animal grazing reduces the need for the fertilizers and fuel used by farm machinery in crop cultivation, things that aggravate climate change.

Livestock grazing has other noteworthy environmental benefits as well. Compared to cropland, perennial pastures used for grazing can decrease soil erosion by 80 percent and markedly improve water quality, Minnesota's Land Stewardship Project research has found. Even the United Nations report acknowledges, "There is growing evidence that both cattle ranching and pastoralism can have positive impacts on biodiversity."

15

As the contrast between the environmental impact of traditional farming and industrial farming shows, efforts to minimize greenhouse gases need to be much more sophisticated than just making blanket condemnations of certain foods. Farming methods vary tremendously, leading to widely variable global warming contributions for every food we eat. Recent research in Sweden shows that, depending on how and where a food is produced, its carbon dioxide emissions vary by a factor of 10.

And it should also be noted that farmers bear only a portion of the blame for greenhouse gas emissions in the food system. Only about one-fifth of the food system's energy use is farm-related, according to University of Wisconsin research. And the Soil Association in Britain estimates that only half of food's total greenhouse impact has any connection to farms. The rest comes from processing, transportation, storage, retailing and food preparation. The seemingly innocent potato chip, for instance, turns out to be a dreadfully climate-hostile food. Foods that are minimally processed, in season and locally grown, like those available at farmers' markets and backyard gardens, are generally the most climate-friendly.

Rampant waste at the processing, retail and household stages compounds the problem. About half of the food produced in the United States is thrown away, according to University of Arizona research. Thus, a consumer could measurably reduce personal global warming impact simply by more judicious grocery purchasing and use.

20

None of us, whether we are vegan or omnivore, can entirely avoid foods that play a role in global warming. Singling out meat is misleading and unhelpful, especially since few people are likely to entirely abandon animal-based foods. Mr. Gore, for one, apparently has no intention of going vegan. The 90 percent of Americans who eat meat and dairy are likely to respond the same way.

Still, there are numerous reasonable ways to reduce our individual contributions to climate change through our food choices. Because it takes more resources to produce meat and dairy than, say, fresh locally grown carrots, it's sensible to cut back on consumption of animal-based foods. More important, all eaters can lower their global warming contribution by following these simple rules: avoid processed foods and those from industrialized farms; reduce food waste; and buy local and in season.

QUESTIONS

1. What is the "overly simplistic conclusion" that Nicolette Hahn Niman challenges? Why is it "overly simplistic" (para. 3)?

2. How successfully does Hahn Niman use sources and statistics to help support her argument? Do you find them convincing? Why or why not?

3. According to this article, what are the chief differences between factory farms and traditional farms? How compelling is the argument for traditional farming methods?

4. How has reading this piece affected your view of sustainable eating?

5. What is your view of the three rules with which the selection concludes? Are they good rules to follow? Why or why not?

---

4 Let Them Eat Dog
A Modest Proposal for Tossing Fido in the Oven

JONATHAN SAFRAN FOER

The following piece, a 2009 article published in the *Wall Street Journal* by novelist Jonathan Safran Foer, explores the taboo against eating dog in American society.

Despite the fact that it's perfectly legal in 44 states, eating "man's best friend" is as taboo as a man eating his best friend. Even the most enthusiastic carnivores won't eat dogs. TV guy and sometimes cooker Gordon Ramsay can get pretty macho with lambs and piglets when doing publicity for something he's selling, but you'll never see a puppy peeking out of one of his pots. And though he once said he'd electrocute his children if they became vegetarian, one can't help but wonder what his response would be if they poached the family pooch.

Dogs are wonderful, and in many ways unique. But they are remarkably unremarkable in their intellectual and experiential capacities. Pigs are every bit as intelligent and feeling, by any sensible definition of the words. They can't hop into the back of a Volvo, but they can fetch, run and play, be mischievous and reciprocate affection. So why don't they get to curl up by the fire? Why can't they at least be spared being tossed on the fire? Our taboo against dog eating says something about dogs and a great deal about us.

The French, who love their dogs, sometimes eat their horses.

The Spanish, who love their horses, sometimes eat their cows.

The Indians, who love their cows, sometimes 5
eat their dogs.

While written in a much different context, George Orwell's words (from "Animal Farm") apply here: "All animals are equal, but some animals are more equal than others."

So who's right? What might be the reasons to exclude canine from the menu? The selective carnivore suggests:

Don't eat companion animals. But dogs aren't kept as companions in all of the places they are eaten. And what about our petless neighbors? Would we have any right to object if they had dog for dinner?

OK, then: Don't eat animals with significant mental capacities. If by "significant mental capacities" we mean what a dog has, then good for the dog. But such a definition would also include the pig, cow and chicken. And it would exclude severely impaired humans.

Then: It's for good reason that the eternal taboos — don't fiddle with your crap, kiss your sister, or eat your companions — are taboo. Evolutionarily speaking, those things are bad for us. But dog eating isn't a taboo in many places, and it isn't in any way bad for us. Properly cooked, dog meat poses no greater health risks than any other meat.

Dog meat has been described as "gamey" "complex," "buttery" and "floral." And there is a proud pedigree of eating it. Fourth-century tombs contain depictions of dogs being slaughtered along with other food animals. It was a fundamental enough habit to have informed language itself: the Sino-Korean character for "fair and proper" (yeon) literally translates into "as cooked dog meat is delicious." Hippocrates[1] praised dog meat as a source of strength. Dakota Indians enjoyed dog liver, and not so long ago Hawaiians ate dog brains and blood. Captain Cook[2] ate dog. Roald Amundsen[3] famously ate his sled dogs. (Granted, he was really hungry.) And dogs are still eaten to overcome bad luck in the Philippines; as medicine in China and Korea; to enhance libido

in Nigeria and in numerous places, on every continent, because they taste good. For centuries, the Chinese have raised special breeds of dogs, like the black-tongued chow, for chow, and many European countries still have laws on the books regarding postmortem examination of dogs intended for human consumption.

◆ ◆ ◆

Of course, something having been done just about everywhere is no kind of justification for doing it now. But unlike all farmed meat, which requires the creation and maintenance of animals, dogs are practically begging to be eaten. Three to four million dogs and cats are euthanized annually. The simple disposal of these euthanized dogs is an enormous ecological and economic problem. But eating those strays, those runaways, those not-quite-cute-enough-to-take and not-quite-well-behaved-enough-to-keep dogs would be killing a flock of birds with one stone and eating it, too.

In a sense it's what we're doing already. Rendering — the conversion of animal protein unfit for human consumption into food for livestock and pets — allows processing plants to transform useless dead dogs into productive members of the food chain. In America, millions of dogs and cats euthanized in animal shelters every year become the food for our food. So let's just eliminate this inefficient and bizarre middle step.

This need not challenge our civility. We won't make them suffer any more than necessary. While it's widely believed that adrenaline makes dog meat taste better — hence the traditional methods of slaughter: hanging, boiling alive, beating to death — we can all agree that if we're going to eat them, we should kill them quickly and painlessly, right? For example, the traditional Hawaiian means of holding the dog's nose shut — in order to conserve blood — must be regarded (socially if not legally) as a no-no. Perhaps we could include dogs under the Humane Methods of Slaughter Act. That doesn't say anything about how they're

10

---

[1] Hippocrates (c. 460–c. 370 B.C.E.), an ancient Greek physician, known as the Father of Western Medicine. —Eds.

[2] Captain James Cook (1728–1779), a British explorer, navigator, and captain in the Royal Navy from 1768 to 1779. —Eds.

[3] Roald Amundsen (1872–1928), a Norwegian explorer who led the first expedition to reach the South Pole in 1911. —Eds.

treated during their lives, and isn't subject to any meaningful oversight or enforcement, but surely we can rely on the industry to "self-regulate," as we do with other eaten animals.

Few people sufficiently appreciate the colossal task of feeding a world of billions of omnivores who demand meat with their potatoes. The inefficient use of dogs — conveniently already in areas of high human population (take note, local-food advocates) — should make any good ecologist blush. One could argue that various "humane" groups are the worst hypocrites, spending enormous amounts of money and energy in a futile attempt to reduce the number of unwanted dogs while at the very same time propagating the irresponsible no-dog-for-dinner taboo. If we let dogs be dogs, and breed without interference, we would create a sustainable, local meat supply with low energy inputs that would put even the most efficient grass-based farming to shame. For the ecologically-minded it's time to admit that dog is realistic food for realistic environmentalists.

For those already convinced, here's a classic Filipino recipe I recently came across. I haven't tried it myself, but sometimes you can read a recipe and just know.

Stewed Dog, Wedding Style.

First, kill a medium-sized dog, then burn off the fur over a hot fire. Carefully remove the skin while still warm and set aside for later

15

(may be used in other recipes). Cut meat into 1" cubes. Marinate meat in mixture of vinegar, peppercorn, salt, and garlic for 2 hours. Fry meat in oil using a large wok over an open fire, then add onions and chopped pineapple and sauté until tender. Pour in tomato sauce and boiling water, add green pepper, bay leaf, and Tabasco. Cover and simmer over warm coals until meat is tender. Blend in purée of dog's liver and cook for additional 5–7 minutes.

There is an overabundance of rational reasons to say no to factory-farmed meat: It is the No. 1 cause of global warming, it systematically forces tens of billions of animals to suffer in ways that would be illegal if they were dogs, it is a decisive factor in the development of swine and avian flus, and so on. And yet even most people who know these things still aren't inspired to order something else on the menu. Why?

Food is not rational. Food is culture, habit, craving and identity. Responding to factory farming calls for a capacity to care that dwells beyond information. We know what we see on undercover videos of factory farms and slaughterhouses is wrong. (There are those who will defend a system that allows for occasional animal cruelty, but no one defends the cruelty, itself.) And despite it being entirely reasonable, the case for eating dogs is likely repulsive to just about every reader of this paper. The instinct comes before our reason, and is more important.

20

QUESTIONS

1. The taboo against eating dogs is not universal. Why is it so strong in our Western culture even when, according to Jonathan Safran Foer, it defies logic? Since, as Safran Foer states, "Three to four million dogs and cats are euthanized annually," (para. 12) why shouldn't we use them instead as food?

2. What are the three reasons the "selective carnivore" gives for why we should not eat dogs? Which do you find most compelling? Why?

3. In paragraph 15, Safran Foer states: "For the ecologically minded it's time to admit that dog

is realistic food for realistic environmentalists." How would you characterize his tone here? Is he serious, or tongue-in-cheek? Explain how you know.

4. Why does Safran Foer include the recipe near the end of his essay? What rhetorical purpose does it serve?

5. In paragraph 19 Safran Foer discusses factory-farmed meat. How does that discussion relate to eating dogs and contribute to his rhetorical purpose?

6. What is the relationship, as Safran Foer sees it, between reason and instinct? Do you agree that instinct, in this case, is more important? Why or why not?

7. What do the title and subtitle suggest about how Safran Foer intends his audience to understand

his essay? To what extent is this essay a satire? What, exactly, does the author satirize?

8. Effective humorists and satirists usually have a very serious point. What is Safran Foer's serious point? How would you state it in one sentence?

5 A Good Food Manifesto for America

WILL ALLEN

The following blog post from Growing Power's website is a plea for sustainable agricultural practices. It was written in 2010 by Will Allen, an urban farmer and former professional basketball player.

I am a farmer. While I find that this has come to mean many other things to other people — that I have become also a trainer and teacher, and to some a sort of food philosopher — I do like nothing better than to get my hands into good rich soil and sow the seeds of hope.

So, spring always enlivens me and gives me the energy to make haste, to feel confidence, to take full advantage of another all-too-short Wisconsin summer. This spring, however, much more so than in past springs, I feel my hope and confidence mixed with a sense of greater urgency. This spring, I know that my work will be all the more important, for the simple but profound reason that more people are hungry.

For years I have argued that our food system is broken, and I have tried to teach what I believe must be done to fix it. This year, and last, we have begun seeing the unfortunate results of systemic breakdown. We have seen it in higher prices for those who can less afford to pay, in lines at local food pantries, churches, and missions, and in the anxious eyes of people who have suddenly become unemployed. We have seen it, too, in nationwide outbreaks of food-borne illness in products as unlikely as spinach and peanuts.

Severe economic recession certainly has not helped matters, but the current economy is not alone to blame. This situation has been spinning

toward this day for decades. And while many of my acquaintances tend to point the finger at the big agro-chemical conglomerates as villains, the fault really is with all of us who casually, willingly, even happily surrendered our rights to safe, wholesome, affordable, and plentiful food in exchange for over-processed and pre-packaged convenience.

Over the past century, we allowed our agriculture to become more and more industrialized, more and more reliant on unsustainable practices, and much more distant from the source to the consumer. We have allowed corn and soybeans, grown on the finest farmland in the world, to become industrial commodities rather than foodstuffs. We have encouraged a system by which most of the green vegetables we eat come from a few hundred square miles of irrigated semi-desert in California.

When fuel prices skyrocket, as they did last year, things go awry. When a bubble like ethanol builds and then bursts, things go haywire. When drought strikes that valley in California, as is happening right now, things start to topple. And when the whole economy shatters, the security of a nation's food supply teeters on the brink of failure.

To many people, this might sound a bit hysterical. There is still food in the suburban supermarket aisles, yes. The shelves are not empty;

490

there are no bread lines. We haven't read of any number of Americans actually starving to death.

No, and were any of those things to happen, you can rest assured that there would be swift and vigorous action. What is happening is that many vulnerable people, especially in the large cities where most of us live, in vast urban tracts where there are in fact no supermarkets, are being forced to buy cheaper and lower-quality foods, to forgo fresh fruits and vegetables, or are relying on food programs — including our children's school food programs — that by necessity are obliged to distribute any kind of food they can afford, good for you or not. And this is coming to haunt us in health care and social costs. No, we are not suddenly starving to death; we are slowly but surely malnourishing ourselves to death. And this fate is falling ever more heavily on those who were already stressed: the poor. Yet there is little action.

Many astute and well-informed people beside myself, most notably Michael Pollan, in a highly persuasive treatise last fall in the *New York Times*, have issued these same warnings and laid out the case for reform of our national food policy. I need not go on repeating what Pollan and others have already said so well, and I do not wish merely to add my voice to a chorus.

I am writing to demand action.   10

It is time and past time for this nation, this government, to react to the dangers inherent in its flawed farm and food policies and to reverse course from subsidizing wealth to subsidizing health.

We have to stop paying the largest farm subsidies to large growers of unsustainable and inedible crops like cotton. We have to stop paying huge subsidies to Big Corn, Big Soy, and Big Chem to use prime farmland to grow fuel, plastics, and fructose. We have to stop using federal and state agencies and institutions as taxpayer-funded research arms for the very practices that got us into this mess.

We have to start subsidizing health and well-being by rewarding sustainable practices in agriculture and assuring a safe, adequate, and wholesome food supply to all our citizens. And we need to start this reform process now, as part of the national stimulus toward economic recovery.

In my organization, Growing Power Inc. of Milwaukee, we have always before tried to be as self-sustaining as possible and to rely on the market for our success. Typically, I would not want to lean on government support, because part of the lesson we teach is to be self-reliant.

But these are not typical times, as we are   15
now all too well aware.

As soon as it became clear that Congress would pass the National Recovery Act, I and members of my staff brainstormed ideas for a meaningful stimulus package aimed at creating green jobs, shoring up the security of our urban food systems, and promoting sound food policies of national scope. The outcome needed to be both "shovel-ready" for immediate impact and sustainable for future growth.

We produced a proposal for the creation of a public-private enabling institution called the Centers for Urban Agriculture. It would incorporate a national training and outreach center, a large working urban farmstead, a research and development center, a policy institute, and a state-of-the-future urban agriculture demonstration center into which all of these elements would be combined in a functioning community food system scaled to the needs of a large city.

We proposed that this working institution — not a "think tank" but a "do tank" — be based in Milwaukee, where Growing Power has already created an operating model on just two acres. But ultimately, satellite centers would become established in urban areas across the nation. Each would be the hub of a local or regional farm-to-market community food system that would provide sustainable jobs, job training, food production, and food distribution to those most in need of nutritional support and security.

This proposal was forwarded in February to our highest officials at the city, state, and federal level, and it was greeted with considerable approval. Unfortunately, however, it soon became clear that the way Congress had structured the stimulus package, with funds earmarked for only particular sectors of the economy, chiefly infrastructure, afforded neither our Congressional representatives nor our local leaders with the discretion to direct any significant funds to this innovative plan. It simply had not occurred to anyone that immediate and lasting job creation was plausible in a field such as community-based agriculture.

I am asking Congress today to rectify that oversight, whether by modifying the current guidelines of the Recovery Act or by designating new and dedicated funds to the development of community food systems through the creation of this national Centers for Urban Agriculture.

Our proposal budgeted the initial creation of this CUA at a minimum of $63 million over two years — a droplet compared to the billions being invested in other programs both in the stimulus plan and from year-to-year in the federal budget.

Consider that the government will fund the Centers for Disease Control at about $8.8 billion this year, and that is above the hundreds of millions more in research grants to other biomedical institutions, public and private. This is money well spent for important work to ensure Americans the best knowledge in protecting health by fighting disease; but surely by now we ought to recognize that the best offense against many diseases is the defense provided by a healthy and adequate diet. Yet barely a pittance of CDC money goes for any kind of preventive care research.

In 2008, the Department of Homeland Security approved spending $450 million for a new National Bio and Agro-Defense Facility at Kansas State University, in addition to the existing Biosecurity Research Institute already there. Again, money well spent to protect our food supply from the potential of a terrorist attack. But note that these hundreds of millions are being spent to protect us from a threat that may never materialize, while we seem to trivialize the very real and material threat that is upon us right now: the threat of malnourishment and undernourishment of very significant numbers of our citizens.

Government programs under the overwhelmed and overburdened departments of Agriculture and of Health and Human Services do their best to serve their many masters, but in the end, government farm and food policies are most often at odds between the needs of the young, the old, the sick, and the poor versus the wants of the super-industry that agriculture has become.

By and large, the government's funding of nutritional health comes down to spending millions on studies to tell us what we ought to eat without in any way guaranteeing that many people will be able to find or afford the foods they recommend. For instance, food stamps ensure only that poor people can buy food; they cannot ensure that, in the food deserts that America's inner cities have become, there will be any good food to buy.

We need a national nutrition plan that is not just another entitlement, that is not a matter of shipping surplus calories to schools, senior centers, and veterans' homes. We need a plan that encourages a return to the best practices of both farming and marketing, that rewards the grower who protects the environment and his customers by nourishing his soil with compost instead of chemicals and who ships his goods the shortest distance, not the longest.

If the main purpose of government is to provide for the common security of its citizens, surely ensuring the security of their food system must be among its paramount duties. And if among our rights are life, liberty, and the pursuit of happiness, we are denied all those rights if our cities become prisons of poverty and malnutrition.

As an African-American farmer, I am calling on the first African-American president of the United States to lead us quickly away from this deepening crisis. Demand, President Obama, that Congress and your own Administration begin without delay the process of reforming our farm and food policies. Start now by correcting the omission in your economic stimulus and recovery act that prevented significant spending on creating new and sustainable jobs for the poor in our urban centers as well as rural farm communities.

It will be an irony, certainly, but a sweet one, if millions of African-Americans whose grandparents left the farms of the South for the factories of the North, only to see those factories close, should now find fulfillment in learning once again to live close to the soil and to the food it gives to all of us.

I would hope that we can move along a continuum to make sure that all our citizens have access to the same fresh, safe, affordable good food regardless of their cultural, social, or economic situation.   *30*

QUESTIONS

1. Where does Will Allen lay blame for the conditions that he describes in paragraph 4?

2. What does Allen suggest are "unsustainable practices" (para. 5)?

3. Allen writes, "To many people, this might sound a bit hysterical" (para. 7). Does it to you? Why or why not?

4. What does Allen mean by "subsidizing health" (para. 11)? What current practices does he identify as unhealthy? Do you agree with him? Explain your response.

5. Allen suggests that access to "fresh, safe, affordable good food" (para. 30) is a right that all Americans should have. Do you agree? How can we work to bring such a condition about?

---

6 from Waste Not

ALIZA ELIAZAROV

The following photo essay is part of a project entitled "Waste Not," by Brooklyn-based photographer Aliza Eliazarov. The food shown in the following photographs has been salvaged from dumpsters in New York City and artfully rearranged as a still life. Still life is a centuries-old art form that typically depicts inanimate objects and is often rich in symbolism. Eliarazov began this project in 2011, and she characterizes it as a quest "to show the beauty in the food that was being wasted" in order to bring awareness to food rescue organizations and the issue of food waste.

Aliza Eliazarov

All food rescued from curbside garbage in front of Caputo's Bakery and Union Market on Court Street — Cobble Hill, Brooklyn.

Aliza Eliazarov

Oyster shells rescued from restaurant Maison Premiere in Brooklyn by Billion Oyster Project to be reseeded to restore oyster beds in New York Harbor.

Aliza Eliazarov

Produce and flowers rescued from curbside trash outside of Union Market at 7th Ave & 13th St. — Park Slope, Brooklyn.

Aliza Eliazarov

Composting organic matter and keeping it out of landfills reduces harmful methane gas emissions that contribute to climate change.

QUESTIONS

1. How do these photos emulate the still life genre? Why do you think Alia Eliazarov composed the subjects of her photographs the way that she did?

2. Select one particular detail from one of the photos — such as the book by Plato, the goblets, the plant that resembles a dead bird, or the composed skull with horns. What is its purpose and effect?

3. Which of the four photographs do you find the most compelling? Why? How appropriate would it be as a public service poster for a school's environmental club? Explain.

4. The first three captions in this photo essay are sentence fragments; the fourth is a complete sentence that makes an assertion. What is the rhetorical purpose of each? How do the first three support the argument made by the fourth?

5. Eliazarov's title, "Waste Not," evokes the familiar adage, "Waste not, want not." How does the visual essay connect both parts of that saying?

6. Overall, what does the visual essay suggest about sustainable eating?

---

7 from Could Insects Be the Wonder Food of the Future?

EMILY ANTHES

The following piece is from a 2014 article written by journalist Emily Anthes and published on the website for *BBC Future*.

At first my meal seems familiar, like countless other dishes I've eaten at Asian restaurants. A swirl of noodles slicked with oil and studded with shredded chicken, the aroma of ginger and garlic, a few wilting chives placed on the plate as a final flourish. And then, I notice the eyes. Dark, compound orbs on a yellow speckled head, joined to a winged, segmented body. I hadn't spotted them right away, but suddenly I see them everywhere — my noodles are teeming with insects.

I can't say I wasn't warned. On this warm May afternoon, I've agreed to be a guinea pig at an experimental insect tasting in Wageningen, a university town in the central Netherlands. My hosts are Ben Reade and Josh Evans from the Nordic Food Lab, a non-profit culinary research institute. Reade and Evans lead the lab's "insect deliciousness" project, a three-year effort to turn insects — the creepy crawlies that most of us squash without a second thought — into tasty treats. . . .

The next morning, Reade and Evans join 450 of the world's foremost experts on entomophagy, or insect eating, at a hotel down the road in Ede. They are here for Insects to Feed the World, a three-day conference to "promote the use of insects as human food and as animal feed in assuring food security."

The attendees are all familiar with the same dire facts. By the year 2050, the planet will be packed with nine billion people. In low- and middle-income countries, the demand for animal products is rising sharply as economies grow; in the next few decades, we'll need to figure out how to produce enough protein for billions more mouths. Simply ramping up our current system is not really a solution. The global livestock industry already takes an enormous toll on the environment. It's a hungry and thirsty beast, gobbling up land and water. It's a potent polluter, thanks to the animal waste and veterinary medicines that seep into soil and water. And it emits more greenhouse gases than planes, trains and automobiles combined.

The insect authorities assembling in Ede believe that entomophagy could be an elegant solution to many of these problems. Insects are chock-full of protein and rich in essential micro-nutrients, such as iron and zinc. They don't need as much space as livestock, emit lower levels of greenhouse gases, and have a sky-high feed conversion rate: a single kilogram of feed yields 12 times more edible cricket protein than beef protein. Some species of insects are drought resistant and may require less water than cows, pigs or poultry.

Insect meal could also replace some of the expensive ingredients (e.g. soybeans and fish-meal) that are fed to farm animals, potentially lowering the cost of livestock products and freeing up feed crops for human consump-tion. As an added bonus, bugs can be raised on refuse, such as food scraps and animal manure, so insect farms could increase the world's supply of protein while reducing and recycling waste. . . .

Turning to insects for nourishment is not a novel idea — the Bible mentions entomophagy, as do texts from Ancient Greece and Rome. But insect eating never became common in Modern Europe. The reasons are unknown, but the spread of agriculture — and, in particular, the domestication of livestock — may have made insects, and undomesticated plants and animals in general, less important as food sources.

Nevertheless, entomophagy remains com-mon in some parts of the world: at least two billion people worldwide eat insects, according to the FAO. Yellow jacket wasp larvae are popular in Japan, cicadas are treasured in Malawi, and weaver ants are devoured in Thailand. Termites, a food favourite in many African nations, can be fried, smoked, steamed, sun-dried or ground into a powder. The list of edible insect species is at 1,900 and growing. . . .

The conference-goers seem to find comfort in telling and re-telling the story of sushi — a strange, foreign dish that showcased raw fish

(raw fish!) and yet became not just acceptable but trendy in the West. . . .

Over my week in the Netherlands, I'd tried other delicacies: locust tabbouleh; chicken crumbed in buffalo worms; bee larvae ceviche; tempura-fried crickets; rose beetle larvae stew; soy grasshoppers; chargrilled sticky rice with wasp paste; buffalo worm, avocado and tomato salad; a cucumber, basil and locust drink; and a fermented, Asian-style dipping sauce made from grasshoppers and mealworms.

None of them had actually tasted bad. The insects themselves were quite bland. The crickets had a slightly fishy aftertaste and the buffalo worms a metallic one. The rose beetle larvae were vaguely reminiscent of smoked ham. Mostly, the insects were carriers for other, stronger flavours in a dish. . . .

Bart Muys, an ecologist at KU Leuven in Belgium, tells the conference-goers that although insects can be reared on relatively tiny plots of land, producing insect meal requires signifi-cantly more energy than fishmeal or soymeal does, largely because the bugs need to be raised in warm conditions. The environmental impact of each production system will vary. The golden rule, Muys warns, is: "Do not claim before you know." . . .

For their part, Evans and Reade reject the notion that insects will be some sort of silver bullet. Bugs, they say, will only be a real part of the solution if we are careful and thoughtful about how we integrate them into the food sys-tem. In their eyes, entomophagy is about more than merely getting a precise amount of protein on a plate — it's about making sure everyone on the planet has access to food that is afford-able, healthy, diverse, environmentally sound and, yes, delicious. "Insects can be a vehicle for something," Reade says. "But it has to be recognised that it's not the insects themselves that are going to make it sustainable. It's the humans."

10

QUESTIONS

1. The stated purpose of the conference Emily Anthes attends is to "promote the use of insects as human food and as animal feed in assuring food security" (para. 3). What do the conference promoters mean by "food security"? To what extent is that term euphemistic?

2. Considering the "dire facts" that Anthes presents in paragraph 4, do you think that eating insects is worthy of consideration as at least a partial solution to sustainable eating? Why or why not?

3. What are some of the pros to entomophagy? What might be some of the cons?

4. Have you visited a country where insects are eaten by people and/or seen entomophagy in practice? What was your reaction?

5. What is the rhetorical purpose of Anthes's reference to sushi in paragraph 9? How effective is it?

6. Why does Anthes introduce the ideas of Bart Muys? What is the significance of his "golden rule" (para. 12)?

7. How would you answer the three questions that Anthes poses in her penultimate paragraph?

8. Anthes concludes with a statement by Reade: "But it has to be recognised that it's not the insects themselves that are going to make it sustainable. It's the humans" (para. 13). What does Reade mean? How does Anthes's choice to conclude with this statement contribute to her overall argument?

8 Lab-Grown Meat May Save a Lot More Than Farm Animals' Lives

BAHAR GHOLIPOUR

The following article was written by Bahar Gholipour, a science journalist and neuroscientist. It was published on the NBC News website in 2017.

Imagine a backyard barbecue where the parents grill burgers and chicken kebabs they've grown from single cells using a home meat-making machine. Meanwhile, the kids are transfixed by grandparents' tales of life in the 20th century, before google was a verb and when meat was brutally carved from animals that looked like their pets.

We're not there, yet. But raising animals for consumption may soon become obsolete. Scientists have shown it's possible to produce animal-free beef, chicken, turkey, and fish. The latest example is lab-grown fried chicken, revealed last month by San Francisco-based startup Memphis Meats. Tasters of the product described it simply as chicken, perhaps a little spongier.

"I was blown away," says Emily Byrd, a spokesperson for the Good Food Institute, a nonprofit dedicated to promoting animal-free meat. "It's almost strange to talk about it because the only way I can describe it is that it was chicken."

Meat is essentially muscle tissue. If it grows naturally from a just few cells into a thick chunk, why can't the same process happen in the lab? Over the past few years, scientists have made progress in figuring out how to use self-renewing cells to grow this tissue outside the body, and some hope to scale it up for mass production soon. You can call it lab-grown, clean, or cultured meat — we have yet to settle on a term — but there's a good chance these products will replace conventional meat because of their potential to reduce environmental cost, increase health benefits for humans, and protect the welfare of the animals.

More Meat, Safer Production

Population growth and changing trends in diet have led to a doubling of meat consumption by humans over the past half-century. By 2050, estimates suggest meat production will have to increase to 455 million tons each year, up from 259 tons today, in order to satisfy the additional demand generated by population and income growth, according to a 2012 report by the United Nations.

But producing that much meat using conventional methods might ruin the planet. Meat and dairy products account for 70 percent of global water consumption, 38 percent of land use, and 19 percent of the world's greenhouse gas emissions, according to the report. The alarming environmental impact of meat production has even led the U.N. to suggest people curb their meat consumption, with a proposed regimen including one meat-free day each week.

Some analyses suggest that growing meat in factories could lessen the environmental footprint of livestock and reduce land and water use, as well as emissions. The lab-grown meat does, however, require creative designs to minimize the electricity and heat required to run the labs.

First, and most important, however, scientists and companies will need to figure out how to make enough lab-grown meat to bring its cost down to that of meat already on grocery shelves. Even the conventional meat industry is warming to the idea. In December, Tyson Foods, the largest U.S. meat company, launched a venture-capital fund to invest in start-ups that work on innovative approaches to protein products.

Historic Changes Are Underway

Winston Churchill predicted in a 1932 essay that within 50 years we'd be growing edible animal parts to "escape the absurdity of growing a whole chicken." He was just barely off. In 2002, a NASA-funded project successfully grew fillets from goldfish cells, but it wasn't until a little later that lab-grown meat started to look viable.

It started with a hamburger grown entirely outside an animal's body by Mark Post, professor of vascular physiology at Maastricht University in the Netherlands.

To grow the burger, he and his team used stem cells extracted from cow muscle tissue in a procedure similar to a biopsy. The cells were then put in a solution of bovine serum taken from unborn calves and then received food, hormones, and other elements naturally needed to grow. Over a few weeks, the cells multiplied and formed thin strips of muscle. It took about 20,000 of these strips to make one patty.

That project cost about $330,000. But the burger, the first of its kind, also required expert care of skilled technicians and expensive laboratory supplies. Post, who later formed the company Mosa Meat, has since announced that the price of his historic burger has fallen to $30 per pound.

Taste testers approved of his product and said it was "very meaty" — perhaps too meaty. It turns out much of red meat's taste actually comes from its fat content, which was nonexistent in the lab-grown burger. This complicates the job of meat creators; growing two types of tissues, each with different needs, outside their natural medium is difficult.

Rapidly Growing Biotechnology

Growing meat in the lab is possible because of breakthroughs in stem cell research and tissue engineering — two fields that have attracted scientific interest because of their immense potential in medicine. Uses now range from growing human tissue for transplantation to creating organs-on-chips for testing new drugs.

"Stem cell science and tissue engineering are at a stage that you can try other applications," says Shulamit Levenberg, a tissue engineer at Technion-Israel Institute of Technology in Haifa.

In her research, Levenberg created muscle grafts that can generate blood vessels to better survive when transplanted into the body. To do this requires a special expertise, one that also comes in handy for producing tasty lab-grown meat made of both muscle and fat, she says.

Such creative applications of tissue engineering are catching on. In 2015, the first cultured meat conference took place in the Netherlands and was attended by about 100 people, many of whom came from medical research fields only peripherally related to lab-grown meat production.

Meat of the Future

All this movement in new foods technology has triggered regulatory authorities to find ways of modernizing the rules set 25 years ago, when these new meat products were still science fiction.

In March, The National Academies of Sciences, Engineering, and Medicine in Washington, D.C. released a report on the issue. "The rapid and often unforeseen advances" in biotechnology over the past decade spurred the committee to predict all future products of biotechnology that may arise over the next five to 10 years. Animal-free meat and dairy production was one field identified as having "high growth potential."

Commercial interest in lab-grown meat may lead to other scientific breakthroughs as

20

it introduces new challenges for biomedical researchers. To reduce the price, for example, scientists will have to discover new ways to grow cells more efficiently, says Liz Specht, a senior scientist at Good Food Institute.

Taking an open source approach may help the field move forward, says Erin Kim of New Harvest, a research institute dedicated to funding the development of cultured meat and other cellular agriculture products. She and her colleagues are opening the field to interested researchers by helping to create "starter cell" lines they can buy to experiment on, much like researchers currently do with mice. This has led to the creation of a turkey cell line, which was used last year to grow a small turkey nugget by North Carolina State University graduate student Marie Gibbons.

It's possible that advances propelled by lab-grown meat could one day translate back into medical science.

"We are still limited in our understanding about how to grow larger pieces of tissue or functional organs," Levenberg says. "If the two parallel approaches — the medical and the food industry — work on it together, there are more chances solutions will be found."

QUESTIONS

1. In paragraph 4, Bahar Gholipour states that "there's a good chance these products will replace conventional meat because of their potential to reduce environmental cost, increase health benefits for humans, and protect the welfare of the animals." To what extent is it a "good chance" that we will change our eating habits as she says?

2. To support her argument, Gholipour refers to a United Nations report, to a NASA-funded project, and to a National Academies of Science, Engineering, and Medicine report. What is the rhetorical effect of using these sources? How does each of them contribute to her argument?

3. What is the rhetorical effect of the author's reference to Winston Churchill?

4. Gholipour believes that a major factor standing in the way of lab-grown meat is its high cost, and suggests that people will be ready when it is brought "down to that of meat already on grocery shelves" (para. 8). Do you agree? Why or why not?

5. What are some advantages to using lab-grown meat as food? What might be likely some objections? Do the pros outweigh the cons? Explain.

MAKING CONNECTIONS

1. Other than by length, how do the "rules" offered by Michael Pollan differ from those offered by Nicolette Hahn Niman? Which writer offers the most reasonable suggestions, in your view? Which set of "rules" would appeal most to James McWilliams, to Will Allen, and to Emily Anthes?

2. Compare Nicolette Hahn Niman's perspective on factory farms with that of Bahar Gholipour. Then compare her position on the eating of meat with that of James McWilliams. How would Gholipour respond to Hahn Niman? How would Hahn Niman respond to McWilliams? Refer to their texts in your answers.

3. Which writer develops the most persuasive argument regarding factory farms, Nicolette Hahn Niman or Will Allen? Compare them with one another.

4. In "A Good Food Manifesto for America," Will Allen writes, "For years I have argued that our food system is broken . . . " (para. 3). Which two writers

in the Conversation present the most convincing arguments concerning how to "fix" the system Allen discusses? Explain with reference to their texts.

5. Of the three approaches to alternative food — by Jonathan Safran Foer, Emily Anthes, and Bahar Gholipour — which do you think has the greatest chance of adoption? Which has the least? Explain your response.

6. How might other writers in the Conversation respond to Johathan Safran Foer's argument?

7. Which of the arguments presented in the Conversation are supported by the visual and textual information in the photo essay by Aliza Eliazarov? Explain.

8. The selections in this conversation present arguments of fact, arguments of value, and arguments of policy. Which selection would you regard as the best example of each? Explain why.

ENTERING THE CONVERSATION

As you respond to the following prompts, support your argument with references to at least three of the sources in this Conversation on Sustainable Eating. For help using sources, see Chapter 4.

1. Imagine that there is a well-known grassroots campaign that wants Congress to legislate against lab-grown meat production. Write an editorial for your school newspaper that supports or challenges this proposed ban. Refer to three of the sources in the Conversation as you support your argument.

2. Each of the writers in this Conversation is a contemporary, living writer. Write a letter addressed to one of them in which you defend, challenge, or qualify his or her position regarding sustainable eating. Refer to three of the other sources to support your position.

3. Imagine that your school's environmental club wants to place posters of animals in a factory farm in the hallways of the elementary, middle, and high schools in your district. Compose a speech that you would deliver to your school board in order to defend or challenge that practice. Refer to three of the sources in the Conversation to support your position.

4. In his essay, "Waste," farmer, professor, writer, and conservationist Wendell Berry states:

> But our waste problem is not the fault only of producers. It is the fault of an economy that is wasteful from top to bottom — a symbiosis of an unlimited greed at the top and a lazy, passive, and self-indulgent consumptiveness at the bottom — and all of us are involved in it. If we wish to correct this economy, we must be careful to understand and to demonstrate how much waste of human life is involved in our waste of the material goods of Creation. . . . The mess that surrounds us, then, must be understood not just as a problem in itself but as a symptom of a greater and graver problem: the centralization of our economy, the gathering of the productive property and power into fewer and fewer hands, and the consequent destruction, everywhere, of the local economies of household, neighborhood, and community.

Write an essay that defends, challenges, or qualifies Berry's position about waste in America. In your response, refer to Aliza Eliazarov's "Waste Not" and two of the other selections in this chapter in addition to your own observation and experience.

5. Imagine that the largest employer in your town is what many of these writers would call a "factory farm." In the voice of the owner of the farm, write a defense of your business, addressed to one of the writers in the Conversation. Refer to three of the other sources in your letter.

6. Your school has been selected to pilot an "alternative food" project, which will offer canine, insect, or lab-grown meat as a staple food. The project will offer free lunch for everyone during the trial period. Write an argument for your school paper for or against the adoption of the project.

7. Following Jonathan Safran Foer's lead, write your own "modest proposal" about sustainable eating.

8. Write a letter about sustainable eating to your local school board regarding the food offered in school cafeterias. Consider the factors that the board should consider before making dietary decisions for students.

from Silent Spring

RACHEL CARSON

I. A Fable for Tomorrow

There was once a town in the heart of America where all life seemed to live in harmony with its surroundings. The town lay in the midst of a checkerboard of prosperous farms, with fields of grain and hillsides of orchards where, in spring, white clouds of bloom drifted above the green fields. In autumn, oak and maple and birch set up a blaze of color that flamed and flickered across a backdrop of pines. Then foxes barked in the hills and deer silently crossed the fields, half hidden in the mists of the fall mornings.

Along the roads, laurel, viburnum and alder, great ferns and wildflowers delighted the travel-er's eye through much of the year. Even in win-ter the roadsides were places of beauty, where countless birds came to feed on the berries and on the seed heads of the dried weeds rising above the snow. The countryside was, in fact, famous for the abundance and variety of its bird life, and when the flood of migrants was pouring through in spring and fall people traveled from great distances to observe them. Others came to fish the streams, which flowed clear and cold out of the hills and contained shady pools where trout lay. So it had been from the days many years ago when the first settlers raised their houses, sank their wells, and built their barns.

Then a strange blight crept over the area and everything began to change. Some evil spell had settled on the community: mysterious maladies swept the flocks of chickens; the cattle and sheep sickened and died. Everywhere was a shadow of death. The farmers spoke of much illness among their families. In the town the doctors had become more and more puzzled by new kinds of sickness appearing among their patients. There had been several sudden and unexplained deaths, not only among adults but even among children, who would be stricken suddenly while at play and die within a few hours.

There was a strange stillness. The birds, for example — where had they gone? Many people spoke of them, puzzled and disturbed. The feed-ing stations in the backyards were deserted. The few birds seen anywhere were moribund; they trembled violently and could not fly. It was a spring without voices. On the mornings that had once throbbed with the dawn chorus of robins, catbirds, doves, jays, wrens, and scores of other bird voices there was now no sound; only silence lay over the fields and woods and marsh.

On the farms the hens brooded, but no chicks 5 hatched. The farmers complained that they were unable to raise any pigs — the litters were small and the young survived only a few days. The apple trees were coming into bloom but no bees droned among the blossoms, so there was no pollination and there would be no fruit.

The roadsides, once so attractive, were now lined with browned and withered vegetation as though swept by fire. These, too, were silent, deserted by all living things. Even the streams were now lifeless. Anglers no longer visited them, for all the fish had died.

In the gutters under the eaves and between the shingles of the roofs, white granular powder still showed a few patches; some weeks before it had fallen like snow upon the roofs and the lawns, the fields and streams.

No witchcraft, no enemy action had silenced the rebirth of new life in this stricken world. The people had done it themselves.

◆ ◆ ◆

This town does not actually exist, but it might easily have a thousand counterparts in America or elsewhere in the world. I know of no community that has experienced all the misfortunes I describe. Yet every one of these disasters has actually happened somewhere, and many real communities have already suffered a substantial number of them. A grim specter has crept upon us almost unnoticed, and this imagined tragedy may easily become a stark reality we all shall know.

---

1. What is the primary purpose of the section title, "A Fable for Tomorrow," and the opening sentence, "There was once a town in the heart of America where all life seemed to live in harmony with its surroundings"?

   a. to establish the fairy-tale quality of the description that follows
   b. to suggest that the first part of the writer's argument has mythical aspects
   c. to draw the reader into feeling comfortable with the simple, childlike story
   d. to set up the tone and tradition of a fable, indicating that there is a lesson to be learned
   e. to provide a false beginning that the writer can contradict as she builds her argument

2. The organizational pattern can best be described as

   a. cause and effect
   b. comparison and contrast
   c. problem and solution
   d. classification
   e. narration

3. The "flood of migrants" in the second paragraph refers to

   a. birds
   b. visitors
   c. fish
   d. foxes
   e. deer

4. Carson's reference to "the first settlers" at the end of paragraph 2 functions to

   a. illustrate the human interference with the natural order previously described
   b. contradict the argument about harmony established in the first sentence of the passage
   c. establish a long and prosperous history of human interaction with the area

   d. signify a shift from the discussion of nature to the discussion of people
   e. expand the argument to include human structures, such as "houses," "wells," and "barns"

5. The word "moribund" in paragraph 4 most likely means

   a. quiet
   b. infertile
   c. small
   d. afraid
   e. dying

6. The writer's use of first person in paragraph 9, beginning with "I know of no community," serves to

   a. shift from an impersonal tone to a confessional tone
   b. undermine the prior discussion by admitting lack of expertise
   c. establish an urgent, honest persona
   d. assert authority that cannot be questioned
   e. strengthen the argument by providing personal examples

7. What is the primary purpose of paragraph 9?

   a. to move the argument from hypothetical situation to reality
   b. to shift from the original argument to a counterargument
   c. to challenge the authority of those who might disagree
   d. to contradict the point established in the first paragraph
   e. to expand the argument from general discussion to specific examples

8. Each of the following pairs of images contributes to the author's argument EXCEPT

   a. "white clouds of bloom" (para. 1) and "no bees droned among the blossoms" (para. 5)

   b. "wildflowers delighted the traveler's eye" (para. 2) and "browned and withered vegetation" (para. 6)

   c. "blaze of color that flamed" (para. 1) and "shadow of death" (para. 3)

   d. "shady pools where trout lay" (para. 2) and "streams were now lifeless" (para. 6)

   e. "deer silently crossed the fields" (para. 1) and "seed heads of the dried weeds" (para. 2)

9. The speaker's attitude toward her subject may best be described as

   a. angry and argumentative

   b. concerned and logical

   c. formal and distant

   d. nostalgic and outraged

   e. formal and authoritative

---

from Nature

RALPH WALDO EMERSON

I. Nature

To go into solitude, a man needs to retire as much from his chamber as from society. I am not solitary whilst I read and write, though nobody is with me. But if a man would be alone, let him look at the stars. The rays that come from those heavenly worlds, will separate between him and what he touches. One might think the atmosphere was made transparent with this design, to give man, in the heavenly bodies, the perpetual presence of the sublime. Seen in the streets of cities, how great they are! If the stars should appear one night in a thousand years, how would men believe and adore; and preserve for many generations the remembrance of the city of God which had been shown! But every night come out these envoys of beauty, and light the universe with their admonishing smile.

The stars awaken a certain reverence, because though always present, they are inaccessible; but all natural objects make a kindred impression, when the mind is open to their influence. Nature never wears a mean appearance. Neither does the wisest man extort her secret, and lose his curiosity by finding out all her perfection. Nature never became a toy to a wise spirit. The flowers, the animals, the mountains, reflected the wisdom of his best hour, as much as they had delighted the simplicity of his childhood.

When we speak of nature in this manner, we have a distinct but most poetical sense in the mind. We mean the integrity of impression made by manifold natural objects. It is this which distinguishes the stick of timber of the wood-cutter, from the tree of the poet. The charming landscape which I saw this morning, is indubitably made up of some twenty or thirty farms. Miller owns this field, Locke that, and Manning the woodland beyond. But none of them owns the landscape. There is a property in the horizon which no man has but he whose eye can integrate all the parts, that is, the poet. This is the best part of these men's farms, yet to this their warranty-deeds give no title.

To speak truly, few adult persons can see nature. Most persons do not see the sun. At least they have a very superficial seeing. The sun illuminates only the eye of the man, but shines into the eye and the heart of the child. The lover of nature is he whose inward and outward senses are still truly adjusted to each other; who has retained the spirit of infancy even into the era of manhood. His intercourse with heaven and earth, becomes part of his daily food. In the presence of nature, a wild delight runs through the man, in spite of real sorrows. Nature says, — he is my creature, and maugre[1] all his impertinent griefs, he shall be glad with me. Not the sun or the summer alone, but every hour and season yields its tribute of delight; for every hour and change corresponds to and authorizes a different state of the mind, from breathless noon to grimmest midnight. Nature is a setting that fits equally well a comic or a mourning piece. In good health, the air is a cordial of incredible virtue. Crossing a bare common, in snow puddles, at twilight, under a clouded sky, without having in my thoughts any occurrence of special good fortune, I have enjoyed a perfect exhilaration. I am glad to the brink of fear. In the woods too, a man casts off his years, as the snake his slough, and at what period soever of life, is always a child. In the woods, is perpetual youth. Within these plantations of God, a decorum and sanctity reign, a perennial festival is dressed, and the guest sees not how he should tire of them in a thousand years. In the woods, we return to reason and faith. There I feel that nothing can befall me in life, — no disgrace, no calamity, (leaving me my eyes,) which nature cannot repair. Standing on the bare ground, — my head bathed by the blithe air, and uplifted into infinite space, — all mean egotism vanishes. I become a transparent eye-ball; I am nothing; I see all; the currents of the Universal Being circulate through me; I am part or particle of God. The name of the nearest friend sounds then foreign and accidental: to be brothers, to be acquaintances, — master or servant, is then a trifle and a disturbance. I am the lover of uncontained and immortal beauty. In the wilderness, I find something more dear and connate[2] than in streets or villages. In the tranquil landscape, and especially in the distant line of the horizon, man beholds somewhat as beautiful as his own nature.

The greatest delight which the fields and woods minister, is the suggestion of an occult relation between man and the vegetable. I am not alone and unacknowledged. They nod to me, and I to them. The waving of the boughs in the storm, is new to me and old. It takes me by surprise, and yet is not unknown. Its effect is like that of a higher thought or a better emotion coming over me, when I deemed I was thinking justly or doing right. 5

Yet it is certain that the power to produce this delight, does not reside in nature, but in man, or in a harmony of both. It is necessary to use these pleasures with great temperance. For, nature is not always tricked in holiday attire, but the same scene which yesterday breathed perfume and glittered as for the frolic of the nymphs, is overspread with melancholy today. Nature always wears the colors of the spirit. To a man laboring under calamity, the heat of his own fire hath sadness in it. Then, there is a kind of contempt of the landscape felt by him who has just lost by death a dear friend. The sky is less grand as it shuts down over less worth in the population.

---

[1]Despite. —Eds.

[2]Sympathetic. —Eds.

1. Throughout the passage, the author's attitude toward nature is one of

   a. objective practicality
   b. veiled disdain
   c. respectful awe
   d. childlike curiosity
   e. restrained ambivalence

2. What is the primary rhetorical function of the sentence "If the stars should appear one night in a thousand years, how would men believe and adore; and preserve for many generations the remembrance of the city of God which had been shown!" (end of para. 1)?

   a. to draw a comparison between God and the heavens to persuade the audience to practice religion
   b. to express the author's passion for stars and other phenomena of the night sky
   c. to suggest that without stars, humanity would have more faith in God
   d. to compare human-built structures such as cities to the grandeur and beauty of natural objects
   e. to illustrate the sublime aspects of nature, which the author believes most humans take for granted

3. The author's references to childhood in paragraph 4 serve to

   a. underscore his argument that only a pure, innocent spirit can truly understand nature
   b. illustrate the argument that those who love nature are simple and naive
   c. provide evidence of the youthful surface appearance of nature
   d. contrast with the imagery of wise adults who have abandoned childish thinking
   e. assert the idea that loss of innocence is the natural progression through life

4. Near the end of paragraph 4, the author's statement "I become a transparent eye-ball" functions as

   a. hyperbole, to marginalize the experience of being in the woods
   b. an illustration of the danger of being consumed by nature
   c. an image, to reinforce the significance of the author's eyesight
   d. metaphor for the clarity of perception in one who abandons oneself to nature
   e. a symbol for the loneliness of one who is solitary in nature

5. Which of the following explains the author's purpose for writing "The name of the nearest friend sounds then foreign and accidental" (end of para. 4)?

   a. to indicate his enjoyment of friends and their unique interests
   b. to expand the discussion of farmers Miller, Locke, and Manning in paragraph 3
   c. to juxtapose the trivial distinctions among people with the divine unity of nature
   d. to clarify the connection between the diversity of humans and the holiness of nature
   e. to provide an anecdote showing the difficulty of remembering human details while in nature

6. Throughout the passage, the author uses the following techniques to illustrate nature EXCEPT

   a. personification
   b. scientific detail
   c. metaphor
   d. imagery
   e. personal anecdote

7. The writer characterizes himself as someone who is

   a. factual and objective
   b. emotional and open-minded
   c. self-centered and condescending
   d. critical and blunt
   e. observant and contemplative

8. The speaker refers to the smile as "admonishing" (para. 1) to suggest

   a. the universe looks down imperiously on the insignificance of humanity
   b. humankind looks to the stars more as objects of conquest than of contemplation
   c. the stars symbolize the indifferent attitude of nature toward humanity
   d. the stars provide a benign and necessary reminder of the value of nature
   e. the stars scold humanity for neglecting nature in the streets of cities

THE ENVIRONMENT

Now that you have examined a number of readings and other texts focusing on nature, explore one dimension of this topic by synthesizing your own ideas and the selections. Consider doing more research or using readings from other classes as you prepare for the following projects.

1. Take a walk in a favorite natural place close to where you live — in the woods, or out on the prairie, or along the beach, or in the desert. Then write to one of the authors in this chapter, comparing your impressions of nature with those he or she presents.

2. Research a local environmental issue — the development of open land, hunting or fishing regulations, wildlife protection, auto emissions, or another important concern. Then write a letter to the editor of your local newspaper in which you take a position on the issue. Refer to at least three sources from the chapter to support your position.

3. Write an essay in which you compare the ways in which two authors in this chapter use research to support their arguments.

4. Write a personal essay that answers this chapter's essential question: What is our responsibility to the natural environment? Refer in your essay to at least three sources from the chapter for support.

5. Write an essay evaluating and comparing the classic appeals to ethos, pathos, and logos used by two or more of the authors in this chapter.

6. Write an essay explaining how one of the visual texts illustrates a major idea espoused by one of the authors in this chapter.

7. Imagine what a person living fifty years in the future might say to us now about the effect we have had on the environment. Employing both exposition and argument, write a "report from the future" warning our society about the consequences of our treatment of the natural world.

8. Select one of the following statements about nature and the environment, and write an essay that explores its validity. To support your essay, refer to your personal experience and to the selections in this chapter.

   a. The West of which I speak is but another name for the Wild; and what I have been preparing to say is, that in Wildness is the preservation of the World.

   — Henry David Thoreau

   b. Sometimes we forget that nature also means us. Termites build mounds; we build cities. All of our being — juices, flesh and spirit — is nature.

   — Diane Ackerman

   c. A true conservationist is a man who knows that the world is not given by his fathers but borrowed from his children.

   — John James Audubon

   d. To waste, to destroy our natural resources, to skin and exhaust the land instead of using it so as to increase its usefulness, will result in undermining in the days of our children the very prosperity which we ought by right to hand down to them amplified and developed.

   — Theodore Roosevelt

   e. We seem to be in a period in which the conservation of anything is disparaged — the conservation of books, the conservation of ideas, the conservation of time, the conservation of darkness, the conservation of love, the conservation of intelligence — it all gets very short shrift in contemporary society. And I think that in the environmental movement, in the curious way in which it overlaps the women's movement and other social movements of the late twentieth century, what we are really seeing is an insistence on the moral dimension of life. When I say the moral dimension, I mean issues of integrity and dignity and responsibility.

   — Barry Lopez

9. View former vice president Al Gore's documentary film *An Inconvenient Truth* (2006) or its sequel, *An Inconvenient Sequel: Truth to Power* (2017). Write a review of the film in the voice of one of the writers you've read in this chapter.

10. View one of the following three films — *Fast Food Nation*; *Supersize Me*; or *Food, Inc.* — and

compare it with the voices you have read in the Conversation on Sustainable Eating.

11. View the documentary film *From Billions to None*. Referring to the film, to Barry Yeoman's essay of the same title, "From Billions to None," and to another selection from this chapter, write an essay that argues for or against resurrection science.

12. View the documentary film *No Impact Man*. Do you find its argument persuasive? How does it address this chapter's essential question?

13. In 1977, artist Andy Warhol said, "I'm a city boy. In the big cities, they've set it up so you can go to a park and be in a miniature countryside; but in the countryside they don't have any patches of big city, so I get very homesick." Write an essay in which you consider Warhol's perspective in relation to those of Ralph Waldo Emerson, Aldo Leopold, E. O. Wilson, and others included in this chapter.

14. Writers Aldo Leopold, Lewis Thomas, Bill McKibben, and E. O. Wilson all discuss a "choice" that confronts humanity regarding the environment. Indicate each of the choices they discuss, and evaluate which one makes the most sense and offers the best solution.

15. Joel Achenbach concludes his article, "Why Science Is So Hard to Believe," with the following statement: "For some people, the tribe is more important than the truth; for the best scientists, the truth is more important than the tribe" (para. 30). Write an essay that defends, challenges, or qualifies this quotation, referring to the texts by E.O. Wilson, Bill McKibben, and one other writer included in this chapter.

16. "The future we've been warned about is beginning to saturate the present," writes Jon Mooallem in his article, "Our Climate Future Is Actually Our Climate Present" (para. 7). Consider the meaning and implications of that statement and explore its validity as it pertains to the relationship that we have with our environment.

17. "The ethical solution is to diagnose and disconnect extraneous political ideology, then shed it in order to move toward the common ground where economic progress and conservation are treated as one and the same goal," writes E. O. Wilson in his book, *The Future of Life*. Having read the selections included in this chapter, how likely do you think it is that we will achieve the ethical solution that Wilson suggests? Refer specifically to at least three of the texts to support your answer.

18. ExxonMobil, self-described as "the world's largest publicly traded international oil and gas company, providing energy that helps underpin growing economies and improve living standards around the world," has made the following statements on its website:

Managing long-term climate risks

Rising greenhouse-gas emissions pose significant risks to society and ecosystems. Since most of these emissions are energy-related, any integrated approach to meeting the world's growing energy needs over the coming decades must incorporate strategies to address the risk of climate change.

Managing climate change risks

Our strategy to reduce greenhouse-gas emissions is focused on increasing energy efficiency in the short term, implementing proven emission-reducing technologies in the near and medium term, and developing breakthrough, game-changing technologies for the long term. Technological innovation will play a central role in our ability to increase supply, improve efficiency, and reduce emissions. Approximately 90 percent of the greenhouse-gas emissions generated by petroleum products are released when customers use our products, and the remaining 10 percent are generated by industry operations. Therefore, technology is also needed to reduce energy-related emissions by end users.

In a time when we still hear many people — even some public officials — questioning the reality of climate change and global warming, it might seem surprising to discover the perspective above coming from a large energy company. What do these statements suggest about climate change? About global warming? About the relationship between economic concerns and environmental protection? Finally, what do they suggest about the essential question posed at the beginning of this chapter: What is our responsibility to the natural environment? Refer to several texts from this chapter as you answer these questions.

8
Community

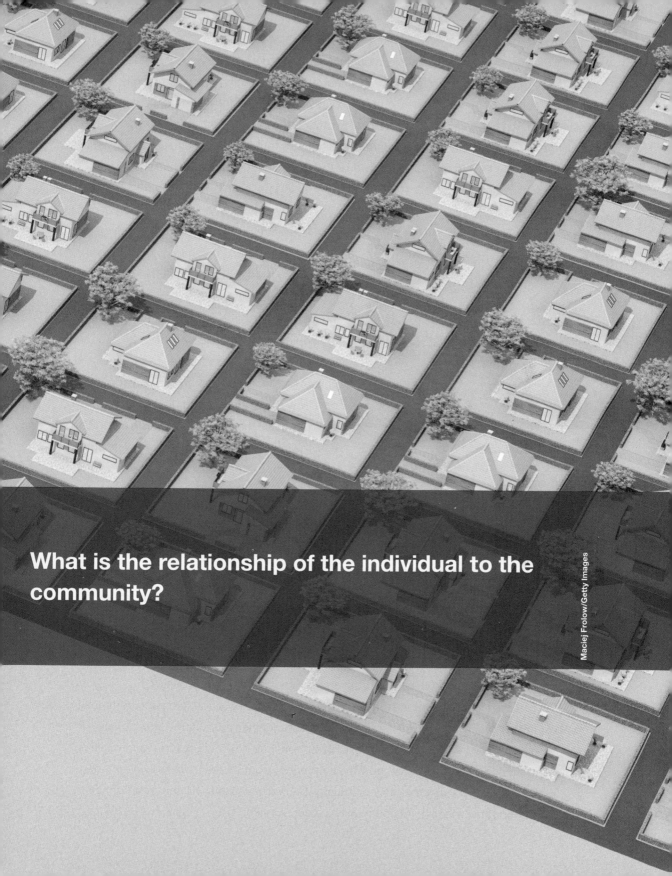

What is the relationship of the individual to the community?

How can an individual maintain integrity and pursue personal dreams while contributing to the overall society? This is the central question facing every community. In the United States, we pride ourselves on rugged individualism and the pioneering spirit; at the same time, we believe in collective values. In other parts of the world, people perceive the balance of the individual and the community differently, but the history and literature of most societies depict the struggle of the individual to live life in good faith or conscience while being part of a community.

In the twenty-first century, the speed of our lives and an increasingly global perspective are redefining what a community is. The word *community* itself is changing, coming to mean a group of like-minded people sharing common interests, when in the past it referred to a group of people of various skills and interests cooperating with one another to survive. Geography and uniformity, once the main criteria of a community, now bow to technology and diversity, which today underlie the definition of ethnic communities, the intelligence community, or online communities, for example. Consider the notion of the "gated community." Is the phrase an expression of a different kind of community, one defined not by inclusion but rather by exclusion?

Matt Rourke/AP Images

▲
──────────

Brennon Jones, shown here, originally provided free haircuts for homeless people on the street in Philadelphia, though he was planning to stop during winter due to the weather. A local barber shop owner named Sean Johnson intervened, giving a new shop to Jones so that he could continue to donate his services to anyone in need. **How does this story define the relationship between the individual and the community?**

We find — and forge — communities based on geography, ethnicity, race, religion, marital status, occupation, class, economic status, gender, political affiliation, shared interest, or even language. Are those features more important than values, principles, and ideals? Or do we belong to various communities based on distinct criteria? How can we belong to several communities simultaneously?

The readings in this chapter explore the balance of individual concerns and community values, and they examine how different types of communities arise, some intentionally, some coincidentally. As you discuss these ideas, consider how people form communities, how individuals gain membership, how the community contributes to an individual's identity, and how outsiders perceive the community. Such discussions will help you formulate questions about the meaning of community in your own life.

Letter from Birmingham Jail

MARTIN LUTHER KING JR.

Martin Luther King Jr. (1929–1968) was one of the most influential leaders of the civil rights movement of the 1950s and 1960s. Dr. King was born in Atlanta, Georgia, and grew up in the Ebenezer Baptist Church, where his father and grandfather were ministers. He earned a BA at Morehouse College, a divinity degree at Crozer Theological Seminary, and a PhD in theology at Boston University, all by the age of 26. In 1957, he founded the Southern Christian Leadership Conference and later led numerous protests against segregation by practicing the Gandhian doctrine of nonviolent resistance. In 1963, while King was in Birmingham, Alabama, eight clergymen published a letter in the *Post-Herald* criticizing his presence and his strategies. From the cell where he was jailed for demonstrating, King responded by writing what has come to be known as "Letter from Birmingham Jail."

Howard Sochurek/The LIFE Picture Collection/Getty Images

The following is the public statement directed to Martin Luther King Jr. by eight Alabama clergymen that occasioned King's letter.

We the undersigned clergymen are among those who, in January, issued "an appeal for law and order and common sense," in dealing with racial problems in Alabama. We expressed understanding that honest convictions in racial matters could properly be pursued in the courts, but urged that decisions of those courts should in the meantime be peacefully obeyed.

Since that time there has been some evidence of increased forbearance and a willingness to face facts. Responsible citizens have undertaken to work on various problems which cause racial friction and unrest. In Birmingham, recent public events have given indication that we all have opportunity for a new constructive and realistic approach to racial problems.

However, we are now confronted by a series of demonstrations by some of our Negro citizens, directed and led in part by outsiders. We recognize the natural impatience of people who feel that their hopes are slow in being realized. But we are convinced that these demonstrations are unwise and untimely.

We agree rather with certain local Negro leadership which has called for honest and open negotiation of racial issues in our area. And we believe this kind of facing of issues can best be accomplished by citizens of our own metropolitan area, white and Negro, meeting with their knowledge and experience of the local situation. All of us need to face that responsibility and find proper channels for its accomplishment.

Just as we formerly pointed out that "hatred and violence have no sanction in our religious and political traditions," we also point out that such actions as incite to hatred and violence, however technically peaceful those actions may be, have not contributed to the resolution of our local problems. We do not believe that these days of new hope are days when extreme measures are justified in Birmingham.

We commend the community as a whole, and the local news media and law enforcement officials in particular, on the calm manner in which these demonstrations have been handled. We urge the public to continue to show restraint should the demonstrations continue, and the law enforcement officials to remain calm and continue to protect our city from violence.

We further strongly urge our own Negro community to withdraw support from these demonstrations, and to unite locally in working peacefully for a better Birmingham. When rights are consistently denied, a cause should be pressed in the courts and in negotiations among local leaders, and not in the streets. We appeal to both our white and Negro citizenry to observe the principles of law and order and common sense.

> BISHOP C. C. J. CARPENTER, D.D., LL.D., Episcopalian Bishop of Alabama
>
> BISHOP JOSEPH A. DURICK, D.D., Auxiliary Bishop, Roman Catholic Diocese of Mobile, Birmingham
>
> RABBI MILTON L. GRAFMAN, Temple Emanu-El, Birmingham, Alabama
>
> BISHOP PAUL HARDIN, Methodist Bishop of the Alabama–West Florida Conference
>
> BISHOP NOLAN B. HARMON, Bishop of the North Alabama Conference of the Methodist Church
>
> REV. GEORGE M. MURRAY, D.D., LL.D., Bishop Coadjutor, Episcopal Diocese of Alabama
>
> REV. EDWARD V. RAMAGE, Moderator, Synod of the Alabama Presbyterian Church in the United States
>
> REV. EARL STALLINGS, Pastor, First Baptist Church, Birmingham, Alabama
>
> *April 12, 1963*

My Dear Fellow Clergymen:

While confined here in the Birmingham city jail, I came across your recent statement calling my present activities "unwise and untimely." Seldom do I pause to answer criticism of my work and ideas. If I sought to answer all the criticisms that cross my desk, my secretaries would have little time for anything other than such correspondence in the course of the day, and I would have no time for constructive work. But since I feel that you are men of genuine good will and that your criticisms are sincerely set forth, I want to try to answer your statement in what I hope will be patient and reasonable terms.

I think I should indicate why I am here in Birmingham, since you have been influenced by the view which argues against "outsiders coming in." I have the honor of serving as president of the Southern Christian Leadership Conference, an organization operating in every southern state, with headquarters in Atlanta, Georgia. We have some eighty-five affiliated organizations across the South, and one of them is the Alabama Christian Movement for Human Rights. Frequently we share staff, educational, and financial resources with our affiliates. Several months ago the affiliate here in Birmingham asked us to be on call to engage in a nonviolent direct-action program if such were

In this photograph, taken in 1963, Martin Luther King Jr. speaks to reporters at a press conference about the planned marches protesting bus and restaurant segregation in Birmingham, Alabama.

What does King's face express to you? In what ways does it communicate the persona King presents in "Letter from Birmingham Jail"?

©Flip Schulke/CORBIS/Corbis via Getty Images

deemed necessary. We readily consented, and when the hour came we lived up to our promise. So I, along with several members of my staff, am here because I was invited here. I am here because I have organizational ties here.

But more basically, I am in Birmingham because injustice is here. Just as the prophets of the eighth century B.C. left their villages and carried their "thus saith the Lord" far beyond the boundaries of their home towns, and just as the Apostle Paul left his village of Tarsus and carried the gospel of Jesus Christ to the far corners of the Greco-Roman world, so am I compelled to carry the gospel of freedom beyond my own home town. Like Paul, I must constantly respond to the Macedonian call for aid.

Moreover, I am cognizant of the interrelatedness of all communities and states. I cannot sit idly by in Atlanta and not be concerned about what happens in Birmingham. Injustice anywhere is a threat to justice everywhere. We are caught in an inescapable network of mutuality, tied in a single garment of destiny. Whatever affects one directly, affects all indirectly. Never again can we afford to live with the narrow, provincial "outside agitator" idea. Anyone who lives inside the United States can never be considered an outsider anywhere within its bounds.

You deplore the demonstrations taking place 5 in Birmingham. But your statement, I am sorry to say, fails to express a similar concern for the conditions that brought about the demonstrations. I am sure that none of you would want to rest content with the superficial kind of social analysis that deals merely with effects and does not grapple with underlying causes. It is unfortunate that demonstrations are taking place in Birmingham, but it is even more unfortunate that the city's white power structure left the Negro community with no alternative.

In any nonviolent campaign there are four basic steps: collection of the facts to determine whether injustices exist; negotiation; self-purification; and direct action. We have gone through all these steps in Birmingham. There can be no gainsaying the fact that racial injustice engulfs this community. Birmingham is probably the most thoroughly segregated city in the United States. Its ugly record of brutality is widely known. Negroes have experienced grossly unjust treatment in the courts. There have been more unsolved bombings of Negro homes and churches in Birmingham than in any other city in the nation. These are the hard, brutal facts of the case. On the basis of these conditions, Negro leaders sought to negotiate with the city fathers. But the latter consistently refused to engage in good-faith negotiation.

Butch Dill/AP Images

This sculpture of a young protester confronted by a police officer and a snarling dog stands in Kelly Ingram Park, an important staging ground for civil rights demonstrations in the 1960s. Today, it is located beside the Birmingham Civil Rights Institute. **What does this sculpture communicate about the context in which King wrote "Letter from Birmingham Jail"?**

Then, last September, came the opportunity to talk with leaders of Birmingham's economic community. In the course of the negotiations, certain promises were made by the merchants — for example, to remove the stores' humiliating racial signs. On the basis of these promises, the Reverend Fred Shuttlesworth and the leaders of the Alabama Christian Movement for Human Rights agreed to a moratorium on all demonstrations. As the weeks and months went by, we realized that we were the victims of a broken promise. A few signs, briefly removed, returned; the others remained.

As in so many past experiences, our hopes had been blasted, and the shadow of deep disappointment settled upon us. We had no alternative except to prepare for direct action, whereby we would present our very bodies as a means of laying our case before the conscience of the local and the national community. Mindful of the difficulties involved, we decided to undertake a process of self-purification. We began a series of workshops on nonviolence, and we repeatedly asked ourselves: "Are you able to accept blows without retaliating?" "Are you able to endure the ordeal of jail?" We decided to schedule our

direct-action program for the Easter season, realizing that except for Christmas, this is the main shopping period of the year. Knowing that a strong economic withdrawal program would be the by-product of direct action, we felt that this would be the best time to bring pressure to bear on the merchants for the needed change.

Then it occurred to us that Birmingham's mayoral election was coming up in March, and we speedily decided to postpone action until after election day. When we discovered that the Commissioner of Public Safety, Eugene "Bull" Connor, had piled up enough votes to be in the runoff, we decided again to postpone action until the day after the runoff so that the demonstrations could not be used to cloud the issues. Like many others, we wanted to see Mr. Connor defeated, and to this end we endured postponement after postponement. Having aided in this community need, we felt that our direct-action program could be delayed no longer.

You may well ask, "Why direct action? Why sit-ins, marches, and so forth? Isn't negotiation a better path?" You are quite right in calling for negotiation. Indeed, this is the very purpose of

10

Dave Granlund/Cagle Cartoons, Inc.

This cartoon by Dave Granlund was published in 2011. **Explain why you think that this viewpoint is more or less relevant today than in 2011.**

direct action. Nonviolent direct action seeks to create such a crisis and foster such a tension that a community which has constantly refused to negotiate is forced to confront the issue. It seeks so to dramatize the issue that it can no longer be ignored. My citing the creation of tension as part of the work of the nonviolent-resister may sound rather shocking. But I must confess that I am not afraid of the word "tension." I have earnestly opposed violent tension, but there is a type of constructive, nonviolent tension which is necessary for growth. Just as Socrates felt that it was necessary to create a tension in the mind so that individuals could rise from the bondage of myths and half-truths to the unfettered realm of creative analysis and objective appraisal, so must we see the need for nonviolent gadflies to create the kind of tension in society that will help men rise from the dark depths of prejudice and racism to the majestic heights of understanding and brotherhood.

The purpose of our direct-action program is to create a situation so crisis-packed that it will inevitably open the door to negotiation. I therefore concur with you in your call for negotiation. Too long has our beloved Southland been bogged down in a tragic effort to live in monologue rather than dialogue.

One of the basic points in your statement is that the action that I and my associates have taken in Birmingham is untimely. Some have asked: "Why didn't you give the new city administration time to act?" The only answer that I can give to this query is that the new Birmingham administration must be prodded about as much as the outgoing one, before it will act. We are sadly mistaken if we feel that the election of Albert Boutwell as mayor will bring the millennium to Birmingham. While Mr. Boutwell is a much more gentle person than Mr. Connor, they are both segregationists, dedicated to maintenance of the status quo. I have hoped that Mr. Boutwell will be reasonable enough to see the futility of massive resistance to desegregation. But he will not see this without pressure from devotees of civil rights. My friends, I must say to you that we have not made a single gain in civil rights without determined legal and nonviolent pressure. Lamentably, it is an historical fact that privileged groups seldom give up their privileges voluntarily. Individuals may see the moral light and voluntarily give up their unjust posture, but,

The Granger Collection, New York

In this photograph, Dr. King is removes a burned cross from the lawn of his home in Atlanta, Georgia, while his son Martin Luther King III stands nearby.
In what ways does this image illustrate paragraph 14 of "Letter from Birmingham Jail"?

as Reinhold Niebuhr[1] has reminded us, groups tend to be more immoral than individuals.

We know through painful experience that freedom is never voluntarily given by the oppressor; it must be demanded by the oppressed. Frankly, I have yet to engage in a direct-action campaign that was "well timed" in the view of those who have not suffered unduly from the disease of segregation. For years now I have heard the word "Wait!" It rings in the ear of every Negro with piercing familiarity. This "Wait" has almost always meant "Never." We must come to see, with one of our distinguished jurists, that "justice too long delayed is justice denied."

We have waited for more than 340 years for our constitutional and God-given rights. The nations of Asia and Africa are moving with jet-like speed toward gaining political independence, but we still creep at horse-and-buggy pace toward gaining a cup of coffee at a lunch counter. Perhaps it is easy for those who have never felt the stinging darts of segregation to say, "Wait." But when you have seen vicious mobs lynch your mothers and fathers at will and drown your sisters and brothers at whim; when you have seen hate-filled policemen curse, kick, and even kill your black brothers and sisters;

when you see the vast majority of your twenty million Negro brothers smothering in an airtight cage of poverty in the midst of an affluent society; when you suddenly find your tongue twisted and your speech stammering as you seek to explain to your six-year-old daughter why she can't go to the public amusement park that has just been advertised on television, and see tears welling up in her eyes when she is told that Funtown is closed to colored children, and see ominous clouds of inferiority beginning to form in her little mental sky, and see her beginning to distort her personality by developing an unconscious bitterness toward white people; when you have to concoct an answer for a five-year-old son who is asking, "Daddy, why do white people treat colored people so mean?"; when you take a cross-country drive and find it necessary to sleep night after night in the uncomfortable corners of your automobile because no motel will accept you; when you are humiliated day in and day out by nagging signs reading "white" and "colored"; when your first name becomes "nigger," your middle name becomes "boy" (however old you are) and your last name becomes "John," and your wife and mother are never given the respected title "Mrs."; when you are harried by day and haunted by night by the fact that you are a Negro, living constantly at tiptoe stance, never quite knowing what

---

[1]Niebuhr (1892–1971) was a U.S. clergyman and a Protestant theologian. —Eds.

to expect next, and are plagued with inner fears and outer resentments; when you are forever fighting a degenerating sense of "nobodiness" — then you will understand why we find it difficult to wait. There comes a time when the cup of endurance runs over, and men are no longer willing to be plunged into the abyss of despair. I hope, sirs, you can understand our legitimate and unavoidable impatience.

You express a great deal of anxiety over our willingness to break laws. This is certainly a legitimate concern. Since we so diligently urge people to obey the Supreme Court's decision of 1954 outlawing segregation in the public schools, at first glance it may seem rather paradoxical for us consciously to break laws. One may well ask: "How can you advocate breaking some laws and obeying others?" The answer lies in the fact that there are two types of laws: just and unjust. I would be the first to advocate obeying just laws. One has not only a legal but a moral responsibility to obey just laws. Conversely, one has a moral responsibility to disobey unjust laws. I would agree with St. Augustine that "an unjust law is no law at all."

Now, what is the difference between the two? How does one determine whether a law is just or unjust? A just law is a man-made code that squares with the moral law or the law of God. An unjust law is a code that is out of harmony with the moral law. To put it in the terms of St. Thomas Aquinas: An unjust law is a human law that is not rooted in eternal law and natural law. Any law that uplifts human personality is just. Any law that degrades human personality is unjust. All segregation statutes are unjust because segregation distorts the soul and damages the personality. It gives the segregator a false sense of superiority and the segregated a false sense of inferiority. Segregation, to use the terminology of the Jewish philosopher Martin Buber, substitutes an "I-it" relationship for an "I-thou" relationship and ends up relegating persons to the status of things. Hence segregation is not only politically, economically, and sociologically unsound, it is morally wrong and sinful. Paul Tillich[2] has said that sin is separation. Is not segregation an existential expression of man's tragic separation, his awful estrangement, his terrible sinfulness? Thus it is that I can urge men to obey the 1954 decision of the Supreme Court, for it is morally right; and I can urge them to disobey segregation ordinances, for they are morally wrong.

15 Let us consider a more concrete example of just and unjust laws. An unjust law is a code that a numerical or power majority group compels a minority group to obey but does not make binding on itself. This is *difference* made legal. By the same token, a just law is a code that a majority compels a minority to follow and that it is willing to follow itself. This is *sameness* made legal.

Let me give another explanation. A law is unjust if it is inflicted on a minority that, as a result of being denied the right to vote, had no part in enacting or devising the law. Who can say that the legislature of Alabama which set up that state's segregation laws was democratically elected? Throughout Alabama all sorts of devious methods are used to prevent Negroes from becoming registered voters, and there are some counties in which, even though Negroes constitute a majority of the population, not a single Negro is registered. Can any law enacted under such circumstances be considered democratically structured?

Sometimes a law is just on its face and unjust in its application. For instance, I have been arrested on a charge of parading without a permit. Now, there is nothing wrong in having an ordinance which requires a permit for a parade. But such an ordinance becomes unjust when it is used to maintain segregation and to deny citizens the First-Amendment privilege of peaceful assembly and protest.

20 I hope you are able to see the distinction I am trying to point out. In no sense do I advocate evading or defying the law, as would the rabid

---

[2]Tillich (1886–1965) was a German American philosopher and a Christian theologian. —Eds.

In this photograph, civil rights leaders Reverend Ralph Abernathy and Dr. Martin Luther King Jr. are on their way to protest a Circuit Court injunction against their anti-segregation campaign. They are followed by journalists, and men kneel as they pass. When they reached the court house, they were arrested, and it was during this time that King wrote "Letter from Birmingham Jail."

What message do King and Abernathy communicate through the clothes they are wearing? What message do the kneeling men convey? How are these messages reflected in King's letter?

Photo by Charles Moore/Getty Images

segregationist. That would lead to anarchy. One who breaks an unjust law must do so openly, lovingly, and with a willingness to accept the penalty. I submit that an individual who breaks a law that conscience tells him is unjust, and who willingly accepts the penalty of imprisonment in order to arouse the conscience of the community over its injustice, is in reality expressing the highest respect for law.

Of course, there is nothing new about this kind of civil disobedience. It was evidenced sublimely in the refusal of Shadrach, Meshach, and Abednego to obey the laws of Nebuchadnezzar, on the ground that a higher moral law was at stake. It was practiced superbly by the early Christians, who were willing to face hungry lions and the excruciating pain of chopping blocks rather than submit to certain unjust laws of the Roman Empire. To a degree, academic freedom is a reality today because Socrates practiced civil

disobedience. In our own nation, the Boston Tea Party represented a massive act of civil disobedience.

We should never forget that everything Adolf Hitler did in Germany was "legal" and everything the Hungarian freedom fighters did in Hungary was "illegal." It was "illegal" to aid and comfort a Jew in Hitler's Germany. Even so, I am sure that, had I lived in Germany at the time, I would have aided and comforted my Jewish brothers. If today I lived in a Communist country where certain principles dear to the Christian faith are suppressed, I would openly advocate disobeying that country's antireligious laws.

I must make two honest confessions to you, my Christian and Jewish brothers. First, I must confess that over the past few years I have been gravely disappointed with the white moderate. I have almost reached the regrettable conclusion that the Negro's great stumbling block in his stride toward freedom is not the White Citizen's Counciler or the Ku Klux Klanner, but the white moderate, who is more devoted to "order" than to justice; who prefers a negative peace which is the absence of tension to a positive peace which is the presence of justice; who constantly says, "I agree with you in the goal you seek, but I cannot agree with your methods of direct action"; who paternalistically believes he can set the timetable for another man's freedom; who lives by a mythical concept of time and who constantly advises the Negro to wait for a "more convenient season." Shallow understanding from people of good will is more frustrating than absolute misunderstanding from people of ill will. Lukewarm acceptance is much more bewildering than outright rejection.

I had hoped that the white moderate would understand that law and order exist for the purpose of establishing justice and that when they fail in this purpose they become the dangerously structured dams that block the flow of social progress. I had hoped that the white moderate would understand that the present tension in the South is a necessary phase of the transition from an obnoxious negative peace, in which the Negro passively accepted his unjust plight, to a substantive and positive peace, in which all men will respect the dignity and worth of human personality. Actually, we who engage in nonviolent direct action are not the creators of tension. We merely bring to the surface the hidden tension that is already alive. We bring it out in the open, where it can be seen and dealt with. Like a boil that can never be cured so long as it is covered up but must be opened with all its ugliness to the natural medicines of air and light, injustice must be exposed, with all the tension its exposure creates, to the light of human conscience and the air of national opinion, before it can be cured.

In your statement you assert that our actions, 25 even though peaceful, must be condemned because they precipitate violence. But is this a logical assertion? Isn't this like condemning a robbed man because his possession of money precipitated the evil act of robbery? Isn't this like condemning Socrates because his unswerving commitment to truth and his philosophical inquiries precipitated the act by the misguided populace in which they made him drink hemlock? Isn't this like condemning Jesus because his unique God-consciousness and never-ceasing devotion to God's will precipitated the evil act of crucifixion? We must come to see that, as the federal courts have consistently affirmed, it is wrong to urge an individual to cease his efforts to gain his basic constitutional rights because the quest

This photograph was taken at the arrest of Reverend Abernathy and Dr. King as they led a line of civil rights demonstrators in Birmingham.
How does this image depict a clash of communities?

AP Images

may precipitate violence. Society must protect the robbed and punish the robber.

I had also hoped that the white moderate would reject the myth concerning time in relation to the struggle for freedom. I have just received a letter from a white brother in Texas. He writes: "All Christians know that the colored people will receive equal rights eventually, but it is possible that you are in too great a religious hurry. It has taken Christianity almost two thousand years to accomplish what it has. The teachings of Christ take time to come to earth." Such an attitude stems from a tragic misconception of time, from the strangely irrational notion that there is something in the very flow of time that will inevitably cure all ills. Actually, time itself is neutral; it can be used either destructively or constructively. More and more I feel that the people of ill will have used time much more effectively than have the people of good will. We will have to repent in this generation not merely for the hateful words and actions of the bad people, but for the appalling silence of the good people. Human progress never rolls in on wheels of inevitability; it comes through the tireless efforts of men willing to be co-workers with God, and without this hard work, time itself becomes an ally of the forces of social stagnation. We must use time creatively, in the knowledge that the time is always ripe to do right. Now is the time to make real the promise of democracy and transform our pending national elegy into a creative psalm of brotherhood. Now is the time to lift our national policy from the quicksand of racial injustice to the solid rock of human dignity.

You speak of our activity in Birmingham as extreme. At first I was rather disappointed that fellow clergymen would see my nonviolent efforts as those of an extremist. I began thinking about the fact that I stand in the middle of two opposing forces in the Negro community. One is a force of complacency, made up in part of Negroes who, as a result of long years of oppression, are so drained of self-respect and a sense of "somebodiness" that they have adjusted to segregation; and in part of a few middle-class Negroes who, because of a degree of academic and economic security and because in some ways they profit by segregation, have become insensitive to the problems of the masses. The other force is one of bitterness and hatred, and it comes perilously close to advocating violence. It is expressed in the various black nationalist groups that are springing up across the nation, the largest and best-known being Elijah Muhammad's Muslim movement. Nourished by the Negro's frustration over the continued existence of racial discrimination, this movement is made up of people who have lost faith in America, who have absolutely repudiated Christianity, and who have concluded that the white man is an incorrigible "devil."

I have tried to stand between these two forces, saying that we need emulate neither

In this photograph, taken during the civil rights campaign in Birmingham in 1963, demonstrators kneel in prayer as police officers look on. **How does the way the photographer framed this image reflect King's rhetoric in "Letter from Birmingham Jail"?**

Charles Moore/Getty Images

the "do-nothingism" of the complacent nor the hatred and despair of the black nationalist. For there is the more excellent way of love and non-violent protest. I am grateful to God that, through the influence of the Negro church, the way of non-violence became an integral part of our struggle.

If this philosophy had not emerged, by now many streets of the South would, I am convinced, be flowing with blood. And I am further convinced that if our white brothers dismiss as "rabble-rousers" and "outside agitators" those of us who employ nonviolent direct action, and if they refuse to support our nonviolent efforts, millions of Negroes will, out of frustration and despair, seek solace and security in black-na-tionalist ideologies — a development that would inevitably lead to a frightening racial nightmare.

Oppressed people cannot remain oppressed forever. The yearning for freedom eventually man-ifests itself, and that is what has happened to the American Negro. Something within has reminded him of his birthright of freedom, and something without has reminded him that it can be gained. Consciously or unconsciously, he has been caught up by the *Zeitgeist*,[3] and with his black brothers of Africa and his brown and yellow brothers of Asia, South America, and the Caribbean, the United States Negro is moving with a sense of great urgency toward the promised land of racial justice. If one recognizes this vital urge that has engulfed the Negro community, one should readily under-stand why public demonstrations are taking place. The Negro has many pent-up resentments and latent frustrations, and he must release them. So let him march; let him make prayer pilgrimages to the city hall; let him go on freedom rides — and try to understand why he must do so. If his repressed emotions are not released in nonviolent ways, they will seek expression through violence; this is not a threat but a fact of history. So I have not said to my people, "Get rid of your discontent." Rather, I have tried to say that this normal and healthy

discontent can be channeled into the c_____ outlet of nonviolent direct action. And _____ approach is being termed extremist.

But though I was initially disappo_____ being categorized as an extremist, as _____ to think about the matter I gradually _____ measure of satisfaction from the label. _____ Jesus an extremist for love: "Love your enemies, bless them that curse you, do good to them that hate you, and pray for them which despitefully use you, and persecute you." Was not Amos an extremist for justice: "Let justice roll down like waters and righteousness like an ever-flowing stream." Was not Paul an extremist for the Christian gospel: "I bear in my body the marks of the Lord Jesus." Was not Martin Luther an extremist: "Here I stand; I cannot do otherwise, so help me God." And John Bunyan: "I will stay in jail to the end of my days before I make a butch-ery of my conscience." And Abraham Lincoln: "This nation cannot survive half slave and half free." And Thomas Jefferson: "We hold these truths to be self-evident, that all men are created equal. . . ." So the question is not whether we will be extremists, but what kind of extremists we will be. Will we be extremists for hate or for love? Will we be extremists for the preservation of injustice or for the extension of justice? In that dramatic scene on Calvary's hill three men were crucified. We must never forget that all three were crucified for the same crime — the crime of extremism. Two were extremists for immorality, and thus fell below their environment. The other, Jesus Christ, was an extremist for love, truth, and goodness, and thereby rose above his environment. Perhaps the South, the nation, and the world are in dire need of creative extremists.

I had hoped that the white moderate would see this need. Perhaps I was too optimistic; per-haps I expected too much. I suppose I should have realized that few members of the oppressor race can understand the deep groans and pas-sionate yearnings of the oppressed race, and still fewer have the vision to see that injustice must be

30

---

[3]German, "spirit of the time." —Eds.

ted out by strong, persistent, and determined action. I am thankful, however, that some of our white brothers in the South have grasped the meaning of this social revolution and committed themselves to it. They are still all too few in quantity, but they are big in quality. Some — such as Ralph McGill, Lillian Smith, Harry Golden, James McBridge Dabbs, Ann Braden, and Sarah Patton Boyle — have written about our struggle in eloquent and prophetic terms. Others have marched with us down nameless streets of the South. They have languished in filthy, roach-infested jails, suffering the abuse and brutality of policemen who view them as "dirty nigger-lovers." Unlike so many of their moderate brothers and sisters, they have recognized the urgency of the moment and sensed the need for powerful "action" antidotes to combat the disease of segregation.

Let me take note of my other major disappointment. I have been so greatly disappointed with the white church and its leadership. Of course, there are some notable exceptions. I am not unmindful of the fact that each of you has taken some significant stands on this issue. I commend you, Reverend [Earl] Stallings, for your Christian stand on this past Sunday, in welcoming Negroes to your worship service on a nonsegregated basis. I commend the Catholic leaders of this state for integrating Spring Hill College several years ago.

But despite these notable exceptions, I must honestly reiterate that I have been disappointed with the church. I do not say this as one of those negative critics who can always find something wrong with the church. I say this as a minister of the gospel, who loves the church; who was nurtured in its bosom; who has been sustained by its spiritual blessings and who will remain true to it as long as the cord of life shall lengthen.

When I was suddenly catapulted into the leadership of the bus protest in Montgomery, Alabama, a few years ago, I felt we would be supported by the white church. I felt that the white ministers, priests, and rabbis of the South would be among our strongest allies. Instead, some have been outright opponents, refusing to understand the freedom movement and misrepresenting its leaders; all too many others have been more cautious than courageous and have remained silent behind the anesthetizing security of stained-glass windows.

In spite of my shattered dreams, I came to Birmingham with the hope that the white

35

Shown here is a painting entitled *Bus* by Jacob Lawrence, who is best known for his Migration series depicting African Americans' flight from the Jim Crow south to the north in the early twentieth century. **What do Lawrence's style decisions — such as composition, lines, color, or framing, for example — communicate about segregation?**

religious leadership of this community would see the justice of our cause and, with deep moral concern, would serve as the channel through which our just grievances could reach the power structure. I had hoped that each of you would understand. But again I have been disappointed.

I have heard numerous southern religious leaders admonish their worshipers to comply with a desegregation decision because it is the law, but I have longed to hear white ministers declare: "Follow this decree because integration is morally right and because the Negro is your brother." In the midst of blatant injustices inflicted upon the Negro, I have watched white church men stand on the sideline and mouth pious irrelevancies and sanctimonious trivialities. In the midst of a mighty struggle to rid our nation of racial and economic injustice, I have heard many ministers say: "Those are social issues, with which the gospel has no real concern." And I have watched many churches commit themselves to a completely otherworldly religion which makes a strange, un-Biblical distinction between body and soul, between the sacred and the secular.

I have traveled the length and breadth of Alabama, Mississippi, and all the other southern states. On sweltering summer days and crisp autumn mornings I have looked at the South's beautiful churches with their lofty spires pointing heavenward. I have beheld the impressive outlines of her massive religious-education buildings. Over and over I have found myself asking: "What kind of people worship here? Who is their God? Where were their voices when the lips of Governor [Ross] Barnett dripped with words of interposition and nullification? Where were they when Governor [George] Wallace gave a clarion call for defiance and hatred? Where were their voices of support when bruised and weary Negro men and women decided to rise from the dark dungeons of complacency to the bright hills of creative protest?"

Yes, these questions are still in my mind. In deep disappointment I have wept over the laxity of the church. But be assured that my tears have been tears of love. There can be no deep disappointment where there is not deep love. Yes, I love the church. How could I do otherwise? I am in the rather unique position of being the son, the grandson, and the great-grandson of preachers. Yes, I see the church as the body of Christ. But, oh! How we have blemished and scarred that body through social neglect and through fear of being nonconformists.

There was a time when the church was very powerful — in the time when the early Christians rejoiced at being deemed worthy to suffer for what they believed. In those days the church was not merely a thermometer that recorded the ideas and principles of popular opinion; it was a thermostat that transformed the mores of society. Whenever the early Christians entered a town, the people in power became disturbed and immediately sought to convict the Christians for being "disturbers of the peace" and "outside agitators." But the Christians pressed on, in the conviction that they were "a colony of heaven," called to obey God rather than man. Small in number, they were big in commitment. They were too God-intoxicated to be "astronomically intimidated." By their effort and example they brought an end to such ancient evils as infanticide and gladiatorial contests.

Things are different now. So often the contemporary church is a weak, ineffectual voice with an uncertain sound. So often it is an archdefender of the status quo. Far from being disturbed by the presence of the church, the power structure of the average community is consoled by the church's silent — and often even vocal — sanction of things as they are.

But the judgment of God is upon the church as never before. If today's church does not recapture the sacrificial spirit of the early church, it will lose its authenticity, forfeit the loyalty of millions, and be dismissed as an irrelevant social club with no meaning for the twentieth century. Every day I meet young people whose disappointment with the church has turned into outright disgust.

Perhaps I have once again been too optimistic. Is organized religion too inextricably bound to the status quo to save our nation and the world? Perhaps I must turn my faith to the inner spiritual church, the church within the church, as the true *ekklesia* and the hope of the world. But again I am thankful to God that some noble souls from the ranks of organized religion have broken loose from the paralyzing chains of conformity and joined us as active partners in the struggle for freedom. They have left their secure congregations and walked the streets of Albany, Georgia, with us. They have gone down the highways of the South on tortuous rides for freedom.

Yes, they have gone to jail with us. Some have been dismissed from their churches, have lost the support of their bishops and fellow ministers. But they have acted in the faith that right defeated is stronger than evil triumphant. Their witness has been the spiritual salt that has preserved the true meaning of the gospel in these troubled times. They have carved a tunnel of hope through the dark mountain of disappointment.

I hope the church as a whole will meet the challenge of this decisive hour. But even if the church does not come to the aid of justice, I have no despair about the future. I have no fear about the outcome of our struggle in Birmingham, even

seeing connections

Shown here is a famous photograph of a seventeen-year-old civil rights activist being attacked by a police dog in Birmingham on May 3, 1963. The image was printed on the front page of the *New York Times* the following day. Just over a month later, President John F. Kennedy announced he was sending new civil rights legislation to Congress in what has become known as his Civil Rights Address. The landmark Civil Rights Act was passed the following year — it ended segregation in public places and banned employment discrimination on the basis of race, color, religion, sex, or national origin.

Why might this photo have helped bring about a turning point in the civil rights movement? How does this photo inform your understanding of King's message in "Letter from Birmingham Jail"?

BILL HUDSON/AP Images

if our motives are at present misunderstood. We will reach the goal of freedom in Birmingham and all over the nation, because the goal of America is freedom. Abused and scorned though we may be, our destiny is tied up with America's destiny. Before the pilgrims landed at Plymouth, we were here. Before the pen of Jefferson etched the majestic words of the Declaration of Independence across the pages of history, we were here. For more than two centuries our fore-bears labored in this country without wages: they made cotton king; they built the homes of their masters while suffering gross injustice and shameful humiliation — and yet out of a bottom-less vitality they continued to thrive and develop. If the inexpressible cruelties of slavery could not stop us, the opposition we now face will surely fail. We will win our freedom because the sacred heritage of our nation and the eternal will of God are embodied in our echoing demands.

Before closing I feel impelled to mention one other point in your statement that has troubled me profoundly. You warmly commended the Birmingham police force for keeping "order" and "preventing violence." I doubt that you would have so warmly commended the police force if you had seen its dogs sinking their teeth into unarmed, nonviolent Negroes. I doubt that you would so quickly commend the policemen if you were to observe their ugly and inhumane treatment of Negroes here in the city jail; if you were to watch them push and curse old Negro women and young Negro girls; if you were to see them slap and kick old Negro men and young boys; if you were to observe them, as they did on two occa-sions, refuse to give us food because we wanted to sing our grace together. I cannot join you in your praise of the Birmingham police department.

It is true that the police have exercised a degree of discipline in handling the demonstra-tors. In this sense they have conducted themselves rather "nonviolently" in public. But for what purpose? To preserve the evil system of segrega-tion. Over the past few years I have consistently

preached that nonviolence demands that the means we use must be as pure as the ends we seek. I have tried to make clear that it is wrong to use immoral means to attain moral ends. But now I must affirm that it is just as wrong, or perhaps even more so, to use moral means to preserve immoral ends. Perhaps Mr. Connor and his police-men have been rather nonviolent in public, as was Chief Pritchett in Albany, Georgia, but they have used the moral means of nonviolence to maintain the immoral end of racial injustice. As T. S. Eliot has said, "The last temptation is the greatest trea-son: To do the right deed for the wrong reason."

I wish you had commended the Negro sit-inners and demonstrators of Birmingham for their sublime courage, their willingness to suffer, and their amazing discipline in the midst of great provocation. One day the South will recognize its real heroes. They will be the James Merediths, with the noble sense of purpose that enables them to face jeering and hostile mobs, and with the agonizing loneliness that characterizes the life of the pioneer. They will be old, oppressed, battered Negro women, symbolized in a seventy-two-year-old woman in Montgomery, Alabama, who rose up with a sense of dignity and with her people decided not to ride segregated buses, and who responded with ungrammatical profundity to one who inquired about her weariness: "My feets is tired, but my soul is at rest." They will be the young high school and college students, the young ministers of the gospel and a host of their elders, courageously and nonviolently sitting in at lunch counters and willingly going to jail for conscience' sake. One day the South will know that when these disinherited children of God sat down at lunch counters, they were in reality standing up for what is best in the American dream and for the most sacred values in our Judaeo-Christian heritage, thereby bringing our nation back to those great wells of democracy which were dug deep by the founding fathers in their formulation of the Constitution and the Declaration of Independence.

45

seeing connections

Shown here are the Martin Luther King Jr. memorial in Washington, D.C., the statue of Martin Luther King Jr. in Birmingham's Kelly Ingram Park, and a bust sculpture of Martin Luther King Jr. **How does each of these representations of King portray him? What aspects of his persona in "Letter from Birmingham Jail" does each suggest? Which rendering best captures and reflects King's rhetorical style, and why?**

Library of Congress

Library of Congress

©Flip Schulke/CORBIS/Corbis/Getty Images

Never before have I written so long a letter. I'm afraid it is much too long to take your precious time. I can assure you that it would have been much shorter if I had been writing from a comfortable desk, but what else can one do when he is alone in a narrow jail cell, other than write long letters, think long thoughts, and pray long prayers?

If I have said anything in this letter that overstates the truth and indicates an unreasonable impatience, I beg you to forgive me. If I have said anything that understates the truth and indicates my having a patience that allows me to settle for anything less than brotherhood, I beg God to forgive me.

I hope this letter finds you strong in the faith. 50 I also hope that circumstances will soon make it possible for me to meet each of you, not as an integrationist or a civil-rights leader but as a fellow clergyman and a Christian brother. Let us all hope that the dark clouds of racial prejudice will soon pass away and the deep fog of misunderstanding will be lifted from our fear-drenched communities, and in some not too distant tomorrow the radiant stars of love and brotherhood will shine over our great nation with all their scintillating beauty.

Yours for the cause of Peace and Brotherhood,
Martin Luther King Jr.

[1963]

QUESTIONS FOR DISCUSSION

1. Martin Luther King Jr. writes as a member of several communities, some overlapping, some in conflict. What are the communities? Focusing on two or three, explain how he defines himself within each.

2. What is the meaning of *ekklesia* (para. 43)? What does King mean when he invokes "the true *ekklesia*"?

3. How does King balance the twin appeals to religion and patriotism throughout "Letter from Birmingham Jail"? Do you think he puts more emphasis on religion or patriotism? Why do you think he makes that choice?

4. In the later 1960s, Alice Walker wrote an essay titled "The Civil Rights Movement: What Good Was It?" How would you answer her question today?

5. How does King emphasize the concept of time throughout the letter? Consider word or phrase markers (e.g., "seldom" or "when"), actual dates and historical references, and different measures of time. What purpose does this focus on time serve?

6. In his letter, King alludes to alternate approaches to change, specifically that of Malcolm X and his followers. What message does this contrast convey? How effective a strategy do you think it is with regard to his primary audience, who are fellow clergymen?

7. Throughout the letter, King juxtaposes opposites to highlight tension between what is and what should be. Focusing on two examples, what points does he raise?

QUESTIONS ON RHETORIC AND STYLE

1. What is King's tone in the opening paragraph? How might you make an argument for its being ironic?

2. Why does King arrange paragraphs 2–4 in the order that he does? How would reversing the order change their impact?

3. How do King's allusions to biblical figures and events appeal to both ethos and pathos?

4. Why does King go into such detail to explain the basic principles and process of the nonviolent protest movement?

5. In sentence 2 of paragraph 14, what is the effect of juxtaposing the rate of change in Asian and African cultures with the rate of change in American culture?

6. In the long sentence in paragraph 14 (beginning with "But when you have seen"), why does King arrange the "when" clauses in the order that he does? Try repositioning them, and then discuss the difference in effect.

7. What rhetorical strategies are used in paragraph 25? Identify at least four.

CENTRAL ESSAY   529

8. What are the chief rhetorical strategies used in paragraph 31? Identify at least five.

9. Why does King wait until paragraph 45 to address the alleged commendable behavior of the Birmingham police in "preventing violence"?

10. Trace one of the following patterns of figurative language throughout King's letter: darkness and light, high and low, sickness and health.

11. King uses repetition of single words or phrases, of sentence structures, and of sounds. Focusing on a passage of one or more paragraphs, discuss the effect of this use of repetition.

12. Considering the final three paragraphs as King's conclusion, discuss whether you believe it is rhetorically effective.

SUGGESTIONS FOR WRITING

1. Write an essay analyzing the style of this letter, paying close attention to how the stylistic devices and resources of language contribute to achieving King's purpose.

2. King spends nearly half of his letter addressing counterarguments before he launches into his main argument to the clergymen. Write an essay analyzing this argument. What are his major claims, his assumptions, the types of evidence he uses?

3. Compare and contrast the rhetorical strategies King employs in "Letter from Birmingham Jail" with those he uses in another piece, such as the "I Have a Dream" speech or the introduction to *Why We Can't Wait* (which appeared on the 1989 AP Language exam). Why are certain strategies more appropriate for a speech than for an essay or a letter?

4. Select a quotation from King's letter, and explain (1) why you find it compelling or (2) on what grounds you would challenge it. Cite evidence from your own experience or reading to support your position. Possible quotations to focus on include:

   a. "Injustice anywhere is a threat to justice everywhere." (para. 4)

   b. ". . . freedom is never voluntarily given by the oppressor; it must be demanded by the oppressed." (para. 13)

   c. "Shallow understanding from people of good will is more frustrating than absolute misunderstanding from people of ill will." (para. 23)

5. Describe a time when your participation in, or loyalty to, two different communities conflicted. Explain the nature of the conflict and how you resolved it.

6. Based on your reading of "Letter from Birmingham Jail," what do you think King's position would be on the social protest movements in America today? Write an op-ed or a speech in the same rhetorical tradition of King's "Letter," explaining your interpretation of his view in general or in response to a particular protest march.

Where I Lived, and What I Lived For

HENRY DAVID THOREAU

Henry David Thoreau (1817–1862) was a philosopher, poet, essayist, and naturalist as well as an outspoken social critic. He was born in Concord, Massachusetts, and was educated at Harvard. He worked in a variety of professions, from land surveyor to teacher to pencil maker. Strongly influenced by his neighbor and friend Ralph Waldo Emerson, Thoreau considered himself a fierce patriot who honored his country and its ideals, if not always its government. He spoke out against the Mexican–American War, and slavery — specifically the Fugitive Slave Act — and defended the abolitionist John Brown. He is best known for *Walden; or, Life in the Woods*, published in 1854, which is his account of living in a cabin on Walden Pond for two years. This selection is from the second chapter of *Walden*.

Library of Congress

I went to the woods because I wished to live deliberately, to front only the essential facts of life, and see if I could not learn what it had to teach, and not, when I came to die, discover that I had not lived. I did not wish to live what was not life, living is so dear; nor did I wish to practice resignation, unless it was quite necessary. I wanted to live deep and suck out all the marrow of life, to live so sturdily and Spartan-like as to put to rout all that was not life, to cut a broad swath and shave close, to drive life into a corner, and reduce it to its lowest terms, and, if it proved to be mean, why then to get the whole and genuine meanness of it, and publish its meanness to the world; or if it were sublime, to know it by experience, and be able to give a true account of it in my next excursion. For most men, it appears to me, are in a strange uncertainty about it, whether it is of the devil or of God, and have *somewhat hastily* concluded that it is the chief end of man here to "glorify God and enjoy him forever."[1]

Still we live meanly, like ants; though the fable tells us that we were long ago changed into men; like pygmies we fight with cranes;[2] it is error upon error, and clout upon clout, and our best virtue has for its occasion a superfluous and evitable wretchedness. Our life is frittered away by detail. An honest man has hardly need to count more than his ten fingers, or in extreme cases he may add his ten toes, and lump the rest. Simplicity, simplicity, simplicity! I say, let your affairs be as two or three, and not a hundred or a thousand; instead of a million count half a dozen, and keep your accounts on your thumb-nail. In the midst of this chopping sea of civilized life, such are the clouds and storms and quicksands and thousand-and-one items to be allowed for, that a man has to live, if he would not founder and go to the bottom and not make his port at all, by dead reckoning, and he must be a great calculator indeed who succeeds. Simplify, simplify. Instead of three meals a day, if it be necessary eat but one; instead of a

---

[1] The first question and answer in the Westminster Catechism, a statement of religious doctrine that came out of the Protestant Reformation, is "Q: What is the chief end of man? A: To glorify God and enjoy him forever." —Eds.

[2] Allusions to the Greek fable of the Myrmidons (ant-people), and to Book III of the *Iliad*, respectively. The *Iliad* draws a parallel between the Trojan War and the mythological war between the cranes and the pygmies. —Eds.

William Hamilton The New Yorker Collection/The Cartoon Bank

How does this cartoon comment on both Thoreau's philosophy and on modern times?

"My secretary is FedExing the Thoreau."

hundred dishes, five; and reduce other things in proportion. Our life is like a German Confederacy, made up of petty states, with its boundary forever fluctuating, so that even a German cannot tell you how it is bounded at any moment. The nation itself, with all its so-called internal improvements, which, by the way are all external and superficial, is just such an unwieldy and overgrown establishment, cluttered with furniture and tripped up by its own traps, ruined by luxury and heedless expense, by want of calculation and a worthy aim, as the million households in the land; and the only cure for it, as for them, is in a rigid economy, a stern and more than Spartan simplicity of life and elevation of purpose. It lives too fast. Men think that it is essential that the *Nation* have commerce, and export ice, and talk through a telegraph, and ride thirty miles an hour, without a doubt, whether *they* do or not; but whether we should live like baboons or like men, is a little uncertain. If we do not get out sleepers,[3] and forge rails, and devote days and nights to the work, but go to tinkering upon our *lives* to improve *them*, who will build railroads? And if railroads are not

built, how shall we get to heaven in season? But if we stay at home and mind our business, who will want railroads? We do not ride on the railroad; it rides upon us. Did you ever think what those sleepers are that underlie the railroad? Each one is a man, an Irishman, or a Yankee man. The rails are laid on them, and they are covered with sand, and the cars run smoothly over them. They are sound sleepers, I assure you. And every few years a new lot is laid down and run over, so that, if some have the pleasure of riding on a rail, others have the misfortune to be ridden upon. And when they run over a man that is walking in his sleep, a supernumerary sleeper in the wrong position, and wake him up, they suddenly stop the cars, and make a hue and cry about it, as if this were an exception. I am glad to know that it takes a gang of men for every five miles to keep the sleepers down and level in their beds as it is, for this is a sign that they may sometimes get up again.

Why should we live with such hurry and waste of life? We are determined to be starved before we are hungry. Men say that a stitch in time saves nine, and so they take a thousand stitches today to save nine tomorrow. As for *work*, we haven't any of any consequence. We

[3] Here, *sleepers* means "railroad ties." —Eds.

seeing connections

Claude Monet's *The Gare Saint-Lazare*, painted in 1877, exemplifies the innovative and lyrical ways the artist used light, color, and texture — yet it depicts a busy train station in Paris, full of steam and machinery. Look carefully at the details of the painting, paying particular attention to Monet's use of color and to how both people and objects are portrayed. **What might Monet, who painted this twenty years after the publication of *Walden*, say to Thoreau about modern life? How might this painting be seen as a defense of Thoreau's argument in "Where I Lived, and What I Lived For"? How might it be interpreted as a challenge to Thoreau's position?**

Musee d'Orsay, Paris, France/Bridgeman Images

have the Saint Vitus' dance,[4] and cannot possibly keep our heads still. If I should only give a few pulls at the parish bell-rope, as for a fire, that is, without setting the bell, there is hardly a man on his farm in the outskirts of Concord, notwithstanding that press of engagements which was his excuse so many times this morning, nor a boy, nor a woman, I might almost say, but would foresake all and follow that sound, not mainly to save property from the flames, but, if we will confess the truth, much more to see it burn, since burn it must, and we, be it known, did not set it on fire — or to see it put out, and have a hand in it, if that is done as handsomely; yes, even if it were the parish church itself. Hardly a man takes a half-hour's nap after dinner, but when he wakes he holds up his head and asks, "What's the news?" as if the rest of mankind had stood his sentinels. Some give directions to be waked every half-hour, doubtless for no other purpose; and then, to pay for it, they tell what they have dreamed. After a night's sleep the news is as indispensable as the breakfast. "Pray tell me anything new that has happened to a man anywhere on this globe" — and he reads it over his coffee and rolls, that a man has had his eyes gouged out this morning on the Wachito River; never dreaming the while that he lives in the dark unfathomed mammoth cave of this world, and has but the rudiment of an eye himself.

[4] A disease that causes the victim to twitch uncontrollably. St. Vitus is the patron saint of dancers. —Eds.

seeing connections

Carefully read "The World Is Too Much with Us," an 1802 sonnet by English Romantic poet William Wordsworth. In this poem, Wordsworth's speaker characterizes humanity as obsessed with "getting and spending." He also longs for the early times, revealing his wish for a closer connection to nature.

What ideas from this poem do you see reflected in Thoreau's argument? What conclusions might a contemporary reader draw after reading both pieces?

The World Is Too Much with Us

WILLIAM WORDSWORTH

The world is too much with us; late and soon,
Getting and spending, we lay waste our powers:
Little we see in Nature that is ours;
We have given our hearts away, a sordid boon!
This Sea that bares her bosom to the moon;   5
The winds that will be howling at all hours,
And are up-gathered now like sleeping flowers;
For this, for everything, we are out of tune;
It moves us not. — Great God! I'd rather be
A Pagan suckled in a creed outworn;   10
So might I, standing on this pleasant lea,
Have glimpses that would make me less forlorn;
Have sight of Proteus rising from the sea;
Or hear old Triton[1] blow his wreathèd horn.

---

[1] In Greek mythology, both Proteus and Triton were gods of the sea and sons of Poseidon. —Eds.

For my part, I could easily do without the post-office. I think that there are very few important communications made through it. To speak critically, I never received more than one or two letters in my life — I wrote this some years ago — that were worth the postage. The penny-post is, commonly, an institution through which you seriously offer a man that penny for his thoughts which is so often safely offered in jest. And I am sure that I never read any memorable news in a newspaper. If we read of one man robbed, or murdered, or killed by accident, or one house burned, or one vessel wrecked or one steamboat blown up, or one cow run over on the Western Railroad, or one mad dog killed, or one lot of grasshoppers in the winter — we never need read of another. One is enough. If you are acquainted with the principle, what do you care for a myriad instances and applications? To a philosopher all *news*, as it is called, is gossip, and they who edit and read it are old women over their tea. Yet not a few are greedy after this gossip. There was such a rush, as I hear, the other day at one of the offices to learn the foreign news by the last arrival, that several large squares of plate glass belonging to the establishment were broken by the pressure — news which I seriously think a ready wit might write a twelvemonth, or twelve years, beforehand with sufficient accuracy. As for Spain, for instance, if you know how to throw in Don Carlos and the Infanta, and Don Pedro and Seville and Granada, from time to time in the right proportions — they may have changed the names a little since I saw the papers — and serve up a bullfight when other entertainments fail, it will be true to the letter, and give us as good an idea of the exact state or ruin of things in Spain as the most succinct and lucid reports under this head in the newspapers; and as for England, almost the last significant scrap of news from that quarter was the revolution of 1649; and if you have learned the history of her crops for an average year, you never need attend to that thing again, unless your speculations are of a merely pecuniary character. If one may judge who rarely looks into the newspapers, nothing new does ever happen in foreign parts, a French revolution not excepted.

What news! how much more important to know what that is which was never old! "Kieou-pe-yu (great dignitary of the state of Wei) sent a man to Khoung-tseu to know his news. Khoung-tseu caused the messenger to be seated near him, and questioned him in these terms: What is your master doing? The messenger answered with respect: My master desires to diminish the number of his faults, but he cannot come to the end of them. The messenger being gone, the philosopher remarked: What a worthy messenger! What a worthy messenger!" The preacher, instead of vexing the ears of drowsy farmers on their day of rest at the end of the week — for Sunday is the fit conclusion of an ill-spent week, and not the fresh and brave beginning of a new one — with this one other draggle-tail of a sermon, should shout with thundering voice, "Pause! Avast! Why so seeming fast, but deadly slow?"

Shams and delusions are esteemed for soundless truths, while reality is fabulous. If men would steadily observe realities only, and not allow themselves to be deluded, life, to compare it with such things as we know, would be like a fairy tale and the Arabian Nights' Entertainments. If we respected only what is inevitable and has a right to be, music and poetry would resound along the streets. When we are unhurried and wise, we perceive that only great and worthy things have any permanent and absolute existence, that petty fears and petty pleasures are but the shadow of the reality. This is always exhilarating and sublime. By closing the eyes and slumbering, and consenting to be deceived by shows, men establish and confirm their daily

5

Michael Rubinkam/AP Images

In 2015, Juniata College senior Dylan Miller built the hut shown in this photo for his senior research project on simple living. He wanted to live like Thoreau, rather than just read about the life he lived. The hut was deep in the woods in Huntingdon, Pennsylvania, and had no heating, plumbing or electricity. **How authentic do you think Miller's experience was? Do you think he learned things he could not have from merely reading Thoreau? Explain.**

seeing connections

This illustration accompanied a critique of Thoreau entitled "Pond Scum," written by Kathryn Schulz and published by the *New Yorker* in 2015. It was accompanied by the caption, "Why, given his hypocrisy, sanctimony, and misanthropy, has Thoreau been so cherished?"

How does this image express the sentiments of the caption? Do you see the qualities mentioned in the caption reflected in "Where I Lived, and What I Lived For?" Explain, using specific details from the reading to support your response.

Eric Nyquist

life of routine and habit everywhere, which still is built on purely illusory foundations. Children, who play life, discern its true law and relations more clearly than men, who fail to live it worthily, but who think that they are wiser by experience, that is, by failure. I have read in a Hindoo book, that "there was a king's son, who, being expelled in infancy from his native city, was brought up by a forester, and, growing up to maturity in that state, imagined himself to belong to the barbarous race with which he lived. One of his father's ministers having discovered him, revealed to him what he was, and the misconception of his character was removed, and he knew himself to be a prince. So soul," continues the Hindoo philosopher, "from the circumstances in which

it is placed, mistakes its own character, until the truth is revealed to it by some holy teacher and then it knows itself to be *Brahme*."[5] I perceive that we inhabitants of New England live this mean life that we do because our vision does not penetrate the surface of things. We think that that *is* which *appears* to be. If a man should walk through this town and see only the reality, where, think you, would the "Milldam"[6] go to? If he should give us an account of the realities he beheld there, we should not recognize the place in his description. Look at the meetinghouse, or a courthouse, or a jail, or a shop, or a dwelling-house, and say what

---

[5] One of the three main Hindu gods, now spelled *Brahma*. —Eds.
[6] Concord's business center. —Eds.

seeing connections

Carefully read the following excerpt from an 1865 essay by James Russell Lowell, a contemporary — but not a fan — of Thoreau.

How would you summarize Lowell's main argument? How effective is his critique of Thoreau's work?

from Thoreau

JAMES RUSSELL LOWELL

Thoreau seems to have prized a lofty way of thinking (often we should be inclined to call it a remote one) not so much because it was good in itself as because he wished few to share it with him. It seems now and then as if he did not seek to lure others up "above our lower region of turmoil," but to leave his own name cut on the mountain peak as the first climber. This itch of originality infects his thought and style. To be misty is not to be mystic. He turns common-places end for end, and fancies it makes something new of them. . . .

But it is much easier for a man to impose on himself when he measures only with himself. A greater familiarity with ordinary men would have done Thoreau good, by showing him how many fine qualities are common to the race. The radical vice of his theory of life was that he confounded physical with spiritual remoteness from men. A man is far enough withdrawn from his fellows if he keep himself clear of their weaknesses. He is not so truly withdrawn as exiled, if he refuse to share in their strength. "Solitude," says Cowley, "can be well fitted and set right but upon a very few persons. They must have enough knowledge of the world to see the vanity of it, and enough virtue to despise all vanity." It is a morbid self-consciousness that pronounces the world of men empty and worthless before trying it, the instinctive evasion of one who is sensible of some innate weakness, and retorts the accusation of it before any has made it but himself. To a healthy mind, the world is a constant challenge of opportunity. Mr. Thoreau had not a healthy mind, or he would not have been so fond of prescribing.

that thing really is before a true gaze, and they would all go to pieces in your account of them. Men esteem truth remote, in the outskirts of the system behind the farthest star, before Adam and after the last man. In eternity there is indeed something true and sublime. But all these times and places and occasions are now and here. God himself culminates in the present moment, and will never be more divine in the lapse of all the ages. And we are enabled to apprehend at all what is sublime and noble only by the perpetual instilling and drenching of the reality that surrounds us. The universe constantly and obediently answers to our conceptions; whether we travel fast or slow, the track is laid for us. Let us spend our lives in conceiving then. The poet or the artist never yet had so fair and noble a design but some of his posterity at least could accomplish it.

Let us spend one day as deliberately as Nature, and not be thrown off the track by every nutshell and mosquito's wing that falls on the rails. Let us rise early and fast, or breakfast, gently and without perturbation; let company come and let company go, let the bells ring and the children cry — determined to make a day of it. Why should we knock under and go with the stream? Let us not be upset and overwhelmed in that terrible rapid and whirlpool called a dinner, situated in the meridian shallows. Weather this danger and you are safe, for the rest of the way is downhill. With unrelaxed nerves, with morning vigor, sail by it, looking another way, tied to the mast like Ulysses. If the engine whistles, let it whistle till it is hoarse for its pains. If the bell rings, why should we run? We will consider what kind of music they are like. Let us settle ourselves and work and wedge our feet downward through the mud and slush of opinion, and prejudice, and tradition, and delusion, and appearance, that alluvion[7] which covers the globe, through Paris and London, through New York and Boston and Concord, through Church and State, through poetry and philosophy and religion, till we come to a hard bottom and rocks in place, which we can call *reality*, and say, This is, and no mistake; and then begin, having a *point d'appui*,[8] below freshet and frost and fire, a place where you might found a wall or a state, or set a lamppost safely, or perhaps a gauge, not a Nilometer, but a Realometer, that future ages might know how deep a freshet of shams and appearances had gathered from time to time. If you stand right fronting and face to face to a fact, you will see the sun glimmer on both its surfaces, as if it were a cimeter,[9] and feel its sweet edge dividing you through the heart and marrow, and so you will happily conclude your mortal career. Be it life or death, we crave only reality. If we are really dying, let us hear the rattle in our throats and feel cold in the extremities; if we are alive, let us go about our business.

Time is but the stream I go afishing in. I drink at it; but while I drink I see the sandy bottom and detect how shallow it is. Its thin current slides away but eternity remains. I would drink deeper; fish in the sky, whose bottom is pebbly with stars. I cannot count one. I know not the first letter of the alphabet. I have always been regretting that I was not as wise as the day I was born. The intellect is a cleaver; it discerns and rifts its way into the secret of things. I do not wish to be any more busy with my hands than is necessary. My head is hands and feet. I feel all my best faculties concentrated in it. My instinct tells me that my head is an organ for burrowing, as some creatures use their snout and fore paws, and with it I would mine and burrow my way through these hills. I think that the richest vein is somewhere hereabouts, so by the divining-rod and thin rising vapors, I judge; and here I will begin to mine.

[1854]

---

[7] The flow of water against a shore. —Eds.

[8] French, "foundation." —Eds.

[9] Also known as a *scimeter* or *scimitar*, a curved bladed sword traditionally used in the Middle East. —Eds.

QUESTIONS FOR DISCUSSION

1. What is Henry David Thoreau calling for early in paragraph 2 when he writes, "Simplicity, simplicity, simplicity!"?

2. Thoreau writes, "We do not ride on the railroad; it rides upon us" (para. 2). Consider an electronic device (such as a laptop computer, a smartphone, a tablet, or an MP3 player). What would Thoreau say about it? Has this device helped to simplify our lives, or has it had a negative impact on them?

3. What does Thoreau mean when he says, "As for *work*, we haven't any of any consequence" (para. 3)? What is his definition of *work*?

4. How do you interpret this assertion: "Shams and delusions are esteemed for soundless truths, while reality is fabulous" (para. 6)? Use that as a topic sentence, and develop it with examples from your own experience.

5. Do you think Thoreau's advice and sentiments in this essay are meant as recommendations for living one's entire life or as suggestions for periodically reflecting on life's true meaning? Is he suggesting isolation as a lifestyle?

6. In today's terms, how would you characterize Thoreau's politics? Is he very conservative or very progressive? Is he somewhere in between?

QUESTIONS ON RHETORIC AND STYLE

1. In the first paragraph, how does Thoreau use antitheses to describe his purpose in going to live in the woods?

2. Paragraph 2 opens with a simile and continues its lengthy development with more similes and an extended metaphor. Identify these and explain their effect.

3. Throughout the text, Thoreau uses repetition, particularly parallel structure. Identify three or four examples and analyze their effect. Try to find ones that illustrate different effects.

4. Thoreau opens paragraph 3 with a rhetorical question. How effectively does the rest of the paragraph answer it — or does he intend to "answer" the question?

5. What does Thoreau mean by the phrase "starved before we are hungry" in the second sentence of paragraph 3? What other examples of paradox do you find in this excerpt from *Walden*?

6. Compare the probable rhetorical effect of paragraph 4 at the time it was written with its effect today.

7. What is the purpose of the parable in paragraph 5? In telling this story, what assumptions does Thoreau make about his audience?

8. In paragraph 6, Thoreau sets forth a series of "if . . . then" statements to support his opening sentence. Explain the deductive logic in at least one of these statements, specifying the major and minor premises and conclusion. Note that the assumption may be unexpressed.

9. What is the meaning of the allusion to Ulysses in paragraph 7?

10. In what ways do the ideas Thoreau presents in paragraph 6 become the foundation for the beliefs he expresses in paragraph 7? For instance, how do the ideas explained in paragraph 6 lead to his exhortation, "If the engine whistles, let it whistle till it is hoarse for its pains" (para. 7)?

11. Sometimes, even the slightest stylistic feature can work effectively as a rhetorical strategy. What is the effect of the alliterative phrase "freshet and frost and fire" in paragraph 7?

12. In the concluding paragraph, Thoreau develops two metaphors regarding time and the intellect. What are they? What is their effect?

SUGGESTIONS FOR WRITING

1. In paragraph 5, Thoreau writes, "What news! how much more important to know what that is which was never old!" Write an essay in which you evaluate Thoreau's own writing according to this thought. Consider how this essay appeals to two audiences: Thoreau's contemporaries and today's readers.

2. In this essay, Thoreau extols the virtues of individualism and self-sufficiency. Discuss how living according to these virtues can jeopardize the community; consider specific circumstances when such jeopardy might occur.

3. Write a response to Thoreau, telling him how modern technology has influenced how we communicate. Acknowledge how he did or did not anticipate our modern condition.

4. Using the reflective style of Thoreau, write your own philosophical essay entitled "Where I Live, and What I Live For" (note present tense).

National Prejudices

OLIVER GOLDSMITH

Born in Ireland, Oliver Goldsmith (1731–1774) was a member of the intellectual circle surrounding Dr. Samuel Johnson. Goldsmith is most widely known for the novel *The Vicar of Wakefield* (1766) and the play *She Stoops to Conquer* (1771). Both deal with a series of misfortunes that end happily. He was also the author of the nursery tale "Goody Two-Shoes," from which we derive the source of the common expression. "National Prejudices," the essay that follows, might seem surprisingly critical for a writer whose works are known to have a sunny disposition. It was published anonymously in the *British Magazine* in August 1760, and while some scholars doubt its authorship, most regard it as Goldsmith's work.

As I am one of that sauntering tribe of mortals, who spend the greatest part of their time in taverns, coffee-houses, and other places of public resort, I have thereby an opportunity of observing an infinite variety of characters, which, to a person of a contemplative turn, is a much higher entertainment than a view of all the curiosities of art or nature. In one of these my late rambles, I accidentally fell into the company of half-a-dozen gentlemen, who were engaged in a warm dispute about some political affair; the decision of which, as they were equally divided in their sentiments, they thought proper to refer to me, which naturally drew me in for a share of the conversation.

Amongst a multiplicity of other topics, we took occasion to talk of the different characters of the several nations of Europe; when one of the gentlemen, cocking his hat, and assuming such an air of importance as if he had possessed all the merit of the English nation in his own person, declared that the Dutch were a parcel of avaricious wretches; the French a set of flattering sycophants; that the Germans were drunken sots,

Getty Images/Getty Images

In this 2003 photograph, Neal Rowland stands in front of the restaurant he owns in Beaufort, North Carolina. To show his anger at the French government's delay in joining American forces in Iraq, he changed French fries to "Freedom fries" on his menu and hung a banner proclaiming "Home of Freedom Fries" outside.
How does this act illustrate what Goldsmith would call national prejudice?

John Moore/Getty Images

In this photograph, taken during the Republican National Convention in July 2016, a delegate holds a sign with a twist on Trump's campaign slogan, "Make America Great Again."
How does this image reflect Goldsmith's main point?

and beastly gluttons; and the Spaniards proud, haughty, and surly tyrants: but that in bravery, generosity, clemency, and in every other virtue, the English excelled all the world.

This very learned and judicious remark was received with a general smile of approbation by all the company — all, I mean, but your humble servant; who, endeavouring to keep my gravity as well as I could, and reclining my head upon my arm, continued for some time in a posture of affected thoughtfulness, as if I had been musing on something else, and did not seem to attend to the subject of conversation; hoping, by this means, to avoid the disagreeable necessity of explaining myself, and thereby depriving the gentleman of his imaginary happiness.

But my pseudo-patriot had no mind to let me escape so easily: not satisfied that his opinion should pass without contradiction, he was determined to have it ratified by the suffrage of everyone in the company; for which purpose, addressing himself to me with an air of inexpressible confidence, he asked me if I was not of the same way of thinking. As I am never forward in giving my opinion, especially when I have reason to believe that it will not be agreeable; so, when I am obliged to give it, I always hold it for a maxim to speak my real sentiments. I therefore told him, that, for my own part, I should not have ventured to talk in such peremptory strain, unless I had made the tour of Europe, and examined the manners of the several nations with great care and accuracy; that, perhaps a more impartial judge would not scruple to affirm, that the Dutch were more frugal and industrious, the French more temperate and polite, the Germans more hardy and patient of labour and fatigue, and the Spaniards more staid and sedate, than the English; who, though undoubtedly brave and generous, were at the same time rash, headstrong, and impetuous, too apt to be elated with prosperity, and to despond in adversity.

I could easily perceive, that all the company began to regard me with a jealous eye before I had finished my answer; which I had no sooner done than the patriotic gentleman observed, with a contemptuous sneer, that he was greatly surprised how some people could have the conscience to live in a country which they did not love, and to enjoy the protection of a government, to which in their hearts they were inveterate enemies. Finding that by this modest declaration of my sentiments, I had forfeited the good opinion of my companions, and given them occasion to call my political principles in question, and well knowing that it was in vain to argue

5

with men who were so very full of themselves, I threw down my reckoning, and retired to my own lodgings, reflecting on the absurd and ridiculous nature of national prejudice and prepossession.

Among all the famous sayings of antiquity, there is none that does greater honour to the author, or affords greater pleasure to the reader (at least if he be a person of a generous and benevolent heart), than that of the philosopher, who being asked what countryman he was, replied that he was a citizen of the world. How few are there to be found in modern times who can say the same, or whose conduct is consistent with such a profession! We are now become so much Englishmen, Frenchmen, Dutchmen, Spaniards, or Germans, that we are no longer citizens of the world; so much the natives of one particular spot, or members of one petty society, that we no longer consider ourselves as the general inhabitants of the globe, or members of that grand society which comprehends the whole human kind.

Did these prejudices prevail only among the meanest and lowest of the people, perhaps they might be excused, as they have few, if any opportunities of correcting them by reading, travelling, or conversing with foreigners; but the misfortune is, that they infect the minds, and influence the conduct even of our gentlemen; of those, I mean, who have every title to this appellation but an exemption from prejudice, which, however, in my opinion, ought to be regarded as the characteristical mark of a gentleman: for let a man's birth be ever so high, his station ever so exalted, or his fortune ever so large, yet, if he is not free from the national and all other prejudices, I should make bold to tell him, that he had a low and vulgar mind, and had no just claim to the character of a gentleman. And, in fact, you will always find, that those are most apt to boast of national merit, who have little or no merit of their own to depend on; than which, to be sure, nothing is more natural: the slender vine twists around the sturdy oak for no other reason in the world, but because it has not strength sufficient to support itself.

Should it be alleged in defense of national prejudice, that it is the natural and necessary growth of love to our country, and that therefore the former cannot be destroyed without hurting the latter; I answer that this is a gross fallacy and delusion. That it is the growth of love to our country, I will allow; but that it is the natural

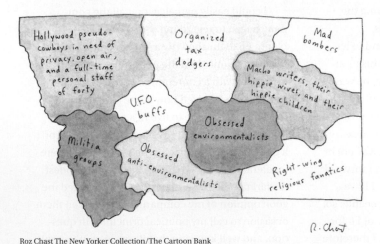

Roz Chast The New Yorker Collection/The Cartoon Bank

Look carefully at this 1996 *New Yorker* cartoon by Roz Chast.
How does she comment on assumptions Americans may make about regions other than their own?

Following the ISIS-related London Bridge terrorist attack in June 2017, members of the 1,000 Roses London project donated roses to members of the public. The women pictured above are participating in the project by passing out roses to pedestrians on London Bridge.

In what ways might this image reflect a modern-day take on Goldsmith's warning against national prejudices?

Barcroft Media/Getty Images

and necessary growth of it, I absolutely deny. Superstition and enthusiasm too are the growth of religion; but whoever took it in his head to affirm, that they are the necessary growth of this noble principle? They are, if you will, the bastard sprouts of this heavenly plant; but not its natural and genuine branches, and may safely enough be lopt off, without doing any harm to the parent stock: nay, perhaps, 'till once they are lopt off, this goodly tree can never flourish in perfect health and vigour.

Is it not very possible that I may love my own country, without hating the natives of other countries? That I may exert the most heroic bravery, the most undaunted resolution, in defending its laws and liberty, without despising all the rest of the world as cowards and poltroons? Most certainly it is: and if it were not — but what need I suppose what is absolutely impossible? — but if it were not I must own I should prefer the title of the ancient philosopher, namely, a citizen of the world, to that of an Englishman, a Frenchman, a European, or to any other appellation whatever.

[1760]

EXPLORING THE TEXT

1. How does Oliver Goldsmith establish his ethos in the opening paragraphs — that is, what gives him the authority to speak on the subject of national prejudices? What is the effect of referring to himself as a member of the "sauntering tribe" (para. 1) and as the "humble servant" of his audience (para. 3)?

2. What does Goldsmith mean by the description of the critic in the conversation as "my pseudo-patriot" (para. 4)? Why does he refer to the critic as a "patriotic gentleman" (para. 5)?

3. How does the language Goldsmith uses to report the responses of the "company" in paragraph 5 convey his attitude toward those men?

4. How does Goldsmith's position, as he articulates it in paragraph 6, differ from that of others in the conversation?

5. A "gentleman" in the eighteenth century — when this essay was written — typically referred to a man who held a high social position because of noble birth rather than personal accomplishment. How does his metaphor illuminate or dramatize his attitude toward the gentlemen in question: "the slender vine twists around the sturdy oak for no other reason in the world, but because it has not strength sufficient to support itself" (para. 7)?

6. In what ways is Goldsmith's analysis in paragraphs 8 and 9 a rebuttal of the argument the "pseudo-patriot" makes in paragraph 4? Include in your analysis the analogy and figurative language Goldsmith uses.

7. In paragraph 6, Goldsmith writes, "[W]e no longer consider ourselves as the general inhabitants

of the globe, or members of that grand society which comprehends the whole human kind." To what extent do you believe that this statement characterizes American society today? Provide specific evidence from current events.

Health and Happiness

ROBERT D. PUTNAM

Robert D. Putnam (b. 1941) is the Peter and Isabel Malkin Professor of Public Policy at Harvard University, former dean of the John F. Kennedy School of Government, and founder of the Saguaro Seminar, a program dedicated to fostering civic engagement in America. He received his undergraduate degree from Swarthmore College, won a Fulbright Fellowship to Balliol College at Oxford University, and earned both his MA and PhD from Yale University. He was the 2006 recipient of the Skytte Prize, the most prestigious international award for scholarly achievement in political science. Among the ten books Putnam has authored or co-authored, his most influential include: *Bowling Alone: The Collapse and Revival of American Community* (1995), *Better Together: Restoring the American Community* (2003), *American Grace: How Religion Divides and Unites Us* (2010), and *Our Kids: The American Dream in Crisis* (2015). *Bowling Alone* argues that our civic, social, associational, and political connections — what are called "social capital" — have decreased dramatically during the latter half of the twentieth century. The following chapter from the book analyzes the impact of social connectedness on physical and psychological health. This enormously popular book is based on extensive research and introduced a wide audience to Putnam's groundbreaking ideas.

Of all the domains in which I have traced the consequences of social capital, in none is the importance of social connectedness so well established as in the case of health and well-being. Scientific studies of the effects of social cohesion on physical and mental health can be traced to the seminal work of the nineteenth-century sociologist Émile Durkheim, *Suicide*. Self-destruction is not merely a personal tragedy, he found, but a sociologically predictable consequence of the degree to which one is integrated into society — rarer among married people, rarer in more tightly knit religious communities, rarer in times of national unity, and more frequent when rapid social change disrupts

the social fabric. Social connectedness matters to our lives in the most profound way.

In recent decades public health researchers have extended this initial insight to virtually all aspects of health, physical as well as psychological. Dozens of painstaking studies from Alameda (California) to Tecumseh (Michigan) have established beyond reasonable doubt that social connectedness is one of the most powerful determinants of our well-being. The more integrated we are with our community, the less likely we are to experience colds, heart attacks, strokes, cancer, depression, and premature death of all sorts. Such protective effects have been confirmed for close family ties, for friendship networks, for participation in social events, and even for simple affiliation with religious and other civic associations. In other words, both *machers** and *schmoozers* enjoy these remarkable health benefits.

After reviewing dozens of scientific studies, sociologist James House and his colleagues have concluded that the *positive* contributions to health made by social integration and social support rival in strength the *detrimental* contributions of well-established biomedical risk factors like cigarette smoking, obesity, elevated blood pressure, and physical inactivity. Statistically speaking, the evidence for the health consequences of social connectedness is as strong today as was the evidence for the health consequences of smoking at the time of the first surgeon general's report on smoking. If the trends in social disconnection are as pervasive as I argued in section II, then "bowling alone" represents one of the nation's most serious public health challenges.[1]

Although researchers aren't entirely sure why social cohesion matters for health, they have a number of plausible theories. First, social networks furnish tangible assistance, such as money, convalescent care, and transportation, which reduces psychic and physical stress and provides a safety net. If you go to church regularly, and then you slip in the bathtub and miss a Sunday, someone is more likely to notice. Social networks also may reinforce healthy norms — socially isolated people are more likely to smoke, drink, overeat, and engage in other health-damaging behaviors. And socially cohesive communities are best able to organize politically to ensure first-rate medical services.[2]

Finally, and most intriguingly, social capital   5
might actually serve as a physiological triggering mechanism, stimulating people's immune systems to fight disease and buffer stress. Research now under way suggests that social isolation has measurable biochemical effects on the body.

---
*Yiddish: a mover and shaker. —Eds.

Animals who have been isolated develop more extensive atherosclerosis (hardening of the arteries) than less isolated animals, and among both animals and humans loneliness appears to decrease the immune response and increase blood pressure. Lisa Berkman, one of the leading researchers in the field, has speculated that social isolation is "a chronically stressful condition to which the organism respond[s] by aging faster."[3]

Some studies have documented the strong correlation between connectedness and health at the community level. Others have zeroed in on individuals, both in natural settings and in experimental conditions. These studies are for the most part careful to account for confounding factors — the panoply of other physiological, economic, institutional, behavioral, and demographic forces that might also affect an individual's health. In many cases these studies are longitudinal: they check on people over many years to get a better understanding of what lifestyle changes might have caused people's health to improve or decline. Thus researchers have been able to show that social isolation *precedes* illness to rule out the possibility that the isolation was caused by illness. Over the last twenty years more than a dozen large studies of this sort in the United States, Scandinavia, and Japan have shown that *people who are socially disconnected are between two and five times more likely to die from all causes, compared with matched individuals who have close ties with family, friends, and the community.*[4]

A recent study by researchers at the Harvard School of Public Health provides an excellent overview of the link between social capital and physical health across the United States.[5] Using survey data from nearly 170,000 individuals in all fifty states, these researchers found, as expected, that people who are African American, lack health insurance, are overweight, smoke, have a low income, or lack a college education are at greater risk for illness than are more socioeconomically advantaged individuals. But these researchers also found an astonishingly strong relationship between poor health and low social capital. States whose residents were most likely to report fair or poor health were the same states in which residents were most likely to distrust others.[6] Moving from a state with a wealth of social capital to a state with very little social capital (low trust, low voluntary group membership) increased one's chances of poor to middling health by roughly 40–70 percent. When the researchers accounted for individual residents' risk factors, the relationship between social capital and individual health remained. Indeed, the researchers concluded that if one wanted to improve one's health, moving to a high-social-capital state would do almost as much good as quitting smoking. These authors' conclusion is complemented by our own analysis. We found a strong positive relationship between a comprehensive index of public health

and the Social Capital Index, along with a strong negative correlation between the Social Capital Index and all-cause mortality rates.[7] (See table 1 for the measure of public health and health care and figure 1 for the correlations of public health and mortality with social capital.)

The state-level findings are suggestive, but far more definitive evidence of the benefits of community cohesion is provided by a wealth of studies that examine individual health as a function of individual social-capital resources. Nowhere is the connection better illustrated than in Roseto, Pennsylvania.[8] This small Italian American community has been the subject of nearly forty years of in-depth study, beginning in the 1950s when medical researchers noticed a happy but puzzling phenomenon. Compared with residents of neighboring towns, Rosetans just didn't die of heart attacks. Their (age-adjusted) heart attack

Table 1: Which State Has the Best Health and Health Care?

Morgan-Quitno Healthiest State Rankings (1993–1998):	
1. Births of low birth weight as a percent of all births (–)	12. Estimate rate of new cancer cases (–)
2. Births to teenage mothers as a percent of live births (–)	13. AIDS rate (–)
3. Percent of mothers receiving late or no prenatal care (–)	14. Sexually transmitted disease rate (–)
4. Death rate (–)	15. Percent of population lacking access to primary care (–)
5. Infant mortality rate (–)	16. Percent of adults who are binge drinkers (–)
6. Estimated age adjusted death rate by cancer (–)	17. Percent of adults who smoke (–)
7. Death rate by suicide (–)	18. Percent of adults overweight (–)
8. Percent of population not covered by health insurance (–)	19. Days in past month when physical health was "not good" (–)
9. Change in percent of population uninsured (–)	20. Community hospitals per 1,000 square miles (+)
10. Health care expenditures as a percent of gross state product (–)	21. Beds in community hospitals per 100,000 population (+)
11. Per capita personal health expenditures (–)	22. Percent of children aged 19–35 months fully immunized (+)
	23. Safety belt usage rate (+)

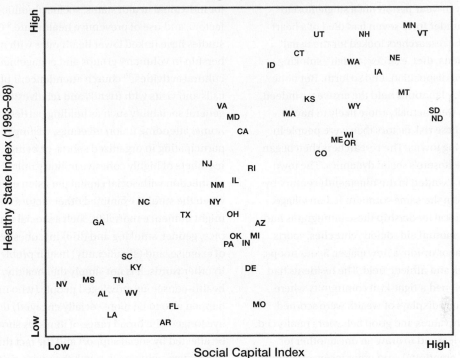

Public health is better in high-social-capital states

Healthy State Index (1993–98) · High / Low

Social Capital Index · Low / High

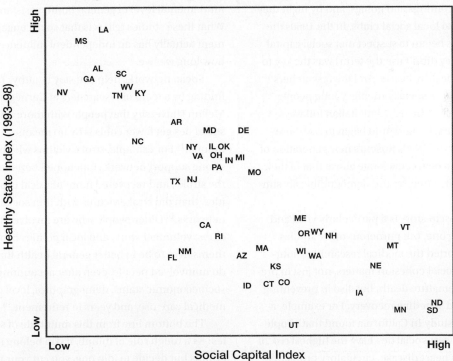

Mortality is lower in high-social-capital states

Healthy State Index (1993–98) · High / Low

Social Capital Index · Low / High

Figure 1: Health Is Better in High-Social-Capital States

rate was less than half that of their neighbors; over a seven-year period not a single Roseto resident under forty-seven had died of a heart attack. The researchers looked for the usual explanations: diet, exercise, weight, smoking, genetic predisposition, and so forth. But none of these explanations held the answer — indeed, Rosetans were actually more likely to have some of these risk factors than were people in neighboring towns. The researchers then began to explore Roseto's social dynamics. The town had been founded in the nineteenth century by people from the same southern Italian village. Through local leadership these immigrants had created a mutual aid society, churches, sports clubs, a labor union, a newspaper, Scout troops, and a park and athletic field. The residents had also developed a tight-knit community where conspicuous displays of wealth were scorned and family values and good behaviors reinforced. Rosetans learned to draw on one another for financial, emotional, and other forms of support. By day they congregated on front porches to watch the comings and goings, and by night they gravitated to local social clubs. In the 1960s the researchers began to suspect that social capital (though they didn't use the term) was the key to Rosetans' healthy hearts. And the researchers worried that as socially mobile young people began to reject the tight-knit Italian folkways, the heart attack rate would begin to rise. Sure enough, by the 1980s Roseto's new generation of adults had a heart attack rate above that of their neighbors in a nearby and demographically similar town.

The Roseto story is a particularly vivid and compelling one, but numerous other studies have supported the medical researchers' intuition that social cohesion matters, not just in preventing premature death, but also in preventing disease and speeding recovery. For example, a long-term study in California found that people with the fewest social ties have the highest risk of dying from heart disease, circulatory problems, and cancer (in women), even after accounting for individual health status, socioeconomic factors, and use of preventive health care.[9] Other studies have linked lower death rates with membership in voluntary groups and engagement in cultural activities;[10] church attendance;[11] phone calls and visits with friends and relatives;[12] and general sociability such as holding parties at home, attending union meetings, visiting friends, participating in organized sports, or being members of highly cohesive military units.[13] The connection with social capital persisted even when the studies examined other factors that might influence mortality, such as social class, race, gender, smoking and drinking, obesity, lack of exercise, and (significantly) health problems. In other words, it is not simply that healthy, health-conscious, privileged people (who might happen also to be more socially engaged) tend to live longer. The broad range of illnesses shown to be affected by social support and the fact that the link is even tighter with death than with sickness tend to suggest that the effect operates at a quite fundamental level of general bodily resistance. What these studies tell us is that social engagement actually has an independent influence on how long we live.

Social networks help you stay healthy. The finding by a team of researchers at Carnegie Mellon University that people with more diverse social ties get fewer colds is by no means unique.[14] For example, stroke victims who had strong support networks functioned better after the stroke, and recovered more physical capacities, than did stroke victims with thin social networks.[15] Older people who are involved with clubs, volunteer work, and local politics consider themselves to be in better general health than do uninvolved people, even after accounting for socioeconomic status, demographics, level of medical care use, and years in retirement.[16]

The bottom line from this multitude of studies: As a rough rule of thumb, if you belong to no groups but decide to join one, you cut your risk

10

of dying over the next year *in half*. If you smoke and belong to no groups, it's a toss-up statistically whether you should stop smoking or start joining. These findings are in some ways heartening: it's easier to join a group than to lose weight, exercise regularly, or quit smoking.

But the findings are sobering, too. As we saw in section II, there has been a general decline in social participation over the past twenty-five years. Figure 2 shows that this same period witnessed a significant decline in self-reported health, despite tremendous gains in medical diagnosis and treatment. Of course, by many objective measures, including life expectancy, Americans are healthier than ever before, but these self-reports indicate that we are feeling worse.[17] These self-reports are in turn closely linked to social connectedness, in the sense that it is precisely less connected Americans who are feeling worse. These facts alone do not *prove* that we are suffering physically from our growing

disconnectedness, but taken in conjunction with the more systematic evidence of the health effects of social capital, this evidence is another link in the argument that the erosion of social capital has measurable ill effects.

We observed in chapter 14 the remarkable coincidence that during the same years that social connectedness has been declining, depression and even suicide have been increasing. We also noted that this coincidence has deep generational roots, in the sense that the generations most disconnected socially also suffer most from what some public health experts call "Agent Blue." In any given year 10 percent of Americans now suffer from major depression, and depression imposes the fourth largest total burden of any disease on Americans overall. Much research has shown that social connections inhibit depression. Low levels of social support directly predict depression, even controlling for other risk factors, and high levels of social support

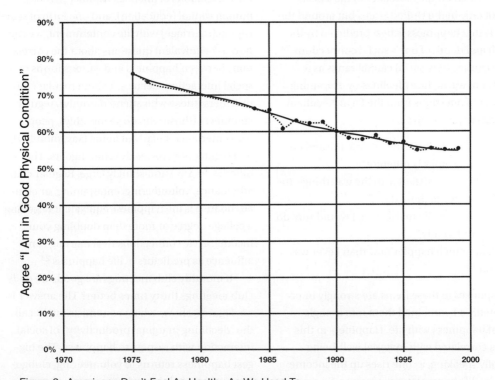

Figure 2: Americans Don't Feel As Healthy As We Used To

lessen the severity of symptoms and speed recovery. Social support buffers us from the stresses of daily life. Face-to-face ties seem to be more therapeutic than ties that are geographically distant. In short, even within the single domain of depression, we pay a very high price for our slackening social connectedness.[18]

Countless studies document the link between society and psyche: people who have close friends and confidants, friendly neighbors, and supportive co-workers are less likely to experience sadness, loneliness, low self-esteem, and problems with eating and sleeping. Married people are consistently happier than people who are unattached, all else being equal. These findings will hardly surprise most Americans, for in study after study people themselves report that good relationships with family members, friends, or romantic partners — far more than money or fame — are prerequisites for their happiness.[19] The single most common finding from a half century's research on the correlates of life satisfaction, not only in the United States but around the world, is that happiness is best predicted by the breadth and depth of one's social connections.[20]

We can see how social capital ranks as a producer of warm, fuzzy feelings by examining a number of questions from the DDB Needham Life Style survey archives:

"I wish I could leave my present life and do something entirely different."

"I am very satisfied with the way things are going in my life these days."

"If I had my life to live over, I would sure do things differently."

"I am much happier now than I ever was before."

Responses to these items are strongly inter-correlated, so I combined them into a single index of happiness with life. Happiness in this sense is correlated with material well-being. Generally speaking, as one rises up the income hierarchy, life contentment increases. So money

can buy happiness after all. But not as much as marriage. Controlling for education, age, gender, marital status, income, and civic engagement, the marginal "effect" of marriage on life contentment is equivalent to moving roughly seventy percentiles up the income hierarchy — say, from the fifteenth percentile to the eighty-fifth percentile.[21] In round numbers, getting married is the "happiness equivalent" of quadrupling your annual income.[22]

What about education and contentment? Education has important indirect links to happiness through increased earning power, but controlling for income (as well as age, gender, and the rest), what is the marginal correlation of education itself with life satisfaction? In round numbers the answer is that four additional years of education — attending college, for example — is the "happiness equivalent" of roughly doubling your annual income.

Having assessed in rough-and-ready terms the correlations of financial capital (income), human capital (education), and one form of social capital (marriage) with life contentment, we can now ask equivalent questions about the correlations between happiness and various forms of social interaction. Let us ask about regular club members (those who attend monthly), regular volunteers (those who do so monthly), people who entertain regularly at home (say, monthly), and regular (say, biweekly) churchgoers. The differences are astonishingly large. Regular club attendance, volunteering, entertaining, or church attendance is the happiness equivalent of getting a college degree or more than doubling your income. Civic connections rival marriage and affluence as predictors of life happiness.[23]

If monthly club meetings are good, are daily club meetings thirty times better? The answer is no. Figure 3 shows what economists might call the "declining marginal productivity" of social interaction with respect to happiness. The biggest happiness returns to volunteering, clubgoing, and entertaining at home appear to come

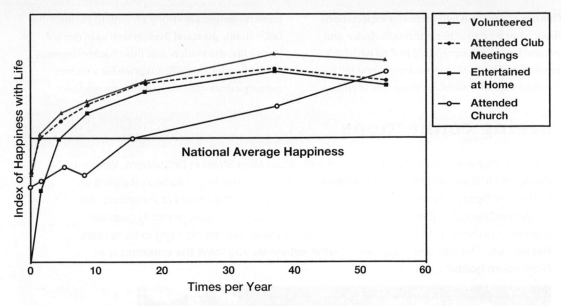

Figure 3: Social Connectedness (at Least in Moderation) Fosters Happiness

between "never" and "once a month." There is very little gain in happiness after about one club meeting (or party or volunteer effort) every three weeks. After fortnightly encounters, the marginal correlation of additional social interaction with happiness is actually negative — another finding that is consistent with common experience! Churchgoing, on the other hand, is somewhat different, in that at least up through weekly attendance, the more the merrier.

This analysis is, of course, phrased intentionally in round numbers, for the underlying calculations are rough and ready. Moreover the direction of causation remains ambiguous. Perhaps happy people are more likely than unhappy people to get married, win raises at work, continue in school, attend church, join clubs, host parties, and so on. My present purpose is merely to illustrate that social connections have profound links with psychological well-being. The Beatles got it right: we all "get by with a little help from our friends."

In the decades since the Fab Four topped the charts, life satisfaction among adult Americans

has declined steadily. Roughly half the decline in contentment is associated with financial worries, and half is associated with declines in social capital: lower marriage rates and decreasing connectedness to friends and community. Not all segments of the population are equally gloomy. Survey data show that the slump has been greatest among young and middle-aged adults (twenty to fifty-five). People over fifty-five — our familiar friends from the long civic generation — are actually *happier* than were people their age a generation ago.[24]

Some of the generational discrepancy is due to money worries: despite rising prosperity, young and middle-aged people feel less secure financially. But some of the disparity is also due to social connectedness. Young and middle-aged adults today are simply less likely to have friends over, attend church, or go to club meetings than were earlier generations. Psychologist Martin Seligman argues that more of us are feeling down because modern society encourages a belief in personal control and autonomy more than a commitment to duty and common enterprise.

20

This transformation heightens our expectations about what we can achieve through choice and grit and leaves us unprepared to deal with life's inevitable failures. Where once we could fall back on social capital — families, churches, friends — these no longer are strong enough to cushion our fall.[25] In our personal lives as well as in our collective life, the evidence of this chapter suggests, we are paying a significant price for a quarter century's disengagement from one another.

seeing connections

In this photograph, cows and their owners walk down Main Street in Brattleboro, Vermont, during its 2016 annual Strolling of the Heifers parade. Inspired by the famous Running of the Bulls in Spain — in which a herd of bulls is released onto the streets of Pamplona and people run alongside them — the Stroll is a parade of friendly calves, perfectly groomed, dressed up in hats and flowers, and led by young people who are planning to be farmers. **Having read "Health and Happiness," what values do you think the community in Brattleboro holds?**

Christian Science Monitor/Getty Images

Notes

1. For comprehensive overviews of the massive literature on health and social connectedness, see James S. House, Karl R. Landis, and Debra Umberson, "Social Relationships and Health," *Science* 241 (1988): 540–545; Lisa F. Berkman, "The Role of Social Relations in Health Promotion," *Psychosomatic Medicine* 57 (1995): 245–254; and Teresa E. Seeman, "Social Ties and Health: The Benefits of Social Integration," *Annual of Epidemiology* 6 (1996): 442–451. Other useful recent overviews include Benjamin C. Amick III, Sol Levine, Alvin R. Tarlov, and Diana Chapman Walsh, eds., *Society and Health* (New York: Oxford University Press, 1995), esp. Donald L. Patrick and Thomas M. Wickizer, "Community and Health," 46–92; Richard G. Wilkinson, *Unhealthy Societies: From Inequality to Well-Being* (New York: Routledge, 1996); Linda K. George, "Social Factors and Illness," in *Handbook of Aging and the Social Sciences*, 4th ed., Robert

H. Binstock and Linda K. George, eds. (New York: Academic Press, 1996), 229–252; Frank W. Young and Nina Glasgow, "Voluntary Social Participation and Health," *Research on Aging* 20 (1998): 339–362; Sherman A. James, Amy J. Schulz, and Juliana van Olphen, "Social Capital, Poverty, and Community Health: An Exploration of Linkages," in *Using Social Capital*, Saegert, Thompson, and Warren, eds.

2. B. H. Kaplan, J. C. Cassel, and S. Gore, "Social Support and Health," *Medical Care* (supp.) 15, no. 5 (1977): 47–58; L. F. Berkman, "The Relationship of Social Networks and Social Support to Morbidity and Mortality," in S. Cohen and S. L. Syme, eds., *Social Support and Health* (Orlando, Fla.: Academic Press, 1985), 241–262; J. S. House, D. Umberson, and K. R. Landis, "Structures and Processes of Social Support," *Annual Review of Sociology* 14 (1988): 293–318; Ichiro Kawachi, Bruce P. Kennedy, and Roberta Glass, "Social Capital and Self-Rated Health: A Contextual Analysis," *American Journal of Public Health* 89 (1999): 1187–1193.

3. Lisa Berkman, "The Changing and Heterogeneous Nature of Aging and Longevity: A Social and Biomedical Perspective," *Annual Review of Gerontology and Geriatrics* 8 (1988): 37–68; Lisa Berkman and Thomas Glass, "Social Integration, Social Networks, Social Support, and Health," in *Social Epidemiology*, Lisa F. Berkman and Ichiro Kawachi, eds. (New York, Oxford University Press, 2000), 137–174; T. E. Seeman, L. F. Berkman, and D. Blazer, et al., "Social Ties and Support and Neuroendocrine Function: The MacArthur Studies of Successful Aging," *Annals of Behavioral Medicine* 16 (1994): 95–106; Sheldon Cohen, "Health Psychology: Psychological Factors and Physical Disease from the Perspective of Human Psychoneuroimmunology," *Annual Review of Psychology* 47 (1996): 113–142.

4. Berkman and Glass, "Social Integration, Social Networks, Social Support, and Health."

5. Kawachi et al., "Social Capital and Self-Rated Health."

6. The Pearson's *r* coefficient between the fraction reporting they were in fair or poor health and the (demographically weighted) state mistrust ranking (low, medium, high) was 0.71; the *r* coefficient between fraction of population in fair/poor health and the (demographically weighted) state "helpfulness" ranking (low, medium, high) was -0.66.

7. The Pearson's *r* coefficient between the Social Capital Index and the Morgan-Quitno health index (1991–98) across the fifty states equals 0.78, which is strong by conventional social science standards; the comparable correlation between the Social Capital Index and the age-adjusted all-cause mortality rate is -.81. Thanks to Ichiro Kawachi for providing this measure of death rates.

8. Thanks to Kimberly Lochner for bringing the history of Roseto to my attention and for introducing me to the literature on the health effects of social connectedness. The key studies of Roseto are J. G. Bruhn and S. Wolf, *The Roseto Story: An Anatomy of Health* (Norman, Okla.: University of Oklahoma Press, 1979); S. Wolf and J. G. Bruhn, *The Power of Clan: The Influence of Human Relationships on Heart Disease* (New Brunswick, N.J.: Transaction Publishers, 1993); B. Egolf, J. Lasker, S. Wolf, and L. Potvin, "The Roseto Effect: A Fifty-Year Comparison of Mortality Rates," *American Journal of Epidemiology* 125, no. 6 (1992): 1089–1092.

9. L. F. Berkman and S. L. Syme, "Social Networks, Host Resistance and Mortality: A Nine Year Follow-up of Alameda County Residents," *American Journal of Epidemiology* 109 (1979): 186–204.

10. J. House, C. Robbins, and H. Metzner, "The Association of Social Relationships and Activities with Mortality: Prospective Evidence from the Tecumseh Community Health Study," *American Journal of Epidemiology* 116, no. 1 (1982): 123–140. This finding held for men only.

11. House, Robbins, and Metzner (1982); this finding held for women only. T. E. Seeman, G. A. Kaplan, L. Knudsen, R. Cohen, and J. Guralnik, "Social Network Ties and Mortality among the Elderly in the Alameda County Study," *American Journal of Epidemiology* 126, no. 4 (1987): 714–723; this study found that social isolation predicted mortality only in people over sixty.

12. D. Blazer, "Social Support and Mortality in an Elderly Community Population," *American Journal of Epidemiology* 115, no. 5 (1982): 684–694; K. Orth-Gomer and J. V. Johnson, "Social Network Interaction and Mortality," *Journal of Chronic Diseases* 40, no. 10 (1987): 949–957.

13. L. Welin, G. Tibblin, K. Svardsudd, B. Tibblin, S. Ander-Peciva, B. Larsson, and L. Wilhelmsen, "Prospective Study of Social Influences on Mortality," The *Lancet*, April 20, 1985, 915–918; Frederick J. Manning and Terrence D. Fullerton, "Health and Well-Being in Highly Cohesive Units of the U.S. Army," *Journal of Applied Social Psychology* 18 (1988): 503–519.

14. Sheldon Cohen et al., "Social Ties and Susceptibility to the Common Cold," *Journal of the American Medical Association* 277 (June 25, 1997): 1940–1944.

15. A. Colantonio, S. V. Kasl, A. M. Ostfeld, and L. Berkman, "Psychosocial Predictors of Stroke Outcomes in an Elderly Population," *Journal of Gerontology* 48, no. 5 (1993): S261–S268.

16. Young and Glasgow, "Voluntary Social Participation and Health."

17. Angus Deaton and C. H. Paxson, "Aging and Inequality in Income and Health," *American Economic Review* 88 (1998): 252, report "there has been no improvement, and possibly some deterioration, in health status across cohorts born after 1945, and there were larger improvements across those born before 1945."

18. R. C. Kessler et al., "Lifetime and 12-Month Prevalence of DSM-III-R Psychiatric Disorders in the United States," *Archives of General Psychiatry* 51 (1994): 8–19; C. J. Murray and A. D. Lopez, "Evidence-Based Health Policy — Lessons from the Global Burden of Disease Study," *Science* 274 (1996): 740–743; L. I. Pearlin et al., "The Stress Process"; G. A. Kaplan et al., "Psychosocial Predictors of Depression"; A. G. Billings and R. H. Moos, "Life Stressors and Social Resources Affect Posttreatment Outcomes among Depressed Patients," *Journal of Abnormal Psychiatry* 94 (1985): 140–153; C. D. Sherbourne, R. D. Hays, and K. B. Wells, "Personal and Psychosocial Risk Factors for Physical and Mental Health Outcomes and Course of Depression among Depressed Patients," *Journal of Consulting and Clinical Psychology* 63 (1995): 345–355; T. E. Seeman and L. F. Berkman, "Structural Characteristics of Social Networks and Their Relationship with Social Support in the Elderly: Who Provides Support," *Social Science and Medicine* 26 (1988): 737–749. I am indebted to Julie Donahue for her fine work on this topic.

19. L. I. Pearlin, M. A. Lieberman, E. G. Menaghan, and J. T. Mullan, "The Stress Process," *Journal of Health and Social Behavior* 22, no. 4 (1981): 337–356; A. Billings and R. Moos, "Social Support and Functioning among Community and Clinical Groups: A Panel Model," *Journal of Behavioral Medicine* 5, no. 3 (1982): 295–311; G. A. Kaplan, R. E. Roberts, T. C. Camacho, and J. C. Coyne, "Psychosocial Predictors of Depression," *American Journal of Epidemiology* 125, no. 2 (1987), 206–220; P. Cohen, E. L. Struening, G. L. Muhlin, L. E. Genevie, S. R. Kaplan, and H. B. Peck, "Community Stressors, Mediating Conditions and Well-being in Urban Neighborhoods," *Journal of Community Psychology* 10 (1982): 377–391; David G. Myers, "Close Relationships and Quality of Life," in D. Kahneman, E. Diener, and N. Schwartz,

eds., *Well-being: The Foundation of Hedonic Psychology* (New York: Russell Sage Foundation, 1999).

20. Michael Argyle, *The Psychology of Happiness* (London: Methuen, 1987); Ed Diener, "Subjective Well-being," *Psychological Bulletin* 95 (1984): 542–575; Ed Deiner, "Assessing Subjective Well-being," *Social Indicators Research*, 31 (1994): 103–175; David G. Myers and Ed Deiner, "Who Is Happy?" *Psychological Science* 6 (1995): 10–19; Ruut Veenhoven, "Developments in Satisfaction-Research," *Social Indicators Research*, 37 (1996): 1–46; and works cited there.

21. In these data and in most studies the effect of marriage on life happiness is essentially identical among men and women, contrary to some reports that marriage has a more positive effect on happiness among men.

22. Income in successive Life Style surveys is measured in terms of income brackets, defined in dollars of annual income. To enhance comparability over time, we have translated each of these brackets in each annual survey into its mean percentile ranking in that year's income distribution. The effect of income measured in percentiles on contentment is not linear, but that is offset by the fact that the translation of income in dollars to income percentiles is also not linear. Thus the "happiness equivalent" of any particular change in income is accurate in its order of magnitude, but not in detail.

23. The results here are based on multiple regression analyses on the DDB Needham Life Style sample, including age, gender, education, income, marital status, as well as our various measures of civic engagement. The results are essentially identical for men and women, except that the effects of education and of social connections on happiness are slightly greater among women. Income, education, and social connections all have a greater effect among single people than among married people. For example, the effects of club meetings on the happiness of single people is twice as great as on the happiness of married people. In other words, absent marriage, itself a powerful booster of life contentment, other factors become more important. Conversely, even among the poor, uneducated, and socially isolated, marriage provides a fundamental buffer for contentment.

24. Author's analysis of DDB Needham Life Style and Harris poll data.

25. Martin E. P. Seligman, "Boomer Blues," *Psychology Today*, October 1988, 50–55.

[1995]

EXPLORING THE TEXT

1. Robert D. Putnam opens with consideration of suicide. Why does he use suicide, perhaps the most profound expression of isolation, as a way to introduce an analysis of social connectedness?

2. What is the purpose of Note 1 from the perspective of both the audience and the author?

3. What theories does Putnam review to explain the positive effects of social connectedness and the negative effects of its absence?

4. What evidence do the Notes present to support Putnam's claim that Lisa Berkman is "one of the leading researchers in the field" (para. 5)?

5. What evidence does Putnam provide in his discussion of the "astonishingly strong relationship between poor health and low social capital" (para. 7)?

6. Putnam discusses at length a classic study of the Italian American community in Roseto, Pennsylvania (para. 8). What have researchers learned from this example?

7. In this chapter, Putnam uses several graphs and charts. Discuss how they function in presenting his arguments — that is, do they add information that is not in the written text, do they confirm it, do they expand on it? Consider each figure individually.

8. What is the causal relationship between marriage and happiness? Between education and happiness? Between money and happiness? Which, according to Putnam, is strongest? What evidence does he provide?

9. Does Putnam's allusion to the musical group the Beatles and his quotation from one of their famous songs (para. 20) strike you as out of place or as a welcome lighter note? Is it effective or ineffective in the context of this essay?

10. Select three sequential paragraphs at random for analysis. Look at the syntax, diction, and point of view. What rhetorical strategies does Putnam use to make technical and specialized research accessible to a more general audience?

11. After looking over all of Putnam's notes for this chapter, classify them into three or four different purposes. Specifically, how do these notes complement the written and visual text in the chapter without interrupting the flow of the analysis?

12. Discuss why you agree or disagree with the position of psychologist Martin Seligman, as described by Putnam: "more of us are feeling down because modern society encourages a belief in personal control and autonomy more than a commitment to duty and common enterprise" (para. 22).

13. If you were asked to develop a series of suggestions for a "healthier environment" in the area where you live, what would you recommend? Base your suggestions on Putnam's research.

14. Identify one or two of the ways people establish social connectedness — for example, by belonging to an organized religion, volunteering, participating in associations, or spending time with friends. What role(s) do you think social media might play in increasing social capital?

Mother Tongue

AMY TAN

Best-selling author Amy Tan (b. 1952) has written several novels, including *The Joy Luck Club* (1989), *The Kitchen God's Wife* (1991), *The Bonesetter's Daughter* (2001), and *The Valley of Amazement* (2013). Known for her portrayal of mother–daughter relationships, Tan draws on her Chinese heritage to depict the clash of traditional Chinese culture with modern-day American customs. Tan grew up in California, has an MA in linguistics, and worked as a business writer before turning to fiction. She was also a member of the Rock Bottom Remainders, a band — including Dave Barry and Stephen King — that played for charity events. Tan collected many of her nonfiction writings in *The Opposite of Fate: A Book of Musings* (2003). Among these is "Mother Tongue," an essay in which Tan explores "all the Englishes" that are part of her identity. Her most recent book is *Where the Past Begins: A Writer's Memoir* (2017).

I am not a scholar of English or literature. I cannot give you much more than personal opinions on the English language and its variations in this country or others.

I am a writer. And by that definition, I am someone who has always loved language. I am fascinated by language in daily life. I spend a great deal of my time thinking about the power of language — the way it can evoke an emotion, a visual image, a complex idea, or a simple truth. Language is the tool of my trade. And I use them all — all the Englishes I grew up with.

Recently, I was made keenly aware of the different Englishes I do use. I was giving a talk to a large group of people, the same talk I had already given to half a dozen other groups. The nature of the talk was about my writing, my life, and my book, *The Joy Luck Club*. The talk was going along well enough, until I remembered one major difference that made the whole talk sound wrong. My mother was in the room. And it was perhaps the first time she had heard me give a lengthy speech, using the kind of English I have never used with her. I was saying things like "The intersection of memory upon imagination" and "There is an aspect of my fiction that relates to thus-and-thus" — a speech filled with carefully wrought grammatical phrases, burdened, it suddenly seemed to me, with nominalized forms, past perfect tenses, conditional phrases, all the forms of standard English that I had learned in school and through books, the forms of English I did not use at home with my mother.

Just last week, I was walking down the street with my mother, and I again found myself conscious of the English I was using, the English I do use with her. We were talking about the price of new and used furniture and I heard myself saying this: "Not waste money that way."

My husband was with us as well, and he didn't notice any switch in my English. And then I realized why. It's because over the twenty years we've been together I've often used that same kind of English with him, and sometimes he even uses it with me. It has become our language of intimacy, a different sort of English that relates to family talk, the language I grew up with.

So you'll have some idea of what this family talk I heard sounds like, I'll quote what my mother said during a recent conversation which I videotaped and then transcribed. During this conversation, my mother was talking about a political gangster in Shanghai who had the same last name as her family's, Du, and how the gangster in his early years wanted to be adopted by her family, which was rich by comparison. Later, the gangster became more powerful, far richer than my mother's family, and one day showed up at my mother's wedding to pay his respects. Here's what she said in part:

"Du Yusong having business like fruit stand. Like off the street kind. He is Du like Du Zong — but not Tsung-ming Island people. The local people call putong, the river east side, he belong to that side local people. That man want to ask Du Zong father take him in like become own family. Du Zong father wasn't look down on him, but didn't take seriously, until that man big like become a mafia. Now important person, very hard to inviting him. Chinese way, came only to show respect, don't stay for dinner. Respect for making big celebration, he shows up. Mean gives lots of respect. Chinese custom. Chinese social life that way. If too important won't have to stay too long. He come to my wedding. I didn't see, I heard it. I gone to boy's side, they have YMCA dinner. Chinese age I was nineteen."

5

In 2006 the sign outside a popular Philadelphia restaurant told customers they must order in English.

How does Amy Tan prompt her audience to consider the definition of English?

You should know that my mother's expressive command of English belies how much she actually understands. She reads the *Forbes* report, listens to *Wall Street Week*, converses daily with her stockbroker, reads all of Shirley MacLaine's books with ease — all kinds of things I can't begin to understand. Yet some of my friends tell me they understand 50 percent of what my mother says. Some say they understand 80 to 90 percent. Some say they understand none of it, as if she were speaking pure Chinese. But to me, my mother's English is perfectly clear, perfectly natural. It's my mother tongue. Her language, as I hear it, is vivid, direct, full of observation and imagery. That was the language that helped shape the way I saw things, expressed things, made sense of the world.

◆ ◆ ◆

Lately, I've been giving more thought to the kind of English my mother speaks. Like others, I have described it to people as "broken" or "fractured" English. But I wince when I say that. It has always bothered me that I can think of no other way to describe it other than "broken," as if it were damaged and needed to be fixed, as if it lacked a certain wholeness and soundness. I've heard other terms used, "limited English," for example. But they seem just as bad, as if everything is limited, including people's perceptions of the limited English speaker.

I know this for a fact, because when I was growing up, my mother's "limited" English limited *my* perception of her. I was ashamed of her English. I believed that her English reflected the quality of what she had to say. That is, because she expressed them imperfectly her thoughts were imperfect. And I had plenty of empirical evidence to support me: the fact that people in department stores, at banks, and at restaurants did not take her seriously, did not give her good service, pretended not to understand her, or even acted as if they did not hear her.

My mother has long realized the limitations of her English as well. When I was fifteen, she used to have me call people on the phone to pretend I was she. In this guise, I was forced to ask for information or even to complain and yell at people who had been rude to her. One time it was a call to her stockbroker in New York. She had cashed out her small portfolio and it just so happened we were going to go to New York the next week, our very first trip outside California. I had to get on the phone and say in an adolescent voice that was not very convincing, "This is Mrs. Tan." 10

And my mother was standing in the back whispering loudly, "Why he don't send me check, already two weeks late. So mad he lie to me, losing me money."

And then I said in perfect English, "Yes, I'm getting rather concerned. You had agreed to send the check two weeks ago, but it hasn't arrived."

Then she began to talk more loudly. "What he want, I come to New York tell him front of his boss, you cheating me." And I was trying to calm her down, make her be quiet, while telling the stockbroker, "I can't tolerate any more excuses. If I don't receive the check immediately, I am going to have to speak to your manager when I'm in New York next week." And sure enough, the following week there we were in front of this astonished stockbroker, and I was sitting there red-faced and quiet, and my mother, the real Mrs. Tan, was shouting at his boss in her impeccable broken English.

We used a similar routine just five days ago, for a situation that was far less humorous. My mother had gone to the hospital for an appointment, to find out about a benign brain tumor a CAT scan had revealed a month ago. She said she had spoken very good English, her best English, no mistakes. Still, she said, the hospital did not apologize when they said they had lost

the CAT scan and she had come for nothing. She said they did not seem to have any sympathy when she told them she was anxious to know the exact diagnosis, since her husband and son had both died of brain tumors. She said they would not give her any more information until the next time and she would have to make another appointment for that. So she said she would not leave until the doctor called her daughter. She wouldn't budge. And when the doctor finally called her daughter, me, who spoke in perfect English — lo and behold — we had assurances the CAT scan would be found, promises that a conference call on Monday would be held, and apologies for any suffering my mother had gone through for a most regrettable mistake.

I think my mother's English almost had an effect on limiting my possibilities in life as well. Sociologists and linguists probably will tell you that a person's developing language skills are more influenced by peers. But I do think that the language spoken in the family, especially in immigrant families which are more insular, plays a large role in shaping the language of the child. And I believe that it affected my results on achievement tests, IQ tests, and the SAT. While my English skills were never judged as poor, compared to math, English could not be considered

15

Chelsea Beck

This illustration was created for a story on National Public Radio's website about the benefits of bilingualism.
How might this image be seen as a portrayal of the experiences that Amy Tan describes in "Mother Tongue"?

my strong suit. In grade school I did moderately well, getting perhaps B's, sometimes B-pluses, in English and scoring perhaps in the sixtieth or seventieth percentile on achievement tests. But those scores were not good enough to override the opinion that my true abilities lay in math and science, because in those areas I achieved A's and scored in the ninetieth percentile or higher.

This was understandable. Math is precise; there is only one correct answer. Whereas, for me at least, the answers on English tests were always a judgment call, a matter of opinion and personal experience. Those tests were constructed around items like fill-in-the-blank sentence completion, such as "Even though Tom was _____, Mary thought he was _____." And the correct answer always seemed to be the most bland combinations of thoughts, for example, "Even though Tom was shy, Mary thought he was charming," with the grammatical structure "even though" limiting the correct answer to some sort of semantic opposites, so you wouldn't get answers like, "Even though Tom was foolish, Mary thought he was ridiculous." Well, according to my mother, there were very few limitations as to what Tom could have been and what Mary might have thought of him. So I never did well on tests like that.

The same was true with word analogies, pairs of words in which you were supposed to find some sort of logical, semantic relationship — for example, "*Sunset* is to *nightfall* as _____ is to _____." And here you would be presented with a list of four possible pairs, one of which showed the same kind of relationship: *red* is to *stoplight, bus* is to *arrival, chills* is to *fever, yawn* is to *boring.* Well, I could never think that way. I knew what the tests were asking, but I could not block out of my mind the images already created by the first pair, "*sunset* is to *nightfall*" — and I would see a burst of colors against a darkening sky, the moon rising, the lowering of a curtain of stars. And all the other pairs of words — red, bus, stoplight, boring — just threw up a mass of confusing images, making it impossible for me to sort out something as logical as saying: "A sunset precedes nightfall" is the same as "a chill precedes a fever." The only way I would have gotten that answer right would have been to imagine an associative situation, for example, my being disobedient and staying out past sunset, catching a chill at night, which turns into feverish pneumonia as punishment, which indeed did happen to me.

◆ ◆ ◆

I have been thinking about all this lately, about my mother's English, about achievement tests. Because lately I've been asked, as a writer, why there are not more Asian Americans represented in American literature. Why are there few Asian Americans enrolled in creative writing programs? Why do so many Chinese students go into engineering? Well, these are broad sociological questions I can't begin to answer. But I have noticed in surveys — in fact, just last week — that Asian students, as a whole, always do significantly better on math achievement tests than in English. And this makes me think that there are other Asian-American students whose English spoken in the home might also be described as "broken" or "limited." And perhaps they also have teachers who are steering them away from writing and into math and science, which is what happened to me.

Fortunately, I happen to be rebellious in nature and enjoy the challenge of disproving assumptions made about me. I became an English-major my first year in college, after being enrolled as pre-med. I started writing nonfiction as a freelancer the week after I was told by my former boss that writing was my worst skill and I should hone my talents toward account management.

But it wasn't until 1985 that I finally began 20 to write fiction. And at first I wrote using what I thought to be wittily crafted sentences, sentences that would finally prove I had mastery over the English language. Here's an example from the

seeing connections

The work shown here, created by British artist Anya Gallaccio in 1997, is a color screen-print on white paper depicting portraits of figures in the art world. Its title is *Broken English*. Notice that some portraits overlap or are upside down, with the glue showing at the back. **What does this work suggest about the contemporary state of English identity, including the English language? Would Amy Tan agree with the message it conveys? Based on your reading of Tan's essay, explain why or why not.**

©Anya Gallaccio, courtesy Lehmann Maupin Gallery, New York/©Tate, London 2017.

first draft of a story that later made its way into *The Joy Luck Club*, but without this line: "That was my mental quandary in its nascent state." A terrible line, which I can barely pronounce.

Fortunately, for reasons I won't get into today, I later decided I should envision a reader for the stories I would write. And the reader I decided upon was my mother, because these were stories about mothers. So with this reader in mind — and in fact she did read my early drafts — I began to write stories using all the Englishes I grew up with: the English I spoke to my mother, which for lack of a better term might be described as "simple"; the English she used with me, which for lack of a better term might be described as "broken"; my translation of her

Chinese, which could certainly be described as "watered down"; and what I imagined to be her translation of her Chinese if she could speak in perfect English, her internal language, and for that I sought to preserve the essence, but neither an English nor a Chinese structure. I wanted to capture what language ability tests can never reveal: her intent, her passion, her imagery, the rhythms of her speech, and the nature of her thoughts.

Apart from what any critic had to say about my writing, I knew I had succeeded where it counted when my mother finished reading my book and gave me her verdict: "So easy to read."

[2003]

QUESTIONS FOR DISCUSSION

1. In paragraph 1, Amy Tan opens her essay by stating, "I am not a scholar of English or literature," but in paragraph 2 she states, "I am a writer." What is the difference between them, according to Tan? How does she establish ethos through this juxtaposition?

2. What are the "different Englishes" (para. 3) Tan describes in this essay? How does each of these relate to the idea of community? Specifically, how does language offer entrance to a community — and, conversely, how does it work to exclude people from a community?

3. How does Tan's facility with English reverse the traditional power dynamic of parent and child? In what ways does this reversal shift the roles parents can assume in the larger community?

4. At several points in her essay, Tan relates anecdotes. How do they further her argument? Be sure to consider the anecdotes regarding Tan giving a speech, the stockbroker, the CAT scan, and Tan's experience with the SAT. What would be the impact of omitting one of them?

5. Tan divides the essay into three sections. How does this structure contribute to the argument she is developing?

6. What does Tan mean when she says, "I think my mother's English almost had an effect on limiting my possibilities in life as well" (para. 15)? To what extent do you think that speaking a nonstandardized English (through grammatical differences or an accent) limits possibilities for people in the United States today?

7. Keep an observational journal for several days, noting the judgments people make on the basis of how a person speaks or writes, what Tan calls "fractured" or "broken English" — a description that suggests something is damaged and needs fixing. Consider your peers, a business environment, or the media. Then write an essay explaining the relationship you have observed between language, power, and community. To what extent does someone's facility with a language (or, in some contexts, with bilingualism) confer power? Did you observe situations where one's position of authority makes his or her language acceptable? Did you note anyone who "code-switched," or shifted his or her way of speaking to accommodate a different audience or community?

---

from A Paradise Built in Hell
The Extraordinary Communities That Arise in Disaster

REBECCA SOLNIT

Rebecca Solnit (b. 1961) is a writer, historian, and activist who has authored over twenty books on feminism, the environment, history, politics, and art. She is currently a contributing editor at *Harper's*. Solnit grew up in Novato, California, moved to Paris, France, to study at age 17, then returned to California to finish college at San Francisco State University. She earned an MA in journalism from the University of California, Berkeley in 1984 and has been writing since. Her most famous books include *River of Shadows: Eadweard Muybridge and the Technological Wild West* (2004), for which she received a Guggenheim, the National Book Critics Circle Award in criticism, and the Lannan Literary Award; *The Faraway Nearby* (2013); *Men Explain Things to Me* (2015), a national bestseller; and its follow-up, *The Mother of All Questions* (2017), which continues Solnit's commentary on feminism, misogyny, gender, and the literary canon. The following chapter is taken from the introduction to her 2009 book *A Paradise Built in Hell*.

Who are you? Who are we? In times of crisis, these are life-and-death questions. Thousands of people survived Hurricane Katrina because grandsons or aunts or neighbors or complete strangers reached out to those in need all through the Gulf Coast and because an armada of boat owners from the surrounding communities and as far away as Texas went into New Orleans to pull stranded people to safety. Hundreds of people died in the aftermath of Katrina because others, including police, vigilantes, high government officials, and the media, decided that the people of New Orleans were too dangerous to allow them to evacuate the septic, drowned city or to rescue them, even from hospitals. Some who attempted to flee were turned back at gunpoint or shot down. Rumors proliferated about mass rapes, mass murders, and mayhem that turned out later to be untrue, though the national media and New Orleans's police chief believed and perpetuated those rumors during the crucial days when people were dying on rooftops and elevated highways and in crowded shelters and hospitals in the unbearable heat, without adequate water, without food, without medicine and medical attention. Those rumors led soldiers and others dispatched as rescuers to regard victims as enemies. Beliefs matter — though as many people act generously despite their beliefs as the reverse.

Katrina was an extreme version of what goes on in many disasters, wherein how you behave depends on whether you think your neighbors or fellow citizens are a greater threat than the havoc wrought by a disaster or a greater good than the property in houses and stores around you. (Citizen, in this book, means members of a city or community, not people in possession of legal citizenship in a nation.) What you believe shapes how you act. How you act results in life or death, for yourself or others, as in everyday life, only more so. Katrina was, like most disasters, also marked by altruism: of young men who took it upon themselves to supply water, food, diapers, and protection to the strangers stranded with them; of

people who rescued or sheltered neighbors; of the uncounted hundreds or thousands who set out in boats — armed, often, but also armed with compassion — to find those who were stranded in the stagnant waters and bring them to safety; of the two hundred thousand or more who (via the Internet site HurricaneHousing.org in the weeks after) volunteered to house complete strangers, mostly in their own homes, persuaded more by the pictures of suffering than the rumors of monstrosity; of the uncounted tens of thousands of volunteers who came to the Gulf Coast to rebuild and restore.

In the wake of an earthquake, a bombing, or a major storm, most people are altruistic, urgently engaged in caring for themselves and those around them, strangers and neighbors as well as friends and loved ones. The image of the selfish, panicky, or regressively savage human being in times of disaster has little truth to it. Decades of meticulous sociological research on behavior in disasters, from the bombings of World War II to floods, tornadoes, earthquakes, and storms across the continent and around the world, have demonstrated this. But belief lags behind, and often the worst behavior in the wake of a calamity is on the part of those who believe that others will behave savagely and that they themselves are taking defensive measures against barbarism. From earthquake-shattered San Francisco in 1906 to flooded New Orleans in 2005, innocents have been killed by people who believed or asserted that their victims were the criminals and they themselves were the protectors of the shaken order. Beliefs matter.

"Today Cain is still killing his brother" proclaims a faded church mural in the Lower Ninth Ward of New Orleans, which was so devastated by the failure of the government levees. In quick succession, the Book of Genesis gives us the creation of the universe, the illicit acquisition of knowledge, the expulsion from Paradise, and the slaying of Abel by Cain, a second fall from grace into jealousy, competition, alienation, and violence. When God asks Cain where his brother is, Cain asks back, "Am

I my brother's keeper?" He is refusing to say what God already knows: that the spilled blood of Abel cries out from the ground that has absorbed it. He is also raising one of the perennial social questions: are we beholden to each other, must we take care of each other, or is it every man for himself?

Most traditional societies have deeply entrenched commitments and connections between individuals, families, and groups. The very concept of society rests on the idea of networks of affinity and affection, and the freestanding individual exists largely as an outcast or exile. Mobile and individualistic modern societies shed some of these old ties and vacillate about taking on others, especially those expressed through economic arrangements — including provisions for the aged and vulnerable, the mitigation of poverty and desperation — the keeping of one's brothers and sisters. The argument against such keeping is often framed as an argument about human nature: we are essentially selfish, and because you will not care for me, I cannot care for you. I will not feed you because I must hoard against starvation, since I too cannot count on others. Better yet, I will take your wealth and add it to mine — if I believe that my well-being is independent of yours or pitted against yours — and justify my conduct as natural law. If I am not my brother's keeper, then we have been expelled from paradise, a paradise of unbroken solidarities.

Thus does everyday life become a social disaster. Sometimes disaster intensifies this; sometimes it provides a remarkable reprieve from it, a view into another world for our other selves. When all the ordinary divides and patterns are shattered, people step up — not all, but the great preponderance — to become their brothers' keepers. And that purposefulness and connectedness bring joy even amid death, chaos, fear, and loss. Were we to know and believe this, our sense of what is possible at any time might change. We speak of self-fulfilling prophecies, but any belief that is acted on makes the world in its image. Beliefs matter. And so do the facts

5

In this photograph, which has become one of the most recognizable images of the rescue effort in the aftermath of Hurricane Harvey in 2017, Houston police officer Daryl Hudeck carries a woman and her baby to safety after rescuing them from the floodwaters that destroyed their home.

What does this image suggest about the role of institutional powers in response to disasters? In what way might it be read as a challenge to Solnit's main argument?

David J. Phillip/AP Images

behind them. The astonishing gap between common beliefs and actualities about disaster behavior limits the possibilities, and changing beliefs could fundamentally change much more. Horrible in itself, disaster is sometimes a door back into paradise, the paradise at least in which we are who we hope to be, do the work we desire, and are each our sister's and brother's keeper.

I landed in Halifax, Nova Scotia, shortly after a big hurricane tore up the city in October of 2003. The man in charge of taking me around told me about the hurricane — not about the winds that roared at more than a hundred miles an hour and tore up trees, roofs, and telephone poles or about the seas that rose nearly ten feet, but about the neighbors. He spoke of the few days when everything was disrupted, and he lit up with happiness as he did so. In his neighborhood all the people had come out of their houses to speak with each other, aid each other, improvise a community kitchen, make sure the elders were okay, and spend time together, no longer strangers, "Everybody woke up the next morning and everything was different," he mused. "There was no electricity, all the stores were closed, no one had access to media. The consequence was that everyone poured out into the street to bear witness. Not quite a street party, but everyone out at once — it was a sense of happiness to see everybody even though we didn't know each other." His joy struck me powerfully.

A friend told me of being trapped in a terrible fog, one of the dense tule fogs that overtakes California's Central Valley periodically. On this occasion the fog mixed with dust from the cotton fields created a shroud so perilous that the highway patrol stopped all traffic on the highway.

For two days she was stranded with many others in a small diner. She and her husband slept upright, shoulder to shoulder with strangers, in the banquettes of the diner's booths. Although food and water began to run short, they had a marvelous time. The people gathered there had little in common, but they all opened up, began to tell each other the stories of their lives, and by the time the road was safe, my friend and her husband were reluctant to leave. But they went onward, home to New Mexico for the holidays, where everyone looked at them perplexedly as they told the story of their stranding with such ebullience. That time in the diner was the first time ever her partner, a Native American, had felt a sense of belonging in society at large. Such redemption amid disruption is common.

It reminded me of how many of us in the San Francisco Bay Area had loved the Loma Prieta earthquake that took place three weeks before the Berlin Wall fell in 1989. Or loved not the earthquake but the way communities had responded to it. It was alarming for most of us as well, devastating for some, and fatal for sixty people (a very low death count for a major earthquake in an area inhabited by millions). When the subject of the quake came up with a new acquaintance, she too glowed with recollection about how her San Francisco neighborhood had,

Win McNamee/Getty Images

This photograph shows Houston neighborhood residents cleaning up after Hurricane Harvey in 2017. **What aspects of Solnit's argument does this image illustrate?**

during the days the power was off, cooked up all its thawing frozen food and held barbecues on the street; how gregarious everyone had been, how people from all walks of life had mixed in candlelit bars that became community centers. Another friend recently remembered with unextinguished amazement that when he traveled the several miles from the World Series baseball game at Candlestick Park in the city's southeast to his home in the central city, someone was at every blacked-out intersection, directing traffic. Without orders or centralized organization, people had stepped up to meet the needs of the moment, suddenly in charge of their communities and streets.

When that earthquake shook the central *10* California coast on October 17, 1989, I was surprised to find that the person I was angry at no longer mattered. The anger had evaporated along with everything else abstract and remote, and I was thrown into an intensely absorbing present. I was more surprised to realize that most of the people I knew and met in the Bay Area were also enjoying immensely the disaster that shut down much of the region for several days, the Bay Bridge for months, and certain unloved elevated freeways forever — if *enjoyment* is the right word for that sense of immersion in the moment and solidarity with others caused by the rupture in everyday life, an emotion graver than happiness but deeply positive. We don't even have a language for this emotion, in which the wonderful comes wrapped in the terrible, joy in sorrow, courage in fear. We cannot welcome disaster, but we can value the responses, both practical and psychological.

For weeks after the big earthquake of 1989, friendship and love counted for a lot, long-term plans and old anxieties for very little. Life was situated in the here and now, and many inessentials had been pared away. The earthquake was unnerving, as were the aftershocks that continued for months. Most of us were at least a little on edge, but many of us were enriched rather than impoverished, overall, at least emotionally. A more somber version of that strange pleasure in disaster emerged after September 11, 2001, when many Americans seemed stirred, moved, and motivated by the newfound sense of urgency, purpose, solidarity, and danger they had encountered. They abhorred what had happened, but they clearly relished who they briefly became.

What is this feeling that crops up during so many disasters? After the Loma Prieta quake, I began to wonder about it. After 9/11, I began to see how strange a phenomenon it was and how deeply it mattered. After I met the man in Halifax who lit up with joy when he talked about the great hurricane there, I began to study it. After I began to write about the 1906 earthquake as its centennial approached, I started to see how often this peculiar feeling arose and how much it remade the world of disaster. After Hurricane Katrina tore up the Gulf Coast, I began to understand the limits and possibilities of disasters. This book is about that emotion, as important as it is surprising, and the circumstances that arouse it and those that it generates. These things count as we enter an era of increasing and intensifying disaster. And more than that, they matter as we enter an era when questions about everyday social possibilities and human nature arise again, as they often have in turbulent times.

When I ask people about the disasters they have lived through, I find on many faces that retrospective basking as they recount tales of Canadian ice storms, midwestern snow days, New York City blackouts, oppressive heat in southern India, fire in New Mexico, the great earthquake in Mexico City, earlier hurricanes in Louisiana, the economic collapse in Argentina, earthquakes in California and Mexico, and a strange pleasure overall. It was the joy on their faces that surprised me. And with those whom I read rather than spoke to, it was the joy in their words that surprised me. It should not be so, is not so, in the familiar version of what disaster brings, and yet it is there, arising from rubble, from ice, from fire, from storms and floods. The joy matters as a measure of otherwise neglected

New York Daily News Archive/Getty Images

This photograph of the New York City skyline was taken in 2003, on the morning after a massive power failure caused the largest outage in U.S. history. Fifty million people across seven states and parts of Canada were left without electricity, including all of New York City. **What might Solnit say about the photographer's choice to document the city from a distance?**

desires, desires for public life and civil society, for inclusion, purpose, and power.

Disasters are, most basically, terrible, tragic, grievous, and no matter what positive side effects and possibilities they produce, they are not to be desired. But by the same measure, those side effects should not be ignored because they arise amid devastation. The desires and possibilities awakened are so powerful they shine even from wreckage, carnage, and ashes. What happens here is relevant elsewhere. And the point is not to welcome disasters. They do not create these gifts, but they are one avenue through which the gifts arrive. Disasters provide an extraordinary window into social desire and possibility, and what manifests there matters elsewhere, in ordinary times and in other extraordinary times.

Most social change is chosen — you want to belong to a co-op, you believe in social safety nets or community-supported agriculture. But disaster doesn't sort us out by preferences; it drags us into emergencies that require we act, and act altruistically, bravely, and with initiative in order to survive or save the neighbors, no matter how we vote or what we do for a living. The positive emotions that arise in those unpromising circumstances demonstrate that social ties and meaningful work are deeply desired, readily improvised, and intensely rewarding. The very structure of our economy and society prevents

these goals from being achieved. The structure is also ideological, a philosophy that best serves the wealthy and powerful but shapes all of our lives, reinforced as the conventional wisdom disseminated by the media, from news hours to disaster movies. The facets of that ideology have been called individualism, capitalism, and Social Darwinism and have appeared in the political philosophies of Thomas Hobbes and Thomas Malthus, as well as the work of most conventional contemporary economists, who presume we seek personal gain for rational reasons and refrain from looking at the ways a system skewed to that end damages much else we need for our survival and desire for our well-being. Disaster demonstrates this, since among the factors determining whether you will live or die are the health of your immediate community and the justness of your society. We need ties, but they along with purposefulness, immediacy, and agency also give us joy — the startling, sharp joy I found in accounts of disaster survivors. These accounts demonstrate that the citizens any paradise would need — the people who are brave enough, resourceful enough, and generous enough — already exist. The possibility of paradise hovers on the cusp of coming into being, so much so that it takes powerful forces to keep such a paradise at bay. If paradise now arises in hell, it's because in the suspension of the usual

15

order and the failure of most systems, we are free to live and act another way....

Since postmodernism reshaped the intellectual landscape, it has been problematic to even use the term *human nature*, with its implication of a stable and universal human essence. The study of disasters makes it clear that there are plural and contingent natures — but the prevalent human nature in disaster is resilient, resourceful, generous, empathic, and brave. The language of therapy speaks almost exclusively of the consequence of disaster as trauma, suggesting a humanity that is unbearably fragile, a self that does not act but is acted upon, the most basic recipe of the victim. Disaster movies and the media continue to portray ordinary people as hysterical or vicious in the face of calamity. We believe these sources telling us we are victims or brutes more than we trust our own experience. Most people know this other human nature from experience, though almost nothing official or mainstream confirms it. This book [*A Paradise Built in Hell*] is an account of that rising from the ruins that is the ordinary human response to disaster and of what that rising can mean in other arenas — a subject that slips between the languages we have been given to talk about who we are when everything goes wrong.

But to understand both that rising and what hinders and hides it, there are two other important subjects to consider. One is the behavior of the minority in power, who often act savagely in a disaster. The other is the beliefs and representations of the media, the people who hold up a distorting mirror to us in which it is almost impossible to recognize these paradises and our possibilities. Beliefs matter, and the overlapping beliefs of the media and the elites can become a second wave of disaster — as they did most dramatically in the aftermath of Hurricane Katrina. These three subjects are woven together in almost every disaster, and finding the one that matters most — this glimpse of paradise — means understanding the forces that obscure, oppose, and sometimes rub out that possibility.

This social desire and social possibility go against the grain of the dominant stories of recent decades. You can read recent history as a history of privatization not just of the economy but also of society, as marketing and media shove imagination more and more toward private life and private satisfaction, as citizens are redefined as consumers, as public participation falters and with it any sense of collective or individual political power, as even the language for public emotions and satisfactions withers. There is no money

SUSAN WALSH/AP Images

◄

In this photograph from 2005, President George W. Bush surveys the immediate aftermath of Hurricane Katrina from Air Force One. **How does this image relate to Solnit's point about the behavior of people in positions of power?**

in what is aptly called free association: we are instead encouraged by media and advertising to fear each other and regard public life as a danger and a nuisance, to live in secured spaces, communicate by electronic means, and acquire our information from media rather than each other. But in disaster people come together, and though some fear this gathering as a mob, many cherish it as an experience of a civil society that is close enough to paradise. In contemporary terms, *privatization* is largely an economic term, for the consignment of jurisdictions, goods, services, and powers — railways, water rights, policing, education — to the private sector and the vagaries of the marketplace. But this economic privatization is impossible without the privatization of desire and imagination that tells us we are not each other's keeper. Disasters, in returning their sufferers to public and collective life, undo some of this privatization, which is a slower, subtler disaster all its own. In a society in which participation, agency,

purposefulness, and freedom are all adequately present, a disaster would be only a disaster.

Few speak of paradise now, except as something remote enough to be impossible. The ideal societies we hear of are mostly far away or long ago or both, situated in some primordial society before the Fall or a spiritual kingdom in a remote Himalayan vastness. The implication is that we here and now are far from capable of living such ideals. But what if paradise flashed up among us from time to time — at the worst of times? What if we glimpsed it in the jaws of hell? These flashes give us, as the long ago and far away do not, a glimpse of who else we ourselves may be and what else our society could become. This is a paradise of rising to the occasion that points out by contrast how the rest of the time most of us fall down from the heights of possibility, down into diminished selves and dismal societies. Many now do not even hope for a better society, but they recognize it when they encounter it, and

▼

In what ways does Rebecca Solnit's description of community response to disaster match the trend shown in this image? Where does the image differ, and how effectively does Solnit address those differences in this excerpt from *A Paradise Built in Hell*?

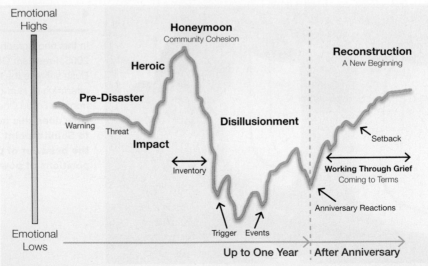

Data from the U.S. Department of Health and Human Services.

that discovery shines out even through the name-lessness of their experience. Others recognize it, grasp it, and make something of it, and long-term social and political transformations, both good and bad, arise from the wreckage. The door to this era's potential paradises is in hell.

The word *emergency* comes from *emerge*, to rise out of, the opposite of merge, which comes from *mergere*, to be within or under a liquid, immersed, submerged. An emergency is a sep-aration from the familiar, a sudden emergence into a new atmosphere, one that often demands we ourselves rise to the occasion. *Catastrophe* comes from the Greek *kata*, or down, and *streiphen*, or turning over. It means an upset of what is expected and was originally used to mean a plot twist. To emerge into the unexpected is not always terrible, though these words have evolved to imply ill fortune. The word *disaster* comes from the Latin compound of *dis-*, or away, without, and *astro*, star or planet; literally, without a star. It originally suggested misfortune due to astrologi-cally generated trouble, as in the blues musician Albert King's classic "Born Under a Bad Sign."

In some of the disasters of the twentieth century — the big northeastern blackouts in 1965

20

and 2003, the 1989 Loma Prieta earthquake in the San Francisco Bay Area, 2005's Hurricane Katrina on the Gulf Coast — the loss of electrical power meant that the light pollution blotting out the night sky vanished. In these disaster-struck cities, people suddenly found themselves under the canopy of stars still visible in small and remote places. On the warm night of August 15, 2003, the Milky Way could be seen in New York City, a heavenly realm long lost to view until the black-out that hit the Northeast late that afternoon. You can think of the current social order as something akin to this artificial light: another kind of power that fails in disaster. In its place appears a rever-sion to improvised, collaborative, cooperative, and local society. However beautiful the stars of a suddenly visible night sky, few nowadays could find their way by them. But the constellations of solidarity, altruism, and improvisation are within most of us and reappear at these times. People know what to do in a disaster. The loss of power, the disaster in the modem sense, is an affliction, but the reappearance of these old heavens is its opposite. This is the paradise entered through hell.

[2009]

EXPLORING THE TEXT

1. What is the paradox at the heart of Rebecca Solnit's basic argument in this essay?

2. Solnit spends an entire paragraph on the Biblical story of Cain and Abel. How does this scriptural reference contribute to her argument? How does it inform your reading of her assertion that "If I am not my brother's keeper, then we have been expelled from paradise, a paradise of unbroken solidarities" (para. 5)?

3. Searching for the right word to describe the emotional shift that occurs within a community after a disaster, Solnit admits that "*enjoyment*" doesn't truly speak to "an emotion graver than happiness but deeply positive" (para. 10). What might be an appropriate word — in English or perhaps another language — or phrase? Or, if words don't work, can you express what Solnit is

getting at with a visual image or a short musical excerpt?

4. Solnit takes the "power elites" and the media to task, criticizing not only their behavior in the face of disaster but the beliefs they spread: "[W]e are . . . encouraged by media and advertising to fear each other and regard public life as a danger and a nuisance, to live in secured spaces, communicate by electronic means, and acquire our information from media rather than each other" (para. 18). To what extent do you agree with this analysis?

5. Solnit basically builds her argument inductively and empirically. Trace how she develops her argument using this strategy. How effective do you think it is?

6. What two views of human nature does Solnit contrast throughout this essay? How are they

related to community? Pay special attention to paragraph 5, where she discusses that "[t]he very concept of [traditional] society rests on the idea of networks of affinity and affection, and the freestanding individual exists largely as an outcast or exile."

7. What exactly what you think Solnit means by her use of the word "paradise"? What does she mean by her assertion, "If paradise now arises in hell, it's because in the suspension of the usual order and the failure of most systems, we are free to live and act another way" (para. 15)?

8. Solnit repeats the phrase, "beliefs matter" a number of times throughout this essay. What do you think is her purpose? How effective is this repetition as a rhetorical strategy? Take note of her first use of the sentence in the initial paragraph.

9. In paragraph 18, Solnit makes the following claims about the effect individualism and capitalism have had on the current social order: "But this economic privatization is impossible without the privatization of desire and imagination that tells us we are not each other's keeper. Disasters, in returning their sufferers to public and collective life, undo some of this privatization, which is a slower, subtler disaster all its own. In a society in which participation, agency, purposefulness, and freedom are all adequately present, a disaster would be only a disaster." Using examples from

your own experience, observation of current events, and/or knowledge of history, develop a position supporting, challenging, or qualifying this argument.

10. In the last two paragraphs, Solnit examines the origin of three words — emergency, catastrophe, and disaster; what is the relationship she finds among these? Then, she describes the way stars become visible in the night sky when electrical power fails. How does she connect that discussion with the previous one about the three terms? What relationship does this comparison have to her overall argument?

11. Critics of Solnit accuse her of taking a romanticized view when she describes disasters as giving rise to temporary utopias characterized by a spirit of generosity and cooperation. To what extent do you agree with this criticism? Although you can refer to the disasters she focuses on, you might also use examples, perhaps on a lesser scale than an earthquake or terrorist attack, from your experience or observation on a local level.

12. One reviewer of *A Paradise Built in Hell* wrote that Solnit "has a rare gift: the ability to turn the act of cognition, of arriving at a coherent point of view, into compelling moral drama." How does Solnit demonstrate this ability in this excerpt from the book?

Small Change
Why the Revolution Will Not Be Tweeted

MALCOLM GLADWELL

Author of five best-selling books, Malcolm Gladwell (b. 1963) grew up in Ontario, Canada, the son of an English university professor father and a Jamaican therapist mother. He has been a staff writer with the *New Yorker* magazine since 1996, and in 2005 he was named one of *Time* magazine's 100 Most Influential People. His books include *The Tipping Point: How Little Things Can Make a Big Difference* (2000); *Blink: The Power of Thinking without Thinking* (2005); *Outliers: The Story of Success* (2008); *What the Dog Saw* (2009), a compilation of articles published in the *New Yorker*; and *David and Goliath: Underdogs, Misfits, and the Art of Battling Giants* (2013). His writing often explores the implications of research in the social sciences and psychology. The following article, which appeared in the *New Yorker* in 2010, compares the intricate network of activists who brought about the civil rights movement with the social media networks that have sprung up on the Internet.

At four-thirty in the afternoon on Monday, February 1, 1960, four college students sat down at the lunch counter at the Woolworth's in downtown Greensboro, North Carolina. They were freshmen at North Carolina A. & T., a black college a mile or so away.

"I'd like a cup of coffee, please," one of the four, Ezell Blair, said to the waitress.

"We don't serve Negroes here," she replied.

The Woolworth's lunch counter was a long L-shaped bar that could seat sixty-six people, with a standup snack bar at one end. The seats were for whites. The snack bar was for blacks. Another employee, a black woman who worked at the steam table, approached the students and tried to warn them away. "You're acting stupid, ignorant!" she said. They didn't move. Around five-thirty, the front doors to the store were locked. The four still didn't move. Finally, they left by a side door. Outside, a small crowd had gathered, including a photographer from the Greensboro *Record*. "I'll be back tomorrow with A. & T. College," one of the students said.

By next morning, the protest had grown to twenty-seven men and four women, most from the same dormitory as the original four. The men were dressed in suits and ties. The students had brought their schoolwork, and studied as they sat at the counter. On Wednesday, students from Greensboro's "Negro" secondary school, Dudley High, joined in, and the number of protesters swelled to eighty. By Thursday, the protesters numbered three hundred, including three white women, from the Greensboro campus of the University of North Carolina. By Saturday, the sit-in had reached six hundred. People spilled out onto the street. White teenagers waved Confederate flags. Someone threw a firecracker. At noon, the A. & T. football team arrived. "Here comes the wrecking crew," one of the white students shouted.

By the following Monday, sit-ins had spread to Winston-Salem, twenty-five miles away, and Durham, fifty miles away. The day after that, students at Fayetteville State Teachers College and at Johnson C. Smith College, in Charlotte, joined in, followed on Wednesday by students at St. Augustine's College and Shaw University, in Raleigh. On Thursday and Friday, the protest crossed state lines, surfacing in Hampton and Portsmouth, Virginia, in Rock Hill, South Carolina, and in Chattanooga, Tennessee. By the end of the month, there were sit-ins throughout the South, as far west as Texas. "I asked every student I met what the first day of the sitdowns had been like on his campus," the political theorist Michael Walzer wrote in *Dissent*. "The answer was always the same: 'It was like a fever. Everyone wanted to go.'" Some seventy thousand students eventually took part. Thousands were arrested and untold thousands more radicalized. These events in the early sixties became a civil-rights war that engulfed the South for the rest of the decade — and it happened without e-mail, texting, Facebook, or Twitter.

◆ ◆ ◆

5 The world, we are told, is in the midst of a revolution. The new tools of social media have reinvented social activism. With Facebook and Twitter and the like, the traditional relationship between political authority and popular will has been upended, making it easier for the powerless to collaborate, coördinate, and give voice to their concerns. When ten thousand protesters took to the streets in Moldova in the spring of 2009 to protest against their country's Communist government, the action was dubbed the Twitter Revolution, because of the means by which the demonstrators had been brought together. A few months after that, when student protests rocked Tehran, the State Department took the unusual step of asking Twitter to suspend scheduled maintenance of its Web site, because the Administration didn't want such a critical organizing tool out of service at the height of the demonstrations. "Without Twitter the people of Iran would not have felt empowered

and confident to stand up for freedom and democracy," Mark Pfeifle, a former national-security adviser, later wrote, calling for Twitter to be nominated for the Nobel Peace Prize. Where activists were once defined by their causes, they are now defined by their tools. Facebook warriors go online to push for change. "You are the best hope for us all," James K. Glassman, a former senior State Department official, told a crowd of cyber activists at a recent conference sponsored by Facebook, A. T. & T., Howcast, MTV, and Google. Sites like Facebook, Glassman said, "give the U.S. a significant competitive advantage over terrorists. Some time ago, I said that Al Qaeda was 'eating our lunch on the Internet.' That is no longer the case. Al Qaeda is stuck in Web 1.0. The Internet is now about interactivity and conversation."

These are strong, and puzzling, claims. Why does it matter who is eating whose lunch on the Internet? Are people who log on to their Facebook page really the best hope for us all? As for Moldova's so-called Twitter Revolution, Evgeny Morozov, a scholar at Stanford who has been the most persistent of digital evangelism's critics, points out that Twitter has scant internal significance in Moldova, a country where very few Twitter accounts exist. Nor does it seem to have been a revolution, not least because the protests — as Anne Applebaum suggested in the *Washington Post* — may well have been a bit of stagecraft cooked up by the government. (In a country paranoid about Romanian revanchism, the protesters flew a Romanian flag over the Parliament building.) In the Iranian case, meanwhile, the people tweeting about the demonstrations were almost all in the West. "It is time to get Twitter's role in the events in Iran right," Golnaz Esfandiari wrote, this past summer, in *Foreign Policy*. "Simply put: There was no Twitter Revolution inside Iran." The cadre of prominent bloggers, like Andrew Sullivan, who championed the role of social media in Iran, Esfandiari continued, misunderstood the situation. "Western

journalists who couldn't reach — or didn't bother reaching? — people on the ground in Iran simply scrolled through the English-language tweets post with tag #iranelection," she wrote. "Through it all, no one seemed to wonder why people trying to coordinate protests in Iran would be writing in any language other than Farsi."

Some of this grandiosity is to be expected. Innovators tend to be solipsists. They often want to cram every stray fact and experience into their new model. As the historian Robert Darnton has written, "The marvels of communication technology in the present have produced a false consciousness about the past — even a sense that communication has no history, or had nothing of importance to consider before the days of television and the Internet." But there is something else at work here, in the outsized enthusiasm for social media. Fifty years after one of the most extraordinary episodes of social upheaval in American history, we seem to have forgotten what activism is.

◆ ◆ ◆

Greensboro in the early nineteen-sixties was the 10 kind of place where racial insubordination was routinely met with violence. The four students who first sat down at the lunch counter were terrified. "I suppose if anyone had come up behind me and yelled 'Boo,' I think I would have fallen off my seat," one of them said later. On the first day, the store manager notified the police chief, who immediately sent two officers to the store. On the third day, a gang of white toughs showed up at the lunch counter and stood ostentatiously behind the protesters, ominously muttering epithets such as "burr-head nigger." A local Ku Klux Klan leader made an appearance. On Saturday, as tensions grew, someone called in a bomb threat, and the entire store had to be evacuated.

The dangers were even clearer in the Mississippi Freedom Summer Project of 1964, another of the sentinel campaigns of the civil-rights movement. The Student Nonviolent

Coordinating Committee recruited hundreds of Northern, largely white unpaid volunteers to run Freedom Schools, register black voters, and raise civil-rights awareness in the Deep South. "No one should go *anywhere* alone, but certainly not in an automobile and certainly not at night," they were instructed. Within days of arriving in Mississippi, three volunteers — Michael Schwerner, James Chaney, and Andrew Goodman — were kidnapped and killed, and, during the rest of the summer, thirty-seven black churches were set on fire and dozens of safe houses were bombed; volunteers were beaten, shot at, arrested, and trailed by pickup trucks full of armed men. A quarter of those in the program dropped out. Activism that challenges the status quo — that attacks deeply rooted problems — is not for the faint of heart.

What makes people capable of this kind of activism? The Stanford sociologist Doug McAdam compared the Freedom Summer dropouts with the participants who stayed, and discovered that the key difference wasn't, as might be expected, ideological fervor. "*All* of the applicants — participants and withdrawals alike — emerge as highly committed, articulate supporters of the goals and values of the summer program," he concluded. What mattered more was an applicant's degree of personal connection to the civil-rights movement. All the volunteers were required to provide a list of personal contacts — the people they wanted kept apprised of their activities — and participants were far more likely than dropouts to have close friends who were also going to Mississippi. High-risk activism, McAdam concluded, is a "strong-tie" phenomenon.

This pattern shows up again and again. One study of the Red Brigades, the Italian terrorist group of the nineteen-seventies, found that seventy per cent of recruits had at least one good friend already in the organization. The same is true of the men who joined the mujahideen in Afghanistan. Even revolutionary actions that look spontaneous, like the demonstrations in East Germany that led to the fall of the Berlin Wall, are, at core, strong-tie phenomena. The opposition movement in East Germany consisted of several hundred groups, each with roughly a dozen members. Each group was in limited contact with the others: at the time, only thirteen per cent of East Germans even had a phone. All they knew was that on Monday nights, outside St. Nicholas Church in downtown Leipzig, people gathered to voice their anger at the state. And the primary determinant of who showed up was "critical friends" — the more friends you had who

Nashville Public Library

◀

This photograph, taken in 1960, shows the violent response to sit-in protests at segregated lunch counters in Nashville, Tennessee. **In what ways does this image illustrate Gladwell's point about what makes activism successful?**

were critical of the regime, the more likely you were to join the protest.

So one crucial fact about the four freshmen at the Greensboro lunch counter — David Richmond, Franklin McCain, Ezell Blair, and Joseph McNeil — was their relationship with one another. McNeil was a roommate of Blair's in A. & T.'s Scott Hall dormitory. Richmond roomed with McCain one floor up, and Blair, Richmond, and McCain had all gone to Dudley High School. The four would smuggle beer into the dorm and talk late into the night in Blair and McNeil's room. They would all have remembered the murder of Emmett Till in 1955, the Montgomery bus boycott that same year, and the showdown in Little Rock in 1957. It was McNeil who brought up the idea of a sit-in at Woolworth's. They'd discussed it for nearly a month. Then McNeil came into the dorm room and asked the others if they were ready. There was a pause, and McCain said, in a way that works only with people who talk late into the night with one another, "Are you guys chicken or not?" Ezell Blair worked up the courage the next day to ask for a cup of coffee because he was flanked by his roommate and two good friends from high school.

◆ ◆ ◆

The kind of activism associated with social media *15* isn't like this at all. The platforms of social media are built around weak ties. Twitter is a way of following (or being followed by) people you may never have met. Facebook is a tool for efficiently managing your acquaintances, for keeping up with the people you would not otherwise be able to stay in touch with. That's why you can have a thousand "friends" on Facebook, as you never could in real life.

This is in many ways a wonderful thing. There is strength in weak ties, as the sociologist Mark Granovetter has observed. Our acquaintances — not our friends — are our greatest source of new ideas and information. The Internet lets us exploit the power of these kinds of distant connections with marvelous efficiency. It's terrific at the diffusion of innovation, interdisciplinary collaboration, seamlessly matching up buyers and sellers, and the logistical functions of the dating world. But weak ties seldom lead to high-risk activism.

In a new book called *The Dragonfly Effect: Quick, Effective, and Powerful Ways to Use Social Media to Drive Social Change,* the business consultant Andy Smith and the Stanford Business School professor Jennifer Aaker tell the story of Sameer Bhatia, a young Silicon Valley entrepreneur who came down with acute myelogenous leukemia. It's a perfect illustration of social media's strengths. Bhatia needed a bone-marrow transplant, but he could not find a match among his relatives and friends. The odds were best with a donor of his ethnicity, and there were few South Asians in the national bone-marrow database. So Bhatia's business partner sent out an e-mail explaining Bhatia's plight to more than four hundred of their acquaintances, who forwarded the e-mail to their personal contacts; Facebook pages and YouTube videos were devoted to the Help Sameer campaign. Eventually, nearly twenty-five thousand new people were registered in the bone-marrow database, and Bhatia found a match.

But how did the campaign get so many people to sign up? By not asking too much of them. That's the only way you can get someone you don't really know to do something on your behalf. You can get thousands of people to sign up for a donor registry, because doing so is pretty easy. You have to send in a cheek swab and — in the highly unlikely event that your bone marrow is a good match for someone in need — spend a few hours at the hospital. Donating bone marrow isn't a trivial matter. But it doesn't involve financial or personal risk; it doesn't mean spending a summer being chased by armed men in pickup trucks. It doesn't require that you confront socially entrenched norms and practices. In fact, it's the kind of commitment that will bring only social acknowledgment and praise.

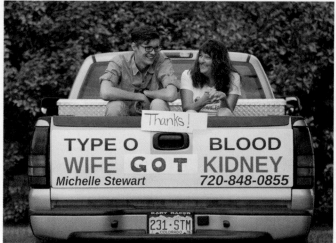

TYPE O BLOOD
WIFE G O T KIDNEY
Michelle Stewart   720-848-0855

Thanks!

231·STM
COLORADO

Kathryn Scott Osler/Getty Images

In 2015, a man from Colorado named Bob Stewart put an advertisement on the back of his truck describing his wife Michelle's need for a new kidney. After the story went viral on social media, a man named Mason Holland responded by donating one of his kidneys. Mason and Michelle are pictured here, sitting in the bed of Bob's truck, after the kidney donation was successful. **Based on your reading of "Small Change," how would Gladwell respond to this type of community activism?**

The evangelists of social media don't understand this distinction; they seem to believe that a Facebook friend is the same as a real friend and that signing up for a donor registry in Silicon Valley today is activism in the same sense as sitting at a segregated lunch counter in Greensboro in 1960. "Social networks are particularly effective at increasing motivation," Aaker and Smith write. But that's not true. Social networks are effective at increasing *participation* — by lessening the level of motivation that participation requires. The Facebook page of the Save Darfur Coalition has 1,282,339 members, who have donated an average of nine cents apiece. The next biggest Darfur charity on Facebook has 22,073 members, who have donated an average of thirty-five cents. Help Save Darfur has 2,797 members, who have given, on average, fifteen cents. A spokesperson for the Save Darfur Coalition told *Newsweek*, "We wouldn't necessarily gauge someone's value to the advocacy movement based on what they've given. This is a powerful mechanism to engage this critical population. They inform their community, attend events, volunteer. It's not something you can measure by looking at a ledger." In other words, Facebook activism succeeds not by motivating people to make a real sacrifice but by motivating them to do the things that people do when they are not motivated enough to make a real sacrifice. We are a long way from the lunch counters of Greensboro.

◆ ◆ ◆

The students who joined the sit-ins across the South during the winter of 1960 described the movement as a "fever." But the civil-rights movement was more like a military campaign than like a contagion. In the late nineteen-fifties, there had been sixteen sit-ins in various cities throughout the South, fifteen of which were formally organized by civil-rights organizations like the N.A.A.C.P. and CORE. Possible locations for activism were scouted. Plans were drawn up. Movement activists held training sessions and retreats for would-be protesters. The Greensboro Four were a product of this groundwork: all were members of the N.A.A.C.P. Youth Council. They had close ties with the head of the local N.A.A.C.P. chapter. They had been briefed on the earlier wave of sit-ins in Durham, and had been part of a series of movement meetings in activist churches. When the sit-in movement spread from Greensboro throughout the South, it did not spread indiscriminately. It spread to those cities which had preexisting "movement centers" — a core of dedicated

20

The January 2017 Women's Marches, which began as a small Facebook group and quickly snowballed to a global movement, were held all on all seven continents. Shown here is a photograph from the Women's March in Antarctica.

What does this photo — and the marches in general — suggest about the power of social media to effect social change?

Courtesy of Linda Zunas

and trained activists ready to turn the "fever" into action.

The civil-rights movement was high-risk activism. It was also, crucially, strategic activism: a challenge to the establishment mounted with precision and discipline. The N.A.A.C.P. was a centralized organization, run from New York according to highly formalized operating procedures. At the Southern Christian Leadership Conference, Martin Luther King, Jr., was the unquestioned authority. At the center of the movement was the black church, which had, as Aldon D. Morris points out in his superb 1984 study, *The Origins of the Civil Rights Movement*, a carefully demarcated division of labor, with various standing committees and disciplined groups. "Each group was task-oriented and coordinated its activities through authority structures," Morris writes. "Individuals were held accountable for their assigned duties, and important conflicts

were resolved by the minister, who usually exercised ultimate authority over the congregation."

This is the second crucial distinction between traditional activism and its online variant: social media are not about this kind of hierarchical organization. Facebook and the like are tools for building *networks*, which are the opposite, in structure and character, of hierarchies. Unlike hierarchies, with their rules and procedures, networks aren't controlled by a single central authority. Decisions are made through consensus, and the ties that bind people to the group are loose.

This structure makes networks enormously resilient and adaptable in low-risk situations. Wikipedia is a perfect example. It doesn't have an editor, sitting in New York, who directs and corrects each entry. The effort of putting together each entry is self-organized. If every entry in Wikipedia were to be erased tomorrow, the content would swiftly be restored, because that's what happens when a network of thousands spontaneously devote their time to a task.

There are many things, though, that networks don't do well. Car companies sensibly use a network to organize their hundreds of suppliers, but not to design their cars. No one believes that the articulation of a coherent design philosophy is best handled by a sprawling, leaderless organizational system. Because networks don't have a centralized leadership structure and clear lines of authority, they have real difficulty reaching consensus and setting goals. They can't think strategically; they are chronically prone to conflict and error. How do you make difficult choices about tactics or strategy or philosophical direction when everyone has an equal say?

The Palestine Liberation Organization originated 25 as a network, and the international-relations scholars Mette Eilstrup-Sangiovanni and Calvert Jones argue in a recent essay in *International Security* that this is why it ran into such trouble as it grew: "Structural features typical of networks — the absence of central authority, the unchecked autonomy of rival groups, and the inability to arbitrate quarrels through formal mechanisms — made the P.L.O. excessively vulnerable to outside manipulation and internal strife."

In Germany in the nineteen-seventies, they go on, "the far more unified and successful left-wing terrorists tended to organize hierarchically, with professional management and clear divisions of labor. They were concentrated geographically in universities, where they could establish central leadership, trust, and camaraderie through regular, face-to-face meetings." They seldom betrayed their comrades in arms during police interrogations. Their counterparts on the right were organized as decentralized networks, and had no such discipline. These groups were regularly infiltrated, and members, once arrested, easily gave up their comrades. Similarly, Al Qaeda was most dangerous when it was a unified hierarchy. Now that it has dissipated into a network, it has proved far less effective.

The drawbacks of networks scarcely matter if the network isn't interested in systemic change — if it just wants to frighten or humiliate or make a splash — or if it doesn't need to think strategically. But if you're taking on a powerful and organized establishment you have to be a hierarchy. The Montgomery bus boycott required the participation of tens of thousands of people who depended on public transit to get to and from work each day. It lasted a *year*. In order to persuade those people to stay true to the cause, the boycott's organizers tasked each local black church with maintaining morale, and put together a free alternative private carpool service, with forty-eight dispatchers and forty-two pickup stations. Even the White Citizens Council, King later said, conceded that the carpool system moved with "military precision." By the time King came to Birmingham, for the climactic showdown with Police Commissioner Eugene (Bull) Connor, he had a budget of a million dollars, and a hundred full-time staff members on the ground, divided into operational units. The operation itself was divided into steadily escalating phases, mapped out in advance. Support was maintained through consecutive mass meetings rotating from church to church around the city.

Boycotts and sit-ins and nonviolent confrontations — which were the weapons of choice for the civil-rights movement — are high-risk strategies. They leave little room for conflict and error. The moment even one protester deviates from the script and responds to provocation, the moral legitimacy of the entire protest is compromised. Enthusiasts for social media would no doubt have us believe that King's task in Birmingham would have been made infinitely easier had he been able to communicate with his followers through Facebook, and contented himself with tweets from a Birmingham jail. But networks are messy: think of the ceaseless pattern of correction and revision, amendment and debate, that characterizes Wikipedia. If Martin Luther King, Jr., had tried to do a wiki-boycott in Montgomery, he would have been steamrollered by the white power structure. And of what use would a digital communication tool be in a town where ninety-eight per cent of the black community could be reached every Sunday morning at church? The things that King needed in Birmingham — discipline and strategy — were things that online social media cannot provide.

◆ ◆ ◆

The bible of the social-media movement is Clay Shirky's *Here Comes Everybody*. Shirky, who teaches at New York University, sets out to demonstrate the organizing power of the Internet, and he begins with the story of Evan, who worked on Wall Street, and his friend Ivanna, after she left her smart phone, an expensive Sidekick, on the back seat of a New York City taxicab. The telephone company transferred the data on Ivanna's lost phone to a new phone, whereupon she and Evan discovered that the Sidekick was now in the hands of a teen-ager from Queens, who was using it to take photographs of herself and her friends.

When Evan e-mailed the teen-ager, Sasha, *30* asking for the phone back, she replied that his "white ass" didn't deserve to have it back. Miffed, he set up a Web page with her picture and a description of what had happened. He forwarded the link to his friends, and they forwarded it to their friends. Someone found the MySpace page of Sasha's boyfriend, and a link to it found its way onto the site. Someone found her address online and took a video of her home while driving by; Evan posted the video on the site. The story was picked up by the news filter Digg. Evan was now up to ten e-mails a minute. He created a bulletin board for his readers to share their stories, but it crashed under the weight of responses. Evan and Ivanna went to the police, but the police filed the report under "lost," rather than "stolen," which essentially closed the case. "By this point millions

of readers were watching," Shirky writes, "and dozens of mainstream news outlets had covered the story." Bowing to the pressure, the N.Y.P.D. reclassified the item as "stolen." Sasha was arrested, and Evan got his friend's Sidekick back.

Shirky's argument is that this is the kind of thing that could never have happened in the pre-Internet age — and he's right. Evan could never have tracked down Sasha. The story of the Sidekick would never have been publicized. An army of people could never have been assembled to wage this fight. The police wouldn't have bowed to the pressure of a lone person who had misplaced something as trivial as a cell phone. The story, to Shirky, illustrates "the ease and speed with which a group can be mobilized for the right kind of cause" in the Internet age.

Shirky considers this model of activism an upgrade. But it is simply a form of organizing which favors the weak-tie connections that give us access to information over the strong-tie connections that help us persevere in the face of danger. It shifts our energies from organizations that promote strategic and disciplined activity and toward those which promote resilience and adaptability. It makes it easier for activists to express themselves, and harder for that expression to have any impact. The instruments of social media are well suited to making the existing social order more efficient. They are not a natural enemy of the status quo. If you are of the opinion that all the world needs is a little buffing around the edges, this should not trouble you. But if you think that there are still lunch counters out there that need integrating, it ought to give you pause.

Shirky ends his story of the Sidekick by asking, portentously, "What happens next?" — no doubt imagining future waves of digital protesters. But he has already answered the question. What happens next is more of the same. A networked, weak-tie world is good at things like helping Wall Streeters get phones back from teen-age girls. *Viva la revolución.*

[2010]

EXPLORING THE TEXT

1. Most of Malcolm Gladwell's readers are familiar with the lunch counter event at Woolworth's in Greensboro, North Carolina, that catalyzed the civil rights movement. Why, then, does he begin by retelling it and providing such detail in the opening section? How does this serve as a foundation for the argument he develops? Consider both what he tells and *how* he tells it.

2. What does Gladwell mean when he writes, "Where activists were once defined by their causes, they are now defined by their tools" (para. 7)? Do you agree or disagree with this idea? Explain why.

3. What is the key point Gladwell makes in the paragraph beginning, "Some of this grandiosity is to be expected" (para. 9)? How does he connect his statement "Innovators tend to be solipsists" with the assertion that ends the paragraph, that "we seem to have forgotten what activism is"?

4. How does Gladwell define "high-risk activism" (paras. 11–12)? Why does he believe that activism based on today's social media cannot qualify as "high risk"? Consider the contrast between "weak ties" and "strong ties" as part of your definition.

5. What is the purpose of the example of Sameer Bhatia, who found a bone marrow donor through social networking (para. 17)? Do you find it persuasive, or is it too exceptional?

6. What distinction does Gladwell make between increasing motivation and increasing participation (para. 19)? Why is this distinction important to his argument?

7. Throughout this essay, Gladwell relies heavily on expert testimony. He cites scholars and researchers as well as business analysts and State Department officials and security advisors. Choose two examples, and discuss how Gladwell uses one to support his argument and the other to examine a counterargument.

8. In order to make his argument against the belief that the "new tools of social media have reinvented social activism" (para. 7), Gladwell must delineate precisely the central qualities of social activism. What are they? Refer to specific passages in the text to support your analysis.

9. Gladwell does not entirely discount the power of social media. What benefits or positive impacts does he grant to social media? Do you find his term "digital evangelism" (para. 8) a critical description, a particularly apt one, or simply a colorful one? Why?

10. Gladwell uses many examples from fairly recent history, such as the fall of the Berlin Wall and protests in Moldova and Tehran, yet he repeatedly returns to the civil rights movement of the 1960s. Why? Does doing so strengthen his argument by adding coherence and depth, or weaken it by relying too much on a single example? Explain your viewpoint.

11. Compare the opening example at the lunch counter with that of the closing one about Evan and Ivanna in terms of such rhetorical strategies as narrative pacing, sensory detail, setting, dialogue, and point of view. Are they more similar or different? In what ways?

12. At key junctures in the essay, Gladwell makes sharp personal comments. In fact, his ending "*Viva la revolución*" (para. 33) could be read as downright sarcastic. What others do you notice? Do these editorial comments add vitality and voice to the essay, or do they undercut the argument with a mocking tone? Explain your response.

13. Choose one of the following assertions that Gladwell makes, and challenge it by referring to an example of social activism in the United States or abroad during the past five years:

    a. "Our acquaintances — not our friends — are our greatest source of new ideas and information" (para. 16).

    b. "[Networks] can't think strategically; they are chronically prone to conflict and error" (para. 24).

    c. "The things that King needed in Birmingham — discipline and strategy — were things that online social media cannot provide" (para. 28).

14. How we use social media has significantly changed since 2010, when Gladwell wrote this essay. To what extent do some of those changes challenge his argument in "Small Change"? Cite specific examples.

Raised to Leave
Some Thoughts on "Culture"

LEE SMITH

Lee Smith (b. 1944) is an award-winning fiction-writer known for her artful portrayal of the Southeastern United States. Smith grew up in the Appalachian Mountain region of southwestern Virginia and, from a young age, wrote and sold stories about her neighbors in the nearby coal boomtown of Grundy. While a senior at Hollins College in Roanoke, Virginia, in 1966, Smith submitted a draft of a coming-of-age novel to a Book-of-the-Month Club contest and was awarded a fellowship. Two years later, that novel, *The Last Day the Dog Bushes Bloomed* (1968), became Smith's first published work of fiction. She has since published twelve more novels, including the best-seller *The Last Girls* (2002), and four short story collections. Smith's numerous awards include two O. Henry Awards, the American Academy of Arts and Letters Award for Fiction, and the very first Sidney Lanier Prize for Southern Literature, awarded in 2013. The following excerpt is from her memoir, *Dimestore: A Writer's Life* (2016).

I was born in a rugged ring of mountains in southwest Virginia — mountains so high, so straight up and down, that the sun didn't even hit our yard until about eleven o'clock. My uncle Bob Venable — they lived across the road — used to predict the weather by sticking his head out the window and hollering back inside, "Sun on the mountaintop, girls!" to my cousins. The only flat land in the county lay in a narrow band along the river where we lived, about a mile from town. Though we all ate out of the garden, real farming was impossible in that hard rock ground. The only thing it produced was coal. We never thought of our jagged mountains as scenic, either, though we all played up in them every day after school. We never saw a tourist, and nobody we knew hiked for fun.

I will never forget the first time I ever saw a jogger: my mother and I were sitting on the front porch stringing beans and watching the cars go up and down Route 460 in front of our house, when suddenly one of these VISTAs we'd been hearing about, a long-haired boy with great legs, came running right up the road. We both stood up, and watched him run out of sight "Well, for heaven's sakes," my mother said. "Where do you reckon he's going, running like that?"

He was going back to where he came from, eventually; but most of us weren't going any-place. We were closed in entirely, cut off from the outside world by our ring of mountains. Many of the children I went to school with had never been out of Buchanan County. People still described my own mother as "not from around here." though she had spent most of her life teaching their children and "trying to civilize you and your daddy!" as she always joked, but it was a challenge.

So I was being raised to leave.

I was not to use double negatives; I was not to say "me and Martha." I was not to trade my pimento cheese sandwiches at school for the lunch I really wanted: cornbread and buttermilk in a mason jar, brought by the kids from the hollers. Me and Martha were not to play in the black river behind our house, dirty with coal that would stain my shorts. I was to take piano lessons from the terrifying Mrs. Ruth Boyd even though I had no aptitude for it. I was to play "Clair de Lune" at my piano recital, wearing an itchy pink net evening dress. 5

How does this cartoon, which was published in the *New Yorker*, comment on the way rural American culture is perceived by others? How would you characterize its tone? Is it tongue-in-cheek, is it satirical, or is it something else?

"The new house is almost ready!"

I was not to like the mountain music that surrounded us on every side, from the men playing banjo and mandolin on the sidewalk outside my daddy's dimestore on Saturdays, to Martha's father playing his guitar down on the riverbank after dinner, to Kitty Wells singing "It Wasn't God Who Made Honky Tonk Angels" on our brand-new radio station, WNRG. But here, my mother ran into serious trouble. For I loved this music. I had been born again to "Angel Band," sung high and sweet at a tent revival that I had to sneak out to go to; and I had a dobro-playing boyfriend, with Nashville aspirations.

Even my mother enjoyed going to the drive-in theater on Saturday evenings in the summer to hear two brothers from over in Dickenson County, Ralph and Carter Stanley, play and sing their bluegrass music on top of the concrete-block concessions stand. "I never will marry, I'll take me no wife; I intend to live single, all of my life," Ralph wailed mournfully, followed by their fast instrumental version of "Shout, Little Lulie." Old people were clogging on the patch of concrete in front of the window where

you bought your Cokes and popcorn; little kids were swinging on the iron-pipe swing set. Whole families ate fried chicken and deviled eggs they'd brought from home, sitting on quilts on the grass. My boyfriend reached over and squeezed my sweaty hand. The Stanley Brothers' nasal voices rose higher than the gathering mist, higher than the lightning bugs that rose from the trees along the river as night came on. When it got full dark, the Stanley Brothers climbed down off the concession stand and we all got into our cars and the movie came on.

I loved that music, just as I loved my grandmother's corn pudding and those scary old stories my Uncle Vern told. But this hillbilly music didn't have anything to do with "culture" as I was constantly being reminded. No, "culture" was someplace else, and when the time came, I would be sent off to get some. Culture lived in big cities like Richmond, and Washington, and Boston and New York — especially in New York, especially in places like Carnegie Hall.

Forty years later, I stood on my hundred-dollar balcony seat in Carnegie Hall and

In this still from the movie *O Brother, Where Art Thou?*, directed by Joel and Ethan Coen, a trio of escaped convicts from rural Mississippi prepare to record a song destined to become a hit. Though the movie is a creative retelling of Horner's epic *Odyssey*, it is also a farcical comedy.

What does this image suggest about Appalachian culture? How does Smith address (or avoid) this portrayal of it?

Buena Vista Pictures/Photofest

screamed as seventy-four-year-old Dr. Ralph Stanley and the rest of the traditional musicians and singers from the phenomenally successful *O Brother, Where Art Thou?* soundtrack played to a sold-out house. Elvis Costello was the emcee; Joel and Ethan Coen, the filmmakers who made the *O Brother* movie, were in the audience, along with T Bone Burnett, its musical director. The Coen Brothers had written this note about the music in the program, aimed at their New York audience: "These songs were for the most part created by people whose lives were hard and horizons narrow. Their lives were not like ours. All that urges their music on us is its humanity. . . . And yet, this soundtrack went platinum without receiving any airplay: pop stations considered it too country, and country stations considered it too . . . country."

On stage at Carnegie Hall, the Fairfield Four sang their stark treatment of "Po' Lazarus."

Dan Tyminski tore it up on "I Am a Man of Constant Sorrow." The Cox family, fresh from Louisiana, brought down the house with "Will There Be Any Stars in My Crown." Reigning bluegrass princess Alison Krauss fiddled up a storm, then sang "When I Co Down to the River to Pray" in tight harmony with Gillian Welch and Emmylou Harris. They sang so sweet, they could have been angels. The little Peasall sisters — Sarah, age thirteen, Hannah, age ten, and Leah, age eight, wore patent-leather shoes and bows in their hair to sing "In the Highways and the Hedges, I'll Be Somewhere Listening for My Name." Gillian's husband, David Rawlings, teamed up with her on "I Want To Sing That Rock and Roll."

But the night belonged to Ralph Stanley, who came our last, all by himself, and took center stage to give his famous a capella rendition of the terrifying "O Death," with all lights black except

10

for a single spotlight trained directly on him. "O Death, O Death, won't you spare me over for another year?" His high, haunting voice filled the huge dark hall. The song lasted for five minutes, followed by almost a full moment of total silence. Then the stage lights went up, the house lights came on, the other performers rushed out on stage, and the standing ovation went on and on.

Although he loves to poke fun at his own success — recently referring to the movie as "O Brother, Where Art Thou *At*" — Dr. Ralph Stanley has come a long way from the top of the concession stand at the Grundy Drive-In Theater. A six-time Grammy nominee and a Grand Ole Opry member, Stanley was the first recipient of the National Endowment for the Humanities' Traditional American Music Award, and he performed at the inaugurations of both Jimmy Carter and Bill Clinton. He has been awarded the Library of Congress Living Legend Medal.

Dr. Ralph's Carnegie Hall appearance symbolized something that has happened to Appalachian culture as a whole. Now, everybody in the region realizes that we don't have to go anyplace else to "get culture." Every little town has its own little festival, celebrating itself with local music, food, and crafts, whether it's called a "blackberry festival," or a "ramp festival," or a "wooly worm contest," or "gingerbread day," or a "hollering contest," or a "fiddling convention." Fueled by a national, politically-correct appreciation of whatever is still ethnically or geographically or culturally distinct, America as a whole is coming to appreciate and value its differences. Everybody understands that our own Appalachian culture is as rich, and as diverse in terms of history, arts, crafts, literature, folklore, and music, for instance, as any area in this country.

But in fact, we are far richer than most. Our formidable geography acted as a natural barrier for so long, keeping others out, holding us in, allowing for the development of our rich folk culture, our distinctive speech patterns, our strong sense of tradition, and out radical individualism. Appalachian people are more rooted than other Southerners. We still live in big, extended families that spoil children and revere old people. We will talk your ears off. We still excel in storytelling — and I mean everybody, not just some old guy in overalls at a folk festival. I mean the woman who cuts your hair, I mean your doctor, I mean your mother. Our great music is country music — which was always working-class, from its beginnings in the old-time string bands and ballads right up through honky-tonk and the high lonesome sound of bluegrass to present-day glitzy Nashville, and then all the way back around to the current revival of more old-time, traditional music.

Look at Dolly Parton, now a national icon: 15 "I had to get rich to sing this poor," she has said, referring to the success of her albums *The Grass Is Blue*, her take on traditional bluegrass, and *Little Sparrow*, which is old-time, or what Dolly calls her "blue mountain music." Look at Lucinda Williams and Steve Earle and Patty Loveless. And the big national stars just keep on coming, like Kenny Chesney, Florida Georgia Line, Eric Church, and Miranda Lambert . . . country music is mainstream American music now.

But what about our literature? No one could deny that there is a veritable explosion of Appalachian writing today. A lot of it is hitting the best-seller lists, too — this means it is being read, and widely read, outside the region. I'm talking about Charles Frazier's Civil War novel *Cold Mountain* and Ron Rash's amazing *Serena*, for instance, both set in western North Carolina; about Barbara Kingsolver's *Prodigal Summer*, which takes place near Emory, Virginia; about Sharyn McCrumb's Ballad Novels and Robert Morgan's *Gap Creek*, which even got "Oprah-fied," as did Gwen Hyman Rubio's eastern Kentucky novel *Icy Sparks*. I'm especially talking about Adriana Trigiani's lively comic novels from

seeing connections

I Got a Gal on Sourwood Mountain, Thomas Hart Benton's 1938 lithograph, depicts a fiddler and people dancing and takes its name from a traditional Appalachian folk song. **Look carefully at the work's composition, lines, and setting. What does the work convey about the importance of music? What does the artist's use of space and perspective suggest about the nature of Appalachian life and culture? Where do you see these themes reflected in Smith's writing?**

my own neck of the woods, *Big Stone Gap, Big Cherry Holler, Milk Glass Moon.*

Big Stone Gap has recently been filmed in Big Stone Gap, Virginia, starring Ashley Judd and directed by Adriana herself. *Cold Mountain* was a hit film even though they shot most of it in Romania, to Charles Frazier's dismay. So was *Walk the Line*, which chronicled the Carter Family and Johnny Cash. *Nashville* is a popular television series. The film *Songcatcher* traced the adventures of a Boston musicologist who comes to visit her crusading sister at a settlement school in Madison County, North Carolina, and sets about "catching" — or transcribing all the local ballads. The darker film *Winter's Bone*, based upon the novel of the same name by Daniel Woodrell and set in Arkansas, deals with the pervasive drug problem in the mountains, as does Ron Rash's *The World Made Straight.*

Newer Appalachian writers such as Silas House, Ann Pancake, and Wiley Cash deal with mountaintop removal mining and other energy and ecological problems besetting the region now. In *Flight Behavior*, Barbara Kingsolver makes it clear that such Appalachian issues are global issues, too. Widespread Appalachian literature courses, festivals, and writing workshops ought to ensure the fine new crop of young writers — and activists — continues.

Clearly, I could go on and on, and I'm not even really getting into visual arts, or poetry, or design, or drama, or documentary film. My point is that mainstream American culture has become "Appalachian-ized." No matter what you think of NASCAR, for instance — arguably our most successful Appalachian export — it's everyplace now.

I'm of two minds about all this. I was country, 20 remember, when country wasn't cool. I don't really like to see my favorite places and people be "discovered." I'd rather hear Sheila Adams sing a ballad on a mountaintop in Sodom, North Carolina, than on her latest CD. I'd rather eat at Cuz's in Pounding Mill, Virginia, than Cracker Barrel.

Even though I sometimes wish I could be back in the simpler, saner, safer world of my childhood, eating a piece of fried chicken on a quilt at the drive-in theater while Ralph Stanley plays music on top of the concession stand, I know I can't. The drive-in is long gone, and so am I. But I'll tell you something else — I was mighty proud to be there the night Dr. Ralph played at Carnegie Hall.

[2016]

EXPLORING THE TEXT

1. Lee Smith opens her memoir with a detailed description of the physical landscape and the characteristics of the community in her hometown as it existed several decades ago. What purpose does that strategy serve?

2. Smith states that she was being "raised to leave" Buchanan County, an Appalachian community (para. 4). What exactly does she mean by that? Why is she being raised to leave? What is it her mother seems to want for her that she believes cannot be found or achieved if Smith remains in Buchanan County?

3. In paragraphs 5 and 6, Smith lists several things she was instructed "not to" do. What is the effect of this repeated structure with its negative message?

4. Why does Smith place the word *culture* in quotation marks in paragraph 8? Is she mocking the idea of "culture" in Appalachia? Is she simply calling attention to the word? Is she redefining it? Something else? Explain, using specific evidence drawn from the text.

5. Smith spends several paragraphs describing the Carnegie Hall performance of musician Ralph Stanley — an event that occurred long after she had left her childhood home. Why would she shift time and place so abruptly and explain in such vivid detail? How does this scene contribute to her larger argument?

6. After she asserts that "mainstream American culture has become 'Appalachian-ized,'" Smith admits that she is "of two minds" about it (paras. 20–21). What does she mean by this? How would you characterize her tone, keeping in mind that she wrote this when she was seventy years old as part of a book reflecting on the community in which she was born and raised?

7. Although this essay is the preface to the memoir *Dimestore: A Writer's Life*, Smith makes an argument. Her argument is not aggressive or confrontational, yet she makes a case against certain assumptions and takes a position. How would you sum up her position in a single sentence? What do you see as the most effective rhetorical strategy she employs to support it, and why?

8. In paragraph 13, Smith says that America, "[f]ueled by a national, politically-correct appreciation of whatever is still ethnically or geographically or culturally distinct," is "coming to appreciate and value its differences." To what extent do you agree with that statement? Develop your response with evidence from your own experience and observation, current events, or your reading.

9. While Smith conveys the culture of Appalachia through several lenses, including its food, community traditions, and literature, she focuses mostly on music. Why do you believe music is the cultural aspect that Smith devotes the most time to in this excerpt? Choose a particular community that you are familiar with — defined by place, age, neighborhood, profession, or something else — and discuss how music defines it.

How Covenants Make Us

DAVID BROOKS

David Brooks (b. 1961) is a political commentator for the *New York Times*. He grew up in New York City and Philadelphia and graduated from the University of Chicago in 1983 with a degree in history. Starting out as a police reporter in Chicago, Brooks went on to a varied journalism career, writing and editing movie reviews, book reviews, news reports, and op-eds for the *Washington Times*, the *Wall Street Journal*, the *Weekly Standard*, *Newsweek*, the *Atlantic Monthly*, NPR, PBS, and the *New York Times*. Brooks edited *Backward and Upward: The New Conservative Writing* (1996) and authored four other books: *Bobos in Paradise: The New Upper Class and How They Got There* (2000), *On Paradise Drive: How We Live Now (And Always Have) in the Future Tense* (2004), *The Social Animal: The Hidden Sources of Love, Character, and Achievement* (2011), and *The Road to Character* (2015). He wrote the following op-ed column for the *New York Times* in 2016.

When you think about it, there are four big forces coursing through modern societies. Global migration is leading to demographic diversity. Economic globalization is creating wider opportunity but also inequality. The Internet is giving people more choices over what to buy and pay attention to. A culture of autonomy valorizes individual choice and self-determination.

All of these forces have liberated the individual, or at least well-educated individuals, but they have been bad for national cohesion and the social fabric. Income inequality challenges economic cohesion as the classes divide. Demographic diversity challenges cultural cohesion as different ethnic groups rub against one another. The emphasis on individual choice challenges community cohesion and settled social bonds.

The weakening of the social fabric has created a range of problems. Alienated young men join ISIS so they can have a sense of belonging. Isolated teenagers shoot up schools. Many people grow up in fragmented, disorganized neighborhoods. Political polarization grows because people often don't interact with those on the other side. Racial animosity stubbornly persists.

Odder still, people are often plagued by a sense of powerlessness, a loss of efficacy. The liberation of the individual was supposed to lead to mass empowerment. But it turns out that people can effectively pursue their goals only when they know who they are — when they have firm identities.

Strong identities can come only when people are embedded in a rich social fabric. They can come only when we have defined social roles — father, plumber, Little League coach. They can come only when we are seen and admired by our neighbors and loved ones in a certain way. As Ralph Waldo Emerson put it, "Other men are lenses through which we read our own minds."

You take away a rich social fabric and what you are left with is people who are uncertain about who they really are. It's hard to live daringly when your very foundation is fluid and at risk.

We're not going to roll back the four big forces coursing through modern societies, so the question is how to reweave the social fabric in the

5

   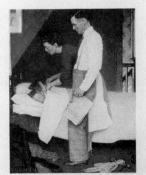

OURS...to fight for

Freedom of Speech *Freedom of Worship*

Freedom from Want *Freedom from Fear*

Pictorial Press Ltd/Alamy Stock Photo. Printed by permission of the Norman Rockwell Family Agency. Copyright ©1943 the Norman Rockwell Family Entities

Norman Rockwell's 1943 illustrations of the "Four Freedoms" — freedom of speech, freedom of worship, freedom from want, and freedom from fear — were used to promote investment in World War II.

What message do these illustrations convey? Do you think Brooks believes American leaders should appeal to such freedoms to "revive patriotism"? Explain why or why not.

seeing connections

In 2011, the Pew Research Center conducted the Global Altitudes Project, a survey of the views of citizens of 23 countries around the world. The graphs included here were created using data Pew gathered from residents of three former Soviet countries: Ukraine, Lithuania, and Russia.

What conclusions can you draw from this data? How might these graphs be used to support, challenge, or qualify Brooks's faith in social covenants?

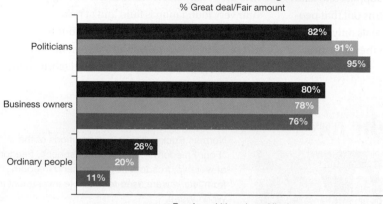

Who Has Benefitted from Changes Since 1991?
% Great deal/Fair amount

Politicians — 82%, 91%, 95%
Business owners — 80%, 78%, 76%
Ordinary people — 26%, 20%, 11%

■ Russia ■ Lithuania ■ Ukraine

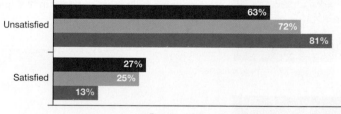

Satisfaction with Democracy

Unsatisfied — 63%, 72%, 81%
Satisfied — 27%, 25%, 13%

■ Russia ■ Lithuania ■ Ukraine

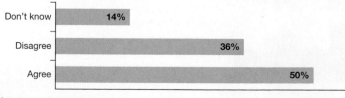

Responses to the Statement,
"It is a great misfortune that the Soviet Union no longer exists"

Don't know — 14%
Disagree — 36%
Agree — 50%

Data from Pew Research Center

face of them. In a globalizing, diversifying world, how do we preserve individual freedom while strengthening social solidarity?

In her new book "Commonwealth and Covenant," Marcia Pally of N.Y.U. and Fordham offers a clarifying concept. What we want, she suggests, is "separability amid situatedness." We want to go off and create and explore and experiment with new ways of thinking and living. But we also want to be situated — embedded in loving families and enveloping communities, thriving within a healthy cultural infrastructure that provides us with values and goals.

Creating situatedness requires a different way of thinking. When we go out and do a deal, we make a contract. When we are situated within something it is because we have made a covenant. A contract protects interests, Pally notes, but a covenant protects relationships. A covenant exists between people who understand they are part of one another. It involves a vow to serve the relationship that is sealed by love: Where you go, I will go. Where you stay, I will stay. Your people shall be my people.

People in a contract provide one another services, but people in a covenant delight in offering gifts. Out of love of country, soldiers offer the gift of their service. Out of love of their craft, teachers offer students the gift of their attention.

The social fabric is thus rewoven in a romantic frame of mind. During another period

10

of national fragmentation, Abraham Lincoln aroused a refreshed love of country. He played upon the mystic chords of memory and used the Declaration of Independence as a unifying scripture and guide.

These days the social fabric will be repaired by hundreds of millions of people making local covenants — widening their circles of attachment across income, social and racial divides. But it will probably also require leaders drawing upon American history to revive patriotism. They'll tell a story that includes the old themes. That we're a universal nation, the guarantor of stability and world order. But it will transcend the old narrative and offer an updated love of America.

In an interview with Bill Maher last month, Senator Cory Booker nicely defined patriotism by contrasting it with mere tolerance. Tolerance, he said, means, "I'm going to stomach your right to be different, but if you disappear off the face of the earth I'm no worse off." Patriotism, on the other hand, means "love of country, which necessitates love of each other, that we have to be a nation that aspires for love, which recognizes that you have worth and dignity and I need you. You are part of my whole, part of the promise of this country."

That emotion is what it means to be situated in a shared national life.

[2016]

EXPLORING THE TEXT

1. What is David Brooks's major claim — that is, what is the thesis of his argument? Is it implicit or explicit? How do the "four big forces coursing through modern societies" (para. 1) relate to that thesis?

2. Brooks explains the "four big forces" in fairly abstract terms, such as "cultural cohesion" and "demographic diversity" (para. 2). What is a concrete example from your own experience or

observation that shows at least two of these forces at work in the way Brooks defines them?

3. In paragraph 5, Brooks asserts, "Strong identities can come only when people are embedded in a rich social fabric." How effectively does he support that claim? To what extent do you believe this is true in general — or in today's society in particular?

4. Brooks draws on the work of scholar Marcia Pally to distinguish between "separability amid

situatedness" (para. 8). According to her, how does the distinction between a contract and covenant contribute to understanding this difference?

5. In the last two paragraphs, Brooks shifts his focus to the topic of patriotism. How does his argument up to this shift contribute to his final point about patriotism? How effective are these final paragraphs in closing out his argument? Explain.

6. In paragraph 13, Brooks discusses Senator Cory Booker's contrast of tolerance with patriotism.

What, according to Booker, is the difference? What purpose does this distinction serve in Brooks's overall argument? Using examples from current events, explain whether you find this distinction meaningful.

7. Essentially, Brooks argues that we've become a nation that prefers and privileges individualism over community. To what extent do you agree with that assessment? Provide specific evidence to support your position.

---

from Tribe
On Homecoming and Belonging

SEBASTIAN JUNGER

Sebastian Junger (b. 1962) is a journalist, author, and filmmaker well known for his best-selling book *The Perfect Storm: A True Story of Men Against the Sea* (1997) and multiple award-winning documentaries about the American war in Afghanistan. Junger grew up in Belmont, Massachusetts, a suburb of Boston, and earned a BA from Wesleyan University in 1984. *The Perfect Storm* earned Junger comparisons to Earnest Hemingway and cemented his reputation as an "adventure journalist." From 2007 to 2008, Junger and photographer Tim Hetherington visited eastern Afghanistan, producing embedded reports that eventually became another best-selling book, *War* (2000). The embedded reporting also led to the creation of two documentaries, *Restrepo* (2010) and *Korengal* (2014), both of which document the deployment of a U.S. Army infantry platoon in Afghanistan. The excerpt below is taken from Junger's 2016 book, *Tribe: On Homecoming and Belonging*.

There's no use arguing that modern society isn't a kind of paradise. The vast majority of us don't, personally, have to grow or kill our own food, build our own dwellings, or defend ourselves from wild animals and enemies. In one day we can travel a thousand miles by pushing our foot down on a gas pedal or around the world by booking a seat on an airplane. When we are in pain we have narcotics that dull it out of existence, and when we are depressed we have pills that change the chemistry of our brains. We understand an enormous amount about

the universe, from subatomic particles to our own bodies to galaxy clusters, and we use that knowledge to make life even better and easier for ourselves. The poorest people in modern society enjoy a level of physical comfort that was unimaginable a thousand years ago, and the wealthiest people literally live the way gods were imagined to have.

And yet.

There are many costs to modern society, starting with its toll on the global ecosystem and working one's way down to its toll on the human psyche, but the most dangerous loss may be to community. If the human race is under threat in some way that we don't yet understand, it will probably be at a community level that we either solve the problem or fail to. If the future of the planet depends on, say, rationing water, communities of neighbors will be able to enforce new rules far more effectively than even local government. It's how we evolved to exist, and it obviously works.

Two of the behaviors that set early humans apart were the systematic sharing of food and altruistic group defense. Other primates did very little of either but, increasingly, hominids did, and those behaviors helped set them on an evolutionary path that produced the modern world. The earliest and most basic definition of community — of tribe — would be the group of people that you would both help feed and help defend. A society that doesn't offer its members the chance to act selflessly in these ways isn't a society in any tribal sense of the word; it's just a political entity that, lacking enemies, will probably fall apart on its own. Soldiers experience this tribal way of thinking at war, but when they come home they realize that the tribe they were actually fighting for wasn't their country, it was their unit. It makes absolutely no sense to make sacrifices for a group that, itself, isn't willing to make sacrifices for you. That is the position American soldiers have been in for the past decade and a half.

There was a period during the run-up to the Iraq War in 2003 when a bumper sticker that read NO BLOOD FOR OIL started appearing on American cars. Implicit in the slogan was the assumption that the Iraq War was over oil, but the central irony of putting such a message on a machine *that runs on oil* seemed lost on most people. There is virtually no source of oil that does not incur enormous damage to either the local population or the environment, and driving a car means that you're unavoidably contributing to that damage. I was deeply

opposed to the Iraq War for other reasons. But the antiwar rhetoric around the topic of oil by people who continued to use it to fuel their cars betrayed a larger hypocrisy that extended across the political spectrum. The public is often accused of being disconnected from its military, but frankly it's disconnected from just about everything. Farming, mineral extraction, gas and oil production, bulk cargo transport, logging, fishing, infrastructure construction — all the industries that keep the nation going are mostly unacknowledged by the people who depend on them most.

As great a sacrifice as soldiers make, American workers arguably make a greater one. Far more Americans lose their lives every year doing dangerous jobs than died *during the entire Afghan War*. In 2014, for example, 4,679 workers lost their lives on the job. More than 90 percent of those deaths were of young men working in industries that have a mortality rate equivalent to most units in the US military. Jobs that are directly observable to the public, like construction, tend to be less respected and less well paid than jobs that happen behind closed doors, like real estate or finance. And yet it is exactly these jobs that provide society's immediate physical needs. Construction workers are more important to everyday life than stockbrokers and yet are far lower down the social and financial ladder.

This fundamental lack of connectedness allows people to act in trivial but incredibly selfish ways. Rachel Yehuda pointed to littering as the perfect example of an everyday symbol of disunity in society. "It's a horrible thing to see because it sort of encapsulates this idea that you're in it alone, that there isn't a shared ethos of trying to protect something shared," she told me. "It's the embodiment of every man for himself. It's the opposite of the military."

In this sense, littering is an exceedingly petty version of claiming a billion-dollar bank bailout or fraudulently claiming disability payments. When you throw trash on the ground, you apparently don't see yourself as truly belonging to the world that you're walking around in. And when you fraudulently claim money from the government, you are ultimately stealing from your friends, family, and neighbors — or somebody else's friends, family, and neighbors. That diminishes you morally far more than it diminishes your country financially. My friend Ellis was once asked by a troubled young boy whether there was any compelling reason for him not to pull the legs off a spider. Ellis said that there was.

"Well, spiders don't feel any pain," the boy retorted.

"It's not the spider I'm worried about," Ellis said.

10

◆ ◆ ◆

The ultimate act of disaffiliation isn't littering or fraud, of course, but violence against your own people. When the Navajo Nation — the *Diné*, in their language — were rounded up and confined to a reservation in the 1860s, a terrifying phenomenon became more prominent in their culture. The warrior skills that had protected the *Diné* for thousands of years were no longer relevant in this dismal new era, and people worried that those same skills would now be turned inward, against society. That strengthened their belief in what were known as skinwalkers, or *yee naaldlooshii*.

Skinwalkers were almost always male and wore the pelt of a sacred animal so that they could subvert that animal's powers to kill people in the community. They could travel impossibly fast across the desert and their eyes glowed like coals and they could supposedly paralyze you with a single look. They were thought to attack remote homesteads at night and kill people and sometimes eat their bodies. People were still scared of skinwalkers when I lived on the Navajo

Reservation in 1983, and frankly, by the time I left, I was too.

Virtually every culture in the world has its version of the skinwalker myth. In Europe, for example, they are called werewolves (literally "man-wolf" in Old English). The myth addresses a fundamental fear in human society: that you can defend against external enemies but still remain vulnerable to one lone madman in your midst. Anglo-American culture doesn't recognize the skinwalker threat but has its own version. Starting in the early 1980s, the frequency of rampage shootings in the United States began to rise more and more rapidly until it doubled around 2006. Rampages are usually defined as attacks where people are randomly targeted and four or more are killed in one place, usually shot to death by a lone gunman. As such, those crimes conform almost exactly to the kind of threat that the Navajo seemed most to fear on the reservation: murder and mayhem committed by an individual who has rejected all social bonds and attacks people at their most vulnerable and unprepared. For modern society, that would mean not in their log hogans but in movie theaters, schools, shopping malls, places of worship, or simply walking down the street.

Seen in that light, it's revealing to look at the kinds of communities where those crimes usually occur. A rampage shooting has never happened in an urban ghetto, for example; in fact, indiscriminate attacks at schools almost always occur in otherwise safe, predominantly white towns. Around half of rampage killings happen in affluent or upper-middle-class communities, and the rest tend to happen in rural towns that are majority-white, Christian, and low-crime. Nearly 600 people have been killed by rampage shooters since the 1980s. Almost by definition, rampage killers are deeply disturbed sociopaths, but that just begs the question why sociopaths in high-crime urban neighborhoods don't turn their guns on other people the way they do in more affluent communities.

Gang shootings — as indiscriminate as they often are — still don't have the nihilistic intent of rampages. Rather, they are rooted in an exceedingly strong sense of group loyalty and revenge, and bystanders sometimes get killed in the process. The first time that the United States suffered a wave of rampage shootings was during the 1930s, when society had been severely stressed and fractured by the Great Depression. Profoundly disturbed, violent individuals might not have felt inhibited by the social bonds that restrained previous generations of potential killers. Rampage killings dropped significantly during World War II, then rose again in the 1980s and have been rising ever since. It may be worth considering whether middle-class American life — for all its material good fortune — has lost some essential sense of unity that might otherwise discourage alienated men from turning apocalyptically violent.

The last time the United States experienced that kind of unity was — briefly — after the

15 terrorist attacks of September 11. There were no rampage shootings for the next two years. The effect was particularly pronounced in New York City, where rates of violent crime, suicide, and psychiatric disturbances dropped immediately. In many countries, antisocial behavior is known to decline during wartime. New York's suicide rate dropped by around 20 percent in the six months following the attacks, the murder rate dropped by 40 percent, and pharmacists saw no increase in the number of first-time patients filling prescriptions for antianxiety and antide- pressant medication. Furthermore, veterans who were being treated for PTSD at the VA experi- enced a significant *drop* in their symptoms in the months after the September 11 attacks.

One way to determine what is missing in day-to-day American life may be to examine what behaviors spontaneously arise when that life is disrupted.

◆ ◆ ◆

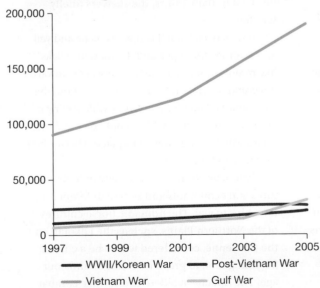

Veterans in Veterans Administration Mental Health Programs for PTSD (1997–2005)

Legend: WWII/Korean War · Post-Vietnam War · Vietnam War · Gulf War

Data from the VA Northeast Program Evaluation Center.

◀

This graph, adapted from a 2007 NPR story on the effect of the Iraq War on Vietnam veterans, shows the number of veterans diagnosed with Post Traumatic Stress Disorder from World War II, the Korean War, the Vietnam War, and later conflicts through 2005.
How might Junger explain the data shown in this graph?

"I talked to my mom only one time from Mars," a Vietnam vet named Gregory Gomez told me about the physical and spiritual distance between his home and the war zone. Gomez is an Apache Indian who grew up in West Texas. Gomez says his grandfather was arrested and executed by Texas Rangers in 1915 because they wanted his land; they strung him from a tree limb, cut his genitals off, and stuffed them in his mouth. Consequently, Gomez says he felt no allegiance to the US government, but he volunteered for service in Vietnam anyway.

"Most of us Indian guys who went to Vietnam went because we were warriors," Gomez told me. "I did not fight for this country. I fought for Mother Earth. I wanted to experience combat. I wanted to see how I'd do."

Gomez was in a Marine Force Recon unit, one of the most elite designations in the US military. He was part of a four-man team that would insert by helicopter into the jungle north of the DMZ for weeks at a time. They had no medic and no air support, and Gomez said that they didn't dare eat C rations because they were afraid their body odor would give them away at close quarters. They ate Vietnamese food and watched enemy soldiers pass just yards away in the dense jungle. "Everyone who has lived through something like that has lived through trauma, and you can never go back," he told me. "You are seventeen or eighteen or nineteen and you just hit that wall. You become very old men."

American Indians, proportionally, provide more soldiers to America's wars than any other demographic group in the country. They are also the product of an ancient culture of warfare that takes great pains to protect the warrior from society, and vice versa. Although those traditions have obviously broken down since the end of the Indian Wars, there may be something to be learned from the principles upon which they stand. When Gomez came home to West Texas he essentially went into hiding for more than a

decade. He didn't drink and he lived a normal life, except that occasionally he'd go to the corner store to get a soda and would wind up in Oklahoma City or East Texas without any idea how he got there.

He finally started seeing a therapist at the VA as well as undergoing traditional Indian rituals. It was a combination that seemed to work: "We do a lot of sweat lodge ceremonies as part of a cleaning and purification," he told me. "The vision quest ceremony is normally a four-day ceremony, and you do fasting so your system is pretty cleaned out. You're detoxified, as it were. You're pretty high."

In the 1980s Gomez underwent an extremely painful ceremony called the Sun Dance — a traditional Lakotah ceremony that was banned for many years by the US government. It was finally made legal again in 1934. At the start of the ceremony, dancers have wooden skewers driven through the skin of their chests. Leather thongs are tied to the skewers and then attached to a tall pole at the center of the dance ground. To a steady drumbeat, the dancers shuffle in a circle and lean back on the thongs until, after many hours, the skewers finally tear free.

"I dance back and I throw my arms and yell and I can see the ropes and the piercing sticks like in slow motion, flying from my chest towards the grandfather tree," Gomez told me about the experience. "And I had this incredible feeling of euphoria and strength, like I could do anything. That's when the healing takes place. That's when life changes take place."

American tribes varied widely in their cultures and economies and so had different relationships to war. The nomadic horse cultures of the Northern Plains, such as the Lakotah and the Cheyenne, considered war to be a chance for young men to prove their honor and courage. The Apache avoided face-to-face combat in favor of raiding expeditions that relied on stealth and endurance. The sedentary Papago,

20

25

whose economy was based largely on agriculture, considered war to be a form of insanity. Men who were forced into combat by attacks from other tribes had to undergo a sixteen-day purification ritual before they could reenter society. The entire community participated in these rituals because every person in the tribe was assumed to have been affected by the war. After the ceremony, the combatants were viewed as superior to their uninitiated peers because — as loathsome and crazy as war was — it was still thought to impart wisdom that nothing else could.

Following both world wars, Indian veterans turned to traditional ceremonies on their reservations to ease the transition to civilian life. The Kiowa Gourd Dance, in particular, was popularized across tribal boundaries in an attempt to heal the psychic wounds of war. During the 1980s, the Vietnam Era Veterans Inter-Tribal Association began holding a yearly summer powwow in Oklahoma that was open to veterans of all races. When they performed the Gourd Dance, captured Vietcong flags were dragged behind them in the same dirt their predecessors had dragged American flags in during the Indian Wars. "Warriors had to be recognized and were charged with the responsibility to take care of others, to practice self-discipline, and to provide leadership," one anthropologist observed about these ceremonies. "The social contract was assumed now as *wichasha yatapika* ('man' plus 'they praise')."

Contemporary America is a secular society that obviously can't just borrow from Indian culture to heal its own psychic wounds. But the spirit of community healing and connection that forms the basis of these ceremonies is one that a modern society might draw on. In all cultures, ceremonies are designed to communicate the experience of one group of people to the wider community. When people bury loved ones, when they wed, when they graduate from college, the respective ceremonies communicate something essential to the people who are watching. The Gourd Dance allowed warriors to recount and act out their battlefield exploits to the people they were protecting. If contemporary America doesn't develop ways to publicly confront the emotional consequences of war, those consequences will continue to burn a hole through the vets themselves.

I once took part in a panel discussion about war with the author Karl Marlantes. Karl is a good friend of mine, and I know that he draws an enormous amount of pride from having led a Marine platoon through some of the heaviest combat of the Vietnam War. At one point a very agitated man stood up and started screaming that he was a Vietnam vet as well, and that Karl and I didn't understand the first thing about war — it was all obscene, down to its smallest detail. Then he stormed out.

"That," Karl finally said into the stunned silence, "is one of the things that's going to happen if you truly let vets speak their mind about the war."

It's entirely possible that gentleman saw little or no combat and simply harbors strong feelings about war. Or he might have done three tours in the heaviest combat there was and remains enormously affected by it. Either way, he is clearly in need of some way to vent his feelings to the wider community. Modern society rarely gives veterans — gives anyone — opportunities to do that. Fortunately, freedom of speech means that, among other things, veterans are entitled to stand on street corners with bullhorns and "disturb the peace." More dignified might be to offer veterans all over the country the use of their town hall every Veterans Day to speak freely about their experience at war. Some will say that war was the best thing that ever happened to them. Others will be so angry that what they say will barely make sense. Still others will be crying so hard that they won't be able to speak at all. But a community ceremony

30

This photograph shows a young American sergeant resting with his radio still pressed to his ear after a five-day-long battle during the Vietnam War.
What does this image add to Junger's description of Vietnam veterans' experiences?

Bettmann/Getty Images

like that would finally return the experience of war to our entire nation, rather than just leaving it to the people who fought. The bland phrase, "I support the troops," would then mean showing up at the town hall once a year to hear these people out.

On Veterans Day 2015, the town hall in Marblehead, Massachusetts, was opened up to just such an event. Several hundred people filed into the hall and listened for more than two hours as veteran after veteran stepped forward to unburden themselves of the war. One of the first to speak was a Korean War vet who had tried to join the Marines at age fifteen. They turned him down but took his three friends, who were all killed in combat and buried next to each other on Okinawa. A couple of years later he paid his respects at their gravesites on his way over to Korea An older woman stood up and said that she'd fought in Vietnam as a man and then had come back and had a sex change. Another Vietnam vet simply read quote after quote from Bush administration officials who — in his opinion — had lied about the Iraq War. My friend Brendan O'Byrne talked about meeting the mother of his friend Juan Restrepo, who had been killed two months into their deployment to Afghanistan. Restrepo's mother asked Brendan if he'd forgiven her son's killer, and he said that no, he hadn't. She told him he had to.

"That's when I began to heal," Brendan told the room. "When I let go of the anger inside me."

◆ ◆ ◆

Today's veterans often come home to find that, although they're willing to die for their country, they're not sure how to live for it. It's hard to know how to live for a country that regularly tears itself apart along every possible ethnic and demographic boundary. The income gap between rich and poor continues to widen, many people live in racially segregated communities, the elderly are mostly sequestered from public life, and rampage shootings happen so regularly that they only remain in the news cycle for a day or two. To make matters worse, politicians occasionally accuse rivals of *deliberately* trying to harm their own country — a charge so destructive to group unity that most past societies would probably have just punished it as a form of treason. It's complete madness, and the veterans know this. In combat, soldiers all but ignore differences of race, religion, and politics within their platoon. It's no wonder many of them get so depressed when they come home.

I know what coming back to America from a war zone is like because I've done it so many times. First there is a kind of shock at the level of comfort and affluence that we enjoy, but that is followed by the dismal realization that we live in a society that is basically at war with itself. People speak with incredible contempt about — depending on their views — the rich, the poor, the educated, the foreign-born, the president, or the entire US government. It's a level of contempt that is usually reserved for enemies in wartime, except that now it's applied to our fellow citizens. Unlike criticism, contempt is particularly toxic because it assumes a moral superiority in the speaker. Contempt is often directed at people who have been excluded from a group or declared unworthy of its benefits. Contempt is often used by governments to provide rhetorical cover for torture or abuse. Contempt is one of four behaviors that, statistically, can predict divorce in married couples. People who speak with contempt for one another will probably not remain united for long.

The most alarming rhetoric comes out of the dispute between liberals and conservatives, and it's a dangerous waste of time because they're both right. The perennial conservative concern about high taxes supporting a nonworking "underclass" has entirely legitimate roots in our evolutionary past and shouldn't be dismissed out of hand. Early hominids lived a precarious existence where freeloaders were a direct threat

to survival, and so they developed an exceedingly acute sense of whether they were being taken advantage of by members of their own group. But by the same token, one of the hallmarks of early human society was the emergence of a culture of compassion that cared for the ill, the elderly, the wounded, and the unlucky. In today's terms, that is a common liberal concern that also has to be taken into account. Those two driving forces have coexisted for hundreds of thousands of years in human society and have been duly codified in this country as a two-party political system. The eternal argument over so-called entitlement programs — and, more broadly, over liberal and conservative thought — will never be resolved because each side represents an ancient and absolutely essential component of our evolutionary past.

So how do you unify a secure, wealthy country that has sunk into a zero-sum political game with itself? How do you make veterans feel that they are returning to a cohesive society that was worth fighting for in the first place? I put that question to Rachel Yehuda of Mount Sinai Hospital in New York City. Yehuda has seen, up close, the effect of such antisocial divisions on traumatized vets. "If you want to make a society

35

Library of Congress

In this photo by Lewis Hines, a shell-shocked World War I soldier who was struck in the head by shrapnel sits in a "Sunshine Room" where there is absolute quiet, harmonious colors, and cheerful surroundings. This was considered an effective treatment for shell shock, known today as Post Traumatic Stress Disorder, or PTSD. **Would Junger consider this an effective treatment? What might he add to the prescription?**

work, then you don't keep underscoring the places where you're different — you underscore your shared humanity," she told me. "I'm appalled by how much people focus on differences. Why are you focusing on how different you are from one another, and not on the things that unite us?"

The United States is so powerful that the only country capable of destroying her might be the United States herself, which means that the ultimate terrorist strategy would be to just leave the country alone. That way, America's ugliest partisan tendencies could emerge unimpeded by the unifying effects of war. The ultimate betrayal of tribe isn't acting competitively — that should be encouraged — but predicating your power on the excommunication of others from the group. That is exactly what politicians of both parties try to do when they spew venomous rhetoric about their rivals. That is exactly what media figures do when they go beyond criticism of their fellow citizens and openly revile them. Reviling people you share a combat outpost with is an incredibly stupid thing to do, and public figures who imagine their nation isn't, potentially, one huge combat outpost are deluding themselves.

In 2009, an American soldier named Bowe Bergdahl slipped through a gap in the concertina wire at his combat outpost in southern Afghanistan and walked off into the night. He was quickly captured by a Taliban patrol, and his absence triggered a massive search by the US military that put thousands of his fellow soldiers at risk. The level of betrayal felt by soldiers was so extreme that many called for Bergdahl to be tried for treason when he was repatriated five years later. Technically his crime was not treason, so the US military charged him with desertion of his post — a violation that still carries a maximum penalty of death.

The collective outrage at Sergeant Bergdahl was based on very limited knowledge but provides a perfect example of the kind of tribal ethos that every group — or country — deploys in order to remain unified and committed to itself. If anything, though, the outrage in the United States may not be broad enough. Bergdahl put a huge number of people at risk and may have caused the deaths of up to six soldiers. But in purely objective terms, he caused his country far less harm than the financial collapse of 2008, when bankers gambled trillions of dollars of taxpayer money on blatantly fraudulent mortgages. These crimes were committed while hundreds of thousands of Americans were fighting and dying in wars overseas. Almost 9 million people lost their jobs during the financial crisis, 5 million families lost their homes, and the unemployment rate doubled to around 10 percent. *40*

For nearly a century, the national suicide rate has almost exactly mirrored the unemployment rate, and after the financial collapse, America's suicide rate increased by nearly 5 percent. In an article published in 2012 in *The Lancet*, epidemiologists who study suicide estimated that the recession cost almost 5,000 additional American lives during the first two years — disproportionately among middle-aged white men. That is close to the nation's losses in the Iraq and Afghan wars combined. If Sergeant Bergdahl betrayed his country — and that's not a hard case to make — surely the bankers and traders who caused the financial collapse did as well. And yet they didn't provoke nearly the kind of outcry that Bergdahl did. Not a single high-level CEO has even been charged in connection with the financial collapse, much less been convicted and sent to prison, and most of them went on to receive huge year-end bonuses. Joseph Cassano of AIG Financial Products — known as "Mr. Credit-Default Swap" — led a unit that required a $99 billion bailout while simultaneously distributing $1.5 billion in year-end bonuses to his employees — including $34 million to himself. Robert Rubin of Citibank received a $10 million bonus in 2008 while serving on the board of directors of a company that required $63 billion in federal funds to keep from failing. Lower down the pay scale, more than 5,000 Wall Street traders received bonuses of $1 million or more despite working for nine of the financial firms that received the most bailout money from the US goverment.

Neither political party has broadly and unequivocally denounced these men for their betrayal of the American people, and yet they are quick to heap scorn on Sergeant Bergdahl. In a country that applies its standard of loyalty in such an arbitrary way, it would seem difficult for others to develop any kind of tribal ethos. Fortunately, that's not the case. Acting in a tribal way simply means being willing to make a substantive sacrifice for your community — be that your neighborhood, your workplace, or your entire country. Obviously, you don't need to be a Navy SEAL in order to do that.

In late 2015, while finishing this book, I saw a family notice in the *New York Times* for a man named Martin H. Bauman, who died peacefully at age eighty-five. The notice explained that Mr. Bauman had joined the army in the 1950s, contracted polio while in the service, graduated college under the GI Bill, and eventually started a successful job placement firm in New York City. The firm found people for top executive positions around the country, but that didn't protect it from economic downturns, and in the 1990s, Bauman's company experienced its first money-losing year in three decades.

According to the *Times* notice, Mr. Bauman called his employees into a meeting and asked them to accept a 10 percent reduction in salary so that he wouldn't have to fire anyone. They all agreed. Then he quietly decided to give up his personal salary until his company was back on safe ground. The only reason his staff found out was because the company bookkeeper told them.

Bauman obviously felt that true leadership — the kind that lives depend on — may require powerful people to put themselves last, and that he was one of those people. I contacted the office manager, Deanna Scharf, and asked her what Mr. Bauman had thought about the behavior of Wall Street executives during the financial collapse of 2008. "Oh, he was very angry," she said. "He was a lifelong Republican, he was a poor kid from the Bronx who made some money, but he was furious with what happened. He didn't understand the greed. He didn't understand if you have a hundred million dollars, why do you need another million?"

Fred Morley/Getty Images

◀

In this photograph, taken during World War II, a milkman delivers milk and firefighters dampen the ruins on a London street destroyed by German bombs.
How does this illustrate Junger's findings about human behavior in times of "disruption"?

Bauman voluntarily served his country, served his employees, and served other handicapped people by establishing a scholarship fund in his name. He clearly understood that belonging to society requires sacrifice, and that sacrifice gives back way more than it costs. ("It was better when it was really bad," someone spray-painted on a wall about the loss of 45 social solidarity in Bosnia after the war ended.) That sense of solidarity is at the core of what it means to be human and undoubtedly helped deliver us to this extraordinary moment in our history.

It may also be the only thing that allows us to survive it.

[2016]

EXPLORING THE TEXT

1. Although paragraph 1 is fairly long and detailed, paragraph 2 consists solely of two words: "And yet." Does this opening intrigue you? How effective is it as in entrance into Sebastian Junger's argument?

2. Why do you think Junger uses the term "tribe" instead of "community"? What connotations does the former term carry?

3. Why does Junger believe that "[A]s great a sacrifice as soldiers make, American workers arguably make a greater one" (para. 6)? How does he support this assertion? To what extent do you agree?

4. How does Junger connect the Navajo myth of "skinwalkers" to issues in other cultures, including the "rampage shootings" in the United States? Do you find this connection plausible? Why or why not? In your response, consider Junger's analysis of gang shootings — according to him, they lack "the nihilistic intent of rampages" (para. 15) — and his reference to the decline in violence in America after 9/11.

5. One criticism leveled at Junger is that he romanticizes tribal cultures. Using his example of Gregory Gomez, on what grounds do you think this is or is not a fair criticism?

6. In paragraph 27, Junger suggests that we need to "publicly confront the emotional consequences of war" by giving veterans an opportunity to voice their anger, fears, pride, regret, confusion, and other deep-seated emotions. He suggests some type of "community ceremony" as a forum for doing that. Do you agree with his claim that such a ceremony "would finally return the experience of war to our entire nation, rather than just leaving it to the people who fought"

(para. 30)? Consider as part of your analysis Junger's belief in the potential of "the unifying effects of war" (para. 37). What form might such a ceremony take in your own local community? In what ways would it help the community? Can you foresee any drawbacks?

7. In paragraph 37, Junger writes that "[t]he ultimate betrayal of tribe isn't acting competitively — that should be encouraged — but predicating your power on the excommunication of others from the group." What does he mean by this? Cite at least one concrete example from this essay as part of your interpretation.

8. Beginning in paragraph 38, Junger draws an analogy between the impact of the desertion of Sergeant Bergdahl and that of the actions of bankers and traders during the financial collapse of 2008. To what extent does this analogy strengthen his argument about the importance of re-establishing a "culture of compassion" (para. 35) in America?

9. Why does Junger find Martin H. Bauman an exemplary citizen who embodied a true sense of community? What purpose does this story serve within Junger's overall argument? How effective is it as a rhetorical strategy for closing out this section of *Tribe*?

10. Junger uses different types of evidence, including statistics, extended stories, analogies, and historical facts. Which kind of evidence do you find the most effective, and why?

11. Defend, challenge, or qualify Junger's assertion that "soldiers all but ignore differences of race, religion, and politics within their platoon" in combat situations (para. 33). Consider both historical evidence and current events in your response.

12. Junger believes that the United States is "a society that is basically at war with itself" (para. 34). What does he mean by that assertion? Explain why your experience and knowledge supports or challenges it.

13. In a review of *Tribe* for the *New York Times*, Matthew B. Crawford criticized Junger for emphasizing community building within the military. "The conclusion one reaches upon finishing *Tribe*," Crawford wrote, "is that we should bring back the draft and have universal, obligatory military service." Based on the excerpt you have just read, does this strike you as a fair criticism? What is the main conclusion you drew from this text?

Why I'm Moving Home

J. D. VANCE

J. D. Vance (b.1984) is an author, venture capitalist, and contributor to CNN. Born and raised in Middletown, Ohio, he went on to attend Ohio State University and Yale Law School. He is perhaps best known for his 2016 memoir *Hillbilly Elegy*, which explores his upbringing, Appalachian values, and the social problems of his lower-middle-class hometown. The book became a best-seller, attracting significant attention from the media during the 2016 U.S. presidential election for its insight into the mindset of white working-class voters. Vance wrote the following article for the *New York Times* in 2017.

In recent months, I've frequently found myself in places hit hard by manufacturing job losses, speaking to people affected in various ways. Sometimes, the conversation turns to the conflict people feel between the love of their home and the desire to leave in search of better work.

It's a conflict I know well: I left my home state, Ohio, for the Marine Corps when I was 19. And while I've returned home for months or even years at a time, job opportunities often pull me away.

Experts have warned for years now that our rates of geographic mobility have fallen to troubling lows. Given that some areas have unemployment rates around 2 percent and others many times that, this lack of movement may mean joblessness for those who could otherwise work.

But from the community's perspective, mobility can be a problem. The economist Matthew Kahn has shown that in Appalachia, for instance, the highly skilled are much likelier to leave not just their hometowns but also the region as a whole. This is the classic "brain drain" problem: Those who are able to leave very often do.

The brain drain also encourages a uniquely modern form of cultural detachment. Eventually, the young people who've moved out marry — typically to partners with similar economic prospects. They raise children in increasingly segregated neighborhoods, giving rise to something the conservative scholar Charles Murray calls "super ZIPs." These super ZIPs are veritable bastions of opportunity and optimism, places where divorce and joblessness are rare.

As one of my college professors recently told me about higher education, "The sociological role we play is to suck talent out of small towns and redistribute it to big cities." There have always been regional and class inequalities in our society, but the data tells us that we're living through a unique period of segregation.

This has consequences beyond the purely material. Jesse Sussell and James A. Thomson of the RAND Corporation argue that this geographic sorting has heightened the polarization that now animates politics. This polarization reflects itself not just in our voting patterns, but also in our political culture: Not long before the election, a friend forwarded me a conspiracy theory about Bill and Hillary Clinton's involvement in a pedophilia ring and asked me whether it was true.

It's easy to dismiss these questions as the ramblings of "fake news" consumers. But the more difficult truth is that people naturally trust the people they know — their friend sharing a story on Facebook — more than strangers who work for faraway institutions. And when we're surrounded by polarized, ideologically homogeneous crowds, whether online or off, it becomes easier to believe bizarre things about them. This problem runs in both directions: I've heard ugly words uttered about "flyover country" and some of its inhabitants from well-educated, generally well-meaning people.

I've long worried whether I've become a part of this problem. For two years, I'd lived in Silicon Valley, surrounded by other highly educated transplants with seemingly perfect lives. It's jarring to live in a world where every person feels his life will only get better when you came from a world where many rightfully believe that things have become worse. And I've suspected that this optimism blinds many in Silicon Valley to the real struggles in other parts of the country. So I decided to move home, to Ohio.

It wasn't an easy choice. I scaled back my commitments to a job I love because of the relocation. My wife and I worry about the quality of local public schools, and whether she (a San Diego native) could stand the unpredictable weather.

But there were practical reasons to move: I'm founding an organization to combat Ohio's opioid epidemic. We chose Columbus because I travel a lot, and I need to be centrally located in the state and close to an airport. And the truth is that not every motivation is rational: Part of me loves Ohio simply because it's home.

I recently asked a friend, Ami Vitori Kimener, how she thought about her own return home. A Georgetown graduate, Ami left a successful career in Washington to start new businesses in Middletown, Ohio. Middletown is in some ways a classic Midwestern city: Once thriving, it was hit hard by the decline of the region's manufacturing base in recent decades. But the town is showing early signs of revitalization, thanks in part to the efforts of those like Ami.

Talking with Ami, I realized that we often frame civic responsibility in terms of government taxes and transfer payments, so that our society's least fortunate families are able to provide basic necessities. But this focus can miss something important: that what many communities need most is not just financial support, but talent and energy and committed citizens to build viable businesses and other civic institutions.

Of course, not every town can or should be saved. Many people should leave struggling places in search of economic opportunity, and many of them won't be able to return. Some people will move back to their hometowns; others, like me, will move back to their home state. The calculation will undoubtedly differ for each person, as it should. But those of us who are lucky enough to choose where we live would do well to ask ourselves, as part of that calculation, whether the choices we make for ourselves are necessarily the best for our home communities — and for the country.

[2016]

EXPLORING THE TEXT

1. What does J. D. Vance mean when he asserts that the geographical mobility many Americans take for granted as a way to improve their economic potential might be good for the individual but is a problem for the community?

2. Vance points out that moving away from one's home community often creates a "brain drain" that leads to "a uniquely modern form of cultural detachment" (para. 5). Why does he believe that moving to places that are "bastions of opportunity and optimism, places where divorce and joblessness are rare" (para. 5) has negative consequences?

3. What kind of evidence does Vance provide to support his argument about the political polarization and "segregation" (para. 6) that results from brain drain? How effective is this evidence?

4. Vance also cites the experience of a friend who went to a prestigious college — Georgetown University — before returning to her Ohio home community, which was suffering from economic downturn. What purpose does this anecdote serve in Vance's argument? How does he relate it to his own decision to move home?

5. In the final paragraph, Vance acknowledges that "not every town can or should be saved." How does the final paragraph illustrate the rhetorical strategy of concession and refutation? How effective do you find in as a conclusion to his argument?

6. How does Vance establish his ethos? To what extent do you think that he is defending, rather than merely explaining, his choice to move back to the area where he was born and raised?

7. At the end of his essay, Vance seems to be arguing that individual achievement can undermine both our local and the larger national community. Do you agree or disagree with this interpretation of Vance's position? Use evidence from your own experience and knowledge to support your response.

8. Do you expect that your pursuit of an education and your future career will take you away from your home community? Could you imagine yourself leaving for a time and then choosing to return? Why or why not?

A GoFundMe Campaign Is Not Health Insurance

TED CLOSSON

Ted Closson (b. 1975) is a writer and artist. He earned a BA at the University of Maine at Augusta in 2009 and an MFA from the University of Houston in 2012. His comics and visual work have been published in the *Alphabet Anthology, Black Warrior Review*, the *Rumpus*, and the *Good Men Project*. After the U.S. House of Representatives voted on whether to repeal and replace the Affordable Care Act, also known as Obamacare, in May of 2017, Closson published the following graphic essay on *The Nib,* an online platform for political cartoons and nonfiction comics.

IN MY EXPERIENCE, AMERICANS HELP ONE ANOTHER.

WE MAY DISAVOW COMMUNITY IN MANY PLACES,

BUT IT'S HOW WE ACTUALLY GET THROUGH MOST OF OUR TROUBLES.

WE EULOGIZE IT IN LITERATURE AND ART INSTEAD OF POLITICAL THEORY.

Ted Closson, "A GoFundMe Campaign Is Not Health Insurance," *The Nib*, May 25th, 2017. Copyright © 2017 by Ted Closson. Used with permission. (Images also appear on pp. 605–14.)

I MET SHANE FOR THE FIRST TIME IN A COLLEGE COMICS WRITING COURSE.

HE WAS SOFT SPOKEN; WROTE SWEET, STRANGE STORIES CENTERED ON LIFE IN HOUSTON AND SUPERHEROES; AND FOUNDED ZINEFEST...

...AN EVENT DEDICATED TO PROMOTING ZINES, MINI-COMICS, AND OTHER FORMS OF SMALL PRESS ART,

OTHER VOICES   605

ZINEFEST HAD GROWN INTO A COMMUNITY REPRESENTATIVE OF HOUSTON'S CREATIVE UNDERCURRENTS.

IT WAS ABOUT THE PEOPLE WHO CREATED THEM, WHO READ THEM, LOVED THEM.

IT WAS ABOUT MORE THAN ZINES AND COMICS.

INSPIRED IN PART BY HIS EXAMPLE, FOR MY MFA THESIS, I CREATED A MINIATURE COMICS CONVENTION AND INVITED CREATORS FROM ALL AROUND HOUSTON THAT I KNEW.

-INCLUDING SHANE.

HE GOT ME A CARD
TO CELEBRATE
THE OCCASION.

I REMEMBER
HUGGING HIM.

THANKING HIM.

I WAS
SO FAR
FROM
HOME.

NO ONE FROM
MY FAMILY COULD
BE THERE FOR
MY SHOW.

SHANE MADE IT
A LITTLE EASIER.

I GRADUATED AND
LEFT THE CITY,
BUT HE AND I WERE
STILL PRESENT IN
EACH OTHER'S LIVES.

WE CELEBRATED
SUCCESSES, REPOSTED
EACH OTHER'S MEMES,
FUNDED ONE ANOTHER'S
KICKSTARTERS.

WE SUPPORTED
EACH OTHER
AS PEOPLE
ONLINE DO.

AND YET SOMEHOW I MISSED THINGS...

ofundr

World's #1 Personal Fundraising V

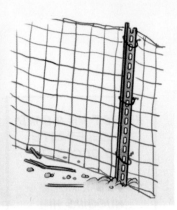

I KNEW HE HAD MOVED.

I ASSUMED IT WAS TO TRY SOMETHING NEW.

SO MANY PEOPLE WERE SEEKING A PLACE FOR THEMSELVES AFTER COLLEGE.

I NEVER THOUGHT ANYTHING OF IT.

I'D LEFT THE CITY MYSELF BECAUSE I COULDN'T AFFORD IT.

FREE CLINIC

BUT I NEVER KNEW HE WAS A DIABETIC-

-NEVER HEARD HIM RELATE IT TO ANYONE, OR TALK ABOUT THE STRUGGLE TO FIND MEDICATION.

SHANE LEFT THE
URBAN SAFETY NET
HE HAD COBBLED TOGETHER
IN TEXAS BECAUSE
HE NEEDED TO GO
HELP HIS MOTHER
IN MENA, ARKANSAS.

SHE WAS DYING.

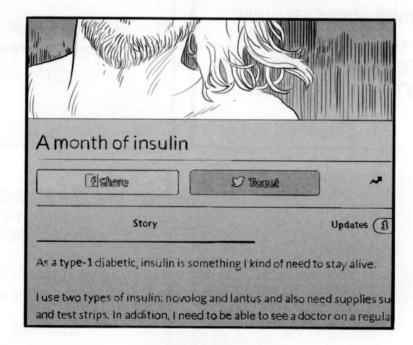

A month of insulin

[f] Share   [🐦] Tweet

Story   Updates ①

As a type-1 diabetic, insulin is something I kind of need to stay alive.

I use two types of insulin: novolog and lantus and also need supplies su
and test strips. In addition, I need to be able to see a doctor on a regula

WITHOUT A JOB,
WAITING FOR ACA INSURANCE TO KICK IN,
IN ARKANSAS SHANE TURNED TO THE
CROWDFUNDING SITE GOFUNDME
TO CAMPAIGN FOR HIS INSULIN
WHILE HE CARED
FOR HIS MOTHER.

HE WAS $50 SHY OF HIS GOAL FOR OVER TWO WEEKS.

MANY OF HIS FRIENDS WERE UNAWARE THE CAMPAIGN EVEN EXISTED.

SHANE PASSED AWAY ON MARCH 18TH OF COMPLICATIONS FROM TYPE-1 DIABETES.

HIS MOTHER HAD PASSED TWO DAYS BEFORE.

I'VE SINCE READ UP ON DIABETIC KETOACIDOSIS.

THE SYMPTOMS ARE HORRIFIC.

VOMITING, ABDOMINAL PAIN, SHORTNESS OF BREATH, AND CONFUSION.

SHANE DIED IN HORRIBLE PAIN.

THIS IS HEALTHCARE
IN THE UNITED STATES.

A PIECEMEAL SYSTEM,
COBBLED TOGETHER FROM
THE MARKETPLACES,
GOVERNMENT GRANTS
TO CLINICS, MEDICARE,
MEDICAID, PRIVATE AND
PERSONAL DONATIONS,
WORKPLACE INSURANCE,
AND ON AND ON.

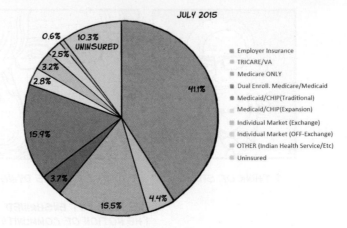

JULY 2015

0.6%
10.3% UNINSURED
2.5%
3.2%
2.8%
41.1%
15.9%
3.7%
15.5%
4.4%

- Employer Insurance
- TRICARE/VA
- Medicare ONLY
- Dual Enroll. Medicare/Medicaid
- Medicaid/CHIP(Traditional)
- Medicaid/CHIP(Expansion)
- Individual Market (Exchange)
- Individual Market (OFF-Exchange)
- OTHER (Indian Health Service/Etc)
- Uninsured

THIS IS HOW WE CARE FOR
OURSELVES AND EACH OTHER.

I THINK OF
MY BROTHER,
BETWEEN JOBS
IN RURAL MAINE*
WITHOUT INSURANCE.

*A STATE THAT
HAS REFUSED TO
EXPAND MEDICAID
UNDER THE
CURRENT GOVERNOR

MY SISTER, WITH HER
HEART PROBLEMS.

MY SPOUSE, WITH A
FAMILY HISTORY
OF DIABETES.

I THINK OF SHANE. I THINK OF SHANE DYING. I THINK OF $50.

WE HAVE NOT ENSHRINED
THE NOTION OF COMMUNITY
INTO OUR FOUNDING DOCUMENTS
AS MANY OTHER NATIONS HAVE.

(MANY OF WHOM, I IMAGINE,
OFFER A BETTER QUALITY
OF LIFE AND HEALTHCARE
TO THEIR CITIZENS)

BUT THESE
THINGS ARE NOT
ALIEN TO US.

AS AMERICANS,
WE UNDERSTAND
THE FUNCTION
OF COMMUNITY.

HOW WE
PROVIDE FOR
EACH OTHER.

I SEE MY FRIEND'S PASSING AS EMBLEMATIC OF OUR FAILURE TO REMAIN TRUE TO OUR SPIRIT AS A NATION,

...TO CIVIC VIRTUE,

...TO THE SOCIAL CONTRACT,

AND MOST IMPORTANT, TO OURSELVES AS A COMMUNITY.

COMMUNITY SHOULD HAVE BEEN A FACET OF SHANE'S MEDICAL CARE

AND IT WASN'T.

IN TRYING TO STAY ALIVE HE LEVERAGED EVERY KIND OF COMMUNITY HE COULD:

NETWORKS OF CLINICS, FRIENDS ONLINE, SOCIAL MEDIA CAMPAIGNS, HEALTHCARE MARKETPLACES.

BUT BECAUSE CARING FOR EACH OTHER ISN'T A QUALITY OF THE AMERICAN HEALTHCARE SYSTEM,

HE'S DEAD.

CARE IS NOT DEFINED BY ITS ABSENCE,

BUT BY ITS PRESENCE.

[2017]

EXPLORING THE TEXT

1. Ted Closson opens with three images that establish his beliefs about community in modern-day society. What are those beliefs? How does he argue that they are not in conflict with one another?

2. What aspects of the very first frame — in which Closson asserts that "in [his] experience, Americans help one another" — immediately jump out at you? What values does the image appeal to?

3. How does the speaker introduce the character of Shane? What did he find compelling about Shane?

4. In what ways is Zinefest a celebration of community? How does Closson replicate this model in his Master's thesis that is a "miniature comics convention" (p. 606)?

5. How would you characterize Closson's tone on (p. 607)? Is it sad, straightforward, nostalgic, optimistic, or something else? Consider his statement that he and Shane "supported each other as people online do" and the ways that the two of them "were still present in each other's lives."

6. Is Closson critical of the crowdfunding site GoFundMe when he explains that Shane failed to secure the funding he needed? Do you think he sees this as a failure of community?

7. On page 606 (panel 9), Closson depicts Shane from three different perspectives, each time with a comment. How effective are the shifting visual perspectives as a rhetorical strategy in this case?

8. How do the visual images on page 613 dramatize the assertions Closson makes? Would you say that the visual images are themselves assertions, or are they evidence to support the written claims?

9. Closson might have ended his graphic essay with the simple statement "He's dead" (p. 614). But he continues with a final panel about "care." Why is this a better choice — or is it? What is gained by the final images?

10. Closson asserts that "[c]ommunity should have been a facet of Shane's medical care . . . and it wasn't" (p. 613). Do you think that Closson is suggesting that health care overall should be one "community" that is part of the federal government?

11. Throughout this graphic essay, Closson uses a limited color palette to illustrate his narrative. Does this choice strengthen or ultimately weaken his argument? Explain.

12. Without question, Closson uses compelling visual images and a heartrending story line in powerful appeals to pathos. To what extent do you think he also builds a logical case for a better, more humane health-care system? Do you feel he relies too heavily on emotional appeals? Why or why not?

VISUAL TEXTS

Freedom from Want

NORMAN ROCKWELL

Norman Rockwell (1894–1978) was an American artist best known for his depictions of everyday life and positive American values. His first cover for the *Saturday Evening Post* appeared in 1916, and over three hundred followed during the next forty-seven years. In the early 1960s, he began working for *Look* magazine, where he turned to more political concerns such as civil rights. This 1943 painting appeared in the *Saturday Evening Post* as part of Rockwell's Four Freedoms series. These illustrations depict the "four essential human freedoms" delineated in President Franklin Delano Roosevelt's Message to Congress on January 6, 1941: freedom of speech and expression, freedom of every person to worship God in his own way, freedom from want, and freedom from fear. The Thanksgiving scene shows Rockwell's interpretation of freedom from want, which, in Roosevelt's words, "means economic understandings which will secure to every nation a healthy peacetime life for its inhabitants — everywhere in the world." This painting appeared in the magazine with the headline, "Ours . . . to fight for."

EXPLORING THE TEXT

1. What is the perspective of the viewer? Where are the participants in the painting looking? As a viewer, do you feel you are an observer or a participant in the community depicted in the painting? Why?

2. How does the painting embody the descriptors Roosevelt used — "healthy" and "peacetime"?

3. In the 1940s, who would likely have felt included in the world shown in this painting? Who might have felt excluded? How does the composition of the image contribute to your thinking on this issue?

4. Did Norman Rockwell succeed in depicting Roosevelt's vision of "economic understandings which will secure to every nation a healthy peacetime life for its inhabitants — everywhere in the world"? Explain.

Printed by permission of the Norman Rockwell Family Agency Copyright ©1943 the Norman Rockwell Family Entities

[1943]

The Black Experience Is Everywhere

NISSAN MOTOR COMPANY

The following advertisement from the Nissan Motor Company appeared in *Vibe* magazine in March 2007.

[2007]

EXPLORING THE TEXT

1. This ad claims, "The Black Experience is everywhere." Do you think that claim is true, or is it a fiction concocted for the advertisement? Do you think that the scene in this ad is believable? Consider the meaning of the barbershop in African American culture. Explain.

2. The ultimate purpose of any advertisement is to sell more products, but modern advertising often is more sly than that. Imagine that you are the creator of this ad, but it has not yet been approved by your boss. Write up a brief explanation of the rationale behind this ad and its benefit to the company. Be sure to answer the question: how will this sell more cars?

3. Do you find this advertisement flattering, offensive, inspiring, exploitive, or simply provocative? Why? Notice that the company motto is "SHIFT_ respect." How does that affect your reading?

4. Using the Toulmin model described in Chapter 3, examine the argument put forth in this ad.

5. What does this ad have to say about the meaning of community in the twenty-first century?

CONVERSATION

Building Online Communities

Each of the following texts presents a view of the nature of online communities: their form and function, their problems and potential, and the ways in which they are similar to and different from face-to-face communities.

SOURCES

1 **Laura Hudson** / from *Curbing Online Abuse Isn't Impossible. Here's Where We Start.*
2 ***Online Harassment*** (graphs)
3 **Emma Sterland** / *Online Forums Are a Lifeline for Isolated Parents of Disabled Children*
4 **Sven Birkerts** / from *Changing the Subject: Art and Attention in the Internet Age*
5 **Dex Torricke-Barton** / from *How the Internet Is Uniting the World*
6 **Daniel Mallory Ortberg** / from *Companions of My Heart: On Making Friends on the Internet*
7 **Jenna Wortham** / from *Is Social Media Disconnecting Us from the Big Picture?*
8 **Emerson Csorba** / *The Constant Sharing Is Making Us Competitive and Depressed*

After using the questions to discuss individual selections, synthesize the pieces through one of the suggested assignments on pages 638–39.

1 from Curbing Online Abuse Isn't Impossible. Here's Where We Start.

LAURA HUDSON

Laura Hudson is a senior editor and writer for *Wired* magazine. She often writes about social media and pop culture for publications that include the *Guardian*, the *Los Angeles Times* and *Complex*. The following piece appeared in *Wired* in 2014.

Too often . . . we talk about online abuse like we talk about bad weather: We shake our heads, shrug, and assume there's nothing we can do. The behavior is so prevalent that it's seen as an inextricable part of online culture. As a widely read article in January's *Pacific Standard* noted, "Internet harassment is routinely dismissed as 'harmless locker-room talk,' perpetrators as 'juvenile pranksters,' and victims as 'overly sensitive complainers.'" What else, in other words, would you expect from the Internet? But the Internet is now where we socialize, where we work. It's where we meet our spouses, where we build

our reputations. Online harassment isn't just inconvenient, nor is it something we can walk away from with ease. It's abhorrent behavior that has real social, professional, and economic costs. And the big social networks where most Americans spend time online — Facebook, YouTube, Twitter, and the rest — aren't doing nearly enough to address the problem. . . .

Boasting more than 67 million active players each month, the battle-arena game *League of Legends* is perhaps the most popular videogame in the world. But two years ago its publisher, Riot Games, noticed that a significant number of players had quit the game and cited noxious behavior as the reason. In response, the company assembled a "player behavior team," bringing together staff members with PhDs in psychology, cognitive science, and neuroscience to study the issue of harassment by building and analyzing behavioral profiles for tens of millions of users.

This process led them to a surprising insight — one that "shaped our entire approach to this problem," says Jeffrey Lin, Riot's lead designer of social systems, who spoke about the process at last year's Game Developers Conference. "If we remove all toxic players from the game, do we solve the player behavior problem? We don't." That is, if you think most online abuse is hurled by a small group of maladapted trolls, you're wrong. Riot found that persistently negative players were only responsible for roughly 13 percent of the game's bad behavior. The other 87 percent was coming from players whose presence, most of the time, seemed to be generally inoffensive or even positive. These gamers were lashing out only occasionally, in isolated incidents — but their outbursts often snowballed through the community. Banning the worst trolls wouldn't be enough to clean up *League of Legends,* Riot's player behavior team realized. Nothing less than community-wide reforms could succeed. . . .

The team also found that it's important to enforce the rules in ways that people understand. When Riot's team started its research, it noticed that the recidivism rate was disturbingly high; in fact, based on number of reports per day, some banned players were actually getting worse after their bans than they were before. At the time, players were informed of their suspension via emails that didn't explain why the punishment had been meted out. So Riot decided to try a new system that specifically cited the offense. This led to a very different result: Now when banned players returned to the game, their bad behavior dropped measurably. . . .

Really, freedom of speech is beside the point. 5 Facebook and Twitter want to be the locus of communities, but they seem to blanch at the notion that such communities would want to enforce norms — which, of course, are defined by shared values rather than by the outer limits of the law. Social networks could take a strong and meaningful stand against harassment simply by applying the same sort of standards in their online spaces that we already apply in our public and professional lives. That's not a radical step; indeed, it's literally a normal one. Wishing rape or other violence on women or using derogatory slurs, even as "jokes," would never fly in most workplaces or communities, and those who engaged in such vitriol would be reprimanded or asked to leave. Why shouldn't that be the response in our online lives?

To truly shift social norms, the community, by definition, has to get involved in enforcing them. This could mean making comments of disapproval, upvoting and downvoting, or simply reporting bad behavior. The best online forums are the ones that take seriously their role as communities, including the famously civil MetaFilter, whose moderation is guided by a "don't be an asshole" principle. On a much larger scale, Microsoft's Xbox network implemented a community-powered reputation system for its new Xbox One console. Using feedback from players, as well as a variety of other metrics, the system determines whether a user gets rated green ("Good Player"), yellow ("Needs Improvement"), or red ("Avoid Me").

In another initiative by Riot's player-behavior team, *League of Legends* launched a disciplinary system called the Tribunal, in which a jury of fellow players votes on reported instances of bad behavior. Empowered to issue everything from email warnings to longer-term bans, users have cast tens of millions of votes about the behavior of fellow players. When Riot asked its staff to audit the verdicts, it found that the staff unanimously agreed with users in nearly 80 percent of cases. And this system is not just punishing players; it's rehabilitating them, elevating more than 280,000 censured gamers to good standing. Riot regularly receives apologies from players who have been through the Tribunal system, saying they hadn't understood how offensive their behavior was until it was pointed out to them. Others have actually asked to be placed in a Restricted Chat Mode, which limits the number of messages they can send in games — forcing a choice to communicate with their teammates instead of harassing others.

A telling example is Riot's most famous and high-profile punishment thus far, which targeted a player in the professional *League of Legends* community (where top performers can pull down six figures a year). After repeated Tribunal punishments, and with a harassment score placing him among the 0.7 percent worst North American players, Christian Rivera was banned for a year from competitive play. Even more telling was Rivera's later epiphany: "It took Riot's interjection for me to realize that I could be a positive influence, not just in *League* but with everything," he said in a subsequent interview. "I started to enjoy the game more, this time not at anyone's expense."

What would our social networks look like if their guidelines and enforcement reflected real-life community norms? If Riot's experiments are any guide, it's unlikely that most or even many users would deem a lot of the casual abuse, the kind that's driving so many people out of online spaces, to be acceptable. Think about how social networks might improve if — as on the gaming sites and in real life — users had more power to reject abusive behavior. Of course, different online spaces will require different solutions, but the outlines are roughly the same: Involve users in the moderation process, set defaults that create hurdles to abuse, give clearer feedback for people who misbehave, and — above all — create a norm in which harassment simply isn't tolerated.

Ultimately, online abuse isn't a technological 10 problem; it's a social problem that just happens to be powered by technology. The best solutions are going to be those that not only defuse the Internet's power to amplify abuse but also encourage crucial shifts in social norms, placing bad behavior beyond the pale. When people speak up about online harassment, one of the most common responses is "Well, what did you expect from the Internet?" If we truly want to change our online spaces, the answer from all of us has got to be: *more*.

QUESTIONS

1. Laura Hudson opens by citing several counterarguments against taking online abuse seriously. What are they? How does she refute them as she develops her thesis?

2. According to the research Hudson cites, who are gamers responsible for most of the online abuse? Are these mainly "a small group of maladapted trolls" (para. 3)?

3. Why is simply banning players found guilty of online abuse not an effective strategy?

4. Hudson opens paragraph 5 with the sentence, "Really, freedom of speech is beside the point."

What does she mean by this statement? Consider the context of online spaces in your response.

5. What actions does Hudson believe are necessary to "truly shift social norms" (para. 6) in online communities? What are the most effective ways to change behavior and foster an environment where "harassment simply isn't tolerated" (para. 9)?

6. Hudson argues that "online abuse isn't a technological problem; it's a social problem that just happens to be powered by technology" (para. 10). How effectively does she support this argument?

2 Online Harassment

The following graphs were created using data published by Pew Research Center in 2014 as part of a report on the results of a study on online harassment.

Percentage of Internet Users Who Experience Online Harassment

■ Have not experienced harassment
■ Have experienced less severe forms of harassment
■ Have experienced more severe forms of harassment

Data from Pew Research Center.

Online Experiences

When asked to think of their online and offline experiences, the percentage of Internet users who agreed or disagreed with the following statements:

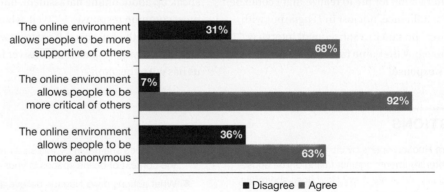

Data from Pew Research Center.

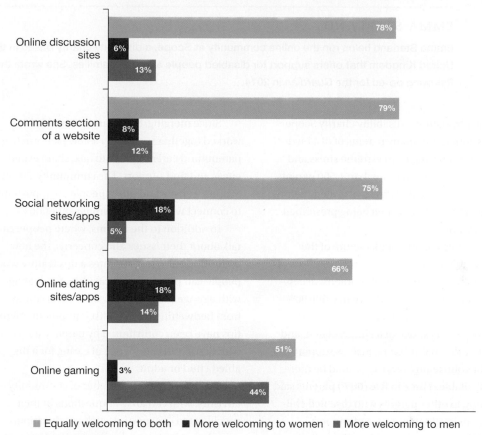

The Hospitality of Online Communities

The percentage of all Internet users who believed the following online communities were more welcoming to men, more welcoming to women, or equally welcoming to both:

Online discussion sites
- 78%
- 6%
- 13%

Comments section of a website
- 79%
- 8%
- 12%

Social networking sites/apps
- 75%
- 18%
- 5%

Online dating sites/apps
- 66%
- 18%
- 14%

Online gaming
- 51%
- 3%
- 44%

■ Equally welcoming to both   ■ More welcoming to women   ■ More welcoming to men

Data from Pew Research Center.

QUESTIONS

1. Do you see any contradictions in the data reported in these graphs? If so, what are they? If not, what cohesive message does the data send?

2. According to the three graphs, what are the most significant differences between the experiences of men and of women online?

3. What do these graphs suggest are the most significant problems with online communities?

4. To what extent does the information in these graphs reflect your own experience?

3 Online Forums Are a Lifeline for Isolated Parents of Disabled Children

EMMA STERLAND

Emma Sterland helps run the online community at Scope, a disability charity based in the United Kingdom that offers support for disabled people and their families. She wrote the following op-ed for the *Guardian* in 2014.

A study by national disability charity Scope has found that many parents of disabled children are suffering from extreme stress and isolation. The survey of more than 1,500 parents, found that almost half (47%) have visited their GP due to anxiety, with 57% then being prescribed antidepressants.

The findings paint a stark picture of the emotional toll of a lack of support. Two thirds of parents (69%) said they'd had problems accessing local services over the past year, while 90% expressed concerns about cuts.

Many parents spoke of feeling isolated, and said that emotional support, such as support groups or counselling services should be more widely available. Three in five (60%) parents said that talking to other parents with disabled children was an invaluable source of support.

Earlier this year, Netbuddy — the online community I helped set up and run for parents of disabled children — became part of Scope.

Since its launch four years ago, Netbuddy 5 provided a place for people to share experiences, swap practical tips and exchange information. In a climate of cuts to support and services, for many it became a lifeline.

Social networks such as Mumsnet and Facebook have become firmly established as platforms for like-minded people to connect. But, for parents of disabled children, the benefits of being part of a community that understands and empathises with the challenges they face can run even deeper.

Since merging, Scope and Netbuddy have worked together to develop a new platform to give parents and carers a place to talk, share experiences and find support. The community sits on Scope's website and offers people an opportunity to connect with others in similar situations.

In addition to the forums, where people can talk about their issues and concerns, the new community also incorporates a tips feature where people can pick up practical ideas for dealing with a range of everyday issues — everything from bedwetting to specialist equipment. All the tips have been contributed by parents and carers, with first-hand experience of caring for a disabled child or adult.

The site also has a number of community advisors, who can answer questions in their specific area of expertise, such as education, speech and language therapy, technology and behavioural issues. Helping to run the community is a team of volunteers — parents of disabled children themselves, who see the value in supportive networks such as these.

Heather Harvey, whose 13-year old son 10 Nicholas has autism and learning disabilities, was a parent volunteer at Netbuddy and is now a community champion for the new community at Scope.

"A lot of parents don't know where to start when they find out their child is disabled," she says. "They don't know what support is available, what they're entitled to, or what to do when they can't access the help they need. Talking to other parents of disabled children, who have been in your situation, is incredibly helpful.

"My son Nicholas was placed in a school that wasn't right for him. It got to the stage where he was doing nothing but lying on the floor of the school he was at, screaming and lashing out because he was so scared. But no-one would listen to me.

"I was so stressed that I lost a lot of weight and got alopecia and my hair fell out. I saw my GP and he suggested anti-depressants, but I didn't want to take them.

"I asked online for advice from other parents of disabled children, and a woman called Jane got in touch. She had been in exactly the same situation as me and her child had just got a place in a brilliant school nearby.

"She helped me through how to get Nicholas 15 a place there. It was a battle, but we did it and the change in him has been incredible.

"I like helping other parents now. It's rewarding to give people hope when you're able to say, I've been there, I've done that, and I've come other the other end."

QUESTIONS

1. Emma Sterland begins by sharing data about the emotional well-being of parents of disabled children. What effect does this statistical information have on you as a reader? How does it relate to Sterland's thesis?

2. According to Sterland, what makes Netbuddy important to the community it aims to support?

3. Given the special population that Netbuddy serves, what concerns about privacy might make families reluctant to participate? Would anonymity help, or is sharing personal experience key to the appeal of the site?

4. Sterland does not discuss whether research has been done to analyze Netbuddy's success at addressing the problems she identifies in her opening paragraphs. To what extent does this omission weaken her overall argument?

4 from Changing the Subject
Art and Attention in the Internet Age

SVEN BIRKERTS

Author of ten books, Sven Birkerts is best known for *The Gutenberg Elegies: The Fate of Reading in an Electronic Age* (1994). He is the director of the Bennington College Writing Seminars and editor of the literary journal *AGNI*. The following excerpt is from his 2015 book, *Changing the Subject: Art and Attention in the Internet Age*, which examines the effects of digital media on society.

rant my argument, that we are experiencing an unprecedented explosion of data; that our technological know-how, speeded up by the nearly independent self-governing know-how of the machines we have created, has put us in the situation of the sorcerer's apprentice in Disney's *Fantasia* — who for all his frenetic exertions was unable to keep up with the flood he had unleashed. Technology has now so far outstripped the human capacity to integrate its output that the essential human premise of context is under siege. Media thinker George W. S. Trow entided his book-length meditation on our information age — his warning cry — *Within the Context of No Context.* That was back in 1980, but no phrase has ever seemed more apt.

Our new circumstance has not brought us to mass psychosis — not yet, anyway — but rather, paradoxically, has led to what appears at first glance to be a technological solution of sorts. Computers, the main source of this proliferation, have also become our primary contextualizing tool, gathering, organizing, and aggregating to create quasi contexts for groupings of data. Search engines like Google work with links and tags to bring us the material we need. We live inside a ceaseless dynamic of cybersowing and cyberreaping. Our range of access has grown immeasurably. What could be wrong with that?

This is a key question. And how we answer it depends in part on what we think should be the place of the individual in the mass-information society. Critics might argue that the large-scale effects of this inundation are a fundamental abstraction, a distancing from reality — letting our machines garner and prioritize our materials for us — *and* a crucial psychological abdication. We seem to be asserting that "it," the world, the universe of data, is altogether too much for us. And as the data flow ultimately determines so much about our lives — fiscal, social, intellectual — this surrender of our power is no small thing.

Consider in this regard — and as necessary contrast — cyber-writer Kevin Kelly's much-discussed essay "Scan This Book!" in the *New York Times Magazine* several years back. Kelly's gist is that we now have the technological ability to digitize all of the world's texts, and thus are close to creating a searchable universal digital library, a radically expanded version of what is already possible with Google and the World Wide Web. The article describes massive digitizing endeavors that are already scanning the complete holdings of major libraries into databases.

But excited as Kelly is about this totalized merging of information, he is nearly rhapsodic about the next step and its implications. "The real magic," he writes, "will come . . . as each word in each book is cross-linked, clustered, cited, extracted, indexed, analyzed, annotated, remixed, reassembled and woven deeper into the culture than ever before. In the new world of books, every bit informs another; every page reads all other pages." The logistics are a bit hard to grasp on first pass, but the direction is clear enough. Significant, too, is the fact that the statistical frequency with which these links and tags are activated will create automatic hierarchies, algorithmic pathways of preferred usage that will map and prioritize certain ideas and connections. If we accede to the defining metaphor of our time, that computers model a neural functioning, then it follows that a universal database is akin to a vast extended brain of sorts. The next stage of analogy is obvious: collective intelligence. After all, in the much-cited phrase of neuropsychologist Donald Hebb, "neurons that fire together wire together," and all the latest theories of neural functioning see memory and intelligence as a product of electrical impulses traveling across a field of synapses, with repetition determining the power and vividness of what we experience as contents.

The implications are staggering in a Huxleian "brave new world" kind of way. Universal digital library, universal brain. One collective mind thinking in determined hierarchies. Pure science fiction — I hope. Kelly is also the author of a book titled, significantly, *Out of Control: The New Biology of Machine, Social Systems, and the Economic World,* which essentially proposes the social organization of bees as a kind of template for human societies in the information age. For him the future is about moving ever closer to unitary, interconnected human experience, the opposite of the subjective individualism around which much of our post-Enlightenment Western culture has been premised.

We may look to dismiss Kelly as a New Age piper, but his vision is just the extreme projection of what is happening all around us in somewhat less dramatic but still obvious forms. I mean a drift toward electronic merging, social hiving — with all the systemic leveling of idiosyncrasy that implies. The explosion (for once the word is not hyperbolic) of cell phone usage is certainly a move in that direction, creating a crosshatched density of communications entirely different from what we had when the telephone was a home appliance. Universal access is no longer an unlikely surmise; it is fast becoming an expectation, and it is changing our social behavior accordingly — if you want to count you have to be connected.

And consider the rapid expansion of *Wikipedia,* with its open-source collaborative procedure for generating and refining subject entries on a mind-numbing array of topics (more compendious by many magnitudes than the old *Encyclopedia Britannica*). The honey of knowledge gathered by the far-flung swarm. It is a concrete realization of a decentralized, nonhierarchical model, a pioneer instance of an all-inclusive one-stop source for knowledge that was hitherto scattered among innumerable texts, and deemed the province of its myriad anointed authorities.

Again, what could be wrong with a communally generated compendium of knowledge — provided that it *is* knowledge and not unverifiable hearsay? From one perspective — that of a Kevin Kelly, certainly — nothing at all. It seems a stirring instance of people working together, pyramid building but with no taskmaster and no pharaoh. And it could be viewed as a kind of apotheosis of human progress. But for those foot draggers among us who

worry about the fate of the individual, the *idea* of the individual — who get stuck on the adjective *human* in *human progress* and who believe *systems* and *selves* to be opposing terms — it can be seen as a further migration toward the groupthink ethos.

Information, then, ideas, references — anything we used to go to separate books for, and therefore understood as the product of individual insight, scholarship, and labor — more and more all this seems to come at us from a single neutral omnipotent source. How can this not threaten the idea of authorship and completely undermine the old understanding that knowledge is not a unilateral absolute, but an intricately worked accumulation, a structure comprising one stone laid upon the next? 10

Digital consolidation, along with the uniformity of the procedures of access, works aggressively against the former system of contexts. The picture of information that we derived from the *idea* of discrete books gives way to the picture of information as something derived from a glowing terminal. And if we lose nothing in terms of access to information from this digital centralization, we do begin to forget what the production of knowledge is really about. We become like children who "forget," or maybe have never even learned, that milk comes from cows — imagining it somehow originates in the cartons Mother buys at the store.

On the broadest, most general level, then, two related things are happening. One is that the massive neural net promotes the collapse of formerly stable-seeming contexts, dissolving us into etherized constituencies, affinity groups. We gradually give up our investment in the idea of a center, and as we do we start to lose the centuries-old understanding that relates the individual through the community to the larger social systems, what is called "the social contract." The other development, a kind of compensation, is the flourishing of virtual modes of interconnectedness. We look to offset the alienation caused by the electronic system through specific uses of the system. We may be more removed than ever from the immediacies of physical community, but we discover hitherto unimaginable kinship networks — people the world over who share our passion for clawhammer banjo styles.

It gets ever harder to stay free of the electronic grid and its dual dynamic, which shatters old supporting structures while at the same time fostering the new model of disengaged engagement.

QUESTIONS

1. What does Sven Birkerts mean by this statement: "We live inside a ceaseless dynamic of cybersowing and cyberreaping" (para. 2)? What concerns him about this situation?

2. Citing the work of "cyberwriter" Kevin Kelly, Birkerts worries about the impact of "automatic hierarchies, algorithmic pathways of preferred usage" (para. 5), and other results of digitizing information. Why? He acknowledges the virtues of access, yet he cautions that "a universal database is akin to a vast extended brain of sorts" (para. 5). Why is that a problem?

3. What does Birkerts mean by his description of "social hiving" (para. 7)? To what extent do you agree that social hiving is a liability to the "subjective individualism" (para. 6) that is at the heart of our society?

4. Birkerts takes a somewhat defensive tone when he concludes that in the digital world, "if you want to count you have to be connected" (para. 7). Based

on your own experience, explain whether you agree with this assertion.

5. What does Birkerts find admirable about Wikipedia? What is objectionable? How does he connect his concern about it with the belief that "*systems* and *selves* [are] opposing terms" (para. 9)?

6. By the end of this excerpt, Birkerts predicts a dystopian view where the technology is "dissolving us into etherized constituencies, affinity groups" (para. 12) where the individual loses ground. To what extent do you share his concern?

7. Birkerts writes from a philosophical standpoint of abstract ideas with some specific examples (e.g., the cell phone). How would his ideas apply to an online community such as a dating site or an online faith community?

---

5 from How the Internet Is Uniting the World

DEX TORRICKE-BARTON

Dex Torricke-Barton served as a media consultant for the United Nations Alliance of Civilizations, a project of the UN Secretary-General from 2008 to 2010. From 2012 to 2016 he was executive communications leader for Facebook and speechwriter for founder and CEO Mark Zuckerberg. After then serving as Head of Communications for SpaceX, he left in 2016 to work on projects that focus on social change. The following piece is from a post he published on the online platform *Medium* in 2015.

On August 25, a Syrian refugee was photographed selling pens on the streets of Beirut, clutching his sleeping daughter.

Abdul Halim Attar was desperate. A single father of two, he came to Lebanon to keep his children safe. And so he appeared in heartbreaking images posted online by an Icelandic journalist, Gissur Simonarson. He looked exhausted and distraught.

Gissur asked the internet to help find the man and started a crowdfunding campaign for him on Indiegogo. He used the hashtag #buypens to promote it on social media.

In less than 24 hours, Abdul was located by people who recognized him. Gissur made contact. And more than $117,000 was donated by people all over the world. Enough to change the lives of Abdul and his family, and hundreds of other refugees.

In a time of turmoil, Abdul's story seems a   5
rare story of hope. But the extraordinary thing is that it's just one example of a much larger global shift taking place today.

The internet is uniting the world. And it's going to change all our lives.

A New Type of Community: The Tools and Knowledge of One Nation Belong to All Nations

When you look at today's headlines, it's easy to scoff at the idea that the world is coming together, or the internet has a meaningful role to play. . . .

Today, 3 billion people have access to the internet. Hundreds of millions of people are now part of online communities. Around 1.5 billion people use Facebook, more than a billion people use Google and 900 million people use WhatsApp.

Admittedly, more than 4 billion people aren't online. Right now the middle classes enjoy most of the benefits of connectivity. But that doesn't lessen the internet's impact.

The internet is the largest community in   10
history — *as big as the global population in 1960*. It crosses every border and culture. And enough people are connected that the internet has become a planetary infrastructure for communications and collaboration. The tools and knowledge of one nation now belong to all nations.

And an internet that connects the middle classes is immensely powerful.

Throughout history, the middle class has been the greatest driver of social, economic and political change. The middle classes are opposed to the inequitable concentration of power and resources, against violence, and supporters of civil liberties and the rule of law.

But the internet isn't just serving the existing middle class — it's expanding it. Research by Deloitte also finds that if more people were connected in developing countries, 160 million people could escape poverty, 140 million new jobs be created and 600 million children receive education.

This is how the internet creates the foundation for a more united world.

As the internet drives social and economic   15
progress, it strengthens the middle class in all nations and brings them into a global middle class, connected by shared tools and knowledge. And as the international community descends into chaos, a rising planetary community is changing lives and communities everywhere — and bringing the world together.

This is happening in three main ways.

Planetary Thinking: Global Empathy Leads to Global Interests

First, the internet is changing the way the world thinks.

In 1938, British Prime Minister Neville Chamberlain famously declared German aggression towards Czechoslovakia as "a quarrel in a faraway country between people of whom we know nothing."

Prague is less than 800 miles from London.

Today, planetary scale internet services   20
allow us to connect with people everywhere to a degree never previously possible. With Facebook and Twitter, you can build friendships and

relationships that cross borders, and share news and information from anywhere. With Instagram, you have a real-time window on the world, with more than 80 million photos shared daily. All of us can see the stars from the vantage point of an astronaut on the International Space Station, join a UN aid worker in a refugee camp in South Sudan, or follow the lives of people from Gaza to Tokyo.

Prague is not so distant now.

Of course, it's difficult to measure what impact this has on people's thinking. But here's what we know.

A century ago, Britain and France were lobbing shells at German soldiers on the frontlines of Europe. Today, online friendship networks tie together millions of Brits, French and Germans, and countless other peoples with historical enmity.

At moments of crisis, the internet erupts in solidarity — at moments of joy, in celebration. After the earthquake in Nepal or recent floods in Myanmar, millions rallied online in support of countries historically marginalized within the international community. This summer, hundreds of thousands of Europeans demanded action on the #refugeecrisis. For Pride Month in June, more than 26 million people changed their Facebook profile pictures to support the LGBT community. . . .

Where mass movements once stood for local or national interests, now online communities are moved by global interests far beyond people's immediate lives and communities. There are no more faraway countries. [25]

Planetary Action: As the World Thinks, the World Acts

And far from simply generating empathy, the internet is mobilizing action.

There are countless examples, large and small, of what this looks like.

The extraordinary story of Abdul, the Syrian refugee, is repeated almost daily thanks to online communities. In July, donations poured in for a Filipino schoolboy pictured doing his homework on the streets. A crying Greek pensioner, unable to withdraw money during the debt crisis, was sponsored by a generous Australian. A New York bus monitor received more than $700,000 from 30,000 people in 84 countries after a YouTube video showed her being bullied.

All these individual acts of compassion are changing people's lives. But the internet also drives action for much larger causes.

This summer, the tragic image of a drowned Syrian boy mobilized the internet to demand action on the refugee crisis. [30]

As politicians admitted, it was this single image — amidst a vast humanitarian crisis — that pushed governments to act. And the internet itself mobilized using hashtags such as #refugeeswelcome and #refugeecrisis, raising funds for refugees and fighting intolerance against them.

The internet has also shown its ability to demand dramatic political change. . . .

In 2014, the ALS ice bucket challenge became a global phenomenon, with more than 17 million videos watched on Facebook by more than 440 million people — and more than $100 million raised. And even if other causes attract less attention, fundraising and awareness campaigns for global issues from climate change to Ebola all depend on the internet.

Certainly, many of these acts of change are momentary. After a brief surge, movements disintegrate. The internet's attention moves on.

For change to endure, action must assume a stronger and more permanent form. [35]

Planetary Institutions

Institutions are instruments for long-term change. . . .

The institutions of the future bear little resemblance to the past, because we are dealing with a new form of human community. In an age where knowledge is our most valuable resource, and the planetary community the most powerful actor, the most effective global institutions are those which harness the power of online networks of citizens, activists and experts.

Innovative civil society organizations and NGOs like Avaaz, Amnesty International and Global Citizen have shown their ability to quickly mobilize thousands of people to sign petitions, write letters and demand action from leaders and governments. These are relatively lean organizations that have invested in online innovation and building strong online networks of supporters.

Where multinational corporations once defined global trade and enterprise, the internet has enabled a new class of "micro multinationals" — small, highly dispersed teams of skilled individuals working across borders to build products and companies.

And some of the most powerful institutions 40 of global collaboration are built on the power of the crowd — with weak hierarchies and emphasis on individuals choosing how to contribute to shared missions. Wikipedia or Ushahidi, the crowd-mapping and reporting tool, are perfect examples. . . .

A More United Earth

So this is how the internet is uniting the world — in thought, action and institutions.

The history of humanity is a story of people coming together in new and different ways. We began as bands of hunter gatherers. But one day we came out of the plains of Africa to make the world our own. Our communities have never stopped growing in size and complexity.

Now technology gives us the chance to take the next big step — to build one great human community.

This will not be a utopian future. As millions of people begin to work together to advance a new world, many more will remain mired in the old. Sectarianism and nationalism are not going away anytime soon. Change creates new tensions and problems in society, which must be carefully managed — or progress can be easily reversed. And to build a truly representative planetary community, we must connect the entire world. We're not there yet.

But for the very first time in history, instead 45 of listening to leaders speak on behalf of the world, the world shall speak for itself. The problems of every nation shall be our problems — but so will the opportunities and solutions that we can all build together. Every leader, movement, business and organization has a chance to harness the power of this planetary community to move the entire world forward.

Everyone connected is part of the next chapter in the story of humanity. All of us have a chance to write it together. A united earth is coming.

QUESTIONS

1. How does Dex Torricke-Barton begin his post? How effectively do you think he uses this opening to transition to the bold claim that "[t]he internet is uniting the world. And it's going to change all our lives" (para. 6)?

2. Why does Torricke-Barton focus on the impact of the Internet on the middle class? What is the particular importance he sees in that connection?

3. What does Torricke-Barton mean when he claims, "There are no more faraway countries" (para. 25)? Explain whether you agree or disagree.

4. What counterargument does Torricke-Barton acknowledge about the ability of the Internet to mobilize action?

5. Who are the "micro multinationals" (para. 39)? Why does Torricke-Barton believe they are so important?

6. What are the "three main ways" that the Internet is "bringing the world together" (para. 15), according to Torricke-Barton? Which do you find most compelling, and why?

7. Return to the opening section of the essay and identify one large-scale assertion that Torricke-Barton makes. How effectively does he develop an argument to support it?

8. In paragraph 44, Torricke-Barton admits that a "utopian future" is not entirely likely. What dangers

can you foresee for a dystopian future? How optimistic are you that technology "gives us the chance . . . to build one great human community" (para. 43), and why?

from Companions of My Heart
On Making Friends on the Internet

DANIEL MALLORY ORTBERG

Author and editor Daniel Mallory Ortberg (b. 1986) is the co-founder of *The Toast*, a feminist general interest site, and author of *Texts from Jane Eyre* (2014), a *New York Times* best seller. In 2015, he took on the role of "Dear Prudence," the advice columnist for *Slate* magazine. The following is an excerpt from an essay he published in *Slate* magazine in 2016.

No one from the internet has ever murdered me. No one has ever murdered me, full stop, for which I'm extremely grateful, but I'm particularly gratified that I have never been murdered by anyone I've met from the internet, as that was a real concern for those of us who grew up in the freewheeling AOL chat rooms of the late '90s and early aughts. Chat rooms seemed to children of the 1990s as New York seemed to Midwesterners in the 1980s: a carnival of murderers trawling for prey. No one, the thinking went, was who they said they were online; 90 percent of instant messages were exchanged between murderers trying to convince one another to buy a ticket to Chicago, all of them blissfully unaware they were talking to fellow murderers with the identically murderous intentions.

In 1998, my friend Briana told me that she was planning on meeting a girl named Talia that she'd met through a Hanson fan group who lived a few towns over, and I remember taking the news like a funeral invitation. *Oh*, I thought, *Briana is going to die, because the only people on*

the internet are Us and Murderers, and Talia isn't Us, so Talia must be a murderer, and I will have to carry on Briana's legacy as best as I can, with only half of this Best Friends necklace to remember her by. As we were all gratified to learn, Talia wasn't a murderer, she was also a 12-year-old girl, and she and Briana became quite good friends, and I think Briana gave her a Best Friends necklace too. I don't say this to criticize Briana. We all have to decide for ourselves how many Best Friends necklaces we are willing to share with friends. (The correct number is one, obviously.)

The internet went on to do me the very great favor of expanding the circle of Us and constricting the circle of Potential Online Murderers. I have found a multiplicity of Us there — I did not meet Nicole in a classroom (*could* not have; she went to an excellent, prestigious college and I did not) or at a grocery store, or through friends, and in fact I could not have found the same friendship with her that I have anywhere else. I could not have met her as she grew up in Canada, or as she started raising a family three states over in

Utah; I could only find her through the magnetic pull of our shared obsessions broadcast over the internet. I have not always been a romantically confident person, but my conviction in my own ability to befriend others, given the slightest encouragement, knows no limits. "Two things are going to happen tonight," I once told a stranger, who later became a friend, at a party: "We are going to fight about that jacket you're wearing, and then we are going to become best friends." Both of those events came to pass exactly in the order I had predicted. Every friend I have ever made, I have been at least partly convinced that we were formed for one another in the Halls of Mandos. Every moment in my life before I had met Nicole had prepared me to meet Nicole. We knocked on all the same doors, and eventually we came to the same room.

The internet did not merely generate our friendship but sustained it; for the next three years, as we ran the *Toast* together, I woke up most mornings to a series of cheerfully efficient messages about data-server costs and went to bed only after having flung several links to fake-documentary trailers like "Pooljumpers" in her direction. In between, the running dialogue covered everything from edits we disagreed on, to trips to meet one another's families, and everything we'd found on the internet that day that we loved or hated or couldn't believe or all three. . . .

We had only one rule: We could complain 5 about one another's fitness as a business partner as much as we liked, but we could only complain about each other to one another. We kept to it, too. After three years, I still find myself looking eagerly for her next message, which is never too far behind the last one. We no longer run the *Toast* together, but the only thing that's changed is she no longer has to remind me to check my email anymore. She just lets me forget.

A great many of my friends now have come from the internet; viciously brilliant souls with robust texting plans, and I regularly cram them into my guest room and force them to watch television and share the inner workings of their hearts with me when they come to town. (If one cannot be a brain in a jar, one should at least be within couch-length of one's dearest friends at least once in a while.) I fight with them about their jackets, and then we become permanently ensconced in one another's hearts. None of us exchange jewelry, but I believe we care for one another just the same.

QUESTIONS

1. Though the first two paragraphs of this essay are rather shocking to read, they are intended to be humorous and perhaps even satirical. How do they prepare you for the rest of the essay? In what ways is Daniel Mallory Ortberg playing with stereotypes of the kinds of communities and connections the Internet fosters?

2. Ortberg launches into a story of his meeting with Nicole, who became a best friend off the Internet as well. What point is he making as he describes their meeting? How has the Internet "not merely generate[d] . . . but sustained" their friendship (para. 4)?

3. In the closing paragraph, Ortberg sings the praises of his Internet friends. How effectively has he dispelled the commonly held notions he introduced in the opening of his essay?

7 from Is Social Media Disconnecting Us from the Big Picture?

JENNA WORTHAM

Jenna Wortham is an award-winning journalist and staff writer for the *New York Times Magazine*. She often writes about the intersection of technology and culture. She published the following article in the *New York Times Magazine* in 2016.

Maybe I shouldn't have been surprised that Donald Trump could be elected president, but I was. I live in Brooklyn and work in Manhattan, two of the most liberal places in the country. But even online, I wasn't seeing many signs of support for him. How did that blindness occur? Social media is my portal into the rest of the world — my periscope into the communities next to my community, into how the rest of the world thinks and feels. And it completely failed me.

In hindsight, that failure makes sense. I've spent nearly 10 years coaching Facebook — and Instagram and Twitter — on what kinds of news and photos I don't want to see, and they all behaved accordingly. Each time I liked an article, or clicked on a link, or hid another, the algorithms that curate my streams took notice and showed me only what they thought I wanted to see. That meant I didn't realize that most of my family members, who live in rural Virginia, were voicing their support for Trump online, and I didn't see any of the pro-Trump memes that were in heavy circulation before the election. I never saw a Trump hat or a sign or a shirt in my feeds, and the only Election Day selfies I saw were of people declaring their support for Hillary Clinton.

To be clear, I'm not blaming the algorithms for what I assume to be their role in augmenting my worldview. They did exactly what I told them to do, blocking out racist, misogynist and anti-immigrant comments, hiding anyone who didn't support Black Lives Matter, all with such deftness that I had no idea that a candidate who ran a campaign on exactly those values had gained enough popularity to win the election. But considering that more than 40 percent of our country's population consumes news on Facebook, finding alternative perspectives shouldn't have been that hard. I knew about Eli Pariser's theory on filter bubbles, or the idea that online personalization distorts the type of information we see, and even so, I still chose to let algorithms shape how I perceive the world. Everything I could want to see is available at my fingertips, and yet I didn't look. . . .

Most social media — like Facebook and Instagram — is curated by software built to manage the high influx of information flowing into it, but there have still been a few islands of digital wilderness, a Galápagos of sorts, where culture thrived untouched. They included Vine (whose closure was announced in October) and Snapchat, and even Tumblr, which were homes for marginalized ideas, theories and lifestyles.

The video-sharing app Vine was the first place I got a glimpse of cultures beyond my own, including those of the Middle East. I was able to see how some women there wanted us to see them: prospering, aware. A young woman living in Saudi Arabia who goes by the name Amy Roko used Vine to show clips of herself living her life — her version of normalcy — at the mall, 5 goofing off at home. In her most viral video, she stares into the camera, her face covered in a niqab, save for her perfectly outlined eyes. "[expletive] called me ugly," she snaps. "I said, [expletive] where?" The emphasis on the last word becomes the punch line as she whips off one niqab to reveal a second underneath. I was thrilled to realize that women living there could have a sense of humor similar to my own.

Vine was born as an app and intended to be a social community. But Vine links could be shared independent of the network, and people did so with abandon, meaning that Vines appeared scattershot around the web, defying the sorting mechanism of streams and feeds. They could land on your screen via text message, direct message, email.

Roko's Vine was a riff on one originally posted by a young black American named Brionna London, who was miffed that someone thought she needed makeup to be pretty. You can draw a straight line from brown women in Saudi Arabia to black women in America, a marvel unto itself, a window into the way the internet flattens space and time — a vivid example of its fulfilling its promise to bridge divides. At Vine's peak, it had more than 200 million monthly users who watched videos billions of times, and it excelled at showing these sorts of commonalities: that, say, black kids in New Orleans lived and looked a lot like white kids in Florida. (At the very least, they shared a similar humor and taste in music, which gave me hope that they would share a sense of humanity as well.). . .

In its earlier days, Snapchat offered its own version of cultural exchange. The app had an incredible series on "city life" that gave users direct windows into different worlds. People submitted short video diaries about life in their cities, which the company compiled into a single video, viewable by anyone using the app. I remember feeling delighted watching people in Istanbul and São Paulo showing off their routines and customs. But the company is now prioritizing "live stories," which feature more mainstream events like the Super Bowl and music festivals. The effect is still fascinating, but less intimate. Snapchat seems to be betting that people are more interested in the familiar.

The future of Tumblr, the blogging platform whose endless warren of rabbit holes about gender theory, critical feminist thought and identity politics is unlike any other on the internet, is the most uncertain. Yahoo, its parent company, succumbed to financial struggles and has announced plans to be acquired by Verizon, raising questions about the future of its properties.

What we're seeing with Snapchat, Tumblr and Vine reflects a larger shift in the social-media economy. User-generated content, by and large, is not lucrative at a scale that satisfies investors, and as a result, most social-media companies are changing direction toward other revenue streams. One of the more significant shifts is the move into social messaging. Semiprivate messaging applications — group text threads and applications like WhatsApp (which is owned by Facebook) and Slack — have grown in popularity as people move away from public arenas for conversation, a shift caused in part by spikes in unchecked harassment on major social networks. New features are introduced daily, it seems, to make messaging with your friends more "fun." . . . These new messaging features work to bind private groups tighter together, by making it more fun to talk to one another than to engage with the world at large.

What happens when we would rather look inward? I have found something of an answer

10

in a short story called "The Great Silence," by Ted Chiang, about humankind's search for signs of alien life. The story is narrated by a parrot in Arecibo, Puerto Rico, home to one of the largest radio telescopes in the world. "Their desire to make a connection is so strong that they've created an ear capable of hearing across the universe," the creature begins. "But I and my fellow parrots are right here. Why aren't they interested in listening to our voices?" The paradox is not to be missed: We are more interested in locating alien species than understanding the humanity among the species we already live

with. The story ends on a somber note. "Human activity has brought my kind to the brink of extinction," the narrator explains. "They didn't do it maliciously. They just weren't paying attention."

Chiang's lesson hits hard in this new political and cultural moment. Social media seemed to promise a way to better connect with people; instead it seems to have made it easier to tune out the people we don't agree with. But if we can't pay attention to one another, we might as well not live on the same planet at all.

QUESTIONS

1. In the opening paragraph, Jenna Wortham states, "Social media is my portal into the rest of the world — my periscope into the communities next to my community, into how the rest of the world thinks and feels." To what extent does social media play a similar role in your life?

2. What does Wortham mean when she says that she has spent nearly ten years "coaching" various social media platforms "on what kinds of news and photos [she doesn't] want to see" (para. 2)?

3. What does Wortham man by the term "curated" (paras. 2 and 4) as it applies to social media?

4. What qualities of the video-sharing app Vine does Wortham praise? What does she mean when she characterizes it as "born as an app and intended to be a social community" (para. 6)?

5. How does Wortham support her argument that social media is a "window into the way the Internet flattens space and time" (para. 7)? What is an

example from your own experience that illustrates such a "window"?

6. Wortham asserts that the uncertain futures of Snapchat, Tumblr, and Vine reflect "a larger shift in the social-media economy" (para. 10). How does this claim relate to her larger point?

7. At the end of the article, Wortham refers to a short story by Ted Chiang. Assuming that her readers are likely to be unfamiliar with it, she summarizes its plot, quotes from it, and discusses what she believes to be its central paradox. How effectively does this segment of her article support her criticism of social media?

8. What, essentially, is Wortham's principal concern about the direction social media in general are going? Based on your own experience and observations, do you agree or disagree with her assessment? Explain.

8 The Constant Sharing Is Making Us Competitive and Depressed

EMERSON CSORBA

An entrepreneur, consultant, and educational policy advisor, Emerson Csorba is a fellow of the Royal Society of Arts and Canada's Public Policy Forum. In a debate with Noa Gafni Slaney, CEO of Impact Squared, Csorba contributed the following piece as part of the *New York Times*'s Room for Debate forum on "digital connectedness" in 2016.

The relationships we form are superficial at best, and the social comparison that these connections fosters can be psychologically damaging.

Over the past three years, I have conducted hundreds of one-on-one interviews with early and mid-career professionals on how they see their lives and careers developing in an uncertain world. Through these discussions, a theme of "ruthless comparison" emerges, where we become acutely aware of how our friends and colleagues portray themselves online. Noa Gafni Slaney highlights campaigns such as the ALS Ice Bucket Challenge and Lean In, where the collective action of celebrities and average citizens creates a social pressure for others to engage in a particular socially conscious activity. While useful in generating real-life action, this pressure to engage is in large part based on social comparison: a need to portray oneself in a particular light to appear to be a person committed to doing good. These online actions are increasingly required to "keep up with the Joneses" in a connected world.

Although many interviewees were aware that these self-representations are illusory, they nevertheless felt pressured to engage in this competition, sharing their achievements and experiences over social media to show others how they are keeping up. This fuels a perpetual competition, focused on the sharing of successes and other updates, regardless of how accurately these portrayals represent real life — and they rarely do.

This sharing has psychological consequences. A handful of studies, including one recently conducted by the University of Michigan, suggest that increased Facebook usage contributes to anxiety and even depression. By constantly seeing what others are doing, and in paying attention to their lives as they seem to be unfolding in real-time, our anxiety and uncertainty as to whether we are leading lives that fulfill our own potential deepens.

This vicious cycle is difficult to escape; it requires a significant amount of confidence in oneself to both remain connected and see past the charade we collectively engage in. For every +SocialGood campaign that legitimately builds in-person dialogue, there are countless online campaigns fuelled by individual or corporate need to "curate" images that compare favorably with those of society's influencers. Based on my interviews with early and mid-career professionals, many individuals are at a crossroads in how to act in their online worlds. Skeptical of the authenticity' of online activity, they nevertheless feel trapped in a society where sharing is celebrated.

Indeed, we must be weary of the comparisons that our connectedness encourages, knowing that these comparisons are often psychologically exhausting and, in some cases, harmful.

5

QUESTIONS

1. What does Emerson Csorba mean when he says that "a theme of 'ruthless comparison' emerges" (para. 2) in the context of online spaces?

2. What does Csorba claim is the problem with self-representation online for early and mid-career professionals? How does it contribute to "anxiety and even depression" (para. 4)?

3. Based on his research, Csorba concludes that although people are "[s]keptical of the authenticity of online activity, they nevertheless feel trapped in a society where sharing is celebrated" (para. 5). To what extent does your own experience with social media — and its role in your academic life — reflect or challenge this dilemma?

MAKING CONNECTIONS

1. Which of these texts most strongly supports the viewpoint that Sven Birkerts expresses, and why?

2. How might Dex Torricke-Barton or Laura Hudson use the data from the Pew Research Center as evidence in their arguments?

3. In what ways does Emma Sterland's op-ed challenge Emerson Csorba's viewpoint?

4. How would Hudson advise the professionals that Csorba refers to in his editorial? What would she likely have to say about the anxiety they feel to "share" in in the name of social interaction while really being motivated by what they see as competition and exaggeration?

5. What cautions might Jenna Wortham offer Torricke-Barton in response to his optimistic claims about the unifying potential he sees in the Internet?

6. In what ways would Daniel Mallory Ortberg likely agree with Wortham?

ENTERING THE CONVERSATION

As you respond to the following prompts, support your argument with references to at least three of the sources in this Conversation on Building Online Communities. For help using sources, see Chapter 4.

1. Smart phones, email, social networking sites, blogs, and other electronic communication have made our world smaller and increased the pace at which we live life. Have these inventions also given us a new sense of community or opened up communities that would otherwise be closed to us? Have they lowered or expanded our standards of what *community* means?

2. Write an essay explaining whether you believe that online communities are more effective as a way to maintain relationships we already have or to develop new relationships.

3. What are your two most serious concerns about the types of communities that the digital environment fosters? How would you address each of them? Use at least three of the sources in this Conversation to develop your position.

4. Suppose that a relative or friend who is in middle school asks your advice about how to become involved in social media; that is, the middle schooler wants to know which online communities are best for him or her, what are the merits and/or liabilities of joining those communities, and what he or she should watch out for as potential dangers. Respond via email, Instagram, or a text with your advice. Keep your audience in mind as you write.

5. Polarization, fake news, self-aggrandizement — these are all criticisms of online communities that reinforce a person's existing ideas rather than introducing (even discussing) new perspectives. What measures can someone your age take to combat such self-serving and insular thinking and foster online communities that are safe and respectful spaces for discussing even the most controversial subjects?

6. Sven Birkerts offers the most philosophical position about the impact of the internet to create what he calls "the new model of disengaged engagement" (para. 13). Write a response to him explaining why you largely support or challenge his perspective.

7. In her groundbreaking book *It's Complicated: The Social Lives of Networked Teens*, researcher danah boyd argues: "Far from being a panacea, the internet simply sheds new light on the divisive social dynamics that plague contemporary society." What do you think she means by this? In a well-written essay that draws from at least three sources in this Conversation, defend, challenge, or qualify her position.

8. In a 2017 article for the *New Yorker* magazine, journalist Nathan Heller wrote that in the early 2000s, "e-mail was the most wanton kind of media," but today that is no longer the case:

[P]eople now have indecent texts at home, manic Slack threads in the workplace, and, for just about every venue, crankish, boastful Facebook, filled with babies and bad news. As the scandals of the past few years show, however, indecorum hasn't left our inboxes, and the lives behind the @ symbol may still have something to hide. For many of us, that seems all right. The urgent project at the moment isn't adding more information to the cultural file; it is understanding how meaning is produced, how stories wrought from narrow data samples seed and grow in the public imagination. . . . As a sign of twenty-first-century progress, it can't come too soon.

Discuss to what extent you believe Heller's comments are accurate and what measures you believe would be most likely to increase the civility of online communication. Use your own experience and at least two of the sources from this conversation to develop your position.

from Letter from Birmingham Jail

MARTIN LUTHER KING JR.

One of the basic points in your statement is that the action that I and my associates have taken in Birmingham is untimely. Some have asked: "Why didn't you give the new city administration time to act?" The only answer that I can give to this query is that the new Birmingham administration must be prodded about as much as the outgoing one, before it will act. We are sadly mistaken if we feel that the election of Albert Boutwell as mayor will bring the millennium to Birmingham. While Mr. Boutwell is a much more gentle person than Mr. Connor, they are both segregationists, dedicated to maintenance of the status quo. I have hoped that Mr. Boutwell will be reasonable enough to see the futility of massive resistance to desegregation. But he will not see this without pressure from devotees of civil rights. My friends, I must say to you that we have not made a single gain in civil rights without determined legal and nonviolent pressure. Lamentably, it is an historical fact that privileged groups seldom give up their privileges voluntarily. Individuals may see the moral light and voluntarily give up their unjust posture, but, as Reinhold Niebuhr[1] has reminded us, groups tend to be more immoral than individuals.

We know through painful experience that freedom is never voluntarily given by the oppressor; it must be demanded by the oppressed. Frankly, I have yet to engage in a direct-action campaign that was "well timed" in the view of those who have not suffered unduly from the disease of segregation. For years now I have heard the word "Wait!" It rings in the ear of every Negro with piercing familiarity. This "Wait" has almost always meant "Never." We must come to see, with

one of our distinguished jurists, that "justice too long delayed is justice denied."

We have waited for more than 340 years for our constitutional and God-given rights. The nations of Asia and Africa are moving with jet-like speed toward gaining political independence, but we still creep at horse-and-buggy pace toward gaining a cup of coffee at a lunch counter. Perhaps it is easy for those who have never felt the stinging darts of segregation to say, "Wait." But when you have seen vicious mobs lynch your mothers and fathers at will and drown your sisters and brothers at whim; when you have seen hate-filled policemen curse, kick, and even kill your black brothers and sisters; when you see the vast majority of your twenty million Negro brothers smothering in an airtight cage of poverty in the midst of an affluent society; when you suddenly find your tongue twisted and your speech stammering as you seek to explain to your six-year-old daughter why she can't go to the public amusement park that has just been advertised on television, and see tears welling up in her eyes when she is told that Funtown is closed to colored children, and see ominous clouds of inferiority beginning to form in her little mental sky, and see her beginning to distort her personality by developing an unconscious bitterness toward white people; when you have to concoct an answer for a five-year-old son who is asking, "Daddy, why do white people treat colored people so mean?"; when you take a cross-country drive and find it necessary to sleep night after night in the uncomfortable corners of your automobile because no motel will accept you; when you are humiliated day in and day out by nagging signs reading "white" and "colored"; when your first name becomes "nigger," your middle name becomes "boy"

---

[1]Niebuhr (1892–1971) was a U.S. clergyman and a Protestant theologian. —Eds.

(however old you are) and your last name becomes "John," and your wife and mother are never given the respected title "Mrs."; when you are harried by day and haunted by night by the fact that you are a Negro, living constantly at tip-toe stance, never quite knowing what to expect next, and are plagued with inner fears and outer resentments; when you are forever fighting a degenerating sense of "nobodiness"` then you will understand why we find it difficult to wait. There comes a time when the cup of endurance runs over, and men are no longer willing to be plunged into the abyss of despair. I hope, sirs, you can understand our legitimate and unavoid-able impatience.

---

1. What stylistic device of King's is most evident throughout the selection?

   a. parallelism

   b. hyperbole

   c. colloquialism

   d. invective

   e. apostrophe

2. Which of the following claims does King leave *unsupported* by evidence?

   I. that, generally, groups act more immorally than individuals

   II. that, historically, those with privilege rarely give it up without being forced

   III. that the racial injustice in the South is too urgent and too long delayed to wait any longer

   a. I only

   b. II only

   c. II and III only

   d. I and II only

   e. I, II, and III

3. To what specific criticism is King responding in this excerpt?

   a. the claim that nonviolence is not effective in creating social change

   b. the claim that King's followers actually provoke violence by their actions

   c. the claim that the protests that King is helping to lead are poorly timed

   d. the claim that satisfactory advances in civil rights had already been made

   e. none of the above

4. The antithesis in the first sentence of paragraph 2 creates a(n)

   a. mandate for immediate action

   b. sense of the painful experiences of oppression

   c. reminder of the strength and power of the oppressor

   d. uncompromising threat to the oppressors

   e. none of the above

5. In paragraph 2, the words in quotation marks represent the language of

   a. those who have been in power

   b. the leaders of the civil rights movement

   c. the American people regarding political change

   d. King in the past to refer to the strategies of the civil rights movement

   e. church leaders to their church members

6. The long list of injustices and brutalities in paragraph 3 primarily provides

   a. evidence for the gains that the civil rights movement has made through putting pressure on leaders

   b. evidence to convince the readers to join the civil rights movement

   c. evidence for King's claim that the civil rights movement is an urgent matter and cannot wait

   d. examples of King's painful personal experiences

   e. an extended metaphor to illustrate the pain of oppression

7. King's use of second person in the paragraph 3 serves primarily as

   a. an appeal to reason

   b. an attempt to establish authority

c. an identification with shared values

d. an incitement to violence

e. an appeal to pathos

8. In the second sentence of paragraph 3, King uses figurative language to

a. suggest that Asia and Africa follow the example set by the United States.

b. contrast the modern political progress being made on other continents with the status of civil rights in America

c. show parallels between Asia, Africa, and America in order to build global solidarity with civil rights movements among the continents

d. emphasize the similarities between the independence movements in Asia and Africa, with the civil rights movement in the United States

e. show the inevitable movement toward civil rights worldwide

9. King's use of the first-person plural serves primarily to

a. create an adversarial dichotomy between the civil rights movement and the audience

b. portray all Americans as a united group

c. refer to the civil rights movement as a unified force

d. allow him to identify with civil rights activists as well as Americans as a whole

e. muddy the issues by never allowing the reader to clearly identify whom King intends to include in the "we" group

10. What form of parallelism is used throughout the paragraph 3 in the list of injustices King presents?

a. anaphora

b. antithesis

c. zeugma

d. epistrophe

e. chiasmus

---

from **Where I Lived and What I Lived For**

HENRY DAVID THOREAU

Shams and delusions are esteemed for soundless truths, while reality is fabulous. If men would steadily observe realities only, and not allow themselves to be deluded, life, to compare it with such things as we know, would be like a fairy tale and the Arabian Nights' Entertainments. If we respected only what is inevitable and has a right to be, music and poetry would resound along the streets. When we are unhurried and wise, we perceive that only great and worthy things have any permanent and absolute existence, that petty fears and petty pleasures are but the shadow of the reality. This is always exhilarating and sublime. By closing the eyes and slumbering, and consenting to be deceived by shows, men establish and confirm their daily life of routine and habit everywhere, which still is built on purely illusory foundations. Children, who play life, discern its true law and relations more clearly than men, who fail to live it worthily, but who think that they are wiser by experience, that is, by failure. I have read in a Hindoo book, that "there was a king's son, who, being expelled in infancy from his native city, was brought up by a forester, and, growing up to maturity in that state, imagined himself to belong to the barbarous race with which he lived. One of his father's ministers having discovered him, revealed to him what he was, and the misconception of his character was removed, and he knew himself to be a prince. So soul," continues the Hindoo philosopher, "from the circumstances in which it is placed, mistakes its own character, until the truth is revealed to it by some holy teacher and then it knows itself to be *Brahme*."[1] I perceive that we inhabitants of New England live this mean life that we do because our vision does not penetrate the surface of things. We think that that *is* which *appears* to be. If a man should walk through this town and see only the reality, where, think you, would the "Milldam"[2] go to? If he should give us

---

[1]One of the three main Hindu gods, now spelled *Brahma*. —Eds.
[2]Concord's business center. —Eds.

...count of the realities he beheld there, we should not recognize the place in his description. Look at the meetinghouse, or a courthouse, or a jail, or a shop, or a dwelling-house, and say what that thing really is before a true gaze, and they would all go to pieces in your account of them. Men esteem truth remote, in the outskirts of the system behind the farthest star, before Adam and after the last man. In eternity there is indeed something true and sublime. But all these times and places and occasions are now and here. God

himself culminates in the present moment, and will never be more divine in the lapse of all the ages. And we are enabled to apprehend at all what is sublime and noble only by the perpetual instilling and drenching of the reality that surrounds us. The universe constantly and obediently answers to our conceptions; whether we travel fast or slow, the track is laid for us. Let us spend our lives in conceiving then. The poet or the artist never yet had so fair and noble a design but some of his posterity at least could accomplish it.

---

1. In the sentence that begins, "By closing the eyes . . . " the speaker uses sleep as a metaphor for

   a. the eternal divinity of mankind
   b. laziness
   c. willing submission to the expectations of a daily routine based on false assumptions
   d. the necessary imposition of daily routine onto the consciousness of humankind
   e. nothing; the speaker is referring literally to sleep that all humans need

2. In context, the word "fabulous" in the first sentence could best be said to mean

   a. mythical
   b. lovely
   c. frightening
   d. extraordinary
   e. true

3. The rhetorical technique used to make the ironic assertion in the first sentence is

   a. appeal to emotion
   b. apostrophe
   c. syllogism
   d. antithesis
   e. analogy

4. The tone of the second sentence is

   a. melancholy and somewhat hopeless
   b. urgent yet ironic
   c. critical and judgmental
   d. confident yet disingenuous
   e. none of the above

5. In the sentence that begins "This is always exhilarating," the word "This" refers to:

   a. the reality of daily life
   b. "When we are unhurried and wise"
   c. "permanent and absolute existence"
   d. "closing the eyes"
   e. sleep as a metaphor for self-delusion

6. At the end of the passage, there is a shift from arguing for an immersion in reality toward

   a. deluding oneself with fables
   b. belief in the Divine
   c. questioning our perceptions of reality
   d. criticizing poets and artists for condoning and promoting fictions
   e. creating new possibilities by conceiving ideas based in reality

7. According to the passage, which of the following inferences can be made about the speaker's concept of reality?

   a. It is heavily based on what humans perceive through the senses, unfiltered by preconceptions.
   b. It is almost unrecognizable because humans are accustomed to perce...
   c. It is not limited to the life of the also includes timeless truths...
   d. Divinity can be found only... the current moment, n... past.
   e. All of the above...

643

The purpose of the story from the "Hindoo book" is

   a. to demonstrate that even a worthy student needs a teacher

   b. to demonstrate that adults should trust the perceptions of children

   c. to re-create the sense of the sublime for the reader

   d. to support the idea that all humans should live worthily

   e. to question the reader's worthiness in pursuit of the sublime

9. Based on the arguments in the passage, which of the following statements best represents the speaker's ideas about art, music, and poetry?

   a. They are dangerous misrepresentations of reality that can lead humans astray in their perceptions.

   b. They promote mythologies, but are largely harmless in their impact.

   c. They are the most truthful representations of reality.

   d. They most faithfully document facts.

   e. They are trivialities not worthy of a person seeking to observe reality only.

10. In the lines following the sentence begin. "I perceive that," what is the rhetorical effect of the use of "we" and the references to New England and, more specifically, to Concord, Massachusetts?

   a. The speaker refers to himself in the plural to refer to the self he was, the self he is, and the self he will be.

   b. The speaker flatters the audience, eliciting good will from them.

   c. The speaker places himself as a member of the audience who also needs to spend more time immersing himself in reality.

   d. The speaker creates a sense of separation between "we" and "they," implying an adversarial relationship with his opponents.

   e. The speaker attempts to unify the audience into a community of action.

11. The overall tone of the passage is best described as

   a. satirically distant and cavalier

   b. angry yet controlled

   c. critical yet hopeful

   d. melancholy and nostalgic

   e. enraged and unforgiving

COMMUNITY

Now that you have examined a number of texts that focus on community, explore this topic yourself by synthesizing your own ideas and the readings. You might want to do more research or use readings from other classes as you write.

1. Write about the discussion that might ensue among several of the writers you have studied in this chapter if they were to focus on the following question: What are the characteristics of a productive and successful community at the start of the twenty-first century?

2. Creating a community of like-minded people is the principle behind the development of many charter schools. Select a charter school in your area, and examine it as an intentional community, defined as "a group of people who have chosen to live together with a common purpose, working cooperatively to create a lifestyle that reflects their shared core values."

3. Are hate groups, such as the Ku Klux Klan, communities? Many would argue yes, that they fit most definitions of *community*, despite the fact that they are counterproductive. Choose a controversial community (such as the punk community, a country club, or a secret society), examine its structure and purpose, and argue for or against its value to its members and to the larger community.

4. Many colleges and universities are developing what they call living-learning communities, in which students choose to live together as a group centered around a theme, which could be anything from Chinese culture to women in science. Some critics believe such groupings are limiting because the students are not exposed to different viewpoints and interests. Others object because they believe segregation based on race, ethnicity, or religion does not contribute to the mission of higher education. What do you think of living-learning communities? Will you choose to live in one when you go to college? Why or why not?

5. Examine a community that is organized around shared values but not geographic proximity. What holds that community together? What do members gain from it? Why does it continue?

6. Following is a description of a coffeehouse called Java from the novel *Queen of Dreams* by Chitra Banerjee Divakaruni.

   > Java demands nothing from them [customers] except their money. It allows them to remain unknown. . . . And yet they have community, too, as much of it as they want: the comfortable company of a roomful of nameless-faceless folks just like themselves, happy to be alone, to gaze into middle distance, to notice no one.

   Discuss this concept of community, explain how it can function for some, and describe examples of it that you have seen.

7. Write an essay about making the transition from one community to another and how that change affects your sense of self. The transition might be from one country to another or simply from one neighborhood or group of friends to another. Include descriptions of the communities as well as your own emotional responses. You might also include photographs as part of the essay.

8. The author Kurt Vonnegut Jr. wrote, "What should young people do with their lives today? Many things, obviously. But the most daring thing is to create stable communities in which the terrible disease of loneliness can be cured." Write a speech that you would deliver to a group of your peers (identify which group) that uses Vonnegut's idea as your main point and recommends ways to "create stable communities."

9
Sports

COMMUNITY

Now that you have examined a number of texts that focus on community, explore this topic yourself by synthesizing your own ideas and the readings. You might want to do more research or use readings from other classes as you write.

1. Write about the discussion that might ensue among several of the writers you have studied in this chapter if they were to focus on the following question: What are the characteristics of a productive and successful community at the start of the twenty-first century?

2. Creating a community of like-minded people is the principle behind the development of many charter schools. Select a charter school in your area, and examine it as an intentional community, defined as "a group of people who have chosen to live together with a common purpose, working cooperatively to create a lifestyle that reflects their shared core values."

3. Are hate groups, such as the Ku Klux Klan, communities? Many would argue yes, that they fit most definitions of *community*, despite the fact that they are counterproductive. Choose a controversial community (such as the punk community, a country club, or a secret society), examine its structure and purpose, and argue for or against its value to its members and to the larger community.

4. Many colleges and universities are developing what they call living-learning communities, in which students choose to live together as a group centered around a theme, which could be anything from Chinese culture to women in science. Some critics believe such groupings are limiting because the students are not exposed to different viewpoints and interests. Others object because they believe segregation based on race, ethnicity, or religion does not contribute to the mission of higher education. What do you think of living-learning communities? Will you choose to live in one when you go to college? Why or why not?

5. Examine a community that is organized around shared values but not geographic proximity. What holds that community together? What do members gain from it? Why does it continue?

6. Following is a description of a coffeehouse called Java from the novel *Queen of Dreams* by Chitra Banerjee Divakaruni.

   > Java demands nothing from them [customers] except their money. It allows them to remain unknown. . . . And yet they have community, too, as much of it as they want: the comfortable company of a roomful of nameless-faceless folks just like themselves, happy to be alone, to gaze into middle distance, to notice no one.

   Discuss this concept of community, explain how it can function for some, and describe examples of it that you have seen.

7. Write an essay about making the transition from one community to another and how that change affects your sense of self. The transition might be from one country to another or simply from one neighborhood or group of friends to another. Include descriptions of the communities as well as your own emotional responses. You might also include photographs as part of the essay.

8. The author Kurt Vonnegut Jr. wrote, "What should young people do with their lives today? Many things, obviously. But the most daring thing is to create stable communities in which the terrible disease of loneliness can be cured." Write a speech that you would deliver to a group of your peers (identify which group) that uses Vonnegut's idea as your main point and recommends ways to "create stable communities."

9
Sports

COMMUNITY

Now that you have examined a number of texts that focus on community, explore this topic yourself by synthesizing your own ideas and the readings. You might want to do more research or use readings from other classes as you write.

1. Write about the discussion that might ensue among several of the writers you have studied in this chapter if they were to focus on the following question: What are the characteristics of a productive and successful community at the start of the twenty-first century?

2. Creating a community of like-minded people is the principle behind the development of many charter schools. Select a charter school in your area, and examine it as an intentional community, defined as "a group of people who have chosen to live together with a common purpose, working cooperatively to create a lifestyle that reflects their shared core values."

3. Are hate groups, such as the Ku Klux Klan, communities? Many would argue yes, that they fit most definitions of *community*, despite the fact that they are counterproductive. Choose a controversial community (such as the punk community, a country club, or a secret society), examine its structure and purpose, and argue for or against its value to its members and to the larger community.

4. Many colleges and universities are developing what they call living-learning communities, in which students choose to live together as a group centered around a theme, which could be anything from Chinese culture to women in science. Some critics believe such groupings are limiting because the students are not exposed to different viewpoints and interests. Others object because they believe segregation based on race, ethnicity, or religion does not contribute to the mission of higher education. What do you think of living-learning communities? Will you choose to live in one when you go to college? Why or why not?

5. Examine a community that is organized around shared values but not geographic proximity. What holds that community together? What do members gain from it? Why does it continue?

6. Following is a description of a coffeehouse called Java from the novel *Queen of Dreams* by Chitra Banerjee Divakaruni.

> Java demands nothing from them [customers] except their money. It allows them to remain unknown. . . . And yet they have community, too, as much of it as they want: the comfortable company of a roomful of nameless-faceless folks just like themselves, happy to be alone, to gaze into middle distance, to notice no one.

Discuss this concept of community, explain how it can function for some, and describe examples of it that you have seen.

7. Write an essay about making the transition from one community to another and how that change affects your sense of self. The transition might be from one country to another or simply from one neighborhood or group of friends to another. Include descriptions of the communities as well as your own emotional responses. You might also include photographs as part of the essay.

8. The author Kurt Vonnegut Jr. wrote, "What should young people do with their lives today? Many things, obviously. But the most daring thing is to create stable communities in which the terrible disease of loneliness can be cured." Write a speech that you would deliver to a group of your peers (identify which group) that uses Vonnegut's idea as your main point and recommends ways to "create stable communities."

9
Sports

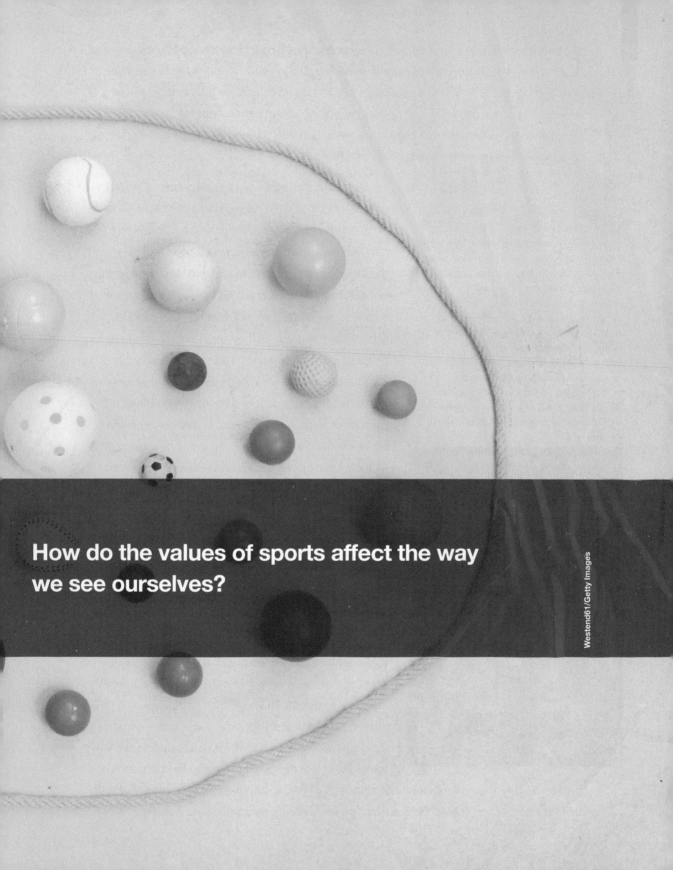

How do the values of sports affect the way we see ourselves?

Love them or hate them, sports are a central part of our modern world. Athletes are cultural icons; sports dominate television, radio, even film. Once the purview of men and boys, the subject of sports — opinions on its ethics, its future, its place in society — is now open to everyone. And in some ways, the line separating the professional from the spectator has blurred. Weekend athletes train like professionals; even couch potatoes participate in fantasy leagues.

▼
_____

During the 1968 Olympics, Americans Tommie Smith and John Carlos won gold and bronze, respectively, for the Men's 200 Meter Final. At the medal ceremony, both men gave the black power salute during the national anthem. Afterward, they were subject to harsh criticism for making such an overtly political gesture. However, public opinion has since changed, and their protest is now considered courageous.

Can you think of any political statements or gestures made by modern-day athletes? Do you think public opinion about their meaning and effectiveness will change in the future? Explain why or why not.

Rolls Press/Popperfoto/Getty Images

We speak the language of sports. We are asked to play to win, play by the rules, play fair, be team players, be good sports. We're taught to be good losers; we're reminded that the best defense is a good offense — and the other way around. We're told that life is a game of chance, but that we can sometimes level the playing field. These exhortations are as at home in a grade school kickball game as they are in politics and business. Why are we so comfortable with this shorthand?

The questions raised by sports are out of proportion to the tiny number of people who play professional sports and are front and center in the news — earning salaries that top those of movie stars. At their best, sports pros are hailed as role models; at their worst, as scourges on society. Is our attraction to professional athletes healthy? Do we learn from their grit, from their strength and commitment to training, or do they encourage unhealthy narcissism and dangerous habits?

The selections in this chapter explore many of the questions raised by our interest in sports and the effect of that interest on everyday life. The readings look at the star power of our professional athletes and the thrill of tapping into our own potential for athletic achievement. They ask questions about ethics; they make us think about whether our passion for both following and participating in sports is a way for us to, at least temporarily, avoid the demands of real life. Finally, they ask whether the language of the playing field and the model of the professional athlete enliven communication and help us become better people.

The Silent Season of a Hero

GAY TALESE

Gay Talese (b. 1932) began life on the small island of Ocean City, New Jersey. As the son of a southern Italian immigrant growing up Catholic in a Protestant town, Talese identified himself as an outsider. He is known for writing the "unnoticed story," reporting the angle ignored by others or the news that others thought was not newsworthy. Recognized for his elegant style, Talese is considered one of the founders of *New Journalism*, a term coined in the 1960s to describe the work of writers such as Talese, Tom Wolfe, and Hunter S. Thompson. New Journalism is characterized by the use of elements of fiction to get at the story behind the story. New Journalists set scenes, include dialogue, and accept their own presence as part of the drama of the story. The following selection appeared in *Esquire* in 1966.

David Gahr/Getty Images

"I would like to take the great DiMaggio fishing,"
the old man said. "They say his father was a fisher-
man. Maybe he was as poor as we are and would
understand."

　　　— Ernest Hemingway, *The Old Man and the Sea*

It was not quite spring, the silent season before the search for salmon, and the old fishermen of San Francisco were either painting their boats or repairing their nets along the pier or sitting in the sun talking quietly among themselves, watching the tourists come and go, and smiling, now, as a pretty girl paused to take their picture. She was about 25, healthy and blue-eyed and wearing a turtleneck sweater, and she had long, flowing blonde hair that she brushed back a few times before clicking her camera. The fishermen, looking at her, made admiring comments, but she did not understand because they spoke a Sicilian dialect; nor did she understand the tall gray-haired man in a dark suit who stood watching her from behind a big bay window on the second floor of DiMaggio's Restaurant that overlooks the pier.

He watched until she left, lost in the crowd of newly arrived tourists that had just come down the hill by cable car. Then he sat down again at the table in the restaurant, finishing his tea and lighting another cigarette, his fifth in the last half hour. It was 11:30 in the morning. None of the other tables was occupied, and the only sounds came from the bar, where a liquor salesman was laughing at something the headwaiter had said. But then the salesman, his briefcase under his arm, headed for the door, stopping briefly to peek into the dining room and call out, "See you later, Joe." Joe DiMaggio turned and waved at the salesman. Then the room was quiet again.

At 51, DiMaggio was a most distinguished-looking man, aging as gracefully as he had played on the ball field, impeccable in his tailoring, his nails manicured, his 6-foot-2 body seeming as lean and capable as when he posed for the portrait that hangs in the restaurant and shows him in Yankee Stadium, swinging from the heels at a pitch thrown 20 years ago. His gray hair was thinning at the crown, but just barely, and his face was lined in the right places, and his expression, once as sad and haunted as a matador's, was more in repose these days, though, as now, tension had returned and he chain-smoked and occasionally paced the floor and looked out the window at the people below. In the crowd was a man he did not wish to see.

The man had met DiMaggio in New York. This week he had come to San Francisco and had telephoned several times, but none of the calls had been returned because DiMaggio suspected that the man, who had said he was doing research on some vague sociological project, really wanted to delve into DiMaggio's private life and that of DiMaggio's former wife, Marilyn Monroe. DiMaggio would never tolerate this. The memory of her death is still very painful to him, and yet, because he keeps it to himself, some people are not sensitive to it. One night in a supper club, a woman who had been drinking approached his table, and when he did not ask her to join him, she snapped:

"All right, I guess I'm *not* Marilyn Monroe." 5

He ignored her remark, but when she repeated it, he replied, barely controlling his anger, "No — I wish you were, but you're not."

The tone of his voice softened her, and she asked, "Am I saying something wrong?"

"You already have," he said. "Now will you please leave me alone?"

His friends on the wharf, understanding him as they do, are very careful when discussing him with strangers, knowing that should they inadvertently betray a confidence, he will not denounce them but rather will never speak to them again; this comes from a sense of propriety not inconsistent in the man who also, after Marilyn Monroe's death, directed that fresh flowers be placed on her grave "forever."

Some of the older fishermen who have known 10 DiMaggio all his life remember him as a small boy who helped clean his father's boat, and as a young man who sneaked away and used a broken oar as a bat on the sandlots nearby. His father, a small mustachioed man known as Zio Pepe, would become infuriated and call him *lagnuso*, lazy, *meschino*, good-for-nothing, but in 1936 Zio Pepe was among those who cheered when Joe

DiMaggio returned to San Francisco after his first season with the New York Yankees and was carried along the wharf on the shoulders of the fishermen.

The fishermen also remember how, after his retirement in 1951, DiMaggio brought his second wife, Marilyn, to live near the wharf, and sometimes they would be seen early in the morning fishing off DiMaggio's boat, the *Yankee Clipper*, now docked quietly in the marina, and in the evening they would be sitting and talking on the pier. They had arguments, too, the fishermen knew, and one night Marilyn was seen running hysterically, crying, as she ran, along the road away from the pier, with Joe following. But the fishermen pretended they did not see this; it was none of their affair. They knew that Joe wanted her to stay in San Francisco and avoid the sharks in Hollywood, but she was confused and torn then — "She was a child," they said — and even today DiMaggio loathes Los Angeles and many of the people in it. He no longer speaks to his onetime friend, Frank Sinatra, who had befriended Marilyn in her final years, and he also is cool to Dean Martin and Peter Lawford and Lawford's former wife, Pat, who once gave a party at which she introduced Marilyn Monroe to Robert Kennedy, and the two of them danced often that night, Joe heard, and he did not take it well. He was possessive of her that year, his close friends say, because Marilyn and he had planned to remarry; but before they could she was dead, and DiMaggio banned the Lawfords and Sinatra and many Hollywood people from her funeral. When Marilyn Monroe's attorney complained that DiMaggio was keeping her friends away, DiMaggio answered coldly, "If it weren't for those friends persuading her to stay in Hollywood, she would still be alive."

Joe DiMaggio now spends most of the year in San Francisco, and each day tourists, noticing the name on the restaurant, ask the men on the wharf if they ever see him. Oh, yes, the men say, they see him nearly every day; they have not seen him yet this morning, they add, but he should be arriving shortly. So the tourists continue to walk along the piers past the crab vendors, under the circling sea gulls, past the fish-'n'-chip stands, sometimes stopping to watch a large vessel steaming toward the Golden Gate Bridge, which, to their dismay, is painted red. Then they visit the Wax Museum, where there is a life-size figure of DiMaggio in uniform, and walk across the street and spend a quarter to peer through the silver telescopes focused on the island of Alcatraz, which is no longer a federal prison. Then they return to ask the men if DiMaggio has been seen. Not yet, the men say, although they notice his blue Impala parked in the lot next to the restaurant. Sometimes tourists will walk into the restaurant and have lunch and will see him sitting calmly in a corner signing autographs and being extremely gracious with everyone. At other times, as on this particular morning when the man from New York chose to visit, DiMaggio was tense and suspicious.

When the man entered the restaurant from the side steps leading to the dining room, he saw DiMaggio standing near the window, talking with an elderly maître d' named Charles Friscia. Not wanting to walk in and risk intrusion, the man asked one of DiMaggio's nephews to inform Joe of his presence. When DiMaggio got the message, he quickly turned and left Friscia and disappeared through an exit leading down to the kitchen.

Astonished and confused, the visitor stood in the hall. A moment later Friscia appeared and the man asked, "Did Joe leave?"

"Joe who?" Friscia replied.   15

"Joe DiMaggio!"

"Haven't seen him," Friscia said.

"You haven't *seen* him! He was standing right next to you a second ago!"

"It wasn't me," Friscia said.

"You were standing next to him. I saw you. In   20 the dining room."

"You must be mistaken," Friscia said, softly, seriously. "It wasn't me."

"You *must* be kidding," the man said angrily, turning and leaving the restaurant. Before he could get to his car, however, DiMaggio's nephew came running after him and said, "Joe wants to see you."

RWK/AP Images

This photograph, taken less than a month after *Esquire* published "The Silent Season of a Hero," shows Joe DiMaggio teaching young boys how to swing a baseball bat in a clinic at San Francisco's Golden Gate Park.

How does this image portray DiMaggio? To what extent do you see this portrayal reflected in Talese's essay?

He returned, expecting to see DiMaggio waiting for him. Instead he was handed a telephone. The voice was powerful and deep and so tense that the quick sentences ran together.

"You are invading my rights. I did not ask you to come. I assume you have a lawyer. You must have a lawyer, get your lawyer!"

"I came as a friend," the man interrupted. 25

"That's beside the point," DiMaggio said. "I have my privacy. I do not want it violated. You'd better get a lawyer. . . ." Then, pausing, DiMaggio asked, "Is my nephew there?"

He was not.

"Then wait where you are."

A moment later DiMaggio appeared, tall and red-faced, erect and beautifully dressed in his dark suit and white shirt with the gray silk tie and the gleaming silver cuff links. He moved with his big steps toward the man and handed him an airmail envelope unopened that the man had written from New York.

"Here," DiMaggio said. "This is yours." 30

Then DiMaggio sat down at a small table. He said nothing, just lit a cigarette and waited, legs crossed, his head held high and back so as to reveal the intricate construction of his nose, a fine sharp tip above the big nostrils and tiny bones built out from the bridge, a great nose.

"Look," DiMaggio said, more calmly, "I do not interfere with other people's lives. And I do not expect them to interfere with mine. There are things about my life, personal things, that I refuse to talk about. And even if you asked my brothers, they would be unable to tell you about them because they do not know. There are things about me, so many things, that they simply do not know. . . ."

"I don't want to cause trouble," the man said. "I think you're a great man, and . . ."

"I'm not great," DiMaggio cut in. "I'm not great," he repeated softly. "I'm just a man trying to get along."

Then DiMaggio, as if realizing that he was 35 intruding upon his own privacy, abruptly stood up. He looked at his watch.

"I'm late," he said, very formal again. "I'm 10 minutes late. You're making me late."

The man left the restaurant. He crossed the street and wandered over to the pier, briefly watching the fishermen hauling their nets and talking in the sun, seemingly very calm and contented. Then, after he turned and was headed back toward the parking lot, a blue Impala stopped in front of him and Joe DiMaggio leaned out the window and asked, "Do you have a car?" His voice was very gentle.

"Yes," the man said.

"Oh," DiMaggio said. "I would have given you a ride."

Joe DiMaggio was not born in San Francisco 40 but in Martinez, a small fishing village 25 miles northeast of the Golden Gate. Zio Pepe had settled there after leaving Isola delle Femmine, an islet off Palermo where the DiMaggios had been fishermen for generations. But in 1915, hearing of the luckier waters off San Francisco's wharf, Zio Pepe left Martinez, packing his boat with furniture and family, including Joe, who was one year old.

San Francisco was placid and picturesque when the DiMaggios arrived, but there was a competitive undercurrent and struggle for power along the pier. At dawn the boats would sail out to where the bay meets the ocean and the sea is rough, and later the men would race back with their hauls, hoping to beat their fellow fishermen to shore and sell it while they could. Twenty or 30 boats would sometimes be trying to gain the channel shoreward at the same time, and a fisherman had to know every rock in the water, and later know every bargaining trick along the shore, because the dealers and restaurateurs would play one fisherman off against the other, keeping the prices down. Later the fishermen became wiser and organized, predetermining the maximum amount each fisherman would catch, but there were always some men who, like the fish, never learned, and so heads would sometimes be broken, nets slashed, gasoline poured onto their fish, flowers of warning placed outside their doors.

AP Images

◀ In what ways does this 1937 photo of DiMaggio and his father, a retired fisherman, reflect DiMaggio's relationship to his father — and his father's career — as Talese portrays it? What might Talese point out about it?

But these days were ending when Zio Pepe arrived, and he expected his five sons to succeed him as fishermen, and the first two, Tom and Michael, did; but a third, Vincent, wanted to sing. He sang with such magnificent power as a young man that he came to the attention of the great banker, A. P. Giannini, and there were plans to send him to Italy for tutoring and the opera. But there was hesitation around the DiMaggio household and Vince never went; instead, he played ball with the San Francisco Seals and sports writers misspelled his name.

It was DeMaggio until Joe, at Vince's recommendation, joined the team and became a sensation, being followed later by the youngest brother, Dominic, who was also outstanding. All three later played in the big leagues, and some writers like to say that Joe was the best hitter, Dom the best fielder, Vince the best singer, and Casey Stengel once said: "Vince is the only player I ever saw who could strike out three times in one game and not be embarrassed. He'd walk into the clubhouse whistling. Everybody would be feeling sorry for him, but Vince always thought he was doing good."

After he retired from baseball Vince became a bartender, then a milkman, now a carpenter. He lives 40 miles north of San Francisco in a house he partly built, has been happily married for 34 years, has four grandchildren, has in the closet one of Joe's tailor-made suits that he has never had altered to fit, and when people ask him if he envies Joe he always says, "No, maybe Joe would like to have what I have." The brother Vincent most admired was Michael, "a big earthy man, a dreamer, a fisherman who wanted things but didn't want to take from Joe, or to work in the restaurant. He wanted a bigger boat, but wanted to earn it on his own. He never got it." In 1953, at the age of 44, Michael fell from his boat and drowned.

Since Zio Pepe's death at 77 in 1949, Tom at 62, the oldest brother — two of his four sisters are older — has become nominal head of the family and manages the restaurant that was opened in 1937 as Joe DiMaggio's Grotto. Later Joe sold out his share, and now Tom is the co-owner with Dominic. Of all the brothers, Dominic, who was known as the "Little Professor" when he played with the Boston Red Sox, is the most successful in business. He lives in a fashionable Boston

45

CENTRAL ESSAY 653

suburb with his wife and three children and is president of a firm that manufactures fiber cushion materials and grossed more than $3,500,000 last year.

Joe DiMaggio lives with his widowed sister, Marie, in a tan stone house on a quiet residential street not far from Fisherman's Wharf. He bought the house almost 30 years ago for his parents, and after their deaths he lived there with Marilyn Monroe. Now it is cared for by Marie, a slim and handsome dark-eyed woman who has an apartment on the second floor, Joe on the third. There are some baseball trophies and plaques in the small room off DiMaggio's bedroom, and on his dresser are photographs of Marilyn Monroe, and in the living room downstairs is a small painting of her that DiMaggio likes very much; it reveals only her face and shoulders and she is wearing a wide-brimmed sun hat, and there is a soft, sweet smile on her lips, an innocent curiosity about her that is the way he saw her and the way he wanted her to be seen by others — a simple girl, "a warm, big-hearted girl," he once described her, "that everybody took advantage of."

The publicity photographs emphasizing her sex appeal often offend him, and a memorable moment for Billy Wilder, who directed her in *The Seven-Year Itch*, occurred when he spotted DiMaggio in a large crowd of people gathered on Lexington Avenue in New York to watch a scene in which Marilyn, standing over a subway grating to cool herself, had her skirts blown high by a sudden wind blow. "What the hell is going on here?" DiMaggio was overheard to have said in the crowd, and Wilder recalled, "I shall never forget the look of death on Joe's face."

He was then 39, she was 27. They had been married in January of that year, 1954, despite disharmony in temperament and time; he was tired of publicity, she was thriving on it; he was intolerant of tardiness, she was always late. During their honeymoon in Tokyo an American general had introduced himself and asked if, as a patriotic gesture, she would visit the troops in

Korea. She looked at Joe. "It's your honeymoon," he said, shrugging, "go ahead if you want to."

She appeared on 10 occasions before 100,000 servicemen, and when she returned, she said, "It was so wonderful, Joe. You never heard such cheering."

"Yes, I have," he said. 50

Across from her portrait in the living room, on a coffee table in front of a sofa, is a sterling-silver humidor that was presented to him by his Yankee teammates at a time when he was the most talked-about man in America, and when Les Brown's band had recorded a hit that was heard day and night on the radio.

▼

Shown here from left to right are San Diego Padres manager Lefty O'Doul, Marilyn Monroe, and Joe DiMaggio. This photograph was taken shortly after the couple's wedding in 1954, during a stopover in Honolulu on the way to Tokyo.

What do you notice about this image? How does it add to your understanding of the story Talese tells about DiMaggio's marriage to Marilyn Monroe?

Bettmann/Getty Images

> From Coast to Coast, that's all you hear
>   Of Joe the One-Man Show.
> He's glorified the horsehide sphere,
>   Jolting Joe DiMaggio . . .
> Joe . . . Joe . . . DiMaggio . . .
>   we want you on our side . . .

The year was 1941, and it began for DiMaggio in the middle of May after the Yankees had lost four games in a row, seven of their last nine, and were in fourth place, five and a half games behind the leading Cleveland Indians. On May 15, DiMaggio hit only a first-inning single in a game that New York lost to Chicago 13–1; he was barely hitting .300, and had greatly disappointed the crowds that had seen him finish with a .352 average the year before and .381 in 1939.

He got a hit in the next game, and the next, and the next. On May 24, with the Yankees losing 6–5 to Boston, DiMaggio came up with runners on second and third and singled them home, winning the game, extending his streak to 10 games. But it went largely unnoticed. Even DiMaggio was not conscious of it until it had reached 29 games in mid-June. Then the newspapers began to dramatize it, the public became aroused, they sent him good-luck charms of every description, and DiMaggio kept hitting, and radio announcers would interrupt programs to announce the news, and then the song again: "Joe . . . Joe . . . DiMaggio . . . we want you on our side . . ."

Sometimes DiMaggio would be hitless his first three times up, the tension would build, it would appear that the game would end without his getting another chance — but he always would, and then he would hit the ball against the left-field wall, or through the pitcher's legs, or between two leaping infielders. In the forty-first game, the first of a doubleheader in Washington, DiMaggio tied an American League record that George Sisler had set in 1922. But before the second game began, a spectator sneaked onto the field and into the Yankees' dugout and stole DiMaggio's favorite bat. In the second game, using another of his bats, DiMaggio lined out twice and flied out. But in the seventh inning, borrowing one of his old bats that a teammate was using, he singled and broke Sisler's record, and he was only three games away from surpassing the major-league record of 44 set in 1897 by Willie Keeler while playing for Baltimore when it was a National League franchise.

An appeal for the missing bat was made through the newspapers. A man from Newark admitted the crime and returned it with regrets. And on July 2 at Yankee Stadium, DiMaggio hit a home run into the left-field stands. The record was broken.

He also got hits on the next 11 games, but on July 17 in Cleveland, at a night game attended by 67,468, he failed against two pitchers, Al Smith and Jim Bagby, Jr., although Cleveland's hero was really its third baseman, Ken Keltner, who in the first inning lunged to his right to make a spectacular backhanded stop of a drive and, from the foul line behind third base, threw DiMaggio out. DiMaggio received a walk in the fourth inning. But in the seventh he again hit a hard shot at Keltner, who again stopped it and threw him out. DiMaggio hit sharply toward the shortstop in the eighth inning, the ball taking a bad hop, but Lou Boudreau speared it off his shoulder and threw to the second baseman to start a double play and DiMaggio's streak was stopped at 56 games. But the New York Yankees were on their way to winning the pennant by 17 games, and the World Series too, and so in August, in a hotel suite in Washington, the players threw a surprise party for DiMaggio and toasted him with champagne and presented him with his Tiffany silver humidor that is now in San Francisco in his living room. . . .

◆ ◆ ◆

Marie was in the kitchen making toast and tea when DiMaggio came down for breakfast; his gray hair was uncombed but, since he wears it short, it was not untidy. He said good morning to Marie, sat down, and yawned. He lit a cigarette. He wore a blue wool bathrobe over his pajamas.

55

CENTRAL ESSAY 655

New York Daily News Archive/Getty Images

This photograph shows New York Yankees fans rushing onto the field after Joe DiMaggio's hitting streak reached 48 games in July, 1941. His legendary hitting streak that summer would eventually reach 56, a record that remains unbroken today. **How does this image inform your interpretation of DiMaggio's response to Marilyn Monroe's claim that he had "never heard such cheering" (para. 49)?**

It was 8:00 A.M. He had many things to do today and he seemed cheerful. He had a conference with the president of Continental Television, Inc., a large retail chain in California of which he is a partner and vice-president; later he had a golf date, and then a big banquet to attend, and, if that did not go on too long and if he were not too tired afterward, he might have a date.

Picking up the morning paper, not rushing to the sports page, DiMaggio read the front-page news, the people problems of 1966; Kwame Nkrumah was overthrown in Ghana, students were burning their draft cards (DiMaggio shook his head), the flu epidemic was spreading through the whole state of California. Then he flipped inside through the gossip columns, thankful they did not have him in there today — they had printed an item about his dating "an electrifying airline hostess" not long ago, and they also spotted him at dinner with Dori Lane, "the frantic frugger" in Whisky à Go Go's glass cage — and then he turned to the sports page and read a story about how the injured Mickey Mantle may never regain his form.

It happened all so quickly, the passing of Mantle, or so it seemed; he had succeeded DiMaggio, who had succeeded Ruth, but now there was no great young power hitter coming up, and the Yankee management, almost desperate, had talked Mantle out of retirement, and on September 18, 1965, they gave him a "day" in New York during which he received several thousand dollars' worth of gifts — an automobile, two quarter horses, free vacation trips to Rome, Nassau, Puerto Rico — and DiMaggio had flown to New York to make the introduction before 50,000: it had been a dramatic day, an almost holy day for the believers who had jammed the grandstands early to witness the canonization of a new stadium saint. Cardinal [Francis] Spellman was on the committee, President [Lyndon] Johnson sent a telegram, the day was officially proclaimed by the Mayor of New York, an orchestra assembled in the center field in front of the trinity of monuments to Ruth, [Lou] Gehrig, [Miller] Huggins; and high in the grandstands, billowing in the breeze of early autumn, were white banners that read: "Don't Quit, Mick," "We Love the Mick."

The banner had been held by hundreds of young boys whose dreams had been fulfilled so often by Mantle, but also seated in the grandstands were older men, paunchy and balding, in whose middle-aged minds DiMaggio was still vivid and invincible, and some of them remembered how one month before, during a pregame exhibition at Old-Timers' Day in Yankee Stadium, DiMaggio had hit a pitch into the left-field seats, and suddenly thousands of people had jumped wildly to their feet, joyously screaming — the great DiMaggio had returned, they were young again, it was yesterday.

But on this sunny September day at the stadium, the feast day of Mickey Mantle, DiMaggio was not wearing No. 5 on his back or a black cap to cover his graying hair; he was wearing a black suit and white shirt and blue tie, and he stood in one corner of the Yankees' dugout waiting to be introduced by Red Barber, who was standing near home plate behind a silver microphone. In the outfield Guy Lombardo's Royal Canadians were playing soothing, soft music; and moving slowly back and forth over the sprawling green grass between the left-field bullpen and the infield were two carts driven by grounds keepers and containing dozens and dozens of large gifts for Mantle — a 6-foot, 100-pound Hebrew National salami, a Winchester rifle, a mink coat for Mrs. Mantle, a set of Wilson golf clubs, a year's supply of Chunky Candy. DiMaggio smoked a cigarette, but cupped it in his hands as if not wanting to be caught in the act by teen-aged boys near enough to peek down into the dugout. Then, edging forward a step, DiMaggio poked his head out and looked up. He could see nothing above except the packed, towering green grandstands that seemed a mile high and moving, and he could see no clouds or blue sky, only a sky of faces. Then the announcer called out his name — *"Joe DiMaggio!"* — and suddenly there was a blast of cheering that grew louder and louder, echoing and reechoing within the big steel canyon, and DiMaggio stomped out his cigarette and climbed up the dugout steps and onto the soft

60

green grass, the noise resounding in his ears, he could almost feel the breeze, the breath of 50,000 lungs upon him, 100,000 eyes watching his every move, and for the briefest instant as he walked he closed his eyes.

Then in his path he saw Mickey Mantle's mother, a smiling woman wearing an orchid, and he gently reached out for her elbow, holding it as he led her toward the microphone next to the other dignitaries lined up on the infield. Then he stood, very erect and without expression as the cheers softened and the stadium settled down.

Mantle was still in the dugout, in uniform, standing with one leg on the top step, and lined on both sides of him were the other Yankees who, when the ceremony was over, would play the Detroit Tigers. Then into the dugout, smiling, came Senator Robert Kennedy, accompanied by two tall curly-haired assistants with blue eyes, Fordham freckles. Jim Farley was the first on the field to notice the Senator, and Farley muttered, loud enough for others to hear, "Who the hell invited *him*?"

Toots Shor and some of the other committeemen standing near Farley looked into the dugout, and so did DiMaggio, his glance seeming cold, but he remained silent. Kennedy walked up and down within the dugout, shaking hands with the Yankees, but he did not walk onto the field.

"Senator," said Yankees' manager Johnny Keane, "why don't you sit down?" Kennedy quickly shook his head, smiled. He remained standing, and then one Yankee came over and asked about getting relatives out of Cuba, and Kennedy called over one of his aides to take down the details in a notebook.

65

On the infield the ceremony went on, Mantle's gifts continued to pile up — a Mobilette motorbike, a Sooner Schooner wagon barbecue, a year's supply of Chock Full O' Nuts coffee, a year's supply of Topps Chewing Gum — and the Yankee players watched, and Maris seemed glum.

"Hey, Rog," yelled a man with a tape recorder, Murray Olderman, "I want to do a 30-second tape with you."

seeing connections

The following excerpt is from *Joe DiMaggio: The Hero's Life* (2000), a *New York Times* bestseller by journalist Richard Ben Cramer.
What similarities do you find between Cramer's writing and Talese's? How do the two writers' perspectives differ? How does Cramer's rhetoric reflect those differences?

from Joe DiMaggio

RICHARD BEN CRAMER

I remember the last public day of Joe's life, the last day of that splendid Yankee season, a sunny Sunday in the Bronx, September 27, 1998 — Joe DiMaggio Day, the mayor had proclaimed it. The Clipper was coming back to Yankee Stadium. . . .

That was the last distant view he permitted. I didn't go anywhere near him that day — didn't try to intrude, try to ask questions. We'd been through all that. Joe didn't want to help with biography. He didn't want to help anybody know his life. It was a smart move by a smart man — canny, anyway. In latter years he cultivated the distance that set him apart from every other person of fame. He was revered for his mystery. We cheered him for never giving himself entirely to us. . . .

For sixty years writers had to make up what Joe cared about. As Joe himself once explained:

"They used to write stories about me like they were interviewing me, and never even talked to me." But now, most of the guys who knew him — who could cobble up a good DiMaggio quote — were gone.

So Mike Lupica, from the *Daily News* (Joe's favorite among the new generation), would settle that day for the wistful "So many memories. So many seasons." . . .

The fact was, DiMaggio . . . never spent an instant in his life to marvel at the beauty of anything. Except maybe a broad. Which wasn't marveling — that was wanting. Wanting he did. That was why he'd hauled himself out of bed at four in the morning, coughing up blood from the cancer he wouldn't speak about . . . to get to the airport, to fly to New York in time for his day. That was want. That was DiMaggio. If you lost track of that hunger, that toughness, you lost his core.

5

Maris swore angrily, shook his head.

"Why don't you ask Richardson? He's a better talker than me."

"Yes, but the fact that it comes from you . . ." 70

Maris swore again. But finally he went over and said in an interview that Mantle was the finest player of his era, a great competitor, a great hitter.

Fifteen minutes later, standing behind the microphone at home plate, DiMaggio was telling the crowd, "I'm proud to introduce the man who succeeded me in center field in 1951," and from every corner of the stadium, the cheering, whistling, clapping came down. Mantle stepped

forward. He stood with his wife and children, posed for the photographers kneeling in front. Then he thanked the crowd in a short speech, and, turning, shook hands with the dignitaries standing nearby. Among them now was Senator Kennedy, who had been spotted in the dugout five minutes before by Red Barber, and been called out and introduced. Kennedy posed with Mantle for a photographer, then shook hands with the Mantle children, and with Toots Shor and James Farley and others. DiMaggio saw him coming down the line and at the last second he backed away, casually, hardly anybody noticing it, and Kennedy seemed not to notice it either, just swept past, shaking more hands. . . .

Finishing his tea, putting aside the newspaper, DiMaggio went upstairs to dress, soon he was waving good-bye to Marie and driving toward his business appointment in downtown San Francisco with his partners in the retail television business. DiMaggio, while not a millionaire, has invested wisely and has always had, since his retirement from baseball, executive positions with big companies that have paid him well. He also was among the organizers of the Fisherman's National Bank of San Francisco last year, and, though it never came about, he demonstrated an acuteness that impressed those businessmen who had thought of him only in terms of baseball. He has had offers to manage big-league baseball teams but always has rejected them, saying, "I have enough trouble taking care of my own problems without taking on the responsibilities of 25 ball players."

So his only contact with baseball these days, excluding public appearances, is his unsalaried job as a batting coach each spring in Florida with the New York Yankees, a trip he would make once again on the following Sunday, three days away, if he could accomplish what for him is always the dreaded responsibility of packing, a task made no easier by the fact that he lately had fallen into the habit of keeping his clothes in two places — some hang in his closet at home, some hang in the back room of a saloon called Reno's.

Reno's is a dimly lit bar in the center of San   75
Francisco. A portrait of DiMaggio swinging a bat hangs on the wall, in addition to portraits of other star athletes, and the clientele consists mainly of the sporting crowd and newspapermen, people who know DiMaggio quite well and around whom he speaks freely on a number of subjects and relaxes as he can in few other places. The owner of the bar is Reno Barsocchini, a broad-shouldered and handsome man of 51 with graying wavy hair who began as a fiddler in Dago Mary's tavern 35 years ago. He later became

a bartender there and elsewhere, including DiMaggio's Restaurant, and now he is probably DiMaggio's closest friend. He was the best man at the DiMaggio-Monroe wedding in 1954, and when they separated nine months later in Los Angeles, Reno rushed down to help DiMaggio with the packing and drove him back to San Francisco. Reno will never forget the day.

Hundreds of people were gathered around the Beverly Hills home that DiMaggio and Marilyn had rented, and photographers were perched in the trees watching the windows, and others stood on the lawn and behind the rose bushes waiting to snap pictures of anybody who walked out of the house. The newspapers that day played all the puns — "Joe Fanned on Jealousy"; "Marilyn and Joe — Out at Home" — and the Hollywood columnists, to whom DiMaggio was never an idol, never a gracious host, recounted instances of incompatibility, and Oscar Levant said it all proved that no man could be a success in two national pastimes. When Reno Barsocchini arrived, he had to push his way through the mob, then bang on the door for several minutes before being admitted. Marilyn Monroe was upstairs in bed. Joe DiMaggio was downstairs with his suitcases, tense and pale, his eyes bloodshot.

Reno took the suitcase and golf clubs out to DiMaggio's car, and then DiMaggio came out of the house, the reporters moving toward him, the lights flashing.

"Where are you going?" they yelled.

"I'm driving to San Francisco," he said, walking quickly.

"Is that going to be your home?"   80

"That is my home and always has been."

"Are you coming back?"

DiMaggio turned for a moment, looking up at the house.

"No," he said, "I'll never be back."

Reno Barsocchini, except for a brief falling-   85
out over something he will not discuss, has been DiMaggio's trusted companion ever since, joining

him whenever he can on the golf course or on the town, otherwise waiting for him in the bar with other middle-aged men. They may wait for hours sometimes, waiting and knowing that when he arrives he may wish to be alone; but it does not seem to matter, they are endlessly awed by him, moved by the mystique, he is a kind of male Garbo. They know that he can be warm and loyal if they are sensitive to his wishes, but they must never be late for an appointment to meet him. One man, unable to find a parking place, arrived a half hour late once, and DiMaggio did not talk to him again for three months. They know, too, when dining at night with DiMaggio, that he generally prefers male companions and occasionally one or two young women, but never wives; wives gossip, wives complain, wives are trouble, and men wishing to remain close to DiMaggio must keep their wives at home.

When DiMaggio strolls into Reno's bar, the men wave and call out his name and Reno Barsocchini smiles and announces, "Here's the Clipper!" — the "Yankee Clipper" being a nickname from his baseball days.

"Hey Clipper, Clipper," Reno had said two nights before, "where you been, Clipper? . . . Clipper, how 'bout a belt?"

DiMaggio refused the offer of a drink, ordering instead a pot of tea, which he prefers to all other beverages except before a date, when he will switch to vodka.

"Hey, Joe," a sports writer asked, a man researching a magazine piece on golf, "why is it that a golfer, when he starts getting older, loses his putting touch first? Like [Sam] Snead and [Ben] Hogan, they can still hit a ball well off the tee, but on the greens they lose the strokes."

"It's the pressure of age," DiMaggio said, turn- 90 ing around on his barstool. "With age you get jittery. It's true of golfers, it's true of any man when he gets into his 50s. He doesn't take chances like he used to. The younger golfer, on the greens, he'll stroke his putts better. The older man, he becomes hesitant. A little uncertain. Shaky.

When it comes to taking chances, the younger man, even when driving a car, will take chances that the older man won't."

"Speaking of chances," another man said, one of the group that had gathered around DiMaggio, "did you see that guy on crutches in here last night?"

"Yeah, had his leg in a cast," a third said. "Skiing."

"I would never ski," DiMaggio said. "Men who ski must be doing it to impress a broad. You see these men, some of them 40, 50, getting onto skis. And later you see them all bandaged up, broken legs."

"But skiing's a very sexy sport, Joe. All the clothes, the tight pants, the fireplaces in the ski lodge, the bear rug — Christ nobody goes to ski. They just go out there to get it cold so they can warm it up."

"Maybe you're right," DiMaggio said. "I might 95 be persuaded."

"Want a belt, Clipper?" Reno asked.

DiMaggio thought for a second, then said, "All right — first belt tonight."

Now it was noon, a warm sunny day. DiMaggio's business meeting with the television retailers had gone well; he had made a strong appeal to George Shahood, president of Continental Television, Inc., which has eight retail outlets in Northern California, to put prices on color television sets and increase the sales volume, and Shahood had conceded it was worth a try. Then DiMaggio called Reno's bar to see if there were any messages, and now he was in Lefty O'Doul's car being driven along Fisherman's Wharf toward the Golden Gate Bridge en route to a golf course 30 miles upstate. Lefty O'Doul was one of the great hitters in the National League in the early thirties, and later he managed the San Francisco Seals when DiMaggio was the shining star. Though O'Doul is now 69, 18 years older than DiMaggio, he nevertheless possesses great energy and spirit, is a hard-drinking, boisterous man with a big belly and roving eye; and when DiMaggio, as they drove along the highway toward the golf club, noticed a lovely blonde at the wheel of a car nearby and exclaimed, "Look at *that* tomato!" O'Doul's head suddenly spun around, he took his eyes off the road, and yelled, "Where, *where*?" O'Doul's golf game is less than what it was — he used to have a two-handicap — but he still shoots in the 80s, as does DiMaggio.

DiMaggio's drives range between 250 and 280 yards when he doesn't sky them, and his putting is good, but he is distracted by a bad back that both pains him and hinders the fullness of his swing. On the first hole, waiting to tee off, DiMaggio sat back watching a foursome of college boys ahead swinging with such freedom. "Oh," he said with a sigh, "to have *their* backs."

DiMaggio and O'Doul were accompanied   100 around the golf course by Ernie Nevers, the former football star, and two brothers who are in the hotel and movie-distribution business. They moved quickly up and down the green hills in electric golf carts, and DiMaggio's game was exceptionally good for the first nine holes. But then he seemed distracted, perhaps tired, perhaps even reacting to a conversation of a few minutes before. One of the movie men was praising the film *Boeing, Boeing*, starring Tony Curtis

and Jerry Lewis, and the man asked DiMaggio if he had seen it.

"No," DiMaggio said. Then he added, swiftly, "I haven't seen a film in eight years."

DiMaggio hooked a few shots, was in the woods. He took a No. 9 iron and tried to chip out. But O'Doul interrupted DiMaggio's concentration to remind him to keep the face of the club closed. DiMaggio hit the ball. It caromed off the side of his club, went skipping like a rabbit through the high grass down toward a pond. DiMaggio rarely displays any emotion on a golf course, but now, without saying a word, he took his No. 9 iron and flung it into the air. The club landed in a tree and stayed up there.

"Well," O'Doul said casually, "there goes *that* set of clubs."

DiMaggio walked to the tree. Fortunately the club had slipped to the lower branch, and DiMaggio could stretch up on the cart and get it back.

"Every time I get advice," DiMaggio muttered   105 to himself, shaking his head slowly and walking toward the pond, "I shank it."

Later, showered and dressed, DiMaggio and the others drove to a banquet about 10 miles from the golf course. Somebody had said it was going to be an elegant dinner, but when they

Richard Drew/AP Images

◀

After retiring from baseball, Joe DiMaggio was a spokesman for several commercial products. He was most famous for his 1978 pitch for Mr. Coffee, an early automatic coffee maker. He appeared in print and television ads, like the one shown here. **To what extent does Gay Talese's essay address this aspect of DiMaggio's later career? How does this image of DiMaggio add to — or subtract from — your impression of him?**

arrived they could see it was more like a county fair; farmers were gathered outside a big barnlike building, a candidate for sheriff was distributing leaflets at the front door, and a chorus of homely ladies was inside singing "You Are My Sunshine."

"How did we get sucked into this?" DiMaggio asked, talking out of the side of his mouth, as they approached the building.

"O'Doul," one of the men said. "It's his fault. Damned O'Doul can't turn *anything* down."

"Go to hell," O'Doul said.

Soon DiMaggio and O'Doul and Ernie Nevers *110* were surrounded by the crowd, and the woman who had been leading the chorus came rushing over and said, "Oh, Mr. DiMaggio, it certainly is a pleasure having you."

"It's a pleasure being here, ma'am," he said, forcing a smile.

"It's too bad you didn't arrive a moment sooner. You'd have heard our singing."

"Oh, I heard it," he said, "and I enjoyed it very much."

"Good, good," she said. "And how are your brothers, Dom and Vic?"

"Fine. Dom lives near Boston. Vince is in *115* Pittsburgh."

"Why, *hello* there, Joe," interrupted a man with wine on his breath, patting DiMaggio on the back, feeling his arm. "Who's gonna take it this year, Joe?"

"Well, I have no idea," DiMaggio said.

"What about the Giants?"

"Your guess is as good as mine."

"Well, you can't count the Dodgers out," the *120* man said.

"You sure can't," DiMaggio said.

"Not with all that pitching."

"Pitching is certainly important," DiMaggio said.

Everywhere he goes the question seems the same, as if he has some special vision into the future of new heroes, and everywhere he goes, too, older men grab his hand and feel his arm and predict that he could still go out there and hit one, and the smile on DiMaggio's face is genuine. He tries hard to remain as he was — he diets, he

takes steambaths, he is careful; and flabby men in the locker rooms of golf clubs sometimes steal peeks at him when he steps out of the shower, observing the tight muscles across his chest, the flat stomach, the long sinewy legs. He has a young man's body, very pale and little hair; his face is dark and lined, however, parched by the sun of several seasons. Still he is always an impressive figure at banquets such as this — an "immortal" sports writers called him, and that is how they have written about him and others like him, rarely suggesting that such heroes might ever be prone to the ills of mortal men, carousing, drinking, scheming; to suggest this would destroy the myth, would disillusion small boys, would infuriate rich men who own ball clubs and to whom baseball is a business dedicated to profit and in pursuit of which they trade mediocre players' flesh as casually as boys trade players' pictures on bubble-gum cards. And so the baseball hero must always act the part, must preserve the myth, and none does it better than DiMaggio, none is more patient when drunken old men grab an arm and ask, "Who's gonna take it this year, Joe?"

Two hours later, dinner and the speeches over, *125* DiMaggio was slumped in O'Doul's car headed back to San Francisco. He edged himself up, however, when O'Doul pulled into a gas station in which a pretty red-haired girl sat on a stool, legs crossed, filing her fingernails. She was about 22, wore a tight black skirt and tighter white blouse.

"Look at *that*," DiMaggio said.

"Yeah," O'Doul said.

O'Doul turned away when a young man approached, opened the gas tank, began wiping the windshield. The young man wore a greasy white uniform on the front of which was printed the name "Burt." DiMaggio kept looking at the girl, but she was not distracted from her fingernails. Then he looked at Burt, who did not recognize him. When the tank was full, O'Doul paid and drove off. Burt returned to his girl; DiMaggio slumped down in the front seat and did not open his eyes again until they arrived in San Francisco.

This cartoon appeared in the *New York Daily News* in 2005, six years after DiMaggio's death. **What comment does the cartoon make about the differences between players like DiMaggio and more contemporary players? In what ways does Talese comment — directly or indirectly — on those differences?**

MAY 3, 1936

A KID FROM SAN FRANCISCO WAITS IN THE ON-DECK CIRCLE— HE'S COMING TO BAT FOR HIS **FIRST** TIME AS A **YANKEE**— HE WENT **3** FOR **6** THAT DAY

AS ANOTHER SEASON COMMENCES, WE REMEMBER THIS MAN... AND TRY TO FORGET TODAY'S AGE OF STEROIDS."

ONCE UPON A TIME A TALL, THIN 21-YR-OLD WITH A SERIOUS DEMEANOR WAS INTRODUCED TO **NEW YORK** FANS... HE DISPLAYED HIS ART ON A BASEBALL FIELD WITH A WIDE STANCE AND CLASSIC SWING... SOON, HE BECAME A FIXED PICTURE TO FANS ALL OVER... ALMOST THE PERFECT PLAYER WHO COULD FIELD, THROW, RUN THE BASES AND HIT... THIS FELLOW MADE ALL TOUGH PLAYS LOOK EASY, AND WITH GRACE AND GREAT CLASS... HE KEPT STRONG AND AGILE BY EATING RIGHT AND ALWAYS RESPECTING HIS BODY. DID HE NEED **STEROIDS?** ARE YOU KIDDING? —B(Nagib)

New York Daily News Archive/Getty Images

"Let's go see Reno," DiMaggio said.

"No, I gotta go see my old lady," O'Doul said. So he dropped DiMaggio off in front of the bar, and a moment later Reno's voice was announcing in the smoky room, "Hey, here's the Clipper!" The men waved and offered to buy him a drink. DiMaggio ordered a vodka and sat for an hour at the bar talking to a half-dozen men around him. Then a blonde girl who had been with friends at the other end of the bar came over, and somebody introduced her to DiMaggio. He bought her a drink, offered her a cigarette. Then he struck a match and held it. His hand was unsteady.

"Is that me that's shaking?" he asked.

"It must be," said the blonde. "I'm calm."

Two nights later, having collected his clothes out of Reno's back room, DiMaggio boarded a jet; he slept crossways on three seats, then came down the steps as the sun began to rise in Miami. He claimed his luggage and golf clubs, put them into the trunk of a waiting automobile, and less than an hour later he was being driven into Fort Lauderdale, past palm-lined streets, toward the Yankee Clipper Hotel.

"All my life it seems I've been on the road traveling," he said, squinting through the windshield into the sun. "I never get a sense of being in any one place."

Arriving at the Yankee Clipper Hotel, DiMaggio checked into the largest suite. People rushed through the lobby to shake hands with him, to ask for his autograph, to say, "Joe, you look great." And early the next morning, and for the next 30 mornings, DiMaggio arrived punctually at the baseball park and wore his uniform with the famous No. 5, and the tourists seated in the sunny grandstands clapped when he first appeared on the field each time, and then they watched with nostalgia as he picked up a bat and played "pepper" with the younger Yankees, some of whom were not even born when, 25 years ago this summer, he hit in 56 straight games and became the most celebrated man in America.

But the younger spectators in the Fort Lauderdale park, and the sports writers, too, were more interested in Mantle and Maris, and nearly every day there were news dispatches reporting how Mantle and Maris felt, what they did, what they said, even though they said and did very little except walk around the field frowning when photographers asked for another picture and when sports writers asked how they felt.

After seven days of this, the big day arrived — Mantle and Maris would swing a bat — and a dozen sports writers were gathered around the big batting cage that was situated beyond the left-field fence; it was completely enclosed in wire, meaning that no baseball could travel more than 30 or 40 feet before being trapped in rope; still Mantle and Maris would be swinging, and this, in spring, makes news.

seeing connections

Joe DiMaggio features prominently in the lyrics to "Mrs. Robinson," a song written by Paul Simon for the soundtrack of *The Graduate*, a 1967 movie in which a middle-aged woman named Mrs. Robinson seduces a recent college graduate. The song, performed by Simon and Garfunkel, ends with a stanza that asks, "Where have you gone, Joe DiMaggio / Our nation turns its lonely eyes to you" — and later answers with, "Joltin' Joe has left and gone away," followed by the word "hey" repeated several times.

Though Joe DiMaggio has appeared on several Sports Illustrated covers, the two shown here — from 1993 and 2011 — both recall the final stanza of "Mrs. Robinson." **How do each of these two covers use the lyrics to comment on DiMaggio's life and career? In what ways can you connect each cover's visual rhetoric to the written rhetoric of "The Silent Season of a Hero"?**

SI Cover/Contributor/Getty Images

SI Cover/Contributor/Getty Images

Mantle stepped in first. He wore black gloves to help prevent blisters. He hit right-handed against the pitching of a coach named Vern Benson, and soon Mantle was swinging hard, smashing line drives against the nets, going *ahhh ahhh* as he followed through with his mouth open.

Then Mantle, not wanting to overdo it on his first day, dropped his bat in the dirt and walked out of the batting cage. Roger Maris stepped in. He picked up Mantle's bat.

"This damn thing must be 38 ounces," Maris said. He threw the bat down into the dirt, left the cage, and walked toward the dugout on the other side of the field to get a lighter bat. 140

DiMaggio stood among the sports writers behind the cage, then turned when Vern Benson, inside the cage, yelled, "Joe, wanna hit some?"

"No chance," DiMaggio said.

"Com'on Joe," Benson said.

The reporters waited silently. Then DiMaggio walked slowly into the cage and picked up Mantle's bat. He took his position at the plate but obviously it was not the classic DiMaggio stance; he was holding the bat about two inches from the knob, his feet were not so far apart, and when DiMaggio took a cut at Benson's first pitch, fouling it, there was none of that ferocious follow-through, the blurred bat did not come whipping all the way around, the No. 5 was not stretched full across his broad back.

DiMaggio fouled Benson's second pitch, then he connected solidly with the third, the fourth, the fifth. He was just meeting the ball easily, however, not smashing it, and Benson called out, "I didn't know you were a choke hitter, Joe." 145

"I am now," DiMaggio said, getting ready for another pitch.

He hit three more squarely enough, and then he swung again and there was a hollow sound.

"Ohhh," DiMaggio yelled, dropping his bat, his fingers stung. "I was waiting for that one." He left the batting cage, rubbing his hands together. The reporters watched him. Nobody said anything. Then DiMaggio said to one of them, not in anger or in sadness, but merely as a simply stated fact, "There was a time when you couldn't get me out of there."

[1966]

QUESTIONS FOR DISCUSSION

1. How does Gay Talese create a picture of Joe DiMaggio at loose ends that nevertheless suggests his heroism?

2. What does Talese tell us about the position of sports in American popular culture?

3. Talese describes DiMaggio as "a kind of male Garbo," referring to the legendary, reclusive film star Greta Garbo (para. 85). The comparison suggests that DiMaggio's detachment was a masculine ideal. Does this ideal still resonate? How does it square with the image of today's superstar athletes? Does our media-crazy era demand more engagement from our heroes? Are we still capable of being "moved by the mystique" (para. 85)?

4. Talese has said that his work is a highly personal response to the world as an Italian American outsider. What evidence do you find that it is an outsider's voice? How does the authorial voice of an outsider add nuance to the profile of Joe DiMaggio?

5. Why is spring the silent season? Consider the essay title from the perspective of fishing and baseball.

QUESTIONS ON RHETORIC AND STYLE

1. What is the effect of juxtaposing details of Joe DiMaggio's legendary baseball prowess with details of his everyday life in San Francisco as a retired athlete?

2. Why does "The Silent Season of a Hero" open with a quotation from Ernest Hemingway's *The Old Man and the Sea*? Cite specific passages from Talese's essay to support your answer.

3. The "tall gray-haired man in a dark suit" in the first paragraph is obviously Joe DiMaggio, but Talese waits until the end of paragraph 2 to name him. What is the effect of delaying identification of the essay's subject?

4. Characterize the narrator. Does he step forward at any time? Who is the "man from New York" (para. 12)? Who is asked by the narrator to comment on DiMaggio?

5. Although DiMaggio was a baseball player, the essay sometimes sounds as if it's about a fisherman. Trace both the language of baseball and the language of fishing. Which is predominant?

6. Talese suggests — but doesn't come out and say — that Joe DiMaggio and Marilyn Monroe were competitive about their celebrity. How does Talese use Monroe's mythical status to develop his portrait of DiMaggio? Is he sympathetic to her? Does his profile of DiMaggio deepen our understanding of Monroe, or does she remain as tantalizingly out of reach as she seems to have been to DiMaggio? Explain your responses.

7. Several parts of the essay — especially paragraphs 3 and 41 — evoke Hemingway. How do the images and language of those allusions create another level of meaning? How do they add to the portrait of DiMaggio?

8. What is the overall tone of the essay? How does Talese achieve his tone? How does the tone add a layer of meaning?

9. Talese notes that sportswriters have called DiMaggio an "immortal" (para. 124). How does the essay both support and debunk that myth?

10. Explain the assumptions Talese makes about his audience based on his portrait of DiMaggio as an aging hero.

SUGGESTIONS FOR WRITING

1. Write an essay in which you analyze the strategies that Talese uses in paragraphs 116–124 to add complexity and nuance to his portrayal of Joe DiMaggio.

2. In this profile of the Yankees player, Talese doesn't hide the fact that DiMaggio smokes, drinks alcohol, and is dismissive of women. Write an essay in which you examine the responsibility of sportswriters. Should they airbrush their subjects to ensure that they meet their obligations as role models? Or should sportswriters give us the unvarnished truth?

3. Examine the parts of the selection that are about Marilyn Monroe, especially the anecdote about her performing for the troops in Korea (paras. 48–50). Write an essay about how, in the absence of details about why her marriage to DiMaggio failed, the language suggests that perhaps the marriage could not accommodate two egos as strong as DiMaggio's and Monroe's. Read other accounts of the marriage to see if they support or contradict Talese's, and refer to them in your essay.

4. Find and read "Frank Sinatra Has a Cold," Talese's profile of Frank Sinatra. Compare and contrast it with "The Silent Season of a Hero." How is the author's voice similar or different? Compare the treatment of DiMaggio and Sinatra as embodiments of a masculine ideal.

5. Paragraphs 53–56 recount DiMaggio's 1941 hitting streak, which ended at a record-breaking fifty-six games. During this streak, the New York Yankees went from fourth place in the American League to victory in the World Series. The missing bat — returned by a rueful fan — seems to have been the magic charm. Compare this account with other tales of heroes who depend on the power of a sword, a shield, or some other special piece of equipment.

from How I Learned to Ride the Bicycle
Reflections of an Influential Nineteenth Century Woman

FRANCES WILLARD

Frances Willard (1839–1898) is little known today, but in her own time she was famous. Born in western New York, she grew up on the prairie near Janesville, Wisconsin. She spent her childhood free of the usual constraints endured by girls of the time. From the age of sixteen on, however, she wore the long skirts, corsets, and high-heeled shoes required of women. She became a teacher and later served as president of Evanston College for Ladies. At thirty-five, Willard found the causes that would become her life's work: the women's movement and the temperance movement. The best-known and most dynamic president of the Women's Christian Temperance Union (WCTU), Willard was an outstanding educator, astute politician, pioneer suffragist, and strong advocate for the emancipation of women. When Willard was fifty-three, she was in poor health, and her doctor encouraged her to take outdoor exercise. Lady Henry Somerset, head of the British Women's Temperance Union, gave her a bicycle, which was nicknamed Gladys. In 1893, Willard wrote *How I Learned to Ride the Bicycle: Reflections of an Influential Nineteenth Century Woman*, which tells how she met the challenge of learning how to ride a bicycle.

Library of Congress

Preliminary

From my earliest recollections, and up to the ripe age of fifty-three, I had been an active and diligent worker in the world. This sounds absurd; but having almost no toys except such as I could manufacture, my first plays were but the outdoor work of active men and women on a small scale. Born with an inveterate opposition to staying in the house, I very early learned to use a carpenter's kit and a gardener's tools, and followed in my mimic way the occupations of the poulterer and the farmer, working my little field with a wooden plow of my own making, and felling saplings with an ax rigged up from the old iron of the wagon-shop. Living in the country, far from the artificial restraints and conventions by which most girls are hedged from the activities that would develop a good physique, and endowed with the companionship of a mother

who let me have my own sweet will, I "ran wild" until my sixteenth birthday, when the hampering long skirts were brought, with their accompanying corset and high heels; my hair was clubbed up with pins, and I remember writing in my journal, in the first heartbreak of a young human colt taken from its pleasant pasture, "Altogether, I recognize that my occupation is gone."

From that time on I always realized and was obedient to the limitations thus imposed, though in my heart of hearts I felt their unwisdom even more than their injustice. My work then changed from my beloved and breezy outdoor world to the indoor realm of study, teaching, writing, speaking, and went on almost without a break or pain until my fifty-third year, when the loss of my mother accentuated the strain of this long period in

seeing connections

The corset was a ubiquitous feature of women's clothing since the sixteenth century, but beginning in the mid-nineteenth century its design changed to accommodate changing fashions while still maintaining the visual effect of a narrow waist. These new corsets required women to be laced into them so tightly that the garment altered their natural body shape and restricted their range of movement. Tight lacing, as the practice was called, resulted in women whose waists had been trained to as little as thirteen inches in circumference. Women who refused to lace tightly or wear corsets and chose functional clothing were referred to as loose women — a term that still suggests improper immoral behavior today. Shown here are an advertisement for a Victorian-era corset and a photograph of a woman wearing that style. It was this kind of corset that the young Frances Willard was expected to wear once she turned sixteen.

What might Willard have considered the worst effects of the corset? How do these images shed light on why it might have taken Willard so long to learn to ride bicycle?

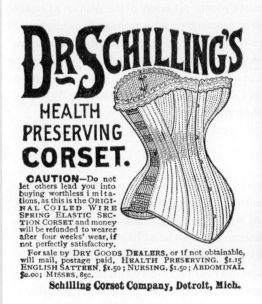

Library of Congress

which mental and physical life were out of balance, and I fell into a mild form of what is called nerve-wear by the patient and nervous prostration by the lookers-on. Thus ruthlessly thrown out of the usual lines of reaction on my environment, and sighing for new worlds to conquer, I determined that I would learn the bicycle.

An English naval officer had said to me, after learning it himself, "You women have no idea of the new realm of happiness which the bicycle has opened to us men." Already I knew well enough that tens of thousands who could never afford to own, feed, and stable a horse, had by this bright invention enjoyed the swiftness of motion which is perhaps the most fascinating feature of material life, the charm of a wide outlook upon the natural world, and that sense of mastery which is probably the greatest attraction in horseback-riding. But the steed that never tires, and is "mettlesome" in the fullest sense of the word, is full of tricks and capers, and to hold his head steady and make him prance to suit you is no small accomplishment. I had often mentioned in my temperance writings that the bicycle was perhaps our strongest ally in winning young men away from public-houses, because it afforded them a pleasure far more enduring, and an exhilaration as much more delightful as the natural is than the unnatural. From my observation of my own brother and hundreds of young men who have been my pupils, I have always held that a boy's heart is not set in him to do evil any more than a girl's, and that the reason our young men fall into evil ways is largely because we have not had the wit and wisdom to provide them with amusements suited to their joyous youth, by means of which they could invest their superabundant animal spirits in ways that should harm no one and help themselves to the best development and the cleanliest ways of living. So as a temperance reformer I always felt a strong attraction toward the bicycle, because it is the vehicle of so much harmless pleasure, and because the skill required in handling it obliges those who mount to keep clear heads and steady hands. Nor could I see a reason in the world why a woman should not ride the silent steed so swift and blithesome. . . .

Since Balaam's beast[1] there has been but little authentic talking done by the four-footed; but that is no reason why the two-wheeled should not speak its mind, and the first utterance I have to chronicle in the softly flowing vocables of my bicycle is to the following purport. I heard it as we trundled off down the Priory incline at the suburban home of Lady Henry Somerset, Reigate, England; it said: "Behold, I do not fail you; I am not a skittish beastie, but a sober, well-conducted roadster. I did not ask you to mount or drive, but since you have done so you must now learn the laws of balance and exploitation. I did not invent these laws, but I have been built conformably to them, and you must suit yourself to the unchanging regulations of gravity, general and specific, as illustrated in me. Strange as the paradox may seem, you will do this best by not trying to do it at all. You must make up what you are pleased to call your mind — make it up speedily, or you will be cast in yonder mud-puddle, and no blame to me and no thanks to yourself. Two things must occupy your thinking powers to the exclusion of every other thing: first, the goal; and, second, the momentum requisite to reach it. Do not look down like an imbecile upon the steering-wheel in front of you — that would be about as wise as for a nauseated voyager to keep his optical instruments fixed upon the rolling waves. It is the curse of life that nearly every one looks down. But the microscope will never set you free; you must glue your eyes to the telescope for ever and a day. Look up and off and on and out; get forehead and foot into line, the latter acting as a rhythmic spur in the flanks of your equilibriated equine; so shall you win, and that right speedily.

"It was divinely said that the kingdom of God 5 is within you. Some make a mysticism of this declaration, but it is hard common sense; for the lesson you will learn from me is this: every kingdom over which we reign must be first formed within us on what the psychic people call the 'astral plane,' but what I as a bicycle look upon as the common parade-ground of individual thought."

The Process

Courtiers wittily say that horseback riding is the only thing in which a prince is apt to excel, for the reason that the horse never flatters and would as soon throw him as if he were a groom. Therefore it is only by actually mastering the art of riding that a prince can hold his place with the noblest of the four-footed animals.

Happily there is now another locomotive contrivance which is no flatterer, and which

---

[1] Balaam is a biblical figure whose donkey, miraculously given the power of speech, saves his life. —Eds.

4332—"Sew on your own buttons, I'm going for a ride."

Library of Congress

This photograph, from 1899, shows a woman pointing to her husband and child as she says, "Sew on your own buttons, I'm going for a ride."
What does this caption suggest about the consequences of women riding bicycles? How might it reflect some of the reasons Willard was eager to learn to ride one?

peasant and prince must master, if they do this at all, by the democratic route of honest hard work. Well will it be for rulers when the tough old Yorkshire proverb applies to them as strictly as to the lowest of their subjects: "*It's dogged as does it.*" We all know the old saying, "Fire is a good servant, but a bad master." This is equally true of the bicycle: if you give it an inch — nay, a hair — it will take an ell — nay, an evolution — and you a contusion, or like enough, a perforated kneecap. . . .

Gradually, item by item, I learned the location of every screw and spring, spoke and tire, and every beam and bearing that went to make up Gladys. This was not the lesson of a day, but of many days and weeks, and it had to be learned before we could get on well together. To my mind the infelicities of which we see so much in life grow out of lack of time and patience thus to study and adjust the natures that have agreed in

the sight of God and man to stand by one another to the last. They will not take the pains, they have not enough specific gravity, to balance themselves in their new environment. Indeed, I found a whole philosophy of life in the wooing and the winning of my bicycle.

Just as a strong and skilful swimmer takes the waves, so the bicycler must learn to take such waves of mental impression as the passing of a gigantic hay-wagon, the sudden obtrusion of black cattle with wide-branching horns, the rattling pace of high-stepping steeds, or even the swift transit of a railway-train. At first she will be upset by the apparition of the smallest poodle, and not until she has attained a wide experience will she hold herself steady in presence of the critical eyes of a coach-and-four.[2] But all this is a part of that

_____
[2] A stagecoach pulled by four horses. —Eds.

seeing connections

Shown here are two advertisements for bicycles from the 1890s. As you look at them, consider the differences in the way bicycles were marketed to men and women during this time period.

What did advertisers consider important selling points for each gender? Does Frances Willard's piece reflect the mindset conveyed by these ads? What connections do you see to contemporary advertisements for women's athletic gear? What connections do you see to Willard's experience of learning to ride a bicycle?

Library of Congress

PHOTOTEQUE PERRIN/Private Collection/Bridgeman Images

equilibration of thought and action by which we conquer the universe in conquering ourselves.

I finally concluded that all failure was from a wobbling will rather than a wobbling wheel. I felt that indeed the will is the wheel of the mind — its perpetual motion having been learned when the morning stars sang together. When the wheel of the mind went well then the rubber wheel hummed merrily; but specters of the mind there are as well as of the wheel. In the aggregate of perception concerning which we have reflected and from which we have deduced our generalizations upon the world without, within, above, there are so many ghastly and fantastical images that they must obtrude themselves at certain intervals, like filmy bits of glass in the turn of the kaleidoscope. Probably every accident of which I had heard or read in my half-century tinged the uncertainty that by the correlation of forces passed over into the tremor that I felt when we

10

This cartoon, published by the humor magazine *Puck* in 1895, shows the "new woman" in pantaloons — suitable for bicycle riding — standing up bravely to three mice. The "old woman" in the portrait behind her has jumped on a chair in fright at the sight of a mouse. The surrounding images show the "new woman" on her bicycle performing various everyday tasks. At the bottom, the cartoon has been captioned: "The 'new woman' and her bicycle — there will be several varieties of her."

How would you characterize the tone of this cartoon's overall message? How do these images of the "new woman" support Willard's reasons for learning to ride a bicycle?

PUCK.

THE "NEW WOMAN" AND HER BICYCLE.——THERE WILL BE SEVERAL VARIETIES OF HER.

Library of Congress

began to round the terminus bend of the broad Priory walk. And who shall say by what original energy the mind forced itself at once from the contemplation of disaster and thrust into the very movement of the foot on the pedal a concept of vigor, safety, and success? I began to feel that myself plus the bicycle equaled myself plus the world, upon whose spinning-wheel we must all learn to ride, or fall into the sluiceways of oblivion and despair. That which made me succeed with the bicycle was precisely what had gained me a measure of success in life — it was the hardihood of spirit that led me to begin, the persistence of will that held me to my task, and the patience that was willing to begin again when the last stroke had failed. And so I found high moral uses in the bicycle and can commend it as a teacher without pulpit or creed. He who succeeds, or, to be more exact in handing over my experience, she who succeeds in gaining the mastery of such an animal as Gladys, will gain the mastery of life, and by exactly the same methods and characteristics. . . .

seeing connections

What does this chart, taken from the U.S. Census Bureau's 2012 American Community Survey, suggest about the popularity — and even the future — of bicycle riding? What societal dynamics does Willard speak to (either directly or indirectly) that might be a factor in the message this data conveys?

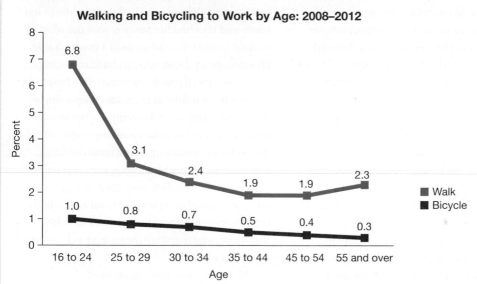

Walking and Bicycling to Work by Age: 2008–2012

Data from U.S. Census Bureau, American Community Survey, 2008–2012.

In Conclusion

If I am asked to explain why I learned the bicycle I should say I did it as an act of grace, if not of actual religion. The cardinal doctrine laid down by my physician was, "Live out of doors and take congenial exercise;" but from the day when, at sixteen years of age, I was enwrapped in the long skirts that impeded every footstep, I have detested walking and felt with a certain noble disdain that the conventions of life had cut me off from what in the freedom of my prairie home had been one of life's sweetest joys. Driving is not real exercise; it does not renovate the river of blood that flows so sluggishly in the veins of those who from any cause have lost the natural adjustment of brain to brawn. Horseback-riding, which does promise vigorous exercise, is expensive. The bicycle meets all the conditions and will ere long come within the reach of all. Therefore, in obedience to the laws of health, I learned to ride. I also wanted to help women to a wider world, for I hold that the more interests women and men can have in common, in thought, word, and deed, the happier will it be for the home. Besides, there was a special value to women in the conquest of the bicycle by a woman in her fifty-third year, and one who had so many comrades in the white-ribbon army[3] that her action would be widely influential. Then there were three minor reasons:

I did it from pure natural love of adventure — a love long hampered and impeded, like a brook that runs underground,

[3] A symbol worn by members of the Women's Christian Temperance Union, which was founded by Willard and others in 1874. —Eds.

but in this enterprise bubbling up again with somewhat of its pristine freshness and taking its merry course as of old.

Second, from a love of acquiring this new implement of power and literally putting it underfoot.

Last, but not least, because a good many people thought I could not do it at my age.

It is needless to say that a bicycling costume *15* was a prerequisite. This consisted of a skirt and blouse of tweed, with belt, rolling collar, and loose cravat,[4] the skirt three inches from the ground; a round straw hat, and walking-shoes with gaiters.[5] It was a simple, modest suit, to which no person of common sense could take exception.

As nearly as I can make out, reducing the problem to actual figures, it took me about three months, with an average of fifteen minutes' practice daily, to learn, first, to pedal; second, to turn; third, to dismount; and fourth, to mount independently this most mysterious animal. January 20th will always be a red-letter bicycle day, because although I had already mounted several times with no hand on the rudder, some

good friend had always stood by to lend moral support; but summoning all my force, and, most forcible of all, what Sir Benjamin Ward Richardson[6] declares to be the two essential elements — decision and precision — I mounted and started off alone. From that hour the spell was broken; Gladys was no more a mystery: I had learned all her kinks, had put a bridle in her teeth, and touched her smartly with the whip of victory. Consider, ye who are of a considerable chronology: in about thirteen hundred minutes, or, to put it more mildly, in twenty-two hours, or, to put it most mildly of all, in less than a single day as the almanac reckons time — but practically in two days of actual practice — amid the delightful surroundings of the great outdoors, and inspired by the bird-songs, the color and fragrance of an English posy-garden, in the company of devoted and pleasant comrades, I had made myself master of the most remarkable, ingenious, and inspiring motor ever yet devised upon this planet.

Moral: *Go thou and do likewise!*

[1895]

---

[4] A necktie. —Eds.

[5] A garment similar to leggings, worn to cover or protect the ankle and lower leg. —Eds.

[6] Sir Benjamin Ward Richardson (1828–1896) was a prominent British physician and writer, best known for his work on public hygiene. —Eds.

QUESTIONS FOR DISCUSSION

1. Why does Frances Willard expand her recommendation to learn to ride a bicycle to boys as well as girls? Men as well as women?

2. Willard's matter-of-fact account of why and how she learned to ride a bicycle is intended as an argument. What aspects of the rhetorical situation make a strong argument necessary? What counterarguments does she present?

3. What are the qualities Willard finds in herself as she learns to ride a bicycle? How does she use this self-discovery to develop her argument that "the mastery of such an animal as Gladys, will gain the mastery of life" (para. 10)?

4. How does Willard frame learning to ride a bicycle as a parable on life, especially the life of a woman?

5. In paragraph 6 Willard repeats an old adage that "horseback riding is the only thing in which a prince is apt to excel, for the reason that the horse never flatters and would as soon throw him as if he were a groom." How does she relate that statement to the process of learning to ride the bicycle? Do you find it convincing? To what extent might this adage apply to a modern skill, such as learning to drive a car or learning to code?

6. It is hard for us to imagine the nineteenth-century controversy over bicycle riding for women. British novelist John Galsworthy summed up the bicycle's role in the eventual demise of the Victorian woman:

> The bicycle . . . has been responsible for more movement in manners and morals than anything [else]. . . . Under its influence, wholly or in part, have wilted chaperones, long and narrow skirts, tight corsets, hair that would come down, black stockings, thick ankles, large hats, prudery and fear of the dark; under its influence, wholly or in part, have blossomed weekends, strong nerves, strong legs, strong language, knickers, knowledge of make and shape, knowledge of woods and pastures, equality of sex, good digestion and professional occupation — in four words, the emancipation of women.

What might the arguments against women's bicycle riding have been? How might Willard and other feminists have addressed these arguments?

7. During her two decades of leadership of the WCTU, Willard effectively organized women for direct political action — without violating the notion of women's "proper" roles — by referring to women as guardians and defenders of their homes and families and by focusing on women's traditional concerns. How does her account of learning to ride a bicycle support those principles? What evidence does her account provide of her skill at inspiring fundamentally conservative, apolitical churchwomen to take political action?

8. Why does Willard call the exhortation at the end of the piece the "Moral"?

QUESTIONS ON RHETORIC AND STYLE

1. Throughout the excerpt, Willard anthropomorphizes her bicycle — that is, she gives it human qualities, including a name ("Gladys"), a mind of its own, and a voice. What is the effect of this strategy? What does her bicycle have to say to her? How would you characterize its "voice," and how does Willard create it? Why do you think Willard devoted nearly two full paragraphs to the voice of her bicycle?

2. In paragraph 3, how does Willard use the comment from the naval officer to establish ethos? Why do you think she chose to quote him in particular?

3. Look carefully at paragraph 4 and analyze the way Willard use figurative language — particularly analogies — to encourage and instruct her readers.

4. In paragraphs 6 and 7 Willard quotes sayings, proverbs and accepted wisdom. What is the purpose of those quotes and citations?

5. Trace the analogies Willard makes between bicycle riding and other activities. How does each one help her achieve her purpose? What is their cumulative effect?

6. Acknowledging the weight of public opinion against her ideas is a strategy Willard often utilized as head of the WCTU. What other rhetorical strategies does she employ that you have seen present-day politicians use? Give at least one example.

7. Though Willard often attributes human qualities to "Gladys," her bicycle, she also encourages her audience to imagine Gladys as a horse. In paragraph 16, for instance, Willard has "put a bridle in [Gladys's] teeth, and touched her smartly with the whip of victory." Why do you think Willard asked her readers to imagine Gladys as a horse?

8. Willard gives three major reasons and three minor reasons why learning to ride a bicycle was important. What are those reasons? What is the effect of her hierarchy? Why do you think she organized her material this way?

9. Analyze the syntax of the final sentence of paragraph 16. What is the effect of delaying the subject and the verb until the end of that very long sentence?

10. You may have noticed that Willard's diction changes, moving between colloquial and formal. Track the changes throughout this excerpt and see if you can find a pattern: What is she talking about when her word choices are more formal? When does her diction slip into more conversational territory? What do these shifts tell you about her purpose? How do they help her achieve that purpose?

SUGGESTIONS FOR WRITING

1. Write an essay in which you support, challenge, or qualify Willard's assertion that "the more interests women and men can have in common, in thought, word, and deed, the happier will it be for the home" (para. 11).

2. Each of the following statements addresses the role of the bicycle in society. Select one that interests you, and write an essay defending, challenging, or qualifying its assertion. To support your argument, refer to your own experience, your knowledge of history, and to Willard's writing.

   a. I find buying a bicycle is a great way to stay in touch with people.

   — Jan Chipchase

   b. Riding a bicycle is the summit of human endeavor — an almost neutral environmental effect coupled with the ability to travel substantial distances without disturbing anybody. The bike is the perfect marriage of technology and human energy.

   — Jeremy Corbyn

   c. To me the bicycle is in many ways a more satisfactory invention than the automobile. It is consonant with the independence of man because it works under his own power entirely. There is no combustion of some petroleum product from Venezuela to set the pedals going. Purely mechanical instruments like watches and bicycles are to be preferred to engines that depend on the purchase of power from foreign sources. You can be more independent, and therefore more of a man, in a sailing vessel than in a power-driven boat. . . . The price of power, on the other hand, is enslavement.

   — Louis J. Halle

   d. If physical mobility is an essential condition of freedom, the bicycle has probably been the greatest single device for achieving what [Karl] Marx has called the full realization of being human invented since Gutenberg, and the only one without obvious drawbacks.

   — Eric Hobsbawm

   e. Cycling is possibly the greatest and most pleasurable form of transport ever invented. It's like walking, only with one-tenth of the effort. Ride through a city and you can understand its geography in a way that no motorist, contained by one-way signs and traffic jams, will ever be able to. . . . It truly is one of the greatest feelings of freedom one can have in a metropolitan environment.

   — Daniel Pemberton

   f. When man invented the bicycle he reached the peak of his attainments. Here was a machine of precision and balance for the convenience of man. And (unlike subsequent inventions for man's convenience) the more he used it, the fitter his body became. Here, for once, was a product of man's brain that was entirely beneficial to those who used it, and of no harm or irritation to others. Progress should have stopped when man invented the bicycle.

   — Elizabeth West

3. One could argue that the fashions of Willard's day intentionally limited women's range of motion and, certainly, one of the strongest objections to women's bicycling had to do with the moral implications of a pursuit that necessitated more practical clothing. Research the clothing reforms that began during the late nineteenth century as a result of the growing popularity of the bicycle and, in a well-written essay, develop a position on the role women's fashion played in securing equal rights for women in America.

4. Willard was a founder and head of the WCTU, a women's political action group that opposed alcohol consumption. Research the temperance movement, including its history and basic tenets, and write a synthesis essay in which you examine the extent to which the movement helped protect women and children. Use at least three sources to support your response.

5. Write an essay in which you examine the process by which you learned a new skill. Make sure to write about both the steps you took and the effect on your life of learning the skill.

The Proper Place for Sports

THEODORE ROOSEVELT

Theodore Roosevelt (1858–1919) was only forty-two when he became the twenty-sixth president of the United States following William McKinley's assassination in 1901. During his first term he spearheaded the construction of the Panama Canal, and during his second he won the Nobel Peace Prize — the first American to do so — for his mediation in the Russo-Japanese War of 1904–05. Prior to holding office, he commanded the famed Rough Riders, an all-volunteer cavalry that led the charge on San Juan Hill in the Spanish-American War, for which he was awarded the Congressional Medal of Honor. Roosevelt led what he called the "strenuous life," which included being a cowboy in the Wild West, going on safari in Africa, and exploring the Amazon basin. His letters to his children, originally published in 1919, capture Roosevelt's view that "for unflagging interest and enjoyment, a household of children, if things go reasonably well, certainly makes all other forms of success and achievement lose their importance by comparison." In the following 1903 letter to his son Ted, Roosevelt puts participation in sports in perspective.

Dear Ted:

In spite of the "Hurry! Hurry!" on the outside of your envelope, I did not like to act until I had consulted Mother and thought the matter over; and to be frank with you, old fellow, I am by no means sure that I am doing right now. If it were not that I feel you will be so bitterly disappointed, I would strongly advocate your acquiescing in the decision to leave you off the second squad this year. I am proud of your pluck, and I greatly admire football — though it was not a game I was ever able to play myself, my qualities resembling Kermit's rather than yours. But the very things that make it a good game make it a rough game, and there is always the chance of your being laid up. Now, I should not in the least object to your being laid up for a season if you were striving for something worth while, to get on the Groton school team, for instance, or on your class team when you entered Harvard — for of course I don't think you will have the weight to entitle you to try

▼

How does this 1912 drawing by George Bellows depict Roosevelt's assessment of football in paragraph 1?

Mead Art Museum, Amherst College, MA, USA/Bridgeman Images

for the 'varsity. But I am by no means sure that it *is* worth your while to run the risk of being laid up for the sake of playing in the second squad when you are a fourth former, instead of when you are a fifth former. I do not know that the risk is balanced by the reward. However, I have told the Rector that as you feel so strongly about it, I think that the chance of your damaging yourself in body is outweighed by the possibility of bitterness of spirit if you could not play. Understand me, I should think mighty little of you if you permitted chagrin to make you bitter on some point where it was evidently right for you to suffer the chagrin. But in this case I am uncertain, and I shall give you the benefit of the doubt. If, however, the coaches at any time come to the conclusion that you ought not to be in the second squad, why you must come off without grumbling.

I am delighted to have you play football. I believe in rough, manly sports. But I do not believe in them if they degenerate into the sole end of any one's existence. I don't want you to sacrifice standing well in your studies to any over-athleticism; and I need not tell you that character counts for a great deal more than either intellect or body in winning success in life. Athletic proficiency is a mighty good servant, and like so many other good servants, a mighty bad master. Did you ever read Pliny's letter to Trajan, in which he speaks of [it] being advisable to keep the Greeks absorbed in athletics, because it distracted their minds from all serious pursuits, including soldiering, and prevented their ever being dangerous to the Romans? I have not a doubt that the British officers in the Boer War had their efficiency partly reduced because they had sacrificed their legitimate duties to an inordinate and ridiculous love of sports. A man must develop his physical prowess up to a certain point; but after he has reached that point there are other things that count more. In my regiment nine-tenths of the men were better horsemen than I was, and probably two-thirds of them better shots than I was, while on the average they were certainly hardier and more enduring. Yet after I had had them a very short while they all knew, and I knew too, that nobody else could command them as I could. I am glad you should play football; I am glad that you should box; I am glad that you should ride and shoot and walk and row as well as you do. I should be very

PETER NEWARK'S PICTURES/Private Collection/Bridgeman Images

Ted Roosevelt, the recipient of the letter here, was Theodore Roosevelt's oldest son. He is third from the left in this family photograph.

What can you read about Roosevelt's family dynamics from this picture, and how are those dynamics reflected throughout the letter?

This detail from an 1898 painting by W. G. Road shows Theodore Roosevelt in a popular pose — leading the Rough Riders during the Spanish-American war.

How does the artist characterize him here? How is this characterization different from the way Roosevelt comes across in his letter?

PETER NEWARK'S PICTURES/Private Collection/Bridgeman Images

sorry if you did not do these things. But don't ever get into the frame of mind which regards these things as constituting the end to which all your energies must be devoted, or even the major portion of your energies.

Yes, I am going to speak at Groton on prize day. I felt that while I was President, and while you and Kermit were at Groton I wanted to come up there and see you, and the Rector wished me to speak, and so I am very glad to accept.

By the way, I am working hard to get Renown accustomed to automobiles. He is such a handful now when he meets them that I seriously mind encountering them when Mother is along. Of course I do not care if I am alone, or with another man, but I am uneasy all the time when I am out with Mother. Yesterday I tried Bleistein over the hurdles at Chevy Chase. The first one was new, high and stiff, and the old rascal never rose six inches, going slap through it. I took him at it again and he went over all right.

I am very busy now, facing the usual endless   5 worry and discouragement, and trying to keep steadily in mind that I must not only be as resolute as Abraham Lincoln in seeking to achieve decent ends, but as patient, as uncomplaining, and as even-tempered in dealing, not only with knaves, but with the well-meaning foolish people, educated and uneducated, who by their unwisdom give the knaves their chance.

[1903]

EXPLORING THE TEXT

1. Theodore Roosevelt is credited with having said, "In short, in life, as in a football game, the principle to follow is: Hit the line hard; don't foul and don't shirk, but hit the line hard!" In what ways does the letter to Ted offer similar advice? How is the advice tempered for his young son? Does the letter contradict the "hit the line hard" quotation in any way? Explain your response.

2. Roosevelt argues against sports if they "degenerate into the sole end of any one's existence" (para. 2). What examples does he give to support his argument? Are they effective? Do they withstand the test of time? Can you apply his argument to participation in sports today? If so, how?

3. What assumptions about his son underlie Roosevelt's argument?

4. Characterize the letter's tone. Do some parts seem more presidential than fatherly? Identify and explain.

5. How does the first paragraph of the letter balance appeals to logos and pathos?

6. Analyze the following two sentences, considering the effects of Roosevelt's diction. In which ways does the language support or undermine his argument?

> Understand me, I should think mighty little of you if you permitted chagrin to make you bitter on some point where it was evidently right for you to suffer the chagrin. (para. 1)

> I don't want you to sacrifice standing well in your studies to any over-athleticism; and I need not tell you that character counts for a great deal more than either intellect or body in winning success in life. (para. 2)

7. Roosevelt begins the letter by saying he did not hurry his response because he wanted to confer with Ted's mother. He doesn't mention her again until paragraph 4. What is the effect of this rhetorical decision?

8. How does Roosevelt achieve his measured response to what was obviously a sense of urgency in the letter to which he is responding? Look particularly at the ways he uses the word *if*.

9. Think about this letter in light of the current generation of parents, considered by many to be overly involved in their children's lives. Could one accuse Roosevelt of being an early-twentieth-century helicopter parent?

An Innocent at Rinkside

WILLIAM FAULKNER

William Faulkner (1897–1962) grew up in Oxford, Mississippi. Except for some time in the Canadian and then the British Royal Air Force during World War I, a bookstore in New York City, and a newspaper in New Orleans, Faulkner seldom left Oxford. His fiction — including *The Sound and the Fury* (1929), *Light in August* (1932), *Absalom, Absalom!* (1936), and *Intruder in the Dust* (1962), among others — takes place in the imaginary Yoknapatawpha County and features a revolving cast of recurring characters. Faulkner won the Nobel Prize in Literature in 1949. The piece presented here, offering Faulkner's impressions of his first National Hockey League game, appeared in *Sports Illustrated* in 1955.

The vacant ice looked tired, though it shouldn't have. They told him it had been put down only a few minutes ago following a basketball game, and after the hockey match it would be taken up again to make room for something else. But it looked not expectant but resigned, like the mirror simulating ice in the Christmas store window, not before the miniature fir trees and reindeer and cosy lamplit cottage were arranged upon it, but after they had been dismantled and cleared away.

Then it was filled with motion, speed. To the innocent, who had never seen it before, it seemed discorded and inconsequent, bizarre and paradoxical like the frantic darting of the weightless bugs which run on the surface of stagnant pools. Then it would break, coalesce through a kind of kaleidoscopic whirl like a child's toy, into a pattern, a design almost beautiful, as if an inspired choreographer had drilled a willing and patient and hard-working troupe of dancers — a pattern, a design which was trying to tell him something, say something to him urgent and important and true in that second before, already bulging with the motion and the speed, it began to disintegrate and dissolve.

Then he learned to find the puck and follow it. Then the individual players would emerge.

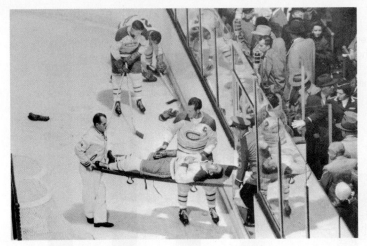

Bettmann/Getty Images

Faulkner says that part of the excitement of the game is that "actual male blood could flow" (para. 4). Pictured here is Bernie "Boom-Boom" Geoffrion, one of the hockey stars Faulkner mentions, being carried off the ice on a stretcher after taking a hit to the ribs.
To what extent does this photo reflect Faulkner's description in paragraphs 4 and 5?

They would not emerge like the sweating bare-handed behemoths from the troglodyte mass of football, but instead as fluid and fast and effortless as rapier thrusts or lightning — Richard with something of the passionate glittering fatal alien quality of snakes, Geoffrion like an agile ruthless precocious boy who maybe couldn't do anything else but then he didn't need to; and others — the veteran Laprade, still with the know-how and the grace. But he had time too now, or rather time had him, and what remained was no longer expendable that recklessly, heedlessly, successfully; not enough of it left now to buy fresh passion and fresh triumph with.

Like the Rapier

Excitement: men in rapid, hard, close physical conflict, not just with bare hands, but armed with the knife blades of skates and the hard, fast, deft sticks which could break bones when used right. He had noticed how many women were among the spectators, and for just a moment he thought that perhaps this was why — that here actual male blood could flow, not from the crude impact of a heavier fist but from the rapid and delicate stroke of weapons, which, like the European rapier or the frontier pistol, reduced mere size and brawn to its proper perspective to the passion and the

will. But only for a moment because he, the innocent, didn't like that idea either. It was the excitement of speed and grace, with the puck for catalyst, to give it reason, meaning.

He watched it — the figure-darted glare of ice, ⁵ the concentric tiers rising in sections stipulated by the hand-lettered names of the individual fanclub idols, vanishing upward into the pall of tobacco smoke trapped by the roof — the roof which stopped and trapped all that intent and tense watching, and concentrated it downward upon the glare of ice frantic and frenetic with motion; until the byproduct of the speed and the motion — their violence — had no chance to exhaust itself upward into space and so leave on the ice only the swift glittering changing pattern. And he thought how perhaps something is happening to sport in America (assuming that by definition sport is something you do yourself, in solitude or not, because it is fun), and that something is the roof we are putting over it and them. Skating, basketball, tennis, track meets and even steeplechasing have moved indoors; football and baseball function beneath covers of arc lights and in time will be rain- and coldproofed too. There still remain the proper working of a fly over trout water or the taking of a rise of birds in front of a dog or the right placing of a bullet in a deer or even a bigger animal

In this 2015 photo, Anaheim Ducks Winger Andrew Cogliano checks Los Angeles Kings Defenseman Brayden McNabb into the boards. In the process, Cogliano's stick hit McNabb in the nose so hard it started to bleed. Look carefully at the fans in the stands.

How do the faces of the fans illustrate Faulkner's descriptions?

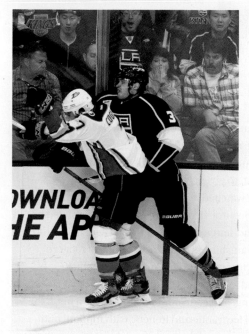

Icon Sportswire/Getty Images

Views on Hockey Fighting Ban

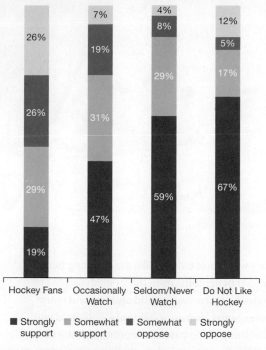

Data from the Environics Institute.

This chart shows the results of a 2012 survey on Canadians' level of support for a fighting ban in hockey.

To what extent does this chart support Faulkner's assertion that we "like to watch" (para. 6)?

which will hurt you if you don't. But not for long: in time that will be indoors too beneath lights and the trapped pall of spectator tobacco, the concentric sections bearing the name and device of the lion or the fish as well as that of the Richard or Geoffrion of the scoped rifle or four-ounce rod.

The Same Little Boys

But (to repeat) not for long, because the innocent did not quite believe that either. We — Americans — like to watch; we like the adrenalic discharge of vicarious excitement or triumph or success. But we like to do also: the discharge of the personal excitement of the triumph and the fear to be had from actually setting the horse at the stone wall or pointing the overcanvased sloop or finding by actual test if you can line up two sights and one buffalo in time. There must have been little boys in that throng too, frantic with the slow excruciating passage of time, panting for the hour when they would be Richard or Geoffrion or Laprade — the same little Negro boys whom the innocent has seen shadow-boxing in front of a photograph of Joe Louis in his own Mississippi town, the same little Norwegian boys he watched staring up the snowless slope of the Holmenkollen jump one July day in the hills above Oslo.

seeing connections

Look carefully at these three linocuts, completed by Russian artist Masabikh Akhunov in 1971. Clockwise from the top, the pieces are entitled *Face-off*, *Attack*, and *Victory*.

How do the images — and their titles — capture the atmosphere Faulkner describes in "An Innocent at Rinkside"? Do you believe that a hockey fan can truly be called innocent? Use the images here and Faulkner's essay to explain your answer.

Gamborg Collection/Bridgeman Images

Gamborg Collection/Bridgeman Images

Gamborg Collection/Bridgeman Images

[1955]

EXPLORING THE TEXT

1. How does William Faulkner bring to life a game that many people have only seen on television?

2. Find examples of figurative language — similes and metaphors in particular. What is the effect of these literary devices, which are more common in fiction and poetry than in sportswriting?

3. Faulkner refers to himself as "the innocent" and in the third person. Why do you think he has avoided the first person? Do you think this is an effective technique? Explain your response.

4. What statement does Faulkner make about the future of sports? To what extent have his predictions come true?

5. What do you think Faulkner's sports biases are? How can you tell?

The Cruelest Sport

JOYCE CAROL OATES

Joyce Carol Oates was born in Lockport, New York, in 1938. With a typewriter she received at age fourteen, Oates wrote "novel after novel" in high school and college in order to train herself to be a writer. Oates, who received a BA from Syracuse University and an MA in English from the University of Wisconsin, is currently the Roger S. Berlind Distinguished Professor of the Humanities at Princeton. She is the youngest author to receive the National Book Award — for her novel *them* (1969). Novelist, playwright, poet, and journalist, Oates is highly prolific, having published more than fifty novels, including *Black Water* (1992), *We Were the Mulvaneys* (1996), and *The Falls* (2004), nearly forty short story collections, and eleven novellas over the course of her career. Her work often addresses the violence and suspense lurking beneath ordinary life. This essay was originally published in the *New York Review of Books* in February 1992.

And if the body does not do fully as much as the soul?

And if the body were not the soul, what is the
soul?
— Walt Whitman, "*I Sing the Body Electric*"

A boxer's victory is gained in blood.
— Greek inscription

Professional boxing is the only major American sport whose primary, and often murderous, energies are not coyly deflected by such artifacts as balls and pucks. Though highly ritualized, and as rigidly bound by rules, traditions, and taboos as any religious ceremony, it survives as the most primitive and terrifying of contests: two men, near-naked, fight each other in a brightly lit, elevated space roped in like an animal pen (though the ropes were originally to keep rowdy spectators out); two men climb into the ring from which only one, symbolically, will climb out. (Draws do occur in boxing, but are rare, and unpopular.)

Boxing is a stylized mimicry of a fight to the death, yet its mimesis is an uncertain convention, for boxers do sometimes die in the ring, or as a consequence of a bout; their lives are sometimes, perhaps always, shortened by the stress and punishment of their careers (in training camps no less than in official fights). Certainly, as in the melancholy case of Muhammad Ali, the most acclaimed and beloved heavyweight in boxing history, the quality of the boxer's post-retirement life is frequently diminished. For the great majority of boxers, past and present, life in the ring is nasty, brutish, and short — and not even that remunerative.

Yet, for inhabitants of the boxing world, the ideal conclusion of a fight is a knockout, and not a decision; and this, ideally, not the kind in which a man is counted "out" on his feet, still less a TKO ("technical knockout" — from injuries), but a knockout in the least ambiguous sense — one man collapsed and unconscious, the other leaping about the ring with his gloves raised in victory, the very embodiment of adolescent masculine fantasy. Like a tragedy in which no one dies, the fight lacking a classic knockout seems unresolved, unfulfilled: the strength, courage, ingenuity, and desperation of neither boxer have been adequately measured. Catharsis is but partial, the Aristotelian principle of an action complete in itself has been thwarted. (Recall the fury of young Muhammad Ali at the too-readily-defeated Sonny Liston in their second, notorious title fight, of 1965: instead of going to a neutral corner, Ali stood over his fallen opponent with his fist cocked, screaming, "Get up and fight, sucker!")

This is because boxing's mimesis is not that of a mere game, but a powerful analogue of human struggle in the rawest of life-and-death terms. When the analogue is not evoked, as, in most fights, it is not, the action is likely to be unengaging, or dull; "boxing" is the art, but "fighting" is the passion. The delirium of the crowd at one of those matches called "great" must be experienced first-hand to be believed (Frazier–Ali I, 1971, Hagler–Hearns, 1986, for instance); identification with the fighters is so intense, it is as if barriers between egos dissolve, and one is in the presence of a Dionysian rite of cruelty, sacrifice, and redemption. "The nearest thing to death," Ali described it, after his third title match with Joe Frazier, in 1975, which he won when the fight was stopped after the fourteenth round. Or: "This is some way to make a living, isn't it?" as the superlightweight Saoul Mamby said, badly battered after a title fight with the champion Billy Costello, in 1984.

A romance of (expendable) maleness — in which The Fight is honored, and even great champions come, and go.

5

◆ ◆ ◆

For these reasons, among others, boxing has long been America's most popularly despised sport: a "so-called" sport, even a "meta-" or an "anti-" sport: a "vicious exploitation of maleness"[1] as prostitution and pornography may be said to be a vicious exploitation of femaleness. It is not, contrary to common supposition, the most dangerous sport (the American Medical Association, arguing for boxing's abolition, acknowledges that it is statistically less dangerous than speedway racing, thoroughbred racing, downhill skiing, professional football, et al.), but it is the most spectacularly and pointedly cruel sport, its intention being to stun one's opponent's brain; to affect the orgasmic communal "knockout" that is the culminating point of the rising action of the ideal fight. The humanitarian argues that boxing's

very intentions are obscene, which sets it apart, theoretically at least, from purer (i.e., Caucasian) establishment sports bracketed above.

Boxing is only possible if there is an endless supply of young men hungry to leave their impoverished ghetto neighborhoods, more than willing to substitute the putative dangers of the ring for the more evident, possibly daily, dangers of the street; yet it is rarely advanced as a means of eradicating boxing that poverty itself be abolished; that it is the social conditions feeding boxing that are obscene. The pious hypocrisy of Caucasian moralists vis-à-vis the sport that has become almost exclusively the province of black and ethnic minorities has its analogue in a classic statement of President Bush's of some months ago, that he is worried about the amount of "filth" flooding America by way of televised hearings and trials: not that the Clarence Thomas–Anita Hill hearing and the William Kennedy Smith rape trial revealed "filth" at the core of certain male–female relations in our society, but that public airings of such, the very hearings and trials, are the problem. Ban the spectacle, and the obscenity will cease to exist.

◆ ◆ ◆

Black boxers from the time of Jack Johnson (the first and most flamboyant of the world's black heavyweight champions, 1908–1915) through Joe Louis, Sugar Ray Robinson, Muhammad Ali, Larry Holmes, Sugar Ray Leonard, and Mike Tyson have been acutely conscious of themselves as racially *other* from the majority of their audiences, whom they must please in one way or another, as black villains, or honorary whites. (After his pulverizing defeat of the "good, humble Negro" Floyd Patterson, in a heavyweight title match in 1962, Sonny Liston gloated in his role as black villain; when he lost so ingloriously to Muhammad Ali, a brash new-style black who drew upon Jack Johnson, Sugar Ray Robinson, and even the campy professional wrestler Gorgeous George for his own public persona, Liston lost his mystique, and his career soon ended.)

---

[1] See Gerald Early's brilliantly corrosive essays on boxing in *Tuxedo Junction: Essays on American Culture* (Ecco, 1989).

To see race as a predominant factor in American boxing is inevitable, but the moral issues, as always in this paradoxical sport, are ambiguous. Is there a moral distinction between the spectacle of black slaves in the Old South being forced by their white owners to fight, for purposes of gambling, and the spectacle of contemporary blacks fighting for multimillion-dollar paydays, for TV coverage from Las Vegas and Atlantic City? When, in 1980, in one of the most cynically promoted boxing matches in history, the aging and ailing Muhammad Ali fought the young heavyweight champion Larry Holmes, in an "execution" of a fight that was stopped after ten rounds, did it alleviate the pain, or the shame, that Ali was guaranteed $8 million for the fight? (Of which, with characteristic finesse, promoter Don King cheated him of nearly $1 million.) Ask the boxers.

Boxing today is very different from the boxing of the past, which allowed a man to be struck repeatedly while trying to get to his feet (Dempsey–Willard, 1919), or to be knocked down seven times in three wholly one-sided rounds (Patterson–Johansson I, 1959), or so savagely and senselessly struck in the head with countless unanswered blows that he died in a coma ten days later (Griffith–Paret, 1962); the more immediate danger, for any boxer fighting a Don King opponent, is that the fight will be stopped prematurely, by a zealous referee protective of King's investment.

As boxing is "reformed," it becomes less satisfying on a deep, unconscious level, more nearly resembling amateur boxing; yet, as boxing remains primitive, brutal, bloody, and dangerous, it seems ever more anachronistic, if not in fact obscene, in a society with pretensions of humanitarianism. Its exemplary figure is that of the warrior, of some mythopoeic time before weapons were invented; the triumph of physical genius, in a technologically advanced world in which the physical counts for very little, set beside intellectual skills. Even in the gritty world of the underclass, who, today, would choose to fight with mere *fists*? Guns abound, death to one's opponents at a safe distance is possible even for children. Mike Tyson's boast, after his defeat of the twelve-to-one underdog Carl Williams in a heavyweight title defense of 1989, "I want to fight, fight, fight and

Shannon Wheeler/The New Yorker Collection/The Cartoon Bank

"I won't lie. It doesn't look good."

◀

Joyce Carol Oates notes that as boxing is "'reformed,' it becomes less satisfying on a deep, unconscious level, more nearly resembling amateur boxing; yet, as boxing remains primitive, brutal, bloody, and dangerous, it seems ever more anachronistic, if not in fact obscene, in a society with pretensions of humanitarianism" (para. 11).
How does this cartoon comment on what Oates considers "obscene" about boxing?

destruct the world," strikes a poignantly hollow note, even if we knew nothing of subsequent disastrous events in Tyson's life and career.[2]

Consider the boxing trainer's time-honored adage: *They all go if you hit them right.*

These themes are implicit in Thomas Hauser's *Muhammad Ali: His Life and Times* and *The Black Lights: Inside the World of Professional Boxing*, but it is only in the latter work that theoretical, historical, and psychological issues are considered — Hauser sees boxing as "the red light district of professional sports," in which individuals of exceptional talent, courage, and integrity nonetheless prevail. His Ali is the heftier and more ambitious of the two, befitting its prodigious subject — the most famous athlete of all time, until recent years the most highly paid athlete of all time. An authorized biography, it would appear to be definitive, and is certainly exhaustive; Hauser spent thousands of hours with his subject, as well as approximately two hundred other people, and was given access to Ali's medical records. The text arranges these testimonies into a chronological history in which (is this New Age biography?) the author's voice alternates with, but rarely comments upon, still less criticizes, what these others have said. Compassionate, intelligent, fair-minded, *Muhammad Ali: His Life and Times* might have benefited from further editing and paraphrase. Specific subjects (an imminent fight, financial deals, Ali's marital problems, Ali's health problems, the Nation of Islam, et al.) become lost in a welter of words; frequently, it is difficult to locate dates, even for important fights. And no ring record of Ali in the appendix! — a baffling omission, as if Ali's performance as an athlete were not the primary reason for the book.

As it happens, Hauser's succinct commentary on the Ali phenomenon and his shrewd analysis of the boxing world, including Don King's role

in it, in his earlier book, *The Black Lights*, can provide, for the reader of the biography, a kind of companion gloss; the books are helpfully read in tandem. It is a remark of Ali's, in 1967, that gives *The Black Lights* its ominous title:

> They say when you get hit and hurt bad you see black lights — the black lights of unconsciousness. But I don't know nothing about that. I've had twenty-eight fights and twenty-eight wins. I ain't never been stopped.

Muhammad Ali, born Cassius Marcellus Clay in Louisville, Kentucky, on January 17, 1942, grandson of a slave, began boxing at the age of twelve, and, by eighteen, had fought 108 amateur bouts. How is it possible that the young man who, in his twenties, would astonish the world not just with the brilliance of his boxing but the sharpness of his wit seems to have been a dull-average student in high school who graduated 376th out of a class of 391? In 1966, his score on a mental aptitude test was an Army IQ of 78, well below military qualification. In 1975, Ali confessed to a reporter that he "can't read too good" and had not read ten pages of all the material written about him. I remember the television interview in which, asked what else he might have done with his life, Ali paused, for several seconds, clearly not knowing how to reply. All he'd ever known, he said finally, was boxing.

Mental aptitude tests cannot measure genius except in certain narrow ranges, and the genius of the body, the play of lightning-swift reflexes coupled with unwavering precision and confidence, eludes comprehension. All great boxers possess this genius, which scrupulous training hones, but can never create. "Styles make fights," as Ali's great trainer Angelo Dundee says, and "style" was young Ali's trademark. Yet even after early wins over such veterans as Archie Moore and Henry Cooper, the idiosyncrasies of Ali's style aroused skepticism in boxing experts. After winning the Olympic gold medal in 1960, Ali was described by A. J. Leibling as "skittering . . . like a

15

---

[2] See Montieth Illingworth, *Mike Tyson: Money, Myth and Betrayal* (Birch Lane, 1991), p. 330.

pebble over water." Everyone could see that this brash young boxer held his hands too low; he leaned away from punches instead of properly slipping them; his jab was light and flicking; he seemed to be perpetually on the brink of disaster. As a seven-to-one underdog in his first title fight with Sonny Liston, the twenty-two-year-old challenger astounded the experts with his performance, which was like none other they had ever seen in the heavyweight division; he so outboxed and demoralized Liston that Liston "quit on his stool" after the sixth round. A new era in boxing had begun, like a new music.

> Ali rode the crest of a new wave of athletes — competitors who were both big and fast. . . . Ali had a combination of size and speed that had never been seen in a fighter before, along with incredible will and courage. He also brought a new style to boxing. Jack Dempsey changed fisticuffs from a kind of constipated science where fighters fought in a tense defensive style to a wild sensual assault. Ali revolutionized boxing the way black basketball players have changed basketball today. He changed what happened in the ring, and elevated it to a level that was previously unknown.
>
> — Larry Merchant,
> quoted in *Muhammad Ali*

◆ ◆ ◆

In the context of contemporary boxing — the sport is in one of its periodic slumps — there is nothing more instructive and rejuvenating than to see again these old, early fights of Ali's, when, as his happy boast had it, he floated like a butterfly and stung like a bee and threw punches faster than opponents could see — like the "mystery" right to the temple of Liston that felled him, in the first minute of the first round of their rematch. These early fights, the most brilliant being against Cleveland Williams, in 1966, predate by a decade the long, grueling, punishing fights of Ali's later career, whose accumulative effects hurt Ali irrevocably, resulting in what doctors call, carefully, his "Parkinsonianism" — to distinguish it from Parkinson's disease. There is a true visceral shock in observing a heavyweight with the grace, agility, swiftness of hands and feet, defensive skills, and ring cunning of a middleweight Ray Robinson, or a featherweight Willie Pep — like all great athletes, Ali has to be seen to be believed.

In a secular, yet pseudo-religious and sentimental nation like the United States, it is quite natural that sports stars emerge as "heroes" — "legends" — "icons." Who else?

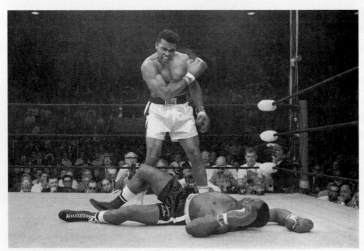

John Rooney/AP Images

In paragraph 17, Joyce Carol Oates describes Ali's ability to "[throw] punches faster than opponents could see — like the 'mystery' right to the temple of Liston that felled him, in the first minute of the first round of their rematch." This photo was taken shortly after Ali threw that "'mystery' right." **How does this photo illustrate some, but not all, of the qualities that Oates attributes to Ali? What's missing, both in this particular bout and in the photo?**

George Santayana described religion as "another world to live in" and no world is so set off from the disorganization and disenchantment of the quotidian than the world, or worlds, of sports. Hauser describes, in considerable detail, the transformation of the birth of Ali out of the unexpectedly stubborn and idealistic will of young Cassius Clay: how, immediately following his first victory over Liston, he declared himself a convert to the Nation of Islam (more popularly known as the Black Muslims) and "no longer a Christian." He repudiated his "slave name" of Cassius Marcellus Clay to become Muhammad Ali (a name which, incidentally, *The New York Times*, among other censorious white publications, would not honor through the 1960s). Ali became, virtually overnight, a spokesman for black America as no other athlete, certainly not the purposefully reticent Joe Louis, had ever done — "I don't have to be what you want me to be," he told white America. "I'm free to be me." Two years later, refusing to be inducted into the army to fight in Vietnam, Ali, beleaguered by reporters, uttered one of the memorable incendiary remarks of that era: "Man, I ain't got no quarrel with them Vietcong."

How ingloriously white America responded to Ali: the government retaliated by overruling a judge who had granted Ali the status of conscientious objector, fined Ali $10,000, and sentenced him to five years in prison; he was stripped of his heavyweight title and deprived of his license to box. Eventually, the U.S. Supreme Court would overturn the conviction, and, as the tide of opinion shifted in the country, in the early 1970s as the Vietnam War wound down Ali returned triumphantly to boxing again, and regained the heavyweight title not once but twice. Years of exile during which he'd endured the angry self-righteousness of the conservative white press seemed, wonderfully, not to have embittered him. He had become a hero. He had entered myth.

◆ ◆ ◆

Yet the elegiac title of Angelo Dundee's chapter in Dave Anderson's *In the Corner*[3] — "We Never Saw Muhammad Ali at His Best" — defines the nature of Ali's sacrifice for his principles, and the loss to boxing. When, after the three-and-a-half-year layoff, Ali returned to the ring, he was of course no longer the seemingly invincible boxer he'd been; he'd lost his legs, thus his primary line of defense. Like the maturing writer who learns to replace the incandescent head-on energies of youth with what is called technique, Ali would have to descend into his physical being and experience for the first time the punishment ("the nearest thing to death") that is the lot of the great boxer willing to put himself to the test. As Ali's personal physician at that time, Ferdie Pacheco, said,

> [Ali] discovered something which was both very good and very bad. Very bad in that it led to the physical damage he suffered later in his career; very good in that it eventually got him back the championship. He discovered that he could take a punch.

The secret of Ali's mature success, and the secret of his tragedy: *he could take a punch.*

For the remainder of his twenty-year career, Muhammad Ali took punches, many of the kind that, delivered to a nonboxer, would kill him or her outright — from Joe Frazier in their three exhausting marathon bouts, from George Foreman, from Ken Norton, Leon Spinks, Larry Holmes. Where in his feckless youth Ali was a dazzling figure combining, say, the brashness of Hotspur and the insouciance of Lear's Fool, he became in these dark, brooding, increasingly willed fights the closest analogue boxing contains to Lear himself; or, rather, since there is no great fight without two great boxers, the title matches

---

[3] See both Dave Anderson, *In the Corner: Great Boxing Trainers Talk about Their Art* (Morrow, 1991), and Ronald K. Fried, *Corner Men: Great Boxing Trainers* (Four Walls, Eight Windows, 1991). Irresistibly readable and informative books of interviews: Angelo Dundee, Eddie Futch, Ray Arcel, Charley Goldman, Lou Duva, Emanuel Steward, Kevin Rooney, et al.

Ali–Frazier I (which Frazier won by a decision) and Ali–Frazier III (which Ali won, just barely, when Frazier virtually collapsed after the fourteenth round) are boxing's analogues to *King Lear* — ordeals of unfathomable human courage and resilience raised to the level of classic tragedy. These somber and terrifying boxing matches make us weep for their very futility; we seem to be in the presence of human experience too profound to be named — beyond the strategies and diminishments of language. The mystic's dark night of the soul, transmogrified as a brutal meditation of the body.

And Ali–Foreman, Zaire, 1974: the occasion of the infamous "rope-a-dope" defense, by which the thirty-two-year-old Ali exhausted his twenty-six-year-old opponent by the inspired method of, simply, and horribly, allowing him to punch himself out on Ali's body and arms. This is a fight of such a magical quality that even to watch it closely is not to see how it was done, its fairy-tale reversal in the eighth round executed. (One of Norman Mailer's most impassioned books, *The Fight*, is about this fight; watching a tape of Ali on the ropes enticing, and infuriating, and frustrating, and finally exhausting his opponent by an offense in the guise of a defense, I pondered what sly lessons of masochism Mailer absorbed from being at ringside that day, what deep-imprinted resolve to outwear all adversaries.)

♦ ♦ ♦

These hard-won victories began irreversible loss: progressive deterioration of Ali's kidneys, hands, reflexes, stamina. By the time of that most depressing of modern-day matches, Ali–Holmes, 1980, when Ali was thirty-eight years old, Ferdie Pacheco had long departed the Ali camp, dismissed for having advised Ali to retire; those who supported Ali's decision to fight, like the bout's promoter, Don King, had questionable motives. Judging from Hauser's information, it is a wonder that Ali survived this fight at all: the fight was, in Sylvester Stallone's words, "like watching an autopsy on a man who's still alive." (In *The Black Lights*, Hauser describes the bedlam that followed this vicious fight at Caesar's Palace, Las Vegas, where gamblers plunged in an orgy of gambling, as in a frenzy of feeding, or copulation: "Ali and Holmes had done their job.") Incredibly, Ali was allowed to fight once more, with Trevor Berbick, in December 1981, before retiring permanently.

Hauser's portrait of Ali is compassionate and unjudging: Is the man to be blamed for having

THEMBA HADEBE/AP Images

In this 2007 photo, Muhammad Ali's daughter, Laila Ali, defends her world championship title against Gwendolyn O'Neill. Ali knocked O'Neill out in the first minute of the first round.
What might Joyce Carol Oates think of this aspect of Ali's legacy — that is, a daughter who is a world champion boxer?

been addicted to his body's own adrenaline, or are others to be blamed for indulging him — and exploiting him? The brash rap-style egoism of young Cassius Clay underwent a considerable transformation during Ali's long public career, yet strikes us, perhaps, as altered only in tone: "Boxing was just to introduce me to the world," Ali has told his biographer. Mystically involved in the Nation of Islam, Ali sincerely believes himself an international emissary for peace, love, and understanding (he who once wreaked such violence upon his opponents!); and who is to presume to feel sorry for one who will not feel sorry for himself?

◆ ◆ ◆

The Black Lights: Inside the World of Professional Boxing describes a small, self-contained arc — a few years in the career of a boxer named Billy Costello, at one time a superlightweight titleholder from Kingston, New York. Like *Muhammad Ali*, it is a sympathetic study of its primary subject, Costello, his manager Mike Jones, and their families and associates; yet, in the interstices of a compelling narrative taking us through the preparation for a successful title defense of 1984, it illuminates aspects of the boxing world generally unknown to outsiders — the routine and discipline of the boxer in training; the complex role of the fight manager; the exhausting contractual negotiations; the state of this "red-light district" —

> Professional boxing is no longer worthy of civilized society. It's run by self-serving crooks, who are called promoters. . . . Except for the fighters, you're talking about human scum. . . . Professional boxing is utterly immoral. It's not capable of reformation. I now favor the abolition of professional boxing. You'll never clean it up. Mud can never be clean.
>
> — Howard Cosell, quoted in
> *The Black Lights*

25

Like others sympathetic with boxers, who are in fact poorly paid, nonunionized workers with no benefits in a monopolistic business without antitrust control, Hauser argues strongly for a national association to regulate the sport; a federal advisory panel to protect boxers from exploitation. His portrait of Billy Costello allows us to see why a young man will so eagerly risk injuries in the ring, which is perceived as a lifeline, and not a place of exploitation; why he will devote himself to the rigors of training in a sport in which, literally, one's entire career can end within a few seconds.

Black Lights ends dramatically, with Costello retaining his title against a thirty-seven-year-old opponent, Saoul Mamby, and with his hope of moving up in weight and making more money. Since its publication in 1986, the book has become a boxing classic; it is wonderfully readable, and, unlike *Ali*, judiciously proportioned. Yet to end the book with this victory is surely misleading, and even, to this reader, perplexing. The "black lights of unconsciousness" would be experienced by Billy Costello shortly, in a bout with a dazzlingly arrogant and idiosyncratic Ali-inspired young boxer named, at that time, "Lightning" Lonnie Smith, who would KO Costello in one of those nightmares all boxers have, before a hometown audience in Kingston. Following that devastating loss, Costello would fight the aging Alexis Arguello, one of the great lightweights of contemporary times, who would beat him savagely and end his career. To end with a tentative victory and not supply at least a coda to take us to the collapse of Billy Costello's career deprives *Black Lights* of the significance it might have had — for boxing is about failure far more than it is about success. In the words of the battered Saoul Mamby, "I'll miss it. I love boxing. Everything passed too soon."

[1992]

EXPLORING THE TEXT

1. What does Joyce Carol Oates think about boxing?

2. What do the two epigraphs — one from Walt Whitman and the other a Greek inscription — suggest about how Oates will approach the subject of boxing?

3. Oates alludes to Thomas Hobbes, a seventeenth-century philosopher, who described the life of humankind as "nasty, brutish, and short," to characterize the life of a boxer (para. 2), adding "and not even that remunerative." What is the effect of this allusion? What other literary allusions does Oates make? How do they help her develop her ideas about boxing?

4. What rhetorical strategies does Oates use in paragraph 6 to respond to the counterargument that boxing is "America's most popularly despised sport"?

5. In paragraph 9, Oates states that American boxing is about race, but that the moral issues are ambiguous, posing a rhetorical question about whether there is a moral distinction between "the

spectacle of black slaves in the Old South being forced by their white owners to fight . . . and the spectacle of contemporary blacks fighting for multimillion-dollar paydays. . . ." Do you think there is a moral distinction? Does Oates answer the question? If so, how does her answer differ from yours?

6. Explain why Oates finds the sport of boxing paradoxical. Give examples to support your answer.

7. Oates cites African American writer Gerald Early (para. 6), who compared boxing's exploitation of maleness to prostitution and pornography's exploitation of femaleness. Do you agree? Explain why or why not.

8. Look carefully at paragraph 21, in which Oates creates a parallel between Muhammad Ali's later fights with Joe Frazier and Shakespeare's dark tragedy, *King Lear*. What is the effect of this comparison? How does the allusion help you understand the complexity of the sport of boxing and Oates's feelings about it?

Barbaro, The Heart in the Winner's Circle

JANE SMILEY

Jane Smiley (b. 1949) is a Pulitzer Prize–winning novelist. Born in Los Angeles, Smiley grew up in a suburb of St. Louis. After attending Vassar College, she received her MA and PhD from the University of Iowa and went on to teach creative writing at Iowa State University for fifteen years. Her novel *A Thousand Acres* (1991) won the Pulitzer Prize for Fiction. She has written fourteen novels, including *The Greenlanders* (1988), *Ordinary Love and Good Will* (1989), *Moo* (1995), *Horse Heaven* (2000), *Private Life* (2010), *Some Luck* (2014), *Early Warning* (2015), and *Golden Age* (2015). Smiley is also the author of five young adult novels, two story collections, and five nonfiction books, including *Thirteen Ways of Looking at the Novel* (2005) and *The Man Who Invented the Computer* (2010). The piece that follows was the *Washington Post*'s obituary for Barbaro, a racehorse who died in 2007. He won the Kentucky Derby in 2006 but broke two legs a few weeks later in the Preakness Stakes, which resulted in his death.

Nine years ago, I had a thoroughbred mare who came down with colic in the night, and was too far gone to save by the time she was found at 6 A.M. After she was euthanized, I remember staring at her body, which was stretched out in the grass, running my hands over her. Her coat was shining. Her haunch was rounded and firm. Her feet and legs were perfect.

French painter Edgar Degas (1834–1917), known mainly for his paintings of dancers, depicted horses and horseracing almost as often. It's been noted that he made horses seem more elegant than they were in real life, yet more accurate than the photography of the time made available.

How does this 1911 painting, which hangs in the Musée d'Orsay in Paris, portray the beauty that Smiley describes in thoroughbreds like Barbaro?

Musee d'Orsay, Paris, France/Bridgeman Images

Only that one thing had been wrong, that twist in her gut, but it was enough, and it killed her. So it is with all horses.

They are engineered so close to the margins of what is physically possible that when one thing fails, it can cause the failure of the whole animal.

So it was with Barbaro, who was euthanized yesterday. When we saw his pictures over the last months, his ears were up, he was attentive and beautiful and interested. He looked pretty good, except for those casts.

His vets warned us all along that the odds were against him, but we didn't really believe them. They had hope, too. How could a horse who appeared so full of life break his leg and be so suddenly close to death? His head was fine. His back was fine. His lungs and heart and chest were fine. In fact, after a while, his broken leg was fairly fine. It was another leg that was so worrisome, since the weight of his body constantly bearing down on the delicate structures inside his foot eventually damaged and destroyed them.

◆ ◆ ◆

A horse's hoof is wondrous structure — the outside horn is lined with delicate membranes and blood vessels that feed and support the bones of the foot. The bones of the foot are analogous to a person's fingertips, since a horse's knee is analogous to a person's wrist. The racehorse carries a thousand pounds at 35 to 40 miles per hour using a few slender bones supported by an apparatus of ligaments and tendons that have no analogues in human anatomy. Every part of the system depends on every other part. What happened to Barbaro was that the engineering couldn't take it. When it was right, as in the Kentucky Derby, it was perfectly right, and when it became wrong, it became irredeemably wrong.

Some observers have been angered by the outpouring of sympathy toward Barbaro, but there is something extra large about the death of a horse.

And the death of a thoroughbred seems to me to be even more shocking, because thoroughbreds have been bred to press on and prevail where other breeds of horse throw in the towel. When we saw Barbaro in last May's Kentucky Derby fly away from the field so

OTHER VOICES

gracefully and effortlessly, he was doing some-thing thoroughbreds have been bred to do for 300 years — to sense the encroaching fatigue of three-quarters of a mile at top speed and want only to run faster, to push ahead and take the lead.

We say that thoroughbreds have "blood," meaning the DNA of desert Arab horses, and "heart," meaning fortitude, desire and competitive spirit.

It was heart that we saw in Barbaro, not only on Derby Day, but also on Preakness Day, when he stood injured in the middle of the track, touching his toe to the ground and snatching it up again, somehow impatient, somehow not truly aware of the pain, somehow still ready to get going.

I watched the Preakness with some lifelong racing people. When Barbaro was injured, we turned the TV off. All of us had seen it before; everyone who loves racing has seen it all too many times. It is the paradox of racing. His dynamic beauty and his exceptional heart were gifts Barbaro inherited from his racing

forebears, who had the luck and toughness to run and win and prove themselves worthy of reproducing.

And then, during his medical saga, he showed that he was intelligent, too. According to a friend of mine who talked to trainer Michael Matz in the summer, Barbaro knew when he needed some pain relief — he would stand by the sling and shake it until they put him in it, and when he was tired of it, he would shake himself so that it rattled, signaling he was ready to be taken out. And then he would go to his stall and lie down.

Did he want to survive? It seemed as though he did.

In a great racehorse, the heart and mind do the running, and the body tries to hold up.

Yes, to those who don't care about horses, terrible things are happening all over the world these days, and they demand from many people an unprecedented level of endurance, but we horse lovers say: This, too? That this beautiful and innocent animal should also die?

10

Garry Jones/AP Images

In this 2006 photo, Barbaro, having fractured his leg during the Preakness, is steadied by a track worker as jockey Edgar Prado looks on in shock and dismay. Barbaro was euthanized eight months later despite an unlimited budget for the best veterinary care. As Smiley describes it, "he stood injured in the middle of the track, touching his toe to the ground and snatching it up again, somehow impatient, somehow not truly aware of the pain, somehow still ready to get going" (para. 9).

What does this photo illustrate that Smiley does not talk about in her obituary for Barbaro? What is the effect of leaving such details out?

In this photo demonstrators protest horseracing before the 140th running of the Belmont Stakes on June 7, 2008. The protest, organized by PETA, came after a race horse named Eight Belles was euthanized immediately after breaking her leg in that year's Kentucky Derby. **What position do you think Smiley would take on PETA's demand that horseracing be banned? Explain your answer.**

When I think of Barbaro, I like to think also of some of the tough ones — John Henry, Seabiscuit, a horse I bred a mare to once named Loyal Pal. Among the three of them, they ran hundreds of times. They managed to avoid the bad steps and the bad luck, to go to the races as if a race were a trot in the park, coming back afterward to a bucket of grain and a long nap.

15 Sometimes, thousands of fans thrilled to their exploits. Sometimes, the only ones watching were the owner, the trainer and a few punters. Like Barbaro, they did it because they were born and bred to do it, because a thoroughbred loves to run, and because they didn't know what it meant not to keep on trying.

[2007]

EXPLORING THE TEXT

1. How is Jane Smiley's piece both similar to and different from an obituary?

2. How does Smiley establish ethos?

3. Why do you think Smiley uses the personal pronoun in paragraph 4?

4. Why do you think Smiley provides anatomical information about horses in paragraph 5? What is the effect of that information?

5. What do you think Smiley means by "the paradox of racing" (para. 10)?

6. What purpose do the rhetorical questions in paragraphs 12 and 14 serve?

7. To whom does Smiley seem to be responding in paragraph 14? What issue might she be commenting on when she says "to those who don't care about horses"?

8. Is Smiley convincing when she says she knows what a horse is thinking: "a thoroughbred loves to run" (para. 15)? Explain your answer.

Man and Superman

MALCOLM GLADWELL

Malcolm Gladwell (b. 1963) was born in England and raised in rural Ontario, Canada. He graduated from the University of Toronto, Trinity College. From 1986 to 1996 he worked at the *Washington Post*, where he covered business and science and was the newspaper's New York City bureau chief. Since 1996 he has been a staff writer with the *New Yorker* magazine. Gladwell's books include *The Tipping Point: How Little Things Can Make a Big Difference* (2000); *Blink: The Power of Thinking without Thinking* (2005); *Outliers: The Story of Success* (2008); *What the Dog Saw* (2009), a compilation of articles published in the *New Yorker;* and *David and Goliath: Underdogs, Misfits, and the Art of Battling Giants* (2013). The piece presented here appeared in the *New Yorker* in 2013.

Toward the end of "The Sports Gene" (Penguin/Current), David Epstein makes his way to a remote corner of Finland to visit a man named Eero Mäntyranta. Mäntyranta lives in a small house next to a lake, among the pine and spruce trees north of the Arctic Circle. He is in his seventies. There is a statue of him in the nearby village. "Everything about him has a certain width to it," Epstein writes. "The bulbous nose in the middle of a softly rounded face. His thick fingers, broad jaw, and a barrel chest covered by a red knit sweater with a stern-faced reindeer across the middle. He is a remarkable-looking man." What's most remarkable is the color of his face. It is a "shade of cardinal, mottled in places with purple," and evocative of "the hue of the red paint that comes from this region's iron-rich soil."

Mäntyranta carries a rare genetic mutation. His DNA has an anomaly that causes his bone marrow to overproduce red blood cells. That accounts for the color of his skin, and also for his extraordinary career as a competitive cross-country skier. In cross-country skiing, athletes propel themselves over distances of ten and twenty miles — a physical challenge that places intense demands on the ability of their red blood cells to deliver oxygen to their muscles. Mäntyranta, by virtue of his unique physiology, had something like sixty-five per cent more red blood cells than the normal adult male. In the 1960, 1964, and 1968 Winter Olympic Games, he won a total of seven medals — three golds, two silvers, and two bronzes — and in the same period he also won two world-championship victories in the thirty-kilometre race. In the 1964 Olympics, he beat his closest competitor in the fifteen-kilometre race by forty seconds, a margin of victory, Epstein says, "never equaled in that event at the Olympics before or since."

In "The Sports Gene," there are countless tales like this, examples of all the ways that the greatest athletes are different from the rest of us. They respond more effectively to training. The shape of their bodies is optimized for certain kinds of athletic activities. They carry genes that put them far ahead of ordinary athletes.

Epstein tells the story of Donald Thomas, who on the seventh high jump of his life cleared 7' 3.25" — practically a world-class height. The next year, after a grand total of eight months of training, Thomas won the world championships. How did he do it? He was blessed, among other things, with unusually long legs and a strikingly long Achilles tendon — ten and a quarter inches in length — which acted as a kind of spring, catapulting him high into the air when he planted his foot for a jump. (Kangaroos have long tendons as well, Epstein tells us, which is what gives them their special hop.)

Why do so many of the world's best distance runners come from Kenya and Ethiopia? The answer, Epstein explains, begins with weight. A runner needs not just to be skinny but — more specifically — to have skinny calves and ankles, because every extra pound carried on your extremities costs more than a pound carried on your torso. That's why shaving even a few ounces off a pair of running shoes can have a significant effect. Runners from the Kalenjin tribe, in Kenya — where the majority of the country's best runners come from — turn out to be skinny in exactly this way. Epstein cites a study comparing Kalenjins with Danes; the Kalenjins were shorter and had longer legs, and their lower legs were nearly a *pound* lighter. That translates to eight per cent less energy consumed per kilometre. (For evidence of the peculiar Kalenjin lower leg, look up pictures of the great Kenyan miler Asbel Kiprop, a tall and elegant man who runs on what appear to be two ebony-colored pencils.) According to Epstein, there's an evolutionary explanation for all this: hot and dry environments favor very thin, long-limbed frames, which are easy to cool, just as cold climates favor thick, squat bodies, which are better at conserving heat.

Distance runners also get a big advantage from living at high altitudes, where the body is typically forced to compensate for the lack of oxygen by producing extra red blood cells. Not *too* high up, mind you. In the Andes, for example, the air is too rarefied for the kind of workouts necessary to be a world-class runner. The optimal range is six to nine thousand feet. The best runners in Ethiopia and Kenya come from the ridges of the Rift Valley, which, Epstein writes, are "plumb in the sweet spot." When Kenyans compete against Europeans or North Americans, the Kenyans come to the track with an enormous head start.

What we are watching when we watch élite sports, then, is a contest among wildly disparate groups of people, who approach the starting line with an uneven set of genetic endowments and natural advantages. There will be Donald Thomases who barely have to train, and there will be Eero Mäntyrantas, who carry around in their blood, by dumb genetic luck, the ability to finish forty seconds ahead of their competitors. Élite sports supply, as Epstein puts it, a "splendid stage for the fantastic menagerie that is human biological diversity." The menagerie is what makes sports fascinating. But it has also burdened high-level competition with a contradiction. We want sports to be fair and we take elaborate measures to make sure that no one competitor has an advantage over any other. But how can a fantastic menagerie ever be a contest among equals?

◆ ◆ ◆

During the First World War, the U.S. Army noticed a puzzling pattern among the young men drafted into military service. Soldiers from some parts of the country had a high incidence of goitre — a lump on their neck caused by the swelling of the thyroid gland. Thousands of recruits could not button the collar of their uniform. The average I.Q. of draftees, we now suspect, also varied according to the same pattern. Soldiers from coastal regions seemed more "normal" than soldiers from other parts of the country.

The culprit turned out to be a lack of iodine. Iodine is an essential micronutrient. Without it, the human brain does not develop normally and the thyroid begins to enlarge. And in certain parts of the United States in those years there wasn't enough iodine in the local diet. As the economists James Feyrer, Dimitra Politi, and David Weil write, in a recent paper for the National Bureau of Economic Research:

> Ocean water is rich in iodine, which is why endemic goiter is not observed in coastal areas. From the ocean, iodine is transferred to the soil by rain. This process, however, only reaches the upper layers of soil, and it can take thousands of years to

complete. Heavy rainfall can cause soil erosion, in which case the iodine-rich upper layers of soil are washed away. The last glacial period had the same effect: iodine-rich soil was substituted by iodine-poor soil from crystalline rocks. This explains the prevalence of endemic goiter in regions that were marked by intense glaciation, such as Switzerland and the Great Lakes region.

After the First World War, the U.S. War Department published a report called "Defects Found in Drafted Men," which detailed how the incidence of goitre varied from state to state, with rates forty to fifty times as high in places like Idaho, Michigan, and Montana as in coastal areas.

The story is not dissimilar from Epstein's account of Kenyan distance runners, in whom accidents of climate and geography combine to create dramatic differences in abilities. In the early years of the twentieth century, the physiological development of American children was an example of the "fantastic menagerie that is human biological diversity."

In this case, of course, we didn't like the fantastic menagerie. In 1924, the Morton Salt Company, at the urging of public-health officials, began adding iodine to its salt, and initiated an advertising campaign touting its benefits. That practice has been applied successfully in many developing countries in the world: iodine supplementation has raised I.Q. scores by as much as thirteen points — an extraordinary increase. The iodized salt in your cupboard is an intervention in the natural order of things. When a student from the iodine-poor mountains of Idaho was called upon to compete against a student from iodine-rich coastal Maine, we thought of it as our moral obligation to redress their natural inequality. The reason debates over élite performance have become so contentious in recent years, however, is that in the world of sport there is little of that clarity. What if those two students were

10

competing in a race? Should we still be able to give the naturally disadvantaged one the equivalent of iodine? We can't decide.

Epstein tells us that baseball players have, as a group, remarkable eyesight. The ophthalmologist Louis Rosenbaum tested close to four hundred major- and minor-league baseball players over four years and found an average visual acuity of about 20/13; that is, the typical professional baseball player can see at twenty feet what the rest of us can see at thirteen feet. When Rosenbaum looked at the Los Angeles Dodgers, he found that half had 20/10 vision and a small number fell below 20/9, "flirting

This cartoon, by artist Bary Blitt, appeared with "Man and Superman" when it was originally published by the *New Yorker*.
What argument does this cartoon make, and how does it relate to Gladwell's essay?

Barry Blitt

with the theoretical limit of the human eye," as Epstein points out. The ability to consistently hit a baseball thrown at speeds approaching a hundred miles an hour, with a baffling array of spins and curves, requires the kind of eyesight commonly found in only a tiny fraction of the general population.

Eyesight can be improved — in some cases dramatically — through laser surgery or implantable lenses. Should a promising young baseball player cursed with normal vision be allowed to get that kind of corrective surgery? In this instance, Major League Baseball says yes. Major League Baseball also permits pitchers to replace the ulnar collateral ligament in the elbow of their throwing arm with a tendon taken from a cadaver or elsewhere in the athlete's body. Tendon-replacement surgery is similar to laser surgery: it turns the athlete into an improved version of his natural self.

But when it comes to drugs Major League Baseball — like most sports — draws the line. An athlete cannot use a drug to become an improved version of his natural self, even if the drug is used in doses that are not harmful, and is something that — like testosterone — is no more than a copy of a naturally occurring hormone, available by prescription to anyone, virtually anywhere in the world.

Baseball is in the middle of one of its periodic doping scandals, centering on one of the game's best players, Alex Rodriguez. Rodriguez is among the most disliked players of his generation. He tried to recover from injury and extend his career through illicit means. (He has appealed his recent suspension, which was based on these allegations.) It is hard to think about Rodriguez, however, and not think about Tommy John, who, in 1974, was the first player to trade in his ulnar collateral ligament for an improved version. John used modern medicine to recover from injury and extend his career. He won a hundred and sixty-four games after his transformation, far more than he did before science intervened. He had one of the longest careers in baseball history, retiring at the age of forty-six. His bionic arm enabled him to win at least twenty games a season, the benchmark of pitching excellence. People loved Tommy John. Maybe Alex Rodriguez looks at Tommy John — and at the fact that at least a third of current major-league pitchers have had the same surgery — and is genuinely baffled about why baseball has drawn a bright moral line between the performance-enhancing products of modern endocrinology and those offered by orthopedics.

15

John Gress/Getty Images

New York Yankees star Alex Rodriguez — known as A-Rod — was suspended for 211 games in 2013 for taking performance-enhancing drugs. This photo shows a sign held up at a Yankees game in Chicago in 2013.
How does Gladwell feel about Rodriguez? In what ways does he sympathize with him? What does this photo suggest about baseball fans' sympathy — or lack of sympathy — for Rodriguez?

The other great doping pariah is Lance Armstrong. He apparently removed large quantities of his own blood and then re-infused himself before competition, in order to boost the number of oxygen-carrying red blood cells in his system. Armstrong wanted to be like Eero Mäntyranta. He wanted to match, through his own efforts, what some very lucky people already do naturally and legally. Before we condemn him, though, shouldn't we have to come up with a good reason that one man is allowed to have lots of red blood cells and another man is not?

"I've always said you could have hooked us up to the best lie detectors on the planet and asked us if we were cheating, and we'd have passed," Lance Armstrong's former teammate Tyler Hamilton writes in his autobiography, "The Secret Race" (co-written with Daniel Coyle; Bantam). "Not because we were delusional — we knew we were breaking the rules — but because we didn't think of it as cheating. It felt fair to break the rules."

◆ ◆ ◆

"The Secret Race" deserves to be read alongside "The Sports Gene," because it describes the flip side of the question that Epstein explores. What if you aren't Eero Mäntyranta?

Hamilton was a skier who came late to cycling, and he paints himself as an underdog. When he first met Armstrong — at the Tour DuPont, in Delaware — he looked around at the other professional riders and became acutely conscious that he didn't look the part. "You can tell a rider's fitness by the shape of his ass and the veins in his legs, and these asses were bionic, smaller and more powerful than any I'd ever seen," he writes. The riders' "leg veins looked like highway maps. Their arms were toothpicks. . . . They were like racehorses." Hamilton's trunk was oversized. His leg veins did not pop. He had a skier's thighs. His arms were too muscled, and he pedalled with an ungainly "potato-masher stroke."

When Hamilton joined Armstrong on the U.S. Postal Service racing team, he was forced to relearn the sport, to leave behind, as he puts it, the romantic world "where I used to climb on my bike and simply hope I had a good day." The makeover began with his weight. When Michele Ferrari, the key Postal Service adviser, first saw Hamilton, he told him he was too fat, and in cycling terms he was. Riding a bicycle quickly is a function of the power you apply to the pedals divided by the weight you are carrying, and it's easier to reduce the weight than to increase the power. Hamilton says he would come home from a workout, after burning thousands of calories, drink a large bottle of seltzer water, take two or three sleeping pills — and hope to sleep through dinner and, ideally, breakfast the following morning. At dinner with friends, Hamilton would take a large bite, fake a sneeze, spit the food into a napkin, and then run off to the bathroom to dispose of it. He knew that he was getting into shape, he says, when his skin got thin and papery, when it hurt to sit down on a wooden chair because his buttocks had disappeared, and when his jersey sleeve was so loose around his biceps that it flapped in the wind. At the most basic level, cycling was about physical transformation: it was about taking the body that nature had given you and forcibly changing it.

"Lance and Ferrari showed me there were more variables than I'd ever imagined, and they all mattered: wattages, cadence, intervals, zones, joules, lactic acid, and, of course, hematocrit," Hamilton writes. "Each ride was a math problem: a precisely mapped set of numbers for us to hit. . . . It's one thing to go ride for six hours. It's another to ride for six hours following a program of wattages and cadences, especially when those wattages and cadences are set to push you to the ragged edge of your abilities."

Hematocrit, the last of those variables, was the number they cared about most. It refers to the percentage of the body's blood that is made up of oxygen-carrying red blood cells. The higher the hematocrit, the more endurance you have. (Mäntyranta had a very high hematocrit.) The paradox of endurance sports is that an athlete can never work as hard as he wants, because if he pushes himself too far his hematocrit will fall. Hamilton had a natural hematocrit of forty-two per cent — which is on the low end of normal. By the third week of the Tour de France, he would be at thirty-six per cent, which meant a six-per-cent decrease in his power — in the force he could apply to his pedals. In a sport where power differentials of a tenth of a per cent can be decisive, this "qualifies as a deal breaker."

▼
―――――――――

What does this 1969 cover of *Sports Illustrated* tell us about the history of performance-enhancing drugs and society's opinions on it? How does Malcolm Gladwell give the controversy a different spin?

For the members of the Postal Service squad, the solution was to use the hormone EPO and blood transfusions to boost their hematocrits as high as they could without raising suspicion. (Before 2000, there was no test for EPO itself, so riders were not allowed to exceed a hematocrit of fifty per cent.) Then they would add maintenance doses over time, to counteract the deterioration in their hematocrit caused by races and workouts. The procedures were precise and sophisticated. Testosterone capsules were added to the mix to aid recovery. They were referred to as "red eggs." EPO (a.k.a. erythropoietin), a naturally occurring hormone that increases the production of red blood cells, was Edgar — short for Edgar Allan Poe. During the Tour de France, and other races, bags of each rider's blood were collected in secret locations at predetermined intervals, then surreptitiously ferried from stage to stage in refrigerated containers for strategic transfusions. The window of vulnerability after taking a drug — the interval during which doping could be detected — was called "glowtime." Most riders who doped (and in the Armstrong era, it now appears, nearly all the top riders did) would take two thousand units of Edgar subcutaneously every couple of days, which meant they "glowed" for a dangerously long time. Armstrong and his crew practiced microdosing, taking five hundred units of Edgar nightly and injecting the drug directly into the vein, where it was dispersed much more quickly.

"The Secret Race" is full of paragraphs like this: 25

> The trick with getting Edgar in your vein, of course, is that you have to get it in the vein. Miss the vein — inject it in the surrounding tissue — and Edgar stays in your body far longer; you might test positive. Thus, microdosing requires a steady hand and a good sense of feel, and a lot of practice; you have to sense the tip of the needle piercing the wall of the vein, and draw back the plunger to get a little bit of blood so you know you're in. In this, as in other things, Lance was

seeing connections

After a 2014 documentary exposed Russia's state-sponsored doping program and cover-up dating back to at least 2011, a scandal erupted in the athletic community. Among other things, this scandal resulted in the removal of 111 Russian athletes slated to compete in the 2016 Olympics. As of 2017, some Russian athletes stripped of their 2008 and 2012 medals still refused to return them to the International Olympic Committee. **These cartoons were published shortly before the 2016 Olympics began. Consider the message each cartoon conveys. To what extent do these images represent opposing viewpoints? Which one best reflects Gladwell's position as expressed in "Man and Superman," and why?**

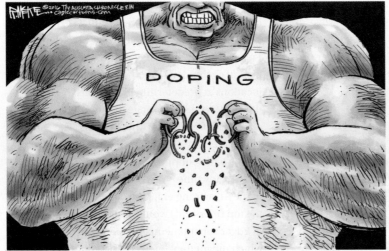

Rick McKee/The Augusta Chronicle

Jeff Koterba/Omaha World-Herald, NE/Cagle Cartoons, Inc.

blessed: he had veins like water mains. Mine were small, which was a recurring headache.

Hamilton was eventually caught and was suspended from professional cycling. He became one of the first in his circle to implicate Lance Armstrong, testifying before federal investigators and appearing on "60 Minutes." He says that he regrets his years of using performance-enhancing drugs. The lies and duplicity became an unbearable burden. His marriage fell apart. He sank into a depression. His book is supposed to serve as his apology. At that task, it fails. Try as he might — and sometimes he doesn't seem to be trying very hard — Hamilton cannot explain why a sport that has no problem with the voluntary induction of anorexia as a performance-enhancing measure is so upset about athletes infusing themselves with their own blood.

"Dope is not really a magical boost as much as it is a way to control against declines," Hamilton writes. Doping meant that cyclists finally could train as hard as they wanted. It was the means by which pudgy underdogs could compete with natural wonders. "People think

doping is for lazy people who want to avoid hard work," Hamilton writes. For many riders, the opposite was true:

> EPO granted the ability to suffer more; to push yourself farther and harder than you'd ever imagined, in both training and racing. It rewarded precisely what I was good at: having a great work ethic, pushing myself to the limit and past it. I felt almost giddy: this was a new landscape. I began to see races differently. They weren't rolls of the genetic dice, or who happened to be on form that day. They didn't depend on who you were. They depended on what you did — how hard you worked, how attentive and professional you were in your preparation.

This is a long way from the exploits of genial old men living among the pristine pines of northern Finland. It is a vision of sports in which the object of competition is to use science, intelligence, and sheer will to conquer. Hamilton and Armstrong may simply be athletes who regard this kind of achievement as worthier than the gold medals of a man with the dumb luck to be born with a random genetic mutation.

[2013]

EXPLORING THE TEXT

1. Characterize the evidence Malcolm Gladwell uses in "Man and Superman." What type of evidence does he depend on the most? Do you find his evidence convincing? Explain why or why not.

2. What is Gladwell's thesis? Is it explicit or implicit? At what point in the essay does Gladwell reveal his thesis? Why do you think he states (or doesn't state) it when he does?

3. How does Gladwell acknowledge the counterargument?

4. Gladwell provides examples of the ways that great athletes differ from the rest of us. What are they? How do these examples serve Gladwell's argument? How convincing do you find these as evidence for his central claim?

5. Describe the overall tone of "Man and Superman." How does this tone reflect Gladwell's assumptions about his audience? How does it reveal his attitude toward the subject of the piece?

6. What is Gladwell's attitude toward the idea of a "fantastic menagerie"? In what way does that attitude change from paragraph 7 to paragraph 11? How does the phrase serve two different aspects of his argument?

7. "Man and Superman" shifts gears between paragraphs 16 and 17, moving from gifted athletes to underperforming ones. How does that shift support Gladwell's core argument? How does the essay's tone and use of evidence change?

8. In paragraphs 22–24, Gladwell writes about hematocrit — an important quantifier for endurance athletes. How does he make this scientific and statistical information accessible to the average reader? What rhetorical strategies does he use to bring the statistics to life?

9. In paragraph 27, Gladwell describes cyclist Tyler Hamilton's perspective on the benefits of using the hormone erythropoietin, or EPO. According to Gladwell, Hamilton "began to see races differently. They weren't rolls of the genetic dice, or who happened to be on form that day. They didn't depend on who you were. They depended on *what you did* — how hard you worked, how attentive and professional you were in your preparation." What is your take on this claim — that is, do you think taking EPO is justified or do you think it's cheating? Explain your answer.

10. Do you think "the object of competition is to use science, intelligence, and sheer will to conquer natural difference" (para. 28)? Write an essay in which you defend, challenge, or qualify this claim.

The Meaning of Serena Williams
On Tennis and Black Excellence

CLAUDIA RANKINE

Claudia Rankine (b. 1963) is an award-winning poet, essayist, playwright, and editor. Born in Kingston, Jamaica, Rankine earned a BA from Williams College and an MFA from Columbia University. Her first four books of poetry were *Nothing in Nature is Private* (1994), *The End of the Alphabet* (1998), *Plot* (2001), and *Don't Let Me Be Lonely: An American Lyric* (2004). Her fifth book, *Citizen: An American Lyric* (2014), won numerous national awards, including the 2014 Los Angeles Times Book Award and the 2015 National Book Critics Circle Award for poetry (while also being nominated for criticism, a distinction no other book has achieved). *Citizen* also holds the distinction of being the only poetry book to be a *New York Times* best seller in the nonfiction category. A recipient of a 2016 MacArthur "Genius" Grant, Rankine is currently Frederick Iseman Professor of Poetry at Yale University and serves as a chancellor of the Academy of American Poets. When the following article was published in the *New York Times* in August 2015, tennis superstar Serena Williams had just won her sixth Wimbledon Title.

There is no more exuberant winner than Serena Williams. She leaps into the air, she laughs, she grins, she pumps her fist, she points her index finger to the sky, signaling she's No. 1. Her joy is palpable. It brings me to my feet, and I grin right back at her, as if I've won something, too. Perhaps I have.

There is a belief among some African-Americans that to defeat racism, they have to work harder, be smarter, be *better*. Only after they give 150 percent will white Americans recognize black excellence for what it is. But of course, once recognized, black excellence is then supposed to perform with good manners and forgiveness in the face of any racist slights or attacks. Black excellence is not supposed to be emotional as it pulls itself together to win after questionable calls. And in winning, it's not supposed to swagger, to leap and pump its fist, to state boldly, in the words of Kanye West, "That's what it is, black excellence, baby."

Imagine you have won 21 Grand Slam singles titles, with only four losses in your 25 appearances in the finals. Imagine that you've achieved two "Serena Slams" (four consecutive Slams in a row), the first more than 10 years ago and the second this year. A win at this year's U.S. Open would be your fifth and your first calendar-year Grand Slam — a feat last achieved by Steffi Graf in 1988, when you were just 6 years old. This win would also break your tie for the most U.S. Open titles in the Open era, surpassing the legendary Chris Evert, who herself has called you "a phenomenon that once every hundred years comes around." Imagine that you're the player John McEnroe recently described as "the greatest player, I think, that ever lived." Imagine that, despite all this, there were so many bad calls against you, you were given as one reason video replay needed to be used on the courts. Imagine that you have to contend with critiques of your body that perpetuate racist notions that black women are hypermasculine and unattractive. Imagine being asked to comment at a news conference before a tournament because the president of the Russian Tennis Federation, Shamil Tarpischev, has described you and your sister as "brothers" who are "scary" to look at. Imagine.

The word "win" finds its roots in both joy and grace. Serena's grace comes because she won't be forced into stillness; she won't accept those racist projections onto her body without speaking back; she won't go gently into the white light of victory. Her excellence doesn't mask the struggle it takes to achieve each win. For black people, there is an unspoken script that demands the humble absorption of racist assaults, no matter the scale, because whites need to believe that it's no big deal. But Serena refuses to keep to that script. Somehow, along the way, she made a decision to be excellent while still being Serena. She would feel what she feels in front of everyone, in response to

How does this Nike ad address the descriptions of Serena Williams as the greatest female athlete of all time? Do you find it convincing? Would Claudia Rankine?

anyone. At Wimbledon this year, for example, in a match against the home favorite Heather Watson, Serena, interrupted during play by the deafening support of Watson, wagged her index finger at the crowd and said, "Don't try me." She will tell an audience or an official that they are disrespectful or unjust, whether she says, simply, "No, no, no" or something much more forceful, as happened at the U.S. Open in 2009, when she told the lineswoman, "I swear to God I am [expletive] going to take this [expletive] ball and shove it down your [expletive] throat." And in doing so, we actually see her. She shows us her joy, her humor and, yes, her rage. She gives us the whole range of what it is to be human, and there are those who can't bear it, who can't tolerate the humanity of an ordinary extraordinary person.

In the essay "Everybody's Protest Novel," [5] James Baldwin wrote, "our humanity is our burden, our life; we need not battle for it; we need only to do what is infinitely more difficult — that is, accept it." To accept the self, its humanity, is to discard the white racist gaze. Serena has freed herself from it. But that doesn't mean she won't be emotional or hurt by challenges to her humanity. It doesn't mean she won't battle for the right to be excellent. There is nothing wrong with Serena, but surely there is something wrong with the expectation that she be "good" while she is achieving greatness. Why should Serena not respond to racism? In whose world should it be answered with good manners? The notable difference between black excellence and white excellence is white excellence is achieved without having to battle racism. Imagine.

Two years ago, recovering from cancer and to celebrate my 50th birthday, I flew from LAX to J.F.K. during Serena's semifinal match at the U.S. Open with the hope of seeing her play in the final. I had just passed through a year when so much was out of my control, and Serena epitomized not so much winning as the pure drive to win. I couldn't quite shake the feeling (I still can't quite shake it) that my body's frailty, not the cancer but the depth of my exhaustion, had been brought on in part by the constant onslaught of racism, whether something as terrible as the killing of Trayvon Martin or something as mundane as the guy who let the door slam in my face. The daily grind of being rendered invisible, or being attacked, whether physically or verbally, for being visible, wears a body down. Serena's strength and focus in the face of the realities we shared oddly consoled me.

That Sunday in Arthur Ashe Stadium at the women's final, though the crowd generally seemed pro-Serena, the man seated next to me was cheering for the formidable tall blonde Victoria Azarenka. I asked him if he was American. "Yes," he said.

"We're at the U.S. Open. Why are you cheering for the player from Belarus?" I asked.

"Oh, I just want the match to be competitive," he said.

After Serena lost the second set, at the opening [10] of the third, I turned to him again, and asked him, no doubt in my own frustration, why he was still cheering for Azarenka. He didn't answer, as was his prerogative. By the time it was clear that Serena was likely to win, his seat had been vacated. I had to admit to myself that in those moments I needed her to win, not just in the pure sense of a fan supporting her player, but to prove something that could never be proven, because if black excellence could cure us of anything, black people — or rather this black person — would be free from needing Serena to win.

◆ ◆ ◆

"You don't understand me," Serena Williams said with a hint of impatience in her voice. "I'm just about winning." She and I were facing each other on a sofa in her West Palm Beach home this July. She looked at me with wariness as if to say, Not you, too. I wanted to talk about the tennis records that she is presently positioned either to tie or to break and had tried more than once to steer the conversation toward them. But she was clear: "It's not about getting 22 Grand Slams," she insisted. Before winning a calendar-year Grand Slam and matching Steffi Graf's record of 22 Slams, Serena would have to win seven matches and defend her U.S. Open title; those were the victories that she was thinking about.

She was wearing an enviable pink jumpsuit with palm trees stamped all over it as if to reflect the trees surrounding her estate. It was a badass outfit, one only someone of her height and figure could rock. She explained to me that she learned not to look ahead too much by looking ahead. As she approached 18 Grand Slam wins in 2014, she said, "I went too crazy. I felt I had to even up with Chris Evert and Martina Navratilova." Instead, she didn't make it past the fourth round at the Australian Open, the second at the French Open or the third at Wimbledon. She tried to change her tactics and focused on getting only to the quarterfinals of the U.S. Open. Make it to the second week and see what happens, she thought. "I started thinking like that, and then I got to 19. Actually I got to 21 just like that, so I'm not thinking about 22." She raised her water

▼
_____

How does this 1932 Vanity Fair cover portray the game of tennis — and the woman playing it? Which elements of such traditional images of tennis has Serena Williams upended, and which elements remain the same?

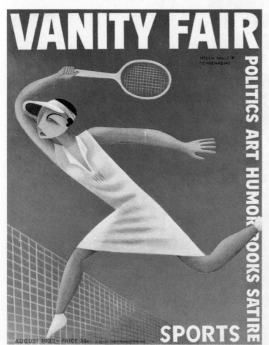

Miguel Covarrubias/Getty Images

bottle to her lips, looking at me over its edge, as if to give me time to think of a different line of questioning.

Three years ago she partnered with the French tennis coach Patrick Mouratoglou, and I've wondered if his coaching has been an antidote to negotiating American racism, a dynamic that informed the coaching of her father, Richard Williams. He didn't want its presence to prevent her and Venus from winning. In his autobiography, "Black and White: The Way I See It," he describes toughening the girls' "skin" by bringing "busloads of kids from the local schools into Compton to surround the courts while Venus and Serena practiced. I had the kids call them every curse word in the English language, including 'Nigger,' " he writes. "I paid them to do it and told them to 'do their worst.'" His focus on racism meant that the sisters were engaged in two battles on and off the court. That level of vigilance, I know from my own life, can drain you. It's easier to shut up and pretend it's not happening, as the bitterness and stress build up.

Mouratoglou shifted Serena's focus to records (even if, as she prepares for a Slam, she says she can't allow herself to think about them). Perhaps it's not surprising that she broke her boycott against Indian Wells, where the audience notoriously booed her with racial epithets in 2001, during their partnership. Serena's decisions now seem directed toward building her legacy. Mouratoglou has insisted that she can get to 24 Grand Slams, which is the most won by a single player — Margaret Court — to date. Serena laughed as she recalled one of her earliest conversations with Mouratoglou. She told him: "I'm cool. I want to play tennis. I hate to lose. I want to win. But I don't have numbers in my head." He wouldn't allow that. "Now we are getting numbers in your head," he told her.

I asked how winning felt for her. I was imagining winning as a free space, one where the unconscious racist shenanigans of umpires, or

15

seeing connections

"Citizen," Claudia Rankine's 2014 book-length prose poem, includes a section that focuses on Serena Williams. In it, Rankine asks, "What does a victorious or defeated black woman's body in a historically white space look like?" In answer, she writes that Serena and her sister Venus Williams "brought to mind Zora Neale Hurston's 'I feel most colored when I am thrown against a sharp white background.' This appropriated line, stenciled on canvas by Glenn Ligon, who used plastic letter stencils, smudging oil sticks, and graphite to transform the words into abstractions, seemed to be ad copy for some aspect of life for all black bodies."

How does the work provide a visual representation of Rankine's point about black women's bodies? How is that view reflected (or deflected) in "The Meaning of Serena Williams"?

Glenn Ligon, *Untitled (Four Etchings)*, 1992. Suite of 4 softground etching, aquatint, spit bite, and sugarlift on paper. Edition of 45 and 10 APs. Each: 25 × 17 inches (63.5 × 43.2 cm) © Glenn Ligon; Image courtesy of the artist, Luhring Augustine, New York, Regen Projects, Los Angeles, and Thomas Dane Gallery, London.

the narratives about her body, her "unnatural" power, her perceived crassness no longer mattered. Unless racism destroyed the moment of winning so completely, as it did at Indian Wells, I thought it had to be the rare space free of all the stresses of black life. But Serena made it clear that she doesn't desire to dissociate from her history and her culture. She understands that even when she's focused only on winning, she is still representing. "I play for me," Serena told me, "but I also play and represent something much greater than me. I embrace that. I love that. I want that. So ultimately, when I am out there on the court, I am playing for me."

Her next possible victory is at the U.S. Open, the major where she has been involved in the most drama — everything from outrageous line calls to probations and fines. Serena admitted to losing her cool in the face of some of what has gone down there. In 2011, for example, a chair umpire, Eva Asderaki, ruled against Serena for yelling "Come on" before a point was completed, and as Serena described it to me, she "clutched her pearls" and told Asderaki not to look at her. But she said in recent years she finally felt embraced by the crowd. "No more incidents?" I asked. Before she could answer, we both laughed, because of course it's not wholly in her control. Then suddenly Serena stopped. "I don't want any incidents there," she said. "But I'm always going to be myself. If anything happens, I'm always going to be myself, true to myself."

I'm counting on it, I thought. Because just as important to me as her victories is her willingness to be an emotionally complete person while also being black. She wins, yes, but she also loses it. She jokes around, gets angry, is frustrated or joyous, and on and on. She is fearlessly on the side of Serena, in a culture that has responded to living while black with death.

◆ ◆ ◆

DON EMMERT/Getty Images

This photograph shows Serena Williams complaining about one of the four very questionable calls made by chair umpire Mariana Alves in the 2004 US Open quarterfinals. In the most controversial call, Alves overruled the line judge to give a set point to Williams's opponent, Jennifer Capriati, who ended up winning the match.

What elements of this photo does Rankine capture in her profile of Serena Williams? What elements might Rankine point out are missing or are underemphasized?

In what ways does this image of Maria Sharapova reinforce the claims Rankine makes in paragraph 21?

Adam Pretty/Getty Images

This July, the London School of Marketing (L.S.M.) released its list of the most marketable sports stars, which included only two women in its Top 20: Maria Sharapova and Serena Williams. They were ranked 12th and 20th. Despite decisively trailing Serena on the tennis court (Serena leads in their head-to-head matchups 18-2, and has 21 majors and 247 weeks at No. 1 to Sharapova's five majors and 21 weeks at number 1), Sharapova has a financial advantage off the court. This month Forbes listed her as the highest-paid female athlete, worth more than $29 million to Serena's $24 million.

When I asked Chris Evert about the L.S.M. list, she said, "I think the corporate world still loves the good-looking blond girls." It's a preference Evert benefited from in her own illustrious career. I suggested that this had to do with race. Serena, on occasion, has herself been a blonde. But of course, for millions of consumers, possibly not the right kind of blonde. "Maria was very aware of business and becoming a business-woman at a much younger stage," Evert told me, adding, "She works hard." She also suggested that any demonstration of corporate preference is about a certain "type" of look or image, not whiteness in general. When I asked Evert what she made of Eugenie Bouchard, the tall, blond Canadian who has yet to really distinguish herself in the sport, being named the world's most marketable athlete by the British magazine *SportsPro* this spring, she said, with a laugh, "Well, there you have it." I took her statement to be perhaps a moment of agreement that Serena probably could not work her way to Sharapova's spot on Forbes's list.

"If they want to market someone who is white [20] and blond, that's their choice," Serena told me when I asked her about her ranking. Her impatience had returned, but I wasn't sure if it was with me, the list or both. "I have a lot of partners who are very happy to work with me." JPMorgan Chase, Wilson Sporting Goods, Pepsi and Nike are among the partners she was referring to. "I can't sit here and say I should be higher on the list because I have won more." As for Sharapova, her nonrival rival, Serena was diplomatic: "I'm happy for her, because she worked hard, too. There is enough at the table for everyone."

Larry Busacca/PW/Getty Images

This photograph shows Serena Williams performing onstage with Beyoncé on the closing night of "The Formation World Tour" in 2016.
What aspects of Serena's public persona are captured here? How are they reflected in Rankine's profile?

There is another, perhaps more important, discussion to be had about what it means to be chosen by global corporations. It has to do with who is worthy, who is desirable, who is associated with the good life. As long as the white imagination markets itself by equating whiteness and blondness with aspirational living, stereotypes will remain fixed in place. Even though Serena is the best, even though she wins more Slams than anyone else, she is only superficially allowed to embody that in our culture, at least the marketable one.

But Serena was less interested in the ramifications involved in being chosen, since she had no power in this arena, and more interested in understanding her role in relation to those who came before her: "We have to be thankful, and we also have to be positive about it so the next black person can be No. 1 on that list," she told me. "Maybe it was not meant to be me. Maybe it's meant to be the next person to be amazing, and I'm just opening the door. Zina Garrison, Althea Gibson, Arthur Ashe and Venus opened so many doors for me. I'm just opening the next door for the next person."

I was moved by Serena's positioning herself in relation to other African-Americans. A crucial component of white privilege is the idea that your accomplishments can be, have been, achieved on your own. The private clubs that housed the tennis courts remained closed to minorities well into the second half of the 20th century. Serena reminded me that in addition to being a phenomenon, she has come out of a long line of African-Americans who battled for the right to be excellent in a such a space that attached its value to its whiteness and worked overtime to keep it segregated.

Serena's excellence comes with the ability to imagine herself achieving a new kind of history for all of us. As long as she remains healthy, she will most likely tie and eventually pass Graf's 22 majors, regardless of what happens at the U.S. Open this year. I want Serena to win, but I know better than to think her winning can end something she didn't start. But Serena is providing a new script, one in which winning doesn't carry the burden of curing racism, in which we win just to win — knowing that it is simply her excellence, baby.

[2015]

EXPLORING THE TEXT

1. Why might Claudia Rankine have entitled her piece "The Meaning of Serena Williams: On Tennis and Black Excellence" rather than, say, "Serena Williams: The Greatest Player"? What does the title imply about the subject of the essay? Does Rankine's essay ultimately define the "meaning" of Serena? Explain why or why not.

2. How does Rankine define "black excellence," which she first mentions in paragraph 2? What evidence does she provide to illustrate that definition? How does this term relate to her central argument?

3. In paragraph 3, Rankine asks the reader to "imagine" several responses to Serena Williams's playing technique and physical appearance. The last sentence of the paragraph is a single word: "Imagine." What is the effect of this repeated call to "imagine"? How does it help characterize Serena Williams? What does it tell us about the speaker, Claudia Rankine?

4. What literary elements of fiction, such as dialogue, characterization, and point of view, among others, does Rankine use to develop her portrait of Serena? Why do you think Rankine employs these strategies? What is their overall effect?

5. In paragraph 5, Rankine poses some questions: "Why should Serena not respond to racism? In whose world should it be answered with good manners?" How does the essay answer those questions?

6. Reread the anecdote in paragraphs 7–10 where Rankine asks an American man at the U.S. Open why he is cheering for a player from Belarus in a match against Serena Williams. How does this anecdote support her argument? What do you think Rankine means when she says "black people — or rather this black person — would be free from needing Serena to win" (para. 10)?

7. What does Rankine consider the most egregious effects of racism? How does she describe the effect on herself? How does she believe they affect Serena Williams?

8. What surprises Rankine about Serena Williams? How does Serena occasionally upset Rankine's preconceived ideas? Rankine could easily have left this out of the profile — why does she show her readers that Serena's responses do not always conform to Rankine's expectations?

9. Consider some of the sources that Rankine uses. What do they have in common? What purpose do you think they serve in the piece?

Uprooted to Brooklyn, and Nourished by Cricket

MICHAEL POWELL

Michael Powell is a sports columnist for the *New York Times.* Powell grew up in New York City, earned a BA in history from the State University of New York at Purchase in 1978, and graduated from the Columbia University Graduate School of Journalism in 1984. Over his career, Powell has covered city politics and government, business, and sports for a variety of periodicals, including *New York Newsday* and the *Washington Post*. The following article on the role of cricket in the lives of Bangladeshi immigrants to the United States was published in the *New York Times* in 2016.

They are the Bangladeshi boys of summer. Tareq Manawer, a strapping, charismatic boy, learned in Bangladesh to craft branches into makeshift bats. Ashekin Rozon practiced his swing with his brother in their cramped and humid bedroom in Dhaka, until their parents yelled to stop. Then there is Raju Rahman, a good-looking teenager who grew up hitting balls in the Bangladesh city Rajshahi. One night, when Raju was 13, his father returned from a place called Brooklyn and asked: Are you ready to move to America? Can you help me a little bit to support our family?

"I said, Yes!" Raju told me with a grin. "I wanted to see why everyone calls this the dream country."

These boys form the core of the Brooklyn International High School cricket team. The sport has spread its tendrils in many corners of New York, as young South Asian and West Indian students embrace a sport — distant kin to baseball — that is dominant in the lands of their birth.

Most of them arrived here in their early teens. 5 At first, they spoke little English, although the older boys are now fluent. They live in far-flung immigrant nooks, in walk-up apartments in the Brooklyn neighborhoods of Kensington and Crown Heights and Flatbush, and in the Queens neighborhoods of Jamaica and Long Island City. All work after-school jobs. And they ended up at Brooklyn International, which, housed in an old torpedo factory, is small (370 students) and takes in only teenagers who have been in this country four years or fewer.

The school is a place of cacophonous hope for students from 41 nations: You hear Fula, Burmese, Arabic, Spanish, Thai, Tibetan, Tajik, Urdu, Russian, Karen and Wolof, not to mention Bengali, in its hallways. Those are just half of the languages spoken there. Ninety-one percent of the students graduate, and 81 percent go to college, rates well above the city average.

The place offers an implicit rebuke to fear of the other.

With students from new global precincts comes a demand for new sports. In 2008, the city's Education Department formed what officials believe is still the only public high school cricket league in the nation. The league began with 14 teams and 230 players. Today it has 32 teams and 575 players, and the battles to win a championship — Queens schools are the established powers — often reach a fevered pitch.

The Bangladeshi students at Brooklyn International asked Scott Jackson, a teacher of history and of English as a second language and a former Peace Corps volunteer, to help them form a cricket team. He was fluent in baseball and basketball, and not so much in cricket.

"Two English buddies helped me with the 10 rules," he told me. "We started watching games together at an Australian bar in NoLIta."

Jackson eventually moved on to coach the school's bowling team, which is itself a mélange of Bengalis, Dominicans and Chinese, and each nationality has its own bowling style.

Paul Allen, 53, the gym teacher and athletic director, took over the cricket team in 2010 and became enraptured. An obsessive sort, he recently watched Afghanistan play Bangladesh in the early morning, in what he said was a riveting match. During cricket season he leaves his home in Merrick, on Long Island, at 5:30 a.m. to hold practices on a concrete field near the school.

Allen was a kicker for Ohio State, which is how this cricket team of Bangladeshis and a single Sri Lankan came by its name: the Buckeyes.

His 2016 team was built around Tareq the tall slugger; Ashekin the expert bowler and batter; and Raju, the one who holds it all together, as hitter, pitcher and captain.

"I love cricket, but I don't really know it," 15 Allen says. "When you have a kid like Raju as captain, it's relaxing."

Cricket is an obsession in the Indian subcontinent, Britain, the West Indies, southern

Africa, Australia and New Zealand. Some matches between national teams — known as test matches — can last five days. (I recall decades ago watching a test match in a pub in Sydney, Australia; it was clear we could drink ourselves bleary-eyed and sober up 10 times over before that match ended.)

New York's high school cricket teams play a different and increasingly popular version, known as Twenty20, that was introduced 13 years ago in Wales and England. It is faster and quicker, which is not to be confused with fast or quick.

Its rhythms share a kinship with baseball. Games run three hours or so. There are pitchers, known in cricket parlance as bowlers. Each side bats for a single long inning; one batter might hit continuously for an hour or more. If the teams are tied, they have a bowl-off, in which pitchers take turns trying to knock over wooden wickets.

The more powerful teens, Tareq and Raju and Ashekin, can drive the ball beyond the far bounds of the field, the equivalent of a baseball home run. That is good for six runs. Put too many balls in the air, however, and you are at risk of getting caught. More often, Buckeyes batters try to accumulate runs on ground balls and line drives.

A cricket field is an oval. Batters can angle drives in any direction, including behind them. [20]

The fielders, except the catcher, play bare-handed. The boys try to perfect the basket motion needed to catch the hard wooden ball, which resembles trying to catch an egg toss.

A Universal Language

I picked up with the Buckeyes just as the regular season drew to a close in June. So it was that I found myself watching a tight playoff match with the Bulldogs of Long Island City High School.

The shadows had grown long and time short for the Buckeyes. Raju, the team's finest hitter, defended his team's wicket for more than an hour, flicking and angling balls into the gaps. Now and then he leaned back and smacked the ball, sending it bouncing toward Avenue U and the Marine Park salt marshes.

His was a fine display. Yet the Buckeyes remained runs behind. Then Raju missed and was called out; the opposing players mocked him in Bengali and Urdu. He shook his head as if in disbelief and shot them a fierce look.

The rivals heaped scorn on his swing as well [25] as the girls in his high school and maybe his mother; afterward, he would say only that it was Bengali smack talk.

Alexander Hassenstein/Getty Images

In this photo Yusra Mardini, a swimmer from Syria, represents her country as part of an Olympic team of stateless refugees. The 18-year-old Mardini swam part of the dangerous journey from war-torn Syria to Greece. **What might Michael Powell see as the benefits — for both athletes and fans — of an Olympic team for refugees?**

Pictured here, in a photograph that appeared with "Uprooted to Brooklyn and Nourished by Cricket" in the *New York Times*, are some of the young men from the team Powell profiles: Mohammed Asraf Hossain, Zedah Islam, and Sarujen Siyakumar. **What does this image reveal about the young men and their relationships — to each other as well as to the sport of cricket?**

Raju has a considerable sense of self-possession but he remains a teenager, which is to say patience is not endless. He jawed at them and walked threateningly toward the opposing bench.

Allen, a naturally caffeinated coach, squinted from afar in disbelief.

He sprinted onto the field and tugged at Raju, sending him walking and tripping toward his own bench. "I have to worry about my captain losing his temper because someone said a bad word to him?" Allen yelled. "Wake up! I need you."

In truth, the entire team needed Raju. A season of fine play, of unlikely comebacks and competitive near-death experiences, was on the line that evening.

A heavy weight of responsibility falls upon a cricket captain. He plays chemist, mixing hot and cold, power and finesse.

Raju sets the batting order and selects the bowlers. Tareq and Ashekin are the pace bowlers, the equivalent of fastball pitchers. (The bowled ball usually bounces once before reaching the batter.) Raju and his angular and lithe friend, Sarujen Sivakumar — the lone Sri Lankan on the team — are spin bowlers. They are the R. A. Dickey knuckleballers of this staff, their bowled balls dipping and diving like drunken fireflies.

"Yah, yah, I'm Mr. Spin," Sarujen says, laughing at himself and making cutting motions with his wrist. "I am all soft stuff."

Sarujen's parents fled a brutal war in Sri Lanka. His mother gave birth to Sarujen in Beirut, Lebanon. When he was 3, his family decamped again to Istanbul. His parents refused to send him to a Turkish-language school; their goal was always to move to the United States, and they wanted Sarujen to learn English.

They tutored him informally, with the help of friends and Sinhalese expatriates, most of whom spoke to him in English. Sarujen learned cricket in the hilly back streets of that old Ottoman city, with a tennis ball and a worn wooden bat.

When Sarujen was 13, his family got word that a relative in New York City would pay to sponsor their entry into the United States. With the help of the International Rescue Committee, his family settled in the Bronx. His father found a job at Lehman College; Sarujen found Brooklyn International.

He recalls that first day. "It was the first time in my life I had sat in a classroom," he says softly. "I had lots of nerves, lots and lots, but I couldn't show that. I wanted them to look at me as a friendly, cool student."

In this still from the Bollywood film *Lagaan: Once Upon a Time in India* (2001), a farmer from a drought-stricken village wears homemade cricket gear in a game against a British oppressor.

What does the image say about the ways cricket crosses racial and socioeconomic lines? How does that message relate to Michael Powell's article?

His ability to speak English helped, as did his easy manner. Soon enough, he had made friends of many nationalities. He grinned. "I was cool with everyone."

Although Bangladeshi players from other schools often see him as one of their own, he speaks not a word of Bengali. "I want to wear a hat: 'Speak English.'"

His lack of Bengali can work to his favor. When playing Long Island City High, opposing players rained Bengali taunts on him as he pitched. He readied his dipper, a pitch that upon bouncing curves away from or toward a bowler.

"I'm like, 'Keep talking,'" he says. "I have no idea what you are saying." 40

More Than Winning

As the Buckeye cricketers met for early morning practice on that concrete baseball field, trucks rumbled up the ramp to the Manhattan Bridge, and construction cranes perched storklike. This once rough-and-tumble corner of Brooklyn has gone upscale.

Housing economics have changed the face of high school cricket.

Long Island City, once an industrial neighborhood of warehouses and rowhouses, has torqued upper middle class. As its population of working-class Bangladeshis and Pakistanis

departs for less expensive neighborhoods, the high school's talent stream has begun to dry up. By contrast, Francis Lewis High School in Fresh Meadows has recorded an influx of South Asians and fielded its first cricket team in 2015.

During a practice in June, Allen tutored batters while Raju ran the larger practice; Raju's girlfriend, Tahhrin Shadid, the team manager, handed out water bottles in the sticky heat. Game days presented a challenge because the playoffs fell in the midst of Ramadan, a time when many Muslims fast.

Practicality triumphed; most boys sipped 45 and nibbled, to stay aware in class and to hit and field cricket balls afterward. It was a delicate dance. Some parents already were not happy that their children played sports; as was true of earlier generations of immigrants, some preferred that their children study and work. The games in Marine Park lie miles from the apartments of families. It was rare to spot a mother or father at games.

The Marine Park field is a rutted and crowded meadow that tilts decidedly toward the south and the marshes; batted grounders in that direction bounce a long distance. During the playoffs, the cricket teams were so tightly packed that the fielders from separate games overlapped each other.

Pictured here is a painting entitled *England v West Indies* by Margaret Baird. Baird was considered a "naive" painter, a term that describes the work of artists who are often uninhibited by formal training in perspective and composition.
What is naive about this painting? What do you see in it that echoes or reinforces what Powell considers the positive aspects of the sport?

MARGARET BAIRD (CONTEMPORARY ARTIST)/Private Collection/Bridgeman Images

The Buckeyes ended up replaying a game against Long Island City High School. In the first try, the Long Island City coach showed up late, and under the city's rules his team should have lost batting time. It did not lose that time, and the Buckeyes lost the game.

But Allen won an appeal and a new game was ordered. Allen felt the soreness of guilt. In cricket, the metaphysical is woven into the material rules: The "Spirit of Cricket" mandates that the game be played not only within the laws but the spirit of the game. "Any action seen to abuse this spirit," the rules state, "causes injury to the game itself."

Allen worried that his appeal was spiritually incorrect. He had wrested victory from another team. Before the second game, he apologized to the Long Island City Bulldogs.

"As a coach, I might want to do all I can to win," he said. "As a teacher I made a poor judgment." 50

Allen apologized as well to his own team, invoking Siddhartha and the virtues of a meditative life. "I told them I took the fun out of the game by focusing so hard on making the finals as the only acceptable result," he said.

Raju smiled and shook his head. The Buckeyes were not surprised. "I've never worked with a coach quite like Paul," he said.

Which brings us back to that playoff game.

Raju made out, but that did not doom his team. Once he calmed down, Raju returned to his team's bench beneath a row of oak trees and encouraged the other players to buck up. The Buckeye batters went on a long run. As late-day shadows crossed the field, they pushed their 95th run across and claimed victory. The final score was 95-94.

The following week they played Franklin Delano Roosevelt. That game, too, was hard-fought. Roosevelt blasted out to a quick start, scoring 156 runs. Again, Raju, Tareq and Ashekin, the three batting pillars, came rumbling back. They simply fell short, 12 runs off the pace. 55

The Buckeyes were knocked out of the playoffs.

Three months later, in September, I ran into Raju and Sarujen at Melody Lanes, a bowling alley in Sunset Park. They are now seniors with college dreams. Since he was 9, Sarujen has used a camera to film his life, from Istanbul to the Bronx. At night, he adds his narration.

OTHER VOICES   717

Sometimes his voice is funny, sometimes wistful, sometimes sad.

"I have my eye on N.Y.U.," he confides to me. "They have a great film program. I hope they provide a package."

Raju works six evenings a week managing a restaurant in Crown Heights and stays up past midnight doing homework. He plans to apply to John Jay College of Criminal Justice; he wants to become a police officer. "In my country, police are part of the corruption, they are not safe," he said. "Here I can try to do something for people."

Are you happy here? I asked. He offered that smile. "If you work hard here, you can do whatever you want," he said. "Yes, this is my dream country. I'm living my dream."

That night I exchanged emails with Allen. We had talked earlier about life's paradoxes, not the least that a Jewish American such as himself formed such a tight bond with Muslim Bangladeshi immigrant teenagers. "We were a very close squad," he wrote. "All the kids felt like they had a role, that they liked each other."

"That is why I as a teacher have no regrets that we did not make the final," he continued, "which as you might know I WANT SO MUCH TO DO."

He signed off: "Oh well, L'Shana Haba'ah."

That was Hebrew for "Next Year in Jerusalem." It was a phrase of longing and hope for next year and next season.

[2016]

EXPLORING THE TEXT

1. In what ways is "Uprooted to Brooklyn, and Nourished by Cricket" about more than the sport of cricket? How does Michael Powell connect cricket to other subjects? What overall effect does drawing those connections have on Powell's message?

2. What is Powell's central argument about the value of team sports? Of cricket, in particular?

3. What elements of fiction does Powell use to characterize Tareq, Raju, and Ashekin, the three boys who "form the core of the Brooklyn International High School cricket team" (para. 4)? How do you think focusing on these three boys serves the purpose of Powell's piece?

4. How does Powell appeal to pathos in this piece?

5. To what does Powell allude in the article's first line: "the Bangladeshi boys of summer"? How does that line set the tone of the rest of the piece?

6. What does Powell mean when he says that Brooklyn International High School is a "place of cacophonous hope" (para. 6)? Why does it "[offer] an implicit rebuke to fear of the other" (para. 7)?

7. How does Powell sketch coach Paul Allen? How do his views of cricket, a sport that is popular in many parts of the world but relatively new to the United States, reveal the kind of person he is? Why is it somewhat ironic that the team he coaches is named the Buckeyes, after the team he played on at Ohio State?

8. What connection does Powell make between the young players' cricket skills and their futures in the United States?

9. Joseph O'Neill's acclaimed 2008 novel *Netherland* is, in part, about the efforts of Chuck Ramkissoon, an Indian immigrant from Trinidad, to start a professional cricket league in the United States. A champion of the game, he says, "All people, Americans, whoever, are at their most civilized when they're playing cricket . . . What's the first thing that happens when Pakistan and India make peace? They play a cricket match. Cricket is instructive, Hans. It has a moral angle . . . it is a lesson in civility." How does Powell illustrate the "moral angle" and "lesson in civility" of cricket in this piece? What implicit connections does he draw between these values and current events?

How Black Books Lit My Way Along the Appalachian Trail

RAHAWA HAILE

Rahawa Haile (b. 1985) is an Eritrean American writer of short stories and essays. Her writing has been published in the *Awl*, the *Guardian*, the *Toast*, the *Village Voice*, and numerous other magazines. In 2016, Haile hiked the Appalachian Trail, a 2,190-mile hiking-only trail stretching from Georgia to Maine. She published the following article about her experience on *BuzzFeed* in February 2017.

For many, the Appalachian Trail is a footpath of numbers. There are miles to Maine. The daily chance of precipitation. Distance to the next campsite with a reliable water source. Here, people cut the handles off of toothbrushes to save grams. Eat cold meals in the summer months to shave weight by going stoveless. They whittle medicine kits down to bottles of ibuprofen. Carry two pairs of socks. One pair of underwear. Abandon enclosed shelters entirely and opt for a tarp. Everything pulls double duty when you are hauling it 2,189 miles over mountains whose trails consist of slick roots and sharp rocks. Pants zip off into shorts. (That second pair of socks can be worn as mittens.) Floss today is thread tomorrow for stitching deteriorating shoes when the next town with a decent outfitter is 80 miles away. Few nonessentials are carried on this trail, and when they are — an enormous childhood teddy bear, a father's bulky camera — it means one thing: The weight of this item is worth considerably more than the weight of its absence.

Everyone had something out here. The love I carried was books. Exceptional books. Books by black authors, their photos often the only black faces I would talk to for weeks. These were writers who had endured more than I'd ever been asked to, whose strength gave me strength in turn. I wanted to show them beauty from heights that a history of terror had made clear were never intended to be theirs. I sought out these titles wherever I could.

It sounds easy enough, but bookshops were virtually nonexistent in Southern trail towns, post offices were open only for a handful of hours each week, and fewer establishments held mail for hikers the farther north we ventured. The pursuit of traveling with at least one book a week rapidly devolved into a game of "Where can I ship the contents of my blackness? How much of it can I permit myself to carry at a time?"

Pack: 40 ounces. Tent: 26. A pound to "love myself when I am laughing . . . and then again when I am looking mean and impressive."[1] Seven ounces of James Baldwin. Thirteen of Octavia Butler. Nine violent ounces of home, the from-from, "originally, I mean." 7,628 feet: the elevation of Asmara, Eritrea. Rain jacket: 5.5 ounces. Options for ZZ Packer. Blues for Toni Morrison. Dragons for Langston Hughes. A river for Jamaica Kincaid. Nine ounces, eight ounces, ten ounces, six. Fifteen: the number of years I spent watching my African grandmother die in the flatness of Florida. Gloves: 1.3 ounces. Warsan Shire: 2.4. Keys to a place I call home: none. Colson Whitehead: 1 pound. Assets: zero. Resting mass of light: none. Headlamp:

---

[1] A famous quote by Harlem Renaissance writer Zora Neale Hurston. —Eds.

This illustration appeared with Haile's essay when it was first published.

What aspects of its visual rhetoric do you see reflected in Haile's writing?

BuzzFeed, Inc.

3.9 ounces. Their names: endless. Trayvon, Renisha, Sandra, Tamir.[2] Spork: 0.6 ounces. Water filter: 3 ounces. Down jacket: seven ounces. Fuel canister: four. Current atmospheric carbon dioxide levels: greater than 400 ppm. Average elevation above sea level in Miami: six feet. Therapists I can no longer afford: one. Kiese Laymon: 9.6 ounces. Amiri Baraka: 1.4 pounds. The amount black women earn for every white male dollar: 63 cents. Bandana: 1.12 ounces. Pack towel: 0.5 ounces. The number of times I've told myself to put a gun to my

head between 2013 and 2016: 8,000–10,000. Bear bagging kit: 3 ounces. Aracelis Girmay: 6.4 ounces. Roxane Gay: 4.8. Emergency whistle: 0.14, orange, should I find myself in the midst of hunting season.

I started to leave books at shelters along the AT so that other hikers could read them as well. Some books were left at hostels. Zora Neale Hurston is in Walasi-Yi, mile 30.7, where roughly a quarter of all thru-hikers decide to call it quits. Yaa Gyasi was last seen at Peru Peak in Vermont. Ladan Osman is at Crazy Larry's in Damascus waiting for next year's Trail Days. Responses to my project from hikers consisted of either effusive praise or dead silence. I chose as many short story, essay, and poetry collections as possible to encourage exploration. I thought about what the author or protagonist of the title might have wanted to see. I got to a view. I held them to the light. I told them, firmly, "This is yours." This country had done an exceptional job making clear what wasn't — equality, safety, justice, financial mobility, the right to vote. In America, the word "progress" was rooted in fluidity. It had always been progress *for now.*

If there exists one stereotype about the Appalachian Trail among minorities — and, on a larger scale, hiking in the United States in general — it concerns its undeniable (but, it is important to note, not entirely unapologetic) whiteness. The whiteness in and of itself is not a bad thing. The AT is without question the kindest, most welcoming, least aggressively homogeneous space I'm likely to encounter in America in the next four years. Thru-hikers aren't gathered in the woods for six months to assert the superiority of their racial composition. They're there to embrace nature, challenge themselves, get stoned, sprain ankles, avoid rattlesnakes, fuck, pursue adventure, and otherwise treasure the joys that find them along the way, large or small. Many are simply looking to heal.

That they happen to overwhelmingly be white is largely a coincidence for those on the

5

---

[2] Trayvon Martin (1995–2012), Renisha McBride (1994–2013), Sandra Bland (1987–2015), and Tamir Rice (2002–2014) were young African Americans. Martin and McBride were shot and killed by white men, Bland died in police custody, and Rice was shot and killed by a police officer. —Eds.

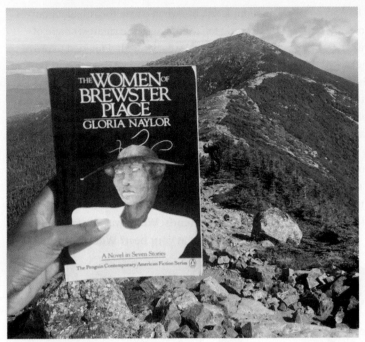

The author of this essay, Rahawa Haile, took this photograph herself while she was hiking the Appalachian Trail. **What does the juxtaposition of the novel by African American writer Gloria Naylor with the rocky path on the trail communicate? What is both in place and out of place, according to Rahawa Haile?**

COURTESY RAHAWA HAILE

trail ("I never noticed it until I saw you," a hiker once told me), a weird fact of life. It is anything but circumstantial for observers of color on the outside looking in.

Racial diversity matters uniquely on a trail that's considered a great equalizer in most other respects. Individuals have no identity but one: hiker. For many, who you were or what you came from wasn't important, because everyone was sharing the same stretches of bad weather and sore feet. It was the hiking community's way of saying all were welcome, and from what I gathered over the six months of my hike, they were. Even me. *Especially* me. Here, all were purportedly safe. "Look at how we've grown." The unintended consequence of colorblindness was benign erasure, a discomfort with looking at how we hadn't.

There is no divorcing the lack of diversity in the outdoors from a history of violence against the black body, systemic racism, and income inequality. A thing I found myself repeatedly explaining to hikers who asked about my books and my experience wasn't that I feared them, but that there was no such thing as freedom from vulnerability for me anywhere in this land. That I might be tolerated in trail towns that didn't expect to see a black hiker, but I'd rarely if ever feel at ease.

Few seemed to understand that simply because hikers had not targeted me did not mean I had ceased being a target. That I viewed every road crossing as a cue to raise shields, eyes open, ears alert. That in the back of my mind there lived my mother's voice: *or else.* Here, they were free, truly free, whereas I was only a little freer than before. That the difference between the two held centuries of slaughters in its maw. That we all carried fears. That some fears never slept.

My presence brought more Confederate flags than expected into focus for white eyes, and that saddened them when they were sad enough as it was. I explained that casual physical mobility had never been a luxury for those

10

OTHER VOICES   721

who shared my hue. That the reasons few people looked like me on the Appalachian Trail were steeped in violence, lynchings, rapes, countless hate crimes, and a fear of the aforementioned that persists to this day. That the world kept going even when, for months, we watched our foot placement instead of the news. That there were few fellow hikers in early July who could understand what it felt like to hear about a rash of black deaths. "I came out here to get away from all that," a hiker said to me. Fair enough. (And yet.) That solitude might be hard to find on the trail but isolation would always come far too easily to some.

People ask me why I chose the Appalachian Trail, and I tell them it was the clearest shape of freedom for who I was before it. I needed to prove it was possible not to give up on myself, day in and day out, when giving up felt like the most natural thing in the world. It is a cliché that one of the draws of thru-hiking is that it shows you what it means to feel infinite. I can confirm that one does not walk 2,000 miles across the face of this country as a black woman without building up an incredible sense of self. I have seen what I can be. I have heard the voices stop.

I've asked friends: When was the last time you saw yourself at your best? When did you

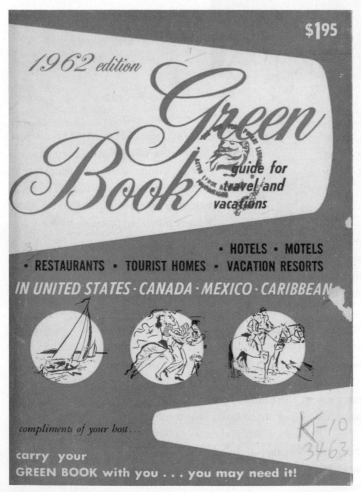

This is the 1962 edition of an annual guide for African American vacationers that gave information on restaurants, hotels, gas stations, and other places that allowed black patrons during the Jim Crow era.

Why does it say, "Carry your green book with you . . . you may need it!"? How might this be used to support one of the points Haile makes in her essay?

Schomburg Center for Research in Black Culture, Jean Blackwell Hutson Research and Reference Division, The New York Public Library.

last wish you could? I can't tell you my last time. What I know is that I moved to New York City in 2008 at the start of the recession, and after a few years a vanishing began. That's how it goes. You stop being yourself without even knowing it. You withdraw. You retreat like a glacier, slowly, until people wonder if there was ever anything more to their memory of you than an inconvenient pile of rocks. You tell yourself things will get better until there's barely anything left to remind. And then you decide what you can still fight for.

Active literary citizenship can take many forms, particularly during times of transition. There's more to writers than writing and more to readers than reading; you are not your byline.

For years, my fight has been promoting writers of color. In 2015, I ran Short Story of the Day, a project where I shared one short story a day by underrepresented writers. This year, I created a library of black excellence along the Appalachian Trail. It cost approximately $250 to build. It symbolized a great deal more. I hold no expectations of it lasting. Erosion is part of the point. Pages will be ripped out

seeing connections

Read the opening of *Wild*, a best-selling memoir by Cheryl Strayed about hiking the Pacific Crest Trail in the 1990s, after the unexpected death of her mother and the breakup of her first marriage.

Compare and contrast the tone and purpose of this excerpt to the tone and purpose of Haile's essay.

from Wild

CHERYL STRAYED

The trees were tall, but I was taller, standing above them on a steep mountain slope in northern California. Moments before, I'd removed my hiking boots and the left one had fallen into those trees, first catapulting into the air when my enormous backpack toppled onto it, then skittering across the gravelly trail and flying over the edge. It bounced off of a rocky outcropping several feet beneath me before disappearing into the forest canopy below, impossible to retrieve. I let out a stunned gasp, though I'd been in the wilderness thirty-eight days and by then I'd come to know that anything could happen and that everything would. But that doesn't mean I wasn't shocked when it did. . . .

I was alone. I was barefoot. I was twenty-six years old and an orphan too. *An actual stray*, a stranger had observed a couple of weeks before,

when I'd told him my name and explained how very loose I was in the world. . . .

In the years before I pitched my boot over the edge of that mountain, I'd been pitching myself over the edge too. I'd ranged and roamed and railed — from Minnesota to New York to Oregon and all across the West — until at last I found myself, bootless, in the summer of 1995, not so much loose in the world as bound to it.

It was a world I'd never been to and yet had known was there all along, one I'd staggered to in sorrow and confusion and fear and hope. A world I thought would both make me into the woman I knew I could become and turn me back into the girl I'd once been. A world that measured two feet wide and 2,663 miles long.

A world called the Pacific Crest Trail.

for fires. Rain and moisture will destroy the rest. For all I know, a trail maintainer has already stuffed a book or two of mine among her gear and grumbled about having to pack out the trash hikers leave behind. What matters is that I tried, and that it kept me whole, and that was good enough.

There are countless articles on post-trail depression about how to deal with the crash that follows. People almost immediately regain the weight they lost. Their bad habits and nervous tics return with a vengeance. Once again, they must look the country in the face, at its politics, its intolerance, and it is nothing, nothing at all like the trail where every day was about community and one step after another. People face their personal shortcomings. They have to find a way to eat. A place to sleep that isn't a hammock. The means to procure both. They must find new methods of battling inertia. Discover meaningful forms of momentum. Eschew self-destruction.

I revisit passages from the books I carried in search of my own light. Many start planning their next long trek. Who could blame them? At some point, most long-distance hikers ask themselves whether it was worth the "what now?" There's no one answer. I can tell you that kindness is everywhere, not as an excuse for the hatred that courses through this country's veins, but out of hope for the progress that is destined to replace it. I can tell you there are many ways to fight, even when things feel hopeless. That the risk may not be worth it. That there might come a time when you won't have a choice either way. That you matter. That you are worthy of love. That you deserve recognition of your humanity from all. That you have nothing to prove to those who would see you as less. That visibility is vulnerability, but that it also paves the way toward action for those who see themselves in you. That your existence, whether you see it or not, helps others be brave.

I can encourage first steps, even the smallest of starts. They are the only thing of which I am certain.

[2017]

EXPLORING THE TEXT

1. How is this essay about hiking the Appalachian Trail a nontraditional piece of outdoors or nature writing? Why do you think Rahawa Haile spends so little time writing about the scenery? What do you think is the real subject of her essay?

2. What are the reasons Haile carries books by black writers with her on the trail? Find at least three.

3. Analyze the rhetorical strategies Haile uses in paragraph 3. What is the effect of the paragraph as a whole? Did it remind you of anything else you've read?

4. At some point the essay shifts gears from Haile's practice of reading and leaving behind books by black authors to her lived experience as a black woman, both on the Trail and off. Where and how does the essay make the transition?

5. What are some of the ways Haile establishes her credibility? Do we end up seeing her as a hiker and nature lover, a social commentator, or a bit of both? Explain your answer.

6. Look carefully at the essay's last paragraph. How does Haile implicate the reader in her observations?

7. In a "behind the story" account for the *Columbia Journalism Review*, Elon Green writes about another of Haile's essays about her hike, "Going It Alone." Green says he was surprised at first to find that her story was more about race than it was about nature. Then he realizes that when "Bill Bryson hiked the trail for what would become 1998's *A Walk in the Woods*, it was the pale-faced, bearded Iowan's privilege to not be constantly reminded of his skin color." How does Haile grapple with being constantly reminded of her skin color? What realizations does she come to about hiking and race?

The Twelfth Player in Every Football Game

NEW YORK WORLD

The following cartoon appeared in the *New York World* in 1897 as a commentary about violence in football. It was reprinted in the *New Yorker* in 2011, accompanying an article by Ben McGrath entitled "Does Football Have a Future?: The N.F.L. and the Concussion Crisis."

THE TWELFTH PLAYER IN EVERY FOOTBALL GAME.

[1897]

EXPLORING THE TEXT

1. Consider the words and the image separately. What is the relationship between them? Does the image support the words or vice versa?

2. What point does the cartoon make about the relationship between football and violence? Do you agree with the cartoon's thesis? Explain your response.

3. According to Ben McGrath, it was Yale football coach Walter Camp, the "so-called Father of American Football, whose preference for order over chaos led to the primary differentiating element between the new sport [football] and its parent, English rugby: a line of scrimmage, with discrete plays, or downs, instead of scrums," and who, in the 1890s, tried to present football as "an upper-class training ground, not as a middle-class spectator sport." What do you suppose Walter Camp would think of the National Football League (NFL) now? Do you think this cartoon has resonance today? Explain your answer.

4. A cartoon can be analyzed through the rhetorical triangle. Consider the cartoon's subject, the artist, and the audience separately; then analyze the relationships among those three elements. Also consider the context: the time and place of the work's creation, and how and where it is viewed. What do you think are differences and similarities between today's audience and the audience when the cartoon was originally published in 1897?

5. There is a tradition in football of the "12th Player," which supposedly began in 1921 when E. King Gill, a player on the Texas A&M football squad who had left the team to play basketball, came down from the stands and suited up for a game in which many of his former teammates had been injured. His willingness to do what he could for his team led to the idea that the fans within a stadium become the "12th Player" on an eleven-player team; their support — and sometimes distracting noise — can be very influential. In this cartoon the twelfth player is Death. How does it contrast with the present-day tradition of the twelfth player? Might this cartoon have resonance today, despite the current meaning of the "12th Player"?

Yes!

SPORTS ILLUSTRATED

Sports Illustrated ran this cover on July 19, 1999, after soccer player Brandi Chastain made the winning penalty kick in the 1999 World Cup.

Robert Beck/Sports Illustrated Classic/Getty Images

[1999]

EXPLORING THE TEXT

1. What argument does this photo make? Why do you think *Sports Illustrated* chose to use it for a cover?

2. When this photo appeared, reactions ranged from appalled (a woman in a bra!) to ecstatic (a strong, athletic woman!). Do you think there is a double standard when it comes to images of women in sports? What is your response to the photo?

3. Consider the layout of the *Sports Illustrated* cover. How much space does the photograph of Chastain take up? What is the effect of obscuring part of the title of the magazine? How is the cover's text balanced by the image of Chastain?

4. Chastain's take on the incident was this: "Momentary insanity, nothing more, nothing less. I wasn't thinking about anything. . . . This is the greatest moment of my life on the soccer field." In what ways does the photo communicate Chastain's explanation? Do you think a male athlete would be asked to explain his response? Why or why not?

5. Chastain has written a book entitled *It's Not about the Bra: Play Hard, Play Fair, and Put the Fun Back into Competitive Sports* (2004). How does this photo help Chastain establish ethos? Do you think this iconic photo makes her more credible or less credible? Explain your response.

6. When asked about the popularity of her teammates — and their attractiveness — Chastain responded by saying, "There are those people who come purely for soccer. There are those people who come purely for the event. And there are those people who come because they like us, to look at us. Those are three great reasons to come." Which do you think is the most important reason people watch women's sports? Is it different for men's sports? Why or why not?

Paying College Athletes

Following are eight selections that comment directly or indirectly on the issue of whether college athletes should be paid.

SOURCES

1   **Kareem Abdul-Jabbar** / from *College Athletes of the World, Unite*
2   **Rosalyn R. Ross** / *Paying Student Athletes Is More Than Just a Question of Compensation*
3   **Ekow N. Yankah** / *Why N.C.A.A. Athletes Shouldn't Be Paid*
4   **Joe Nocera** / from *A Way to Start Paying College Athletes*
5   **John R. Thelin** / *Here's Why We Shouldn't Pay College Athletes*
6   **Broke College Athlete** (photograph)
7   **Shane Battier** / from *Let Athletes Be Students*
8   **Patrick Hruby** / from *Does Racial Resentment Fuel Opposition to Paying College Athletes?*

After using the questions to discuss individual selections, synthesize the pieces through one of the suggested assignments on pages 747–49.

1   from College Athletes of the World, Unite

KAREEM ABDUL-JABBAR

Kareem Abdul-Jabbar, a retired professional basketball player who remains the NBA's all-time leading scorer, wrote the following essay for *Jacobin* magazine in 2014.

When I played basketball for UCLA, I learned the hard way how the NCAA's refusal to pay college athletes impacted our daily lives. Despite the hours I put in every day, practicing, learning plays, and traveling around the country to play games, and despite the millions of dollars our team generated for UCLA — both in cash and in recruiting students to attend the university — I was always too broke to do much but study, practice, and play.

What little money I did have came from spring break and summer jobs. For a couple summers, Mike Frankovich, president of Columbia Pictures and a former UCLA quarterback, hired me to do publicity for his movies, most memorably *Cat Ballou* (which was nominated for five Academy Awards).

In 1968, I needed to earn enough summer money to get through my senior year. So, instead of playing in the Summer Olympics, I took a job in New York City with Operation Sports Rescue, in which I traveled around the city encouraging kids to go to college. Spring breaks I worked as a groundskeeper on the UCLA campus or in their steam plant repairing plumbing and electrical problems. No partying in Cabo San Lucas for me. Pulling weeds and swapping fuses was my glamorous life.

Despite my jobs, every semester was a financial struggle. So in order to raise enough money to get through my junior and senior years, I let Sam Gilbert, the wealthy godfather of a friend of mine, scalp my season tickets to his rich friends. This brought me a couple thousand dollars. Spread out over a year, it was still barely enough to survive. I was walking out on the court a hero, but into my bedroom a pauper.

Naturally, I felt exploited and dissatisfied. In my first year, our freshman team beat the varsity team, who had just won the NCAA championship. We were the best team in the country, yet I was too broke to go out and celebrate. The more privileged students on academic scholarships were allowed to make money on the side, just not the athletes.

And unlike those with academic scholarships, if we were injured and couldn't play anymore, we lost our scholarships but still had medical bills to worry about. We were only as valuable as our ability to tote that ball and lift that score.

Coach Wooden told us that there was no changing the NCAA's minds, that they were "immovable, like the sun rising in the east." I never personally encountered any players who cheated or shaved points, but I could see why some resorted to illegally working an extra job or accepting monetary gifts in order to get by.

The worst part is that nothing much has changed since my experience as a college athlete almost forty years ago. Well, one thing has changed: the NCAA, television broadcasters, and the colleges and universities are making a lot more money.

- The NCAA rakes in nearly $1 billion annually from its March Madness contract with CBS and Turner Broadcasting.
- The NCAA president made $1.7 million in 2012.
- The ten highest paid coaches in this year's March Madness earn between $2,627,806 and $9,682,032.

Management argues that student-athletes receive academic scholarships and special

training worth about $125,000. While that seems like generous compensation, it comes with some serious restrictions:

- College athletes on scholarship are not allowed to earn money beyond the scholarship. Yet students on academic scholarships are allowed to earn extra money.
- The NCAA allows the scholarship money to be applied only toward tuition, room and board, and required books. On average, this is about $3,200 short of what the student needs.
- Academic scholarships provide for school supplies, transportation, and entertainment. Athletic scholarships do not.
- Athletic scholarships can be taken away if the player is injured and can't contribute to the team anymore. He or she risks this possibility every game.
- The injustice worsens when we realize that the millionaire coaches are allowed to go out and earn extra money outside their contracts. Many do, acquiring hundreds of thousands of dollars a year beyond their already enormous salaries.

In this light, not only is the compensation inadequate to the effort and risk compared to academic scholarships, but there is a real chance that players may end up without an education, yet deeply in debt. Players who are seriously injured could technically make use of the NCAA's catastrophic injury relief. This sounds fair and compassionate, except the policy doesn't apply unless the medical expenses exceed $90,000 — which most claims don't. If the student's medical bills are $80,000, they're on the hook for it themselves.

To protect against career-ending injuries, the NCAA also offers Student-Athlete Disability Insurance. Unfortunately, this only pays if the athlete can't return to the sport at all. But most injuries can be repaired to some extent, even if the athlete is no longer as good and gets cut from the team. Only a dozen such claims have been successful over the past twenty years.

Life for student-athletes is no longer the quaint Americana fantasy of the homecoming bonfire and a celebration at the malt shop. It's big business in which everyone is making money — everyone except the eighteen to twenty-one-year-old kids who every game risk permanent career-ending injuries.

It's the kind of injustice that just shouldn't sit right with American workers who face similar uncertainty every day.

Unfortunately, those with a stranglehold on the profits aren't likely to give up their money just because it's the right thing to do. Instead, they will trickle some out in a show of fairness and hope that it's enough to keep the peasants from storming the castle. That's what happened in a settlement earlier this year, when college football and basketball players whose likenesses have been used in sports video games — generating millions of dollars for other people — finally received compensation.

The NCAA's power is further eroding thanks to the push to unionize college athletes, a necessary step in securing a living wage in the future. Without the power of collective bargaining, student-athletes will have no leverage in negotiating for fair treatment. History has proven that management will not be motivated to do the right thing just because it's right. Unions aren't all perfect, but they have done more to bring about equal opportunities and break down class barriers than any other institution.

We're angry when we see a vulnerable group exploited for profit by big companies, when executives rake in big bucks while powerless workers barely scrape by. We were furious when it was reported that Nike made billions in 2001, while at the same time employing, through subcontracted companies, twelve-year-old Cambodian girls working sixteen-hour days for pennies an hour to make $120 shoes.

We were outraged again in 2006, when the Labor and Worklife Program at Harvard Law School reported that about two hundred children as young as eleven years old were sewing clothing for Hanes, Walmart, JC Penney, and Puma in a factory in Bangladesh.

The children sometimes were forced to work nineteen to twenty-hour shifts, slapped and beaten if they took too long in the bathroom, and paid pennies for their efforts. According to the report, "The workers say that if they could earn just thirty-six cents an hour, they could climb out of misery and into poverty, where they could live with a modicum of decency."

Thirty-six cents an hour.

While such horrific and despicable conditions are rarer in the United States, we still have to be vigilant against all forms of exploitation so that by condoning one form, we don't implicitly condone others. Which is why, in the name of fairness, we must bring an end to the indentured servitude of college athletes and start paying them what they are worth.

The August decision by a federal judge to issue an injunction against NCAA rules that ban athletes from earning money from the use of their names and likenesses in video games, also included television broadcasts. This in itself could do much to bring about the end of NCAA tyranny.

The NCAA is appealing the decision so the case could drag out for years. In the meantime, the student-athletes continue to play Oliver Twist approaching the Mr Bumbles of collegiate sports, begging, "Please, sir, I want some more."

15

20

QUESTIONS

1. What were the consequences of the NCAA's refusal to pay college athletes for Kareem Abdul-Jabbar?

2. What is Abdul-Jabbar's major claim in this piece? What appeals does he make to support it?

3. How does Abdul-Jabbar refute the counterargument? Is this the most effective counterargument he could choose to refute? Explain why or why not.

4. Abdul-Jabbar makes several different comparisons — for instance, he likens student athletes to exploited workers, including child laborers. How effectively do these comparisons support his claim? Which comparison do you consider most effective? Explain why.

5. In what ways does Abdul-Jabbar see hope for the future?

2   Paying Student Athletes Is More Than Just a Question of Compensation

ROSALYN R. ROSS

The following piece appeared in the *Sports Fan Journal* in 2015.

To pay student athletes or not to pay student athletes? That is the question and an inciting one at that.

One of the more recent, high-profile and very public dust-ups on the topic happened via Twitter when two ESPN personalities had a difference of opinion as to whether well wishes or cash would be more comforting to Georgia running back Nick Chubb in the face of a devastating injury and an uncertain future as a football player.

When you put it that plainly, though, the answer feels embarrassingly obvious. A kid has a chance to make millions of dollars doing something he loves if he's in peak physical form, except now his peak physical form is in jeopardy. And so are his millions. So, yeah, cash might be preferable here.

A look at the bigger picture, however, reveals a far more tangled web of questions and complex issues, the surface of which even a month's worth of tweets couldn't scratch. For example, about the cash, how much money is enough money?

What would be a fair salary for these student athletes? Is this salary in lieu of tuition, room, board and stipend or in addition to? Will football players be paid more than lacrosse players since football is likely a bigger revenue driver for the school? For that same reason, should more be paid out for men's sports that women's? Will star players be paid more than everyone else on the team?

With such provocative questions on the table, 5 one would think onlookers would be treated to a healthy debate on the topic. Disappointingly, those with the strongest opinions on the matter have proven lazy, rarely rising to anything more than emotional responses to an emotionally charged set of circumstances. Ultimately the sides break down to *"I feel like college athletes should get paid because they make millions for their respective schools and they should be compensated"* and *"A free education is compensation enough."*

Unfortunately, the heavier burden lies mostly with those seeking a change to the system. It's as though a ruling has been made on the field, and now they'll need to present enough evidence to overturn the call. That will prove nearly impossible. They'll be trying to mount a campaign against the "college degree as cure-all" rhetoric that is part of the very fabric of our society. For years, the NCAA has been pitching America on the idea that no greater opportunity can be afforded a student athlete than that of a free college education. And not just them — America never stops selling America on the value of an education. Our current president believes educating our youth to be the best investment we can make in our future.

It's hard to ignore the racial and socioeconomic matters at hand in the pay-for-play argument. The call for wages in college athletics rings loudest when the story line juxtaposes a poor black kid with a struggling family back home who's putting his future earning potential on the line every week and a fat cat conference administrator making a half a million dollars a year while universities rake in obscene amounts of money for participating in a bowl game or going to the Final Four. It's an ugly reality of the college athletics construct for sure, but those who wish to right the ship should be careful of a reliance on such narratives and tread lightly. The questions are weightier down that path.

What systems will be put in place to help a kid who has never been exposed to significant amounts of money manage his finances? If a kid from an underprivileged background leaves college at 22 years old having collected a salary for four years but not having earned a degree and doesn't go pro, will we still celebrate the victory of the salary he was able to earn or mourn the loss of opportunity from the degree that he didn't?

Yes, of course, that happens now without the paycheck or the proverbial pat on the back.

Contrarily, many of the pundits who have the platform to express their feelings about why we should just pay those poor, academically challenged, athletically gifted black kids now without the facade of them being students first are folks who know very well just how fleeting a career as a professional athlete can be. There are the folks who report on the many instances of professional athletes going broke and having nothing to fall back on when their playing days are done. And they are the same folks who go home from their jobs on air to tell their own kids and nieces and nephews and cousins and godchildren how, more than anything else, a college education gives them the best options down the road.

And with that, the questions get tougher and more uncomfortable.

Just what is it about these poor black kids, then, that renders that advice irrelevant? Are these protestations of sympathy nothing more than a thinly veiled lack of expectation and an extension of our society's minimizing of opportunity for Americans who look a certain way and come from certain neighborhoods?

It's easy to start pointing fingers and say that we've known for a long time that many of these kids struggle in school and see sports as their only way out of their poverty. The people advocating for the college athlete as a full-time, paid position may see themselves as do-gooders helping kids who need the money most and logical thinkers who are brave enough to let them off the hook and exist fully in their capitalism.

It's entirely possible, though, that these guys are just the latest in a long line of folks to blame for not encouraging these kids to see their education in all its glorious and long-term potential.

Maybe they're right to want to get our student athletes paid, but at what cost?

QUESTIONS

1. What questions does Rosalyn R. Ross raise about paying student athletes?

2. Why does Ross think that the debate on the topic of paying college athletes has been "lazy" (para. 5)?

3. What is Ross's view on what she calls the "'college degree as cure-all' rhetoric that is part of the very fabric of our society" (para. 6)?

4. Ross ends by asking the reader a question about the "cost" of paying student athletes (para. 15). What cost is Ross talking about? What is your answer to her question?

3 Why N.C.A.A. Athletes Shouldn't Be Paid

EKOW N. YANKAH

Ekow N. Yankah, a professor at Cordozo School of Law, wrote the following article for the *New Yorker* magazine in 2015.

Two weeks ago, as Americans were settling into the harvest comfort of football Saturdays, the United States Court of Appeals for the Ninth Circuit issued a ruling in the antitrust suit against the National Collegiate Athletic Association. The decision drew blood on both sides. The court sided with the players in affirming that the N.C.A.A. is not immune to antitrust regulation, but simultaneously reversed a lower-court ruling that would have granted former athletes as much as five thousand dollars a year in deferred compensation — essentially back pay — for the use of their images in video games and other commercial ventures. At the same time, the court required that the N.C.A.A. increase scholarship payouts to cover the full cost of college attendance, thus making mandatory an option that the N.C.A.A. first permitted a few years ago.

These legal niceties did very little to address the deeper question of fairness. The N.C.A.A. ideal of amateurism in college athletics has come to border on farce. In the highest-revenue sports — football and basketball — the argument in favor of paying players is so searingly obvious as to seem undeniable. These athletes collectively generate tens if not hundreds of millions of dollars annually for their schools. Many college coaches are the highest-paid public employees in their states — a five-million-dollar salary is no longer eye-popping — and that paycheck doesn't include gifts from boosters, who will occasionally pay for a coach's house to make sure that he stays happy.

But this understates the exploitation. The athletes in major football and men's basketball programs are disproportionately black, many from poor and educationally disadvantaged backgrounds. For too many of them, the N.C.A.A. is the only game in town. In some dispiriting cases, the students are so unprepared that academic failure seems inevitable. In worse cases still, their scholarships are cynically undermined by the schools themselves. Coaches steer students into empty classes (what one recent report from the University of North Carolina at Chapel Hill characterized as a "shadow curriculum") or supply so-called academic support that amounts to cheating. It hardly seems coincidental, then, that sports with less African-American participation, such as baseball and hockey, maintain robust minor-league systems without the national gnashing of teeth.

And yet I believe that the drive to pay college athletes is a grave mistake — not because it misdiagnoses the disease but because it suggests that the only cure is to put the patient out of his misery. It fails, first of all, to recognize the value of sports as a part of education. This value can be seen in the countless student athletes, from gymnasts to softball players, who pour hours of work into training and competing with no hope of going pro. (Similarly, many of those in even the biggest sports show dedication long after it is clear that they will never be professionals.)

This value is again revealed in the fact that many N.C.A.A. teams are vastly more popular than their professional counterparts. My beloved Michigan Wolverines pack the Big House with more than a hundred thousand spectators each football Saturday; the Detroit Lions, meanwhile, do not. (I know, I know — it's the Lions. That's why their stadium is smaller.) Minor-league arenas attract even fewer spectators. Fans are not only seeking athletic excellence as such — the biggest and fastest players in descending order. Our connection to the athletes is deeper. These student athletes walk the same halls, have the same professors, and sweat the same midterms that we did, however long ago. At the University of Illinois at Urbana–Champaign, where I once taught, the inscription on the statue of Alma Mater reads, "To thy happy children of the future, those of the past send greetings." It's easy to dismiss that sentiment as saccharine, but it gets at an important truth: we are embedded in our cultures and social groups, and we revel in their excellence.

Paying student athletes erodes that association. If a high-school football prodigy reported that he chose Michigan not for its academic quality, tradition, or beautiful campus but because it outbid all other suitors, a connection to the university's values would be lost. This is not naïve

idealism. Auburn fans still bristle at accusations that Cam Newton auctioned them his services; prideful Michigan fans still smart over the sanctions surrounding Chris Webber, and over stinging comments intimating that he might just as well have attended a rival school. These episodes reveal what happens when college sports are reduced to a market; that this occurs all too often already is no reason to surrender to it.

The law plays a critical role here, and the Ninth Circuit's ruling can be a constructive step. It recognizes that the N.C.A.A. is subject to antitrust regulation — unlike, say, Major League Baseball — and refuses to put a monetary value on college sports. In the future, Congress could, through antitrust and commerce legislation, promote a more just landscape in college and professional sports. Professional leagues, in particular, could be encouraged to invest more seriously in their minor-league programs — the N.B.A. Development League is at least the right idea — and drop the relevant age restrictions. This would mean that the extraordinary few could go pro out of high school, and some other highfliers, could enter the developmental leagues, paid whatever the market will bear. College sports might well lose some spectacular stars, but the stars alone were never really the point.

None of this would be easy to accomplish, of course, given the money that is at stake, and there would be casualties. Some of the players who might at least have been exposed to college would forgo it entirely. We might lose the story of the exceptional athlete, often poor and dark-skinned, who goes to school solely to play sports but then sees the world widen before him. Nor should we imagine that those who opt for the developmental leagues have made it; minor-league baseball and the lower tiers of European soccer remind us how thankless and poorly compensated such a life can be. But this is no less true for those who skip college to pursue music or theatre, and, more to the point, there is no reason to think that we wouldn't hear stories of intellectual discovery among slightly less athletically gifted athletes from the same streets. Even if we cannot save sports (or music, or theatre) from its high-risk nature, we can go some way toward making sure that a few élite college programs are not unduly feeding off it.

At sports bars, when I hear people dismiss these (or other) ideas for preserving college

amateurism, I realize that it's not simply a question of their being overwhelmed by the practical difficulties involved. It is, rather, another manifestation of that corrosive American belief that anything that has value must also have a price. The recent ruling, though, hints at a path ahead, a way to cheer for our student athletes without being held hostage to money, exploitation, racism, or cynicism.

QUESTIONS

1. What reasons does Ekow N. Yankah give for not paying college athletes?

2. According to Yankah, what are some of the connections we make to college athletes and to college teams?

3. What solution does Yankah offer for promoting a "more just landscape in college and professional sports" (para. 7)? How has the American justice system paved the way toward that solution?

4. What parallels does Yankah make between sports and music or theater? Explain why you agree or disagree with that comparison.

5. How does Yankah feel about what he calls the "American belief that anything that has value must also have a price" (para. 9)? How does this claim relate to his central argument?

4 from A Way to Start Paying College Athletes

JOE NOCERA

The following excerpt is from an op-ed piece written for the *New York Times* in 2016 by sports and business columnist Joe Nocera.

I wrote my first article for the *New York Times* about the N.C.A.A. four years ago. Appearing in the magazine, it was headlined "Let's Start Paying College Athletes." Although I had been a college basketball fan all my life, I had never paid much attention to the inner workings of the N.C.A.A. But my research woke me up to the inequities faced by college football and men's basketball players, and compelled me to begin writing regularly about how the N.C.A.A. and the college sports establishment exploit the players who generate the billions that the grownups pocket.

The conceit for the original article was to imagine that the N.C.A.A.'s "amateurism"

model — which, of course, enables that exploitation — had magically disappeared, finally allowing athletes to be paid. My charge was to devise a scheme that would divert some revenue to them without bankrupting university athletic departments or destroying the fabric of college sports. What I came up with was a system that revolved around a salary cap. . . .

Here's how it would work:

Every Division I men's basketball and football team would have a salary cap, just as the pros do — except the amounts would be vastly lower. In basketball, the cap would be $650,000. In football, it would be $3 million. It is ludicrous to argue that the Power 5 programs cannot afford this; the combined $3.65 million is barely half the $7 million that Michigan Coach Jim Harbaugh made this season. (I would also drop the number of scholarships in college football to 60, which is closer to the size of an N.F.L. team, from 85 in the top tier.)

Second, I would impose a minimum salary: $25,000 per player in each sport. This would obviously not make the athletes rich, but it would give them enough to live like typical college students. [5]

Now to the free-market aspect: The minimum salaries consume only half the cap. The rest of the money would be used as a recruiting tool, so that a star player could be offered additional money as an inducement to go to a particular university. One university might want to offer a star halfback $40,000, while another might offer him $60,000. The player would make a choice based not on a recruiter's sweet-talking promises — or not solely on that — but on cold, hard cash.

I can see you recoiling at this notion. But let me ask: Is offering cash compensation really that much worse than the current system, in which universities build lavish facilities and spend absurd sums on their "programs" to lure good players? Doesn't it make more sense to give some of that money to the players? It would actually be less expensive.

It would also have other benefits. Universities could hit up boosters to put money into a fund — tax-deductible under current law — to pay the players' salaries. That would diminish their incentive to sneak money and benefits to athletes under the table.

And the contracts between players and universities — yes, contracts, just as in any other important economic transaction — could go well beyond compensation.

They could require a player to spend, say, three years in college, reducing reliance on one-and-dones. The players and their parents might insist on certain academic benefits or the right to pursue a particular major. (My system would also necessitate agents to advise athletes. This is a good thing, not a bad one.) [10]

And to those who say that paying some players more than others would create dissension on a college team, I would reply that huge salary disparities are a fact of life in the pros, and they seem to manage somehow.

(Although I did not think of this when I wrote my original article, it seems clear to me now that college sports should also adopt the Olympic model, so that athletes in any sport, not just football and men's basketball, could endorse products and be paid for their autographs and the right to use their image. That seems like a pretty basic right.)

Salary caps, of course, violate antitrust law — unless they are negotiated at arm's length by an organization representing the athletes. That is why pro basketball, hockey and football depend on players' unions: If the unions disappear, so do the salary caps.

For college athletes, such an organization already exists: It is called the National College Players Association, headed by Ramogi Huma, the longtime activist who was the driving force behind the effort to unionize Northwestern's football players. As an advocacy group, the N.C.P.A. lacks power; under my approach, it would be given the power to collectively negotiate on behalf of college athletes.

The N.C.P.A. would negotiate with the N.C.A.A. and the Power 5 over the salary cap and minimum salaries, which would probably increase over time. It would also have a seat at the table when the conferences and the N.C.A.A. negotiate with the networks over television rights. The players would get a certain percentage of all TV and marketing revenues — I'm thinking 10 percent at first, though that, too, would probably rise — which would be held in a fund by the N.C.P.A. and disbursed to a player after he left school. How much the player would get would depend on how often his team played on television, and under which TV contract. [15]

Yes, that sounds complicated, but it's really not that different from the way music royalties are distributed.

This same fund would pay for lifetime health insurance for football and men's basketball players. Former college athletes would be assured health insurance no matter what, relieving the universities of what ought to be their moral responsibility. The N.C.P.A. could also vet agents — as the pro unions do — and, for pro prospects, offer insurance against career-ending injury.

My plan has one other element. Although college eligibility would remain at the current four years, the scholarships themselves would give players eight years to complete a degree. (My original article suggested six years, but I now think eight years makes more sense.) Playing football or men's basketball is a full-time job and then some. The appeal of college athletics, in no small part, is that the players are students at the universities, so they would still have to take classes. But their loads should be reduced during their years of eligibility, and once their playing days are over, they should be able to finish their education free. That's only fair.

What's more, a huge percentage of athletes, including bench warmers, are convinced that they are bound for professional glory. Many athletes do not bother with their studies because they think they will get rich once they enter the pros. By the time they realize that's not going to happen, it's too late. My plan would make it possible for them to return to college and get the education that would allow them to find another path to a successful life.

Is my plan perfect? Of course not. The most 20 obvious problem is whether my scheme violates Title IX[1] by carving out football and men's basketball players for special treatment. My belief is that athletes in the revenue sports play a different role on campus than other athletes: Many of them have been admitted to the university, after all, because they will generate revenue through their play. But I also realize that this is a point that would most likely have to be litigated.

There is also the question of what smaller colleges will do. Four years ago, I thought that the increasing cost of big-time college sports would cause smaller schools to reconsider the role of football, an expensive sport to put on. I thought they might decide to de-emphasize sports, perhaps forming a subset of Division I that did not view itself as in competition with the Power 5 conferences.

But I've been proved wrong about this. After the cost-of-attendance payments were approved, the non-Power 5 universities were nearly unanimous in vowing to find ways to pay them to their athletes despite the strain on their athletic budgets. Now my best guess is that if a salary cap were put in place, the non-Power 5 universities would find ways to pay for salaries as well. I don't think that's the best outcome, but it is outweighed by the net good that would result from a salary cap.

---

[1] A federal law from the Education Amendments Act of 1972 that states: "No person in the United States shall, on the basis of sex, be excluded from participation in, be denied the benefits of, or be subjected to discrimination under any education program or activity receiving Federal financial assistance." —Eds.

QUESTIONS

1. What is Joe Nocera's solution to the "inequities faced by college football and men's basketball players" (para. 1)?

2. How does Nocera address the counterargument?

3. What are some of the practical matters that Nocera addresses in this piece?

4. What does Nocera consider to be the moral responsibility universities bear for their student athletes?

5. According to Nocera, how does his plan to compensate student athletes benefit both the players and their universities?

5 · Here's Why We Shouldn't Pay College Athletes

JOHN R. THELIN

John R. Thelin is a professor of educational policy studies at the University of Kentucky and the author of *A History of American Higher Education* (2011). The following op-ed was published in *Time* magazine in 2016.

College basketball is going to be dominating winter sports until the NCAA's March Madness championships finally end in April. Meanwhile, between games there's another contest taking place: debates about whether colleges should pay athletes in two big-time sports — football and men's basketball. This replaces 1980s television beer commercials pitting "tastes great" versus "less filling" factions among sports fans.

So, to start the "play for pay" games, let's assume that salaries replace scholarships in big-time men's college sports. What happens, for example, to the college player if he were paid $100,000 per year?

A full athletic scholarship (a "grant-in-aid") at an NCAA Division I university is about $65,000 if you enroll at a college with high tuition. This includes such private colleges as Stanford, Duke, Northwestern, University of Southern California, Syracuse, and Vanderbilt. The scholarship is $45,000 for tuition and $20,000 for room, board and books. At state universities, the scholarship would be lower if you were an "in state" student — because tuition would be about $13,000. But if Michigan coach Jim Harbaugh recruits nationwide and wants a high school player from California or Texas, the University of Michigan out-of-state tuition bumps up to about the same as that charged by the private colleges.

That's the old model. In the new era, a coach could offer a recruit a salary instead of a scholarship. Does a $100,000 salary give the student-athlete a better deal than the $65,000 scholarship?

The $100,000 salary is impressive. A future Heisman Trophy winner might command more, but $100,000 is not bad for an 18-year-old high school recruit. But since it's a salary, not a scholarship, it is subject to federal and state income taxes. Tuition and college expenses would not be deductible because the income level surpasses the IRS eligibility limit.

So, a student-athlete paid a salary would owe $23,800 in federal income tax and $6,700 in state taxes, a total of $30,500. In cities that levy an employee payroll tax, the salaried student's taxes go up about $2,400 per year. Income taxes then are $32,900. And, as an employee, the player would have to pay at least $2,000 in other taxes, such as Social Security, for a total of $34,900. This leaves the college player with $65,100. Since college bills come to $65,000, the player has $100 left.

By comparison, how bad was the scholarship model? According to the federal tax code, the $45,000 tuition award is deductible, but room and board are not. The student-athlete will be able to deduct book expenses and qualify for a tax credit under the American Opportunity Tax Credit (AOTC), reducing his tax. The bottom line is that the student-athlete gets a $200 refund in federal taxes and pays $820 in state taxes, for a total tax bill of $620. There's no local payroll tax because he was not an employee. This means $64,380 of the $65,000 scholarship can go toward paying academic expenses of $65,000.

How does the salary compare to the scholarship for student purchasing power? The $100,000 salary gives the college sports "employee" an advantage of $720 per year, the difference between his net salary of $65,100 versus the

5

scholarship player's net of $64,380. That's not great news for the salaried player. It's bad news for the athletics department which paid $100,000 in salary rather than $65,000 in scholarship, driving up expenses $35,000.

What's clear is that paying salaries for college players is a taxing situation. Each case will vary by state. The case above used a moderate tax state, Kentucky. Massachusetts (a.k.a. "Taxachusetts") will be more painful. In following all the "pay for play" contests, the skilled players will be dueling accountants and agents.

There's a crucial human dimension to the "numbers game." Star high school athletes are talented. Coaches and sports journalists reinforce this perception. But players and their families often overestimate a player's market worth. They fail to recognize how many equally talented players are competing for a salary. Many

10

All-State players may be surprised that college coaches are not willing to pay them $100,000 or even $50,000.

High school and college players understandably use the National Football League and the National Basketball Association salaries as the gold standard. Multimillion-dollar contracts make professional sports part of the American Dream. But since the NFL and NBA are the pinnacle, it's good to add the full range of professional sports leagues when a college player plans his financial future. Former college stars on professional indoor football squads make about $225 per game — with a $25 bonus if the team wins. Outside the NBA, players in the professional developmental league — one step from making a NBA squad — make about $43,000 per year. The college scholarship model may not be so bad for student-athletes after all.

QUESTIONS

1. How would you describe the tone of "Here's Why We Shouldn't Pay College Athletes"? What does the tone suggest about John R. Thelin's audience? Do you think the tone helps Thelin's argument or hinders it? Explain why.

2. How does Thelin's use of quantitative evidence help him develop his argument?

3. What, according to Thelin, are the consequences of overestimating college athletes' market value?

6 Broke College Athlete

Nigel Hayes, pictured here on College Game Day in 2016, played basketball for the University of Wisconsin Badgers from 2013 to 2017 and was named the pre-season Big Ten Player of the Year in 2016. He averaged 15.7 points and 5.8 rebounds per game as a junior.

Ross Jacobson—State Journal/Wisconsin State Journal

QUESTIONS

1. What is the first thing you notice about Nigel Hayes's sign? What's included? What's missing? In what ways does his sign show consideration for his audience?

2. What ethos does Hayes bring to the message on his sign? Must the viewer know who he is, or does the poster have credibility on its own? Explain your answer.

3. What statement do you think Hayes is making here? Explain whether you agree or disagree with his actions.

7 from Let Athletes Be Students

SHANE BATTIER

The following piece, written by retired professional basketball player Shane Battier, was published in 2016 by the *Players' Tribune* — a "new media company that provides athletes with a platform to connect directly with their fans, in their own words."

More or less every person not directly employed by the NCAA will readily admit that there needs to be serious reforms made to college athletics. Unfortunately, that's about as far as the conversation usually gets, because saying you *want* reform is one thing, but once you start discussing the details, it gets murky and uncomfortable. But, hey, you don't grow unless you are uncomfortable.

How can student-athletes be properly compensated for the value they bring a university? Should they be paid or are there appropriate alternatives? Which players then? Which sports? If a school doesn't have the resources to provide payment, then what? And thinking broader, what does success look like given the current state of affairs? Is the current model sustainable? Should we start from scratch?

All of these are legitimate questions with no clear solutions. There are solid arguments on all sides of these issues.

One metric for success the NCAA likes to tout is graduation rates and eligibility. In 2015, a report indicated that the Graduation Success Rate among student-athletes was 67%, two percentage points higher than the overall student rate.

On the surface, this is laudable, but when you *5* examine it further, it doesn't really paint a full picture of the outcomes that schools are providing for their student-athletes.

How many students found a job in their preferred field after graduation?

How many of them were guided into a major that they had a passion for while in school?

You hate to ask, but how many of those degrees were simply the path of least resistance?

And ultimately, what percentage of athletes felt prepared to take on the world once their eligibility was up and they no longer had advisors and coaches mapping out their lives?

While graduation rates are celebrated exter- *10* nally as a measure of success, the message many programs give to student-athletes is simple: Stay eligible and win. That's success. . . .

I've always thought that there are simple steps that programs can take to give their student-athletes better chances at success after college is over. And the tools to do so are right at their school's disposal.

For starters, I do think that it's essential to have student-athletes spend less time practicing their sport, and more time living the college experience and discovering what it means to be a productive member of society. You don't necessarily learn these lessons in a classroom. You learn them navigating your group projects, interacting with your classmates and discovering what it takes to become an adult. Producing a well-rounded human being should be one of the highest goals of our institutions of higher education. The first core value listed on the NCAA's website states that the organization believes in and is committed to: "The collegiate model of athletics in which students participate as an avocation, balancing their academic, social and athletics experiences."

Exactly.

The real value of attending college isn't just the degree that looks pretty sitting in a frame in your office, it's also creating meaningful connections that pay dividends for your future. Any person in any industry can attest to how vital connections and networks are to progressing in a career.

I would argue that the true value of any [15] degree is the alumni network that shares that same degree. The saying, "It's not what you know, but who you know," is becoming more true every day. Networking matters. Maybe more than ever. For the most part, alumni networks strictly benefit the universities and athletic program budgets that inspire them. But what if universities began leveraging alumni networks for the benefit of the athletes. I'm talking about programs that match up athletes with alumni capable of providing genuine mentorship, networking opportunities and internships. That's the kind of thing that will actually give student-athletes practical directions in careers outside of their sports.

Now, I can probably guess your reservations about this idea. You might be envisioning no-show jobs and $200 handshakes. That's how the booster-athlete relationship is often portrayed. I even hate the term booster. The connotations are so negative. But this fear of improper benefits — which still occur despite current rules — does the athlete a huge disservice. Because a dinner with an expert in the field you hope to go into *is* truly life-changing. It provides a young person with guidance that can help them once they're on their own, without the help of an army of academic advisors. The concern over a college kid getting steak dinner bought for them shouldn't outweigh the concern over them leaving school with more uncertainty about their future than when they arrived.

Schools being proactive about setting up meetings and whiteboard sessions between their student-athletes and alumni is a simple — and free — way to increase the value of a college education.

I think setting up such an arrangement would ultimately pay dividends in terms of graduation rates because athletes won't just be working towards a degree. They'll actually have an idea of what their degrees mean, and who they can call once they get them. As the founder of the Shane Battier Take Charge Foundation, I deal directly with the issues surrounding the gap in educational opportunities and access in our underserved areas. The No. 1 reason why minorities in economically depressed areas give up their pursuit of college degrees is not because of finances or support. We have found that those who abandon the path of a college degree do so because they simply do not see the value and implications of earning a degree. It is an inspiration problem. Supplying inspiration by showing college athletes what is possible will not solve the issue of graduation rates by itself (especially with minority students) but it'd be a hell of a place to start.

Of course, setting up a program such as this would mean that schools would need to budget the time for student-athletes to pursue such opportunities. They'd have to put in the work to learn what the student is actually interested in outside of their sport, and design opportunities based on what they find out. But what if that became a top selling point for a coach/school when talking to high school prospects. It would be worth the effort for both the students and the university to pursue such a course.

Right now, universities are pitched to reg- [20] ular students and student-athletes alike basically as, If you come here, you're set for life. But ultimately, that's a stretch. Anybody who has attended college knows that what you do with your life isn't determined by where you go, but what you do, how you go about it, who you meet while you're doing it and how you foster those relationships.

That is why I think the alumni base should be utilized more as an added benefit for student-athletes. It would be a way to recruit kids not just based on top coaches, trainers and facilities, but also because of the potential to have relationships facilitated with a rich alumni network that will set the student up for success in their post-career. Every school has an area of expertise — an industry they are proud to trumpet.

If athletes don't show passion for topics outside of their sports, then that is on them, and that's fine. It has been my experience that there are more athletes that are interested in preparing for life after college to create a fulfilling successful life for themselves. The NCAA likes to parade the number of athletes who *don't* play in the professional ranks and its numbers are spot-on. Let's use the unbelievably strong resources of our universities: their networks. Universities have the

tools at their disposal to make this happen. It just takes a little bit of creative thinking, and a willingness to place importance on something less tangible than a transcript.

We're in a different economy now. A degree does not equal success. So it's on the college programs to stop selling that myth and to be more proactive about ensuring their athletes find success after they graduate. That doesn't mean paying their athletes while they're in school. It means making sure somebody else does for many years after they graduate.

QUESTIONS

1. What is Shane Battier's view of what he considers the strongest message many programs give to college athletes: "Stay eligible and win" (para. 10)? What would he consider a better message?

2. What steps does Battier suggest for helping student athletes achieve success after college?

3. Why does Battier think that "a dinner with an expert in the field you hope to go into *is* truly life-changing" (para. 16)?

4. Why does Battier think that minority students from economically depressed areas give up on their college educations? What solution does he suggest?

5. Overall, what can you infer about Battier's position on paying college athletes? What aspects of this article support your inference?

---

8 from Does Racial Resentment Fuel Opposition to Paying College Athletes?

PATRICK HRUBY

Patrick Hruby is a contributing editor at *VICE Sports*, where the following article appeared in 2017.

As a political scientist, Tatishe Nteta studies how racial resentment affects attitudes toward public policy. But it took Colin Cowherd for him to realize that the same dynamic also might be influencing the ongoing debate over paying college athletes.

It was the spring of 2014, and Nteta, a professor at the University of Massachusetts, Amherst, was listening to sports talk radio while driving to work. Cowherd, then an ESPN host, was

discussing a federal antitrust lawsuit brought by former University of California, Los Angeles basketball star Ed O'Bannon against the National Collegiate Athletic Association — a much-publicized case that sought to allow past and present campus athletes to be compensated for the use of their names, images, and likeness.

"I don't think paying all college athletes is great, not every college is loaded and most 19-year-olds [are] gonna spend it — and let's be honest, they're gonna spend it on weed and kicks," Cowherd said. "And spare me the 'they're being extorted' thing.

"Listen, 90 percent of these college guys are gonna spend it on tats, weed, kicks, Xboxes, beer and swag. They are, get over it!"

Weed and kicks. Tats and swag. To Nteta's 5 ears, this sounded familiar, like the coded language sometimes used by politicians to indirectly talk about race. "To be fair to Cowherd, he didn't explicitly racialize this," Nteta says. "He simply said college athletes. But from the blowback he got from civil rights groups, it was clear that he was talking about young black men."

This piqued Nteta's curiosity. In politics, researchers know that negative racial attitudes can impact support for government initiatives like health care and welfare. For example, if you're white, and you believe that African-Americans tend to be, say, lazy, and you *also* think a particular program is likely to benefit blacks, you're far more likely to oppose that program.

"So the question was," Nteta says, "does race play a role in opposition to or support for this overarching issue of paying college athletes?"

Two and a half years later, Nteta and his colleagues have done enough work to produce a tentative answer: *Yes.* When it comes to arguments over NCAA amateurism, race definitely seems to matter.

How so? In a study recently published in *Political Research Quarterly,* Nteta and fellow professors Kevin Wallsten, Melinda Tarsi, and Lauren McCarthy analyzed responses to public opinion survey questions from 2014 and additional follow-up polling, and concluded that:

- Whites were more likely than blacks to oppose college athlete pay-for-play.
- Harboring negative racial views about blacks was the single strongest predictor of white opposition to paying athletes — more important than age, education level, political affiliation, sports fandom, or

even if respondents had played college sports themselves.
- The more negatively white respondents felt about blacks, the more they opposed pay-for-play.
- Racially resentful whites who were primed to think about African-American athletes before answering questions were more likely to oppose paying athletes than racially resentful whites who were primed to think about white athletes.

"It's not race and only race," Nteta says. 10 "There are a number of reasons why people will support or oppose policy options here. But race can't be divorced from the story. Race is one of the central reasons why whites are opposed to pay-for-play."

At first glance, that conclusion may seem counterintuitive. Off-base. Even offensive. After all, the players in big-time college football and men's basketball — the two sports at the center of pay-for-play arguments — are predominantly African-American. And they're *popular.* Majority white fan bases tune in to their broadcasts, buy tickets to their games, and loudly cheer for their performances; they wear replica jerseys essentially celebrating black athletic excellence. Where, exactly, is the racial animus?

Nteta has a more nuanced view. . . .

Perception is key. As studied and defined by social scientists, "racial resentment" is not the same thing as traditional racism. The latter — used to justify both South African apartheid and American slavery and Jim Crow — is rooted in a belief that blacks are genetically inferior to whites. By contrast, the former is "not outright hatred, but negative views about blacks justified by a belief that other races don't share the values of my group." Nteta says. "It's like when [former FOX News host] Bill O'Reilly said on his radio show that he went to dinner with [African-American television host and civil rights activist] Al Sharpton in Harlem and it was just like any other restaurant, with people being respectful and eating their food."

Nteta laughs. "As if that was a surprise."

After hearing Cowherd, Nteta and his colleagues looked at previous public opinion polls on college sports. When it came to pay-for-play, they showed a clear racial divide. A 2014 *Washington Post*/ABC News poll found that 51 percent of non-whites favored paying campus athletes, while only 24 percent of whites agreed; similarly, 66 percent of non-whites supported athlete unionization, compared to 38 percent of whites. A 2015 HBO *Real Sports*/Marist poll found that 59 percent of African-Americans believed college athletes should be paid; by contrast, 74 percent of whites believed the opposite.

How to explain the split? Nteta and company knew from NCAA demographic data that blacks made up the largest share of athletes in Division I college football (47 percent in 2013–14) and men's basketball (58 percent), the two highest-profile campus sports. The numbers in the six largest athletic conferences from 2007–11 were even higher, with African-Americans accounting for 57 percent of football players and 64 percent of men's basketball players. If whites perceived young black men to be the primary beneficiaries of pay-for-play, and if those same whites *also* harbored negative attitudes toward African-Americans in general, then perhaps college athletics and public policy had more in common than anyone realized.

"Whenever you see those kinds of splits, you know there may be a place for blacks' self-interest and whites' racial resentment." Nteta says.

That was the theory. To test it, Nteta, Wallsten, and McCarthy came up with a short series of questions about people's feelings toward the NCAA and college athletes, what schools they had received their undergraduate degrees from, their interest in college sports, if they had been college athletes themselves, and whether they agreed or disagreed that college athletes should receive salaries in addition to their scholarships. The researchers also selected three questions used by political scientists to measure racial resentment among whites:

15

- Do you support the statement "the Irish, Italians, Jews, and many other minorities overcame prejudice, and worked their way up. Blacks should do the same without any special favors"?
- Do you agree with the statement "it is really a matter of some people not trying hard enough; if blacks would only try harder, they could be as well-off as whites"?
- Do you agree with the statement "generations of slavery and discrimination have created conditions that make it difficult for blacks to work their way out of the lower class"?

The questions were added to a portion of the 2014 Cooperative Congressional Election Study, an online public opinion poll conducted by YouGov before and after the midterm elections. Analyzing responses from 1,000 survey recipients — 674 of them self-identifying as white — Nteta and his colleagues found that nearly 58 percent of whites opposed paying college athletes.

That wasn't a surprise. What *was* surprising were the nitty-gritty correlations. Sentiment toward the NCAA had no statistically significant effect on how whites felt about pay-for-play, nor did sentiment toward college athletes. Identifying as a Democrat or a Republican didn't matter. Neither did political ideology. Higher interest in campus sports actually dovetailed with *increased* support for athlete compensation.

Meanwhile, racial resentment was the strongest predictor of opposition to pay-for-play — the more resentful whites were, the less they supported it. The finding was clear, but two questions remained. First, were white respondents thinking of African-Americans when they thought about college athletes? Second, "the problem was that even though you find racial resentment matters, you couldn't dismiss the reverse causation argument," Nteta says. "You can say negative attitudes towards blacks

20

influence opinions on pay, but someone else can say that opinions on pay are actually influencing opinions on blacks."

To address those issues, the researchers conducted a second online survey last spring through Amazon's Mechanical Turk. In the new poll, the pay-for-play question was accompanied by one of two images of college athletes: either an "all white faces" treatment of three head shots of young white men in athletic uniforms, or a "mixed faces" treatment featuring two of the same white faces and one African-American face.

Nteta and his colleagues found that whites with low levels of racial resentment who saw the "mixed faces" treatment were generally supportive of pay-for-play — but whites with high resentment levels who saw the same treatment were strongly opposed. Moreover, the gap between those groups was bigger than the one between high and low-resentment level whites who saw the "all white faces" treatment. . . .

To get more data — and to better understand how racial resentment and other factors influence attitudes toward play-for-play — Nteta and his colleagues included a larger set of questions on a 2016 election survey, information they are just beginning to analyze. Ultimately, he says, the goal is not to reduce everything to race, or to call people like Cowherd racists. Rather, it's to help both the public and college sports decision-makers see their own possible biases, unwitting and otherwise, so they can better evaluate the fundamental fairness of the NCAA's economic system.

"Until we recognize that one of the reasons   25 there's opposition to paying college athletes is because of negative views of the group that is seen as benefitting, we will never be able to have an adult conversation about the real, true merits of the policy," Nteta says. "If we sweep race under the rug, we will never get to a place where we can have a real debate."

QUESTIONS

1. According to Patrick Hruby, what inspired Tatishe Nteta to study the ways that racial resentment affects the issue of paying college athletes?

2. What conclusions did Nteta reach after conducting his study? What were some surprising results of the study?

3. According to Hruby, how should Nteta's study be used? Why does Hruby think that the discussion of race must be part of the decision-making process when considering whether or not to pay college athletes?

MAKING CONNECTIONS

1. Several pieces in this Conversation mention the 2014 Ninth Circuit decision that upheld an earlier ruling that the National Collegiate Athletic Association (NCAA) violated antitrust laws. However, the court also determined that "amateurism" serves a purpose for the NCAA, rejecting a proposal that would have allowed college athletes to receive up to $5,000 a year. In "College Athletes of the World, Unite," Kareem Abdul-Jabbar writes, "The August [2014] decision by a federal judge to issue an injunction against NCAA rules that ban athletes from earning money

from the use of their names and likenesses in video games also included television broadcasts. This in itself could do much to bring about the end of NCAA tyranny" (para. 21). Which of the writers in this Conversation would agree that the NCAA's rules are tyrannical and that the injunction is a step forward for college sports? Explain why.

2. In 2016 Nigel Hayes tweeted: "The @bigten made nearly $450 million. My scholarship is about $160,00[0]. If only there was enough money to pay us. . . [.]" How might John R. Thelin and Shane Battier respond to this tweet?

3. In "College Athletes of the World, Unite," Kareem Abdul-Jabbar mentions a 2014 settlement that resulted in "college football and basketball players whose likenesses have been used in sports video games — generating millions of dollars for other people — finally receiv[ing] compensation" (para. 14). What would Ekow Yankah think of such compensation? Would he agree that these concessions are essentially, as Abdul-Jabbar says, "a show of fairness . . . enough to keep the peasants from storming the castle" (para. 14)? Why or why not?

4. Shane Battier argues that a "[college] degree doesn't equal success" (para. 22) and that college programs should stop selling that myth. In what ways does Rosalyn Ross see eye to eye with Battier on that question? Where do their views differ?

5. In "Paying Student Athletes Is More than Just a Question of Compensation," Rosalyn Ross asks: "Just what is it about these poor black kids, then, that renders [the advice to get a college education] irrelevant" (para. 12)? How would Patrick Hruby

respond? What details from his article might he use to make his point?

6. Jay Bilas, a lawyer and sports analyst for ESPN. com, says,

"I don't believe college athletes should be paid as employees. Rather, I believe barriers should be removed that limit an athlete from receiving fair compensation for his or her image and likeness. There is no legitimate reason why a college athlete should be denied the opportunity to enter into legitimate, legally binding contracts to, among other things, hire an agent, do paid appearances, appear in advertisements, endorse shoes and apparel or otherwise profit from their [sic] names and likenesses. It would not sink college sports, substantially limit the NCAA's massive television profits or negatively affect the education of the athletes or any other student. It would simply be fair."

How would Joe Nocera respond to Bilas? What might Nigel Hayes say?

ENTERING THE CONVERSATION

As you respond to each of the following prompts, support your argument with references to at least three of the sources in this Conversation on paying college athletes. For help using sources, see Chapter 4.

1. Write an essay explaining why college athletes should or should not be paid. Be sure to consider athletes who participate in sports that are not revenue producing.

2. In a 2017 essay entitled "Don't Just Shut Up and Play," published online in *The Players' Tribune*, Nigel Hayes wrote:

[Paying student athletes] shouldn't even be a controversial notion. After all, I'm a finance major. It's just the simple law of supply and demand, sprinkled with principles of the American market economy. Isn't it interesting that collegiate athletics is one of the only American industries that doesn't feel the need to abide by those same rules?

(*Psst*, I learned that in college, *while* playing basketball.)

Write an essay in which you support, challenge, or qualify his statement.

3. What is your solution? Write an essay in which you propose a system in which college athletes would be fairly compensated for the commitment they make to the athletic programs at their colleges and universities.

4. Dr. Boyce Watkins, a blogger on *Huffington Post,* wrote:

With March Madness upon us, perhaps it's time to think about what it means to be an American. We should also reconsider what it means to be a college student. As it stands, the 700-plus men and women signed on to play in the largest post-season extravaganza in professional sports (wait, did I say "professional"?) are treated neither as Americans nor as college students. Instead, they are expected to exist in a peculiar socio-economic purgatory created by March Madness that we might call pseudo-amateurism.

In pseudo-amateurism, you get to live the lifestyle of a professional: your schedule is rigorously controlled like an animal at the zoo. You are given massive amounts of media training so you can protect your brand in the public eye. You are expected to practice several times per day, and even on weekends. Oh, and that academic thing? You can do that too, as long as it doesn't interfere with your full-time job.

Write an essay in which you support, challenge, or qualify Watkins's definition of "pseudo-amateurism."

5. Research the legal issues involved with paying college athletes, particularly the September 2016 Ninth Circuit Court of Appeals ruling in *O'Bannon v. NCAA*. Consider these those issues and create a roundtable discussion among the writers here in which they update or expand their articles to address the Ninth Circuit ruling.

6. University of Kentucky coach John Calipari is known — and often criticized — for his school's "one and done" reputation. That is, students are not discouraged from playing their one required year in college and then going professional, and he has called one year of playing for Kentucky a "gap year." He considers his players "prodigies," noting that "[e]very kid is different — mentally, physically and in skill set. . . . My job is to develop players, young men who are ready to move on to success. These kids all have a genius just like Bill Gates or Steve Jobs when they didn't stay in college." Write an essay responding to Calipari's "one and done" philosophy in which you support, challenge, or qualify his position on student athletes, using the sources from this Conversation to support your argument.

7. In a scene from the cartoon *South Park*, called "Stu-dent ATH-O-LEETS," Eric T. Cartman is a representative of a "prestigious institution." He asks a university president how he gets away with not paying his "slaves." Watch the clip online, and write the transcript of an imagined roundtable discussion of it with the authors of the texts in this Conversation.

from **The Silent Season of a Hero**

GAY TALESE

Picking up the morning paper, not rushing to the sports page, DiMaggio read the front-page news, the people problems of 1966; Kwame Nkrumah was overthrown in Ghana, students were burning their draft cards (DiMaggio shook his head), the flu epidemic was spreading through the whole state of California. Then he flipped inside through the gossip columns, thankful they did not have him in there today — they had printed an item about his dating "an electrifying airline hostess" not long ago, and they also spotted him at dinner with Dori Lane, "the frantic frugger" in Whisky à Go Go's glass cage — and then he turned to the sports page and read a story about how the injured Mickey Mantle may never regain his form.

It happened all so quickly, the passing of Mantle, or so it seemed; he had succeeded DiMaggio, who had succeeded Ruth, but now there was no great young power hitter coming up, and the Yankee management, almost desperate, had talked Mantle out of retirement, and on September 18, 1965, they gave him a "day" in New York during which he received several thousand dollars' worth of gifts — an automobile, two quarter horses, free vacation trips to Rome, Nassau, Puerto Rico — and DiMaggio had flown to New York to make the introduction before 50,000: it had been a dramatic day, an almost holy day for the believers who had jammed the grandstands early to witness the canonization of a new stadium saint. Cardinal [Francis] Spellman was on the committee, President [Lyndon] Johnson sent a telegram, the day was officially proclaimed by the Mayor of New York, an orchestra assembled in the center field in front of the trinity of monuments to Ruth, [Lou] Gehrig, [Miller] Huggins; and high in the grandstands, billowing in the breeze of early autumn, were white banners that read: "Don't Quit, Mick," "We Love the Mick."

The banner had been held by hundreds of young boys whose dreams had been fulfilled so often by Mantle, but also seated in the grandstands were older men, paunchy and balding, in whose middle-aged minds DiMaggio was still vivid and invincible, and some of them remembered how one month before, during a pregame exhibition at Old-Timers' Day in Yankee Stadium, DiMaggio had hit a pitch into the left-field seats, and suddenly thousands of people had jumped wildly to their feet, joyously screaming — the great DiMaggio had returned, they were young again, it was yesterday.

But on this sunny September day at the stadium, the feast day of Mickey Mantle, DiMaggio was not wearing No. 5 on his back or a black cap to cover his graying hair; he was wearing a black suit and white shirt and blue tie, and he stood in one corner of the Yankees' dugout waiting to be introduced by Red Barber, who was standing near home plate behind a silver microphone. In the outfield Guy Lombardo's Royal Canadians were playing soothing, soft music; and moving slowly back and forth over the sprawling green grass between the left-field bullpen and the infield were two carts driven by grounds keepers and containing dozens and dozens of large gifts for Mantle — a 6-foot, 100-pound Hebrew National salami, a Winchester rifle, a mink coat for Mrs. Mantle, a set of Wilson golf clubs, a year's supply of Chunky Candy. DiMaggio smoked a cigarette, but cupped it in his hands as if not wanting to be caught in the act by teen-aged boys near enough to peek down into the dugout. Then, edging forward a step, DiMaggio poked his head out and looked up. He could see nothing above except the packed, towering green grandstands that seemed a mile high and moving, and he could see no clouds or blue sky, only a sky of faces. Then the announcer called out his name — *"Joe DiMaggio!"* — and suddenly there was a blast of cheering that grew louder and louder, echoing and reechoing within the big steel canyon, and DiMaggio stomped out his cigarette and climbed up the dugout steps and onto the soft green grass, the noise resounding in his ears, he could almost feel the breeze, the breath of 50,000 lungs upon him, 100,000 eyes watching his every move, and for the briefest instant as he walked he closed his eyes.

Then in his path he saw Mickey Mantle's mother, a smiling woman wearing an orchid, and he gently reached out for her elbow, holding it as he led her toward the microphone next to the other dignitaries lined up on the infield. Then he stood, very erect and without expression as the cheers softened and the stadium settled down.

5

---

1. The first paragraph characterizes DiMaggio as:

a. empathetic and appreciative

b. curious and eager

c. self-absorbed and leisurely

d. indifferent and uncaring

e. analytical and introspective

2. A more conventional way to punctuate the first sentence of the passage would be to replace the semi-colon with:

a. a comma

b. a colon

c. a period

d. a hyphen

e. an ellipsis

3. The language of the first sentence of paragraph two ("It happened so quickly . . . a new stadium saint") does all of the following EXCEPT:

a. emphasizes how "quickly" the events occurred by including them in one sentence.

b. undermines the importance of the event placing "day" in quotations.

c. reinforces the Yankees' desperation by listing the gifts and other details of the ceremony.

d. suggests how strong the fans' hopes were by using religious diction.

e. introduces a humorous note by including a sly pun in the phrase "the passing of Mantle."

4. In paragraph 2, all of the following contribute to the same pattern EXCEPT:

a. "an almost holy day"

b. "the canonization"

c. "a new stadium saint"

d. "officially proclaimed"

e. "the trinity of monuments"

5. At the end of paragraph 3, "it was yesterday" refers to:

a. the day Mickey Mantle was celebrated

b. the days when DiMaggio was "vivid and invincible"

c. the day of the pregame exhibition

d. the day "thousands of people had jumped wildly to their feet"

e. "this sunny September day" (para. 4)

6. The transition between paragraphs 3 and 4 implicitly contrasts:

a. the fans of Mickey Mantle with the fans of Joe DiMaggio

b. Mickey Mantle's achievements with Joe DiMaggio's

c. the memories of the young DiMaggio with the image of the current man

d. the enthusiasm surrounding the baseball game with the solemnity of the ceremony

e. the banners made by the fans with the gifts provided by the Yankees

7. The imagery in the first part of paragraph 4 ("But on this sunny September day . . . only a sky of faces") presents the stadium as:

a. idyllic

b. extravagant

c. chaotic

d. clandestine

e. anticipatory

8. The reason DiMaggio "closed his eyes" at the end of paragraph 4 is mostly likely:

a. to alleviate the pressure of being the focus of attention

b. to escape the expectations of the crowd

c. to remember his purpose at the ceremony

d. to suppress his jealousy with the lavish attention Mantle receives

e. to savor once again the moment in the spotlight

9. The final paragraph characterizes DiMaggio as:

a. aging and infirm

b. authoritative and egotistic

c. kindly and respectful

d. distracted and remote

e. detached and frustrated

10. Taken as a whole, the purpose of the passage is:

a. to contrast the skills of two athletes

b. to criticize the celebrity culture of sports

c. to depict the decline of a sport

d. to characterize a well-known athlete

e. to analyze the relationship between fans and athletes

---

from How I Learned to Ride the Bicycle

FRANCES WILLARD

Since Balaam's beast[1] there has been but little authentic talking done by the four-footed; but that is no reason why the two-wheeled should not speak its mind, and the first utterance I have to chronicle in the softly flowing vocables of my bicycle is to the following purport. I heard it as we trundled off down the Priory incline at the suburban home of Lady Henry Somerset, Reigate, England; it said: "Behold, I do not fail you; I am not a skittish beastie, but a sober, well-conducted roadster. I did not ask you to mount or drive, but since you have done so you must now learn the laws of balance and exploitation. I did not invent these laws, but I have been built conformably to them, and you must suit yourself to the unchanging regulations of gravity, general and specific, as illustrated in me. Strange as the paradox may seem, you will do this best by not trying to do it at all. You must make up what you are pleased to call your mind — make it up speedily, or you will be cast in yonder mud-puddle, and no blame to me and no thanks to yourself. Two things must occupy your thinking powers to the exclusion of every other thing: first, the goal; and, second, the momentum requisite to reach it. Do not look down like an imbecile upon the steering-wheel in front of you — that would be about as wise as for a nauseated voyager to keep his optical instruments fixed upon the rolling waves. It is the curse of life that nearly every one looks down. But the microscope will never set you free; you must glue your eyes to the telescope for ever and a day. Look up

and off and on and out; get forehead and foot into line, the latter acting as a rhythmic spur in the flanks of your equilibriated equine; so shall you win, and that right speedily.

"It was divinely said that the kingdom of God is within you. Some make a mysticism of this declaration, but it is hard common sense; for the lesson you will learn from me is this: every kingdom over which we reign must be first formed within us on what the psychic people call the 'astral plane,' but what I as a bicycle look upon as the common parade-ground of individual thought."

The Process

Courtiers wittily say that horseback riding is the only thing in which a prince is apt to excel, for the reason that the horse never flatters and would as soon throw him as if he were a groom. Therefore it is only by actually mastering the art of riding that a prince can hold his place with the noblest of the four-footed animals.

Happily there is now another locomotive contrivance which is no flatterer, and which peasant and prince must master, if they do this at all, by the democratic route of honest hard work. Well will it be for rulers when the tough old Yorkshire proverb applies to them as strictly as to the lowest of their subjects: "*It's dogged as does it.*" We all know the old saying, "Fire is a good servant, but a bad master." This is equally true of the bicycle: if you give it an inch — nay, a hair — it will take an ell — nay, an evolution — and you a contusion, or, like enough, a perforated knee-cap. . . .

Gradually, item by item, I learned the location of every screw and spring, spoke and tire, and every beam and bearing that went to

[1] Balaam is a biblical figure whose donkey, miraculously given the power of speech, saves his life. — Eds.

5

make up [my bike] Gladys. This was not the lesson of a day, but of many days and weeks, and it had to be learned before we could get on well together. To my mind the infelicities of which we see so much in life grow out of lack of time and patience thus to study and adjust the natures that have agreed in the sight of God and man to stand by one another to the last. They will not take the pains, they have not enough specific gravity, to balance themselves in their new environment. Indeed, I found a whole philosophy of life in the wooing and the winning of my bicycle.

Just as a strong and skilful swimmer takes the waves, so the bicycler must learn to take such waves of mental impression as the passing of a gigantic hay-wagon, the sudden obtrusion of black cattle with wide-branching horns, the rattling pace of high-stepping steeds, or even the swift transit of a railway-train. At first she will be upset by the apparition of the smallest poodle, and not until she has attained a wide experience will she hold herself steady in presence of the critical eyes of a coach-and-four. But all this is a part of that equilibration of thought and action by which we conquer the universe in conquering ourselves.

1. The speaker's tone in the first sentence can best be described as
   a. analytical and objective
   b. fanciful and humorous
   c. combative and defensive
   d. didactic and serious
   e. thoughtful and empathetic

2. In the second sentence, "it" refers to
   a. "Balaam's beast"
   b. "the first utterance"
   c. "my bicycle"
   d. "the following purport"
   e. "the Priory incline"

3. The speaker of the passage in quotations ("Behold, I do not fail you. . . the common parade-ground of individual thought") is
   a. Frances Elizabeth Willard
   b. Lady Henry Somerset
   c. God
   d. a bicycle
   e. a policeman

4. The main purpose of the second paragraph is to suggest that riding a bicycle
   a. is a religious experience
   b. demands both common sense and faith
   c. is more difficult than it might appear
   d. requires mental determination
   e. allows a woman more power than she previously had

5. The rhetorical function of the third paragraph can best be described as
   a. a humorous digression
   b. an analogy
   c. a counter-argument
   d. an anecdote
   e. a speculative claim

6. The Yorkshire proverb in the fourth paragraph comments on
   a. the dangers of flattery
   b. the limits of democracy
   c. the value of hard work
   d. the discrepancies of class
   e. the risks of fire

7. The speaker's primary purpose in the first four paragraphs is to
   a. Reassure that bicycle riding is an achievable goal
   b. Use bicycle riding as a metaphor for political commentary
   c. Amuse the reader with exaggerated descriptions
   d. Instruct about the hazards of bicycle riding
   e. Comment on the social inequalities of her time

8. In paragraph 5, the central metaphor compares the speaker's experience with her bicycle to
   a. a marriage
   b. a house
   c. a scientific equation
   d. a religious experience
   e. a classroom

9. In the context of the final paragraph, "equilibration" means
   a. conflict
   b. juxtaposition
   c. balance
   d. triumph
   e. friction

SPORTS

Now that you have examined a number of texts that focus on sports, explore this topic yourself by synthesizing your own ideas and the readings. You may want to do additional research or use readings from other classes as you write.

1. Sportswriter Grantland Rice famously wrote: "For when the One Great Scorer comes to mark against your name, He writes — not that you won or lost — but how you played the Game." Do you agree with that philosophy? Write an essay in which you support, challenge, or qualify Rice's assertion.

2. "The Proper Place for Sports" by Theodore Roosevelt appears on page 677. Kathleen Dalton, a historian and high school history teacher, subtitled her 2002 biography of Theodore Roosevelt, *The Strenuous Life*. In an interview, she explained that Roosevelt used that phrase to summarize his philosophy of life.

   > He urged Americans to turn their backs on the soft, easy indoor life they had been leading and embrace the challenges of the twentieth century with a spirit of adventure and courage. He praised physical activity — sports, mountain climbing, exploring, and fighting if necessary — and strenuous endeavor of all kinds, including building an empire and making America a major moral force in the world. He criticized spectators and urged them to participate in sports rather than merely watch them. He also argued that you could lead a strenuous life by working politically to make your country a better place or by writing a book or a poem or by being a caring mother who raised good kids.

   Dalton added that the subtitle has a direct connection to Roosevelt's own life. That is, Roosevelt

   > followed his own advice and lived his own kind of rugged strenuous life. He threw himself completely into each new endeavor — wrestling, bronco busting, mountain climbing, chopping trees, or exploring a dangerous uncharted river. He also led a strenuous life of struggle by making a new man of himself again and again: he resisted illness and built a stronger body, he proved himself a true man by holding his own among western ranch hands and cowboys, he made himself a writer and reformer, and he made himself a leader and a political prophet without losing his sense of ethics.

   Write about your own philosophy of life. In your essay, explain your thoughts on how to improve humankind, and examine the ways you have practiced what you preach.

3. Write an essay in which you discuss the connection between sports and character. Do you think that athletes should be role models? Develop your response with at least three examples — pro or con — of athletes mentioned in the readings in this chapter.

4. Working in groups, research the ways in which sports such as boxing, football, car racing, and soccer have made reforms to preserve the health and safety of their participants. Create a visual, such as a timeline or graph, that indicates the timing of the changes as well as their effectiveness. Show for which sport the change has been most effective and/or most radical.

5. Write an essay comparing the ways the media projects images of male and female athletes. Which images create more pressure to conform — images of male athletes or images of female athletes?

6. Write a personal narrative in which you describe the effect sports has had on your connection to family, community, or school. Has the experience been positive or negative?

7. Do some research on Title IX, the law that bans sex discrimination at schools receiving federal funds. What effect has this legislation had on participation in high school, college, and professional sports? Develop a thesis and then write about it, supporting it with your research sources. Be sure to consider the law's effect on male and female role models.

8. The following excerpt is from George Orwell's essay "The Sporting Spirit," published in 1945:

> I am always amazed when I hear people saying that sport creates goodwill between nations, and that if only the common peoples of the world could meet one another at football or cricket, they would have no inclination to meet on the battlefield. Even if one didn't know from concrete examples (the 1936 Olympics, for instance) that international sporting contests lead to orgies of hatred, one could deduce it from general principles. . . . At the international level sport is frankly mimic warfare.

In an essay, agree or disagree with Orwell's view of sports.

9. Read *The Old Man and the Sea* by Ernest Hemingway. Write an essay discussing whether you think Joe DiMaggio would have been a good fishing companion for the old man.

10

Money

What is the role of money in our everyday lives?

Hardly a day goes by without people hearing something about the economy, and more specifically, about money. Just what is this grand presence that money inserts into our lives? Generally, "the economy" refers to the production, trade, and consumption of goods and services. And economics is the study of that process.

It is generally broken into macroeconomics and microeconomics: the former refers to the economy at large, and the latter refers to the economic considerations and transactions that we make in our everyday lives.

For most of us, our experience with money begins first with consumption of goods, and then with work. We perform labor in order to earn the money we need to purchase goods and pay for services, especially those that are necessary to life. And yet it's not so simple. How do we choose what work to do? What counts as important work? Should work do more than pay the bills — should it satisfy the soul? And what exactly do we mean by "necessary for life"?

Our national mythology — the American Dream — is based on the belief that hard work will not go unrewarded. Yet recently that dream seems increasingly difficult to realize. We consume more and more but produce less and less. For the first time in history, we are participating in a truly global economy. Ultimately, what will be the outcome of such extreme shifts?

Julie Dermansky/Getty Images

Occupy Wall Street was a protest movement that began in New York City's financial district in 2011. Decrying social and economic inequality stemming from corporate greed, the movement quickly grew and spread to other cities, despite criticism that it lacked a clear agenda. In this photograph, retired Philadelphia police captain Ray Lewis joins the protesters in New York City on November 20, 2011.
Based on this image, what position do you think Lewis takes on the nature of money? Do you agree with him? Why or why not?

The authors and artists whose work you find in this chapter offer different perspectives on the role that money plays in our economy and in our everyday lives. In the central work, Barbara Ehrenreich tells of her experience trying to make a living earning minimum wage; and in our classic essay, Jonathan Swift poses a novel solution to the woes of the destitute in eighteenth-century Ireland. Eric Schlosser (p. 796) asks whether we can enjoy the fruits of labor without exploiting the laborers, and Carmen Maria Machado looks at the nature of work itself, and how it is felt and perceived on both sides of the register. Other authors in this chapter consider the plight of the poor and the sustainability of the American Dream. Finally, we enter a conversation by posing a question about the cost of a college education: Should a U.S. college education be free?

from **Serving in Florida**

BARBARA EHRENREICH

Best-selling author Barbara Ehrenreich (b. 1941) started out as a scientist. But after receiving her PhD in biology from Rockefeller University, she pursued a career in the academic world only briefly before starting to write for magazines such as *Time* and the *Progressive*. A social critic with a decidedly liberal bent, her sardonic sensibility often animates her writing. Some of her recent books include *Nickel and Dimed: On (Not) Getting By in America* (2001), *Bait and Switch: The (Futile) Pursuit of the American Dream* (2005), *Bright-Sided: How the Relentless Promotion of Positive Thinking Has Undermined America* (2009), and *Living with a Wild God: A Nonbeliever's Search for the Truth about Everything* (2014). To research her most famous book, *Nickel and Dimed*, a study of the working poor in the United States, Ehrenreich worked undercover as a server, maid, and salesclerk; and she tried to live on the wages she received. The following excerpt from "Serving in Florida," a chapter in *Nickel and Dimed*, describes Ehrenreich's experience working in a restaurant named Jerry's.

Picture a fat person's hell, and I don't mean a place with no food. Instead there is everything you might eat if eating had no bodily consequences — the cheese fries, the chicken-fried steaks, the fudge-laden desserts — only here every bite must be paid for, one way or another, in human discomfort. The kitchen is a cavern, a stomach leading to the lower intestine that is the garbage and dishwashing area, from which issue bizarre smells combining the edible and the offal: creamy carrion, pizza barf, and that unique and enigmatic Jerry's scent, citrus fart. The floor is slick with spills, forcing us to walk through the kitchen with tiny steps, like Susan McDougal[1] in leg irons. Sinks everywhere are clogged with scraps of lettuce, decomposing lemon wedges, water-logged toast crusts. Put your hand down on any counter and you risk being stuck to it by the film of ancient syrup spills, and this is unfortunate because hands are utensils here, used for scooping up lettuce onto the salad plates, lifting out pie slices, and even moving hash browns from one plate to another. The regulation poster in the single unisex rest room admonishes us to wash our hands thoroughly, and even offers instructions for doing so, but there is always some vital substance missing — soap, paper towels, toilet paper — and I never found all three at once. You learn to stuff your pockets with napkins before going in there, and too bad about the customers, who must eat, although they don't realize it, almost literally out of our hands.

The break room summarizes the whole situation: there is none, because there are no breaks at Jerry's. For six to eight hours in a row, you never sit except to pee. Actually, there are three folding chairs at a table immediately adjacent

[1]Susan McDougal was imprisoned in 1996 for contempt of court, fraud, and conspiracy in connection with the failed Whitewater land deal involving President Bill Clinton and First Lady Hillary Rodham Clinton. The Clintons were never charged with any wrongdoing. —Eds.

to the bathroom, but hardly anyone ever sits in this, the very rectum of the gastroarchitectural system. Rather, the function of the peri-toilet area is to house the ashtrays in which servers and dishwashers leave their cigarettes burning at all times, like votive candles, so they don't have to waste time lighting up again when they dash back here for a puff. Almost everyone smokes as if their pulmonary well-being depended on it — the multinational mélange of cooks; the dishwashers, who are all Czechs here; the servers, who are American natives — creating an atmosphere in which oxygen is only an occasional pollutant. My first morning at Jerry's, when the hypoglycemic shakes set in, I complain to one of my fellow servers that I don't understand how she can go so long without food. "Well, I don't understand how *you* can go so long without a cigarette," she responds in a tone of reproach. Because work is what you do for others; smoking is what you do for yourself. I don't know why the antismoking crusaders have never grasped the element of defiant self-nurturance that makes the habit so endearing to its victims — as if, in the American workplace, the only thing people have to call their own is the tumors they are nourishing and the spare moments they devote to feeding them.

Now, the Industrial Revolution is not an easy transition, especially, in my experience, when you have to zip through it in just a couple of days. I have gone from craft work straight into the factory, from the air-conditioned morgue of the Hearthside directly into the flames. Customers arrive in human waves, sometimes disgorged fifty at a time from their tour buses, peckish and whiny. Instead of two "girls" on the floor at once, there can be as many as six of us running around in our brilliant pink-and-orange Hawaiian shirts. Conversations, either with customers or with fellow employees, seldom last more than twenty seconds at a time. On my first day, in fact, I am hurt by my sister servers' coldness. My mentor for the day is a supremely competent, emotionally uninflected twenty-three-year-old, and the others, who gossip a little among themselves about the real reason someone is out sick today and the size of the bail bond someone else has had to pay, ignore me completely. On my second day, I find out why. "Well, it's good to see *you* again," one of them says in greeting. "Hardly anyone comes back after the first day." I feel powerfully vindicated — a survivor — but it would take a long time, probably months, before I could hope to be accepted into this sorority.

CBS Photo Archive/Getty Images

This photograph shows Andy Wiederhorn, CEO of Fatburger, working undercover as a line cook on an episode of *Undercover Boss*, a reality show on CBS. **What are some possible outcomes of Andy's experience working side-by-side with the line cooks? If the boss at Jerry's, the diner where Ehrenreich works, went undercover at his own restaurant, what might be his possible response to the experience?**

I start out with the beautiful, heroic idea of handling the two jobs at once, and for two days I almost do it: working the breakfast/lunch shift at Jerry's from 8:00 till 2:00, arriving at the Hearthside a few minutes late, at 2:10, and attempting to hold out until 10:00. In the few minutes I have between jobs, I pick up a spicy chicken sandwich at the Wendy's drive-through window, gobble it down in the car, and change from khaki slacks to black, from Hawaiian to rust-colored polo. There is a problem, though. When, during the 3:00–4:00 dead time, I finally sit down to wrap silver, my flesh seems to bond to the seat: I try to refuel with a purloined cup of clam chowder, as I've seen Gail and Joan do dozens of times, but Stu catches me and hisses "No *eating*!" although there's not a customer around to be offended by the sight of food making contact with a server's lips. So I tell Gail I'm going to quit, and she hugs me and says she might just follow me to Jerry's herself.

But the chances of this are minuscule. She has left the flophouse and her annoying roommate and is back to living in her truck. But, guess what, she reports to me excitedly later that evening, Phillip has given her permission to park overnight in the hotel parking lot, as long as she keeps out of sight, and the parking lot should be totally safe since it's patrolled by a hotel security guard! With the Hearthside offering benefits like that, how could anyone think of leaving? This must be Phillip's theory, anyway. He accepts my resignation with a shrug, his main concern being that I return my two polo shirts and aprons.

Gail would have triumphed at Jerry's, I'm sure, but for me it's a crash course in exhaustion management. Years ago, the kindly fry cook who trained me to waitress at a Los Angeles truck stop used to say: Never make an unnecessary trip; if you don't have to walk fast, walk slow; if you don't have to walk, stand. But at Jerry's the effort of distinguishing necessary from unnecessary and urgent from whenever would itself be too much of an energy drain. The only thing to do is to treat each shift as a one-time-only emergency: you've got fifty starving people out there, lying scattered on the battlefield, so get out there and feed them! Forget that you will have to do this again tomorrow, forget that you will have to be alert enough to dodge the drunks on the drive home tonight — just burn, burn, burn! Ideally, at some point you enter what servers call a "rhythm" and psychologists term a "flow state," where signals pass from the sense organs directly to the muscles, bypassing the cerebral cortex, and a Zen-like emptiness sets in.

5

"Sorry, I don't tip. I find it degrading."

B. Smaller

Barbara Smaller The New Yorker Collection/The Cartoon Bank

◄

Look closely at this cartoon, which appeared in the *New Yorker* in 1997.
What details has the artist chosen to include? To what extent does this image embody Ehrenreich's description of life as a food service worker?

I'm on a 2:00–10:00 P.M. shift now, and a male server from the morning shift tells me about the time he "pulled a triple"—three shifts in a row, all the way around the clock—and then got off and had a drink and met this girl, and maybe he shouldn't tell me this, but they had sex right then and there and it was like *beautiful*.

But there's another capacity of the neuro-muscular system, which is pain. I start tossing back drugstore-brand ibuprofens as if they were vitamin C, four before each shift, because an old mouse-related repetitive-stress injury in my upper back has come back to full-spasm strength, thanks to the tray carrying. In my ordinary life, this level of disability might justify a day of ice packs and stretching. Here I comfort myself with the Aleve commercial where the cute blue-collar guy asks: If you quit after working four hours, what would your boss say? And the not-so-cute blue-collar guy, who's lugging a metal beam on his back, answers: He'd fire me, that's what. But fortunately, the commercial tells us, we workers can exert the same kind of authority over our painkillers that our bosses exert over us. If Tylenol doesn't want to work for more than four hours, you just fire its ass and switch to Aleve.

True, I take occasional breaks from this life, going home now and then to catch up on e-mail and for conjugal visits (though I am careful to "pay" for everything I eat here, at $5 for a dinner, which I put in a jar), seeing *The Truman Show* with friends and letting them buy my ticket. And I still have those what-am-I-doing-here moments at work, when I get so homesick for the printed word that I obsessively reread the six-page menu. But as the days go by, my old life is beginning to look exceedingly strange. The e-mails and phone messages addressed to my former self come from a distant race of people with exotic concerns and far too much time on their hands. The neighborly market I used to cruise for produce now looks forbiddingly like a Manhattan yuppie emporium. And when I sit down one morning in my real home to pay bills from my past life, I am dazzled

▼
━━━━━━━━

What story does this map tell about minimum wage and income inequality? How might Ehrenreich use details from "Serving in Florida" in response to this image?

State-Mandated Minimum Wages for Tipped Employees

Legend:
- ■ $10.01+
- ■ $9.01–$10
- ■ $7.01–$9
- ■ $5.01–$7
- ■ $3.01–$5
- ■ $2–$3

Data from US Department of Labor.

by the two- and three-figure sums owed to outfits like Club Body Tech and Amazon.com.

Management at Jerry's is generally calmer and more "professional" than at the Hearthside, with two exceptions. One is Joy, a plump, blowsy woman in her early thirties who once kindly devoted several minutes of her time to instructing me in the correct one-handed method of tray carrying but whose moods change disconcertingly from shift to shift and even within one. The other is B.J., aka B.J. the Bitch, whose contribution is to stand by the kitchen counter and yell, "Nita, your order's up, move it!" or "Barbara, didn't you see you've got another table out there? Come *on*, girl!" Among other things, she is hated for having replaced the whipped cream squirt cans with big plastic whipped-cream-filled baggies that have to be squeezed with both hands — because, reportedly, she saw or thought she saw employees trying to inhale the propellant gas from the squirt cans, in the hope that it might be nitrous oxide. On my third night, she pulls me aside abruptly and brings her face so close that it looks like she's planning to butt me with her forehead. But instead of saying, "You're fired," she says, "You're doing fine." The only trouble is I'm spending time chatting with customers: "That's how they're getting you." Furthermore I am letting them "run me," which means harassment by sequential demands: you bring the catsup and they decide they want extra Thousand Island; you bring that and they announce they now need a side of fries, and so on into distraction. Finally she tells me not to take her wrong. She tries to say things in a nice way, but "you get into a mode, you know, because everything has to move so fast."[2]

I mumble thanks for the advice, feeling like I've just been stripped naked by the crazed enforcer of some ancient sumptuary law: No chatting for *you*, girl. No fancy service ethic allowed for the serfs. Chatting with customers is for the good-looking young college-educated servers in the downtown carpaccio and ceviche joints, the kids who can make $70–$100 a night. What had I been thinking? My job is to move orders from tables to kitchen and then trays from kitchen to tables. Customers are in fact the major obstacle to the smooth transformation of information into food and food into money — they are, in short, the enemy. And the painful thing is that I'm beginning to see it this way myself. There are the traditional asshole types — frat boys who down multiple Buds and then make a fuss because the steaks are so emaciated and the fries so sparse — as well as the variously impaired — due to age, diabetes, or literacy issues — who require patient nutritional counseling. The worst, for some reason, are the Visible Christians — like the ten-person table, all jolly and sanctified after Sunday night service, who run me mercilessly and then leave me $1 on a $92 bill. Or the guy with the crucifixion T-shirt (SOMEONE TO LOOK UP TO) who complains that his baked potato is too hard and his iced tea too icy (I cheerfully fix both) and leaves no tip at all. As a general rule, people wearing crosses or WWJD? ("What Would Jesus Do?") buttons look at us disapprovingly no matter what we do, as if they were confusing waitressing with Mary Magdalene's original profession.

I make friends, over time, with the other "girls" who work my shift: Nita, the tattooed twenty-something who taunts us by going around saying brightly, "Have we started making money yet?" Ellen, whose teenage son cooks on the graveyard shift and who once managed a restaurant in Massachusetts but won't try out for management here because she prefers being a "common worker" and not "ordering people around." Easy-going fifty-ish Lucy, with the raucous laugh, who limps toward the end of the shift because of something that has gone wrong with her leg, the exact nature of which cannot be determined without health insurance. We talk about the usual girl things — men, children,

10

[2] In *Workers in a Lean World: Unions in the International Economy* (Verso, 1997), Kim Moody cites studies finding an increase in stress-related workplace injuries and illness between the mid-1980s and the early 1990s. He argues that rising stress levels reflect a new system of "management by stress" in which workers in a variety of industries are being squeezed to extract maximum productivity, to the detriment of their health.

Artist Fernando Botero, whose 1968 painting *El Patron* is shown here, is known for work that defies viewer expectations of scale and perspective. **Describe the tone and mood of the painting. What message does it convey, and how does it relate to that of "Serving in Florida"? What aspects of Ehrenreich's experiences and reportage do you see reflected here?**

FISCHER FINE ART/Private Collection/Bridgeman Images

and the sinister allure of Jerry's chocolate peanut-butter cream pie — though no one, I notice, ever brings up anything potentially expensive, like shopping or movies. As at the Hearthside, the only recreation ever referred to is partying, which requires little more than some beer, a joint, and a few close friends. Still, no one is homeless, or cops to it anyway, thanks usually to a working husband or boyfriend. All in all, we form a reliable mutual-support group: if one of us is feeling sick or overwhelmed, another one will "bev" a table or even carry trays for her. If one of us is off sneaking a cigarette or a pee, the others will do their best to conceal her absence from the enforcers of corporate rationality.[3]

But my saving human connection — my oxytocin [hormone] receptor, as it were — is George, the nineteen-year-old Czech dishwasher who has been in this country exactly one week. We get talking when he asks me, tortuously, how much cigarettes cost at Jerry's. I do my best to explain that they cost over a dollar more here than at a regular store and suggest that he just take one from the half-filled packs that are always lying around on the break table. But that would be unthinkable. Except for the one tiny earring signaling his allegiance to some vaguely alternative point of view, George is a perfect straight arrow — crew-cut, hardworking, and hungry for eye contact. "Czech Republic," I ask, "or Slovakia?" and he seems delighted that I know the difference. "Vaclav Havel," I try, "Velvet Revolution, Frank Zappa?" "Yes, yes, 1989," he says, and I realize that for him this is already history.

My project is to teach George English. "How are you today, George?" I say at the start of each shift. "I am good, and how are you today, Barbara?" I learn that he is not paid by Jerry's but by the "agent" who shipped him over — $5 an hour, with the agent getting the dollar or so difference between that and what Jerry's pays

[3]Until April 1998, there was no federally mandated right to bathroom breaks. According to Marc Linder and Ingrid Nygaard, authors of *Void Where Prohibited: Rest Breaks and the Right to Urinate on Company Time* (Cornell University Press, 1997), "The right to rest and void at work is not high on the list of social or political causes supported by professional or executive employees, who enjoy personal workplace liberties that millions of factory workers can only dream about. . . . While we were dismayed to discover that workers lacked an acknowledged right to void at work, [the workers] were amazed by outsiders' naïve belief that their employers would permit them to perform this basic bodily function when necessary. . . . A factory worker, not allowed a break for six-hour stretches, voided into pads worn inside her uniform; and a kindergarten teacher in a school without aides had to take all twenty children with her to the bathroom and line them up outside the stall door while she voided."

dishwashers. I learn also that he shares an apartment with a crowd of other Czech "dishers," as he calls them, and that he cannot sleep until one of them goes off for his shift, leaving a vacant bed. We are having one of our ESL sessions late one afternoon when B.J. catches us at it and orders "Joseph" to take up the rubber mats on the floor near the dishwashing sinks and mop underneath. "I thought your name was George," I say loud enough for B.J. to hear as she strides off back to the counter. Is she embarrassed? Maybe a little, because she greets me back at the counter with "George, Joseph — there are so many of them!" I say nothing, neither nodding nor smiling, and for this I am punished later, when I think I am ready to go and she announces that I need to roll fifty more sets of silverware, and isn't it time I mixed up a fresh four-gallon batch of blue-cheese dressing? May you grow old in this place, B.J., is the curse I beam out at her when I am finally permitted to leave. May the syrup spills glue your feet to the floor.

I make the decision to move closer to Key West. First, because of the drive. Second and third, also because of the drive: gas is eating up $4–$5 a day, and although Jerry's is as high-volume as you can get, the tips average only 10 percent, and not just for a newbie like me. Between the base pay of $2.15 an hour and the obligation to share tips with the busboys and dishwashers, we're averaging only about $7.50 an hour. Then there is the $30 I had to spend on the regulation tan slacks worn by Jerry's servers — a setback it could take weeks to absorb. (I had combed the town's two downscale department stores hoping for something cheaper but decided in the end that these marked-down Dockers, originally $49, were more likely to survive a daily washing.) Of my fellow servers, everyone who lacks a working husband or boyfriend seems to have a second job: Nita does something at a computer eight hours a day; another welds. Without the forty-five-minute commute, I can picture myself working two jobs and still having the time to shower between them.

Shown here is a 2011 cover of *TIME* magazine. How do the cover image and text relate to each other? What connections can you make between it and Ehrenreich's argument?

So I take the $500 deposit I have coming from my landlord, the $400 I have earned toward the next month's rent, plus the $200 reserved for emergencies, and use the $1,100 to pay the rent and deposit on trailer number 46 in the Overseas Trailer Park, a mile from the cluster of budget hotels that constitute Key West's version of an industrial park. Number 46 is about eight feet in width and shaped like a barbell inside, with a narrow region — because of the sink and the stove — separating the bedroom from what might optimistically be called the "living" area, with its two-person table and half-sized couch. The bathroom is so small my knees rub against the shower stall when I sit on the toilet, and you can't just leap out of the bed, you have to climb down to the foot of it in order to find a patch of floor space to stand on. Outside, I am within a few yards of

15

seeing connections

The graphs shown here use data from the Luxembourg Income Study Database.
What do the data in each of these graphs indicate about the economic realities underpinning Ehrenreich's article? How might she use the graphs to emphasize the overall point that she argues?

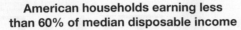

American households earning less than 60% of median disposable income

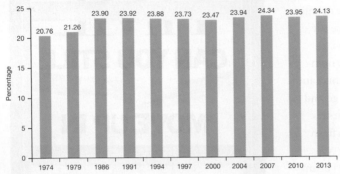

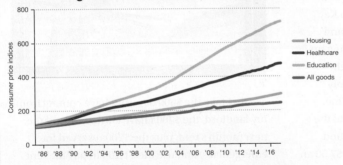

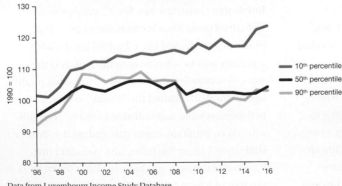

Data from Luxembourg Income Study Database.

a liquor store, a bar that advertises "free beer tomorrow," a convenience store, and a Burger King — but no supermarket or, alas, laundromat. By reputation, the Overseas park is a nest of crime and crack, and I am hoping at least for some vibrant multicultural street life. But desolation rules night and day, except for a thin stream of pedestrians heading for their jobs at the Sheraton or the 7-Eleven. There are not exactly people here but what amounts to canned labor, being preserved between shifts from the heat.

In line with my reduced living conditions, a new form of ugliness arises at Jerry's. First we are confronted — via an announcement on the computers through which we input orders — with the new rule that the hotel bar, the Driftwood, is henceforth off-limits to restaurant employees. The culprit, I learn through the grapevine, is the ultraefficient twenty-three-year-old who trained me — another trailer home dweller and a mother of three. Something had set her off one morning, so she slipped out for a nip and returned to the floor impaired. The restriction mostly hurts Ellen, whose habit it is to free her hair from its rubber band and drop by the Driftwood for a couple of Zins before heading home at the end of her shift, but all of us feel the chill. Then the next day, when I go for straws, I find the dry-storage room locked. It's never been locked before; we go in and out of it all day — for napkins, jelly containers, Styrofoam cups for takeout. Vic, the portly assistant manager who opens it for me, explains that he caught one of the dishwashers attempting to steal something and, unfortunately, the miscreant will be with us until a replacement can be found — hence the locked door. I neglect to ask what he had been trying to steal but Vic tells me who he is — the kid with the buzz cut and the earring, you know, he's back there right now.

I wish I could say I rushed back and confronted George to get his side of the story. I wish I could say I stood up to Vic and insisted that George be given a translator and allowed to defend himself or announced that I'd find a lawyer who'd handle the case pro bono. At the very least I should have testified as to the kid's honesty. The mystery to me is that there's not much worth stealing in the dry-storage room, at least not in any fenceable quantity: "Is Gyorgi here, and am having 200 — maybe 250 — catsup packets. What do you say?" My guess is that he had taken — if he had taken anything at all — some Saltines or a can of cherry pie mix and that the motive for taking it was hunger.

So why didn't I intervene? Certainly not because I was held back by the kind of moral paralysis that can mask as journalistic objectivity. On the contrary, something new — something loathsome and servile — had infected me, along with the kitchen odors that I could still sniff on my bra when I finally undressed at night. In real life I am moderately brave, but plenty of brave people shed their courage in POW camps, and maybe something similar goes on in the infinitely more congenial milieu of the low-wage American workplace. Maybe, in a month or two more at Jerry's, I might have regained my crusading spirit. Then again, in a month or two I might have turned into a different person altogether — say, the kind of person who would have turned George in.

seeing connections

Shortly after graduating from college in 2010, Adam W. Shepard penned the book *Scratch Beginnings* as a direct response to Ehrenreich's *Nickel and Dimed*. The book chronicles a social experiment in which Shepard was dropped off in a city he had never lived in — Charleston, South Carolina — with just $25, a sleeping bag, a tarp, an empty gym bag, and the clothes he was wearing. His goal was to have a car, $2,500, and a job as well as to live in a furnished apartment within 365 days. He did not use his college education or credit history to improve his conditions, and he did not beg for money. When he ended his experiment after ten months, Shepard had moved into an apartment, bought a pickup truck, and saved $3,500. Included here is an excerpt from the epilogue of *Scratch Beginnings*. **After reading carefully, paraphrase Shepard's main point. Then compare and contrast his rhetorical strategies with those of Ehrenreich in Nickel and Dimed. How persuasive do you find Shepard's argument? Explain.**

from Scratch Beginnings

ADAM W. SHEPARD

[I]t is important that I acknowledge that poverty will be around forever. I don't say this as a downer, but rather as a simple reality. While I have more sympathy for the poor now than when I started, I also understand that poverty is going to be around for reasons beyond a person's unlucky childhood. Even after countless lessons learned, some people will always find it easier to remain apathetic and make bad decisions, to lie down rather than getting up to fight. . . .

You can say what you want about my project, how it was flawed because of this or that. What if I had picked Jacksonville or Mobile or Savannah out of the hat instead of Charleston? And what if I had kids to tow around or what if I wouldn't have struck the luck that I did in working with the greatest mover on the planet? Fair enough, but I've heard it all from the people who have critiqued my book along the way. I hope, though, that the criticisms of this book don't take away from the fact that my story is by no means unique. The point stands that we can do something about our plight, or not. It is what it is. Get out and do something. After all, what is the alternative? Scrape by forever, complaining the whole time about how we've been done wrong? I'm telling you, it doesn't have to be that way.

So, here I go, to retreat into my white-collar world. . . .

I'll work my way up that infamous corporate ladder or perhaps go into business for myself, hopefully finding something that I am passionate about along the way.

That's how it's supposed to be. A blank canvas and unlimited upside potential. It's the foundation of the American Dream.

[2001]

QUESTIONS FOR DISCUSSION

1. Does Barbara Ehrenreich seem to be exaggerating the workplace as she describes it in this selection? If you have worked in a restaurant, does her description of the environment match your experience?

2. What is Ehrenreich's attitude toward her coworkers? Does she appreciate them? Is she condescending? How do you react to her observations?

3. As Ehrenreich pays bills left over from her "real life," she reflects, "[My] old life is beginning to look exceedingly strange" (para. 8). At the end of the excerpt, she asks, "So why didn't I intervene [with George]?" (para. 18). Does the experience of "serving in Florida" change Ehrenreich? Cite specific passages to support your response.

4. According to Ehrenreich, who is to blame for the situation of those who work at low-paying jobs in restaurants? Are there heroes and villains, or does the workplace itself change the people who are part of it?

5. Overall, what is your attitude toward Ehrenreich and her method of research? Does choosing to live as one of the working poor for a short time — as a kind of visitor or tourist — give her an accurate picture of their lives? Explain whether you find her presentation of them respectful, convincing, sympathetic, patronizing, superficial, or some combination of these. Cite specific passages.

6. Ehrenreich's essay delivers strong implications about the U.S. economy. What is the relationship between the macroeconomy and the microeconomy in this selection? Which is more prominent? Identify places where she addresses each. What implications does her essay make about each?

QUESTIONS ON RHETORIC AND STYLE

1. Ehrenreich opens the selection with "Picture a fat person's hell . . ." (para. 1). What is the intended effect? Does she want to shock or disgust the reader? Is she being humorous?

2. Ehrenreich describes the kitchen in terms of bodily organs and functions. What response is she trying to evoke? Is she successful? (See paras. 1 and 2.)

3. Ehrenreich provides fairly extensive commentary in footnotes. What is the effect of this strategy? In the footnotes, is her tone different from the one she uses in the body of the piece? Explain.

4. Ehrenreich uses lively, emotionally charged language throughout. Identify one passage and analyze the diction, especially the connotations of the words. Suggestions include the paragraph beginning "Now, the Industrial Revolution is not an easy transition . . ." (para. 3) or "I make friends, over time, with the other 'girls' who work my shift . . ." (para. 11).

5. Ehrenreich occasionally uses crude expressions. Are they appropriate? What is her intended effect in shifting to diction that is not only informal but, some would say, crass?

6. In this selection Ehrenreich is both outsider and insider; that is, she is the writer observing the environment in which she is playing a role. How does she make this narrative stance work? Does she shift abruptly between describing what is going on and commenting about it, or does she move smoothly between the two? Discuss by citing specific passages.

7. Discuss specific instances of humor in this selection. Is it primarily ironic humor? Aggressively sarcastic? Affectionately amusing? Cite specific passages in your response.

8. What elements of fiction does Ehrenreich employ? Consider such elements as figurative language, dialogue, narrative commentary, and description of people and settings.

9. In this selection, Ehrenreich does not state a thesis or indicate directly what her purpose is; instead, she works by inference and implication. What is her purpose? State it directly in a sentence that begins, "In this selection, Ehrenreich . . . ."

10. At times, Ehrenreich seems to raise tangential issues. When she describes her coworker

smoking, for instance, she writes: "Because work is what you do for others; smoking is what you do for yourself. I don't know why the antismoking crusaders have never grasped the element of defiant self-nurturance that makes the habit so endearing to its victims — as if, in the American workplace, the only thing people have to call their own is the tumors they are nourishing and the spare moments they devote to feeding them"

(para. 2). What is the effect of this commentary? What is its relevance to Ehrenreich's overall purpose?

11. How does Ehrenreich establish her ethos in this selection? What part does her relationship with George play in her appeal to ethos?

12. Who is Ehrenreich's audience? Base your answer on the tone you detect in specific passages.

SUGGESTIONS FOR WRITING

1. Using Ehrenreich as a model, describe a negative work experience (for example, you may have found a boss to be arrogant or you may have encountered prejudice or bias). You can narrate — and comment — but also use dialogue, as Ehrenreich does, to make the situation come alive for your readers.

2. In "Evaluation," the final chapter of *Nickel and Dimed*, Ehrenreich observes:

> Some odd optical property of our highly polarized and unequal society makes the poor almost invisible to their economic superiors. The poor can see the affluent easily enough — on television, for example, or on the covers of magazines. But the affluent rarely see the poor or, if they do catch sight of them in some public space, rarely know what they're seeing, since — thanks to consignment stores and, yes, Wal-Mart — the poor are usually able to disguise themselves as members of the more comfortable classes.

Write an essay supporting or challenging Ehrenreich's analysis.

3. *Nickel and Dimed* takes place from 1998 to 2000. Write an essay explaining whether the author's experience would be the same or different in today's economy.

4. Write an editorial for a newspaper on a topic related to the issues Ehrenreich raises — for example, a minimum wage, health care, working conditions.

5. How much is the minimum wage? Develop a budget for living for one month as a single person earning the minimum wage (plus tips if applicable) in your geographical area. What kind of living accommodations could you afford? How much money would you have available for food? What would your transportation costs be?

A Modest Proposal

JONATHAN SWIFT

Perhaps best known for *Gulliver's Travels* (1726), which has mistakenly come to be thought of as a children's novel, Jonathan Swift (1667–1745) was born in Ireland to English parents. He was educated at Trinity College, was ordained a minister, and was appointed dean of Saint Patrick's Cathedral in Dublin in 1713. For years he addressed the political problems of his day by publishing pamphlets on contemporary social issues, some of them anonymously. For one, it is believed that a reward of 300 pounds was offered to anyone who would "discover" the authorship. Among these pamphlets is the well-known essay "A Modest Proposal for Preventing the Children of Poor People in Ireland from Being a Burden to Their Parents or Country, and for Making Them Beneficial to the Publick," widely known as "A Modest Proposal." As a model of elegant prose and cogent argument, it has gained deserved fame. After reading it, you will understand what *Swiftian* means and why Swift is regarded as one of the world's premier satirists.

National Portrait Gallery, London, UK/Bridgeman Images

It is a melancholy object to those who walk through this great town or travel in the country, when they see the streets, the roads, and cabin doors, crowded with beggars of the female sex, followed by three, four, or six children, all in rags and importuning every passenger for an alms. These mothers instead of being able to work for their honest livelihood, are forced to employ all their time in strolling to beg sustenance for their helpless infants: who as they grow up either turn thieves for want of work, or leave their dear native country to fight for the pretender[1] in Spain, or sell themselves to the Barbadoes.

I think it is agreed by all parties that this prodigious number of children in the arms, or on the backs, or at the heels of their mothers, and frequently of their fathers, is in the present deplorable state of the kingdom a very great additional grievance; and, therefore, whoever could find out a fair, cheap, and easy method of making these children sound, useful members of the commonwealth, would deserve so well of the public as to have his statue set up for a preserver of the nation.

But my intention is very far from being confined to provide only for the children of professed beggars; it is of a much greater extent, and shall take in the whole number of infants at a certain age who are born of parents in effect as little able to support them as those who demand our charity in the streets.

As to my own part, having turned my thoughts for many years upon this important subject, and maturely weighed the several schemes of our projectors, I have always found them grossly mistaken in their computation. It is true, a child just dropped from its dam may be supported by her milk for a solar year, with

[1] James Francis Edward, son of deposed Catholic King James II. His claim to the throne was not considered legitimate; thus, he was a pretender to the throne. —Eds.

From the wording of the full title, what assumptions can you infer Swift makes about the motivations of his audience?

A MODEST

PROPOSAL

For preventing the

CHILDREN

O F

POOR PEOPLE

From being a Burthen to

Their Parents or Country,

A N D

For making them Beneficial to the
PUBLICK.

By Dr. SWIFT.

Dublin, Printed by *S. Harding :*
London, Re-printed ; and fold by *J. Roberts*
in *Warwick-lane*, and the Pamphlet-Shops.
M.DCC.XXIX.

Private Collection/Bridgeman Images

little other nourishment; at most not above the value of 2s., which the mother may certainly get, or the value in scraps, by her lawful occupation of begging; and it is exactly at one year old that I propose to provide for them in such a manner as instead of being a charge upon their parents or the parish, or wanting food and raiment for the rest of their lives, they shall on the contrary contribute to the feeding, and partly to the clothing, of many thousands.

There is likewise another great advantage in my scheme, that it will prevent those voluntary abortions, and that horrid practice of women murdering their bastard children, alas! too frequent among us! sacrificing the poor innocent babes I doubt more to avoid the expense than the shame, which would move tears and pity in the most savage and inhuman breast.

The number of souls in this kingdom being usually reckoned one million and a half, of these I calculate there may be about 200,000 couple whose wives are breeders; from which number I subtract 30,000 couple who are able to maintain their own children (although I apprehend there cannot be so many, under the present distress of the kingdom); but this being granted, there will remain 170,000 breeders. I again subtract 50,000 for those women who miscarry, or whose children die by accident or disease within the year. There only remain 120,000 children of poor parents annually born. The question therefore is, how this number shall be reared and provided for? which, as I have already said, under the present situation of affairs, is utterly impossible by all the methods hitherto proposed. For we can neither employ them in handicraft of agriculture; we neither build houses (I mean in the country) nor cultivate land; they can very seldom pick up a livelihood by stealing, till they arrive at six years old, except where they are of towardly parts, although I confess they learn the rudiments much earlier; during which time they can, however, be properly looked upon only as probationers; as I have been informed by a principal gentleman in the county of Cavan, who protested to me that he never knew above one or two instances under the age of six, even in a part of the kingdom so renowned for the quickest proficiency in that art.

I am assured by our merchants, that a boy or a girl before twelve years old is no salable commodity; and even when they come to this age they will not yield above 3£ or 3£ 2s. 6d.[2] at most on the exchange; which cannot turn to account either to the parents or kingdom, the charge of nutriment and rags having been at least four times that value.

5

---

[2] 3 pounds, 2 shillings, 6 pence (denominations of English money). —Eds.

I shall now therefore humbly propose my own thoughts, which I hope will not be liable to the least objection.

I have been assured by a very knowing American of my acquaintance in London, that a young healthy child well nursed is at a year old a most delicious, nourishing, and wholesome food, whether stewed, roasted, baked, or broiled; and I make no doubt that it will equally serve in a fricassee or a ragout.

I do therefore humbly offer it to public consideration that of the 120,000 children already computed, 20,000 may be reserved for breed, whereof only one-fourth part to be males; which is more than we allow to sheep, black cattle, or swine; and my reason is, that these children are seldom the fruits of marriage, a circumstance not much regarded by our savages; therefore one male will be sufficient to serve four females. That the remaining 100,000 may, at a year old, be offered in sale to the persons of quality and fortune through the kingdom; always advising the mother to let them suck plentifully in the last month, so as to render them plump and fat for a good table. A child will make two dishes at an entertainment for friends; and when the family dines alone, the fore and hind quarter will make a reasonable dish, and seasoned with a little pepper or salt will be very good boiled on the fourth day, especially in winter.

I have reckoned upon a medium that a child just born will weigh 12 pounds, and in a solar year, if tolerably nursed, will increase to 28 pounds.

I grant this food will be somewhat dear, and therefore very proper for landlords, who, as they have already devoured most of the parents, seem to have the best title to the children.

Infants' flesh will be in season throughout the year, but more plentiful in March, and a little before and after: for we are told by a grave author, an eminent French physician, that fish being a prolific diet, there are more children born in Roman Catholic countries about nine months after Lent than at any other season; therefore, reckoning a year after Lent, the markets will be more glutted than usual, because the number of popish infants is at least three to one in this kingdom: and therefore it will have one other collateral advantage, by lessening the number of papists among us.

I have already computed the charge of nursing a beggar's child (in which list I reckon all cottagers, laborers, and four-fifths of the farmers) to be about 2s. per annum, rags included; and I believe no gentleman would repine to give 10s. for the carcass of a good fat child, which, as I have said, will make four dishes of excellent nutritive meat, when he has only some particular friend or his own family to dine with him. Thus the squire will learn to be a good landlord, and grow popular among the tenants; the mother will have 8s. net profit, and be fit for work till she produces another child.

Those who are more thrifty (as I must confess the times require) may flay the carcass; the skin of which artificially dressed will make admirable gloves for ladies, and summer boots for fine gentlemen.

As to our city of Dublin, shambles may be appointed for this purpose in the most convenient parts of it, and butchers we may be assured will not be wanting: although I rather recommend buying the children alive, and dressing them hot from the knife as we do roasting pigs.

A very worthy person, a true lover of his country, and whose virtues I highly esteem, was lately pleased in discoursing on this matter to offer a refinement upon my scheme. He said that many gentlemen of this kingdom, having of late destroyed their deer, he conceived that the want of venison might be well supplied by the bodies of young lads and maidens, not exceeding fourteen years of age nor under twelve; so great a number of both sexes in every country being now ready to starve for want of work and service; and these to be disposed of by their parents, if alive, or otherwise by their nearest relations. But with due deference to so excellent a friend and so deserving a patriot, I cannot be altogether in his sentiments; for as to the males, my American acquaintance assured me from frequent

The image above, from *Hutchinson's Story of the British Nation* (1923), subtitled "a glorious and vivid panorama of the mightiest empire in history — one quarter of the earth," depicts "Irish Life, circa 1710." **What do the details from this image imply about both the Irish and the British? To what extent does this suggest the attitudes of each group toward the other have shifted between Swift's time and the early twentieth century? How might Swift respond to this depiction?**

STAPLETON COLLECTION/Private Collection/Bridgeman Images

experience that their flesh was generally tough and lean, like that of our schoolboys by continual exercise, and their taste disagreeable; and to fatten them would not answer the charge. Then as to the females, it would, I think, with humble submission be a loss to the public, because they soon would become breeders themselves: and besides, it is not improbable that some scrupulous people might be apt to censure such a practice (although indeed very unjustly), as a little bordering upon cruelty; which, I confess, has always been with me the strongest objection against any project, how well soever intended.

But in order to justify my friend, he confessed that this expedient was put into his head by the famous Psalmanazar, a native of the island Formosa,[3] who came from thence to London about twenty years ago: and in conversation told my friend, that in his country when any young person happened to be put to death, the executioner sold the carcass to persons of quality as a prime dainty; and that in his time the body of a plump girl of fifteen, who was crucified for an attempt to poison the emperor, was sold to his imperial majesty's prime minister of state, and other great mandarins of the court, in joints from the gibbet, at 400 crowns. Neither indeed can I deny, that if the same use were made of several plump young girls in this town, who without one single groat to their fortunes cannot stir abroad without a chair, and appear at the playhouse and assemblies in foreign fineries which they never will pay for, the kingdom would not be the worse.

Some persons of a desponding spirit are in great concern about the vast number of poor people, who are aged, diseased, or maimed, and I have been desired to employ my thoughts what course may be taken to ease the nation of so grievous an encumbrance. But I am not in the least pain upon that matter, because it is very well known that they are every day dying and rotting by cold and famine, and filth and vermin, as fast as can be reasonably expected. And as to the young laborers, they are now in as hopeful condition: They cannot get work, and consequently pine away for want of nourishment, to a degree that if at any time they are accidentally hired to common labor, they have not strength to perform it; and thus the country and themselves are happily delivered from the evils to come.

I have too long digressed, and therefore shall 20 return to my subject. I think the advantages by the proposal which I have made are obvious and many, as well as of the highest importance.

---

[3]Taiwan. Psalmanazar was later found to be a fraud. His book on Formosa and its culture described cannibalistic religious rituals. —Eds.

For first, as I have already observed, it would greatly lessen the number of papists, with whom we are yearly overrun, being the principal breeders of the nation as well as our most dangerous enemies; and who stay at home on purpose to deliver the kingdom to the Pretender, hoping to take their advantage by the absence of so many good Protestants, who have chosen rather to leave their country than stay at home and pay tithes against their conscience to an Episcopal curate.

Secondly, The poor tenants will have something valuable of their own, which by law may be made liable to distress and help to pay their landlord's rent, their corn and cattle being already seized, and money a thing unknown.

Thirdly, Whereas the maintenance of 100,000 children from two years old and upward, cannot be computed at less than 10s. a-piece per annum, the nation's stock will be thereby increased £50,000 per annum, beside the profit of a new dish introduced to the tables of all gentlemen of fortune in the kingdom who have any refinement in taste. And the money will circulate among ourselves, the goods being entirely of our own growth and manufacture.

Fourthly, The constant breeders beside the gain of 8s. sterling per annum by the sale of their children, will be rid of the charge of maintaining them after the first year.

Fifthly, This food would likewise bring great custom to taverns where the vintners will certainly be so prudent as to procure the best receipts for dressing it to perfection, and consequently have their houses frequented by all the fine gentlemen, who justly value themselves upon their knowledge in good eating; and a skilful cook who understands how to oblige his guests, will contrive to make it as expensive as they please.

Sixthly, This would be a great inducement to marriage, which all wise nations have either encouraged by rewards or enforced by laws and penalties. It would increase the care and tenderness of mothers toward their children, when

What impressions about eighteenth-century British society can you gather from this lithograph entitled "Shopping in Sedan Chairs in the Last Century, Queen Charlotte's visit to Pears for soap for her complexion, 1789"? What specific details in Swift's essay validate these impressions?

LOOK AND LEARN (VALERIE JACKSON HARRIS COLLECTION)/Private Collection/Bridgeman Images

25

they were sure of a settlement for life to the poor babes, provided in some sort by the public, to their annual profit instead of expense. We should see an honest emulation among the married women, which of them would bring the fattest child to the market. Men would become as fond of their wives during the time of their pregnancy as they are now of their mares in foal, their cows in calf, their sows when they are ready to farrow; nor offer to beat or kick them (as is too frequent a practice) for fear of a miscarriage.

Many other advantages might be enumerated. For instance, the addition of some thousand carcasses in our exportation of barreled beef, the propagation of swine's flesh, and improvement in the art of making good bacon, so much wanted among us by the great destruction of pigs, too frequent at our table; which are no way comparable in taste or magnificence to a well-grown, fat, yearling child, which roasted whole will make a considerable figure at a lord mayor's feast or any other public entertainment. But this and many others I omit, being studious of brevity.

Supposing that 1,000 families in this city would be constant customers for infants' flesh, besides others who might have it at merry-meetings, particularly at weddings and christenings, I compute that Dublin would take off annually about 20,000 carcasses; and the rest of the kingdom (where probably they will be sold somewhat cheaper) the remaining 80,000.

I can think of no one objection that will possibly be raised against this proposal unless it should be urged that the number of people will be thereby much lessened in the kingdom. This I freely own, and it was indeed one principal design in offering it to the world. I desire the reader will observe, that I calculate my remedy for this one individual kingdom of Ireland and for no other that ever was, is, or I think ever can be upon earth. Therefore let no man talk to me of other expedients: of taxing our absentees at 5s. a pound: of using neither clothes nor household furniture except what is of our own growth and manufacture: of utterly rejecting the materials and instruments that promote foreign luxury: of curing the expensiveness of pride, vanity, idleness, and gaming in our women: of introducing a vein of parsimony, prudence, and temperance: of learning to love our country, in the want of which we differ even from Laplanders and the inhabitants of Topinamboo[4]: of quitting our animosities and factions; nor acting any longer like the Jews, who were murdering one another at the very moment their city was taken: of being a little cautious not

to sell our country and conscience for nothing: of teaching landlords to have at least one degree of mercy toward their tenants: lastly, of putting a spirit of honesty, industry, and skill into our shop-keepers; who, if a resolution could now be taken to buy only our native goods, would immediately unite to cheat and exact upon us in the price, the measure, and the goodness, nor could ever yet be brought to make one fair proposal of just dealing, though often and earnestly invited to it.

Therefore I repeat, let no man talk to me of these and the like expedients, till he has at least some glimpse of hope that there will be ever some hearty and sincere attempt to put them in practice.

But as to myself, having been wearied out for many years with offering vain, idle, visionary thoughts, and at length utterly despairing of success, I fortunately fell upon this proposal; which, as it is wholly new, so it has something solid and real, of no expense and little trouble, full in our own power, and whereby we can incur no danger in disobliging England. For this kind of commodity will not bear exportation, the flesh being of too tender a consistence to admit a long continuance in salt, although perhaps I could name a country which would be glad to eat up our whole nation without it.

After all, I am not so violently bent upon my own opinion as to reject any offer proposed by wise men, which shall be found equally innocent, cheap, easy, and effectual. But before something of that kind shall be advanced in contradiction to my scheme, and offering a better, I desire the author or authors will be pleased maturely to consider two points. First, as things now stand, how they will be able to find food and raiment for 100,000 useless mouths and backs. And secondly, there being a round million of creatures in human figure throughout this kingdom, whose subsistence put into a common stock would leave them in debt 2,000,000£, sterling, adding those who are beggars by profession to the bulk of farmers, cottagers, and laborers, with the wives and children who are beggars in effect; I desire those politicians who dislike my overture, and

---

[4] "Laplanders" refers to Norwegians, and "Topinamboo" is a region in Brazil. —Eds.

30

seeing connections

Political cartoonist R.J. Matson borrows Swift's trope in this cartoon suggesting that if the legislature wants to achieve full employment, they might cut the minimum wage to $1.00.
Do you find Matson's argument powerful? Is it "Swiftian"? Why or why not?

A MODEST PROPOSAL TO THE MISSOURI LEGISLATURE:
FOR FULL EMPLOYMENT, CUT THE MINIMUM WAGE!

RJ Matson, CagleCartoons.com

may perhaps be so bold as to attempt an answer, that they will first ask the parents of these mortals, whether they would not at this day think it a great happiness to have been sold for food at a year old in the manner I prescribe, and thereby have avoided such a perpetual scene of misfortunes as they have since gone through by the oppression of landlords, the impossibility of paying rent without money or trade, the want of common sustenance, with neither house nor clothes to cover them from the inclemencies of the weather, and the most inevitable prospect of entailing the like or greater miseries upon their breed for ever.

I profess, in the sincerity of my heart, that I have not the least personal interest in endeavoring to promote this necessary work, having no other motive than the public good of my country, by advancing our trade, providing for infants, relieving the poor, and giving some pleasure to the rich. I have no children by which I can propose to get a single penny; the youngest being nine years old, and my wife past childbearing.

[1729]

QUESTIONS FOR DISCUSSION

1. What were the social conditions in Ireland that occasioned the writing of Jonathan Swift's essay? Does the essay indicate what Swift considers to be the causes of these conditions? Does the government — the state — have a responsibility for the condition of its poor? Does Swift target anybody in particular with his satire? How can you tell?

2. To what extent would a modern audience feel offended by Swift's proposal? Explain your reasoning.

3. Of the six advantages Swift enumerates (paras. 21–26), which one might be considered the most sardonic? Explain.

4. Explain how Swift uses the essay to satirize both his subject and the vehicle he employs — that is, a political proposal itself.

5. What is Swift's overall purpose? Why did he choose such a provocative approach?

6. The modern reader may notice the misogyny in Swift's essay. Does it affect your opinion of the essay? Does it make Swift's criticism of society less powerful?

7. Several eighteenth-century writers made allusions to "A Modest Proposal" in the titles of their satiric essays. For example, Philip Skelton made his irony obvious by calling an essay "Some Proposals for the Revival of Christianity." Why do you think Swift's title was considered such a useful satiric tool?

8. By publishing such an outrageous text, what might Swift have hoped to bring about among the people of Ireland?

QUESTIONS ON RHETORIC AND STYLE

1. How does Swift want the reader to view his speaker? That is, how would Swift want his reader to describe the persona he adopts?

2. At what point in the essay did you recognize that Swift's proposal is meant to be satiric? Do you think a modern audience would get the joke faster than Swift's contemporaries did?

3. Note Swift's diction in the first seven paragraphs. How does it show quantification and dehumanization? Explain the purpose of Swift's specific word choices.

4. At the beginning of the essay, Swift explains the anticipated results before revealing the actual proposal. Explain the rhetorical purpose of such a strategy.

5. In paragraph 9, why doesn't Swift end the sentence after the word *food*? Explain the purpose and effect of the modifiers included there.

6. Identify examples of appeals to values such as thrift and patriotism. Explain the rhetorical strategy behind each example.

7. Consider the additional proposal that Swift mentions in paragraph 17. Explain the rhetorical strategy at work in that paragraph.

8. Which targets does Swift ironically identify in paragraphs 21 and 22? Note the rhetorical progression of paragraphs 21–26. By using such a method, what is Swift satirizing?

9. What are the assumptions behind each of Swift's claims in paragraphs 21–26? Explain them.

10. Read carefully paragraphs 29–31. What are the "expedients" that Swift discusses there? How does irony serve his rhetorical purpose in this section?

11. To what do the "vain, idle, visionary thoughts" (para. 31) refer? What is Swift's tone here?

12. How does the final paragraph of the essay contribute to Swift's rhetorical purpose?

SUGGESTIONS FOR WRITING

1. "A Modest Proposal" is remarkably consistent in its ironic voice throughout. There are, however, some places where Swift's own voice intrudes. Write an essay showing how these breaks in tone reveal Swift's own attitude toward his subject.

2. Read carefully paragraphs 20–26. Then write an essay explaining how Swift uses resources of language to develop his positions. Consider diction, voice, pacing, and other rhetorical features to support your position.

3. Write an essay explaining the influence of Swift on a contemporary example of satire. One example, by political commentator Christopher Buckley

about mad cow disease, was published in the *New Yorker* (April 15, 1996) and titled "A Moodest Proposal." Another example might be the satiric news program *The Colbert Report*.

4. Write a response to Swift in the voice of an economist sympathetic to Swift's views, or in the voice of someone who takes the proposal seriously, challenging Swift's argument.

5. Write your own "modest proposal" about an economic condition in today's society. Be sure to specify who your audience is — whether you intend your piece to be published in a national magazine, your local newspaper, or your school newspaper.

from The Gospel of Wealth

ANDREW CARNEGIE

Following is a selection from *The Gospel of Wealth*, an extended essay that American industrialist Andrew Carnegie (1835–1919) wrote in 1889, a time when wealth was increasingly being concentrated in the hands of an elite group of industrialists, including Carnegie himself. *The Gospel of Wealth*, which outlines Carnegie's belief that the rich have a responsibility to use their wealth to create a better society, was first published in the *North American Review*, a highly regarded literary magazine.

Those who would administer wisely must, indeed, be wise, for one of the serious obstacles to the improvement of our race is indiscriminate charity. It were better for mankind that the millions of the rich were thrown into the sea than so spent as to encourage the slothful, the drunken, the unworthy. Of every thousand dollars spent in so-called charity to-day, it is probable that $950 is unwisely spent; so spent, indeed, as to produce the very evils which it proposes to mitigate or cure. A well-known writer of philosophic books admitted the other day that he had given a quarter of a dollar to a man who approached him as he was coming to visit the house of his friend. He knew nothing of the habits of this beggar; knew not the use that would be made of this money, although he had every reason to suspect that it would be spent improperly. This man professed to be a disciple of Herbert Spencer;[1] yet the quarter-dollar given that night will probably work more injury than all the money which its thoughtless donor will ever be able to give in true charity will do good. He only gratified his own feelings, saved himself from annoyance, — and this was probably one of the most selfish and very worst actions of his life, for in all respects he is most worthy.

In bestowing charity, the main consideration should be to help those who will help themselves; to provide part of the means by which those who desire to improve may do so; to give those who desire to rise the aids by which they may rise; to assist, but rarely or never to do all. Neither the individual nor the race is improved by alms-giving. Those worthy of assistance, except in rare cases, seldom require assistance. The really valuable men of the race never do, except in cases of accident or sudden change. Every one has, of course, cases of individuals brought to his own knowledge where temporary assistance can do genuine good, and these he will not overlook. But the amount which can be wisely given by the individual for individuals is necessarily limited by his lack of knowledge of the circumstances connected with each. He is the only true reformer who is as careful and as anxious not to aid the unworthy as he is to aid the worthy, and, perhaps, even more so, for in alms-giving more injury is probably done by rewarding vice than by relieving virtue.

---

[1]British philosopher and scientist Herbert Spencer (1820–1903) was an early proponent of evolution and coined the term "survival of the fittest." He is notorious for the concept of social Darwinism, which tried to apply the notion of "survival of the fittest" to human civilization. The logical conclusion was that the poor were less "fit" for survival, so helping them was counterproductive for society as a whole. Social Darwinism was also used to justify racism, eugenics, and Nazism. —Eds.

seeing connections

From 1871 to 1918, the satirical and humorous *Puck Magazine* was published in New York City, and its stance on social issues was powerful. In a cartoon from the magazine shown here, entitled "A Christmas Reminder," Puck tugs at Andrew Carnegie as he looks over blueprints of a "Plan for the Carnegie Library." After examining the image closely, answer the following questions.

1. **What is Puck trying to say to Carnegie?**

2. **What details in the image support your interpretation of Puck's message?**

3. **Think about the position Carnegie established in this passage from *The Gospel of Wealth*. Where does *Puck* magazine stand in relation to Carnegie on the matter of how to distribute excess wealth in philanthropic ways?**

4. **To what extent do you agree with the magazine's message on how best to practice philanthropy?**

A CHRISTMAS REMINDER.

Library of Congress

The rich man is thus almost restricted to following the examples of Peter Cooper, Enoch Pratt of Baltimore, Mr. Pratt of Brooklyn, Senator Stanford, and others, who know that the best means of benefiting the community is to place within its reach the ladders upon which the aspiring can rise — parks, and means of recreation, by which men are helped in body and mind; works of art, certain to give pleasure and improve the public taste; and public institutions of various kinds, which will improve the general condition of the people; — in this manner returning their surplus wealth to the mass of their fellows in the forms best calculated to do them lasting good.

Thus is the problem of Rich and Poor to be solved. The laws of accumulation will be left free; the laws of distribution free. Individualism will continue, but the millionaire will be but a trustee for the poor; intrusted for a season with

Alice Beach Winter's image of a young girl with a factory in the background appeared with the caption "Why Must I Work?" on the cover of the May 1912 issue of *The Masses*, a magazine for the working class. **How might Carnegie have responded to such an image? What do you think Winter would say to Carnegie in response to his "Gospel of Wealth"?**

Library of Congress

a great part of the increased wealth of the community, but administering it for the community far better than it could or would have done for itself. The best minds will thus have reached a stage in the development of the race in which it is clearly seen that there is no mode of disposing of surplus wealth creditable to thoughtful and earnest men into whose hands it flows save by using it year by year for the general good. This day already dawns. Men may die without incurring the pity of their fellows, still sharers in great business enterprises from which their capital cannot be or has not been withdrawn, and is left chiefly at death for public uses, yet the man who dies leaving behind him millions of available wealth, which was his to administer during life, will pass away "unwept, unhonored, and unsung," no matter to what uses he leaves the dross which he cannot take with him. Of such as these public verdict will then be: "The man who dies thus rich dies disgraced."

Such, in my opinion, is the true Gospel concerning Wealth, obedience to which is destined some day to solve the problem of the Rich and the Poor, and to bring "Peace on earth, among men Good-Will."

[1889]

EXPLORING THE TEXT

1. In his opening sentence Andrew Carnegie speaks of "indiscriminate charity" as "one of the serious obstacles to the improvement of [the human] race." What does Carnegie mean by this? What was your first impression of this sentence—that is, to what extent do you agree with Carnegie's assertion? Did your position change by the time you reached the end of the excerpt? Explain.

2. How does Carnegie characterize the donor he discusses in the first paragraph? Why does he say that giving money to the beggar was "probably one of the most selfish and very worst actions of his life" (para. 1)?

3. If Carnegie believes that "in alms-giving more injury is probably done by rewarding vice than by relieving virtue" (para. 2), then what is his recommendation for "the best means of benefiting the community" (para. 3)? Do you agree or disagree with his analysis?

4. Carnegie claims that the best way to improve the situation of the poor "is to place within its reach the ladders upon which the aspiring can rise." The "ladders" he mentions are "parks, and means of recreation, by which men are helped in body and mind" (para. 3). Do you think that this is an effective plan? Explain. What assumption(s) about the relationship between rich and poor does this viewpoint suggest?

5. When Carnegie claims that "the millionaire will be but a trustee for the poor" (para. 4), what assumption about the relationship between the rich and the poor is he making?

6. What overall responsibility does wealth confer, according to Carnegie's assertion that "the man who dies leaving behind him millions of available wealth, which was his to administer during life, will pass away 'unwept, unhonored, and unsung,' no

matter to what uses he leaves the dross which he cannot take with him" (para. 4)?

7. Carnegie's title, "The Gospel of Wealth," refers to the New Testament of the Bible, and his concluding sentence quotes the Gospel of Luke (Luke 2:14). What attitude toward money and wealth is suggested by those references in the title and conclusion? To what extent do you think that Carnegie's philosophy is consistent with the spirit of the title and concluding quotation?

The Atlanta Exposition Address

BOOKER T. WASHINGTON

Born a slave in West Virginia, Booker T. Washington (1856–1915) was an influential educator and the founder of Tuskegee Normal and Industrial Institute in Alabama. After emancipation, he worked for several years — first in a in salt furnace and later in a coal mine — before leaving home to attend the Hampton Institute in Virginia, which was then an industrial school for African Americans and Native Americans. There, he paid his tuition and board by working as a janitor. Graduating with honors in 1875, Washington returned to his hometown of Malden, where he taught until 1881. Stressing the importance of learning a trade and developing self-confidence, Washington's pragmatism appealed to African Americans living in the post-Reconstruction South. He was criticized by the NAACP and other organizations for promoting accommodation rather than resistance to Southern white supremacy. He worked behind the scenes, however, to sponsor civil rights suits and advocate on behalf of Historically Black Colleges and Universities. Washington delivered the following speech in 1895 before the Cotton States and International Exposition in Atlanta to promote the economic ascendancy of the South.

Mr. President and Gentlemen of the Board of Directors and Citizens.

One-third of the population of the South is of the Negro race. No enterprise seeking the material, civil, or moral welfare of this section can disregard this element of our population and reach the highest success. I but convey to you, Mr. President and Directors, the sentiment of the masses of my race when I say that in no way have the value and manhood of the American Negro been more fittingly and generously recognized than by the managers of this magnificent Exposition at every stage of its progress. It is

a recognition that will do more to cement the friendship of the two races than any occurrence since the dawn of our freedom.

Not only this, but the opportunity here afforded will awaken among us a new era of industrial progress. Ignorant and inexperienced, it is not strange that in the first years of our new life we began at the top instead of at the bottom; that a seat in Congress or the state legislature was more sought than real estate or industrial skill; that the political convention of stump speaking had more attractions than starting a dairy farm or truck garden.

NEW YORK PUBLIC LIBRARY/New York Public Library, USA/Bridgeman Images

These three photographs of Washington giving a speech appeared together in a 1916 book entitled *Booker T. Washington, Builder of a Civilization* by Emmett Jay Scott and Lyman Beecher Stowe. **How do these photographs characterize Washington? To what extent do they affect your interpretation of the tone of "The Atlanta Exposition Address"?**

A ship lost at sea for many days suddenly sighted a friendly vessel. From the mast of the unfortunate vessel was seen a signal, "Water, water; we die of thirst!" The answer from the friendly vessel at once came back, "Cast down your bucket where you are." A second time the signal, "Water, water; send us water!" ran up from the distressed vessel, and was answered, "Cast down your bucket where you are." And a third and fourth signal for water was answered, "Cast down your bucket where you are." The captain of the distressed vessel, at last heeding the injunction, cast down his bucket, and it came up full of fresh, sparkling water from the mouth of the Amazon River. To those of my race who depend on bettering their condition in a foreign land or who underestimate the importance of cultivating friendly relations with the Southern white man, who is their next-door neighbour, I would say: "Cast down your bucket where you are" — cast it down in making friends in every manly way of the people of all races by whom we are surrounded.

Cast it down in agriculture, mechanics, in commerce, in domestic service, and in the professions. And in this connection it is well to bear in mind that whatever other sins the South may be called to bear, when it comes to business pure and simple, it is in the South that the Negro is given a man's chance in the commercial world, and in nothing is this Exposition more eloquent than in emphasizing this chance. Our greatest danger is that in the great leap from slavery to freedom we may overlook the fact that the masses of us are to live by the productions of our hands, and fail to keep in mind that we shall prosper in proportion as we learn to dignify and glorify common labour and put brains and skill into the common occupations of life; shall prosper in proportion as we learn to draw the line between the superficial and the substantial, the ornamental gewgaws of life and the useful. No race can prosper till it learns that there is as much dignity in tilling a field as in writing a poem. It is at the bottom of life we must begin, and not at the top. Nor should we permit our grievances to overshadow our opportunities.

To those of the white race who look to the incoming of those of foreign birth and strange tongue and habits for the prosperity of the South, were I permitted I would repeat what I say to my own race, "Cast down your bucket where you are." Cast it down among the eight millions of Negroes whose habits you know, whose fidelity and love you have tested in days when to have proved treacherous meant the ruin of your firesides. Cast down your bucket among these people who have, without strikes and labour

5

wars, tilled your fields, cleared your forests, builded your railroads and cities, and brought forth treasures from the bowels of the earth, and helped make possible this magnificent representation of the progress of the South. Casting down your bucket among my people, helping and encouraging them as you are doing on these grounds, and to education of head, hand, and heart, you will find that they will buy your surplus land, make blossom the waste places in your fields, and run your factories. While doing this, you can be sure in the future, as in the past, that you and your families will be surrounded by the most patient, faithful, law-abiding, and unresentful people that the world has seen. As we have proved our loyalty to you in the past, in nursing your children, watching by the sickbed of your mothers and fathers, and often following them with tear-dimmed eyes to their graves, so in the future, in our humble way, we shall stand by you with a devotion that no foreigner can approach, ready to lay down our lives, if need be, in defence of yours, interlacing our industrial, commercial, civil, and religious life with yours in a way that shall make the interests of both races one. In all things that are purely social we can be as separate as the fingers, yet one as the hand in all things essential to mutual progress.

There is no defence or security for any of us except in the highest intelligence and development of all. If anywhere there are efforts tending to curtail the fullest growth of the Negro, let these efforts be turned into stimulating, encouraging, and making him the most useful and intelligent citizen. Effort or means so invested will pay a thousand per cent interest. These efforts will be twice blessed — "blessing him that gives and him that takes."

There is no escape through law of man or God from the inevitable: —

> The laws of changeless justice bind
>   Oppressor with oppressed;
> And close as sin and suffering joined
>   We march to fate abreast.

Lifting the Veil of Ignorance, by sculptor Charles Keck, is located at Tuskegee University in Alabama. **How does the sculptor characterize Washington? What aspects of Washington's address at the Atlanta Exposition are captured in this depiction?**

Library of Congress

Nearly sixteen millions of hands will aid you in pulling the load upward, or they will pull against you the load downward. We shall constitute one-third and more of the ignorance and crime of the South, or one-third its intelligence and progress; we shall contribute one-third to the business and industrial prosperity of the South, or we shall prove a veritable body of death, stagnating, depressing, retarding every effort to advance the body politic.

Gentlemen of the Exposition, as we present to you our humble effort at an exhibition of our progress, you must not expect overmuch. Starting thirty years ago with ownership here and there in a few quilts and pumpkins and chickens (gathered from miscellaneous sources), remember the path that has led from these to the inventions and production of agricultural implements, buggies, steam-engines, newspapers, books, statuary, carving, paintings, the management of drug-stores and banks, has not been trodden without contact with thorns and thistles. While we take pride in what we exhibit as a result of our independent efforts, we do not for a moment forget that our part in this exhibition would fall far short of your expectations but for the constant help that has come to our educational life, not only from the Southern states, but especially from Northern philanthropists, who have made their gifts a constant stream of blessing and encouragement.

The wisest among my race understand that the agitation of questions of social equality is the extremest folly, and that progress in the enjoyment of all the privileges that will come to us must be the result of severe and constant struggle rather than of artificial forcing. No race that has anything to contribute to the markets of the world is long in any degree ostracized. It is important and right that all privileges of the law be ours, but it is vastly more important that we be prepared for the exercises of these privileges. The opportunity to earn a dollar in a factory just now is worth infinitely more than the opportunity to spend a dollar in an opera-house.

seeing connections

After a scheduled meeting in 1901 at the White House, President Roosevelt invited Washington to stay and dine with him. It was an impromptu dinner, and the cartoon below appeared shortly following the event.

What details does the artist include, and how do they reveal an argumentative position? What issues does the cartoon raise for its turn-of-the-century audience? Consider the image from the perspective of that audience. What is the artist suggesting?

EQUALITY

DINNER GIVEN AT THE WHITE HOUSE BY PRESIDENT ROOSEVELT TO BOOKER T. WASHINGTON, OCTOBER 17TH, 1901.

The Frent Collection/Getty Images

In conclusion, may I repeat that nothing in thirty years has given us more hope and encouragement, and drawn us so near to you of the white race, as this opportunity offered by the Exposition; and here bending, as it were, over the altar that represents the results of the struggles of your race and mine, both starting practically empty-handed three decades ago, I pledge that in your effort to work out the great and intricate problem which God has laid at the doors of the South, you shall have at all times the patient, sympathetic help of my race; only let this be constantly in mind, that, while from representations in these buildings of the product of field, of forest, of mine, of factory, letters, and art, much good will come, yet far above and beyond material benefits will be that higher good, that, let us pray God, will come, in a blotting out of sectional differences and racial animosities and suspicions, in a determination to administer absolute justice, in a willing obedience among all classes to the mandates of law. This, then, coupled with our material prosperity, will bring into our beloved South a new heaven and new earth.

[1895]

EXPLORING THE TEXT

1. What are Booker T. Washington's goals as articulated in this speech? What does he believe is the best way to achieve them?

2. What appeals to ethos does Washington make in the opening paragraphs? What additional appeals to ethos does he make as the speech proceeds?

3. What is the point of the story Washington tells in paragraph 3 about a "ship lost at sea"? What is the rhetorical effect?

4. This speech has come to be known by the sentence "Cast down your bucket where you are" (para. 3). What does Washington mean by this exhortation?

5. In what types of work does Washington want African Americans to engage? Are such jobs as readily available now as they were at the time of his speech? To what extent do his ideas apply in our current economy?

6. How do you interpret Washington's concluding statement in paragraph 5: "In all things that are purely social we can be as separate as the fingers, yet one as the hand in all things essential to mutual progress"?

7. Why is the Shakespeare quotation in paragraph 6 ("'blessing him that gives and him that takes'") appropriate to the point Washington is making?

8. Discuss two possible — and contrasting — interpretations of Washington's assertion: "The opportunity to earn a dollar in a factory just now is worth infinitely more than the opportunity to spend a dollar in an opera-house" (para. 10). In today's age of globalization and outsourcing, when many of our factory jobs have gone to foreign workers, does this statement still apply? Rewrite the sentence, replacing "factory" with a contemporary place of employment. Does the new sentence effectively update the idea? Why or why not?

9. Where in this speech does Washington implicitly argue against racial stereotypes and advocate American values of rugged individualism and a strong work ethic? How have racial stereotypes changed since then? Is our work ethic as strong now as it once was?

10. Discuss the importance of the occasion and audience of this speech. How do these factors influence its form and content?

11. In an introduction to Washington's autobiography, *Up from Slavery*, Henry Louis Gates Jr. and Nellie McKay make the following observation: "To some, Washington's autobiography seems to paper over centuries of accumulated white responsibility for the evils of slavery, and instead of demanding the reform of white American institutions, it calls for African American conformity to the dominant myth of individualism in the United States. To other readers, however, Washington's message in *Up from Slavery* puts its priorities exactly where they had to be — on the necessity of self-help within the African American community." Which view is closer to yours? Cite specific passages to support your position.

On Dumpster Diving

LARS EIGHNER

Lars Eighner (b. 1948) was born in Corpus Christi, Texas, and grew up primarily in Houston. As a child, he studied creative writing at the Corpus Christi Fine Arts Colony, and after graduating from Lamar High School, he attended the University of Texas at Austin. After losing his job at the state asylum in Austin, Eighner became homeless for three years. "On Dumpster Diving," an account of being homeless with his dog, Lizbeth, was published as "My Daily Dives in the Dumpster" in *Harper's* magazine in 1991 and was revised to become part of Eighner's 1993 memoir, *Travels with Lizbeth: Three Years on the Road and on the Streets*. Eighner's work has appeared in the *Threepenny Review*, *Harper's*, the *Washington Post*, the *Utne Reader*, and the *New York Times Book Review*.

Long before I began Dumpster diving I was impressed with Dumpsters, enough so that I wrote the Merriam-Webster research service to discover what I could about the word "Dumpster." I learned from them that "Dumpster" is a proprietary word belonging to the Dempster Dumpster company.

Since then I have dutifully capitalized the word although it was lowercased in almost all of the citations Merriam-Webster photocopied for me. Dempster's word is too apt. I have never heard these things called anything but Dumpsters. I do not know anyone who knows the generic name for these objects. From time to time, however, I hear a wino or hobo give some corrupted credit to the original and call them Dipsy Dumpsters.

I began Dumpster diving about a year before I became homeless.

I prefer the term "scavenging" and use the word "scrounging" when I mean to be obscure. I have heard people, evidently meaning to be polite, using the word "foraging," but I prefer to reserve that word for gathering nuts and berries and such which I do also according to the season and the opportunity. "Dumpster diving" seems to me to be a little too cute and, in my case, inaccurate because I lack the athletic ability to lower myself into the Dumpsters as the true divers do, much to their increased profit.

I like the frankness of the word "scavenging," 5 which I can hardly think of without picturing a big black snail on an aquarium wall. I live from the refuse of others. I am a scavenger. I think it a sound and honorable niche, although if I could I would naturally prefer to live the comfortable consumer life, perhaps — and only perhaps — as a slightly less wasteful consumer owing to what I have learned as a scavenger.

While my dog Lizbeth and I were still living in the house on Avenue B in Austin, as my savings ran out, I put almost all my sporadic income into rent. The necessities of daily life I began to extract from Dumpsters. Yes, we ate from Dumpsters. Except for jeans, all my clothes came from Dumpsters. Boom boxes, candles, bedding, toilet paper, medicine, books, a typewriter, a virgin male love doll, change sometimes amounting to many dollars: I acquired many things from the Dumpsters.

I have learned much as a scavenger. I mean to put some of what I have learned down here, beginning with the practical art of Dumpster diving and proceeding to the abstract.

What is safe to eat?

After all, the finding of objects is becoming something of an urban art. Even respectable employed people will sometimes find something tempting sticking out of a Dumpster or standing beside one. Quite a number of people, not all of them of the bohemian type, are willing to brag that they found this or that piece in the trash. But eating from Dumpsters is the thing that separates the dilettanti from the professionals.

Eating safely from the Dumpsters involves three principles: using the senses and common sense to evaluate the condition of the found materials, knowing the Dumpsters of a given area and checking them regularly, and seeking always to answer the question "Why was this discarded?"

Perhaps everyone who has a kitchen and a regular supply of groceries has, at one time or another, made a sandwich and eaten half of it before discovering mold on the bread or got a mouthful of milk before realizing the milk had turned. Nothing of the sort is likely to happen to a Dumpster diver because he is constantly reminded that most food is discarded for a reason. Yet a lot of perfectly good food can be found in Dumpsters.

Canned goods, for example, turn up fairly often in the Dumpsters I frequent. All except the most phobic people would be willing to eat from a can even if it came from a Dumpster. Canned goods are among the safest of foods to be found in Dumpsters, but are not utterly foolproof.

Although very rare with modern canning methods, botulism is a possibility. Most other forms of food poisoning seldom do lasting harm to a healthy person. But botulism is almost certainly fatal and often the first symptom is death. Except for carbonated beverages, all canned goods should contain a slight vacuum and suck air when first punctured. Bulging, rusty, dented cans and cans that spew when punctured should be avoided, especially when the contents are not very acidic or syrupy.

Heat can break down the botulin, but this requires much more cooking than most people do to canned goods. To the extent that botulism occurs at all, of course, it can occur in cans on pantry shelves as well as in cans from Dumpsters. Need I say that home-canned goods found in Dumpsters are simply too risky to be recommended.

From time to time one of my companions, aware of the source of my provisions, will ask, "Do you think these crackers are really safe to eat?" For some reason it is most often the crackers they ask about.

This question always makes me angry. Of course I would not offer my companion anything I had doubts about. But more than that I wonder why he cannot evaluate the condition of the crackers for himself. I have no special knowledge and I have been wrong before. Since he knows where the food comes from, it seems to me he ought to assume some of the responsibility for deciding what he will put in his mouth.

For myself I have few qualms about dry foods such as crackers, cookies, cereal, chips, and pasta if they are free of visible contaminates and still dry and crisp. Most often such things are found in the original packaging, which is not so much a positive sign as it is the absence of a negative one.

Raw fruits and vegetables with intact skins seem perfectly safe to me, excluding of course the obviously rotten. Many are discarded for minor imperfections which can be pared away. Leafy vegetables, grapes, cauliflower, broccoli, and similar things may be contaminated by liquids and may be impractical to wash.

Candy, especially hard candy, is usually safe if it has not drawn ants. Chocolate is often discarded only because it has become discolored as the cocoa butter de-emulsified. Candying after all is one method of food preservation because pathogens do not like very sugary substances.

All of these foods might be found in any Dumpster and can be evaluated with some confidence largely on the basis of appearance. Beyond these are foods which cannot be correctly evaluated without additional information.

I began scavenging by pulling pizzas out of the Dumpster behind a pizza delivery shop. In general prepared food requires caution, but in

The term *freegan* refers to activists who choose to work and purchase very little in the consumer culture, and instead live off the waste created by society. Here, a freegan checks garbage in the evenings outside upscale grocery stores to find food. **What place would Eighner's essay have in the freegan lifestyle? Do you think freegans are making an effective statement? Why or why not?**

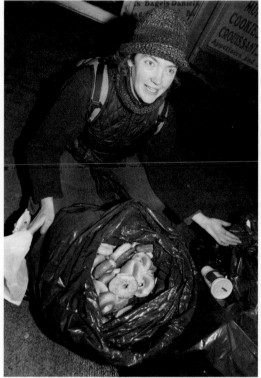

DON EMMERT/Getty Images

this case I knew when the shop closed and went to the Dumpster as soon as the last of the help left.

Such shops often get prank orders, called "bogus." Because help seldom stays long at these places pizzas are often made with the wrong topping, refused on delivery for being cold, or baked incorrectly. The products to be discarded are boxed up because inventory is kept by counting boxes: A boxed pizza can be written off; an unboxed pizza does not exist.

I never placed a bogus order to increase the supply of pizzas and I believe no one else was

scavenging in this Dumpster. But the people in the shop became suspicious and began to retain their garbage in the shop overnight.

While it lasted I had a steady supply of fresh, sometimes warm pizza. Because I knew the Dumpster I knew the source of the pizza, and because I visited the Dumpster regularly I knew what was fresh and what was yesterday's.

The area I frequent is inhabited by many 25 affluent college students. I am not here by chance; the Dumpsters in this area are very rich. Students throw out many good things, including food. In particular they tend to throw everything out when they move at the end of a semester, before and after breaks, and around midterm when many of them despair of college. So I find it advantageous to keep an eye on the academic calendar.

The students throw food away around the breaks because they do not know whether it has spoiled or will spoil before they return. A typical discard is a half jar of peanut butter. In fact non-organic peanut butter does not require refrigeration and is unlikely to spoil in any reasonable time. The student does not know that, and since it is Daddy's money, the student decides not to take a chance.

Opened containers require caution and some attention to the question "Why was this discarded?" But in the case of discards from student apartments, the answer may be that the item was discarded through carelessness, ignorance, or wastefulness. This can sometimes be deduced when the item is found with many others, including some that are obviously perfectly good.

Some students, and others, approach defrosting a freezer by chucking out the whole lot. Not only do the circumstances of such a find tell the story, but also the mass of frozen goods stays cold for a long time and items may be found still frozen or freshly thawed.

Yogurt, cheese, and sour cream are items that are often thrown out while they are still good. Occasionally I find a cheese with a spot of mold, which of course I just pare off, and because it is obviously why such a cheese was discarded, I treat it with less suspicion than an apparently perfect cheese found in similar circumstances. Yogurt is often discarded, still sealed, only because the expiration date on the carton had passed. This is one of my favorite finds because yogurt will keep several days, even in warm weather.

Students throw out canned goods and staples 30 at the end of semesters and when they give up college at midterm. Drugs, pornography, spirits, and the like are often discarded when parents are expected — Dad's day, for example. And spirits also turn up after big party weekends, presumably discarded by the newly reformed. Wine and spirits, of course, keep perfectly well even once opened.

My test for carbonated soft drinks is whether they still fizz vigorously. Many juices or other beverages are too acid or too syrupy to cause much concern provided they are not visibly contaminated. Liquids, however, require some care.

One hot day I found a large jug of Pat O'Brien's Hurricane mix. The jug had been opened, but it was still ice cold. I drank three large glasses before it became apparent to me that someone had added the rum to the mix, and not a little rum. I never tasted the rum and by the time I began to feel the effects I had already ingested a very large quantity of the beverage. Some divers would have considered this a boon, but being suddenly and thoroughly intoxicated in a public place in the early afternoon is not my idea of a good time.

I have heard of people maliciously contaminating discarded food and even handouts, but mostly I have heard of this from people with vivid imaginations who have had no experience with the Dumpsters themselves. Just before the pizza shop stopped discarding its garbage at night, jalapeños began showing up on most of the discarded pizzas. If indeed this was meant to discourage me it was a wasted effort because I am a native Texan.

For myself, I avoid game, poultry, pork, and egg-based foods whether I find them raw or cooked. I seldom have the means to cook what I find, but when I do I avail myself of plentiful supplies of beef which is often in very good condition. I suppose fish becomes disagreeable before it becomes dangerous. The dog is happy to have any such thing that is past its prime and, in fact, does not recognize fish as food until it is quite strong.

Home leftovers, as opposed to surpluses from 35 restaurants, are very often bad. Evidently, especially among students, there is a common type of personality that carefully wraps up even the smallest leftover and shoves it into the back of the refrigerator for six months or so before discarding it. Characteristic of this type are the reused jars and margarine tubs which house the remains.

I avoid ethnic foods I am unfamiliar with. If I do not know what it is supposed to look like when it is good, I cannot be certain I will be able to tell if it is bad.

No matter how careful I am I still get dysentery at least once a month, oftener in warm weather. I do not want to paint too romantic a picture. Dumpster diving has serious drawbacks as a way of life.

◆ ◆ ◆

I learned to scavenge gradually, on my own. Since then I have initiated several companions into the trade. I have learned that there is a predictable series of stages a person goes through in learning to scavenge.

At first the new scavenger is filled with disgust and self-loathing. He is ashamed of being seen and may lurk around, trying to duck behind things, or he may try to dive at night.

(In fact, most people instinctively look away 40 from a scavenger. By skulking around, the novice calls attention to himself and arouses suspicion. Diving at night is ineffective and needlessly messy.)

Every grain of rice seems to be a maggot. Everything seems to stink. He can wipe the egg yolk off the found can, but he cannot erase the stigma of eating garbage out of his mind.

That stage passes with experience. The scavenger finds a pair of running shoes that fit and look and smell brand new. He finds a pocket calculator in perfect working order. He finds pristine ice cream, still frozen, more than he can eat or keep. He begins to understand: People do throw away perfectly good stuff, a lot of perfectly good stuff.

At this stage, Dumpster shyness begins to dissipate. The diver, after all, has the last laugh. He is finding all manner of good things which are his for the taking. Those who disparage his profession are the fools, not he.

He may begin to hang onto some perfectly good things for which he has neither a use nor a market. Then he begins to take note of the things which are not perfectly good but are nearly so. He mates a Walkman with broken earphones and one that is missing a battery cover. He picks up things which he can repair.

At this stage he may become lost and never recover. Dumpsters are full of things of some potential value to someone and also of things which never have much intrinsic value but are interesting. All the Dumpster divers I have known come to the point of trying to acquire everything they touch. Why not take it, they reason, since it is all free.

This is, of course, hopeless. Most divers come to realize that they must restrict themselves to items of relatively immediate utility. But in some cases the diver simply cannot control himself. I have met several of these pack-rat types. Their ideas of the values of various pieces of junk verge on the psychotic. Every bit of glass may be a diamond, they think, and all that glistens, gold.

I tend to gain weight when I am scavenging. Partly this is because I always find far more pizza and doughnuts than water-packed tuna, nonfat yogurt, and fresh vegetables. Also I have not developed much faith in the reliability of Dumpsters as a food source, although it has been proven to me many times. I tend to eat as if I have no idea where my next meal is coming from. But mostly I just hate to see food go to waste and so I eat much more than I should. Something like this drives the obsession to collect junk.

As for collecting objects, I usually restrict myself to collecting one kind of small object at a time, such as pocket calculators, sunglasses, or campaign buttons. To live on the street I must anticipate my needs to a certain extent: I must pick up and save warm bedding I find in August because it will not be found in Dumpsters in November. But even if I had a home with extensive storage space I could not save everything that might be valuable in some contingency.

I have proprietary feelings about my Dumpsters. As I have suggested, it is no accident that I scavenge from Dumpsters where good finds are common. But my limited experience with Dumpsters in other areas suggests to me that it is the population of competitors rather than the affluence of the dumpers that most affects the feasibility of survival by scavenging. The large number of competitors is what puts me off the idea of trying to scavenge in places like Los Angeles.

Curiously, I do not mind my direct competition, other scavengers, so much as I hate the can scroungers.

People scrounge cans because they have to have a little cash. I have tried scrounging cans with an able-bodied companion. Afoot a can scrounger simply cannot make more than a few dollars a day. One can extract the necessities of life from the Dumpsters directly with far less effort than would be required to accumulate the equivalent value in cans.

Can scroungers, then, are people who *must* have small amounts of cash. These are drug addicts and winos, mostly the latter because the amounts of cash are so small.

Spirits and drugs do, like all other commodities, turn up in Dumpsters and the scavenger will from time to time have a half bottle of a rather

45

50

good wine with his dinner. But the wino cannot survive on these occasional finds; he must have his daily dose to stave off the DTs. All the cans he can carry will buy about three bottles of Wild Irish Rose.

I do not begrudge them the cans, but can scroungers tend to tear up the Dumpsters, mixing the contents and littering the area. They become so specialized that they can see only cans. They earn my contempt by passing up change, canned goods, and readily hockable items.

There are precious few courtesies among scavengers. But it is a common practice to set aside surplus items: pairs of shoes, clothing, canned goods, and such. A true scavenger hates to see good stuff go to waste and what he cannot use he leaves in good condition in plain sight.

Can scroungers lay waste to everything in their path and will stir one of a pair of good shoes to the bottom of the Dumpster, to be lost or ruined in the muck. Can scroungers will even go through individual garbage cans, something I have never seen a scavenger do.

Individual garbage cans are set out on the public easement only on garbage days. On other days going through them requires trespassing close to a dwelling. Going through individual garbage cans without scattering litter is almost impossible. Litter is likely to reduce the public's tolerance of scavenging. Individual garbage cans are simply not as productive as Dumpsters; people in houses and duplexes do not move as often and for some reason do not tend to discard as much useful material. Moreover, the time required to go through one garbage can that serves one household is not much less than the time required to go through a Dumpster that contains the refuse of twenty apartments.

But my strongest reservation about going through individual garbage cans is that this seems to me a very personal kind of invasion to which I would object if I were a householder. Although many things in Dumpsters are obviously meant never to come to light, a Dumpster is somehow less personal.

I avoid trying to draw conclusions about the people who dump in the Dumpsters I frequent. I think it would be unethical to do so, although I know many people will find the idea of scavenger ethics too funny for words.

seeing connections

Dumpster diving for high-end makeup and beauty products is a controversial trend. Beauty bloggers sometimes film their dumpster dive outings — called live dives — and post them to YouTube. These videos often end with a sweeping shot of the beauty "haul" laid out neatly in rows.

What position do you believe Eighner would take on this issue? Support your response with evidence from his essay.

Dumpsters contain bank statements, bills, correspondence, and other documents, just as anyone might expect. But there are also less obvious sources of information. Pill bottles, for example. The labels on pill bottles contain the name of the patient, the name of the doctor, and the name of the drug. AIDS drugs and antipsychotic medicines, to name but two groups, are specific and seldom prescribed for any other disorders. The plastic compacts for birth control pills usually have complete label information.

Despite all of this sensitive information, I have had only one apartment resident object to my going through the Dumpster. In that case it turned out the resident was a university athlete who was taking bets and who was afraid I would turn up his wager slips.

Occasionally a find tells a story. I once found a small paper bag containing some unused condoms, several partial tubes of flavored sexual lubricant, a partially used compact of birth control pills, and the torn pieces of a picture of a young man. Clearly she was through with him and planning to give up sex altogether.

Dumpster things are often sad — abandoned teddy bears, shredded wedding books, despaired-of sales kits. I find many pets lying in state in Dumpsters. Although I hope to get off the streets so that Lizbeth can have a long and comfortable old age, I know this hope is not very realistic. So I suppose when her time comes she too will go into a Dumpster. I will have no better place for her. And after all, for most of her life her livelihood has come from the Dumpster. When she finds something I think is safe that has been spilled from the Dumpster I let her have it. She already knows the route around the best Dumpsters. I like to think that if she survives me she will have a chance of evading the dog catcher and of finding her sustenance on the route.

Silly vanities also come to rest in the Dumpsters. I am a rather accomplished needleworker. I get a lot of materials from the Dumpsters. Evidently sorority girls, hoping to impress someone, perhaps themselves, with their mastery of a womanly art, buy a lot of embroider-by-number kits, work a few stitches horribly, and eventually discard the whole mess. I pull out their stitches, turn the canvas over, and work an original design. Do not think I refrain from chuckling as I make original gifts from these kits.

I find diaries and journals. I have often thought of compiling a book of literary found objects. And perhaps I will one day. But what I find is hopelessly commonplace and bad without being, even unconsciously, camp. College students also discard their papers. I am horrified to discover the kind of paper which now merits an A in an undergraduate course. I am grateful, however, for the number of good books and magazines the students throw out.

In the area I know best I have never discovered vermin in the Dumpsters, but there are two kinds of kitty surprise. One is alley cats which I meet as they leap, claws first, out of Dumpsters. This is especially thrilling when I have Lizbeth in tow. The other kind of kitty surprise is a plastic garbage bag filled with some ponderous, amorphous mass. This always proves to be used cat litter.

City bees harvest doughnut glaze and this makes the Dumpster at the doughnut shop more interesting. My faith in the instinctive wisdom of animals is always shaken whenever I see Lizbeth attempt to catch a bee in her mouth, which she does whenever bees are present. Evidently some birds find Dumpsters profitable, for birdie surprise is almost as common as kitty surprise of the first kind. In hunting season all kinds of small game turn up in Dumpsters, some of it sadly, not entirely dead. Curiously, summer and winter, maggots are uncommon.

The worst of the living and near-living hazards of the Dumpsters are the fire ants. The food that they claim is not much of a loss, but they are vicious and aggressive. It is very easy to brush against some surface of the Dumpster and pick up half a dozen or more fire ants, usually in

Fresno Bee/Getty Images

Daniel Northern, a homeless man in California, is shown here bringing his dogs in for free vaccinations. **To what extent does the image reflect Eighner's situation and his position on his experiences?**

some sensitive area such as the underarm. One advantage of bringing Lizbeth along as I make Dumpster rounds is that, for obvious reasons, she is very alert to ground-based fire ants. When Lizbeth recognizes the signs of fire ant infestation around our feet she does the Dance of the Zillion Fire Ants. I have learned not to ignore this warning from Lizbeth, whether I perceive the tiny ants or not, but to remove ourselves at Lizbeth's first pas de bourrée.[1] All the more so because the ants are the worst in the months I wear flip-flops, if I have them.

(Perhaps someone will misunderstand the above. Lizbeth does the Dance of the Zillion Fire Ants when she recognizes more fire ants than she cares to eat, not when she is being bitten. Since I have learned to react promptly, she does not get bitten at all. It is the isolated patrol of fire ants that falls in Lizbeth's range that deserves pity. Lizbeth finds them quite tasty.)

By far the best way to go through a Dumpster is to lower yourself into it. Most of the good stuff tends to settle at the bottom because it is usually weightier than the rubbish. My more athletic companions have often demonstrated to me 70

that they can extract much good material from a Dumpster I have already been over.

To those psychologically or physically unprepared to enter a Dumpster, I recommend a stout stick, preferably with some barb or hook at one end. The hook can be used to grab plastic garbage bags. When I find canned goods or other objects loose at the bottom of a Dumpster I usually can roll them into a small bag that I can then hoist up. Much Dumpster diving is a matter of experience for which nothing will do except practice.

Dumpster diving is outdoor work, often surprisingly pleasant. It is not entirely predictable; things of interest turn up every day and some days there are finds of great value. I am always very pleased when I can turn up exactly the thing I most wanted to find. Yet in spite of the element of chance, scavenging more than most other pursuits tends to yield returns in some proportion to the effort and intelligence brought to bear. It is very sweet to turn up a few dollars in change from a Dumpster that has just been gone over by a wino.

The land is now covered with cities. The cities are full of Dumpsters. I think of scavenging as a modern form of self-reliance. In any event, after ten years of government service, where

---
[1] A transitional ballet step. —Eds.

everything is geared to the lowest common denominator, I find work that rewards initiative and effort refreshing. Certainly I would be happy to have a sinecure again, but I am not heartbroken not to have one anymore.

I find from the experience of scavenging two rather deep lessons. The first is to take what I can use and let the rest go by. I have come to think that there is no value in the abstract. A thing I cannot use or make useful, perhaps by trading, has no value however fine or rare it may be. I mean useful in a broad sense — so, for example, some art I would think useful and valuable, but other art might be otherwise for me.

I was shocked to realize that some things are not worth acquiring, but now I think it is so. Some material things are white elephants that eat up the possessor's substance.

75

The second lesson is of the transience of material being. This has not quite converted me to a dualist, but it has made some headway in that direction. I do not suppose that ideas are immortal, but certainly mental things are longer-lived than other material things.

Once I was the sort of person who invests material objects with sentimental value. Now I no longer have those things, but I have the sentiments yet.

Many times in my travels I have lost everything but the clothes I was wearing and Lizbeth. The things I find in Dumpsters, the love letters and ragdolls of so many lives, remind me of this lesson. Now I hardly pick up a thing without envisioning the time I will cast it away. This I think is a healthy state of mind. Almost everything I have now has already been cast out at least once, proving that what I own is valueless to someone.

Anyway, I find my desire to grab for the gaudy bauble has been largely sated. I think this is an attitude I share with the very wealthy — we both know there is plenty more where what we have came from. Between us are the rat-race millions who have confounded their selves with the objects they grasp and who nightly scavenge the cable channels looking for they know not what.

I am sorry for them. 80

[1991]

EXPLORING THE TEXT

1. What is the effect of Lars Eighner's attention to language in the first five paragraphs? Does this opening appeal more to ethos, logos, or pathos? Explain.

2. In paragraph 7, Eighner identifies the rhetorical direction he plans to follow. What is the effect of such information?

3. Note the technical and clinical nature of much of the first part (paras. 1–37) of the essay. In paragraph 19, for example, Eighner writes of de-emulsification and the behavior of pathogens. What is the effect of such scientific language and information?

4. The wealth of goods that Eighner is able to salvage from Dumpsters would suggest that our society is wasteful — at least on the micro level. What might be the effect of such wasteful habits on the macroeconomy?

5. Identify and explain two examples of irony in the section about students (paras. 25–30). What does this section suggest about their relationship to the economy at large?

6. Paragraph 37 concludes, "I do not want to paint too romantic a picture. Dumpster diving has serious drawbacks as a way of life." What is the effect of these sentences? What is their rhetorical purpose?

7. Note the careful distinction Eighner makes between the "true scavenger" and the "can scrounger" (paras. 50–56). What purpose does it serve?

8. Eighner addresses homelessness in America. How successfully does he debunk the stereotype of homeless people as indolent and uneducated?

9. Explain the irony in paragraph 73 where Eighner writes, "I think of scavenging as a modern form of self-reliance."

10. Explain the irony in the closing passage (paras. 78–80). In the sentence "This I think is a healthy state of mind," what does *this* refer to? Do you agree with Eighner's claim? Explain.

11. How would you characterize Eighner's attitudes toward wealth and materialism as revealed especially in paragraphs 74–80? What implications do they have regarding the economy at large?

12. Eighner is obviously an intelligent man who writes well. What does it suggest about our economy that such a person as he could become homeless and resort to Dumpster diving? Does our society have an obligation to help those in similar situations? Explain.

from In the Strawberry Fields

ERIC SCHLOSSER

Eric Schlosser (b. 1959) was raised in New York and Los Angeles. He graduated from Princeton University with a degree in American history and studied British history at Oxford University. In addition to working as a correspondent for the *Atlantic*, Schlosser has published articles in such periodicals as the *New Yorker*, the *Nation*, *Rolling Stone*, and *Vanity Fair*. His 2001 book about the food industry, *Fast Food Nation: The Dark Side of the All-American Meal*, became a best seller and was adapted into a film in 2006. Schlosser also participated in the making of the 2009 documentary film *Food, Inc.* His most recent book is *Command and Control: Nuclear Weapons, the Damascus Accident, and the Illusion of Safety* (2013). His 2003 best seller, *Reefer Madness: Sex, Drugs, and Cheap Labor in the American Black Market*, grew out of his articles on the enforcement of marijuana laws and illegal immigration in California. It includes "In the Strawberry Fields," an earlier version of which appeared in the *Atlantic Monthly* in 1995.

La Fruta del Diablo

It was mid-April when I visited Watsonville, and heavy rains had recently flooded hundreds of acres. Bright blue plastic barrels from a Smuckers plant were scattered across local strawberry fields and embedded in the mud. Many fields that hadn't been flooded still had been damaged by the rains. I met with strawberry workers at an old labor camp — a small slum set amid rolling hills and strawberry fields not far from town. For most of the year this bleak collection of gray wooden barracks housed about 350 residents, mainly strawberry workers and their families. But at the peak of the harvest hundreds more crammed into its forty apartments. In the mid-1990s there'd been a major outbreak of tuberculosis at the camp, fueled by its crowded living quarters and poor building design. The bedrooms occupied a central corridor of the barracks; none had a window. The tenants paid $500 a month for their two-bedroom apartments and felt lucky to have a roof over their heads. As I walked around the camp, there were children everywhere, running and playing in the courtyards, oblivious of the squalor.

The sky was overcast, more bad weather was coming, and a year's income for these workers would be determined in the next few months. Half a dozen strawberry pickers, leaning against parked cars, told me that at this point in the season they usually worked in the fields eight or ten hours a day. Only one of them was employed at the moment. Every morning the others visited the strawberry farm on a nearby hillside, inquired about work, and were turned away. The foreman, who had hired them for years, said to try again next week.

Harvest work in the strawberry fields, like most seasonal farmwork in California, is considered "at will." There is no contract, no seniority, no obligation beyond the day-to-day. A grower hires and fires workers as necessary, without need for explanation. It makes no difference whether the migrant has been an employee for six days or for six years. The terms of employment are laid down on a daily basis. If a grower wants slow and careful work, wages are paid by the hour. If a grower wants berries quickly removed from the field, the wages are piece-rate, providing an incentive to move fast. A migrant often does not know how long the workday will last or what the wage rate will be until he or she arrives at the field that morning. There might be two weeks of ten-hour days followed by a week of no work at all, depending upon the weather and the market.

This system did not arise because growers are innately mean and heartless. Harvests are unpredictable from beginning to end. Many growers try to guarantee their workers a certain amount of income each week. Among other things, it makes good business sense to have reliable and capable workers returning each year. And yet there is no denying where the power lies.

The strawberry has long been known to migrants as *la fruta del diablo* — the fruit of the devil. Picking strawberries is some of the lowest-paid, most difficult, and therefore least desirable farmwork in California. Strawberries are fragile and bruise easily. They must be picked with great care, especially the berries that will be sold fresh at the market. Market berries are twisted, not pulled, off the stem to preserve a green cap on top. Workers must select only berries of the proper size, firmness, shape, and color. They must arrange the berries neatly in baskets to catch the shopper's eye. Learning how to pick strawberries correctly can take weeks. The worker is often responsible not only for gathering

and packing the fruit but also for tending the plants. The drip irrigation system has to be continually checked. Shoots and runners have to be removed. Rotting berries have to be tossed away, or they will spoil the rest. When a piece-rate wage is being paid, workers must perform these tasks and pick berries as fast as they can. There is a strong undercurrent of anxiety in a field being harvested at piece-rate. Workers move down the furrows pushing small wheelbarrows; they pause, bend over, brush away leaves to their left and right, pick berries, place them in boxes, check the plants, and move on, all in one fluid motion. Once their boxes are filled, they rush to have them tallied at the end of the field, rush back, and begin the process again.

Strawberry plants are four or five inches high and grow from beds eight to twelve inches high. You must bend at the waist to pick the fruit, which explains why the job is so difficult. Bending over that way for an hour can cause a stiff back; doing so for ten to twelve hours a day, weeks at a time, can cause excruciating pain and lifelong disabilities. Most strawberry pickers suffer back pain. As would be expected, the older you get, the more your back hurts. Farmworkers, like athletes, also decline in speed as they age. The fastest strawberry pickers tend to be in their late teens and early twenties. Most migrants quit picking strawberries in their mid-thirties, although some highly skilled women do work longer. Age discrimination is commonplace in the fields — it is purely a question of efficiency.

The hourly wages vary considerably, depending on the grower, the type of strawberry being picked, the time of year, and often, the skill of the worker. Wages are higher in Watsonville and the Salinas than in Southern California, because of the greater distance from Mexico. Growers producing top-quality berries for the fresh market may pay as much as $8 or $10 an hour. At the height of the season, when berries are plentiful and growers pay a piece-rate of $1.25 a box, the fastest workers can earn more than $150 a day.

Hourly Wages of Nonsupervisory Crop and Livestock Workers Compared to Nonsupervisory Workers in the Nonfarm Economy

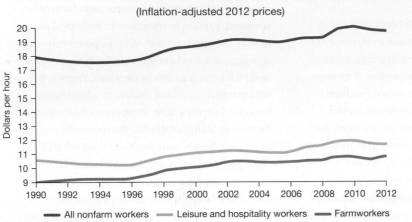

(Inflation-adjusted 2012 prices)

Data from the U.S. Department of Agriculture.

Consider the information depicted in this graph, which compares the hourly wages of various types of workers. **What conclusions can you draw from the graph? How does it relate to Schlosser's claims in the selection from "In the Strawberry Fields"?**

But wages at that level only last for a month or so, and even during that period most workers can't attain them. When a crew of thirty picks at a piece-rate, three or four will earn $10 an hour, five or six will earn at or below the state minimum wage, $6.75 an hour, and the rest will earn somewhere in between.

The availability of work, not the pay scale, is of greatest concern to migrants. Despite the hardships that accompany the job, there is an oversupply of people hoping to pick strawberries. The fear of unemployment haunts all farmworkers in California today. Each harvest brings a new struggle to line up enough jobs for a decent income. The average migrant spends half the year working and a few months looking for work.

Another constant worry is finding a place to sleep. Santa Cruz and Monterey counties have some of the highest housing costs in the country. Long popular with tourists and wealthy retirees, the area has also attracted commuters from Silicon Valley. The residents of Watsonville and Salinas are determined to preserve the local farm economy, despite enormous pressure from developers. Agricultural land that currently sells for $40,000 an acre could be sold for many

times that amount if it were rezoned; there are strawberry fields overlooking the Pacific Ocean. The determination to preserve agricultural land has not, however, extended to providing shelter for agricultural workers. Since 1980 the acreage around Watsonville and Salinas devoted to strawberries has more than doubled and the tonnage of strawberries produced there has nearly quadrupled. But the huge influx of migrant workers required to pick these berries has been forced to compete for a supply of low-income housing that's been inadequate for decades.

The few remaining labor camps for single men are grim places. I toured one that was a group of whitewashed buildings surrounded by chain-link fences and barbed wire. Desolate except for a rosebush in front of the manager's office, it looked like a holding pen or an old minimum-security prison. A nearby camp was reputed to be one of the best of its kind. Inside the barracks, the walls were freshly painted and the concrete floor was clean. A typical room was roughly twelve feet by ten feet, unheated, and occupied by four men. Sheets of plywood separated the steel cots. For $80 a week, a price far too high for most migrants, you got a bed and two meals a day. I've seen nicer horse barns.

10

Nevertheless, the labor camps are often preferable to the alternatives. When migrants stay in residential neighborhoods, they must pool their resources. In Watsonville three to four families will share a small house, seven or eight people to a room. Migrants routinely pay $100 to $200 a month to sleep in a garage with anywhere from four to ten other people. A survey of garages in Soledad found 1,500 inhabitants — a number roughly equal to one-eighth of the town's official population. At the peak of the harvest the housing shortage becomes acute. Migrants at the labor camps sometimes pay to sleep in parked cars. The newest migrant workers, who lack family in the area and haven't yet learned the ropes, often sleep outdoors in the wooded sections of Prunedale, trespassing, moving to a different hiding place each night. On hillsides above the Salinas Valley, hundreds of strawberry pickers have been found living in caves.

Locked into Dependence

The immigration history of Guadalupe, California, can be read in the names and faces adorning headstones at its small cemetery. The Swiss and Italian and Portuguese surnames belong to families who settled in the Santa Maria Valley around the turn of the last century, growing beans and sugar beets, running cattle, and raising dairy herds. The Chinese, Japanese, and Filipino names belong to the first wave of farmworkers, some of whom managed to acquire land of their own. Spanish surnames greatly outnumber the rest, marking the recent graves along with plastic flowers and the images of saints. There is a sepulchral custom in Guadalupe, practiced for generations: most of the headstones bear sepia-tinted photographs of the deceased. Walking through the graveyard, one sees at a glance the slightly different ethnic traits and the subtle variations in skin color — long the basis of economic status and rivalry. Now all these faces stare in the same direction from the same place, arranged like crops in long, straight rows.

For most of the twentieth century, the Santa Maria Valley had a diverse farm economy. Although migrants were a large seasonal presence, the area lacked the huge industrial farms that dominated the landscape elsewhere in California. The acreage around Guadalupe was devoted primarily to field crops and irrigated pasture. The cattle ranches and dairy farms were owned and managed by local families. Fruits and vegetables, though an important source of revenue, occupied a small portion of the agricultural land.

Then, from the early 1970s to the late 1980s, the Santa Maria Valley was transformed. As field crops and dairy products became less profitable, farmers either switched to high-value crops or quit farming. Much of the land was bought by outside corporations, such as Mobil and the Bank of America. Irrigated pastures became strawberry fields (dotted with oil wells) on leased land. The number of migrant workers soared. In 1960 Guadalupe's population was 18 percent Latino; today it is about 85 percent Latino. The middle classes fled to the nearby city of Santa Maria, leaving behind a rural underclass.

Juan Vicente Palerm has spent the last two decades studying the social and economic changes in the Santa Maria Valley. The director of the University of California's Institute for Mexico and the United States, Palerm is an anthropologist by training. His early fieldwork traced the lives of Spanish guest workers in northern Europe — migrants imported by treaty to labor in the factories and fields. He is an imposing figure, with the graying beard of a patriarch, and has a remarkable grasp not only of labor market dynamics, but also of how every crop in the valley is planted, tended, marketed, and sold. I spent a day with Palerm and one of his graduate students, Manolo Gonzalez (who picked strawberries for a year as part of his research), driving the side streets of Guadalupe, touring the fields, and discussing how the growers of California and the peasants of rural Mexico created an agricultural system that has locked them into mutual dependence.

By relying on poor migrants from Mexico, California growers established a wage structure that discouraged American citizens from seeking farmwork. The wages offered at harvest were too low to sustain a family in the United States, but they were up to ten times as high as any wages Mexican peasants could earn in their native villages. A system evolved in which the cheap labor of Mexican migrants subsidized California agriculture, while remittances from that farm-work preserved rural communities in Mexico that otherwise might have collapsed. For decades the men of Mexican villages have traveled north to the fields of California, leaving behind women, children, and the elderly to look after their small farms. Migrant work in California has long absorbed Mexican surplus labor, while Mexico has in effect paid for the education, health care, and retirement of California's farmworkers.

Whenever migrants decided to settle in California, however, they disrupted the smooth workings of this system, by imposing higher costs on the state — especially if they married and raised children. That is why the Immigration and Naturalization Service (INS) used to round up and deport illegal immigrants in California immediately after the harvest. Nevertheless, millions of Mexican farmworkers have settled in the United States over the years, most of them becoming American citizens. Although agricultural employment has long been a means of entering U.S. society, low wages and poor working conditions have made it an occupation that most immigrants and their children hope to escape. Farm labor is more physically demanding and less financially rewarding than almost any other kind of work. A migrant who finds a job in a factory can triple his or her income. As a result, the whole system now depends upon a steady supply of illegal immigrants to keep farm wages low and to replace migrants who have either retired to Mexico or found better jobs in California.

Juan Vicente Palerm believes that today there are not only more migrants shuttling back and forth from Mexico but also more Mexican farmworkers settling permanently in California. Throughout the state towns like Guadalupe, Calexico, Cutler, and McFarland are becoming enclaves of rural poverty. In the Santa Maria Valley the increased production of fruits and vegetables, higher yields per acre, and an extended growing season have created thousands of full- and part-time jobs for farmworkers. Broccoli fields now occupy more than 20,000 acres, requiring a large supply of resident workers for a staggered harvest that lasts most of the year. Celery and cauliflower production has also increased the number of full-time jobs. Perhaps 40 percent of the farm labor in the valley is currently performed by workers who live there. Many farmworkers now own houses. But the strawberry fields have drawn thousands of poor migrants to the area. Only 12 percent of the work force at a strawberry farm can claim year-round employment. And cultivating the fruit is so labor-intensive — twenty-five times as labor-intensive as cultivating broccoli — that strawberry production now employs more farmworkers than the production of all the vegetables grown in the valley combined. Most strawberry pickers hope to find jobs in the neighboring vegetable fields, where the wages are better and the work is less arduous. Turnover rates are extremely high in the strawberry work force. But there is no impending shortage of potential migrants. The rural population of Mexico has tripled since the 1940s. "In terms of absolute numbers," Palerm says, "there are far more Mexican peasants today than ever before."

Twenty-five years ago academic texts declared that California agriculture — with its large-scale irrigation, sophisticated farming practices, corporate structure, and low-wage, imported labor — was unique. That is no longer true. Southern Spain is fast becoming the "California of Europe," borrowing many of the same techniques to grow the same high-value crops and relying on illegal immigrants from North Africa. Southern Italy and Mediterranean France are adopting the system as well. Mexico, Guatemala, and Chile, with the aid of foreign investors, are recreating California's industrialized agriculture in Latin America, producing some crops that now compete with those grown in the United States. Improvements in transportation systems and cooling technology have created an international market for commodities that until recent years were rarely exported. Juan Vicente Palerm believes that the cultivation of fruits and vegetables for processing will increasingly shift from California to Mexico, where labor costs are much lower. Mexico will produce the frozen vegetables for TV dinners, while California grows artichokes, broccoli, strawberries, and asparagus for the fresh market. The harvest of these specialty crops, however, cannot easily be mechanized: their high value is closely linked to their unblemished appearance. The prosperity of California agriculture increasingly depends on uninterrupted access to Mexico's peasantry.

Most of the strawberry workers in the Santa Maria Valley are Mixtec Indians — some of the poorest and most exploited people in the Western Hemisphere. Soil erosion and declining

20

crop yields in the mountains of western Oaxaca have forced the Mixtecs to become migrant workers. According to Michael Kearney, a professor of anthropology at the University of California at Riverside, their choice is simple: "Migrate or starve." Mixtecs now dominate the lowest-paid jobs in California agriculture. In Tijuana you often see wives and children of Mixtec farmworkers, small and dark and beautiful, dressed in the bright colors of their native villages, selling Chiclets to tourists on the street.

Until the 1970s almost all the Mexican farmworkers in California were mestizos with strong links to communities already in the state. The new migrants present social workers with unusual challenges. In addition to the ninety-two dialects of Mixtec, there are at least half a dozen other pre-Columbian languages spoken by the indigenous peoples of Oaxaca. Perhaps one-fifth of the Mixtec farmworkers in California speak little English or Spanish. Throughout their migratory route Mixtecs are the victims of robbery and discrimination. In central Mexico they must run a gauntlet of officials demanding bribes. In Tijuana they are preyed upon by smugglers, rapists, and thieves. In the Imperial Desert, east of San Diego, they risk their lives crossing the border. Two

Andrew Lichtenstein/Getty Images

Volunteer union organizers from the United Farm Workers of America (UFW) are seen here speaking with migrant workers in California strawberry fields in 1997. The majority of strawberry pickers voted against unionization.
Based on the details in Schlosser's essay, what may have led them to decide not to unionize?

or three migrants now die there from exposure every week.

In Guadalupe many of the settled farmworkers resent the new arrivals from Oaxaca. Illegal immigrants often crossed picket lines during the 1980s, helping to drive the UFW from the valley. Adjusted for inflation, the hourly wages have declined, and there is widespread underemployment. Labor contractors now actively recruit illegals, who work for less money and raise fewer objections than legal residents. At harvest time Guadalupe's population of roughly 5,700 swells by as much as one-third, placing greater demands on local services. Palerm's researchers once discovered twenty-two people living in a two-bedroom apartment.

Despite the hardships of the long journey, Mixtecs hoping to sustain their native villages have a strong incentive to find work in California. Wages in Oaxaca are about two or three dollars a day. Wages in the strawberry fields of Baja California are about five dollars a day. A Mixtec farmworker in the Santa Maria Valley, making ten dollars an hour at the peak of the strawberry harvest, can earn more in one day than he or she could earn back home in a month. . . .

Bowing Down to the Market

One morning in San Diego County, I met a strawberry grower named Doug. We sat and talked in a trailer on the edge of his field. Doug's father and his grandfather had both been sent to an internment camp for Japanese Americans during World War II. Upon their release, the grandfather bought a used truck. At first he worked for other farmers, then he leased some land. He spoke no English and so Doug's father, still a teenager, assumed an important role in the business. The two grew vegetables with success and eventually shifted to strawberries, shipping and processing the fruit as well. On the land where their original farm once stood, there are now condominiums, a park, and a school. Doug grows strawberries a few miles inland. His fields are surrounded by chain-link fences topped with barbed wire. An enormous real estate development, with hundreds of Spanish-style condo units, is creeping up the hills toward his farm. Many of the farmers nearby have already sold their land. Doug has spent most of his life in strawberry fields, learning every aspect of the business first-hand, but now isn't sure he wants his children to do the same.

"Farming's not a glamorous business," Doug said. "Farmers don't have a high status in this community. In fact, we're resented by most people." With all the hassles today from the state and from his neighbors, he sometimes asks himself, "Hey, why do this?" Selling the land would make him instantly rich. Instead, he worries about water costs, about theft, about the strawberries from New Zealand he saw in the market the other day. Rain had wiped out a quarter of his early-season berries, just when the market price was at its peak. Doug cannot understand the hostility toward growers in California. After all, agriculture preserves open land. He thinks Americans don't appreciate how lucky they are to have cheap food. He doesn't understand why anyone would impede strawberry production by limiting his access to migrants. "My workers are helping themselves," he said. "I've picked strawberries, and let me tell you, there is no harder work. I respect these people. They work damn hard. And my jobs are open to anyone who wants to apply." Every so often college kids visit the ranch, convinced that picking strawberries would be a nice way to earn some extra money. Doug laughed. "They don't last an hour out here."

We stepped from the trailer into bright sunshine. Workers moved down the furrows under close supervision. Doug takes great pride in being a third-generation grower. He is smart, well educated, meticulous, and it showed in his field. But I wondered if Doug and his workers would still be there in a few years.

Doug picked a berry and handed it to me, a large Chandler that was brilliantly red. I took a

25

bite. The strawberry was warm and sweet and fragrant, with a slightly bitter aftertaste from the soil.

That evening I inadvertently met some of Doug's workers. Ricardo Soto, a young lawyer at CRLA, had brought me to the edge of an avocado orchard to visit a hidden encampment of migrant workers. Perhaps one-third of the farmworkers in northern San Diego County — about 7,000 people — are now homeless. An additional 9,000 of their family members are homeless, too. Many are living outdoors. The shortage of low-income housing became acute in the early 1980s, and large shantytowns began to appear, some containing hundreds of crude shacks. As suburbs encroached on agricultural land in northern San Diego County, wealthy commuters and strawberry pickers became neighbors. At one large shantytown I visited, women were doing their laundry in a stream not far from a walled compound with tennis courts, a pool, and a sign promising country club living. The suburbanites do not like living beside Mexican farmworkers. Instead of providing low-income housing, local authorities have declared states of emergency, passed laws to forbid curbside hiring, and bulldozed many of the large encampments. San Diego growers appalled by the living conditions of their migrants have tried to build farmworker housing near the fields — only to encounter fierce resistance from neighboring homeowners. Although the shantytowns lower nearby property values, permanent farmworker housing might reduce property values even more. "When people find out you want to build housing for your migrants," one grower told me, "they just go ballistic."

The new encampments are smaller and built to avoid detection. At the end of a driveway, near a chain-link fence, I met a young Mixtec who lived in such an encampment. His name was Francisco, and he was eighteen years old. He looked deeply exhausted. He had just picked strawberries for twelve hours at Doug's farm. I asked what he thought of Doug as a boss. "Not bad," he said politely.

The previous year Francisco had picked strawberries from April until July. He had saved $800 during that period and had wired all of it to his mother and father in the village of San Sebastian Tecomaxtlahuaca. This was Francisco's second season in the fields, but he had not seen much of San Diego County. He was too afraid of getting caught. His days were spent at the farm, his nights at the encampment. He picked strawberries six days a week, sometimes seven, for ten or twelve hours a day. "When there's work," Francisco said, "you have to work." Each morning he woke up around four-thirty and walked for half an hour to reach Doug's field.

At dusk, thirteen tired men in dirty clothes approached us. They were all from Francisco's village. They worked together at Doug's farm and stayed at the same encampment. They knew one another's families back home and looked after one another here. The oldest was forty-three and the youngest looked about fifteen. All the men were illegals. All were sick with coughs, but none dared to see a doctor. As the sun dropped behind the hills, clouds of mosquitoes descended, and yet the migrants seemed too tired to notice. They lay on their backs, on their sides, resting on the hard ground as though it were a sofa.

Francisco offered to show me their encampment. We squeezed through a hole in the chain-link fence and through gaps in rusting barbed wire, and climbed a winding path enclosed by tall bushes. It felt like a medieval maze. As we neared the camp, I noticed beer cans and food wrappers littering the ground. We came upon the first shack — short and low, more like a tent, just silver trash bags draped over a wooden frame. A little farther up the path stood three more shacks in a small clearing. They were built of plywood and camouflaged. Branches and leaves had been piled on their roofs. The landowner did not know the migrants lived here,

30

and the encampment would be difficult to find. These migrants were hiding out, like criminals or Viet Cong. Garbage was everywhere. Francisco pointed to his shack, which was about five feet high, five feet wide, and seven feet long. He shared it with two other men. He had a good blanket. But when it rained at night the roof leaked, and the men would go to work soaking wet the next day and dry off in the sun. Francisco had never lived this way before coming to San Diego. At home he always slept in a bed.

Beyond the sheds, bushes crowded the path again, and then it reached another clearing, where two battered lawn chairs had been placed at the edge of the hill. There was a wonderful view of strawberry fields, new houses, and the lights of the freeway in the distance.

Driving back to my motel that night, I thought about the people of Orange County, one of the richest counties in the nation — big on family values, yet bankrupt from financial speculation, unwilling to raise taxes to pay for their own children's education, unwilling to pay off their debts, whining about the injustice of it, and blaming all their problems on illegal immigrants. And I thought about Francisco, their bogeyman, their scapegoat, working ten hours a day at one of the hardest jobs imaginable, and sleeping on the ground every night, for months, so that he could save money and send it home to his parents.

seeing connections

Examine this cartoon carefully and answer the following questions.

1. In this cartoon, what positions on immigration do you see portrayed?

2. What, ultimately, is the cartoonist's position?

3. Where do you see the tensions depicted in this poster reflected in Schlosser's essay? Cite specific passages in your response.

4. What resolution, if any, would you see as a possibility in the future for immigration and the workforce described in Schlosser's argument?

Source: Otherwords

We have been told for years to bow down ^{35} before "the market." We have placed our faith in the laws of supply and demand. What has been forgotten, or ignored, is that the market rewards only efficiency. Every other human value gets in its way. The market will drive wages down like water, until they reach the lowest possible level. Today that level is being set not in Washington or New York or Sacramento but in the fields of Baja California and the mountain villages of Oaxaca. That level is about five dollars a day. No deity that

men have ever worshipped is more ruthless and more hollow than the free market unchecked; there is no reason why shantytowns should not appear on the outskirts of every American city. All those who now consider themselves devotees of the market should take a good look at what is happening in California. Left to its own devices, the free market always seeks a work force that is hungry, desperate, and cheap — a work force that is anything but free.

Notes (by Paragraph)

8 *spends half the year working:* According to the latest NAWS survey, the average farmworker spent 47 percent of his or her time in the United States doing farmwork, 19 percent residing but not working, and 8 percent in nonfarm work. See "NAWS, 1997–98," p. 24.

9 *Since 1980, the acreage around Watsonville and Salinas:* In 1980 there were 4,270 acres of strawberries in the area that produced about 96,000 tons of strawberries. In 2000 there were 11,570 acres that produced about 365,000 tons of strawberries. See "California Strawberry Acreage and Yield by Major Areas, 1972 through 1994," California Strawberry Commission, and the Agricultural Commission crop reports for Monterey County and Santa Cruz County, 2000.

11 *A survey of garages in Soledad:* Meuter interview.
hundreds of strawberry pickers have been found living in caves: A decade ago, a large encampment was found near a strawberry farm in Prunedale. Smaller encampments are discovered from time to time in the area. See Roya Camp, "Shanty Camp Draws Aid; Field Workers Found Living in Makeshift Caves," *Salinas Californian,* August 28, 1991; Everett Messick and Susan Ferris, "Authorities to Move Laborers Out of Caves; Seeks Housing for 200 Migrants in Castroville, Salinas Areas," *Monterey Herald,* August 29, 1991; "Back Wages Sought for Farmworkers," *Watsonville Register-Pajaronian,* September 3, 1991.

14 *Guadalupe's population was 18 percent Latino:* Cited in Juan Vicente Palerm, "Farm Labor Needs and Farmworkers in California, 1970 to 1989," *California Agricultural Studies, 91–92,* Labor Market Information Division, State Employment Development Department, April 1991, p. 21.
today it is about 85 percent Latino: According to the U.S. Census Bureau, Guadalupe's population was

84.5 percent Latino in 2000. The actual proportion was most likely higher, given the perennial undercount of Latinos by the census.

16 *up to ten times as high as any wages Mexican peasants could earn:* See Juan Vicente Palerm with Jose Ignacio Urquiola, "A Binational System of Agricultural Production: The Case of the Mexican Bajio and California," in Daniel G. Aldrich, Jr., and Lorenzo Meyer, eds., *Mexico and the United States: Neighbors in Crisis* (San Bernardino, Calif.: Borgo Press, 1993), p. 327.
preserved rural communities in Mexico that otherwise might have collapsed: According to Michael Kearney, a professor of anthropology at the University of California, Northridge, some villages in Oaxaca now derive 80 percent of their annual income from remittances sent home by migrant workers in California. Interview with Michael Kearney. See also "Binational System," pp. 311, 346; Michael Kearney, "Mixtec Ethnicity: Social Identity, Political Consciousness, and Political Activism," *Latin American Research Review* 25 (2): 74–77.

18 *Juan Vicente Palerm believes:* Palerm interview.
Perhaps 40 percent of the farm labor: Cited in Palerm, "Immigrant and Migrant Farmworkers in the Santa Maria Valley, California," Center for Survey Methods Research, Bureau of the Census, 1994, p. 11.
twenty-five times as labor-intensive as cultivating broccoli: Broccoli production requires 80 man-hours per acre; strawberry production requires about 2,000 man-hours per acre. See "Immigrant and Migrant," pp. 4, 6.
The rural population of Mexico: Palerm interview.

20 *"Migrate or starve":* Kearney interview.

[1995]

EXPLORING THE TEXT

1. Note Eric Schlosser's title, "In the Strawberry Fields." Compare the imagery evoked by the Beatles song "Strawberry Fields Forever" and the ceremonial place in New York City's Central Park with Schlosser's description in paragraphs 1 and 2.

2. How does Schlosser use the resources of language to characterize the work of the strawberry pickers in paragraph 6?

3. What are some of the particular hardships facing the strawberry pickers? Which one does Schlosser say is the worst?

4. Explain the rhetorical shift that Schlosser makes from the section "La Fruta del Diablo" to the section "Locked into Dependence."

5. According to Schlosser, how has the need for money changed the land and the population?

6. Schlosser concludes paragraphs 16 and 17 with claims. Analyze his arguments according to the Toulmin model as explained in Chapter 3.

7. What aspects of strawberry production differ significantly from the production of broccoli, celery, or cauliflower (para. 18)? How does this affect the lives of the workers?

8. Explain the nature of the economic imperative that concludes the section "Locked into Dependence" (para. 23).

9. How do you feel about the conditions described in the selection? Does reading it influence your attitude toward eating strawberries? Toward migrant workers? Explain.

10. Why does Schlosser conclude with narration and personal experience?

11. How would you characterize Schlosser's tone in the concluding paragraphs (34–35)? Do you agree with his conclusions? Why or why not?

12. Select an example of a general statement, such as the one that concludes the first section: "On hillsides above the Salinas Valley, hundreds of strawberry pickers have been found living in caves" (para. 11). Then read the endnote that corresponds to the sentence. Explain the relationship between the endnote and the text. What is the rhetorical function of the endnote? Overall, what effect do the endnotes have on ethos and logos? Explain.

The Singer Solution to World Poverty

PETER SINGER

Peter Singer (b. 1946) is an Australian moral philosopher most well-known for his pro-vegetarian book *Animal Liberation* (1975). The son of Austrian Jews who fled Vienna after the Nazi takeover in 1938, Singer studied law, history, and philosophy at the University of Melbourne, where he earned a BA in 1967 and an MA in 1969. He went on to earn another post-graduate degree from the University of Oxford in 1971. He currently teaches bioethics at Princeton University and philosophy and ethics at the University of Melbourne. Singer is the author of over fifteen books and the coauthor and editor of many other volumes. His most recent books include *The Life You Can Save: Acting Now to End World Poverty* (2009), *The Most Good You Can Do: How Effective Altruism Is Changing Ideas About Living Ethically* (2015), and *Ethics in the Real World: 82 Brief Essays on Things That Matter* (2016). The following essay first appeared in the *New York Times* in 1999.

In the Brazilian film *Central Station*, Dora is a retired schoolteacher who makes ends meet by sitting at the station writing letters for illiterate people. Suddenly she has an opportunity to pocket $1,000. All she has to do is persuade a homeless 9-year-old boy to follow her to an address she has been given. (She is told he will be adopted by wealthy foreigners.) She delivers the boy, gets the money, spends some of it on a television set and settles down to enjoy her new acquisition. Her neighbor spoils the fun, however, by telling her that the boy was too old to be adopted — he will be killed and his organs sold for transplantation. Perhaps Dora knew this all along, but after her neighbor's plain speaking, she spends a troubled night. In the morning Dora resolves to take the boy back.

Suppose Dora had told her neighbor that it is a tough world, other people have nice new TV's too, and if selling the kid is the only way she can get one, well, he was only a street kid. She would then have become, in the eyes of the audience, a monster. She redeems herself only by being prepared to bear considerable risks to save the boy.

At the end of the movie, in cinemas in the affluent nations of the world, people who would have been quick to condemn Dora if she had not rescued the boy go home to places far more comfortable than her apartment. In fact, the average family in the United States spends almost one-third of its income on things that are no more necessary to them than Dora's new TV was to her. Going out to nice restaurants, buying new clothes because the old ones are no longer stylish, vacationing at beach resorts — so much of our income is spent on things not essential to the preservation of our lives and health. Donated to one of a number of charitable agencies, that money could mean the difference between life and death for children in need.

All of which raises a question: In the end, what is the ethical distinction between a Brazilian who sells a homeless child to organ peddlers and an American who already has a TV and upgrades to a better one — knowing that the money could be donated to an organization that would use it to save the lives of kids in need?

Of course, there are several differences   5 between the two situations that could support different moral judgments about them. For one thing, to be able to consign a child to death when he is standing right in front of you takes a chilling kind of heartlessness; it is much easier to ignore an appeal for money to help children you will never meet. Yet for a utilitarian philosopher like myself — that is, one who judges whether acts are right or wrong by their consequences — if the upshot of the American's failure to donate the money is that one more kid dies on the streets of a Brazilian city, then it is, in some sense, just as bad as selling the kid to the organ peddlers. But one doesn't need to embrace my utilitarian ethic to see that, at the very least, there is a troubling incongruity in being so quick to condemn Dora for taking the child to the organ peddlers while, at the same time, not regarding the American consumer's behavior as raising a serious moral issue.

▼

Does this cartoon, published in a 2014 issue of the *New Yorker*, ultimately support or challenge Singer's main argument? How would Singer respond to it?

Carolita Johnson The New Yorker Collection/The Cartoon Bank

"Do you have a minute for a problem whose solution has eluded humanity since the dawn of civilization?"

♦ ♦ ♦

In his 1996 book, *Living High and Letting Die*, the New York University philosopher Peter Unger presented an ingenious series of imaginary examples designed to probe our intuitions about whether it is wrong to live well without giving substantial amounts of money to help people who are hungry, malnourished or dying from easily treatable illnesses like diarrhea. Here's my paraphrase of one of these examples:

Bob is close to retirement. He has invested most of his savings in a very rare and valuable old car, a Bugatti, which he has not been able to insure. The Bugatti is his pride and joy. In addition to the pleasure he gets from driving and caring for his car, Bob knows that its rising market value means that he will always be able to sell it and live comfortably after retirement. One day when Bob is out for a drive, he parks the Bugatti near the end of a railway siding and goes for a walk up the track. As he does so, he sees that a runaway train, with no one aboard, is running down the railway track. Looking farther down the track, he sees the small figure of a child very likely to be killed by the runaway train. He can't stop the train and the child is too far away to warn of the danger, but he can throw a switch that will divert the train down the siding where his Bugatti is parked. Then nobody will be killed — but the train will destroy his Bugatti. Thinking of his joy in owning the car and the financial security it represents, Bob decides not to throw the switch. The child is killed. For many years to come, Bob enjoys owning his Bugatti and the financial security it represents.

Bob's conduct, most of us will immediately respond, was gravely wrong. Unger agrees. But then he reminds us that we, too, have opportunities to save the lives of children. We can give to organizations like UNICEF or Oxfam America. How much would we have to give one of these organizations to have a high probability of saving the life of a child threatened by easily preventable diseases? (I do not believe that children are more worth saving than adults, but since no one can argue that children have brought their poverty on themselves, focusing on them simplifies the issues.) Unger called up some experts and used the information they provided to offer some plausible estimates that include the cost of raising money, administrative expenses and the cost of delivering aid where it is most needed. By his calculation, $200 in donations would help a sickly 2-year-old transform into a healthy 6-year-old — offering safe passage through childhood's most dangerous years. To show how practical philosophical argument can be, Unger even tells his readers that they can easily donate funds by using their credit card and calling one of these toll-free numbers: (800) 367-5437 for Unicef; (800) 693-2687 for Oxfam America.

Now you, too, have the information you need to save a child's life. How should you judge yourself if you don't do it? Think again about Bob and his Bugatti. Unlike Dora, Bob did not have to look into the eyes of the child he was sacrificing for his own material comfort. The child was a complete stranger to him and too far away to relate to in an intimate, personal way. Unlike Dora, too, he did not mislead the child or initiate the chain of events imperiling him. In all these respects, Bob's situation resembles that of people able but unwilling to donate to overseas aid and differs from Dora's situation.

If you still think that it was very wrong of Bob 10 not to throw the switch that would have diverted the train and saved the child's life, then it is hard to see how you could deny that it is also very wrong not to send money to one of the organizations listed above. Unless, that is, there is some morally important difference between the two situations that I have overlooked.

Is it the practical uncertainties about whether aid will really reach the people who need it? Nobody who knows the world of overseas aid can doubt that such uncertainties exist. But Unger's figure of $200 to save a child's life was reached after he had made conservative assumptions about the proportion of the money donated that will actually reach its target.

Leo Cullum The New Yorker Collection/The Cartoon Bank

"I'm donating a portion of your tip to charity."

What does this cartoon suggest about wealth in American society? How do its implications inform your understanding of Singer's argument?

One genuine difference between Bob and those who can afford to donate to overseas aid organizations but don't is that only Bob can save the child on the tracks, whereas there are hundreds of millions of people who can give $200 to overseas aid organizations. The problem is that most of them aren't doing it. Does this mean that it is all right for you not to do it?

Suppose that there were more owners of priceless vintage cars — Carol, Dave, Emma, Fred and so on, down to Ziggy — all in exactly the same situation as Bob, with their own siding and their own switch, all sacrificing the child in order to preserve their own cherished car. Would that make it all right for Bob to do the same? To answer this question affirmatively is to endorse follow-the-crowd ethics — the kind of ethics that led many Germans to look away when the Nazi atrocities were being committed. We do not excuse them because others were behaving no better.

We seem to lack a sound basis for drawing a clear moral line between Bob's situation and that of any reader of this article with $200 to spare who does not donate it to an overseas aid agency. These readers seem to be acting at least as badly as Bob was acting when he chose to let the runaway train hurtle toward the unsuspecting child. In the light of this conclusion, I trust that many readers will reach for the phone and donate that $200. Perhaps you should do it before reading further.

◆ ◆ ◆

Now that you have distinguished yourself morally 15 from people who put their vintage cars ahead of a child's life, how about treating yourself and your partner to dinner at your favorite restaurant? But wait. The money you will spend at the restaurant could also help save the lives of children overseas! True, you weren't planning to blow $200 tonight, but if you were to give up dining out just for one month, you would easily save that amount. And what is one month's dining out, compared to a child's life? There's the rub. Since there are a lot of desperately needy children in the world, there will always be another child whose life you could save for another $200. Are you therefore obliged to keep giving until you have nothing left? At what point can you stop?

Hypothetical examples can easily become farcical. Consider Bob. How far past losing the Bugatti should he go? Imagine that Bob had got his foot stuck in the track of the siding, and if he diverted the train, then before it rammed the car it would also amputate his big toe. Should he still throw the switch? What if it would amputate his foot? His entire leg?

As absurd as the Bugatti scenario gets when pushed to extremes, the point it raises is a serious one: only when the sacrifices become very significant indeed would most people be prepared to say that Bob does nothing wrong when he decides not to throw the switch. Of course, most people could be wrong; we can't decide moral issues by taking opinion polls. But consider for yourself the level of sacrifice that you would demand of Bob, and then think about how much money you would have to give away in order to make a sacrifice that is roughly equal to that. It's almost certainly much, much more than $200. For most middle-class Americans, it could easily be more like $200,000.

Isn't it counterproductive to ask people to do so much? Don't we run the risk that many will shrug their shoulders and say that morality, so conceived, is fine for saints but not for them?

I accept that we are unlikely to see, in the near or even medium-term future, a world in which it is normal for wealthy Americans to give the bulk of their wealth to strangers. When it comes to praising or blaming people for what they do, we tend to use a standard that is relative to some conception of normal behavior. Comfortably off Americans who give, say, 10 percent of their income to overseas aid organizations are so far ahead of most of their equally comfortable fellow citizens that I wouldn't go out of my way to chastise them for not doing more. Nevertheless, they should be doing much more, and they are in no position to criticize Bob for failing to make the much greater sacrifice of his Bugatti.

At this point various objections may crop up. Someone may say: "If every citizen living in the affluent nations contributed his or her share I wouldn't have to make such a drastic sacrifice, because long before such levels were reached, the resources would have been there to save the lives of all those children dying from lack of food or medical care. So why should I give more than

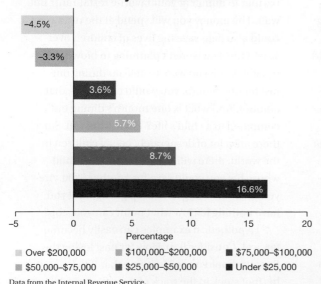

Change in Percentage of Income Given to Charity from 2006–2012

Data from the Internal Revenue Service.

This graph depicts a relationship between income and charitable giving.
What conclusions about charity can you draw from this data? How might this graph be used to challenge — or support — Singer's argument?

my fair share?" Another, related, objection is that the Government ought to increase its overseas aid allocations, since that would spread the burden more equitably across all taxpayers.

Yet the question of how much we ought to give is a matter to be decided in the real world — and that, sadly, is a world in which we know that most people do not, and in the immediate future will not, give substantial amounts to overseas aid agencies. We know, too, that at least in the next year, the United States Government is not going to meet even the very modest United Nations–recommended target of 0.7 percent of gross national product; at the moment it lags far below that, at 0.09 percent, not even half of Japan's 0.22 percent or a tenth of Denmark's 0.97 percent. Thus, we know that the money we can give beyond that theoretical "fair share" is still going to save lives that would otherwise be lost.

20

While the idea that no one need do more than his or her fair share is a powerful one, should it prevail if we know that others are not doing their fair share and that children will die preventable deaths unless we do more than our fair share? That would be taking fairness too far.

Thus, this ground for limiting how much we ought to give also fails. In the world as it is now, I can see no escape from the conclusion that each one of us with wealth surplus to his or her essential needs should be giving most of it to help people suffering from poverty so dire as to be life-threatening. That's right: I'm saying that you shouldn't buy that new car, take that cruise, redecorate the house or get that pricey new suit. After all, a $1,000 suit could save five children's lives.

So how does my philosophy break down in dollars and cents? An American household

seeing connections

Read the following excerpt by Karl Marx, considered the father of socialism. Written in 1844 and never published during his lifetime, this passage appeared in a section entitled "Human requirements and division of labour under the rule of private property." **To what extent could the ideas presented here be used to support a counterargument to Singer's position? How convincing do you find Marx's central point?**

from Human Requirements and Division of Labour Under the Rule of Private Property

KARL MARX

Political economy, this science of *wealth,* is therefore simultaneously the science of renunciation, of want, of *saving* and it actually reaches the point where it *spares* man the *need* of either fresh air or physical *exercise.* This science of marvellous industry is simultaneously the science of *asceticism,* and its true ideal is the *ascetic* but *extortionate* miser and the *ascetic* but *productive* slave . . . .

Thus political economy — despite its worldly and voluptuous appearance — is a true moral science, the most moral of all the sciences. Self-renunciation, the renunciation of life and of all human needs, is its principal thesis. The less you eat, drink and buy books; the less you go to the theatre, the dance hall, the public house; the less you think, love, theorise, sing, paint, fence, etc., the more you *save* — the *greater* becomes your treasure which neither moths nor rust will devour — your capital.

with an income of $50,000 spends around $30,000 annually on necessities, according to the Conference Board, a nonprofit economic research organization. Therefore, for a household bringing in $50,000 a year, donations to help the world's poor should be as close as possible to $20,000. The $30,000 required for necessities holds for higher incomes as well. So a household making $100,000 could cut a yearly check for $70,000. Again, the formula is simple: whatever money you're spending on luxuries, not necessities, should be given away.

Now, evolutionary psychologists tell us that human nature just isn't sufficiently altruistic to make it plausible that many people will sacrifice so much for strangers. On the facts of human nature, they might be right, but they would be wrong to draw a moral conclusion from those facts. If it is the case that we ought to do things that, predictably, most of us won't do, then let's

face that fact head-on. Then, if we value the life of a child more than going to fancy restaurants, the next time we dine out we will know that we could have done something better with our money. If that makes living a morally decent life extremely arduous, well, then that is the way things are. If we don't do it, then we should at least know that we are failing to live a morally decent life — not because it is good to wallow in guilt but because knowing where we should be going is the first step toward heading in that direction.

When Bob first grasped the dilemma that faced him as he stood by that railway switch, he must have thought how extraordinarily unlucky he was to be placed in a situation in which he must choose between the life of an innocent child and the sacrifice of most of his savings. But he was not unlucky at all. We are all in that situation.

[1999]

EXPLORING THE TEXT

1. Peter Singer opens his essay by describing a situation from a movie, yet it could be argued that seeing movies is, in fact, a luxury that one advocating his position should forgo. Does this interpretation undermine Singer's argument? Explain.

2. How would you answer the question that Singer poses at the end of paragraph 4? What answer does Singer imply is the right one? Explain.

3. What is the assumption underlying Singer's assertion regarding the "troubling incongruity" he discusses in paragraph 5?

4. Singer discusses the hypothetical example of Bob and his Bugatti from Peter Unger's book, *Living High and Letting Die*. Is this a rhetorical strategy that strengthens or weakens Singer's argument? Explain your response.

5. The inclusion of toll-free phone numbers might seem unusual in an essay. What purpose is served by his inclusion of that information from Unger's book? What does it suggest about the nature of Singer's argument?

6. Singer concludes paragraph 10 by stating that there might be "some morally important difference between the two situations that I have overlooked." How would you characterize his tone here? Is he being disingenuous? Is he being frank and serious? Explain.

7. Note the places where Singer addresses the counterargument. Where does he concede, and where does he refute? How do those sections contribute to his argument?

8. When does Singer use the pronoun *we*? When does he shift to *you*? How do these rhetorical shifts reflect and contribute to appeals to ethos and pathos? What purpose do they serve in his overall argument?

9. What is the primary rhetorical strategy Singer uses in paragraphs 14 and 15? Why does he use it in that particular place in the argument?

10. What is the rhetorical purpose and effect of the statement, "That's right" in paragraph 21?

11. In what paragraph does Singer assert his major claim, or thesis? Identify it by quoting him and then

paraphrasing what you consider to be his main idea.

12. This selection appeared in the *New York Times Magazine* in 1999. What does that fact tell you about the audience to whom Singer is appealing? To what extent do you think he is effective in reaching them?

13. Consider the American public as Singer's audience. Does Singer's argument account for the life situations of everyone? What about people who work in the restaurant industry, the auto industry, the clothing industry? How would Singer's solution affect their lives?

14. What is the challenge that Singer poses in paragraph 23? How are we as human beings capable of accepting that challenge? Is it reasonable that we should be expected to do so? Explain.

Luxury Shopping, from the Other Side of the Register

CARMEN MARIA MACHADO

Carmen Maria Machado is a writer whose stories, essays, and criticism have appeared in the *New Yorker*, the *Paris Review*, *Tin House*, *Granta*, and many other publications. Machado was raised an hour north of Philadelphia in Allentown, Pennsylvania, and went on to earn an MFA from the Iowa Writers' Workshop. She is the author of a book of stories entitled *Her Body and Other Parties* (2017). She is currently an Artist in Residence at the University of Pennsylvania. The following essay appeared in the *New Yorker* in 2013.

This holiday season, I'm working in sales at a store in a giant luxury mall, just outside Philadelphia and near one of the richest Zip Codes in the United States. Major employers in the area include defense contractors and pharmacy conglomerates. Every day, I park my run-down car among BMWs and hybrids. The mall's interior is decked out for Christmas: light-studded garlands are strung in the eaves; colossal reindeer grace the entrances like sphinxes; security officers zoom by on Segways. The mall rats who hover around the doors smoking cigarettes wear brands of designer jeans I've only ever heard about in songs. Some of the stores resemble modern-art exhibits, and I'm still not entirely sure what they sell because I'm too afraid to approach the willowy, elegant salespeople to ask.

My work, truthfully, is not bad, nor are the customers. This is not going to be an essay excoriating the behavior of the rich, who have been, at their best, perfectly friendly, and, at their utmost worst, uninterested in my presence. But there is something shocking about working in a place like this, especially around the holidays. It is the presence of money — lots of it, more than I have ever seen in one place before — and the ease with which it moves around me.

Every day, I serve a parade of affluent customers: a perfectly coiffed eleven-year-old girl, carrying half a dozen shopping bags, who launched into a deeply nuanced assessment of her own skin, for which she ended up purchasing fifty dollars' worth of high-end creams; a man in his late twenties, no older than I am, wearing a pair of shoes that cost more than my monthly rent. Then there was the kindly middle-aged woman who stopped by on a whim and picked up everything I suggested without a moment's hesitation. She checked out, having spent hundreds of dollars, thanked me, and was gone. Hours later, this last interaction in particular was still hovering around me like smoke as I drove home through the too-early dark. When I entered my apartment, I was still trying to figure out why it had made me feel so strange. As I recounted

▼
_____

How effectively does this cartoon illustrate Machado's argument—particularly her depiction of the interaction in paragraph 3? How do you think the cartoonist would respond to the details in that paragraph?

"Stop complaining. Who isn't broke?"

the day's events to my partner, I put my finger on it. "She had just walked in," I said, "just because. And she didn't look at the price of anything, not for a second. It just looked so easy."

I once dated someone from money, and it felt confusing and alien in the same way: she kept what my roommate called "banker's son's hours" (courtesy of Alice Cooper's "Generation Landslide")[1], threw elaborate parties where she never asked guests to chip in, and spent money as reflexively as she breathed. I am not, and have never been, in poverty, but I have been varying shades of poor: tiny-nonprofit-salary-in-an-expensive-urban-area poor, graduate-student

[1]A reference to lyrics from the song "Generation Landslide" by Alice Cooper ("Sister's out till five doing banker's son's hours") — and to the privilege it suggests people with inherited wealth enjoy. —Eds.

poor, can't-find-a-job-out-of-school-during-a-recession poor. In the mall, the mingling of my financial status and my customers' abundant wealth results in a kind of daily culture shock to which I have yet to adapt. And on top of exhaustion and stress, I find myself feeling oddly antisocial. When I come home at the end of each day, it's difficult to talk, to interact. I have always loved the aesthetic of Christmas, but this year I find myself utterly immune to all of it. I simply don't care. I experience a varying mixture of depression, anxiety about the cost of gas and food and my student loans and other necessary expenses, and a kind of overwhelming disassociation that makes everything difficult — and, at times, impossible.

I'm not alone. In July, Stephen Gandel, of *Fortune*, wrote about how economic growth for budget retailers — places like Target and Walmart — has stagnated, while luxury shopping continues to rise. A chart accompanying the piece showed sales from the first quarter of 2013 rising more than nine per cent for high-end retailers, and zero per cent for discount stores. This confirms what we already know: the wealthy have reaped far more of the benefits of the economic recovery than the poor and middle-class.

And now, just after Black Friday, I'm able to see this all in action. Much has been written about those who participate in Black Friday on the buying end. Less attention has been paid to those on the other side of the register. Retail workers earned a median wage of just over ten dollars per hour in 2010, according to the Bureau of Labor Statistics, and during the holiday season they must contend with particularly frenzied customers. But the tough work and low pay distract from a larger question: Even if the crowds were large but orderly, even if we paid all retail workers a living wage and didn't make them work on Thanksgiving, what does it mean to them—what does it *do* to them—to see so much money moving in such unbelievable quantities?

5

Carolyn Cole/Getty Images

Jennifer Jones (left) and Alicia Sgro (right) were at the Walmart in Valley Stream, Long Island on Black Friday when they were caught in a stampede of customers that injured them and killed a Walmart employee. **What comments on American culture does this story and its accompanying photo invite? How does Machado's account reflect them?**

As it turns out, it may do quite a bit. Kathleen Vohs, a marketing professor at the University of Minnesota, has done extensive studies on how the presence of money affects the brain. In her study "The Psychological Consequences of Money," published in *Science* in 2006, she found that "money-priming" — that is, exposing people to money, or representations of money, or even words having to do with money — is enough to temporarily reduce a person's ability to perceive physical and emotional sensations and to make them "disinterested" in others. To deduce this, she exposed people to money in various forms — essays about wealth, word scrambles containing phrases like "a high-paying salary," even Monopoly bills. She then asked them to do various tasks: helping a stranger pick up spilled pencils, donating to a charity, pulling out a chair, or assisting someone asking for aid. She found that money-primed people may be less inclined to help others, and likelier to eschew social intimacy. The study hypothesized, and then confirmed, that "when reminded of money, people would want to be free from dependency and would also prefer that others not depend on them."

In other words, the study suggests that constant exposure to money, even if it's not your own, can desensitize you to the needs of others. And what is a mall but a giant box of money? What's more, selling high-end products during a high-volume shopping season seems to make a difference. Vohs explained to me that while any amount or representation of money will trip off this tendency toward disinterest, the effect is amplified when you use larger quantities of money and raise the frequency of the monetary interactions. So retail workers ringing up hundreds or even thousands of dollars of purchases would be more "primed," and thus more likely to experience this involuntary tendency toward self-isolation. Everyone is exposed to money in some capacity or another on a daily basis, but the life of a retail worker, in this regard, is unique.

On top of that, constant exposure to wealth in conjunction with one's own financial struggles may affect people's happiness. For a study published in the journal *Psychological Science* in 2011, researchers looked at data gathered from 1972 to 2008 by the General Social Survey, a poll of people randomly chosen from the U.S. population. They examined respondents' incomes alongside overall levels of U.S. income equality over time; they also studied how people rated their happiness and judged how fair and

Michael Maslin/The New Yorker Collection/The Cartoon Bank

"O.K., we'll meet back here in about five hundred dollars."

This *New Yorker* cartoon by Michael Maslin depicts a mall during the holiday season.
What message does the caption send? Would you say that Maslin's depiction supports any part of Machado's argument? If so, which part?

trustworthy they felt other Americans were. For the richest twenty per cent, levels of income equality did not affect their happiness, or their sense of others' fairness and trustworthiness. But for the rest, inequality was correlated with, in general, "a diminished sense of well-being" and a sense that other people were less fair and trustworthy.

Those of us who work in retail during the holiday season have plenty to worry about: managing unruly holiday crowds, anticipating potential unemployment in January, and buying gifts of our own when we're being paid ten dollars an hour. Treating workers better and paying them 10 more is the first step toward addressing our woes, but this would solve only part of the problem, absent a societal shift in how we value money and the things it buys.

As I found out at 3 A.M. on Black Friday, the light in the mall looks the same in the middle of the night as it does at twilight, or noon. I stood across from a teen-age girl who had come into my store with her family. I was bleary-eyed and exhausted; she looked just as worn out. She asked me a question. I answered. "I'm tired," she told me, as if she were confessing some secret. I nodded. "Yeah," I said. "I'm tired, too."

[2013]

EXPLORING THE TEXT

1. Carmen Maria Machado speaks of money and "the ease with which it moves around me" (para. 2). Does it sometimes seem odd, perhaps ironic, that while there seems to be money everywhere, it is so difficult for her to obtain? What effect does the presence — and absence — of money have regarding her perspective on work?

2. Machado writes, "I am not, and have never been, in poverty, but I have been varying shades of poor" (para. 4). What does she mean by this? How does she distinguish the "varying shades of poor" from poverty, and how does that difference inform her argument?

3. In paragraph 5, Machado refers to a chart in Stephen Gandel's piece for *Fortune*, which shows that the wealthy have benefited more from economic recovery than anyone else in America. According to her, it "confirms what we already know." What does that statement suggest about how Machado regards her audience? What effect does such a statement have on her argument?

4. According to Machado, how is the retail worker's relationship to money unique? To what extent do you agree with her portrayal of that relationship?

5. Where in the essay does Machado return to the idea of the effect of money in great quantity? What purpose does returning to this idea serve within her overall argument?

6. What evidence does Machado use to support her claims in paragraphs 7 and 9? How does she use that evidence to support her claims? How effective is this evidence in strengthening her argument?

7. Based on the entire essay, how would you characterize the "problem" that Machado refers to in paragraph 10? Why does she claim that "treating workers better and paying them more . . . would solve only part of" that problem? Explain whether you agree or disagree with her diagnosis of the problem and with her assertion that better compensation for retail workers is only a partial solution. Draw on your own experience, the history of workers' rights in America, or current events in your response.

8. What are the purpose and effect of the rhetorical strategies Machado employs in her conclusion? What rhetorical appeal does she rely on the most, and how effective is it?

A Guaranteed Income for Every American

CHARLES MURRAY

Charles Murray (b.1943) is a political scientist and author. In his influential and controversial book, *Losing Ground: American Social Policy 1950–1980* (1984), Murray argued most welfare state policies were doomed to be ineffective. Even more controversial, in *The Bell Curve* (1994) cowritten with Richard Herrnstein, Murray argued that human intelligence is influenced by inherited and environmental factors and is a better predictor of income, job performance, and crime participation than socioeconomic status. Murray's writings have also been published in *Commentary*, the *Washington Post*, the *Wall Street Journal*, and the *New York Times*. In the following article published by the conservative American Enterprise Institute, Murray argues that a universal basic income would benefit society.

When people learn that I want to replace the welfare state with a universal basic income, or UBI, the response I almost always get goes something like this: "But people will just use it to live off the rest of us!" "People will waste their lives!" Or, as they would have put it in a bygone age, a guaranteed income will foster idleness and vice. I see it differently. I think that a UBI is our only hope to deal with a coming labor market unlike any in human history and that it represents our best hope to revitalize American civil society.

The great free-market economist Milton Friedman originated the idea of a guaranteed income just after World War II. An experiment using a bastardized version of his "negative income tax"[1] was tried in the 1970s, with disappointing results. But as transfer payments continued to soar while the poverty rate remained stuck at more than 10% of the population, the appeal of a guaranteed income persisted: If you want to end poverty, just give people money. As of 2016, the UBI has become a live policy option. Finland is planning a pilot project for a UBI next year, and Switzerland is voting this weekend on a referendum to install a UBI.

The UBI has brought together odd bedfellows. Its advocates on the left see it as a move toward

---

[1]A system, first proposed by economist Milton Friedman in the early 1960s, in which people earning less than a fixed amount are paid by the government instead of paying taxes to the government. —Eds.

In this British Conservative Party poster from 1931, note how the cartoonist delivers and supports his message with the details in the drawing and text. **In what ways might Murray argue with this depiction? To what extent does Murray's essay address the fears inherent in this poster's message?**

The Conservative Party Archive/Getty Images

social justice; its libertarian supporters (like Friedman) see it as the least damaging way for the government to transfer wealth from some citizens to others. Either way, the UBI is an idea whose time has finally come, but it has to be done right.

First, my big; caveat: A UBI will do the good things I claim only if it replaces all other transfer payments and the bureaucracies that oversee them. If the guaranteed income is an add-on to the existing system, it will be as destructive as its critics fear.

Second, the system has to be designed with certain key features. In my version, every American citizen age 21 and older would get a $13,000 annual grant deposited electronically into a bank account in monthly installments. Three thousand dollars must be used for health insurance (a complicated provision I won't try to explain here), leaving every adult with $10,000 in disposable annual income for the rest of their lives.

People can make up to $30,000 in earned income without losing a penny of the grant. After $30,000, a graduated surtax reimburses part of the grant, which would drop to $6,500 (but no lower) when an individual reaches $60,000 of earned income. Why should people making good incomes retain any part of the UBI? Because they will be losing Social Security and Medicare, and they need to be compensated.

The UBI is to be financed by getting rid of Social Security, Medicare, Medicaid, food stamps, Supplemental Security Income, housing subsidies, welfare for single women and every other kind of welfare and social-services program, as well as agricultural subsidies and corporate welfare. As of 2014, the annual cost of a UBI would have been about $200 billion cheaper than the current system. By 2020, it would be nearly a trillion dollars cheaper.

Finally, an acknowledgment: Yes, some people will idle away their lives under my UBI plan. But that is already a problem. As of 2015, the Current Population Survey tells us that 18% of unmarried males and 23% of unmarried women ages 25 through 54 — people of prime working age — weren't even in the labor force. Just about all of them were already living off other people's money. The question isn't whether a UBI will discourage work, but whether it will make the existing problem significantly worse.

I don't think it would. Under the current system, taking a job makes you ineligible for many welfare benefits or makes them subject to extremely high marginal tax rates. Under my

5

version of the UBI, taking a job is pure profit with no downside until you reach $30,000 — at which point you're bringing home way too much ($40,000 net) to be deterred from work by the imposition of a surtax.

Some people who would otherwise work will surely drop out of the labor force under the UBI, but others who are now on welfare or disability will enter the labor force. It is prudent to assume that net voluntary dropout from the labor force will increase, but there is no reason to think that it will be large enough to make the UBI unworkable.

Involuntary dropout from the labor force is another matter, which brings me to a key point: We are approaching a labor market in which entire trades and professions will be mere shadows of what they once were. I'm familiar with the retort: People have been worried about technology destroying jobs since the Luddites, and they have always been wrong. But the case for "this time is different" has a lot going for it.

10 When cars and trucks started to displace horse-drawn vehicles, it didn't take much imagination to see that jobs for drivers would replace jobs lost for teamsters, and that car mechanics would be in demand even as jobs for stable boys vanished. It takes a better imagination than mine to come up with new blue-collar occupations that will replace more than a fraction of the jobs (now numbering 4 million) that taxi drivers and truck drivers will lose when driverless vehicles take over. Advances in 3-D printing and "contour craft" technology will put at risk the jobs of many of the 14 million people now employed in production and construction.

The list goes on, and it also includes millions of white-collar jobs formerly thought to be safe. For decades, progress in artificial intelligence lagged behind the hype. In the past few years, AI has come of age. Last spring, for example, a computer program defeated a grandmaster in the classic Asian board game of Go a decade sooner than had been expected. It wasn't done

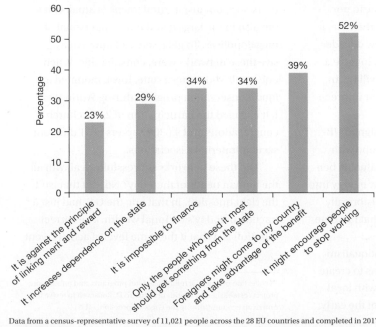

Which of the Following Arguments Against Basic Income Do You Find Convincing?

Percentage values:
- It is against the principle of linking merit and reward: 23%
- It increases dependence on the state: 29%
- It is impossible to finance: 34%
- Only the people who need it most should get something from the state: 34%
- Foreigners might come to my country and take advantage of the benefit: 39%
- It might encourage people to stop working: 52%

Data from a census-representative survey of 11,021 people across the 28 EU countries and completed in 2017 by Dalia Research.

Shown here are the results of a poll on arguments against universal basic income. **How does Murray's argument address the various criteria analyzed in this graph? Does the poll address anything Murray left out? After looking at the poll results, does your view of Murray's argument shift? Explain.**

David Parkins

This cartoon appeared with an article on UBI by *The Economist* in 2016. **Compare and contrast what is happening in the foreground with the action in the background. What position on UBI does the cartoonist take? To what extent is this image intended as satire, and how do you know? How effective is it?**

by software written to play Go but by software that taught itself to play — a landmark advance. Future generations of college graduates should take note.

Exactly how bad is the job situation going to be? An Organization for Economic Cooperation and Development study concluded that 9% of American jobs are at risk. Two Oxford scholars estimate that as many as 47% of American jobs are at risk. Even the optimistic scenario portends a serious problem. Whatever the case, it will need to be possible, within a few decades, for a life well lived in the U.S. not to involve a job as traditionally defined. A UBI will be an essential part of the transition to that unprecedented world.

The good news is that a well-designed UBI can do much more than help us to cope with disaster. It also could provide an invaluable benefit: injecting new resources and new energy into an American civic culture that has historically been one of our greatest assets but that has deteriorated alarmingly in recent decades.

A key feature of American exceptionalism has been the propensity of Americans to create voluntary organizations for dealing with local problems. Tocqueville was just one of the early

European observers who marveled at this phenomenon in the 19th and early 20th centuries. By the time the New Deal[2] began, American associations for providing mutual assistance and aiding the poor involved broad networks, engaging people from the top to the bottom of society, spontaneously formed by ordinary citizens.

These groups provided sophisticated and effective social services and social insurance of every sort, not just in rural towns or small cities but also in the largest and most impersonal of megalopolises. To get a sense of how extensive these networks were, consider this: When one small Midwestern state, Iowa, mounted a food-conservation program during World War I, it engaged the participation of 2,873 church congregations and 9,630 chapters of 31 different secular fraternal associations.

Did these networks successfully deal with all the human needs of their day? No. But that isn't the right question. In that era, the U.S. had just a fraction of today's national wealth. The correct question is: What if the same level of activity went

15

---

[2]A collection of financial reforms, federal programs, and public work projects established by President Franklin D. Roosevelt to revive the American economy during the Great Depression. —Eds.

into civil society's efforts to deal with today's needs — and financed with today's wealth?

The advent of the New Deal and then of President Lyndon Johnson's Great Society[3] displaced many of the most ambitious voluntary efforts to deal with the needs of the poor. It was a predictable response. Why continue to contribute to a private program to feed the hungry when the government is spending billions of dollars on food stamps and nutrition programs? Why continue the mutual insurance program of your fraternal organization once Social Security is installed? Voluntary organizations continued to thrive, but most of them turned to needs less subject to crowding out by the federal government.

This was a bad trade, in my view. 20 Government agencies are the worst of all mechanisms for dealing with human needs. They are necessarily bound by rules applied uniformly to people who have the same problems on paper but who will respond differently to different forms of help. Whether religious or secular, nongovernmental organization are inherently better able to tailor their services to local conditions and individual cases.

Under my UBI plan, the entire bureaucratic apparatus of government social workers would disappear, but Americans would still possess their historic sympathy and social concern. And the wealth in private hands would be greater than ever before. It is no pipe dream to imagine the restoration, on an unprecedented scale, of a great American tradition of voluntary efforts to meet human needs. It is how Americans, left to themselves, have always responded. Figuratively, and perhaps literally, it is in our DNA.

Regardless of what voluntary agencies do (or fail to do), nobody will starve in the streets. Everybody will know that, even if they can't find

any job at all, they can live a decent existence if they are cooperative enough to pool their grants with one or two other people. The social isolates who don't cooperate will also be getting their own monthly deposit of $833.

Some people will still behave irresponsibly and be in need before that deposit arrives, but the UBI will radically change the social framework within which they seek help: Everybody will know that everybody else has an income stream. It will be possible to say to the irresponsible what can't be said now: "We won't let you starve before you get your next deposit, but it's time for you to get your act together. Don't try to tell us you're helpless, because we know you aren't."

The known presence of an income stream would transform a wide range of social and personal interactions. The unemployed guy living with his girlfriend will be told that he has to start paying part of the rent or move out, changing the dynamics of their relationship for the better. The guy who does have a low-income job can think about marriage differently if his new family's income will be at least $35,000 a year instead of just his own earned $15,000.

Or consider the unemployed voting man 25 who fathers a child. Today, society is unable to make him shoulder responsibility. Under a UBI, a judge could order part of his monthly grant to be extracted for child support before he ever sees it. The lesson wouldn't be lost on his male friends.

Or consider teenage girls from poor neighborhoods who have friends turning 21. They watch — and learn — as some of their older friends use their new monthly income to rent their own apartments, buy nice clothes or pay for tuition, while others have to use the money to pay for diapers and baby food, still living with their mothers because they need help with day care.

These are just a few possible scenarios, but multiply the effects of such interactions by the millions of times they would occur throughout

[3]A collection of federal programs established by President Lyndon B. Johnson to combat poverty and racial discrimination during the civil rights era. —Eds.

FABRICE COFFRINI/Getty Images

This photograph, taken from above Plainpalais Place in Geneva, Switzerland, shows the largest poster ever created. Printed by a campaign group supporting universal basic income in Switzerland in 2016, it ultimately did not achieve its goal of convincing people to vote for one in the referendum that took place shortly afterward. **Who do you think is the intended audience for this poster? How would Murray answer the question it poses?**

the nation every day. The availability of a guaranteed income wouldn't relieve individuals of responsibility for the consequences of their actions. It would instead, paradoxically, impose responsibilities that didn't exist before, which would be a good thing.

Emphasizing the ways in which a UBI would encourage people to make better life choices still doesn't do justice to its wider likely benefits. A powerful critique of the current system is that the most disadvantaged people in America have no reason to think that they can be anything else. They are poorly educated, without job skills, and live in neighborhoods where prospects are bleak. Their quest for dignity and self-respect often takes the form of trying to beat the system.

The more fortunate members of society may see such people as obstinately refusing to take advantage of the opportunities that exist. But when seen from the perspective of the man who has never held a job or the woman who wants a stable family life, those opportunities look fraudulent.

My version of a UBI would do nothing to stage-manage their lives. In place of little bundles of benefits to be used as a bureaucracy specifies, they would get $10,000 a year to use as they wish. It wouldn't be charity — every citizen who has turned 21 gets the same thing, deposited monthly into that most respectable of possessions, a bank account.

A UBI would present the most disadvantaged among us with an open road to the middle class if they put their minds to it. It would say to people who have never had reason to believe it before: "Your future is in your hands." And that would be the truth.

[2016]

EXPLORING THE TEXT

1. What inferences can you make about Murray's intended audience? Does he imagine his readers as politically conservative, liberal, or both? Use evidence from the text of the article to support your answer.

2. Charles Murray begins by giving voice to opponents of his idea, who might complain: "But people will just use it to live off the rest of us!" (para. 1). How does that compare with your first impression of giving "free money" to everyone?

Why do you believe he begins his essay in this way?

3. In paragraph 2, Murray says, "If you want to end poverty, just give people money." How effectively does such a seemingly simple statement appeal to the reader? To what extent is this statement an oversimplification of the problem and a potential solution to it?

4. When Murray wrote this piece, Switzerland had not yet voted on a referendum to install a universal basic income, or UBI. Just days later, the country's voters rejected the referendum, with just 23 percent of people voting in its favor. How does that fact affect Murray's argument? How might Murray address this event, were he to revise or update this essay?

5. Briefly paraphrase Murray's "big caveat" and the key features of his plan for a UBI in America. How would they ensure, in Murray's view, that the UBI would be "done right" (para. 3)?

6. How — and where — does Murray acknowledge counterarguments? How do they fit into the overall structure of his argument? How convincingly does he address these counterarguments?

7. Discussing the long history of worry over the inimical effects of technology on people's jobs, Murray states that "'this time is different'" (para. 11). What evidence does he assemble to support this claim? Do you agree with him? Explain why or why not.

8. What is the purpose and effect of the information that Murray supplies in paragraphs 16–20?

9. In paragraph 20, Murray makes a strong claim that will likely appeal to conservative readers: "Government agencies are the worst of all mechanisms for dealing with human needs." Defend, challenge, or qualify this claim, drawing on personal experience, history, and current events to support your response.

10. In paragraph 21, Murray asserts that if we adopt his UBI plan, "the entire bureaucratic apparatus of government social workers would disappear." Does Murray's plan address what would become of the thousands of people who would be out of work by the disappearance of that apparatus? How does this affect the cogence of his argument?

11. How compelling do you find the examples that Murray provides in paragraphs 24–26? Identify the

rhetorical appeals that they make. How effectively do they support his position?

12. Identify and explain the paradox in paragraph 27. What is paradoxical about it?

13. The idea of the UBI has a long history. As Akash Kapur writes in a 2017 article for the *Financial Times*,

> "Thomas More, the godfather of utopia, envisioned something like a guaranteed income for the residents of his idealized world. Versions of the concept have also found favor among thinkers as varied as John Stuart Mill, Thomas Paine, Friedrich Hayek, Milton Friedman and John Kenneth Galbraith. In the late 1960s . . . Richard Nixon presented a basic income bill, labelling it 'the most significant piece of social legislation in our nation's history.'"

Kapur also notes that while the bill passed in the House of Representatives, it later died in the Senate and never became law. Given this information, why do you think UBI is not more well-known and more highly promoted? To what extent do you think pieces such as Murray's will bring the idea more serious attention from both the American public and legislators?

14. What do you see as the most compelling benefit of UBI as Murray presents it? Are you in favor of his proposal? Why or why not?

15. In *Agrarian Justice* (1797), Thomas Paine proposed a universal basic income. His stated purpose:

> To create a national fund, out of which there shall be paid to every person, when arrived at the age of twenty-one years, the sum of fifteen pounds sterling, as a compensation in part, for the loss of his or her natural inheritance, by the introduction of the system of landed property: And also, the sum of ten pounds per annum, during life, to every person now living, of the age of fifty years, and to all others as they shall arrive at that age.

How does Paine's proposal compare with Murray's? Why do you think that the idea of a universal basic income has been discussed — yet not put into practice — for over two hundred years?

The Gig Economy Celebrates Working Yourself to Death

JIA TOLENTINO

Jia Tolentino (b. 1988) is a contributing writer for the *New Yorker* and formerly the deputy editor of the feminist website *Jezebel*. A graduate of the University of Virginia and the MFA Program at the University of Michigan, Tolentino writes on a wide range of topics, including music, race, feminism, and the media. Her writing has appeared in the *New York Times Magazine*, the *Awl*, *Pitchfork*, the *Fader*, *Time*, and *Slate*. The following essay was published in the *New Yorker* in 2017.

Last September, a very twenty-first-century type of story appeared on the company blog of the ride-sharing app Lyft. "Long-time Lyft driver and mentor, Mary, was nine months pregnant when she picked up a passenger the night of July 21st," the post began. "About a week away from her due date, Mary decided to drive for a few hours after a day of mentoring." You can guess what happened next.

Mary, who was driving in Chicago, picked up a few riders, and then started having contractions. "Since she was still a week away from her due date," Lyft wrote, "she assumed they were simply a false alarm and continued driving." As the contractions continued, Mary decided to drive to the hospital. "Since she didn't believe she was going into labor yet," Lyft went on, "she stayed in driver mode, and sure enough — ping! — she received a ride request en route to the hospital."

"Luckily," as Lyft put it, the passenger requested a short trip. After completing it, Mary went to the hospital, where she was informed that she was in labor. She gave birth to a daughter, whose picture appears in the post. (She's wearing a "Little Miss Lyft" onesie.) The post concludes with a call for similar stories: "Do you have an exciting Lyft story you'd love to share? Tweet us your story at @lyft_CHI!"

Mary's story looks different to different people. Within the ghoulishly cheerful Lyft public-relations machinery, Mary is an exemplar of hard work and dedication — the latter being, perhaps,

hard to come by in a company that refuses to classify its drivers as employees. Mary's entrepreneurial spirit — taking ride requests while she was in labor! — is an "exciting" example of how seamless and flexible app-based employment can be. Look at that hustle! You can make a quick buck with Lyft anytime, even when your cervix is dilating.

Lyft does not provide its drivers paid maternity leave or health insurance. (It offers to connect drivers with an insurance broker, and helpfully notes that "the Affordable Care Act offers many choices to make sure you're covered.") A third-party platform called SherpaShare, which some drivers use to track their earnings, found, in 2015, that Lyft drivers in Chicago net about eleven dollars per trip. Perhaps, as Lyft suggests, Mary kept accepting riders while experiencing contractions because "she was still a week away from her due date," or "she didn't believe she was going into labor yet." Or maybe Mary kept accepting riders because the gig economy has further normalized the circumstances in which earning an extra eleven dollars can feel more important than seeking out the urgent medical care that these quasi-employers do not sponsor. In the other version of Mary's story, she's an unprotected worker in precarious circumstances. "I can't pretend to know Mary's economic situation," Bryan Menegus at Gizmodo wrote, when the story first appeared. "Maybe she's an heiress who happens to love the freedom of chauffeuring strangers from place to place on

5

her own schedule. But that Lyft, for some reason, thought that this would reflect kindly on them is perhaps the most horrifying part."

It does require a fairly dystopian strain of doublethink[1] for a company to celebrate how hard and how constantly its employees must work to make a living, given that these companies are themselves setting the terms. And yet this type of faux-inspirational tale has been appearing more lately, both in corporate advertising and in the news. Fiverr, an online freelance marketplace that promotes itself as being for "the lean entrepreneur" — as its name suggests, services advertised on Fiverr can be purchased for as low as five dollars — recently attracted ire for an ad campaign called "In Doers We Trust." One ad, prominently displayed on some New York City subway cars, features a woman staring at the camera with a look of blank determination. "You eat a coffee for lunch," the ad proclaims. "You follow through on your follow through. Sleep deprivation is your drug of choice. You might be a doer."

Fiverr, which had raised a hundred and ten million dollars in venture capital by November 2015, has more about the "In Doers We Trust" campaign on its Web site. In one video, a peppy female voice over urges "doers" to "always be available," to think about beating "the trust-fund kids," and to pitch themselves to everyone they see, including their dentist. A Fiverr press release about "In Doers We Trust" states, "The campaign positions Fiverr to seize today's emerging Zeitgeist of entrepreneurial flexibility, rapid experimentation, and doing more with less. It pushes against bureaucratic overthinking, analysis-paralysis, and excessive whiteboarding." This is the jargon through which the essentially cannibalistic nature of the gig economy is dressed up as an aesthetic. No one wants to eat coffee for lunch or go on a bender of sleep

Jia Tolentino refers to this particular advertisement in her essay.

How would you characterize the intended audience for this ad? If you had not read Tolentino's argument, how would you react to it? Is Tolentino's interpretation of this ad is a fair one? Explain.

deprivation — or answer a call from a client while having sex, as recommended in the video. It's a stretch to feel cheerful at all about the Fiverr marketplace, perusing the thousands of listings of people who will record any song, make any happy-birthday video, or design any book cover for five dollars. I'd guess that plenty of the people who advertise services on Fiverr would accept some "whiteboarding" in exchange for employer-sponsored health insurance.

At the root of this is the American obsession with self-reliance, which makes it more acceptable to applaud an individual for working himself to death than to argue that an individual working himself to death is evidence of a flawed economic system. The contrast between the gig economy's rhetoric (everyone is always connecting, having fun, and killing it!) and the conditions that allow it to exist (a lack of dependable employment that

---

[1]The ability to accept multiple contradictory positions as simultaneously being true. The term was coined by George Orwell in his dystopian novel *1984*. —Eds.

www.polyp.org

How does this four-frame cartoon by Polyp, a British political cartoonist, depict working life in the present day? In what ways does this cartoon relate to the culture of the "gig economy" as Tolentino portrays it?

pays a living wage) makes this kink in our thinking especially clear. Human-interest stories about the beauty of some person standing up to the punishments of late capitalism are regular features in the news, too. I've come to detest the local-news set piece about the man who walks ten or eleven or twelve miles to work — a story that's been tiled from Oxford, Alabama; from Detroit, Michigan; from Plano, Texas. The story is always written as a tearjerker, with praise for the person's uncomplaining attitude; a cat is usually donated to the subject in the end. Never mentioned or even implied is the shamefulness of a job that doesn't permit a worker to afford his own commute.

There's a painful distance between the chipper narratives surrounding labor and success in America and the lived experience of workers. A similar conflict drove Nathanael West, in 1934, to publish the novel "A Cool Million," which satirized the Horatio Alger bootstrap fables that remained popular into the Great Depression.

"Alger is to America what Homer was to the Greeks," West once wrote. His protagonist in "A Cool Million," Lemuel Pitkin, is an innocent, energetic striver, tasked with saving his mother's house from foreclosure. A series of Alger-esque plot twists ensue. But Pitkin, rather than triumphing, ends up losing his teeth, his eye, his leg, his scalp, and finally his thumb. Morris Dickstein, in his book "Dancing in the Dark: A Cultural History of the Great Depression," notes, "The novel ends with Lem as a vaudeville clown being beaten nightly until he simply falls apart." A former President named Shagpoke Whipple gives a speech valorizing Pitkin's fate, extolling "the right of every American boy to go into the world and . . . make his fortune by industry." Whipple describes Pitkin's dismemberment — "lovingly," Dickstein adds — and tells his audience that, through Pitkin's hard work and enthusiastic martyrdom, "America became again American."

[2017]

EXPLORING THE TEXT

1. What is your response to Jia Tolentino's opening anecdote? Do you agree with her description of the Lyft campaign as "ghoulishly cheerful" (para. 4)? Why or why not?

2. How would you describe Tolentino's tone in paragraph 4? How does the rhetorical shift between paragraphs 4 and 5 affect the tone? How effectively does this shift serve Tolentino's purpose?

3. What are two reasons that Lyft suggests for Mary's continued acceptance of rides? What third reason does Tolentino proffer? How do they differ?

4. What is the rhetorical function of the quotation from Bryan Menegus in paragraph 5? How does it contribute to Tolentino's argument?

5. How would you characterize the appeal of Fiverr's "In Doers We Trust" campaign that Tolentino discusses in paragraph 6?

6. The language of Fiverr's marketing campaign is, Tolentino states, "the jargon through which the essentially cannibalistic nature of the gig economy is dressed up as an aesthetic" (para. 7). What does she mean by this? How does her word choice in this sentence reveal her attitude toward the gig economy in general?

7. In paragraph 8, Tolentino states that "the American obsession with self-reliance" is responsible for "mak[ing] it more acceptable to applaud an individual for working himself to death than [arguing] that an individual working himself to death is evidence of a flawed economic system." The American ideal of "self-reliance" is best expressed in Ralph Waldo Emerson's essay of that name, published in 1841. In it, Emerson states:

> Society everywhere is in conspiracy against the manhood of every one of its members. Society is a joint-stock company, in which the members agree, for the better securing of his bread to each shareholder, to surrender the liberty and culture of the eater. The virtue in most request

is conformity. Self-reliance is its aversion. It loves not realities and creators, but names and customs. Whoso would be a man must be a nonconformist. He who would gather immortal palms must not be hindered by the name of goodness, but must explore if it be goodness. Nothing is at last sacred but the integrity of your own mind.

What connection do you see between Emerson's idea as expressed above and Fiverr's marketing campaign? To what extent does Fiverr distort or manipulate Emerson's idea? To what extent does Tolentino?

8. What is the nature of the contrast that Tolentino explores in paragraph 8? What paradox underlies this paragraph? What else could be responsible for the phenomenon that Tolentino criticizes?

9. What rhetorical strategies does Tolentino employ to conclude her article? What is the effect of the example of Nathanael West's satirical novel, *A Cool Million*?

10. Identify Tolentino's major claim in this article. Provide a quotation, other than the title itself, that states this claim, as well as examples of evidence she uses to support it. How effective is her overall argument? Explain.

11. Based on this essay, how would you define the gig economy, as Jia Tolentino sees it? Do you agree with the stance she takes on its place in and effect on modern society? Explain.

from **House Rules**
How Homeownership Became the Engine of American Inequality

MATTHEW DESMOND

Matthew Desmond is a prize-winning sociologist who currently teaches at Harvard University. His first book, *On the Fireline* (2008), covered the lives of wildland firefighters. His next two books, *Racial Domination, Racial Progress* (2009) and *The Racial Order* (2015), were both coauthored with fellow scholar Mustafa Emirbayer. Desmond's most recent book, *Evicted* (2016), discusses the economics of urban housing and garnered Desmond the 2017 Pulitzer Prize for Nonfiction. The recipient of a 2015 MacArthur Fellowship, Desmond has also written for the *New York Times*, the *New Yorker*, and the *Chicago Tribune*. He wrote the following article for the *New York Times Magazine* in 2017.

The son of a minister, Ohene Asare grew up poor. His family immigrated from Ghana when he was 8 and settled down in West Bridgewater, Mass., a town 30 miles south of Boston, where he was one of the few black students at the local public school. "It was us and this Jewish family," Asare remembered. "It was a field day." His white classmates bullied him, sometimes using racial slurs. His father transferred Asare when he was 14 to Milton Academy, which awarded Asare a scholarship that covered tuition and board. His parents still had to take out loans worth about $20,000 for his living expenses. But the academy set Asare up for future success. He and his wife, Régine Jean-Charles, whom he got to know at Milton, are in their late 30s. She is a tenured professor of romance languages and literature at Boston College, and Asare is a founder of Aesara, a consulting and technology company.

Two years ago, the couple bought a new home. Set on a half-acre lot that backs up to conservation land in Milton, Mass., the 2,350-square-foot split-level has four bedrooms, three bathrooms, an open-concept kitchen and dining area, a finished basement, hardwood floors and beautiful touches throughout, like the Tennessee marble fireplace and hearth. It cost $665,000. "This is the nicest house I've ever lived in," Asare told me.

Asare and Jean-Charles have four children and earn roughly $290,000 a year, which puts them in the top 5 percent of household incomes in the country. After renting for the first years of their marriage, they participated in a home buyers' program administered by the nonprofit Neighborhood Assistance Corporation of America. The program allowed Asare and Jean-Charles to purchase their first home in 2009 for $360,000 with a 10 percent down payment, half of what is typically required. In 2015, they sold it for $430,000. There is a reason so many Americans choose to develop their net worth through homeownership: It is a proven wealth builder and savings compeller. The average homeowner boasts a net worth ($195,400) that is 36 times that of the average renter ($5,400).

Asare serves on the advisory board for HomeStart, a nonprofit focused on ending and preventing homelessness. Like most organizations, HomeStart is made up of people at various rungs on the economic ladder. Asare sits near the top; his salary exceeds that of anyone on staff at the nonprofit he helps advise. When Crisaliz Diaz was a staff member at HomeStart, she was at the other end of the ladder. She earned $38,000 a year, putting her near the bottom third of American household incomes. A 26-year-old Latina with thick-rimmed glasses, Diaz rents a small two-bedroom apartment in Braintree, Mass., an outer suburb of Boston. Her two sons, Xzayvior and Mayson — Zay and May, she calls them — share a room plastered with Lego posters and Mickey Mouse stickers. Her apartment is spare and clean, with ceiling tiles you can push up and views of the parking lot and busy street.

When Diaz moved in four years ago, the rent was $1,195 a month, heat included, but her landlord has since raised the rent to $1,385 a month, which takes 44 percent of her paycheck. Even with child-support payments and side jobs, she still doesn't bring in enough to pay her regular bills. She goes without a savings account and regularly relies on credit cards to buy toilet paper and soap. "There's no stop to it," she told me. "It's just a consistent thing."

Diaz receives no housing assistance. She has applied to several programs, but nothing has come through. The last time Boston accepted new applications for rental-assistance Section 8 vouchers was nine years ago, when for a few precious weeks you were allowed to place your name on a very long waiting list. Boston is not atypical in that way. In Los Angeles, the estimated wait time for a Section 8 voucher is 11 years. In Washington, the waiting list for housing vouchers is closed indefinitely, and over 40,000 people have applied for public housing alone. While many Americans assume that most poor families live in subsidized housing, the opposite is true; nationwide, only one in four households that qualifies for rental assistance receives it. Most are like Diaz, struggling without government help in the private rental market, where housing costs claim larger and larger chunks of their income.

Almost a decade removed from the foreclosure crisis that began in 2008, the nation is facing one of the worst affordable-housing shortages in generations. The standard of "affordable" housing is that which costs roughly 30 percent or less of a family's income. Because of rising housing costs and stagnant wages, slightly more than half of all poor renting families in the country spend more than 50 percent of their income on housing costs, and at least one in four spends more than 70 percent. Yet America's national housing policy gives affluent homeowners large benefits; middle-class homeowners, smaller benefits; and most renters, who are disproportionately poor, nothing. It is difficult to think of another social policy that more successfully multiplies America's inequality in such a sweeping fashion.

Consider Asare and Diaz. As a homeowner, Asare benefits from tax breaks that Diaz does not, the biggest being the mortgage-interest deduction — or MID, in wonk-speak. All homeowners in America may deduct mortgage interest on their first and second homes. In 2015, Asare and Jean-Charles claimed $21,686 in home interest and other real estate deductions, which saved them $470 a month. That's roughly 15 percent of Diaz's monthly income. That same year, the federal government dedicated nearly $134 billion to homeowner subsidies. The MID accounted for the biggest chunk of the total, $71 billion, with real estate tax deductions, capital gains exclusions and other expenditures accounting for the rest. That number, $134 billion, was larger than the entire budgets of the Departments of Education, Justice and Energy combined for that year. It is a figure that exceeds half the entire gross domestic product of countries like Chile, New Zealand and Portugal.

Recently, Gary Cohn, the chief economic adviser to President Trump, heralded his boss's first tax plan as a "once-in-a-generation opportunity to do something really big." And indeed, Trump's plan represents a radical transformation in how we will fund the government, with its biggest winners being corporations and wealthy families. But no one in his administration, and only a small (albeit growing) group of people in either party, is pushing to reform what may very well be the most regressive piece of social policy in America. Perhaps that's because the mortgage-interest deduction overwhelmingly benefits the sorts of upper-middle-class voters who make up the donor base of both parties and who generally fail to acknowledge themselves to be beneficiaries of federal largess. "Today, as in the past," writes the historian Molly Michelmore in her book "Tax and Spend," "most of the recipients of federal aid are not the suspect 'welfare queens' of the popular imagination but rather middle-class homeowners, salaried professionals and retirees." A 15-story public housing tower and a mortgaged suburban home are both government-subsidized, but only one looks (and feels) that way. It is only by recognizing this fact that we can begin to understand why there is so much poverty in the United States today.

◆ ◆ ◆

When we think of entitlement programs, Social Security and Medicare immediately come to mind. But by any fair standard, the holy trinity of United States social policy should also include the mortgage-interest deduction — an enormous benefit that has also become politically untouchable. 10

The MID came into being in 1913, not to spur homeownership but simply as part of a general policy allowing businesses to deduct interest payments from loans. At that time, most Americans didn't own their homes and only the rich paid income tax, so the effects of the mortgage deduction on the nation's tax proceeds were fairly trivial.

That began to change in the second half of the 20th century, though, because of two huge transformations in American life. First, income tax was converted from an elite tax to a mass tax: In 1932, the Bureau of Internal Revenue (precursor to the I.R.S.) processed fewer than two million individual tax returns, but 11 years later, it processed over 40 million. At the same time, the federal government began subsidizing homeownership through large-scale initiatives like the G.I. Bill and mortgage insurance. Homeownership grew rapidly in the postwar period, and so did the MID.

By the time policy makers realized how extravagant the MID had become, it was too late to do much about it without facing significant backlash. Millions of voters had begun to count on getting that money back. Even President Ronald Reagan, who oversaw drastic cuts to housing programs benefiting low-income Americans, let the MID be. Subsequent politicians followed suit, often eager to discuss reforms to Social Security and Medicare but reluctant to touch the MID, even as the program continued to grow more costly: By 2019, MID expenditures are expected to exceed $96 billion.

"Once we're in a world with a MID," says Todd Sinai, a professor of real estate and public policy at the University of Pennsylvania's Wharton School, "it is very hard to get to a world without the MID." That's in part because the benefit helps to prop up home values. It's impossible to say how much, but a widely cited 1996 study estimated that eliminating the MID and property-tax deductions would result in a 13 to 17 percent reduction in housing prices nationwide, though that estimate varies widely by region and more recent analyses have found smaller effects. The MID allows home buyers to collect more after-tax savings if they take on more mortgage debt, which incentivizes them to pay more for properties than they could have otherwise. By inflating home values, the MID benefits Americans who already own homes — and makes joining their ranks harder.

The owner-renter divide is as salient as any other in this nation, and this divide is a historical result of statecraft designed to protect and promote inequality. Ours was not always a nation of homeowners; the New Deal fashioned it so, particularly through the G.I. Bill of Rights. The G.I.

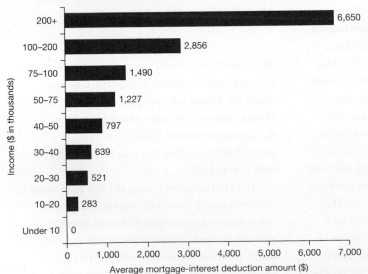

Average Mortgage-Interest Deduction by Income

Income ($ in thousands):

Income bracket	Average mortgage-interest deduction amount ($)
200+	6,650
100–200	2,856
75–100	1,490
50–75	1,227
40–50	797
30–40	639
20–30	521
10–20	283
Under 10	0

Data from U.S. Senate Joint Committee on Taxation, "Present Law, Data, and Analysis Relating to Tax Incentives for Homeownership" (2011).

This bar graph charts the average value of the mortgage-interest deduction (MID) by income bracket. **What conclusions can you draw from the data presented here? Where in Desmond's essay would this image have the most rhetorical impact? Explain.**

Bill was enormous, consuming 15 percent of the federal budget in 1948, and remains unmatched by any other single social policy in the scope and depth of its provisions, which included things like college tuition benefits and small-business loans. The G.I. Bill brought a rollout of veterans' mortgages, padded with modest interest rates and down payments waived for loans up to 30 years. Returning soldiers lined up and bought new homes by the millions. In the years immediately following World War II, veterans' mortgages accounted for over 40 percent of all home loans.

But both in its design and its application, the G.I. Bill excluded a large number of citizens. To get the New Deal through Congress, Franklin Roosevelt needed to appease the Southern arm of the Democratic Party. So he acquiesced when Congress blocked many nonwhites, particularly African-Americans, from accessing his newly created ladders of opportunity. Farm work, housekeeping and other jobs disproportionately staffed by African-Americans were omitted from programs like Social Security and unemployment insurance. Local Veterans Affairs centers and other entities loyal to Jim Crow did their parts as well, systematically denying nonwhite veterans access to the G.I. Bill. If those veterans got past the V.A., they still had to contend with the banks, which denied loan applications in nonwhite neighborhoods because the Federal Housing Administration refused to insure mortgages there. From 1934 to 1968, the official F.H.A. policy of redlining made homeownership virtually impossible in black communities. "The consequences proved profound," writes the historian Ira Katznelson in his perfectly titled book, "When Affirmative Action Was White." "By 1984, when G.I. Bill mortgages had mainly matured, the median white household had a net worth of $39,135; the comparable figure for black households was only $3,397, or just 9 percent of white holdings. Most of this difference was accounted for by the absence of homeownership."

15   This legacy has been passed down to subsequent generations. Today a majority of first-time home buyers get down-payment help from their parents; many of those parents pitch in by refinancing their own homes. As black homeowners, Asare and Jean-Charles are exceptions to the national trend: While most white families own a home, a majority of black and Latino families do not. Differences in homeownership rates remain the prime driver of the nation's racial wealth gap. In 2011, the median white household had a net worth of $111,146, compared with $7,113 for the median black household and $8,348 for the median Hispanic household. If black and Hispanic families owned homes at rates similar to whites, the racial wealth gap would be reduced by almost a third.

Racial exclusion was Roosevelt's first concession to pass the New Deal; his second, to avoid a tax revolt, was to rely on regressive and largely hidden payroll taxes to fund generous social-welfare programs. A result, the historian Michelmore observes, is that we "never asked ordinary taxpayers to pay for the economic security many soon came to expect as a matter of right." In providing millions of middle-class families stealth benefits, the American government rendered itself invisible to those families, who soon came to see their success as wholly self-made. We forgot because we were not meant to remember. . . .

◆ ◆ ◆

Today as in years past, MID reform is generally considered a lost cause. There have been gestures at reform — Representative Keith Ellison, a Minnesota Democrat, keeps reintroducing a bill that would replace the MID with a 15 percent tax credit on interest paid up to $500,000 — but they have gone nowhere. . . .

Capping the MID at $500,000 would have virtually no effect on homeownership rates. And according to the economist Glaeser, it would have only "modest effects on home prices" in supply-constrained cities like San Francisco and virtually no effect in cities with plenty of available land, like Houston. "Most homeowners wouldn't even feel it," Glaeser says, pointing out further that encouraging homeownership typically means moving people from multifamily buildings to single-family homes, which increases traffic congestion and pollution. But capping the MID at half a million dollars could cause properties in the $625,000 to $1.25 million range to drop in value.

Would we be O.K. with that? Would we support 20 reform that provided desperately needed housing relief to millions of low-income Americans if it meant that the net worth of those who owned expensive homes took a hit? The answer is almost certainly no, at least for owners of houses valued north of $500,000. Wealth granted by a bizarre government subsidy is still wealth, and once people have it, they'd prefer to keep it. When it comes to public housing for the rich, it becomes hard to break the cycle of welfare dependency. It's why some Democratic leaders who represent districts with high housing prices, like Representative

Nancy Pelosi (San Francisco) and Senator Chuck Schumer (New York), have been outspoken critics of MID reform, even if they are consistent backers of other equality-promoting initiatives.

We tend to speak about the poor as if they didn't live in the same society, as if our gains and their losses weren't intertwined. Conservatives explain poverty by pointing to "individual factors," like bad decisions or the rise of single-parent families; liberals refer to "structural causes," like the decline of manufacturing or the historical legacies of racial discrimination. Usually pitted against each other, each perspective serves a similar function: letting us off the hook by asserting that there is a deep-rooted, troubling problem — more than one in six Americans does not make enough to afford basic necessities — that most of us bear no responsibility for.

It's around this point that the conversation gets snagged in the weeds with questions about home prices, political ramifications or the

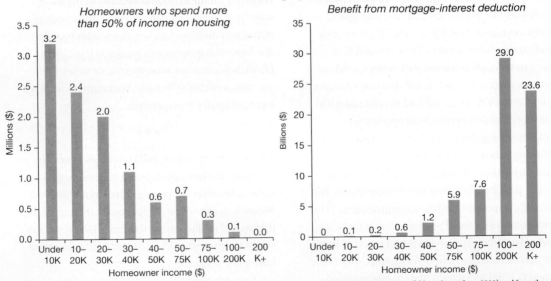

Who Benefits from the Mortgage-Interest Deduction?

Data from U.S. Senate Joint Committee on Taxation, "Estimates of Federal Tax Expenditures for Fiscal Years 2012–2017," (data shown from 2012) and from the U.S. Census Bureau American Housing Survey.

This figure shows the percentage of households who benefit from the MID alongside the housing cost burden, derived from annual income statistics.

How does this information correlate with the evidence Desmond presents in his essay?

administrative hurdles of reform — escape routes that allow us to lose sight of people like Cris Diaz, low-income renters who are not entitled to any housing assistance and who are giving most of their income to landlords and utility companies. To drive down poverty and promote economic mobility, the United States will need to make a major investment in affordable housing. You don't need to reform the MID to pay for that — there are plenty of other ways to raise revenue — but you have to pay for it somehow. Whatever our position on homeowner tax benefits, we should have an answer for people like Diaz.

Trump's preliminary 2018 budget includes a 13.2 percent reduction to the Department of Housing and Urban Development and the elimination of the Interagency Council on Homelessness, cuts that will almost certainly result in the loss of hundreds of thousands of housing vouchers and leave more families rent-burdened and homeless. President Barack Obama's 2017 budget proposal estimated that it would take $1 billion a year over the next 10 years to eliminate family homelessness in America — not decrease it or slice it in half, but end it. That's less than 1 percent of what we currently spend on homeowner subsidies. And yet a bill designed to provide every child in America with a home was pronounced dead on arrival in Congress. Up to this point, bills proposing modest reforms to the mortgage-interest deduction have met the same fate.

Poverty and homelessness are political creations. Their amelioration is within our grasp and budget. But those of us most likely to vote and contribute to political campaigns are least likely to support MID reform — either because it wouldn't affect our lives or because it would, by asking us to take less so that millions of Americans could be given the opportunity to climb out of poverty. It's just that we usually don't dial our elected officials when our less-fortunate neighbors are hurting, because we are not.

And yet over the course of our history, there have been times when Americans embraced a ²⁵ politics of sacrifice. During World War II, families volunteered to pay more taxes, ration food and give blood to serve a higher purpose. And even today, in what can feel like an age of insecurity and self-preservation, some Americans have shown a willingness to take a personal financial hit to promote social mobility and equality. Take the people of Seattle: For 36 years, they have agreed to be taxed more to raise revenue for affordable-housing programs. Last August, 70 percent of Seattle voters agreed to the largest housing levy yet, one expected to raise $290 million over the next seven years. Contributions to the levy are based on home values; a family living in a $400,000 home (the city's median value in 2015) pays an additional $122 a year in taxes. With that money, Seattle will fund emergency rental assistance, loans to first-time home buyers and the construction of housing units that must remain affordable for at least 50 years. Previous housing levies have generated over 13,000 affordable apartment units and enabled 900 low-income families to buy homes. The 2016 Housing Levy will do more because the residents of Seattle decided to invest in economic diversity and residential stability, sacrificing a pinch to help those in need.

Asare and Jean-Charles would welcome MID reform, even if it meant that they would have less in the bank at the end of the year. "There are people who sacrificed for me to be here," Asare told me. One of them was a boy named Chris Jackson, whom Asare met during his tormented years in the West Bridgewater school system. When Asare wouldn't fight back, Jackson, a fellow black student, would stick up for him. "I watched him fight and fight, get into trouble," Asare remembers. "And I'd be like, 'No, stop.' But he wouldn't, because what was right was right." Asare paused to collect himself, a hand fingering the space above his freshly shaved head. "That kind of compassion, that kind of brotherhood, is what I would ask of people: that we don't give according to what people are willing to receive;

seeing connections

The photographs and captions shown here both appeared with Desmond's original article in the *New York Times* magazine. Look carefully at each image and read each caption closely before answering the following questions.

1. **Compare and contrast the two photographs. What details in each are noteworthy?**

2. **What argumentative value does each photograph and its original caption lend to Desmond's article?**

3. **What considerations would you say the *New York Times* magazine editors may have taken into account in choosing these particular photographs to accompany Desmond's article?**

Damon Casarez/Redux

OHENE ASARE AND RÉGINE JEAN-CHARLES
  Homeowners
LOCATION Milton, Mass.
OCCUPATION Asare is an owner of the consulting and technology company Aesara; Jean-Charles is a tenured professor at Boston College.
DWELLING TYPE Single-family house
BEDROOMS Four
OCCUPANTS Seven (the couple and their four children, Bediako, 9; Kwaku 8; Farah-Adwoa, 3; and Afia, 1; and an au pair)
PRICE OF HOME $665,000, in 2015
DOWN PAYMENT $150,000 ("We sold a house," Asare

says, "and we also had savings from stock sales.")
TOTAL HOUSEHOLD INCOME $290,000
MONTHLY MORTGAGE PAYMENT $3,540
AVERAGE MONTHLY EXPENSES $2,800 (including after-school program and child care)

ASARE SAYS: "It's a nice neighborhood. We know our neighbors. It's all people who have been there a while. They're tradesmen, but they've been there forever. There are no chain fences; the grass rolls one house to the next. People work together. We all tapped maple syrup on our trees this year. Everyone is into keeping the property value high, and there's almost a pressure to keep it up."

Damon Casarez/Redux

CRISALIZ DIAZ Renter

LOCATION Braintree, Mass.

OCCUPATION Formerly a housing advocate at the nonprofit HomeStart, Diaz got a new job as a leasing consultant this year, but she was recently let go.

DWELLING TYPE Apartment

BEDROOMS Two

OCCUPANTS Three (Diaz and her two sons, Xzayvior, 8, and Mayson, 3)

TOTAL HOUSEHOLD INCOME $38,000 at HomeStart

MONTHLY RENT Previously $1,385; recently renewed at $1,450.

AVERAGE MONTHLY EXPENSES $1,500 (including after-school program and day care)

DIAZ SAYS: "I'm worried about eviction, because technically if you put my income to my cost of living, I have so many expenses. If we have to leave, we would have to stay with family. I'm not too prideful for a shelter — I grew up in a shelter system — but I don't want my boys to grow up like that. I'd rather stay with family and explain to my boys that Mommy just needs to get on her feet. People who are living in a middle-to-lower-class system, there's no progressing. You're stuck in that system. I don't have subsidies. I work, but I feel stuck in this cycle and can barely make ends meet."

we give according to the standard for what they should have."

◆ ◆ ◆

In February, Diaz's landlord increased her rent by $65 a month, to $1,450. The timing couldn't have been worse: Diaz had recently taken a new job as a leasing consultant at a small property management firm. The pay wasn't better, but she had reduced her commute to 30 minutes from two hours. "I get to see my kids before it gets dark," she said. But transitioning between the jobs caused her to go without income for

a couple of weeks. With no savings to fall back on, she couldn't pay the increased rent and was summoned to eviction court. A month later, Diaz walked through the metal detector at the Quincy District Courthouse. "Where do you go for evictions?" she asked a clerk, who pointed to a crowd of tenants shuffling toward the same room. Some wore heavy-heeled work boots and worn jeans; some leaned on canes and walkers; some bounced babies. Diaz took a seat on a long wooden bench and looked at the clock. She had had to use her lunch break to make court and only had 45 minutes.

Once a rarity in America, eviction has become commonplace in our cities, disrupting families, schools and entire neighborhoods. Forty people a day are evicted in Milwaukee; each day in New York City brings 60 marshal evictions. An eviction could plunge Diaz and her boys into homelessness and poverty. Studies have found that evicted families lose not only their homes but their jobs, possessions and neighbors too; they relocate to substandard housing in distressed communities; they have higher rates of depression and suicide. Even if poor families avoid eviction, they still suffer, because so much of their money goes to housing costs, forcing them to buy fewer school supplies, clothes, books — and food.

In some markets, there are virtually no affordable units left. The median annual rent for a two-bedroom apartment is currently $39,600 in Boston, $49,200 in New York City and $54,720 in San Francisco. Families priced out of large cities have moved to smaller ones, and now those cities are experiencing some of the steepest rent increases in the nation. The poor used to live on the other side of the tracks. Now they live in different towns and counties entirely.

And yet we continue to give the most help to those who least need it — affluent home-owners — while providing nothing to most rent-burdened tenants. If this is our design, our social contract, then we should at least own up to it; we should at least stand up and profess, "Yes, this is the kind of nation we want." Before us, there are two honest choices: We can endorse this inequality-maximizing arrangement, or we can reject it. What we cannot do is look a mother like Diaz in the face and say, "We'd love to help you, but we just can't afford to." Because that is, quite simply, a lie.

After her name was called, Diaz stepped outside the courtroom to talk with her landlord's attorney, a white man in wire glasses. She had secured emergency assistance from the state. It wasn't enough. But the lawyer told Diaz that if she "zeroed out" by next month, paying all her back rent and April's rent in full, he would dismiss the case. Diaz wrote out a check for $583 — a start, and what amounted to $357 less than what Asare and Jean-Charles receive from the MID in two months — and raced back to work. In April, she was let go.

Thinking about the long, hard road ahead for Diaz, I remembered a conversation I had with her six months earlier. Around her small dining table, Diaz and I had calculated her monthly budget, which left her with –$221 after all the bills were paid. The process seemed to reduce her to a sadder, emptied-out version of herself. "Eventually I'm going to have to figure something out," she said softly, "whether it's a second job or a third job. I don't know."

I looked down at my empty plate, smeared with tomato sauce from the meatball sub Diaz had made me. "Do you know what the mortgage-interest deduction is?" I asked.

"I don't," she said. "I'm sorry."

After I explained what it is, she asked, "Why don't they spend it on lower-income housing?" I shrugged. After a moment, I asked, "What would you do if you only had to pay 30 percent of your income on rent?"

Diaz looked around. Her eyes paused on one of Zay's homework assignments stuck to the refrigerator. Titled "Someone Special," its words wiggled forward in a child's handwriting: "My mom is special because she helps me figure out addition and subtraction. We always cook together. We cook some spaghetti." On the other side of the fridge, held up by a clown-fish magnet, was a bill from the Massachusetts Registry of Motor Vehicles.

"That would be life," she said.

[2017]

EXPLORING THE TEXT

1. What is the purpose of Matthew Desmond's opening anecdote about Ohene Asare? How does it prepare the reader for what follows?

2. What is the effect of the information that concludes paragraph 3? Did you think that the difference between the average homeowner and the average renter could be that great? Why or why not?

3. Desmond writes that "many Americans assume that most poor families live in subsidized housing" (para. 6). Do you think that is true? Did you assume that? How does such a statement affect Desmond's ethos?

4. Reread paragraphs 7–9 carefully. What, according to Desmond, is the mortgage-interest deduction, or MID? How does he characterize it? Cite two examples where he makes a strong claim about it. How effectively does he support those claims?

5. Why, according to Desmond, has the MID been "politically untouchable" (para. 10)? Should it be so? Why or why not?

6. In paragraph 13, Desmond states: "The MID allows home buyers to collect more after-tax savings if they take on more mortgage debt, which incentivizes them to pay more for properties than they could have otherwise." Is Desmond claiming that our government is encouraging debt? Explain.

7. How do Desmond's references to the GI Bill, the New Deal, and economic statistics in paragraphs 14–16 contribute to his overall argument? What function do they serve?

8. What are the "stealth benefits" that Desmond discusses in paragraph 17? Why does he use that phrase to characterize them?

9. Desmond suggests that when we hear the word, "welfare," we think of the poor. To what extent does he characterize the MID as a form of welfare for the rich? Explain.

10. What is Desmond's attitude toward liberals' and conservatives' positions on the MID? Why is it that resistance to MID reform should come from both sides of the political spectrum?

11. What is the effect of the "escape routes" that Desmond discusses in paragraph 22?

12. Desmond makes a strong claim when he asserts that "poverty and homelessness are political creations" (para. 24). How effectively does he support that claim?

13. What is the purpose of the rhetorical shift between paragraphs 24 and 25? How does Desmond use it to appeal to the reader?

14. Are you surprised at the figures in paragraph 29? How might the MID affect those figures?

15. How do you respond to the challenge that Desmond proposes in paragraph 30?

16. Desmond begins and ends his articles with anecdotes. How would you compare and contrast the two? How do they contribute to Desmond's argument?

17. Were you surprised to learn that Diaz did not even know what the MID is? What does that suggest about the nature of the MID, and the need for reform?

18. Identify places in the essay where Desmond makes claims of fact, value, and policy. How effectively does he move through all three?

VISUAL TEXTS

Night of the Rich

DIEGO RIVERA

Diego Rivera (1886–1957) was a prominent Mexican painter whose large frescoes helped establish the Mexican mural movement. Rivera studied art at the Academy of San Carlos in Mexico City, and then later in Madrid and Paris, where he witnessed the beginning of Cubism in paintings by artists like Pablo Picasso. He returned to Mexico in 1921 and painted murals through a government-sponsored program. In 1923, Rivera joined the Mexican Communist Party, and his murals thereafter tended to reflect revolutionary and communist themes. Rivera was also known for his tumultuous personal life. He was still married to the novelist and model Guadalupe Marín when he met art student Frida Kahlo, whom he married in 1929. Rivera and Kahlo, who herself would become an extremely influential painter and feminist icon, divorced in 1939 and remarried in 1940. Rivera's large and distinctive murals can be found in cities such as Mexico City, San Francisco, Detroit, and New York City, and are known for their use of storytelling, character, and controversial communist, socialist, and atheist themes.

EXPLORING THE TEXT

1. What types of people are represented in the mural? How can you tell one type from another?

2. Consider the shape of this mural. Why do you think Diego Rivera chose it? How does it help communicate his message?

3. What argument does "Night of the Rich" make? What evidence does Rivera provide to support it?

4. Following a revolutionary period in Mexico (1910–1919), Diego Rivera was one of several artists commissioned by the Mexican government to create murals that would show a sense of pride in the new national identity. How do this mural's images idealize aspects of Mexico that might have been previously ignored?

5. This mural is located in the Ministry of Education in Mexico City. The text above the mural is believed to come from a Spanish ballad entitled "Asi Sera La Revolucion Proletaria" by Jose Guerrero and, loosely translated, means that the fruits of the orchard are worth more than money. How does the mural illustrate those words?

[1928]

Panama Papers

HAZEL FLOREZ

Hazel Florez is a London-based artist whose work blends elements of folk art, symbolism, and surrealism with current events, philosophy, and literature. Her pieces are hand-drawn and often combine a range of media. The title *Panama Papers* refers to the 2015 scandal in which 11.5 million documents containing private financial and legal information for wealthy politicians and public figures around the world were anonymously leaked from a Panamanian law firm.

Panama Papers, 2016, (pen, pencil, collage on card)/Florez, Hazel/Hazel Florez/
Private Collection/Bridgeman Images

[2016]

EXPLORING THE TEXT

1. This piece contains vivid iconography, such as the two Panama hats. Look for other familiar or symbolic images. What purpose does each serve? How are they connected to the revelations of the Panama Papers? How does Hazel Florez comment on those revelations?

2. This piece was created with pen and ink, pencil, and collage. Why do you think Florez chose the media she did?

3. What do you think the two islands represent? What does the imagery of the World Bank symbols over the islands suggest?

4. How does the slogan at the bottom — "MAN WAS BORN FREE AND EVERYWHERE

HE IS IN CHAINS . . ." — add to Florez's argument?

5. According to Florez, the center of this piece shows a "winged beast with three human eyes." She identifies the beast as what professor Richard Peet called, in his book by the same name, an "Unholy Trinity" of the World Bank, the World Trade Organization, and the International Monetary Fund. Peet has criticized these institutions for implementing programs beneficial to corporations and investors, but disastrous for poor countries. How does Florez's portrayal of the "Unholy Trinity" in this work offer her view of these institutions?

The Cost of College

Each of the following texts presents a viewpoint on the cost of a college education in America.

SOURCES

1 **Sara Goldrick-Rab and Nancy Kendall** / *Make the First Two Years of College Free: A Cost-Effective Way to Expand Access to Higher Education in America*
2 **Matt Bruenig** / *The Case Against Free College*
3 **The Value of a College Education** and **The Effect of Student Loan Debt on Major Life Decisions** (graphs)
4 **Bernie Sanders** / *Make College Free for All*
5 **Keith Ellison** / *The Argument for Tuition-Free College*
6 **Thomas Sowell** / *No Way That Going to College Can, or Should Be, Free*
7 **Anya Kamenetz** / *Is Free College Really Free?*

After you have read, studied, and synthesized these pieces, enter the Conversation by responding to one of the prompts on pages 857–58.

Make the First Two Years of College Free
A Cost-Effective Way to Expand Access to Higher Education in America

SARA GOLDRICK-RAB AND NANCY KENDALL

Sara Goldrick-Rab is a professor of higher education policy and sociology at Temple University, and Nancy Kendall is an associate professor of education policy studies at the University of Wisconsin-Madison. The following article was published in 2014.

Almost half a century ago, the U.S. federal government expanded financial aid to college students to make college more affordable — but today the odds of getting a degree are more tightly linked to family income than ever before. Getting a college degree remains a good investment, but the current distribution of federal and state financial aid dollars leaves many families of modest means out in the cold. Between 1992 and 2004, the odds that a high school graduate who took at least Algebra II would decide not to go to college went up among all income-groups except the very wealthiest. Sadly, students from families of modest means have also become more likely to drop out from public colleges and universities — leaving with debts, not degrees.

The fact that so many students cannot realize their full potential is a loss for them and also for the country and the world. Clearly, it is time for the United States to refocus public financial aid efforts — and the most straightforward change would be to make the first two years free for all qualified students at community colleges and public universities. This would control rising costs and improve access to higher education for the majority of Americans.

Why U.S. Financial Aid Fails to Make College Affordable

How can it be that growing amounts of financial aid leave college unaffordable for so many? In the current system, aid based on economic need or academic merit goes to students who choose to pursue associate or bachelors' degrees at institutions of all kinds, public, private, and for-profit. Over time, costs of attendance in all sectors have skyrocketed, but this is particularly true in the for-profit sector where students are encouraged to make heavy use of public aid but often stop their studies short of a degree. Financial aid does not cover as much of the costs as it once did. What is more, even though students from the poorest families are likely to receive grants rather than loans, these students still often end up paying a lot themselves, carrying a proportionately higher burden of costs than students from better-off families.

The bottom line is that the U.S. federal government thinly spreads a financial aid pool of about $170 billion a year across many types of students and schools, and in the end leaves many low-income families paying too much. Such families shell out about 40% of family income for a member to attend community college, and for four-year colleges the bill can add up to 59% of a low-income family's earnings. Even a middle-class family earning $81,000 a year may be asked to spend or borrow a quarter of that annual income to finance one child's attendance at a public four-year university. The cost is far higher for most private colleges.

Not only do families face high costs, it is not easy to obtain aid. People must navigate through a highly bureaucratic and time-consuming process with repeated applications and verifications mandated by multiple layers of government. Students and families often come away unhappy and with too little to pay for college expenses without

working very long hours or racking up startlingly high debts. The experience heightens distrust of government and educational institutions.

Doing More by Covering Costs for Two College Years

Financial support for college attendance in America does not have to be so inefficient, poorly targeted, and frustrating. With the same resources already being spent, the U.S. federal and state governments could work together to create a far simpler approach with much better outcomes for students, families, and the country. By focusing public resources on helping qualified students complete their first two years at public colleges and universities, a simple message could be delivered to students from all family backgrounds: If you earn your high school degree, the country will ensure that you can obtain a 13th and 14th year of education at no cost to you beyond doing a modest amount of work while you attend college.

This plan would allow existing financial aid resources to be effectively redeployed to help all qualified students go to college. Ensuring broader access would help the United States regain a leading role in college attainment—something the country badly needs to do to ensure an educated citizenry and a well-prepared work force.

Here are the specifics of how the two-year college plan would work:

- All eligible students would be able to attend any public two- or four-year college or university to which they could gain admittance at no financial cost for the first two years.
- The federal government would redeploy existing financial aid funds to cover first and second-year tuition for all students, and to provide additional funding for colleges that do a good job of educating relatively large numbers of low-income students.
- Per-student funding would be set at a higher level than the average tuition currently charged by community colleges, and at just a slightly lower level than the average charged by four-year

5

public colleges and universities. Institutions participating in the public program would not be able to charge tuition or additional fees to the covered first and second-year students.

- The states would also contribute to the program by redirecting financial aid funds to cover the cost of books and supplies for first and second-year students.
- Students' living expenses would be covered through a public stipend equal to fifteen hours a week of employment at a living wage in the given local area, supplemented by federal work-study funding and access to federal

loans equaling up to five hours a week of employment.

The appeal of this new model for U.S. public financial aid to college students is that it would redirect public financial aid resources to control costs, increase quality, decrease achievement gaps, and improve graduation rates by working in partnership with the community colleges and public universities that serve the majority of low- and middle-income students. The system would become much more transparent and cost-effective for everyone — and above all for working families and U.S. taxpayers.

QUESTIONS

1. What do you think is the most compelling fact included in the first paragraph? What does that information suggest about higher education in America?

2. Summarize why "growing amounts of financial aid leave college unaffordable," as Sara Goldrick-Rab and Nancy Kendall put it in paragraph 3. What do you think is the most serious reason?

3. How would the plan put forth by Goldrick-Rab and Kendall simplify economic cost and encourage college enrollment and completion?

4. How do the authors define "qualified students" in paragraphs 6 and 7? Do you agree with their idea of what it means to be qualified? Explain.

5. Which of the specifics of the plan, designated by bullet points, do you find most compelling? Why?

6. The authors conclude with four reasons that their model would appeal to Americans. Rank them in order of importance. Why would you prioritize them in that order?

7. Goldrick-Rab and Kendall assert that their plan would be "cost effective for everyone — and above all for working families and U.S. taxpayers" (para. 9). Can you imagine any possible objections to such a plan? What are they, and who might voice those objections?

2   The Case Against Free College

MATT BRUENIG

Matt Bruening covers politics and economics on his blog and in the *Washington Post*, the *Los Angeles Times*, the *Atlantic*, and the *New Republic*, among other publications. Bruening wrote the following article in 2015 for an issue of *Dissent*, a quarterly journal about politics and culture first established in 1954.

In the United States, as in much of the rest of the world, college students receive three kinds of public benefits: tuition subsidies, living grants, and public loans. Through various combinations

of this benefit troika, almost all students are able to finance their college education. Some on the left are very unhappy with the precise mix of student benefits currently on offer. Student debt activists, among others, complain that tuition subsidies and living grants make up too little of the student benefit bundle, while public loans make up too much of it.

Recently, this complaint has begun to coalesce into a number of movements and proposals for "free college." I put the phrase in quotes because it means different things to different people. For some, "free college" means subsidizing tuition to zero. For others, it means subsidizing tuition to zero and providing living grants high enough to completely cover room and board. For still others, it appears to mean putting in place some mix of means-tested tuition subsidies, living grants, and even subsidized work-study jobs that, combined with expected parental assistance, allow nearly all students to leave college with little to no debt.

One could write at great length about these different conceptions of "free" and the policy proposals that have formed around them. For instance, since people who do not attend college also have housing and food costs, is it really correct to say room and board is a cost of attending college? Why do none of these conceptions consider as a cost of college all of the potential wages students forego by choosing to study rather than work? Does parental assistance with college really help to make it free or is it more properly understood as a family wealth transfer that students then pay towards their higher education?

Of greater importance than all of those questions, however, is the more basic question about the fairness of free college as an idea. Those clamoring for free college make normative claims about the nature of a just and good society. As currently argued, however, these claims are largely uncompelling. Without a dramatic overhaul of how we understand student benefits, making college more or entirely free would most likely boost the wealth of college attendees without securing any important egalitarian gains.

The main problem with free college is that most students come from disproportionately well-off backgrounds and already enjoy disproportionately well-off futures, which makes them relatively uncompelling targets for public transfers. At age nineteen, only around 20 percent of children from the poorest 2 percent of families in the country attend college. For the richest 2 percent of families, the same number is around 90 percent. In between these two extremes, college attendance rates climb practically straight up the income ladder: the richer your parents are, the greater the likelihood that you are in college at age nineteen. The relatively few poor kids who do attend college heavily cluster in two-year community colleges and cheaper, less selective four-year colleges, while richer kids are likely to attend more expensive four-year institutions. At public colleges (the type we'd likely make free), students from the poorest fourth of the population currently pay no net tuition at either two-year or four-year institutions, while also receiving an average of $3,080 and $2,320 respectively to offset some of their annual living expenses. Richer students currently receive much fewer tuition and living grant benefits.

Given these class-based differences in attendance levels, institutional selection, and current student benefit levels, making college free for everyone would almost certainly mean giving far more money to students from richer families than from poorer ones. Of course, providing more generous student benefits might alter these class-based skews a bit by encouraging more poor and middle-class people to go to college or to attend more expensive institutions. But even reasonably accounting for those kinds of responses, the primary result of such increased student benefit generosity would be to fill the pockets of richer students and their families.

Student benefit campaigners tend not to focus on these sorts of distributive questions, preferring instead to gesture towards a supposed student debt crisis to prove that those who attended college really are a hurting class needing higher benefits. While there are certain

5

extreme cases of students with very high debts, and certain college sectors such as for-profits that are truly immiserating specific groups of students, the reality remains that college graduates are generally on track for much better financial outcomes than non-attendees. Even in the wake of the Great Recession, which hit young people harder than anyone else, those with bachelor's degrees had median personal incomes $17,500 higher than young high school graduates. Just one year of this income premium would be enough to wipe out the median debt of a public four-year-college graduate, which currently stands slightly above $10,000.

Although extending extra benefits to such a disproportionately well-off group is a deeply suspicious idea, the way American student benefit campaigners talk about it is somehow worse still. Due to the toxic American mix of aversion to welfare benefits, love of individual rights, and faith in meritocracy, the typical line you hear about free college is that it should be a right of students because they have worked hard and done everything right. The implicit suggestion of such rhetoric is that students are really owed free college as the reward for not being like those less virtuous high school graduates who refuse to do what it takes to better themselves through education.

Needless to say, such thinking is extremely damaging to a broader egalitarian project, even more so in some ways than its goal of setting aside a part of our national income for the inegalitarian aim of making college free. If we are actually going to push a free college agenda, it should not be under a restrictive students' rights banner, but instead under a general pro-welfare banner. The goal of free college should not be to help students *per se*, but instead to bind them to a broader welfare benefit system. By presenting their tuition subsidies and living grants as indistinguishable from benefits for the disabled, the poor, the elderly, and so on, it may be possible to encourage wealthier students to support the welfare state and to undermine students' future claims of entitlement to the high incomes that college graduates so often receive. After all, the college income premium would only be possible through the welfare benefits to which the rest of society—including those who never went to college—has contributed.

Without understanding and presenting student benefits as welfare handouts, a free college agenda has no real egalitarian purpose. Giving extra money to a class of disproportionately well-off people without securing any reciprocal benefit to poor and working-class people who so often do not attend college, all while valorizing the college student as a virtuous person individually deserving of such benefits, would be at worst destructive, and at best, totally pointless.

10

QUESTIONS

1. Matt Bruenig claims at the outset that "almost all students are able to finance their college education" (para. 1). Does the selection contain evidence to support that claim? Does this claim ring true to you? Explain why or why not.

2. How would you answer the questions that Bruenig poses in paragraph 3? What do those questions imply about the debate surrounding educational costs?

3. Bruenig discusses the idea of fairness as it relates to the larger discussion surrounding college costs.

How would you paraphrase his position regarding fairness? How does the idea of fairness help shape his overall argument?

4. In paragraphs 5–7, Bruenig uses evidence to support his position. How could that same evidence be used to support an opposing position? Explain.

5. Bruenig claims that "making college free for everyone would almost certainly mean giving far more money to students from richer families than

from poorer ones" (para. 6). How adequately does his evidence and reasoning support that claim?

6. Bruenig repeats the phrase "disproportionately well-off" in paragraphs 8 and 10. What larger point does this repetition emphasize?

7. In paragraph 9, Bruenig asserts that "the goal of free college should not be to help students *per se*,

but instead to bind them to a broader welfare benefit system." How does this claim illustrate his point about the economics of education in America? Explain.

8. Identify areas where you agree with Bruenig and areas where you disagree. Which side of his argument are you on?

3 The Value of a College Education and The Effect of Student Loan Debt on Major Life Decisions (graphs)

The following graphs use data from a report entitled "The Relationship Between Student Debt, Experiences and Perceptions of College Worth," issued in 2015 by Gallup, Inc., an American research and consulting company founded in 1935 and best known for its public opinion polls.

The Value of a College Education

Responses of those who graduated college between 2006 and 2015 to the statement, "my education from [university name] was worth the cost."

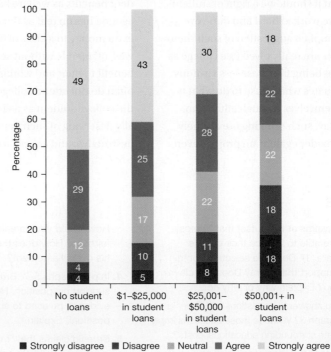

Data from the Gallup-Purdue Index 2015 Report.

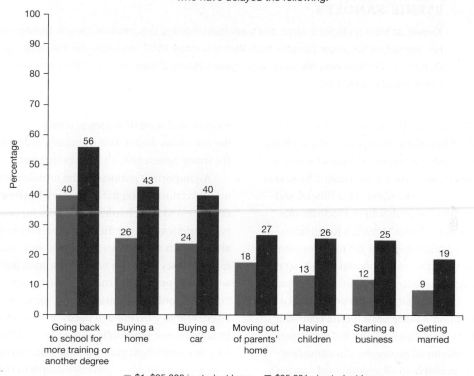

The Effect of Student Loan Debt on Major Life Decisions

*Percentage of recent alumni who took out student loans as undergraduates
who have delayed the following:*

Data from the Gallup-Purdue Index 2015 Report.

■ $1–$25,000 in student loans ■ $25,001+ in student loans

QUESTIONS

1. According to the first graph, what conclusions can you draw about the relationship between the amount of student loan debt and a person's satisfaction with the worth of his or her education? Overall, what does it suggest about the perceived value of higher education?

2. What might account for the fact that even among those with no debt, only 49 percent strongly agree that their college education was worth the cost? What might account for the fairly even spread of satisfaction for those with the greatest level of debt?

3. Based on the second graph, what conclusions can you draw about the relationship between student debt and delaying typical milestones of adulthood? What do these data suggest about the priorities and values of college graduates? To what extent do the data indicate a difference in priorities and values between those who have less than $25,000 in debt and those who have more than $25,000? Explain.

4. Are you surprised by any of the information in either of the graphs? Explain.

5. How might "free college" affect the findings indicated by the charts?

4 Make College Free for All

BERNIE SANDERS

Known as both an independent and a socialist-leaning progressive, Bernie Sanders (b. 1941) has served as the junior Senator from Vermont since 2007. He wrote the following op-ed in October of 2015, during his campaign against Hillary Clinton for the 2016 Democratic Party presidential nomination.

In 1877, Rutherford B. Hayes became the first president to make a strong case for universally available public education. "Universal suffrage should rest upon universal education," he said in his inaugural address, adding that "liberal and permanent provision should be made for the support of free schools." Hayes, a Republican, didn't worry that some poor kid might benefit from access to "free stuff," nor did he believe that the children of wealthy elites should be excluded from the universal nature of the program. For him, education was the basis for full economic and political participation, and full participation was the basis for all prosperity. An education should be available to all regardless of anyone's station.

Today, there is universal access to free, public schools across the United States for kindergarten through 12th grade. That didn't happen by presidential decree. It took populist pressure from the progressive movement, beginning in the 1890s, to make widespread access to free public schools a reality. By 1940, half of all young people were graduating from high school. As of 2013, that number was 81 percent. But that achievement is no longer enough. A college degree is the new high school diploma.

In the 1950s and 1960s, it was possible to graduate from high school and move right into a decent-paying job with good benefits. Strong unions offered apprenticeships, and a large manufacturing sector provided opportunities for those without an advanced degree. A couple with a sole breadwinner could buy a home, raise a family and send their kids to college. That was the American dream. Unfortunately, today, for too many Americans, it's not a possibility.

An important pathway to the middle class now runs through higher education, but rising costs are making it harder and harder for ordinary Americans to get the education they want and need. In 1978, it was possible to earn enough money to pay for a year of college tuition just by working a summer job that paid minimum wage. Today, it would take a minimum wage worker an entire year to earn enough to cover the annual in-state tuition at a public university. And that's why so many bright young people don't go to college, don't finish or graduate deeply in debt. With $1.3 trillion in student loans, Americans are carrying more student debt than credit card or auto-loan debt. That's a tragedy for our young people and for our nation.

In my view, education is essential for personal 5 and national well-being. We live in a highly competitive, global economy, and if our economy is to be strong, we need the best-educated workforce in the world. We won't achieve that if, every year, hundreds of thousands of bright young people cannot afford to go to college while millions more leave school deeply in debt. We need to ensure that every young person in this country who wishes to go to college can get the education that he or she desires, without going into debt and regardless of his or her family's income.

It may seem hard to believe, but there was a time when higher education was pretty close to free in this country, at least for many Americans.

After World War II, the GI Bill gave free education to more than 2 million veterans, many of whom would otherwise never have been able to go to college. This benefited them, and it was good for the economy and the country, too. In fact, scholars say that this investment was a major reason for the high productivity and economic growth our nation enjoyed during the postwar years. And, in certain states, such as California and New York, tuition was so low that college was practically free for much of the 20th century. That is no longer the case in America, but free college is still a priority in many parts of the world.

In Finland, Denmark, Ireland, Iceland, Norway, Sweden and Mexico, public colleges and universities remain tuition-free. They're free throughout Germany, too, and not just for Germans or Europeans but for international citizens as well. That's why every year, more than 4,600 students leave the United States and enroll in German universities. For a token fee of about $200 per year, an American can earn a degree in math or engineering from one of the premier universities in Europe. Governments in these countries understand what an important investment they are making, not just in the individuals who are able to acquire knowledge and skills but for the societies these students will serve as teachers, architects, scientists, entrepreneurs and more.

It is time to build on the progressive movement of the past and make public colleges and universities tuition-free in the United States — a development that will be the driver of a new era of American prosperity. We will have a stronger economy and a stronger democracy when all young people with the ambition and the talent can reach their full potential, regardless of their circumstances at birth.

QUESTIONS

1. How does the reference to President Rutherford B. Hayes serve to introduce Bernie Sanders's subject and attitude?

2. In paragraph 2, Sanders asserts that "a college degree is the new high school diploma." What is his larger point? How does this analogy support his position?

3. According to Sanders, how has the pathway to the American Dream changed?

4. Identify the sentence that most clearly states Sanders's thesis. How adequately does he support it through evidence and reasoning?

5. In paragraph 7, Sanders addresses college education in other countries. What is his purpose in doing so?

6. Does Sanders appeal most frequently to ethos, logos, or pathos in his article? Identify where he appeals to each and explain your answer.

7. Paraphrase Sanders's main position and analyze it using the Toulmin model. How effective is his argument? How persuasive is it?

5   The Argument for Tuition-Free College

KEITH ELLISON

Keith Maurice Ellison (b. 1963) has been the U.S. Representative for Minnesota's Fifth Congressional District since 2007 and Deputy Chair of the Democratic National Committee since 2017. He wrote the following op-ed for the *American Prospect* in 2016.

In 1862, President Abraham Lincoln signed the Land Grant College Act into law, laying the groundwork for the largest system of publicly funded universities in the world. Some of America's greatest colleges, including the University of Minnesota, were created by federal land grants, and were known as "democracy's colleges" or "people's colleges."

But that vision of a "people's college" seems awfully remote to a growing number of American students crushed under soaring tuitions and mounting debt. One hundred and fifty years after Lincoln made his pledge, it's time to make public colleges and universities free for every American.

This idea is easier than it looks. For most of our nation's history, public colleges and universities have been much more affordable than they are today, with lower tuition, and financial aid that covered a much larger portion of the costs. The first step in making college accessible again, and returning to an education system that serves every American, is addressing the student loan debt crisis.

The cost of attending a four-year college has increased by 1,122 percent since 1978. Galloping tuition hikes have made attending college more expensive today than at any point in U.S. history. At the same time, debt from student loans has become the largest form of personal debt in America—bigger than credit card debt and auto loans. Last year, 38 million American students owed more than $1.3 trillion in student loans.

Once, a degree used to mean a brighter   5 future for college graduates, access to the middle class, and economic stability. Today, student loan debt increases inequality and makes it harder for low-income graduates, particularly those of color, to buy a house, open a business, and start a family.

The solution lies in federal investments to states to lower the overall cost of public colleges and universities. In exchange, states would commit to reinvesting state funds in higher education. Any public college or university that benefited from the reinvestment program would be required to limit tuition increases. This federal-state partnership would help lower tuition for all students. Schools that lowered tuition would receive additional federal grants based on the degree to which costs are lowered.

Reinvesting in higher education programs like Pell Grants and work-study would ensure that Pell and other forms of financial aid that students don't need to pay back would cover a greater portion of tuition costs for low-income students. In addition, states that participate in this partnership would ensure that low-income students who attend state colleges and universities could afford non-tuition expenses like textbooks and housing fees. This proposal is one way to ensure that no student graduates with loans to pay back.

If the nation can provide hundreds of billions of dollars in subsidies to the oil and gas industry and billions of dollars more to Wall Street, we can afford to pay for public higher education. A tax on financial transactions like derivatives and stock trades would cover the cost. Building a truly affordable higher education system is an investment that would pay off economically.

Eliminating student loan debt is the first step, but it's not the last. Once we ensure that student loan debt isn't a barrier to going to college, we should reframe how we think about higher education. College shouldn't just be debt free—it should be free. Period.

We all help pay for our local high schools   10 and kindergartens, whether or not we send our kids to them. And all parents have the option of choosing public schools, even if they can afford private institutions. Free primary and secondary schooling is good for our economy, strengthens our democracy, and most importantly, is critical for our children's health and future. Educating our kids is one of our community's most important responsibilities, and it's a right that every one of us enjoys. So why not extend public schooling to higher education as well?

Some might object that average Americans should not have to pay for students from wealthy families to go to school. But certain things should be guaranteed to all Americans, poor or rich. It's not a coincidence that some of the most important social programs in our government's history have applied to all citizens, and not just to those struggling to make ends meet.

Universal programs are usually stronger and more stable over the long term, and they're less frequently targeted by budget cuts and partisan attacks. Public schools have stood the test of time—let's make sure public colleges and universities do, too.

The United States has long been committed to educating all its people, not only its elites.

This country is also the wealthiest in the history of the world. We can afford to make college an option for every American family.

QUESTIONS

1. What is Keith Ellison's purpose in referring to Abraham Lincoln? How effectively does this reference bolster his argument?

2. Ellison writes that "mak[ing] public colleges and universities free for every American" (para. 2) is "easier than it looks" (para. 3). How convincingly does he support this claim?

3. In paragraphs 6 and 7, Ellison offers a plan for making public higher education free. How well does he explain his plan? Does his solution seem practical and reasonable? Why or why not?

4. Identify the analogy in paragraph 8. How does it contribute to Ellison's argument?

5. Identify at least three assertions that Ellison makes throughout this op-ed. What evidence does he use to support them?

6. Where does Ellison address a counterargument? What might be some other counterarguments that would challenge Ellison's position?

7. In paragraph 9, Ellison states: "College shouldn't just be debt free — it should be free. Period." What is your position on this issue? Explain why you do or do not agree with Ellison.

6 No Way That Going to College Can, or Should Be, Free

THOMAS SOWELL

Thomas Sowell (b. 1930) is a conservative economist, political philosopher, and author. He has written over forty books on economics, politics, and American culture. The following article appeared in the *East Bay Times* in 2016.

Many people of mature years are amazed at how many young people have voted for Sen. Bernie Sanders, and are enthusiastic about the socialism he preaches.

Many of those older people have lived long enough to have seen socialism fail, time and again, in countries around the world. Venezuela, with all its rich oil resources, is currently on the verge of economic collapse, after its heady fling with socialism.

But, most of the young have missed all that, and their dumbed-down education is far more likely to present the inspiring rhetoric of socialism than to present its dismal track record.

Socialism is a wonderful vision — a world of the imagination far better than any place anywhere in the real world, at any time over the thousands of years of recorded history.

Who would not want to live in a world where college was free, along with many other things, and where government protected us from the shocks of life and guaranteed our happiness?

Free college of course has an appeal to the young, especially those who have never studied economics. But college cannot possibly be free. It would not be free even if there was no such thing as money.

Consider the costs of just one professor teaching just one course. He or she has probably spent more than 20 years being educated, from kindergarten to the Ph.D., before ending up standing in front of a class and trying to convey knowledge picked up in all those years. That means being fed, clothed and housed all those years, along with other expenses.

All the people who grew the food, manufactured the clothing and built the housing used by this one professor, for at least two decades, had to be compensated for their efforts, or those efforts would not continue. And of course someone has to produce food, clothing and shelter for all the students in this one course, as well as books, computers and other requirements or amenities.

Add up all these costs — and multiply by 100 or so — and you have a rough idea of what going to college costs. Whether these costs are paid by using money in a capitalist economy or by some other mechanism in a feudal economy, a socialist economy, or whatever, there are heavy costs to pay.

Moreover, under any economic system, those costs are either going to be paid or there are not going to be any colleges.

Those young people who understand this, whether clearly or vaguely, are not likely to be deterred from wanting socialism. Because what they really want is for somebody else to pay for their decision to go to college.

A market economy is one in which whoever makes a decision is the one who pays for that decision. It forces people to be sure that what they want to do is really worth what it is going to cost.

Even the existing subsidies of college have led many people to go to college who have very little interest in, or benefit from, going to college.

Whether judging by test results, by number of hours per week devoted to studying or by on-campus interviews, it is clear that today's college students learn a lot less than college students once did. If college becomes "free," even more people can attend college without bothering to become educated or acquiring any economically meaningful skills.

More fundamentally, making all sorts of other things "free" means more of those things being wasted as well. Even worse, it means putting more of the decisions that shape our lives into the hands of politicians and bureaucrats who control the purse strings.

Obamacare has given us a foretaste of what that means.

Worst of all, government giveaways polarize society into segments, each trying to get what it wants at somebody else's expense, creating bitterness that can tear a society apart. Some seem to blithely assume that "the rich" can be taxed to pay for what they want — as if "the rich" won't see what is coming and take their wealth elsewhere.

QUESTIONS

1. At the beginning of his article, Thomas Sowell refers to Bernie Sanders's 2016 presidential campaign. Is his logic in this paragraph sound? If not, what kind of logical fallacy does he employ? How effectively does it serve to introduce his argument?

2. How does Sowell characterize today's students? In what ways do his diction and tone in paragraphs 1–6 reveal his attitude toward the education that young people have received?

3. Briefly summarize the economic costs that Sowell discusses. How does he use that information to support his position?

4. What are the assumptions underlying Sowell's points in paragraphs 11 and 16? What do they suggest about Sowell's intended audience?

5. Paraphrase Sowell's main position and analyze it using the Toulmin model. How effective is his argument? How persuasive is it?

---

7   Is Free College Really Free?

ANYA KAMENETZ

Anya Kamenetz is lead education blogger for National Public Radio (NPR) and the author of several books about the future of education, including *Generation Debt* (2006), *DIY U: Edupunks, Edupreneurs, and the Coming Transformation of Higher Education* (2010), and *The Test* (2015). The following report was published on NPR's website in 2017.

"Free" is a word with a powerful appeal. And in the past year or so it has been tossed around a lot, followed by another word: "college."

Both Bernie Sanders and Hillary Clinton spent a lot of time talking about free tuition. And this week, the promise has been taken up by one of the largest public university systems in the country: New York state's.

Gov. Andrew Cuomo unveiled a proposal that would offer free tuition at state-run colleges for students from families earning less than $125,000 a year. Called the Excelsior Scholarship, his plan — which needs approval by the Legislature — would grant full rides to qualifying students as long as they attend one of the state's public two- or four-year colleges.

Cuomo's proposal, in the lexicon of "free-college" policymaking, is what's called a "last dollar" program.

As NPR Ed explained this summer, that means students who are already eligible for federal Pell Grants must use them to pay for school. After that money is gone, the state pledges to fill in the gap.

This method is the cheapest for the state, since students can draw on federal money first before taking state aid. With this type of plan, a larger share of funds from the new program is likely to go mainly to families who are relatively well off.

As Robert Kelchen, a higher education scholar at Seton Hall University, explains on his blog:

> The benefits of the program would go to two groups of students. The first group is fairly obvious: middle-income and upper-middle-income families. In New York, $125,000 falls at roughly the 80th percentile of family income — an income level where families may not be able to pay tuition

without borrowing, but college enrollment rates are quite high.

The other group that may benefit, says Kelchen, are lower-income students who are enticed by the clarity of the promise of "free."

But New York's proposal, like others, is likely to be controversial.

In reality there's no free college, just as there's [10] no free lunch. The real policy discussion is about how to best distribute the burden of paying for it — between individual families and the public at large — and, secondly, how to hold down the cost of providing it. All while leveraging the power of "free" responsibly.

Fueling a Bubble

For many conservatives, the answer is simple. An education makes individuals richer, and individuals should bear the cost. "The state should not subsidize intellectual curiosity," said Ronald Reagan, back when he was running for governor of California. In recent times, the conservative position is perhaps best expressed by economist Richard Vedder, director of the Center for College Affordability and Productivity.

In his books, articles and public appearances, Vedder argues that federal student aid is creating a bubble that allows colleges to raise prices indefinitely, and the only way to stop the cycle is to cut off public funding.

Kevin Carey, now the director of the higher education policy program at the nonpartisan New America Foundation, made pretty much the same argument in the New Republic in 2012. He compared public universities to apple vendors:

> You, the apple vendor, look at the situation and say, "Hey, the market price of an apple is still $1. Wouldn't it be great if I could charge $1 for apples, but still get 40 cents from the government for every apple I sell?" . . . So you start raising prices by 3, 4, or 5 percent above inflation annually.

In a world with no public subsidy at all for education, the only option left for free tuition would be something like the Starbucks plan — large corporations or wealthy donors footing the bill. And that kind of "free" comes, generally, with a significant catch — like requiring students to work for a certain employer.

The Public Piggy Bank

At the other end of the political spectrum are [15] those who see a large public obligation to pay for the education of citizens, to promote democracy, meritocracy and equal rights, among other things. They just can't agree on how.

Once upon a time, public university in this country actually was free, for the most part. In the 19th and early 20th centuries, from New York to California, states opted to charge no tuition or nominal fees.

Here's the catch. Until World War II, college was also pretty sparsely attended. In 1940, only about 5 percent of the population, most of them white men, had a bachelor's degree. And the U.S. was the most educated nation in the world! The small numbers made tuition relatively cheap to subsidize.

But starting with the GI Bill, the United States moved to a new model of "mass" higher education. The expansion continued through the 1960s, with the Higher Education Act of 1965 establishing federal student-aid programs.

Suddenly, most high school graduates — men, women, black, white, new immigrants — aspired to a college degree. In defiance of the laws of economics, as the supply of college graduates went up, so did the demand for them, year after year. A college degree pretty much always meant you made more money.

Graduates also paid more taxes, so the gov- [20] ernment got its money back in the long term — $6 for every dollar spent on the GI Bill, by some estimates.

No Such Thing

Starting in the 1970s, there was a backlash to all this free money. In the economic slump, federal and state subsidies to higher education tightened. Enrollments declined. Loans, which were cheaper for the government, began to replace grants.

Public universities responded to the decreased state subsidies by raising tuition. They responded to the increased availability of loan financing by raising tuition. They responded to the continued robust demand for higher education by raising tuition. They responded to the pressure to expand, adding new programs and majors and building bigger campuses, by raising tuition. Since 1978, public university tuition has climbed every single year, two or three times faster than inflation. Average student loan debt for a bachelor's degree: $29,400.

Sara Goldrick-Rab of Temple University sums up the results of all this in a paper she wrote for the Lumina Foundation:

> Talented students are forgoing college because of the costs, students who start college are unable to complete because they cannot afford to continue, and even students who finish degrees may not realize all of the expected returns because of sizable debt burdens.

The United States is no longer the most educated nation in the world — it's the 12th. Most of the countries ahead of it have lower-cost public university options than the U.S. Perhaps most damning, the high cost of college in this country helps ensure that in too many cases, wealth trumps merit.

The success rate in college for the lowest-achieving but highest-income students is slightly better than the success rate for the highest-achieving, lowest-income students.

Found Money

Out-of-control college costs are hurting the most vulnerable. There are many different efforts to pacify the giant octopus.

The new proposals bank on the fact that the federal government already spends lots of money on student aid: $47 billion in grants a year, $101 billion in loans (which are repaid), and another $20 billion in tax credits. The total of state, federal and private money going to defray the cost of tuition — that's distinct from state appropriations directly to institutions — is $247 billion per year.

Seems like with that kind of dough, there ought to be ways of buying better access and more equity.

There's substantial evidence that low-income students are less likely to even aspire to college because they think it's too expensive. It affects things like their choice of math classes as early as sixth grade.

That's why so many of these programs have the word "promise" or "hope" in the name. The student-aid bureaucracy is complicated to navigate. "Free college" is a promise everyone can understand.

Redeeming America's Promise calls for offering a full scholarship to a public two- or four-year college to every academically qualified student from families making no more than $160,000 a year. Part of the money, they say, could come from Pell Grants and tax credits, which would no longer be needed. (This math has been challenged.)

Goldrick-Rab, a scholar who studies access to higher education, argued in her paper last year for the Lumina Foundation that the federal student-aid budget would and should go to pay for two years of universal free public college for all comers, including books, supplies, even a living stipend for those who need it.

The Fine Print

Unfortunately, most attempts to defray the cost of college come with unintended consequences.

For a good example, look no further than Georgia's HOPE Scholarship. This statewide program, dating from 1993, offers high school graduates who meet certain requirements scholarships at a state university. At one time, about a dozen states had created similar models.

According to this early look at the impact   35
of the HOPE program, by Susan Dynarski for the National Bureau of Economic Research, "Georgia's program has likely increased the college attendance rate of all 18- to 19-year-olds by 7.0 to 7.9 percentage points."

Not too shabby. However, "the evidence suggests that Georgia's program has widened the gap in college attendance between blacks and whites and between those from low and high-income families."

Wait a minute. So a free tuition plan, instead of helping low-income and minority students, actually left them further behind? Yes, and that result has been seen in other states. It happens because these state programs require certain high school GPAs and test scores, and require that students maintain a certain GPA in college. And proportionately more middle-class white kids meet those bars.

Nothing Left to Lose

Most of the conversations about free college, as we've seen, are really about moving around piles of government money and other funds.

Some folks are starting to talk about whether we can meaningfully lower the cost of delivering a college education, instead of or in addition to paying for it differently. Most of those conversations have something to do with technology.

Some thought Massive Open Online   40
Courses would be the Holy Grail: free, high quality college for everyone! But in that case, "free" led to lower commitment. Completion rates for MOOCs hover around 5 to 7 percent.

Blended programs, which are self-paced and combine online learning with assistance from real people by phone or in person, seem to be able to hold down costs and get good results at the same time. Like Western Governors University, a nonprofit whose teacher-prep program was the National Council of Teacher Quality's first-ranked program in the country in 2014. It manages to charge less than the average public university without taking any public subsidy.

The unique thing about education, and what makes it so hard to control the price, is that it's not just a service or a good. It's a process, and the learner takes an active role in creating its value. A college education may never be free, but for many people it will remain priceless.

QUESTIONS

1. How does Anya Kamenetz characterize Governor Cuomo's proposal for higher education in the state of New York? Why does she put quotation marks around the word "free" (para. 1)?

2. In this article, Kamenetz refers to Bernie Sanders, Hillary Clinton, and Andrew Cuomo. She also quotes from Robert Kelchen, Ronald Reagan, Kevin Carey, Richard Vedder, and Sara Goldrick-Rab's thoughts on the topic of free higher education. How do these references and quotations contribute to Kamenetz's argument?

3. How does the analogy of the apple vendor (para. 12) contribute to the development of Kamenetz's argument?

4. How would you summarize the information included in the section titled, "The Public Piggy Bank"? What connotations does the phrase carry? How does it aid your understanding of the article's purpose?

5. In paragraph 22, Kamenetz says, "The success rate in college for the lowest-achieving but

highest-income students is slightly better than the success rate for the highest-achieving, lowest-income students." What does that suggest about social conditions in the United States? Does this information support — or undermine — the argument for "free college"? Explain.

6. In her discussion of Redeeming America's Promise in paragraph 28, Kamenetz refers to "academically qualified students" without explaining what that would mean. What do you think it likely means in the context of the article? What do you think it should mean? Explain.

7. What are some of the "unintended consequences" that Kamenetz discusses in the section entitled "The Fine Print"? How do they relate to the concluding section, "Nothing Left to Lose"?

8. Kamenetz opens paragraph 34 by saying, "Wait a minute. So a free tuition plan, instead of helping low-income and minority students, actually left them further behind?" What is the effect of this rhetorical question? What does it reveal about her attitude toward the achievement gap?

MAKING CONNECTIONS

1. A thread that runs through several of the selections in this Conversation is the nature of what it means for a student to be "qualified." In their article, Sara Goldrick-Rab and Nancy Kendall argue that the first two years of college should be free for "qualified students," while Thomas Sowell decries the results of "dumbed-down education." Anya Kamenetz discusses a proposal that would offer scholarships to "every academically qualified student." What does it mean for a student to be qualified? Do each of these writers use the word with the same meaning in mind? What do you think it should mean? Compare and contrast how at least three of these writers use the idea in their pieces.

2. Anya Kamenetz makes reference to Sara Goldrick-Rab twice in her piece. How might Goldrick-Rab respond to Kamenetz? Write a reply in her voice.

3. How might Sara Goldrick-Rab and Nancy Kendall, Matt Bruenig, Bernie Sanders, Keith Ellison, Thomas Sowell and Anya Kamenetz respond to the data in the Gallup graphs? Write a one- to two-sentence response from each author.

4. Which selection presents the strongest voice in favor of "free college"? Which presents the strongest case against it? Compare and contrast the two. What aspects of the rhetoric in each piece make the argument strong?

5. Thomas Sowell and Anya Kamenetz refer to Bernie Sanders in their articles. Compare and contrast the ways that each writer uses the reference to develop his or her argument. Then, write a response to one of them in the voice of Bernie Sanders.

ENTERING THE CONVERSATION

As you respond to the following prompts, support your argument with references to at least three sources in this Conversation on the cost of college education in America. For help using sources, see Chapter 4.

1. Write an essay identifying the major issues discussed in the selections and taking a position on what you view as the most important idea. Which of the selections most nearly share a perspective on the topic? Which ones most obviously present opposing positions?

2. Among the selections in the Conversation, which one do you think will exert the greatest influence on the ongoing debate regarding whether a U.S. college education should be freely available? Write an essay that explains why.

3. Thomas Sowell states: "If college becomes 'free,' even more people can attend college without bothering to become educated or acquiring any economically meaningful skills" (para. 14). Consider the implications of the statement, and write an essay that defends, challenges, or qualifies it.

4. In a National Education Association article titled "It's Time to Push for Free College," authors Max Page and Dan Clawson state: "Free is not enough. It has to be free *quality* education." Review how several of the writers in this Conversation approach the notion of "quality." Consider what they — and you — mean by the words "quality" and "qualified" as they apply to education and to

students. Write an essay that develops a strong position on the extent to which a free education should be tied to standards of quality.

5. Are we perhaps asking the wrong question? Instead of focusing on whether college should be free, should we be asking, "Why does college cost so much?" Review how the selections in this Conversation have addressed this question. Do some research on the growing cost of college over the last few decades. Write an essay that develops a position on whether the high cost of a college education is justified, and what might and should be done to make it more affordable and fair.

from Serving in Florida

BARBARA EHRENREICH

Picture a fat person's hell, and I don't mean a place with no food. Instead there is everything you might eat if eating had no bodily consequences — the cheese fries, the chicken-fried steaks, the fudge-laden desserts — only here every bite must be paid for, one way or another, in human discomfort. The kitchen is a cavern, a stomach leading to the lower intestine that is the garbage and dishwashing area, from which issue bizarre smells combining the edible and the offal: creamy carrion, pizza barf, and that unique and enigmatic Jerry's scent, citrus fart. The floor is slick with spills, forcing us to walk through the kitchen with tiny steps, like Susan McDougal[1] in leg irons. Sinks everywhere are clogged with scraps of lettuce, decomposing lemon wedges, water-logged toast crusts. Put your hand down on any counter and you risk being stuck to it by the film of ancient syrup spills, and this is unfortunate because hands are utensils here, used for scooping up lettuce onto the salad plates, lifting out pie slices, and even moving hash browns from one plate to another. The regulation poster in the single unisex rest room admonishes us to wash our hands thoroughly, and even offers instructions for doing so, but there is always some vital substance missing — soap, paper towels, toilet paper — and I never found all three at once. You learn to stuff your pockets with napkins before going in there, and too bad about the customers, who must eat, although they don't realize it, almost literally out of our hands.

The break room summarizes the whole situation: there is none, because there are no breaks at Jerry's. For six to eight hours in a row, you never sit except to pee. Actually, there are three folding chairs at a table immediately adjacent to the bathroom, but hardly anyone ever sits in this, the very rectum of the gastroarchitectural system. Rather, the function of the peri-toilet area is to house the ashtrays in which servers and dishwashers leave their cigarettes burning at all times, like votive candles, so they don't have to waste time lighting up again when they dash back here for a puff. Almost everyone smokes as if their pulmonary well-being depended on it — the multinational mélange of cooks; the dishwashers, who are all Czechs here; the servers, who are American natives — creating an atmosphere in which oxygen is only an occasional pollutant. My first morning at Jerry's, when the hypoglycemic shakes set in, I complain to one of my fellow servers that I don't understand how she can go so long without food. "Well, I don't understand how *you* can go so long without a cigarette," she responds in a tone of reproach. Because work is what you do for others; smoking is what you do for yourself. I don't know why the antismoking crusaders have never grasped the element of defiant self-nurturance that makes the habit so endearing to its victims — as if, in the American workplace, the only thing people have to call their own is the tumors they are nourishing and the spare moments they devote to feeding them.

Now, the Industrial Revolution is not an easy transition, especially, in my experience, when you have to zip through it in just a couple of days. I have gone from craft work straight into the factory, from the air-conditioned morgue of the Hearthside directly into the flames. Customers arrive in human waves, sometimes disgorged fifty at a time from their tour buses, peckish and whiny. Instead of two "girls" on the floor at once,

---

[1]Susan McDougal was imprisoned in 1996 for contempt of court, fraud, and conspiracy in connection with the failed Whitewater land deal involving President Bill Clinton and First Lady Hillary Rodham Clinton. The Clintons were never charged with any wrongdoing. —Eds.

there can be as many as six of us running around in our brilliant pink-and-orange Hawaiian shirts. Conversations, either with customers or with fellow employees, seldom last more than twenty seconds at a time. On my first day, in fact, I am hurt by my sister servers' coldness. My mentor for the day is a supremely competent, emotionally uninflected twenty-three-year-old, and the others, who gossip a little among themselves about the real reason someone is out sick today and the size of the bail bond someone else has had to pay, ignore me completely. On my second day, I find out why. "Well, it's good to see *you* again," one of them says in greeting. "Hardly anyone comes back after the first day." I feel powerfully vindicated — a survivor — but it would take a long time, probably months, before I could hope to be accepted into this sorority.

---

1. The second-person point of view Barbara Ehrenreich uses in paragraph 1 serves to

   a. introduce the characters
   b. effect an appeal to logos
   c. establish the narrator's ethos
   d. create immediacy for the reader
   e. provide contrast to the physical description

2. Sentences 2 and 3 contain each of the following EXCEPT

   a. metaphor
   b. analogy
   c. allusion
   d. paradox
   e. simile

3. Which of the following is the BEST possible reason for Ehrenreich's comparison of cigarettes to votive candles in the sentence that begins "Rather, the function of the peri-toilet area" (para. 2)?

   a. to create a detailed picture
   b. to create an ironic contrast
   c. to reveal the narrator's biases
   d. to extend a complex metaphor
   e. to illustrate the sarcastic tone

4. The most likely purpose of Ehrenreich's mention of the Industrial Revolution in paragraph 3 is to compare

   a. the diner work force to early industrial union strikers
   b. Jerry, the boss at the diner, to a ruthless factory foreman
   c. her former place of employment to a cottage industry
   d. the pace of work at the diner with that of technological progress
   e. the food in the diner to the products manufactured in a factory

5. Which of the following best illustrates the meaning of the phrase "emotionally uninflected" (para. 3) in the context of this essay?

   a. obstinate
   b. hyperbolic
   c. stolid
   d. presumptuous
   e. decisive

6. In this passage, the speaker implies that

   a. The tedium of work is relieved by conversation with the diners
   b. The managers do not treat the women workers as adults
   c. The workers are truthful about their reasons for missing work
   d. The mood of the women workers is brightened by their attire
   e. The workers regard each other with concern and respect

7. In this context, the phrase "powerfully vindicated" (para. 3) is best interpreted as meaning

   a. completely set free
   b. entirely justified
   c. strongly affirmed
   d. roundly condemned
   e. completely dismayed

8. The diction in each of the following reveals

   a. The floor is slick with spills, forcing us to walk through the kitchen with tiny steps . . ."
   b. " . . .the only thing people have to call their own is the tumors they are nourishing . . ."
   c. "Instead of two 'girls' on the floor at once, there can be as many as six of us . . ."

d. "It would take a long time, probably months, before I could hope to be accepted into this sorority."

e. "Almost everyone smokes as if their pulmonary well-being depended on it—"

9. As seen in the first and last paragraphs of this selection, the overall structure can best be described as a

a. movement from the abstract to the concrete

b. series of specific details followed by generalizations

c. collage of loosely related events

d. claim followed by scientific evidence

e. detailed account of daily activities

10. In the passage, Ehrenreich's attitude can be characterized as each of the following EXCEPT

a. solemn

b. sardonic

c. blunt

d. scornful

e. critical

11. Each of the following is figurative EXCEPT

a. "the air-conditioned morgue of the Hearthside"

b. "the very rectum of the gastroarchitectural system"

c. "when the hypoglycemic shakes set in"

d. "disgorged fifty at a time from their tour buses"

e. "have gone from craft work straight into the factory"

12. The speaker holds which of the following assumptions about her audience?

a. They have likely worked in a similar place of business

b. They are likely small business owners or entrepreneurs

c. They are responsible for the poor workplace conditions she describes

d. They are relatively unfamiliar with the conditions that she describes

e. They are officials charged with improving the workplace environment

from A Modest Proposal

JONATHAN SWIFT

It is a melancholy object to those who walk through this great town or travel in the country, when they see the streets, the roads, and cabin doors, crowded with beggars of the female sex, followed by three, four, or six children, all in rags and importuning every passenger for an alms. These mothers instead of being able to work for their honest livelihood, are forced to employ all their time in strolling to beg sustenance for their helpless infants: who as they grow up either turn thieves for want of work, or leave their dear native country to fight for the pretender[1] in Spain, or sell themselves to the Barbadoes.

I think it is agreed by all parties that this prodigious number of children in the arms, or on the backs, or at the heels of their mothers, and frequently of their fathers, is in the present deplorable state of the kingdom a very great additional grievance; and, therefore, whoever could find out a fair, cheap, and easy method of making these children sound, useful members of the commonwealth, would deserve so well of the public as to have his statue set up for a preserver of the nation.

But my intention is very far from being confined to provide only for the children of professed beggars; it is of a much greater extent, and shall take in the whole number of infants at a certain age who are born of parents in effect as little able to support them as those who demand our charity in the streets.

[1]James Francis Edward, son of deposed Catholic King James II. His claim to the throne was not considered legitimate; thus, he was a pretender to the throne. —Eds.

As to my own part, having turned my thoughts for many years upon this important subject, and maturely weighed the several schemes of our projectors, I have always found them grossly mistaken in their computation. It is true, a child just dropped from its dam may be supported by her milk for a solar year, with little other nourishment; at most not above the value of 2s., which the mother may certainly get, or the value in scraps, by her lawful occupation of begging; and it is exactly at one year old that I propose to provide for them in such a manner as instead of being a charge upon their parents or the parish, or wanting food and raiment for the rest of their lives, they shall on the contrary contribute to the feeding, and partly to the clothing, of many thousands.

There is likewise another great advantage in 5
my scheme, that it will prevent those voluntary abortions, and that horrid practice of women murdering their bastard children, alas! too frequent among us! sacrificing the poor innocent babes I doubt more to avoid the expense than the shame, which would move tears and pity in the most savage and inhuman breast.

The number of souls in this kingdom being usually reckoned one million and a half, of these I calculate there may be about 200,000 couple whose wives are breeders; from which number I subtract 30,000 couple who are able to maintain their own children (although I apprehend there cannot be so many, under the present distress of the kingdom); but this being granted, there will remain 170,000 breeders. I again subtract 50,000 for those women who miscarry, or whose children die by accident or disease within the year. There only remain 120,000 children of poor parents annually born. The question therefore is, how this number shall be reared and provided for? which, as I have already said, under the present situation of affairs, is utterly impossible by all the methods hitherto proposed. For we can neither employ them in handicraft of agriculture; we neither build houses (I mean in

the country) nor cultivate land; they can very seldom pick up a livelihood by stealing, till they arrive at six years old, except where they are of towardly parts, although I confess they learn the rudiments much earlier; during which time they can, however, be properly looked upon only as probationers; as I have been informed by a principal gentleman in the county of Cavan, who protested to me that he never knew above one or two instances under the age of six, even in a part of the kingdom so renowned for the quickest proficiency in that art.

I am assured by our merchants, that a boy or a girl before twelve years old is no salable commodity; and even when they come to this age they will not yield above 3£ or 3£ 2s. 6d.[2] at most on the exchange; which cannot turn to account either to the parents or kingdom, the charge of nutriment and rags having been at least four times that value.

I shall now therefore humbly propose my own thoughts, which I hope will not be liable to the least objection.

I have been assured by a very knowing American of my acquaintance in London, that a young healthy child well nursed is at a year old a most delicious, nourishing, and wholesome food, whether stewed, roasted, baked, or broiled; and I make no doubt that it will equally serve in a fricassee or a ragout.

I do therefore humbly offer it to public con- 10
sideration that of the 120,000 children already computed, 20,000 may be reserved for breed, whereof only one-fourth part to be males; which is more than we allow to sheep, black cattle, or swine; and my reason is, that these children are seldom the fruits of marriage, a circumstance not much regarded by our savages; therefore one male will be sufficient to serve four females. That the remaining 100,000 may, at a year old,

---

[2]3 pounds, 2 shillings, 6 pence (denominations of English money). —Eds.

be offered in sale to the persons of quality and fortune through the kingdom; always advising the mother to let them suck plentifully in the last month, so as to render them plump and fat for a good table. A child will make two dishes at an entertainment for friends; and when the family dines alone, the fore and hind quarter will make a reasonable dish, and seasoned with a little pepper or salt will be very good boiled on the fourth day, especially in winter.

---

1. The speaker of Swift's proposal appeals to each of the following values EXCEPT

  a. pity

  b. economy

  c. avarice

  d. pragmatism

  e. reason

2. In paragraph 4, "schemes of our projectors" is best interpreted to mean

  a. policies mandated by dictators

  b. grossly miscalculated statistics

  c. misguided suggestions of the populace

  d. strategies contrived by the state

  e. speeches delivered to the public

3. The speaker employs each of the following to support his argument EXCEPT

  a. statistical data

  b. reference to authority

  c. professional tone

  d. self-interest

  e. oxymoron

4. The rhetorical strategy of the phrase "which would move tears and pity in the most savage and inhuman breast" (para. 5) is best described as

  a. anachronism

  b. euphemism

  c. appeal to pathos

  d. inverted syntax

  e. dramatic irony

5. The speaker lists each of the following as an advantage of his proposal EXCEPT

  a. it would reduce burden in the parents' household

  b. it would subsidize the feeding and clothing of many households

  c. it would reduce the occurrence of voluntary abortions

  d. it would contribute to a more equitable distribution of resources

  e. it would provide entertainment and sustenance for family and friends

6. The tone of the speaker might be best described as

  a. condescending and indifferent

  b. reasoned and objective

  c. ironic and satiric

  d. illogical and arrogant

  e. irrational and aggressive

7. Which of the following best describes the effect of the phrase, "except where they are of towardly parts" (para. 6)?

  a. it refutes a counterargument to strengthen the speaker's position

  b. it qualifies a characterization of Irish children

  c. it offers an exception to the terms of the proposal

  d. it provides a concession to opposing position

  e. it presents an exception for the speaker's audience

8. In paragraph 9, what purpose does the phrase, "whether stewed, roasted, baked, or boiled" serve?

  a. it implies that the Irish are already treated like the English

  b. it alludes to the preparation of potatoes in the great famine

  c. it offers a culinary qualification for cooks and chefs

  d. it offers a mock qualification to soften the bluntness of the proposal

  e. it emphasizes the food shortage suffered by the Irish peasants

9. Swift's intention in paragraph 6 can be best characterized as a wish to

a. see slavery adopted as a policy less severe than his own ironic proposal

b. persuade lords and ladies to partake of a more equitable, varied, and balanced diet

c. achieve a precipitous and immediate reduction in the Irish population

d. prove the accuracy of his calculations and statistical data

e. present a brutalized sensitivity to expose the flaws of existing policy

10. Which of the following is most effective in assuaging feelings of disgust for Swift's readers?

a. the technical aspect of the facts and figures

b. the speaker's avoidance of the grotesque

c. the blunt candor of the proposal

d. the ironic stance of the author

e. the speaker's avoidance of hypocrisy

11. The speaker's rhetorical method in the passage involves a movement from

a. melancholy description to optimistic outlook

b. uneasy perspective to manipulative motive

c. reasoned deliberation to eager anticipation

d. outraged disgust to pensive reflection

e. sympathetic concern to sardonic scorn

12. The speaker implies that Americans are

a. prodigal

b. savage

c. intelligent

d. cultured

e. assiduous

13. The tone of the author might be best described as

a. sartorial

b. culinary

c. solemn

d. satiric

e. didactic

MONEY

Now that you have examined a number of texts focusing on money, explore one dimension of this topic by synthesizing your own ideas and those in the readings. You might want to do more research or use readings from other classes as you prepare for the following assignments.

1. Two of the major subjects discussed in the chapter are known best by their acronyms: UBI and MID. The universal basic income and the mortgage-interest deduction are economic issues, of course, but political issues as well. As we learn in "A Guaranteed Income for Every American" by Charles Murray, and Matthew Desmond's article, "House Rules: How Homeownership Became the Engine of American Inequality," UBI is an idea that appeals to the left and the right — to both sides of the political spectrum in America, while MID reform is resisted on both sides. Write an essay about how perspectives regarding these two programs illuminate the political divide that we face in America.

2. How has the pursuit of money been portrayed in popular culture, either in the past or today? You might consider films such as *Wall Street: Money Never Sleeps* (2010), *Inside Job* (2010), *Margin Call* (2011), *The Wolf of Wall Street* (2013), *The Big Short* (2015), or *It's a Wonderful Life* (1947); periodicals such as the *Onion*; or television programs such as *The Daily Show*. Select one genre, such as movies, comedy shows, or cartoons. Do they extol the virtues of capitalism? Do they ennoble work? Do they satirize economics and economists? Explain using examples.

3. In *The City of God*, philosopher St. Augustine tells the story of a pirate captured by Alexander the Great. "The Emperor asked him, 'How dare you molest the seas?' The pirate replied, 'How dare you molest the whole world? Because I do it with a small boat, I am called a pirate and a thief. You, with a great fleet, molest the world

and are called an emperor.'" St. Augustine "approved of the pirate's response." In our time, there are many who bemoan the greed with which our financial system is riddled, while observing at the same time the punishments meted out to the poor for minor offenses. Consider the implications of the pirate's response and St. Augustine's thought. Write an essay in which you evaluate the application of the story to our nation's current economic situation, using the works presented in this chapter for support.

4. Two of the selections in this chapter address poverty in America. In "The Singer Solution to World Poverty" (p.806), Peter Singer advocates that "each one of us with wealth surplus to his or her essential needs should be giving most of it to help people suffering from poverty so dire as to be life-threatening. . . . Again, the formula is simple: whatever money you're spending on luxuries, not necessities, should be given away" (paras. 21–22). In "A Guaranteed Income for Every American," Charles Murray simply states: "If you want to end poverty, just give people money" (para. 2). Write an essay in which you compare and contrast the validity of the proposals put forth by both of these writers as a means of eliminating poverty.

5. Write a response to Barbara Ehrenreich, Eric Schlosser, Carmen Maria Machado, or Matthew Desmond in the voice of a financially successful or powerful contemporary person, such as Kanye West or Bill Gates, for example. Indicate areas of common ground as well as disagreement.

6. One common method of distributing money to make up for the negative effects of wealth inequality is through what we call welfare. When we hear or read the word, "welfare," most of us are likely to think of programs for the poor — programs to address poverty. But as Charles Murray points out in his article, we also have corporate welfare in America, and Matthew Desmond discusses welfare for the rich in his piece. Research welfare in America — as it applies to assistance to the poor and also as it applies to the kinds of programs discussed by Murray and Desmond. Write an essay about the nature of welfare in America. Consider how welfare in all of its iterations affects the circumstances that Americans face as illustrated by the selections in this chapter. In your essay, refer to two other pieces in the chapter.

7. Write an argument defending or challenging the large salaries paid to athletes, movie stars, or corporate executives. Develop a logical argument with clearly drawn reasons — or write your response as a satire.

8. In the following excerpts, Adam Smith and Henry David Thoreau consider price and cost as features of economy. Write an essay in which you compare the two and evaluate which speaks more accurately and eloquently to our time. In your essay, refer to at least three of the selections presented in this chapter as support.

   a. The real price of everything, what everything is really worth to the man who has acquired it, and who wants to dispose of it or exchange for something else, is the toil and trouble which it can save for himself, and which it can impose on other people.
   — Adam Smith, *The Wealth of Nations*, 1776

   b. If it is asserted that civilization is a real advance on the condition of man, — and I think that it is, though only the wise improve their advantages, — it must be shown that it has produced better dwellings without making them more costly; and the cost of a thing is the amount of what I will call life which is required to be exchanged for it, immediately or in the long run.
   — Henry David Thoreau, *Walden*, 1854

9. Which of the following quotations most accurately captures your attitude toward work and the economy? Write an essay about why the quotation speaks to you. In your essay, refer to the selections presented in this chapter.

   a. Never work just for money or for power. They won't save your soul or help you sleep at night.
   — Marian Wright Edelman

   b. Work for something because it is good, not just because it stands a chance to succeed.
   — Vaclav Havel

   c. Every man is rich or poor according to the degree to which he can afford the necessaries, conveniences, and amusements of human life.
   — Adam Smith

   d. It is easier for a camel to pass through the eye of a needle, than for a rich man to enter into the kingdom of God.
   — Matthew 19:24

   e. Capital is dead labor that, vampire-like, lives only by sucking living labor, and lives the more, the more labor it sucks.
   — Karl Marx

   f. I am opposed to millionaires, but it would be dangerous to offer me the position.
   — Mark Twain

   g. I'd like to live as a poor man with lots of money.
   — Pablo Picasso

   h. There's no way that Michael Jackson or whoever Jackson should have a million thousand droople billion dollars and then there's people starving. There's no way! There's no way that these people should own planes and there people don't have houses. Apartments. Shacks. Drawers. Pants! I know you're rich. I know you got 40 billion dollars, but can you just keep it to one house? You only need one house. And if you only got two kids, can you just keep it to two rooms? I mean why have 52 rooms and you know there's somebody with no room?! It just don't make sense to me. It don't.
   — Tupac Shakur

i. The great enemy of freedom is the alignment of political power with wealth. This alignment destroys the commonwealth — that is, the natural wealth of localities and the local economies of household, neighborhood, and community — and so destroys democracy, of which the commonwealth is the foundation and practical means.

                    — Wendell Berry

j. Money often costs too much.

                    — Ralph Waldo Emerson

k. Money doesn't talk, it swears.

                    — Bob Dylan

l. I love money. I love everything about it. I bought some pretty good stuff. Got me a $300 pair of socks. Got a fur sink. An electric dog polisher. A gasoline powered turtleneck sweater. And, of course, I bought some dumb stuff, too.

                    — Steve Martin

m. Money was never a big motivation for me, except as a way to keep score. The real excitement is playing the game.

                    — Donald Trump

10. In *The Souls of Black Folk* (1903), African American intellectual W.E.B. DuBois took Booker T. Washington to task. Acknowledging that Washington "stands as the one recognized spokesman of his ten million fellows and one of the most notable figures in a nation of seventy million," DuBois criticizes him for promoting "a gospel of Work and Money to such an extent as apparently almost completely to overshadow the higher aims of life." Read Chapter 3 of DuBois's *The Souls of Black Folk* called "Of Mr. Booker T. Washington and Others," and then explain whether you agree with Washington or DuBois. You might also want to read Dudley Randall's poem "Booker T. and W.E.B.," which captures and comments on the debate between Washington and DuBois.

11. This chapter has two featured visual texts — Diego Rivera's mural, "Night of the Rich," and "Panama Papers," a collage by Hazel Florez. Find another work of visual art that you consider worthy of inclusion with these two. Explain how it fits with them and illustrates the themes explored in this chapter.

12. Imagine that some of the authors represented in this chapter were to meet for a conversation about money. Write a dialogue among Barbara Ehrenreich, Lars Eighner, Carmen Maria Machado, and Jia Tolentino. Characterize each speaker according to what you know about them from reading their selections.

13. Write an ironic response to one of the selections in the chapter. You might consider, for example, "Dining in Florida;" "The Gospel of Greed;" "In the Corporate Office;" "Luxury Shopping, from This Side of the Register;" (or "Luxury Shopping, Online"); or "The Gig Economy: Equal Opportunity for All."

14. Look again at the fiverr ad to which Jia Tolentino refers in her essay (p. 825). Find an ad that would fit an argument made in another of the selections as well as that one does there. Explain the relationship between the text and the ad, and also how the ad contributes to the argument that the text develops.

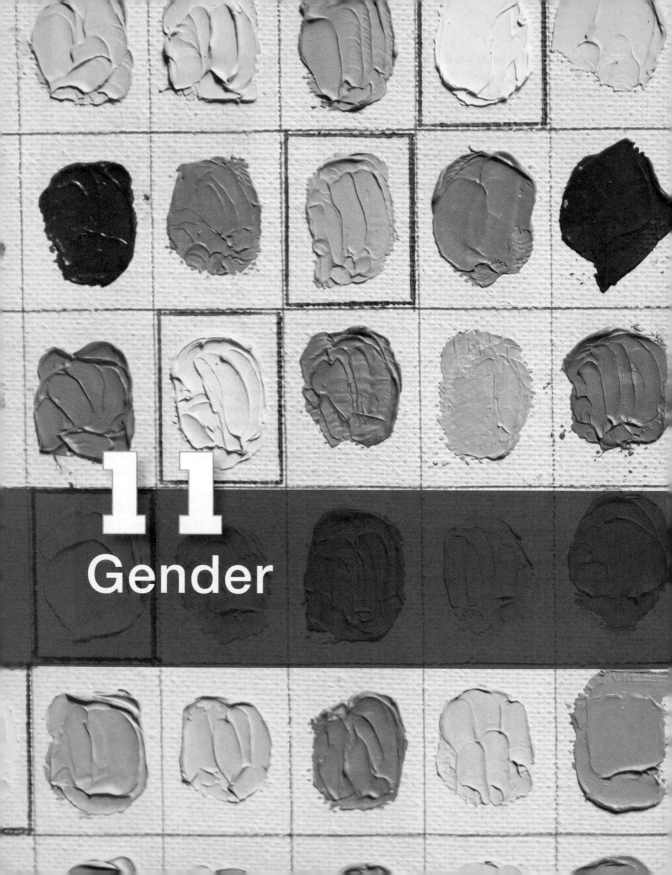

11

Gender

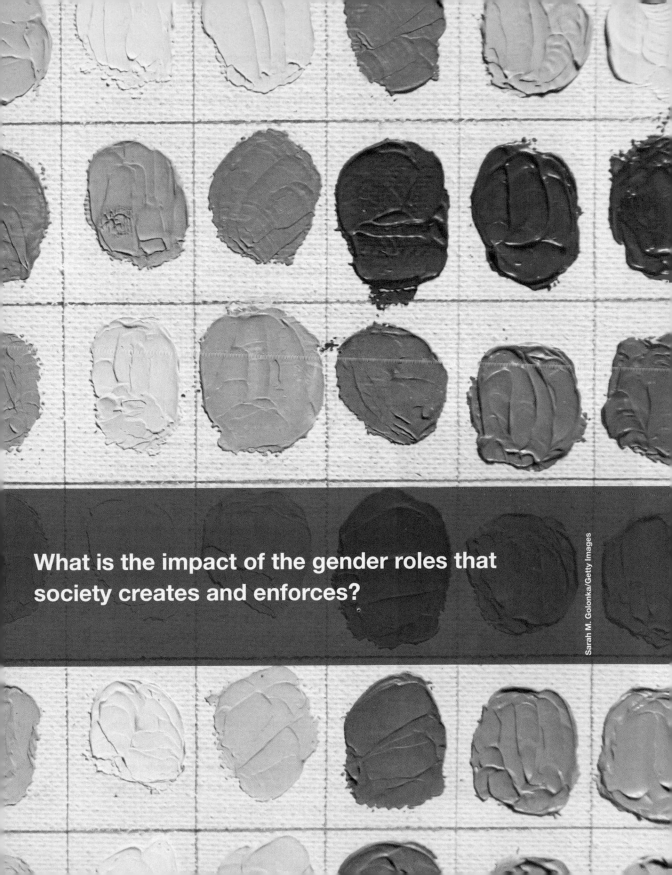

What is the impact of the gender roles that society creates and enforces?

"Why can't a woman be more like a man?" asks the exasperated Henry Higgins in *My Fair Lady* when he fails to understand his indomitable pupil, Eliza Doolittle. Why, indeed! The question of gender differences and roles has baffled and angered us, delighted and confused us.

What is the distinction between sex and gender? The former refers to biological identity; the latter has come to mean behavior that is learned. Some "socially constructed" gender roles result from beliefs about the proper way to behave. When do gender roles become stereotypes of what it means to be a woman or a man? These ideas vary according to culture and time. A look at men in the eighteenth century wearing wigs of curls tells us that what is considered appropriate in one context is wholly inappropriate in another.

What other forces define gender roles? How does ethnicity contribute to the expectations of what is masculine or feminine behavior? How does setting — a small town, an athletic field, a formal dinner — affect a group's expectations?

Such issues take on even greater importance in the context of bias. When do socially constructed roles hinder individual expression or choice? Why are certain professions dominated by men and others by women? How do beliefs about sex or gender affect public policy, including education?

These are the questions taken up in this chapter, starting with an exploration into what "scientific evidence" has been marshaled to "prove" the intellectual superiority of men over women. Other selections focus on the social pressure to behave "like a man" and the communication differences between men and women. The serious economic and even medical consequences of beliefs about gender are also considered.

The fictional Professor Higgins was, in fact, asking a rhetorical question, but the authors presented in this chapter answer his question in specific and provocative ways that are bound to challenge — and deepen — our thinking about gender roles.

This poster was created in 1943, shortly after the United States entered World War II. At the beginning of the war, women made up just 24 percent of the workforce, but by 1945 that number had increased to 36 percent.
How does this poster challenge traditional gender roles? In what ways does it reinforce them?

Library of Congress

In Search of Our Mothers' Gardens

ALICE WALKER

Alice Walker (b. 1944) is a novelist, a poet, an essayist, a civil rights activist, and a self-described eco-pacifist, best known for her depictions of the struggles and strengths of African American women. The youngest of eight children born to sharecropper parents, Walker grew up in the small town of Eatonton, Georgia. After high school, she attended Spelman College in Georgia, then transferred to Sarah Lawrence College in New York, which she graduated from in 1965. Her first novel, *The Third Life of Grange Copeland*, was published in 1969, followed by her poetry collection *Revolutionary Petunias and Other Poems* (1973). In 1982, she published *The Color Purple*, her most celebrated work, which won the Pulitzer Prize and was adapted into both a movie (directed by Steven Spielberg) and a Tony Award-winning Broadway musical. Walker is also known for her essays, in which she coined the term *womanist*. Claiming a more inclusive connotation than "feminist," which Walker criticized as focusing on the experiences of white, heterosexual women, she writes that a womanist is "committed to survival and wholeness of entire people, male *and* female. Not a separatist. . . . Traditionally a universalist." Walker has taught at Wellesley College, Yale University, the University of California at Berkeley, and many other institutions. She continues to support environmental causes and is an advocate for international women's rights. The following essay is from *In Search of Our Mothers' Gardens: Womanist Prose* (1983), a collection of works written between 1966 and 1982.

Monica Morgan/Getty Images

> Creation often
> needs two hearts
> one to root
> and one to flower
> One to sustain . . .
> the fragile bloom
> that in the glory
> of its hour
> affirms a heart
> unsung, unseen.
> — Marilou Awiakta, "Motheroot"

> *I described her own nature and temperament. Told how they needed a larger life for their expression. . . . I pointed out that in lieu of proper channels, her emotions had overflowed into paths that dissipated them. I talked, beautifully I thought, about an art that would be born, an art that would open the way for women the likes of her. I asked her to hope, and build up an inner life against the coming of that day. . . . I sang, with a strange quiver in my voice, a promise song.*
> — Jean Toomer, "Avey," *Cane*

> *The poet speaking to a prostitute who falls asleep while he's talking —*

When the poet Jean Toomer[1] walked through the South in the early twenties, he discovered a curious thing: black women whose spirituality was so intense, so deep, so *unconscious,* that they were themselves unaware of the richness they held. They stumbled blindly through their lives: creatures so abused and mutilated in body, so dimmed and confused by pain, that they considered themselves unworthy even of hope. In the selfless abstractions their bodies became to the men who used them, they became more than "sexual objects," more even than mere women: they became "Saints." Instead of being perceived as whole persons, their bodies became shrines: what was thought to be their minds became temples suitable for worship. These crazy Saints stared out at the world, wildly, like lunatics — or quietly, like suicides; and the "God" that was in their gaze was as mute as a great stone.

Who were these Saints? These crazy, loony, pitiful women?

Some of them, without a doubt, were our mothers and grandmothers.

In the still heat of the post-Reconstruction South, this is how they seemed to Jean Toomer: exquisite butterflies trapped in an evil honey, toiling away their lives in an era, a century, that did not acknowledge them, except as "the *mule* of the world."[2] They dreamed dreams that no one knew — not even themselves, in any coherent fashion — and saw visions no one could understand. They wandered or sat about the countryside crooning lullabies to ghosts, and drawing the mother of Christ in charcoal on courthouse walls.

They forced their minds to desert their bodies *5* and their striving spirits sought to rise, like frail whirlwinds from the hard red clay. And when those frail whirlwinds fell, in scattered particles, upon the ground, no one mourned. Instead, men lit candles to celebrate the emptiness that

remained, as people do who enter a beautiful but vacant space to resurrect a God.

Our mothers and grandmothers, some of them: moving to music not yet written. And they waited.

They waited for a day when the unknown thing that was in them would be made known; but guessed, somehow in their darkness, that on the day of their revelation they would be long dead. Therefore to Toomer they walked, and even ran, in slow motion. For they were going nowhere immediate, and the future was not yet within their grasp. And men took our mothers and grandmothers, "but got no pleasure from it." So complex was their passion and their calm.

To Toomer, they lay vacant and fallow as autumn fields, with harvest time never in sight: and he saw them enter loveless marriages, without joy; and become prostitutes, without resistance; and become mothers of children, without fulfillment.

For these grandmothers and mothers of ours were not Saints, but Artists; driven to a numb and bleeding madness by the springs of creativity in them for which there was no release. They were Creators, who lived lives of spiritual waste, because they were so rich in spirituality — which is the basis of Art — that the strain of enduring their unused and unwanted talent drove them insane. Throwing away this spirituality was their pathetic attempt to lighten the soul to a weight their work-worn, sexually abused bodies could bear.

What did it mean for a black woman to be *10* an artist in our grandmothers' time? In our great-grandmothers' day? It is a question with an answer cruel enough to stop the blood.

Did you have a genius of a great-great-grandmother who died under some ignorant and depraved white overseer's lash? Or was she required to bake biscuits for a lazy backwater tramp, when she cried out in her soul to paint watercolors of sunsets, or the rain falling on the green and peaceful pasturelands? Or was her body broken and forced to bear children (who were more often than not sold away from

---

[1] Jean Toomer (1894–1967) was an African American writer during the Harlem Renaissance, best known for the novel *Cane* (1923). —Eds.
[2] A reference to a line of dialogue from *Their Eyes Were Watching God,* a 1937 novel by Harlem Renaissance writer Zora Neale Hurston. —Eds.

seeing connections

Billie Holiday (1915–1959) was arguably the most influential jazz singer of all time. One seldom reads about her accomplishments as a musician without also learning of her impoverished childhood, the abuse she endured, and her heroin addiction. Shown here is a publicity photograph of the singer taken in 1939 alongside a painting by contemporary artist Kaaria Mucherera entitled *Billie Holiday*.

Compare and contrast these two portrayals of Billie Holiday. How does each image characterize the singer? What aspects of Walker's argument does each one capture? Which one is the more compelling visual, and why?

Michael Ochs Archives/Getty Images

KAARIA MUCHERERA/Private Collection. Bridgeman Images

her) — eight, ten, fifteen, twenty children — when her one joy was the thought of modeling heroic figures of rebellion, in stone or clay?

How was the creativity of the black woman kept alive, year after year and century after century, when for most of the years black people have been in America, it was a punishable crime for a black person to read or write? And the freedom to paint, to sculpt, to expand the mind with action did not exist. Consider, if you can bear to imagine it, what might have been the result if singing, too, had been forbidden by law. Listen to the voices of Bessie Smith, Billie Holiday, Nina Simone, Roberta Flack, and Aretha Franklin, among others, and imagine those voices muzzled for life. Then you may begin to comprehend the

lives of our "crazy," "Sainted" mothers and grandmothers. The agony of the lives of women who might have been Poets, Novelists, Essayists, and Short-Story Writers (over a period of centuries), who died with their real gifts stifled within them.

And, if this were the end the story, we would have cause to cry out in my paraphrase of Okot p'Bitek's[3] great poem:

> O, my clanswomen
> Let us all cry together!
> Come,
> Let us mourn the death of our mother,
> The death of a Queen

---

[3] Okot p'Bitek (1931–1982) was a Ugandan poet best known for the poem "Song of Lawino." —Eds.

The ash that was produced
By a great fire!
O, this homestead is utterly dead
Close the gates
With *lacari* thorns,
For our mother
The creator of the Stool is lost!
And all the young women
Have perished in the wilderness!

But this is not the end of the story, for all the young women — our mothers and grandmothers, *ourselves* — have not perished in the wilderness. And if we ask ourselves why, and search for and find the answer, we will know beyond all efforts to erase it from our minds, just exactly who, and of what, we black American women are.

One example, perhaps the most pathetic, most misunderstood one, can provide a backdrop for our mothers' work: Phillis Wheatley, a slave in the 1700s.

Virginia Woolf, in her book *A Room of One's Own,* wrote that in order for a woman to write fiction she must have two things, certainly: a room of her own (with key and lock) and enough money to support herself.

What then are we to make of Phillis Wheatley, a slave, who owned not even herself? This sickly, frail black girl who required a servant of her own at times — her health was so precarious — and who, had she been white, would have been easily considered the intellectual superior of all the women and most of the men in the society of her day.

Virginia Woolf wrote further, speaking of course not of our Phillis, that "any woman born with a great gift in the sixteenth century [insert "eighteenth century," insert "black woman," insert "born or made a slave"] would certainly have gone crazed, shot herself, or ended her days in some lonely cottage outside the village, half witch, half wizard [insert "Saint"], feared and mocked at. For it needs little skill and psychology to be sure that a highly gifted girl who had tried to use her gift for poetry would have been so

15

This engraving of poet and former slave Phillis Wheatley was likely done by a slave named Scipio Moorhead around 1773.
How does this detail about the authorship of the engraving relate to Walker's central message? How does Moorhead's depiction of Wheatley align with Walker's?

Library of Congress

thwarted and hindered by contrary instincts [add "chains, guns, the lash, the ownership of one's body by someone else, submission to an alien religion"], that she must have lost her health and sanity to a certainty."

The key words, as they relate to Phillis, are "contrary instincts." For when we read the poetry of Phillis Wheatley — as when we read the novels of Nella Larsen[4] or the oddly false-sounding autobiography of that freest of all black women writers, Zora Hurston — evidence of "contrary instincts" is everywhere. Her loyalties were

---

[4] Nella Larsen (1891–1964) was a Harlem Renaissance writer who published two novels: *Quicksand* (1928) and *Passing* (1929). —Eds.

completely divided, as was, without question, her mind.

But how could this be otherwise? Captured at seven, a slave of wealthy, doting whites who instilled in her the "savagery" of the Africa they "rescued" her from, one wonders if she was even able to remember her homeland as she had known it, or as it really was.

Yet, because she did try to use her gift for poetry in a world that made her a slave, she was "so thwarted and hindered by . . . contrary instincts, that she . . . lost her health. . . ." In the last years of her brief life, burdened not only with the need to express her gift but also with a penniless, friendless "freedom" and several small children for whom she was forced to do strenuous work to feed, she lost her health, certainly. Suffering from malnutrition and neglect and who knows what mental agonies, Phillis Wheatley died.

So torn by "contrary instincts" was black, kidnapped, enslaved Phillis that her description of "the Goddess" — as she poetically called the Liberty she did not have — is ironically, cruelly humorous. And, in fact, has held Phillis up to ridicule for more than a century. It is usually read prior to hanging Phillis's memory as that of a fool. She wrote:

> The Goddess comes, she moves divinely fair,
> Olive and laurel binds her *golden* hair.
> Wherever shines this native of the skies,
> Unnumber'd charms and recent graces rise.
> [My italics]

It is obvious that Phillis, the slave, combed the "Goddess's" hair every morning; prior, perhaps, to bringing in the milk, or fixing her mistress's lunch. She took her imagery from the one thing she saw elevated above all others.

With the benefit of hindsight we ask, "How could she?"

But at last, Phillis, we understand. No more snickering when your stiff, struggling, ambivalent lines are forced on us. We know now that you

were not an idiot or a traitor; only a sickly little black girl, snatched from your home and country and made a slave; a woman who still struggled to sing the song that was your gift, although in a land of barbarians who praised you for your bewildered tongue. It is not so much what you sang, as that you kept alive, in so many of our ancestors, *the notion of song*.

◆ ◆ ◆

Black women are called, in the folklore that so aptly identifies one's status in society, "the *mule* of the world," because we have been handed the burdens that everyone else — *everyone else* — refused to carry. We have also been called "Matriarchs," "Superwomen," and "Mean and Evil Bitches." Not to mention "Castraters" and "Sapphire's Mama." When we have pleaded for understanding, our character has been distorted; when we have asked for simple caring, we have been handed empty inspirational appellations, then stuck in the farthest corner. When we have asked for love, we have been given children. In short, even our plainer gifts, our labors of fidelity and love, have been knocked down our throats. To be an artist and a black woman, even today, lowers our status in many respects, rather than raises it: and yet, artists we will be.

Therefore we must fearlessly pull out of ourselves and look at and identify with our lives the living creativity some of our great-grandmothers were not allowed to know. I stress *some* of them because it is well known that the majority of our great-grandmothers knew, even without "knowing" it, the reality of their spirituality, even if they didn't recognize it beyond what happened in the singing at church — and they never had any intention of giving it up.

◆ ◆ ◆

How they did it — those millions of black women who were not Phillis Wheatley, or Lucy Terry or Frances Harper or Zora Hurston or Nella Larsen or Bessie Smith; or Elizabeth Catlett, or Katherine

This photograph, taken by Dorothea Lange, shows a sharecropper's wife in front of her family's home in 1937. **How does Lange portray her subject? What does this image add to your understanding of Walker's description of her childhood experiences?**

Library of Congress

Dunham,[5] either — brings me to the title of this essay, "In Search of Our Mothers' Gardens," which is a personal account that is yet shared, in its theme and its meaning, by all of us. I found, while thinking about the far-reaching world of the creative black woman, that often the truest answer to a question that really matters can be found very close.

◆ ◆ ◆

In the late 1920s my mother ran away from home to marry my father. Marriage, if not running away, was expected of seventeen-year-old girls. By the time she was twenty, she had two children and was pregnant with a third. Five children later, I was born. And this is how I came to know my mother: she seemed a large, soft, loving-eyed woman who was rarely impatient in our home. Her quick, violent temper was on view only a few times a year, when she battled with the white landlord who had the misfortune to suggest to her that her children did not need to go to school.

She made all the clothes we wore, even my brothers' overalls. She made all the towels and 30

sheets we used. She spent the summers canning vegetables and fruits. She spent the winter evenings making quilts enough to cover all our beds.

During the "working" day, she labored beside — not behind — my father in the fields. Her day began before sunup, and did not end until late at night. There was never a moment for her to sit down, undisturbed, to unravel her own private thoughts; never a time free from interruption — by work or the noisy inquiries of her many children. And yet, it is to my mother — and all our mothers who were not famous — that I went in search of the secret of what has fed that muzzled and often mutilated, but vibrant, creative spirit that the black woman has inherited, and that pops out in wild and unlikely places to this day.

But when, you will ask, did my overworked mother have time to know or care about feeding the creative spirit?

The answer is so simple that many of us have spent years discovering it. We have constantly looked high, when we should have looked high — and low.

For example: in the Smithsonian Institution in Washington, D.C., there hangs a quilt unlike any other in the world. In fanciful, inspired, and

_____

[5] African American writers, musicians, and artists who were influential throughout the eighteenth, nineteenth, and twentieth centuries. —Eds.

seeing connections

Shown here is a quilt made by Emma Civey Stahl around 1875, most likely in Illinois. Three of the vignettes depict Civil War soldiers, and another three feature scenes from the American suffrage movement. In the close-up included here, a woman leaves her husband and child at home to go to a suffragette meeting. A "WOMAN'S RIGHTS" banner flies in the foreground.

What story does this quilt tell? How might it illustrate Walker's point about "looking high — and low" (para. 33)?

© The Metropolitan Museum of Art/Art Resource, NY

© The Metropolitan Museum of Art/Art Resource, NY

yet simple and identifiable figures, it portrays the story of the Crucifixion. It is considered rare, beyond price. Though it follows no known pattern of quilt-making, and though it is made of bits and pieces of worthless rags, it is obviously the work of a person of powerful imagination and deep spiritual feeling. Below this quilt I saw a note that says it was made by "an anonymous Black woman in Alabama, a hundred years ago."

If we could locate this "anonymous" black woman from Alabama, she would turn out to be one of our grandmothers — an artist who left her mark in the only materials she could afford, and in the only medium her position in society allowed her to use.

As Virginia Woolf wrote further, in *A Room of One's Own:*

Yet genius of a sort must have existed among women as it must have existed among the working class. [Change this to "slaves" and "the wives and daughters of sharecroppers."] Now and again an Emily Brontë or a Robert Burns [change this to "a Zora Hurston or a Richard Wright"] blazes out and proves its presence. But certainly it never got itself on to paper. When, however, one reads of a witch being ducked, of a woman possessed by devils [or "Sainthood"], of a wise woman selling herbs [our root workers], or even a very remarkable man who had a mother, then I think we are on the track of a lost novelist, a

35

suppressed poet, of some mute and inglorious Jane Austen. . . . Indeed, I would venture to guess that Anon, who wrote so many poems without signing them, was often a woman. . . .

And so our mothers and grandmothers have, more often than not anonymously, handed on the creative spark, the seed of the flower they themselves never hoped to see: or like a sealed letter they could not plainly read.

And so it is, certainly, with my own mother. Unlike "Ma" Rainey's songs, which retained their creator's name even while blasting forth from Bessie Smith's mouth, no song or poem will bear my mother's name. Yet so many of the stories that I write, that we all write, are my mother's stories. Only recently did I fully realize this: that through years of listening to my mother's stories of her life, I have absorbed not only the stories themselves, but something of the manner in which she spoke, something of the urgency that involves the knowledge that her stories — like her life — must be recorded. It is probably for this reason that so much of what I have written is about characters whose counterparts in real life are so much older than I am.

But the telling of these stories, which came from my mother's lips as naturally as breathing, was not the only way my mother showed herself as an artist. For stories, too, were subject to being distracted, to dying without conclusion. Dinners must be started, and cotton must be gathered before the big rains. The artist that was and is my mother showed itself to me only after many years. This is what I finally noticed:

Like Mem, a character in *The Third Life of Grange Copeland,* my mother adorned with flowers whatever shabby house we were forced to live in. And not just your typical straggly country stand of zinnias, either. She planted ambitious gardens — and still does — with over fifty different varieties of plants that bloom profusely from early March until late November. Before she left home for the fields, she watered her flowers, chopped up the grass, and laid out new beds. When she returned from the fields she might divide clumps of bulbs, dig a cold pit, uproot and replant roses, or prune branches from her taller bushes or trees — until night came and it was too dark to see.

Whatever she planted grew as if by magic, and her fame as a grower of flowers spread over three counties. Because of her creativity with her flowers, even my memories of poverty are seen through a screen of blooms — sunflowers, petunias, roses, dahlias, forsythia, spirea, delphiniums, verbena . . . and on and on.

And I remember people coming to my mother's yard to be given cuttings from her flowers; I hear again the praise showered on her because whatever rocky soil she landed on, she turned into a garden. A garden so brilliant with colors, so original in its design, so magnificent with life and creativity, that to this day people drive by our house in Georgia — perfect strangers and imperfect strangers — and ask to stand or walk among my mother's art.

I notice that it is only when my mother is working in her flowers that she is radiant, almost to the point of being invisible — except as Creator: hand and eye. She is involved in work her soul must have. Ordering the universe in the image of her personal conception of Beauty.

Her face, as she prepares the Art that is her gift, is a legacy of respect she leaves to me, for all that illuminates and cherishes life. She has handed down respect for the possibilities — and the will to grasp them.

For her, so hindered and intruded upon in so many ways, being an artist has still been a daily part of her life. This ability to hold on, even in very simple ways, is work black women have done for a very long time.

This poem is not enough, but it is something, for the woman who literally covered the holes in our walls with sunflowers:

They were women then
My mama's generation
Husky of voice — Stout of
Step

seeing connections

This 1996 lithograph by African American artist Faith Ringgold (b. 1930) is in the collection of the Philadelphia Museum of Art. Entitled *The Sunflower Quilting Bee at Arles* (1991), it depicts eight prominent African American women throughout American history standing together, each holding a section of a quilt that celebrates their achievements. From the upper left, these women are entrepreneur Madam C. J. Walker (1867–1919), abolitionist Sojourner Truth (c. 1797–1883), journalist Ida B. Wells (1862–1931), civil rights activist Fannie Lou Hamer (1917–1977), abolitionist Harriet Tubman (c. 1822–1913), civil rights activist Rosa Parks (1913–2005), educator Mary McLeod Bethune (1875–1955), and civil rights activist Ella Baker (1903–1986). The ninth figure holding the quilt, on the lower left, is Willia Marie Simone, a fictional character created by Ringgold. The artist Vincent van Gogh (1853–1890), who was known for his paintings of sunflowers and lived in the French city of Arles, stands to the right and slightly in the background.

Look carefully at this lithograph, and then answer the following questions.

1. **How would you describe the mood of the piece, and how is that mood reflected in Ringgold's artistic style?**

2. **How does Ringgold characterize each of the women, and why do you think she chose these eight in particular? How do you interpret the inclusion of the fictional Willia Marie Simone?**

3. **Why do you believe Ringgold chose this particular setting? What might the inclusion of Vincent Van Gogh signify?**

4. **How does this image reflect the themes of Alice Walker's essay?**

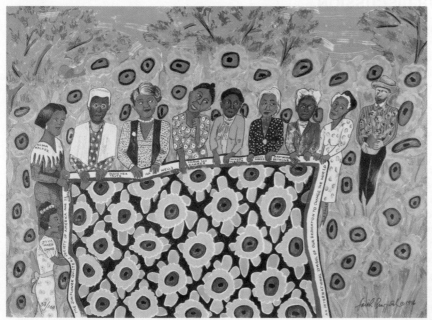

The Philadelphia Museum of Art/Art Resource, NY

With fists as well as

Hands

How they battered down

Doors

And ironed

Starched white

Shirts

How they led

Armies

Headragged Generals

Across mined

Fields

Booby-trapped

Kitchens

To discover books

Desks

A place for us

How they knew what we

Must know

Without knowing a page

Of it

Themselves.

Guided by my heritage of a love of beauty and a respect for strength — in search of my mother's garden, I found my own.

And perhaps in Africa over two hundred years ago, there was just such a mother; perhaps she painted vivid and daring decorations in oranges and yellows and greens on the walls of her hut; perhaps she sang — in a voice like Roberta Flack's — *sweetly* over the compounds of her village; perhaps she wove the most stunning mats or told the most ingenious stories of all the village storytellers. Perhaps she was herself a poet — though only her daughter's name is signed to the poems that we know.

Perhaps Phillis Wheatley's mother was also an artist.

Perhaps in more than Phillis Wheatley's 50 biological life is her mother's signature made clear.

[1972]

QUESTIONS FOR DISCUSSION

1. The title of this essay is "In Search of Our Mothers' Gardens." What do you think that Alice Walker intends to signal at the very outset by her use of the first person plural ("our") rather than the singular pronoun "(my")?

2. The poem "Motheroot" appears before the essay as a kind of dedication. What images in the poem set the stage for an essay on mothers and motherhood?

3. In the opening quotation by Jean Toomer, as the speaker describes his conversation with a prostitute, he points out that "in lieu of proper channels, her emotions had overflowed into paths that dissipated them." What do you take this to mean? How does this description set the stage for the central ideas in Walker's essay?

4. Why does Walker examine Virginia Woolf's phrase "contrary instincts" (paras. 18–25) so closely? In what ways does it resonate for Walker several decades after it was written?

5. What is it about Phillis Wheatley that fascinates Walker? Consider the conclusion of the essay (paras. 49–50) as you formulate your response.

6. What does Walker mean when she asserts, "To be an artist and a black woman, even today, lowers our status in many respects, rather than raises it: and yet, artists we will be" (para. 26)? Do you agree? Explain why or why not.

7. Walker describes her mother in some detail in this essay. Which of her mother's qualities does she emphasize? In what ways does her mother encourage Walker to become a writer? How might this essay be considered her mother's legacy?

8. Walker asks — or suggests that her readers might ask — how her "overworked mother" (para. 32) was even aware of the desire for creative expression. She responds: "The answer is so simple that many of us have spent years discovering it. We have constantly looked high,

when we should have looked high — and low" (para. 33). What does Walker mean by "that paradox"?

9. Throughout the essay, Walker identifies her foremothers with a range of terms, such as "'Saints'" and "crazy, loony, pitiful women" (para. 2); "Artists" (para. 9); "pathetic . . . misunderstood" (para. 15); and "Creator[s]" (para. 9). Does she ever settle on a description that encompasses the ambitions and abilities of all of these women? What does this wide range suggest about how she views these women?

10. Walker asks, "What did it mean for a black woman to be an artist in our grandmothers' time? In our great-grandmothers' day?" (para. 10). How does Walker answer this question in the essay? Is answering the question the purpose of her essay?

11. How do you interpret Walker's last line: "Perhaps in more than Phillis Wheatley's biological life is her mother's signature made clear" (para. 50)? In what ways might this statement relate to Walker's own journey as a writer?

12. Published in 1972, this essay has remained enormously popular for nearly fifty years. What do you think accounts for its lasting appeal?

QUESTIONS ON RHETORIC AND STYLE

1. Walker uses figurative language extensively throughout the essay. For instance, she writes: "And so our mothers and grandmothers have, more often than not anonymously, handed on the creative spark, the seed of the flower they themselves never hoped to see: or like a sealed letter they could not plainly read" (para. 37). Identify at least two other examples of figurative language and discuss their effect.

2. Paragraph 28 signals a rhetorical shift in the essay. How would you characterize the structure of the essay before and after this shift? What purpose does this shift serve in Walker's argument?

3. Merriam-Webster defines "intertextuality" as "the complex interrelationship between a text and other texts taken as basic to the creation or interpretation of the text." Walker uses intertextuality throughout her essay — from the poem by Okot p'Bitek to passages from Jean Toomer and Virginia Woolf. Choose one of these instances and analyze how Walker uses the secondary text to develop her own argument. Does she use intertextuality mainly to establish her own ethos or to appeal to reason by citing a series of examples that support her central claim?

4. What is Walker's attitude toward Virginia Woolf? Why is she drawn to her? Does she admire her? Is she critical of her? A little of both? Explain.

5. Walker concludes with an untitled poem that she wrote specifically for "In Search of Our Mothers' Gardens." How effective is this poem as a rhetorical strategy?

6. One way to interpret Walker's inclusion of her own experiences is that she is developing herself as an authority, implicitly asserting that her experiences are evidence drawn from expert testimony. To what extent do you agree with this interpretation of this rhetorical strategy? Explain.

7. Phillis Wheatley is, arguably, as strong a presence in this essay as is Walker herself. In what ways does Walker use the conventional view of Wheatley as the counterargument — which she concedes and refutes — to build her own argument?

8. Walker writes explicitly about "our mothers and grandmothers" (para. 3) — that is, the female ancestors of African American women. Is her audience primarily African American women, or do you think that she writes for a broader, more diverse audience? Cite specific passages and rhetorical moves to support your position.

9. Critics have described this essay as a "quest narrative," meaning a personal journey — a "search" — that takes on mythic qualities as it becomes the story of a community. To what extent do you think that is an appropriate description?

SUGGESTIONS FOR WRITING

1. From the very title of this essay, Walker develops the garden (and plants and flowers) as both a literal setting and a powerful symbol. Write an essay analyzing how she uses this imagery to develop her argument.

2. The subtitle of the essay collection *In Search of Our Mothers' Gardens* is *Womanist Prose*. In the introduction to the collection, Walker offers four definitions of the term "womanist," including:

   1. From *womanish*. (Opp. Of "girlish," i.e., frivolous, irresponsible, not serious.) A black feminist or feminist of color. From the black folk expression of mothers to female children, "You acting womanish," i.e., like a woman. Usually referring to outrageous, audacious, courageous or *willful* behavior. Wanting to know more and in greater depth than is considered "good" for one. Interested in grown-up doings. Acting grown up. Being grown up. Interchangeable with another black folk expression: "You trying to be grown." Responsible. In charge. *Serious*. . . .

   4. Womanist is to feminist as purple is to lavender.

   How might these definitions of womanist prose be applied to "In Search of Our Mothers' Gardens"? Provide specific examples from the text.

3. In a review of the essay collection in which "In Search of Our Mothers' Gardens" first appeared, one critic wrote that Walker "strives to maintain an awareness of and openness to mystery" in her writing. To that reviewer, this quality "is deeper than any politics, race, or geographical location." Write an essay analyzing how "In Search of Our Mothers' Gardens" demonstrates an openness to mystery, and why this is an important part of what gives the essay its rhetorical power.

4. Critics debate whether using personal experience is an effective way to address social issues — that is, whether such an approach is a strategy likely to effect change. Discuss what you believe to be the effect of the highly personal nature of Walker's approach in this essay on the social criticism that is the heart of her argument.

5. Walker's short story "Everyday Use" strikes many of the same chords as "In Search of Our Mother's Garden," though the methods of fiction differ from those of nonfiction. Compare and contrast the similarities in themes and ideas of the two works.

6. In two places in this essay (paras. 18 and 36), Walker quotes from Virginia Woolf's *A Room of One's Own* and comments parenthetically. Do a dramatic reading with two voices that interprets Walker's use of Woolf as evidence for her argument. Record this reading (with or without music in the background). Write an explanation of your interpretation of Walker's attitude toward Woolf and how the recording illustrates it.

7. Throughout "In Search of Our Mothers' Gardens," Walker mentions African American women of note, including Nina Simone, Bessie Smith, Nella Larsen, Elizabeth Catlett, Katherine Dunham, and Zora Neale Hurston. Research one of them and develop a multimedia presentation on how your choice illustrates the points Walker makes in her essay.

Professions for Women

VIRGINIA WOOLF

A prolific novelist, critic, and essayist, Virginia Woolf (1882–1941) was born in London. Her novels, particularly *Mrs. Dalloway* (1925) and *To the Lighthouse* (1927), are renowned for their penetrating psychological insight. Her novels are known for their use of interior monologue, or stream of consciousness. Woolf is also noted for her nonfiction, especially for such works as *The Common Reader* (1925), *A Room of One's Own* (1929), and *Three Guineas* (1938). Having struggled with depression for much of her life, she drowned herself in 1941. "Professions for Women," delivered as a talk in 1931 to the Women's Service League, was included in *The Death of the Moth and Other Essays* (1942).

Culture Club/Getty Images

When your secretary invited me to come here, she told me that your Society is concerned with the employment of women and she suggested that I might tell you something about my own professional experiences. It is true I am a woman; it is true I am employed; but what professional experiences have I had? It is difficult to say. My profession is literature; and in that profession there are fewer experiences for women than in any other, with the exception of the stage — fewer, I mean, that are peculiar to women. For the road was cut many years ago — by Fanny Burney, by Aphra Behn, by Harriet Martineau, by Jane Austen, by George Eliot — many famous women, and many more unknown and forgotten, have been before me, making the path smooth, and regulating my steps. Thus, when I came to write, there were very few material obstacles in my way. Writing was a reputable and harmless occupation. The family peace was not broken by the scratching of a pen. No demand was made upon the family purse. For ten and sixpence one can buy paper enough to write all the plays of Shakespeare — if one has a mind that way. Pianos and models, Paris, Vienna and Berlin, masters and mistresses, are not needed by a writer. The cheapness of writing paper is, of course, the reason why women have succeeded as writers before they have succeeded in the other professions.

But to tell you my story — it is a simple one. You have only got to figure to yourselves a girl in a bedroom with a pen in her hand. She had only to move that pen from left to right — from ten o'clock to one. Then it occurred to her to do what is simple and cheap enough after all — to slip a few of those pages into an envelope, fix a penny stamp in the corner, and drop the envelope into the red box at the corner. It was thus that I became a journalist; and my effort was rewarded on the first day of the following month — a very glorious day it was for me — by a letter from an editor containing a cheque for one pound ten shillings and sixpence. But to show you how little I deserve to be called a professional woman, how little I know of the struggles and difficulties of such lives, I have to admit that instead of spending that sum upon bread and butter, rent, shoes and stockings, or butcher's bills, I went out and bought a cat — a beautiful cat, a Persian cat, which very soon involved me in bitter disputes with my neighbours.

Roger Fry painted this portrait of Virginia Woolf in 1917. Fry, an English post-Impressionist painter and critic, was part of the Bloomsbury Group that included Woolf, her husband Leonard Woolf, her sister Vanessa Bell, and other prominent artists and writers of the time. **How does Fry characterize Woolf? How does Woolf's portrayal of herself in "Professions for Women[1]" compare with this painting?**

On Loan to Leeds Museums and Galleries (Leeds Art Gallery)/Bridgeman Images

What could be easier than to write articles and to buy Persian cats with the profits? But wait a moment. Articles have to be about something. Mine, I seem to remember, was about a novel by a famous man. And while I was writing this review, I discovered that if I were going to review books I should need to do battle with a certain phantom. And the phantom was a woman, and when I came to know her better I called her after the heroine of a famous poem, The Angel in the House.[1] It was she who used to come between me

[1] "The Angel in the House" is a nineteenth-century poem about a self-sacrificing heroine; for many, she represented the ideal Victorian woman. —Eds.

and my paper when I was writing reviews. It was she who bothered me and wasted my time and so tormented me that at last I killed her. You who come of a younger and happier generation may not have heard of her — you may not know what I mean by the Angel in the House. I will describe her as shortly as I can. She was intensely sympathetic. She was immensely charming. She was utterly unselfish. She excelled in the difficult arts of family life. She sacrificed herself daily. If there was chicken, she took the leg; if there was a draught she sat in it — in short she was so constituted that she never had a mind or a wish of her own, but preferred to sympathize always with the minds and wishes of others. Above all — I need not say it — she was pure. Her purity was supposed to be her chief beauty — her blushes, her great grace. In those days — the last of Queen Victoria — every house had its Angel. And when I came to write I encountered her with the very first words. The shadow of her wings fell on my page; I heard the rustling of her skirts in the room. Directly, that is to say, I took my pen in my hand to review that novel by a famous man, she slipped behind me and whispered: "My dear, you are a young woman. You are writing about a book that has been written by a man. Be sympathetic; be tender; flatter; deceive; use all the arts and wiles of our sex. Never let anybody guess that you have a mind of your own. Above all, be pure." And she made as if to guide my pen. I now record the one act for which I take some credit to myself, though the credit rightly belongs to some excellent ancestors of mine who left me a certain sum of money — shall we say five hundred pounds a year? — so that it was not necessary for me to depend solely on charm for my living. I turned upon her and caught her by the throat. I did my best to kill her. My excuse, if I were to be had up in a court of law, would be that I acted in self-defence. Had I not killed her she would have killed me. She would have plucked the heart out of my writing. For, as I found, directly I put pen to paper, you cannot review even a novel without having a mind of your own, without expressing what you think to be the truth about human relations, morality, sex. And all these questions, according to the Angel of the House, cannot be dealt with freely and openly by women; they must charm, they must conciliate, they must — to put it bluntly — tell lies if they are to succeed. Thus, whenever I felt the shadow of her wing or the radiance of her halo upon my page, I took up the inkpot and flung it at her. She died hard. Her fictitious nature was of great assistance to her. It is far harder to kill a phantom than a reality. She was always creeping back when I thought I had despatched her. Though I flatter myself that I killed her in the end, the struggle was severe; it took much time that had better have been spent upon learning Greek grammar; or in roaming the world in search of adventures. But it was a real experience; it was an experience that was found to befall all women writers at that time. Killing the Angel in the House was part of the occupation of a woman writer.

But to continue my story. The Angel was dead; what then remained? You may say that what remained was a simple and common object — a young woman in a bedroom with an inkpot. In other words, now that she had rid herself of falsehood, that young woman had only to be herself. Ah, but what is "herself"? I mean, what is a woman? I assure you, I do not know. I do not believe that you know. I do not believe that anybody can know until she has expressed herself in all the arts and professions open to human skill. That indeed is one of the reasons why I have come here — out of respect for you, who are in process of showing us by your experiments what a woman is, who are in process of providing us, by your failures and successes, with that extremely important piece of information.

But to continue the story of my professional experiences. I made one pound ten and six by my first review; and I bought a Persian cat with the proceeds. Then I grew ambitious. A Persian cat is all very well, I said; but a Persian cat is not enough. I must have a motor car. And it was thus that I became a novelist — for it is a very strange thing that people will give you a motor car if you will tell them a story. It is a still stranger thing that there is nothing so delightful in the world as telling stories. It is far pleasanter than writing reviews of famous novels. And yet, if I am to obey your secretary and tell you my professional experiences as a novelist, I must tell you about a very strange experience that befell me as a novelist. And to understand it you must try first to imagine a novelist's state of mind. I hope I am not giving away professional

STAPLETON COLLECTION/Victoria & Albert Museum, London, UK/Bridgeman Images

This color engraving by Franz Xaver Winterhalter shows Queen Victoria with her husband, Prince Albert, and five of their nine children. Victoria ruled the British Empire from 1837 to her death in 1876, the longest monarchy in British history. Some say that Victoria, known for her strict moral standards, embodied the ideal of the Angel in the House. **How does this work portray Victoria as that model? Are there any ways in which this depiction of her challenges the idea of the Angel in the House?**

secrets if I say that a novelist's chief desire is to be as unconscious as possible. He has to induce in himself a state of perpetual lethargy. He wants life to proceed with the utmost quiet and regularity. He wants to see the same faces, to read the same books, to do the same things day after day, month after month, while he is writing, so that nothing may break the illusion in which he is living — so that nothing may disturb or disquiet the mysterious nosings about, feelings round, darts, dashes and sudden discoveries of that very shy and illusive spirit, the imagination. I suspect that this state is the same both for men and women. Be that as it may, I want you to imagine me writing a novel in a state of trance. I want you to figure to yourselves a girl sitting with a pen in her hand, which for minutes, and indeed for hours, she never dips into the inkpot. The image that comes to my mind when I think of this girl is the image of a fisherman lying sunk in dreams on the verge of a deep lake with a rod held out over the water. She was letting her imagination sweep unchecked round every rock and cranny of the world that lies submerged in the depths of our unconscious being. Now came the experience, the experience that I believe to be far commoner with women writers than with men. The line raced through the girl's fingers. Her imagination had rushed away. It had sought the pools, the depths, the dark places where the largest fish slumber. And then there was a smash. There was an explosion. There was foam and confusion. The imagination had dashed itself against something hard. The girl was roused from her dream. She was indeed in a state of the most acute and difficult

seeing connections

This still is from the 2004 film version of *The Stepford Wives*, based on the 1972 satirical thriller novel by Ira Levin. Its plot follows a working woman who has recently moved from the city to the suburbs with her husband and children. In her new neighborhood, she meets a group of suburban men and their happily subservient, beautiful wives — and she gradually becomes convinced that they are somehow being brainwashed into submission. Here, Nicole Kidman plays one of the happy homemakers.

What do you notice about Kidman's pose and expression that suggest the film is a criticism or parody of "The Angel in the House"?

DreamWorks/Photofest

distress. To speak without figure she had thought of something, something about the body, about the passions which it was unfitting for her as a woman to say. Men, her reason told her, would be shocked. The consciousness of what men will say of a woman who speaks the truth about her passions had roused her from her artist's state of unconsciousness. She could write no more. The trance was over. Her imagination could work no longer. This I believe to be a very common experience with women writers — they are impeded by the extreme conventionality of the other sex. For though men sensibly allow themselves great freedom in these respects, I doubt that they realize or can control the extreme severity with which they condemn such freedom in women.

These then were two very genuine experiences of my own. These were two of the adventures of my professional life. The first — killing the Angel in the House — I think I solved. She died. But the second, telling the truth about my own experiences as a body, I do not think I solved. I doubt that any woman has solved it yet. The obstacles against her are still immensely powerful — and yet they are very difficult to define. Outwardly, what is simpler than to write

books? Outwardly, what obstacles are there for a woman rather than for a man? Inwardly, I think, the case is very different; she has still many ghosts to fight, many prejudices to overcome. Indeed it will be a long time still, I think, before a woman can sit down to write a book without finding a phantom to be slain, a rock to be dashed against. And if this is so in literature, the freest of all professions for women, how is it in the new professions which you are now for the first time entering?

Those are the questions that I should like, had I time, to ask you. And indeed, if I have laid stress upon these professional experiences of mine, it is because I believe that they are, though in different forms, yours also. Even when the path is nominally open — when there is nothing to prevent a woman from being a doctor, a lawyer, a civil servant — there are many phantoms and obstacles, as I believe, looming in her way. To discuss and define them is I think of great value and importance; for thus only can the labour be shared, the difficulties be solved. But besides this, it is necessary also to discuss the ends and the aims for which we are fighting, for which we are doing battle with these formidable obstacles. Those aims cannot be taken for granted; they

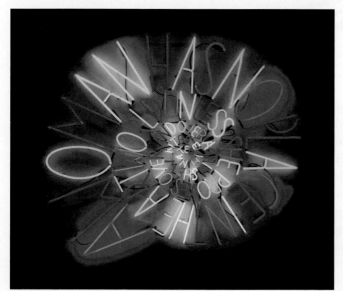

Photo courtesy of Deborah Kass/Art Resource, NY

This piece by American artist Deborah Kass is constructed from neon lights. It reads: "A WOMAN HAS NO PLACE IN THE ART WORLD UNLESS SHE PROVES OVER AND OVER AGAIN SHE WON'T BE ELIMINATED."

How does the medium of this work support the artist's message? Based on your reading of "Professions for Women," to what extent would Woolf agree?

seeing connections

This 1884 cartoon from the British satire publication *Punch* shows a woman who has won a seat in the House of Commons thanks to women's suffrage. Its caption references "The Angel in 'the House.'" The woman in the center has dropped her knitting project — a "bluestocking," which was an unflattering term for women who were highly educated or intellectual.

What is the cartoonist's stance on women's suffrage? How does this image address many of the issues in "Professions for Women"?

JUNE 14, 1884.]   PUNCH, OR THE LONDON CHARIVARI.   279

"THE ANGEL IN 'THE HOUSE;'" OR, THE RESULT OF FEMALE SUFFRAGE.
(A Troubled Dream of the Future.)

Print Collector/Getty Images

must be perpetually questioned and examined. The whole position, as I see it — here in this hall surrounded by women practising for the first time in history I know not how many different professions — is one of extraordinary interest and importance. You have won rooms of your own in the house hitherto exclusively owned by men. You are able, though not without great labour and effort, to pay the rent. You are earning your five hundred pounds a year. But this freedom is only a beginning; the room is your own, but it is still bare. It has to be furnished; it has to be decorated; it has to be shared. How are you going to furnish it, how are you going to decorate it? With whom are you going to share it, and upon what terms? These, I think, are questions of the utmost importance and interest. For the first time in history you are able to ask them; for the first time you are able to decide for yourselves what the answers should be. Willingly would I stay and discuss those questions and answers — but not tonight. My time is up; and I must cease.

[1931]

QUESTIONS FOR DISCUSSION

1. According to Virginia Woolf, what are the two main obstacles to women's professional identity? Are these still the two main obstacles, or does the contemporary woman face different hurdles? Explain.

2. Research the origin of "The Angel in the House" (para. 3). Why is this an appropriate or effective frame of reference for Woolf?

3. What do you think Woolf means in paragraph 5 when she asserts that "a novelist's chief desire is to be as unconscious as possible"? Do you agree that someone who writes fiction should be "unconscious"? Why do you think a novelist would want to be "unconscious" or would benefit from being "unconscious"?

4. In paragraphs 5 and 6, Woolf explores the consequences of being unable to tell "the truth" about her own "experiences as a body." What does she mean? Why does she believe that surmounting this obstacle is more difficult — perhaps impossible at the time she was writing — than "killing the Angel in the House"?

5. In her conclusion, Woolf apologizes to a certain extent for dwelling on her own experience, and then points out that her "professional experiences . . . are, though in different forms,"

(para. 7) also the experiences of her audience. What exactly is she asking of her audience here?

6. In an online essay, Barbara Wahl Ledingham makes the following assertion about the relevance of Woolf's essay to women in the twenty-first century:

> We must claim and have knowledge of our feminists, our artists, our mothers, our leaders, and our organizers, women like Susan B. Anthony . . . or Margaret Sanger. . . . All of these women acted despite persecution. Their sacrifice is responsible for many of the rights we take for granted today, but the biggest challenge is confronting our own Angel in the House, our own inner phantom, the one that keeps us from . . . defining and owning our own lives.

> With a kind of uncanny prescience, Woolf's words follow us seventy years later, haunting us with their veracity and timelessness. They are a gauge by which to measure not only our exterior accomplishments but also our inner state, and they serve as a warning not to lose consciousness or become apathetic about either realm.

After summarizing what Ledingham is saying, explain why you agree or disagree with her analysis.

QUESTIONS ON RHETORIC AND STYLE

1. How does Woolf present herself in the opening paragraph? What relationship is she establishing with her audience?

2. Identify an example in the opening paragraph of each of the following, and explain its effect: understatement, parallel structure, rhetorical question, irony, and metonymy.

3. What is the effect of the personal anecdote in paragraph 2? Does the anecdote appeal mainly to logos or pathos? Why is it especially effective for Woolf's audience?

4. What does Woolf mean in the following description of the Angel in the House: "The shadow of her wings fell on my page; I heard the rustling of her skirts in the room" (para. 3)?

5. Discuss the effect of the short, simple sentences that Woolf uses in paragraph 3. How do they

contribute to her tone as she describes the Angel in the House?

6. In paragraph 3, Woolf tells how she did her "best to kill [the Angel in the House]." Examine the words and images she uses to describe this act. Do you believe the violence of her descriptions to be appropriate? Explain why or why not.

7. How does the shift in person in paragraph 4 serve Woolf's purpose? In what ways is this a transitional paragraph?

8. What is the effect in paragraph 5 of Woolf's referring to a novelist as *he*? Should Woolf have used *she* as though she were referring to herself? Why or why not?

9. Summarize the extended analogy Woolf develops in paragraph 5 to describe "a girl sitting with a pen in her hand." Explain its effect.

10. Would you characterize the language at the end of paragraph 5, where Woolf writes about "the body," to be delicate and genteel or euphemistic? Explain, keeping in mind the historical context of the work.

11. By the time of this speech, Woolf's extended essay *A Room of One's Own* was well known as a feminist manifesto: Woolf claimed that every woman requires a separate income and a room of her own if she is to become an independent, productive woman. How does Woolf embellish this metaphor of a room of one's own in paragraph 7? What is the effect?

12. What is Woolf's overall tone in this speech? Because the tone evolves and shifts throughout the text, determining the overall tone is complex. Identify passages where Woolf displays various tones, sometimes in order to assume a specific persona, and then develop a description of the overall tone. You will probably need to use two words (possibly joined with *but* or *yet*) or a phrase rather than a single word. Does Woolf display anger, bitterness, resignation, aggression, apology, or combativeness? Or does she show a combination of these emotions or others?

SUGGESTIONS FOR WRITING

1. Write an essay analyzing the rhetorical strategies Woolf uses in this speech to reach her specific audience. Pay attention to the way she uses the tools of the novelist, such as characterization, scene setting, highly textured and specific descriptive detail, and figurative language.

2. Imagine that you have been invited to deliver a speech entitled "Professions for Women" to an audience of your peers, male and female. Cite Woolf to support your speech's thesis, or propose a counterargument to Woolf's position. Also, be sure to describe the audience and occasion of your speech.

3. If you have read any of Woolf's fiction (either her short stories or the novels *Mrs. Dalloway* or *To the Lighthouse*, for example), discuss how this essay informs them.

4. In *A Room of One's Own*, Woolf asks, what if Shakespeare had had a sister? She calls her Judith and considers whether circumstances would have encouraged or allowed Judith to write great plays. Write an essay comparing and contrasting the ideas and style of that essay with those in "Professions for Women."

5. In the conclusion of her speech, Woolf says, "Even when the path is nominally open — when there is nothing to prevent a woman from being a doctor, a lawyer, a civil servant — there are many phantoms and obstacles, as I believe, looming in her way" (para. 7). Write an essay in which you defend, challenge, or modify that statement with regard to women today in the United States *or* to women in another country where gender equality might be more problematic. Pay particular attention to what you see as the "phantoms and obstacles."

Letters

JOHN AND ABIGAIL ADAMS

John Adams (1735–1826), one of America's Founding Fathers, was the second president of the United States. His wife, Abigail Smith Adams (1744–1818), was also dedicated to the cause of independence and wrote frequently to him on the conditions of wartime Boston, which was held by the British for most of the American Revolutionary War. The city was liberated by George Washington's army just before these letters were written. In the following two letters, Abigail writes to her husband in Philadelphia, where he is serving in the Continental Congress, and John responds as both husband and politician. Abigail presses her husband to "remember the ladies" as he and his colleagues are discussing freedom from tyranny. Given the time period, her exhortation did not refer to women's suffrage but rather to laws regarding such matters as inheritance and spousal abuse.

From Abigail to John

Braintree, March 31, 1776

I wish you would ever write me a Letter half as long as I write you; and tell me if you may where your Fleet are gone? What sort of Defence Virginia can make against our common Enemy? Whether it is so situated as to make an able Defence? Are not the Gentery Lords and the common people vassals, are they not like the uncivilized Natives Brittain represents us to be? I hope their Riffel Men who have shewen themselves very savage and even Blood thirsty; are not a specimen of the Generality of the people.

I . . . am willing to allow the Colony great merrit for having produced a Washington but they have been shamefully duped by a Dunmore.[1]

I have sometimes been ready to think that the passion for Liberty cannot be Eaquelly Strong in the Breasts of those who have been accustomed to deprive their fellow Creatures of theirs. Of this I am certain that it is not founded upon that generous and christian principal of doing to others as we would that others should do unto us.

Do not you want to see Boston; I am fearfull of the small pox, or I should have been in before this time. I got Mr. Crane to go to our House and see what state it was in. I find it has been occupied by one of the Doctors of a Regiment, very dirty, but no other damage has been done to it. The few things which were left in it are all gone. Cranch has the key which he never deliverd up. I have wrote to him for it and am determined to get it cleand as soon as possible and shut it up. I look upon it a new acquisition of property, a property which one month ago I did not value at a single Shilling, and could with pleasure have seen it in flames.

The Town in General is left in a better state than we expected, more oweing to a percipitate flight than any Regard to the inhabitants, tho some individuals discoverd a sense of honour and justice and have left the rent of the Houses in which they were, for the owners and the furniture unhurt, or if damaged sufficent to make it good.

Others have committed abominable Ravages. The Mansion House of your President is safe and

5

---

[1]The Fourth Earl of Dunmore (John Murray) was the British colonial governor of Virginia from 1771 to 1776. He opposed independence for the colonies and was forced to return to England. —Eds.

the furniture unhurt whilst both the House and Furniture of the Solisiter General have fallen a prey to their own merciless party. Surely the very Fiends feel a Reverential awe for Virtue and patriotism, whilst they Detest the paricide[2] and traitor.

I feel very differently at the approach of spring to what I did a month ago. We knew not then whether we could plant or sow with safety, whether when we had toild we could reap the fruits of our own industery, whether we could rest in our own Cottages, or whether we should not be driven from the sea coasts to seek shelter in the wilderness, but now we feel as if we might sit under our own vine and eat the good of the land.

I feel a gaieti de Coar[3] to which before I was a stranger. I think the Sun looks brighter, the Birds sing more melodiously, and Nature puts on a more chearfull countanance. We feel a temporary peace, and the poor fugitives are returning to their deserted habitations.

Tho we felicitate ourselves, we sympathize with those who are trembling least the Lot of Boston should be theirs. But they cannot be in similar circumstances unless pusilanimity and cowardise should take possession of them. They have time and warning given them to see the Evil and shun it. — I long to hear that you have declared an independency — and by the way in the new Code of Laws which I suppose it will be necessary for you to make I desire you would Remember the Ladies, and be more generous and favourable to them than your ancestors. Do not put such unlimited power into the hand of the Husbands. Remember all Men would be tyrants if they could. If perticuliar care and attention is not paid to the Ladies we are determined to foment a Rebelion, and will not hold ourselves bound by any Laws in which we have no voice, or Representation.

That your Sex are Naturally Tyrannical is a Truth so thoroughly established as to admit of

How does this image portray Abigail Adams? What does it imply about her role in American history?

Louis S. Glanzman/Getty Images

no dispute, but such of you as wish to be happy willingly give up the harsh title of Master for the more tender and endearing one of Friend. Why then, not put it out of the power of the vicious and the Lawless to use us with cruelty and indignity with impunity. Men of Sense in all Ages abhor those customs which treat us only as the vassals of your Sex. Regard us then as Beings placed by providence under your protection and in immitation of the Supreem Being make use of that power only for our happiness.

10

---

[2]A son who murdered his father, also known as a *patricide*. —Eds.
[3]French (correctly spelled *gaieté de coeur*), happiness of heart. —Eds.

From John to Abigail

April 14, 1776

You justly complain of my short Letters, but the critical State of Things and the Multiplicity of Avocations must plead my Excuse. You ask where the Fleet is. The inclosed Papers will inform you. You ask what Sort of Defence Virginia can make. I believe they will make an able Defence. Their Militia and minute Men have been some time employed in training them selves and they have Nine Battallions of regulars as they call them, maintained among them, under good Officers, at the Continental Expence. They have set up a Number of Manufactories of Fire Arms, which are busily employed. They are tolerably supplied with Powder, and are successfull and assiduous, in making Salt Petre. Their neighbour-ing Sister or rather Daughter Colony of North Carolina, which is a warlike Colony, and has several Battallions at the Continental Expence, as well as a pretty good Militia, are ready to assist them, and they are in very good Spirits, and seem determined to make a brave Resistance. — The Gentry are very rich, and the common People very poor.

This Inequality of Property, gives an Aristocratical Turn to all their Proceedings, and occasions a strong Aversion in their Patricians, to Common Sense. But the Spirit of these Barons, is coming down, and it must submit.

It is very true, as you observe they have been duped by Dunmore. But this is a Common Case. All the Colonies are duped, more or less, at one Time and another. A more egregious Bubble was never blown up, than the Story of Commissioners coming to treat with the Congress. Yet it has gained Credit like a Charm, not only without but against the clearest Evidence. I never shall forget the Delusion, which seized our best and most sagacious Friends the dear Inhabitants of Boston, the Winter before last. Credulity and the Want of Foresight, are Imperfections in the human Character, that no Politician can sufficiently guard against.

You have given me some Pleasure, by your Account of a certain House in Queen Street. I had burned it, long ago, in Imagination. It rises now to my View like a Phoenix. — What shall I say of the Solicitor General? I pity his pretty Children, I pity his Father, and his sisters. I wish I could be clear that it is no moral Evil to pity him and his Lady. Upon Repentance they will certainly have a large Share in the Compassions of many. But . . . let Us take Warning and give it to our Children. Whenever Vanity, and Gaiety, a Love of Pomp and Dress, Furniture, Equipage, Buildings, great Company, expensive Diversions, and elegant Entertainments get the better of the Principles and Judgments of Men or Women there is no knowing where they will stop, nor into what Evils, natural, moral, or political, they will lead us.

Your Description of your own Gaiety de Coeur, charms me. Thanks be to God you have just Cause to rejoice — and may the bright Prospect be obscured by no Cloud.

As to Declarations of Independency, be patient. Read our Privateering Laws, and our Commercial Laws. What signifies a Word.

As to your extraordinary Code of Laws, I cannot but laugh. We have been told that our Struggle has loosened the bands of Government every where. That Children and Apprentices were disobedient — that schools and Colledges were grown turbulent — that Indians slighted their Guardians and Negroes grew insolent to their Masters.

But your Letter was the first Intimation that another Tribe more numerous and powerfull than all the rest were grown discontented. — This is rather too coarse a Compliment but you are so saucy, I wont blot it out.

Depend upon it, We know better than to repeal our Masculine systems. Altho they are in full Force, you know they are little more than Theory. We dare not exert our Power in its full Latitude. We are obliged to go fair, and softly, and in Practice you know We are the subjects. We have only the Name of Masters, and rather

15

HBO/Photofest

This still from the 2008 HBO miniseries *John Adams* shows Paul Giamatti as John Adams and Laura Linney as Abigail Adams.
Do their images here match your characterization of them, based on the details from their letters? What qualities might the creators of the miniseries have considered as they cast these two actors?

than give up this, which would compleatly subject Us to the Despotism of the Peticoat, I hope General Washington, and all our brave Heroes would fight. I am sure every good Politician would plot, as long as he would against Despotism, Empire, Monarchy, Aristocracy, Oligarchy, or Ochlocracy.[4] — A fine Story indeed.

—————
[4]Mob rule. —Eds.

I begin to think the Ministry as deep as they are wicked. After stirring up Tories, Landjobbers, Trimmers, Bigots, Canadians, Indians, Negroes, Hanoverians, Hessians, Russians, Irish Roman Catholicks, Scotch Renegadoes, at last they have stimulated the[e] to demand new Priviledges and threaten to rebell.

EXPLORING THE TEXT

1. What ethos does Abigail Adams establish in the opening paragraph? How do the questions contribute to the persona she presents?

2. Abigail describes Boston in considerable detail. What is the general impression she tries to convey? Why do you think she chose the details she did?

3. When Abigail exhorts John Adams to "Remember the Ladies," she also points out that "all Men would be tyrants if they could" (para. 9) and that "your Sex are Naturally Tyrannical" (para. 10). How does she make such statements without sounding accusatory or alienating her husband? Explain.

4. When John tells Abigail that he "cannot but laugh" (para. 17) at her suggestions for laws, is

he dismissing her? Is he disrespectful to her? Explain.

5. Is the last paragraph of John's letter written tongue-in-cheek, or is he serious? What does he mean by "the Despotism of the Peticoat" (para. 19)? How do you interpret this ending?

6. Describe the overall tone of each of these letters. Based on the tone and the information in the letters, describe the relationship between John and Abigail Adams. What evidence of intimacy do you find in each letter?

7. Imagine that Abigail and John Adams had access to email, and rewrite these two letters as email correspondence.

Biographical Notice of Ellis and Acton Bell

CHARLOTTE BRONTË

Charlotte Brontë (1816–1831) was an English novelist, poet, and the eldest of the three Brontë sisters, whose novels have become classics of English literature. Charlotte first published her works, including her best-known novel *Jane Eyre* (1847), under the pen name Currer Bell. Her sisters Emily (1818–1848) and Anne (1820–1849) also published their novels under male pen names: Ellis Bell and Acton Bell, respectively. Before the Brontë sisters revealed their identities to the public, there was much speculation that their writings were actually the work of a single author. In 1850, Emily's novel *Wuthering Heights* (1847) and Anne's novel *Agnes Grey* (1847) were reprinted together in a single volume. Since both sisters had recently died, Charlotte Brontë took the opportunity to write the following preface. In it, she clarifies the reasons why the Brontë sisters adopted masculine pseudonyms early in their careers.

It has been thought that all the works published under the names of Currer, Ellis, and Acton Bell were, in reality, the production of one person. This mistake I endeavoured to rectify by a few words of disclaimer prefixed to the third edition of "Jane Eyre." These, too, it appears, failed to gain general credence, and now, on the occasion of a reprint of "Wuthering Heights" and "Agnes Grey," I am advised distinctly to state how the case really stands.

Indeed, I feel myself that it is time the obscurity attending those two names — Ellis and Acton — was done away. The little mystery, which formerly yielded some harmless pleasure, has lost its interest; circumstances are changed. It becomes, then, my duty to explain briefly the origin and authorship of the books written by Currer, Ellis, and Acton Bell.

About five years ago, my two sisters and myself, after a somewhat prolonged period of separation, found ourselves reunited, and at home. Resident in a remote district, where education had made little progress, and where, consequently, there was no inducement to seek social intercourse beyond our own domestic circle, we were wholly dependent on ourselves and each other, on books and study, for the enjoyments and occupations of life. The highest stimulus, as well as the liveliest pleasure we had known from childhood upwards, lay in attempts at Literary composition; formerly we used to show each other what we wrote, but of late years this habit of communication and consultation had been discontinued; hence it ensued, that we were mutually ignorant of the progress we might respectively have made.

One day, in the autumn of 1845, I accidentally lighted on a MS. volume of verse in my sister Emily's handwriting. Of course, I was not surprised, knowing that she could and did write verse: I looked it over, and something more than surprise seized me — a deep conviction that these were not common effusions, nor at all like the poetry women generally write. I thought them condensed and terse, vigorous and genuine. To my ear they had also a peculiar music — wild, melancholy, and elevating.

My sister Emily was not a person of demonstrative character, nor one on the recesses of whose mind and feelings even those nearest and dearest to her could, with impunity, intrude unlicensed; it took hours to reconcile her to the discovery I had made, and days to persuade her that such poems merited publication. I knew, however, that a mind

5

BRIAN SEED/National Portrait Gallery, London, UK/Bridgeman Images

This detail from an 1834 portrait of the Brontë sisters shows (from left to right) Emily, Charlotte and Anne. It was painted by their brother Patrick Branwell, who originally included — and subsequently erased — himself. **How is the depiction of the three sisters in this image reflected in the "Biographical Notice of Ellis and Acton Bell"?**

like hers could not be without some latent spark of honourable ambition, and refused to be discouraged in my attempts to fan that spark to flame.

Meantime, my younger sister quietly produced some of her own compositions, intimating that, since Emily's had given me pleasure, I might like to look at hers. I could not but be a partial judge, yet I thought that these verses, too, had a sweet, sincere pathos of their own.

We had very early cherished the dream of one day becoming authors. This dream, never relinquished even when distance divided and absorbing tasks occupied us, now suddenly acquired strength and consistency: it took the character of a resolve. We agreed to arrange a small selection of our poems, and, if possible, to get them printed. Averse to personal publicity, we veiled our own names under those of Currer, Ellis, and Acton Bell; the ambiguous choice being dictated by a sort of conscientious scruple at assuming Christian names positively masculine, while we did not like to declare ourselves women, because — without at that time suspecting that our mode of writing and thinking was not what is called "feminine" — we had a vague impression that authoresses are liable to be looked on with prejudice; we had noticed how critics sometimes use for their chastisement the weapon of personality, and for their reward, a flattery, which is not true praise.

The bringing out of our little book was hard work. As was to be expected, neither we nor our poems were at all wanted; but for this we had been prepared at the outset; though inexperienced ourselves, we had read the experience of others. The great puzzle lay in the difficulty of getting answers of any kind from the publishers to whom we applied. Being greatly harassed by this obstacle, I ventured to apply to the Messrs. Chambers, of Edinburgh,[1] for a word of advice; *they* may have forgotten the circumstance, but *I* have not, for from them I received a brief and business-like, but civil and sensible reply, on which we acted, and at last made a way.

The book was printed: it is scarcely known, and all of it that merits to be known are the poems of Ellis Bell. The fixed conviction I held, and hold, of the worth of these poems has not indeed received the confirmation of much favourable criticism; but I must retain it notwithstanding.

Ill-success failed to crush us: the mere effort to succeed had given a wonderful zest to existence; it 10

[1]Robert and William Chambers, editors of *Chamber's Edinburgh Journal,* a popular utilitarian publication in the 1830s. —Eds.

must be pursued. We each set to work on a prose tale: Ellis Bell produced "Wuthering Heights," Acton Bell "Agnes Grey," and Currer Bell also wrote a narrative in one volume. These MSS. were perseveringly obtruded upon various publishers for the space of a year and a half; usually, their fate was an ignominious and abrupt dismissal.

At last "Wuthering Heights" and "Agnes Grey" were accepted on terms somewhat impoverishing to the two authors; Currer Bell's book found acceptance nowhere, nor any acknowledgment of merit, so that something like the chill of despair began to invade her heart. As a forlorn hope, she tried one publishing house more — Messrs. Smith, Elder and Co. Ere long, in a much shorter space than that on which experience had taught her to calculate — there came a letter, which she opened in the dreary expectation of finding two hard, hopeless lines, intimating that Messrs. Smith, Elder and Co. "were not disposed to publish the MS.," and, instead, she took out of the envelope a letter of two pages. She read it trembling. It declined, indeed, to publish that tale, for business reasons, but it discussed its merits and demerits so courteously, so considerately, in a spirit so rational, with a discrimination so enlightened, that this very refusal cheered the author better than a vulgarly expressed acceptance would have done. It was added, that a work in three volumes would meet with careful attention.

I was then just completing "Jane Eyre," at which I had been working while the one-volume tale was plodding its weary round in London: in three weeks I sent it off; friendly and skilful hands took it in. This was in the commencement of September, 1847; it came out before the close of October following, while "Wuthering Heights" and "Agnes Grey," my sisters' works, which had already been in the press for months, still lingered under a different management.

They appeared at last. Critics failed to do them justice. The immature but very real powers revealed in "Wuthering Heights" were scarcely recognised; its import and nature were misunderstood; the identity of its author was misrepresented; it was said that this was an earlier and ruder attempt of the same pen which had produced "Jane Eyre." Unjust and grievous error! We laughed at it at first, but I deeply lament it now. Hence, I fear, arose a prejudice against the book. That writer who could attempt to palm off an inferior and immature production under cover of one successful effort, must indeed be unduly eager after the secondary and sordid result of authorship, and pitiably indifferent to its true and honourable meed. If reviewers and the public truly believed this, no wonder that they looked darkly on the cheat.

Yet I must not be understood to make these things subject for reproach or complaint; I dare not do so; respect for my sister's memory forbids me. By her any such querulous manifestation would have been regarded as an unworthy and offensive weakness.

It is my duty, as well as my pleasure, to acknowledge one exception to the general rule of criticism. One writer, endowed with the keen vision and fine sympathies of genius, has discerned the real nature of "Wuthering Heights," and has, with equal accuracy, noted its beauties, and touched on its faults.[2] Too often do reviewers remind us of the mob of Astrologers, Chaldeans, and Soothsayers gathered before the "writing on the wall," and unable to read the characters or make known the interpretation. We have a right to rejoice when a true seer comes at last, some man in whom is an excellent spirit, to whom have been given light, wisdom, and understanding; who can accurately read the "Mene, Mene, Tekel, Upharsin"[3] of an original mind (however unripe, however inefficiently cultured and partially expanded that mind may be); and who can say with confidence, "This is the interpretation thereof."

15

---

[2] A reference to Sydney Dobell's September 1850 review in the *Palladium*. —Eds.
[3] A reference to the Old Testament story of Belshazzar's feast, during which no one but Daniel can read God's writing on the wall. —Eds.

This nineteenth-century lithograph shows Charlotte Brontë working on the novel *Jane Eyre* as her father Patrick looks on in the background.

What stands out about this image? What do you make of the inclusion of Patrick Brontë?

STAPLETON COLLECTION/Private Collection/Bridgeman Images

Yet even the writer to whom I allude shares the mistake about the authorship, and does me the injustice to suppose that there was equivoque[4] in my former rejection of this honour (as an honour I regard it). May I assure him that I would scorn in this and in every other case to deal in equivoque; I believe language to have been given us to make our meaning clear, and not to wrap it in dishonest doubt?

"The Tenant of Wildfell Hall," by Acton Bell, had likewise an unfavourable reception. At this I cannot wonder. The choice of subject was an entire mistake. Nothing less congruous with the writer's nature could be conceived. The motives which dictated this choice were pure, but, I think, slightly morbid. She had, in the course of her life, been called on to contemplate, near at hand, and for a long time, the terrible effects of talents misused and faculties abused: hers was naturally a sensitive, reserved, and dejected nature; what she saw sank very deeply into her mind; it did her harm. She brooded over it till she believed it to be a duty to reproduce every detail (of course with fictitious characters, incidents, and situations), as a warning to others. She hated her work, but would pursue it. When reasoned with on the subject, she regarded such reasonings as a temptation to self-indulgence. She must be honest; she must not varnish, soften, nor conceal. This well-meant resolution brought on her misconstruction, and some abuse, which she bore, as it was her custom to bear whatever was unpleasant, with mild, steady patience. She was a very sincere and practical Christian, but the tinge of religious melancholy communicated a sad shade to her brief, blameless life.

Neither Ellis nor Acton allowed herself for one moment to sink under want of encouragement; energy nerved the one, and endurance upheld the other. They were both prepared to try again; I would fain think that hope and the sense of power were yet strong within them. But a great change approached; affliction came in that shape which to anticipate is dread; to look back on, grief. In the very heat and burden of the day, the labourers failed over their work.

My sister Emily first declined. The details of her illness are deep-branded in my memory, but to dwell on them, either in thought or narrative, is not in my power. Never in all her life had she lingered over any task that lay before her, and she did not linger now. She sank rapidly. She made haste to leave us. Yet, while physically she perished, mentally she grew stronger than we had yet known her. Day by day, when I saw with what a front she met suffering, I looked on her with an anguish of wonder and love. I have seen nothing like it; but, indeed, I have never seen her parallel

[4]An expression that may have multiple meanings. —Eds.

CHRIS BEETLES LTD/Private Collection/Bridgeman Images

How does this early twentieth-century caricature, entitled *Script Writing at the Brontës'*, characterize each Brontë sibling? How does it comment on their personalities and on their work?

in anything. Stronger than a man, simpler than a child, her nature stood alone. The awful point was, that while full of ruth for others, on herself she had no pity; the spirit was inexorable to the flesh; from the trembling hand, the unnerved limbs, the faded eyes, the same service was exacted as they had rendered in health. To stand by and witness this, and not dare to remonstrate, was a pain no words can render.

Two cruel months of hope and fear passed painfully by, and the day came at last when the terrors and pains of death were to be undergone by this treasure, which had grown dearer and dearer to our hearts as it wasted before our eyes. Towards the decline of that day, we had nothing of Emily but her mortal remains as consumption left them. She died December 19, 1848.

We thought this enough: but we were utterly and presumptuously wrong. She was not buried ere Anne fell ill. She had not been committed to

20

the grave a fortnight, before we received distinct intimation that it was necessary to prepare our minds to see the younger sister go after the elder. Accordingly, she followed in the same path with slower step, and with a patience that equalled the other's fortitude. I have said that she was religious, and it was by leaning on those Christian doctrines in which she firmly believed, that she found support through her most painful journey. I witnessed their efficacy in her latest hour and greatest trial, and must bear my testimony to the calm triumph with which they brought her through. She died May 28, 1849.

What more shall I say about them? I cannot and need not say much more. In externals, they were two unobtrusive women; a perfectly secluded life gave them retiring manners and habits. In Emily's nature the extremes of vigour and simplicity seemed to meet. Under an unsophisticated culture, inartificial tastes, and an

▲
——————

Shown here is a photograph of Haworth parsonage, the Brontë family home, during
the nineteenth century. All of the Brontë siblings died young, with Charlotte living the
longest — age 38 — and their father surviving them all. The illnesses that caused the deaths
of Branwell, Emily, Anne, and Charlotte herself were likely partly due to the fact that the
vast cemetery surrounding the church and parsonage contaminated the family's drinking
water.

**What is Charlotte Brontë's tone as she talks about the deaths of her sisters? How
might living beside a cemetery, and outliving all of her siblings, have affected her
view of death?**

unpretending outside, lay a secret power and fire
that might have informed the brain and kindled
the veins of a hero; but she had no worldly wisdom; her powers were unadapted to the practical
business of life; she would fail to defend her most
manifest rights, to consult her most legitimate
advantage. An interpreter ought always to have
stood between her and the world. Her will was not
very flexible, and it generally opposed her interest. Her temper was magnanimous, but warm and
sudden; her spirit altogether unbending.

Anne's character was milder and more subdued; she wanted the power, the fire, the originality of her sister, but was well endowed with
quiet virtues of her own. Long-suffering, self-
denying, reflective, and intelligent, a constitutional reserve and taciturnity placed and kept
her in the shade, and covered her mind, and

especially her feelings, with a sort of nun-like
veil, which was rarely lifted. Neither Emily nor
Anne was learned; they had no thought of filling
their pitchers at the well-spring of other minds;
they always wrote from the impulse of nature,
the dictates of intuition, and from such stores
of observation as their limited experience had
enabled them to amass. I may sum up all by
saying, that for strangers they were nothing,
for superficial observers less than nothing; but
for those who had known them all their lives
in the intimacy of close relationship, they were
genuinely good and truly great.

This notice has been written because I felt it a
sacred duty to wipe the dust off their gravestones,
and leave their dear names free from soil.

CURRER BELL.

September 19, 1850.

EXPLORING THE TEXT

1. In this "Biographical Notice" which serves as a preface to the second edition of *Wuthering Heights* and *Agnes Grey*, Charlotte Brontë shares her purpose in the first paragraph: "to state how the case really stands." What is "the case" that she seeks to rectify? Why does she believe it is necessary to do so?

2. What is Brontë's point in paragraph 3? What does she mean when she describes herself and her sisters as being "mutually ignorant of the progress we might respectively have made"?

3. In the context of Brontë's stated purpose, what does she suggest by describing her sister Emily's poetry as being not "at all like the poetry women generally write" (para. 4)? What qualities can you infer Bronte believes characterize poetry by women?

4. In paragraph 6, Brontë introduces her "younger sister" Anne — though without naming her — and describes her poetry as having "a sweet, sincere pathos." How does Brontë depict Anne, particularly in comparison to her sister Emily? What is her attitude toward each of her sisters? Cite specific passages to support your interpretation.

5. Brontë recounts how the three sisters shared a "dream of one day becoming authors," and that the dream "took the character of a resolve" (para. 7). Why, then, do they choose to assume male pseudonyms? As you respond, note the shift in this paragraph from the use of "authors" to "authoresses."

6. Brontë indicates she and her sisters were frustrated not only by rejection of their work but by another "obstacle" (para. 8). What is that obstacle, and how does addressing it in this preface serve Brontë's purpose?

7. In paragraphs 10 and 11, Brontë refers to herself as "Currer Bell"; then she shifts to "I" (para. 12). What is her purpose in this movement from third to first person, from the pseudonym to "I"?

8. Brontë not only explains that critics assumed *Wuthering Heights* and *Jane Eyre* were written by the same author, but she describes the emotional distress the Brontë sisters experienced as a result. In light of this detail, what do you make of Brontë's insistence that she intends neither a "reproach or complaint" because "respect for [Emily's] memory forbids me" (para. 14)? What ethos is she trying to establish?

9. Overall, how does C. Brontë characterize the literary marketplace, both publishers and critics? Cite textual evidence to support your response.

10. In the closing paragraphs of her "Biographical Notice," Brontë directly contrasts her two sisters, including in her account of their deaths. What are the chief differences she emphasizes? Consider her depiction of Emily as "stronger than a man, simpler than a child," who by nature "stood alone" (para. 19) and of Anne as being "well endowed with quiet virtues of her own" (para. 23). What purpose does this contrast serve in the development of Brontë's argument?

11. In paragraph 23, Brontë says that "neither Emily nor Anne was learned; they had no thought of filling their pitchers at the well-spring of other minds; they always wrote from the impulse of nature . . . as their limited experience had enabled them to amass." What does this suggest about the role of and resources available to women in society at the time?

12. While Brontë states her intention to debunk the myth that Acton, Ellis, and Currer Bell were, in fact, one male person, this text has also been read as an attempt to establish a different myth about the three sisters — one that Charlotte Brontë controls. What parts of the text might be used to support such an interpretation?

13. Brontë concludes with a single sentence that attests she has been motivated by a "sacred duty to wipe the dust off [Emily and Anne's] gravestones, and leave their dear names free from soil" (para. 24). To what extent do you believe that she has achieved that purpose in this text?

14. How would you describe this text? Is it an indignant defense, an insightful biography, a loving tribute, a misguided criticism, a dramatic exposé, an objective explanation, a veiled social commentary, an ambivalent appreciation, or something else? Try to formulate an adjective-noun description, and support your position with evidence from the reading.

15. Even after the publication of this text, Brontë continued to publish her novels under the name Currer Bell. Why do you think she made that choice? What might have been her motivations — artistic, economic, and political?

I Want a Wife

JUDY BRADY

Judy Brady (1937–2017) was born in San Francisco and earned a BFA in painting from the University of Iowa in 1962. She has been active in political and environmental movements as an editor and author. She edited *Women and Cancer* (1990) and *One in Three: Women with Cancer Confront an Epidemic* (1991). Brady's work has also appeared in periodicals such as *Greenpeace* magazine and the *Women's Review of Books*. Since appearing in the premiere issue of *Ms.* magazine in 1972, "I Want a Wife" has become a classic piece of feminist writing and humor. It was reprinted as "I [Still] Want a Wife" in *Ms.* in 1990.

I belong to that classification of people known as wives. I am A Wife. And, not altogether incidentally, I am a mother.

Not too long ago a male friend of mine appeared on the scene fresh from a recent divorce. He had one child, who is, of course, with his ex-wife. He is looking for another wife. As I thought about him while I was ironing one evening, it suddenly occurred to me that I, too, would like to have a wife. Why do I want a wife?

I would like to go back to school so that I can become economically independent, support myself, and, if need be, support those dependent upon me. I want a wife who will work and send me to school. And while I am going to school I want a wife to take care of my children. I want a wife to keep track of the children's doctor and dentist appointments. And to keep track of mine, too. I want a wife to make sure my children eat properly and are kept clean. I want a wife who will wash the children's clothes and keep them mended. I want a wife who is a good nurturant attendant to my children, who arranges for their schooling, makes sure that they have an adequate social life with their peers, takes them to the park, the zoo, etc. I want a wife who takes care of the children when they are sick, a wife who arranges to be around when the children need special care, because, of course, I cannot miss classes at school. My wife must arrange to lose time at work and not lose the job. It may mean a small cut in my wife's income from time to time, but I guess I can tolerate that. Needless to say, my wife will arrange and pay for the care of the children while my wife is working.

This 1954 screenprint is entitled *The American Wife Presenting Perfect Thanksgiving Turkey*. **How does this image illustrate one of Brady's central points? Pay close attention to the extended family waiting in the background.**

GRAPHICA ARTIS/Private Collection/Bridgeman Images

I want a wife who will take care of my physical needs. I want a wife who will keep my house clean. A wife who will pick up after my children, a wife who will pick up after me. I want a wife who will keep my clothes clean, ironed, mended, replaced when need be, and who will see to it that my personal things are kept in their proper place so that

I can find what I need the minute I need it. I want a wife who cooks the meals, a wife who is a good cook. I want a wife who will plan the menus, do the necessary grocery shopping, prepare the meals, serve them pleasantly, and then do the cleaning up while I do my studying. I want a wife who will care for me when I am sick and sympathize with my pain and loss of time from school. I want a wife to go along when our family takes a vacation so that someone can continue to care for me and my children when I need a rest and change of scene.

I want a wife who will not bother me with rambling complaints about a wife's duties. But I want a wife who will listen to me when I feel the need to explain a rather difficult point I have come across in my course of studies. And I want a wife who will type my papers for me when I have written them.

I want a wife who will take care of the details of my social life. When my wife and I are invited out by my friends, I want a wife who will take care of the babysitting arrangements. When I meet people at school that I like and want to entertain, I want a wife who will have the house clean, will prepare a special meal, serve it to me and my friends, and not interrupt when I talk about things that interest me and my friends. I want a wife who will have arranged that the children are fed and ready for bed before my guests arrive so that the children do not bother us. I want a wife who takes care of the needs of my guests so that they feel comfortable, who makes sure that they have an ashtray, that they are passed the hors d'oeuvres, that they are offered a second helping of the food, that their wine glasses are replenished when necessary, that their coffee is served to them as they like it. And I want a wife who knows that sometimes I need a night out by myself.

I want a wife who is sensitive to my sexual needs, a wife who makes love passionately and eagerly when I feel like it, a wife who makes sure that I am satisfied. And, of course, I want a wife who will not demand sexual attention when I am not in the mood for it. I want a wife who assumes the complete responsibility for birth control, because I do not want more children. I want a wife

What do the various images on this 1972 cover of *Ms.* magazine represent? How might they illustrate the idea of "The Housewife's Moment of Truth"? Where do you see that "moment of truth" represented in Brady's essay?

who will remain sexually faithful to me so that I do not have to clutter up my intellectual life with jealousies. And I want a wife who understands that my sexual needs may entail more than just strict adherence to monogamy. I must, after all, be able to relate to people as fully as possible.

If, by chance, I find another person more suitable as a wife than the wife I already have, I want the liberty to replace my present wife with another one. Naturally, I will expect a fresh new life; my wife will take the children and be solely responsible for them so that I am left free.

When I am through with school and have a job, I want my wife to quit working and remain at home so that my wife can more fully and completely take care of a wife's duties.

My God, who *wouldn't* want a wife?   10

seeing connections

The graph shown here uses data from a 2015 *Huffington Post* article that examined the "expectation gap." The article claimed that despite the fact that men have taken on more parenting and household duties than ever before, "the cultural expectation that women do all the traditional stuff hasn't really budged."

Has the expectation gap widened since the time that "I Want a Wife" was written, or has it narrowed? Explain your answer, using the data in these graphs as evidence.

Working Parents' Views on Balancing Work and Family

Based on survey of those working 20+ hours/week with children under 18 years

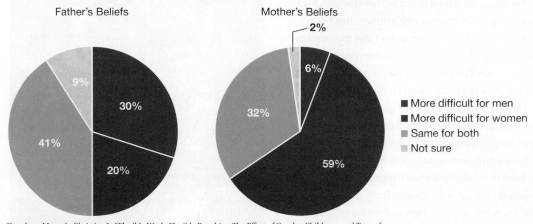

Data from Munsch, Christine L. "Flexible Work, Flexible Penalties: The Effect of Gender, Childcare, and Type of Request on the Flexibility Bias." *Social Forces*, vol. 94, Issue 4, June 2016, pp. 1567–1591.

[1972]

EXPLORING THE TEXT

1. How does the opening paragraph set the tone for the entire essay? Note details such as the form and progression of sentences, the use of capitalization, and the qualifying phrases.

2. What is the effect of Judy Brady repeating the sentence (or clause) "I want a wife" again and again? What is the effect of Brady's use of pronouns in referring to herself and "her" wife?

3. What is the overall structure of Brady's argument? Consider breaking this essay into a straightforward syllogism or analyzing it using the Toulmin model presented in Chapter 3.

4. How would you describe the progression of the paragraphs? Does Brady go from most to least or from least to most, or does she follow another organizational principle? Why is her choice effective?

5. What elements of satire does Brady use? How does she, for instance, use hyperbole? Understatement? Humor? Irony? Others?

6. Although Brady never uses the term *sexism* (or *feminism*), what gender inequities does she catalog in this essay?

7. Even though this essay was published in 1971, when the feminist movement was a strong political force, it has remained popular for decades. Why? Some of the details seem dated, such as the references to a typewriter and ashtrays. Do you think that the situation Brady describes is still relevant? Or is the essay mainly a historical document that is a reminder of times past?

8. How might you apply the same rhetorical strategies that Brady uses in this essay to another one entitled "I Want a Husband"?

Women's Brains

STEPHEN JAY GOULD

Paleontologist and evolutionary biologist Stephen Jay Gould (1941–2002) was a professor of geology and zoology at Harvard University from 1967 until his death. His major scientific work was the theory of punctuated equilibrium, a theory of evolutionary biology that builds on the work of Charles Darwin by suggesting that evolution occurs sporadically, rather than gradually over a long period of time. Gould is the author of numerous scientific texts, including *The Mismeasure of Man* (1981); *Wonderful Life: The Burgess Shale and the Nature of History* (1989); his magnum opus, *The Structure of Evolutionary Theory* (2002); and *The Hedgehog, the Fox, and the Magister's Pox: Mending the Gap between Science and the Humanities* (2003). Gould also wrote for a more general audience in his column in *Natural History*, where the following essay originally appeared in 1980.

In the Prelude to *Middlemarch*, George Eliot lamented the unfulfilled lives of talented women:

> Some have felt that these blundering lives are due to the inconvenient indefiniteness with which the Supreme Power has fashioned the natures of women: if there were one level of feminine incompetence as strict as the ability to count three and no more, the social lot of women might be treated with scientific certitude.

Eliot goes on to discount the idea of innate limitation, but while she wrote in 1872, the leaders of European anthropometry were trying to measure "with scientific certitude" the inferiority of women. Anthropometry, or measurement of the human body, is not so fashionable a field these days, but it dominated the human sciences for much of the nineteenth century and remained popular until intelligence testing replaced skull measurement as a favored device for making invidious comparisons among races, classes, and sexes. Craniometry, or measurement of the skull, commanded the most attention and respect. Its unquestioned leader, Paul Broca (1824–80), professor of clinical surgery at the Faculty of Medicine in Paris, gathered a school of disciples and imitators around himself. Their work, so meticulous and apparently irrefutable, exerted great influence and won high esteem as a jewel of nineteenth-century science.

Broca's work seemed particularly invulnerable to refutation. Had he not measured with the most scrupulous care and accuracy? (Indeed, he had. I have the greatest respect for Broca's meticulous procedure. His numbers are sound. But science is an inferential exercise, not a catalog of facts. Numbers, by themselves, specify nothing. All depends upon what you do with them.) Broca depicted himself as an apostle of objectivity, a man who bowed before facts and cast aside superstition and sentimentality. He declared that "there is no faith, however respectable, no interest, however legitimate, which must not accommodate itself to the progress of human knowledge and bend before truth." Women, like it or not, had smaller brains than men and, therefore, could not equal them in intelligence. This fact, Broca argued, may reinforce a common prejudice in male society, but it is also a scientific truth. L. Manouvrier, a black sheep in Broca's fold, rejected the inferiority of women and wrote with feeling about the burden imposed upon them by Broca's numbers:

> Women displayed their talents and their diplomas. They also invoked philosophical authorities. But they were opposed by *numbers* unknown to Condorcet or to John Stuart Mill. These numbers fell upon poor women like a sledge hammer, and they were accompanied by commentaries and sarcasms more ferocious than the most misogynist imprecations of certain church fathers. The theologians had asked if women had a soul. Several centuries later, some scientists were ready to refuse them a human intelligence.

Broca's argument rested upon two sets of data: the larger brains of men in modern societies, and a supposed increase in male superiority through time. His most extensive data came from autopsies performed personally in four Parisian hospitals. For 292 male brains, he calculated an average weight of 1,325 grams; 140 female brains averaged 1,144 grams for a difference of 181 grams, or 14 percent of the male weight. Broca understood, of course, that part of this difference could be attributed to the greater height of males. Yet he made no attempt to measure the effect of size alone and actually stated that it cannot account for the entire difference because we know, a priori, that women are not as intelligent as men (a premise that the data were supposed to test, not rest upon):

> We might ask if the small size of the female brain depends exclusively upon the small size of her body. Tiedemann has proposed this explanation. But we must not forget that women are, on the average, a little less intelligent than men, a

difference which we should not exaggerate but which is, nonetheless, real. We are therefore permitted to suppose that the relatively small size of the female brain depends in part upon her physical inferiority and in part upon her intellectual inferiority.

In 1873, the year after Eliot published *Middlemarch*, Broca measured the cranial capacities of prehistoric skulls from L'Homme Mort cave. Here he found a difference of only 99.5 cubic centimeters between males and females, while modern populations range from 129.5 to 220.7. Topinard, Broca's chief disciple, explained the increasing discrepancy through time as a result of differing evolutionary pressures upon dominant men and passive women:

> The man who fights for two or more in the struggle for existence, who has all the responsibility and the cares of tomorrow, who is constantly active in combating the environment and human rivals, needs more brain than the woman whom he must protect and nourish, the sedentary woman, lacking any interior occupations, whose role is to raise children, love, and be passive.

In 1879, Gustave Le Bon, chief misogynist of Broca's school, used these data to publish what must be the most vicious attack upon women in modern scientific literature (no one can top Aristotle). I do not claim his views were representative of Broca's school, but they were published in France's most respected anthropological journal. Le Bon concluded:

> In the most intelligent races, as among the Parisians, there are a large number of women whose brains are closer in size to those of gorillas than to the most developed male brains. This inferiority is so obvious that no one can contest it for a moment; only its degree is worth discussion. All psychologists who have studied the intelligence of women, as well as poets and novelists, recognize today that they represent the most inferior forms

of human evolution and that they are closer to children and savages than to an adult, civilized man. They excel in fickleness, inconstancy, absence of thought and logic, and incapacity to reason. Without doubt there exist some distinguished women, very superior to the average man, but they are as exceptional as the birth of any monstrosity, as, for example, of a gorilla with two heads; consequently, we may neglect them entirely.

seeing connections

In her 2015 book *Inferior: How Science Got Women Wrong—and the New Research That's Rewriting the Story*, Angela Saini relays an anecdote of the correspondence between Caroline Kennard, an American woman, and prominent scientist Charles Darwin. Kennard wrote Darwin a letter asking him to confirm that women were men's intellectual equals. Saini then describes Darwin's response below.

How does Darwin's analysis of women's intellectual abilities compare to the analyses of the scientists Gould writes about? To what extent do you believe Darwin's reasoning is still the basis for some of our current social norms and political debates?

---

from **Inferior**

How Science Got Women Wrong—and the New Research That's Rewriting the Story

ANGELA SAINI

"I certainly think that women though generally superior to men [in] moral qualities are inferior intellectually," [Darwin] tells her, "and there seems to me to be a great difficulty from the laws of inheritance, (if I understand these laws rightly) in their becoming the intellectual equals of man."

It doesn't end there. For women to overcome this biological inequality, he adds, they would have to become breadwinners like men. And this wouldn't be a good idea because it might damage young children and the happiness of households. Darwin is telling Kennard that women aren't just intellectually inferior to men, but they're better off not aspiring to a life beyond their homes. It's a rejection of everything Kennard and the women's movement at the time were fighting for.

Darwin's personal correspondence echoes what's expressed quite plainly in his published work. . . .

Darwin writes that if women had somehow managed to develop some of the same remarkable qualities as men, it may have been because they were dragged along on men's coattails by the fact that children happen to inherit a bit of everything from both parents in the womb. Girls, by this process, manage to steal some of the superior qualities of their fathers. "It is, indeed, fortunate that the law of the equal transmission of characters to both sexes has commonly prevailed throughout the whole class of mammals; otherwise it is probable that man would have become as superior in mental endowment to woman, as the peacock is in ornamental plumage to the peahen." It's only a stroke of biological luck, he implies, that has stopped women from being even more inferior to men than they already are.

Nor did Le Bon shrink from the social implications of his views. He was horrified by the proposal of some American reformers to grant women higher education on the same basis as men:

> A desire to give them the same education, and, as a consequence, to propose the same goals for them, is a dangerous chimera. . . . The day when, misunderstanding the inferior occupations which nature has given her, women leave the home and take part in our battles; on this day a social revolution will begin, and everything that maintains the sacred ties of the family will disappear.

Sound familiar?[1]

I have reexamined Broca's data, the basis for all this derivative pronouncement, and I find his numbers sound but his interpretation ill-founded, to say the least. The data supporting his claim for increased difference through time can be easily dismissed. Broca based his contention on the samples from L'Homme Mort alone — only seven male and six female skulls in all. Never have so little data yielded such far-ranging conclusions.

In 1888, Topinard published Broca's more extensive data on the Parisian hospitals. Since Broca recorded height and age as well as brain size, we may use modern statistics to remove their effect. Brain weight decreases with age, and Broca's women were, on average, considerably older than his men. Brain weight increases with height, and his average man was almost half a foot taller than his average woman. I used multiple regression, a technique that allowed me to assess simultaneously the influence of height and age upon brain size. In an analysis of the data for women, I found that, at average male height and age, a woman's brain would weigh 1,212 grams. Correction for height and age reduces Broca's measured difference of 181 grams by more than a third, to 113 grams.

I don't know what to make of this remaining difference because I cannot assess other factors known to influence brain size in a major way. Cause of death has an important effect: degenerative disease often entails a substantial diminution of brain size. (This effect is separate from the decrease attributed to age alone.) Eugene Schreider, also working with Broca's data, found that men killed in accidents had brains weighing, on average, 60 grams more than men dying of infectious diseases. The best modern data I can find (from American hospitals) records a full 100-gram difference between death by degenerative arteriosclerosis and by violence or accident. Since so many of Broca's subjects were very elderly women, we may assume that lengthy degenerative disease was more common among them than among the men.

More importantly, modern students of brain size still have not agreed on a proper measure for eliminating the powerful effect of body size. Height is partly adequate, but men and women of the same height do not share the same body build. Weight is even worse than height, because most of its variation reflects nutrition rather than intrinsic size — fat versus skinny exerts little influence upon the brain. Manouvrier took up this subject in the 1880s and argued that muscular mass and force should be used. He tried to measure this elusive property in various ways and found a marked difference in favor of men, even in men and women of the same height. When he corrected for what he called "sexual mass," women actually came out slightly ahead in brain size.

Thus, the corrected 113-gram difference is surely too large; the true figure is probably close to zero and may as well favor women as men. And 113 grams, by the way, is exactly the average difference between a 5 foot 4 inch and a 6 foot 4 inch male in Broca's data. We would not (especially us short folks) want to ascribe greater intelligence to tall men. In short, who knows what to do with Broca's data? They certainly don't permit any confident claim that men have bigger brains than women.

10

---

[1]When I wrote this essay, I assumed that Le Bon was a marginal, if colorful, figure. I have since learned that he was a leading scientist, one of the founders of social psychology, and best known for a seminal study on crowd behavior, still cited today (*La psychologie des foules*, 1895), and for his work on unconscious motivation.

This photograph, taken in 1980, shows both men and women rallying to support as well as stop the passage of the Equal Rights Amendment (ERA). First introduced to Congress in 1923, the bill was intended to guarantee equal rights for all regardless of sex. As of 2017, the ERA had not yet been ratified.

How does this 1980 photograph illustrate fairly contemporary differing opinions of women's place in society? How do the viewpoints represented here — including the fact that they differ — relate to Gould's argument?

Bettmann/Getty Images

To appreciate the social role of Broca and his school, we must recognize that his statements about the brains of women do not reflect an isolated prejudice toward a single disadvantaged group. They must be weighed in the context of a general theory that supported contemporary social distinctions as biologically ordained. Women, blacks, and poor people suffered the same disparagement, but women bore the brunt of Broca's argument because he had easier access to data on women's brains. Women were singularly denigrated but they also stood as surrogates for other disenfranchised groups. As one of Broca's disciples wrote in 1881: "Men of the black races have a brain scarcely heavier than that of white women." This juxtaposition extended into many other realms of anthropological argument, particularly to claims that, anatomically and emotionally, both women and blacks were like white children — and that white children, by the theory of recapitulation,

represented an ancestral (primitive) adult stage of human evolution. I do not regard as empty rhetoric the claim that women's battles are for all of us.

Maria Montessori did not confine her activities to educational reform for young children. She lectured on anthropology for several years at the University of Rome, and wrote an influential book entitled *Pedagogical Anthropology* (English edition, 1913). Montessori was no egalitarian. She supported most of Broca's work and the theory of innate criminality proposed by her compatriot Cesare Lombroso. She measured the circumference of children's heads in her schools and inferred that the best prospects had bigger brains. But she had no use for Broca's conclusions about women. She discussed Manouvrier's work at length and made much of his tentative claim that women, after proper correction of the data, had slightly larger brains than men. Women, she concluded, were intellectually superior, but

OTHER VOICES

seeing connections

These graphs illustrate some gender-specific trends in parent Google searches in 2014. **What does each of these images convey about present-day hopes and expectations for girls and boys? To what extent do these images show the relevance of Gould's message to twenty-first century society?**

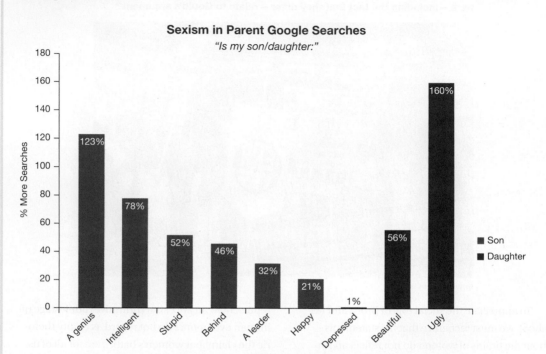

Sexism in Parent Google Searches

"Is my son/daughter:"

Data from the National Center for Health Statistics and the Department of Education Office of Civil Rights.

"Is my son/daughter:"

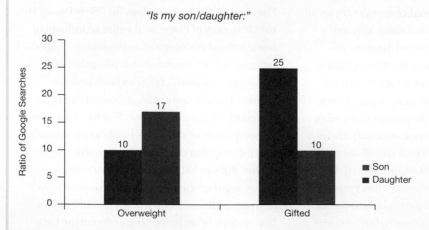

Data from the National Center for Health Statistics and the Department of Education Office of Civil Rights.

men had prevailed heretofore by dint of physical force. Since technology has abolished force as an instrument of power, the era of women may soon be upon us: "In such an epoch there will really be superior human beings, there will really be men strong in morality and in sentiment. Perhaps in this way the reign of women is approaching, when the enigma of her anthropological superiority will be deciphered. Woman was always the custodian of human sentiment, morality and honor."

This represents one possible antidote to "scientific" claims for the constitutional inferiority of certain groups. One may affirm the validity of biological distinctions but argue that the data have been misinterpreted by prejudiced men with a stake in the outcome, and that disadvantaged groups are truly superior. In recent years, Elaine Morgan has followed this strategy in her *Descent of Woman*, a speculative reconstruction of human prehistory from the woman's point of view — and as farcical as more famous tall tales by and for men.

I prefer another strategy. Montessori and Morgan followed Broca's philosophy to reach a more congenial conclusion. I would rather label

15

the whole enterprise of setting a biological value upon groups for what it is: irrelevant and highly injurious. George Eliot well appreciated the special tragedy that biological labeling imposed upon members of disadvantaged groups. She expressed it for people like herself — women of extraordinary talent. I would apply it more widely — not only to those whose dreams are flouted but also to those who never realize that they may dream — but I cannot match her prose. In conclusion, then, the rest of Eliot's prelude to *Middlemarch*:

> The limits of variation are really much wider than anyone would imagine from the sameness of women's coiffure and the favorite love stories in prose and verse. Here and there a cygnet is reared uneasily among the ducklings in the brown pond, and never finds the living stream in fellowship with its own oary-footed kind. Here and there is born a Saint Theresa, foundress of nothing, whose loving heartbeats and sobs after an unattained goodness tremble off and are dispersed among hindrances instead of centering in some long-recognizable deed.

[1980]

EXPLORING THE TEXT

1. Stephen Jay Gould's argument focuses on research about women's brain size, but — more importantly — what does he say about the nature of scientific inquiry — that is, about how scientists think?

2. In paragraph 3, Gould states, "I have the greatest respect for Broca's meticulous procedure. His numbers are sound." Despite this praise, Gould goes on to refute Broca's findings. What vulnerability does Gould find in Broca's conclusions? Does Gould's praise of Broca strengthen or weaken his own argument? Explain.

3. At the end of paragraph 7, Gould adds a footnote reassessing an earlier point. Does this admission add or detract from his credibility?

4. Paragraphs 9–12 work as a unit to develop a single point that is integral to the overall essay. What is

this point? How do paragraphs 9–12 develop the point?

5. What does Gould mean when he says, "Women were singularly denigrated but they also stood as surrogates for other disenfranchised groups" (para. 13)?

6. What do you think Gould's purpose is in saying, "I do not regard as empty rhetoric the claim that women's battles are for all of us" (para. 13)? Is he being patronizing? Does such a personal comment undermine his scientific credibility? Explain.

7. Gould builds two parallel arguments: one on scientific method, another on speculative conclusions. In which passages does he question the scientific method(s) rather than the findings themselves? How does Gould weave these sources together in order to make his own point?

8. What purposes do the quotations in this essay from George Eliot's novel *Middlemarch* serve? Why does Gould, when introducing the quotation from Broca in paragraph 5, refer to Eliot? Why are quotations from Eliot, whose real name was Mary Anne Evans, especially appropriate for Gould's essay?

9. Why is questioning Maria Montessori's research and conclusions an effective strategy? What criticism might Gould be guarding against in doing so?

10. How do the individuals Gould cites — Paul Broca, L. Manouvrier, Gustave Le Bon, and Maria Montessori — contribute to the development of his argument? Does each make a separate point, or do they reinforce one another? Could Gould have eliminated any of them without damaging his argument? Explain your reasoning.

11. In the final two paragraphs, how does Gould bring together both of his arguments — that is, his argument against the actual scientific research and his argument about the conclusions drawn from that research?

12. This essay has a strong appeal to logos, as would be expected of a scientific argument. How does Gould also appeal to pathos? How does that appeal add to the persuasiveness of his argument?

13. Gould's essay was published in 1980, and it centers on research conducted a century before that. What case might you make that Gould's true subject was not women but assumptions about the abilities of certain groups?

14. Consider another myth or stereotype about women based on biology that has prevailed at some point in history — perhaps one that continues to have some credibility, such as women are more emotional, more intuitive, better at child care, or worse at math and science. What scientific evidence can you cite to challenge the myth?

Just Walk on By
A Black Man Ponders His Power to Alter Public Space

BRENT STAPLES

An author and editorial writer for the *New York Times*, Brent Staples (b. 1951) grew up in Pennsylvania in a family of nine children. He received his BA from Widener University and his PhD in psychology from the University of Chicago. His memoir, *Parallel Time: Growing Up in Black and White* (1994), won the Anisfield-Wolf Book Award, which recognizes books that contribute to a deeper understanding of racism and of human diversity. The following essay originally appeared in *Ms.* magazine in 1986.

My first victim was a woman — white, well dressed, probably in her early twenties. I came upon her late one evening on a deserted street in Hyde Park, a relatively affluent neighborhood in an otherwise mean, impoverished section of Chicago. As I swung onto the avenue behind her, there seemed to be a discreet, uninflammatory distance between us. Not so. She cast back a worried glance. To her, the youngish black man — a broad six feet two inches with a beard and billowing hair, both hands shoved into the pockets of a bulky military jacket — seemed menacingly close.

After a few more quick glimpses, she picked up her pace and was soon running in earnest. Within seconds she disappeared into a cross street.

That was more than a decade ago. I was twenty-two years old, a graduate student newly arrived at the University of Chicago. It was in the echo of that terrified woman's footfalls that I first began to know the unwieldy inheritance I'd come into — the ability to alter public space in ugly ways. It was clear that she thought herself the quarry of a mugger, a rapist, or worse. Suffering a bout of insomnia, however, I was stalking sleep, not defenseless wayfarers. As a softy who is scarcely able to take a knife to a raw chicken — let alone hold it to a person's throat — I was surprised, embarrassed, and dismayed all at once. Her flight made me feel like an accomplice in tyranny. It also made it clear that I was indistinguishable from the muggers who occasionally seeped into the area from the surrounding ghetto. That first encounter, and those that followed, signified that a vast, unnerving gulf lay between nighttime pedestrians — particularly women — and me. And I soon gathered that being perceived as dangerous is a hazard in itself. I only needed to turn a corner into a dicey situation, or crowd some frightened, armed person in a foyer somewhere, or make an errant move after being pulled over by a policeman. Where fear and weapons meet — and they often do in urban America — there is always the possibility of death.

In that first year, my first away from my hometown, I was to become thoroughly familiar with the language of fear. At dark, shadowy intersections in Chicago, I could cross in front of a car stopped at a traffic light and elicit the *thunk, thunk, thunk, thunk* of the driver — black, white, male, or female — hammering down the door locks. On less traveled streets after dark, I grew accustomed to but never comfortable with people who crossed to the other side of the street rather than pass me. Then there were the standard unpleasantries with police, doormen, bouncers, cabdrivers, and others whose business is to screen out troublesome individuals *before* there is any nastiness.

I moved to New York nearly two years ago and I have remained an avid night walker. In central Manhattan, the near-constant crowd cover minimizes tense one-on-one street encounters. Elsewhere — visiting friends in Soho, where sidewalks are narrow and tightly spaced buildings shut out the sky — things can get very taut indeed.

Black men have a firm place in New York mugging literature. Norman Podhoretz in his

5

Films such as the 1974 *Death Wish*, a Charles Bronson vehicle directed by Michael Winner, place the black man as mugger firmly in the public imagination.
What other messages do the casting, costuming, and framing of this shot convey?

Paramount Pictures/Photofest

famed (or infamous) 1963 essay, "My Negro Problem — And Ours," recalls growing up in terror of black males; they "were tougher than we were, more ruthless," he writes — and as an adult on the Upper West Side of Manhattan, he continues, he cannot constrain his nervousness when he meets black men on certain streets. Similarly, a decade later, the essayist and novelist Edward Hoagland extols a New York where once "Negro bitterness bore down mainly on other Negroes." Where some see mere panhandlers, Hoagland sees "a mugger who is clearly screwing up his nerve to do more than just *ask* for money." But Hoagland has "the New Yorker's quick-hunch posture for broken-field maneuvering," and the bad guy swerves away.

I often witness that "hunch posture," from women after dark on the warren-like streets of Brooklyn where I live. They seem to set their faces on neutral and, with their purse straps strung across their chests bandolier style, they forge ahead as though bracing themselves against being tackled. I understand, of course, that the danger they perceive is not a hallucination. Women are particularly vulnerable to street violence, and young black males are drastically overrepresented among the perpetrators of that violence. Yet these truths are no solace against the kind of alienation that comes of being ever the suspect, against being set apart, a fearsome entity with whom pedestrians avoid making eye contact.

It is not altogether clear to me how I reached the ripe old age of twenty-two without being conscious of the lethality nighttime pedestrians attributed to me. Perhaps it was because in Chester, Pennsylvania, the small, angry industrial town where I came of age in the 1960s, I was scarcely noticeable against a backdrop of gang warfare, street knifings, and murders. I grew up one of the good boys, had perhaps a half-dozen fistfights. In retrospect, my shyness of combat has clear sources.

Many things go into the making of a young thug. One of those things is the consummation of the male romance with the power to intimidate. An infant discovers that random flailings send the baby bottle flying out of the crib and crashing to the floor. Delighted, the joyful babe repeats those motions again and again, seeking to duplicate the feat. Just so, I recall the points at which some of my boyhood friends were finally seduced by the perception of themselves as tough guys. When a mark cowered and surrendered his money without resistance, myth and reality merged — and paid off. It is, after all, only manly to embrace the power to frighten and intimidate. We, as men, are not supposed to give an inch of our lane on the highway; we are to seize the fighter's edge in work and in play and even in love; we are to be valiant in the face of hostile forces.

Unfortunately, poor and powerless young men seem to take all this nonsense literally. As a boy, I saw countless tough guys locked away; I have since buried several, too. They were babies, really — a teenage cousin, a brother of twenty-two, a childhood friend in his midtwenties — all gone down in episodes of bravado played out in the streets. I came to doubt the virtues of intimidation early on. I chose, perhaps even unconsciously, to remain a shadow — timid, but a survivor.

The fearsomeness mistakenly attributed to me in public places often has a perilous

10

Joe Raedle/Getty Images

◀

Following Officer Darren Wilson's shooting of Michael Brown, an unarmed black teenager, in 2014, demonstrators protested by marching with their hands up — a physical manifestation of their change, "Hands up, don't shoot." **How does Staples's essay address the concept of obvious displays of nonthreatening behavior?**

flavor. The most frightening of these confusions occurred in the late 1970s and early 1980s when I worked as a journalist in Chicago. One day, rushing into the office of a magazine I was writing for with a deadline story in hand, I was mistaken for a burglar. The office manager called security and, with an ad hoc posse, pursued me through the labyrinthine halls, nearly to my editor's door. I had no way of proving who I was. I could only move briskly toward the company of someone who knew me.

Another time I was on assignment for a local paper and killing time before an interview. I entered a jewelry store on the city's affluent Near North Side. The proprietor excused herself and returned with an enormous red Doberman pinscher straining at the end of a leash. She stood, the dog extended toward me, silent to my questions, her eyes bulging nearly out of her head. I took a cursory look around, nodded, and bade her good night. Relatively speaking, however, I never fared as badly as another black male journalist. He went to nearby Waukegan, Illinois, a couple of summers ago to work on a story about a murderer who was born there. Mistaking the reporter for the killer, police hauled him from his car at gunpoint and but for his press credentials would probably have tried to book him. Such episodes are not uncommon. Black men trade tales like this all the time.

In "My Negro Problem — And Ours," Podhoretz writes that the hatred he feels for blacks makes itself known to him through a variety of avenues — one being his discomfort with that "special brand of paranoid touchiness" to which he says blacks are prone. No doubt he is speaking here of black men. In time, I learned to smother the rage I felt at so often being taken for a criminal. Not to do so would surely have led to madness — via that special "paranoid touchiness" that so annoyed Podhoretz at the time he wrote the essay.

I began to take precautions to make myself less threatening. I move about with care, particularly late in the evening. I give a wide berth to nervous people on subway platforms during the wee hours, particularly when I have exchanged business clothes for jeans. If I happen to be entering a building behind some people who appear skittish, I may walk by, letting them clear the lobby before I return, so as not to seem to be following them. I have been calm and extremely congenial on those rare occasions when I've been pulled over by the police.

And on late-evening constitutionals along streets less traveled by, I employ what has proved to be an excellent tension-reducing measure: I whistle melodies from Beethoven and Vivaldi and the more popular classical composers. Even steely New Yorkers hunching toward nighttime destinations seem to relax, and occasionally they even join in the tune. Virtually everybody seems to sense that a mugger wouldn't be warbling bright, sunny selections from Vivaldi's *Four Seasons*. It is my equivalent of the cowbell that hikers wear when they know they are in bear country.

[1986]

EXPLORING THE TEXT

1. What is the impact of the opening sentence, "My first victim was a woman . . ." (para. 1)? How is Brent Staples using the term "victim"? How does the meaning of the sentence and the term change as you read and reread the essay?

2. In what ways does the description at the beginning resemble a scene from a novel? What mood does Staples set with the details and specific words he chooses? Pay close attention to modifiers and verbs.

3. Staples opens paragraph 2 with the short, simple sentence "That was more than a decade ago," an objective statement that indicates the passage of time. Does this sentence jolt you as a reader? Disappoint you? Explain why you think it is or is not an effective follow-up to the opening paragraph.

4. What examples does Staples provide to illustrate "the language of fear" (para. 3)?

5. In what ways does Staples acknowledge that the "victim's" response is not unwarranted? What explanations does he provide for her behavior? To what extent does he blame her? Does he want us as readers to blame or be more sympathetic toward her?

6. What is Staples's purpose in quoting Norman Podhoretz and Edward Hoagland? Are they providing support for his viewpoint, a contrasting viewpoint, expert testimony, or something else?

7. Is Staples being ironic when he writes, "I began to take precautions to make myself less threatening" (para. 13)? Cite specific parts of the text to support your viewpoint.

8. Is the final paragraph intended to be flippant? Humorous? Explain whether you find it an effective conclusion to the essay.

9. How would you describe the overall tone of this essay? You might consider a phrase rather than a single word to capture the complexity of this piece. Support your reading with specific references to Staples's language.

10. In 1994, Staples incorporated this essay into his memoir, *Parallel Time*, but he revised it substantially. Following are the first two paragraphs from that revised version. Compare those paragraphs with the originals. Why do you think Staples made the changes he did? In your opinion, did they improve the essay?

At night, I walked to the lakefront whenever the weather permitted. I was headed home from the lake when I took my first victim. It was late fall, and the wind was cutting. I was wearing my navy pea jacket, the collar turned up, my hands snug in the pockets. Dead leaves scuttled in shoals along the streets. I turned out of Blackstone Avenue and headed west on 57th Street, and there she was, a few yards ahead of me, dressed in business clothes and carrying a briefcase. She looked back at me once, then again, and picked up her pace. She looked back again and started to run. I stopped where I was and looked up at the surrounding windows. What did this look like to people peeking out through their blinds? I was out walking. But what if someone had thought they'd seen something they hadn't and called the police. I held back the urge to run. Instead, I walked south to The Midway, plunged into its darkness, and remained on The Midway until I reached the foot of my street.

I'd been a fool. I'd been walking the streets grinning good evening at people who were frightened to death of me. I did violence to them by just being. How had I missed this? I kept walking at night, but from then on I paid attention.

11. Staples first wrote this essay in 1986. Do you think the essay is dated? Explain why you do or do not feel that many people in today's society continue to perceive young African American males as threatening.

Losing My Religion for Equality

JIMMY CARTER

Jimmy Carter (b. 1924) is an American politician and human rights activist. A member of the Democratic Party, he served as the Governor of Georgia prior to his election as President of the United States in 1976. In 2002, Carter was awarded the Nobel Peace Prize for his work with the Carter Center, a non-governmental organization dedicated to advancing human rights and the qualitiy of life for people around the world. The following article, originally published in 2009, first went viral on social media in 2015.

I have been a practising Christian all my life and a deacon and Bible teacher for many years. My faith is a source of strength and comfort to me, as religious beliefs are to hundreds of millions of people around the world. So my decision to sever my ties with the Southern Baptist Convention, after six decades, was painful and difficult. It was, however, an unavoidable decision when the convention's leaders, quoting a few carefully selected Bible verses and claiming that Eve was created second to Adam and was responsible for original sin, ordained that women must be "subservient" to their husbands and prohibited from serving as deacons, pastors or chaplains in the military service.

This view that women are somehow inferior to men is not restricted to one religion or belief. Women are prevented from playing a full and equal role in many faiths. Nor, tragically, does its influence stop at the walls of the church, mosque, synagogue or temple. This discrimination, unjustifiably attributed to a Higher Authority, has provided a reason or excuse for the deprivation of women's equal rights across the world for centuries.

At its most repugnant, the belief that women must be subjugated to the wishes of men excuses slavery, violence, forced prostitution, genital mutilation and national laws that omit rape as a crime. But it also costs many millions of girls and women control over their own bodies and lives, and continues to deny them fair access to education, health, employment and influence within their own communities.

The impact of these religious beliefs touches every aspect of our lives. They help explain why in many countries boys are educated before girls; why girls are told when and whom they must marry; and why many face enormous and unacceptable risks in pregnancy and childbirth because their basic health needs are not met.

In some Islamic nations, women are   5
restricted in their movements, punished for permitting the exposure of an arm or ankle, deprived of education, prohibited from driving a car or competing with men for a job. If a woman is raped, she is often most severely punished as the guilty party in the crime.

The same discriminatory thinking lies behind the continuing gender gap in pay and why there are still so few women in office in the West. The root of this prejudice lies deep in our histories, but its impact is felt every day. It is not women and girls alone who suffer. It damages all of us. The evidence shows that investing in women and girls delivers major benefits for society. An educated woman has healthier children. She is more likely to send them to school. She earns more and invests what she earns in her family.

It is simply self-defeating for any community to discriminate against half its population. We need to challenge these self-serving and outdated attitudes and practices — as we are seeing

TSJ MERLYN LICENSING BV/Gallo Images/Getty Images

The Elders, an "independent group of global leaders" including Jimmy Carter and Nelson Mandela — pictured here at its launch in 2007 — was created to support the "shared interests of humanity."
What does this photo contribute to your understanding of the ethos Carter brings to "Losing My Religion for Equality"? Why does Carter believe this group can be effective in challenging discrimination against women?

in Iran where women are at the forefront of the battle for democracy and freedom.

I understand, however, why many political leaders can be reluctant about stepping into this minefield. Religion, and tradition, are powerful and sensitive areas to challenge. But my fellow Elders and I, who come from many faiths and backgrounds, no longer need to worry about winning votes or avoiding controversy — and we are deeply committed to challenging injustice wherever we see it.

The Elders are an independent group of eminent global leaders, brought together by former South African president Nelson Mandela, who offer their influence and experience to support peace building, help address major causes of human suffering and promote the shared interests of humanity. We have decided to draw particular attention to the responsibility of religious and traditional leaders in ensuring equality and human rights and have recently published a statement that declares: "The justification of discrimination against women and girls on grounds of religion or tradition, as if it were prescribed by a Higher Authority, is unacceptable."

We are calling on all leaders to challenge and change the harmful teachings and practices, no matter how ingrained, which justify discrimination against women. We ask, in particular, that leaders of all religions have the courage to acknowledge and emphasise the positive messages of dignity and equality that all the world's major faiths share.

The carefully selected verses found in the Holy Scriptures to justify the superiority of men owe more to time and place — and the determination of male leaders to hold onto their influence — than eternal truths. Similar biblical excerpts could be found to support the approval of slavery and the timid acquiescence to oppressive rulers.

I am also familiar with vivid descriptions in the same Scriptures in which women are revered as pre-eminent leaders. During the years of the early Christian church women served as deacons, priests, bishops, apostles, teachers and prophets. It wasn't until the fourth century that dominant Christian leaders, all men, twisted and distorted Holy Scriptures to perpetuate their ascendant positions within the religious hierarchy.

The truth is that male religious leaders have had — and still have — an option to interpret holy teachings either to exalt or subjugate women. They have, for their own selfish ends, overwhelmingly chosen the latter. Their continuing choice provides the foundation or justification for much of the pervasive persecution and abuse of women throughout the world. This is in clear

10

AFP Contributor/Getty Images

Women dressed as characters from *The Handmaid's Tale* — a dystopian novel about a theocratic society in which women are forced to bear children for an elite sector of society — have been seen in several protests concerning women's rights, particularly health care.
What message do these costumes and protests send? How effective are they? Based on Carter's argument in "Losing My Religion for Equality," how would he be likely to respond to this protest strategy?

violation not just of the Universal Declaration of Human Rights but also the teachings of Jesus Christ, the Apostle Paul, Moses and the prophets, Muhammad, and founders of other great religions — all of whom have called for proper and equitable treatment of all the children of God. It is time we had the courage to challenge these views.

[2009]

EXPLORING THE TEXT

1. How does Jimmy Carter establish his ethos in this piece? To what extent does he rely upon the ethos that being a former U.S. president automatically brings? What strategies does he use to position himself as a credible spokesperson on this particular issue?

2. The essay was originally published by *The Age*, an Australian newspaper. What evidence indicates that Carter assumes he is speaking to a wider audience?

3. How would you describe the logic of Carter's argument in paragraphs 2–4? You might try expressing his logic as a deductive syllogism or by using the Toulmin model.

4. What purpose does paragraph 5 serve in Carter's overall argument?

5. What evidence does Carter provide to support his assertion that gender bias "damages all of us" (para. 6)?

6. Carter, of course, never explicitly addresses the most obvious counterargument — that women are indeed inferior to men — though he does consider why gender discrimination based in religion is rarely challenged. Why do you think he does not address that counterargument? To what extent does this choice impact the effectiveness of his argument?

7. Carter briefly explains who the group "The Elders" are in paragraph 9. What is their purpose? You can read more about the group, its origins, and its purposes on the organization's website. To what extent does citing the work of this group encourage religious leaders not to feel themselves targets of his criticism?

8. How does Carter's diction change in the final two paragraphs as he characterizes negative behaviors that assert the inferiority of women? Provide specific examples to support your response.

9. In 2015, an analysis of why this article went viral appeared in the *Brisbane Times*, noting that Carter's essay had been viewed more than 1.9 million times. Why do you think the article gained such a wide audience?

Why Can't a Smart Woman Love Fashion?

CHIMAMANDA NGOZI ADICHIE

Chimamanda Ngozi Adichie (b. 1977) is one of her generation's most promising Nigerian writers. Adichie's first novel, *Purple Hibiscus* (2003), was awarded the Commonwealth Writers' Prize for Best First Book. Her second novel, *Half of a Yellow Sun* (2006), which is set during the Biafran civil war in Nigeria (1967–1970), won the Orange Broadband Prize for Fiction in 2007; the novel is dedicated to her two grandfathers, who died in the war. Adichie was awarded a MacArthur Foundation Fellowship in 2008, and *The Thing Around Your Neck*, her first collection of short stories, was published to acclaim in 2009. Her third novel, *Americanah*, was selected as one of the ten best books of 2013 by the *New York Times Book Review* and won a National Book Critics Circle Award. Adichie reached new audiences when a portion of her 2013 TEDx Talk entitled "We Should All Be Feminists" was heavily sampled in the Beyoncé song "****Flawless" later that year. Her essay *Dear Ijeawele, or A Feminist Manifesto in Fifteen Suggestions* was conceived as a letter to a friend who had sought her advice on raising a feminist daughter and later published as a book in 2017. Adichie currently divides her time between the United States and Nigeria, where she grew up and attended medical school at the University of Nigeria for two years before coming to America. She has also earned an MFA in creative writing from Johns Hopkins University and an MA in African studies from Yale University. Adichie describes fellow Nigerian writer Chinua Achebe as her hero, and many consider her his literary heir. The following article, "Why Can't a Smart Woman Love Fashion?," was published in *Elle* magazine in 2014.

As a child, I loved watching my mother get dressed for Mass. She folded and twisted and pinned her *ichafu*[1] until it sat on her head like a large flower. She wrapped her george — heavy beaded cloth, alive with embroidery, always in bright shades of red or purple or pink — around her waist in two layers. The first, the longer piece, hit her ankles, and the second formed an elegant tier just below her knees. Her sequined blouse caught the light and glittered. Her shoes and handbag always matched. Her lips shone with gloss. As she moved, so did the heady scent of Dior Poison. I loved, too, the way she dressed me in pretty little-girl clothes, lace-edged socks pulled up to my calves, my hair arranged in two puffy bunny-tails. My favorite memory is of a sunny Sunday morning, standing in front of her dressing table, my mother clasping her necklace around my neck, a delicate gold wisp with a fish-shape pendant, the mouth of the fish open as though in delighted surprise.

For her work as a university administrator, my mother also wore color: skirt suits, feminine swingy dresses belted at the waist, medium-high heels. She was stylish, but she was not unusual. Other middle- class Igbo[2] women also invested in gold jewelry, in good shoes, in appearance. They searched for the best tailors to make clothes for them and their children. If they were lucky

enough to travel abroad, they shopped mostly for clothes and shoes. They spoke of grooming almost in moral terms. The rare woman who did not appear well dressed and well lotioned was frowned upon, as though her appearance were a character failing. "She doesn't look like a person," my mother would say.

As a teenager, I searched her trunks for crochet tops from the 1970s. I took a pair of her old jeans to a seamstress who turned them into a miniskirt. I once wore my brother's tie, knotted like a man's, to a party. For my 17th birthday, I designed a halter maxidress, low in the back, the collar lined with plastic pearls. My tailor, a gentle man sitting in his market stall, looked baffled while I explained it to him. My mother did not always approve of these clothing choices, but what mattered to her was that I made an effort. Ours was a relatively privileged life, but to pay attention to appearance — and to look as though one did — was a trait that cut across class in Nigeria.

When I left home to attend university in America, the insistent casualness of dress alarmed me. I was used to a casualness with care — T-shirts ironed crisp, jeans altered for the best fit — but it seemed that these students had rolled out of bed in their pajamas and come straight to class. Summer shorts were so short they seemed like underwear, and how, I wondered, could people wear rubber flip-flops to school?

Still, I realized quickly that some outfits I might have casually worn on a Nigerian university campus would simply be impossible now. 5

---

[1] A traditional Nigerian head scarf. —Eds.
[2] The Igbo are an ethnic group from south-central and southeastern Nigeria. —Eds.

This work by the Guerrilla Girls, an anonymous radical feminist art collective highlights the historical difficulties faced by women artists.

How does the Guerilla Girls' message about female artists dovetail with Adichie's perception of how and why American artists and intellectuals have had trouble being taken seriously?

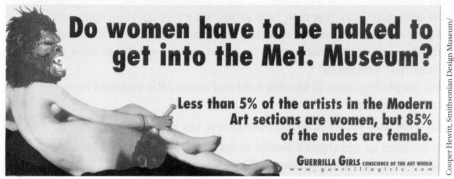

Do women have to be naked to get into the Met. Museum?

Less than 5% of the artists in the Modern Art sections are women, but 85% of the nudes are female.

GUERRILLA GIRLS CONSCIENCE OF THE ART WORLD
www.guerrillagirls.com

Cooper Hewitt, Smithsonian Design Museum/ Art Resource, NY

I made slight amendments to accommodate my new American life. A lover of dresses and skirts, I began to wear more jeans. I walked more often in America, so I wore fewer high heels, but always made sure my flats were feminine. I refused to wear sneakers outside a gym. Once, an American friend told me, "You're overdressed." In my short-sleeve top, cotton trousers, and high wedge sandals, I did see her point, especially for an undergraduate class. But I was not uncomfortable. I felt like myself.

My writing life changed that. Short stories I had been working on for years were finally receiving nice, handwritten rejection notes. This was progress of sorts. Once, at a workshop, I sat with other unpublished writers, silently nursing our hopes and watching the faculty — published writers who seemed to float in their accomplishment. A fellow aspiring writer said of one faculty member, "Look at that dress and makeup! You can't take her seriously." I thought the woman looked attractive, and I admired the grace with which she walked in her heels. But I found myself quickly agreeing. Yes, indeed, one could not take this author of three novels seriously, because she wore a pretty dress and two shades of eye shadow.

I had learned a lesson about Western culture: Women who wanted to be taken seriously were supposed to substantiate their seriousness with a studied indifference to appearance. For serious women writers in particular, it was better not to dress well at all, and if you did, then it was best to pretend that you had not put much thought into it. If you spoke of fashion, it had to be either with apology or with the slightest of sneers. The further your choices were from the mainstream, the better. The only circumstance under which caring about clothes was acceptable was when making a statement, creating an image of some sort to be edgy, eclectic, counterculture. It could not merely be about taking pleasure in clothes.

A good publisher had bought my novel. I was 26 years old. I was eager to be taken seriously. And so began my years of pretense. I hid my high heels. I told myself that orange, flattering to my skin tone, was too loud. That my large earrings were too much. I wore clothes I would ordinarily consider uninteresting, nothing too bright or too fitted or too unusual. I made choices thinking only about this: How should a serious woman writer be? I didn't want to look as if I tried too hard. I also wanted to look older. Young and

seeing connections

In 2015 Matilda Kahl, a creative director in New York City, wrote a personal essay entitled, "Why I Wear the Exact Same Thing to Work Every Day," describing her decision to wear a "work uniform" comprised of a simple white top, black pants, and a black ribbon tied in a bow under her collar every day. "For men," she wrote, "it's a very common approach, even mandatory in most professions. Nevertheless, I received a lot of mixed reactions for usurping this idea for myself." One man famous for a work uniform was Steve Jobs, the CEO of Apple from 1997 through 2011.

After examining the photographs of Matilda Kahl and Steve Jobs included here, answer the questions below.

1. **Why do you think Kahl received mixed reactions to her uniform?**

2. **Can Kahl's decision be considered similar to Adichie's approach of wearing bright, well-tailored, and avant-garde outfits? Explain.**

3. **What do you think Adichie's position on Kahl's uniform would be? What about her position on Jobs's uniform?**

Matilda Kahl

Tim Mosenfelder/Getty Images

female seemed to me a bad combination for being taken seriously.

Once, I brought a pair of high heels to a literary event but left them in my suitcase and wore flats instead. An old friend said, "Wear what you want to; it's your work that matters." But he was a man, and I thought that was easy for him to say. Intellectually, I agreed with him. I would have said the same thing to someone else. But it took years before I truly began to believe this.

I am now 36 years old. During my most   10
recent book tour, I wore, for the first time, clothes that made me happy. My favorite outfit was a pair of ankara-print shorts, a damask top, and yellow high-heel shoes. Perhaps it is the confidence that comes with being older. Perhaps it is the good fortune of being published and read seriously, but I no longer pretend not to care about clothes. Because I do care. I love embroidery and texture. I love lace and full skirts and cinched waists. I love black, and I love color. I love heels, and I love flats. I love exquisite detailing. I love shorts and long maxidresses and feminine jackets with puffy sleeves. I love colored trousers. I love shopping. I love my two wonderful tailors in Nigeria, who often give me suggestions and with whom I exchange sketches. I admire well-dressed women and often make a point to tell them so. Just because. I dress now thinking of what I like, what I think fits and flatters, what puts me in a good mood. I feel again myself — an idea that is no less true for being a bit hackneyed.

I like to think of this, a little fancifully, as going back to my roots. I grew up, after all, in a world in which a woman's seriousness was not incompatible with an interest in appearance; if anything, an interest in appearance was expected of women who wanted to be taken seriously.

My mother made history as the first woman to be registrar of the University of Nigeria at Nsukka; her speeches at senate meetings were

This photograph of Chimamanda Ngozi Adichie was taken at a 2017 Times Talks event in which she participated. The talk was entitled, "On Raising a Feminist."

How might this photograph of Adichie be used to emphasize her main points in this essay?

Donna Ward/Getty Images

famous for their eloquence and brilliance. Now, at 70, she still loves clothes. Our tastes, though, are very different. She wishes I were more conventional. She would like to see me wearing jewelry that matches and long hair weaves. (In her world, better one real-gold set than 20 of what she calls "costume"; in her world, my kinky hair is "untidy.") Still, I am my mother's daughter, and I invest in appearance.

[2014]

EXPLORING THE TEXT

1. Adichie opens the essay with a description of childhood memories of her mother. Why is this an effective opening to her argument?

2. Adichie waits until the second paragraph to reveal that her mother is a university administrator. What is the effect of withholding this information rather than including it in the opening line?

3. What does Adichie mean by her statement that her mother, like other middle-class Igbo women in Nigeria, "spoke of grooming almost in moral terms" (para. 2)? How does this statement relate to her point that paying attention to appearance "was a trait that cut across class in Nigeria" (para. 3)?

4. What is the distinction Adichie makes between the "insistent casualness of dress" of U.S. students and her own "casualness with care" (para. 4)? Do you believe this is a significant distinction? Explain.

5. How does her "writing life" (para. 6) alter her attitude toward the way she dresses? Do you think she was right to make such changes? Explain why or why not.

6. In paragraph 7, Adichie makes a number of assertions about Western culture's attitude toward women's appearance, including her belief that Americans generally assume that paying attention to fashion suggests a lack of professionalism or intelligence. To what extent do you agree with any or all of these assertions?

7. What does Adichie mean when she remembers, "And so began my years of pretense" (para. 8)? Can you recall a time when you dressed more as you thought you should rather than as you wanted to? Was it worth it?

8. When Adichie writes of her own feelings about fashion, she uses words like "pleasure" and "love" — the latter a word she repeats many times in paragraph 10. How might these descriptions defy such common attitudes toward fashionable clothes as fitting in, feeling up to date and part of current trends, or being admired?

9. In the penultimate paragraph, Adichie contrasts Nigerian society's attitude toward women's appearance with that of American society. What do you make of her assessment? Is it an astute observation, an oversimplification, or something else? Explain by citing specific examples.

10. At the end of her essay, Adichie points out that she and her mother continue to differ in their taste in clothing, yet they both "invest in appearance" (para. 12). How do you interpret her use of the word "invest"? To what extent does it conflict with the more emotional language she uses in paragraph 10?

11. Ultimately, how does Chimamanda Ngozi Adichie answer the question she poses in her title?

12. In 2016, Adichie became the face of the British brand Boots's new beauty campaign. In an article on Adichie's turn as a beauty brand ambassador, journalist Chaédria LaBouvier praised her as a fashion icon, asserting that she uses "beauty and style in direct, political ways that subvert dehumanizing expectations" — a relationship to fashion LaBouvier refers to as "weaponized glamour." To what extent does LaBouvier's statement reveal a false dichotomy between brains and appearance?

---

from Why I Am Not a Feminist
A Feminist Manifesto

JESSA CRISPIN

Jessa Crispin (b. 1978) is a critic best known for editing *Bookslut*, a literary blog founded in 2002 that has since received mention in the *New York Times Book Review* and the *Washington Post*. Crispin has also written for the *Guardian*, the *Chicago Sun-Times*, and the *Toronto Globe and Mail*. She has published three books: *The Dead Ladies Project: Exiles, Expats, and Ex-Countries* (2015), *The Creative Tarot: A Modern Guide to an Inspired Life* (2016), and *Why I Am Not a Feminist: A Feminist Manifesto* (2017), a rejection of modern-day, mainstream feminism that calls on the movement to remember its radical roots. "Women Do Not Have to Be Feminists" is the second chapter of *Why I Am Not a Feminist*.

There is a tendency to look at women who have rejected feminism and decide they must be pitiable. Poor silly cows, they don't know what's best for them. Choosing dependency and subjugation, choosing sad lives of imprisonment and enslavement. When will they awake from their slumber?

It's always going to be easier to pity someone for making different choices than you than to try to understand why they made the choices they did. Otherwise you might have to question your own choices and deal with the possible regret of not having chosen differently. You proselytize to rid yourself of doubt, not to spread the good news.

We speak for these women instead of listening to them. This must be their character: they must be lazy, deluded, greedy, stupid. These must be their reasons: they must have daddy issues, they must be gold diggers, they must think men are actually superior to women due to some sort of religious indoctrination, they must be doing this because they think it makes them hotter to guys. This must be who they are: uneducated, lower class, evangelical Christians, pampered suburban moms, twits.

It's really not that difficult to see why someone might choose not to be a feminist. To understand that, all we really have to do is take a look at what the feminist revolution has, and has not, offered to women.

◆ ◆ ◆

When we all decided to be feminists, it was because we were looking at what was denied to us. We had historically been shut out of masculine spaces, like public life, the workplace, and education. Our traditional realm, of the home and the family and the nursery, looked like prisons.

◆ ◆ ◆

What feminism thought it was offering its followers, then, was escape. It was an expanded life. A life of independence, of adventure, of work.

But in order to believe that, we have to forget that women have always worked. Many women have always had to. The unmarried, the widowed, the poor, the disadvantaged have always worked. When feminists decided to fight for the right to work, what they meant was the right to become doctors, lawyers, and so on. Women have always scrubbed toilets and floors, have always been paid to touch other people's bodies as nurses and assistants and sex workers.

Nor were women fighting to work in the jobs of poor men, the laborers and miners and slaughterhouse workers. Right from the beginning, the assumption was that work was a good thing, a fulfilling thing, that we were missing out on. Not a soul and body–destroying thing that can kill you off young or make you wish it would.

Some women have historically had an out from the realm of work. That out was through men. If they found the right man with the right situation, they could exit this soul-destroying work world and retreat to the relative comfort of the house. The house might be a prison, but when freedom looks like wiping up someone else's vomit and urine under migraine-inducing fluorescent lighting, can you actually blame someone for asking to be let back into their cell?

Poor women are not the only women who would prefer not to work, of course. Highly educated women working in ambitious fields also decide to check out. That "opting out" as the feminists call it, is considered something of a betrayal. Women should work! To help their sisters out! And yet, opting in means prioritizing long hours at jobs over any sense of community or family. Because in this age of precarity, work and money are so elusive that cutting back hours can mean a slide into irrelevance or unemployability for many.

This is part of the problem of creating a unified front for feminism: the median feminist is generally going to be a middle-class, educated white woman. Her desires and needs cannot stand in for the needs of all women. And yet

"I don't want to be empowered—I want to be sassy."

This cartoon by Barbara Smaller appeared in the *New Yorker* in 2012. **Do you think the message of this cartoon is one that supports Crispin's argument? Why or why not?**

we've focused on facilitating her dreams for much of recent feminist history. Our goals have been things that would make her life easier, like equal pay, removing barriers to higher education, delaying childbearing through birth control and fertility treatment developments.

The workplace and capitalistic society has become increasingly hostile. Not only to women, but to men, too. By keeping the focus on how women are doing in the marketplace, rather than how human beings exist under this system of competition and precarity, our thinking remains very small. How are women faring in the job market in comparison to men? Does that really matter when due to overwhelming student loan debt, sharply decreased job stability, the gutting of social services and work benefits, rapacious CEOs and boards of directors, and globalization, the world of work and money is hurting everyone?

But sure, stick with it, sisters! We must prevail because of . . . something.

◆ ◆ ◆

One thing we are told we must persevere for is independence. The independence of women is important. Independence from men, sure. If only because dependence on men is not what it used

to be. The deal was, I give up my freedom and my body and you offer me protection from the outside world. That arrangement would last until you died.

Now of course, romance is as unstable as the job market, and just as competitive and demeaning. Unless you decide to black widow a few rich guys in a row, looking to men to provide the stability and protection you desire is unlikely to work out in a lifelong kind of way.

So it's important to have a Plan B. But why is our Plan B to manage all of it on our own? To have to, as individuals, make our money, set up our homes, bear and raise children, cook our meals, develop and maintain a sense of style and taste, decide how we spend our free time, and on and on until we die. In the name of freedom, we broke out of communities and towns and tribes and created families and blood lineage. In the name of freedom, we broke out of families and blood lineage to create a nuclear household. In the name of freedom, we broke out of nuclear households to become individuals. And yet at no point along that way did we put serious consideration into creating a social equivalent of the support system those larger groups provided to us.

True, a lot of those systems were built explicitly for the oppression of women. Community

15

can often seem like a system for controlling behavior and insisting on conformity; family can often seem like a method of keeping women docile and tamed. But we're all so eager to over-correct. We toss out entire systems because they once hurt us, without taking a moment to reflect on how, so often, they helped us.

Now independence is hailed as a feminist virtue. The ability to stand on one's own, outside of family or men. And now we have all the freedom and independence we desire, like the freedom to go bankrupt, to be socially isolated, to be home-less without any social support network, to labor all your life with nothing to show for it. As long as feminism is still infected with the Protestant economic determinist mindset — the idea that your station in life is determined by how virtuous you are or what you deserve — we'll continue to put our time and energy into breaking down social structures rather than creating new, more empathetic ones.

And so of course a significant number of women are going to look at this atomized, cap-italistic world that feminism offers to them like a gift and ask if they can take it back to the store and exchange it for something a little bit more old-fashioned. Women everywhere! Leave the comfortable confines of traditional life and enter this brand new world of struggle, despair, and uncertainty! Thanks, . . . but no.

Not every woman, or man, is ambitious. Not every woman is determined to make her mark on the world. Not every woman gets satisfaction out of working eighty hours a week just to watch some young Harvard asshole get promoted above her to a job she didn't really want but would pay her a little better. Not every woman longs to par-ticipate in . . . the consumerist culture we live in, filling the holes in her heart and soul with shoes and limited edition crop tops from Topshop. It's feminism's s fault that these are the two options we have available to women. Either you can let a man take care of the financial and outer world side of things while you spend time with your

20

children and shop for overpriced organic blue-berries, or you can work until you die to buy stuff you don't need and fight for every square inch you exist on. Either that pays off for you in the end or it doesn't.

◆ ◆ ◆

When — let's call them "traditional" — women "feel sorry" for feminists, they're doing pretty much what we do to them. We are using pity as a self-defense mechanism. We feel sorry for

▼
————————

In this photograph, a model for designer Prabal Gurung's Fall/Winter 2017 fashion show wears a t-shirt bearing the slogan, "GIRLS JUST WANT TO HAVE FUNDAMENTAL RIGHTS."
Does this image ultimately support Crispin's argument or refute it? Consider the rhetorical situation of the image as you explain your answer.

The Washington Post/Getty Images

someone so we don't have to assign value to anything they say or do or believe. We do not have to listen to their complaints about our beliefs.

And yet if we were able to sit down, without judgment, and ask what we're not offering these women, we might actually be able to get some-where. Not along the lines of conversion. We need to stop thinking that way. Instead, we could see the limitations of our own project; that we're not as smart as we think we are; that maybe the ways these women are unhappy line up with the ways we are unhappy.

If you look at what is missing from today's society, much of it falls within traditional fem-inine values and pursuits. Carving out space within the masculine realm, in the work and public spheres, meant in part abandoning the feminine spheres of home, care, and commu-nity. There was no equal effort to make space for men in the feminine pursuits. As a result, what you see is a kind of hyper-masculinized world, where women are participating — and abso-lutely expected to participate in this world by feminists — in patriarchal values.

Feminism has been marred by these patri-archal values. It has been warped in the name of greed and power. Feminism was seduced by all the pleasures the patriarchal world has to offer and overwhelmed by the enormous amount of work it would take to break it apart. So we adapted feminism's goals in order to live more comfortable lives.

In order to succeed in a patriarchal world, we 25 took on the role of patriarchs ourselves. In order to win in this world, we had to exhibit the charac-teristics the patriarchal world values and discard what it does not.

In order to get ahead in this culture, we also shape ourselves to what men value in women, which is sexuality and beauty. Never before has there been such pressure to maintain our sexual availability throughout our lives, and women celebrities who keep their figures, who are still hot after all these years, are praised as role mod-els by feminists.

We've been cut off from traditions and rituals, from family and intergenerational connections, from communities and a sense of belonging. We saw these things as unpaid labor that we were forced to do, rather than something worth pre-serving. It is true that we were forced into these roles, but it's also true that these things have value and should be maintained. It goes beyond

JUSTIN TALLIS/Getty Images

In this photograph, protesters dressed in both two- and one-piece bathing suits protest France's ban on burkinis, or full-body bathing suits designed to allow observant Muslim women to swim in public places. **Do you consider this demonstration to be a form of what Jessa Crispin calls "rescue and protection" (para. 28) or a consideration of the needs of women from all walks of life? Explain your answer.**

seeing connections

Carefully read this excerpt from *Feminism Is for Everybody*, a 2001 book by feminist activist and scholar bell hooks, and then answer the following questions.

1. **What is hooks's main argument in this excerpt?**

2. **In what ways does hooks support Crispin's critique of contemporary feminism? In what ways does she challenge it?**

3. **Compare and contrast both the rhetoric and message of Crispin and hooks. How does each writer use rhetorical strategies to achieve her purpose?**

from Feminism Is for Everybody

BELL HOOKS

While it was in the interest of mainstream white supremacist capitalist patriarchy to suppress visionary feminist thinking . . . reformist feminists were also eager to silence these forces. Reformist feminism became their route to class mobility. They could break free of male domination in the workforce and be more self-determining in their lifestyles. While sexism did not end, they could maximize their freedom within the existing system. And they could count on there being a lower class of exploited subordinated women to do the dirty work they were refusing to do. By accepting and indeed colluding with the subordination of working-class and poor women, they not only ally themselves with the existing patriarchy and its concomitant sexism, they give themselves the right to lead a double life, one where they are the equals of men in the workforce and at home when they want to be. . . .

Lifestyle feminism ushered in the notion that there could be as many versions of feminism as there were women. Suddenly the politics was being slowly removed from feminism. And the assumption prevailed that no matter what a woman's politics, be she conservative or liberal, she too could fit feminism into her existing lifestyle. Obviously this way of thinking has made feminism more acceptable because its underlying assumption is that women can be feminists without fundamentally challenging and changing themselves or the culture. . . .

Feminist politics is losing momentum because feminist movement has lost clear definitions. We have those definitions. Let's reclaim them. Let's share them. Let's start over. Let's have T-shirts and bumper stickers and postcards and hip-hop music, television and radio commercials, ads everywhere and billboards, and all manner of printed material that tells the world about feminism. We can share the simple yet powerful message that feminism is a movement to end sexist oppression.

squabbling over who does the housework and childcare in a nuclear family, to the question of how do we feel like we belong somewhere? How do we begin to value giving as much as we value taking? How do we participate in and contribute to the world, outside of the jobs we have? How do we think of our place in society, beyond being an individual or being part of a couple or nuclear family? These will be the challenges of feminism moving forward.

◆ ◆ ◆

Our job, as feminists, should not be recruitment. It should not be conversion. It should be listening to the wants and needs of women that might differ from our own. The condescending attitude of Western feminists toward women in Muslim countries — this idea that these women need to be rescued from their head scarves and their traditions — is a good illustration of that. Never mind the fact that rescue and protection are masculine, patriarchal ideas. Our attempts at conversion are asking women to devalue what they find valuable about their existence, to take on our values of independence, success, and sexuality.

And yet despite our attempts at converting women to our values, we rarely seem to pause and ask ourselves if these things actually make us happy. If this way of life is the best we can do.

To question this is not to run screaming back to the kitchen, to allow men to make our decisions for us and go back to our subjugation. It is to ask if maybe there were things we discarded that we should go back and reclaim. It's to ask if maybe we need to pause for a moment and rethink not only our strategy but also our goals.

There are questions we need to ask ourselves. They're going to make us uncomfortable. The first: Has feminism created a better world? Not just for you personally, but for both women and men in all levels of society. The next: Has feminism created the space for men to take on traditionally feminine traits at the same level it has created the space for women to take on traditionally masculine traits? And lastly: If we say we want a better world for women, are the current goals and ideas of feminism likely to create that world?

[2017]

EXPLORING THE TEXT

1. Jessa Crispin begins with an analysis of our tendency to pity — rather than listen to — people whose choices are different from our own. At the end of paragraph 2, she explains this dynamic: "You proselytize to rid yourself of doubt." What does she mean by this? Do your own experiences support this analysis? Explain.

2. Crispin claims that women became feminists because their "traditional realm . . . looked like prisons," and they sought "an expanded life" (paras. 5–6). How effectively does she support this claim? To what extent do you believe it represents a fair assessment of women in generations past?

3. How, according to Crispin, are the patriarchy and capitalism related? What effect does this connection have on the focus of her argument?

4. When Crispin points out that the "workplace and capitalistic society has become increasingly hostile" to both women and men (para. 12), what point is she developing? Is she casting doubt on the goals of mainstream feminism as she has defined them (e.g., "an expanded life" [para. 6])?

5. In paragraph 12, Crispin asserts: "By keeping the focus on how women are doing in the marketplace, rather than how human beings exist under this system of competition and precarity, our thinking remains very small." She then follows this statement with a series of rhetorical questions. How effectively do these questions support Crispin's bold statement?

6. In paragraphs 14–16, Crispin focuses on the concept of independence. How would you characterize her tone in these paragraphs? To what extent is she arguing that independence might actually be detrimental to women? Are you swayed by her argument? Why or why not?

7. In paragraph 28, Crispin refers to the "condescending attitude of Western feminists toward women in Muslim countries." How valid do you believe this characterization is? Explain.

8. Throughout the text, Crispin asks questions, often several together in one sentence, at other times in a series. How effective do you find this rhetorical strategy? Consider the final paragraph as you develop your response.

9. One reviewer of Crispin's book noted that Crispin's rhetoric "makes for an effective, rousing call to action, even if it's at odds with the kind of

unromantic, swagger-less work of social change that Crispin, a former Planned Parenthood staffer, advocates. But the irony of her dismissal of 'pop culture feminism,' as it were, is that her book is such a prime example of it: accessible, entertaining, and cathartic in its expression of an often unspoken rage." To what extent do you agree with this assessment of Crispin's rhetoric? Cite specific language to support your response.

10. Who do you think is the intended audience for *Why I Am Not a Feminist*? Cite specific examples and passages from this excerpt to support your response.

11. Crispin's "manifesto," as her book's title calls it, has been called a "rant" and a "polemic." One critic characterized the book as being "another rant into the void, another intervention for the sake of intervention that offers no concrete strategy for meaningful change." Based on "Women Do Not Have to Be Feminists," do you believe this is

a fair assessment? How would you characterize Crispin's argument? Is it a polemic, a thoughtful proposal for change, or something else?

12. In a 2017 interview, Crispin described her book as a work that's "basically about how the popular feminist movement has gotten so off track with such terrible things done in its name that I don't want to associate myself with it. Feminism now seems to be defined as success is defined: as being as good at capitalism as men are. I feel very estranged from it." How effectively does she argue this claim in "Women Do Not Have to Be Feminists"?

13. In this chapter, and the book in general, Crispin argues that the political and economic goals of feminism have been so diluted that today, it has more to do with the marketplace than with substantive change. Does your view of contemporary feminism support or challenge Crispin's?

Doubly Denied

CRISTINA HENRÍQUEZ

Christina Henríquez (b. 1977) is the author of one short fiction collection, *Come Together, Fall Apart* (2006), and two novels: *The World in Half* (2009) and *The Book of Unknown Americans* (2014), which the *Daily Beast* named its 2014 novel of the year. Henríquez has also contributed to the *New Yorker* and the anthologies *This Is Not Chick Lit* (2006), *Thirty Ways of Looking at Hillary: Reflections by Women Writers* (2008), and *Double Bind: Women on Ambition* (2017), in which the following essay appears.

I called my mother. I said, "Am I ambitious?"
She said, "You? Yes."
"Really?"
"You don't think so?"
"What's your evidence?" I asked.   5
"Well, you've been successful. You're good at what you do."
"Okay."
"You've wanted things. You wanted to go to graduate school, for example, and you did it."
"But is that because I'm ambitious?"
"Isn't it?"   10
"I'm not sure," I said.

♦ ♦ ♦

I emailed a friend. I wrote: "Question. Would you say I'm ambitious?"
She wrote back: "sure. i mean, you've accomplished a hell of a lot in your thirty-something years, so you're definitely something. why??"
I wrote: "I have to write an essay about ambition, and I can't figure out if I am ambitious."
Her response: "maybe you're committed. is   15
that how you spell that? anyway. you're the real deal—you work regularly, you stay in touch with the world of literature. you clearly HAVE ambition. or ambitions."

◆ ◆ ◆

I asked my husband as we sat on the couch one night, watching television, "What's the most ambitious thing I've ever done?"

He looked at me for a few seconds, thinking. Then he said, "What's the definition of ambitious?"

Exactly.

◆ ◆ ◆

It was only a word, but I kept dancing around it. If someone had asked, I might have said I was tenacious, or that I worked hard, or that I was diligent, or determined, but I never would have said I was ambitious. My mother was right. I had wanted things out of life, but simple desire doesn't necessarily mean a person is ambitious. Ambition, it seemed, was something that other people possessed — men mostly, or Hillary Clinton — but it wasn't something that felt quite like me. But why not?

I lay in bed at night thinking about it. I conjured up memories of when I was just starting college and the thought was forming that maybe, possibly I would like to be a writer, and that maybe, possibly, I had what it would take to make that happen. What kind of writer, I didn't know (in an admissions interview I had been asked what I liked to write and my response was, "Letters"), but a fantasy was taking root in my mind about a life where writing was at the center, a vision that included things like scarves and coffee and stacks of well-worn books, and me, by candlelight, scribbling into the night.

I went to Northwestern University, halfway across the country from Delaware, where I lived, and I used to wander along the edge of Lake Michigan and through the majestic, neo-Gothic Deering Library, awed by where I had ended up. I knew by then that I loved writing, but I still didn't know exactly what I would do with it. Would I actually write books? That seemed like a wild, far-off dream.

Not long into my freshman year, though, I learned that Northwestern had an undergraduate writing program. It was highly competitive, and each year students applied with the hopes that they, and their work, would be deemed worthy. At the end of my sophomore year, I submitted a manuscript, a few very short stories, and waited to learn my fate. I don't remember how the news was delivered, but when it came, I do remember feeling that I had been punched in the gut. I didn't get in.

I could have stopped there, I guess. I could have interpreted the rejection as the universe's way of telling me that I should find something else to do. But although I was devastated (I wrote entry after tearful journal entry about it), I was stubborn, too. I applied to the program again the following year. That time, I was accepted.

A similar story played out when I was leaving college. My wild dream of writing books for a living had solidified by then, and I thought the best course would be to go to graduate school to learn how to do that. I knew almost nothing about graduate programs, so I found a copy of *U.S. News & World Report* and looked up the most recent rankings of graduate writing programs, chose five in the top ten, and applied. Every single one turned me down.

For the next two years, I worked in the publicity department at a university press. During my lunch break I wrote stories — one about people stuck in an elevator, one about cliff-jumping during the summer, one about a man who cuts off his pinky finger — and at the end of the day, I went home to my studio apartment and wrote more, banging out stories on the manual typewriter I had bought at a church sale. When the stories were finished, I put them in envelopes and mailed them to a former professor, who read them and gave me feedback that he jotted down and mailed back to me. I sent stories to magazines, ridiculous pipe dreams like the *New Yorker* and the *Atlantic* and *Zoetrope* and *BOMB*, and all of them got rejected. Incredibly, none of it put

20

25

In this photograph, sixteen-year-old Starr Andrews competes at the 2018 U.S. Figure Skating Championships for the first time. Openly ambitious, Andrews told reporters before the event that she wanted to earn a spot on the podium (and thus a trip to the Olympics). Skating to her own rendition of a Whitney Houston song, she performed so well she earned a standing ovation from the audience. Although she did not ultimately earn a spot on the Olympic team, she captured the attention of judges and fans alike.

Choose a section of Henríquez's essay that you think best applies to Andrews's career as an elite athlete. What aspects of that passage resonate, and why?

Tony Avelar/AP Images

me off course. Eventually I applied to graduate programs again. Different ones this time, and I submitted different material. I hoped — God, I hoped — it would be enough.

It was. The first school I heard back from was the Iowa Writers' Workshop, the top-ranked program in the country, telling me I had gotten in.

Was it tenacity? Resilience? Just plain hard-headedness? Or could it have been ambition, churning somewhere inside of me all that time? And if so, why was it so difficult for me to simply call it what it was?

◆ ◆ ◆

Growing up, I can't recall any discussion of ambition in my house — at least, not in an overt way. I was the oldest of three, and though expectations were high (A's were good, A-pluses were better), my parents gave all of us wide berth to explore our interests. They opened doors, as many as they could, and then left it up to us whether we would walk through. In grade school, they rented me a violin when I said I wanted to learn. They bought me the books I wanted to read from every Scholastic book fair. They went out of their way to plan trips so that my brother and sister and I would have the benefit of encountering new places. They allowed my natural enthusiasm — and from that my ambition — to flourish on its own, in its time, and then let me follow it in any direction I chose. In certain ways, this seems like one of the best gifts a parent could give a child.

And yet, when it came time for me to start thinking about college, I do remember my father telling me, "I think you should apply to Princeton."

I remember I laughed.

This was at the time when bulging envelopes filled with glossy folders and brochures touting the glories of schools all over the country arrived daily in the mailbox. I lay on my bed and pored over them, captivated by photographs of happy students walking through leaves and sitting on grassy lawns in the sun.

"I'm serious," he said. "It's a good school."

I thought he was nuts, of course, but when I look back on it now, I see that my father was trying to teach me something. He must have known how improbable it was for me to go to Princeton. (Northwestern, where I ended up going, was enough of a long shot.) *But it's important,* he seemed to be telling me, *to reach for things that might seem beyond your grasp.* The only way to *get* further is to *reach* further, after all. To be ambitious is to connect yourself to the future. It's a movement outward, forward, toward something new.

It's not surprising that it's a lesson I learned from my father. When he was eighteen, my father came from Panama to the United States to study chemical engineering at the University of Delaware. It was the first time he had been away from home, and he traveled by himself with a trunk and a suitcase and a student visa in his pocket. He came with hope and fear and what surely can only be described as ambition. To be an immigrant, after all, to uproot your life, to walk away from everything you have known with the goal of going somewhere new and with the hope of finding something better is to be, necessarily, ambitious.

But if his leaving Panama seemed the very embodiment of ambition, my father also brought with him certain attitudes that seemed to undermine it, at least where women were concerned. He was raised in a culture that operates within the structure of traditional gender roles, which meant, for example, that he expected my mother to serve him dinner every night, no matter how late he arrived home from work, and that he had to adjust when she wanted to get a job after my

This chart uses data from an article entitled "Changing Companies' Minds About Women," published in *McKinsey Quarterly* in 2011. The article states, "By addressing the mind-sets holding women back, corporate leaders can reshape the talent pipeline . . . increasing the number of women role models at the top and, in turn, making it likelier that more women will retain their ambition."

What might Cristina Henríquez consider most important for corporate leaders to know about ambition?

Ambition in the Workplace

Percentage of those who agree/strongly agree with the desire to advance to the next level of their careers

Young men age 24–34	98%
Young women age 24–34	92%
Women of all ages in entry-level roles	79%
Women of all ages in early to middle management	83%

Data from McKinsey Analysis survey of 1,000 women and 525 men currently working in large corporations or professional-services firms, 2011.

brother, sister, and I were grown. I saw all of that, of course. And seeing it against the backdrop of my father's personal story, I received two messages about ambition, both of which came through loud and clear: the importance of striving and the importance of staying put.

◆ ◆ ◆

A year after my first book had been published, more than a decade after my father brought up Princeton, I had my first child. I lived halfway across the country from my parents by then, so as often as I could I called my mother on the webcam. I was in the throes of new motherhood, lonely and feeling much of the time like I had been sideswiped by a truck. In those early months, I struggled, as many new parents do, to get through the days. My husband was back at work, and I shuffled around in my bathrobe, which I didn't even have the energy to tie, and nursed my daughter while I gazed down at her long eyelashes and full cheeks, and fell asleep on the couch when I could, and stared in the mirror at the deep blue circles under my eyes, and tried to make sense of what had happened to me. My mother was my savior. Over the computer, she sympathized and told me how hard it had been for her at the beginning. She recounted being home with young children, being far from family, the consuming loneliness when my father was traveling for work, as he often did. She told me in no uncertain terms how important it was to be doing what I was doing, how important it was to have this time to bond with my daughter. She believed, she said to me more than once, that when they could, when financially it was a viable option, at least one parent should stay home to be with their children. She was trying to comfort me, I know, to assure me that I was doing something good, even noble. But she was sending another message, too: It was what I was *supposed* to be doing.

I had decided by then that I was going to try to stay home with my daughter. I was in the middle of my first novel, but I could write while she napped, I reasoned. I could write at night. And later, when my daughter was in preschool, I could use that time to write, too. I wouldn't get the book finished quite as fast, but that was okay. Eventually I would complete it. Eventually I would get back on track.

Except that I never did.

Writing during naptimes was a bust. It was laughable that I thought that would work. Evenings were a bust, too. Most nights, all I could do was stuff a new breast pad into my nursing bra before collapsing in bed. And preschool, of course, was still years away. Oh, they go fast! everyone always tells you. Maybe, but I needed the time *right then*.

The longer I went without writing, the more   40
frustrated I became. I was crazy about my daughter, utterly in love. But I missed connecting to that part of myself I had honed over so many years. And I couldn't figure out a way to get writing back into my life. Or not, I should say, a way that didn't involve leaving my daughter for periods of time. "Hire someone," my husband told me. "Your work is important." But I couldn't bring myself to do it. I kept hearing my mother's voice in my head, telling me how vital it was to be at home. If I didn't do that, would I have failed? But if I didn't continue writing, wouldn't I be failing in another way? Had I turned into a walking cliché of the woman who wants it all?

When people asked me what I did, sometimes I said that I was writer, but more and more I started answering that I was a stay-at-home mother. "I'm surprised to even hear you describe yourself that way," a friend of mine said. But wasn't it the truth? The overwhelming majority of my time was spent taking care of my child or taking care of the house. Writing was just something I was squeezing in — a quick paragraph while I sat in the car in a parking lot because my daughter had fallen asleep in her car seat, a page or two on a weekend morning when my husband was around — if I was doing it at all.

The imbalance altered my sense of identity and, along with it, my concept of my own ambition. *Ambition* is a word that most people associate with professional life, after all. Ask someone if they see themselves as ambitious, and if they answer yes, most of the time they will tell you about something related to their career. And yet, motherhood exists outside of the bounds of professionalism in our country. It's not a job, society tells mothers, at least not a real one. And because it's not viewed that way, the concept of ambition gets divorced from the concept of motherhood. Insofar as I identified as a stay-at-home mother, I didn't identify as someone who had — at least not anymore — much ambition at all.

Eventually, I did hire a sitter. I asked her to come only three mornings a week — a compromise with myself. It was enough time to slowly, slowly finish my second book. But the decision was fraught. I was happy to be writing again, even in limited doses, but I felt awful every time I walked out the door. "Why?" my husband kept asking me, genuinely confounded. It would be different, I told him, if I were going to an office and getting a regular paycheck. At least then I would have something to show for it.

"But you *will* have something to show for it one day," he argued.

"But what if it takes me ten years to finish this book?" 45

"So? That's like me saying what if I only got paid once every ten years? It doesn't mean I wouldn't go to work every day."

It was all so cut-and-dry for him, which I found incredible and also made me a little resentful. Why was it so easy for him to walk out the door each morning, while I felt trapped inside this dense tangle of choices and guilt and expectation and desire? But I saw his point. What if I really didn't finish a book or get paid again for another ten years? What if I never published a book and never got paid? What if I kept writing merely because I wanted to? Because I had this fire in me that wouldn't die out, and I wanted to

feed it? Because every time I sat down to write I had the thought that I wanted to create something great? Wasn't that ambition? The urge to reach for something beyond what I had accomplished in the past, to strive toward new heights? Why did I feel like I needed the promise of some financial reward or public acknowledgment before I could claim my own ambition, before I could say, yes, I want to do this thing? Was I looking for permission to be ambitious, to really grab hold of it, because I didn't believe I deserved to claim it otherwise? Had I been shying away from the word all this time because I didn't feel I deserved it, not unless someone else told me I did?

◆ ◆ ◆

Years and years ago, when I applied to Northwestern and got in, a friend of mine who hadn't been accepted said to me, "You know the only reason they let you in is because you're Hispanic, right?" I can only assume he meant it as a joke, though it came across as anything but. Affirmative action. Quotas. Dumb luck. These are the reasons I got what I got. It could not have been that I had worked hard for years, toiling over papers in my room, staying up late to study. It could not have been that I was naturally curious, a high school student who was reading Dylan Thomas and Samuel Beckett and the letters of Zelda Fitzgerald in her spare time. It could not have been my record of community service nor my strong GPA. It could not have been that I wrote one hell of an admissions essay. It could not have been, simply, me.

A woman is denied her ambition on the grounds of gender. Ambition is active, not passive; it's forceful, not meek; it's stubborn, not yielding. It's everything that society tells women not to be. It's unfeminine, for goodness sake! And yet to be a woman of color — even a woman of some color, like me — is to be told all of that and more. A woman of color who exhibits ambition and who makes good on that ambition to achieve something, no matter how big or how small, is often told — subtly, overtly, it doesn't

seeing connections

Look closely at *Mother Stumped*, a 1986 a painting by artist Edward Ruscha (left) and *The Child's Bath*, an 1893 painting by artist Mary Cassatt (right).

Compare and contrast these two portrayals of motherhood, painted almost 100 years apart. How does each of them illustrate the questions Henríquez ponders in "Doubly Denied"?

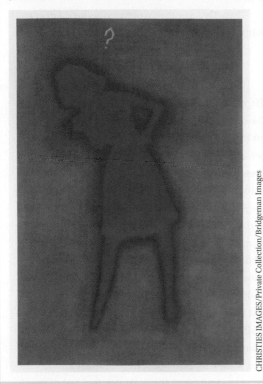

CHRISTIES IMAGES/Private Collection/Bridgeman Images

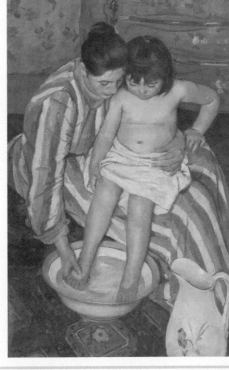

The Art Institute of Chicago, IL, USA/Bridgeman Images

matter — that she didn't actually achieve much at all, and that what she did achieve, she didn't deserve. To be a woman of color is to be doubly denied.

This is how things get taken from you. Somewhere along the way, a seed was planted, and a part of me began to believe that maybe my accomplishments — academic degrees and published books — were not much more than a matter of luck or a helping hand. In my better moments, I knew that was stupid. But at times when I was feeling low, or vulnerable, or unsure of who I was anymore, the seed bloomed like ivy,

threatening to strangle. At those times, I began to believe it: that I got what I got because of forces beyond my control, not because of any particular talent or skill or ambition, and certainly not because I deserved it.

50

◆ ◆ ◆

The other night I visited a book club — approximately twenty middle-age women who had read my novel and invited me to join them. We sat in the host's beautiful living room with its stone fireplace, and ate candy corn and drank wine. After we discussed my book, one of the women asked me what I was working on next. I mentioned that I was trying to finish an essay about ambition. I said, "Do you all think you're ambitious?"

Immediately, a petite woman with red hair spoke up. "I absolutely think I'm ambitious." She went on to tell the group how she had known, since she was twelve years old, that she wanted to be a lawyer, and how she let nothing stand in the way of achieving that goal. She told us about her daughter, who she described as driven, and who had just been accepted to a prestigious PhD program. "Have you had explicit conversations with her," I asked, "about her own ambition? About claiming it?" Yes, the woman told me. She paused. "But I'm of an age now where I want grandchildren," she said almost apologetically, "and I would like them before I'm too old to do anything with them." The rest of the women nodded. I could see where this was going. All along, she'd been sending her daughter one message, and now she didn't want to send a second — one about how she hoped her daughter would take time to start a family — that seemed counter to the first.

"But maybe we're too limited in our definition of ambition," another woman said. "I had a lot of ambition, but I didn't necessarily succeed in anything I did. I failed at most of it, but I still consider myself ambitious."

Can failure be part of ambition, too? All along I had been thinking that achievement was the end point. I thought of ambition, I realized, like a curve on a graph where desire was the point of origin, striving was a sweep upward in the middle, and achievement was the result. But maybe I'd been thinking about it wrong.

Another woman said, "I don't know. I wanted to stay home with my kids, so I turned my ambition toward them. My kids are older now, but I remember back then worrying that by staying home with them I was putting aside my ambition. But now the way I see it is that I just redirected it."

"I think that's true," someone else said. "And I think that's the difference between men and women. Men measure ambition by their professional achievements, whereas women measure it by how much of a difference they've made in the world."

"Exactly," another woman offered. "I don't think of it as ambition so much as passion."

"Like finding your purpose."

"Right. And going after it."

I smiled. Here we were, dancing around the word again, only now we were all doing the dance together. It was a slippery concept for everyone, apparently, one that was hard to get a handle on. And yet, as I sat there among these women, I felt a certain clarity that I hadn't before. Maybe it was something they had said, or maybe it was because I had spent so much time in the weeks leading up to that moment considering ambition and scrutinizing it, untangling all of my associations with the word. I thought about how, not long before, I had asked everybody I knew whether they saw me as ambitious. But I didn't need anyone or anything else, I realized — not a person, not a book deal, not a paycheck — to tell me what I already knew. I do want things — sometimes I want all the things — and often those things feel out of reach, but I stretch my arms out for them regardless, in my way. My ambition was there, and it had always been there, subdued at some times and thunderous at others, but never absent. I only needed to look within myself to see it.

The conversation went on for a while, but near the end of it one of the women threw the question back at me. "Do you think you're ambitious?" she asked.

I turned to her. "Yes," I answered without hesitation. "I think I am."

[2017]

EXPLORING THE TEXT

1. In what ways is the title of this essay a fitting one for Cristina Henríquez's argument? Cite specific passages to support your response.

2. As Henríquez describes her younger self as someone who aspires to become a writer, she uses words such as "fantasy" (para. 20), "far-off dream" (para. 21), and "ridiculous pipe dreams" (para. 25). To what extent do you think that this description of her self-perception is at odds with her actual behavior?

3. How does Henríquez's father influence her decisions? What contradictions does she see between what he says and does? Between his expectations for her mother and for her?

4. In paragraph 34, Henríquez asserts: "To be an immigrant, after all, to uproot your life, to walk away from everything you have known with the goal of going somewhere new and with the hope of finding something better is to be, necessarily, ambitious." Do you agree with this claim? Explain why or why not.

5. How does Henríquez respond to her mother's advice in paragraph 36? What does this response reveal about her attitude toward the relationship between motherhood and female ambition?

6. How does Henríquez portray her husband? Is he supportive, oblivious to the conflicts she feels, or something else? How do his responses develop her main argument about ambition? Be specific as you draw inferences from her descriptions of his attitudes and actions.

7. Do you agree with Henríquez's point that ambition is largely associated with professional rather than personal or private life? How does this point affect your understanding of the book group member's claim that "Men measure ambition by their professional achievements, whereas women measure it by how much of a difference they've made in the world" (para. 56)? Explain.

8. When Henríquez describes the book club, particularly the lawyer who expresses her eagerness for grandchildren, is she suggesting that women are pitted against one another, or that they are conflicted about being "ambigious"? Or is she just reporting a range of viewpoints?

9. Much of Henríquez's argument pivots on the definition of "ambitious." What are different definitions that she explores? What is her preferred definition? In the final paragraph, when she tells the book club participants "without hesitation" (para. 62) that she is ambitious, do you agree?

10. Robin Romm, editor of the collection in which Henríquez's essay appears, describes the paradox at the heart of feminism to be women's "pervasive sense that striving and achieving had to be approached delicately or you risked the negative judgment of others. The ideal was achievement with an air of self-sacrifice or gentleness." Does your understanding and experience of women's experiences today support or challenge this explanation?

11. One reviewer of *Double Bind* characterized its essays as "specific, moving, and real" critiques of "a culture drunk on the dreams of girls and hostile to the aspirations of women." How does "Doubly Denied" perform this sort of critique? What examples can you think of — from your own experience, knowledge of current events or popular culture, or reading — that illustrate this conflict between idealization of youthful dreams and the fulfillment of adult goals?

12. How would you define ambition in the context of your own life? Would you describe yourself as ambitious? Would your parents consider you ambitious? Would your peers? To what extent does an attitude toward ambition as generally positive — or negative — depend upon cultural and generational factors?

Why *Wonder Woman* Is a Masterpiece of Subversive Feminism

ZOE WILLIAMS

Zoe Williams (b. 1973) is an English columnist, journalist, and author who has written political commentary, interviews, and reviews for the *Guardian* since 2000. Williams has contributed to many other periodicals, including *Marie Claire*, *Glamour*, and *Good Housekeeping*, and she has made frequent appearances on television and radio in the UK. The following article was published in the *Guardian* in June 2017, just after the release of *Wonder Woman*, the superhero movie starring Gal Godot.

The chances are you will read a feminist take-down of *Wonder Woman* before you see the film. And you'll probably agree with it. Wonder Woman is a half-god, half-mortal super-creature; she is without peer even in superhero leagues. And yet, when she arrives in London to put a stop to the war to end all wars, she instinctively obeys a handsome meathead who has no skills apart from moderate decisiveness and pretty eyes. This is a patriarchal figment. Then, naturally, you begin to wonder why does she have to fight in knickers that look like a fancy letterbox made of leather? Does her appearance and its effect on the men around her really have to play such a big part in all her fight scenes? Even my son lodged a feminist critique: if she were half god, he said, she would have recognised the god Ares immediately—unless he were a better god than her (being a male god).

I agree with all of that, but I still loved it. I didn't love it as a guilty pleasure. I loved it with my whole heart. Wonder Woman, or Diana Prince, as her civilian associates would know her, first appeared as a character in DC Comics in 1941, her creator supposedly inspired by the feminism of the time, and specifically the contraception pioneer Margaret Sanger. Being able to stop people getting pregnant would be a cool superpower, but, in fact, her skills were: bullet-pinging with bracelets; lassoing; basic psychology; great strength and athleticism; and being half-god (the result of unholy con-gress between Zeus and Hyppolyta). The 1970s TV version lost a lot of the poetry of that, and was just all-American cheesecake. Gal Gadot's Wonder Woman made her cinematic debut last year in *Batman v Superman*, and this first live-action incarnation makes good on the char-acter's original premise, the classical-

warrior element amped up and textured. Her might makes sense.

Yes, she is sort of naked a lot of the time, but this isn't objectification so much as a cultural reset: having thighs, actual thighs you can kick things with, not thighs that look like arms, is a feminist act. The whole Diana myth, women safe-guarding the world from male violence not with nurture but with better violence, is a feminist act. Casting Robin Wright as Wonder Woman's aunt, reimagining the battle-axe as a battler, with an

In paragraph 2, Williams claims that the TV incarnation of Wonder Woman, starring Linda Carter, was just "all-American cheesecake." **Based on this still from the television show, do you agree with Williams's assessment? Explain why or why not.**

ABC/Photofest

axe, is a feminist act. A female German chemist trying to destroy humans (in the shape of Dr. Poison, a proto-Mengele before Nazism existed) might be the most feminist act of all.

Women are repeatedly erased from the history of classical music, art and medicine. It takes a radical mind to pick up that being erased from the history of evil is not great either. Wonder Woman's casual rebuttal of a sexual advance, her dress-up montage ("it's itchy," "I can't fight in this," "it's choking me") are also feminist acts. *Wonder Woman* is a bit like a BuzzFeed list: 23 Stupid Sexist Tropes in Cinema and How to Rectify Them. I mean that as a compliment.

Yet *Wonder Woman* is not a film about empowerment so much as a checklist of all the cliches by which women are disempowered. So it leaves you feeling a bit baffled and deflated — how can we possibly be so towering a threat that Hollywood would strive so energetically, so rigorously, for our belittlement? At the same time, you are conflicted about what the fightback should look like. Because, as every reviewer has pointed out, *Wonder Woman* is by no means perfect.

The woman who can fight is not new; from Sigourney Weaver's Ripley in *Alien*, to Linda Hamilton's Sarah Connor in *The Terminator*,

5

this idea has a long pedigree. Connor was a farfetched feminist figure because her power was concentrated in her ambivalent maternal love — like a hypothetical tiger mother, which doesn't do a huge amount for female agency. She is still an accessory for male power, just on the other side of the mother/whore dichotomy. Ripley, being the same gender as her foe, recast action as a cat-fight, with all the sexist bullshit that entails (hot, sweaty woman saying "bitch" a lot — a classic pornography trope).

But the underlying problem is that the male fighter is conceived as an ego ideal for a male audience, who would imagine themselves in the shirt of Bruce Willis or mankini of Superman and get the referred thrill of their heroism. If you are still making the film for a male gaze, the female warrior becomes a sex object, and her fighting curiously random, like pole dancing — movement that only makes sense as display, and even then, only just. That was always the great imponderable of Lara Croft (as she appeared in the video-game, not the film): the listlessness of her combat, the slightly dreamlike quality of it. Even as it was happening, it was hard to remember why. When Angelina Jolie made her flesh, I thought she brought something subversive to the role; something deliberated, knowing and a bit scornful,

Warner Bros./Photofest

What qualities make this version of Wonder Woman — from the 2017 film starring Gal Gadot and directed by Patty Jenkins — different from the previous incarnations of Wonder Woman?

as though looking into the teenage gamer's soul and saying: "You don't know whether that was a dragon, a dinosaur or a large dog. You are just hypnotised by my buttocks."

The fighter as sex symbol stirs up a snakepit of questions: are you getting off on the woman or the violence? An unbreakable female lead can be liberating to the violent misogynist tendency since the violence against her can get a lot more ultra, and nobody has to feel bad about it, because she'll win.

This is tackled head on in *Wonder Woman*. The tension, meanwhile, between the thrill of the action, which is what combat is all about, and the objectification, which is what women are all about, is referenced when Wonder Woman hurls someone across a room and an onlooker says: "I'm both frightened, and aroused." A word on the fighting: there's a lot of hurling, tons of lassoing, much less traditional fighting, where people harm one another with punches. This is becoming a

sub-genre in films: "the kind of fighting that is ladylike." It almost always involves bows and arrows, for which, as with so many things, we can thank Jennifer Lawrence in *The Hunger Games*. The way Lawrence fights is so outrageously adroit and natural that she makes it look as though women have been doing it all along, and men are only learning.

I find it impossible to imagine the feminist action-movie slam-dunk; the film in which every sexist Hollywood convention, every miniature slight, every outright slur, every incremental diss was slain by a lead who was omnipotent and vivid. That film would be long and would struggle for jokes. Just trying to picture it leaves you marvelling at the geological slowness of social progress in this industry, which finds it so hard to create female characters of real mettle, even when they abound in real life. Wonder Woman, with her 180 languages and her near-telepathic insights, would stand more chance of unpicking

10

seeing connections

Look carefully at this still from the movie *The Hunger Games*, which shows Jennifer Lawrence as Katniss Everdeen, and at this still from the television show *The Walking Dead*, in which Norman Reedus portrays a character named Daryl.
Why do you think Lawrence's portrayal prompted Williams to say that "the kind of fighting that is ladylike . . . involves bows and arrows" (para. 9)? After considering the image from *The Walking Dead*, do you agree with Williams on this point? Explain.

Lionsgate

AMC/Photofest

this baffler than Superman or Batman. But the answer, I suspect, lies in the intersection between the market and the culture; the more an artform costs, the less it will risk, until the most expensive of them — blockbusters — can't change at all. In an atmosphere of such in-built ossification, the courage of Wonder Woman is more stunning even than her lasso.

[2017]

EXPLORING THE TEXT

1. What is the effect of the opening two sentences of this article? Do they present a challenge? A warning? What do they signal about Zoe Williams's understanding of her audience?

2. What does Williams mean by "a patriarchal figment" (para. 1)?

3. In the second paragraph, Williams briefly explains the history of Wonder Woman, including her origin as a character in DC Comics. What purpose does this paragraph serve in developing Williams's argument?

4. Acknowledging that Wonder Woman, or Diana Prince, is "sort of naked a lot of the time," Williams claims that "this isn't objectification so much as a cultural reset" (para. 3). What evidence does she present to support that statement? How persuasive do you find it?

5. Williams asserts that *Wonder Woman* "is not a film about empowerment so much as a checklist of all the cliches by which women are disempowered" (para. 5). Which clichés might she be referring to? Identify at least three in this film or other films about women.

6. In paragraph 5, Williams makes the point that audiences are likely "conflicted about what the fightback should look like" — the fightback to the belittlement of women. She further acknowledges that *Wonder Woman* "is by no means perfect." What is her rhetorical strategy here? Is she damning with faint praise? Offering a qualified compliment? Acknowledging a counterargument?

7. What point is Williams making when she describes the "tension . . . between the thrill of the action, which is what combat is all about, and the objectification, which is what women are all about" (para. 9)? How does her mention of the *Hunger Games* protagonist, Katniss Everdeen (played by Jennifer Lawrence), support and illustrate that point?

8. Williams concludes with consideration of "the intersection between the market and the culture" (para. 10). How does this discussion strengthen her claim that the film *Wonder Woman* is, as the headline states, "a masterpiece of subversive feminism"?

9. Throughout the article, Williams uses the term "feminist" — particularly in paragraphs 3 and 4, where she refers to "feminist act(s)." Given the context and content of the essay, how does Williams define feminism?

VISUAL TEXTS

Chancellor Séguier at the Entry of Louis XIV into Paris in 1660

CHARLES LE BRUN

and

The Chancellor Séguier on Horseback

KEHINDE WILEY

Charles Le Brun (1619–1690) was responsible for the production of paintings, sculpture, and decorative objects commissioned by the French government during the reign of Louis XIV. The monarch had extravagant tastes and favored artists whose work reflected the opulence of the period. Although known as a fine portrait painter, Le Brun preferred a narrative style, believing that a painting told a story through symbols, costumes, and gestures — as in the one shown here depicting Pierre Séguier, Duke of Villemor, the Lord Chief Justice of France. He and his entourage are shown entering Paris in August 1660 to celebrate the marriage of Louis XIV and his wife, Maria Theresa, daughter of the king of Spain. Those shown would be counselors, treasurers, secretaries, court ushers, and the like who took part in the procession.

Kehinde Wiley was born in 1977 in Los Angeles, lives in New York City, and maintains studios in several cities worldwide, including Beijing and Dakar. He holds a BFA from the San Francisco Art Institute and an MFA from Yale. Wiley is a photo-realist painter whose work is inspired by traditional portraitists, such as Sir Joshua Reynolds, Thomas Gainsborough, Titian, and Jean-Auguste-Dominique Ingres. His paintings are in the permanent collections of the Columbus Museum of Art, the Studio Museum in Harlem, the Walker Art Center, the Miami Art Museum, and the Detroit Institute of Arts, among others. To create paintings such as the one shown here, Wiley often seeks out average African American men and asks them to select a painting from one of the old masters such as Titian or Ingres. Then they strike a pose from one of those paintings. In an interview with *Art in America*, Wiley said of his work, "Black masculinity has been codified in a fixed way. I'm not trying to provide a direct corrective, but . . . there is a certain desire in my work to tie the urban street and the way it's been depicted with elements that are not necessarily coded as masculine."

Reunion des Musees Nationaux/Art Resource, NY

[c.1661]

Courtesy Sean Kelly Gallery, New York, Roberts & Tilton, Culver City, California, and
Rhona Hoffman Gallery, Chicago

[2005]

VISUAL TEXTS

945

EXPLORING THE TEXTS

1. The men in Charles Le Brun's painting are dressed in the height of fashion for their day. How would you characterize it? Note differences between the eminence on horseback and the others. What specific elements of dress seem to define the male image? Note the hair, hats, and shoes.

2. The entourage pictured in Le Brun's painting was intended as a sign to the cheering Parisians that a new epoch of peace and glory had dawned. What elements of this painting attest to affluence and power?

3. What symbols of African American culture or hip-hop culture does Kehinde Wiley include in his painting?

4. Wiley applies the visual vocabulary and conventions of glorification, wealth, and prestige to his subject matter. In this painting, what is the fashion code? How does the appearance of these men define the image of today's young, urban African American male?

5. What is the effect of Wiley's melding of the prototypes of French Classicism and hip-hop street style? Is Wiley being critical of one or the other — or both? Is he celebrating or criticizing (or both) what one reviewer called "the hyper-masculine posturing of hip-hop culture"?

6. In a review of one of Wiley's shows, an art critic asks, "Do his big, flashy pictures of young African-American men recast as the kings, dandies, prophets, and saints of European portraiture subvert the timeworn ruses of Western art and its hierarchies of race, class and sex?" Based on these two paintings, how would you answer that question? To expand your response, you might look at other paintings by Wiley on his website, www.kehindewiley.com.

We Can Do It!

J. HOWARD MILLER
and

The March

ABIGAIL GRAY SWARTZ

The iconic image known as "Rosie the Riveter" began as a poster for the Westinghouse Electric and Manufacturing Company in 1943. After a United Press International photographer snapped a picture of a woman on the job, freelance artist J. Howard Miller, hired to make posters supporting the war effort, created a poster of a determined-looking woman proclaiming, "We can do it!" Who exactly "Rosie" was is uncertain, though Geraldine Hoff Doyle, a metal worker in a factory in Ann Arbor, Michigan, is often cited as the inspiration. This poster, along with many others, urged American women to support the war effort by taking up jobs left vacant by men who were fighting overseas. Though it was originally intended as an appeal to patriotic duty rather than a feminist call to arms, the original Rosie has been interpreted, appropriated, and reinvented in many different contexts and genres over the past seventy-five years. Since then, different versions of "Rosie" have been depicted on magazine covers; two U.S. Postal Service stamps; and commercial goods, including mugs and T-shirts.

In 2017, a contemporary Rosie appeared on the cover of the *New Yorker* magazine. A painting by Maine-based artist Abigail Gray Swartz, this cover features a woman of color, in a pose and outfit echoing the original Rosie, wearing the pink hat that has come to symbolize the Women's March. The Women's March — a protest with participants in all fifty of the U.S. states, thirty-two countries around the world, and on all seven continents — is a movement that describes itself as "committed to equality, diversity, and inclusion and those who understand women's rights as human rights."

UNIVERSAL IMAGES GROUP/Bridgeman Images

[1943]

PRICE $8.99   THE

FEB. 6, 2017

YORKER

Abagail Gray Swartz/The New Yorker

[2017]

EXPLORING THE TEXTS

1. Carefully examine and consider J. Howard Miller's "We Can Do It!" poster in the social and historical context of its time. What message(s) do the placement of the image, the pose of the central figure, her facial expression, the colors used, and the interaction of text and image convey?

2. In what ways does the woman that Miller depicts reflect the feminine ideals of the 1940s, and in what ways might you interpret her as a challenge to those ideals? As you respond to this question, consider the makeup that the figure is clearly wearing: is it a tactic to keep women — even those working on behalf of the war effort — worrying about their appearance? Or is it "war paint" — what some have called a public assertion of women's power?

3. In *Faces of Feminism: An Activist's Reflections on the Women's Movement*, author Sheila Tobias describes Miller's Rosie:

   > She is "Rosie the Riveter," with movie-star looks, hair pulled up in a colorful bandana, sleeves rolled up high, ready to take rivet gun in hand. Everyone knows Rosie. She had not worked before the war. With "her man away fighting," however, and "not much else to do," she was cajoled into taking care of those dirty wartime jobs — out of patriotism or boredom (or both). Attired in new-found overalls and bandana, she riveted away for the duration of the war, dreaming of a time when she could return to her home and tend to her domestic chores.

   To what extent do you agree with this description?

4. Compare and contrast Swartz's Rosie painting with Miller's poster. What are the two most striking differences between them? Is the 2017 Rosie a challenge to the 1942 Rosie? A reinvention? A tribute? A repudiation? A satire? Something else entirely? A combination of several of these? Support your position with concrete details from both images.

5. One article about the *New Yorker* covered declared that, in Swartz's painting, Rosie the Riveter "got an update. And it is pretty darn intersectional." *Intersectionality* is a term that takes into account that cultural patterns of oppression are not only interrelated but bound together and influenced by intersecting systems of society (e.g., by race, gender, class, ethnicity). Feminist discussions of intersectionality encourage recognition of a more multilayered view and acknowledge that the issues most germane to white, middle-class women constitute a limited perspective. To what extent do you think the concept of intersectionality captures the appeal of the image? Why?

CONVERSATION

Redefining Masculinity

The following six texts comment directly or indirectly on definitions and images of masculinity in today's society.

SOURCES

1 **Leonard McCombe** / *Marlboro Man* (photo)
2 **Paul Theroux** / *Being a Man*
3 **Stephanie Coontz** / from *The Myth of Male Decline*
4 **Kali Holloway** / from *Toxic Masculinity Is Killing Men: The Roots of Men and Trauma*
5 **Roberto A. Ferdman** / *The Perils of Being Manly*
6 **Frank Miniter** / *The Hard, Adrenaline-Soaked Truth about "Toxic Masculinity"*
7 **Emily Bobrow** / from *The Man Trap*
8 **Andrew Reiner** / *Talking to Boys the Way We Talk to Girls*

After you have read, studied, and synthesized these pieces, enter the conversation by responding to one of the prompts on page 970.

1 | Marlboro Man

LEONARD McCOMBE

This iconic photograph, taken by Leonard McCombe, was used by the Philip Morris Company to transform Marlboro cigarettes from having a feminine image that was "Mild as May," to an image that was more rugged and appealing to men. When this campaign began in 1955, sales were at $5 billion; by 1957, they had jumped to $20 billion despite growing health concerns over cigarettes. McCombe took this photo of Clarence Hailey Long, a ranch foreman in Texas, in 1949.

QUESTIONS

1. How does the composition of the photograph contribute to its effect? Why is the focus exclusively on the face rather than a longer shot that would include the entire body?

2. What is the effect of the subject's gaze not meeting the eyes of the viewer?

3. *Life* magazine assigned McCombe to do a story that dispelled the glamorous image of cowboys seen in Hollywood movies of the period and, instead, documented the hardworking life of ranchers. What stereotypes about cowboys or the West does the photo exploit — or combat?

4. Why do you think that this photo caught the eye of legendary advertising executive Leo Burnett as a good choice for his campaign to transform the image of Marlboro cigarettes?

Leonard McCombe/Getty Images

2 Being a Man

PAUL THEROUX

In the following essay, part of the collection *Sunrise with Seamonsters* (1985), American novelist and travel writer Paul Theroux (b. 1941) examines society's views of masculinity.

There is a pathetic sentence in the chapter "Fetishism" in Dr. Norman Cameron's book *Personality Development and Psychopathology*. It goes, "Fetishists are nearly always men; and their commonest fetish is a woman's shoe." I cannot read that sentence without thinking that it is just one more awful thing about being a man — and perhaps it is an important thing to know about us.

I have always disliked being a man. The whole idea of manhood in America is pitiful, in my opinion. This version of masculinity is a little like having to wear an ill-fitting coat for one's entire life (by contrast, I imagine femininity to be an oppressive sense of nakedness). Even the expression "Be a man!" strikes me as insulting and abusive. It means: Be stupid, be unfeeling, obedient, soldierly and stop thinking. Man means "manly" — how can one think about men without considering the terrible ambition of manliness? And yet it is part of every man's life. It is a hideous and crippling lie; it not only insists on difference and connives at superiority, it is also by its very nature destructive — emotionally damaging and socially harmful.

The youth who is subverted, as most are, into believing in the masculine ideal is effectively separated from women and he spends the rest of his life finding women a riddle and a nuisance. Of course, there is a female version of this male affliction. It begins with mothers encouraging little girls to say (to other adults) "Do you like my new dress?" In a sense, little girls are traditionally urged to please adults with a kind of coquettishness, while boys are enjoined to behave like monkeys towards each other. The nine-year-old coquette proceeds to become womanish in a subtle power game in which she learns to be sexually indispensable, socially decorative and always alert to a man's sense of inadequacy.

Femininity — being lady-like — implies needing a man as witness and seducer; but masculinity celebrates the exclusive company of men. That is why it is so grotesque; and that is also why there is no manliness without inadequacy — because it denies men the natural friendship of women.

It is very hard to imagine any concept of manliness that does not belittle women, and it begins very early. At an age when I wanted to meet girls — let's say the treacherous years of thirteen to sixteen — I was told to take up a sport, get more fresh air, join the Boy Scouts, and I was urged not to read so much. It was the 1950s and if you asked too many questions about sex you were sent to camp — boy's camp, of course: the nightmare. Nothing is more unnatural or prison-like than a boy's camp, but if it were not for them we would have no Elks' Lodges, no pool rooms, no boxing matches, no Marines.

And perhaps no sports as we know them. Everyone is aware of how few in number are the athletes who behave like gentlemen. Just as high school basketball teaches you how to be a poor loser, the manly attitude towards sports seems to be little more than a recipe for creating bad marriages, social misfits, moral degenerates, sadists, latent rapists and just plain louts. I regard high school sports as a drug far worse than marijuana, and it is the reason that the average tennis champion, say, is a pathetic oaf.

Any objective study would find the quest for manliness essentially right-wing, puritanical, cowardly, neurotic and fueled largely by a fear of women. It is also certainly philistine. There is no book-hater like a Little League coach. But indeed all the creative arts are obnoxious to the manly ideal, because at their best the arts are pursued by uncompetitive and essentially solitary people. It makes it very hard for a creative youngster, for any boy who expresses the desire to be alone seems to be saying that there is something wrong with him.

It ought to be clear by now that I have something of an objection to the way we turn boys into men. It does not surprise me that when the President of the United States [Ronald Reagan] has his customary weekend off he dresses like a cowboy — it is both a measure of his insecurity and his willingness to please. In many ways, American culture does little more for a man than prepare him for modeling clothes in the L. L. Bean catalogue. I take this as a personal insult because for many years I found it impossible to admit to myself that I wanted to be a writer. It was my guilty secret, because being a writer was incompatible with being a man.

There are people who might deny this, but that is because the American writer, typically, has been so at pains to prove his manliness that we have come to see literariness and manliness as mingled qualities. But first there was a fear that writing was not a manly profession — indeed, not a profession at all. (The paradox in American letters is that it has always been easier for a woman to write and for a man to be published.) Growing up, I had thought of sports as wasteful and humiliating, and the idea of manliness was a bore. My wanting to become a writer was not a flight from that oppressive role-playing, but I quickly saw that it was at odds with it. Everything in stereotyped manliness goes against the life of the mind. The Hemingway personality is too tedious to go into here, and in any case his exertions are well-known, but certainly it was not until this aberrant behavior was examined by feminists in the 1960s that any male writer dared question the pugnacity in Hemingway's fiction. All the bullfighting

and arm wrestling and elephant shooting diminished Hemingway as a writer, but it is consistent with a prevailing attitude in American writing: one cannot be a male writer without first proving that one is a man.

It is normal in America for a man to be 10 dismissive or even somewhat apologetic about being a writer. Various factors make it easier. There is a heartiness about journalism that makes it acceptable — journalism is the manliest form of American writing and, therefore, the profession the most independent-minded women seek (yes, it is an illusion, but that is my point). Fiction-writing is equated with a kind of dispirited failure and is only manly when it produces wealth — money is masculinity. So is drinking. Being a drunkard is another assertion, if misplaced, of manliness. The American male writer is traditionally proud of his heavy drinking. But we are also a very literal-minded people. A man proves his manhood in America in old-fashioned ways. He kills lions, like Hemingway; or he hunts ducks, like Nathanael West; or he makes pronouncements like, "A man should carry enough knife to defend himself with," as James Jones once said to a *Life* interviewer. Or he says he can drink you under the table. But even tiny drunken William Faulkner loved to mount a horse and go fox hunting, and Jack Kerouac roistered up and down Manhattan in a lumberjack shirt (and spent every night of *The Subterraneans*[1] with his mother in Queens). And we are familiar with the lengths to which Norman Mailer[2] is prepared, in his endearing way, to prove that he is just as much a monster as the next man.

When the novelist John Irving was revealed as a wrestler, people took him to be a very serious writer; and even a bubble reputation like Erich (*Love Story*) Segal's was enhanced by the news that he ran the marathon in a respectable time.

---

[1] A 1960 film based on Jack Kerouac's novel about the lifestyle of 1950s Beats. —Eds.
[2] An American journalist and novelist. —Eds.

How surprised we would be if Joyce Carol Oates were revealed as a sumo wrestler or Joan Didion active in pumping iron. "Lives in New York City with her three children" is the typical woman writer's biographical note, for just as the male writer must prove he has achieved a sort of muscular manhood, the woman writer — or rather her publicists — must prove her motherhood.

There would be no point in saying any of this if it were not generally accepted that to be a man is somehow — even now in feminist-influenced America — a privilege. It is on the contrary an unmerciful and punishing burden. Being a man is bad enough; being manly is appalling (in this sense, women's lib has done much more for men than for women). It is the sinister silliness of men's fashions, and a clubby attitude in the arts. It is the subversion of good students. It is the so-called "Dress Code" of the Ritz-Carlton Hotel in Boston, and it is the institutionalized cheating in college sports. It is the most primitive insecurity.

And this is also why men often object to feminism but are afraid to explain why: of course women have a justified grievance, but most men believe — and with reason — that their lives are just as bad.

QUESTIONS

1. Much of this essay consists of negative descriptions of what it means to Paul Theroux to be masculine or a man. Why does he offer such strong images and assertions?

2. Do you agree or disagree with Theroux when he writes, "It is very hard to imagine any concept of manliness that does not belittle women, and it begins very early" (para. 5)? Explain.

3. How does Theroux prepare his readers for the turn the essay takes in paragraph 12 when he says,

"There would be no point in saying any of this if it were not generally accepted that to be a man is somehow — even now in feminist-influenced America — a privilege"? What does this statement reveal about Theroux's overall purpose in this piece?

4. Theroux's essay was written in 1983. Which of his points are outdated? Which ones do you think remain true today?

3 from **The Myth of Male Decline**
The Roots of Men and Trauma

STEPHANIE COONTZ

Stephanie Coontz (b. 1944) is Director of Research and Public Education for the Council on Contemporary Families, a nonprofit, nonpartisan association of family researchers based at the University of Texas at Austin. She also teaches history and family studies at Evergreen State College in Olympia, Washington. The following excerpt is taken from an op-ed Coontz wrote for the *New York Times* in 2012.

Scroll through the titles and subtitles of recent books, and you will read that women have become "The Richer Sex," that "The Rise of Women Has Turned Men Into Boys," and that we may even be seeing "The End of Men." Several of the authors of these books posit that we are on the verge of a "new majority of female breadwinners," where middle-class wives lord over their husbands while demoralized single men take refuge in perpetual adolescence.

How is it, then, that men still control the most important industries, especially technology, occupy most of the positions on the lists of the richest Americans, and continue to make more money than women who have similar skills and education? And why do women make up only 17 percent of Congress?

These books and the cultural anxiety they represent reflect, but exaggerate, a transformation in the distribution of power over the past half-century. Fifty years ago, every male American was entitled to what the sociologist R. W. Connell called a "patriarchal dividend" — a lifelong affirmative-action program for men.

The size of that dividend varied according to race and class, but all men could count on women's being excluded from the most desirable jobs and promotions in their line of work, so the average male high school graduate earned more than the average female college graduate working the same hours. At home, the patriarchal dividend gave husbands the right to decide where the family would live and to make unilateral financial decisions. Male privilege even trumped female consent to sex, so marital rape was not a crime.

The curtailment of such male entitlements   5
and the expansion of women's legal and economic rights have transformed American life, but they have hardly produced a matriarchy. Indeed, in many arenas the progress of women has actually stalled over the past 15 years. . . .

If the ascent of women has been much exaggerated, so has the descent of men. Men's irresponsibility and bad behavior is now a stock theme in popular culture. But there has always been a subset of men who engage in crude, coercive and exploitative behavior. What's different today is that it's harder for men to get away with such behavior in long-term relationships. Women no longer feel compelled to put up with it and the legal system no longer condones it. The result is that many guys who would have been obnoxious husbands, behaving badly behind closed doors, are now obnoxious singles, trumpeting their bad behavior on YouTube.

Their boorishness may be pathetic, but it's much less destructive than the masculine misbehavior of yore. Most men are in fact behaving better than ever. Domestic violence rates have been halved since 1993, while rapes and sexual assaults against women have fallen by 70 percent in that time. In recent decades, husbands have doubled their share of housework and tripled their share of child care. And this change is not confined to highly educated men.

Among dual-earner couples, husbands with the least education do as much or more housework than their more educated counterparts. Men who have made these adjustments report happier marriages — and better sex lives.

◆ ◆ ◆

One thing standing in the way of further progress for many men is the same obstacle that held women back for so long: overinvestment in their gender identity instead of their individual personhood. Men are now experiencing a set of limits — externally enforced as well as self-imposed — strikingly similar to the ones Betty Friedan set out to combat in 1963, when she identified a "feminine mystique" that constrained women's self-image and options.

Although men don't face the same discrim-   10
inatory laws as women did 50 years ago, they do face an equally restrictive gender mystique.

Just as the feminine mystique discouraged women in the 1950s and 1960s from improving their education or job prospects, on the assumption that a man would always provide for them, the masculine mystique encourages men to neglect their own self-improvement on the assumption that sooner or later their "manliness" will be rewarded.

According to a 2011 poll by the Pew Research Center, 77 percent of Americans now believe that a college education is necessary for a woman to get ahead in life today, but only 68 percent think that is true for men. And just as the feminine mystique exposed girls to ridicule and harassment if they excelled at "unladylike" activities like math or sports, the masculine mystique leads to bullying and ostracism of boys who engage in "girlie" activities like studying hard and behaving well in school. One result is that men account for only 2 percent of kindergarten and preschool teachers, 3 percent of dental assistants and 9 percent of registered nurses.

The masculine mystique is institutionalized in work structures, according to three new studies forthcoming in the *Journal of Social Issues*. Just as women who display "masculine" ambitions or behaviors on the job are often penalized, so are men who engage in traditionally female behaviors, like prioritizing family involvement. Men who take an active role in child care and housework at home are more likely than other men to be harassed at work.

Men who request family leave are often viewed as weak or uncompetitive and face a greater risk of being demoted or downsized. And men who have ever quit work for family reasons end up earning significantly less than other male employees, even when controlling for the effects of age, race, education, occupation, seniority and work hours. Now men need to liberate themselves from the pressure to prove their masculinity. Contrary to the fears of some pundits, the ascent of women does not portend the end of men. It offers a new beginning for both. But women's progress by itself is not a panacea for America's inequities. The closer we get to achieving equality of opportunity between the sexes, the more clearly we can see that the next major obstacle to improving the well-being of most men and women is the growing socioeconomic inequality within each sex.

QUESTIONS

1. Stephanie Coontz begins by addressing a counterargument. What is that counterargument, and how does she address it?

2. How does Coontz define the term "'patriarchal dividend'" (para. 3)? To what extent do you agree that there is such a benefit?

3. What evidence does Coontz provide to support her contention that "[M]ost men are in fact behaving better than ever" (para. 7)?

4. What does Coontz mean by her claim that the real problem is men's "overinvestment in their gender identity" (para. 9)? Is it the same as "the masculine mystique" (para. 11)? Explain.

5. How effectively does Coontz support her claim that the "masculine mystique is institutionalized in work structures" (para. 13)?

6. To what extent do you agree with Coontz's assertion that "the ascent of women does not portend the end of men' and instead "offers a new beginning for both" (para. 14)? Explain, using examples from your own experience and knowledge.

 4 from **Toxic Masculinity Is Killing Men**

KALI HOLLOWAY

Kali Holloway is a senior writer and associate editor of media and culture at *AlterNet*, a news magazine and online community founded in 1998 that, according to its website, aims to "inspire action and advocacy on the environment, human rights and civil liberties, social justice, media, health care issues, and more." The following excerpt is taken from an essay Holloway wrote for AlterNet in 2015. It was later published on Salon, a news and opinion website.

The three most destructive words that every man receives when he's a boy is when he's told to "be a man."

— Joe Ehrmann, coach and former NFL player

If we are honest with ourselves, we have long known that masculinity kills men, in ways both myriad and measurable. While social constructions of femininity demand that women be thin, beautiful, accommodating . . . social constructions of masculinity demand that men constantly prove and re-prove the very fact that they are, well, men.

Both ideas are poisonous and potentially destructive, but statistically speaking, the number of addicted and afflicted men and their comparatively shorter lifespans proves masculinity is actually the more effective killer, getting the job done faster and in greater numbers. Masculinity's death tolls are attributed to its more specific manifestations: alcoholism, workaholism and violence. Even when it does not literally kill, it causes a sort of spiritual death, leaving many men traumatized, dissociated and often unknowingly depressed. (These issues are heightened by race, class, sexuality and other marginalizing factors, but here let's focus on early childhood and adolescent socialization overall.) To quote poet Elizabeth Barrett Browning, "tis not in death that men die most." And for many men, the process begins long before manhood.

The emotionally damaging "masculinization" of boys starts even before boyhood, in infancy. Psychologist Terry Real, in his 1998 book *I Don't Want to Talk About It: Overcoming the Secret Legacy of Male Depression*, highlights numerous studies which find that parents often unconsciously begin projecting a kind of innate "manliness" — and thus, a diminished need for comfort, protection and affection — onto baby boys as young as newborns. This, despite the fact that gendered behaviors are absent in babies; male infants actually behave in ways our society defines as "feminine." As Real explains, "[l]ittle boys and little girls start off . . . equally emotional, expressive, and dependent, equally desirous of physical affection. At the youngest ages, both boys and girls are more like a stereotypical girl. If any differences exist, little boys are, in fact, slightly more sensitive and expressive than little girls. They cry more easily, seem more easily frustrated, appear more upset when a caregiver leaves the room."

Yet both mothers and fathers imagine inherent sex-related differences between baby girls and boys. Even when researchers controlled for babies' "weight, length, alertness, and strength," parents overwhelmingly reported that baby girls were more delicate and "softer" than baby boys; they imagined baby boys to be bigger and generally "stronger." When a group of 204 adults was shown video of the same baby crying and given differing information about the baby's sex, they judged the "female" baby to be scared, while the "male" baby was described as "angry."

Intuitively, these differences in perception create correlating differences in the kind of parental caregiving newborn boys receive. In the words of the researchers themselves, "it would seem reasonable to assume that a child who is thought to be afraid is held and cuddled more than a child who is thought to be angry." That theory is bolstered by other studies Real cites, which consistently find that "from the moment of birth, boys are spoken to less than girls, comforted less, nurtured less." To put it bluntly, we begin emotionally shortchanging boys right out of the gate, at the most vulnerable point in their lives.

It's a pattern that continues throughout childhood and into adolescence. . . .

Undeniably, these kinds of lessons impart deeply damaging messages to both girls and

boys, and have lifelong and observable consequences. But whereas, as Terry Real says, "girls
are allowed to maintain emotional expressive-
ness and cultivate connection," boys are not only
told they should suppress their emotions, but
that their manliness essentially depends on them
doing so. Despite its logic-empty premise, our
society has fully bought into the notion that the
relationship between maleness and masculinity is somehow incidental and precarious, and
embraced the myth that "boys must be turned
into men . . . that boys, unlike girls, must achieve
masculinity."

Little boys internalize this concept early;
when I spoke to Real, he indicated that research
suggests they begin to hide their feelings from as
young as 3 to 5 years old. "It doesn't mean that
they have fewer emotions. But they're already
learning the game — that it's not a good idea to
express them," Real says. Boys, conventional
wisdom holds, are made men not by merely
aging into manhood, but through the crushing
socialization just described. But Real points out
what should be obvious about cisgender boys:
"[they] do not need to be turned into males. They
are males. Boys do not need to develop their
masculinity."

It is impossible to downplay the concurrent
influence of images and messages about masculinity embedded in our media. TV shows and
movies inform kids — and all of us, really — not so
much about who men (and women) are, but who
they should be. While much of the scholarship
about gender depictions in media has come from
feminists deconstructing the endless damaging
representations of women, there's been far less
research specifically about media-perpetuated
constructions of masculinity. But certainly, we all
recognize the traits that are valued among men
in film, television, videogames, comic books, and
more: strength, valor, independence, the ability
to provide and protect.

While depictions of men have grown more
complicated, nuanced and human over time
(we're long past the days of "Father Knows Best"
and "Superman" archetypes), certain "masculine" qualities remain valued over others. As
Amanda D. Lotz writes in her 2014 book, *Cable
Guys: Television and Masculinities in the 21st
Century*, though depictions of men in media have
become more diverse, "storytelling has nevertheless performed significant ideological work
by consistently supporting . . . male characters
it constructs as heroic or admirable, while deni-
grating others. So although television series may
have displayed a range of men and masculinities,
they also circumscribed a 'preferred' or 'best'
masculinity through attributes that were consistently idealized."

We are all familiar with these recurring
characters. They are fearless action heroes;
[violent] psychopaths in *Grand Theft Auto*;
shlubby, housework-averse sitcom dads with
inexplicably beautiful wives; bumbling stoner
twentysomethings who still manage to "nail" the
hot girl in the end; and still, the impenetrable
Superman. Even sensitive, loveable everyguy
Paul Rudd somehow "mans up" before the
credits roll in his films. Here, it seems important
to mention a National Coalition on Television
Violence study which finds that on average,
18-year-old American males have already witnessed some 26,000 murders on television,
"almost all of them committed by men." Couple
those numbers with violence in film and other
media, and the figures are likely astronomical.

The result of all this — the early denial of
boys' feelings, and our collective insistence that
they follow suit — is that boys are effectively cut
off from their emotions, and with them, their
deepest and most vulnerable selves. Historian
Stephanie Coontz has labeled this effect the
"*masculine mystique.*" It leaves little boys, and
later, men, emotionally disembodied, afraid to

10

show weakness and often unable to fully access, recognize or cope with their feelings.

In his book, *Why Men Can't Feel*, Marvin Allen states, "[T]hese messages encourage boys to be competitive, focus on external success, rely on their intellect, withstand physical pain, and repress their vulnerable emotions. When boys violate the code, it is not uncommon for them to be teased, shamed, or ridiculed." The cliche about men not being in touch with their emotions says nothing about inherent markers of maleness. It instead identifies behavioral outcomes that have been rigorously taught, often by well-meaning parents and society at large. As Terry Real said when I spoke to him, this process of disconnecting boys from their "feminine" — or more accurately, "human" — emotional selves is deeply harmful. "Every step . . . is injurious," says Real. "It's traumatic. It's traumatic to be forced to abdicate half of your own humanity." . . .

Masculinity is both difficult to achieve and impossible to maintain, a fact that Real notes is evident in the phrase "fragile male ego." Because men's self-esteem often rests on so shaky a construct, the effort to preserve it can be all-consuming. Avoiding the shame that's left when it is peeled away can drive some men to dangerous ends. This is not to absolve people of responsibility for their actions, but it does drive home the forces that underlie and inform behaviors we often attribute solely to individual issues, ignoring their root causes.

James Gilligan, former director of the Center 15 for the Study of Violence at Harvard Medical School, has written numerous books on the subject of male violence and its source. In a 2013 *interview with MenAlive*, a men's health blog, Gilligan spoke of his study findings, stating, "I have yet to see a serious act of violence that was not provoked by the experience of feeling shamed and humiliated, disrespected and

ridiculed, and that did not represent the attempt to prevent or undo that 'loss of face' — no matter how severe the punishment, even if it includes death."

Too often, men who are suffering do so alone, believing that revealing their personal pain is tantamount to failing at their masculinity. "As a society, we have more respect for the walking wounded," Terry Real writes, "those who deny their difficulties, than we have for those who 'let' their conditions 'get to them.'" And yet, the cost, both human and in real dollars, of not recognizing men's trauma is far greater than attending to those wounds, or avoiding creating them in the first place. It's critical that we begin taking more seriously what we do to little boys, how we do it, and the high emotional cost exacted by masculinity, which turns emotionally whole little boys into emotionally debilitated adult men.

When masculinity is defined by absence, when it sits, as it does, on the absurd and fallacious idea that the only way to be a man is to not acknowledge a key part of yourself, the consequences are both vicious and soul crushing. The resulting displacement and dissociation leaves men yet more vulnerable, susceptible, and in need of crutches to help allay the pain created by our demands of manliness. As Terry Real writes, "A depressed woman's internalization of pain weakens her and hampers her capacity for direct communication. A depressed man's tendency to extrude pain . . . may render him psychologically dangerous."

We have set an unfair and unachievable standard, and in trying to live up to it, many men are slowly killing themselves. We have to move far beyond our outdated ideas of masculinity, and get past our very ideas about what being a man is. We have to start seeing men as innately so, with no need to prove who they are, to themselves or anyone else.

QUESTIONS

1. What does Kali Holloway mean by what she calls the "social constructions of masculinity" (para. 1)?

2. Holloway enumerates a list of medical problems these expectations of masculinity contribute to, but she also asserts that they can cause "a sort of spiritual death" (para. 2). What does she mean?

3. In paragraphs 3–5, Holloway recounts ways that parents, often unintentionally, support and enforce socially constructed gender roles for male children from a young age. What are two of the most pernicious of these roles? From your own observation or experience, how pervasive is this "emotionally shortchanging" of boys, as Holloway calls it?

4. To what extent do you agree with Holloway's analysis of "media-perpetuated constructions of masculinity" (para. 9)? Use examples from today's media (e.g., television, film, video games, celebrity lifestyles) to support your viewpoint.

5. In her discussion of behaviors and attitudes that are "taught," Holloway corrects herself after referring to the disconnection of boys from their feminine selves with the caveat, "or more accurately, 'human. . .'" (para. 13). Do you think that this clarification ultimately undermines — or strengthens — Holloway's case that the expectations of "being a man" are "poisonous and potentially destructive" (para. 2)?

6. In paragraph 18, Holloway asserts: "We have to get past our very ideas about what being a man is. We have to start seing men as innately so." How do you interpret this claim?

5   The Perils of Being Manly

ROBERTO A. FERDMAN

Roberto Ferdman is a reporter for Wonkblog at the *Washington Post*, where he writes about food, economics, and other topics. He was previously a writer for Quartz, where he specialized in Latin American business and economics. He wrote the following article for the *Washington Post* in 2016.

A few years ago, I found myself in the emergency room. I had hurt my ankle playing basketball, and the pain was unbearable. I remember sitting there, waiting for someone to see me, thinking to myself that it must be broken, or fractured, or something similarly severe.

"I'm going touch your ankle in a few places," the doctor said shortly after I was brought in. "I want you to describe the pain on a scale from 1 to 10."

He pressed down onto various parts of my foot, each one more painful than the last. And yet, the numbers I uttered barely nudged, moving up from 5 to 5.5, and then from 5.5 to 6. I never said anything higher than that.

When the X-rays were in, the doctor showed them to me and told me two things. The first was that I had fractured my ankle. The second was that there was no way the pain was less than an 8. He joked that if I had sought medical care somewhere else, somewhere less precautionary in its practices, I might have been sent away with a prescription for a mild painkiller and a bag of ice.

Machismo, the driver of so many questionable decisions made by men, is a fickle thing. Sometimes, a little bit of it — a tinge of toughness — doesn't seem to hurt. In sport, for instance. Or maybe negotiation. Other times, it turns out, it can do more harm than good. Like, say, when it comes to caring for one's health.

5

"Everyone has a story about how a male friend or family member has been reluctant to go to the doctor," said Diana Sanchez, who teaches psychology at Rutgers University. "But it's more than that — it's also what happens when they actually go see a doctor."

"There are all sorts of adverse consequences associated with masculinity," she added.

A downside to being too much of a dude

Sanchez first became interested in the subject both because of the discrepancy in the life expectancy for men and women (men tend to die about five years earlier than women) and because of a personal experience with a family member who waited too long to see a doctor. She wondered whether the two might somehow be related. And she figured that there must be a way to find out.

Eventually, she, along with Mary S. Himmelstein, a doctoral candidate at Rutgers, devised two studies to explore the extent to which masculinity affects decisions about health care. And together they suggest that the effect could be fairly significant.

In the first of the two studies, which was pub- 10 lished in the *Journal of Health Psychology* in late 2014, they gathered two groups — one of them comprising university students, the other not. They measured the importance of manliness to the individuals in each group, using a scale called the Contingencies of Self-Worth (CSW for short), which was developed by researchers at Ohio State University. (The process involves questions that force the participants to rate the significance of bravery and self-reliance to their respective genders as well as to them personally). They also asked questions about health care, including ones that gauged the frequency with which the participants sought out preventive care and the regularity with which they delayed care.

What they found is that for both men and women, those who exhibited the most machismo (deriving self-worth from things such as bravery and self-reliance) were also the least likely to seek preventive care and the most likely to delay care.

"Masculine men, in particular, tend to avoid the doctor," Sanchez said. "Obviously, that's not a good thing."

In the second study, which was published in the journal *Preventive Medicine* in December, the researchers used three experiments to approximate what happens when people actually end up going to the doctor.

In the first two, the researchers tested the relationship between masculinity and male doctor preference, measuring each in the roughly 150 participants (all male) and finding that the two exhibited a strong correlation.

In the third, they explored what happens 15 when men see male doctors. They had 246 individuals (all male) complete a prescreening, during which the researchers also measured masculinity, and then had them come in and discuss their ailments with either male or female medical students (all of whom were unaware of each patient's masculinity score).

The results were fairly straightforward. Per the study:

> In accordance with predictions, men with higher scores in masculinity reported fewer symptoms in the lab compared to their prescreen reports when reporting to a male interviewer relative to a female interviewer.

This chart, plucked from the study, does a good job of showing the results, too:

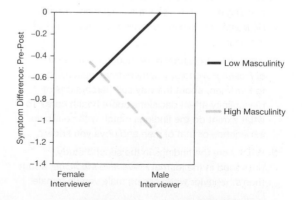

Men, in short, are less likely to seek preventive care than women and more likely to put off seeing a doctor when in need of medical care. They also prefer to seek out male doctors, but they tend to underreport pain and injuries to male doctors, thereby compromising the chances of receiving optimal care. And all of this, it should be said, is particularly true among those men who prescribe to masculine ideologies.

"Masculine men tend to not go to the doctor, and when they do, they tend to pick male doctors whom they then underreport their ailments to," Sanchez said.

A dangerous game

There is some humor in Sanchez's research. It's because of their own foolishness, after all, that some men — those who swear by archaic, rigid, animalistic understandings of their own sex — could be compromising their health. The cycle the two successive studies suggest certainly paints such a picture.

But there is also, hopefully, some humility *20* to be had. The consequences of delaying care when experiencing health issues is no joke. Nor are those that might arise from communicating poorly (or, really, inadequately) with your doctor.

"I think these findings will really resonate with a lot of people," Sanchez said. "But I also think people should take this seriously. This is something doctors should be aware of."

I spoke with three doctors, all of whom acknowledged that what Sanchez has found makes sense. They said that it's well known and problematic that men are less likely to seek preventive care than women. They agreed, based on their experience, that men, generally speaking, tended to approach visits to the doctor differently than women.

"All of this seems plausible," said Peter Hoenig, a doctor who has worked as a generalist in Massachusetts for more than 30 years.

But he also cautioned, as did others, against brandishing too wide a brushstroke. The complexities of individuals, they noted, seemed to far outweigh the quirks of gender ideology.

"Be careful of putting too much weight on *25* machismo," Hoenig said. "It is pretty light clothing and sheds easily."

"For several years, I worked as an emergency physician in a worn-out industrial city," he added. "It was not uncommon for a 300-pound-heavy, tattooed motorcycle guy to faint at the sight of a needle and a little old lady with pink pajamas to endure minor surgery without anesthesia in order to get home quickly to be with her poodle."

QUESTIONS

1. What is the purpose of Roberto A. Ferdman's opening anecdote about the emergency room? How effective is it in illustrating a central point of the article?

2. What does the study published in the *Journal of Health Psychology* demonstrate, according to Ferdman, about the way self-perceptions of masculinity affect decisions about health care? To what extent do the findings match with your own experience or that of men and boys you know?

3. What were the findings in the second study, published in the journal *Preventive Medicine*, about men's behavior when seeing male versus female doctors? Be sure to discuss the graph included with Ferdman's article in your response.

4. What is the definition of "masculinity" that the researchers used? What is meant by such terms as "masuline ideologies" (para. 17) or "masculine men" (para. 12)?

5. The article ends with a warning not to put "too much weight on machismo" (para. 25) from "a doctor who has worked as a generalist in Massachusetts for more than 30 years" (para. 23). How strong do you find this challenge to the research being reported?

6 The Hard, Adrenaline-Soaked Truth about "Toxic Masculinity"

FRANK MINITER

An author and investigative journalist, Frank Miniter has served as a senior editor at *Outdoor Life* magazine and executive editor of *American Hunter* magazine. He is the author of the bestseller *The Ultimate Man's Survival Guide: Recovering the Lost Art of Manhood* (2009). He wrote the following piece for *Forbes* magazine in 2017.

Have you felt the touch of "toxic masculinity" lately? Maybe you just didn't realize when its steely grip grabbed you by the back of the neck, say some academics at Duke and more.

Wait a second, you say, what is toxic masculinity?

Quite right, we need a definition. This is a relatively new and controversial academic idea. Urban Dictionary took a swing at it and came up with this:

n.) *A false idea that men are expected to be as manly as possible even though they're definitely not regularly expected to drink gallon sized beers in under three seconds, grow out gravely beards by mere thought alone, kill sharks with their bare hands . . . .*

The Good Men Project blog does a better job: "Toxic masculinity is a narrow and repressive description of manhood, designating manhood as defined by violence, sex, status and aggression."

So right, it's a negative thing that must be 5 repressed, as if manliness is a psychological disorder that only leads to aggression and violence, say these academics.

Basically, they say telling young men to "man up" or "grow a pair" is making young men do violent things. They say old-school patriarchal elements of society are pushing them to prove themselves to their peers in destructive ways. Man's caveman traits, they argue, run toxic with adrenaline unless our young men can swear off being men.

Never mind that these academics are ignoring thousands of years of things like Christian virtues, Confucian principles, knightly conduct and gentlemanly codes developed and used to channel boys' natural aggression in positive ways as mentors show them how to be stand-up men living a chivalric code. All that is passé.

Actually, it's worse than passé. That portion of human history is too loaded with things these academics want to wipe away — and, to some extent, they already have diminished, which is the actual reason colleges are dealing with boys who never learned to be gentlemen.

Now, instead of taking an honest look at what makes men, some colleges have opted to condemn manliness.

CampusReform.org is reporting that "Oregon 10 State University invited students to attend a 'healthy masculinities conference' where they will 'engage in collective imagining to construct new futures for masculinities, unrestricted by power, privilege, and oppression.'"

Advertisements for Oregon State's "masculinities conference" ask: "Join us in a collective examination of the histories and legacies that shape present day masculinities. Through a day of presentations, panels, workshops, and artistic expression, learn how to engage systems of power."

Meanwhile, Ithaca College is holding a workshop called "MLK Week: Educational Workshop — From the Batman to J. Cole: Masculinity and Violence." Students are going to study "hegemonic masculinity and its role as the wheel that rotates a cycle of violence." This workshop's goal it to help "willing individuals to begin to recognize, acknowledge, own, and disrupt the toxicity of manhood in order to end violence."

Duke University even has a "Men's Project" sponsored by the university's Women's Center. It says it will "examine the ways we present — or don't present — our masculinities, so we can better understand how masculinity exists on our campus — often in toxic ways — and begin the work of unlearning violence." (Okay, don't even let yourself imagine the fallout that would occur if a Duke's Men's Center sponsored a "Women's Project" in order to help women understand and solve their issues. First of all, come on, a Men's Center at Duke! Secondly, well, come on.)

Certainly, sexual assault and worse are a problem on college campuses, but these academics are trying to cure a problem with more of what is causing a societal problem. They are trying to further emasculate young men instead of, you know, teaching them to be gentlemen.

If teaching young men how to be gentlemen sounds stodgy to someone, then point out to them that becoming a gentleman is about finding real, heart-thumping ways to test yourself that will help you become your best self. There is an ancient formula behind this process used by every society and institution we all agree made or makes people of character. In my book *This Will Make a Man of You* I show how the same method, a process now being misunderstood

and destroyed, has always been used to help men (and now an increasing number of women) prove themselves in positive ways as they thereby become upstanding members of society.

Even the mad streets of Pamplona, Spain, during an *encierro* (the running of the bulls) does this every July by helping youth test themselves in something real. Running with the bulls, like any real rite of passage, requires you to face a physical test, a dangerous trial. You need to follow certain rules to make it through. The rules make your chances of surviving uninjured higher, but they also make it safer for everyone. For example, if you break the rules by grabbing a bull's tail and so make the bull stop and turn around in the street then that bull will begin to gore people. Not doing this — and many other things — shows respect for the bull, for yourself and for those in the street with you. That understood respect is the beginning of a real gentlemanly code of honor.

This is hard for people who avoid reality to comprehend. It is about proving yourself in some real thing, a thing that will require you to struggle and live up to something greater than yourself — places like karate dojos, boot camp and, yes, volunteering at a soup kitchen can do this if done with your mind open. Those are growing experiences.

A group of academics telling boys not to be men will only make the problems associated with young men who haven't learned to be gentleman worse.

15

QUESTIONS

1. In paragraphs 3 and 4, Frank Miniter provides two definitions of "'toxic masculinity.'" Which of these do you think is more accurate? How would you define the term?

2. Miniter claims that, basically, "manliness" has been defined as a "psychological disorder" (para. 5) that promotes violent, destructive

behaivaior. What evidence does he present to support this claim?

3. Miniter's target in this article is the academic world, particularly colleges. What is his basic criticism of programs such as the three he discusses? How do they "emasculate" (para. 14) young men? How valid do you find his objections?

4. What is Miniter's definition of a "gentleman"? What associations do you have with this word?

5. In paragraph 16, Miniter describes the running of the bulls in Spain. How does this example serve as evidence for the case he is making?

6. What constitues "growing experiences" (para. 17), according to Miniter?

7. What questions might you raise in response to Miniter's argument?

7 from The Man Trap

EMILY BOBROW

Emily Bobrow is a journalist whose work has appeared in the *New York Times*, the *Wall Street Journal*, the *Economist*, and the *New York Review of Books*, among others. The following excerpt is from a 2017 article Bobrow wrote for *1843*, the *Economist*'s culture and lifestyle magazine.

Eric, a corporate litigator at a big law firm in Philadelphia, says the hustle to make partner keeps him at the office around 50 hours a week. "The goal-posts keep moving," he says with a sigh. With a mortgage, two young children in private school and a wife who decided to stay at home to raise them (her own salary as an attorney barely covered the cost of a nanny), he admits he feels a bit "stuck." "No one tells you how these things work out in real life. Then you suddenly find yourself on the treadmill and you just gotta keep going." In an ideal world he would split the parenting and housework evenly with his wife, he says, but his job makes this impossible. He recalls having to miss a recent parent-teacher conference because of a scheduled call with a client. "I didn't even bother to say I had a conflict because I knew I would get a scowl or an eye roll, as if I was high-maintenance."

Many jobs have grown more demanding in recent decades. Low earners often juggle just-in-time schedules that change weekly and with little notice. High-earning professionals are expected to put in longer hours than ever before, toiling in offices long into the night. In 1979 16% of salaried American workers punched in at least 50 hours a week. By 2014 that number was 21%.

Research from Youngjoo Cha of Indiana University and Kim Weeden of Cornell has found that since the 1990s the workers who stay shackled to their desks the longest tend to be rewarded with the highest wages and the most promotions. Previously, those who worked long hours tended to be low earners; now, the reverse is true. An average man in a typical full-time job made around $26 an hour in 2015; those working at least 50 hours a week earned nearly $33. Increasingly punishing expectations at work reinforce a more gendered division of labour at home. They encourage women to shift into part-time employment, and men to rely on women to look after the children. Many employers also presume from the outset that mothers will — and should — put their families first. . . . This helps explain why economists have found that in America having one child reduces a woman's earnings by roughly 6%; having two depresses them by 15%. By contrast, fatherhood spurs men to work around 80 more hours a year, on average, which bumps up men's earnings by around 6%; this bonus is largest among highly educated professionals. It hardly seems to matter that between 1965 and 2000 men doubled the time they spent changing nappies and keeping house. Mothers often work fewer hours than they would prefer, and fathers work longer hours than they would like.

Many fathers feel obliged to live up to their bosses' demands in part because breadwinning, and being a good provider more generally, is still often seen as a fundamental feature of fatherhood. Even couples who meet at Harvard Business School can find themselves navigating an awkward and unspoken expectation that the man will earn more. Sean Grover, a therapist in Manhattan who is writing a book about the bumpy transition into parenthood, says that "very traditional ideas begin to resurface" when some career-minded young women start to think about settling down. "When we scratch the surface, they confess they want someone to take care of them, someone who can provide for them. It's something we really wrestle with."

These expectations are shifting rapidly: only 28% of respondents to a 2013 Pew Research survey in America agreed with the statement, "It's generally better for a marriage if the husband earns more than his wife," down from 40% in 1997. But few are completely impervious to centuries of socialisation. Steve, a screenwriter in his early 40s in Brooklyn, says it was "definitely weird" when he earned half what his wife made during their first years of marriage. "We're all modern and progressive and we want our marriage to be 50-50, but in times of stress she'd sometimes say, 'You're supposed to be taking care of us.'" This tension was subtle, he adds, and they never had real money problems. "But whenever things got to her she'd play a card that it wasn't supposed to be her problem because she's the wife. For a man there's no card like that."

Many men also worry that their appeal to their partners is wrapped up in their professional success. Robert, a 32-year-old digital-media entrepreneur in San Francisco, says he envies friends who are a bit more frugal with their money. "If we were more prudent, then maybe I wouldn't have to work so hard," he says. "But it's hard to communicate that when your fiancée sees you as a great success who's providing for us."

Women rightly complain that they are often shunted onto a mommy track with lower wages, fewer promotions and less prestige, whether they like it or not. But many men are just as frustrated by the elusiveness of a daddy track. Brian, a TV presenter in his late 30s in New Jersey, says that when he wanted to take time off after the birth of his second child, "it was a nightmare just trying to figure out what I was entitled to. It's so rare for anyone to take any kind of paternity leave that no one knew how it worked." He finally discovered he could use some of his sick days. He suspects few men take advantage of this policy "because they think it's somehow frowned upon."

His colleagues are right to be cautious. Research shows that parents who take family leave or request a flexible schedule to tend to young children often face harsh penalties, like lower long-term earnings, fewer promotions and poorer performance reviews. Mothers suffer from this too, but fathers often get an extra hit for defying cultural expectations. Studies show that both men and women tend to see fathers who ask for paternity leave as weak and inadequate. A survey of professional workers in Australia found that men are twice as likely as women to have their request to work flexibly rejected. One man recalled a manager telling him that "part-time is traditionally only something we make work for women." Research on middle-class workers in America found that fathers who are open about their child-care responsibilities are often bullied and harassed by their colleagues for not being manly enough. More than a third of 1,000 American male respondents in a recent Deloitte survey said taking paternity leave would "jeopardise their position" at work. Given this stigma, it is perhaps unsurprising that nearly three-quarters of the workers who have taken advantage of California's law to provide paid leave to new parents are women.

Patrick, a broadcast journalist in Atlanta in his early 40s, learned early in his career not to expect his employer to make allowances for his domestic duties. His wife, an obstetrician-gynaecologist, was working a double shift at the hospital, so he had to shoulder much of the child care for their three young children. When he tried to explain to his producer why he wasn't able to work over the weekend, he received a chilling response: "He said 'Patrick, everyone has a family. Nobody cares about yours.'" It's hard to imagine a male manager saying that to a woman.

Some fathers privately admit that their long hours at the office leave them unsure of their role at home. "If I've been travelling or I've been on trial and working 7am to midnight every night six days a week, my wife says it's actually more stressful when I'm back because she has her routine," says Eric. "Sometimes you feel like a visitor in your own house." *10*

QUESTIONS

1. Although Emily Bobrow offers some statistical evidence of wage earnings and hours spent at work, she mainly focuses on societal attitudes. Specifically, what are three societal issues that she believes are contributing to men's frustration and discontent?

2. Why do you think that traditional gender expectations become more pervasive when people become parents? What does Bobrow mean by "the daddy track" (para. 8)? What do you think might change this attitude or behavior?

3. Paragraph 4 discusses the impact that having children has on earnings for both men and women and on the relationships between work

expectations and "a more gendered division of labour at home." What are the cause-and-effect relationships at work here?

4. In what ways does Bobrow point out that institutional changes — or policies — have outpaced or are in conflict with gendered expectations, both in terms of the way people see themselves and the way others see them? Pay particular attention to paragraph 9 ("His colleagues are right to be cautious").

5. To what extent are the issues that are the focus of this article the exclusive realm of highly educated professionals? In what ways might the same issues apply to men who work in blue-collar professions?

8 Talking to Boys the Way We Talk to Girls

ANDREW REINER

Andrew Reiner, a faculty member in the Honors College of Towson University in Maryland, writes on the erosion of civility and community in society. He has written for the *Chicago Tribune*, the *Washington Post*, and the *Chronicle of Higher Education*. The following essay appeared in the *New York Times* in 2017.

At a Father's Day breakfast, my 5-year-old son and his classmates sang a song about fathers, crooning about "my dad who's big and strong" and "fixes things with his hammer" and, above all else, "is really cool."

Now, there's nothing wrong with most of these qualities in and of themselves. But when

these lyrics are passed down as the defining soundtrack to masculine identity, we limit children's understanding not just of what it means to be a father but of what it means to be a man — and a boy, as well.

When fathers appear in children's picture books, they're angling for laughs, taking their sons on adventures or modeling physical strength or stoic independence. There is the rare exception in children's books where a father baldly demonstrates — without symbolic gestures — his love for his son (a few are "Guess How Much I Love You" and "Oh, Oh, Baby Boy!"). Just as women's studies classes have long examined the ways that gendered language undermines women and girls, a growing body of research shows that stereotypical messages are similarly damaging to boys.

A 2014 study in Pediatrics found that mothers interacted vocally more often with their infant daughters than they did their infant sons. In a different study, a team of British researchers found that Spanish mothers were more likely to use emotional words and emotional topics when speaking with their 4-year-old daughters than with their 4-year-old sons. Interestingly, the same study revealed that daughters were more likely than sons to speak about their emotions with their fathers when talking about past experiences. And during these reminiscing conversations, fathers used more emotion-laden words with their 4-year-old daughters than with their 4-year-old sons.

What's more, a 2017 study led by Emory University researchers discovered, among other things, that fathers also sing and smile more to their daughters, and they use language that is more "analytical" and that acknowledges their sadness far more than they do with their sons. The words they use with sons are more focused on achievement — such as "win" and "proud." Researchers believe that these discrepancies in fathers' language may contribute to "the consistent findings that girls outperform boys in school achievement outcomes."

After visits to the emergency room for accidental injuries, another study found, parents of both genders talk differently to sons than they do to daughters. They are nearly four times more likely to tell girls than boys to be more careful if undertaking the same activity again. The same

study cited earlier research which found that parents of both genders used "directives" when teaching their 2- to 4-year-old sons how to climb down a playground pole but offered extensive "explanations" to daughters.

Even boys' literacy skills seem to be impacted by the taciturn way we expect them to speak. In his book "Manhood in America," Michael Kimmel, the masculine studies researcher and author, maintains that "the traditional liberal arts curriculum is seen as feminizing by boys." Nowhere is this truer than in English classes where, as I've witnessed after more than 20 years of teaching, boys and young men police each other when other guys display overt interest in literature or creative writing assignments. Typically, nonfiction reading and writing passes muster because it poses little threat for boys. But literary fiction, and especially poetry, are mediums to fear. Why? They're the language of emotional exposure, purported feminine "weakness" — the very thing our scripting has taught them to avoid at best, suppress, at worst.

Women often say they want men to be emotionally transparent with them. But as the vulnerability and shame expert Brené Brown reveals in her book, "Daring Greatly," many grow uneasy or even recoil if men take them up on their offer.

Indeed, a Canadian study found that college-aged female respondents considered men more attractive if they used shorter words and sentences and spoke less. This finding seems to jibe with Dr. Brown's research, suggesting that the less men risk emoting verbally, the more appealing they appear.

Such squelching messages run counterintuitively to male wiring, it turns out: Guys are born more emotionally sensitive than girls.

For three decades the research of Edward Tronick explored the interplay between infants and their mothers. He and his colleagues in the department of newborn medicine at Harvard Medical School discovered that mothers unconsciously interacted with their infant sons more attentively and vigilantly than they did with their infant daughters because the sons needed more support for controlling their emotions. Some of their research found that boys' emotional reactivity was eventually "restricted or perhaps more change-worthy than the reactivity of girls," Dr. Tronick noted in an email. Mothers initiated this — through physical withdrawal.

"So the 'manning up' of infant boys begins early on in their typical interactions," Dr. Tronick said, "and long before language plays its role."

Judy Chu, a human biologist, conducted a two-year study of 4- and 5-year-old boys and found that they were as astute as girls at reading other people's emotions and at cultivating close, meaningful friendships. In her book "When Boys Become Boys" she maintains that by the time the boys reached first grade, sometimes earlier, they traded their innate empathy for a learned stoicism and greater emotional distance from friends. Interestingly, they adopted this new behavior in public, exclusively, but not at home or when their parents were around.

Why do we limit the emotional vocabulary of boys?

We tell ourselves we are preparing our sons 15 to fight (literally and figuratively), to compete in a world and economy that's brutish and callous. The sooner we can groom them for this dystopian future, the better off they'll be. But the Harvard psychologist Susan David insists the opposite is true: "Research shows that people who suppress emotions have lower-level resilience and emotional health."

How can we change this? We can start, says Dr. David, by letting boys experience their emotions, all of them, without judgment — or by offering them solutions. This means helping them learn the crucial lessons that "Emotions aren't good or bad" and that "their emotions aren't bigger than they are. They aren't something to fear."

Say to boys: "I can see that you're upset," or ask them, "What are you feeling?" or "What's going on for you right now?" There doesn't have to be any grand plan beyond this, she says. "Just show up for them. Get them talking. Show that you want to hear what they're saying."

QUESTIONS

1. What, according to Andrew Reiner, is "the defining soundtrack to masculine identity" (para. 2)?

2. In paragraph 4, Reiner reports on several studies of how parents interact verbally with their infants and young children. What conclusions do you draw from this research?

3. Reiner reports on a research study at Emory University that concludes that "discrepancies in fathers' language may contribute to 'the consistent findings that girls outperform boys in school achievement outcomes'" (para. 5). What other variables would you want to consider before making a definitive statement on the relationship between fathers' language and children's school performance?

4. In his article, Reiner places a number of words in quotation marks — not because he is quoting someone else but to indicate a meaning other than the most expected one: e.g., "analytical" (para. 5), "directives," and "explanations" (para. 6). What do you think he means by each of these terms?

5. In paragraph 7, Reiner comments on why boys tend not to like the literature studied in their English classes. To what extent do you agree with his analysis, based on your own experience?

6. What evidence does Reiner offer to support his statement that men are "born more emotionally sensitive than girls" (para. 10)?

7. Reiner concludes by offering a suggestion for changing what he calls the tendency to "limit the emotional vocabulary of boys" (para. 14). Would you characterize these suggestions as solid, oversimplified, or something else?

MAKING CONNECTIONS

1. In what ways does the research reported by Kali Holloway or Emily Bobrow support or challenge the more personal commentary of Paul Theroux?

2. How might Stephanie Coontz respond to Frank Miniter's argument that young men need to be schooled in how to be "gentlemen"?

3. To what extent do you think that the iconic image of the Marlboro Man would be an appropriate visual to accompany the article by Roberto Ferdman?

4. On the face of it, Andrew Reiner and Theroux seem at odds; yet despite their quite different perspectives, they share a number of concerns. What are the most obvious differences in their arguments? What are the more subtle commonalities?

5. How might Miniter respond to Bobrow's statement, "Some fathers privately admit that their long hours at the office leave them unsure of their role at home" (para. 11)?

6. Based on her article, what two questions might Holloway ask Reiner?

ENTERING THE CONVERSATION

As you respond to each of the following prompts, support your argument with references to at least three of the sources in this Conversation on Redefining Masculinity. For help using sources, see Chapter 4.

1. Suppose you are part of a community group deciding whether to implement single-sex classrooms in grades 9–12 in an effort to raise the academic achievement level and character development of boys. Develop a position on this proposal informed by at least three of the readings in this Conversation.

2. Many of the texts in this Conversation explore the negative consequences of the different ways we talk and interact with boys and men as well as the expectations women have of men and men have of themselves. What do you see as the most promising approaches to bring about change? Base your position on at least three of the readings as well as your own experience and knowledge.

3. At the start of Kali Holloway's article, she cites Joe Ehrmann, coach and former NFL player: "The three most destructive words that every man receives when he's a boy is when he's told to 'be a man.'" Write an essay suporting, challenging, or qualifying Ehrmann's statement. Develop it with at least three of the sources and your own experience and observation.

4. Is there such a thing as "toxic masculinity"? If so, what does it mean? If not, why do you think that the term has become so commonly used (though, perhaps, not clearly defined) in our society today? Develop your position with at least three of the sources from this Conversation.

5. How much of an impact does the media — whether it be television, film, social media, video games, or graphic novels — have on our society's view of men's behavior and attitudes? Develop your position by referring to the image of the Marlboro Man and at least two other sources along with contemporary examples.

6. In this Conversation on what it means to be "a man" or "masculine," some authors have written about society in general, while others have alluded to differences based on other factors, including ethnicity, socioecoomic status, and race. To what extent do you think it is fair to generalize discussions of socially constructed gender roles for men across society? Develop your position with at least two of the texts in the Conversation, your own experience, and at least one source you research on your own.

from In Search of Our Mothers' Gardens

ALICE WALKER

In the late 1920s my mother ran away from home to marry my father. Marriage, if not running away, was expected of seventeen-year-old girls. By the time she was twenty, she had two children and was pregnant with a third. Five children later, I was born. And this is how I came to know my mother: she seemed a large, soft, loving-eyed woman who was rarely impatient in our home. Her quick, violent temper was on view only a few times a year, when she battled with the white landlord who had the misfortune to suggest to her that her children did not need to go to school.

She made all the clothes we wore, even my brothers' overalls. She made all the towels and sheets we used. She spent the summers canning vegetables and fruits. She spent the winter evenings making quilts enough to cover all our beds.

During the "working" day, she labored beside-not behind-my father in the fields. Her day began before sunup, and did not end until late at night. There was never a moment for her to sit down, undisturbed, to unravel her own private thoughts; never a time free from interruption-by work or the noisy inquiries of her many children. And yet, it is to my mother-and all our mothers who were not famous-that I went in search of the secret of what has fed that muzzled and often mutilated, but vibrant, creative spirit that the black woman has inherited, and that pops out in wild and unlikely places to this day.

But when, you will ask, did my overworked mother have time to know or care about feeding the creative spirit?

The answer is so simple that many of us 5 have spent years discovering it. We have constantly looked high, when we should have looked high — and low.

For example: in the Smithsonian Institution in Washington, D.C., there hangs a quilt unlike any other in the world. In fanciful, inspired, and yet simple and identifiable figures, it portrays the story of the Crucifixion. It is considered rare, beyond price. Though it follows no known pattern of quilt-making, and though it is made of bits and pieces of worthless rags, it is obviously the work of a person of powerful imagination and deep spiritual feeling. Below this quilt I saw a note that says it was made by "an anonymous Black woman in Alabama, a hundred years ago."

If we could locate this "anonymous" black woman from Alabama, she would turn out to be one of our grandmothers — an artist who left her mark in the only materials she could afford, and in the only medium her position in society allowed her to use.

As Virginia Woolf wrote further, in *A Room of One's Own:*

> Yet genius of a sort must have existed among women as it must have existed among the working class. [Change this to "slaves" and "the wives and daughters of sharecroppers."] Now and again an Emily Brontë or a Robert Burns [change this to "a Zora Hurston or a Richard Wright"] blazes out and proves its presence. But certainly it never got itself on to paper. When, however, one reads of a witch being ducked, of a woman possessed by devils [or "Sainthood"], of a wise woman selling herbs [our root workers], or even a very remarkable man who had a mother, then I think we are on the track of a lost novelist, a suppressed poet, of some mute and inglorious Jane Austen. . . . Indeed, I would venture to guess that Anon, who wrote so many poems without signing them, was often a woman. . . .

And so our mothers and grandmothers have, more often than not anonymously, handed on the creative spark, the seed of the flower they themselves never hoped to see: or like a sealed letter they could not plainly read.

And so it is, certainly, with my own mother. 10 Unlike "Ma" Rainey's songs, which retained their creator's name even while blasting forth from Bessie Smith's mouth, no song or poem will bear my mother's name. Yet so many of the stories that I write, that we all write, are my mother's stories. Only recently did I fully realize this: that through years of listening to my mother's stories of her life, I have absorbed not only the stories themselves, but something of the manner in which she spoke, something of the urgency that involves the knowledge that her stories — like her life — must be recorded. It is probably for this reason that so much of what I have written is about characters whose counterparts in real life are so much older than I am.

---

1. The primary rhetorical strategies used in paragraph 2 are

   a. antithesis and subordination
   b. imagery and appeals to pathos
   c. metaphors and allusions
   d. anaphora and simple syntax
   e. irony and hyperbole

2. In the context of the passage as a whole, the activities in paragraph 2 are primarily examples of the mother's

   a. creativity
   b. dutifulness
   c. self-discipline
   d. conformity
   e. love

3. The quotation marks around "working" (para. 3) primarily suggest that

   a. the author does not consider the activity true work
   b. her mother's work continued beyond those hours spent in the fields
   c. her mother did not value the work she did
   d. her father did not value the work her mother did
   e. her mother was not paid well for her work in the fields

4. In the first four paragraphs, the author establishes a tension primarily between her mother's

   a. short temper and loving character
   b. responsibility to her children and need for time to herself
   c. formal working life and the work of other "mothers who were not famous"
   d. seemingly mundane activities and her "creative spirit"
   e. strong-will and the sexist expectations of males in her life

5. The author uses the example of the quilt in the museum (paras. 6–7) primarily to show

   a. how art by Black women should be recognized by formal establishments
   b. that religious art can be found in unexpected contexts
   c. that anonymous artists are often more talented than well-known artists
   d. that art can be produced by women with limited opportunities
   e. that the definition of what qualifies as art is controversial

6. We can infer that the bracketed phrases within the Virginia Woolf quotation were written by

   a. Virginia Woolf
   b. The author of the overall passage
   c. An editor
   d. An employee of the Smithsonian Institute
   e. The author's mother

7. In the context of the passage as a whole, the primary rhetorical purpose of the quotation from Virginia Woolf is

   a. to argue that creativity is not bound by gender, race, or class
   b. to suggest that artists are often outsiders in society
   c. to criticize the treatment of artists within American society
   d. to validate the assumption that the quilt in the Smithsonian was created by a woman
   e. to expose and explore traditional definitions of art

8. An explicit example of "the seed of the flower" (para. 10) is

   a. the stories the author writes
   b. the quilt in the Smithsonian
   c. Ma Rainey's songs

d. the novels of Jane Austen

e. the clothes the author's mother made

9. Taken as a whole, the primary purpose of the passage is

   a. to provide a character sketch of the author's mother

   b. to explain the author's method of writing

c. to criticize the art establishment for its exclusion of non-traditional art

d. to argue against discrimination based on sex and gender in the art world

e. to analyze a manifestation of the creative impulse

---

from **Professions for Women**

VIRGINIA WOOLF

When your secretary invited me to come here, she told me that your Society is concerned with the employment of women and she suggested that I might tell you something about my own professional experiences. It is true I am a woman; it is true I am employed; but what professional experiences have I had? It is difficult to say. My profession is literature; and in that profession there are fewer experiences for women than in any other, with the exception of the stage — fewer, I mean, that are peculiar to women. For the road was cut many years ago — by Fanny Burney, by Aphra Behn, by Harriet Martineau, by Jane Austen, by George Eliot — many famous women, and many more unknown and forgotten, have been before me, making the path smooth, and regulating my steps. Thus, when I came to write, there were very few material obstacles in my way. Writing was a reputable and harmless occupation. The family peace was not broken by the scratching of a pen. No demand was made upon the family purse. For ten and sixpence one can buy paper enough to write all the plays of Shakespeare — if one has a mind that way. Pianos and models, Paris, Vienna and Berlin, masters and mistresses, are not needed by a writer. The cheapness of writing paper is, of course, the reason why women have succeeded as writers before they have succeeded in the other professions.

But to tell you my story — it is a simple one. You have only got to figure to yourselves a girl in a bedroom with a pen in her hand. She had only to move that pen from left to right — from ten o'clock to one. Then it occurred to her to do what is simple and cheap enough after all — to slip a few of those pages into an envelope, fix a penny stamp in the corner, and drop the envelope into the red box at the corner. It was thus that I became a journalist; and my effort was rewarded on the first day of the following month — a very glorious day it was for me — by a letter from an editor containing a cheque for one pound ten shillings and sixpence. But to show you how little I deserve to be called a professional woman, how little I know of the struggles and difficulties of such lives, I have to admit that instead of spending that sum upon bread and butter, rent, shoes and stockings, or butcher's bills, I went out and bought a cat — a beautiful cat, a Persian cat, which very soon involved me in bitter disputes with my neighbours.

What could be easier than to write articles and to buy Persian cats with the profits? But wait a moment. Articles have to be about something. Mine, I seem to remember, was about a novel by a famous man. And while I was writing this review, I discovered that if I were going to review books I should need to do battle with a certain phantom. And the phantom was a woman, and when I came to know her better I called her after the heroine of a famous poem, The Angel in the House.[1] It was

---

[1] "The Angel in the House" is a nineteenth-century poem about a self-sacrificing heroine; for many, she represented the ideal Victorian woman. —Eds.

she who used to come between me and my paper when I was writing reviews. It was she who bothered me and wasted my time and so tormented me that at last I killed her. You who come of a younger and happier generation may not have heard of her — you may not know what I mean by the Angel in the House. I will describe her as shortly as I can. She was intensely sympathetic. She was immensely charming. She was utterly unselfish. She excelled in the difficult arts of family life. She sacrificed herself daily. If there was chicken, she took the leg; if there was a draught she sat in it — in short she was so constituted that she never had a mind or a wish of her own, but preferred to sympathize always with the minds and wishes of others. Above all — I need not say it — she was pure. Her purity was supposed to be her chief beauty — her blushes, her great grace. In those days — the last of Queen Victoria — every house had its Angel. And when I came to write I encountered her with the very first words. The shadow of her wings fell on my page; I heard the rustling of her skirts in the room. Directly, that is to say, I took my pen in my hand to review that novel by a famous man, she slipped behind me and whispered: "My dear, you are a young woman. You are writing about a book that has been written by a man. Be sympathetic; be tender; flatter; deceive; use all the arts and wiles of our sex. Never let anybody guess that you have a mind of your own. Above all, be pure." And she made as if to guide my pen. I now record the one act for which I take some credit to myself, though the credit rightly belongs to some excellent ancestors of mine who left me a certain sum of money — shall we say five hundred pounds a year? — so that it was not necessary for me to depend solely on charm for my living. I turned upon her and caught her by the throat. I did my best to kill her. My excuse, if I were to be had up in a court of law, would be that I acted in self-defence. Had I not killed her she would have

killed me. She would have plucked the heart out of my writing. For, as I found, directly I put pen to paper, you cannot review even a novel without having a mind of your own, without expressing what you think to be the truth about human relations, morality, sex. And all these questions, according to the Angel of the House, cannot be dealt with freely and openly by women; they must charm, they must conciliate, they must — to put it bluntly — tell lies if they are to succeed. Thus, whenever I felt the shadow of her wing or the radiance of her halo upon my page, I took up the inkpot and flung it at her. She died hard. Her fictitious nature was of great assistance to her. It is far harder to kill a phantom than a reality. She was always creeping back when I thought I had despatched her. Though I flatter myself that I killed her in the end, the struggle was severe; it took much time that had better have been spent upon learning Greek grammar; or in roaming the world in search of adventures. But it was a real experience; it was an experience that was found to befall all women writers at that time. Killing the Angel in the House was part of the occupation of a woman writer.

But to continue my story. The Angel was dead; what then remained? You may say that what remained was a simple and common object — a young woman in a bedroom with an inkpot. In other words, now that she had rid herself of falsehood, that young woman had only to be herself. Ah, but what is "herself"? I mean, what is a woman? I assure you, I do not know. I do not believe that you know. I do not believe that anybody can know until she has expressed herself in all the arts and professions open to human skill. That indeed is one of the reasons why I have come here — out of respect for you, who are in process of showing us by your experiments what a woman is, who are in process of providing us, by your failures and successes, with that extremely important piece of information.

1. In the first paragraph, the writer's primary purpose is to

   a. establish her background to show why she is an appropriate choice of speaker
   b. connect her work to the work of previous great women to illustrate her expertise
   c. illustrate why writing is an easy occupation that all women can pursue
   d. downplay her accomplishments to create a humble, trustworthy persona
   e. set up a point about the "cheapness" of writing that she will later argue against

2. What is the literary device illustrated in the statement "No demand was made upon the family purse" (para. 1)?

   a. metonymy
   b. hyperbole
   c. allusion
   d. apostrophe
   e. onomatopoeia

3. In the second paragraph, Virginia Woolf distinguishes herself from other professional women in that

   a. writing and publishing come very easily and naturally to her
   b. she purchases luxury items rather than necessities with her earnings
   c. she makes the effort to mail her writing to a publisher, which results in a paycheck
   d. she spent several hours a day writing when she was a girl, preparing herself for the writer's life
   e. her Persian cat causes disagreements with her neighbors, interfering with the peace needed to write

4. Paragraph 3 includes all of the following rhetorical strategies EXCEPT

   a. metaphor
   b. personification
   c. rhetorical question
   d. allusion
   e. antithesis

5. Through the mention of "The Angel in the House" (para. 3), Woolf suggests that

   a. a woman's role in society is to be self-sacrificing, charming, and pure
   b. battling a woman's natural inclinations is necessary for success as a writer
   c. societal expectations for women impede a woman's ability to write honestly
   d. women of all ages face obstacles to their work in an unchanging society
   e. an internal phantom whispers to a woman writer and guides her pen

6. The organizational pattern of this essay can best be described as

   a. description of purpose to personal anecdote to symbolic story
   b. specific information to qualification of points to qualified opinion
   c. history to personal anecdotes to projection into the future
   d. personal reflection to fictional example to personal experience
   e. general overview of problem to illustrative anecdotes to solution

7. All of the following statements characterize the author's struggle to become a writer except

   a. "The family peace was not broken by the scratching of a pen." (para. 1)
   b. "The shadow of her wings fell on my page; I heard the rustling of her skirts in the room." (para. 3)
   c. "'Never let anybody guess that you have a mind of your own.'" (para. 3)
   d. "My excuse, if I were to be had up in a court of law, would be that I acted in self-defence." (para. 3)
   e. "It is far harder to kill a phantom than a reality." (para. 3)

8. Throughout the essay, the author's attitude toward her audience is one of

   a. disdain and sarcasm
   b. politeness and condescension
   c. concern and criticism
   d. honesty and admiration
   e. hopefulness and skepticism

GENDER

Now that you have examined a number of readings and other texts that focus on gender, including gender stereotypes and their consequences, explore one dimension of this topic by synthesizing your own ideas and the readings. You might want to do more research or use readings from other classes as you prepare for the following projects.

1. From popular magazines and newspapers, collect ads that reflect stereotypes about the roles of men and women, as well as ads that show men and women in a more progressive light. You might work in groups to collect and analyze the ads. Make lists of both kinds of ads. Determine which kinds of products show men and women in stereotyped roles and which show men and women breaking gender stereotypes. Which stereotypes are more common in these ads — stereotypes about women or about men? Then, working individually, write a report that discusses what the ads show about American values, beliefs, and attitudes toward gender roles.

2. Write a personal narrative in which you describe a gender role that your family or friends expected of you but that you either refused to play or struggled against. Explain the origin and nature of the expectation, as well as your reasons for not wanting to fulfill it. Include a discussion of the reactions you have gotten as you challenged the role or expectation.

3. To explore the idea that gender roles are socially constructed rather than biologically determined, do some research into other cultures and times. Report on a role that our society believes is gender-specific (for example, the nurturing mother, the protective male) but that another culture or people from another time period viewed quite differently.

4. The Internet is arguably gender-neutral. When you do not know other users' backgrounds, physical traits, style of dress, and so on, you have to judge them only by their words. Some observers believe that the anonymity of the Internet allows people to move outside of expected gender roles. Does the Internet

affect you that way? Are you more willing to be confrontational online, for example? Are you funnier? Does your online voice resemble who you are in person? Write an essay exploring how gender does or does not influence your online communication style.

5. Write a roundtable conversation that you might have with three authors in this chapter about *one* of the following quotations:

   a. The curse of too many women has been that they have this privilege of refuge in the home.
   — Pearl Buck

   b. There are two kinds of spiritual law, two kinds of conscience, one in man and another, altogether different, in women. They do not understand each other. — Henrik Ibsen

   c. The discovery is, of course, that "man" and "woman" are fictions, caricatures, cultural constructs. As models they are reductive, totalitarian, inappropriate to human becoming. As roles they are static, demeaning to the female, dead-ended for males and females both. — Andrea Dworkin

   d. You see a lot of smart guys with dumb women but you hardly ever see a smart woman with a dumb guy. — Erica Jong

6. Examine a popular movie in terms of gender roles, and write about it. In what ways do the characters reflect conventional roles, and in what ways do they step out of those roles?

7. Write a "myth-buster" essay. Take a stereotype based on gender (such as "women are bad drivers" or "men are more prone to violent behavior than women"), and debunk it by conducting research. Use quantitative information as well as anecdotal or personal

experience as evidence. Consider how this myth originated and who benefits from perpetuating it.

8. In his book *Men Are from Mars, Women Are from Venus*, John Gray writes, "A man's sense of self is defined through his ability to achieve results. . . . A woman's sense of self is defined through her feelings and the quality of her relationships." Write an essay supporting, challenging, or modifying these statements. Use examples from your own experience and selections from this chapter.

9. Several of the authors in this Conversation on Redefining Masculinity raise questions about the reading required in school. Working in groups, develop a list of books the girls like, and a list of books the boys like; then try to reach a consensus on at least two or three selections that both groups find interesting. Write an essay analyzing the process and explaining the results. As part of your inquiry, you might visit www.guysread.com.

10. In a 2005 *New York Times* op-ed entitled "Mind over Muscle," columnist David Brooks asserted: "One thing is for sure: in 30 years the notion that we live in an oppressive patriarchy that discriminates against women will be regarded as a quaint anachronism." Write an essay explaining why you agree or disagree with Brooks's prediction.

11. In *Why I Am Not a Feminist: A Feminist Manifesto*, author Jessa Crispin writes: "In order to succeed in a patriarchal world, we took on the role of patriarchs ourselves. In order to win in this world, we had to exhibit the characteristics the patriarchal world values and discard what it does not." Think of someone who you would call a feminist in the most positive sense of the word — someone you know personally or know from history or current events. Write an essay analyzing the extent to which this person falls prey to Crispin's criticism.

12
Justice

To what extent do our laws and politics reflect the values of a just society?

Different in every culture, evolving throughout history, justice is difficult to pin down. Perhaps it is the process that determines what is fair, perhaps it is a means of protecting human rights, perhaps it is the embodiment of morality, or perhaps it is something else. The ancient Greek philosopher Plato argued that it is the harmonious condition of both the individual and the state, while many religions hold that God dispenses justice. Enlightenment thinkers such as John Locke believed in natural law, or the idea that humans are entitled to certain unalienable rights — a concept enshrined in America's founding documents. The idea of a social contract, in which people consent to be governed in exchange for the protection of their natural rights, is integral to any discussion of justice. Utilitarian thinkers such as John Stuart Mill subscribed to the idea of a basic moral standard: that what is right has the best consequences for the most people. Modern-day conversations about justice incorporate distributive justice, which focuses not on rights but on favorable and fair distribution of wealth, power, respect; social justice, which is concerned with equality, including equality of opportunity; retributive justice, concerned with punishment for wrongdoing; and restorative justice, which addresses the needs of both victims and offenders.

▼
―――――――

This photograph shows a panel from four linen tapestries by Judith Poxson Fawkes, entitled *Oregon Justice, Judicial Heritage, Oregon Environment* (1997), that hang in the Mark O. Hatfield U.S. Courthouse in Portland, Oregon. In this panel, justice takes a familiar, traditional pose: blindfolded, with scales in one hand and a sword in the other. **What unconventional features does Fawkes add to this portrayal of justice? How do those elements connect the concept of justice with environmentalism?**

Library of Congress

This chapter's texts examine, directly and indirectly, the ways our laws and politics function in relation to the ideal of a just society. Abraham Lincoln's Gettysburg Address is an exemplar of even-handedness, honoring the dead on both sides of the Civil War. In "Politics and the English Language," George Orwell reminds us that to communicate clearly and precisely is to be honest and fair. In this chapter's Classic Essay, Henry David Thoreau explores the connection between political action and moral duty, one that Barack Obama's speech on the fiftieth anniversary of the Selma to Montgomery marches emphasizes by honoring the "warriors of justice" whose activism and sacrifice propelled the civil rights movement to victory. In "Justice and the Passion for Vengeance," Robert Solomon faces head-on the human urge for revenge, while Naomi Shihab Nye's letter, "To Any Would-Be Terrorist," reminds us that the path to a fair and just society lies in sharing our art, friendship, and culture with others. In this chapter's Central Essay, Ta-Nehisi Coates discusses the controversial and sometimes deadly role police serve, raising questions explored by many of the authors included here.

Justice is not, however, a lofty ideal discussed solely by judges, philosophers, or politicians. Everyone craves it, and everyone thinks about it. We all recall — and have voiced — the cry, "It's not fair." We look to those who wield power and authority — whether they are parents, teachers, elected officials, or public figures — to right what we perceived as wrongs. And, of course, everyone has been told once or twice to accept the fact that life's just not fair. While this is true, it is not an invitation to disregard what is right. "A Theory of Justice," an essay by twentieth-century philosopher John Rawls, imagines a society of free citizens holding equal basic rights and cooperating in an egalitarian economic system; the result is civic unity despite diversity of views. Rawls's theory perhaps serves as a model to strive for in our families, in our classrooms, and in our democratic society.

from **Between the World and Me**

TA-NEHISI COATES

Ta-Nehisi Coates (b. 1975) is an award-winning author, journalist, comic book writer, and educator. Originally from Baltimore, Coates attended Howard University before leaving school to start a career in journalism. He has since worked for *Philadelphia Weekly*, the *Village Voice*, *Time*, the *New York Times*, the *Washington Post*, and the *Atlantic*, where he is a national correspondent. A 2015 MacArthur fellow, Coates is the author of three nonfiction books: *The Beautiful Struggle* (2008), *Between the World and Me* (2015), which won the 2015 National Book Award, and *We Were Eight Years in Power* (2017), a collection of essays published during the Obama presidency. Since 2016, Coates has also written *Black Panther* comics for Marvel.

The excerpt below is taken from *Between the World and Me*, a nonfiction book in the form of a letter Coates wrote to his teenage son about the reality of being a black man in America today. Near the beginning of this letter, Coates introduces "the Dream," a concept he returns to often over the course of the book:

> *I have seen that dream all my life. It is perfect houses with nice lawns. It is Memorial Day cookouts, block associations, and driveways. The Dream is tree houses and the Cub Scouts. The Dream smells like peppermint but tastes like strawberry shortcake. And for so long I have wanted to escape into the Dream, to fold my country over my head like a blanket. But this has never been an option because the Dream rests on our backs, the bedding made from our bodies. And . . . the Dream persists by warring with the known world.*

Paul Marotta/Getty Images

Shortly before you were born, I was pulled over by the PG County[1] police, the same police that all the D.C. poets had warned me of. They approached on both sides of the car, shining their flashing lights through the windows. They took my identification and returned to the squad car. I sat there in terror. By then I had added to the warnings of my teachers what I'd learned about PG County through reporting and reading the papers. And so I knew that the PG County police had killed Elmer Clay Newman,

then claimed he'd rammed his own head into the wall of a jail cell. And I knew that they'd shot Gary Hopkins and said he'd gone for an officer's gun. And I knew they had beaten Freddie McCollum half-blind and blamed it all on a collapsing floor. And I had read reports of these officers choking mechanics, shooting construction workers, slamming suspects through the glass doors of shopping malls. And I knew that they did this with great regularity, as though moved by some unseen cosmic clock. I knew that they shot at moving cars, shot at the unarmed, shot through the backs of men and claimed that it had been

---

[1]Prince George's County, Maryland. —Eds.

they who'd been under fire. These shooters were investigated, exonerated, and promptly returned to the streets, where, so emboldened, they shot again. At that point in American history, no police department fired its guns more than that of Prince George's County. The FBI opened multiple investigations — sometimes in the same week. The police chief was rewarded with a raise. I replayed all of this sitting there in my car, in their clutches. Better to have been shot in Baltimore, where there was the justice of the streets and someone might call the killer to account. But these officers had my body, could do with that body whatever they pleased, and should I live to explain what they had done with it, this complaint would mean nothing. The officer returned. He handed back my license. He gave no explanation for the stop.

Then that September I picked up *The Washington Post* and saw that the PG County police had killed again. I could not help but think that this could have been me, and holding you — a month old by then — I knew that such loss would not be mine alone. I skimmed the headline — their atrocities seemed so common back then. The story spread second day, and reading slightly closer, I saw it was a Howard student who had been killed. I thought perhaps I knew him. But I paid it no further mind. Then on the third day a photo appeared with the story, and I glimpsed at and then focused on the portrait, and I saw him there. He was dressed in his formal clothes, as though it were his senior prom, and frozen in the amber of his youth. His face was lean, brown, and beautiful, and across that face, I saw the open, easy smile of Prince Carmen Jones.

I cannot remember what happened next. I think I stumbled back. I think I told your mother what I'd read. I think I called the girl with the long dreads and asked her if it could be true. I think she screamed. What I remember for sure is, what I felt: rage and the old gravity of West Baltimore, the gravity that condemned me to the schools, the streets, the void. Prince Jones had made it

through, and still they had taken him. And even though I already knew that I would never believe any account that justified this taking, I sat down to read the story. There were very few details. He had been shot by a PG County officer, not in PG County, not even in D.C., but somewhere in Northern Virginia. Prince had been driving to see his fiancée. He was killed yards from her home. The only witness to the killing of Prince Jones was the killer himself. The officer claimed that Prince had tried to run him over with his jeep, and I knew that the prosecutors would believe him.

Days later, your mother and I packed you into the car, drove down to Washington, left you with your aunt Kamilah, and went to the service for Prince at Rankin Chapel on Howard's campus, where I'd once sat amazed at the parade of activists and intellectuals — Joseph Lowery, Cornel West, Calvin Butts — who preached at that pulpit. I must have seen a great number of old friends there, though I cannot recall precisely who. What I remember is all the people who spoke of Prince's religious zeal, his abiding belief that Jesus was with him. I remember watching the president of the university stand and weep. I remember Dr. Mabel Jones, Prince's mother, speaking of her son's death as a call to move from her comfortable suburban life into activism. I heard several people ask for forgiveness for the officer who'd shot Prince Jones down. I only vaguely recall my impressions of all this. But I know that I have always felt great distance from the grieving rituals of my people, and I must have felt it powerfully then. The need to forgive the officer would not have moved me, because even then, in some inchoate form, I knew that Prince was not killed by a single officer so much as he was murdered by his country and all the fears that have marked it from birth.

At this moment the phrase "police reform" has come into vogue, and the actions of our publicly appointed guardians have attracted attention presidential and pedestrian. You may have heard the talk of diversity, sensitivity training,

5

and body cameras. These are all fine and applicable, but they understate the task and allow the citizens of this country to pretend that there is real distance between their own attitudes and those of the ones appointed to protect them. The truth is that the police reflect America in all of its will and fear, and whatever we might make of this country's criminal justice policy, it cannot be said that it was imposed by a repressive minority. The abuses that have followed from these policies — the sprawling carceral state, the random detention of black people, the torture of suspects — are the product of democratic will. And so to challenge the police is to challenge the American people who send them into the ghettos armed with the same self-generated fears that compelled the people who think they are white to flee the cities and into the Dream. The problem with the police is not that they are fascist pigs but that our country is ruled by majoritarian pigs.

I knew some of this even then, sitting in Rankin Chapel, even if I could not yet express it. So forgiving the killer of Prince Jones would have seemed irrelevant to me. The killer was the direct expression of all his country's beliefs. And raised conscious, in rejection of a Christian God, I could see no higher purpose in Prince's death. I believed, and still do, that our bodies are

our selves, that my soul is the voltage conducted through neurons and nerves, and that my spirit is my flesh. Prince Jones was a one of one, and they had destroyed his body, scorched his shoulders and arms, ripped open his back, mangled lung, kidney, and liver. I sat there feeling myself a heretic, believing only in this one-shot life and the body. For the crime of destroying the body of Prince Jones, I did not believe in forgiveness. When the assembled mourners bowed their heads in prayer, I was divided from them because I believed that the void would not answer back.

Weeks wore on. Nauseating details slowly dribbled out. The officer was a known liar. A year earlier he had arrested a man on false evidence. Prosecutors had been forced to drop every case in which the officer was involved. The officer was demoted, restored, then put out on the street to continue his work. Now, through additional reports, a narrative began to take shape. The officer had been dressed like an undercover drug dealer. He'd been sent out to track a man whose build was five foot four and 250 pounds. We know from the coroner that Prince's body was six foot three and 211 pounds. We know that the other man was apprehended later. The charges against him were dropped. None of this mattered. We know that his superiors sent this

Andrew Burton/Getty Images

This photograph was taken at a march in support of Maryland state attorney Marilyn Mosby's announcement that charges would be filed against the Baltimore police officers involved in the death of Freddie Gray in 2015.
What is your response to the claim this banner makes? Do you think Coates would agree? Explain your answer with evidence from the reading.

officer to follow Prince from Maryland, through Washington, D.C., and into Virginia, where the officer shot Prince several times. We know that the officer confronted Prince with his gun drawn, and no badge. We know that the officer claims he shot because Prince tried to run him over with his jeep. We know that the authorities charged with investigating this shooting did very little to investigate the officer and did everything in their power to investigate Prince Jones. This investigation produced no information that would explain why Prince Jones would suddenly shift his ambitions from college to cop killing. This officer, given maximum power, bore minimum responsibility. He was charged with nothing. He was punished by no one. He was returned to his work.

There were times when I imagined myself, like Prince, tracked through many jurisdictions by a man in a criminal's costume. And I was horrified, because I knew what I would have done with such a man confronting me, gun drawn, mere feet from my own family's home. *Take care of my baby,* your grandmother had said, which was to say *Take care of your new family.* But I now knew the limits of my caring, the reach of its powers, etched by an enemy old as Virginia. I thought of all the beautiful black people I'd seen at The Mecca,[2] all their variation, all their hair, all their language, all their stories and geography, all their stunning humanity, and none of it could save them from the mark of plunder and the gravity of our particular world. And it occurred to me then that you would not escape, that there were awful men who'd laid plans for you, and I could not stop them. Prince Jones was the superlative of all my fears. And if he, good Christian, scion of a striving class, patron saint of the twice as good, could be forever bound, who then could not? And the plunder was not just of Prince alone. Think of all the love poured into him. Think of the tuitions for Montessori and

_____
[2]Coates's term for Howard University. —Eds.

music lessons. Think of the gasoline expended, the treads worn carting him to football games, basketball tournaments, and Little League. Think of the time spent regulating sleepovers. Think of the surprise birthday parties, the daycare, and the reference checks on babysitters. Think of *World Book* and *Childcraft.* Think of checks written for family photos. Think of credit cards charged for vacations. Think of soccer balls, science kits, chemistry sets, racetracks, and model trains. Think of all the embraces, all the private jokes, customs, greetings names, dreams, all the shared knowledge and capacity of a black family injected into that vessel of flesh and bone. And think of how that vessel was taken, shattered on the concrete, and all its holy contents, all that had gone into him, sent flowing back to the earth. Think of your mother who had no father. And your grandmother, who was abandoned by her father. And your grandfather, who was left behind by his father. And think of how Prince's daughter was now drafted into those solemn ranks and deprived of her birthright — that vessel which was her father, which brimmed with twenty-five years of love and was the investment of her grandparents and was to be her legacy.

Now at night, I held you and a great fear, wide as all our American generations, took me. Now I personally understood my father and the old mantra — "Either I can beat him or the police." I understood it all — the cable wires, the extension cords, the ritual switch. Black people love their children with a kind of obsession. You are all we have, and you come to us endangered. I think we would like to kill you ourselves before seeing you killed by the streets that America made. That is a philosophy of the disembodied, of a people who control nothing, who can protect nothing, who are made to fear not just the criminals among them but the police who lord over them with all the moral authority of a protection racket. It was only after you that I understood this love, that I understood the grip of my mother's hand. She knew that the galaxy itself could kill me, that all of me could be shattered and all of her legacy spilled upon the curb like bum wine. And no one would be brought to account for this destruction, because my death would not be the fault of any human but the fault of some unfortunate but immutable fact of "race," imposed upon an innocent country by the inscrutable judgment of invisible gods. The earthquake cannot be subpoenaed. The typhoon will not bend under indictment. They sent the killer of Prince Jones back to his work, because he was not a killer at all. He was a force of nature, the helpless agent of our world's physical laws.

This entire episode took me from fear to a rage that burned in me then, animates me now, and will likely leave me on fire for the rest of my days. I still had my journalism. My response was, in this moment, to write. I was lucky I had even that. Most of us are forced to drink our travesties straight and smile about it. I wrote about the history of the Prince George's County police. Nothing had ever felt so essential to me. Here is what I knew at the outset: The officer who killed Prince Jones was black. The politicians who empowered this officer to kill were black. Many of the black politicians, many of them twice as good, seemed unconcerned. How could this be? It was like I was back at Moorland[3] again, called by great mysteries. But by then I didn't need any call slips; the Internet had bloomed into an instrument of research. That must strike you as novel. For all of your life, whenever you've had a question you have been able to type that question out on a keyboard, watch it appear in a rectangular space bordered by a corporate logo, and within seconds revel in the flood of potential answers. But I still remember when typewriters were useful, the dawn of the Commodore 64, and days when a song you loved would have its moment on the radio and then disappear into

the nothing. I must have gone five years without hearing the Mary Jane Girls sing "All Night Long." For a young man like me, the invention of the Internet was the invention of space travel.

My curiosity, in the case of Prince Jones, opened a world of newspaper clippings, histories, and sociologies. I called politicians and questioned them. I was told that the citizens were more likely to ask for police support than to complain about brutality. I was told that the black citizens of PG County were comfortable and had "a certain impatience" with crime. I had seen these theories before, back when I was researching in Moorland, leafing through the various fights within and without the black community. I knew that these were theories, even in the mouths of black people, that justified the jails springing up around me, that argued for ghettos and projects, that viewed the destruction of the black body as incidental to the preservation of order. According to this theory "safety" was a higher value than justice, perhaps the highest value. I understood. What I would not have given, back in Baltimore, for a line of officers, agents of my country and my community, patrolling my route to school! There were no such officers, and whenever I saw the police it meant that something had already gone wrong. All along I knew that there were some, those who lived in the Dream, for whom the conversation was different. Their "safety" was in schools, portfolios, and skyscrapers. Ours was in men with guns who could only view us with the same contempt as the society that sent them.

And the lack of safety cannot help but constrain your sense of the galaxy. It never occurred to me, for instance, that I could, or should even want to, live in New York. I did love Baltimore. I loved Charlie Rudo's and the sidewalk sales at Mondawmin. I loved sitting out on the porch with your uncle Damani waiting for Frank Ski to play "Fresh Is the Word." I always thought I was destined to go back home after college — but not simply because I loved home but because

10

---

[3]Moorland-Spingarn Research Center at Howard University. —Eds.

Nate Beeler, The Columbus Dispatch/Cagle Cartoons, Inc.

This cartoon by Nate Beeler appeared in the Columbus Dispatch on July 8, 2016, the day after a shooter killed five Dallas police officers in an attack that also left nine other officers and two bystanders wounded. **How does Beeler express his position in this cartoon? How does it compare to Coates's position in this excerpt from *Between the World and Me*?**

I could not imagine much else for myself. And that stunted imagination is something I owe to my chains. And yet some of us really do see more.

I met many of them at The Mecca — like your uncle Ben, who was raised in New York, which forced him to understand himself as an African American navigating among Haitians, Jamaicans, Hasidic Jews, and Italians. And there were others like him, others who, having gotten a boost from a teacher, an aunt, an older brother, had peered over the wall as children, and as adults became set on seeing the full view. These black people felt, as did I, that their bodies could be snatched back at a whim, but this set in them a different kind of fear that propelled them out into the cosmos. They spent semesters abroad. I never knew what they did or why. But perhaps I always sensed I was going down too easy. Perhaps that explains every girl I've ever loved, because every girl I've ever loved was a bridge to somewhere else. Your mother, who knew so much more of the world than me, fell in love with New York through culture, through *Crossing Delancey, Breakfast at Tiffany's, Working Girl,* Nas, and Wu-Tang. Your mother secured a job, and I

followed, stowed away almost, because no one in New York, at that time, was paying for me to write much of anything. What little I did make, reviewing an album or a book, covered approximately two electric bills every year.

We arrived two months before September 11, 2001. I suppose everyone who was in New York that day has a story. Here is mine: That evening, I stood on the roof of an apartment building with your mother, your aunt Chana, and her boyfriend, Jamal. So we were there on the roof, talking and taking in the sight — great plumes of smoke covered Manhattan Island. Everyone knew someone who knew someone who was missing. But looking out upon the ruins of America, my heart was cold. I had disasters all my own. The officer who killed Prince Jones, like all the officers who regard us so warily, was the sword of the American citizenry. I would never consider any American citizen pure. I was out of sync with the city. I kept thinking about how southern Manhattan had always been Ground Zero for us. They auctioned our bodies down there, in that same devastated, and rightly named, financial district. And there was once a burial ground for the auctioned there. They built

Scott Olson/Getty Images

What message does this image of a protester, whose mouth is covered with a strip of tape that reads "#BLACKLIVESMATTER," send? How does that message relate to Coates's narrative?

a department store over part of it and then tried to erect a government building over another part. Only a community of right-thinking black people stopped them. I had not formed any of this into a coherent theory. But I did know that Bin Laden was not the first man to bring terror to that section of the city. I never forgot that. Neither should you. In the days after, I watched the ridiculous pageantry of flags, the machismo of firemen, the overwrought slogans. Damn it all. Prince Jones was dead. And hell upon those who tell us to be twice as good and shoot us no matter. Hell for ancestral fear that put black parents under terror. And hell upon those who shatter the holy vessel.

I could see no difference between the officer who killed Prince Jones and the police who died, or the firefighters who died. They were not human to me. Black, white, or whatever, they were the menaces of nature; they were the fire, the comet, the storm, which could — with no justification — shatter my body.

I saw Prince Jones, one last time, alive and whole. He was standing in front of me. We were in a museum. I felt in that moment that his death had just been an awful dream. No, a premonition. But I had a chance. I would warn him. I walked

over, gave him a pound, and felt that heat of the spectrum, the warmth of The Mecca. I wanted to tell him something. I wanted to say — Beware the plunderer. But when I opened my mouth, he just shook his head and walked away.

◆ ◆ ◆

We lived in a basement apartment in Brooklyn, which I doubt you remember, down the street from Uncle Ben and his wife, your aunt Janai. These were not great times. I remember borrowing two hundred dollars from Ben, and it feeling like a million. I remember your grandfather coming to New York, taking me out for Ethiopian, after which I walked him to the West Fourth Street subway station. We said our goodbyes and walked away. He called me back. He had forgotten something. He handed me a check for $120. I tell you this because you must understand, no matter the point of our talk, that I didn't always have things, but I had people — *I always had people*. I had a mother and father who I would match against any other. I had a brother who looked out for me all through college. I had The Mecca that directed me. I had friends who would leap in front of a bus for me. You need to know that I was

15

loved, that whatever my lack of religious feeling, I have always loved my people and that broad love is directly related to the specific love I feel for you. I remember sitting out on Ben's stoop on Friday nights, drinking Jack Daniel's, debating the mayor's race or the rush to war. My weeks felt aimless. I pitched to various magazines with no success. Your aunt Chana lent me another two hundred dollars; I burned it all on a scam bartending school. I delivered food for a small deli in Park Slope. In New York, everyone wanted to know your occupation. I told people that I was "trying to be a writer."

Some days I would take the train into Manhattan. There was so much money everywhere, money flowing out of bistros and cafés, money pushing the people, at incredible speeds, up the wide avenues, money drawing intergalactic traffic through Times Square, money in the limestones and brownstones, money out on West Broadway where white people spilled out of wine bars with sloshing glasses and without police. I would see these people at the club, drunken, laughing, challenging breakdancers to battles. They would be destroyed and humiliated in these battles. But afterward they would give dap, laugh, order more beers. They were utterly fearless. I did not understand it until I looked out on the street. That was where I saw white parents pushing double-wide strollers down gentrifying Harlem boulevards in T-shirts and jogging shorts. Or I saw them lost in conversation with each other, mother and father, while their sons commanded entire sidewalks with their tricycles. The galaxy belonged to them, and as terror was communicated to our children, I saw mastery communicated to theirs.

And so when I remember pushing you in your stroller to other parts of the city, the West Village for instance, almost instinctively believing that you should see more, I remember feeling ill at ease, like I had borrowed someone else's heirloom, like I was traveling under an assumed name. All this time you were growing into words and feelings; my beautiful brown boy, who would soon come into the knowledge, who would soon comprehend the edicts of his galaxy, and all the extinction-level events that regarded you with a singular and discriminating interest.

You would be a man one day, and I could not save you from the unbridgeable distance between you and your future peers and colleagues, who might try to convince you that everything I know, all the things I'm sharing with you here, are an illusion, or a fact of a distant past that need not be discussed. And I could not save you from the police, from their flashlights, their hands, their nightsticks, their guns. Prince Jones, murdered by the men who should have been his security guards, is always with me, and I knew that soon he would be with you.

In those days I would come out of the house, turn onto Flatbush Avenue, and my face would tighten like a Mexican wrestler's mask, my eyes would dart from corner to corner, my arms loose, limber, and ready. This need to be always on guard was an unmeasured expenditure of energy, the slow siphoning of the essence. It contributed to the fast breakdown of our bodies. So I feared not just the violence of this world but the rules designed to protect you from it, the rules that would have you contort your body to address the block, and contort again to be taken seriously by colleagues, and contort again so as not to give the police a reason. All my life I'd heard people tell their black boys and black girls to "be twice as good," which is to say "accept half as much." These words would be spoken with a veneer of religious nobility, as though they evidenced some unspoken quality, some undetected courage, when in fact all they evidenced was the gun to our head and the hand in our pocket. This is how we lose our softness. This is how they steal our right to smile. No one told those little white children, with their tricycles, to be twice as good. I imagined their parents telling them

20

▼
_____

This photograph shows a woman facing a line of Baltimore police officers in riot gear during the protests that followed the funeral of Freddie Gray, who died from injuries he received in police custody in 2015.

How does the rhetoric of this image convey a message?

Chip Somodevilla/Getty Images

to take twice as much. It seemed to me that our own rules redoubled plunder. It struck me that perhaps the defining feature of being drafted into the black race was the inescapable robbery of time, because the moments we spent readying the mask, or readying ourselves to accept half as much, could not be recovered. The robbery of time is not measured in lifespans but in moments. It is the last bottle of wine that you have just uncorked but do not have time to drink. It is the kiss that you do not have time to share, before she walks out of your life. It is the raft of second chances for them, and twenty-three-hour days for us. . . .

❖ ❖ ❖

I did not want to raise you in fear or false memory. I did not want you forced to mask your joys and bind your eyes. What I wanted for you was to grow into consciousness. I resolved to hide nothing from you.

Do you remember when I first took you to work, when you were thirteen? I was going to see the mother of a dead black boy. The boy had exchanged hard words with a white man and been killed, because he refused to turn down his music. The killer, having emptied his gun, drove his girlfriend to a hotel. They had drinks. They ordered a pizza. And then the next day, at his leisure, the man turned himself in. The man claimed to have seen a shotgun. He claimed to have been in fear for his life and to only have triumphed through righteous violence. "I was the victim and the victor," he asserted, much as generations of American plunderers had asserted before. No shotgun was ever found. The claim still influenced the jury, and the killer was convicted not of the boy's murder but of firing

seeing connections

This mural of Trayvon Martin — a black teenager shot and killed in Florida in 2013 — is located in the Baltimore neighborhood where twenty-five-year-old Freddie Gray was arrested in 2015. Gray died from injuries he received while in police custody, and protests erupted across America as a result. While six police officers were eventually charged with crimes related to Gray's death, none was found guilty. One officer's trial was declared a mistrial, three other officers were found not guilty, and all remaining charges were later dropped. George Zimmerman, who shot Martin, was also tried and acquitted for murder. The hoodie that Martin was wearing at the time of his death became a rallying symbol for those protesting racial profiling and police brutality from that time forward.

Look closely at this mural, and then answer the following questions.

1. **What stands out about the artist's use of color and scale? What effect do those choices have?**

2. **How would you characterize the rhetorical situation of this mural? Why do you think the artist chose to portray Trayvon Martin?**

3. **Compare the rhetorical situation of this image to that of *Between the World and Me*. What differences do you see, and how are those reflected in the rhetoric of each?**

Andrew Burton/Getty Images

Scott Olson/Getty Images

This photograph was taken at a 2017 protest against the acquittal of St. Louis police officer Jason Stockley. He had been charged with first-degree murder for the shooting of Anthony Lamar Smith while on duty in 2011. Evidence in the case suggested that Stockley had planted a gun in Smith's car.

What answer might Coates give to the young man holding the sign in this photo? Support your response with details from the reading.

repeatedly as the boy's friends tried to retreat. Destroying the black body was permissible — but it would be better to do it efficiently.

The mother of this murdered black boy was then taking her case before journalists and writers. We met her in the lobby of her Times Square hotel. She was medium height with brown skin and hair down to her shoulders. It had not even been a week since the verdict. But she was composed and wholly self-possessed. She did not rage at the killer but wondered aloud if the rules she'd imparted had been enough. She had wanted her son to stand for what he believed and to be respectful. And he had died for believing his friends had a right to play their music loud, to be American teenagers. Still, she was left wondering. "In my mind I keep saying, 'Had he not spoke back, spoke up, would he still be here?'"

She would not forget the uniqueness of her son, his singular life. She would not forget that he had a father who loved him, who took him in while she battled cancer. She would not forget that he was the life of the party, that he always had new friends for her to shuttle around in her minivan. And she would have him live on in her work. I told her the verdict angered me. I told her that the idea that someone on that jury thought it plausible there was a gun in the car baffled the mind. She said that she was baffled too, and that I should not mistake her calm probing for the absence of anger. But God had focused her anger away from revenge and toward redemption, she said. God had spoken to her and committed her to a new activism. Then the mother of the murdered boy rose, turned to you, and said, "You exist. You matter. You have value. You have every right to wear your hoodie, to play your music as loud as you want. You have every right to be you. And no one should deter you from being you. You have to be you. And you can never be afraid to be you."

I was glad she said this. I have tried to say the same to you, and if I have not said it with the same direction and clarity, I confess that is because I am afraid. And I have no God to hold me up. And I believe that when they shatter the body they shatter everything, and I knew that all of us — Christians, Muslims, atheists — lived in this fear of this truth. Disembodiment is a kind of terrorism, and the threat of it alters the orbit of all our lives and, like terrorism, this distortion is intentional. Disembodiment. The dragon that compelled the boys I knew, way back, into extravagant theater of ownership. Disembodiment. The

25

demon that pushed the middle-class black survivors into aggressive passivity, our conversation restrained in public quarters, our best manners on display, our hands never out of pockets, our whole manner ordered as if to say, "I make no sudden moves." Disembodiment. The serpent of school years, demanding I be twice as good, though I was but a boy. Murder was all around us and we knew, deep in ourselves, in some silent space, that the author of these murders was beyond us, that it suited some other person's ends. We were right.

◆ ◆ ◆

Here is how I take the measure of my progress in life: I imagine myself as I was, back there in West Baltimore, dodging North and Pulaski, ducking Murphy Homes, fearful of the schools and the streets, and I imagine showing that lost boy a portrait of my present life and asking him what he would make of it. Only once — in the two years after your birth, in the first two rounds of the fight of my life — have I believed he would have been disappointed. I write you at the precipice of my fortieth year, having come to a point in my life — not of great prominence — but far beyond anything that boy could have even imagined. I did not master the streets, because I could not read the body language quick enough. I did not master the schools, because I could not see where any of it could possibly lead. But I did not fall. I have my family. I have my work. I no longer feel it necessary to hang my head at parties and tell people that I am "trying to be a writer." And godless though I am, the fact of being human, the fact of possessing the gift of study, and thus being remarkable among all the matter floating through the cosmos, still awes me.

I have spent much of my studies searching for the right question by which I might fully understand the breach between the world and me. I have not spent my time studying the problem of "race" — "race" itself is just a restatement and retrenchment of the problem. You see this from time to time when some dullard — usually believing himself white — proposes that the way forward is a grand orgy of black and white, ending only when we are all beige and thus the same "race." But a great number of "black" people already are beige. And the history of civilization is littered with dead "races" (Frankish, Italian, German, Irish) later abandoned because they no longer serve their purpose — the organization of people beneath, and beyond, the umbrella of rights.

If my life ended today, I would tell you it was a happy life — that I drew great joy from the study, from the struggle toward which I now urge you. You have seen in this conversation that the struggle has ruptured and remade me several times over — in Baltimore, at The Mecca, in fatherhood, in New York. The changes have awarded me a rapture that comes only when you can no longer be lied to, when you have rejected the Dream. But even more, the changes have taught me how to best exploit that singular gift of study, to question what I see, then to question what I see after that, because the questions matter as much, perhaps more than, the answers....

◆ ◆ ◆

I did not die in my aimless youth. I did not perish   30 in the agony of not knowing. I was not jailed. I had proven to myself that there was another way beyond the schools and the streets. I felt myself to be among the survivors of some great natural disaster, some plague, some avalanche or earthquake. And now, living in the wake of a decimation and having arrived at a land that I once considered mythical, everything seemed cast in a halo — the pastel Parisian scarves burned brighter, the morning odor wafting out of the boulangeries was hypnotic, and the language all around me struck me not so much as language but as dance.

seeing connections

Coates was influenced by *The Fire Next Time*, a book James Baldwin wrote in 1963 that opens with a letter to his fifteen-year-old nephew. In the opening pages, Baldwin offers advice to the young man about how to navigate a world that challenges his worth, urging his nephew to call on his own dignity and power as a human being to help "make America what it must become."

After reading the following excerpt from *The Fire Next Time* carefully, compare and contrast Baldwin's advice to his nephew with that of Coates to his son.

from The Fire Next Time

JAMES BALDWIN

Please try to be clear... about the reality which lies behind the words *acceptance* and *integration*. There is no reason for you to try to become like white people and there is no basis whatever for their impertinent assumption that *they* must accept *you*. The really terrible thing, old buddy, is that *you* must accept *them*. And I mean that very seriously. You must accept them and accept them with love. For these innocent people have no other hope. They are, in effect, still trapped in a history which they do not understand; and until they understand it, they cannot be released from it. They have had to believe for many years, and for innumerable reasons, that black men are inferior to white men. Many of them, indeed, know better, but, as you will discover, people find it very difficult to act on what they know. To act is to be committed, and to be committed is to be in danger. In this case, the danger, in the minds of most white Americans, is the loss of their identity. Try to imagine how you would feel if you woke up one morning to find the sun shining and all the stars aflame. You would be frightened because it is out of the order of nature. Any upheaval in the universe is terrifying because it so profoundly attacks one's sense of one's own reality. Well, the black man has functioned in the white man's world as a fixed star, as an immovable pillar: and as he moves out of his place, heaven and earth are shaken to their foundations.... And if the word *integration* means any-thing,... it means: that we, with love, shall force our brothers to see themselves as they are, to cease fleeing from reality and begin to change it.

Your route will be different. It must be. You knew things at eleven that I did not know when I was twenty-five. When I was eleven my highest priority was the simple security of my body. My life was the immediate negotiation of violence — within my house and without. But already you have expectations, I see that in you. Survival and safety are not enough.

Your hopes — your dreams, if you will — leave me with an array of warring emotions. I am so very proud of you — your openness, your ambition, your aggression, your intelligence. My job, in the little time we have left together, is to match that intelligence with wisdom. Part of that wisdom is understanding what you were given — a city where gay bars are unremarkable, a soccer team on which half the players speak some other language. What I am saying is that it does not all belong to you, that the beauty in you is not strictly yours and is largely the result of enjoying an abnormal amount of security in your black body.

Perhaps that is why, when you discovered that the killer of Mike Brown would go unpunished, you told me you had to go. Perhaps that is why you were crying, because in that moment you understood that even your relatively privileged security can never match a sustained assault launched in the name of the Dream. Our current politics tell you that should you fall victim to such an assault and lose your body, it somehow must be your fault. Trayvon Martin's hoodie got him killed. Jordan Davis's loud music did the same. John Crawford should never have touched the rifle on display. Kajieme Powell should have known not to be crazy. And all of them should have had fathers — even the ones who had fathers, even you. Without its own justifications, the Dream would collapse upon itself. You first learned this from Michael Brown. I first learned it from Prince Jones.

Michael Brown did not die as so many of his defenders supposed. And still the questions behind the questions are never asked. Should assaulting an officer of the state be a capital offense, rendered without trial, with the officer as judge and executioner? Is that what we wish civilization to be? And all the time the Dreamers are pillaging Ferguson for municipal governance. And they are torturing Muslims, and their drones are bombing wedding parties (by accident!), and the Dreamers are quoting Martin Luther King and exulting nonviolence for the weak and the biggest guns for the strong. Each time a police officer engages us, death, injury, maiming is possible. It is not enough to say that this is true of anyone or more true of criminals. The moment the officers began their pursuit of Prince Jones, his life was in danger. The Dreamers accept this as the cost of doing business, accept our bodies as currency, because it is their tradition. As slaves we were this country's first windfall, the down payment on its freedom. After the ruin and liberation of the Civil War came Redemption for the unrepentant South and Reunion, and our bodies became this country's second mortgage. In the New Deal[4] we were their guestroom, their finished basement. And today, with a sprawling prison system, which has turned the warehousing of black bodies into a jobs program for Dreamers and a lucrative investment for Dreamers; today, when 8 percent of the world's prisoners are black men, our bodies have refinanced the Dream of being white. Black life is cheap, but in America black bodies are a natural resource of incomparable value.

[2015]

---

[4]A reference to the discriminatory housing practices codified by the Federal Housing Administration and Home Owners Loan Corporation during the Great Depression. —Eds.

QUESTIONS FOR DISCUSSION

1. Ta-Nehisi Coates begins with a scene where the police stop him in his car. How does he build suspense in this opening paragraph? Specifically, how does he blend what is happening to him externally and what is going through his mind? What makes this strategy effective?

2. In paragraph 5, Coates comments on the concept of "'police reform'" — which he places in quotes. What is his assessment of its value? To what extent might such an appraisal alienate his readers? Why might he be willing to take that chance?

3. What exactly is Coates's worst fear? How does that fear motivate him to write this letter to his son? What does he mean when, speaking of African American children, he writes, "You are all we have, and you come to us endangered" (para. 9)?

4. What does Howard University mean to Coates? How does it become his "Mecca"?

5. How does Coates describe his response to the 9/11 terrorist attacks? What does he mean when he writes, "I was out of sync with the city. I kept thinking about how southern Manhattan had always been Ground Zero for us" (para. 14)?

6. What dimensions of his personality and experience prior to fatherhood does Coates reveal to his son? Why do you think he reminds his son, "I didn't always have things, but I had people — *I always had people*" (para. 17)? What is Coates's larger point here?

7. In paragraph 21, Coates says, "It struck me that perhaps the defining feature of being drafted into the black race was the inescapable robbery of time, because the moments we spent readying the mask, or readying ourselves to accept half as much, could not be recovered. The robbery of time is not measured in lifespans but in moments." How do you interpret this statement? How does it relate to the advice (and warnings) Coates offers to his son elsewhere in the excerpt?

8. What does Coates mean by "the gift of study" (para. 27)? In what ways does it become a lifeline for him?

9. What role does Prince Carmen Jones play in Coates's argument? Who was he as an individual? What larger meaning does his life and death take on for Coates in this excerpt?

10. Coates brings up religion in several passages — to explain, for instance, that he has "no God to hold me up" (para. 26) and, thus, cannot feel the solace of religion that others around him do. Why does Coates take this position? What is it about organized religion that he cannot accept?

11. What does Coates mean by "the Dream" and the "Dreamers" in this excerpt from *Between the World and Me*? To what extent do you think he is using the term ironically?

12. Coates and his wife named their son Samori, after Samori Touré, the nineteenth-century Islamic ruler who resisted French colonial rule in West Africa. What do you think this name suggests about Coates's stance on the responsibilities of parenthood? What historical narrative does this name bring to his son? You might do some research into Touré to develop your response.

13. Coates has been criticized for offering an unyieldingly bleak view of the future for his son. Do you agree with this critique of his message? If so, to what extent do you believe his purpose and message are out of sync? If not, what details from this excerpt challenge the assessment of his writing as relentlessly grim? How would you respond to a similar letter from a parent or elder written to you in a similar tone or conveying a similar message?

QUESTIONS ON RHETORIC AND STYLE

1. What is the rhetorical situation of this letter? Consider the context of a father writing to his teenage son, but then also consider that this letter is not a traditional letter: it is a book-length work that Coates wrote with the intention of publishing, and it is therefore a public document. To what extent are these aspects of the context at odds with each other?

2. How might Coates's reflections on Prince Jones in paragraph 8 be read as a kind of eulogy for his friend? Pay close attention to the language, especially parallel structure and the cadence of Coates's sentences, in your response.

3. Coates describes interviewing an unnamed mother of a "murdered black boy ... taking her case before journalists and writers" (para. 24), a scene that he had taken his then-thirteen-year-old son to witness. What is the impact of recounting this scene in the letter?

4. What effect does Coates's use of figurative language have on the emotional appeal of his argument? Consider at least four examples. For instance, "The earthquake cannot be subpoenaed. The typhoon will not bend under indictment" (para. 9).

5. A master wordsmith, Coates often chooses language with unexpected or unusually precise meaning. He uses the term "galaxy" in paragraph 9, for instance, instead of "world" or even "universe." Why? Trace the use of the words "galaxy," "gravity," and "plunder," throughout the text and discuss how those particular choices serve the purpose of the argument Coates makes.

6. Note how Coates addresses the passage of time throughout this excerpt, indicating multiple shifts with phrases such as "Shortly before you were born" (para. 1), "Days later" (para. 4), "At this moment" (para. 5), "Weeks wore on" (para. 7), and "In those days" (para. 21). What is the effect of continually shifting between present, immediate past, and distant past? How do these structural shifts serve Coates's purpose?

7. Some critics have argued that although *Between the World and Me* is a direct address to his son, Coates is actually crafting his message for a wider (mostly white) audience, as his position would likely be familiar to his family and to other African Americans. Based on this excerpt, who do you think is the audience for *Between the World and Me*? Consider how Coates establishes his ethos, and support your response with specific reference to the text.

8. In the final paragraph, Coates describes the black body as a "natural resource" in America (para. 33). Why do you think he does this? What point is he making? To what extent does this rhetorical strategy help him achieve his purpose?

9. Although Coates is developing a strong and logical argument, he primarily structures it as a narrative, or story. Why do you think this rhetorical strategy is or is not effective?

10. One reviewer described Coates's style as "a departure from the rhetoric of the civil rights movement, or at least the civil rights movement that has been sanitized and commercialized for mass consumption. Because of these departures, Coates's hope feels stark and brutal." Do you agree or disagree with this characterization of his rhetoric? Explain with specific reference to the text.

SUGGESTIONS FOR WRITING

1. Elsewhere in *Between the World and Me,* Coates writes, "Race is the child of racism, not the father." Defend, challenge, or qualify that assertion, using details from this excerpt to support your position.

2. In paragraph 28, Coates tells his son, "I have spent much of my studies searching for the right question by which I might fully understand the breach between the world and me. I have not spent my time studying the problem of 'race' — 'race' itself is just a restatement and retrenchment of the problem." To what extent do you agree with Coates's claim that race "is just a restatement and retrenchment of the problem"? Be sure to support your response with evidence from Coates's writing, personal experience, historical knowledge, and/or analysis of current events.

3. Throughout this text, Coates refers to the "body" and "disembodiment." Trace his discussion of the concept of the body throughout the excerpt, then write an essay explaining how he uses the black body to convey the vulnerability of and challenge to full citizenship, even humanity, of African Americans today. As you develop your response, consider Coates's assertion that "I believed, and still do, that our bodies are our selves, that my soul is the voltage conducted through neurons and nerves, and that my spirit is my flesh" (para. 6). Coates takes the title for his book from the poem "Between the World and Me" by Richard Wright. After reading and analyzing the poem, write an essay explaining why you believe Coates chose that phrase. Would you call it an inspiration, an echo, a reminder, a dare, or something else? How well does it suit Coates's overall argument?

4. In a 2015 interview for *Rolling Stone*, Coates commented that his idea of "the Dream" in *Between the World and Me* is "subverting the notion of the American Dream, subverting Martin Luther King's rendition of 'I Have a Dream.'" In fact, King's famous statement — "The arc of the moral universe is long, but it bends toward justice" — is both echoed and challenged by Coates in an earlier section of *Between the World and Me*, in which he describes his teenage years: "My understanding of the universe was physical, and its moral arc bent toward chaos, then concluded in a box." Write an imagined conversation between Coates and King about race in America today. Include in your conversation what you believe might have been King's response to the excerpt from Coates's book.

5. Many have responded to *Between the World and Me* by criticizing its lack of hopefulness and its pessimism about the future. Melvin Rogers, a professor of African American Studies and Political Science at the University of California, Los Angeles, wrote a review of the book that expressed his concern with the fact that "Coates cannot even tell [his son] it may be okay." Rogers goes on to assert that "the reason why you can't say there isn't hope is not because you are living in a dream or selling a fantasy but because there can be no certain knowledge of the future. Humility, borne of our ignorance of the future, justifies hope." Write an essay supporting, challenging, or qualifying the logic of this assertion. Refer to Coates as well as to your own experience and knowledge as you develop your position.

6. Letters of advice to a younger generation is a practice beyond Baldwin and Coates. Research other examples of it, such as *The Measure of Our Success: A Letter to My Children and Yours* by Marian Wright Edelman (1992), *Letters to a Young Brother: Manifest Your Destiny* by Hill Harper (2007), *Letters to a Young Muslim* by Omar Saif Ghobash (2016), and *Dear Ijeawele, or A Feminist Manifesto in Fifteen Suggestions* by Chimamanda Ngozi Adichie (2017). Using one of these or Coates as your model, write a letter to a person in your family or community at least five years younger than you, offering advice on an issue — political, environmental, personal, economic, educational, religious — that you believe is important to his or her future.

On the Duty of Civil Disobedience

HENRY DAVID THOREAU

Henry David Thoreau (1817–1862) was a philosopher, poet, essayist, and naturalist as well as an outspoken social critic. He was born in Concord, Massachusetts, and was educated at Harvard. He worked in a variety of professions, from land surveyor to teacher to pencil maker. Strongly influenced by his neighbor and friend Ralph Waldo Emerson, Thoreau considered himself a fierce patriot who honored his country and its ideals, if not always its government. He spoke out against the Mexican-American War and slavery — specifically the Fugitive Slave Act — and he defended the abolitionist John Brown. He is best known for *Walden; or, Life in the Woods*, published in 1854, which is his account of living in a cabin on Walden Pond for two years. Originally delivered as a lecture, "On the Duty of Civil Disobedience" is Thoreau's response to his arrest and incarceration for not paying a poll tax. Its influence has been enormous, deeply affecting such twentieth-century figures as Mahatma Gandhi and Martin Luther King Jr.

Library of Congress

I heartily accept the motto, — "That government is best which governs least"; and I should like to see it acted up to more rapidly and systematically. Carried out, it finally amounts to this, which I also believe, — "That government is best which governs not at all"; and when men are prepared for it, that will be the kind of government which they will have. Government is at best but an expedient; but most governments are usually, and all governments are sometimes, inexpedient. The objections which have been brought against a standing army, and they are many and weighty, and deserve to prevail, may also at last be brought against a standing government. The standing army is only an arm of the standing government. The government itself, which is only the mode which the people have chosen to execute their will, is equally liable to be abused and perverted before the people can act through it. Witness the present Mexican war, the work of comparatively a few individuals using the standing government as their tool; for, in the outset, the people would not have consented to this measure.

This American government, — what is it but a tradition, though a recent one, endeavoring to transmit itself unimpaired to posterity, but each instant losing some of its integrity? It has not the vitality and force of a single living man; for a single man can bend it to his will. It is a sort of wooden gun to the people themselves. But it is not the less necessary for this; for the people must have some complicated machinery or other, and hear its din, to satisfy that idea of government which they have. Governments show thus how successfully men can be imposed on, even impose on themselves, for their own advantage. It is excellent, we must all allow. Yet this government never of itself furthered any enterprise, but by the alacrity with which it got out of its way. *It* does not keep the country free. *It* does not settle the West. *It* does not educate. The character inherent in the American people has done all that has been accomplished; and it would have done somewhat more, if the government had not sometimes got in its way. For government is an expedient by which men would fain succeed in letting one another alone; and, as has been said, when it is most expedient, the governed are most let alone by it. Trade and commerce, if they were not made of India-rubber, would never manage to bounce over the obstacles which legislators are continually putting in their way; and, if one were to judge these men wholly by the effects of their actions and not partly by their intentions, they would deserve to be classed and punished with those mischievous persons who put obstructions on railroads.

But, to speak practically and as a citizen, unlike those who call themselves no-government men, I ask for, not at once no government, but *at once* a better government. Let every man make known what kind of government would command his respect, and that will be one step toward obtaining it.

After all, the practical reason why, when the power is once in the hands of the people, a majority are permitted, and for a long period continue, to rule, is not because they are most likely to be in the right, nor because this seems fairest to the minority, but because they are physically the strongest. But a government in which the majority rule in all cases cannot be based on justice, even as far as men understand it. Can there not be a government in which majorities do not virtually decide right and wrong, but conscience? — in which majorities decide only those questions to which the rule of expediency is applicable? Must the citizen ever for a moment, or in the least degree, resign his conscience to the legislator? Why has every man a conscience, then? I think that we should be men first, and subjects afterward. It is not desirable to cultivate a respect for the law, so much as for the right. The only obligation which I have the right to assume, is to do at any time what I think right. It is truly enough said, that a corporation has no conscience; but a corporation of conscientious men is a corporation *with* a conscience. Law never made men a whit more just; and, by means

◀

What aspects of "On the Duty of Civil Disobedience" does this cartoon poke fun at? Do you think it's funny? Explain why or why not.

"If you start granting amnesty to people for following their conscience, pretty soon <u>everyone</u> will be following his conscience."

of their respect for it, even the well-disposed are daily made the agents of injustice. A common and natural result of an undue respect for law is, that you may see a file of soldiers, colonel, captain, corporal, privates, powder-monkeys, and all, marching in admirable order over hill and dale to the wars, against their wills, ay, against their common sense and consciences, which makes it very steep marching indeed, and produces a palpitation of the heart. They have no doubt that it is a damnable business in which they are concerned; they are all peaceably inclined. Now, what are they? Men at all? or small movable forts and magazines, at the service of some unscrupulous man in power? Visit the Navy-Yard, and behold a marine, such a man as an American government can make, or such as it can make a man with its black arts, — a mere shadow and reminiscence of humanity, a man laid out alive and standing, and already, as one may say, buried under arms with funeral accompaniments, though it may be, —

> Not a drum was heard, not a funeral note,
> As his corse to the rampart we hurried;
> Not a soldier discharged his farewell shot
> O'er the grave where our hero we buried.[1]

The mass of men serve the state thus, not as 5 men mainly, but as machines, with their bodies. They are the standing army, and the militia, jailers, constables, posse comitatus, &c. In most cases there is no free exercise whatever of the judgment or of the moral sense; but they put themselves on a level with wood and earth and stones; and wooden men can perhaps be manufactured that will serve the purpose as well. Such command no more respect than men of straw or a lump of dirt. They have the same sort of worth only as horses and dogs. Yet such as these even are commonly esteemed good citizens. Others, — as most legislators, politicians, lawyers, ministers, and office-holders, — serve the state chiefly with their heads; and, as they rarely make any moral distinctions, they are as likely to serve the Devil, without *intending* it, as God. A very few, as heroes, patriots, martyrs, reformers in the great sense, and *men*, serve the state with their consciences also, and so necessarily resist it for the most part; and they are commonly treated as enemies by it. A wise man will only be useful as a man, and will not submit to be "clay," and "stop a hole to keep the wind away,"[2] but leave that office to his dust at least: —

> I am too high-born to be propertied,
> To be a secondary at control,
> Or useful serving-man and instrument
> To any sovereign state throughout the world.[3]

He who gives himself entirely to his fellow-men appears to them useless and selfish; but he who gives himself partially to them is pronounced a benefactor and philanthropist.

How does it become a man to behave toward this American government today? I answer, that he cannot without disgrace be associated with it. I cannot for an instant recognize that political organization as *my* government which is the *slave's* government also.

All men recognize the right of revolution; that is, the right to refuse allegiance to, and to resist, the government, when its tyranny or its inefficiency are great and unendurable. But almost all say that such is not the case now. But such was the case, they think, in the Revolution of '75. If one were to tell me that this was a bad government because it taxed certain foreign commodities brought to its ports, it is most probable that I should not make an ado about it, for I can do without them. All machines have their friction; and possibly this does enough good to counterbalance the evil. At any rate, it is a great evil to make a stir about it. But when the friction comes to have its machine, and oppression and robbery are organized, I say, let us not have such a

---

[1] From an early nineteenth-century song. —Eds.

[2] Hamlet 5.1.236–237. —Eds.
[3] King John 5.1.79–82. —Eds.

machine any longer. In other words, when a sixth of the population of a nation which has undertaken to be the refuge of liberty are slaves, and a whole country is unjustly overrun and conquered by a foreign army, and subjected to military law, I think that it is not too soon for honest men to rebel and revolutionize. What makes this duty the more urgent is the fact, that the country so overrun is not our own, but ours is the invading army.

[William] Paley, a common authority with many on moral questions, in his chapter on the "Duty of Submission to Civil Government," resolves all civil obligation into expediency; and he proceeds to say, "that so long as the interest of the whole society requires it, that is, so long as the established government cannot be resisted or changed without public inconveniency, it is the will of God that the established government be obeyed, and no longer." — "This principle being admitted, the justice of every particular case of resistance is reduced to a computation of the quantity of the danger and grievance on the one side, and of the probability and expense of redressing it on the other." Of this, he says, every man shall judge for himself. But Paley appears never to have contemplated those cases to which the rule of expediency does not apply, in which a people, as well as an individual, must do justice, cost what it may. If I have unjustly wrested a plank from a drowning man, I must restore it to him though I drown myself. This, according to Paley, would be inconvenient. But he that would save his life, in such a case, shall lose it. This people must cease to hold slaves, and to make war on Mexico, though it cost them their existence as a people.

In their practice, nations agree with Paley; but does any one think that Massachusetts does exactly what is right at the present crisis?

> A drab of state, a cloth-'o-silver slut,
> To have her train borne up, and her soul trail in
> the dirt.[4]

---

[4]From a work by Cyril Tourneur (c. 1575–1626). —Eds.

Practically speaking, the opponents to a reform in Massachusetts are not a hundred thousand politicians at the South, but a hundred thousand merchants and farmers here, who are more interested in commerce and agriculture than they are in humanity, and are not prepared to do justice to the slave and to Mexico, *cost what it may*. I quarrel not with far-off foes, but with those who, near at home, cooperate with, and do the bidding of, those far away, and without whom the latter would be harmless. We are accustomed to say, that the mass of men are unprepared; but improvement is slow, because the few are not materially wiser or better than the many. It is not so important that many should be as good as you, as that there be some absolute goodness somewhere; for that will leaven the whole lump. There are thousands who are *in opinion* opposed to slavery and to the war, who yet in effect do nothing to put an end to them; who, esteeming themselves children of Washington and Franklin, sit down with their hands in their pockets, and say that they know not what to do, and do nothing; who even postpone the question of freedom to the question of free-trade, and quietly read the prices-current along with the latest advices from Mexico, after dinner, and, it may be, fall asleep over them both. What is the price-current of an honest man and a patriot today? They hesitate, and they regret, and sometimes they petition; but they do nothing in earnest and with effect. They will wait, well disposed, for others to remedy the evil, that they may no longer have it to regret. At most, they give only a cheap vote, and a feeble countenance and God-speed, to the right, as it goes by them. There are nine hundred and ninety-nine patrons of virtue to one virtuous man. But it is easier to deal with the real possessor of a thing than with the temporary guardian of it.

All voting is a sort of gaming, like checkers or backgammon, with a slight moral tinge to it, a playing with right and wrong, with moral questions; and betting naturally accompanies it. The character of the voters is not staked. I cast

10

my vote, perchance, as I think right; but I am not vitally concerned that that right should prevail. I am willing to leave it to the majority. Its obligation, therefore, never exceeds that of expediency. Even voting *for the right* is *doing* nothing for it. It is only expressing to men feebly your desire that it should prevail. A wise man will not leave the right to the mercy of chance, nor wish it to prevail through the power of the majority. There is but little virtue in the action of masses of men. When the majority shall at length vote for the abolition of slavery, it will be because they are indifferent to slavery, or because there is but little slavery left to be abolished by their vote. *They* will then be the only slaves. Only *his* vote can hasten the abolition of slavery who asserts his own freedom by his vote.

I hear of a convention to be held at Baltimore, or elsewhere, for the selection of a candidate for the Presidency, made up chiefly of editors, and men who are politicians by profession; but I think, what is it to any independent, intelligent, and respectable man what decision they may come to? Shall we not have the advantage of his wisdom and honesty, nevertheless? Can we not count upon some independent votes? Are there not many individuals in the country who do not attend conventions? But no: I find that the respectable man, so called, has immediately drifted from his position, and despairs of his country, when his country has more reason to despair of him. He forthwith adopts one of the candidates thus selected as the only *available* one, thus proving that he is himself *available* for any purposes of the demagogue. His vote is of no more worth than that of any unprincipled foreigner or hireling native, who may have been bought. O for a man who is *a man*, and, as my neighbor says, has a bone in his back which you cannot pass your hand through! Our statistics are at fault: The population has been returned too large. How many *men* are there to a square thousand miles in this country? Hardly one. Does not America offer any inducement for men

to settle here? The American has dwindled into an Odd Fellow, — one who may be known by the development of his organ of gregariousness, and a manifest lack of intellect and cheerful self-reliance; whose first and chief concern, on coming into the world, is to see that the Almshouses are in good repair; and, before yet he has lawfully donned the virile garb, to collect a fund for the support of the widows and orphans that may be; who, in short, ventures to live only by the aid of the Mutual Insurance company, which has promised to bury him decently.

It is not a man's duty, as a matter of course, to devote himself to the eradication of any, even the most enormous wrong; he may still properly have other concerns to engage him; but it is his duty, at least, to wash his hands of it, and, if he gives it no thought longer, not to give it practically his support. If I devote myself to other pursuits and contemplations, I must first see, at least, that I do not pursue them sitting upon another man's shoulders. I must get off him first, that he may pursue his contemplations too. See what gross inconsistency is tolerated. I have heard some of my townsmen say, "I should like to have them order me out to help put down an insurrection of the slaves, or to march to Mexico; — see if I would go"; and yet these very men have each, directly by their allegiance, and so indirectly, at least, by their money, furnished a substitute. The soldier is applauded who refuses to serve in an unjust war by those who do not refuse to sustain the unjust government which makes the war; is applauded by those whose own act and authority he disregards and sets at naught; as if the State were penitent to that degree that it hired one to scourge it while it sinned, but not to that degree that it left off sinning for a moment. Thus, under the name of Order and Civil Government, we are all made at last to pay homage to and support our own meanness. After the first blush of sin comes its indifference; and from immoral it becomes, as it were, *un*moral, and not quite unnecessary to that life which we have made.

The broadest and most prevalent error requires the most disinterested virtue to sustain it. The slight reproach to which the virtue of patriotism is commonly liable, the noble are most likely to incur. Those who, while they disapprove of the character and measures of a government, yield to it their allegiance and support, are undoubtedly its most conscientious supporters, and so frequently the most serious obstacles to reform. Some are petitioning the State to dissolve the Union, to disregard the requisitions of the President. Why do they not dissolve it themselves, — the union between themselves and the States, — and refuse to pay their quota into its treasury? Do not they stand in the same relation to the State, that the State does to the Union? And have not the same reasons prevented the State from resisting the Union, which have prevented them from resisting the State?

How can a man be satisfied to entertain an opinion merely, and enjoy *it*? Is there any enjoyment in it, if his opinion is that he is aggrieved? If you are cheated out of a single dollar by your neighbor, you do not rest satisfied with knowing that you are cheated, or with saying that you are cheated, or even with petitioning him to pay you your due; but you take effectual steps at once to obtain the full amount, and see that you are never

cheated again. Action from principle, the perception and the performance of right, changes things and relations; it is essentially revolutionary, and does not consist wholly with anything which was. It not only divides states and churches, it divides families; ay, it divides the *individual*, separating the diabolical in him from the divine.

Unjust laws exist: Shall we be content to obey them, or shall we endeavor to amend them, and obey them until we have succeeded, or shall we transgress them at once? Men generally, under such a government as this, think that they ought to wait until they have persuaded the majority to alter them. They think that, if they should resist, the remedy would be worse than the evil. But it is the fault of the government itself that the remedy *is* worse than the evil. *It* makes it worse. Why is it not more apt to anticipate and provide for reform? Why does it not cherish its wise minority? Why does it cry and resist before it is hurt? Why does it not encourage its citizens to be on the alert to point out its faults, and *do* better than it would have them? Why does it always crucify Christ, and excommunicate Copernicus and Luther, and pronounce Washington and Franklin rebels?

One would think, that a deliberate and practical denial of its authority was the only offence never contemplated by government; else, why

15

INDIVISION CHARMET/Private Collection/Bridgeman Images

Mahatma Gandhi, a leader of the Indian independence movement, first read "On the Duty of Civil Disobedience" during one of several jail sentences for protesting racist laws in South Africa during the early 1900s. He adopted the term "civil disobedience" to describe the nonviolent protests that eventually led to India's independence from Britain in 1947. Imprisoned, as shown in this photo, many times throughout his life, he once said, "Non-cooperation with evil is as much a duty as is cooperation with good." **How does that claim reflect Thoreau's views in "On the Duty of Civil Disobedience"?**

has it not assigned its definite, its suitable and proportionate penalty? If a man who has no property refuses but once to earn nine shillings for the State, he is put in prison for a period unlimited by any law that I know, and determined only by the discretion of those who placed him there; but if he should steal ninety times nine shillings from the State, he is soon permitted to go at large again.

If the injustice is part of the necessary friction of the machine of government, let it go, let it go: Perchance it will wear smooth, — certainly the machine will wear out. If the injustice has a spring, or a pulley, or a rope, or a crank, exclusively for itself, then perhaps you may consider whether the remedy will not be worse than the evil; but if it is of such a nature that it requires you to be the agent of injustice to another, then, I say, break the law. Let your life be a counter friction to stop the machine. What I have to do is to see, at any rate, that I do not lend myself to the wrong which I condemn.

As for adopting the ways which the State has provided for remedying the evil, I know not of such ways. They take too much time, and a man's life will be gone. I have other affairs to attend to. I came into this world, not chiefly to make this a good place to live in, but to live in it, be it good or bad. A man has not everything to do, but something; and because he cannot do *everything*, it is not necessary that he should do *something* wrong. It is not my business to be petitioning the Governor or the Legislature any more than it is theirs to petition me; and, if they should not hear my petition, what should I do then? But in this case the State has provided no way: Its very Constitution is the evil. This may seem to be harsh and stubborn and unconciliatory; but it is to treat with the utmost kindness and consideration the only spirit that can appreciate or deserves it. So is all change for the better, like birth and death, which convulse the body.

I do not hesitate to say, that those who call themselves Abolitionists should at once

effectually withdraw their support, both in person and property, from the government of Massachusetts, and not wait till they constitute a majority of one, before they suffer the right to prevail through them. I think that it is enough if they have God on their side, without waiting for that other one. Moreover, any man more right than his neighbors constitutes a majority of one already.[5]

I meet this American government, or its representative, the State government, directly, and face to face, once a year — no more — in the person of its tax-gatherer; this is the only mode in which a man situated as I am necessarily meets it; and it then says distinctly, Recognize me; and the simplest, the most effectual, and, in the present posture of affairs, the indispensablest mode of treating with it on this head, of expressing your little satisfaction with and love for it, is to deny it then. My civil neighbor, the tax-gatherer, is the very man I have to deal with, — for it is, after all, with men and not with parchment that I quarrel, — and he has voluntarily chosen to be an agent of the government. How shall he ever know well what he is and does as an officer of the government, or as a man, until he is obliged to consider whether he shall treat me, his neighbor, for whom he has respect, as a neighbor and well-disposed man, or as a maniac and disturber of the peace, and see if he can get over this obstruction to his neighborliness without a ruder and more impetuous thought or speech corresponding with his action. I know this well, that if one thousand, if one hundred, if ten men whom I could name, — if ten *honest* men only, — ay, if *one* honest man, in this State of Massachusetts, *ceasing to hold slaves*, were actually to withdraw from this copartnership, and be locked upon the county jail therefor, it would be the abolition of slavery in America. For it matters not how small

_____
[5] An allusion to a statement by John Knox (1505?–1572), a religious reformer, who said, "A man with God is always in the majority." —Eds.

20

the beginning may seem to be: What is once well done is done forever. But we love better to talk about it. That we say is our mission. Reform keeps many scores of newspapers in its service, but not one man. If my esteemed neighbor, the State's ambassador, who will devote his days to the settlement of the question of human rights in the Council Chamber, instead of being threatened with the prisons of Carolina, were to sit down the prisoner of Massachusetts, that State which is so anxious to foist the sin of slavery upon her sister, — though at present she can discover only an act of inhospitality to be the ground of a quarrel with her, — the Legislature would not wholly waive the subject the following winter.

Under a government which imprisons any unjustly, the true place for a just man is also a prison. The proper place today, the only place which Massachusetts has provided for her freer and less desponding spirits, is in her prisons, to be put out and locked out of the State by her own act, as they have already put themselves out by their principles. It is there that the fugitive slave, and the Mexican prisoner on parole, and the Indian come to plead the wrongs of his race, should find them; on that separate, but more free and honorable ground, where the State places those who are not *with* her, but *against* her, — the only house in a slave State in which a free man can abide with honor. If any think that their influence would be lost there, and their voices no longer afflict the ear of the State, that they would not be as an enemy within its walls, they do not know by how much truth is stronger than error, nor how much more eloquently and effectively he can combat injustice who has experienced a little in his own person. Cast your whole vote, not a strip of paper merely, but your whole influence. A minority is powerless while it conforms to the majority; it is not even a minority then; but it is irresistible when it clogs by its whole weight. If the alternative is to keep all just men in prison, or give up war and slavery, the State will not hesitate which to choose. If a thousand men were not to

pay their tax-bills this year, that would not be a violent and bloody measure, as it would be to pay them, and enable the State to commit violence and shed innocent blood. This is, in fact, the definition of a peaceable revolution, if any such is possible. If the tax-gatherer, or any other public officer, asks me, as one has done, "But what shall I do?" my answer is, "If you really wish to do anything, resign your office." When the subject has refused allegiance, and the officer has resigned his office, then the revolution is accomplished. But even suppose blood should flow. Is there not a sort of blood shed when the conscience is wounded? Through this wound a man's real manhood and immortality flow out, and he bleeds to an everlasting death. I see this blood flowing now.

I have contemplated the imprisonment of the offender, rather than the seizure of his goods, — though both will serve the same purpose, — because they who assert the purest right, and consequently are most dangerous to a corrupt State, commonly have not spent much time in accumulating property. To such the State renders comparatively small service, and a slight tax is wont to appear exorbitant, particularly if they are obliged to earn it by special labor with their hands. If there were one who lived wholly without the use of money, the State itself would hesitate to demand it of him. But the rich man, — not to make any invidious comparison, — is always sold to the institution which makes him rich. Absolutely speaking, the more money, the less virtue; for money comes between a man and his objects, and obtains them for him; and it was certainly no great virtue to obtain it. It puts to rest many questions which he would otherwise be taxed to answer; while the only new question which it puts is the hard but superfluous one, how to spend it. Thus his moral ground is taken from under his feet. The opportunities of living are diminished in proportion as what are called the "means" are increased. The best thing a man can do for his culture when he is rich is to endeavor

This photo was taken at a Canadian protest during the National Day of Action against Islamophobia and White Supremacy. Along with rallies in countries around the world, these protests arose in response to President Donald Trump's travel ban on citizens from seven predominantly Muslim countries. The slogan on the sign shown here — "When injustice becomes law, resistance becomes duty" — is often misattributed to Thoreau.

Why do you think this saying is so often associated with him?

NurPhoto/Getty Images

to carry out those schemes which he entertained when he was poor. Christ answered the Herodians according to their condition. "Show me the tribute-money," said he; — and one took a penny out of his pocket; — if you use money which has the image of Caesar on it, and which he has made current and valuable, that is, *if you are men of the State*, and gladly enjoy the advantages of Caesar's government, then pay him back some of his own when he demands it; "Render therefore to Caesar that which is Caesar's, and to God those things which are God's,"[6] — leaving them no wiser than before as to which was which; for they did not wish to know.

When I converse with the freest of my neighbors, I perceive that, whatever they may say about the magnitude and seriousness of the question, and their regard for the public tranquility, the long and the short of the matter is, that they cannot spare the protection of the existing government, and they dread the consequences to their property and families of disobedience to it. For my own part, I should not like to think that I ever rely on the protection of the State. But, if I deny the authority of the State when it presents its tax-bill, it will soon take and waste all my property, and so harass me and my children without end. This is hard. This makes it impossible for a man to live honestly, and at the same time comfortably, in outward respects. It will not be worth the while to accumulate property; that would be sure to go again. You must hire or squat somewhere, and raise but a small crop, and eat that soon. You must live within yourself, and depend upon yourself always tucked up and ready for a start, and not have many affairs. A man may grow rich in Turkey even, if he will be in all respects a good subject of the Turkish government. Confucius said: "If a state is governed by the principles of reason, poverty and misery are subjects of shame; if a state is not governed by the principles of reason, riches and honors are the subjects of shame." No: Until I want the protection of Massachusetts to be extended to me in some distant Southern port, where my liberty is endangered, or until I am bent solely on building up an estate at home by peaceful enterprise, I can afford to refuse allegiance to Massachusetts, and her right to my property and life. It costs me less in every sense to incur the penalty of disobedience to the State, than it would to obey. I should feel as if I were worth less in that case.

Some years ago, the State met me in behalf of the Church and commanded me to pay a   25

[6]Matt. 22:16–21. —Eds.

certain sum toward the support of a clergyman whose preaching my father attended, but never I myself. "Pay," it said, "or be locked up in the jail." I declined to pay. But, unfortunately, another man saw fit to pay it. I did not see why the school-master should be taxed to support the priest, and not the priest the schoolmaster; for I was not the State's schoolmaster, but I supported myself by voluntary subscription. I did not see why the lyceum should not present its tax-bill, and have the State to back its demand, as well as the Church. However, at the request of the selectmen, I condescended to make some such statement as this in writing: — "Know all men by these pres-ents, that I, Henry Thoreau, do not wish to be regarded as a member of any incorporated society which I have not joined." This I gave to the town clerk; and he has it. The State, having thus learned that I did not wish to be regarded as a member of that church, has never made a like demand on me since; though it said that it must adhere to its orig-inal presumption that time. If I had known how to name them, I should then have signed off in detail from all the societies which I never signed on to; but I did not know where to find a complete list.

I have paid no poll-tax for six years. I was put into a jail once on this account, for one night; and, as I stood considering the walls of solid stone, two or three feet thick, the door of wood and iron, a foot thick, and the iron grating which strained the light, I could not help being struck with the foolishness of that institution which treated me as if I were mere flesh and blood and bones, to be locked up. I wondered that it should have concluded at length that this was the best use it could put me to, and had never thought to avail itself of my services in some way. I saw that, if there was a wall of stone between me and my townsmen, there was a still more difficult one to climb or break through, before they could get to be as free as I was. I did not for a moment feel confined, and the walls seemed a great waste of stone and mortar. I felt as if I alone of all my townsmen had paid my tax. They plainly did

not know how to treat me, but behaved like per-sons who are underbred. In every threat and in every compliment there was a blunder; for they thought that my chief desire was to stand the other side of that stone wall, I could not but smile to see how industriously they locked the door on my meditations, which followed them out again without let or hindrance, and *they* were really all that was dangerous. As they could not reach me, they had resolved to punish my body; just as boys, if they cannot come at some person against whom they have a spite, will abuse his dog. I saw that the State was half-witted, that it was timid as a lone woman with her silver spoons, and that it did not know its friends from its foes, and I lost all my remaining respect for it, and pitied it.

Thus the State never intentionally confronts a man's sense, intellectual or moral, but only his body, his senses. It is not armed with superior wit or honesty, but with superior physical strength. I was not born to be forced. I will breathe after my own fashion. Let us see who is the strongest. What force has a multitude? They only can force me who obey a higher law than I. They force me to become like themselves. I do not hear of *men* being *forced* to live this way or that by masses of men. What sort of life were that to live? When I meet a government which says to me, "Your money or your life," why should I be in haste to give it my money? It may be in a great strait, and not know what to do: I cannot help that. It must help itself; do as I do. It is not worth the while to snivel about it. I am not responsible for the successful working of the machinery of society. I am not the son of the engineer. I perceive that, when an acorn and a chestnut fall side by side, the one does not remain inert to make way for the other, but both obey their own laws, and spring and grow and flourish as best they can, till one, perchance, over-shadows and destroys the other. If a plant cannot live according to its nature, it dies; and so a man.

◆ ◆ ◆

The night in prison was novel and interesting enough. The prisoners in their shirt-sleeves were enjoying a chat and the evening air in the doorway, when I entered. But the jailer said, "Come, boys, it is time to lock up"; and so they dispersed, and I heard the sound of their steps returning into the hollow apartments. My roommate was introduced to me by the jailer, as "a first-rate fellow and a clever man." When the door was locked, he showed me where to hang my hat, and how he managed matters there. The rooms were white-washed once a month; and this one, at least, was the whitest, most simply furnished, and probably the neatest apartment in the town. He naturally wanted to know where I came from, and what brought me there; and, when I had told him, I asked him in my turn how he came there, presuming him to be an honest man, of course; and, as the world goes, I believe he was. "Why," said he, "they accuse me of burning a barn; but I never did it." As near as I could discover, he had probably gone to bed in a barn when drunk, and smoked his pipe there; and so a barn was burnt. He had the reputation of being a clever man, had been there some three months waiting for his trial to come on, and would have to wait as much longer; but he was quite domesticated and contented, since he got his board for nothing, and thought that he was well-treated.

He occupied one window, and I the other; and I saw, that, if one stayed there long, his principal business would be to look out the window. I had soon read all the tracts that were left there, and examined where former prisoners had broken out, and where a grate had been sawed off, and heard the history of the various occupants of that room; for I found that even here there was a history and a gossip which never circulated beyond the walls of the jail. Probably this is the only house in the town where verses are composed, which are afterward printed in a circular form, but not published. I was shown quite a long list of verses which were composed by some young men who had been detected in an attempt to escape, who avenged themselves by singing them.

I pumped my fellow-prisoner as dry as I could, for fear I should never see him again; but at length he showed me which was my bed, and left me to blow out the lamp.

It was like travelling into a far country, such as I had never expected to behold, to lie there for one night. It seemed to me that I never had heard the town-clock strike before, nor the evening sounds of the village; for we slept with the windows open, which were inside the grating. It was to see my native village in the light of the Middle Ages, and our Concord was turned into a Rhine stream, and visions of knights and castles passed before me. They were the voices of old burghers that I heard in the streets. I was an involuntary spectator and auditor of whatever was done and said in the kitchen of the adjacent village-inn, — a wholly new and rare experience to me. It was a closer view of my native town. I was fairly inside of it. I never had seen its institutions before. This is one of its peculiar institutions; for it is a shire town. I began to comprehend what its inhabitants were about.

In the morning, our breakfasts were put through the hole in the door, in small oblong-square tin pans, made to fit, and holding a pint of chocolate, with brown bread, and an iron spoon. When they called for the vessels again, I was green enough to return what bread I had left; but my comrade seized it, and said that I should lay that up for lunch or dinner. Soon after he was let out to work at haying in a neighboring field, whither he went every day, and would not be back till noon; so he bade me good-day, saying that he doubted if he should see me again.

When I came out of prison, — for some one interfered, and paid that tax, — I did not perceive that great changes had taken place on the common, such as he observed who went in a youth, and emerged a tottering and gray-headed man; and yet a change had to my eyes come over the scene, — the town, a State, and country, — greater than any mere time could effect. I saw yet more distinctly the State in which I lived. I saw to what extent the people among whom I lived could be trusted as good neighbors and friends; that their friendship was for summer weather only; that they did not greatly propose to do right; that they were a distinct race from me by their prejudices and superstitions, as the Chinamen and Malays are; that, in their sacrifices to humanity, they ran no risks, not even to their property; that, after all, they were not so noble but they treated the thief as he had treated them, and hoped, by a certain outward observance and a few prayers, and by walking in a particular straight though useless path from time to time, to save their souls. This may be to judge my neighbors harshly; for I believe that many of them are not aware that they have such an institution as the jail in their village.

It was formerly the custom in our village, when a poor debtor came out of jail, for his acquaintances to salute him, looking through their fingers, which were crossed to represent the grating of a jail window. "How do ye do?" My neighbors did not thus salute me, but first looked at me, and then at one another, as if I had returned from a long journey. I was put into jail as I was going to the shoemaker's to get a shoe which was mended. When I was let out the next morning, I proceeded to finish my errand,

and having put on my mended shoe, joined a huckleberry party, who were impatient to put themselves under my conduct; and in half an hour, — for the horse was soon tackled, — was in the midst of a huckleberry field, on one of our highest hills, two miles off, and then the State was nowhere to be seen.

This is the whole history of "My Prisons." 35

♦ ♦ ♦

I have never declined paying the highway tax, because I am as desirous of being a good neighbor as I am of being a bad subject; and, as for supporting schools, I am doing my part to educate my fellow-countrymen now. It is for no particular item in the tax-bill that I refuse to pay it. I simply wish to refuse allegiance to the State, to withdraw and stand aloof from it effectually. I do not care to trace the course of my dollar, if I could, till it buys a man or a musket to shoot one with, — the dollar is innocent, — but I am concerned to trace the effects of my allegiance. In fact, I quietly declare war with the State, after my fashion, though I will still make what use and get what advantage of her I can, as is usual in such cases.

If others pay the tax which is demanded of me, from a sympathy with the State, they do but

Boston Globe/Getty Images

In this photo of an anti-war demonstration, marchers on a "Thoreau Walk" in Boston protest Americans' tax dollars being used to fund the Vietnam War. **Why might this protest have resonated with the antiwar movement?**

what they have already done in their own case, or rather they abet injustice to a greater extent than the State requires. If they pay the tax from a mistaken interest in the individual taxed, to save his property, or prevent his going to jail, it is because they have not considered wisely how far they let their private feelings interfere with the public good.

This, then, is my position at present. But one cannot be too much on his guard in such a case, lest his action be biased by obstinacy, or an undue regard for the opinions of men. Let him see that he does only what belongs to himself and to the hour.

I think sometimes, Why, this people mean well; they are only ignorant; they would do better if they knew how; why give your neighbors this pain to treat you as they are not inclined to? But I think again, this is no reason why I should do as they do, or permit others to suffer much greater pain of a different kind. Again, I sometimes say to myself, When many millions of men, without heat, without ill will, without personal feeling of any kind, demand of you a few shillings only, without the possibility, such is their constitution, of retracing or altering their present demand, and without the possibility, on your side, of appeal to any other millions, why expose yourself to this overwhelming brute force? You do not resist cold and hunger, the winds and the waves, thus obstinately; you quietly submit to a thousand similar necessities. You do not put your head into the fire. But just in proportion as I regard this as not wholly a brute force, partly a human force, and consider that I have relations to those millions as to so many millions of men, and not of mere brute or inanimate things, I see that appeal is possible, first and instantaneously, from them to the Maker of them, and, secondly, from them to themselves. But, if I put my head deliberately into the fire, there is no appeal to fire or to the Maker of fire, and I have only myself to blame. If I could convince myself that I have any right to be satisfied with men as they are, and to treat them according, and not according, in some respects, to my requisitions and expectations of what they and I ought to be, then, like a good Mussulman[7] and fatalist, I should endeavor to be satisfied with things as they are, and say it is the will of God. And, above all, there is this difference between resisting this and a purely brute or natural force, that I can resist this with some effect; but I cannot expect, like Orpheus, to change the nature of the rocks and trees and beasts.

I do not wish to quarrel with any man or   *40* nation. I do not wish to split hairs, to make fine distinctions, or set myself up as better than my neighbors. I seek rather, I may say, even an excuse for conforming to the laws of the land. I am but too ready to conform to them. Indeed, I have reason to suspect myself on this head; and each year, as the tax-gatherer comes round, I find myself disposed to review the acts and position of the general and State governments, and the spirit of the people, to discover a pretext for conformity.

> We must affect our country as our parents;
> And if at any time we alienate
> Our love or industry from doing it honor.
> We must respect effects and teach the soul
> Matter of conscience and religion.
> And not desire of rule or benefit.

I believe that the State will soon be able to take all my work of this sort out of my hands, and then I shall be no better a patriot than my fellow-countrymen. Seen from a lower point of view, the Constitution, with all its faults, is very good; the law and the courts are very respectable; even this State and this American government are, in many respects, very admirable and rare things, to be thankful for, such as a great many have described them; but seen from a point of view a little higher, they are what I have described them; seen from a higher still, and the highest, who shall say what they are, or that they are worth looking at or thinking of at all?

---

[7]Muslim. —Eds.

However, the government does not concern me much, and I shall bestow the fewest possible thoughts on it. It is not many moments that I live under a government, even in this world. If a man is thought-free, fancy-free, imagination-free, that which *is not* never for a long time appearing *to be* to him, unwise rulers or reformers cannot fatally interrupt him.

I know that most men think differently from myself; but those whose lives are by profession devoted to the study of these or kindred subjects, content me as little as any. Statesmen and legislators, standing so completely within the institution, never distinctly and nakedly behold it. They speak of moving society, but have no resting-place without it. They may be men of a certain experience and discrimination, and have no doubt invented ingenious and even useful systems, for which we sincerely thank them; but all their wit and usefulness lie within certain not very wide limits. They are wont to forget that the world is not governed by policy and expediency. Webster never goes behind government, and so cannot speak with authority about it. His words are wisdoms to those legislators who contemplate no essential reform in the existing government; but for thinkers, and those who legislate for all time, he never once glances at the subject. I know of those whose serene and wise speculations on this theme would soon reveal the limits of his mind's range and hospitality. Yet, compared with the cheap professions of most reformers, and the still cheaper wisdom and eloquence of politicians in general, his are almost the only sensible and valuable words, and we thank Heaven for him. Comparatively, he is always strong, original, and, above all, practical. Still his quality is not wisdom, but prudence. The lawyer's truth is not Truth, but consistency, or a consistent expediency. Truth is always in harmony with herself, and is not concerned chiefly to reveal the justice that may consist with wrong-doing. He well deserves to be called, as he has been called, the Defender of the Constitution. There are really

no blows to be given by him but defensive ones. He is not a leader, but a follower. His leaders are the men of '87. "I have never made an effort," he says, "and never propose to make an effort; I have never countenanced an effort, and never mean to countenance an effort, to disturb the arrangement as originally made, by which the various States came into the Union."[8] Still thinking of the sanction which the Constitution gives to slavery, he says, "Because it was a part of the original compact, — let it stand." Notwithstanding his special acuteness and ability, he is unable to take a fact out of its merely political relations, and behold it as it lies absolutely to be disposed of by the intellect, — what, for instance, it behooves a man to do here in America today with regard to slavery, but ventures, or is driven, to make some such desperate answer as the following, while professing to speak absolutely, and as a private man, — from which what new and singular code of social duties might be inferred? "The manner," says he, "in which the governments of those States where slavery exists are to regulate it, is for their own consideration, under their responsibility to their constituents, to the general laws of propriety, humanity, and justice, and to God. Associations formed elsewhere, springing from a feeling of humanity, or any other cause, have nothing whatever to do with it. They have never received any encouragement from me, and they never will."

They who know of no purer sources of truth, who have traced up its stream no higher, stand, and wisely stand, by the Bible and the Constitution, and drink at it there with reverence and humility; but they who behold where it comes trickling into this lake or that pool, gird up their loins once more, and continue their pilgrimage toward its fountain-head.

No man with a genius for legislation has appeared in America. They are rare in the history

---

[8]From an 1845 speech given by Daniel Webster about the admission of Texas to the United States. —Eds.

seeing connections

In this photograph from 2016, San Francisco 49er players Eli Harold (#58), Colin Kaepernick (#7), and Eric Reid (#35) kneel during the national anthem in a protest to bring attention to racism and police violence against African Americans. Kaepernick, who initiated the protest, continued to kneel during the anthem for the remainder of the football season, sparking both controversy and similar protests across athletic disciplines. When asked about Kaepernick's tactics, activist and former professional football player Wade Davis replied, "The actual point of protest is to disrupt how we move about our daily lives. What Kaepernick did was disrupt one of our most treasured sports. . . . The larger conversation is what he is protesting about. The fact that so many don't want to have that specific conversation speaks to the fact that they know what is happening in America is beyond tragic."

To what extent do Davis's and Thoreau's concept of protest align? Do you think Kaepernick's protest exemplifies civil disobedience as Thoreau defines it? Explain why or why not.

Michael Zagaris/Getty Images

of the world. There are orators, politicians, and eloquent men, by the thousand; but the speaker has not yet opened his mouth to speak, who is capable of settling the much-vexed questions of the day. We love eloquence for its own sake, and not for any truth which it may utter, or any heroism it may inspire. Our legislators have not yet learned the comparative value of free-trade and of freedom, of union, and of rectitude, to a nation. They have no genius or talent for comparatively humble questions of taxation and finance, commerce and manufactures and agriculture. If we were left solely to the wordy wit of legislators in Congress for our guidance, uncorrected by the seasonable experience and the effectual complaints of the people, America would not long retain her rank among the nations. For eighteen hundred years, though perchance I have no right to say it, the New Testament has been written; yet where is the legislator who has wisdom and practical talent enough to avail himself of the light which it sheds on the science of legislation?

The authority of government, even such as I am willing to submit to, — for I will cheerfully obey those who know and can do better than I, and in many things even those who neither know nor can do so well, — is still an impure one: To be strictly just, it must have the sanction and consent of the governed. It can have no pure right over my person and property but what I concede to it. The progress from an absolute to a limited monarchy, from a limited monarchy to a democracy, is a progress toward a true respect for the individual. Even the Chinese philosopher was wise enough to regard the individual as the basis of the empire.

45 Is a democracy, such as we know it, the last improvement possible in government? Is it not possible to take a step further towards recognizing and organizing the rights of man? There will never be a really free and enlightened State, until the State comes to recognize the individual as a higher and independent power, from which all its own power and authority are derived, and treats him accordingly. I please myself with imagining a State at last which can afford to be just to all men, and to treat the individual with respect as a neighbor; which even would not think it inconsistent with its own repose, if a few were to live aloof from it, not meddling with it, nor embraced by it, who fulfilled all the duties of neighbors and fellowmen. A State which bore this kind of fruit, and suffered it to drop off as fast as it ripened, would prepare the way for a still more perfect and glorious State, which also I have imagined, but not yet anywhere seen.

[1849]

QUESTIONS FOR DISCUSSION

1. In paragraph 1, what distinction does Henry David Thoreau make between the government and the people? Why does he begin the essay this way? Why does Thoreau not begin the essay with his stay in jail?

2. Why does Thoreau refer to civil disobedience not merely as a right but as a duty?

3. What are the two government policies Thoreau most objects to? Explain his objection.

4. Thoreau writes, "When the majority shall at length vote for the abolition of slavery, it will be because they are indifferent to slavery, or because there is but little slavery left to be abolished by their vote" (para. 11). What does this statement imply about the voting populace? Do you think that Thoreau is accurate in his characterization of the populace? Why or why not?

5. In paragraph 20, Thoreau states that "any man more right than his neighbors constitutes a majority of one already." What does he mean by this? How does this statement support his thesis?

6. In paragraph 23, Thoreau discusses the effects of wealth on character. Paraphrase that discussion. Do you agree with his analysis? Why or why not?

7. What did Thoreau learn from his night in jail (paras. 26–35)? Explain, using specific reference to the text.

8. In paragraph 36, Thoreau distinguishes among different types of taxes. Why? In the same paragraph he says, "I do not care to trace the course of my dollar, if I could, till it buys a man or a musket to shoot one with, — the dollar is innocent, — but I am concerned to trace the effects of my allegiance." What might our dollars buy today that would cause such a reflection and response?

9. Under the circumstances Thoreau describes, do you believe civil disobedience is a duty, as he says? What circumstances in our own society would justify civil disobedience? Explain how Thoreau's essay speaks to our own time. Is the essay dated?

QUESTIONS ON RHETORIC AND STYLE

1. Describe the tone Thoreau establishes in paragraph 2. How does it contribute to the rhetorical effect of the paragraph?

2. What is the effect of the metaphor about friction in paragraphs 8 and 18?

3. Thoreau develops many analogies to support his arguments (e.g., in paras. 8 and 9). Select three, and explain whether you find them convincing. How effectively does each one support the claim Thoreau is using it to support?

4. One characteristic of Thoreau's style is the use of aphorism. For example, in paragraph 4, he writes, "It is not desirable to cultivate a respect for the law, so much as for the right." Find other examples of Thoreau's aphorisms. You might find some in

paragraphs 9–10 and 20–22. What is the rhetorical effect of such statements?

5. How would you describe Thoreau's tone in paragraph 12? How does it contribute to his position?

6. Thoreau uses several rhetorical questions in the essay. Identify three, and explain how each one contributes to the paragraph in which it is found.

7. Which of the three classic rhetorical appeals dominates in paragraph 21, where Thoreau gives the government a human face? Defend your answer.

8. Note how Thoreau qualifies his argument in paragraph 40. How does using this strategy serve his rhetorical purpose?

SUGGESTIONS FOR WRITING

1. "There are nine hundred and ninety-nine patrons of virtue to one virtuous man," states Thoreau (para. 10). Do you agree? Can you think of a "virtuous man" in American public life today? Write an essay about someone you regard as a virtuous man or woman according to Thoreau's characterization of such a person. Refer specifically to the text of Thoreau's essay.

2. Compare and contrast Thoreau's "On the Duty of Civil Disobedience" with Martin Luther King Jr.'s "Letter from Birmingham Jail" (p. 513) by focusing on one of the following: purpose, definition of a just law, or figurative language.

3. Thoreau writes, "We love eloquence for its own sake, and not for any truth which it may utter, or any heroism it may inspire" (para. 44). Defend, challenge, or qualify the accuracy of that statement as it applies to contemporary society. Use examples of public voices from such institutions as the schools, government, religion, industry, or finance to support your position.

4. Thoreau says, "No man with a genius for legislation has appeared in America. They are rare in the history of the world. There are orators, politicians, and eloquent men, by the thousand; but the speaker has not yet opened his mouth to speak, who is capable of settling the much-vexed questions of the day" (para. 44). Surely there are many who would disagree. Write an essay that defends, challenges, or qualifies Thoreau's statement as it applies to his time or our own.

5. Think of a contemporary issue in your local community that might justify the kind of civil disobedience that Thoreau discusses. How would you make the case for civil disobedience in that context? Write a speech directed to a specific audience explaining the gravity of the situation and the justification for your recommended actions.

6. Think of a contemporary issue that some people in our society regard as justification for civil disobedience. Write an argument that explains why civil disobedience would be wrong and offers alternative solutions.

The Gettysburg Address

ABRAHAM LINCOLN

Abraham Lincoln (1809–1865) was the sixteenth president of the United States of America. Born in rural Kentucky and raised in rural Indiana, he settled in Illinois, where he held various jobs before becoming a self-taught lawyer and a member of the state legislature. He was elected president in 1860 and re-elected in 1864 in the midst of the Civil War, which broke out in 1861. On January 1, 1863, Lincoln issued the Emancipation Proclamation, an executive order that freed slaves in ten Southern states and led to the abolition of slavery in America — something he would not live to see. He was assassinated in 1865. Shortly before his death Lincoln delivered the Gettysburg Address, a speech often regarded as one of the most powerful and significant by an American, to commemorate the dead and wounded soldiers at the site of the battle in Gettysburg, Pennsylvania. In addition to being one of the greatest American presidents, Lincoln also was a skilled writer and rhetorician.

Four score and seven years ago our fathers brought forth on this continent a new nation, conceived in liberty, and dedicated to the proposition that all men are created equal.

Now we are engaged in a great civil war, testing whether that nation, or any nation, so conceived and so dedicated, can long endure. We are met on a great battle-field of that war. We have come to dedicate a portion of that field, as a final resting place for those who here gave their lives that that nation might live. It is altogether fitting and proper that we should do this.

But, in a larger sense, we can not dedicate, we can not consecrate, we can not hallow this ground. The brave men, living and dead, who struggled here, have consecrated it, far above our poor power to add or detract. The world will little note, nor long remember what we say here, but it can never forget what they did here. It is for us the living, rather, to be dedicated here to the unfinished work which they who fought here have thus far so nobly advanced. It is rather for us to be here dedicated to the great task remaining before us — that from these honored dead we take increased devotion to that cause for which they gave the last full measure of devotion — that we here highly resolve that these dead shall not have died in vain — that this nation, under God, shall have a new birth of freedom — and that government of the people, by the people, for the people, shall not perish from the earth.

[1863]

EXPLORING THE TEXT

1. What does Abraham Lincoln refer to in the first sentence? Explain the effect of this reference.

2. How would you describe the tone of this speech?

3. When Lincoln delivered the Gettysburg Address, the audience was quite surprised by how short it was: a mere 272 words. Do you think it should have been longer? Why or why not? Notice what he does not mention; for instance, there is no mention of the enemy. Discuss the rhetorical effect of such brevity.

4. Indicate examples of repeated diction. What is the purpose and effect of these repetitions?

5. Identify examples of diction that relate to life and to death. What is the effect of such language?

6. Identify several examples of parallel structures, juxtapositions, and antitheses. Explain the effect of each one.

7. Note the rhetorical shift indicated by "But . . ." in sentence 6. What is its purpose and effect?

8. What is the "great task remaining before us" that Lincoln mentions in sentence 10?

9. In such a short speech, the final sentence is notable for its length (eighty-two words, roughly 30 percent of the total) and complexity. How do the style and rhetoric of the final sentence contribute to the speech as a whole?

10. Considering the importance of the speech, note how ironic it is that Lincoln said, "The world will little note, nor long remember what we say here" (sentence 8). Why do you think this speech has endured?

11. The historian Gary Wills titled his historical and rhetorical analysis of the Gettysburg Address *Lincoln at Gettysburg: The Words That Remade America* (1992). That title, and the book as a whole, makes a strong claim about the speech. Do you think that it is a reasonable claim? Drawing on your knowledge of U.S. history, discuss the extent to which Wills's title accurately characterizes the importance of the speech.

12. Read "The Gettysburg PowerPoint Presentation" by Peter Norvig. It can be found online. What is the object of Norvig's satire? Do you find it effective? Refer to Lincoln's speech as well as your own experience with PowerPoint demonstrations to support your answer.

from Freedom or Death

EMMELINE PANKHURST

Emmeline Pankhurst (1858–1928) was a British activist and a leader of the suffragette movement who helped British women win the right to vote. In 1903, Pankhurst founded the Women's Social and Political Union (WSPU), an all-women suffrage advocacy organization through which Pankhurst and her daughters fought anti-women voting laws with "deeds, not words." When WSPU members were jailed for smashing windows and assaulting police officers, they staged hunger strikes to secure better prison conditions. The WSPU eventually adopted arson as a tactic, increasing the animosity between moderate suffragists and WSPU and eventually causing Pankhurst's daughters Adela and Sylvia to leave the group in 1913. At the start of World War I, Pankhurst called a halt to militant suffrage activism and instead urged women to aid British industrial production in the fight against Germany. In 1918, when the Representation of the People Act granted the vote to women over 30, Pankhurst transformed the WSPU into the Women's Party, which was dedicated to promoting women's equality in public life. She died in 1928, mere weeks before the Representation of the People Act extended the vote to all women over age 21. Although she was criticized for her militant tactics, Pankhurst's work is now recognized as a crucial element in achieving women's suffrage in Britain.

From 1912 to 1913, Pankhurst was arrested twelve separate times, and she spent all of her imprisonments on hunger strike. During the fall of 1913, she embarked on a fundraising tour in the United States, during which she gave the following speech in Hartford, Connecticut. Addressing the Connecticut Women's Suffrage Association — and its leader, Katherine Houghton Hepburn — Pankhurst justifies militant activist tactics in service of women's suffrage. This subject was a particularly sensitive one at that time, as her audience would have known that earlier that year a member of the WSPU named Emily Davison had run in front of the king of England's horse during a Derby race, resulting in her death. While Pankhurst and her supporters considered Davison a martyr for the cause of women's suffrage, the intent behind her actions remains a mystery to this day.

Mrs. Hepburn, Ladies and Gentlemen: Many people come to Hartford to address meetings as advocates of some reform. Tonight it is not to advocate a reform that I address a meeting in Hartford. I do not come here as an advocate, because whatever position the suffrage movement may occupy in the United States of America, in England it has passed beyond the realm of advocacy and it has entered into the sphere of practical politics. It has become the subject of revolution and civil war, and so tonight I am not here to advocate woman suffrage. American suffragists can do that very well for themselves. I am here as a soldier who has temporarily left the field of battle in order to explain — it seems strange it should have to be explained — what civil war is like when civil war is waged by women. I am not only here as a soldier temporarily absent from the field of battle; I am here — and that, I think, is the strangest part of my coming — I am here as a person who, according to the law courts of my country, it has been decided, is of no value to the community at

all; and I am adjudged because of my life to be a dangerous person, under sentence of penal servitude in a convict prison....

If I were a man and I said to you: "I come from a country which professes to have representative institutions and yet denies me, a taxpayer, an inhabitant of the country, representative rights," you would at once understand that that human being, being a man, was justified in the adoption of revolutionary methods to get representative institutions. But since I am a woman it is necessary in the twentieth century to explain why women have adopted revolutionary methods in order to win the rights of citizenship.

You see, in spite of a good deal that we hear about revolutionary methods not being necessary for American women, because American women are so well off, most of the men of the United States quite calmly acquiesce in the fact that half of the community are deprived absolutely of citizen rights, and we women, in trying to make our case clear, always have to make as part of our argument, and urge upon men in our audience the fact — a

Universal History Archive/Getty Images

This photograph, taken in 1911, shows Emmeline Pankhurst addressing a crowd on Wall Street in New York City.

Based on this image, how would you characterize her reception in New York? What does this image add to your impression of the ethos Pankhurst brings to "Freedom or Death"?

very simple fact — that women are human beings. It is quite evident you do not all realize we are human beings or it would not be necessary to argue with you that women may, suffering from intolerable injustice, be driven to adopt revolutionary methods. We have, first of all to convince you we are human beings, and I hope to be able to do that in the course of the evening before I sit down, but before doing that, I want to put a few political arguments before you, — not arguments for the suffrage, because I said when I opened, I didn't mean to do that, — but arguments for the adoption of militant methods in order to win political rights. . . .

Suppose the men of Hartford had a grievance, and they laid that grievance before their legislature, and the legislature obstinately refused to listen to them, or to remove their grievance, what would be the proper and the constitutional and the practical way of getting their grievance removed? Well, it is perfectly obvious at the next general election, when the legislature is elected, the men of Hartford in sufficient numbers would turn out that legislature and elect a new one; entirely change the personnel of an obstinate legislature which would not remove their grievance. It is perfectly simple and perfectly easy for voting communities to get their grievances removed if they act in combination and make an example of the legislature by changing the composition of the legislature and sending better people to take the place of those who have failed to do justice. But let the men of Hartford imagine that they were not in the position of being voters at all, that they were governed without their consent being obtained, that the legislature turned an absolutely deaf ear to their demands, what would the men of Hartford do then? They couldn't vote the legislature out. They would have to choose; they would have to make a choice of two evils; they would either have to submit indefinitely to an unjust state of affairs, or they would have to rise up and adopt some of the antiquated means by which men in the past got their grievances remedied. We know what happened when your forefathers decided that they must have representation for taxation, many, many years

ago. When they felt they couldn't wait any longer, when they laid all the arguments before an obstinate British government that they could think of, and when their arguments were absolutely disregarded, when every other means had failed, they began by the Tea Party at Boston, and they went on until they had won the independence of the United States of America. That is what happened in the old days. . . .

I don't know, Mrs. Hepburn, whether I have used the domestic illustration in Hartford, but it is a very good one; it is quite worth using again. You have two babies very hungry and wanting to be fed. One baby is a patient baby, and waits

5

Here, Emmeline Pankhurst — then fifty-five years old — is shown being arrested outside of Buckingham Palace after trying to present a petition to the king in May of 1914. Newspapers reported that, as she was driven away to jail, she called out, "Arrested at the gates of the palace. Tell the king!" **How does this photograph portray Pankhurst? To what extent is this portrayal reflected in the persona she develops in "Freedom or Death"?**

HIP/Art Resource, NY

indefinitely until its mother is ready to feed it. The other baby is an impatient baby and cries lustily, screams and kicks and makes everybody unpleasant until it is fed. Well, we know perfectly well which baby is attended to first. That is the whole history of politics. Putting sentiment aside, people who really want reforms learn that lesson very quickly. It is only the people who are quite content to go on advocating them indefinitely who play the part of the patient baby in politics. You have to make more noise than anybody else, you have to make yourself more obtrusive than anybody else, you have to fill all the papers more than anybody else, in fact you have to be there all the time and see that they do not snow you under, if you are really going to get your reform realized. That is what we women have been doing, and in the course of our desperate struggle we have had to make a great many people very uncomfortable. . . .

If you are dealing with an industrial revolution, if you get the men and women of one class to rising up against the men and women of another class, you can locate the difficulty; if there is a great industrial strike, you know exactly where the violence is, and every man knows exactly how the warfare is going to be waged; but in our war against the government you can't locate it. You can take Mrs. Hepburn and myself on this platform, and now, without being told, how could you tell that Mrs. Hepburn is a non-militant and that I am a militant? Absolutely impossible. If any gentleman who is the father of daughters in this meeting went into his home and looked around at his wife and daughters, if he lived in England and was an Englishman, he couldn't tell whether some of his daughters were militants or non-militants. When his daughters went out to post a letter, he couldn't tell if they went harmlessly out to make a tennis engagement at that pillar-box by posting a letter, or whether they went to put some corrosive matter in that would burn all the letters up inside of that box. We wear no mark; we belong to every class; we permeate every class of the community from

This postcard from around 1910 depicts a "Suffragette Madonna."
What argument does this image make? What logic supports the argument? How might Pankhurst respond?

PRISMATIC PICTURES/Private Collection/Bridgeman Images

the highest to the lowest; and so you see in the woman's civil war the dear men of my country are discovering it is absolutely impossible to deal with it; you cannot locate it, and you cannot stop it. "Put them in prison," they said; "that will stop it." But it didn't stop it. They put women in prison for long terms of imprisonment, for making a nuisance of themselves — that was the expression when they took petitions in their hands to the door of the House of Commons; and they thought that by sending them to prison, giving them a day's imprisonment, would cause them to

On November 18, 1910, WSPU suffragettes marched on the British House of Commons after Prime Minister H. H. Asquith shelved a bill that would have granted partial suffrage to women. A riot ensued, and over 100 women were arrested. Shown here is a photograph taken on that day — known as "Black Friday." **What story does this image tell? How does it bolster Pankhurst's explanation of her tactics?**

HIP/Art Resource, NY

all settle down again and there would be no further trouble. But it didn't happen so at all: instead of the women giving it up, more women did it, and more and more and more women did it until there were three hundred women at a time, who had not broken a single law, only "made a nuisance of themselves" as the politicians say. Well then they thought they must go a little farther, and so then they began imposing punishments of a very serious kind. The Judge who sentenced me last May to three years penal servitude for certain speeches in which I had accepted responsibility for acts of violence done by other women, said that if I would say I was sorry, if I would promise not to do it again, that he would revise the sentence and shorten it, because he admitted that it was a very heavy sentence, especially as the jury had recommended me to mercy because of the purity of my motives; and he said he was giving a determinate sentence, a sentence that would convince me that I would have to give up my "evil ways" and would also deter other women from imitating me. But it hadn't that effect at all. So far from it having that effect more and more women have been doing these things that I had incited them to do, and were more determined in doing them; so that the long determinate sentence had no effect in crushing the agitation.

Well then they felt they must do something else, and they began to legislate. I want to tell men in this meeting that the British government, which is not remarkable for having very mild laws to administer, has passed more stringent laws to deal with this agitation than it ever found it necessary during all the history of political agitation in my country. They were able to deal with the revolutionaries of the Chartists'[1] time; they were able to deal with the Trades Union agitation; they were able to deal with the **r**evolutionaries later on when the Reform Acts of 1867 and 1884[2] were passed; but the ordinary law has not sufficed to curb insurgent women. They have had to pass special legislation, and now they are on the point of admitting that that special legislation has absolutely failed. They had to dip back into the middle ages to find a means of repressing the women in revolt, and the whole history shows how futile it is for men who have been considered able statesmen to deal with dissatisfied women who are determined to win their citizenship and who will not submit to government until their consent is obtained. That is the whole point of our agitation. The whole argument with the anti-suffragists, or

[1] Members of a mid-nineteenth-century political movement to grant more rights to working class British men. —Eds.
[2] Legislation that extended suffrage to working class men in Britain. —Eds.

Emmeline Pankhurst was one of the most photographed women of her day, and she was known for using theatrical flair to get her message across. This photograph shows Emmeline Pankhurst and her daughter, Christabel, wearing their prison uniforms during a two-month sentence they served in 1908 for inciting a crowd to rush the House of Commons. **What purpose(s) might be served by this image? Who do you think was its intended audience?**

HIP/Art Resource, NY

even the critical suffragist man, is this: that you can govern human beings without their consent. They have said to us, government rests upon force, the women haven't force, so they must submit. Well, we are showing them that government does not rest upon force at all; it rests upon consent. As long as women consent to be unjustly governed, they can be; but directly women say: "We with-hold our consent, we will not be governed any longer so long as that government is unjust," not by the forces of civil war can you govern the very weakest woman. You can kill that woman, but she escapes you then;

you cannot govern her. And that is, I think, a most valuable demonstration we have been making to the world. We have been proving in our own person that government does not rest upon force; it rests upon consent; as long as people consent to government, it is perfectly easy to govern, but directly they refuse then no power on earth can govern a human being, however feeble, who withholds his or her consent; and all of the strange happenings that you have read about over here, have been manifestations of a refusal to consent on the part of the women. When they put us in prison at first, simply for taking petitions, we submitted; we allowed them to dress us in prison clothes; we allowed them to put us in solitary confinement; we allowed them to treat us as ordinary criminals, and put us amongst the most degraded of those criminals; and we were very glad of the experience, because out of that experience we learned of the need for prison reform; we learned of the fearful mistakes that men of all nations have made when it is a question of dealing with human beings; we learned of some of the appalling evils of our so-called civilization that we could not have learned in any other way except by going through the police courts of our country, in the prison vans that take you up to prison; and right through that prison experience. It was valuable experience, and we were glad to get it. But there came a time when we said: "It is unjust to send political agitators to prison in this way for merely asking for justice, and we will not submit any longer." And I am always glad to remind American audiences that two of the first women that came to the conclusion that they would not submit to unjust imprisonment any longer, were two American girls, who are doing some of the most splendid suffrage work in America today up in Washington. I think they are making things extremely lively for the politicians up there, and I don't know whether every American woman knows what those two women, working in conjunction with others, are doing for the enfranchisement of American women at this moment. I am always proud to think that Miss Lucy Burns and Miss Alice Paul served their suffrage apprenticeship in the militant ranks in England, and they were not slow about it either, because one of them came, I believe it was, from Heidelberg, travelling all night, to take part in one of those little processions to Parliament with a petition. She was arrested and thrown into prison with about twenty others, and that group of twenty women were the first women who decided they would not submit themselves to the degradation of wearing prison clothes; and they refused, and they were almost the first to adopt the "Hunger strike" as a protest against the criminal treatment. They forced their way out of prison. Well, then it was that women began to withhold their consent. I have been in audiences where I have seen men smile when they heard the words "Hunger strike," and yet I think there are very few men today who would be prepared to adopt a "Hunger strike" for any cause. It is only people who feel an intolerable sense of oppression who would adopt a means of that kind. I know of no people who did it before us except revolutionaries in Russia — who adopted the hunger strike against intolerable prison conditions. Well, our women decided to terminate those unjust sentences at the earliest possible moment by the terrible means of the hunger strike. It means, you refuse food until you are at death's door, and then the authorities have to choose between letting you die, and letting you go; and then they let the women go.

Now, that went on so long that the government felt they had lost their power, and that they were unable to cope with the situation. Then it was that, to the shame of the British government, they set the example to authorities all over the world of feeding sane, resisting human beings by force. There may be doctors in this meeting; if so, they know it is one thing to treat an insane person, to feed by force an insane person, or a patient who has some form of illness which makes it necessary; but it is quite another thing to feed a sane, resisting human being who resists with every nerve and with every fibre of her body the indignity and the outrage of forcible feeding. Now, that was done in England, and the government thought they had

This poster, made between 1910 and 1919, depicts a suffragette on hunger strike being force-fed in prison. **How does this image appeal to its audience? How are those appeals similar to (or different from) the appeals Pankhurst makes in "Freedom or Death"?**

crushed us. But they found that it did not quell the agitation, that more and more women came in and even passed that terrible ordeal, and that they were not able with all their forcible feeding to make women serve out their unjust sentences. They were obliged to let them go.

Then came the legislation to which I have referred, the legislation which is known in England as the Cat and Mouse Act. It got through the British House of Commons because the Home Secretary assured the House of Commons that he wanted the bill passed in the interests of humanity; he said he was a humane man and he did not like having to resort to forcible feeding; he wanted the House of Commons to give him some way of disposing of them, and this was his way: he said, "Give me the power to let these women go when they are at death's door, and leave them at liberty under license until they have recovered their health again and then bring them back; leave it to me to fix the time of their licenses; leave it in my hands altogether to deal with this intolerable situation, because the laws must be obeyed and people who are sentenced for breaking the law must be compelled to serve their sentences." Well, the House of Commons passed the law. They said: "As soon as the women get a taste of this they will give it up." In fact, it was passed to repress the agitation, to make the women yield — because that is what it has really come to, ladies and gentlemen. It has come to a battle between the women and the government as to who shall yield first, whether they will yield and give us the vote, or whether we will give up our agitation. Well, they little know what women are. Women are very slow to rouse, but once they are aroused, once they are determined, nothing on earth and nothing in heaven will make women give way; it is impossible. And so this Cat and Mouse Act which is being used against women today has failed; and the Home Secretary has taken advantage of the fact that Parliament is not sitting,

to revive and use alongside of it the forcible feeding. At the present time there are women lying at death's door, recovering enough strength to undergo operations, who have had both systems applied to them, and have not given in and won't give in, and who will be prepared, as soon as they get up from their sick-beds, to go on as before. There are women who are being carried from their sick-beds on stretchers into meetings. They are too weak to speak, but they go amongst their fellow-workers just to show that their spirits are unquenched, and that their spirit is alive, and they mean to go on as long as life lasts.

Now, I want to say to you who think women cannot succeed, we have brought the government of England to this position, that it has to face this alternative: either women are to be killed or women are to have the vote. I ask American men in this meeting, what would you say if in your State you were faced with that alternative, that you must either kill them or give them their citizenship, — women, many of whom you respect, women whom you know have lived useful lives, women whom you know, even if you do not know them personally, are animated with the highest motives, women who are in pursuit of liberty and the power to do useful public service? Well, there is only one answer to that alternative; there is only one way out of it, unless you

10

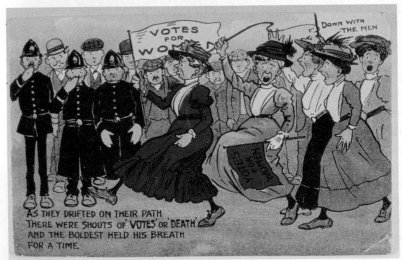

AS THEY DRIFTED ON THEIR PATH
THERE WERE SHOUTS OF VOTES OR DEATH
AND THE BOLDEST HELD HIS BREATH
FOR A TIME.

Snark/Art Resource, NY

In this cartoon, suffragettes carry banners reading "VOTES FOR WOMEN" and "DOWN WITH THE MEN." The text at the bottom of the image says, "AS THEY DRIFTED ON THEIR PATH / THERE WERE SHOUTS OF '**VOTES**' OR '**DEATH**' / AND THE BOLDEST HELD HIS BREATH / FOR A TIME." **How does this cartoon portray the suffragettes? What position does the cartoonist take on their tactics?**

seeing connections

In 2017, white nationalist Richard Spencer was invited to speak at the University of Florida. The planned event inspired a protest denouncing the hatred and bigotry Spencer and his followers espouse. On the day of Spencer's speech, a man named Randy Furniss, wearing a white tee-shirt covered in swastikas, mingled with the crowd of protesters. In one photograph included here, an anonymous man punches Furniss in the jaw. The other image, from a viral video of the event, shows an African American man named Aaron Courtney hugging Furniss in the aftermath of the punch. In the video, Courtney asks him, "Why do you hate me?" and Furniss replies, "I don't know."

Consider these images carefully, and think about how modern-day protests relate to historically successful protest movements.

1. **How would you characterize the purpose of the protests against Spencer speaking at the University of Florida?**
2. **To what extent do you see the actions of such protesters as the kind of militant resistance Pankhurst advocates in "Freedom or Death"?**
3. **What kinds of protest tactics do you believe are most successful in the present day? How do they compare to those that Pankhurst and the WSPU undertook for women's suffrage?**

Brian Blanco/Getty Images

are prepared to put back civilization two or three generations; you must give those women the vote. Now that is the outcome of our civil war.

You won your freedom in America when you had the revolution, by bloodshed, by sacrificing human life. You won the civil war by the sacrifice of human life when you decided to emancipate the negro. You have left it to women in your land, the men of all civilized countries have left it to women, to work out their own salvation. That is the way in which we women of England are doing. Human life for us is sacred, but we say if any life is to be sacrificed it shall be ours; we won't do it ourselves, but we will put the enemy in the position where they will have to choose between giving us freedom or giving us death.

So here am I. I come in the intervals of prison appearance; I come after having been four times imprisoned under the Cat and Mouse Act, probably going back to be rearrested as soon as I set my foot on British soil. I come to ask you to help to win this fight. If we win it, this hardest of all fights, then, to be sure, in the future it is going to be made easier for women all over the world to win their fight when their time comes.

[1913]

EXPLORING THE TEXT

1. At the opening of her speech, Emmeline Pankhurst states that in England, the suffragette movement "has passed beyond the realm of advocacy and it has entered into the sphere of practical politics" (para. 1). What does she mean by this statement? How does it relate to the rhetorical situation?

2. In paragraph 1, Pankhurst introduces an extended metaphor in which she compares suffragettes to soldiers and their movement to battle. How does Pankhurst develop this metaphor throughout the speech? What tone does it establish at the outset?

3. Pankhurst asks the men of her audience to put themselves in the position of women multiple times: "If I were a man and I said to you" (para. 2); "Suppose the men of Hartford had a grievance" (para. 4); and "But let the men of Hartford imagine" (para. 4). What is the effect of this strategy? Why does Pankhurst use this strategy early on in her speech?

4. In paragraph 4, Pankhurst refers to the American Revolution. How does this allusion serve her purpose?

5. What is the "domestic illustration" Pankhurst describes in paragraph 5? How does it contribute to the development of her argument, and what is its intended effect on her audience?

6. What is the purpose and effect of Pankhurst's repetition of the phrase "more and more" in paragraphs 6 and 8?

7. What does Pankhurst mean when she says that "government does not rest upon force at all; it rests upon consent" (para. 7)? What rhetorical strategies does she employ to support this position?

8. How was being put in prison a "valuable" experience for the suffragettes, according to Pankhurst (para. 7)? How does what they "learned" help convey her message to her audience?

9. Consider the section of the speech that addresses the hunger strike and the Cat and Mouse Act (para. 9). What role does this section play in Pankhurst's overall argument? How does she use rhetoric to achieve her purpose in this paragraph?

10. How does Pankhurst use syntax to build to the concluding sentence of paragraph 10?

11. Who is Pankhurst addressing in paragraph 11 when she repeatedly uses the pronoun *you*? Who is the "enemy," according to Pankhurst? How does this paragraph appeal to women and men differently?

12. Examine the last two paragraphs of the speech. How do the paragraphs relate to one another? How do they help achieve Pankhurst's larger purposes?

Politics and the English Language

GEORGE ORWELL

George Orwell (1903–1950) is the pseudonym of Eric Arthur Blair, a writer who was the son of an English civil servant during the Raj, the British rule of India. Orwell was educated in England, but when financial constraints prevented him from attending university, he joined the India Imperial Police Force in Burma, an experience immortalized in his famous essay "Shooting an Elephant." He returned to England five years later, but in 1928 he moved to Paris. There he took on a series of menial jobs, which he described in his first book, *Down and Out in Paris and London* (1933). Later Orwell worked as a schoolteacher, fought on the side of the Republicans in the Spanish Civil War, and began writing for magazines, often speaking out against economic injustice. He finally gained recognition and considerable financial success with his novels *Animal Farm* (1945) and *Nineteen Eighty-Four* (1949). The term *Orwellian* came to describe mechanisms used by totalitarian governments to manipulate the populace in order to enforce conformity. In the following essay, which first appeared in *Horizon* in 1946, Orwell explores the impact of totalitarian thinking on language.

Most people who bother with the matter at all would admit that the English language is in a bad way, but it is generally assumed that we cannot by conscious action do anything about it. Our civilization is decadent and our language — so the argument runs — must inevitably share in the general collapse. It follows that any struggle against the abuse of language is a sentimental archaism, like preferring candles to electric light or hansom cabs to aeroplanes. Underneath this lies the half-conscious belief that language is a natural growth and not an instrument which we shape for our own purposes.

Now, it is clear that the decline of a language must ultimately have political and economic causes: it is not due simply to the bad influence of this or that individual writer. But an effect can become a cause, reinforcing the original cause and producing the same effect in an intensified form, and so on indefinitely. A man may take to drink because he feels himself to be a failure, and then fail all the more completely because he drinks. It is rather the same thing that is happening to the English language. It becomes ugly and inaccurate because our thoughts are foolish, but the slovenliness of our language makes it easier

for us to have foolish thoughts. The point is that the process is reversible. Modern English, especially written English, is full of bad habits which spread by imitation and which can be avoided if one is willing to take the necessary trouble. If one gets rid of these habits one can think more clearly, and to think clearly is a necessary first step towards political regeneration: so that the fight against bad English is not frivolous and is not the exclusive concern of professional writers. I will come back to this presently, and I hope that by that time the meaning of what I have said here will have become clearer. Meanwhile, here are five specimens of the English language as it is now habitually written.

These five passages have not been picked out because they are especially bad — I could have quoted far worse if I had chosen — but because they illustrate various of the mental vices from which we now suffer. They are a little below the average, but are fairly representative samples. I number them so that I can refer back to them when necessary:

> (1) I am not, indeed, sure whether it is not true to say that the Milton who once seemed not unlike a seventeenth-century Shelley had not become,

"It's a good speech—just a couple of points that need obfuscation."

◀

This cartoon by Mike Twohy appeared in the *New Yorker* in 2002.

How does this image use humor to illustrate one of Orwell's main points in "Politics and the English Language"?

out of an experience ever more bitter in each year, more alien [*sic*] to the founder of that Jesuit sect which nothing could induce him to tolerate.

> — Professor Harold Laski (Essay in *Freedom of Expression*)

(2) Above all, we cannot play ducks and drakes with a native battery of idioms which prescribes such egregious collocations of vocables as the Basic *put up with* for *tolerate* or *put at a loss* for *bewilder*.

> — Professor Lancelot Hogben (*Interglossa*)

(3) On the one side we have the free personality: by definition it is not neurotic, for it has neither conflict nor dream. Its desires, such as they are, are transparent, for they are just what institutional approval keeps in the forefront of consciousness; another institutional pattern would alter their number and intensity; there is little in them that is natural, irreducible, or culturally dangerous. But *on the other side*, the social bond itself is nothing but the mutual reflection of these self-secure integrities. Recall the definition of love. Is not this the very picture of a small academic? Where is there a place in this hall of mirrors for either personality or fraternity?

> — Essay on psychology in *Politics* (New York)

(4) All the "best people" from the gentlemen's clubs, and all the frantic fascist captains, united in common hatred of Socialism and bestial horror of the rising tide of the mass revolutionary movement, have turned to acts of provocation, to foul incendiarism, to medieval legends of poisoned wells, to legalize their own destruction of proletarian organizations, and rouse the agitated petty-bourgeoisie to chauvinistic fervor on behalf of the fight against the revolutionary way out of the crisis.

> — Communist pamphlet

(5) If a new spirit *is* to be infused into this old country, there is one thorny and contentious reform which must be tackled, and that is the humanization and galvanization of the B.B.C. Timidity here will bespeak canker and atrophy of the soul. The heart of Britain may be sound and of strong beat, for instance, but the British lion's roar at present is like that of Bottom in Shakespeare's

Midsummer Night's Dream — as gentle as any sucking dove. A virile new Britain cannot continue indefinitely to be traduced in the eyes, or rather ears, of the world by the effete languors of Langham Place, brazenly masquerading as "standard English." When the Voice of Britain is heard at nine o'clock, better far and infinitely less ludicrous to hear aitches honestly dropped than the present priggish, inflated, inhibited, school-ma'amish arch braying of blameless bashful mewing maidens!

> — Letter in *Tribune*

Each of these passages has faults of its own, but, quite apart from avoidable ugliness, two qualities are common to all of them. The first is staleness of imagery; the other is lack of precision. The writer either had a meaning and cannot express it, or he inadvertently says something else, or he is almost indifferent as to whether his words mean anything or not. This mixture of vagueness and sheer incompetence is the most marked characteristic of modern English prose, and especially of any kind of political writing. As soon as certain topics are raised, the concrete melts into the abstract and no one seems able to think of terms of speech that are not hackneyed: prose consists less and less of *words* chosen for the sake of their meaning, and more and more of *phrases* tacked together like the sections of a prefabricated henhouse. I list below, with notes and examples, various of the tricks by means of which the work of prose-construction is habitually dodged:

Dying Metaphors

A newly invented metaphor assists thought by evoking a visual image, while on the other hand a metaphor which is technically "dead" (e.g., *iron resolution*) has in effect reverted to being an ordinary word and can generally be used without loss of vividness. But in between these two classes there is a huge dump of worn-out metaphors which have lost all evocative power and are merely used because they save people the trouble

IT'S ON | THE INTERNET | SO IT MUST | BE TRUE!

©DAVEGRANLUND.COM
POLITICALCARTOONS.COM

Dave Granlund, Politicalcartoons.com

This cartoon was created by Dave Granlund shortly after the 2016 presidential election. **Who does Granlund hold responsible for "fake news"? Who would Orwell consider responsible?**

of inventing phrases for themselves. Examples are: *Ring the changes on, take up the cudgels for, toe the line, ride roughshod over, stand shoulder to shoulder with, play into the hands of, no axe to grind, grist to the mill, fishing in troubled waters, rift within the lute, on the order of the day, Achilles' heel, swan song, hotbed.* Many of these are used without knowledge of their meaning (what is a "rift," for instance?), and incompatible metaphors are frequently mixed, a sure sign that the writer is not interested in what he is saying. Some metaphors now current have been twisted out of their original meaning without those who use them even being aware of the fact. For example, *toe the line* is sometimes written *tow the line.* Another example is *the hammer and the anvil,* now always used with the implication that the anvil gets the worst of it. In real life it is always the anvil that breaks the hammer, never the other way about: a writer who stopped to think what he was saying would be aware of this, and would avoid perverting the original phrase.

Operators or Verbal False Limbs

These save the trouble of picking out appropriate verbs and nouns, and at the same time pad each sentence with extra syllables which give it an appearance of symmetry. Characteristic phrases are *render inoperative, militate against, make contact with, be subjected to, give rise to, give grounds for, have the effect of, play a leading part (role) in, make itself felt, take effect, exhibit a tendency to, serve the purpose of, etc., etc.* The keynote is, the elimination of simple verbs. Instead of being a single word, such as *break, stop, spoil, mend, kill,* a verb becomes a *phrase,* made up of a noun or adjective tacked on to some general-purposes verb such as *prove, serve, form, play, render.* In addition, the passive voice is wherever possible used in preference to the active, and noun constructions are used instead of gerunds (*by examination of* instead of *by examining*). The range of verbs is further cut down by means of the *-ize* and *de-* formations, and the banal statements are given an appearance of profundity by means of the *not un-* formation. Simple conjunctions and prepositions are replaced by such phrases as *with respect to, having regard to, the fact that, by dint of, in view of, in the interests of, on the hypothesis that*; and the ends of sentences are saved from anticlimax by such resounding commonplaces as *greatly to be desired, cannot be left out of account, a development to be expected in the near future, deserving of serious* *consideration, brought to a satisfactory conclusion,* and so on and so forth.

Pretentious Diction

Words like *phenomenon, element, individual* (as noun), *objective, categorical, effective, virtual, basic, primary, promote, constitute, exhibit, exploit, utilize, eliminate, liquidate* are used to dress up simple statements and give an air of scientific impartiality to biased judgments. Adjectives like *epoch-making, epic, historic, unforgettable, triumphant, age-old, inevitable, inexorable, veritable* are used to dignify the sordid processes of international politics, while writing that aims at glorifying war usually takes on an archaic color, its characteristic words being: *realm, throne, chariot, mailed fist, trident, sword, shield, buckler, banner, jackboot, clarion.* Foreign words and expressions such as *cul de sac, ancien régime, deus ex machina, mutatis mutandis, status quo, Gleichschaltung, Weltanschauung* are used to give an air of culture and elegance. Except for the useful abbreviations *i.e., e.g.,* and *etc.,* there is no real need for any of the hundreds of foreign phrases now current in English. Bad writers, and especially scientific, political and sociological writers, are nearly always haunted by the notion that Latin or Greek words are grander than Saxon ones, and unnecessary words like *expedite, ameliorate, predict, extraneous, deracinated, clandestine, subaqueous* and hundreds of others constantly gain ground from their Anglo-Saxon opposite numbers.[1] The jargon peculiar to Marxist writing (*hyena, hangman, cannibal, petty bourgeois, these gentry, lacquey, flunkey, mad dog, White Guard,* etc.) consists largely of words and phrases translated from Russian, German or French; but the normal way of coining a new word is to use a Latin or Greek root

with the appropriate affix and, where necessary, the *-ize* formation. It is often easier to make up words of this kind (*deregionalize, impermissible, extramarital, non-fragmentary* and so forth) than to think up the English words that will cover one's meaning. The result, in general, is an increase in slovenliness and vagueness.

Meaningless Words

In certain kinds of writing, particularly in art criticism and literary criticism, it is normal to come across long passages which are almost completely lacking in meaning.[2] Words like *romantic, plastic, values, human, dead, sentimental, natural, vitality,* as used in art criticism, are strictly meaningless, in the sense that they not only do not point to any discoverable object, but are hardly ever expected to do so by the reader. When one critic writes, "The outstanding feature of Mr. X's work is its living quality," while another writes, "The immediately striking thing about Mr. X's work is its peculiar deadness," the reader accepts this as a simple difference of opinion. If words like *black* and *white* were involved, instead of the jargon words *dead* and *living,* he would see at once that language was being used in an improper way. Many political words are similarly abused. The word *Fascism* has now no meaning except in so far as it signifies "something not desirable." The words *democracy, socialism, freedom, patriotic, realistic, justice* have each of them several different meanings which cannot be reconciled with one another. In the case of a word like *democracy,* not only is there no agreed definition, but the attempt to make one is resisted from all sides. It is almost universally felt that when we call a country democratic we are praising it: consequently the defenders of every kind of régime claim that

---

[1] An interesting illustration of this is the way in which the English flower names which were in use till very recently are being ousted by Greek ones, *snapdragon* becoming *antirrhinum, forget-me-not* becoming *myosotis,* etc. It is hard to see any practical reason for this change of fashion: it is probably due to an instinctive turning-away from the more homely word and a vague feeling that the Greek word is scientific.

[2] Example: "Comfort's catholicity of perception and image, strangely Whitmanesque in range, almost the exact opposite in aesthetic compulsion, continues to evoke that trembling atmospheric accumulative hinting at a cruel, an inexorably serene timelessness. . . . Wrey Gardiner scores by aiming at simple bull's-eyes with precision. Only they are not so simple, and through this contented radness runs more than the surface bitter-sweet of resignation."

it is a democracy, and fear that they might have to stop using the word if it were tied down to any one meaning. Words of this kind are often used in a consciously dishonest way. That is, the person who uses them has his own private definition, but allows his hearer to think he means something quite different. Statements like *Marshal Pétain*[3] *was a true patriot, The Soviet Press is the freest in the world, The Catholic Church is opposed to persecution* are almost always made with intent to deceive. Other words used in variable meanings, in most cases more or less dishonestly, are: *class, totalitarian, science, progressive, reactionary, bourgeois, equality.*

Now that I have made this catalogue of swindles and perversions, let me give another example of the kind of writing that they lead to. This time it must of its nature be an imaginary one. I am going to translate a passage of good English into modern English of the worst sort. Here is a well-known verse from Ecclesiastes:

> I returned and saw under the sun, that the race is not to the swift, nor the battle to the strong, neither yet bread to the wise, nor yet riches to men of understanding, nor yet favour to men of skill; but time and chance happeneth to them all.

Here it is in modern English: 10

> Objective consideration of contemporary phenomena compels the conclusion that success or failure in competitive activities exhibits no tendency to be commensurate with innate capacity, but that a considerable element of the unpredictable must invariably be taken into account.

This is a parody, but not a very gross one. Exhibit (3), above, for instance, contains several patches of the same kind of English. It will be seen that I have not made a full translation. The beginning and ending of the sentence follow the original meaning fairly closely, but in the

middle the concrete illustrations — race, battle, bread — dissolve into the vague phrase "success or failure in competitive activities." This had to be so, because no modern writer of the kind I am discussing — no one capable of using phrases like "objective consideration of contemporary phenomena" — would ever tabulate his thoughts in that precise and detailed way. The whole tendency of modern prose is away from concreteness. Now analyse these two sentences a little more closely. The first contains forty-nine words but only sixty syllables, and all its words are those of everyday life. The second contains thirty-eight words of ninety syllables: eighteen of its words are from Latin roots, and one from Greek. The first sentence contains six vivid images, and only one phrase ("time and chance") that could be called vague. The second contains not a single fresh, arresting phrase, and in spite of its ninety syllables it gives only a shortened version of the meaning contained in the first. Yet without a doubt it is the second kind of sentence that is gaining ground in modern English. I do not want to exaggerate. This kind of writing is not yet universal, and outcrops of simplicity will occur here and there in the worst-written page. Still, if you or I were to write a few lines on the uncertainty of human fortunes, we should probably come much nearer to my imaginary sentence than to the one from Ecclesiastes.

As I have tried to show, modern writing at its worst does not consist in picking out words for the sake of their meaning and inventing images in order to make the meaning clearer. It consists in gumming together long strips of words which have already been set in order by someone else, and making the results presentable by sheer humbug. The attraction of this way of writing is that it is easy. It is easier — even quicker, once you have the habit — to say *In my opinion it is not an unjustifiable assumption that* than to say *I think.* If you use ready-made phrases, you not only don't have to hunt about for words; you also don't have to bother with

---

[3] Henri Phillipe Pétain (1856–1951), head of the French government during the German occupation from 1940 to 1945, was convicted of treason in 1945. —Eds.

the rhythms of your sentences, since these phrases are generally so arranged as to be more or less euphonious. When you are composing in a hurry — when you are dictating to a stenographer, for instance, or making a public speech — it is natural to fall into a pretentious, Latinized style. Tags like *a consideration which we should do well to bear in mind* or *a conclusion to which all of us would readily assent* will save many a sentence from coming down with a bump. By using stale metaphors, similes and idioms, you save much mental effort, at the cost of leaving your meaning vague, not only for your reader but for yourself. This is the significance of mixed metaphors. The sole aim of a metaphor is to call up a visual image. When these images clash — as in *The Fascist octopus has sung its swan song, the jackboot is thrown into the melting pot* — it can be taken as certain that the writer is not seeing a mental image of the objects he is naming; in other words he is not really thinking. Look again at the examples I gave at the beginning of this essay. Professor Laski (1) uses five negatives in fifty-three words. One of these is superfluous, making nonsense of the whole passage, and in addition there is the slip *alien* for akin, making further nonsense, and several avoidable pieces of clumsiness which increase the general vagueness. Professor Hogben (2) plays ducks and drakes with a battery which is able to write prescriptions, and, while disapproving of the everyday phrase *put up with*, is unwilling to look *egregious* up in the dictionary and see what it means; (3), if one takes an uncharitable attitude towards it, is simply meaningless: probably one could work out its intended meaning by reading the whole of the article in which it occurs. In (4), the writer knows more or less what he wants to say, but an accumulation of stale phrases chokes him like tea leaves blocking a sink. In (5), words and meaning have almost parted company. People who write in this manner usually have a general emotional meaning — they dislike one thing and

want to express solidarity with another — but they are not interested in the detail of what they are saying. A scrupulous writer, in every sentence that he writes, will ask himself at least four questions, thus: What am I trying to say? What words will express it? What image or idiom will make it clearer? Is this image fresh enough to have an effect? And he will probably ask himself two more: Could I put it more shortly? Have I said anything that is avoidably ugly? But you are not obliged to go to all this trouble. You can shirk it by simply throwing your mind open and letting the ready-made phrases come crowding in. They will construct your sentences for you — even think your thoughts for you, to a certain extent — and at need they will perform the important service of partially concealing your meaning even from yourself. It is at this point that the special connection between politics and the debasement of language becomes clear.

In our time it is broadly true that political writing is bad writing. Where it is not true, it will generally be found that the writer is some kind of rebel, expressing his private opinions and not a "party line." Orthodoxy, of whatever color, seems to demand a lifeless, imitative style. The political dialects to be found in pamphlets, leading articles, manifestos, White Papers and the speeches of undersecretaries do, of course, vary from party to party, but they are all alike in that one almost never finds in them a fresh, vivid, homemade turn of speech. When one watches some tired hack on the platform mechanically repeating the familiar phrases — *bestial atrocities, iron heel, bloodstained tyranny, free peoples of the world, stand shoulder to shoulder* — one often has a curious feeling that one is not watching a live human being but some kind of dummy: a feeling which suddenly becomes stronger at moments when the light catches the speaker's spectacles and turns them into blank discs which seem to have no eyes behind them. And this is not altogether fanciful. A speaker who uses that kind of phraseology has gone some distance towards turning himself into a machine. The

seeing connections

Timothy Snyder's 2017 book *On Tyranny: Twenty Lessons from the Twentieth Century* argues that we can learn from the mistakes of the past to protect our future freedom. One of his "lessons" from the twentieth century is to "Listen for dangerous words. Be alert to the use of the words *extremism* and *terrorism*. Be alive to the fatal notions of *emergency* and *exception*. Be angry about the treacherous use of patriotic vocabulary."

Read the excerpt from *On Tyranny* and consider the ways in which the content and logic of Snyder's lesson echo Orwell in "Politics and the English Language."

from On Tyranny

Twenty Lessons from the Twentieth Century

TIMOTHY SYNDER

When politicians today invoke *terrorism* they are speaking, of course, of an actual danger. But when they try to train us to surrender freedom in the name of safety, we should be on our guard. There is no necessary tradeoff between the two. Sometimes we do indeed gain one by losing the other, and sometimes not. People who assure you that you can *only* gain security at the price of liberty usually want to deny you both....

Extremism certainly sounds bad, and governments often try to make it sound worse by using the word *terrorism* in the same sentence. But the word has little meaning. There is no doctrine called *extremism*. When tyrants speak of *extremists*, they just mean people who are not in the mainstream — as the tyrants themselves are defining that mainstream at that particular moment. Dissidents of the twentieth century, whether they were resisting fascism or communism, were called *extremists*. Modern authoritarian regimes, such as Russia, use laws on *extremism* to punish those who criticize their policies. In this way the notion of *extremism* comes to mean virtually everything except what is, in fact, extreme: tyranny.

appropriate noises are coming out of his larynx, but his brain is not involved as it would be if he were choosing his words for himself. If the speech he is making is one that he is accustomed to make over and over again, he may be almost unconscious of what he is saying, as one is when one utters the responses in church. And this reduced state of consciousness, if not indispensable, is at any rate favorable to political conformity.

In our time, political speech and writing are largely the defence of the indefensible. Things like the continuance of British rule in India, the Russian purges and deportations, the dropping of the atom bombs on Japan, can indeed be defended, but only by arguments which are too brutal for most people to face, and which do not square with the professed aims of political parties. Thus political language has to consist largely of euphemism, question-begging and sheer cloudy vagueness. Defenceless villages are bombarded from the air, the inhabitants driven out into the countryside, the cattle machine-gunned, the huts set on fire with incendiary bullets: this is called *pacification*. Millions of peasants are robbed of their farms and sent trudging along the roads with no more than they can carry: this is called *transfer of population* or *rectification of frontiers*. People are imprisoned for years without trial, or shot in the back of the neck or sent to die of scurvy in Arctic lumber camps: this is called *elimination of* unreliable elements. Such phraseology is needed if one wants to name things without calling up mental pictures of them. Consider for instance some comfortable English professor defending Russian totalitarianism. He cannot say outright, "I believe in killing off your opponents when you can get good results by doing so." Probably, therefore, he will say something like this:

> While freely conceding that the Soviet régime exhibits certain features which the humanitarian may be inclined to deplore, we must, I think, agree that a certain curtailment of the right to political opposition is an unavoidable concomitant of transitional periods, and that the rigors which the Russian people have been called upon to undergo have been amply justified in the sphere of concrete achievement.

The inflated style is itself a kind of euphemism. A mass of Latin words falls upon the facts like soft snow, blurring the outlines and covering up all the details. The great enemy of clear language is insincerity. When there is a gap between one's real and one's declared aims, one turns as it were instinctively to long words and exhausted idioms, like a cuttlefish squirting out ink. In our age there is no such thing as "keeping out of politics." All issues are political issues, and politics itself is a mass of lies, evasions, folly, hatred and schizophrenia. When the general atmosphere is bad, language must suffer. I should expect to find — this is a guess which I have not sufficient knowledge to verify — that the German, Russian and Italian languages have all deteriorated in the last ten or fifteen years, as a result of dictatorship.

But if thought corrupts language, language can also corrupt thought. A bad usage can spread by tradition and imitation, even among people who should and do know better. The debased language that I have been discussing is in some ways very convenient. Phrases like *a not unjustifiable assumption, leaves much to be desired, would serve no good purpose, a consideration which we should do well to bear in mind*, are a continuous temptation, a packet of aspirins always at one's elbow.

15

Look back through this essay, and for certain you will find that I have again and again committed the very faults I am protesting against. By this morning's post I have received a pamphlet dealing with conditions in Germany. The author tells me that he "felt impelled" to write it. I open it at random, and here is almost the first sentence that I see: "[The Allies] have an opportunity not only of achieving a radical transformation of Germany's social and political structure in such a way as to avoid a nationalistic reaction in Germany itself, but at the same time of laying the foundation of a cooperative and unified Europe." You see, he "feels impelled" to write — feels, presumably, that he has something new to say — and yet his words, like cavalry horses answering the bugle, group themselves automatically into the familiar dreary pattern. This invasion of one's mind by ready-made phrases (*lay the foundations, achieve a radical transformation*) can only be prevented if one is constantly on guard against them, and every such phrase anaesthetizes a portion of one's brain.

I said earlier that the decadence of our language is probably curable. Those who deny this would argue, if they produced an argument at all, that language merely reflects existing social conditions, and that we cannot influence its development by any direct tinkering with words and constructions. So far as the general tone or spirit of a language goes, this may be true, but it is not true in detail. Silly words and expressions have often disappeared, not through any evolutionary process but owing to the conscious action of a minority. Two recent examples were *explore every avenue* and *leave no stone unturned*, which were killed by the jeers of a few journalists. There is a long list of flyblown metaphors which could similarly be got rid of if enough people would interest themselves in the job; and it should also be possible to laugh the *not un-* formation out of existence,[4] to reduce the amount of Latin and

---

[4]One can cure oneself of the *not un-* formation by memorizing this sentence: *A not unblack dog was chasing a not unsmall rabbit across a not ungreen field.*

Greek in the average sentence, to drive out foreign phrases and strayed scientific words, and, in general, to make pretentiousness unfashionable. But all these are minor points. The defence of the English language implies more than this, and perhaps it is best to start by saying what it does *not* imply.

To begin with it has nothing to do with archaism, with the salvaging of obsolete words and turns of speech, or with the setting up of a "standard English" which must never be departed from. On the contrary, it is especially concerned with the scrapping of every word or idiom which has outworn its usefulness. It has nothing to do with correct grammar and syntax, which are of no importance so long as one makes one's meaning clear, or with the avoidance of Americanisms, or with having what is called a "good prose style." On the other hand it is not concerned with fake simplicity and the attempt to make written English colloquial. Nor does it even imply in every case preferring the Saxon word to the Latin one, though it does imply using the fewest and shortest words that will cover one's meaning. What is above all needed is to let the meaning choose the word, and not the other way about. In prose, the worst thing one can do with words is to surrender to them. When you think of a concrete object, you think wordlessly, and then, if you want to describe the thing you have been visualizing you probably hunt about till you find the exact words that seem to fit it. When you think of something abstract you are more inclined to use words from the start, and unless you make a conscious effort to prevent it, the existing dialect will come rushing in and do the job for you, at the expense of blurring or even changing your meaning. Probably it is better to put off using words as long as possible and get one's meaning as clear as one can through pictures or sensations. Afterwards one can choose — not simply *accept* — the phrases that will best cover the meaning, and then switch round and decide

what impression one's words are likely to make on another person. This last effort of the mind cuts out all stale or mixed images, all prefabricated phrases, needless repetitions, and humbug and vagueness generally. But one can often be in doubt about the effect of a word or a phrase, and one needs rules that one can rely on when instinct fails. I think the following rules will cover most cases:

(i) Never use a metaphor, simile or other figure of speech which you are used to seeing in print.

(ii) Never use a long word where a short one will do.

(iii) If it is possible to cut a word out, always cut it out.

(iv) Never use the passive where you can use the active.

(v) Never use a foreign phrase, a scientific word or a jargon word if you can think of an everyday English equivalent.

(vi) Break any of these rules sooner than say anything outright barbarous.

These rules sound elementary, and so they are, but they demand a deep change of attitude in anyone who has grown used to writing in the style now fashionable. One could keep all of them and still write bad English, but one could not write the kind of stuff that I quoted in those five specimens at the beginning of this article.

I have not here been considering the literary use of language, but merely language as an instrument for expressing and not for concealing or preventing thought. Stuart Chase[5] and others have come near to claiming that all abstract words are meaningless, and have used this as a pretext for advocating a kind of political quietism. Since you don't know what Fascism

20

---

[5]Stuart Chase (1888–1985) popularized the field of general semantics in his book *The Tyranny of Words* (1958). General semantics argued that words could never capture the entire essence of a thing; for instance, you can describe a smell, but you cannot directly share the experience with someone else. —Eds.

seeing connections

These graphs use data from a report that Pew Research Center published on the impact of fake news shortly after the 2016 presidential election. However, there is not universal agreement on what fake news means. Merriam Webster, in its explanation of why it will not likely be added to the dictionary, described fake news as a term "frequently used to describe a political story which is seen as damaging to an agency, entity, or person" and noted that though it has seen a recent increase in popularity, the concept has been consistently used since the end of the nineteenth century. Dictionary.com does offer an entry on the term, defining it as "false news stories, often of a sensational nature, created to be widely shared online for the purpose of generating ad revenue via web traffic or discrediting a public figure, political movement, company, etc." The Oxford English Dictionary has not yet created an entry because the definition of the term is still evolving.

After looking closely at the graphs included here, answer the following questions.

1. **Do you see any contradictions in Americans' perception of the impact of fake news on a national versus the personal level? If so, what are they, and to what extent does Orwell's argument account for them? If not, what does this indicate about modern American politics and civic life?**

2. **Taking both Pew's data and Orwell's "Politics and the English Language" into account, how would you define fake news? What do you believe its impact on American politics — and society — will be in the years to come?**

Americans' Views on the Effect of Fake News

% of U.S. adults who say completely made-up news has caused _____ about the basic facts of current events

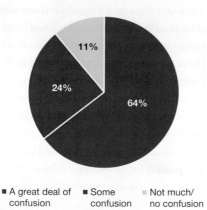

- A great deal of confusion
- Some confusion
- Not much/ no confusion

Data from Pew Research Center.

Americans' Perception of Their Ability to Recognize Fake News

% of U.S. adults who are _____ in their ability to recognize made-up news

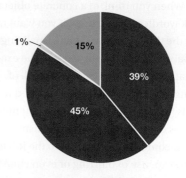

- Very confident
- Somewhat confident
- Don't know/ refused
- Not very/ at all confident

Data from Pew Research Center.

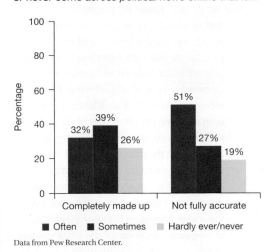

**Frequency of Americans' Encounters
with Fake News**

*% of U.S. adults who often/sometimes/hardly ever
or never come across political news online that is...*

- ■ Often ■ Sometimes ■ Hardly ever/never

Data from Pew Research Center.

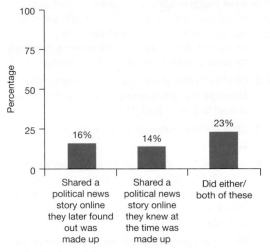

Americans Report Sharing Fake News

% of U.S. adults who say they...

Data from Pew Research Center.

is, how can you struggle against Fascism? One
need not swallow such absurdities as this, but
one ought to recognize that the present political
chaos is connected with the decay of language,
and that one can probably bring about some
improvement by starting at the verbal end. If
you simplify your English, you are freed from the
worst follies of orthodoxy. You cannot speak any
of the necessary dialects, and when you make
a stupid remark its stupidity will be obvious,
even to yourself. Political language — and with
variations this is true of all political parties, from

Conservatives to Anarchists — is designed to
make lies sound truthful and murder respectable, and to give an appearance of solidity to
pure wind. One cannot change this all in a
moment, but one can at least change one's own
habits, and from time to time one can even, if
one jeers loudly enough, send some worn-out
and useless phrase — some *jackboot, Achilles'
heel, hotbed, melting pot, acid test, veritable
inferno* or other lump of verbal refuse — into the
dustbin where it belongs.

[1946]

EXPLORING THE TEXT

1. George Orwell argues against the "belief that
   language is a natural growth and not an instrument
   which we shape for our own purposes" (para. 1).
   Explain why you do or do not agree with Orwell's
   position.

2. Do you agree or disagree with Orwell's opening
   statement that "the English language is in a bad
   way" (para. 1). Support your answer with examples
   from your reading and personal experience.

3. In speeches by contemporary politicians, find
   examples of each type of writing problem that
   Orwell discusses: dying metaphors, operators
   or verbal false limbs, pretentious diction, and
   meaningless words. Explain why the examples
   you've cited are "swindles and perversions," as
   Orwell calls them (para. 9).

4. Why does Orwell object to "ready-made phrases"
   and "mixed metaphors" (para. 12)?

5. In paragraph 12, Orwell says that every writer "ask[s] himself at least four questions, thus: What am I trying to say? What words will express it? What image or idiom will make it clearer? Is this image fresh enough to have an effect?" What do you think of these questions? Do you agree or disagree that they are the most essential questions for writers to ask themselves? Explain why.

6. What does Orwell mean when he asserts, "But if thought corrupts language, language can also corrupt thought" (para. 16)?

7. What is Orwell's thesis? Does he actually state it, or is it implied?

8. In each of the following paragraphs — paragraphs 4, 5, 12, 15, and 16 — Orwell uses at least one metaphor or simile. Identify each figure of speech. Then explain how it works and whether you find it rhetorically effective.

9. What is the purpose of the additional information provided in Orwell's footnotes for paragraphs 7 and 8? Why do you think Orwell chose to put the information in footnotes rather than in the main text?

10. Orwell wrote this essay before he was well known for his novels. He uses the first person, yet he does not directly state his qualifications to speak on language. How does he establish ethos?

11. How would you describe the overall organization of this essay? Examine its movement, from the examples in the opening to the rules near the ending.

12. What is Orwell's purpose in writing this essay? How might the historical context of post–World War II affect that purpose? Cite specific passages to support your response.

13. How would you describe the tone of Orwell's essay? Can you sum it up in one word, or does the essay range from one tone to another? Cite specific passages to support your response.

14. Compare and contrast paragraph 14 in Orwell's essay with the following paragraph from Toni Morrison's 1993 Nobel Prize speech.

> The systematic looting of language can be recognized by the tendency of its users to forgo its nuanced, complex, mid-wifery properties for menace and subjugation. Oppressive language does more than represent violence; it is violence; does more than represent the limits of knowledge; it limits knowledge. Whether it is obscuring state language or the faux-language of mindless media; whether it is the proud but calcified language of the academy or the commodity driven language of science; whether it is the malign language of law-without-ethics, or language designed for the estrangement of minorities, hiding its racist plunder in its literary cheek — it must be rejected, altered and exposed. It is the language that drinks blood, laps vulnerabilities, tucks its fascist boots under crinolines of respectability and patriotism as it moves relentlessly toward the bottom line and the bottomed-out mind. Sexist language, racist language, theistic language — all are typical of the policing languages of mastery, and cannot, do not permit new knowledge or encourage the mutual exchange of ideas.

What ideas do the two passages have in common? In what ways are they different? What do each of the passages have to say about the connection between language and justice?

A Home for American Jurisprudence

EARL WARREN

Earl Warren (1891–1974) was an American judge and politician who served as California's Attorney General from 1939–1943, Governor of California from 1943–1953, and Chief Justice of the United States from 1953–1969. Warren's time on the Supreme Court is best known for several landmark decisions, including desegregating public schools, ending prayer in public school, and requiring one man-one vote rules for the creation of election districts. The decisions Warren oversaw during his tenure, often called the Warren Court, solidified the judiciary's power to check both the legislature and the president. Warren gave the following speech at the seventy-seventh annual American Bar Association (ABA) meeting on the University of Chicago campus in 1954. Given before an audience of lawyers, this speech was also part of the dedication ceremony of the American Bar Center, which has since served as the national headquarters of the ABA. A voluntary association of lawyers and students, the ABA is responsible for setting the academic standards of law schools and the ethical standards of the legal profession. Currently, the ABA has over 400,000 members.

Until today, the buildings which we are here dedicating were mere walls and ceilings, composites of mortar, bricks and steel. Like other structures they could have been adapted to a variety of uses and to purposes either high or low.

Today in the presence of each other and standing before the world, we of the American Bar Association testify to the high purpose which brought them into being and to the fond hopes we have for their usefulness to mankind.

From this day forward we shall call them home, with all that word implies, not only for the organized Bar of the nation, but also for the abiding spirit of American jurisprudence. Not merely a home for lawyers, but also for the law.

It is a happy day for us, but what is even more significant we purpose that it shall be an important one in the life of our nation.

It is fitting that we have this dedicatory service 5 in a house of God. Here in this beautiful chapel which stands so close to our new home, as if to guard it from evil, we give notice to all, that in the world struggle between the forces of freedom and the godless totalitarian state, we rededicate ourselves to the principle that God's way is our way.

It is most fortunate that the site for our home was contributed by and is adjacent to one of the great universities of the world, where unfettered men and women pursue knowledge in every field to establish the truths that will keep us free. It will be a constant reminder to us that in our endeavor to keep our institutions stable and at the same time flexible to meet the changing conditions of every age, we must insist upon man's right to knowledge and the free use thereof; the right to explore at will, to disagree and even to dissent from the opinions of the majority. As evidence of such a purpose, we have carved on one of our walls this quotation from a great lover of freedom: "Give me the liberty to know, to think, to believe, and to utter freely, acording to my conscience, above all other liberties."[1]

It is also a fortuitous circumstance that our new home should be situated in the very heart of America, in this city of cross-roads leading to all parts of the nation, the great City of Chicago. Pilgrims of freedom will beat a path to our shrine, and after being refreshed here, will return to the four corners of the country equipped with knowledge and strengthened in spirit. Perhaps even pilgrims from other lands will come bringing us knowledge of how freedom fares in their particular sections of the globe, prepared to exchange ideas and to learn with us how we can apply to ever-changing conditions the never-changing principles of freedom.

It is from a wonderful vantage point that we will be privileged to thus commune. Our home is close to Lake Michigan, one of the beautiful Great Lakes whose friendly waters alone separate this part of our country from our incomparable Canadian neighbor to the north. They are part of an invisible boundary line from ocean

---

[1] A quote from a speech John Milton gave before Parliament in 1644, defending the right of freedom of speech. —Eds.

to ocean that only a surveyor could define; the most secure boundary line on earth because it is guarded zealously on both sides solely by friendship.

To strangers it should be an inspiration to see these two great countries existing side by side in harmony with each other merely because both are dedicated to freedom, to justice and in peace. It should also be evidence, if evidence is needed, to prove that if we are to achieve a peaceful world, it will be accomplished through ideas rather than armaments; through a sense of justice and mutual friendships rather than with guns and bombs and guided missiles.

We are living in a world of ideas and are *10* going through a world war of ideas. Everywhere there is a contest for the hearts and minds of people. Every political concept is under scrutiny. Our American system, like all others, is on trial both at home and abroad. The way it works; the manner in which it solves the problems of our day; the extent to which we maintain the spirit of our Constitution with its Bill of Rights, will in the long run do more to make it both secure and the object of adulation than the number of hydrogen bombs we stockpile.

We say that ours is a government of laws and not of men. It is with these laws and their administration that the lawyers of America are particularly concerned. It is to improve these laws and to make them better serve the public weal, that we have constructed this Law Center and planned its activities.

We are not like some who are satisfied with their own lot to the point of complacency. We do not believe that perfection in government is ever permanently achieved. We do not believe we can honorably accept our heritage of freedom without assuming the responsibility for preserving it and passing it on unimpaired to those who follow us. We believe that so long as human nature is as it is, there must be a constant struggle to preserve our freedoms. We do not propose to let nature take its course, On the contrary, we are

In this photograph from 1963, dueling billboards on a California highway argue for and against Earl Warren's position as Chief Justice of the Supreme Court. **What do these billboards suggest about the role that lawyers and judges play in dispensing justice? What evidence do you see in Warren's speech to suggest he was a politically divisive figure?**

Bettmann/Getty Images

determined here to create the climate essential to the constant improvement of both the text of our law and its application to the affairs of people.

The law schools of the nation and their students will help us. Fifteen hundred state and local bar associations will be our allies. There are 225,000 lawyers in the country. They too will be our allies. Fifty-two thousand of them are already the bone and sinew of our Association.

We beckon the others to join us in one great crusade, because every true lawyer is interested in the improvement of the administration of justice. That is our cause, and we could do so much together.

We earnestly hope this Center will be the catalyst for our entire profession. Here every lawyer from city, town or country, as an individual or through his local or state bar association could make his presence felt to remedy the defects we have inherited as well as those that continually creep into human institutions. As lawyers we know better than most other people that there are defects in our administration of justice. With adequate research we can strengthen our leadership in remedying them.

Some of these defects we know now. We know that in some parts of our country a citizen cannot have his case tried within four years. We know this situation means a denial of justice to litigants. We know also that millions of people are financially unable to obtain adequate legal advice or to protect their rights in the courts, and that this too is a denial of justice. We know that civil liberties are too often violated and that whenever that occurs, something is chipped away from the foundation of our institutions. We know that in some states a man charged with felony is not guaranteed the services of a lawyer. We realize that that is a remnant of another day.

Every lawyer appreciates the fact that no man accused of a serious offense is capable of representing himself. We all learned as far back as law school days that even a lawyer is incapable of

15

doing so. I am sure that none of us have forgotten the adage that a lawyer who represents himself has a fool for a client.

We are sensitive to the fact that technicalities, anachronisms and lack of uniformity in the law still beset us in the ascertainment of facts and that haphazard methods of appointing judges, inadequate court organization and loose courtroom practices too often cause delay, confusion, inefficiency and consequent unjustifiable expense. We are regretfully aware that lawyer conduct often contributes to these unfortunate conditions. As a profession we do not seek to avoid responsibility for it. We will not sweep the dust under the rug.

Here in our new home, we will honestly face all of our family problems as an integral part of greater problems of justice. We will maintain the American concept of freedom and justice for all. We will rededicate ourselves to constitutional principles. We will urge others to do likewise.

The genius of our American institutions is the spirit that has been breathed into them — the spirit of a free, just and friendly people. As that spirit is strengthened or weakened so is our government strengthened or weakened. We of the American Bar Association would not only maintain that spirit, we would fortify it to meet every emergency that could confront our nation in the confused and turbulent world in which we are living. To that cause we dedicate our American Bar Center. In that cause we dedicate ourselves to "do justly and love mercy and walk humbly with God."

[1954]

EXPLORING THE TEXT

1. How does Earl Warren acknowledge the occasion for this speech in the first three paragraphs, and how does his rhetoric establish his position on the importance of the Center?

2. Although Warren was Chief Justice of the Supreme Court at the time, he makes no mention of it in his speech. What persona does Warren portray, how is

it developed, and how is it related to the purpose of his speech?

3. Who is Warren's immediate audience? How does Warren use rhetoric to appeal to this audience? Consider his diction, appeals, and use of imagery. Be sure to identify specific examples of the strategies he employs and explain their

effectiveness. In what ways does his language suggest that he is aware this speech will be read in the distant future?

4. What is Warren's position on the relationship between American law and foreign law? How would you characterize his attitude toward foreign countries? Explain how he uses language to convey that attitude.

5. In paragraph 3, Warren calls the buildings "home, with all that word implies." What does that word imply? How does Warren's use of the word *home* connect to his position on the role of the Center?

6. What is the connotation of the word *spirit* in paragraph 3? Warren uses the word elsewhere, including in paragraph 19, where he states that "the genius of our American institutions is the spirit that has been breathed into them." Is he using the word *spirit* the same way here as he did in paragraph 3?

7. At the time of the speech, America had was seven years into what is known as the Cold War period with communist Soviet Union, and global tension was high. How does Warren acknowledge this larger context in paragraphs 5–8? How does his language and syntax in these paragraphs serve his purpose in this context?

8. In paragraph 12, Warren says, "There must be a constant struggle to preserve our freedoms. We do not propose to let nature take its course." What does he mean by this?

9. In paragraphs 14–16, Warren discusses the "defects in our administration of justice." Why does he use the word "defect"? How does this discussion contribute to the development of Warren's overall argument?

10. Examine Warren's final three paragraphs. How does he appeal to his audience, and what tone does he strike? What purpose do these paragraphs serve?

11. Warren delivered this speech only three months after the Court's unanimous ruling in Brown v. Board of Education, the landmark case that made segregation in public schools unconstitutional. Warren himself wrote the decision, which found that racial segregation is "inherently unequal." Do you see any evidence of how this aspect of the larger context may have influenced the content, tone, or purpose of Warren's speech here? Be sure to provide textual support and an explanation of how the support proves your analysis.

12. Research whether any buildings near you or your school have had a formal dedication ceremony to commemorate the building's specific purpose. Choose one of these buildings and, after conducting research, take a position on whether the building is currently fulfilling the intent or purpose of its original dedication.

Inaugural Address

JOHN F. KENNEDY

John F. Kennedy (1917–1963) was a Democratic politician who served as the thirty-fifth President of the United States from January 1961 until his assassination in November 1963. Before that, he represented Massachusetts in both the House of Representatives and the Senate. President Kennedy served at the height of the Cold War, and much of his presidency focused on managing relations with the Soviet Union. These tensions nearly boiled over during the 1962 Cuban Missile Crisis, when American spy planes discovered Soviet missile bases in Cuba. Kennedy also presided over the establishment of the Peace Corps and supported the civil rights movement, but his early death prevented him from advancing his domestic agenda. After his assassination, many of his proposals were enacted, including the Civil Rights Act of 1964. Throughout his career, Kennedy was known as an eloquent public speaker, and his average approval rating remains the highest of any past president. He gave the following speech at his presidential inauguration on January 20, 1961.

Vice President Johnson, Mr. Speaker, Mr. Chief Justice, President Eisenhower, Vice President Nixon, President Truman, Reverend Clergy, fellow citizens:

We observe today not a victory of party but a celebration of freedom — symbolizing an end as well as a beginning — signifying renewal as well as change. For I have sworn before you and Almighty God the same solemn oath our forebears prescribed nearly a century and three-quarters ago.

The world is very different now. For man holds in his mortal hands the power to abolish all forms of human poverty and all forms of human life. And yet the same revolutionary beliefs for which our forebears fought are still at issue around the globe — the belief that the rights of man come not from the generosity of the state but from the hand of God.

We dare not forget today that we are the heirs of that first revolution. Let the word go forth from this time and place, to friend and foe alike, that the torch has been passed to a new generation of Americans — born in this century, tempered by war, disciplined by a hard and bitter peace, proud of our ancient heritage — and unwilling to witness or permit the slow undoing of those human rights to which this nation has always been committed, and to which we are committed today at home and around the world.

Let every nation know, whether it wishes us well or ill, that we shall pay any price, bear any burden, meet any hardship, support any friend, oppose any foe to assure the survival and the success of liberty.

This much we pledge — and more.   5

To those old allies whose cultural and spiritual origins we share, we pledge the loyalty of faithful friends. United there is little we cannot do in a host of cooperative ventures. Divided there is little we can do — for we dare not meet a powerful challenge at odds and split asunder.

To those new states whom we welcome to the ranks of the free, we pledge our word that one form of colonial control shall not have passed away merely to be replaced by a far more iron tyranny. We shall not always expect to find them supporting our view. But we shall always hope to find them strongly supporting their own freedom — and to remember that, in the past,

New York Daily News Archive/Getty Images

◄

This photograph shows Chief Justice Earl Warren administering the presidential oath of office to John F. Kennedy during the swearing-in ceremony at the U.S. Capitol on January 20, 1961. Among the notables in attendance are poet Robert Frost; former presidents Dwight D. Eisenhower and Harry S. Truman and their wives, Mamie and Bess; Vice President Lyndon B. Johnson and his wife, Lady Bird; as well as the new first lady, Jacqueline Kennedy. **What details from this photo stand out most to you? What sets Kennedy apart from the other men in attendance? What does this image add to your understanding of the rhetorical situation?**

those who foolishly sought power by riding the back of the tiger ended up inside.

To those people in the huts and villages of half the globe struggling to break the bonds of mass misery, we pledge our best efforts to help them help themselves, for whatever period is required — not because the communists may be doing it, not because we seek their votes, but because it is right. If a free society cannot help the many who are poor, it cannot save the few who are rich.

To our sister republics south of our border, we offer a special pledge — to convert our good words into good deeds — in a new alliance for progress — to assist free men and free governments in casting off the chains of poverty. But this peaceful revolution of hope cannot become the prey of hostile powers. Let all our neighbors know that we shall join with them to oppose aggression or subversion anywhere in the Americas. And let every other power know that this Hemisphere intends to remain the master of its own house.

To that world assembly of sovereign states, the United Nations, our last best hope in an age where the instruments of war have far outpaced the instruments of peace, we renew our pledge of support — to prevent it from becoming merely a forum for invective — to strengthen its shield of the new and the weak — and to enlarge the area in which its writ may run. [10]

Finally, to those nations who would make themselves our adversary, we offer not a pledge but a request: that both sides begin anew the quest for peace, before the dark powers of destruction unleashed by science engulf all humanity in planned or accidental self-destruction.

We dare not tempt them with weakness. For only when our arms are sufficient beyond doubt can we be certain beyond doubt that they will never be employed.

But neither can two great and powerful groups of nations take comfort from our present course — both sides overburdened by the cost of modern weapons, both rightly alarmed by the steady spread of the deadly atom, yet both racing to alter that uncertain balance of terror that stays the hand of mankind's final war.

So let us begin anew — remembering on both sides that civility is not a sign of weakness, and sincerity is always subject to proof. Let us never negotiate out of fear. But let us never fear to negotiate.

Let both sides explore what problems unite us instead of belaboring those problems which divide us. [15]

Let both sides, for the first time, formulate serious and precise proposals for the inspection and control of arms — and bring the absolute power to destroy other nations under the absolute control of all nations.

Let both sides seek to invoke the wonders of science instead of its terrors. Together let us explore the stars, conquer the deserts, eradicate disease, tap the ocean depths and encourage the arts and commerce.

Let both sides unite to heed in all corners of the earth the command of Isaiah — to "undo the heavy burdens . . . [and] let the oppressed go free."

And if a beachhead of cooperation may push back the jungle of suspicion, let both sides join in creating a new endeavor, not a new balance of power, but a new world of law, where the strong are just and the weak secure and the peace preserved.

All this will not be finished in the first one hundred days. Nor will it be finished in the first one thousand days, nor in the life of this Administration, nor even perhaps in our lifetime on this planet. But let us begin. [20]

In your hands, my fellow citizens, more than mine, will rest the final success or failure of our course. Since this country was founded, each generation of Americans has been summoned to give testimony to its national loyalty. The graves of young Americans who answered the call to service surround the globe.

seeing connections

James Rosenquist (1933–2017) was a billboard painter who became a leader in the Pop Art movement, which uses the visual language of popular culture and advertising in fine art. Shown below is a screenprint Rosenquist completed in 1960, entitled *Presidential Election: Kennedy 1960*. Examine it carefully before answering the following questions.

1. What aspects of popular culture and advertising do you see?
2. Why might Kennedy have been a good subject for such a work?
3. In what ways does Rosenquist's characterization of Kennedy echo Kennedy's inaugural address?

VISUAL ARTS LIBRARY/Musee National d'Art Moderne, Centre Pompidou, Paris, France/Bridgeman Images/Art © Estate of James Rosenquist/Licensed by VAGA, New York, NY

Now the trumpet summons us again — not as a call to bear arms, though arms we need — not as a call to battle, though embattled we are — but a call to bear the burden of a long twilight struggle, year in and year out, "rejoicing in hope, patient in tribulation" — a struggle against the common enemies of man: tyranny, poverty, disease and war itself.

Can we forge against these enemies a grand and global alliance, North and South, East and West, that can assure a more fruitful life for all mankind? Will you join in that historic effort?

In the long history of the world, only a few generations have been granted the role of defending freedom in its hour of maximum danger. I do not shrink from this responsibility — I welcome it. I do not believe that any of us would exchange places with any other people or any other generation. The energy, the faith, the devotion which we bring to this endeavor will light our country and all who serve it — and the glow from that fire can truly light the world.

And so, my fellow Americans: ask not what your country can do for you — ask what you can do for your country.

My fellow citizens of the world: ask not what America will do for you, but what together we can do for the freedom of man.

Finally, whether you are citizens of America or citizens of the world, ask of us here the same high standards of strength and sacrifice which we ask of you. With a good conscience our only sure reward, with history the final judge of our deeds, let us go forth to lead the land we love, asking His blessing and His help, but knowing that here on earth God's work must truly be our own.

[1961]

EXPLORING THE TEXT

1. John F. Kennedy's inaugural address is fairly short, comprised of a succession of short paragraphs, some containing only one sentence. How does the structure of the speech reflect Kennedy's understanding of his audience — the people in attendance in Washington that day as well as the millions watching on television? What is the effect of that structure on the persona of the speaker? Keep in mind that, after a close race, Kennedy was taking office as both the first Roman Catholic president and the youngest elected president.

2. What are some of the ways Kennedy appeals to pathos? Find at least three examples of places where he connects emotionally to his audience. How do these appeals serve the purpose of the inaugural address?

3. How does Kennedy establish credibility? Consider how he appeals to ethos both as an American and also as a citizen of the world.

4. Looking carefully at the language choices Kennedy makes in his speech, especially archaic words such as *asunder, foe, writ, forebears*. How do these words set the tone for the speech and relate to its occasion?

5. Kennedy uses figures of speech throughout: *iron tyranny* (para. 7), *sister republics* (para. 9), and *jungle of suspicion* (para. 19), for example. Find several more of these. What is their effect? How do they serve his purpose?

6. Paragraph 23 consists of two rhetorical questions. How does that paragraph signal a shift? To what extent does this shift reflect a change in Kennedy's purpose?

7. Consider Kennedy's use of parallelism: for example, "born in this century, tempered by war, disciplined by a hard and bitter peace, proud of our ancient heritage" (para. 3) and "pay any price, bear any burden, meet any hardship, support any friend, oppose any foe" (para. 4). How do they lend themselves to Kennedy's purpose?

8. The speech has many examples of antithesis (the opposition, or contrast, of ideas or words) in parallel grammatical structures: "If a free society cannot help the many who are poor, it cannot save the few who are rich" (para. 8); "[A]sk not what your country can do for you — ask what you can do for your country" (para. 25). How does this syntax reflect the rhetorical situation?

9. Kennedy uses hortative sentences — language that urges or calls to action, such as "let us" (para. 14) and "let both sides" (para. 15) — throughout most of his speech. However, in paragraphs 25–26, he switches to the imperative — language that commands, such as "ask" and "ask not." What does Kennedy achieve with this switch?

10. Consider the transitional words Kennedy uses. You may notice that many are coordinating conjunctions (so, for, and, but). What is the effect of those particular transition words? How do they reflect the occasion and purpose of Kennedy's speech?

11. How would you characterize the overall tone of the speech? Try to use at least two words to describe it. What details from the speech support your stance?

12. The ancient Greeks and Romans maintained that eloquence is indispensable to politics. Based on your knowledge of American politics, to what extent do you agree? What do you find eloquent about Kennedy's inaugural address?

13. Compare and contrast a political speech from the last ten years with Kennedy's inaugural address. What influence from Kennedy's speech do you see in the speech you chose? How do the rhetorical situation and strategies compare to each other?

Statement on United States Immigration and Refugee Policy

RONALD REAGAN

Ronald Reagan (1911–2004) was an American actor and politician who served as the fortieth President of the United States. After a successful career in Hollywood, Reagan switched from the Democratic Party to the Republican Party in 1962. He served as the 33rd Governor of California from 1967 to 1975, and, after two unsuccessful attempts to win the Republican presidential nomination, won it in 1980 and defeated Democratic incumbent Jimmy Carter in the general election. Reagan's first-term agenda was focused on conservative domestic policies such as tax reduction, deregulation, reduction in government spending, and acceleration of the War on Drugs. After winning reelection in a landslide in 1984, his second term saw the end of the Cold War with the Soviet Union and was marked by the Iran-Contra scandal, in which officials in the Reagan administration facilitated the sale of weapons to Iran in order to fund a right-wing insurrection in Nicaragua while securing the release of U.S. hostages. Reagan departed his second term with one of the highest approval ratings for departing presidents in the modern era. He issued the following statement regarding immigration on July 30, 1981.

Our nation is a nation of immigrants. More than any other country, our strength comes from our own immigrant heritage and our capacity to welcome those from other lands. No free and prosperous nation can by itself accommodate all those who seek a better life or flee persecution. We must share this responsibility with other countries.

The bipartisan select commission which reported this spring concluded that the Cuban influx to Florida made the United States sharply aware of the need for more effective immigration policies and the need for legislation to support those policies.

For these reasons, I asked the Attorney General last March to chair a Task Force on Immigration and Refugee Policy. We discussed the matter when President López Portillo[1] visited me last month, and we have carefully considered the views of our Mexican friends. In addition, the Attorney General has consulted with those concerned in Congress and in affected States and localities and with interested members of the public.

The Attorney General is undertaking administrative actions and submitting to Congress, on behalf of the administration, a legislative package, based on eight principles. These principles are designed to preserve our tradition of accepting foreigners to our shores, but to accept them in a controlled and orderly fashion:

- We shall continue America's tradition as a land that welcomes peoples from other countries. We shall also, with other countries, continue to share in the responsibility of welcoming and resettling those who flee oppression.

- At the same time, we must ensure adequate legal authority to establish control over

---

[1] José López Portillo was President of Mexico from 1976 to 1982. —Eds.

seeing connections

The graphs below show Americans' views on offering asylum to refugees throughout the twentieth century.

How does this data both support and challenge the views Reagan expresses in his statement?

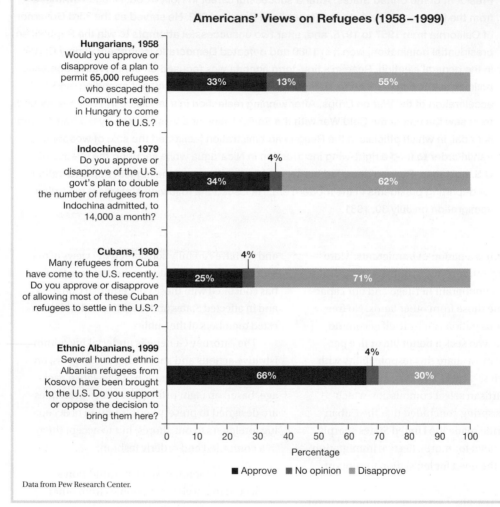

Americans' Views on Refugees (1958–1999)

Hungarians, 1958
Would you approve or disapprove of a plan to permit 65,000 refugees who escaped the Communist regime in Hungary to come to the U.S.?
33% | 13% | 55%

Indochinese, 1979
Do you approve or disapprove of the U.S. govt's plan to double the number of refugees from Indochina admitted, to 14,000 a month?
34% | 4% | 62%

Cubans, 1980
Many refugees from Cuba have come to the U.S. recently. Do you approve or disapprove of allowing most of these Cuban refugees to settle in the U.S.?
25% | 4% | 71%

Ethnic Albanians, 1999
Several hundred ethnic Albanian refugees from Kosovo have been brought to the U.S. Do you support or oppose the decision to bring them here?
66% | 4% | 30%

Percentage

■ Approve ■ No opinion ■ Disapprove

Data from Pew Research Center.

immigration: to enable us, when sudden influxes of foreigners occur, to decide to whom we grant the status of refugee or asylee; to improve our border control; to expedite (consistent with fair procedures and our Constitution) return of those coming here illegally; to strengthen enforcement of our fair labor standards and laws; and to penalize those who would knowingly encourage violation of our laws. The steps we take to further these objectives, however, must also be consistent with our values of individual privacy and freedom.

- We have a special relationship with our closest neighbors, Canada and Mexico. Our immigration policy should reflect this relationship.

- We must also recognize that both the United States and Mexico have historically benefited from Mexicans obtaining employment in the United States. A number of our States have special labor needs, and we should take these into account.

- Illegal immigrants in considerable numbers have become productive members of our society and are a basic part of our work force. Those who have established equities[2] in the United States should be recognized and accorded legal status. At the same time, in so doing, we must not encourage illegal immigration.

- We shall strive to distribute fairly, among the various localities of this country, the impacts of our national immigration and refugee

---

[2] Financial assets. —Eds.

policy, and we shall improve the capability of those agencies of the Federal Government which deal with these matters.

- We shall seek new ways to integrate refugees into our society without nurturing their dependence on welfare.

- Finally, we recognize that immigration and refugee problems require international solutions. We will seek greater international cooperation in the resettlement of refugees and, in the Caribbean Basin, international cooperation to assist accelerated economic development to reduce motivations for illegal immigration.

Immigration and refugee policy is an important part of our past and fundamental to our national interest. With the help of the Congress and the American people, we will work towards a new and realistic immigration policy, a policy that will be fair to our own citizens while it opens the door of opportunity for those who seek a new life in America.

[1981]

EXPLORING THE TEXT

1. Ronald Reagan was one of the most revered and popular presidents of the twentieth century. Thus he begins with an automatic ethos. How does he maintain that ethos throughout this statement?

2. How does Reagan characterize America in the opening paragraph? What are some of the values that he evokes?

3. Consider the rhetorical situation. What is this statement occasioned by? What are the "reasons" Reagan refers to in paragraph 3?

4. What are some indications that the "legislative package" (para. 4) and Reagan's statement itself are both carefully thought out and prepared?

5. What is the intent and purpose of the eight principles contained in the legislation? Briefly summarize them. Which two or three do you see as being the most important in 1981, the date of the statement? Which principles do you see as still important and relevant today? Explain, using examples from current events or your own experiences to support your response.

6. Identify appeals to logos, ethos, and pathos that Reagan makes. Which of them is the most persuasive, and why?

7. Read carefully the final sentence of the statement. To what extent do you think it expresses the nation's attitude toward immigration at the time of its composition? To what extent do you think it does so today? Explain.

from Justice and the Passion for Vengeance

ROBERT C. SOLOMON

Robert C. Solomon (1942–2007) was an American professor of philosophy at the University of Texas at Austin, where he taught for more than 30 years. Born in Detroit, Michigan, Solomon earned an MA in philosophy and a PhD in psychology from the University of Michigan. Solomon was known for his lectures on Søren Kierkegaard, Friedrich Nietzsche, Jean-Paul Sartre, and other existentialist philosophers. He authored and edited over 45 books, including *The Passions* (1976), *About Love* (1988), *Ethics and Excellence* (1992), *A Better Way to Think about Business* (1999), *The Joy of Philosophy* (1999), *Spirituality for the Skeptic* (2002), and In *Defense of Sentimentality* (2004). In following excerpt, from *A Passion for Justice* (1989), Solomon argues for a more nuanced understanding of vengeance.

There is no denying the aesthetic satisfaction, the sense of poetic justice, that pleasures us when evil-doers get the comeuppance they deserve. . . . The satisfaction is heightened when it becomes possible to measure out punishment in exact proportion to the size and shape of the wrong that has been done.
— Arthur Lelyveld, *Punishment: for and against*

I think that the deterrent argument is simply a rationalization. The motive for punishment is revenge — not deterrence. . . . Punishment is hate.
— A. S. Neill, *Punishment: for and against*

However problematic its current role in justice may be, there is no doubt but that vengeance is the original passion for justice. The word *justice* in the Old Testament and in Homer too virtually always refers to revenge. Throughout most of history the concept of justice has been far more concerned with the punishment of crimes and the balancing of wrongs than it has been with the fair distribution of goods and services. "Getting even" is and has always been one of the most basic metaphors of our moral vocabulary, and the frightening emotion of righteous, wrathful anger is just as much a part of the emotional basis for our current sense of justice as benign compassion. Wrongdoing should be punished, and, especially, those who have wronged *us* should be punished, preferably by us or, at least,

in our name. However intense our passion for justice, our resentment of injustice is necessarily its precondition and retributive anger its essential consequence. "Don't get mad, get even" — whether or not it is prudent advice — is conceptually confused. Getting even is just an effective way of being angry, and getting angry typically includes a lively desire for revenge.[1]

Like it or not, I think that we have to agree with Arthur Lelyveld's words in the epigraph at the head of this section. The immense pleasure, and aesthetic satisfaction to which he refers points to the depth of our passion, and the need for proportion indicates the intelligence involved in this supposedly most irrational and uncontrollable emotion. This is not to say, of course, that the motive of revenge is therefore legitimate or acts of revenge always justified. Sometimes vengeance is wholly called for, even obligatory. Sometimes it is not, notably when one is mistaken about the offender or the offense. But to seek vengeance for a grievous wrong, to revenge oneself against evil — that seems to lie at the very foundation of our sense of justice, indeed, of our very sense of ourselves, our dignity and our sense of right and wrong. Even Adam Smith* writes,

---

*Adam Smith (1723–1790) was a Scottish philosopher and economist; his *Theory of Moral Sentiments* used social psychology to explain human ethics. —Eds.

This cartoon by Edward Koren was published in the *New Yorker* in 1999.

How do the visual elements in this image comment on the concept of vengeance? Be sure to look at all of the details in the image.

"*I am not a vengeful man, but I do enjoy a touch of retribution now and then.*"

in his *Theory of the Moral Sentiments*. "The violation of justice is injury . . . it is, therefore, the proper object of resentment, and of punishment." We are not mere observers of the moral life, and the desire for vengeance seems to be an integral aspect of our recognition of evil. But it also contains — or can be cultivated to contain — the elements of its own control, a sense of its limits, a sense of balance. Thus the Old Testament instruction that revenge should be *limited to* "eye for eye, tooth for tooth, hand for hand, foot for foot, burning for burning, wound for wound, stripe for stripe" (the *lex talionis,** Exodus 21:24–5). The New Testament demands even more restraint, the abstention from revenge oneself and the patience to entrust it to God. Both the Old and New Testaments (more the latter than the former) also encourage forgiveness, but there can be no forgiveness if there is not first the desire (and the warrant) for revenge.

The desire for vengeance is not satisfied by harm to others alone no matter how harsh. It is a matter of emotion, and like punishment, it is always for some offense, not just hurting for its own sake. (We should stress here that retaliation and retribution should not be confused with mere reparation or compensation, which may in some cases undo the damage but in no case by themselves count as punishment.) Vengeance, then, always has its reasons (though, to be sure, these can be mistaken, irrelevant, out of proportion or otherwise bad reasons). Vengeance is not merely a matter of rational obligation, but neither is it opposed to a sense of obligation (e.g., in matters of family honor) or rationality (insofar as rationality is to be found in every emotion, even this one). Vengeance means getting even, putting the world back in balance, and these simple phrases already embody a whole philosophy of justice, even if (as yet) unarticulated and unjustified. . . .

These preliminary comments are intended to unearth a number of bad arguments against vengeance (which are often generalized into even

---

*Latin for "the law of retaliation." —Eds.

worse arguments concerning "negative" and violent emotions as a unified class):

(1) *Vengeance is (as such) irrational, and, consequently, it is never legitimate.* Only a moment's reflection is necessary to realize that we all recognize (eventually if not immediately) the difference between justified and unjustified revenge. Vengeance is not just the desire to harm but the desire to harm for a reason, and a reason of a very particular sort. To flunk a student because he has an orange punk hairdo or because he disagreed with one's pet theory in class is not justified, but to expel him for burning down the department library is another matter. But what about the fact that sometimes, while in the grip of the passion for revenge, we fail to recognize or properly exercise the reason and warrant for our vengeance? But the point is the word *sometimes,* for there is nothing essential to vengeance that requires such failure. In indisputably rational contexts a decision-maker mistakes a means for an end, or becomes so distracted in his pursuit of the end that he neglects or simply misses the most appropriate means. In vengeance one can also get caught up in the means or obsessed and distracted by the end, but the logic of reasons and appropriateness is nevertheless present as a standard. Accordingly, the question is not whether vengeance is ever legitimate but rather when it is legitimate.

(2) *There is no "natural" end to vengeance.* But, of course, there is. The idea that vengeance leads to a total loss of inhibition and control ignores the built-in and cultivated satisfactions of revenge, and seems to confuse the fact that mutually vengeful acts tend to escalate with the fact that a single act of vengeance typically has its very specific goals and, consequently, its own built-in standard of satisfaction.[2] I think that we are misled here by the conflation of vengeance, which is always aimed at some particular offense (or series of offenses) and the familiar feud, which is an ongoing form of personal, family or tribal hostility whose origins may well be forgotten. In other words, we conflate hatred (which may or may not be part of vengeance) with vengeance itself. . . .

(3) *Vengeance is always violent.* The bloodthirsty acts of the Clint Eastwood character or the Ninja assassin may hold dramatic sway over our fantasies, but the more usual act of revenge is a negative vote in the next department meeting, a forty-five minute delay in arriving to dinner, or a hurtful comment or letter, delivered with a vicious twist of phrase, perhaps, but rarely the twist of a blade, except, of course, metaphorically. One might, given the current tendency to inflate the meaning of words and numb our sensitivities to moral differences, argue that such acts do indeed constitute "violence," but this certainly drains the substance from this standard objection against vengeance. At stake here is the important if problematic distinction between actually doing harm to an offender and depriving him or her of some essential human good, like liberty, for example. It is probably true that vengeance generally aims at harm whereas the cooler claims of the law tend to prefer punishments by way of deprivation — the payment of fines, for example, or depriving the criminal of certain privileges or freedoms (to drive a car, for example, or to use the university library), or even depriving him of freedom as such. The continuing ruckus over the death penalty is, in part, due to the fact that it is one of the few punishments today that is designed to inflict harm — indeed the ultimate harm — rather than impose some deprivation. But, then, it is obvious that this important distinction will not stand too much scrutiny, and it would be hard to insist for very long that sending a man to prison is not in fact actually harming him. And by the same token, there is much that counts as punishment, and consequently satisfies the desire for revenge, but is not violent.

(4) *It takes the law "into our own hands."* (The use of "in hand" metaphors seem to abound in such discussions.) Historically, punishing the perpetrator for almost any offense against an individual, from an obscene gesture to rape and murder, rested with the family, and it was considered not only inappropriate but unjustifiable intrusion into private matters for the state to step in. It is a relatively recent development — and an obviously very political move — that punishment of such crimes should have become the exclusive province of the state. Moral objections against vengeance and the desire for public order seem to me to have far less to do with this than the state's usual arrogance in abrogating individual rights and its desire for control. Indeed, it is a point worth pondering that major crimes against the person are construed by the law as crimes against the state. When current criminal law reduces the victim of such crimes to a mere bystander (if, that is, the victim has survived the crime), the problem is not that in vengeance we take the law "into our own hands" but rather that without vengeance justice seems not only to be taken out of our hands but eliminated as a consideration altogether. Current concerns with punishment, even those that claim to take "retribution" seriously, seem to serve the law and sanction respect for the law (or reason) rather than the need for justice. Not that the law and respect for the law are unimportant, of course, but one should not glibly identify these with justice and dismiss the passion for vengeance as something quite different and wholly illegitimate.

Retribution is the pivotal term in all arguments about punishment. On the one hand, "backward-looking" retribution is juxtaposed against the "forward-looking" utilitarian concerns of deterrence and rehabilitation. That is, retribution is characterized in terms of its "undoing" a past offense; deterrence and criminal reform are concerned with preventing future offenses. Much of this dispute, I would argue, is purely academic; it is almost impossible to imagine an instance in which both responsibility for the offense and concern for the future are not at stake....

Granger, NYC

This photo shows members of the Hatfield family around 1897, posing with their weapons in their home state of West Virginia. The Hatfields fought a generations-long feud with another rural clan, the McCoys, and the conflict has since come to signify how an inflexible fixation on vengeance can lead to tragedy.
What would Solomon say about the Hatfield-McCoy feud? How might he have explained a family feud that raged across generations?

The rationale of retribution, the "intelligence" embodied in vengeance, is the idea that "the punishment should fit the crime." This is an idea that goes back (at least) to the biblical "eye for an eye" injunction, but it has long been under fire as well. Since ancient times, there has been Socrates' oft-repeated objection — that punishment is the return of evil for evil and so is never legitimate, no matter how horrendous the crime. So conceived, of course, punishment is just another wrong, whether carried out as a personal act of revenge or under the cool, deliberate auspices of the state legal system. (The argument that "murder is wrong, no matter who does it" has often been used as a central argument against capital punishment.) But punishment is not the return of "evil for evil." The German philosopher Hegel* argued, I think convincingly, that this is one sure way to misunderstand the nature of punishment.[3] "Harm for harm" perhaps, but it is justified and legitimate harm in return for unjustified and illegitimate harm. The hard question is, how does one get one harm to "fit" another? What does "an eye for an eye" really mean, and is it ultimately intelligible?

How does one calculate how many years in prison it will take to "equal" the crime of armed robbery, even after we decide to take into account the history and character of the criminal and the circumstances of the crime? In what conceivable sense does time in prison "equal" the harm inflicted by the offender on his victims or on the community? My favorite objection to the "eye for an eye" formulation was leveled against retributivism by Lord Blackstone* back in the eighteenth century. He queried, "What

10

is the equivalent harm when a two-eye'd man knocks out the eye of a one-eye'd man?"[4] Cute, to be sure, but hardly a knock-down argument against the idea that the punishment should fit the crime. Granting the gruesomeness of the concept, we might well feel an embarrassing satisfaction if a vicious criminal who has intentionally blinded his innocent victim were blinded himself in an accident. To be sure, few of us would suggest that the law should inflict such a punishment, but the "fit" is evident enough to us. . . .

The reader will no doubt discern that much of the language with which we describe both our passion for vengeance and the concept of retribution consists largely of an interrelated group of metaphors — notably the images of "equality," "balance," and "fit." These are too often thrown together as one, and too often treated as if they were not metaphors at all but literal truths. I want to wrap up this section by distinguishing and discussing briefly four such metaphors.

(1) The *debt* metaphor: to punish is to "repay" a wrong. There is some dispute . . . whether the notion of legal obligation preceded or rather grew out of this idea of a debt, but with regard to punishment, the metaphorical character of "repayment" is quite clear. The suggestion that there is an implicit contract . . . is just another approach to the same metaphor. To link it with the other metaphors, punishment does not "balance the books" nor does it "erase" the wrong in question, as repayment of a debt surely does. The "debt" metaphor, by the way, is not restricted to capitalist societies; "debt" is not the same as "consumer debt" and applies as well to the New Guinea custom of giving a pig for a wrongful death as to the problem of paying off one's MasterCard. In most societies, debt is a moral measure rather than a monetary arrangement.

(2) The *fit* metaphor is the popular idea that the punishment should "fit" the crime (W. S. Gilbert's *Mikado*: "My object all sublime . . .

---

*Georg Wilhelm Friedrich Hegel (1770–1831) was a German philosopher who espoused absolute idealism, a philosophy based on the idea that the way we experience the world around us is dependent on subjective experience rather than objective reality. —Eds.

*William Blackstone (1723–1780) was a British jurist and politician who wrote a comprehensive explanation of the various laws of England. —Eds.

Louvre, Paris, France/Bridgeman Images

Justice and Divine Vengeance pursuing Crime was painted by Pierre-Paul Prud'hon in 1808. **How does the story this painting tells reflect Solomon's view on the relationship between crime, justice, and vengeance?**

To make the punishment fit the crime"*). Punishment must "fit" the crime, we are told, going back to the easy formulation of the *lextalionis*: "Eye for eye, tooth for tooth," etc. But as many critics of retributivism have pointed out, such punishments are administered — or even make sense — only for a very limited number of crimes, such as intentional murder. But even then, as Albert Camus* has famously pointed out, "For there to be equivalence, the death penalty would have to punish a criminal who had warned his victim of the date at which he would inflict a horrible death on him and who, from that moment onward, had confined him at his mercy for months. Such a monster is not encountered in private life."[5]

Defenders of retributivism gladly weaken the demands of "fit," suggesting, for instance, that it

provides only a general measure, that the crucial concept is "proportion" — so that petty theft is not (as it once was) punished with the harshness of a violent crime. With this, of course, we all agreed, but "proportion" too misleadingly suggests quantification where there often is none, and it summarizes rather than solves the problem of punishment. To be sure, it is somehow fitting to trade a life for a life (or more accurately, "a death for a death"), but is it just? And given the many extenuating circumstances that qualify each and every case, does "fit" make sense? Of course, we recognize the lack of fit: witness our horror, for example, when Afghan tribesmen summarily behead the hapless tourist involved in an automobile accident, even one in which the driver, if given a trial, might have been proclaimed faultless. Eighteenth-century British law, responsible for the burgeoning white population of Australia, was astonishing in its lack of fit and harsh penalties, as were the punishments meted out to those who arrived on the "fatal shore."[6]

(3) The *balance* metaphor: punishment makes things "even" again. It is through

15

*A comedic opera, with music by Arthur Sullivan and lyrics by W.S. Gilbert. —Eds.
*Albert Camus (1913–1960) was a French philosopher and author often associated with existentialism, although he rejected the label. Existentialism explores the relationship between the self and a meaningless, often absurd, world. —Eds.

punishment that one "gets even." In epic literature, it is by punishing the villain that one balances the forces of good and evil. One problem is that this moral balance is often simply equated, in the crudest utilitarian fashion, with a balance of pleasure and pain, as if the application to the villain of an amount of pain equal to the amount of pain he or she has caused balances the scales. (We should remember again the standard allegorical figure of justice, this time with her scales.) Where the crime is strictly pecuniary, it might seem that balance (like the repayment of a debt) might be literally appropriate, but this, of course, isn't so. One can pay back the amount of money stolen or otherwise taken, but this does not yet take into account the offense itself. As soon as one must pay back even an extra penny, the literalness of the "balance" again comes into question. Granted the original sum has been repaid, but now what is the "cost" or the "price" of the crime? Again, my point is not that the metaphor of "balance" isn't applicable or revealing of how we think about justice, but it underscores rather than solves our problems.

(4) The *erasure* metaphor: the idea that we can "annul the evil" through punishment. Vendetta cultures talk about "blood marks" (also "blood debts") not as a sign of guilt but rather of unrevenged wrong. But the obvious question is, can we undo a crime — for instance, rape or murder — in any sense whatever? In financial crimes, again, one can "erase" the debt by paying it back, but not the crime itself. For example, how could the terror suffered in an armed robbery be erased, even if the money were to be politely returned? ("Here you are, Miss; I'm a student at the local police academy and I wanted to experience what the criminal felt like.") Indeed, how can we measure the fear suffered in such crimes, quite apart from any more substantial harm? And yet, the idea of annulment looms large in the history of theories of punishment,

from the ancient world (in which one quite literally made the offender disappear through exile and obliteration, for example) to modern conceptions in Hegel, Bosanquet,[*] and others. The punishment doesn't literally eliminate the crime, of course, but Bosanquet's suggestion that it eliminates it as a precedent has the virtue of showing us how this metaphor too, hardly intelligible when taken literally, can nonetheless be given an intelligible interpretation that is not strictly retributivist but takes future behavior into account as well.[7] . . . .

I have not tried here to defend vengeance as such, but my claim is that vengeance deserves its central place in any theory of justice and, whatever else we are to say about punishment, the desire for revenge must enter into our deliberations along with such emotions as compassion, caring, and love. Any system of legal principles that does not take such emotions into account, which does not motivate itself on their behalf, is not — whatever else it may be — a system of justice. But vengeance as such, I do not deny, is in any case dangerous. As the Chinese used to say (and no doubt still do), "If you seek vengeance, dig two graves." But I think that the dangers and destructiveness of vengeance are much overblown, and its importance for a sense of one's own self-esteem and integrity ignored. Many people believe that vengeance is the primary cause of the world's troubles today, causing unending feuds and vendettas that block every rational effort at resolution and peace. But in addition to my insistence that vengeance is not the same as vendetta and feuds are not the same as vengeance, I would argue that the passionate hostilities of the world that are fueled by revenge are only secondary. In many cases they are caused or at any rate aggravated and rendered

---

[*]Bernard Bosanquet (1848–1923) was a British philosopher whose primary influence was Hegel. —Eds.

seeing connections

Director Quentin Tarantino is known for his violent comedies, which often revolve around the theme of vengeance. Shown here are movie posters for two of his most popular films in this vein: *Inglourious Basterds* (2009), set in Nazi-occupied France, and *Django Unchained* (2012), set in the American south during slavery. Each poster markets the movie with the tagline, "AN INGLORIOUS, UPROARIOUS THRILL-RIDE OF VENGEANCE" and "LIFE, LIBERTY AND THE PURSUIT OF VENGEANCE," respectively. Both movies were met with critical as well as commercial success.

Examine these images carefully, and then answer the following questions.

1. **What does the visual rhetoric of these posters suggest about the relationship between vengeance, popular entertainment, and catharsis?**

2. **What role do you think vengeance plays in the public imagination? Do you think this role is a healthy one? Explain.**

3. **What details from Solomon's argument might explain the success and popularity of films such as *Inglourious Basterds* and *Django Unchained*?**

unresolvable not by passion so much as by supposedly rational ideology. It is ideology that abstracts and elevates personal prejudices to the status of absolute truths and gives vengeance a set of reasons far less negotiable than any feud or mere urge to "get even." Vengeance, at least, has its measure. Ideology, however "reasonable," may not.

Vengefulness, no doubt, is a vice, and because vengeance is so often dangerous and destructive it makes perfectly good sense for moralists to urge us to rise "above" the urge to vengeance.... The argument [for rising above the urge to vengeance] is that instead of following that often narrow path to personal retribution we would much better embrace that expansive form of social consciousness in which we become more aware of the real desperation of others than we are of our own (usually petty) complaints. To transcend revenge is to become keenly aware of the suffering of others with an urgency that eclipses the blows to our own fragile egos and gives our sense of compassion priority over the urge to vengeance. But it is not to give up vengeance as such and, as in tit for tat, it is the ready willingness to retaliate that provides stability to both the social system and one's personal sense of integrity and control. Despite volumes of propaganda to the contrary, experience seems to show that to see oneself as a helpless victim makes one less, and not more, likely to open one's heart to others. But we do not have to be or see ourselves as victims, and it is vengeance or at least fantasies of vengeance that make this possible. Our concept of injustice is inextricably tied up with the concept of blame and with the concept of punishment, and where the injustice is personal, so is the felt need for retribution. In a world in which justice is getting ever more impersonal and statistical, vengeance retains the virtue of being personal. But so, of course, does compassion, which commands not the impersonal but a more expanded sense of the personal. Between vengeance and compassion there is no doubt which is the greater virtue, but vengeance is nevertheless necessary and compassion for one's own offender (the object of one's revenge) is often foolish rather than noble. Justice is not forgiveness nor even forgetting but rather it is getting one's emotional priorities right, putting blame aside in the face of so much other human suffering and thereby giving up vengeance for the sake of larger and more noble emotions.

Notes

1. Aristotle's analysis of anger as including the desire for revenge is in his *Rhetoric*, 1378–80.
2. In Eisenstein's *Ivan the Terrible, Part II*, one of the outraged Russians responds to the slaughter of the innocents by insisting, "even beasts are rational in their anger." Considering the intervening centuries of human slaughter, we might well choose to side with the beasts.
3. Hegel on punishment: *Philosophy of Right,* translated by T. M. Knox (New York: Oxford Univ. Press, 1967), 140–41.
4. Blackstone is quoted in Acton, *The Philosophy of Punishment*, 13.
5. Camus, "Reflections on the Guillotine," in *Resistance, Rebellion and Death* (New York: Vintage, 1961).
6. Robert Hughes, *The Fatal Shore* (New York: Knopf, 1987).
7. Bernard Bosanquet defends a "therapeutic" theory of punishment in his *Philosophical Theory of the State.*

[1989]

EXPLORING THE TEXT

1. In his opening paragraph Solomon states: "However intense our passion for justice, our resentment of injustice is necessarily its precondition and retributive anger its essential consequence." Why does he use words such as "necessarily" and "essential"? Does it seem reasonable that a passion for justice might arise from resentment? Explain.

2. When referring to the epigraph by Arthur Lelyveld, Solomon begins with the words "Like it or not" (para. 2). What assumption does this direct address make? What does it suggest about the relationship between the speaker and reader?

3. In paragraph 2, Solomon states that "to seek vengeance for a grievous wrong, to revenge oneself against evil — that seems to lie at the very foundation of our sense of justice, indeed, of our very sense of ourselves, our dignity and our sense of right and wrong." What is your first response to this claim? To what extent does it match your own conceptions of human nature and of ethics?

4. When referring to the Biblical philosophy of "eye for eye," Solomon italicizes the words *limited to* (para. 2) for emphasis. What point does he make by emphasizing that particular phrase?

5. What, according to Solomon, distinguishes "justified" from "unjustified" revenge (para. 5)? Can you think of a specific example of each?

6. In his discussion of the third "bad" argument against vengeance — *Vengeance is always violent* (para. 7) — Solomon claims that the death penalty inflicts harm rather than deprivation. Might it not be argued that the death penalty in fact inflicts the ultimate deprivation — that of life? Explain.

7. In his discussion of the fourth "bad" argument against vengeance, Solomon writes, "Moral objections against vengeance and the desire for public order seem to me to have far less to do with this than the state's usual arrogance in abrogating individual rights and its desire for control" (para. 8). What does Solomon mean by this? How does this

sentence support the argument Solomon makes in the paragraph?

8. What do the words "retribution," "deterrence," and "rehabilitation" (para. 9) mean in the context of Solomon's overall argument, and how do they relate to his notion of justice? What does Solomon mean by the phrases "'backward-looking'" and "'forward-looking'" retribution (para. 9)? Why is the distinction between them an important facet of his argument?

9. In paragraph 10, Solomon writes, "The rationale of retribution, the 'intelligence' embodied in vengeance, is the idea that 'the punishment should fit the crime.'" What does he mean by this? Why does he cast "intelligence" in quotation marks — that is, what is he suggesting about the nature of retribution, vengeance, and crime?

10. How does the German philosopher Hegel's distinction between "'evil for evil'" and "'harm for harm'" (para. 10) contribute to Solomon's position on retribution and justice?

11. Briefly discuss Solomon's analysis of each of the four metaphors associated with "equality," "balance," and "fit" as they relate to "both our passion for vengeance and the concept of retribution" (para. 12). How does his discussion of language contribute to his overall argument?

12. In paragraph 18, Solomon writes that his "claim is that vengeance deserves its central place in any theory of justice." Based on details from Solomon's essay, how would you characterize the "central place" that Solomon attributes to vengeance?

13. What is the role of compassion, caring, and love in Solomon's conception of justice?

14. Which of the classical appeals — ethos, logos, or pathos — does Solomon rely on most in this essay? Explain, using specific references to the text.

15. Identify places throughout the essay where Solomon makes claims of fact, value, and policy. How effectively does he move through all three?

To Any Would-Be Terrorists

NAOMI SHIHAB NYE

Naomi Shihab Nye (b. 1952) is a Palestinian American poet, novelist, editor, and political activist. Her works for children include the picture book *Sitti's Secrets* (1994) and the novel *Habibi* (1997). Her poetry collections include *Different Ways to Pray* (1980), *Fuel* (1998), *19 Varieties of Gazelle: Poems of the Middle East* (2002), *You and Yours* (2005), *Honeybee* (2008), and *Tender Spot: Selected Poems* (2009). Nye describes herself as "a wandering poet" and has been a visiting writer all over the world. Her many awards include four Pushcart Prizes, the Jane Addams Children's Book award, and the Paterson Poetry Prize. Nye was elected a Chancellor of the Academy of American Poets in 2010, and in 2013 she was awarded both the Robert Creeley Award and the NSK Neustadt Prize for Children's Literature. She published the following essay in 2001, in the aftermath of the 9/11 attacks on the World Trade Center.

I am sorry I have to call you that, but I don't know how else to get your attention. I hate that word. Do you know how hard some of us have worked to get rid of that word, to deny its instant connection to the Middle East? And now look. Look what extra work we have. Not only did your colleagues kill thousands of innocent, international people in those buildings and scar their families forever, they wounded a huge community of people in the Middle East, in the United States and all over the world. If that's what they wanted to do, please know the mission was a terrible success, and you can stop now.

Because I feel a little closer to you than many Americans could possibly feel, or ever want to feel, I insist that you listen to me. Sit down and listen. I know what kinds of foods you like. I would feed them to you if you were right here, because it is very very important that you listen. I am humble in my country's pain and I am furious.

My Palestinian father became a refugee in 1948. He came to the United States as a college student. He is 74 years old now and still homesick. He has planted fig trees. He has invited all the Ethiopians in his neighborhood to fill their little paper sacks with his figs. He has written columns and stories saying the Arabs are not terrorists, he has worked all his life to defy that word. Arabs are businessmen and students and kind neighbors. There is no one like him and there are thousands like him — gentle Arab daddies who make everyone laugh around the dinner table, who have a hard time with headlines, who stand outside in the evenings with their hands in their pockets staring toward the far horizon.

I am sorry if you did not have a father like that. I wish everyone could have a father like that.

My hard-working American mother has spent 5 50 years trying to convince her fellow teachers and choir mates not to believe stereotypes about the Middle East. She always told them, there is a much larger story. If you knew the story, you would not jump to conclusions from what you see in the news. But now look at the news. What a mess has been made. Sometimes I wish everyone could have parents from different countries or ethnic groups so they would be forced to cross boundaries, to believe in mixtures, every day of their lives. Because this is what the world calls us to do. WAKE UP!

The Palestinian grocer in my Mexican-American neighborhood paints pictures of the Palestinian flag on his empty cartons. He paints trees and rivers. He gives his paintings away. He

Following the September 11, 2001 terrorist attack on New York City, Palestinian children held a vigil for the victims outside of the U. S. Consulate in Jerusalem.

What would Naomi Shihab Nye think about this demonstration? Explain.

says, "Don't insult me" when I try to pay him for a lemonade. Arabs have always been famous for their generosity. Remember? My half-Arab brother with an Arabic name looks more like an Arab than many full-blooded Arabs do and he has to fly every week.

My Palestinian cousins in Texas have beautiful brown little boys. Many of them haven't gone to school yet. And now they have this heavy word to carry in their backpacks along with the weight of their papers and books. I repeat, the mission was a terrible success. But it was also a complete, total tragedy and I want you to think about a few things.

1. Many people, thousands of people, perhaps even millions of people, in the United States are very aware of the long unfairness of our country's policies regarding Israel and Palestine. We talk about this all the time. It exhausts us and we keep talking. We write letters to newspapers, to politicians, to each other. We speak out in public even when it is uncomfortable to do so, because that is our responsibility. Many of these people aren't even Arabs. Many happen to be Jews who are equally troubled by the inequity. I promise you this is true. Because I am Arab-American, people always express these views to me and I am amazed how many understand the intricate situation and have strong, caring feelings for Arabs and Palestinians even when they don't have to. Think of them, please: All those people who have been standing up for Arabs when they didn't have to. But as ordinary citizens we don't run the government and don't get to make all our government's policies, which makes us sad sometimes. We believe in the power of the word and we keep using it, even when it seems no one large enough is listening. That is one of the best things about this country: the free power of free words. Maybe we take it for granted too much. Many of the people killed in the World Trade Center probably believed in a free Palestine and were probably talking about it all the time.

But this tragedy could never help the Palestinians. Somehow, miraculously, if other people won't help them more, they are going to have to help themselves. And it will be peace, not violence, that fixes things. You could ask any one of the kids in the Seeds of Peace organization and they would tell you that. Do you ever talk to kids? Please, please, talk to more kids.

2. Have you noticed how many roads there are? Sure you have. You must check out maps

10

and highways and small alternate routes just like anyone else. There is no way everyone on earth could travel on the same road, or believe in exactly the same religion. It would be too crowded, it would be dumb. I don't believe you want us all to be Muslims. My Palestinian grandmother lived to be 106 years old, and did not read or write, but even she was much smarter than that. The only place she ever went beyond Palestine and Jordan was to Mecca, by bus, and she was very proud to be called a Hajji and to wear white clothes afterwards. She worked very hard to get stains out of everyone's dresses — scrubbing them with a stone. I think she would consider the recent tragedies a terrible stain on her religion and her whole part of the world. She would weep. She was scared of airplanes anyway. She wanted people to worship God in whatever ways they felt comfortable. Just worship. Just remember God in every single day and doing. It didn't matter what they called it. When people asked her how she felt about the peace talks that were happening right before she died, she puffed up like a proud little bird and said, in Arabic, "I never lost my peace inside." To her, Islam was a welcoming religion. After

her home in Jerusalem was stolen from her, she lived in a small village that contained a Christian shrine. She felt very tender toward the people who would visit it. A Jewish professor tracked me down a few years ago in Jerusalem to tell me she changed his life after he went to her village to do an oral history project on Arabs. "Don't think she only mattered to you!" he said. "She gave me a whole different reality to imagine — yet it was amazing how close we became. Arabs could never be just a 'project' after that."

Did you have a grandmother or two? Mine never wanted people to be pushed around. What did yours want? Reading about Islam since my grandmother died, I note the "tolerance" that was "typical of Islam" even in the old days. The Muslim leader Khalid ibn al-Walid signed a Jerusalem treaty which declared, "in the name of God, you have complete security for your churches which shall not be occupied by the Muslims or destroyed." It is the new millennium in which we should be even smarter than we used to be, right? But I think we have fallen behind.

3. Many Americans do not want to kill any more innocent people anywhere in the world.

NurPhoto/Getty Images

This photograph shows a crowd at Los Angeles International Airport protesting a 2017 executive order from President Donald Trump that attempted to ban citizens of seven predominantly Muslim countries from entering the United States. **How does this image reflect the plea Nye makes in her letter?**

We are extremely worried about military actions killing innocent people. We didn't like this in Iraq, we never liked it anywhere. We would like no more violence, from us as well as from you. HEAR US! We would like to stop the terrifying wheel of violence, just stop it, right on the road, and find something more creative to do to fix these huge problems we have. Violence is not creative, it is stupid and scary and many of us hate all those terrible movies and TV shows made in our own country that try to pretend otherwise. Don't watch them. Everyone should stop watching them. An appetite for explosive sounds and toppling buildings is not a healthy thing for anyone in any country. The USA should apologize to the whole world for sending this trash out into the air and for paying people to make it.

But here's something good you may not know—one of the best-selling books of poetry in the United States in recent years is the Coleman Barks translation of Rumi, a mystical Sufi poet of the 13th century, and Sufism is Islam and doesn't that make you glad?

Everyone is talking about the suffering that ethnic Americans are going through. Many will no doubt go through more of it, but I would like to thank everyone who has sent me a consolation card. Americans are usually very kind people. Didn't your colleagues find that out during their time living here? It is hard to imagine they missed it. How could they do what they did, knowing that?

4. We will all die soon enough. Why not take   *15* the short time we have on this delicate planet and figure out some really interesting things we might do together? I promise you, God would be happier. So many people are always trying to speak for God—I know it is a very dangerous thing to do. I tried my whole life not to do it. But this one time is an exception. Because there are so many people crying and scarred and confused and complicated and exhausted right now—it is as if we have all had a giant simultaneous breakdown. I beg you, as your distant Arab cousin, as your American neighbor, listen to me. Our hearts are broken, as yours may also feel broken in some ways we can't understand, unless you tell us in words. Killing people won't tell us. We can't read that message. Find another way to live. Don't expect others to be like you. Read Rumi. Read Arabic poetry. Poetry humanizes us in a way that news, or even religion, has a harder time doing. A great Arab scholar, Dr. Salma Jayyusi, said, "If we read one another, we won't kill one another." Read American poetry. Plant mint. Find a friend who is so different from you, you can't believe how much you have in common. Love them. Let them love you. Surprise people in gentle ways, as friends do. The rest of us will try harder too. Make our family proud.

[2001]

EXPLORING THE TEXT

1. Naomi Shihab Nye addresses her letter to "you" and apologizes for using the term "would-be-terrorist," though she says she doesn't "know how else to get your attention" (para. 1). Are terrorists her real audience, or is she speaking primarily to another group of people? Whose attention is she trying to get? How do you know?

2. Nye introduces her Palestinian father in paragraph 3 before mentioning her mother in paragraph 5. How does she characterize each of her parents?

How do these depictions help Nye achieve her purpose?

3. What is it about American popular culture, particularly movies and television, that Nye criticizes? Why does she call it "trash" (para. 12)? To what extent do you agree with her about what she perceives as the cause-and-effect relationship between popular culture and violence?

4. In paragraph 10, Nye describes her Palestinian grandmother, and in paragraph 11 she asks, "Did

you have a grandmother or two?" In what ways does her grandmother represent the wisdom of community elders that Nye appeals to? How does this address to the "would-be terrorist" contribute to her argument?

5. Fundamental to Nye's argument is a set of assumptions about the values she and "any would-be terrorists" share. What are these assumptions?

6. Throughout her open letter, Nye expresses herself in contradictory terms. For instance, she uses the oxymoron "a terrible success" (para. 1) to characterize the World Trade Center attacks, and she says she is "humble" but also "furious" (para. 2). Find at least two other examples and discuss the use of contraries or dualities as a rhetorical strategy. How do they serve Nye's purpose?

7. One of Nye's strategies is using a concrete image as a springboard for a metaphor with broader significance. For example, she mentions her father's fig tree (para. 3), then turns that concrete example into a metaphor for cultural understanding. Identify at least one other example of this technique and discuss how it serves Nye's argument.

8. How would you describe Nye's tone in this letter? Is it consistent throughout, or does it shift? Cite specific details to support your response.

9. In paragraph 9, Nye asserts that "it will be peace, not violence, that fixes things." How persuasively does she argue this position? Is her viewpoint hopeful, idealistic, somewhat naïve, or something else? Explain with specific textual references.

---

from Hellhole

ATUL GAWANDE

Atul Gawande (b. 1955) is an American surgeon, writer, and public health researcher. He practices general and endocrine surgery at Brigham and Women's Hospital in Boston, Massachusetts. He is also Professor in the Department of Health Policy and Management at the Harvard School of Public Health and a Professor of Surgery at Harvard Medical School. Additionally, Gawande serves as the Executive Director of Ariadne Labs, a joint center for health systems innovation, and Chairman of Lifebox, a nonprofit organization making surgery safer globally. A staff writer for the *New Yorker* since 1998, Gawande has written four *New York Times* bestsellers: *Complications: A Surgeon's Notes on an Imperfect Science* (2003); *Better: A Surgeon's Notes on Performance* (2008); *The Checklist Manifesto: How to Get Things Right* (2009); and *Being Mortal: Medicine and What Matters in the End* (2014). Gawande's numerous awards include two National Magazine Awards, a MacArthur Fellowship, and the Lewis Thomas Award for writing about science. The following is an excerpt from "Hellhole," an article on solitary confinement, originally published in the *New Yorker* in 2009.

Human beings are social creatures. We are social not just in the trivial sense that we like company, and not just in the obvious sense that we each depend on others. We are social in a more elemental way: simply to exist as a normal human being requires interaction with other people.

Children provide the clearest demonstration of this fact, although it was slow to be accepted. Well into the nineteen-fifties, psychologists were encouraging parents to give children *less* attention and affection, in order to encourage independence. Then Harry Harlow, a professor of psychology at the University of Wisconsin at

Madison, produced a series of influential studies involving baby rhesus monkeys.

He happened upon the findings in the mid-fifties, when he decided to save money for his primate-research laboratory by breeding his own lab monkeys instead of importing them from India. Because he didn't know how to raise infant monkeys, he cared for them the way hospitals of the era cared for human infants — in nurseries, with plenty of food, warm blankets, some toys, and in isolation from other infants to prevent the spread of infection. The monkeys grew up sturdy, disease-free, and larger than those from the wild. Yet they were also profoundly disturbed, given to staring blankly and rocking in place for long periods, circling their cages repetitively, and mutilating themselves.

At first, Harlow and his graduate students couldn't figure out what the problem was. They considered factors such as diet, patterns of light exposure, even the antibiotics they used. Then, as Deborah Blum recounts in a fascinating biography of Harlow, "Love at Goon Park," one of his researchers noticed how tightly the monkeys clung to their soft blankets. Harlow wondered whether what the monkeys were missing in their Isolettes was a mother. So, in an odd experiment, he gave them an artificial one.

In the studies, one artificial mother was a doll 5 made of terry cloth; the other was made of wire. He placed a warming device inside the dolls to make them seem more comforting. The babies, Harlow discovered, largely ignored the wire mother. But they became deeply attached to the cloth mother. They caressed it. They slept curled up on it. They ran to it when frightened. They refused replacements: they wanted only "their" mother. If sharp spikes were made to randomly thrust out of the mother's body when the rhesus babies held it, they waited patiently for the spikes to recede and returned to clutching it. No matter how tightly they clung to the surrogate mothers, however, the monkeys remained psychologically abnormal.

In a later study on the effect of total isolation from birth, the researchers found that the test monkeys, upon being released into a group of ordinary monkeys, "usually go into a state of emotional shock, characterized by . . . autistic self-clutching and rocking." Harlow noted, "One of six monkeys isolated for three months refused to eat after release and died five days later." After several weeks in the company of other monkeys, most of them adjusted — but not those who had been isolated for longer periods. "Twelve months of isolation almost obliterated the animals socially," Harlow wrote. They became permanently withdrawn, and they lived as outcasts — regularly set upon, as if inviting abuse.

The research made Harlow famous (and infamous, too — revulsion at his work helped spur the animal-rights movement). Other psychologists produced evidence of similarly deep and sustained damage in neglected and orphaned children. Hospitals were made to open up their nurseries to parents. And it became widely accepted that children require nurturing human beings not just for food and protection but also for the normal functioning of their brains.

We have been hesitant to apply these lessons to adults. Adults, after all, are fully formed, independent beings, with internal strengths and knowledge to draw upon. We wouldn't have anything like a child's dependence on other people, right? Yet it seems that we do. We don't have a lot of monkey experiments to call upon here. But mankind has produced tens of thousands of human ones, including in our prison system. And the picture that has emerged is profoundly unsettling.

◆ ◆ ◆

Among our most benign experiments are those with people who voluntarily isolate themselves for extended periods. Long-distance solo sailors, for instance, commit themselves to months at sea. They face all manner of physical terrors: thrashing storms, fifty-foot waves, leaks, illness. Yet, for many, the single most overwhelming difficulty they report is the "soul-destroying loneliness," as one sailor called it. Astronauts have to be screened for their ability to tolerate long stretches in tightly confined isolation, and they come to depend on radio and video communications for social contact.

The problem of isolation goes beyond ordinary loneliness, however. Consider what we've learned from hostages who have been held in solitary confinement—from the journalist Terry Anderson, for example, whose extraordinary memoir, "Den of Lions," recounts his seven years as a hostage of Hezbollah[1] in Lebanon.

Anderson was the chief Middle East correspondent for the Associated Press when, on March 16, 1985, three bearded men forced him from his car in Beirut at gunpoint. He was pushed into a Mercedes sedan, covered head to toe with a heavy blanket, and made to crouch head down in the footwell behind the front seat. His captors drove him to a garage, pulled him out of the car, put a hood over his head, and bound his wrists and ankles with tape. For half an hour, they grilled him for the names of other Americans in Beirut, but he gave no names and they did not beat him or press him further. They threw him in the trunk of the car, drove him to another building, and put him in what would be the first of a succession of cells across Lebanon. He was soon placed in what seemed to be a dusty closet, large enough for only a mattress. Blindfolded, he could make out the distant sounds of other hostages. (One was William Buckley, the C.I.A. station chief who was kidnapped and tortured repeatedly until he weakened and died.) Peering around his blindfold, Anderson could see a bare light bulb dangling from the ceiling. He received three unpalatable meals a day—usually a sandwich

of bread and cheese, or cold rice with canned vegetables, or soup. He had a bottle to urinate in and was allotted one five- to ten-minute trip each day to a rotting bathroom to empty his bowels and wash with water at a dirty sink. Otherwise, the only reprieve from isolation came when the guards made short visits to bark at him for breaking a rule or to threaten him, sometimes with a gun at his temple.

He missed people terribly, especially his fiancée and his family. He was despondent and depressed. Then, with time, he began to feel something more. He felt himself disintegrating. It was as if his brain were grinding down. A month into his confinement, he recalled in his memoir, "The mind is a blank. Jesus, I always thought I was smart. Where are all the things I learned, the books I read, the poems I memorized? There's nothing there, just a formless, gray-black misery. My mind's gone dead. God, help me."

He was stiff from lying in bed day and night, yet tired all the time. He dozed off and on constantly, sleeping twelve hours a day. He craved activity of almost any kind. He would watch the daylight wax and wane on the ceiling, or roaches creep slowly up the wall. He had a Bible and tried to read, but he often found that he lacked the concentration to do so. He observed himself becoming neurotically possessive about his little space, at times putting his life in jeopardy by flying into a rage if a guard happened to step on his bed. He brooded incessantly, thinking back on all the mistakes he'd made in life, his regrets, his offenses against God and family.

His captors moved him every few months. For unpredictable stretches of time, he was granted the salvation of a companion—sometimes he shared a cell with as many as four other hostages—and he noticed that his thinking recovered rapidly when this occurred He could read and concentrate longer, avoid hallucinations, and better control his emotions. "I would rather have had the worst companion than no companion at all," he noted.

10

---

[1] A Shi'ah Muslim militant group and political party based in Lebanon. —Eds.

In September, 1986, after several months of sharing a cell with another hostage, Anderson was, for no apparent reason, returned to solitary confinement, this time in a six-by-six-foot cell, with no windows, and light from only a flickering fluorescent lamp in an outside corridor. The guards refused to say how long he would be there. After a few weeks, he felt his mind slipping away again.

"I find myself trembling sometimes for no reason," he wrote. "I'm afraid I'm beginning to lose my mind, to lose control completely."

One day, three years into his ordeal, he snapped. He walked over to a wall and began beating his forehead against it, dozens of times. His head was smashed and bleeding before the guards were able to stop him.

Some hostages fared worse. Anderson told the story of Frank Reed, a fifty-four-year-old American private-school director who was taken hostage and held in solitary confinement for four months before being put in with Anderson. By then, Reed had become severely withdrawn. He lay motionless for hours facing a wall, semi-catatonic. He could not follow the guards' simplest instructions. This invited abuse from them, in much the same way that once isolated rhesus monkeys seemed to invite abuse from the colony. Released after three and a half years, Reed ultimately required admission to a psychiatric hospital.

"It's an awful thing, solitary," John McCain wrote of his five and a half years as a prisoner of war in Vietnam — more than two years of it spent in isolation in a fifteen-by-fifteen-foot cell, unable to communicate with other P.O.W.s except by tap code, secreted notes, or by speaking into an enamel cup pressed against the wall. "It crushes your spirit and weakens your resistance more effectively than any other form of mistreatment." And this comes from a man who was beaten regularly; denied adequate medical treatment for two broken arms, a broken leg, and chronic dysentery; and tortured to the point

of having an arm broken again. A U.S. military study of almost a hundred and fifty naval aviators returned from imprisonment in Vietnam, many of whom were treated even worse than McCain, reported that they found social isolation to be as torturous and agonizing as any physical abuse they suffered.

And what happened to them *was* physical. EEG studies going back to the nineteen-sixties have shown diffuse slowing of brain waves in prisoners after a week or more of solitary confinement. In 1992, fifty-seven prisoners of war, released after an average of six months in detention camps in the former Yugoslavia, were examined using EEG-like tests. The recordings revealed brain abnormalities months afterward; the most severe were found in prisoners who had endured either head trauma sufficient to render them unconscious or, yes, solitary confinement. Without sustained social interaction, the human brain may become as impaired as one that has incurred a traumatic injury.

On December 4, 1991, Terry Anderson was released from captivity. He had been the last and the longest-held American hostage in Lebanon. I spoke to Keron Fletcher, a former British military psychiatrist who had been on the receiving team for Anderson and many other hostages, and followed them for years afterward. Initially, Fletcher said, everyone experiences the pure elation of being able to see and talk to people again, especially family and friends. They can't get enough of other people, and talk almost non-stop for hours. They are optimistic and hopeful. But, afterward, normal sleeping and eating patterns prove difficult to reestablish. Some have lost their sense of time. For weeks, they have trouble managing the sensations and emotional complexities of their freedom.

For the first few months after his release, Anderson said when I reached him by phone recently, "it was just kind of a fog." He had done many television interviews at the time. "And if you look at me in the pictures? Look at my eyes. You can tell. I look drugged."

Most hostages survived their ordeal, Fletcher said, although relationships, marriages, and careers were often lost. Some found, as John McCain did, that the experience even strengthened them. Yet none saw solitary confinement as anything less than torture. This presents us with an awkward question: If prolonged isolation is — as research and experience have confirmed for decades — so objectively horrifying, so intrinsically cruel, how did we end up with a prison system that may subject more of our own citizens to it than any other country in history has?

◆ ◆ ◆

The main argument for using long-term isolation in prisons is that it provides discipline and prevents violence. When inmates refuse to follow the rules — when they escape, deal drugs, or attack other inmates and corrections officers — wardens must be able to punish and contain the misconduct. Presumably, less stringent measures haven't worked, or the behavior would not have occurred. And it's legitimate to incapacitate violent aggressors for the safety of others. So, advocates say, isolation is a necessary evil, and those who don't recognize this are dangerously naïve.

The argument makes intuitive sense. If the worst of the worst are removed from the general prison population and put in isolation, you'd expect there to be markedly fewer inmate shankings and attacks on corrections officers. But the evidence doesn't bear this out. Perhaps the most careful inquiry into whether supermax prisons decrease violence and disorder was a 2003 analysis examining the experience in three states — Arizona, Illinois, and Minnesota — following the opening of their supermax prisons. The study found that levels of inmate-on-inmate violence were unchanged, and that levels of inmate-on-staff violence changed unpredictably,

25

rising in Arizona, falling in Illinois, and holding steady in Minnesota.

Prison violence, it turns out, is not simply an issue of a few belligerents. In the past thirty years, the United States has quadrupled its incarceration rate but not its prison space. Work and education programs have been cancelled, out of a belief that the pursuit of rehabilitation is pointless. The result has been unprecedented overcrowding, along with unprecedented idleness — a nice formula for violence. Remove a few prisoners to solitary confinement, and the violence doesn't change. So you remove some more, and still nothing happens. Before long, you find yourself in the position we are in today. The United States now has five per cent of the world's population, twenty-five per cent of its prisoners, and probably the vast majority of prisoners who are in long-term solitary confinement.

It wasn't always like this. The wide-scale use of isolation is, almost exclusively, a phenomenon of the past twenty years. In 1890, the United States Supreme Court came close to declaring the punishment to be unconstitutional. Writing for the majority in the case of a Colorado murderer who had been held in isolation for a month, Justice Samuel Miller noted that experience had revealed "serious objections" to solitary confinement: A considerable number of the prisoners fell, after even a short confinement, into a semi-fatuous condition, from which it was next to impossible to arouse them, and others became violently insane; others, still, committed suicide; while those who stood the ordeal better were not generally reformed, and in most cases did not recover sufficient mental activity to be of any subsequent service to the community. Prolonged isolation was used sparingly, if at all, by most American prisons for almost a century. Our first supermax — our first institution specifically designed for mass solitary confinement — was not established until 1983, in Marion, Illinois. In

1995, a federal court reviewing California's first supermax admitted that the conditions "hover on the edge of what is humanly tolerable for those with normal resilience." But it did not rule them to be unconstitutionally cruel or unusual, except in cases of mental illness. The prison's supermax conditions, the court stated, did not pose "a sufficiently high risk to all inmates of incurring a serious mental illness." In other words, there could be no legal objection to its routine use, given that the isolation didn't make *everyone* crazy. The ruling seemed to fit the public mood. By the end of the nineteen-nineties, some sixty supermax institutions had opened across the country. And new solitary-confinement units were established within nearly all of our ordinary maximum-security prisons.

The number of prisoners in these facilities has since risen to extraordinary levels. America now holds at least twenty-five thousand inmates in isolation in supermax prisons. An additional fifty to eighty thousand are kept in restrictive segregation units, many of them in isolation, too, although the government does not release these figures. By 1999, the practice had grown to the point that Arizona, Colorado, Maine, Nebraska, Nevada, Rhode Island, and Virginia kept between five and eight per cent of their prison population in isolation, and, by 2003, New York had joined them as well. Mississippi alone held eighteen hundred prisoners in supermax — twelve per cent of its prisoners over all. At the same time, other states had just a tiny fraction of their inmates in solitary confinement. In 1999, for example, Indiana had eighty-five supermax beds; Georgia had only ten. Neither of these two states can be described as being soft on crime.

Advocates of solitary confinement are left with a single argument for subjecting thousands of people to years of isolation: What else are we supposed to do? How else are we to deal with the violent, the disruptive, the prisoners who are just too dangerous to be housed with others?

As it happens, only a subset of prisoners currently locked away for long periods of isolation would be considered truly dangerous. Many are escapees or suspected gang members; many others are in solitary for nonviolent breaches of prison rules. Still, there are some highly dangerous and violent prisoners who pose a serious challenge to prison discipline and safety. In August, I met a man named Robert Felton, who had spent fourteen and a half years in isolation in the Illinois state correctional system. He is now thirty-six years old. He grew up in the predominantly black housing projects of Danville, Illinois, and had been a force of mayhem from the time he was a child.

His crimes were mainly impulsive, rather than planned. The first time he was arrested was at the age of eleven, when he and a relative broke into a house to steal some Atari video games. A year later, he was sent to state reform school after he and a friend broke into an abandoned building and made off with paint cans, irons, and other property that they hardly knew what to do with. In reform school, he got into fights and screamed obscenities at the staff. When the staff tried to discipline him by taking away his recreation or his television privileges, his behavior worsened. He tore a pillar out of the ceiling, a sink and mirrors off the wall, doors off their hinges. He was put in a special cell, stripped of nearly everything. When he began attacking counsellors, the authorities transferred him to the maximum-security juvenile facility at Joliet, where he continued to misbehave.

Felton wasn't a sociopath. He made friends easily. He was close to his family, and missed them deeply. He took no pleasure in hurting others. Psychiatric evaluations turned up little more than attention-deficit disorder. But he had a terrible temper, a tendency to escalate rather than to defuse confrontations, and, by the time he was released, just before turning eighteen, he had achieved only a ninth-grade education.

Within months of returning home, he was arrested again. He had walked into a Danville sports bar and ordered a beer. The barman took his ten-dollar bill.

"Then he says, 'Naw, man, you can't get no beer. You're underage,'" Felton recounts. "I says, 'Well, give me my ten dollars back.' He says, 'You ain't getting shit. Get the hell out of here.'"

Felton stood his ground. The bartender had a pocket knife on the counter. "And, when he went for it, I went for it," Felton told me. "When I grabbed the knife first, I turned around and spinned on him. I said, 'You think you're gonna cut me, man?'"

The barman had put the ten-dollar bill in a Royal Crown bag behind the counter. Felton grabbed the bag and ran out the back door. He forgot his car keys on the counter, though. So he went back to get the keys — "the stupid keys," he now says ruefully — and in the fight that ensued he left the barman severely injured and bleeding. The police caught Felton fleeing in his car. He was convicted of armed robbery, aggravated unlawful restraint, and aggravated battery, and served fifteen years in prison.

He was eventually sent to the Stateville Correctional Center, a maximum security facility in Joliet. Inside the overflowing prison, he got into vicious fights over insults and the like. About three months into his term, during a shakedown following the murder of an inmate, prison officials turned up a makeshift knife in his cell. (He denies that it was his.) They gave him a year in isolation. He was a danger, and he had to be taught a lesson. But it was a lesson that he seemed incapable of learning.

Felton's Stateville isolation cell had gray walls, a solid steel door, no window, no clock, and a light that was kept on twenty-four hours a day. As soon as he was shut in, he became claustrophobic and had a panic attack. Like Anderson and McCain, he was soon pacing back and forth, talking to himself, studying the insects crawling around his cell, reliving past events from childhood, sleeping for as much as sixteen hours a day. But, unlike them, he lacked the inner resources to cope with his situation.

Many prisoners find survival in physical exercise, prayer, or plans for escape. Many carry out elaborate mental exercises, building entire houses in their heads, board by board, nail by nail, from the ground up, or memorizing team rosters for a baseball season.

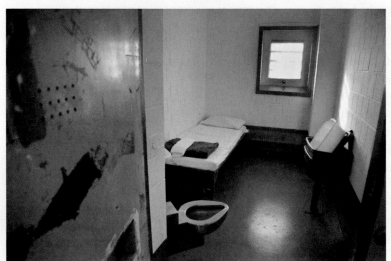

Bebeto Matthews/AP Images

◀

In a *GQ* magazine article entitled "Buried Alive, Stories from Inside Solitary Confinement," inmate Brian Nelson, who spent over 23 years in solitary, said, "I don't know if you can even grasp what it's like just to be in this gray box."
Why might living in the gray box pictured here, a solitary confinement cell at Rikers Island jail in New York, be the equivalent of being buried alive?

McCain recreated in his mind movies he'd seen. Anderson reconstructed complete novels from memory. Yuri Nosenko, a K.G.B[2] defector whom the C.I.A. wrongly accused of being a double agent and held for three years in total isolation (no reading material, no news, no human contact except with interrogators) in a closet-size concrete cell near Williamsburg, Virginia, made chess sets from threads and a calendar from lint (only to have them discovered and swept away).

But Felton would just yell, "Guard! Guard! Guard! Guard! Guard!," or bang his cup on the toilet, for hours. He could spend whole days hallucinating that he was in another world, that he was a child at home in Danville, playing in the streets, having conversations with imaginary people. Small cruelties that others somehow bore in quiet fury — getting no meal tray, for example — sent him into a rage. Despite being restrained with handcuffs, ankle shackles, and a belly chain whenever he was taken out, he managed to assault the staff at least three times. He threw his food through the door slot. He set his cell on fire by tearing his mattress apart, wrapping the stuffing in a sheet, popping his light bulb, and using the exposed wires to set the whole thing ablaze. He did this so many times that the walls of his cell were black with soot.

After each offense, prison officials extended his sentence in isolation. Still, he wouldn't stop. He began flooding his cell, by stuffing the door crack with socks, plugging the toilet, and flushing until the water was a couple of feet deep. Then he'd pull out the socks and the whole wing would flood with wastewater.

"Flooding the cell was the last option for me," Felton told me. "It was when I had nothing else I could do. You know, they took everything out of my cell, and all I had left was toilet water. I'd sit there and I'd say, 'Well, let me see what I can do with this toilet water.'"

40 Felton was not allowed out again for fourteen and a half years. He spent almost his entire prison term, from 1990 to 2005, in isolation. In March, 1998, he was among the first inmates to be moved to Tamms, a new, high-tech supermax facility in southern Illinois.

"At Tamms, man, it was like a lab," he says. Contact even with guards was tightly reduced. Cutoff valves meant that he couldn't flood his cell. He had little ability to force a response — negative or positive — from a human being. And, with that gone, he began to deteriorate further. He ceased showering, changing his clothes, brushing his teeth. His teeth rotted and ten had to be pulled. He began throwing his feces around his cell. He became psychotic.

_____

This illustration accompanied a 2015 *New York Times* editorial entitled "Solitary Confinement Is Cruel and All Too Common."

How does this image reflect the psychological effects Gawande describes in "Hellhole"?

_____
[2] The main security agency for the Soviet Union. —Eds.

Alex Nabaum/The New York Times

It is unclear how many prisoners in sol- 45
itary confinement become psychotic. Stuart
Grassian, a Boston psychiatrist, has interviewed
more than two hundred prisoners in solitary
confinement. In one in-depth study, prepared
for a legal challenge of prisoner-isolation practices, he concluded that about a third developed
acute psychosis with hallucinations. The markers of vulnerability that he observed in his interviews were signs of cognitive dysfunction — a
history of seizures, serious mental illness, mental retardation, illiteracy, or, as in Felton's case,
a diagnosis such as attention-deficit hyperac-
tivity disorder, signalling difficulty with impulse
control. In the prisoners Grassian saw, about a
third had these vulnerabilities, and these were
the prisoners whom solitary confinement had
made psychotic. They were simply not cogni-
tively equipped to endure it without mental
breakdowns.

A psychiatrist tried giving Felton antipsychotic medication. Mostly, it made him
sleep — sometimes twenty-four hours at a
stretch, he said. Twice he attempted suicide. The
first time, he hanged himself in a noose made
from a sheet. The second time, he took a single
staple from a legal newspaper and managed to
slash the radial artery in his left wrist with it. In
both instances, he was taken to a local emergency room for a few hours, patched up, and sent
back to prison.

◆ ◆ ◆

Is there an alternative? Consider what other
countries do. Britain, for example, has had
its share of serial killers, homicidal rapists,
and prisoners who have taken hostages and
repeatedly assaulted staff. The British also
fought a seemingly unending war in Northern
Ireland, which brought them hundreds of Irish
Republican Army prisoners committed to violent resistance. The authorities resorted to a
harshly punitive approach to control, including,

in the mid-seventies, extensive use of solitary confinement. But the violence in prisons
remained unchanged, the costs were phenomenal (in the United States, they reach more
than fifty thousand dollars a year per inmate),
and the public outcry became intolerable.
British authorities therefore looked for another
approach.

Beginning in the nineteen-eighties, they
gradually adopted a strategy that focussed
on preventing prison violence rather than on
delivering an ever more brutal series of punishments for it. The approach starts with the
simple observation that prisoners who are
unmanageable in one setting often behave perfectly reasonably in another. This suggested that
violence might, to a critical extent, be a function
of the conditions of incarceration. The British
noticed that problem prisoners were usually
people for whom avoiding humiliation and
saving face were fundamental and instinctive.
When conditions maximized humiliation and
confrontation, every interaction escalated into a
trial of strength. Violence became a predictable
consequence.

So the British decided to give their most dangerous prisoners more control, rather than less.
They reduced isolation and offered them opportunities for work, education, and special programming to increase social ties and skills. The
prisoners were housed in small, stable units of
fewer than ten people in individual cells, to avoid
conditions of social chaos and unpredictability.
In these reformed "Close Supervision Centres,"
prisoners could receive mental-health treatment
and earn rights for more exercise, more phone
calls, "contact visits," and even access to cooking
facilities. They were allowed to air grievances.
And the government set up an independent
body of inspectors to track the results and enable
adjustments based on the data.

The results have been impressive. The use of 50
long-term isolation in England is now negligible.

In all of England, there are now fewer prisoners in "extreme custody" than there are in the state of Maine. And the other countries of Europe have, with a similar focus on small units and violence prevention, achieved a similar outcome.

In this country, in June of 2006, a bipartisan national task force, the Commission on Safety and Abuse in America's Prisons, released its recommendations after a yearlong investigation. It called for ending long-term isolation of prisoners. Beyond about ten days, the report noted, practically no benefits can be found and the harm is clear — not just for inmates but for the public as well. Most prisoners in long-term isolation are returned to society, after all. And evidence from a number of studies has shown that supermax conditions — in which prisoners have virtually no social interactions and are given no programmatic support — make it highly likely that they will commit more crimes when they are released. Instead, the report said, we should follow the preventive approaches used in European countries.

The recommendations went nowhere, of course. Whatever the evidence in its favor, people simply did not believe in the treatment.

I spoke to a state-prison commissioner who wished to remain unidentified. He was a veteran of the system, having been either a prison warden or a commissioner in several states across the country for more than twenty years. He has publicly defended the use of long-term isolation everywhere that he has worked. Nonetheless, he said, he would remove most prisoners from long-term isolation units if he could and provide programming for the mental illnesses that many of them have.

"Prolonged isolation is not going to serve anyone's best interest," he told me. He still thought that prisons needed the option of isolation. "A bad violation should, I think, land you there for about ninety days, but it should not go beyond that."

He is apparently not alone among prison officials. Over the years, he has come to know commissioners in nearly every state in the country. "I believe that today you'll probably find that two-thirds or three-fourths of the heads of correctional agencies will largely share the position that I articulated with you," he said.

Commissioners are not powerless. They could eliminate prolonged isolation with the stroke of a pen. So, I asked, why haven't they? He told me what happened when he tried to move just one prisoner out of isolation. Legislators called for him to be fired and threatened to withhold basic funding. Corrections officers called members of the crime victim's family and told them that he'd gone soft on crime. Hostile stories appeared in the tabloids. It is pointless for commissioners to act unilaterally, he said, without a change in public opinion.

This past year, both the Republican and the Democratic Presidential candidates came out firmly for banning torture and closing the facility in Guantánamo Bay, where hundreds of prisoners have been held in years-long isolation. Neither Barack Obama nor John McCain, however, addressed the question of whether prolonged solitary confinement is torture. For a Presidential candidate, no less than for the prison commissioner, this would have been political suicide. The simple truth is that public sentiment in America is the reason that solitary confinement has exploded in this country, even as other Western nations have taken steps to reduce it. This is the dark side of American exceptionalism. With little concern or demurral, we have consigned tens of thousands of our own citizens to conditions that horrified our highest court a century ago. Our willingness to discard these standards for American prisoners made it easy to discard the Geneva Conventions prohibiting similar treatment of foreign prisoners of war, to the detriment of America's moral stature in the world. In much

seeing connections

While on a tour of the United States in 1842, English writer Charles Dickens visited a Pennsylvania prison run by Quakers, an experience he recorded in a chapter of *American Notes for General Circulation* entitled "Philadelphia, and Its Solitary Prison." The prison, which came to be known as Eastern State Penitentiary, was built in 1829 and remained open until 1971. It was the first to establish solitary confinement in America, though the practice was aimed at reform rather than punishment. Quakers imposed solitary confinement and mandatory silence out of a belief that such conditions were humane and would prompt spiritual reflection and growth.

Examine the image of a solitary cell from Eastern State Penitentiary and read the excerpt from Dickens's *American Notes for General Circulation* on page 1076 before answering the following questions.

1. **What sense of the effects of solitary confinement does the photo of a cell convey? What does it add to your understanding of the excerpt from *American Notes for General Circulation*?**

2. **How does Dickens characterize solitary confinement? How does his description of prisoners' mental states compare with the details Gawande shares?**

3. **Does the fact that Dickens wrote about Eastern State Penitentiary around 150 years before "Hellhole" was published undermine Gawande's claim that it makes "intuitive sense" to isolate criminals? Explain.**

Library of Congress

from **American Notes for General Circulation**

CHARLES DICKENS

Over the head and face of every prisoner who comes into this melancholy house, a black hood is drawn; and in this dark shroud, an emblem of the curtain dropped between him and the living world, he is led to the cell from which he never again comes forth, until his whole term of imprisonment has expired. He never hears of wife or children; home or friends; the life or death of any single creature. He sees the prison-officers, but with that exception he never looks upon a human countenance, or hears a human voice. He is a man buried alive; to be dug out in the slow round of years; and in the mean time dead to everything but torturing anxieties and horrible despair....

My firm conviction is, that independent of the mental anguish it occasions — an anguish so acute and so tremendous, that all imagination of it must fall far short of the reality — it wears the mind into a morbid state, which renders it unfit for the rough contact and busy action of the world. It is my fixed opinion that those who have undergone this punishment, *must* pass into society again morally unhealthy and diseased....

That it is a singularly unequal punishment, and affects the worst man least, there is no doubt. In its superior efficiency as a means of reformation, compared with that other code of regulations which allows the prisoners to work in company without communicating together, I have not the smallest faith....

It seems to me that the objection that nothing wholesome or good has ever had its growth in such unnatural solitude, and that even a dog or any of the more intelligent among beasts, would pine, and mope, and rust away, beneath its influence, would be in itself a sufficient argument against this system. But when we recollect, in addition, how very cruel and severe it is, and that a solitary life is always liable to peculiar and distinct objections of a most deplorable nature, which have arisen here; and call to mind, moreover, that the choice is not between this system, and a bad or ill-considered one, but between it and another which has worked well, and is, in its whole design and practice, excellent; there is surely more than sufficient reason for abandoning a mode of punishment attended by so little hope or promise, and fraught, beyond dispute, with such a host of evils.

the same way that a previous generation of Americans countenanced legalized segregation, ours has countenanced legalized torture. And there is no clearer manifestation of this than our routine use of solitary confinement — on our own people, in our own communities, in a supermax prison, for example, that is a thirty-minute drive from my door.

◆ ◆ ◆

Robert Felton drifted in and out of acute psychosis for much of his solitary confinement. Eventually, however, he found an unexpected resource. One day, while he was at Tamms, he was given a new defense lawyer, and, whatever expertise this lawyer provided, the more important thing was genuine human contact. He visited regularly, and sent Felton books. Although some were rejected by the authorities and Felton was restricted to a few at a time, he devoured those he was permitted. "I liked political books," he says. "'From Beirut to Jerusalem,' Winston Churchill, Noam Chomsky."

That small amount of contact was a lifeline. Felton corresponded with the lawyer about what he was reading. The lawyer helped him get his G.E.D. and a paralegal certificate through a correspondence course, and he taught Felton how to advocate for himself. Felton began writing letters to politicians and prison officials explaining the misery of his situation, opposing supermax isolation, and asking for a chance to return to the general prison population. (The Illinois Department of Corrections would not comment on Felton's case, but a spokesman stated that "Tamms houses the most disruptive, violent, and problematic inmates.") Felton was persuasive enough that Senator Paul Simon, of Illinois, wrote him back and, one day, even visited him. Simon asked the director of the State Department of Corrections, Donald Snyder, Jr., to give consideration to Felton's objections. But Snyder didn't budge. If there was anyone whom Felton fantasized about taking revenge upon, it was Snyder. Felton continued to file request after request. But the answer was always no.

On July 12, 2005, at the age of thirty-three, Felton was finally released. He hadn't socialized with another person since entering Tamms, at the age of twenty-five. Before his release, he was given one month in the general prison population to get used to people. It wasn't enough. Upon returning to society, he found that he had trouble in crowds. At a party of well-wishers, the volume of social stimulation overwhelmed him and he panicked, headed for a bathroom, and locked himself in. He stayed at his mother's house and kept mostly to himself.

For the first year, he had to wear an ankle bracelet and was allowed to leave home only for work. His first job was at a Papa John's restaurant, delivering pizzas. He next found work at the Model Star Laundry Service, doing pressing. This was a steady job, and he began to settle down. He fell in love with a waitress named Brittany. They moved into a three-room house that her grandmother lent them, and got engaged. Brittany became pregnant.

This is not a story with a happy ending. Felton lost his job with the laundry service. He went to work for a tree-cutting business; a few months later, it went under. Meanwhile, he and Brittany had had a second child. She had found work as a certified nursing assistant, but her income wasn't nearly enough. So he took a job forty miles away, at Plastipak, the plastics manufacturer, where he made seven-fifty an hour inspecting Gatorade bottles and Crisco containers as they came out of the stamping machines. Then his twenty-year-old Firebird died. The bus he had to take ran erratically, and he was fired for repeated tardiness.

When I visited Felton in Danville last August, he and Brittany were upbeat about their prospects. She was working extra shifts at a nursing home, and he was taking care of their children, ages one and two. He had also applied to a six-month training program for heating and air-conditioning technicians.

"I could make twenty dollars an hour after graduation," he said. ₆₀

"He's a good man, Brittany told me, taking his arm and giving him a kiss. ₆₅

But he was out of work. They were chronically short of money. It was hard to be optimistic about Felton's prospects. And, indeed, six weeks after we met, he was arrested for breaking into a car dealership and stealing a Dodge Charger. He pleaded guilty and, in January, began serving a seven-year sentence.

Before I left town — when there was still a glimmer of hope for him — we went out for lunch at his favorite place, a Mexican restaurant called La Potosina. Over enchiladas and Cokes, we talked about his family, Danville, the economy, and, of course, his time in prison. The strangest story had turned up in the news, he said. Donald

Snyder, Jr., the state prison director who had refused to let him out of solitary confinement, had been arrested, convicted, and sentenced to two years in prison for taking fifty thousand dollars in payoffs from lobbyists.

"Two years in prison," Felton marvelled. "He could end up right where I used to be."

I asked him, "If he wrote to you, asking if you would release him from solitary, what would you do?"

Felton didn't hesitate for a second. "If he wrote to me to let him out, I'd let him out," he said.

This surprised me. I expected anger, vindictiveness, a desire for retribution. "You'd let him out?" I said.

"I'd let him out," he said, and he put his fork down to make the point. "I wouldn't wish solitary confinement on anybody. Not even him."

[2009]

EXPLORING THE TEXT

1. How does Atul Gawande establish his ethos in "Hellhole"? Identify places where he appeals to logos and pathos as well. Which one is most prominent? Explain.

2. How does Gawande's discussion of Harry Harlow's study of baby rhesus monkeys prepare the reader for the argument that follows?

3. In paragraph 8, Gawande writes, "We wouldn't have anything like a child's dependence on other people, right?" How would you describe the tone of this question? What rhetorical purpose does it serve?

4. How does Gawande use the experiences of Terry Anderson and John McCain to develop his argument? Select a key quotation from each example. How does that quotation illustrate an important point?

5. Discussing the experiences of hostages, Gawande says that "none saw solitary confinement as anything less than torture. This presents us with an awkward question:…how did we end up with a prison system that may subject more of our citizens to it than any other country in history has?" (para. 23). What is the reader's likely response to this rhetorical question? Why do you think Gawande frames it as a question rather than a statement of fact?

6. In paragraph 25, Gawande concedes that the argument for using long-term isolation "makes intuitive sense." What does he mean by this? To what extent is he suggesting that factual information often runs contrary to intuition? Explain.

7. How does Gawande use the statistical information about incarceration in the United States in paragraph 26? What is its likely intended effect on his audience?

8. What rhetorical strategies does Gawande use to render Robert Felton's experience a compelling and suspenseful part of his essay? How does it contribute to the essay as a whole?

9. According to Gawande, what makes Felton's prison experience different from those of Anderson, McCain, and Nosenko? Why is that difference important to Gawande's argument?

10. How does Britain's experience with incarceration compare with that of the United States? What does Gawande suggest by way of the comparison?

11. Why do you think the state-prison commissioner whom Gawande quotes "wished to remain unidentified" (para. 53)? How compelling do you find his or her statements and attitudes? How does Gawande's use of an unidentified source affect his argument? Explain.

12. In paragraph 57, Gawande claims, "The simple truth is that public sentiment in America is the reason that solitary confinement has exploded in this country, even as other Western nations have taken steps to reduce it." Whom does Gawande blame? To what extent do you believe this to be a fair characterization of American values?

13. Gawande compares today's countenancing of "legalized torture" with a previous generation's practice of "legalized segregation" (para. 57). Is the comparison sound? Is it effective? Explain why or why not.

14. At the end of his essay, Gawande returns to the example of Robert Felton. What is the purpose and effect of concluding the piece this way?

15. Throughout the article, Gawande includes arguments of fact, value, and policy. Identify two of each kind. Which ones are prominent? Which are most effective? Explain.

16. In paragraph 27, Gawande discusses the idea that punishments might be "unconstitutionally cruel or unusual." In the U.S. Constitution, the eighth amendment states: "Excessive bail shall not be required, nor excessive fines imposed, nor cruel and unusual punishments inflicted." In your view, do the punishments described in Gawande's article violate the Constitution? Explain why or why not.

Remarks by the President at the 50th Anniversary of the Selma to Montgomery Marches

BARACK OBAMA

Barack Obama (b. 1961), a Democratic politician and the forty-fourth President of the United States. Originally from Honolulu, Hawaii, Obama graduated from Columbia University in 1983, worked as a community organizer in Chicago until 1988, and then enrolled in Harvard Law School, where he became the first African American president of the *Harvard Law Review*. After graduating, Obama became a civil rights attorney and professor of constitutional law at the University of Chicago Law School from 1992 to 2004. He served in the Illinois State Senate from 1996 until 2004, when he was elected to the U.S. Senate. In 2008, Obama defeated Republican candidate John McCain to become the first African American President of the United States. Nine months later, he was named the 2009 Nobel Peace Prize Laureate. He delivered the following speech at the Edmund Pettus Bridge in Selma, Alabama on March 7, 2015 to mark the fiftieth anniversary of the Selma to Montgomery civil rights marches. These marches, organized in 1965 by nonviolent activists to protest Southern state legislatures' disenfranchisement of African Americans, prompted violent assaults by state troopers and local militias. The violence led to a national outcry and ultimately contributed to the passage of the Voting Rights Act of 1965.

It is a rare honor in this life to follow one of your heroes. And John Lewis is one of my heroes.

Now, I have to imagine that when a younger John Lewis woke up that morning 50 years ago and made his way to Brown Chapel, heroics were not on his mind. A day like this was not on his mind. Young folks with bedrolls and backpacks were milling about. Veterans of the movement trained newcomers in the tactics of non-violence; the right way to protect yourself when attacked. A doctor described what tear gas does to the body, while marchers scribbled down instructions for contacting their loved ones. The air was thick with doubt, anticipation and fear. And they comforted themselves with the final verse of the final hymn they sung:

> "No matter what may be the test, God will take care of you;
> Lean, weary one, upon His breast, God will take care of you."

And then, his knapsack stocked with an apple, a toothbrush, and a book on government — all you need for a night behind bars — John Lewis led them out of the church on a mission to change America.

President and Mrs. Bush, Governor Bentley, Mayor Evans, Sewell, Reverend Strong, members of Congress, elected officials, foot soldiers, friends, fellow Americans:

As John noted, there are places and moments 5 in America where this nation's destiny has been decided. Many are sites of war — Concord and Lexington, Appomattox, Gettysburg. Others are sites that symbolize the daring of America's character — Independence Hall and Seneca Falls, Kitty Hawk and Cape Canaveral.

Selma is such a place. In one afternoon 50 years ago, so much of our turbulent history — the stain of slavery and anguish of civil war; the yoke of segregation and tyranny of Jim Crow; the death of four little girls in Birmingham; and the dream of a Baptist preacher — all that history met on this bridge.

It was not a clash of armies, but a clash of wills; a contest to determine the true meaning of America. And because of men and women like John Lewis, Joseph Lowery, Hosea Williams, Amelia Boynton, Diane Nash, Ralph Abernathy, C.T. Vivian, Andrew Young, Fred Shuttlesworth, Dr. Martin Luther King, Jr., and so many others, the idea of a just America and a fair America, an inclusive America, and a generous America — that idea ultimately triumphed.

As is true across the landscape of American history, we cannot examine this moment in isolation. The march on Selma was part of a broader campaign that spanned generations; the leaders that day part of a long line of heroes.

We gather here to celebrate them. We gather here to honor the courage of ordinary Americans willing to endure billy clubs and the chastening rod; tear gas and the trampling hoof; men and women who despite the gush of blood and splintered bone would stay true to their North Star and keep marching towards justice.

They did as Scripture instructed: "Rejoice 10 in hope, be patient in tribulation, be constant in prayer." And in the days to come, they went back again and again. When the trumpet call sounded for more to join, the people came — black and white, young and old, Christian and Jew, waving the American flag and singing the same anthems full of faith and hope. A white newsman, Bill Plante, who covered the marches then and who is with us here today, quipped that the growing number of white people lowered the quality of the singing. To those who marched, though, those old gospel songs must have never sounded so sweet.

In time, their chorus would well up and reach President Johnson. And he would send them

This photograph shows civil rights marchers kneeling to pray after successfully crossing the Edmund Pettus Bridge in 1965. **What do the photographer's choices in the framing and perspective of this image convey? What does this suggest about how the marches were viewed at the time they happened?**

protection, and speak to the nation, echoing their call for America and the world to hear: "We shall overcome." What enormous faith these men and women had. Faith in God, but also faith in America.

The Americans who crossed this bridge, they were not physically imposing. But they gave courage to millions. They held no elected office. But they led a nation. They marched as Americans who had endured hundreds of years of brutal violence, countless daily indignities — but they didn't seek special treatment, just the equal treatment promised to them almost a century before.

What they did here will reverberate through the ages. Not because the change they won was preordained; not because their victory was complete; but because they proved that nonviolent change is possible, that love and hope can conquer hate.

As we commemorate their achievement, we are well-served to remember that at the time of the marches, many in power condemned rather than praised them. Back then, they were called Communists, or half-breeds, or outside agitators, sexual and moral degenerates, and worse — they were called everything but the name their parents gave them. Their faith was questioned. Their lives were threatened. Their patriotism challenged.

And yet, what could be more American than 15 what happened in this place? What could more profoundly vindicate the idea of America than plain and humble people — unsung, the downtrodden, the dreamers not of high station, not born to wealth or privilege, not of one religious tradition but many, coming together to shape their country's course?

What greater expression of faith in the American experiment than this, what greater form of patriotism is there than the belief that America is not yet finished, that we are strong enough to be self-critical, that each successive generation can look upon our imperfections and decide that it is in our power to remake this nation to more closely align with our highest ideals?

That's why Selma is not some outlier in the American experience. That's why it's not a museum or a static monument to behold from a distance. It is instead the manifestation of a creed written into our founding documents: "We the People . . . in order to form a more perfect union." "We hold these truths to be self-evident, that all men are created equal."

These are not just words. They're a living thing, a call to action, a roadmap for citizenship

Paramount Pictures/Photofest

This still from the movie *Selma* (2014) shows civil rights leaders standing together as marchers kneel with their hands behind their heads.

Compare and contrast the message conveyed by this image and Obama's speech. How does each capture the determination and unity of the civil rights activists?

and an insistence in the capacity of free men and women to shape our own destiny. For founders like Franklin and Jefferson, for leaders like Lincoln and FDR, the success of our experiment in self-government rested on engaging all of our citizens in this work. And that's what we celebrate here in Selma. That's what this movement was all about, one leg in our long journey toward freedom.

The American instinct that led these young men and women to pick up the torch and cross this bridge, that's the same instinct that moved patriots to choose revolution over tyranny. It's the same instinct that drew immigrants from across oceans and the Rio Grande; the same instinct that led women to reach for the ballot, workers to organize against an unjust status quo; the same instinct that led us to plant a flag at Iwo Jima and on the surface of the Moon.

It's the idea held by generations of citizens 20 who believed that America is a constant work in progress; who believed that loving this country requires more than singing its praises or avoiding uncomfortable truths. It requires the occasional disruption, the willingness to speak out for what is right, to shake up the status quo. That's America.

That's what makes us unique. That's what cements our reputation as a beacon of opportunity. Young people behind the Iron Curtain would see Selma and eventually tear down that wall. Young people in Soweto would hear Bobby Kennedy talk about ripples of hope and eventually banish the scourge of apartheid. Young people in Burma went to prison rather than submit to military rule. They saw what John Lewis had done. From the streets of Tunis to the Maidan in Ukraine, this generation of young people can draw strength from this place, where the powerless could change the world's greatest power and push their leaders to expand the boundaries of freedom.

They saw that idea made real right here in Selma, Alabama. They saw that idea manifest itself here in America.

Because of campaigns like this, a Voting Rights Act was passed. Political and economic and social barriers came down. And the change these men and women wrought is visible here today in the presence of African Americans who run boardrooms, who sit on the bench, who serve in elected office from small towns to big cities; from the Congressional Black Caucus all the way to the Oval Office.

Because of what they did, the doors of opportunity swung open not just for black folks, but for every American. Women marched through those doors. Latinos marched through those doors. Asian Americans, gay Americans, Americans with disabilities — they all came through those doors. Their endeavors gave the entire South the chance to rise again, not by reasserting the past, but by transcending the past.

What a glorious thing, Dr. King might say. And 25 what a solemn debt we owe. Which leads us to ask, just how might we repay that debt?

First and foremost, we have to recognize that one day's commemoration, no matter how special, is not enough. If Selma taught us anything, it's that our work is never done. The American experiment in self-government gives work and purpose to each generation.

Selma teaches us, as well, that action requires that we shed our cynicism. For when it comes to the pursuit of justice, we can afford neither complacency nor despair.

Just this week, I was asked whether I thought the Department of Justice's Ferguson report shows that, with respect to race, little has changed in this country. And I understood the question; the report's narrative was sadly familiar. It evoked the kind of abuse and disregard for citizens that spawned the Civil Rights Movement. But I rejected the notion that nothing's changed. What happened in Ferguson may not be unique, but it's no longer endemic. It's no longer sanctioned by law or by custom. And before the Civil Rights Movement, it most surely was.

We do a disservice to the cause of justice by intimating that bias and discrimination are

seeing connections

In the top photograph, President Barack Obama, First Lady Michelle Obama, former President George W. Bush, former First Lady Laura Bush, Congressman John Lewis, and Amelia Boynton Robinson lead a walk across the Edmund Pettus Bridge to mark the fiftieth anniversary of the Selma to Montgomery civil rights marches. In the bottom photograph, Dr. Martin Luther King, Jr., flanked by civil rights activists John Lewis, Reverend Jesse Douglas, James Forman, and Ralph Abernathy, are pictured setting out on the march to Montgomery from Selma.

What connections do you see between these two images? How does the top image show a continuation of the traditions established by the activists in the bottom image?

SAUL LOEB/Getty Images

Steve Schapiro/Corbis/Getty Images

Milt Priggee, www.miltpriggee.com/Cagle Cartoons, Inc.

Cartoonist Milt Priggee drew this to mark the fiftieth anniversary of the Selma to Montgomery marches in 2015.
Why do you think he depicts the Edmund Pettus Bridge as a treadmill? What details from Obama's speech support the position Priggee expresses here? What details challenge it?

immutable, that racial division is inherent to America. If you think nothing's changed in the past 50 years, ask somebody who lived through the Selma or Chicago or Los Angeles of the 1950s. Ask the female CEO who once might have been assigned to the secretarial pool if nothing's changed. Ask your gay friend if it's easier to be out and proud in America now than it was thirty years ago. To deny this progress, this hard-won progress — our progress — would be to rob us of our own agency, our own capacity, our responsibility to do what we can to make America better.

Of course, a more common mistake is to suggest that Ferguson is an isolated incident; that racism is banished; that the work that drew men and women to Selma is now complete, and that whatever racial tensions remain are a consequence of those seeking to play the "race card" for their own purposes. We don't need the Ferguson report to know that's not true. We just need to open our eyes, and our ears, and our hearts to know that this nation's racial history still casts its long shadow upon us.

We know the march is not yet over. We know the race is not yet won. We know that reaching that blessed destination where we are judged,

all of us, by the content of our character requires admitting as much, facing up to the truth. "We are capable of bearing a great burden," James Baldwin once wrote, "once we discover that the burden is reality and arrive where reality is."

There's nothing America can't handle if we actually look squarely at the problem. And this is work for all Americans, not just some. Not just whites. Not just blacks. If we want to honor the courage of those who marched that day, then all of us are called to possess their moral imagination. All of us will need to feel as they did the fierce urgency of now. All of us need to recognize as they did that

30 change depends on our actions, on our attitudes, the things we teach our children. And if we make such an effort, no matter how hard it may sometimes seem, laws can be passed, and consciences can be stirred, and consensus can be built.

With such an effort, we can make sure our criminal justice system serves all and not just some. Together, we can raise the level of mutual trust that policing is built on — the idea that police officers are members of the community they risk their lives to protect, and citizens in Ferguson and New York and Cleveland, they just want the same thing young people here marched for 50 years ago — the protection of the law.

Together, we can address unfair sentencing and overcrowded prisons, and the stunted circumstances that rob too many boys of the chance to become men, and rob the nation of too many men who could be good dads, and good workers, and good neighbors.

With effort, we can roll back poverty and the roadblocks to opportunity. Americans don't accept a free ride for anybody, nor do we believe in equality of outcomes. But we do expect equal opportunity. And if we really mean it, if we're not just giving lip service to it, but if we really mean it and are willing to sacrifice for it, then, yes, we can make sure every child gets an education suitable to this new century, one that expands imaginations and lifts sights and gives those children the skills they need. We can make sure every person willing to work has the dignity of a job, and a fair wage, and a real voice, and sturdier rungs on that ladder into the middle class.

And with effort, we can protect the foundation stone of our democracy for which so many marched across this bridge — and that is the right to vote. Right now, in 2015, 50 years after Selma, there are laws across this country designed to make it harder for people to vote. As we speak, more of such laws are being proposed. Meanwhile, the Voting Rights Act, the culmination of so much blood, so much sweat and tears, the product of so much sacrifice in the face of wanton violence, the Voting Rights Act stands weakened, its future subject to political rancor.

How can that be? The Voting Rights Act was one of the crowning achievements of our democracy, the result of Republican and Democratic efforts. President Reagan signed its renewal when he was in office. President George W. Bush signed its renewal when he was in office. One hundred members of Congress have come here today to honor people who were willing to die for the right to protect it. If we want to honor this day, let that hundred go back to Washington and gather four hundred more, and together, pledge to make it their mission to restore that law this year. That's how we honor those on this bridge.

Of course, our democracy is not the task of Congress alone, or the courts alone, or even the President alone. If every new voter-suppression law was struck down today, we would still have, here in America, one of the lowest voting rates among free peoples. Fifty years ago, registering to vote here in Selma and much of the South meant guessing the number of jellybeans in a jar, the number of bubbles on a bar of soap. It meant risking your dignity, and sometimes, your life.

_____

This photograph was taken at a civil rights march.
What rhetorical strategies does this image use to convey the importance of the marchers' cause? How might this photograph be used to emphasize one of Obama's central points?

35

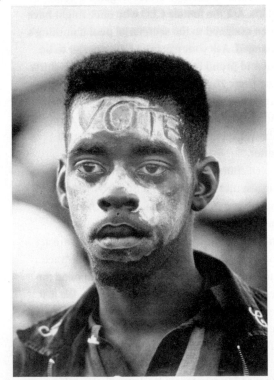

Steve Schapiro/Getty Images

What's our excuse today for not voting? How do we so casually discard the right for which so many fought? How do we so fully give away our power, our voice, in shaping America's future? Why are we pointing to somebody else when we could take the time just to go to the polling places? We give away our power.

Fellow marchers, so much has changed in 50 years. We have endured war and we've fashioned peace. We've seen technological wonders that touch every aspect of our lives. We take for granted conveniences that our parents could have scarcely imagined. But what has not changed is the imperative of citizenship; that willingness of a 26-year-old deacon, or a Unitarian minister, or a young mother of five to decide they loved this country so much that they'd risk everything to realize its promise.

That's what it means to love America. That's what it means to believe in America. That's what it means when we say America is exceptional.

For we were born of change. We broke the old aristocracies, declaring ourselves entitled not by bloodline, but endowed by our Creator with certain inalienable rights. We secure our rights and responsibilities through a system of self-government, of and by and for the people. That's why we argue and fight with so much passion and conviction — because we know our efforts matter. We know America is what we make of it.

Look at our history. We are Lewis and Clark and Sacajawea, pioneers who braved the unfamiliar, followed by a stampede of farmers and miners, and entrepreneurs and hucksters. That's our spirit. That's who we are.

We are Sojourner Truth and Fannie Lou Hamer, women who could do as much as any man and then some. And we're Susan B. Anthony, who shook the system until the law reflected that truth. That is our character.

We're the immigrants who stowed away on ships to reach these shores, the huddled masses yearning to breathe free — Holocaust survivors, Soviet defectors, the Lost Boys of Sudan. We're the hopeful strivers who cross the Rio Grande because we want our kids to know a better life. That's how we came to be.

We're the slaves who built the White House and the economy of the South. We're the ranch hands and cowboys who opened up the West, and countless laborers who laid

40

45

SAUL LOEB/Getty Images

This photograph was taken as President Obama gave his Selma speech.
Analyze the visual rhetoric of this image. How does it reflect Obama's persona and tone?

Obama   Remarks by the President at the 50th Anniversary of the Selma to Montgomery Marches

OTHER VOICES   1085

rail, and raised skyscrapers, and organized for workers' rights.

We're the fresh-faced GIs who fought to liberate a continent. And we're the Tuskeegee Airmen, and the Navajo code-talkers, and the Japanese Americans who fought for this country even as their own liberty had been denied.

We're the firefighters who rushed into those buildings on 9/11, the volunteers who signed up to fight in Afghanistan and Iraq. We're the gay Americans whose blood ran in the streets of San Francisco and New York, just as blood ran down this bridge.

We are storytellers, writers, poets, artists who abhor unfairness, and despise hypocrisy, and give voice to the voiceless, and tell truths that need to be told.

We're the inventors of gospel and jazz and blues, bluegrass and country, and hip-hop and rock and roll, and our very own sound with all the sweet sorrow and reckless joy of freedom.

We are Jackie Robinson, enduring scorn and spiked cleats and pitches coming straight to his head, and stealing home in the World Series anyway.

We are the people Langston Hughes wrote of who "build our temples for tomorrow, strong as we know how." We are the people Emerson wrote of, "who for truth and honor's sake stand fast and suffer long;" who are "never tired, so long as we can see far enough."

That's what America is. Not stock photos or airbrushed history, or feeble attempts to define some of us as more American than others. We respect the past, but we don't pine for the past. We don't fear the future; we grab for it. America is not some fragile thing. We are large, in the words of Whitman, containing multitudes. We are boisterous and diverse and full of energy, perpetually young in spirit. That's why someone like John Lewis at the ripe old age of 25 could lead a mighty march.

And that's what the young people here today and listening all across the country must take away from this day. You are America. Unconstrained by habit and convention. Unencumbered by what is, because you're ready to seize what ought to be.

For everywhere in this country, there are first steps to be taken, there's new ground to cover, there are more bridges to be crossed. And it is you, the young and fearless at heart, the most diverse and educated generation in our history, who the nation is waiting to follow.

Because Selma shows us that America is not the project of any one person. Because the singlemost powerful word in our democracy is the word "We." "We The People." "We Shall Overcome." "Yes We Can." That word is owned by no one. It belongs to everyone. Oh, what a glorious task we are given, to continually try to improve this great nation of ours.

Fifty years from Bloody Sunday, our march is not yet finished, but we're getting closer. Two hundred and thirty-nine years after this nation's founding our union is not yet perfect, but we are getting closer. Our job's easier because somebody already got us through that first mile. Somebody already got us over that bridge. When it feels the road is too hard, when the torch we've been passed feels too heavy, we will remember these early travelers, and draw strength from their example, and hold firmly the words of the prophet Isaiah: "Those who hope in the Lord will renew their strength. They will soar on [the] wings like eagles. They will run and not grow weary. They will walk and not be faint."

We honor those who walked so we could run. We must run so our children soar. And we will not grow weary. For we believe in the power of an awesome God, and we believe in this country's sacred promise.

May He bless those warriors of justice no longer with us, and bless the United States of America. Thank you, everybody.

[2015]

EXPLORING THE TEXT

1. What is the rhetorical situation of this speech? Although the obvious and immediate occasion is the fiftieth anniversary of the march across the Edmund Pettus Bridge in Selma, Alabama, what other elements of context did President Barack Obama likely take into consideration as he crafted this speech?

2. How do the opening three paragraphs set the tone for the speech, particularly in terms of Obama's appeal to a national audience?

3. How does Obama's diction in paragraph 6 establish the significance of the occasion?

4. In paragraph 12, Obama uses a series of contraries; that is, a series of statements, each followed by "but." Examine other examples of contraries or contrasts in the speech. What is their cumulative rhetorical effect? Why is this strategy particularly fitting to the subject at hand?

5. Much of the drama of this speech derives from the strong active verbs such as "questioned," "threatened," and "challenged" (para. 14). Select one passage and analyze how Obama's verb choices convey both energy and urgency.

6. What connection does Obama make between the struggles of Americans and of people in the larger international community? How does he emphasize the relevance of the specific circumstances of American civil rights to a broader movement?

7. Why does Obama bring up the Department of Justice's report on the fatal shooting of Michael Brown, an African American teenager, by a white police officer in Ferguson, Missouri? How effectively does he concede and refute the position that events in Ferguson confirm "racial division is inherent to America" (para. 29)?

8. In paragraph 32, Obama recalls the "moral imagination" of those who marched in Selma in 1965 and calls on Americans today to show the same characteristic. What does he mean by the term "moral imagination"?

9. Obama sharply rebukes Congress for not renewing the Voting Rights Act of 1965, which he characterizes as "one of the crowning achievements of our democracy" (para. 36). How effectively does he make the case that this occasion is the right one to call for its renewal?

How persuasive is he in his support of the implicit claim that voting gives voice to the voiceless?

10. How does Obama use quotations from scripture to develop his position in this speech? Do they serve as appeals to both ethos and pathos? Explain.

11. Throughout the speech, Obama refers to and quotes from American writers, including James Baldwin, Ralph Waldo Emerson, Langston Hughes, and Walt Whitman. In what ways do these authors' words serve as evidence for his argument? You might look up the full passages from which Obama is quoting as you consider how effective these choices are.

12. How does the litany of "We" statements toward the end of speech (para. 57) function rhetorically to achieve Obama's purpose(s)? Consider not only his language but its syntactical pace and rhythm.

13. The 1965 march was also known as Bloody Sunday because of the violent attacks on the civil rights demonstrators. Why do you think that Obama waited until the end of his speech to use this moniker? In your response, be sure to discuss Obama's audience(s) and his central purpose.

14. Although there were people in the audience who participated in the 1965 march, what is the evidence that shows another key audience — one of a younger generation — is also in attendance? In what ways is this speech a call to arms for them?

15. In what ways — from the very outset — does Obama broaden the appeal of his speech beyond African Americans and the civil rights movement of the 1960s? How effectively do you believe he was in doing this? Cite specific passages and references to support your viewpoint.

16. Throughout the speech, Obama refers to the 1965 march on Selma, but he also turns the concept of a march — or journey — into a symbol of the present, perhaps of American history in general. How does he develop a specific event into the concept of a larger journey? Consider his references to miles, races, bridges, travelers, and similar terms. Pay particular attention to the ending of the speech.

17. Ultimately, how does Obama define American exceptionalism? What precisely is it that makes

America "exceptional" (para. 40)? To what extent do you agree with this position?

18. Often analyzed, this speech has been praised for its "soaring rhetoric" and "plain but potent language." Citing specific examples as support, explain the extent to which you believe that these descriptions apply to the speech.

19. Rich in rhetorical strategies, this speech contains a number of different ideas and themes. Select one of the following phrases from the speech and discuss why it is a key idea in the argument(s) Obama makes:

a. "the occasional disruption" (para. 20)

b. "neither complacency nor despair" (para. 27)

c. "to rob us of our own agency" (para. 29)

d. "the fierce urgency of now" (para. 32)

e. "the imperative of citizenship" (para. 39)

f. "truths that need to be told" (para. 48)

g. "America is not some fragile thing" (para. 52)

h. "warriors of justice" (para. 58)

The Irrationality of Natural Life Sentences

JENNIFER LACKEY

Jennifer Lackey is a professor of philosophy at Northwestern University. She is known for her research in epistemology, the branch of philosophy concerned with the theory of knowledge and sometimes defined as "how we know what we know." Lackey's research focuses specifically on testimony, disagreement, memory, and the norms of assertion. She is the author of *Learning from Words: Testimony as a Source of Knowledge* (2008), the co-editor of *The Epistemology of Testimony* (2006) and *The Epistemology of Disagreement: New Essays* (2013), and the editor of *Essays in Collective Epistemology* (2014). She is the Editor-in-Chief of the journal *Episteme* and edits both the international journal *Philosophical Studies* and the *Stanford Encyclopedia of Philosophy*. She published the following op-ed in the *New York Times* in 2016.

I've been teaching philosophy for 15 years, and while I've had some very memorable experiences along the way, I knew early on that my current seminar would be unique. The course itself is on values, and each Monday for nearly three hours my students debate — in an often lively and engaging manner — issues ranging from the existence of universal moral truths to the permissibility of torture and the death penalty. In fact, a few weeks ago, there was a complaint about the level of noise coming from my classroom. The reason for the noise? The utilitarians[1] were rather loudly arguing to the Kantians[2] that sacrificing

one of their classmates to prevent the Paris attacks[3] would clearly have been justified.

The complaint resulted in a guard being stationed in the doorway of my classroom to ensure that there wasn't "a security threat," followed by some breath-holding as I waited to see if I would, once again, be removed from the building. You see, the course I'm teaching is at Stateville Correctional Center — a maximum-security men's prison in a suburb of Chicago — where raised voices aren't typically the result of intense philosophical debate about normative ethical theories. Yet, the room felt no more in need of a guard than do my classes at Northwestern.

[1] Proponents of utilitarianism, which holds that what is morally right is what has the best consequences for the most people. —Eds.
[2] Proponents of the moral theory of Immanuel Kant (1724–1804), which holds that what is morally right is dependent not on consequences but on a person's intent. —Eds.

[3] Terrorist attacks on the city of Paris, France, in November 2015, resulting in the deaths of 137 people. —Eds.

In some respects, this is a striking fact. Just about all of my students at Stateville have been convicted of at least one murder; some have assaulted staff members, and others have spent over a decade in solitary confinement. Some are former gang members, and others were on death row — neighbors with John Wayne Gacy — for almost half of their lives.

In other respects, however, this is not at all surprising. The most obvious is that some end up at Stateville for reasons that are disconnected from culpability — coerced confessions, poor counsel, a racist jury, and so on. But even where these external forces are largely absent, the fact that my classroom seems indistinguishable from those at an elite university turns out not to be that shocking. And here's the simple, yet crucially important reason: People can change, often in profoundly transformative ways.

◆ ◆ ◆

Such transformations can be seen most clearly   5 by considering the two ends of the spectrum of life. On the early side, it is often noted that the prefrontal cortex of the brains of adolescents is still developing, and so they are more likely than adults to act on impulse, engage in dangerous or risky behavior, and misread social cues and emotions. This raises a host of questions about the level of responsibility that juveniles bear for their crimes and the appropriate punishments that should be handed out to them. If the underdeveloped brains of adolescents at least partly explain their criminal behavior, then holding them fully responsible for their actions, and punishing them as adults, seems wildly off the mark.

On the later side of the spectrum, only 1 percent of serious crime is committed by people over the age of 60. According to Jonathan Turley, a professor of public interest law at George Washington University: "Everyone agrees on what is the most reliable predictor of recidivism: age. As people get older, they statistically become less dangerous." Turley refers to this period as "criminal

Shown here is a work by artist Evelyn Williams (1929–2012) entitled *The Prisoner*, completed in 1984. **How does it portray the experience of imprisonment? What about the message this work conveys might Lackey find especially relevant to her argument?**

ESTATE OF EVELYN WILLIAMS (BACS)/Private Collection/Bridgeman Images

menopause," a phenomenon that raises serious questions about the rationale for incarcerating the elderly. Still, researchers project that the elderly prison population in the United States will be over 400,000 in 2030, compared with 8,853 in 1981.

At the early end of the spectrum of life, then, there is the possibility that prisoners *might change*; at the later end, there is the reality that they *have changed*. Both facts bump up against natural life sentences. A sentence of "natural life" means that there are no parole hearings, no credit for time served, no possibility of release.

Short of a successful appeal or an executive pardon, such a sentence means that the convicted will, in no uncertain terms, die behind bars.

◆ ◆ ◆

Many types of arguments have been leveled against natural life sentences. Economic ones focus on the ballooning costs of mass incarceration and the toll this takes on government budgets, especially as the age and medical expenses of prisoners rapidly increase. Legal ones ask whether such sentences are cruel and unusual and therefore violate the Eighth Amendment, particularly for juveniles. Social arguments ask whether natural life sentences discourage reform by providing no incentive for rehabilitation. Moral concerns are grounded in the dignity and rights of prisoners, while psychological objections call attention to the myriad causes of deviant behavior and their responsiveness to appropriate treatment.

But one argument that is surprisingly absent from these conversations is an *epistemic*[4] one that has to do with *us*. For natural life sentences say to all involved that there is no possible piece of information that could be learned between sentencing and death that could bear in any way on the punishment the convicted is said to deserve, short of what might ground an appeal. Nothing. So no matter how much a juvenile is transformed behind bars, and no matter how unrecognizable an elderly prisoner is from his earlier self, this is utterly irrelevant to whether they should be incarcerated. Our absence of knowledge about the future, our ignorance of what is to come, our lack of a crystal ball, is in no way a barrier to determining now what someone's life ought to be like decades from now.

Moreover, prisoners aren't the only ones who can change: victims and their families can come

to see the convicted as being worthy of forgiveness and a second chance, and public attitudes can evolve, moving away from a zealous "war on crime" approach to one that sees much criminal activity as the result of broader social problems that call for reform. Even if we set aside the other arguments against natural life sentences — economic, legal, moral and so on — the question I want to ask here is this: how is it *rational* to screen off the relevance of this information? How, that is, is it rational to say today that there can be no possible evidence in the future that could bear on the punishment that a decades-from-now prisoner deserves?

In any other domain, it would obviously be irrational to make a high-stakes decision about the rest of another person's life that not only rules out the possibility of ever considering additional evidence, but is also meant to be absolutely final.

If I were given the option to heavily invest in one, and only one, career for my 15-year-old based only on her current beliefs, preferences, and character, I would refuse without hesitation. A lot can change in a decade, especially during the critical transition between adolescence and adulthood. Even choices that we expect to significantly constrain our future selves, such as marriage, can be revisited in light of new evidence. This is precisely why divorce is legal. Yet natural life sentences stand out as a glaring exception: They permit binding, life-altering decisions to be made in a state of radical *epistemic impoverishment.*

Of course, when punishment is connected with rehabilitation, it's undeniable that information about changes, especially among prisoners, is relevant. But this is also true for all but the crudest forms of retributive justice. It's a commonplace that information about a person's mental states bears on the punishment deserved, regardless of its consequences. When considering punishments, including at parole hearings,

---

[4] A philosophical framework that explores the nature of human knowledge. —Eds.

10

seeing connections

The graphs included here show data compiled by the Sentencing Project, an organization dedicated to "changing the way Americans think about crime and punishment."
What conclusions can you draw from the information provided by these graphs? Why do you think Lackey decides not to include it as evidence to support her argument?

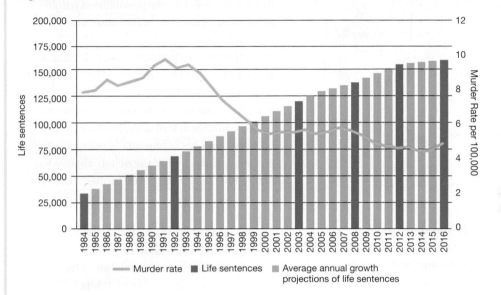

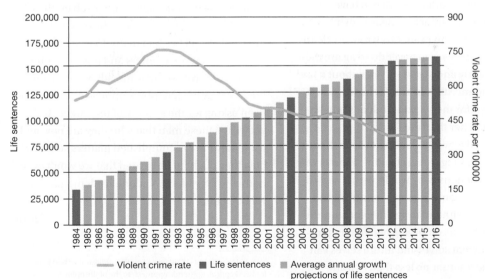

The Sentencing Project

▼ ◆◆◆

Do you think this cartoon trivializes the consequences of life without parole? Explain why or why not.

LIFE WITHOUT PAROLE

Peter Steiner/The New Yorker Collection/The Cartoon Bank

we are often highly sensitive to whether the wrongdoer appreciates the wrongness of the act, feels remorse, and is committed to not being a repeat offender.

Compare two students known to have cheated: The first fully acknowledges that looking at her notes during an exam was wrong, is clearly contrite, and promises to never do so again; the second flagrantly and steadfastly lies about it and shows no evidence that he won't cheat again. It is fairly standard for the second student's punishment to be harsher than the first's.

But if we take two students with such different mental states regarding cheating as deserving of different sanctions, why would we not regard two stages of the same person — one at 19 and another at 49 — with radically different attitudes toward his crime, as deserving of different punishments? Current selves and future selves can vary from one another no less than two altogether distinct people do.

Notice that nothing in the epistemic argument here suggests that no prisoners should, in fact, spend the rest of their natural lives behind bars. Instead, the point is that rationality requires that we leave the epistemic door open to acquiring new information. Put bluntly, the argument says that it is irrational for the possibility of parole to be taken off the table at the outset of any sentence.

If Hume[5] is right that "a wise man proportions his belief to the evidence," then our beliefs about the punishment a person deserves at any given time need to be sensitive to the evidence available at that time. But if we screen off huge amounts of potentially relevant information decades before the beliefs about what a prisoner deserves are even formed, then it is impossible for them to be proportioned to the evidence.

Nearly all of my students at Stateville are serving natural life sentences. At least a handful of them have been incarcerated since they were teenagers, one since he was 14. While I didn't know any of their decades-earlier selves, their current selves are some of the most extraordinary students I've had in my 15 years of teaching. They are painters and poets, mentors and authors, researchers and advocates. They breathe new life into philosophical questions I've been asking for the entirety of my career. And yet we tell these men that who they are now and what they have accomplished matters so little to how they ought to be treated that we won't even bother to consider it. Rationality demands that we do better.

15

[2016]

---

[5] David Hume (1711–1776) was a Scottish philosopher best known for his skeptical, epistemic approach to the philosophic theories of his era. —Eds.

EXPLORING THE TEXT

1. Jennifer Lackey, a professor of philosophy, begins her essay with an anecdote from her "current seminar" (para. 1). Through her description, what does she convey about herself, her students, and the class? How does this opening paragraph prepare the reader for the following paragraph, and why is this strategy effective, given her particular argument?

2. What is Lackey's position on natural life sentences? Identify the reasons she provides to support that position.

3. In paragraph 2, Lackey says that her class at the prison felt "no more in need of a guard" than her classes at the university where she teaches. Examine the paragraphs 3 and 4. How does Lackey reveal an understanding of her audience's reaction to her statement in paragraph 2? How does she then move to her claim that "people can change, often in profoundly transformative ways" (para. 4)?

4. In paragraph 7, Lackey says, "At the early end of the spectrum of life, then, there is the possibility that prisoners *might change*; at the later end, there is the reality that they *have changed*." What is the function of this sentence, and how do her syntax and diction contribute to that function?

5. How does Lackey's syntax in paragraph 9 reflect her purpose? Why does Lackey italicize the terms "epistemic" and "us"?

6. In paragraph 10, Lackey asks, "How is it *rational* to screen off the relevance of this information?" What are the connotations of the word "rational" in this context? How does Lackey use this word, in its various forms, from this point forward? What is the effect of its use in the first instance and the last, specifically?

7. Examine the analogies Lackey makes in paragraph 12. What is the effect of this strategy on the reader? How would you characterize the logic of these analogies?

8. How does Lackey build her claim that "current selves and future selves can vary from one another no less than two altogether distinct people do" (para. 15)?

9. Why does Lackey bring the reader back to her class at Stateville in her closing paragraph? What persuasive appeals does she employ ? Explain how the appeals are created and how they work to achieve the essay's purpose.

10. Identify the types of evidence Lackey uses in her essay and provide one example for each type. Looking at your list, evaluate the strengths and weaknesses of Lackey's evidence. Then, select two other kinds of evidence that Lackey could have also used to support her position and explain why you think they would have been effective.

Truth
Remarks on the Removal of Confederate Monuments in New Orleans

MITCH LANDRIEU

Mitch Landrieu (b. 1960) is a Democratic politician and lawyer who has served as Mayor of New Orleans, Louisiana since 2010. He grew up in New Orleans and went on to earn a degree in political science and theater from the Catholic University of America in Washington, D.C., before attending Loyola University Law School in Chicago, Illinois. He was elected to the Louisiana House of Representatives in 1987, where he served for 16 years before becoming Lieutenant Governor of Louisiana in 2004. In 2015, Landrieu called for the removal of four New Orleans monuments to the "Lost Cause of the Confederacy," erected decades after the Civil War. After several legal challenges were struck down, the first of the four statues was removed on April 24, 2017. Landrieu gave the following speech on May 19, 2017, just blocks away from the final monument, a statue of the Confederate general Robert E. Lee, which was scheduled for removal later that day. His audience was invitation-only, but a transcript of the speech quickly went viral.

Thank you for coming.

The soul of our beloved City is deeply rooted in a history that has evolved over thousands of years; rooted in a diverse people who have been here together every step of the way — for both good and for ill.

It is a history that holds in its heart the stories of Native Americans: the Choctaw, Houma Nation, the Chitimacha. Of Hernando de Soto, Robert Cavelier, Sieur de La Salle, the Acadians, the Islenos, the enslaved people from Senegambia, Free People of Color, the Haitians, the Germans, both the empires of France and Spain. The Italians, the Irish, the Cubans, the south and central Americans, the Vietnamese and so many more.

You see: New Orleans is truly a city of many nations, a melting pot, a bubbling cauldron of many cultures.

There is no other place quite like it in the world that so eloquently exemplifies the uniquely American motto: *e pluribus unum* — out of many we are one.

But there are also other truths about our city that we must confront. New Orleans was America's largest slave market: a port where hundreds of thousands of souls were brought, sold and shipped up the Mississippi River to lives of forced labor, of misery, of rape, of torture.

America was the place where nearly 4,000 of our fellow citizens were lynched, 540 alone in Louisiana; where the courts enshrined "separate but equal"; where Freedom riders coming to New Orleans were beaten to a bloody pulp.

So when people say to me that the monuments in question are history, well what I just described is real history as well, and it is the searing truth.

seeing connections

This photograph, taken in 2015, shows the Door of No Return, a memorial to the people sold into slavery, in Benin, a country located on the west coast of Africa.

What impression do you think this memorial is intended to make? What point does Landrieu make that this image would support?

Eric Lafforgue/Art in All of Us/Getty Images

And it immediately begs the questions: why there are no slave ship monuments, no prominent markers on public land to remember the lynchings or the slave blocks; nothing to remember this long chapter of our lives; the pain, the sacrifice, the shame — all of it happening on the soil of New Orleans.

So for those self-appointed defenders of history and the monuments, they are eerily silent on what amounts to this historical malfeasance, a lie by omission.

There is a difference between remembrance of history and reverence of it. For America and New Orleans, it has been a long, winding road, marked by great tragedy and great triumph. But we cannot be afraid of our truth.

As President George W. Bush said at the dedication ceremony for the National Museum of African American History & Culture, "A great nation does not hide its history. It faces its flaws and corrects them."

So today I want to speak about why we chose to remove these four monuments to the Lost Cause of the Confederacy, but also how and why this process can move us towards healing and understanding of each other.

So, let's start with the facts.

The historic record is clear: the Robert E. Lee, Jefferson Davis, and P.G.T. Beauregard statues were not erected just to honor these men, but as part of the movement which became known as The Cult of the Lost Cause. This "cult" had one goal — through monuments and through other means — to rewrite history to hide the truth, which is that the Confederacy was on the wrong side of humanity.

First erected over 166 years after the founding of our city and 19 years after the end of the Civil War, the monuments that we took down were meant to rebrand the history of our city and the ideals of a defeated Confederacy.

It is self-evident that these men did not fight for the United States of America. They fought against it. They may have been warriors, but in this cause they were not patriots.

These statues are not just stone and metal. They are not just innocent remembrances of a benign history. These monuments purposefully celebrate a fictional, sanitized Confederacy; ignoring the death, ignoring the enslavement, and the terror that it actually stood for.

After the Civil War, these statues were a part of that terrorism as much as a burning cross on someone's lawn; they were erected purposefully to send a strong message to all who walked in their shadows about who was still in charge in this city.

Should you have further doubt about the true goals of the Confederacy, in the very weeks before the war broke out, the Vice President of the Confederacy, Alexander Stephens, made it clear that the Confederate cause was about maintaining slavery and white supremacy.

He said in his now famous "Cornerstone speech" that the Confederacy's "cornerstone rests upon the great truth, that the negro is not equal to the white man; that slavery — subordination to the superior race — is his natural and normal condition. This, our new government, is the first, in the history of the world, based upon this great physical, philosophical, and moral truth."

Now, with these shocking words still ringing in your ears, I want to try to gently peel from your hands the grip on a false narrative of our history that I think weakens us and make straight a wrong turn we made many years ago so we can more closely connect with integrity to the founding principles of our nation and forge a clearer and straighter path toward a better city and more perfect union.

Last year, President Barack Obama echoed these sentiments about the need to contextualize and remember all of our history. He recalled a piece of stone, a slave auction block engraved with a marker commemorating a single moment in 1830 when Andrew Jackson and Henry Clay stood and spoke from it.

This map shows the role each state played during the Civil War and the number of Confederate monuments in each as of 2017.

What is surprising about this map? How might it be used to respond to Landrieu's argument?

Confederate Symbols Across America

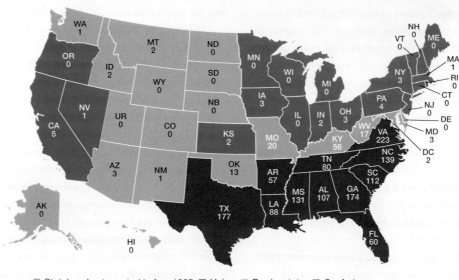

■ Statehood not granted before 1865 ■ Union ■ Border state ■ Confederacy

Data from the Southern Poverty Law Center.

President Obama said, "Consider what this artifact tells us about history… on a stone where day after day for years, men and women…bound and bought and sold and bid like cattle on a stone worn down by the tragedy of over a thousand bare feet. For a long time the only thing we considered important, the singular thing we once chose to commemorate as history with a plaque were the unmemorable speeches of two powerful men."

A piece of stone — one stone. Both stories were history. One story told. One story forgotten or maybe even purposefully ignored.

As clear as it is for me today — for a long time, even though I grew up in one of New Orleans' most diverse neighborhoods, even with my family's long proud history of fighting for civil rights — I must have passed by those monuments a million times without giving them a second thought.

So I am not judging anybody, I am not judging people. We all take our own journey on race.

I just hope people listen like I did when my dear friend Wynton Marsalis helped me see the truth. He asked me to think about all the people who have left New Orleans because of our exclusionary attitudes.

Another friend asked me to consider these four monuments from the perspective of an African American mother or father trying to explain to their fifth grade daughter who Robert E. Lee is and why he stands atop of our beautiful city. Can you do it?

Can you look into that young girl's eyes and convince her that Robert E. Lee is there to encourage her? Do you think she will feel inspired and hopeful by that story? Do these monuments help her see a future with limitless potential? Have you ever thought that if her potential is limited, yours and mine are too?

We all know the answer to these very simple 30 questions.

25

When you look into this child's eyes is the moment when the searing truth comes into focus for us. This is the moment when we know what is right and what we must do. We can't walk away from this truth.

And I knew that taking down the monuments was going to be tough, but you elected me to do the right thing, not the easy thing and this is what that looks like. So relocating these Confederate monuments is not about taking something away from someone else. This is not about politics, this is not about blame or retaliation. This is not a naïve quest to solve all our problems at once.

This is, however, about showing the whole world that we as a city and as a people are able to acknowledge, understand, reconcile and, most importantly, choose a better future for ourselves, making straight what has been crooked and making right what was wrong.

Otherwise, we will continue to pay a price with discord, with division, and yes, with violence.

To literally put the Confederacy on a pedestal in 35 our most prominent places of honor is an inaccurate recitation of our full past, it is an affront to our present, and it is a bad prescription for our future.

History cannot be changed. It cannot be moved like a statue. What is done is done. The Civil War is over, and the Confederacy lost and we are better for it. Surely we are far enough removed from this dark time to acknowledge that the cause of the Confederacy was wrong.

And in the second decade of the 21st century, asking African Americans — or anyone else — to drive by property that they own; occupied by reverential statues of men who fought to destroy the country and deny that person's humanity seems perverse and absurd.

Centuries-old wounds are still raw because they never healed right in the first place.

Here is the essential truth: we are better together than we are apart. Indivisibility is our essence. Isn't this the gift that the people of New Orleans have given to the world?

We radiate beauty and grace in our food, in 40 our music, in our architecture, in our joy of life, in our celebration of death; in everything that we do. We gave the world this funky thing called jazz; the most uniquely American art form that is developed across the ages from different cultures.

Think about second lines, think about Mardi Gras, think about muffaletta, think about the Saints, gumbo, red beans and rice. By God, just think. All we hold dear is created by throwing everything in the pot; creating, producing

Scott Threlkeld/AP Images

This photograph shows the statue of Robert E. Lee being removed in New Orleans in May 2017, just hours after Landrieu gave his speech.
How does this image add to your understanding of the effect the monument had on the city of New Orleans and its residents? What details from Landrieu's speech do you think best articulate this effect?

something better; everything a product of our historic diversity.

We are proof that out of many we are one — and better for it! Out of many we are one — and we really do love it!

And yet, we still seem to find so many excuses for not doing the right thing. Again, remember President Bush's words, "A great nation does not hide its history. It faces its flaws and corrects them."

We forget, we deny how much we really depend on each other, how much we need each other. We justify our silence and inaction by manufacturing noble causes that marinate in historical denial. We still find a way to say "wait, not so fast."

But like Dr. Martin Luther King Jr. said, "wait 45 has almost always meant never."

We can't wait any longer. We need to change. And we need to change now. No more waiting. This is not just about statues, this is about our attitudes and behavior as well. If we take these statues down and don't change to become a more open and inclusive society this would have all been in vain.

While some have driven by these monuments every day and either revered their beauty or failed to see them at all, many of our neighbors and fellow Americans see them very clearly.

Many are painfully aware of the long shadows their presence casts, not only literally but figuratively. And they clearly receive the message that the Confederacy and the cult of the lost cause intended to deliver.

Earlier this week, as the cult of the lost cause statue of P.G.T Beauregard came down, world renowned musician Terence Blanchard stood watch, his wife Robin and their two beautiful daughters at their side.

Terence went to a high school on the edge of City Park named after one of America's greatest heroes and patriots, John F. Kennedy. But to get there he had to pass by this monument to a man who fought to deny him his humanity.

He said, "I've never looked at them as a 50 source of pride . . . it's always made me feel as if they were put there by people who don't respect us. This is something I never thought I'd see in my lifetime. It's a sign that the world is changing."

Yes, Terence, it is, and it is long overdue.

Now is the time to send a new message to the next generation of New Orleanians who can follow in Terence and Robin's remarkable footsteps.

A message about the future, about the next 300 years and beyond; let us not miss this opportunity New Orleans and let us help the rest of the country do the same. Because now is the time for

Justin Sullivan/Getty Images

In this photograph, a man wearing body armor and a mask over his face prepares to take down the monument to Confederate President Jefferson Davis in New Orleans, Louisiana. **What does this image suggest about the emotions surrounding the removal of such monuments? How does Landrieu address them in his speech?**

choosing. Now is the time to actually make this the City we always should have been, had we gotten it right in the first place.

We should stop for a moment and ask ourselves — at this point in our history, after Katrina, after Rita, after Ike, after Gustav, after the national recession, after the BP oil catastrophe and after the tornado — if presented with the opportunity to build monuments that told our story or to curate these particular spaces...would these monuments be what we want the world to see? Is this really our story?

We have not erased history; we are becoming 55 part of the city's history by righting the wrong image these monuments represent and crafting a better, more complete future for all our children and for future generations.

And unlike when these Confederate monuments were first erected as symbols of white supremacy, we now have a chance to create not only new symbols, but to do it together, as one people.

In our blessed land we all come to the table of democracy as equals.

We have to reaffirm our commitment to a future where each citizen is guaranteed the uniquely American gifts of life, liberty and the pursuit of happiness.

That is what really makes America great and today it is more important than ever to hold fast to these values and together say a self-evident truth that out of many we are one. That is why today we reclaim these spaces for the United States of America.

Because we are one nation, not two; indi- 60 visible with liberty and justice for all, not some. We all are part of one nation, all pledging allegiance to one flag, the flag of the United States of America. And New Orleanians are in, all of the way.

It is in this union and in this truth that real patriotism is rooted and flourishes.

Instead of revering a 4-year brief historical aberration that was called the Confederacy we can celebrate all 300 years of our rich, diverse history as a place named New Orleans and set the tone for the next 300 years.

After decades of public debate, of anger, of anxiety, of anticipation, of humiliation and of frustration. After public hearings and approvals from three separate community led commissions. After two robust public hearings and a 6-1 vote by the duly elected New Orleans City Council. After review by 13 different federal and state judges. The full weight of the legislative, executive, and judicial branches of government

Alex Wong/Getty Images

In this photograph, a man from Virginia Beach counter-protests an activist rally calling for the removal of a local Confederate soldier statue.
How does Landrieu address the argument that symbols of the Confederacy are simply aspects of southerners' heritage in his speech?

seeing connections

Standing at seventy-six feet tall, this statue of Christopher Columbus is the focal point of Columbus Circle in New York City. Its presence is the subject of a longstanding, and ongoing, political debate about monuments to controversial historical figures. Those who believe statues celebrating Columbus should be removed cite his treatment of Native Americans, which included land theft, enslavement, and genocide.

What is your view about the place of Christopher Columbus in American history? Do you think this statue should be removed? Explain why or why not.

Spencer Platt/Getty Images

has been brought to bear and the monuments in accordance with the law have been removed.

So now is the time to come together and heal and focus on our larger task. Not only building new symbols, but making this city a beautiful manifestation of what is possible and what we as a people can become.

Let us remember the once exiled, imprisoned 65 and now universally loved Nelson Mandela and what he said after the fall of apartheid. "If the pain has often been unbearable and the revelations shocking to all of us, it is because they indeed bring us the beginnings of a common understanding of what happened and a steady restoration of the nation's humanity."

So before we part let us again state the truth clearly.

The Confederacy was on the wrong side of history and humanity. It sought to tear apart our nation and subjugate our fellow Americans to slavery. This is the history we should never forget and one that we should never again put on a pedestal to be revered.

As a community, we must recognize the significance of removing New Orleans' Confederate monuments. It is our acknowledgment that now is the time to take stock of, and then move past, a painful part of our history. Anything less would render generations of courageous struggle and soul-searching a truly lost cause.

Anything less would fall short of the immortal words of our greatest President Abraham Lincoln, who with an open heart and clarity of purpose calls on us today to unite as one people when he said:

"With malice toward none, with charity for 70 all, with firmness in the right as God gives us to see the right, let us strive on to finish the work we are in, to bind up the nation's wounds, to do all which may achieve and cherish: a just and lasting peace among ourselves and with all nations."

Thank you.

[2017]

EXPLORING THE TEXT

1. In an article for the *New York Times*, columnist Frank Bruni praised Landrieu's speech for its "elevated, hopeful rhetoric" and lauded him for "putting poetry back into public life." Focusing on one section of the speech — at least three or four paragraphs — explain why you agree or disagree with Bruni's characterization of the speech.

2. What is the rhetorical situation in which Landrieu delivered this speech? Pay particular attention to the relationship between his purpose and audience. In paragraph 19, Landrieu uses an analogy: "After the Civil War, these statues were a part of that terrorism as much as a burning cross on someone's lawn...." Does this rhetorical strategy strengthen his argument by dramatizing it, or is his argument weakened by his recollection of an extremely volatile issue?

3. After he quotes former President Barack Obama in paragraph 24, Landrieu follows with four very short statements, most of them sentence fragments. What is the effect of this rhetorical choice? What impact do you think he expects them to have on his audience at this point in the speech?

4. About halfway through the speech, Landrieu boldly asserts, "To literally put the Confederacy on a pedestal in our most prominent places of honor is an inaccurate recitation of our full past, it is an affront to our present, and it is a bad prescription for our future" (para. 35). To what extent does he provide specific evidence for each of these three points? Consider both what came before this statement and what follows it.

5. Landrieu invokes Martin Luther King Jr. and Nelson Mandela as well as former Presidents George W. Bush, Abraham Lincoln, and Barack Obama — all as authorities. How effective are his quotations from these figures as evidence? Consider them individually and collectively as you develop your position.

6. Throughout the speech, Landrieu echoes language from America's founding documents. What rhetorical purpose does this strategy serve? Identify at least four examples to support your response.

7. Where does Landrieu address counterargument(s), particularly those that say the monuments are part of American history and that taking them down is a wrong-headed attempt to erase that history? To what extent does he concede and refute perspectives different from his own in this speech?

8. In this speech, Landrieu mentions the word "truth" thirteen times. Examine several instances and consider the different nuances in how he uses the word. How does the repetition act as a rhetorical strategy — that is, what purpose does it serve in his argument?

9. Landrieu takes on different personae as he asks for healing in this speech: among these are the mayor of a city that has been embroiled in volatile conflict, a white politician in a city with a significant African American population, a proud long-time resident of New Orleans, a concerned citizen. Analyze each of the following passages in terms of the persona the mayor assumes and how he appeals for reconciliation and healing amid controversy:

   a. "So, let's start with the facts." (7 paragraphs)

   b. "As clear as it is for me today..." (4 paragraphs)

   c. "Centuries-old wounds..." (5 paragraphs)

   d. "While some have driven by these monuments..." (5 paragraphs)

   e. "Let us remember what the once exiled, imprisoned, and now universally loved..." (to the end of the speech)

10. How have other countries dealt with the issue of the history of injustice? Research one of the following locations and discuss whether you believe a similar strategy would be an acceptable solution to the controversy over Confederate monuments: Memorial to the Murdered Jews of Europe (Berlin, Germany), the Topography of Terror Museum (Berlin, Germany), the Soviet Statue Graveyard (Tallinn, Estonia).

A Presumption of Guilt

BRYAN STEVENSON

Bryan Stevenson (b. 1959) is an internationally acclaimed lawyer, writer, and activist. He is also founder and director of the Equal Justice Initiative, a non-profit organzation based in Montgomery, Alabama, that offers legal representation to those who may have been wrongly accused and which guarantees the defense of anyone in Alabama on death row. Stevenson is the author of *Just Mercy* (2015), a *New York Times* bestseller and winner of the 2015 Carnegie Medal for Best Non-Fiction, the Dayton Literary Peace Prize, and the NAACP Image Award for Best Non-Fiction. His numerous other awards include the ACLU National Medal of Liberty in 1991 and a MacArthur Fellowship in 1995. Stevenson has served as a visiting professor of law at the University of Michigan School of Law and holds honorary degrees from Harvard, Yale, Princeton, the University of Pennsylvania, and Georgetown University School of Law. He published the following article in the *New York Review of Books* in 2017.

Late one night several years ago, I got out of my car on a dark midtown Atlanta street when a man standing fifteen feet away pointed a gun at me and threatened to "blow my head off." I'd been parked outside my new apartment in a racially mixed but mostly white neighborhood that I didn't consider a high-crime area. As the man repeated the threat, I suppressed my first instinct to run and fearfully raised my hands in helpless submission. I begged the man not to shoot me, repeating over and over again, "It's all right, it's okay."

The man was a uniformed police officer. As a criminal defense attorney, I knew that my survival required careful, strategic thinking. I had to stay calm. I'd just returned home from my law office in a car filled with legal papers, but I knew the officer holding the gun had not stopped me because he thought I was a young professional. Since I was a young, bearded black man dressed casually in jeans, most people would not assume I was a lawyer with a Harvard Law School degree. To the officer threatening to shoot me I looked like someone dangerous and guilty.

I had been sitting in my beat-up Honda Civic for over a quarter of an hour listening to music that could not be heard outside the vehicle. There was a Sly and the Family Stone retrospective playing on a local radio station that had so engaged me I couldn't turn the radio off. It had been a long day at work. A neighbor must have been alarmed by the sight of a black man sitting in his car and called the police. My getting out of my car to explain to the police officer that this was my home and nothing criminal was taking place prompted him to pull his weapon.

Having drawn his weapon, the officer and his partner justified their threat of lethal force by dramatizing their fears and suspicions about me. They threw me on the back of my car, searched it illegally, and kept me on the street for fifteen humiliating minutes while neighbors gathered to view the dangerous criminal in their midst. When no crime was discovered and nothing incriminating turned up in a computerized background check on me, I was told by the two officers to consider myself lucky. While this was said as a taunt, they were right: I was lucky.

People of color in the United States, particularly young black men, are often assumed to be guilty and dangerous. In too many situations, black men are considered offenders incapable of being victims themselves. As a consequence of this country's failure to address effectively its legacy of racial inequality, this presumption of guilt and the history that created it have significantly shaped every institution in American society, especially our criminal justice system.

◆ ◆ ◆

At the Civil War's end, black autonomy expanded but white supremacy remained deeply rooted. States began to look to the criminal justice system to construct policies and strategies to maintain the subordination of African-Americans. Convict leasing, the practice of "selling" the labor of state and local prisoners to private interests for state profit, used the criminal justice system to take away their political rights. State legislatures passed the Black Codes, which created new criminal offenses such as "vagrancy" and "loitering" and led to the mass arrest of black people. Then, relying on language in the Thirteenth Amendment that prohibits slavery and involuntary servitude "except as punishment for crime," lawmakers authorized white-controlled governments to exploit the labor of African-Americans in private lease contracts or on state-owned farms.[1] The legal scholar Jennifer Rae Taylor has observed:

> While a black prisoner was a rarity during the slavery era (when slave masters were individually empowered to administer "discipline" to their human property), the solution to the free black population had become criminalization. In turn, the most common fate facing black convicts was to be sold into forced labor for the profit of the state.

Beginning as early as 1866 in states like Texas, Mississippi, and Georgia, convict leasing spread throughout the South and continued through the late nineteenth and early twentieth centuries. Leased black convicts faced deplorable, unsafe working conditions and brutal violence when they attempted to resist or escape bondage. An 1887 report by the Hinds County, Mississippi, grand jury recorded that six months after 204 convicts were leased to a man named McDonald, twenty were dead, nineteen had escaped, and twenty-three had been returned to the penitentiary disabled, ill, and near death. The penitentiary hospital was filled with sick and dying black men whose bodies bore "marks of the most inhuman and brutal treatment...so poor and emaciated that their bones almost come through the skin."[2]

The explicit use of race to codify different kinds of offenses and punishments was challenged as unconstitutional, and criminal statutes were modified to avoid direct racial references, but the enforcement of the law didn't change. Black people were routinely charged with a wide range of "offenses," some of which whites were never charged with. African-Americans endured these challenges and humiliations and continued to rise up from slavery by seeking education and working hard under difficult conditions, but their refusal to act like slaves seemed only to provoke and agitate their white neighbors. This tension led to an era of lynching and violence that traumatized black people for decades.

◆ ◆ ◆

Between the Civil War and World War II, thousands of African-Americans were lynched in the United States. Lynchings were brutal public murders that were tolerated by state and federal officials. These racially motivated acts, meant to bypass legal institutions in order to intimidate entire populations, became a form of terrorism. Lynching had a profound effect on race relations in the United States and defined the geographic, political, social, and economic conditions of African-Americans in ways that are still evident today.

Of the hundreds of black people lynched after being accused of rape and murder, very few were legally convicted of a crime, and many were demonstrably innocent. In 1918, for example, after a white woman was raped in Lewiston, North Carolina, a black suspect named Peter Bazemore was lynched by a mob before an investigation revealed that the real perpetrator had been a white man wearing blackface makeup.[3] Hundreds more black people were

Shown here is one of a sequence of 60 paintings by Jacob Lawrence (1917–2000) known as *The Migration Series*. Painted in the 1940s, these works chronicle the mass migration of African Americans from the rural south to the urban north primarily between the world wars. Lawrence's caption for this piece reads, "Among the social conditions that existed which was partly the cause of the migration was the injustice done to the Negroes in the courts." **How does this image characterize the court of law? How does it relate to Stevenson's main argument?**

© The Museum of Modern Art/Licensed by SCALA/Art Resource, NY. © 2018 The Jacob and Gwendolyn Knight Lawrence Foundation, Seattle/Artists Rights Society (ARS), New York

with less respect or formality than observers believed due.[4]

Many African-Americans were lynched not because they had been accused of committing a crime or social infraction, but simply because they were black and present when the preferred party could not be located. In 1901, Ballie Crutchfield's brother allegedly found a lost wallet containing $120 and kept the money. He was arrested and about to be lynched by a mob in Smith County, Tennessee, when, at the last moment, he was able to break free and escape. Thwarted in their attempt to kill him, the mob turned their attention to his sister and lynched her instead, though she was not even alleged to have been involved in the theft.

New research continues to reveal the extent of lynching in America. The extraordinary documentation compiled by Professor Monroe Work (1866–1945) at Tuskegee University has been an invaluable historical resource for scholars, as has the joint work of sociologists Stewart Tolnay and E.M. Beck. These two sources are widely viewed as the most comprehensive collections of data on the subject in America. They have uncovered over three thousand instances of lynching between the end of Reconstruction in 1877 and 1950 in the twelve states that had the most lynchings: Alabama, Arkansas, Florida, Georgia, Kentucky, Louisiana, Mississippi, North Carolina, South Carolina, Tennessee, Texas, and Virginia.

◆ ◆ ◆

Recently, the Equal Justice Initiative (EJI) in Montgomery, Alabama — of which I am the founder and executive director — spent five years and hundreds of hours reviewing this research and other documentation, including local newspapers, historical archives, court records, interviews, and reports in African-American newspapers. Our research documented more than four thousand racial terror lynchings between 1877 and 1950 in those twelve states, eight hundred more than had been previously

lynched based on accusations of far less serious crimes, like arson, robbery, nonsexual assault, and vagrancy, many of which would not have been punishable by death even if the defendants had been convicted in a court of law. In addition, African-Americans were frequently lynched for not conforming to social customs or racial expectations, such as speaking to white people reported. We distinguished "racial terror lynchings" from hangings or mob violence that followed some sort of criminal trial or were committed against nonminorities. However heinous, this second category of killings was a crude form of punishment. By contrast, racial terror lynchings were directed specifically at black people, with little bearing on an actual crime; the aim was to maintain white supremacy and political and economic racial subordination.

We also distinguished terror lynchings from other racial violence and hate crimes that were prosecuted as criminal acts, although prosecution for hate crimes committed against black people was rare before World War II. The lynchings we documented were acts of terrorism because they were murders carried out with impunity — sometimes in broad daylight, as Sherrilyn Ifill explains in her important book on the subject, *On the Courthouse Lawn* (2007) — whose perpetrators were never held accountable. These killings were not examples of "frontier justice," because they generally took place in communities where there was a functioning criminal justice system that was deemed too good for African-Americans. Some "public spectacle lynchings" were even attended by the entire local white population and conducted as celebratory acts of racial control and domination.

Records show that racial terror lynchings from Reconstruction until World War II had six particularly common motivations: (1) a wildly distorted fear of interracial sex; (2) as a response to casual social transgressions; (3) after allegations of serious violent crime; (4) as public spectacle, which could be precipitated by any of the allegations named above; (5) as terroristic violence against the African-American population as a whole; and (6) as retribution for sharecroppers, ministers, and other community leaders who resisted mistreatment — the last becoming common between 1915 and 1945.

Our research confirmed that many victims of terror lynchings were murdered without being accused of any crime; they were killed for minor social transgressions or for asserting basic rights. Our conversations with survivors of lynchings also confirmed how directly lynching and racial terror motivated the forced migration of millions of black Americans out of the South. Thousands of people fled north for fear that a social misstep in an encounter with a white person might provoke a mob to show up and take their lives. Parents and spouses suffered what they characterized as "near-lynchings" and sent their loved ones away in frantic, desperate acts of protection.

◆ ◆ ◆

The decline of lynching in America coincided with the increased use of capital punishment often following accelerated, unreliable legal processes in state courts. By the end of the 1930s, court-ordered executions outpaced lynchings in the former slave states for the first time. Two thirds of those executed that decade were black, and the trend continued: as African-Americans fell to just 22 percent of the southern population between 1910 and 1950, they constituted 75 percent of those executed.

Probably the most famous attempted "legal lynching" is the case of the "Scottsboro Boys," nine young African-Americans charged with raping two white women in Alabama in 1931. During the trial, white mobs outside the courtroom demanded the teens' executions. Represented by incompetent lawyers, the nine were convicted by all-white, all-male juries within two days, and all but the youngest were sentenced to death. When the NAACP and others launched a national movement to challenge the cursory proceedings, the legal scholar Stephen Bright has written, "the [white] people of Scottsboro did not understand the reaction. After all, they did not lynch the accused; they gave them a trial."[5] In reality, many defendants of the era learned that the prospect of being executed rather than lynched did little to introduce fairness into the outcome.

Though northern states had abolished public executions by 1850, some in the South maintained the practice until 1938. The spectacles were more often intended to deter mob lynchings than crimes. Following Will Mack's execution by public hanging in Brandon, Mississippi, in 1909, the *Brandon News* reasoned:

> Public hangings are wrong, but under the circumstances, the quiet acquiescence of the people to submit to a legal trial, and their good behavior throughout, left no alternative to the board of supervisors but to grant the almost universal demand for a public execution.

Even in southern states that had outlawed public hangings much earlier, mobs often successfully demanded them.

In Sumterville, Florida, in 1902, a black man named Henry Wilson was convicted of murder in a trial that lasted just two hours and forty minutes. To mollify the mob of armed whites that filled the courtroom, the judge promised a death sentence that would be carried out by public hanging — despite state law prohibiting public executions. Even so, when the execution was set for a later date, the enraged mob threatened, "We'll hang him before sundown, governor or no governor." In response, Florida officials moved up the date, authorized Wilson to be hanged before the jeering mob, and congratulated themselves on having "avoided" a lynching.

In the 1940s and 1950s, the NAACP's Legal Defense Fund (LDF) began what would become a multidecade litigation strategy to challenge the American death penalty — which was used most actively in the South — as racially biased and unconstitutional. It won in *Furman* v. *Georgia* in 1972, when the Supreme Court struck down Georgia's death penalty statute, holding that capital punishment still too closely resembled "self-help, vigilante justice, and lynch law" and "if any basis can be discerned for the selection of these few to be sentenced to die, it is the constitutionally impermissible basis of race."

Southern opponents of the decision immediately decried it and set to writing new laws authorizing the death penalty. Following *Furman*, Mississippi Senator James O. Eastland accused the Court of "legislating" and "destroying our system of government," while Georgia's white supremacist lieutenant governor, Lester Maddox, called the decision "a license for anarchy, rape, and murder." In December 1972, Florida became the first state after *Furman* to enact a new death penalty statute, and within two years, thirty-five states had followed suit. Proponents of Georgia's new death penalty bill unapologetically borrowed the rhetoric of lynching, insisting, as Maddox put it:

> There should be more hangings. Put more nooses on the gallows. We've got to make it safe on the street again.... It wouldn't be too bad to hang some on the court house square, and let those who would plunder and destroy see.

State representative Guy Hill of Atlanta proposed a bill that would require death by hanging to take place "at or near the courthouse in the county in which the crime was committed." Georgia state representative James H. "Sloppy" Floyd remarked, "If people commit these crimes, they ought to burn." In 1976, in *Gregg* v. *Georgia*, the Supreme Court upheld Georgia's new statute and thus reinstated the American death penalty, capitulating to the claim that legal executions were needed to prevent vigilante mob violence.

◆ ◆ ◆

The new death penalty statutes continued to result in racial imbalance, and constitutional challenges persisted. In the 1987 case of *McCleskey* v. *Kemp*, the Supreme Court considered statistical evidence demonstrating that Georgia officials were more than four times as likely to impose a death sentence for the killing of a white person than a black person. Accepting the data as accurate, the Court conceded that racial disparities in sentencing "are an inevitable

20

25

This map shows the number of prisoners executed by each state between 1976 and 2017.
To what extent does this image support Stevenson's central argument?

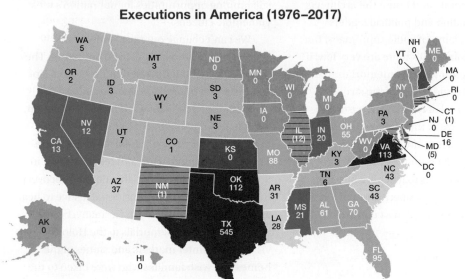

Executions in America (1976–2017)

Legend: 0 | 1-10 | 11-25 | 26-50 | 51-100 | 101+

■ States with no penalty/no executions ≡ States with no penalty but executions prior to implementing

Data from The Death Penalty Information Center.

part of our criminal justice system" and upheld Warren McCleskey's death sentence because he had failed to identify "a constitutionally significant risk of racial bias" in his case.

Today, large racial disparities continue in capital sentencing. African-Americans make up less than 13 percent of the national population, but nearly 42 percent of those currently on death row and 34 percent of those executed since 1976. In 96 percent of states where researchers have examined the relationship between race and the death penalty, results reveal a pattern of discrimination based on the race of the victim, the race of the defendant, or both. Meanwhile, in capital trials today the accused is often the only person of color in the courtroom and illegal racial discrimination in jury selection continues to be widespread. In Houston County, Alabama, prosecutors have excluded 80 percent of qualified African-Americans from serving as jurors in death penalty cases.

More than eight in ten American lynchings between 1889 and 1918 occurred in the South, and more than eight in ten of the more than 1,400 legal executions carried out in this country since 1976 have been in the South, where the legacy of the nation's embrace of slavery lingers. Today death sentences are disproportionately meted out to African-Americans accused of crimes against white victims; efforts to combat racial bias and create federal protection against it in death penalty cases remain thwarted by the familiar rhetoric of states' rights. Regional data demonstrate that the modern American death penalty has its origins in racial terror and is, in the words of Bright, the legal scholar, "a direct descendant of lynching."

In the face of this national ignominy, there is still an astonishing failure to acknowledge, discuss, or address the history of lynching. Many of the communities where lynchings took place have gone to great lengths to erect markers and memorials to the Civil War, to the Confederacy, and to events and incidents in which local power was violently reclaimed by white people. These communities celebrate and honor the architects of racial subordination and political leaders known for their defense of white supremacy. But in these same communities there are very few, if any, significant monuments or memorials that address the history and legacy of the struggle for racial equality and of lynching in particular. Many people who live in these places today have no awareness that race relations in their histories included terror and lynching. As Ifill has argued, the absence of memorials to lynching has deepened the injury to African-Americans and left the rest of the nation ignorant of this central part of our history.

◆ ◆ ◆

The Civil Rights Act of 1964, arguably the signal legal achievement of the civil rights movement, contained provisions designed to eliminate discrimination in voting, education, and employment, but did not address racial bias in criminal justice. Though it was the most insidious engine of the subordination of black people throughout the era of racial terror and its aftermath, the criminal justice system remains the institution in American life least affected by the civil rights movement. Mass incarceration in America today stands as a continuation of past abuses, still limiting opportunities for our nation's most vulnerable citizens.

We can't change our past, but we can acknowledge it and better shape our future. The United States is not the only country with a violent history of oppression. Many nations have been burdened by legacies of racial domination, foreign occupation, or tribal conflict resulting in pervasive human rights abuses or genocide. The commitment to truth and reconciliation in South Africa was critical to that nation's recovery. Rwanda has embraced transitional justice to heal and move forward. Today in Germany, besides a number of large memorials to the Holocaust, visitors encounter markers and stones at the homes of Jewish families who were taken to the concentration camps. But in America, we barely acknowledge the history and legacy of slavery, we have done nothing to recognize the era of lynching, and only in the last few years have a few monuments to the Confederacy been removed in the South.

The crucial question concerning capital punishment is not whether people deserve to die for the crimes they commit but rather whether we

30

Bettmann/Getty Images

In this 1934 photograph, students from Howard University in Washington, D.C., stand outside the Daughters of the American Revolution Museum wearing nooses around their necks as part of a protest against the National Crime Conference's decision not to include lynching in its program.
What might Bryan Stevenson consider the reason it was not addressed at this conference? Do you think Stevenson considers the subject of lynching to have been effectively addressed since then? Explain.

deserve to kill. Given the racial disparities that still exist in this country, we should eliminate the death penalty and expressly identify our history of lynching as a basis for its abolition. Confronting implicit bias in police departments should be seen as essential in twenty-first-century policing.

What threatened to kill me on the streets of Atlanta when I was a young attorney wasn't just a misguided police officer with a gun, it was the force of America's history of racial injustice and the presumption of guilt it created. In America, no child should be born with a presumption of guilt, burdened with expectations of failure and dangerousness because of the color of her or his skin or a parent's poverty. Black people in this nation should be afforded the same protection, safety, and opportunity to thrive as anyone else. But that won't happen until we look squarely at our history and commit to engaging the past that continues to haunt us.

Notes

1. "The Mississippi Black Codes were copied, sometimes word for word, by legislators in South Carolina, Georgia, Florida, Alabama, Louisiana and Texas," writes the historian David M. Oshinsky in *Worse Than Slavery: Parchman Farm and the Ordeal of Jim Crow Justice* (Simon and Schuster, 1996), p. 21.
2. See "Prison Abuses in Mississippi: Under the Lease System Convicts Are Treated with Brutal Cruelty," *Chicago Daily Tribune,* July 11, 1887.
3. See "Southern Farmers Lynch Peter Bazemore," *Chicago Defender,* March 30, 1918, and "Short Shrift for Negro," *Cincinnati Enquirer,* March 26, 1918.
4. Stewart E. Tolnay and E. M. Beck, *A Festival of Violence: An Analysis of Souther Lynchings, 1882–1930* (University of Illinois Press, 1995), p. 47.
5. Stephen B. Bright, "Discrimination, Death and Denial: The Tolerance of Racial Discrimination in Infliction of the Death Penalty," *Santa Clara Law Review,* Vol. 35, No. 2 (1995).

[2017]

EXPLORING THE TEXT

1. Bryan Stevenson, a criminal justice lawyer, begins this essay with an anecdote. What are some of the reasons a writer might use an anecdote, in general? What are the most powerful elements of Stevenson's anecdote? How does this anecdote contribute to Stevenson's overall argument?

2. What is the purpose of the third paragraph? How does Stevenson's syntax help achieve that purpose?

3. Stevenson uses variations of the word "threat" several times in the first four paragraphs and once more in the final paragraph. What is the purpose of this word choice and the cumulative effect of its repetition?

4. In paragraph 5, Stevenson takes the firm position that "as a consequence of this country's failure to address effectively its legacy of racial inequality, this presumption of guilt and the history that created it have significantly shaped every institution in American society, especially our criminal justice system." How does Stevenson develop this argument in the rest of the essay? Consider his use of organization, detail, and ethos.

5. According to Stevenson, what is the relationship between lynching and today's criminal justice system? What rhetorical strategies does Stevenson employ to convey his position on this relationship?

6. About halfway through the essay, Stevenson introduces the term "racial terror lynchings" (para. 13). What method(s) does Stevenson use to define the term? Consider the placement of this section of the essay. How does the discussion of "racial terror lynchings" fit within the rest of the essay?

7. What kind of evidence does Stevenson use in paragraphs 17, 25, and 26? How does he use this evidence to build his argument? What kinds of evidence does Stevenson use in paragraphs 18 through 24? Analyze Stevenson's use of this evidence, especially with regard to organization.

8. What does Stevenson mean when he alludes to the "familiar rhetoric of states' rights" as an obstacle to "combat[ing] racial bias and creat[ing] federal protection against [racial bias] in death penalty cases" (para. 27)? What does this allusion

suggest about his audience? What does it suggest about his attitude toward that "familiar rhetoric"?

9. What points does Stevenson make about Civil War memorials and markers? How do these points relate to his argument?

10. In paragraph 28, Stevenson claims that "many people who live in [the American south] today have no awareness that race relations in their histories included terror and lynching." Defend, challenge, or qualify Stevenson's assertion, using examples drawn from current events, your studies, or personal observations to support your position.

11. We can consider paragraph 29 to be the start of Stevenson's conclusion. What is the purpose of each of the four paragraphs in this section? How do they function as part of the larger conclusion? What rhetorical strategies does Stevenson employ to achieve these purposes and end his essay?

12. How does Stevenson use sources in his essay? Consider the type of sources, their placement, and their relationship to other kinds of evidence he uses. Looking at the list of sources, what aspects stand out to you as important when determining their reliability and validity?

Why Corrupt Bankers Avoid Jail

PATRICK RADDEN KEEFE

Patrick Radden Keefe (b. 1976) is an American writer and investigative journalist whose work has appeared in the *New Yorker*, *Slate*, and the *New York Times Magazine*. He is the author of two books: *Chatter* (2005), which examines global eavesdropping by American security agencies in the wake of the September 11th attacks, and *The Snakehead* (2009), about the Chinatown underworld in New York City. In addition to writing, Keefe is a senior fellow at The Century Foundation, a nonprofit think tank whose mission is to bolster American prosperity and security by promoting effective government, open democracy, and free markets. Keefe wrote the following article for the *New Yorker* in 2017.

In the summer of 2012, a subcommittee of the U.S. Senate released a report so brimming with international intrigue that it read like an airport paperback. Senate investigators had spent a year looking into the London-based banking group HSBC, and discovered that it was awash in skulduggery. According to the three-hundred-and-thirty-four-page report, the bank had laundered billions of dollars for Mexican drug cartels, and violated sanctions by covertly doing business with pariah states. HSBC had helped a Saudi bank with links to Al Qaeda transfer money into the United States. Mexico's Sinaloa cartel, which is responsible for tens of thousands of murders, deposited so much drug money in the bank that the cartel designed special cash boxes to fit HSBC's teller windows. On a law-enforcement

wiretap, one drug lord extolled the bank as *"the place to launder money."*

With four thousand offices in seventy countries and some forty million customers, HSBC is a sprawling organization. But, in the judgment of the Senate investigators, all this wrongdoing was too systemic to be a matter of mere negligence. Senator Carl Levin, who headed the investigation, declared, "This is something that people knew was going on at that bank." Half a dozen HSBC executives were summoned to Capitol Hill for a ritual display of chastisement. Stuart Gulliver, the bank's C.E.O., said that he was "profoundly sorry." Another executive, who had been in charge of compliance, announced during his testimony that he would resign. Few observers would have described the banking sector as a hotbed of ethical compunction, but even by the jaundiced standards of the industry HSBC's transgressions were extreme. Lanny Breuer, a senior official at the Department of Justice, promised that HSBC would be "held accountable."

What Breuer delivered, however, was the sort of velvet accountability to which large banks have grown accustomed: no criminal charges were filed, and no executives or employees were prosecuted for trafficking in dirty money. Instead, HSBC pledged to clean up its institutional culture, and to pay a fine of nearly two billion dollars: a penalty that sounded hefty but was only the equivalent of four weeks' profit for the bank. The U.S. criminal-justice system might be famously unyielding in its prosecution of retail drug crimes and terrorism, but a bank that facilitated such activity could get away with a rap on the knuckles. A headline in the *Guardian* tartly distilled the absurdity: "HSBC 'Sorry' for Aiding Mexican Drug Lords, Rogue States and Terrorists."

In the years since the mortgage crisis of 2008, it has become common to observe that certain financial institutions and other large corporations may be "too big to jail." The Financial Crisis Inquiry Commission, which investigated the causes of the meltdown, concluded that the mortgage-lending industry was rife with "predatory and fraudulent practices." In 2011, Ray Brescia, a professor at Albany Law School who had studied foreclosure procedures, told Reuters, "I think it's difficult to find a fraud of this size . . . in U.S. history." Yet federal prosecutors filed no criminal indictments against major banks or senior bankers related to the mortgage crisis. Even when the authorities uncovered less esoteric, easier-to-prosecute crimes — such as those committed by HSBC — they routinely declined to press charges.

This regime, in which corporate executives have essentially been granted immunity, is relatively new. After the savings-and-loan crisis of the nineteen-eighties, prosecutors convicted

In a riff on the use of the phrase "too big to fail," the theory that the failure of huge financial institutions would be disastrous for the global economy, Keefe mentions that after the financial crisis of 2008, "it has become common to observe that certain financial institutions and other large corporations may be 'too big to jail'" (para. 4).

What is this Occupy Wall Street protester's take on "too big to fail"? To what extent does it align with Keefe's?

Kyodo News/Getty Images

nearly nine hundred people, and the chief executives of several banks went to jail. When Rudy Giuliani was the top federal prosecutor in the Southern District of New York, he liked to march financiers off the trading floor in handcuffs. If the rules applied to mobsters like Fat Tony Salerno, Giuliani once observed, they should apply "to big shots at Goldman Sachs, too." As recently as 2006, when Enron imploded, such titans as Jeffrey Skilling and Kenneth Lay were convicted of conspiracy and fraud.

Something has changed in the past decade, however, and federal prosecutions of white-collar crime are now at a twenty-year low. As Jesse Eisinger, a reporter for ProPublica, explains in a new book, "The Chickenshit Club: Why the Justice Department Fails to Prosecute Executives" (Simon & Schuster), a financial crisis has traditionally been followed by a legal crackdown, because a market contraction reveals all the wishful accounting and outright fraud that were hidden when the going was good. In Warren Buffett's memorable formulation, "You only find out who is swimming naked when the tide goes out." After the mortgage crisis, people in Washington and on Wall Street expected prosecutions. Eisinger reels off a list of potential candidates for criminal charges: Countrywide, Washington Mutual, Lehman Brothers, Citigroup, A.I.G., Bank of America, Merrill Lynch, Morgan Stanley. Although fines were paid, and the Financial Crisis Inquiry Commission referred dozens of cases to prosecutors, there were no indictments, no trials, no jail time. As Eisinger writes, "Passing on one investigation is understandable; passing on every single one starts to speak to something else."

One morning in February, 1975, a fifty-three-year-old businessman named Eli Black took the elevator to the forty-fourth floor of the Pan Am Building, in Manhattan. When he was alone in his corner office, Black slammed his attaché case into one of the big windows overlooking the city until the glass broke. Then he jumped out. Black was the chairman of United Brands, a multibillion-dollar conglomerate. After his death, friends speculated that he had been working too hard, but an alert investigator at the Securities and Exchange Commission, Stanley Sporkin, grew suspicious, noting that people don't just "drop out of windows for no reason." Black, it emerged, had become embroiled in a bribery

scheme. United Brands owned Chiquita, and in exchange for a reduction of the export tax on bananas Black had authorized a two-and-a-half-million-dollar bribe to the President of Honduras.

"White-collar crime," in the definition of the sociologist who coined the term in the nineteen-thirties, is "committed by a person of respectability and high social status in the course of his occupation." Eli Black fit the criteria. But he was dead. Sporkin, determined to secure justice, enlisted a young federal prosecutor in New York, Jed Rakoff, who devised a clever work-around: charge the whole company. Under U.S. law, it was technically possible to hold a company responsible for the actions of a single employee.

With their inventive legal minds and their tenacious pursuit of malefactors, Sporkin and Rakoff are two of the heroes in Eisinger's deeply reported account. United Brands ended up pleading guilty to conspiracy and wire fraud, and though it got off with a token fine of fifteen thousand dollars, Congress later cited the case when it passed the Foreign Corrupt Practices Act, in 1977. Before the United Brands scandal, prosecutors tended to go after white-collar crimes by indicting the executives who committed them; now they charged the firms themselves. But the notion of prosecuting a corporation raises a number of tricky questions. A company, as an eighteenth-century British jurist once remarked, has "no soul to be damned, and no body to be kicked." Corporations can own property, sue people and be sued, even assert First Amendment rights. But you can't put a corporation in jail. So you impose a fine. The trouble is that the employees responsible don't pay the fine: if the company is publicly traded, the shareholders do. These individuals may have benefitted from the felonious conduct if it inflated the value of their stock, but they are innocent of any crime.

The very conception of the modern corporation is that it limits individual liability. Yet, in the decades after the United Brands case,

10

prosecutors often pursued both errant executives and the companies they worked for. When the investment firm Drexel Burnham Lambert was suspected of engaging in stock manipulation and insider trading, in the nineteen-eighties, prosecutors levelled charges not just against financiers at the firm, including Michael Milken, but also against the firm itself. (Drexel Burnham pleaded guilty, and eventually shut down.) After the immense fraud at Enron was exposed, federal authorities pursued its accounting company, Arthur Andersen, for helping to cook the books. Arthur Andersen executives, desperate to cover their tracks, deleted tens of thousands of e-mails and shredded documents by the ton. In 2002, Arthur Andersen was convicted of obstruction of justice, and lost its accounting license. The corporation, which had tens of thousands of employees, was effectively put out of business.

Eisinger describes the demise of Arthur Andersen as a turning point. Many lawyers, particularly in the well-financed realm of white-collar criminal defense, regarded the case as a flagrant instance of government overreach: the problem with convicting a company was that it could have "collateral consequences" that would be borne by employees, shareholders, and other innocent parties. "The Andersen case ushered in an era of prosecutorial timidity," Eisinger writes. "Andersen had to die so that all other big corporations might live."

With plenty of encouragement from high-end lobbyists, a new orthodoxy soon took hold that some corporations were so colossal — and so instrumental to the national economy — that even filing criminal charges against them would be reckless. In 2013, Eric Holder, then the Attorney General, acknowledged that decades of deregulation and mergers had left the U.S. economy heavily consolidated. It was therefore "difficult to prosecute" the major banks, because indictments could "have a negative impact on the national economy, perhaps even the world economy."

The 2013 film *The Wolf of Wall Street* was based on the true story of a white collar criminal with a larger-than-life personality.
What does this poster for the movie — featuring Leonardo DiCaprio in the main role — tell us about the American public's view of Wall Street and white collar crime?

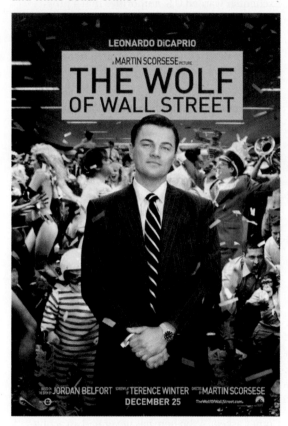

Prosecutors came to rely instead on a type of deal, known as a deferred-prosecution agreement, in which the company would acknowledge wrongdoing, pay a fine, and pledge to improve its corporate culture. From 2002 to 2016, the Department of Justice entered into more than four hundred of these arrangements. Having spent a trillion dollars to bail out the banks in 2008 and 2009, the federal government may have been loath to jeopardize the fortunes of those banks by prosecuting them just a few years later.

OTHER VOICES   1113

But fears of collateral consequences also inhibited the administration of justice in more run-of-the-mill instances of criminal money laundering. Some officials in the Department of Justice wanted to indict HSBC, according to e-mails unearthed by a subsequent congressional investigation. But Britain's Chancellor of the Exchequer warned U.S. authorities that a prosecution could lead to "very serious implications for financial and economic stability." HSBC was granted a deferred-prosecution agreement.

◆ ◆ ◆

Numerous explanations have been offered for the failure of the Obama Justice Department to hold the big banks accountable: corporate lobbying in Washington, appeals-court rulings that tightened the definitions of certain types of corporate crime, the redirecting of investigative resources after 9/11. But Eisinger homes in on a subtler factor: the professional psychology of élite federal prosecutors. "The Chickenshit Club" is about a specific vocational temperament. When James Comey took over as the U.S. Attorney for the Southern District of New York, in 2002, Eisinger tells us, he summoned his young prosecutors for a pep talk. For graduates of top law schools, a job as a federal prosecutor is a brass ring, and the Southern District of New York, which has jurisdiction over Wall Street, is the most selective office of them all. Addressing this ferociously competitive cohort, Comey asked, "Who here has never had an acquittal or a hung jury?" Several go-getters, proud of their unblemished records, raised their hands.

But Comey, with his trademark altar-boy probity,[1] had a surprise for them. "You are members of what we like to call the Chickenshit Club," he said.

Most people who go to law school are risk-averse types. With their unalloyed drive to excel, the élite young attorneys who ascend to the Southern District have a lifetime of good grades to show for it. Once they become prosecutors,

_____
[1] Decency and integrity. —Eds.

they are invested with extraordinary powers. In a world of limited public resources and unlimited wrongdoing, prosecutors make decisions every day about who should be charged and tried, who should be allowed to plead, and who should be let go. This is the front line of criminal justice, and decisions are made unilaterally, with no review by a judge. Even in the American system of checks and balances, there are few fetters on a prosecutor's discretion. A perfect record of convictions and guilty pleas might signal simply that you're a cracker jack attorney. But, as Comey implied, it could also mean that you're taking only those cases you're sure you'll win — the lawyerly equivalent of enrolling in a gut class for the easy A.

You might suppose that the glory of convicting a blue-chip C.E.O. would be irresistible. But taking such a case to trial entails serious risk. In contemporary corporations, the decision-making process is so diffuse that it can be difficult to establish criminal culpability beyond a reasonable doubt. In the United Brands case, Eli Black directly authorized the bribe, but these days the precise author of corporate wrongdoing is seldom so clear. Even after a provision in the Sarbanes-Oxley Act, of 2002, began requiring C.E.O.s and C.F.O.s to certify the accuracy of corporate financial reports, few executives were charged with violating the law, because the companies threw up a thicket of subcertifications to buffer accountability.

As Samuel Buell, who helped prosecute the Enron and Andersen cases and is now a law professor at Duke, points out in his recent book, "Capital Offenses: Business Crime and Punishment in America's Corporate Age," an executive's claim that he believed he was following the rules often poses "a severe, even disabling, obstacle to prosecution." That is doubly so in instances where the alleged crime is abstruse. Even the professionals who bought and sold the dodgy mortgage-backed instruments that led to the financial crisis often didn't understand exactly how they worked. How do you explicate such transactions — and prove criminal intent — to a jury?

Even with an airtight case, going to trial is always a gamble. Lose a white-collar criminal trial and you become a symbol of prosecutorial overreach. You might even set back the cause of corporate accountability. Plus, you'll have a ding on your record. Eisinger quotes one of Lanny Breuer's deputies in Washington telling a prosecutor, "If you lose this case, Lanny will have egg on his face." Such fears can deter the most ambitious and scrupulous of young attorneys.

The deferred-prosecution agreement, by contrast, is a sure thing. Companies will happily enter into such an agreement, and even pay an enormous fine, if it means avoiding prosecution. "That rewards laziness," David Ogden, a Deputy Attorney General in the Obama Administration, tells Eisinger. "The department gets publicity, stats, and big money. But the enormous settlements may or may not reflect that they could actually prove the case." When companies agree to pay fines for misconduct, the agreements they sign are often conspicuously stinting in details about what they did wrong. Many agreements acknowledge criminal conduct by the corporation but do not name a single executive or officer who was responsible. "The Justice Department argued that the large fines signaled just how tough it had been," Eisinger writes. "But since these settlements lacked transparency, the public didn't receive basic information about why the agreement had been reached, how the fine had been determined, what the scale of the wrongdoing was and which cases prosecutors never took up." These pas de deux[2] between prosecutors and corporate chieftains came to feel "stage-managed, rather than punitive."

◆ ◆ ◆

White-collar crime is not the only area in which prosecutors show reluctance to risk a trial. By the time Comey issued his Chickenshit Club admonition, a deeper shift in the administration

20

This painting, completed in 1945 by American artist Ben Shahn, is entitled *Portrait of an Industrialist a.k.a. A Corporate Portrait*.
Look carefully at the details of this image. What do they communicate about the artist's views of businessmen? What might Keefe think of this portrayal?

CHRISTIES IMAGES/Private Collection/Bridgeman Images/Art © Estate of Ben Shahn/Licensed by VAGA, New York, NY

of justice was already under way. Faced with the challenges of entrusting any criminal case to a jury, prosecutors were increasingly skipping trial altogether, negotiating a plea bargain instead. With the introduction of stiff sentencing guidelines, prosecutors routinely "up charged" crimes, requesting maximal prison sentences in the event of a conviction at trial.

Defendants can be risk-averse, too. Offered the choice between, say, pleading guilty and serving three to five years, or going to trial and serving ten if convicted, many opt for the former. But, as with corporate deferred-prosecution agreements, these arrangements grant prosecutors a victory without

---

[2] French for "step of two," often used to refer to a complicated relationship or activity between two parties. —Eds.

testing their evidence in court. Rachel Barkow, a law professor at N.Y.U., has pointed out that when you threaten defendants with Draconian sentences if they refuse to plead guilty "you penalize people who have the nerve to go to trial." Some scholars argue that such prosecutorial bullying may violate the Sixth Amendment right to a trial by jury. (In 2014, a federal judge in Colorado declared that, for most Americans, this constitutional right is now "a myth.")

The criminal trial is increasingly becoming a relic. More than ninety-five per cent of all criminal cases at both the state and the federal level are now resolved in plea bargains. A recent article in the *Times* described vacant courtrooms, out-of-work stenographers, and New York judges who can go a year or more without hearing a single criminal case. It may be no accident that the vanishing of the criminal trial has coincided with Eisinger's story of vanishing corporate accountability. Presenting a case to a jury is a skill, and prosecutors now have fewer opportunities to hone it. The less adept you are in the courtroom, the more intimidated you will be by the prospect of going to trial, making you more likely to opt for a plea agreement instead.

This phenomenon has broader societal consequences. As John Pfaff demonstrates in his recent book, "Locked In," one grave result of the tremendous leverage that prosecutors exert is the rise of mass incarceration. As judges and juries are written out of the criminal-justice equation, an awful paradox has emerged: the poor sign plea bargains and go to jail; the privileged sign deferred-prosecution agreements and avoid it.

This is a curious state of affairs, given that the notion of deferring criminal prosecution was originally introduced to benefit individuals, not corporations. During the nineteen-sixties, pilot programs in New York and Washington, D.C., demonstrated that when charges were suspended for ninety days, so that low-income defendants who had been arrested for nonviolent crimes could obtain counselling and job-placement services, offenders often turned their lives around

to a point where the charges were dropped. This approach was both humane and efficient, in that it diverted people from the costly prison system. Among those who completed the program, few were arrested again. In 1974, following the success of such initiatives, the deferred-prosecution agreement was incorporated into federal law.

It is a pernicious irony that a progressive legal instrument designed to help working-class defendants stay out of jail has been repurposed as a vehicle for facilitating corporate impunity. As the federal judge Emmet Sullivan noted in 2015, "Drug conspiracy defendants are no less deserving of a second chance than bribery conspiracy defendants." Yet these days the Department of Justice seldom offers this form of clemency to the kinds of individuals for whom the practice was conceived.

Perhaps, as Eric Holder has argued, there is simply more at stake when the defendant is a major bank. But what about the collateral consequences of showing less mercy when prosecuting low-income individuals? When you charge someone with a felony and send him to prison, the repercussions radiate outward, through his family and his community. Nearly three million American children have a parent in prison. According to the Rutgers criminologist Todd Clear, low-income neighborhoods in which a large proportion of the population cycles in and out of confinement experience greater familial dysfunction, warped labor markets, and a general lack of "mental and physical health." Entire communities bear the brunt of our zealous approach to less rarefied varieties of crime. Prosecutors and judges seldom regard those collateral costs as a rationale for leniency.

◆ ◆ ◆

One day in the nineteen-sixties, the economist Gary Becker was late for an appointment, and parked on the street illegally, rather than pay for a garage. Calculating the cost of a potential ticket against the likelihood that he would get one, Becker chose to take the risk. He didn't get a ticket, and from that experience he extrapolated the insight that "criminal behavior is rational": people who commit crimes often do so after weighing the relevant variables and deciding that the potential benefits outweigh the potential costs. Not everyone agrees with Becker's thesis, but it holds a certain allure, because if crime is rational, then it should, at least in theory, be deterrable.

The failure to prosecute white-collar executives might be more justifiable if there were any indication that fines and deferred-prosecution agreements deterred corporate wrongdoing. The evidence, however, is not promising. Pfizer has been hit with three successive deferred-prosecution agreements, for illegal marketing, bribing doctors, and other crimes. On each occasion, the company paid a substantial fine and pledged to change — then returned to the same type of behavior. You might think that the price for flouting a deferred-prosecution agreement would be prosecution. But after offering Pfizer a second chance, only to have misconduct continue, the government was apparently happy to offer a third.

Jed Rakoff, the prosecutor who indicted United Brands, became a judge, and he has

30

emerged as an outspoken critic of the prevailing approach to corporate crime. He has argued that companies may come to view even billion-dollar fines as a "cost of doing business." In an article in *The New York Review of Books*, titled "The Financial Crisis: Why Have No High Level Executives Been Prosecuted?," he highlights the farce of obliging a corporation to acknowledge criminal wrongdoing without identifying or prosecuting the managers who were responsible. Rakoff is dubious of obligatory promises from companies to change their corporate culture, and suspects that "sending a few guilty executives to prison for orchestrating corporate crimes might have a far greater effect."

In recent years, the Department of Justice, sensitive to criticism of its kid-glove approach to corporations, did actually indict a string of banks, including Credit Suisse, BNP Paribas, J. P. Morgan, and Barclays. The banks pleaded guilty and, despite all the alarmism about "collateral consequences," they all stayed in business, and there were no major shocks to the global economy.

In "Why They Do It: Inside the Mind of the White-Collar Criminal," the Harvard Business

Mike Twohy/The New Yorker Collection/The Cartoon Bank

◄

This cartoon by Mike Twohy was published in the *New Yorker* in 2008, shortly after the financial collapse that triggered the Great Recession. **What does this image suggest about the extent to which prison sentences for white collar criminals serves as a deterrent? Would Keefe agree with the argument this cartoon makes? Explain.**

School professor Eugene Soltes points out that, in the 2015–16 academic year, ten companies recruiting for new hires at Harvard had recently been convicted of a federal crime or entered into a deferred-prosecution agreement. By now, Soltes suggests, corporate deviance may have become so routine that even pleading guilty to a felony is no big deal. What had once been described as a badge of ignominy that could put a company out of business was now just a bit of unpleasantness: a passing hassle, like a parking ticket.

[2017]

EXPLORING THE TEXT

1. What is your first response to the information that Patrick Radden Keefe supplies regarding the HSBC bank (paras. 1–3)? Are you surprised to learn the nature of the crimes committed? Are you surprised that no one was prosecuted?

2. Keefe reports that the fine for HSBC's crimes was "two billion dollars: a penalty that sounded hefty but was only the equivalent of four weeks' profit for the bank" (para. 3). How closely does the punishment fit the crime? What deterrent value do you think such a penalty might have?

3. Connecticut Congressman Stewart McKinney is noted for having coined the phrase "too big to fail" in 1984, suggesting that corporations and financial institutions are so large and important that their failure could be disastrous for the national, and even the world, economy. What does Keefe's play on that phrase, "too big to jail" (para. 4), suggest about the nature of corporations in America?

4. To what does "this regime" (para. 5) refer? What connotations does that particular word carry?

5. Discussing the "list of potential candidates for criminal charges" (which includes several of the most important highly respected financial institutions in the world), Keefe quotes Jesse Eisinger: "Passing on one investigation is understandable; passing on every single one starts to speak to something else" (para. 6). What are the implications of Eisinger's statement? How does Keefe use it to develop his argument?

6. What role does the anecdote about businessman Eli Black play in Keefe's argument? How does it relate to his purpose and reinforce his overall message?

7. How, according to Keefe, is "white-collar crime" treated differently from other crime in America? What does this difference suggest about the nature of justice and equality in America?

8. What is Keefe's position on the culpability of bank employees? Refer specifically to the text to support your answer. Do you agree with Keefe's position? Explain why or why not.

9. Why does Keefe use the phrase "pas de deux" to describe agreements made between "prosecutors and corporate chieftains" (para. 21)? According to Keefe, how effective is the deferred-prosecution agreement as an instrument of justice?

10. According to Keefe, what is similar in the attitudes toward corporate prosecution held by both U.S. Attorney General Eric Holder and Britain's Chancellor of the Exchequer? What point does Keefe make with this comparison, and how does it serve his main argument?

11. How does the anecdote about then U.S. Attorney James Comey contribute to Keefe's argument?

12. How does Keefe characterize lawyers? How does Keefe use this characterization to explore the "subtler factor" (para. 15) suggested by Eisinger? Does it seem reasonable, as Keefe states that fear of losing a case "can deter the most ambitious and scrupulous of young attorneys" (para. 20)?

13. According to Keefe, what role does the increasing incidence of the "plea bargain" play in our justice system? How has it led to the paradox that he relates in paragraph 25?

14. What is the "pernicious irony" that Keefe discusses (para. 27)? How does the analogy he develops in the following paragraph emphasize that irony?

15. How do the quotations from judge and former prosecutor Jed Rakoff in paragraph 31 support Keefe's assessment of the judicial system?

16. How would you characterize the appeals Keefe makes to his audience in the final two paragraphs of his essay? How effectively do they conclude his argument?

17. Identify arguments of fact, value, and policy throughout Keefe's article. Which of the three is dominant? Explain.

Society Freed Through Justice

GEORGE BIDDLE

George Biddle (1885–1973) was born in Philadelphia and educated at Harvard. He studied art in Paris and in the United States and traveled widely, including touring Mexico with muralist Diego Rivera. At the start of World War I he enlisted in the army. During the Great Depression, Biddle encouraged his childhood friend, the newly elected president Franklin Delano Roosevelt, to create a relief program for artists as part of the New Deal. An arm of the Works Progress Administration (WPA), the Federal Art Project operated from 1935 through 1943, commissioning around 10,000 artists and artisans in the creation of many forms of art — including but not limited to posters, murals, sculpture, museum and theater design, and photography — and resulting in over 200,000 different works of public art. *Society Freed Through Justice* is a mural on the fifth floor of the Robert F. Kennedy Department of Justice Building. Built between 1935 and 1941, the building is decorated with sixty-eight murals by many well-known artists, depicting realistic and allegorical scenes of the role of justice in American society.

Carol M. Highsmith/Library of Congress Prints and Photographs Division[LC-DIG-highsm-02881]

[1936]

EXPLORING THE TEXT

1. Consider the rhetorical situation as described in the headnote. What do you think is the purpose of this mural? What decisions did George Biddle make to achieve that purpose? Consider the shapes and lines he used to create the people and animals as well as the mural's perspective. How is the eye drawn from the foreground to the background?

2. The mural is divided into three sections, each portraying a part of the house in the foreground. The peaked roof of the house is a focal point. What tone does that triangular structure set? Think about the feeling you get from the scene and try to describe the tone in two or three words.

3. What elements of American society has Biddle included in his mural? What seems to be missing? Why do you think Biddle made the choice not to include certain elements?

4. Does *Society Freed Through Justice* ultimately present a utopian view of America, or do you think it offers a critique of society? Explain your answer, using details from the mural to support your position.

5. This photograph of the mural hints at its majestic size (13 ft. 6 in. × 43 ft. 2 in.), which decorates fifth-floor stairway in the Department of Justice Building. What is the effect of art as decoration in a building? Why is a mural especially suited to public spaces?

6. Compare the right and left sides of the mural. What aspects of the American experience — and landscape — does each portray? How do the backgrounds in each differ? How do the two side panels complement and comment on the central panel?

7. "The Sweatshop and Tenement / of Yesterday Can Be the Life / Ordered with Justice for Tomorrow" is inscribed in the grass at the bottom of the mural. What do you think that statement means? How does that inscription relate to images it accompanies? Consider the year it was painted — 1936 — as you formulate your answer.

8. Biddle came from an established and affluent Philadelphia family. He studied art in Europe and the United States, traveled widely, and joined the army at the beginning of World War I. In the 1930s he became interested in social realism and combat art. What artistic influences can you see in his work? What social influences can you see?

Liberty Leading the People

EUGÈNE DELACROIX

and

Injustice Leading Greed and Opportunity

SANDOW BIRK

Eugène Delacroix (1798–1863) was a French artist. His first major work, *The Barque of Dante* (1822), was met by ridicule, yet it was purchased for display. This pattern of initial criticism followed by enthusiastic support would continue throughout his life. *Liberty Leading the People*, one of his most well-known works, commemorates the July Revolution of 1830, which toppled King Charles X of France. Personifying the concept of liberty, a woman leads the people forward over a barricade littered with the corpses of the fallen, holding the flag of the French Revolution in one hand and a bayonetted musket in the other. The woman is considered the image that inspired Marianne, the symbol of France and the French Republic.

Both allegorical and literal, she is a leader, striding across a pile of corpses. She wears a Phrygian cap — a soft hat with the top pulled forward — which was widely recognized at the time as a symbol of the pursuit of freedom. The other figures in the painting represent a mix of social classes: the man in the top hat represents the middle class; the boy in the two-cornered hat is a student; and the boy holding two pistols is a revolutionary.

Sandow Birk (b. 1962) was born in Detroit and grew up in southern California. He went to art school in Los Angeles and also studied in France, England, and New York. Birk's artwork frequently explores themes of violence, graffiti, and politics. Inspired by Delacroix's *Liberty Leading the People*, Birk's *Injustice Leading Greed and Opportunity* depicts a woman heading toward the viewer, holding the Los Angeles flag and a sign that reads, "NO JUSTICE NO PEACE." She, too, steps over corpses. She is accompanied by looters and a young man about to throw a Molotov cocktail. The Los Angeles skyline is visible in the background. Red and blue, the colors of the notorious rival Bloods and Crips gangs, predominate. The newspaper in the foreground shows the headline "Not Guilty," a reference to the four Los Angeles Police Department officers who were acquitted in the beating of a black man, Rodney King, in 1992. Riots broke out in Los Angeles and other cities across the country in response to the verdict.

Louvre-Lens, France/Bridgeman Images

[1830]

Courtesy of the artist and Catharine Clark Gallery, San Francisco, California.

[1992]

EXPLORING THE TEXTS

1. Spend some time looking at both paintings. What are the similarities? What are the differences? Look especially at the figures in the painting. What do they have in common?

2. Consider the titles of the two works. The title of the Eugène Delacroix piece seems to name the woman at the center "Liberty." Where do you think "Injustice" is portrayed in Sandow Birk's painting? Is it the central figure of the woman, or is it something or someone else? Explain your answer.

3. What other symbols can you find in the two paintings? What do you think each symbol represents?

4. Blue and red predominate in both paintings. Consider the colors beyond their connections to the French flag in Delacroix and the gang colors in Birk — for instance, blue traditionally denotes peace and harmony, while red often means danger or intensity. How do the artists use those colors both traditionally and unconventionally?

5. Do you think that Birk's painting honors or criticizes the painting by Delacroix? Explain your answer.

6. Although Delacroix's painting was initially lambasted by critics, it has become a work universally recognized as both a forerunner of eighteenth-century "history painting" and of revolutionary art such as Pablo Picasso's *Guernica*. Much of its power comes from a combination of what the Louvre's website calls "a blend of document and symbol, actuality and fiction, reality and allegory." Look for those qualities in both paintings. What do you find? Do you think Birk's painting will withstand the test of time? Explain why or why not.

CONVERSATION

The Limits of Free Speech

Each of the following texts presents a viewpoint on the limits of the right to free speech, a right guaranteed by the First Amendment to the United States Constitution. The First Amendment states, "Congress shall make no law respecting an establishment of religion, or prohibiting the free exercise thereof; or abridging the freedom of speech, or of the press; or the right of the people peaceably to assemble, and to petition the Government for a redress of grievances."

SOURCES

1 **Thane Rosenbaum** / *Should Neo-Nazis Be Allowed Free Speech?*
2 **Eugene Volokh** / *No, There's No "Hate Speech" Exception to the First Amendment*
3 **Sean Stevens and Nick Phillips** / *Free Speech Is the Most Effective Antidote to Hate Speech*
4 **Lata Nott** / *Free Speech Isn't Always Valuable. That's Not the Point.*
5 **Laura Beth Nielsen** / *The Case for Restricting Hate Speech*
6 **Signe Wilkinson** / *Free Speech* (cartoon)

After you have read, studied, and synthesized these pieces, enter the Conversation by responding to one of the prompts on page 1135.

---

1 Should Neo-Nazis Be Allowed Free Speech?

THANE ROSENBAUM

Thane Rosenbaum, an American writer and law professor at New York University, wrote the following op-ed for the *Daily Beast* in 2014.

ver the past several weeks, free speech has gotten costlier — at least in France and Israel.

In France, Dieudonne M'Bala M'Bala, an anti-Semitic stand-up comic infamous for popularizing the quenelle, an inverted Nazi salute, was banned from performing in two cities. M'Bala M'Bala has been repeatedly fined for hate speech, and this was not the first time his act was perceived as a threat to public order.

Meanwhile, Israel's parliament is soon to pass a bill outlawing the word Nazi for non-educational purposes. Indeed, any slur against another that invokes the Third Reich could land the speaker in jail for six months with a fine of $29,000. The Israelis are concerned about both the rise of anti-Semitism globally, and the trivialization of the Holocaust — even locally.

To Americans, these actions in France and Israel seem positively undemocratic. The First Amendment would never prohibit the quenelle, regardless of its symbolic meaning. And any lover of "Seinfeld" would regard banning the "Soup Nazi" episode as scandalously un-American.

After all, in 1977 a federal court upheld the right of neo-Nazis to goose-step right through the town of Skokie, Illinois, which had a disproportionately large number of Holocaust survivors as residents. And more recently, the Supreme Court upheld the right of a church group opposed to gays serving in the military to picket the funeral of a dead marine with signs that read, "God Hates Fags."

While what is happening in France and Israel ₅ is wholly foreign to Americans, perhaps it's time to consider whether these and other countries may be right. Perhaps America's fixation on free speech has gone too far.

Actually, the United States is an outlier among democracies in granting such generous free speech guarantees. Six European countries, along with Brazil, prohibit the use of Nazi symbols and flags. Many more countries have outlawed Holocaust denial. Indeed, even encouraging racial discrimination in France is a crime. In pluralistic nations like these with clashing cultures and historical tragedies not shared by all, mutual respect and civility helps keep the peace and avoids unnecessary mental trauma.

Yet, even in the United States, free speech is not unlimited. Certain proscribed categories have always existed — libel, slander and defamation, obscenity, "fighting words," and the "incitement of imminent lawlessness" — where the First Amendment does not protect the speaker, where the right to speak is curtailed for reasons of general welfare and public safety. There is no freedom to shout "fire" in a crowded theater. Hate crime statutes exist in many jurisdictions where bias-motivated crimes are given more severe penalties. In 2003, the Supreme Court held that speech intended to intimidate, such as cross burning, might not receive First Amendment protection.

Yet, the confusion is that in placing limits on speech we privilege physical over emotional harm. Indeed, we have an entire legal system, and an attitude toward speech, that takes its cue from a nursery rhyme: "Stick and stones can break my bones but names can never hurt me."

All of us know, however, and despite what we tell our children, names do, indeed, hurt. And recent studies in universities such as Purdue, UCLA, Michigan, Toronto, Arizona, Maryland, and Macquarie University in New South Wales, show, among other things, through brain scans and controlled studies with participants who were subjected to both physical and emotional pain, that emotional harm is equal in intensity to that experienced by the body, and is even more long-lasting and traumatic. Physical pain subsides; emotional pain, when recalled, is relived.

Pain has a shared circuitry in the human ₁₀ brain, and it makes no distinction between being hit in the face and losing face (or having a broken heart) as a result of bereavement, betrayal, social exclusion and grave insult. Emotional distress can, in fact, make the body sick. Indeed, research has shown that pain relief medication can work equally well for both physical and emotional injury.

We impose speed limits on driving and regulate food and drugs because we know that the costs of not doing so can lead to accidents and harm. Why should speech be exempt from public welfare concerns when its social costs can be even more injurious?

In the marketplace of ideas, there is a difference between trying to persuade and trying to injure. One can object to gays in the military without ruining the one moment a father has to bury his son; neo-Nazis can long for the Third Reich without re-traumatizing Hitler's victims; one can oppose Affirmative Action without burning a cross on an African-American's lawn.

Of course, everything is a matter of degree. Juries are faced with similar ambiguities when it comes to physical injury. No one knows for certain whether the plaintiff wearing a neck brace can't actually run the New York Marathon. We tolerate the fake slip and fall, but we feel absolutely helpless in evaluating whether words and gestures intended to harm actually do cause harm. Jurors are as capable of working through these uncertainties in the area of emotional harms as they are in the realm of physical injury.

Free speech should not stand in the way of common decency. No right should be so freely and recklessly exercised that it becomes an impediment to civil society, making it so that others are made to feel less free, their private space and peace invaded, their sensitivities cruelly trampled upon.

QUESTIONS

1. Why does Thane Rosenbaum open his essay with examples from France and Israel? In what ways are their free speech laws different from those of the United States?

2. What do you think Rosenbaum means when he says, "In pluralistic nations like these [six European countries and Brazil] with clashing cultures and historical tragedies not shared by all, mutual respect and civility helps keep the peace and avoids unnecessary mental trauma" (para. 6)? Do you think that description can apply to the United States?

3. How does Rosenbaum classify the categories of free speech that are limited? What does he think of these limitations? What support does he offer for his viewpoint?

4. In paragraph 12, Rosenbaum gives examples of the difference between "trying to persuade and trying to injure." Do you find his examples compelling? Explain your answer.

2 No, There's No "Hate Speech" Exception to the First Amendment

EUGENE VOLOKH

Eugene Volokh is the Gary T. Schwartz Distinguished Professor of Law at the University of California Los Angeles School of Law and an expert on the First Amendment. In 2015, he wrote "No, There's No 'Hate Speech' Exception to the First Amendment" for a regular column, entitled "The Volokh Conspiracy," in the *Washington Post*.

I keep hearing about a supposed "hate speech" exception to the First Amendment, or statements such as, "This isn't free speech, it's hate speech," or "When does free speech stop and hate speech begin?" But there is no hate speech exception to the First Amendment. Hateful ideas (whatever exactly that might mean) are just as protected under the First Amendment as other ideas. One is as free to condemn Islam — or Muslims, or Jews, or blacks, or whites, or illegal aliens, or native-born citizens — as one is to condemn capitalism or Socialism or Democrats or Republicans.

To be sure, there are some kinds of speech that are unprotected by the First Amendment. But those narrow exceptions have nothing to do with "hate speech" in any conventionally used sense of the term. For instance, there is an exception for "fighting words" — face-to-face personal insults addressed to a specific person, of the sort that are likely to start an immediate fight. But this exception isn't limited to racial or religious insults, nor does it cover all racially or religiously offensive statements. Indeed, when the City of St. Paul tried to specifically punish bigoted fighting words, the Supreme Court held that this selective prohibition was unconstitutional (*R.A.V. v. City of St. Paul* (1992)), even though a broad ban on all fighting words would indeed be permissible. (And, notwithstanding CNN anchor Chris Cuomo's Tweet that "hate speech is excluded from protection," and his later claims that by "hate speech" he means "fighting words," the fighting words exception is not generally labeled a "hate speech" exception, and isn't coextensive with any established definition of "hate speech" that I know of.)

The same is true of the other narrow exceptions, such as for true threats of illegal conduct or incitement intended to and likely to produce imminent illegal conduct (i.e., illegal conduct in the next few hours or maybe days, as opposed to some illegal conduct some time in the future). Indeed, threatening to kill someone because he's black (or white), or intentionally inciting someone to a likely and immediate attack on someone because he's Muslim (or Christian or Jewish), can be made a crime. But this isn't because it's "hate speech"; it's because it's illegal to make true threats and incite imminent crimes against anyone and for any reason, for instance because they are police officers or capitalists or just someone who is sleeping with the speaker's ex-girlfriend.

The Supreme Court did, in *Beauharnais v. Illinois* (1952), uphold a "group libel" law that outlawed statements that expose racial or religious groups to contempt or hatred, unless the speaker could show that the statements were true, and were said with "good motives" and for "justifiable ends." But this too was treated by the Court as just a special case of a broader First Amendment exception — the one for libel generally. And *Beauharnais* is widely understood to no longer be good law, given the Court's restrictions on the libel exception. See *New York Times Co. v. Sullivan* (1964) (rejecting the view that libel is categorically unprotected, and holding that the libel exception requires a showing that the libelous accusations be "of and concerning" a particular person); *Garrison v. Louisiana* (1964)

(generally rejecting the view that a defense of truth can be limited to speech that is said for "good motives" and for "justifiable ends"); *Philadelphia Newspapers, Inc. v. Hepps* (1986) (generally rejecting the view that the burden of proving truth can be placed on the defendant); *R.A.V. v. City of St. Paul* (1992) (holding that singling bigoted speech is unconstitutional, even when that speech fits within a First Amendment exception); *Nuxoll ex rel. Nuxoll v. Indian Prairie Sch. Dist. # 204*, 523 F.3d 668, 672 (7th Cir. 2008) (concluding that *Beauharnais* is no longer good law); *Dworkin v. Hustler Magazine Inc.*, 867 F.2d 1188, 1200 (9th Cir. 1989) (likewise); *Am. Booksellers Ass'n, Inc. v. Hudnut*, 771 F.2d 323, 331 n.3 (7th Cir. 1985) (likewise); *Collin v. Smith*, 578 F.2d 1197, 1205 (7th Cir. 1978) (likewise); *Tollett v. United States*, 485 F.2d 1087, 1094 n.14 (8th Cir. 1973) (likewise); Erwin Chemerinsky, *Constitutional Law: Principles and Policies* 1043–45 (4th ed. 2011); Laurence Tribe, *Constitutional Law,* §12–17, at 926; Toni M. Massaro, *Equality and Freedom of Expression: The Hate Speech Dilemma*, 32 Wm. & Mary L. Rev. 211, 219 (1991); Robert C. Post, *Cultural Heterogeneity and Law: Pornography, Blasphemy, and the First Amendment*, 76 Calif. L. Rev. 297, 330–31 (1988).

Finally, "hostile environment harassment law" has sometimes been read as applying civil liability — or administrative discipline by universities — to allegedly bigoted speech in workplaces, universities, and places of public accommodation. There is a hot debate on whether those restrictions are indeed constitutional; they have generally been held unconstitutional when applied to universities, but decisions are mixed as to civil liability based on speech that creates hostile environments in workplaces. . . . But even when those restrictions have been upheld, they have been justified precisely on the rationale that they do not criminalize speech (or otherwise punish it) in society at large, but only apply to particular contexts, such as workplaces. None of them represent a "hate speech" [5] exception, nor have they been defined in terms of "hate speech."

For this very reason, "hate speech" also doesn't have any fixed legal meaning under U.S. law. U.S. law has just never had occasion to define "hate speech" — any more than it has had occasion to define rudeness, evil ideas, unpatriotic speech, or any other kind of speech that people might condemn but that does not constitute a legally relevant category.

Of course, one can certainly argue that First Amendment law *should* be changed to allow bans on hate speech (whether bigoted speech, blasphemy, blasphemy to which foreigners may respond with attacks on Americans or blasphemy or flag burning or anything else). Perhaps some statements of the "This isn't free speech, it's hate speech" variety are deliberate attempts to call for such an exception, though my sense is that they are usually (incorrect) claims that the exception already exists.

I think no such exception should be recognized, but of course, like all questions about what the law ought to be, this is a matter that can be debated. Indeed, people have a First Amendment right to call for speech restrictions, just as they have a First Amendment right to call for gun bans or bans on Islam or government-imposed race discrimination or anything else that current constitutional law forbids. Constitutional law is no more set in stone than any other law.

But those who want to make such arguments should acknowledge that they are calling for a change in First Amendment law, and should explain just what that change would be, so people can thoughtfully evaluate it. Calls for a new First Amendment exception for "hate speech" shouldn't just rely on the undefined term "hate speech" — they should explain just what viewpoints the government would be allowed to suppress, what viewpoints would remain protected, and how judges, juries, and prosecutors are supposed to distinguish the two. Saying "this isn't free speech, it's hate speech" doesn't, I think, suffice.

QUESTIONS

1. What is the purpose of Eugene Volokh's piece?
2. According to Volokh, what kinds of speech are unprotected by the First Amendment?
3. What purpose do the court cases serve in Volokh's argument? How effective do you find them to be?

4. What suggestions does Volokh have for those who would like to change First Amendment law?
5. How would you characterize the tone of this op-ed? Support your response with specific details from the text.

3 Free Speech Is the Most Effective Antidote to Hate Speech

SEAN STEVENS AND NICK PHILLIPS

Sean Stevens is a postdoctoral researcher at New York University, and Nick Phillips is at New York University School of Law. They published the following post in 2016 on the website of the Heterodox Academy, whose mission is "to improve the quality of research and education in universities by increasing viewpoint diversity, mutual understanding, and constructive disagreement."

On December 6, Texas A&M University will play host to Richard Spencer, a leader of the "alt-right" movement, and an open white supremacist. Many will likely view Spencer's presence at Texas A&M as confirmation that Donald Trump's election to the presidency has allowed fringe political views to enter mainstream discussion. When Spencer, or someone like him, makes a statement like "America was, until this last generation, a white country, designed for ourselves and our posterity. It is our creation and our inheritance, and it belongs to us," many people may question why we should remain committed to the First Amendment. This post argues why members of an academic community need to remain steadfast in that commitment, even when faced with a figure like Richard Spencer.

When hardcore racists and xenophobes remain consigned to obscure message boards and poorly attended events, it's fairly easy to believe in freedom of speech and expression. But when organized hatred arrives on campus, such defenses can be perceived as granting unacceptable cover to viewpoints that are widely considered despicable and immoral. To many, such viewpoints don't deserve the protection of the First Amendment. Unfortunately, the impulse to start limiting speech — either with on-the-books campus speech codes or simply through stepped-up social enforcement of speech taboos — is likely to pour gasoline on the fire and make the problem worse.

Research suggests that restrictions perceived to threaten or possibly eliminate behavioral freedoms may trigger "psychological reactance," and increase one's desire to engage in the restricted behavior. For instance, Worchel and colleagues (1975) assessed desire to hear censored material among students at the University of North Carolina. The experimenter informed participants that they would soon be hearing a tape recording of a speech and that the study was interested in how personal characteristics impact a speaker's ability to get their message across. Some participants were then informed that because a student group (either the YM-YWCA or the John Birch Society) on campus was opposed to the content of the speech, the experimenter would not be able to play the taped recording.

Consistent with reactance theory, participants who were informed they could not hear the content of the speech reported a stronger desire to do so. This effect occurred regardless of whether the student group was viewed positively (YM-YWCA) or negatively (the John Birch Society). More recently, Silvia (2005) investigated if interpersonal similarity could override the experience of psychological reactance. In two separate studies, psychological reactance occurred when people felt their attitudinal freedom was threatened when interpersonal similarity was low, but not when interpersonal similarity was high.

More broadly, while ingroup favoritism may depend more on positive affect towards the ingroup, perceived discrimination by an outgroup increases ingroup identification, and can increase anger, hostility and aggression towards outgroups. If we incorporate these findings into our thinking about whether to censor a speaker, the following chain of events does not seem to be an implausible reaction:

1. Censoring a speaker may increase some people's desire to hear that speaker's message, particularly those who perceive the speaker as similar to them in some way.
2. Censoring a speaker may be perceived as threatening to people who perceive the speaker as similar to them.
3. The perception of threat is likely to increase identification with a salient ingroup.
4. Increased ingroup identification in response to threat may result in anger, hostility, and aggression towards outgroups.

In other words, censoring and disinviting a speaker such as Richard Spencer may actually

5

make him and his views more popular. Instead of acting as an antidote to hatred, censorship may pour gasoline onto an already simmering fire. Calls to disinvite, and thus censor, Spencer may produce the unintended consequence of promoting his vile, racist views.

People like Spencer revel in the power of their words to arouse emotions and strong reactions in their opponents. They interpret attempts to silence and exile their voices as fear of the truth they possess. The alt-right movement confidently hoists the pirate flag of rebellion, but it can only claim to be rebellious if it can point to the "powers that be" trying to shut them down.

Meeting hate speech with more speech is hard. It is extremely difficult to engage with people who hold beliefs that call another's humanity into question. But engagement may be the most effective tool we have. Speech codes and disinvitations may feel good in the moment, but they represent an easy way out. Often, what has been made taboo and socially undesirable comes back stronger than before.

We believe a stronger antidote is needed, and that antidote is more speech. To challenge Spencer, this speech can take different forms; and on December 6, some may find it cathartic, empowering and/or exciting to do so. However, we urge that opposition be constructive, not disruptive. Donating to counter causes, such as the Anti-Defamation League, the Simon Wiesenthal Center, and the National Organization for Advancement of Colored People's legal defense fund, that are actively combatting people like Spencer and his ideas is one useful tactic. Indeed, shortly after the announcement that Spencer would be speaking on campus, the psychology department at Texas A&M launched a fundraising campaign to protest Spencer and his racism. Joining this protest and funding groups opposed to Spencer is a form of speech and action that makes Spencer weaker, not strong. Same thing for attending his talk and rebutting his speech during the question and answer period. Speech can be deployed as a scalpel, able to cut through vitriol, rhetoric and mendacity to help counter speech that advocates for harmful ideas and outcomes.

QUESTIONS

1. How would you describe the argument that Sean Stevens and Nick Phillips make?

2. Characterize the evidence Stevens and Phillips use. Do you find it convincing? Explain your answer.

3. Why do Stevens and Phillips believe that censoring hate speech is more harmful than allowing it — that is, what is the logic behind their central argument?

4. What suggestions do they make for combatting hate speech without putting limits on it? Do you think those suggestions are practical? Do you think they would ultimately prove successful? Explain your response, drawing from historical evidence, your own experiences, or current events to support your position.

4 Free Speech Isn't Always Valuable. That's Not the Point.

LATA NOTT

Lata Nott is a lawyer and Executive Director of the Newseum Institute's First Amendment Center in New York City. She wrote the following post for the Newseum Institute's website in 2017.

You may think you love the First Amendment. You may get misty-eyed just thinking about it. It calls to mind Woodward and Bernstein unraveling the Watergate scandal, Dr. King leading the March on Washington, Voltaire proclaiming, "I disapprove of what you say, but I will defend to the death your right to say it." (Voltaire didn't actually say that, but he probably wouldn't mind that you think he did.)

But sooner or later, you will come across something that will make you wonder just what's so great about freedom of speech.

It could be a campus speaker arguing that Hitler might have been onto something. Or a protester burning an American flag. Or your neighbor's teenage son, who just bought a drone on Amazon and is now using it to take pictures of your front yard.

You will not disavow the First Amendment (because you love it, of course). You will squarely place the blame on those idiots who are clearly misinterpreting what it means, who think that free speech is somehow a free pass to be a total jerk. They're the problem, you tell yourself. The First Amendment, when applied *properly*, is great.

Maybe it's time for us to come to terms with the truth: While everybody loves the First Amendment in theory, nobody's all that fond of it in practice.   5

Consider the massive popularity of partisan media, and, as *The Wall Street Journal*'s "Blue Feed, Red Feed" project has shown, the *complete lack of overlap* between liberal and conservative Facebook feeds. We love speakers and media outlets that articulate the thoughts that we were already thinking. We can barely tolerate the ones that contradict our world view. As Nat Hentoff argued in his book, "Free Speech For Me But Not For Thee," most of us struggle with the desire to relentlessly censor one another.

Supreme Court Justice Oliver Wendell Holmes understood this back in 1919: "Persecution for the expression of opinions seems to me perfectly logical. If you...want a certain result with all your heart, you naturally express your wishes in law, and sweep away all opposition." Of course, he followed this with an instruction to resist this natural urge, and to think of speech as a marketplace where all ideas should be allowed to compete so that the best ideas can emerge victorious.

It's nice to think about a bustling marketplace of ideas, but it might be a little tough to hold that cheery picture in your mind when you think about, say, the First Amendment right to sell dog-fighting videos, or to hold up a "Thank God for dead soldiers" banner outside a military funeral. When you picture a marketplace, you can't help but assess the value of the goods for sale. Do we really have to make space for the vendors selling rotten fruit, or that candy that contains trace amounts of lead?

Hate speech may be protected by the First Amendment, but what benefit do we actually derive from it? How much did Milo Yiannopoulos's controversial campus visits contribute to intelligent debate when his speeches primarily revolved around publicly ridiculing audience members and basking in his own outrageousness? If the point of free speech is to encourage that intellectual marketplace, to make us a better society, why should we care about defending speech that we find intellectually worthless?

But there's another way to look at the First Amendment. Maybe we shouldn't think about free expression in terms of value. Free speech isn't always valuable, no matter how loosely you define that word. Sometimes it's hurtful, or nonsensical, or idiotic. What's important is that free expression rights are always indivisible. Remember: The First Amendment protects your speech from *government* censorship. It's meant to keep the power to decide what's valuable expression and what isn't out of the hands of public officials. You are not in competition with the people who disagree with you. In the   10 real conflict, all of us are on the same side: How much control over speech do we want to cede to the people in power?

In other words: Your rights are my rights. This is true even if I hate you. Nevertheless, I have to stand up for your rights to speak, to publish, to protest, even if I think your opinions are junk and you are wrong about everything. Not just in service of a lofty ideal, but also out of my own self-interest.

The same holds true for you, for all of us. You may advocate for hate speech policies that will silence bigots, but once they're passed, these same laws can be used to silence you. You may support laws that are intended to restrict and neuter public protests, but you will find yourself without many options when it comes time to stand up for a cause that you believe in.

You don't have to love the First Amendment. Just acknowledge that we all need it.

QUESTIONS

1. What aspects of human nature does Lata Nott hold responsible for the ways the First Amendment is misinterpreted?

2. What point does Nott make in paragraph 5 when she discusses partisan media? How does this point contribute to her overall argument?

3. How does Nott use rhetorical questions to develop her argument?

4. Why does Nott believe we all need to stand up for the First Amendment even if we don't "love" it?

---

5 The Case for Restricting Hate Speech

LAURA BETH NIELSEN

Laura Beth Nielsen is Director of the Center for Legal Studies and a professor of sociology at Northwestern University as well as a research professor at the American Bar Foundation. She is the author of *License to Harass: Law, Hierarchy, and Offensive Public Speech* (2006), a book about the First Amendment and offensive public speech. The following op-ed was published by the *Los Angeles Times* in 2017.

As a sociologist and legal scholar, I struggle to explain the boundaries of free speech to undergraduates. Despite the 1st Amendment — I tell my students — local, state, and federal laws limit all kinds of speech. We regulate advertising, obscenity, slander, libel, and inciting lawless action to name just a few. My students nod along until we get to racist and sexist speech. Some can't grasp why, if we restrict so many forms of speech, we don't also restrict hate speech. Why, for example, did the Supreme Court on Monday rule that the trademark office cannot reject "disparaging" applications — like a request from an Oregon band to trademark "the Slants" as in Asian "slant eyes."

The typical answer is that judges must balance benefits and harms. If judges are asked to compare the harm of restricting speech — a cherished core constitutional value — to the harm of hurt feelings, judges will rightly choose to protect free expression. But perhaps it's nonsense to characterize the nature of the harm as nothing more than an emotional scratch; that's a reflection of the deep inequalities in our society, and one that demonstrates a profound misunderstanding of how hate speech affects its targets.

Legally, we tell members of traditionally disadvantaged groups that they must live with hate speech except under very limited circumstances. The KKK can parade down Main Street. People can't falsely yell fire in a theater but can yell the N-word at a person of color. College women are told that a crowd of frat boys chanting "no means yes . . ." is something they must tolerate in the name of (someone else's) freedom.

At the same time, our regime of free speech protects the powerful and popular. Many city governments, for instance, have banned panhandling at the behest of their business communities. The legal justification is that the targets of begging (commuters, tourists, and consumers) have important and legitimate purposes for being in public: to get to work or to go shopping. The law therefore protects them from aggressive requests for money.

Consider also the protections afforded to 5 soldiers' families in the case of Westboro Baptist anti-gay demonstrations. When the Supreme Court in 2011 upheld that church's right to stage offensive protests at veterans' funerals, Congress passed the Honoring America's Veterans' Act, which prohibits any protests 300 to 500 feet around such funerals. (The statute made no mention of protecting LGBTQ funeral attendees from hate speech, just soldiers' families).

So soldiers' families, shoppers and workers are protected from troubling speech. People of color, women walking down public streets or just living in their dorm on a college campus are not. The only way to justify this disparity is to argue that commuters asked for money on the way to work experience a tangible harm, while women catcalled and worse on the way to work do not — as if being the target of a request for change is worse than being racially disparaged by a stranger.

In fact, empirical data suggest that frequent verbal harassment can lead to various negative consequences. Racist hate speech has been linked to cigarette smoking, high blood pressure, anxiety, depression and post-traumatic stress disorder, and requires complex coping strategies. Exposure to racial slurs also diminishes academic performance. Women subjected to sexualized speech may develop a phenomenon of "self-objectification," which is associated with eating disorders.

These negative physical and mental health outcomes — which embody the historical roots of race and gender oppression — mean that hate speech is not "just speech." Hate speech is doing something. It results in tangible harms that are serious in and of themselves and that collectively amount to the harm of subordination. The harm of perpetuating discrimination. The harm of creating inequality.

Instead of characterizing racist and sexist hate speech as "just speech," courts and legislatures need to account for this research and, perhaps, allow the restriction of hate speech as do all of the other economically advanced democracies in the world.

Many readers will find this line of thinking 10 repellent. They will insist that protecting hate speech is consistent with and even central to our founding principles. They will argue that regulating hate speech would amount to a serious break from our tradition. They will trivialize the harms that social science research undeniably associates with being the target of hate speech, and call people seeking recognition of these affronts "snowflakes."

But these free-speech absolutists must at least acknowledge two facts. First, the right to speak already is far from absolute. Second, they are asking disadvantaged members of our society to shoulder a heavy burden with serious consequences. Because we are "free" to be hateful, members of traditionally marginalized groups suffer.

QUESTIONS

1. Laura Beth Nielsen's op-ed focuses on the targets of unlimited free speech as well as groups who are "protected from troubling speech" (para. 6). How does she classify them?

2. Why does Nielsen consider unlimited free speech to be an equity issue — that is, an issue that creates an unfair disparity between and among groups of people?

3. How does Nielsen define harm in the context of her argument? How does this definition relate to how she develops her position?

4. How does Nielsen acknowledge the counterargument? How does she refute it?

6   Free Speech

SIGNE WILKINSON

Signe Wilkinson is an American political cartoonist whose work appears in newspapers nationally. The following cartoon was completed in 2017.

Signe Wilkinson/The Cartoonist Group

QUESTIONS

1. Why is Uncle Sam holding the Free Speech umbrella?

2. Look carefully at the people underneath the umbrella. Who are they? What does each represent? To what extent is Wilkinson suggesting these people exist on even moral footing?

3. What is the message of Wilkinson's cartoon? Do you think she is in favor of limiting free speech? Explain your answer.

MAKING CONNECTIONS

1. Laura Beth Nielsen and Thane Rosenbaum refute the notion that while sticks and stones can break bones, names never do lasting harm. What might Lata Nott have to say on the subject?

2. In his op-ed, Eugene Volokh argues that there is no hate speech exception to the First Amendment. He concedes, however, that adding one might be up for debate. How might Rosenbaum or Nielsen debate him? What limitations might they propose, and under what circumstances?

3. Would Rosenbaum find Sean Stevens and Nick Phillips's psychological testing convincing enough to lift limits on free speech? Would Stevens and Phillips be convinced by Rosenbaum's assertion? Explain your answers.

4. Cartoonist Signe Wilkinson satirizes the push and pull of individual needs and rights in the question of limiting free speech. How would Nielsen draw a cartoon illustrating her views?

ENTERING THE CONVERSATION

As you respond to the following prompts, support your argument with references to at least three sources in this Conversation on the limits of free speech. For help using sources, see Chapter 4.

1. Write an essay in which you take a stand on free speech. In what ways, if any, should it be limited? Use at least three of the sources from this Conversation to develop your position.

2. After the terrorist attack on the offices of the French satire magazine *Charlie Hebdo,* Floyd Abrams, a preeminent First Amendment lawyer, wrote the following response in a letter to the *New York Times*:

   > The decision of the *New York Times* to report on the murders in Paris of journalists who worked for *Charlie Hebdo* while not showing a single example of the cartoons that led to their executions is regrettable. There are times for self-restraint, but in the immediate wake of the most threatening assault on journalism in living memory, you would have served the cause of free expression best by engaging in it.

   Write an essay explaining the extent to which you believe it is the responsibility of the press to practice "free expression" at the same time they report on threats to it.

3. In June 2017, the U.S. Supreme Court affirmed in a unanimous decision that phrases or terms that are considered offensive are still protected as free speech under the First Amendment. The court struck down a "disparagement provision"

that the U.S. Patent and Trademark Office used to deny an Asian American rock band a trademark for their name, "The Slants," because they found it offensive. In the decision handed down by the court, Samuel Alito wrote, "It offends a bedrock First Amendment principle: Speech may not be banned on the ground that it expresses ideas that offend." This is called "viewpoint discrimination: that is, giving offense is a viewpoint." This decision has application to the names of sports teams, such as the Washington Redskins, a name that many find offensive. Write an essay in which you consider First Amendment protections for the names of sports teams and whether you believe they fall into the category of "viewpoint discrimination."

4. In an August 2017 post on slate.com, Dahlia Lithwick, a resident of Charlottesville, Virginia, wrote that "to guarantee an escape from conflict, from violence, requires censorship. To have free speech in this moment, when the stakes are so high, is to live with fear. This is not an easy thing to confront — or to accept. If everyone had just stayed home last Wednesday [August 12, 2017] in Charlottesville, there would have been no need to be afraid. There would also have been no dialogue." Write an essay in which you argue for or against the value of "dialogue" in situations in which conflict leads to violence.

from **Between the World and Me**

TA-NEHISI COATES

Here is how I take the measure of my progress in life: I imagine myself as I was, back there in West Baltimore, dodging North and Pulaski, ducking Murphy Homes, fearful of the schools and the streets, and I imagine showing that lost boy a portrait of my present life and asking him what he would make of it. Only once — in the two years after your birth, in the first two rounds of the fight of my life — have I believed he would have been disappointed. I write you at the precipice of my fortieth year, having come to a point in my life — not of great prominence — but far beyond anything that boy could have even imagined. I did not master the streets, because I could not read the body language quick enough. I did not master the schools, because I could not see where any of it could possibly lead. But I did not fall. I have my family. I have my work. I no longer feel it necessary to hang my head at parties and tell people that I am "trying to be a writer." And godless though I am, the fact of being human, the fact of possessing the gift of study, and thus being remarkable among all the matter floating through the cosmos, still awes me.

I have spent much of my studies searching for the right question by which I might fully understand the breach between the world and me. I have not spent my time studying the problem of "race" — "race" itself is just a restatement and retrenchment of the problem. You see this from time to time when some dullard — usually believing himself white — proposes that the way forward is a grand orgy of black and white, ending only when we are all beige and thus the same "race." But a great number of "black" people already are beige. And the history of civilization is littered with dead "races" (Frankish, Italian, German, Irish) later abandoned because they no longer serve their purpose — the organization of people beneath, and beyond, the umbrella of rights.

If my life ended today, I would tell you it was a happy life — that I drew great joy from the study, from the struggle toward which I now urge you. You have seen in this conversation that the struggle has ruptured and remade me several times over — in Baltimore, at The Mecca, in fatherhood, in New York. The changes have awarded me a rapture that comes only when you can no longer be lied to, when you have rejected the Dream. But even more, the changes have taught me how to best exploit that singular gift of study, to question what I see, then to question what I see after that, because the questions matter as much, perhaps more than, the answers. . . .

◆ ◆ ◆

I did not die in my aimless youth. I did not perish in the agony of not knowing. I was not jailed. I had proven to myself that there was another way beyond the schools and the streets. I felt myself to be among the survivors of some great natural disaster, some plague, some avalanche or earthquake. And now, living in the wake of a decimation and having arrived at a land that I once considered mythical, everything seemed cast in a halo — the pastel Parisian scarves burned brighter, the morning odor wafting out of the boulangeries was hypnotic, and the language all around me struck me not so much as language but as dance.

Your route will be different. It must be. You knew things at eleven that I did not know when I was twenty-five. When I was eleven my highest priority was the simple security of my body. My life was the immediate negotiation of violence — within my house and without. But already you have expectations, I see that in

5

you. Survival and safety are not enough. Your hopes — your dreams, if you will — leave me with an array of warring emotions. I am so very proud of you — your openness, your ambition, your aggression, your intelligence. My job, in the little time we have left together, is to match that intelligence with wisdom. Part of that wisdom is understanding what you were given — a city where gay bars are unremarkable, a soccer team on which half the players speak some other language. What I am saying is that it does not all belong to you, that the beauty in you is not strictly yours and is largely the result of enjoying an abnormal amount of security in your black body.

Perhaps that is why, when you discovered that the killer of Mike Brown would go unpunished, you told me you had to go. Perhaps that is why you were crying, because in that moment you understood that even your relatively privileged security can never match a sustained assault launched in the name of the Dream. Our current politics tell you that should you fall victim to such an assault and lose your body, it somehow must be your fault. Trayvon Martin's hoodie got him killed. Jordan Davis's loud music did the same. John Crawford should never have touched the rifle on display. Kajieme Powell should have known not to be crazy. And all of them should have had fathers — even the ones who had fathers, even you. Without its own justifications, the Dream would collapse upon itself. You first learned this from Michael Brown. I first learned it from Prince Jones.

Michael Brown did not die as so many of his defenders supposed. And still the questions behind the questions are never asked. Should assaulting an officer of the state be a capital offense, rendered without trial, with the officer as judge and executioner? Is that what we wish civilization to be? And all the time the Dreamers are pillaging Ferguson for municipal governance. And they are torturing Muslims, and their drones are bombing wedding parties (by accident!), and the Dreamers are quoting Martin Luther King and exulting nonviolence for the weak and the biggest guns for the strong. Each time a police officer engages us, death, injury, maiming is possible. It is not enough to say that this is true of anyone or more true of criminals. The moment the officers began their pursuit of Prince Jones, his life was in danger. The Dreamers accept this as the cost of doing business, accept our bodies as currency, because it is their tradition. As slaves we were this country's first windfall, the down payment on its freedom. After the ruin and liberation of the Civil War came Redemption for the unrepentant South and Reunion, and our bodies became this country's second mortgage. In the New Deal[1] we were their guestroom, their finished basement. And today, with a sprawling prison system, which has turned the warehousing of black bodies into a jobs program for Dreamers and a lucrative investment for Dreamers; today, when 8 percent of the world's prisoners are black men, our bodies have refinanced the Dream of being white. Black life is cheap, but in America black bodies are a natural resource of incomparable value.

[2015]

---

[1]A reference to the discriminatory housing practices codified by the Federal Housing Administration and Home Owners Loan Corporation during the Great Depression. —Eds.

---

1. The author's tone in paragraph 1 is most accurately characterized as

a. self-effacing confidence

b. defensive self-justification

c. ironic humility

d. arrogant superiority

e. thoughtful questioning

2. We can infer from the statement, "I no longer feel it necessary to hang my head at parties and tell people that I am 'trying to be a writer'," that the author

a. has found relief in choosing a career path other than becoming a writer

b. had been embarrassed by his choice of career in the past but is no longer

c. has found reluctant acceptance for his career as a writer

d. has overcome the insecurities he formerly felt at social gatherings

e. has become famous enough so that people no longer ask him what he does

3. In the last sentence of paragraph 1, the author characterizes himself as

a. confident but diminutive

b. unscientific but imaginative

c. unexceptional but impressed

d. unreligious but grateful

e. self-centered but unsurprised

4. In paragraph 2, the primary function of the quotation marks around the words "race" and "black" is to

a. emphasize their importance to his argument

b. imply that they are quoted from other well-known sources

c. challenge the common definitions of the terms

d. highlight that he seeks to stipulate alternative meanings

e. attack those who use the terms improperly

5. In paragraph 2, the phrase "the organization of people beneath, and beyond, the umbrella of rights" serves to

a. answer the question the author has been "searching for"

b. identify what the author has "spent [his] time studying"

c. explain the basis of "the history of civilization"

d. define the function that "race" had performed in the past

e. challenge "Frankish, Italian, German, Irish" concepts of culture

6. In paragraph 3, the use of the word "rapture" derives its force from all the following EXCEPT

a. it subtly develops the perspective presented in the phrase "If my life ended today"

b. it expands on the meaning of "great joy"

c. it contains linguistic echoes of "rupture"

d. it links connotatively to "The Mecca" and "the Dream"

e. it defines a method "to best exploit that singular gift of study"

7. In paragraph 4, we can infer that the "land that I once considered mythical" is

a. America

b. heaven

c. freedom

d. France

e. The Mecca

8. In paragraph 5, the author's "warring emotions" refer to his conflict between

a. his pride in his son's confidence and knowledge of his son's privileged status

b. his desire for peace and his experience of the violence that disrupts it

c. his childhood experiences and his adult perspective on that experience

d. his personal life in his home and his public life in the community

e. his participation in his professional career and his personal family life at home

9. The tone of the first five paragraphs of the passage is best characterized as

a. didactic yet impartial

b. moralistic yet evenhanded

c. blunt yet hopeful

d. condescending yet generous

e. candid yet emotional

from On the Duty of Civil Disobedience

HENRY DAVID THOREAU

I heartily accept the motto, — "That government is best which governs least"; and I should like to see it acted up to more rapidly and systematically. Carried out, it finally amounts to this, which I also believe, — "That government is best which governs not at all"; and when men are prepared for it, that will be the kind of government which they will have. Government is at best but an expedient; but most governments are usually, and all governments are sometimes, inexpedient. The objections which have been brought against a standing army, and they are many and weighty, and deserve to prevail, may also at last be brought against a standing government. The standing army is only an arm of the standing government. The government itself, which is only the mode which the people have chosen to execute their will, is equally liable to be abused and perverted before the people can act through it. Witness the present Mexican war, the work of comparatively a few individuals using the standing government as their tool; for, in the outset, the people would not have consented to this measure.

This American government, — what is it but a tradition, though a recent one, endeavoring to transmit itself unimpaired to posterity, but each instant losing some of its integrity? It has not the vitality and force of a single living man; for a single man can bend it to his will. It is a sort of wooden gun to the people themselves. But it is not the less necessary for this; for the people must have some complicated machinery or other, and hear its din, to satisfy that idea of government which they have. Governments show thus how successfully men can be imposed on, even impose on themselves, for their own advantage. It is excellent, we must all allow. Yet this government never of itself furthered any enterprise, but by the alacrity with which it got out of its way. *It* does not keep the country free.

It does not settle the West. *It* does not educate. The character inherent in the American people has done all that has been accomplished; and it would have done somewhat more, if the government had not sometimes got in its way. For government is an expedient by which men would fain succeed in letting one another alone; and, as has been said, when it is most expedient, the governed are most let alone by it. Trade and commerce, if they were not made of India-rubber, would never manage to bounce over the obstacles which legislators are continually putting in their way; and, if one were to judge these men wholly by the effects of their actions and not partly by their intentions, they would deserve to be classed and punished with those mischievous persons who put obstructions on railroads.

But, to speak practically and as a citizen, unlike those who call themselves no-government men, I ask for, not at once no government, but *at once* a better government. Let every man make known what kind of government would command his respect, and that will be one step toward obtaining it.

After all, the practical reason why, when the power is once in the hands of the people, a majority are permitted, and for a long period continue, to rule, is not because they are most likely to be in the right, nor because this seems fairest to the minority, but because they are physically the strongest. But a government in which the majority rule in all cases cannot be based on justice, even as far as men understand it. Can there not be a government in which majorities do not virtually decide right and wrong, but conscience? — in which majorities decide only those questions to which the rule of expediency is applicable? Must the citizen ever for a moment, or in the least degree, resign his conscience to the legislator? Why has every man a conscience, then? I think that we should be men first, and subjects afterward. It is not desirable to cultivate a respect for the law, so much as for the right. The only obligation which I have the right to assume, is to do at any time what I think right. It is truly enough said, that a corporation has no conscience; but a corporation of conscientious men is a corporation *with* a conscience. Law never made men a whit more just; and, by means of their respect for it, even the well-disposed are daily made the agents of injustice. A common and natural result of an undue respect for law is, that you may see a file of soldiers, colonel, captain, corporal, privates, powder-monkeys, and all, marching in admirable order over hill and dale to the wars, against their wills, ay, against their common sense and consciences, which makes it very steep marching indeed,

and produces a palpitation of the heart. They have no doubt that it is a damnable business in which they are concerned; they are all peaceably inclined. Now, what are they? Men at all? or small movable forts and magazines, at the service of some unscrupulous man in power? Visit the Navy-Yard, and behold a marine, such a man as an American government can make, or such as it can make a man with its black arts, — a mere shadow and reminiscence of humanity, a man laid out alive and standing, and already, as one may say, buried under arms with funeral accompaniments, though it may be, —

Not a drum was heard, not a funeral note. As his corse to the rampart we hurried; Not a soldier discharged his farewell shot O'er the grave where our hero we buried.

---

1. In paragraph 2, which of the following devices contribute to Thoreau's attitude toward the government?

   a. parallelism
   b. metaphor
   c. alliteration
   d. asyndeton
   e. paradox

2. The word "expedient" in the third sentence of the first paragraph suggests that the government is

   a. effective in listening to the needs of its citizens
   b. conscious of the changes it needs to make
   c. efficient with its decision making
   d. merely a quick fix
   e. only successful when its rule is limited

3. Which of the following does Thoreau use to criticize the existing government and encourage the reader to voice his or her opinions?

   a. standing army (para. 1)
   b. wooden gun (para. 2)
   c. corporation (para. 4)
   d. movable forts (para. 4)
   e. funeral accompaniments (para. 4)

4. The speaker in the passage can best be described as a person who

   a. values his opinion above the opinion of others
   b. defines himself by those he associates with
   c. appreciates the government as a compulsory institution
   d. respects those who vocalize their beliefs
   e. believes that the government aptly represents the majority

5. Throughout the passage, the speaker most frequently employs all of the following rhetorical devices EXCEPT

   a. juxtaposition
   b. apostrophe
   c. rhetorical question
   d. definition
   e. aphorism

6. Based on the second half of the fourth paragraph, beginning with "Why has every man a conscience, then?" what is the speaker suggesting about those who do not agree with him?

   a. That they are not men at all.
   b. That they aren't worth the freedom they have.

c. That they don't deserve a conscience.

d. That they have been broken by the government.

e. That they have created the flaws in the current government.

7. Which of the following best captures the main idea of the passage?

a. "I heartily accept the motto, — 'That government is best which governs least'; and I should like to see it acted up to more rapidly and systematically" (para. 1)

b. "Carried out, it finally amounts to this, which I also believe, — 'That government is best which governs not at all'" (para. 1)

c. "Government is at best but an expedient, but most governments are usually, and all governments are sometimes, inexpedient" (para. 1)

d. "Let every man make known what kind of government would command his respect, and that will be one step toward obtaining it" (para. 3)

e. "The only obligation which I have a right to assume, is to do at any time what I think is right" (para. 4)

8. The tone of the passage can best be described as

a. apathetic

b. contemplative

c. sardonic

d. paranoid

e. critical

JUSTICE

Now that you have examined a number of texts focusing on justice, explore one dimension of this topic by synthesizing your own ideas and those in the readings. You might want to do more research or use readings from other classes as you write.

1. Henry David Thoreau's objections to slavery and to what he saw as unjustified war prompted the writing of the essay "On the Duty of Civil Disobedience" (p. 999), which strongly influenced both Mahatma Gandhi and Martin Luther King Jr. In "Freedom or Death" (p. 1017), Emmeline Pankhurst argues for the need for militancy in pursuit of a righteous cause. Reflect on the state of our society today, and write an essay in which you apply Thoreau's and Pankhurst's ideas to our time. Is civil disobedience an appropriate response to perceived injustice today? Why or why not?

2. All of the authors in this chapter address the meaning of justice, though they approach it from different perspectives. Which two do you think offer the most powerful guidance for addressing a controversial issue today — and why? Define the issue as specifically as possible, and refer to the texts as to explain and support your position.

3. When Martin Luther King Jr. wrote, "Injustice anywhere is a threat to justice everywhere," he alluded to the ripple effect of injustice. Where do you see that happening today? You might consider a local or national problem that has global repercussions.

4. Are the terms *equality* and *justice* synonymous? Are they similar but distinct? Is one dependent on the other? Analyze the relationship between the two, using examples from your experience or knowledge of history and current events to support your analysis.

5. What does justice mean in the context of education — especially public education — in America? What three characteristics do you believe would be necessary to create a just K-12 educational system? Be sure to define your terms carefully, and do not equate just with ideal or utopian.

6. Does justice have a time limit? Consider a grave injustice — such as atrocities committed by war criminals, Japanese internment in America during World War II, wrongful convictions in today's prison system, medical research projects conducted on humans without their knowledge or consent — and discuss how justice can be done.

7. Each of the following statements addresses the nature of politics. Select one that interests you, and write an essay defending or challenging its assertion. To support your argument, refer to your knowledge of history and to the selections in this chapter.

    a. Nobody made a greater mistake than he who did nothing because he could do only a little.
    — Edmund Burke

    b. It is certain, in any case, that ignorance, allied with power, is the most ferocious enemy justice can have.
    — James Baldwin

    c. In matters of truth and justice, there is no difference between large and small problems, for issues concerning the treatment of people are all the same.
    — Albert Einstein

    d. Reconciliation should be accompanied by justice, otherwise it will not last. While we all hope for peace it shouldn't be peace at any cost but peace based on principle, on justice.
    — Corazon Aquino

    e. Social justice cannot be attained by violence. Violence kills what it intends to create.
    — Pope John Paul II

    f. I have always found that mercy bears richer fruits than strict justice.
    — Abraham Lincoln

g. For children are innocent and love justice, while most of us are wicked and naturally prefer mercy.

— G.K. Chesterton

h. Law and justice are not always the same. When they aren't, destroying the law may be the first step toward changing it.

— Gloria Steinem

8. Many of the readings in this chapter address injustices. What is an example of an injustice that has been corrected and justice has prevailed? How was justice achieved, and what lessons from that success can be applied universally?

9. If you were choosing a career based on your commitment to fighting injustice in your society — on a local, national, or global level — what would you choose and why? Define the injustice and explain how your chosen career might address it.

10. The nature and concept of justice has been explored in many classic works of literature. Read and discuss how it is treated in *Antigone* by Sophocles, *Beloved* by Toni Morrison, *The Scarlet Letter* by Nathaniel Hawthorne, or a work of your own choosing.

GRAMMAR AS RHETORIC AND STYLE

Part 1: Diction and Syntax

1. Appositives

An appositive is a noun or noun phrase that tells you more about a nearby noun or pronoun. In each sentence below, the appositive is bracketed. The arrow shows the noun or pronoun that the appositive describes.

It's a conflict I know well: I left my home state, **Ohio**, for the Marine Corps when I was 19.

— J. D. Vance (p. 601)

But it was the first song I liked that could soundtrack my entire drive to school, **or the time it took to run five laps**.

— Hua Hsu (p. 340)

And yet we continue to give the most help to those who least need it — **affluent homeowners** — while providing nothing to most rent-burdened tenants.

— Matthew Desmond (p. 836)

That is one of the best things about this country: **the free power of free words**.

— Naomi Shihab Nye (p. 1061)

According to the Rutgers criminologist **Todd Clear**, low-income neighborhoods in which a large proportion of the population cycles in and out of confinement experience greater familial dysfunction, warped labor markets, and a general lack of "mental and physical health."

— Patrick Radden Keefe (p. 1116)

Punctuation and Appositives

The last example given does not use punctuation to set off the appositive from the rest of the sentence, but the others do. Here's why: If the appositive is not essential to the meaning of the sentence but is more of an aside or parenthetical remark, then the writer uses punctuation to set off the appositive. If the appositive *is* essential to the meaning of the sentence, then the writer does *not* set off the appositive with punctuation marks. Include what is essential; exclude what is not. In the first example given, the information in the appositive is provided merely as a parenthetical remark with pauses in the reading indicated by commas, so J. D. Vance sets off the appositive with commas. In the final sentence, the reader does not pause for the essential information provided by the appositive, so Sebastian Junger does not punctuate the appositive.

Choosing Punctuation

If your appositive needs punctuation, you can set off the appositive in one of three ways. First, you can use one or two commas.

> But it was the first song I liked that could soundtrack my entire drive to school, **or the time it took to run five laps**.
>
> — Hua Hsu (p. 340)

> It's a conflict I know well: I left my home state, **Ohio**, for the Marine Corps when I was 19.
> — J. D. Vance (p. 601)

Second, you can use one or two dashes.

> Soldiers from some parts of the country had a high incidence of goitre — **a lump on their neck caused by the swelling of the thyroid gland**.
>
> — Malcolm Gladwell (p. 697)

> And yet we continue to give the most help to those who least need it — **affluent homeowners** — while providing nothing to most rent-burdened tenants.
>
> — Matthew Desmond (p. 836)

Third, you can use a colon.

> That is one of the best things about this country: **the free power of free words**.
> — Naomi Shihab Nye (p. 1061)

Dashes emphasize the appositive more than commas do. Furthermore, if an appositive contains its own internal commas, then one dash, two dashes, or a colon makes it easier to read the complete sentence.

Position of Appositive: Before or after the Noun?

The examples so far have shown an appositive coming *after* the noun or pronoun it details. Although that structure is the most common, an appositive can also come *before* the noun or pronoun as well.

I recently asked a friend, **Ami Vitori Kimener,** how she thought about her own return home. **A Georgetown graduate,** Ami left a successful career in Washington to start a new business in Middletown, Ohio.

— J. D. Vance (p. 602)

In Vance's first sentence, the appositive follows the noun; in the second, it comes before. Whether you put the appositive before or after the noun it details is a stylistic choice. If in doubt, read the sentence aloud with several surrounding sentences to determine which placement sounds better.

Rhetorical and Stylistic Strategy

An appositive serves two rhetorical and stylistic functions:

First, an appositive can *clarify* a term by providing a proper noun or a synonym for the term, by defining or explaining the term, or by getting more specific.

PROPER NOUN	Its hero is Scout's father, **the saintly Atticus Finch**.
	— Francine Prose (p. 227)

SYNONYM	. . . an automaton, **a machine**, can be made to keep a school so.
	— Ralph Waldo Emerson

LONGER DEFINITION	First published in 1970, *I Know Why the Caged Bird Sings* is what we have since learned to recognize as a "survivor" memoir, **a first-person narrative of victimization and recovery**.
	— Francine Prose (p. 226)

EXPLANATION	[O]ne might suppose that teenagers might enjoy the transformative science-fiction aspects of *The Metamorphosis*, **a story about a young man so alienated from *his* "dysfunctional" family that he turns . . . into a giant beetle**.
	— Francine Prose (p. 226)

SPECIFICITY	Yet in other genres — **fiction and memoir** — the news is far more upsetting.
	— Francine Prose (p. 226)

Second, an appositive can *smooth* choppy writing. Note how stilted each of the following items is compared with the preceding versions.

Its hero is Scout's father. His name is Atticus Finch. He is saintly.

An automaton is a machine. An automaton can be made to keep a school so.

I Know Why the Caged Bird Sings was first published in 1970. It is what we have since learned to recognize as a "survivor" memoir. A "survivor" memoir is a first-person narrative. The narrative deals with victimization and recovery.

[O]ne might suppose that teenagers might enjoy the transformative science-fiction aspects of *The Metamorphosis*. *The Metamorphosis* is a story about a young man.

Yet in other genres the news is far more upsetting. Other genres are fiction and memoir.

Exercises

EXERCISE 1

Identify the appositive in each of the following sentences and the word or phrase it details.

1. My father, a truly exceptional man, worked at an ordinary job and was unknown outside the small town where he lived.

2. His rage passes description — the sort of rage that is only seen when rich folk that have more than they can enjoy suddenly lose something that they have long had but have never before used or wanted.

   — J. R. R. Tolkien, *The Hobbit*

3. [W. E. B.] DuBois saw the grandeur and degradation in a single unifying thought — slavery was the West's tragic flaw; yet it was tragic precisely because of the greatness of the civilization that encompassed it.

   — Dinesh D'Souza, "Equality and the Classics"

4. The eruptions in the early part of our century — the time of world wars and emergent modernity — were premonitions of a sort.

   — Sven Birkerts, *The Gutenberg Elegies*

5. Evidently I need this starting point — the world as it appeared before people bent it to their myriad plans — from which to begin dreaming up my own myriad, imaginary hominid agendas.

   — Barbara Kingsolver, "Knowing Our Place"

6. The war America waged in Vietnam, the first to be witnessed day after day by television cameras, introduced the home front to new tele-intimacy with death and destruction.

   — Susan Sontag, *Regarding the Pain of Others*

7. The restaurant's signature dish, a tantalizing fish taco, is also one of the least expensive entrees on the menu.

EXERCISE 2

Provide the correct punctuation for each of the following sentences by using a dash, comma, or colon to separate the appositive from the rest of the sentence. Or, if a sentence does not need punctuation around the appositive, for that sentence write "NP" for "no punctuation." Be ready to explain why your choice of punctuation is the most effective in each case.

1. Several West African countries Nigeria, Ghana, Benin, Cameroon, and Togo were at some time in their history under colonial rule.

2. The mayoral candidate's rally opened to throngs of people an unusually large turnout for a cold, rainy day.

3. The British parliamentary system has two branches the House of Lords and the House of Commons.

4. The fifth canon of rhetoric style includes a writer's choices of diction and syntax.

5. One of our most popular poets Billy Collins is also one of our most gifted.

6. The surgeons reconstructed his hand the most damaged part of his body.

7. The rewards of hard work both physical and mental are often intangible.

8. Nadine Gordimer a white South African author won the Nobel Prize for Literature in 1991 when the country was still under the rule of apartheid.

9. Don't you think that businesses should close on July 4 the birthday of our country?

EXERCISE 3

Combine each of the following pairs of sentences into one more fluent and coherent sentence by using an appositive. Be sure to punctuate correctly.

1. The *Times* is a world-renowned newspaper. It is delivered to my house every day.

2. Dolores Cunningham is the first mayor in our town's history to increase jobs during her four-year term. She is an advocate of the supply-side theory of economics.

3. A major health problem for teenagers is bulimia. Bulimia is a potentially life-threatening eating disorder.

4. My car is in the parking lot. It's an old blue station wagon with a dent in the fender.

5. That call was from Bridget. She's the top student in my calculus class.

6. The Edwardsville Tigers are the only baseball team ever to lose a series that it had led three games to none. They will be forever remembered for this colossal choke.

7. Warren G. Harding defeated James Cox in the 1920 presidential election by 26 percentage points. This was the biggest landslide victory in the history of U.S. presidential elections.

8. The service opened to the choir's rendition of Handel's "Hallelujah Chorus." That performance was a smashing success.

EXERCISE 4

Identify the appositives in the following sentences from "I Know Why the Caged Bird Can't Read," and explain their effect. Note that all are direct quotations.

1. Traditionally, the love of reading has been born and nurtured in high school English class — the last time many students will find themselves in a roomful of people who have all read the same text and are, in theory, prepared to discuss it.

2. The intense loyalty adults harbor for books first encountered in youth is one probable reason for the otherwise baffling longevity of vintage mediocre novels, books that teachers may themselves have read in adolescence. . . .

3. My older son spent the first several weeks of sophomore English discussing the class's summer assignment, *Ordinary People*, a weeper and former bestseller by Judith Guest about a "dysfunctional" family recovering from a teenage son's suicide attempt.

4. Yet in other genres — fiction and memoir — the news is far more upsetting.

5. First published in 1970, *I Know Why the Caged Bird Sings* is what we have since learned to recognize as a "survivor" memoir, a first-person narrative of victimization and recovery.

6. Its hero is Scout's father, the saintly Atticus Finch, a lawyer who represents everything we cherish about justice and democracy and the American Way.

7. The novel has a shadow hero, too, the descriptively named Boo Radley, a gooney recluse who becomes the occasion for yet another lesson in tolerance and compassion.

8. To read the novel is, for most, an exercise in wish-fulfillment and self-congratulation, a chance to consider thorny issues of race and prejudice from a safe distance and with the comfortable certainty that the reader would *never* harbor the racist attitudes espoused by the lowlifes in the novel.

9. The question is no longer what the writer has written but rather who the writer is — specifically, what ethnic group or gender identity an author represents.

10. Meanwhile, aesthetic beauty — felicitous or accurate language, images, rhythm, wit, the satisfaction of recognizing something in fiction that seems fresh and true — is simply too frivolous, suspect, and elitist even to mention.

EXERCISE 5

Each of the following sentences includes one or more appositives. Identify the appositives, explain their effect, and then write a sentence of your own using that sentence as a model.

1. And on the basis of the evidence — the moral and political evidence — one is compelled to say that this is a backward society.

   — James Baldwin, *A Talk to Teachers* (p. 217)

2. So to regard the young child, the young man, requires, no doubt, rare patience: a patience that nothing but faith in the medial forces of the soul can give.

   — Ralph Waldo Emerson, *Education*

3. Her next possible victory is at the U.S. Open, the major where she has been involved in the most drama — everything from outrageous line calls to probations and fines.

   — Claudia Rankine, *The Meaning of Serena Williams* (p. 709)

4. I am also other selves: a late starter, a casualty of the culture wars of the 1960s, an alienated adolescent sopping up pop culture and dreaming of escape, an American kid growing up in the 1950s, playing touch football and watching *I Love Lucy*.

   — Sven Birkerts, *The Gutenberg Elegies*

5. Mr. Somervell — a most delightful man, to whom my debt is great — was charged with the duty of teaching the stupidest boys the most regarded thing — namely, to write mere English.

   — Winston Churchill, *A Roving Commission: My Early Life*

2. Modifiers

A modifier may be a one-word adverb or adjective; a phrase, such as a prepositional phrase or a participial phrase; or a clause, such as an adjective clause. At its best, a modifier describes, focuses, or qualifies the nouns, pronouns, and verbs it modifies. But when a writer overuses or incorrectly uses modifiers, the result may be verbose or even flowery writing.

Here is how David Denby describes the "most hated young woman in America" in "High-School Confidential: Notes on Teen Movies" (p. 322):

> a blonde — well, sometimes a redhead or a brunette, but usually a blonde. She has big hair flipped into a swirl of gold at one side of her face or arrayed in a sultry mane. . . . She's tall and slender, with a waist as supple as a willow, but she's dressed in awful, spangled taste.

These sentences include single-word adjectives (*sultry*, *tall*, *slender*, *supple*, *awful*, *spangled*), a participle followed by two prepositional phrases (*flipped into a swirl of gold*), and several other prepositional phrases (*at one side of her face*; *in a sultry mane*; *with a waist . . .* ; *in awful, spangled taste*). Focusing on all of these words and phrases in this way may make the modification seem heavy, but in the passage itself, the modifiers do *not* amount to overkill because Denby paces them.

Let's look more closely at another Denby sentence with a participial phrase as a modifier (p. 322):

> Sprawling and dull in class, he comes alive in the halls and in the cafeteria.

Here Denby has essentially combined two sentences: "He is sprawling and dull in class. He comes alive in the halls and in the cafeteria." The result is a smoother, single sentence that focuses on the difference between the subject's behavior in and out of class.

Similarly, Fareed Zakaria relies upon modifiers to bring his experiences alive to his readers. For instance, on page 188, he describes the Harvard University course book that his mother brought back to India:

> For me, it was an astonishing document. Instead of a thin pamphlet containing a dry list of subjects, as one would find at Indian universities, it was a bulging volume overflowing with ideas.

Modifiers in the second sentence that describe "an astonishing document" contrast his expectations of something dull and perfunctory with the reality of a book chock-full of interesting information. So, he uses the adjective "thin" and the participial phrase "containing a dry list of subjects," which itself contains another adjective: "dry." This image literally pales before the reality of a "bulging" course book that is "overflowing with ideas."

Rhetorical and Stylistic Strategy

Modifiers can enliven, focus, and qualify ideas. The *placement* of modifiers can add to or detract from these effects. Note the following example by Denby.

> Physically awkward, she walks like a seal crossing a beach, and is prone to drop her books and dither in terror when she stands before a handsome boy.

The modifiers that describe the girl gather steam, and finally, in a prepositional phrase at the end of the sentence, they contrast her with the handsome boy. Note the different effect if the handsome boy comes into the sentence before the awkward girl drops her books and dithers:

> When she stands before the handsome boy, physically awkward, she walks like a seal crossing a beach, and is prone to drop her books and dither in terror.

Announcing the handsome boy early in the sentence undercuts the contrast between the girl and the boy that Denby wants to stress.

In her essay, "Why Can't a Smart Woman Love Fashion?" (p. 920), Chimamanda Ngozi Adichie illustrates how modifiers can reinforce an author's message. Describing the impact of clothing, she includes precise details about her mother's fashion sense (p. 920):

> My favorite memory is of a sunny Sunday morning, standing in front of her dressing table, my mother clasping her necklace around my neck, a delicate gold wisp with a fish-shape pendant, the mouth of the fish open as though in delighted surprise.

The structure of the sentence itself seems to mimic the process of getting dressed. As the modifiers accumulate like layers — "standing in front of her dressing table" (participial phrase), "clasping her necklace" (participial phrase), "a delicate gold wisp with a fish-shape pendant" (adjectives and a prepositional phrase), "delighted surprise" (adjective to add emphasis) — we can feel young Adichie's pleasure in what she experienced as her mother's care and artistry.

Consider the effect of the modifier *now* in this sentence from Mark Twain (p. 315):

> We are conforming in the other way, now, because it is another case of everybody.

The placement of *now* in the middle of the sentence reinforces *the other way* and reminds us that Twain is making a point about the mercurial nature of public opinion.

Cautions

Studying how accomplished writers use modifiers helps us understand how to use them effectively. Following are some cautions to keep in mind when using modifiers in your own writing.

1. *Do not use too many modifiers.* David Denby gives a clear visual image of the evil high-school cheerleader by using a variety of modifiers. However, less experienced writers may overwrite by including too many adjectives, as shown in the following example:

   > The bright yellow compact car with the pun-laden, out-of-state vanity plates was like beautiful, warm sunshine on the gray, dreary Tuesday afternoon.

2. *Do not rely on adjectives when strong verbs are more effective.* Instead of writing, "Elani walked with a confident and quick stride," perhaps say, "Elani strutted" or "Elani strode."

3. *Beware of adding too many qualifiers.* Be especially careful about *really* and *very*.

   - "Troy felt really sad" might be expressed as "Troy felt discouraged" or "despondent." Or it might simply be stated as "Troy felt sad."

- Similarly, "The mockingbird's song is very beautiful" is probably just as well stated as "The mockingbird's song is beautiful" or, introducing a strong verb, as "The mockingbird serenades."

You need not avoid qualifiers altogether, but if you find yourself using them over and over, it's time to check whether they're *really very* effective.

Exercises

EXERCISE 1

Rewrite each of the following sentences to make the modifiers more effective.

1. Dolores offered a rather unique view of the situation.

2. I had difficulty understanding my teacher because he talked so quickly and softly.

3. Michael was so very excited about the beginning of lacrosse season. He could barely sleep.

4. Susan talked with self-assurance about movies she hadn't even seen.

5. The skyline was amazing on the beautiful evening.

EXERCISE 2

Discuss the following passage from Claudia Rankine's "The Meaning of Serena Williams" (p. 706). Focus on the writer's use of modifiers. Look carefully at the adjectives Rankine uses to describe Williams and consider how they suit the purpose of the essay.

She was wearing an enviable pink jumpsuit with palm trees stamped all over it as if to reflect the trees surrounding her estate. It was a badass outfit, one only someone of her height and figure could rock. She explained to me that she learned not to look ahead too much by looking ahead. As she approached 18 Grand Slam wins in 2014, she said, "I went too crazy. I felt I had to even up with Chris Evert and Martina Navratilova." Instead, she didn't make it past the fourth round at the Australian Open, the second at the French Open or the third at Wimbledon. She tried to change her tactics and focused on getting only to the quarterfinals of the U.S. Open. Make it to the second week and see what happens, she thought. "I started thinking like that, and then I got to 19. Actually I got to 21 just like that, so I'm not thinking about 22." She raised her water bottle to her lips, looking at me over its edge, as if to give me time to think of a different line of questioning.

EXERCISE 3

Identify the modifiers, both words and phrases, in the following paragraph from "The Gig Economy Celebrates Working Yourself to Death" by Jia Tolentino (p. 825). Are the modifiers effective, or are they excessive? Cite specific examples to support your view.

It does require a fairly dystopian strain of doublethink for a company to celebrate how hard and how constantly its employees must work to make a living, given that these companies are themselves setting the terms. And yet this type of faux-inspirational tale has been appearing more lately, both in corporate advertising and in the news. Fiverr, an online freelance marketplace that promotes itself as being for "the lean entrepreneur" — as its name suggests, services advertised on Fiverr can be purchased for as low as five dollars — recently attracted ire for an ad campaign called "In Doers We Trust." One ad, prominently displayed on some New York City subway cars, features a woman staring at the camera with a look of blank determination. "You eat a coffee for lunch," the ad proclaims. "You follow through on your follow through. Sleep deprivation is your drug of choice. You might be a doer."

EXERCISE 4

Most of the modifiers have been removed from the following passage from "Hip Hop Planet" by James McBride.

Not since the advent of jazz in the 1930s has an American music exploded across the world with force. Not since the Beatles invaded America and Elvis packed up his shoes has a music crashed against the world with outrage. The culture of song, graffiti, and dance, known as hip hop, has ripped music from its moorings in society it has permeated.

Read the paragraph aloud and listen to its cadence (the combination of the text's rhythm with the rise and fall in the inflection of the speaker's voice).

- **Add the following modifiers:** *blue, overwhelming, suede, swing, such, defiant, popular, every, collectively.* **Use them to improve the paragraph's effectiveness.**
- **Compare your version to the original (see para. 7, p. 302).**
- **Discuss the rhetorical effect of the modifiers in this passage.**

EXERCISE 5

Following are examples of authors' skillful use of modifiers, both single words and phrases. In each, identify the modifier or modifiers and discuss the effect they create. Then write a sentence or passage of your own, emulating the writer's technique.

1. . . . I realize to my horror that rap — music seemingly without melody, sensibility, instruments, verse, or harmony, music with no beginning, end, or middle, music that doesn't even seem to be music — rules the world.

— James McBride (p. 301)

2. He's usually a football player, muscular but dumb, with a face like a beer mug and only two ways of speaking — in a conspiratorial whisper, to a friend; or in a drill sergeant's sudden bellow.

— David Denby (p. 322)

3. Broadly speaking, there are none but corn-pone opinions. And broadly speaking, corn-pone stands for self-approval.

— Mark Twain (p. 316)

4. There was never a moment for her to sit down, undisturbed, to unravel her own private thoughts; never a time free from interruption — by work or the noisy inquiries of her many children.

—Alice Walker (p. 876)

5. We do not believe we can honorably accept our heritage of freedom without assuming the responsibility for preserving it and passing it on unimpaired to those who follow us.

— Earl Warren (p. 1040)

6. With their inventive legal minds and their tenacious pursuit of malefactors, Sporkin and Rakoff are two of the heroes in Eisinger's deeply reported account.

— Patrick Radden Keefe (p. 1112)

7. If the underdeveloped brains of adolescents at least partly explain their criminal behavior, then holding them fully responsible for their actions, and punishing them as adults, seems wildly off the mark.

— Jennifer Lackey (p. 1089)

8. Suffering from malnutrition and neglect and who knows what mental agonies, Phillis Wheatley died.

— Alice Walker (p. 875)

3. Pronouns

As you well know, a pronoun takes the place of a noun (called the *antecedent*). Unlike a noun, however, a pronoun defines the viewpoint in your writing. Are you talking about yourself (first person), are you talking directly to the audience (second person), or are you referring to a person who is neither the speaker nor the audience (third person)? This section considers two points of pronoun usage that affect viewpoint: (1) consistency of pronouns in a sentence or passage and (2) sexist pronouns.

Consistency: Viewpoint and Number

Pronouns must agree with one another and with their antecedents in number and in viewpoint (person). The following table summarizes which personal pronouns are singular and which are plural, as well as which are first person, second person, and third person:

	Number	
Viewpoint	**Singular**	**Plural**
First person	*I, me, my, mine*	*we, us, our, ours*
Second person	*you, your, yours*	*you, your, yours*
Third person	*he, him, his*	*they, them, their, theirs*
	she, her, hers	
	it, its	
	one, one's	

If you use pronouns to refer to an antecedent more than once in a sentence or paragraph, it's important that they be consistent in person and number. Consider the following sentence:

> If, by chance, *you* find another person more suitable as a wife than the wife I already have, I want the liberty to replace *my* present wife with another one.

This sentence shifts viewpoint from second person to first-person singular, and as a result it is confusing to the reader.

When corrected, the sentence maintains a consistent first-person singular viewpoint:

> If, by chance, *I* find another person more suitable as a wife than the wife *I* already have, *I* want the liberty to replace *my* present wife with another one.
>
> — Judy Brady (p. 903)

Consistency is also important when using *indefinite pronouns*. (An indefinite pronoun is one that does not have a specific antecedent.) Consider the singular indefinite pronoun *one* as it is used here:

> One cannot think well, love well, sleep well, if one has not dined well.
>
> — Virginia Woolf

This sentence begins with the singular indefinite pronoun *one* and sticks with *one*. The sentence would be much less effective if it said:

> *One* cannot think well, love well, sleep well, if *you* have not dined well.

Note, though, that Virginia Woolf could have opted to use the second person:

> *You* cannot think well, love well, sleep well, if *you* have not dined well.

Woolf's use of the third person adds a formality to the tone — through the more distanced *one* — while the second-person *you* sounds more conversational.

Sexist Pronoun Usage

When a third-person singular pronoun (*he, she, it*) could refer to either a male or a female, writers have several options: they can combine the male and female pronouns, using *or*; they can use the plural form of the pronoun, being careful to adjust the rest of the sentence accordingly; or they can alternate the gender of the pronouns.

Consider the following sentences from Virginia Woolf's "Professions for Women" (p. 883).

> I hope I am not giving away professional secrets if I say that a *novelist's* chief desire is to be as unconscious as possible. *He* has to induce in *himself* a state of perpetual lethargy.

The pronouns *he* and *himself* in the second sentence refer to the antecedent *novelist* in the first sentence. In using *he* and *himself*, Woolf was not only following standard grammatical practice of the 1930s but also underscoring the reality that during her lifetime most published novelists were indeed male. But the world and the English language have changed, and using the generic *he, his, him, himself* to refer to any individual is not as acceptable today as it was when Woolf wrote. How would writers today handle a discussion of an unidentified novelist? One possibility would be to use the term *his/her* or *his or her*:

> I hope I am not giving away professional secrets if I say that a *novelist's* chief desire is to be as unconscious as possible. *He or she* has to induce in *himself or herself* a state of perpetual lethargy.

If writers need to make only one or two references to an unspecified antecedent, perhaps they can get away with *he or she* and *himself or herself*, though even the two references in this sentence are awkward. But if there are many references to the antecedent, as in the Woolf passage that follows, the *or* construction becomes monotonous or downright annoying:

> I hope I am not giving away professional secrets if I say that a *novelist's* chief desire is to be as unconscious as possible. *He or she* has to induce in *himself or herself* a state of perpetual lethargy. *He or she* wants life to proceed with the utmost quiet and regularity. *He or she* wants to see the same faces, to read the same books, to do the same things day after day, month after month, while *he or she* is writing, so that nothing may break the illusion in which *he or she* is living.

The most straightforward revision would be to change the unspecified singular noun to an unspecified plural noun:

> I hope I am not giving away professional secrets if I say that the chief desire of *novelists* is to be as unconscious as possible. *They* have to induce in *themselves* a state of perpetual lethargy. *They* want life to proceed with the utmost quiet and regularity. *They* want to see the same faces, to read the same books, to do the same things day after day, month after month, while *they* are writing, so that nothing may break the illusion in which *they* are living.

Another possibility for large sections of an essay is to shift between male and female pronouns, using *he* or *him* or *his* for a while, then shifting to *she* or *her* or *hers*, and shifting yet again. Generally, writers seem to like this approach more than readers, who can lose track of what they are reading about, especially if the shift in gender happens too frequently.

Rhetorical and Stylistic Strategy

Although maintaining a consistent viewpoint is a matter of grammatical accuracy, selecting which viewpoint to use is a rhetorical decision. If the writing is formal, then the third person is generally the most appropriate choice. For example, most teachers expect a research paper to be written in the third person. If the essay is more informal and draws on the writer's personal experience, then the first person (singular or plural) works well. The second person — *you* — is generally reserved for informal writing, such as a newspaper column, where the writer is addressing readers as though they are in conversation, or for speeches, where the writer is directly addressing an audience.

In the second part of this section, we focused on sexist pronouns. Why do we recommend that you eliminate pronouns that some people think of as sexist? After all, there is nothing grammatically wrong with Virginia Woolf's use of a male pronoun to refer to an indefinite singular noun such as *novelist*. But language choice sometimes involves more than grammatical correctness. Throughout this book, you are reading about how to appeal to audiences and how to make audiences find you credible. One way to impress readers is to be sensitive to their likes and dislikes — in this case, to their own attitudes toward sexist language. Many of your readers will appreciate any steps you take in your writing to establish common ground with them. In pronoun usage, meet your readers' expectations that an indefinite singular noun might just as easily refer to a woman as to a man.

Remember, grammatical correctness and a writer's purpose go hand in hand.

Exercises

EXERCISE 1

In the following sentences, correct all errors that result from sexist pronouns or inconsistencies in pronoun person or number.

1. Popular culture once provided us with a common vocabulary, but now you have a hard time keeping up with the jargon.

2. For a runner to keep up his pace, one must pay attention to nutrition.

3. If one measures her country's commitment to education by dollars allocated, you can see that it's not our top priority.

4. Baseball fans pay so much attention to percentages that you almost always have a sense of the improbability or likelihood of an event actually occurring.

5. Most of the time a teacher tries to tailor writing assignments to interest his students.

6. Everyone is wondering who the next Democratic presidential candidate will be and if he will be a charismatic leader.

7. A doctor should treat his patients respectfully by listening to them no matter how busy they are.

8. We hoped to get a free pass to the movie, but the mall was so crowded that you didn't have a chance.

9. You should try to stop arguments before they start; otherwise, one might become involved in a conflict that gets more complicated than we thought possible.

10. When one is as strong a student as Chong is, you're not surprised that he passed the bar on his first try.

EXERCISE 2

The following paragraph is taken from the essay "I Want a Wife" by Judy Brady (p. 902). Discuss the effect of the pronouns *I* and *my*. How many times does Brady use them? How does this repetition help to achieve her purpose?

I would like to go back to school so that I can become economically independent, support myself, and, if need be, support those dependent upon me. I want a wife who will work and send me to school. And while I am going to school I want a wife to take care of my children. I want a wife to keep track of the children's doctor and dentist appointments. And to keep track of mine, too. I want a wife to make sure my children eat properly and are kept clean. I want a wife who will wash the children's clothes and keep them mended. I want a wife who is a good nurturant attendant to my children, who arranges for their schooling, makes sure that they have an adequate social life with their peers, takes them to the park, the zoo, etc. I want a wife who takes care of the children when they are sick, a wife who arranges to be around when the children need special care, because, of course, I cannot miss classes at school. My wife must arrange to lose time at work and not lose the job. It may mean a small cut in my wife's income from time to time, but I guess I can tolerate that. Needless to say, my wife will arrange and pay for the care of the children while my wife is working.

EXERCISE 3

The following excerpt is from "Professions for Women" by Virginia Woolf (p. 887). It includes both the first and third person. Rewrite it entirely in the first person — for example, with *I* and *we women*. Then discuss the effect of your changes. Consider the excerpt in the context of the entire essay.

These then were two very genuine experiences of my own. These were two of the adventures of my professional life. The first — killing the Angel in the House — I think I solved. She died. But the second, telling the truth about my own experiences as a body, I do not think I solved. I doubt that any woman has solved it yet. The obstacles against her are still immensely powerful — and yet they are very difficult to define. Outwardly, what is simpler than to write books? Outwardly, what obstacles are there for a woman rather than for a man? Inwardly, I think, the case is very different; she has still many ghosts to fight, many prejudices to overcome. Indeed it will be a long time still, I think, before a woman can sit down to write a book without finding a phantom to be slain, a rock to be dashed against. And if this is so in literature, the freest of all professions for women, how is it in the new professions which you are now for the first time entering?

EXERCISE 4

Think of an example of gender stereotyping that drives you crazy. Perhaps it's a television or movie character, an incident from the news, or a pop culture personality who seems to play to stereotypical expectations of male or female behavior. Write two paragraphs explaining your outrage. In one, use the first person, singular or plural, so that your identity is front and center; then rewrite it in third person so that your gender is not a part of the voice. Discuss the different effects of the two.

4. Direct, Precise, and Active Verbs

Direct, precise, active verbs energize writing. Consider this passage with verbs in bold from "Truth" (p. 1095), the speech former New Orleans mayor Mitch Landrieu gave about the removal of Confederate monuments in his city in 2017:

> I **want to try** to gently **peel** from your hands the grip on the false narrative of your history that I think **weakens** us and **make** straight a wrong turn we **made** many years ago so we **can** more closely **connect** with integrity to the founding principles of our nation and **forge** a clearer and straighter path toward a better city and more perfect union.

The highlighted strong verbs, especially *connect* and *forge*, create a sense of movement and unity that echo Landrieu's stated wish to bring the citizens of his city together on a "path toward a better city and more perfect union." His verb choices also reflect the fact that he knows not all of his listeners agree with him. He describes his efforts to persuade his audience in gentle terms, telling them that he wishes to "try to…peel" false beliefs and assumptions about the history of the south away from them. He could have used more forceful language there — telling them, for instance, "I want to disprove the false narrative of your history" — but this would have probably alienated a number of his listeners.

Now consider another passage, this one from "The Silent Season of a Hero" by Gay Talese (p. 649), with its verbs, verb phrases, and verbals (adjectives made from verbs) in bold type:

> He **watched** until she **left**, **lost** in the crowd of the newly arrived tourists that **had** just **come** down the hill by cable car. Then he **sat** down again at the table in the restaurant, **finishing** his tea and **lighting** another cigarette, his fifth in the last half hour. It **was** 11:30 in the morning. None of the other tables **was occupied**, and the only sounds **came** from the bar, where a liquor salesman **was laughing** at something the headwaiter **had said**. But then the salesman, his briefcase under his arm, **headed** for the door, **stopping** briefly **to peek** into the dining room and **call** out, "**See** you later, Joe." Joe DiMaggio **turned** and **waved** at the salesman. Then the room **was** quiet again.

Talese uses the action verbs, verb phrases, and verbals to give you a sense of the scene's movement and drama. Yet the two shortest sentences — both emphasizing silence and stasis rather than movement — rely on the linking verb *was*.

Once you've learned to recognize effective verbs in your reading, you'll become more aware of them in your own writing. You may find yourself working on the verbs in revisions rather than first drafts, but here are some suggestions for making even your first draft active and precise.

Direct Verbs

Use forms of *to be* and other linking verbs sparingly and with a specific reason. Often you can change a form of *to be* followed by a predicate adjective or a predicate noun (also called nominalization) into an action verb. Consider how the second sentence in each pair below sports a stronger verb than the first:

The motorcyclist of the popular imagination **was a mutation** from a genial daredevil into a diabolical marauder over the course of Independence Day weekend in 1947.

The motorcyclist of the popular imagination **mutated** from a genial daredevil into a diabolical marauder over the course of Independence Day weekend in 1947.

— Troy Patterson (p. 337)

Perhaps that is why, when you **made the discovery** that killer of Mike Brown would go unpunished, you told me you had to go.

Perhaps that is why, when you **discovered** that the killer of Mike Brown would go unpunished, you told me you had to go.

— Ta-Nehisi Coates (p. 995)

Precise Verbs

While there is nothing wrong with the verbs **showed** and **saw** in the first example that follows, consider the precision of the verbs in the second example.

What if paradise showed up among us from time to time — at the worst of times? What if we saw it in the jaws of hell?

What if paradise flashed up among us from time to time — at the worst of times? What if we glimpsed it in the jaws of hell?

— Rebecca Solnit (p. 568)

The verbs in this example capture the drama of Solnit's rhetorical questions by suggesting situations quite out of the ordinary.

Similarly, in the first sentence that follows, **looking forward to** is a perfectly serviceable verb — until you compare it with the more precise verb that the writer selects.

There must have been little boys in that throng too, frantic with the slow excruciating passage of time, looking forward to the hour when they would be Richard or Geoffrion or Laparade. . . .

There must have been little boys in that throng too, frantic with the slow excruciating passage of time, **panting for** the hour when they would be Richard or Geoffrion or Laprade. . . .

— William Faulkner (p. 682)

Active Verbs

In addition to selecting a verb that is direct and creates a precise image, use verbs in the active voice — with an easy-to-picture subject doing something — unless you have a specific purpose for using the passive voice, where the subject is acted upon. Here, for example, in the final part of a sentence from "The Silent Season of a Hero," Gay Talese makes good use of the passive voice (p. 650, para. 10):

Zio Pepe was among those who cheered when Joe DiMaggio returned to San Francisco after his first season with the New York Yankees and **was carried** along the wharf on the shoulders of the fishermen.

In this sentence, DiMaggio is acted upon by the fishermen. Why? Perhaps because Talese wanted *DiMaggio* to remain as the subject instead of switching away from *DiMaggio* and making *the fishermen* the subject.

By and large, though, strong writers stick with the active voice, as Talese does in the following passage (p. 655, para. 54):

> In the forty-first game [of 1941] . . . DiMaggio **tied** an American League record that George Sisler **had set** in 1922.

Talese could have cast that sentence in the passive voice, as follows:

> In the forty-first game . . . an American League record **that had been set** by George Sisler in 1922 **was tied** by DiMaggio.

As is often the case, the use of passive voice in this example makes for a wordy sentence that is harder to follow than a more direct and succinct one.

Exercises

EXERCISE 1

Improve the following sentences by replacing one or more verbs in each with a more effective verb — that is, a more vivid, precise, and active verb.

1. My first college visit will always be remembered by me.
2. There are many technological advances available to make our lives easier.
3. In the middle of the night, sirens could be heard.
4. It was not very long before she regretted buying the expensive handbag.
5. The Graham technique is little esteemed by modern dancers today.
6. The college advisor said she could not make a suggestion about which school to apply to because she didn't know his SAT scores.
7. The team captain is responsible for scheduling practices and communicating with team members.
8. A decision was reached by the arbitration panel.
9. The local sheriff gave a warning to the college students about walking around with open containers.
10. The chief of surgery took the opportunity to thank the volunteers.
11. Do your children have fears about going away to camp?

EXERCISE 2

Identify the verbs and verbals in the following passages. Discuss how these verbs affect the tone of the passages.

> His vets warned us all along that the odds were against him, but we didn't really believe them. They had hope, too. How could a horse who appeared so full of life break his leg and be so suddenly close to death? His head was fine. His back was fine. His lungs and heart and chest were fine. In fact, after a while, his broken leg was fairly fine. It was

another leg that was so worrisome, since the weight of his body constantly bearing down on the delicate structures inside his foot eventually damaged and destroyed them.

— Jane Smiley, "Barbaro, The Heart in the Winner's Circle" (p. 693)

Fellow marchers, so much has changed in 50 years. We have endured war and we've fashioned peace. We've seen technological wonders that touch every aspect of our lives. We take for granted conveniences that our parents could have scarcely imagined. But what has not changed is the imperative of citizenship; that willingness of a 26-year-old deacon, or a Unitarian minister, or a young mother of five to decide they loved this country so much that they'd risk everything to realize its promise.

That's what it means to love America. That's what it means to believe in America. That's what it means when we say America is exceptional.

For we were born of change. We broke the old aristocracies, declaring ourselves entitled not by bloodline, but endowed by our Creator with certain inalienable rights. We secure our rights and responsibilities through a system of self-government, of and by and for the people. That's why we argue and fight with so much passion and conviction — because we know our efforts matter. We know America is what we make of it.

— Barack Obama, "Remarks by the President at the 50th Anniversary
of the Selma to Montgomery Marches" (p. 1085)

EXERCISE 3

Analyze the verbs in the opening paragraph of "The Cruelest Sport" (p. 684). How would you describe the verbs Joyce Carol Oates uses? How do they mirror the subject she is writing about? Do the verbs she uses tip you off that this piece is more complex and academic than usual for sportswriting? Cite specific examples to support your view.

Professional boxing is the only major American sport whose primary, and often murderous, energies are not coyly deflected by such artifacts as balls and pucks. Though highly ritualized, and as rigidly bound by rules, traditions, and taboos as any religious ceremony, it survives as the most primitive and terrifying of contests: two men, near-naked, fight each other in a brightly lit, elevated space roped in like an animal pen (though the ropes were originally to keep rowdy spectators out); two men climb into the ring from which only one, symbolically, will climb out. (Draws do occur in boxing, but are rare, and unpopular.)

EXERCISE 4

Count the verbs in one of the passages in Exercise 2. Then categorize them into linking verbs and more vivid action verbs, and calculate the ratio. Do the same for several paragraphs of your own writing. Are you relying more on linking verbs, or are most of your verbs direct and precise action verbs?

5. Concise Diction

At the start of her essay "Mother Tongue," Amy Tan (p. 555) criticizes herself for writing that is "burdened . . . with nominalized forms, past perfect tenses, conditional phrases." Similarly, George Orwell (p. 1029) lambasts "the *-ize* and *de-* formations," preferring direct verbs. He also cautions against complex or unusual words that "dress up simple statements," preferring economy of language. Both writers argue for clear, authentic writing in the most straightforward language possible.

Nominalization

Nominalization is the process that changes a verb into its noun form. The verb *discuss* becomes *discussion*, for instance; the verb *depend* becomes *dependence*; *recognize* becomes *recognition*. The noun forms often result in wordiness, stiffness, or awkward constructions, as the following examples (with added color) show.

Chimamanda Ngozi Adichie (p. 920) could have written:

Still, I quickly **came to the realization** that some outfits I might have casually worn on a Nigerian university campus would simply be impossible now.

Instead of its noun form *realization*, she chose the verb *realized*:

Still, I **realized** quickly that some outfits I might have casually worn on a Nigerian university campus would simply be impossible now.

Similarly, Jia Tolentino (p. 824) writes:

Last September, a very twenty-first-century type of story **appeared** on the company blog of the ride-sharing app Lyft.

If she had used the nominalized version *appearance*, her sentence would be more wordy and less forceful or clear:

Last September, a very twenty-first-century type of story **made its appearance** on the company blog of the ride-sharing app Lyft.

These changes might seem very minor, but often they have a cumulative effect. In paragraph 39 of "Hellhole," by Atul Gawande (p. 1070), there are several other instances where he could have used the nominalized form but chose a strong verb instead. We've printed that paragraph below with the nominalized forms in brackets. Read the paragraph aloud and think about the effect of the strong, clear verbs as opposed to the nominalized forms.

Many prisoners find survival in physical exercise, prayer, or plans for escape. Many carry out elaborate mental exercises, building entire houses in their heads, board by board, nail by nail, from the ground up, or memorizing **[creating memories of]** team rosters for a baseball season. McCain recreated **[made recreations of]** in his mind movies he'd seen. Anderson reconstructed **[made reconstructions of]** complete novels from memory. Yuri Nosenko . . . made **[created simulated constructions of]** chess sets from threads and **[constructed a]** a calendar from lint (only to have them discovered and swept away).

Showy Vocabulary

Having a large and diverse vocabulary gives a writer many choices and usually results in more precise writing. Inexperienced writers, however, often believe that fancier is better and try to show off words they know. In "Mother Tongue" (p. 560), Amy Tan looks back on a first draft of a story containing this line:

That was my mental **quandary** in its **nascent** state.

With a sense of humor about herself, she tells us that when she first wrote the question-able sentence she believed that a sentence with such elevated vocabulary "would finally prove I had mastery over the English language," but she realized it was "a terrible line" that needed revision. One such revision might read:

That was my dilemma in its earliest state.

The key to figuring out if a word is too showy is to ask yourself if the fancy word — for example, *pernicious* — is more precise than the more ordinary word — for example, *fatal* — or if you think the former is simply more impressive than the latter. *Pernicious* seems appropriate when Patrick Radden Keefe (p. 1116) says:

It is a **pernicious** irony that a progressive legal instrument designed to help working-class defendants stay out of jail has been repurposed as a vehicle for facilitating corporate impunity.

On the other hand, *pernicious* is inappropriate in a sentence such as:

We all heard the pernicious gunshots.

The only reason you might laugh when someone says to you, "Felicitations on your natal day!" is that that expression is so much more pompous than "Happy birthday!" — and much less authentic. Like Tan, you must make your own decisions because these choices are not a matter of hard-and-fast rules but rather of how you assess your audience's expectations and the effect your language will have.

Rhetorical and Stylistic Strategy

Writers who use nominalizations, *de-* and *-ize* verbs, and overly complex or unusual words may think these choices add elegance or complexity to their prose and the ideas they express. However, the opposite is true. A writer who relies on expressions that fall into these categories gives the impression of insecurity and perhaps even insincerity. Whenever possible, follow the aphorism "Less is more": less complexity, less length, and less obscurity will lead you toward clear and readable prose with an authentic voice.

Exercises

EXERCISE 1

Identify awkward or pretentious diction in the following sentences, and revise each sentence as necessary to improve clarity.

1. A person who has a dependence on constant approval from others is usually insecure.
2. Let's have a discussion of the essay you read for homework.
3. Khaya finally came to the realization that she preferred research to teaching.
4. A key step toward losing weight is to make a reduction in the amount of food you consume.
5. A supercilious manager rarely contributes to a felicitous workplace.
6. Recommendations are being made by the faculty for the honor society.
7. Colin filled out his application to work part-time during the holidays.
8. We should give serious consideration to the possibility of traveling to China this summer.
9. The president has every intention of hearing both viewpoints.
10. Before finalizing the meeting, the chair of the group offered a plethora of ideas.
11. Before Derrell made a serious purchase, such as a car, he made a study of the competition.
12. Many benefits accrue from residing in a heterogeneous community.
13. The press release gave an explanation for the senator's stance on homeland security.
14. A recalcitrant attitude has resulted from too many of our colleagues becoming mired in quotidian concerns.
15. Maya has a lot of sympathy for students who experience test anxiety.

EXERCISE 2

In "Politics and the English Language" (p. 1028), George Orwell cites the following paragraph as an example of "bad writing." Revise the paragraph by eliminating pretentious diction and improving clarity.

On the one side we have the free personality: by definition it is not neurotic, for it has neither conflict nor dream. Its desires, such as they are, are transparent, for they are just what institutional approval keeps in the forefront of consciousness; another institutional pattern would alter their number and intensity; there is little in them that is natural, irreducible, or culturally dangerous. But *on the other side*, the social bond itself is nothing but the mutual reflection of these self-secure integrities. Recall the definition of love. Is not this the very picture of a small academic? Where is there a place in this hall of mirrors for either personality or fraternity?

EXERCISE 3

Find a text that contains examples of pretentious and awkward diction — it could be an article in a newspaper, a memo from an organization, or a speech. Identify the examples and explain their effect. Suggest ways to revise that would make the writing clearer. Do you think the writer is intentionally keeping the language obscure? If so, why might that be the case?

Part 2: Syntax and Structure

6. Parallel Structures

Sentences or parts of a sentence are parallel when structures within them take the same form. Parallelism is important at the level of the word, the phrase, and the clause.

Words

> Why should we live with such hurry and waste of life?
>
> — Henry David Thoreau (p. 532)

In this sentence, the words **hurry** and **waste**, both nouns, follow the preposition **with**; **hurry** and **waste** are parallel.

> In eternity there is indeed something true and sublime.
>
> — Henry David Thoreau (p. 536)

In this sentence, the words **true** and **sublime**, both adjectives, modify the pronoun **something**; **true** and **sublime** are parallel.

Phrases

> Men esteem truth remote, in the outskirts of the system behind the farthest star, before Adam and after the last man.
>
> — Henry David Thoreau (p. 536)

To modify the adjective **remote** in this first sentence, Thoreau uses parallel prepositional phrases: **in the outskirts, before the farthest star**, **before Adam**, and **after the last man.**

> The surviving wildlands of the world are not art museums. They are not gardens to be arranged and tended for our delectation. They are not recreation centers or reservoirs or sanatoriums or undeveloped sites of business opportunities — of any kind.
>
> — E. O. Wilson (p. 468)

Wilson uses a series of parallel phrases to emphasize what the wildlands **are not** — they are not museums, they are not gardens, and they are not recreations centers. By listing of all the things that some might think is the purpose of wildlands, Wilson lays the foundation to define just what he believes is their rightful function.

Clauses

> "Where I Lived, and What I Lived For"
>
> — Title of an essay by Henry David Thoreau (p. 531)

The title of Thoreau's essay consists of two parallel dependent, or subordinate, clauses; one begins with **where**, and the other begins with **what**.

[W]e perceive that only great and worthy things have any permanent and absolute existence, that petty fears and petty pleasures are but the shadow of the reality.

— Henry David Thoreau (p. 535)

The preceding example contains two parallel dependent clauses, each beginning with **that** and functioning as an object of the verb **perceive.**

If we are really dying, let us hear the rattle in our throats and feel cold in the extremities; if we are alive, let us go about our business.

— Henry David Thoreau (p. 537)

This example begins with a dependent clause (**If . . . dying**) followed by an independent, or main, clause (**let . . . extremities**); then, after the semicolon, Thoreau presents another dependent-independent construction, parallel to the first.

Alice Walker uses the parallel structure of clauses to underscore the historical disconnect between the dreams and reality of African American women (p. 875):

When we have pleaded for understanding, our character has been distorted; when we have asked for simple caring, we have been handed empty, inspirational appellations, then stuck in the farthest corner. When we have asked for love, we have been given children.

The structure of her sentences in this passage is similar from one to the next: a subordinate clause opening with "**when**," followed by an independent clause. In each case, she contrasts what the women sought and what they realized.

Lack of Parallelism

To fully appreciate the power of the parallelism created by Thoreau and Walker in the preceding examples, consider what happens when supposedly equal elements of a sentence do not follow the same grammatical or syntactical form — that is, when they are not parallel with each other.

Why should we live with such hurry and to waste life?

This version of Thoreau's sentence tries to modify the verb **should live** by coordinating a prepositional phrase, **with such hurry**, with an infinitive phrase, **to waste life**. The two phrases are not parallel with each other, and as a result, the sentence lacks balance and force.

Parallelism can be tricky when the elements — words, phrases, or clauses — are separated by modifiers or other syntactical elements. The following sentence may not at first glance seem to lack parallelism:

Let the word go forth from this time and place, to friend and foe alike, that the torch has been passed to a new generation of Americans—born in this century, tempered by war, disciplined by a hard and bitter peace, proud of our ancient heritage—and people who are unwilling to witness or permit the slow undoing of those human rights to which this nation has always been committed, and to which we are committed today at home and around the world.

In this long and fairly complicated sentence, the seemingly parallel structure of the words that describe "a new generation of Americans" adds to the force of the message. These young citizens were **born, tempered, disciplined, proud,** and, finally, **people who are unwilling.** While the first four descriptors are adjectives, the last one is a phrase that begins with a noun — and this break in parallelism weakens the overall point of the sentence. Note how a subtle change below — from **people who are unwilling** to **unwilling** — changes the rhythm of the sentence and does not disrupt its flow:

> Let the word go forth from this time and place, to friend and foe alike, that the torch has been passed to a new generation of Americans — born in this century, tempered by war, disciplined by a hard and bitter peace, proud of our ancient heritage — and unwilling to witness or permit the slow undoing of those human rights to which this nation has always been committed, and to which we are committed today at home and around the world.
>
> — John F. Kennedy (p. 1043)

Parallelism is often at its most effective at the level of the clause, but, again, it may be difficult to keep track. Let's use an example from Malcolm Gladwell (p. 575). Here it is without parallel structure:

> In other words, Facebook activism succeeds not by motivating people to make a real sacrifice but when people are motivated to do things even though they are not motivated enough to make a real sacrifice.

That sentence makes sense — once you've untangled all the motivations! — but the emphasis Gladwell intends is on the *not*: people are *not* motivated by x *but* by y. In the sentence that actually appears in his essay, he repeats the phrase *by motivating* and thus uses parallel structure to emphasize the contrast:

> In other words, Facebook activism succeeds not by motivating people to make a real sacrifice but by motivating them to do the things that people do when they are not motivated enough to make a real sacrifice.
>
> — Malcolm Gladwell (p. 575)

Rhetorical and Stylistic Strategy

Looking first at the parallel sentences at the beginning of this grammar workshop and then at the rewrites that lack parallelism, you can see that writers use parallelism on the level of the word, phrase, or clause as a rhetorical and stylistic device to emphasize ideas, to contrast ideas, or to connect ideas.

Following are the names, definitions, and examples of specific types of parallelism:

Anaphora: Repetition of a word or phrase at the beginning of successive phrases, clauses, or lines.

> But when you have seen vicious mobs lynch your mothers and fathers at will and drown your sisters and brothers at whim; when you have seen hate-filled policemen curse, kick, and even kill your black brothers and sisters; . . . when you are forever fighting a degenerating sense of "nobodiness" — then you will understand why we find it difficult to wait.
>
> — Martin Luther King Jr. (p. 518)

In this example, form follows function. Just as King is saying that African Americans have had to endure unjust treatment as they waited for full civil rights, this series of parallel clauses makes the reader wait — and wait — for the main point in the independent clause.

Antimetabole: Repetition of words in reverse order.

> We do not ride on the railroad; it rides upon us.
>
> — Henry David Thoreau (p. 532)

> Ask not what your country can do for you; ask what you can do for your country.
>
> — John F. Kennedy (p. 1045)

The example above from President Kennedy is, perhaps, his most famous quote. Part of what makes this quote so "quotable" is that the repetition inherent in antimetabole makes it dramatic and easy to remember. Because the pattern of the two clauses is so similar, the listener only needs to remember one pattern. Because that sentence pattern is repeated, it gives the listener two chances to understand the entire sentence and places extra emphasis on the second part. It is almost as if Kennedy is repeating a point for emphasis. Keep an eye out for antimetabole in modern political soundbites.

Antithesis: Opposition, or contrast, of ideas or words in a parallel construction.

> [F]reedom is never voluntarily given by the oppressor; it must be demanded by the oppressed.
>
> — Martin Luther King Jr. (p. 518)

> One has not only a legal but a moral responsibility to obey just laws. Conversely, one has a moral responsibility to disobey unjust laws.
>
> — Martin Luther King Jr. (p. 519)

> That's one small step for man, one giant leap for mankind.
>
> — Neil Armstrong

In all three of these examples, the parallel structure creates a clear comparison between two things in order to emphasize the difference between them. *Given by the oppressor* is contrasted in meaning and in placement with *demanded by the oppressed*. Notice also how the parallel prepositional phrases *by the oppressor* and *by the oppressed* call attention to the tension between oppressor and oppressed.

Zeugma: Use of two different words in a grammatically similar way that produces different, often incongruous, meanings.

> You are free to execute your laws and your citizens as you see fit.
>
> — *Star Trek: The Next Generation*

> My Palestinian cousins in Texas have beautiful brown little boys. Many of them haven't gone to school yet. And now they have this heavy word to carry in their backpacks along with the weight of their papers and books.
>
> — Naomi Shihab Nye (p. 1061)

In this example, the zeugma is created when the verb *to carry* takes different nouns as its direct object: the boys' *papers,* presumably their school work but also *this heavy word* — Nye's reference to "terrorist." While both of these words are nouns, they do not have the same meanings — *papers* refer to tangible physical objects, while *heavy word* refers to the more abstract concept of language and its emotional impact on children. In this way, Nye uses zeugma to draw a connection between two things that her audience might not otherwise think of as similar, emphasizing that, just like the tangible things these boys carry, negative words can impose a burden that is just as real.

Exercises

EXERCISE 1

Identify the parallel structure in words, phrases, or clauses in each of the following sentences.

1. A penny saved is a penny earned.

2. Was this act the work of a genius or a lunatic?

3. This situation is a problem not only for the students but also for the teachers.

4. Heather learned to work fast, ask few questions, and generally keep a low profile.

5. After you finish your homework and before you check your email, please do your chores.

EXERCISE 2

Correct the faulty parallelism in the following sentences.

1. My new exercise program and going on a strict diet will help me lose the weight I gained over the holidays.

2. As part of his accounting business, Rick has private clients, does some pro bono work, and corporations.

3. Try not to focus on the mistakes that you've made; what you've learned from them should be your focus instead.

4. A new job is likely to cause a person anxiety and working extra hours to make a good impression.

5. A competent physician will assess a patient's physical symptoms, and mental attitude will also be considered.

EXERCISE 3

Identify the parallel structures in the following sentences from Martin Luther King Jr.'s "Letter from Birmingham Jail" (p. 513), and explain their effect.

1. So I, along with several members of my staff, am here because I was invited here. I am here because I have organizational ties here. (para. 2)

2. We are caught in an inescapable network of mutuality, tied in a single garment of destiny. (para. 4)

3. Whatever affects one directly, affects all indirectly. (para. 4)

4. In any nonviolent campaign there are four basic steps: collection of the facts to determine whether injustices exist; negotiation; self-purification; and direct action. (para. 6)

5. An unjust law is a code that a numerical or power majority group compels a minority group to obey but does not make binding on itself. This is *difference* made legal. By the same token, a just law is a code that a majority compels a minority to follow and that it is willing to follow itself. This is *sameness* made legal. (para. 17)

6. Was not Jesus an extremist for love: "Love your enemies, bless them that curse you, do good to them that hate you, and pray for them which despitefully use you, and persecute you." Was not Amos an extremist for justice: "Let justice roll down like waters and righteousness like an ever-flowing stream." Was not Paul an extremist for the Christian gospel: "I bear in my body the marks of the Lord Jesus." Was not Martin Luther an extremist: "Here I stand; I cannot do otherwise, so help me God." And John Bunyan: "I will stay in jail to the end of my days before I make a butchery of my conscience." And Abraham Lincoln: "This nation cannot survive half slave and half free." And Thomas Jefferson: "We hold these truths to be self-evident, that all men are created equal. . . ." (para. 31)

7. If I have said anything in this letter that overstates the truth and indicates an unreasonable impatience, I beg you to forgive me. If I have said anything that understates the truth and indicates my having a patience that allows me to settle for anything less than brotherhood, I beg God to forgive me. (para. 49)

EXERCISE 4

The following paragraph is from Frederick Douglass's speech "The Blessings of Liberty and Education" (p. 198), delivered in 1894 at a dedication ceremony celebrating the opening of the Manassas Industrial School for Colored Youth. Find examples of parallel structure; identify whether the construction is a word, clause, or phrase; and explain its effect.

As man is the highest being on earth, it follows that the vocation of teacher is among the highest known to him. To properly teach it to enduce man's potential and latent greatness, to discover and develop the noblest, highest and best that is in him. In view of this fact, no man whose business it is to teach should ever allow himself to feel that his mission is mean, inferior, or circumscribed. In my estimation, neither politics nor religion present to us a calling higher than this primary business of unfolding and strengthening the powers of the human soul. It is a permanent vocation. Some know the value of education, by having it. I know its value by not having it. It is a want that begins with the beginning of human existence, and continues through all the journey of life. Of all the creatures that live and move and have their being on this green earth, man, at his birth, is the most helpless and the most in need of instruction. He does not know even how to seek his food. His little life is menaced on every hand. The very elements conspire against him. The cattle upon a thousand hills; the wolves and bears in the forest, all come into the world better equipped for life than does man. From first to last, his existence depends upon instruction.

EXERCISE 5

Each of the following sentences is an example of parallelism. Identify the type of parallelism, explain its effect, and then model a sentence of your own on the example.

1. To spend too much time in studies is sloth; to use them too much for ornament is affectation; to make judgment wholly by their rules is the humour of a scholar.

    — Francis Bacon

2. We must learn to live together as brothers or perish together as fools.

    — Martin Luther King Jr.

3. Flowers are as common here . . . as people are in London.

    — Oscar Wilde

4. Where justice is denied, where poverty is enforced, where ignorance prevails, and where any one class is made to feel that society is in an organized conspiracy to oppress, rob, and degrade them, neither persons nor property will be safe.

    — Frederick Douglass

5. He carried a strobe light and the responsibility for the lives of his men.

    — Tim O'Brien

7. Short Simple Sentences and Fragments

Short Simple Sentences

A simple sentence, strictly defined, has a subject and verb: it consists of one independent clause. A simple sentence may have a compound subject, a compound verb, a modifier, and an object or a complement, but it still is one independent clause.

The following examples of simple sentences appear in Barbara Ehrenreich's "Serving in Florida" (p. 759).

There is a problem, though.

But the chances of this are minuscule.

This must be Phillip's theory, anyway. Finally she tells me not to take her wrong.

What had I been thinking?

Sometimes simple sentences can be rather long:

The e-mails and phone messages addressed to my former self come from a distant race of people with exotic concerns and far too much time on their hands.

This example from Ehrenreich consists of twenty-eight words.

Sentence Fragments

A sentence fragment is an incomplete sentence, often the result of careless writing; an effective fragment, however, is an incomplete sentence that readers understand to be complete. Some fragments are missing a subject, a verb, or both; other fragments have a subject and verb but are dependent clauses. Consider the fragments in blue from Danielle Allen's "What is Education For?" (p. 252):

> Is it political equality that concerns us? **Social equality? Or economic equality only?**

The fragments, which ask questions, have neither a subject nor a verb. If we added a subject and verb to make it a complete sentence, it might read like this:

> Is it political equality that concerns us? Is it social equality? Or is it economic equality only?

Posing a question is a common use for fragments, but they can also be used to express doubt, surprise, shock, outrage, or to speak directly to the reader in an appeal to the audience, as in this example from Naomi Shihab Nye (p. 1060):

> The Palestinian grocer in my Mexican-American neighborhood paints pictures of the Palestinian flag on his empty cartons. He paints trees and rivers. He gives his paintings away. He says, "Don't insult me" when I try to pay him for a lemonade. Arabs have always been famous for their generosity. **Remember?**

This one-word fragment, another question, has neither a subject nor a complete verb, nor an object. If we added a subject and complete verb and direct object to make it a complete sentence, it might read like this:

> Arabs have always been famous for their generosity. Don't you remember that?

In the following example, E. O. Wilson concludes a paragraph with a fragment that provokes the reader to consider the implications of the entire paragraph (p. 468):

> We, like all other species, are the product of a highly successful and potentially important line that goes back all the way to the birth of humanity and beyond that for billions of years, to the time when life began. The same is true of the creatures still around us. They are champions, each and all. **Thus far.**

Lest you think that fragments are more common to contemporary than classic writing, consider this example from Thoreau:

> When a man is warmed by the several modes which I have described, what does he want next? **Surely not more warmth of the same kind, as more and richer food, larger and more splendid houses, finer and more abundant clothing, more numerous incessant and hotter fires, and the like.**

Here the fragment is used not to ask, but to answer a rhetorical question. The missing subject, *he*, and verb, *would [not] want*, are understood. The fragment creates a sense of impatience that conveys Thoreau's tone of exasperation.

In the following example from Ta-Nehisi Coates, each of the sentences, except the first, is a fragment. The passage shows how fragments can provide both economy of expression and emphasis (p. 992):

> Disembodiment is a kind of terrorism, and the threat of it alters the orbit of all our lives and, like terrorism, this distortion is intentional. **Disembodiment. The dragon that compelled**

> the boys I knew, way back, into extravagant theater of ownership. Disembodiment. The demon that pushed the middle-class black survivors into aggressive passivity, our conversation restrained in public quarters, our best manners on display, our hands never out of pockets, our whole manner ordered as if to say, "I make no sudden moves." Disembodiment. The serpent of school years, demanding I be twice as good, though I was but a boy.

The antecedent of "it" is "disembodiment." The fragments that follow emphasize the unrelenting effect of "disembodiment," personifying it as dragon, demon, and serpent. Turning each of these fragments (including the repetition of the word "disembodiment" itself) into complete sentences would lessen the dramatic force of Coates's point.

Fragments also suggest the rhythm and patterns of natural speech. Read the following sentences from "Get Off the Treadmill: The Art of Living Well in the Age of Plenty," in which Mark Greif reflects on the "necessities of life" (p. 350):

> For millennia, people have known what the necessities of life are. Food, shelter, and clothes, made or won by labour. Sex and reproduction, tied to the labour of childbirth and work of child rearing. Sleep.

The fragments deliver the tone of a natural mental reflection through casual expression, mimicking the way thoughts pop up in a person's mind as they ponder different aspects of an idea. If Greif had written the passage without using fragments, it might look something like this:

> For millennia, people have known what the necessities of life are. These necessities include food, shelter, and clothes, all of which are made or won by labour. They also include sex and reproduction, since they are tied to the labour of childbirth and work of child rearing. Finally, the necessities of life include sleep.

The result not only spoils the casual, conversational tone Greif wants, but also make the passage wordy and awkward by slowing the reader down for something that does not need to be explained.

Using Short Sentences Rhetorically

A series of simple sentences can become monotonous, but one or two short simple sentences can be rhetorically effective in a number of situations:

- after several long sentences
- as a summary of what the writer has just said
- as a transition between sentences or paragraphs

Essentially, one or two short simple sentences create emphasis by contrast. As a writer, when you juxtapose one or two short simple sentences with several longer ones, you call attention to the short simple ones. Consider this example from Bernie Sanders (p. 848):

> Today, there is universal access to free, public schools across the United States for kindergarten through twelfth grade. That didn't happen by presidential decree. It took populist pressure from the progressive movement, beginning in the 1890s, to make widespread

access to free public schools a reality. By 1940, half of all young people were graduating from high school. As of 2013, that number was 81 percent. But that achievement is no longer enough. A college degree is the new high school diploma.

Notice how the short simple sentences in the second half of the paragraph stand out after the longer sentences of the first part. Their similar structure adds even more emphasis. Also consider the sentences in this example from Claudia Rankine (p. 704):

There is no more exuberant winner than Serena Williams. She leaps into the air, she laughs, she grins, she pumps her fist, she points her index finger to the sky, signaling she's No. 1. Her joy is palpable. It brings me to my feet, and I grin right back at her, as if I've won something, too. Perhaps I have.

Notice how Rankine alternates short simple sentences with longer ones. The longer, second sentence illustrates the "exuberance" mentioned in the first. The shorter ones that follow slow the pace of the paragraph, moving the attention from Williams, the subject, to her effect on the writer, and also on the reader. The shift in structure effects a shift in emphasis that suits Rankine's purpose.

In some instances, writers choose to use sentence fragments, especially short ones. Although most of the time you will avoid fragments, occasionally you might use one for effect. What's important is that you use the fragment as you would use a short simple sentence — *deliberately*, for a special reason:

- to make a transition
- to signal a conclusion
- to economize expression
- to emphasize an important point

A word of caution, however. Use both short simple sentences and fragments sparingly. Used intentionally and infrequently, both can be effective. Overused, they lose their punch or become more of a gimmick than a valuable technique. Also, consider whether your audience will interpret a fragment as a grammatical error. If you are confident that your audience will recognize your deliberate use of a fragment, then use it. But if you think your instructor or reader will assume you made a mistake, then it's better to write a complete sentence. Again, if you use fragments infrequently, then your audience is more likely to know you're deliberately choosing what is technically an incomplete sentence.

Exercises

EXERCISE 1

Identify the simple sentences in the following selection from "In the Strawberry Fields" by Eric Schlosser (p. 798).

The few remaining labor camps for single men are grim places. I toured one that was a group of whitewashed buildings surrounded by chain-link fences and barbed wire. Desolate except for a rosebush in front of the manager's office, it looked like a holding pen or an old minimum-security prison. A nearby camp was reputed to be one of the best of its kind. Inside the barracks, the walls were freshly painted and the concrete floor was clean. A typical room was roughly twelve feet by ten feet, unheated, and occupied by four men. Sheets of plywood separated the steel cots. For $80 a week, a price far too high for most migrants, you got a bed and two meals a day. I've seen nicer horse barns.

Nevertheless, the labor camps are often preferable to the alternatives. When migrants stay in residential neighborhoods, they must pool their resources. In Watsonville three to four families will share a small house, seven or eight people to a room. Migrants routinely pay $100 to $200 a month to sleep in a garage with anywhere from four to ten other people. A survey of garages in Soledad found 1,500 inhabitants — a number roughly equal to one-eighth of the town's official population. At the peak of the harvest the housing shortage becomes acute. Migrants at the labor camps sometimes pay to sleep in parked cars. The newest migrant workers, who lack family in the area and haven't yet learned the ropes, often sleep outdoors in the wooded sections of Prunedale, trespassing, moving to a different hiding place each night. On hillsides above the Salinas Valley, hundreds of strawberry pickers have been found living in caves.

EXERCISE 2

Revise the selection in Exercise 1 by turning it into a series of short simple sentences. Then revise it again to eliminate the simple sentences entirely by turning every sentence into a compound, complex, or compound-complex sentence. How do your revisions change the effect? Read the original excerpt; then read your revisions aloud, and listen to the difference.

EXERCISE 3

Identify the short simple sentences and fragments in the following passage from "Why Can't a Smart Woman Love Fashion?" by Chimamanda Ngozi Adichie (p. 921). Discuss their effect.

A good publisher had bought my novel. I was 26 years old. I was eager to be taken seriously. And so began my years of pretense. I hid my high heels. I told myself that orange, flattering to my skin tone, was too loud. That my large earrings were too much. I wore clothes I would ordinarily consider uninteresting, nothing too bright or too fitted or too unusual. I made choices thinking only about this: How should a serious woman writer be? I didn't want to look as if I tried too hard. I also wanted to look older. Young and female seemed to me a bad combination for being taken seriously.

Once, I brought a pair of high heels to a literary event but left them in my suitcase and wore flats instead. An old friend said, "Wear what you want to; it's your work that matters." But he was a man, and I thought that was easy for him to say. Intellectually, I agreed with him. I would have said the same thing to someone else. But it took years before I truly began to believe this.

I am now 36 years old. During my most recent book tour, I wore, for the first time, clothes that made me happy. My favorite outfit was a pair of ankara-print shorts, a damask top, and yellow high-heel shoes. Perhaps it is the confidence that comes with being older. Perhaps it is the good fortune of being published and read seriously, but I no longer pretend not to care about clothes. Because I do care. I love embroidery and texture. I love lace and full skirts and cinched waists. I love black, and I love color. I love heels, and I love flats. I love exquisite detailing. I love shorts and long maxidresses and feminine jackets with puffy sleeves. I love colored trousers. I love shopping. I love my two wonderful tailors in Nigeria, who often give me suggestions and with whom I exchange sketches. I admire well-dressed women and often make a point to tell them so. Just because. I dress now thinking of what I like, what I think fits and flatters, what puts me in a good mood. I feel again myself — an idea that is no less true for being a bit hackneyed.

EXERCISE 4

Find six examples of short simple sentences or fragments in the selections included in this book. Explain their effect in the context of the paragraphs in which you find them.

---

8. Cumulative, Periodic, and Inverted Sentences

Most of the time, writers of English use the following standard sentence patterns:

Subject/Verb (SV)
My father cried.

— Terry Tempest Williams (p. 429)

Subject/Verb/Subject complement (SVC)
Even the streams were now lifeless.

— Rachel Carson (p. 398)

Subject/Verb/Direct object (SVO)
We believed her.

— Terry Tempest Williams (p. 429)

To make longer sentences, writers often coordinate two or more of the standard sentence patterns or subordinate one sentence pattern to another. (See the grammar workshop on subordination on p. 1186.) Here are examples of both techniques.

Coordinating patterns

          S   V   C
Yet every one of these disasters has actually happened somewhere, and many
          S   V   O
real communities have already suffered a substantial number of them.

— Rachel Carson (p. 398)

Subordinating one pattern to another

```
        S    V                              S    V        O
```
And when they arrived on the edge of Mercury, they carried all the butterflies of a summer
```
        I
```
day in their wombs.

— Terry Tempest Williams (p. 433)

The downside to sticking with standard sentence patterns, coordinating them, or subordinating them is that too many standard sentences in a row become monotonous. So writers break out of the standard patterns now and then by using a more unusual pattern, such as the cumulative sentence, the periodic sentence, or the inverted sentence.

When you use one of these unusual sentence patterns, you call attention to that sentence because its pattern contrasts significantly with those of the sentences surrounding it. You can use unusual sentence patterns to emphasize a point, as well as to control sentence rhythm, increase tension, or create a dramatic impact. In other words, using the unusual pattern helps you avoid monotony in your writing.

Cumulative Sentences

Cumulative, or so-called loose, sentences begin with a standard sentence pattern (shown here in blue) and adds multiple details *after* it. The details can take the form of subordinate clauses or different kinds of phrases. These details accumulate, or pile up — hence, the name *cumulative*.

The women moved through the streets as winged messengers, twirling around each other in slow motion, peeking inside homes and watching the easy sleep of men and women.

— Terry Tempest Williams (p. 433)

Here's another cumulative sentence, this one from Frederick Douglass (p. 204):

Attempts are being made to set aside the amendments of the Constitution; to wrest from us the elective franchise; to exclude us from respectable railroad cars; to draw against us the color line in religious organizations; to exclude us from hotels and to make us a proscribe class.

Look closely at this cumulative sentence by Lewis Thomas (p. 426):

We have grown into everywhere, spreading like a new growth over the entire surface, touching and affecting every other kind of life, incorporating ourselves.

The independent clause in the sentence focuses on the *growth* of humanity. Then the sentence accumulates a string of modifiers about the extent of that growth. Using a cumulative sentence allows Thomas to include all of these modifiers in one smooth sentence, rather than using a series of shorter sentences that repeat *grown*. Furthermore, this accumulation of modifiers takes the reader into the scene just as the writer experiences it, one detail at a time.

Periodic Sentences

Periodic sentences *begin* with multiple details and hold off a standard sentence pattern — or at least its predicate (shown here in blue) — until the end. The following periodic sentence by Lewis Thomas (p. 426) presents its subject, *human beings*, followed by an accumulation of modifiers, with the predicate coming at the end.

> **Human beings,** large terrestrial metazoans, fired by energy from microbial symbionts lodged in their cells, instructed by tapes of nucleic acid stretching back to the earliest live membranes, informed by neurons essentially the same as all the other neurons on earth, sharing structures with mastodons and lichens, living off the sun, **are now in charge, running the place, for better or worse.**

In the following periodic sentence, Ralph Waldo Emerson (p. 408) packs the front of the sentence with phrases providing elaborate detail:

> Crossing a bare common, in snow puddles, at twilight, under a clouded sky, without having in my thoughts any occurrence of special good fortune, **I have enjoyed a perfect exhilaration.**

The vivid descriptions engage us, so that by the end of the sentence we can feel (or at least imagine) the exhilaration Emerson feels. By placing the descriptions at the beginning of the sentence, Emerson demonstrates how nature can ascend from the physical ("snow puddles," "clouded sky") to the psychological ("without . . . thoughts of . . . good fortune"), and finally to the spiritual ("perfect exhilaration").

Could Emerson have written this as a cumulative sentence? He probably could have by moving things around — "I have enjoyed a perfect exhilaration as I was crossing . . ." — and then providing the details. In some ways, the impact of the descriptive detail would be similar.

Whether you choose to place detail at the beginning or end of a sentence often depends on the surrounding sentences. Unless you have a good reason, though, you probably should not put one cumulative sentence after another or one periodic sentence after another. Instead, by shifting sentence patterns, you can vary sentence length and change the rhythm of your sentences.

Finally, perhaps the most famous example of the periodic sentence in modern English prose is the fourth sentence in paragraph 14 of Martin Luther King Jr.'s "Letter from Birmingham Jail" (p. 518):

> But when you have seen vicious mobs lynch your mothers and fathers at will and drown your sisters and brothers at whim; when you have seen hate-filled policemen curse, kick, and even kill your black brothers and sisters; when you see the vast majority of your twenty million Negro brothers smothering in an airtight cage of poverty in the midst of an affluent society; when you suddenly find your tongue twisted and your speech stammering as you seek to explain to your six-year-old daughter why she can't go to the public amusement park that has just been advertised on television, and see tears welling up in her eyes when she is told that Funtown is closed to colored children, and see ominous clouds of inferiority beginning to form in her little mental sky, and see her beginning to distort her personality by developing an unconscious bitterness toward white people; when you have to concoct an answer for a five-year-old son who is asking, "Daddy, why do white people treat colored

people so mean?"; when you take a cross-country drive and find it necessary to sleep night after night in the uncomfortable corners of your automobile because no motel will accept you; when you are humiliated day in and day out by nagging signs reading "white" and "colored"; when your first name becomes "nigger," your middle name becomes "boy" (however old you are) and your last name becomes "John," and your wife and mother are never given the respected title "Mrs."; when you are harried by day and haunted by night by the fact that you are a Negro, living constantly at tiptoe stance, never quite knowing what to expect next, and are plagued with inner fears and outer resentments; when you are forever fighting a degenerating sense of "nobodiness" — then you will understand why we find it difficult to wait.

Inverted Sentences

In every standard English sentence pattern, the subject comes before the verb (SV). But if a writer chooses, he or she can invert the standard sentence pattern and put the verb before the subject (VS). This is called an inverted sentence. Here is an example:

Everywhere was a shadow of death.

— Rachel Carson (p. 397)

Being awarded the Nobel Prize for Literature is something I never could have imagined or seen coming.

— Bob Dylan (p. 361)

Perhaps in more than Phillis Wheatley's biological life is her mother's signature made clear.

— Alice Walker (p. 880)

The inverted sentence pattern slows the reader down, because it is simply more difficult to comprehend inverted word order. Take this example from Emerson's "Nature" (p. 408):

       V   S

In the woods, is perpetual youth.

In this example, Emerson calls attention to "woods" and "youth," minimizing the verb "is" and juxtaposing a place ("woods") with a state of being ("youth"). Consider the difference if he had written:

      S   V

Perpetual youth is in the woods.

This "revised" version is easier to read quickly, and even though the meaning is essentially the same, the emphasis is different. In fact, to understand the full impact, we need to consider the sentence in its context. If you look back at Emerson's essay "Nature," you'll see that his sentence is a short one among longer, more complex sentences. That combination of inversion and contrasting length makes the sentence — and the idea it conveys — stand out. It's clear that what is truly important to Emerson is the "woods," where "perpetual youth" may be found.

A Word about Punctuation

It is important to follow the normal rules of comma usage when punctuating unusual sentence patterns. In a cumulative sentence, the descriptors that follow the main clause need to be set off from it and from one another with commas, as in the example from Terry Tempest Williams on page 428. Likewise, in a periodic sentence, the series of clauses or phrases that precede the subject should be set off from the subject and from one another by commas, as in the Emerson example on page 208. When writing an inverted sentence, you may be tempted to insert a comma between the verb and the subject because of the unusual order — but don't.

Exercises

EXERCISE 1

For each of the following, craft a periodic, cumulative, or inverted sentence by filling in the blanks.

1. Among the tangle of weeds and brush were _____.

2. Hoping, knowing _____, but realizing _____, the candidate _____.

3. All his life he would remember that fateful moment when the fish _____, _____, _____.

4. If you _____ and if you _____, then _____.

5. Into the clouds soared _____.

6. Only when _____ will _____.

EXERCISE 2

In the following paragraph from "Hellhole" by Atul Gawande (p. 1070), the cumulative sentences are in blue. Rewrite them as periodic sentences. How does the sentence structure affect the focus, tone, and meaning of each of the three sentences? Discuss the rhetorical effectiveness of the way that Gawande decided to write them.

Many prisoners find survival in physical exercise, prayer, or plans for escape. **Many carry out elaborate mental exercises, building entire houses in their heads, board by board, nail by nail, from the ground up, or memorizing team rosters for a baseball season.** McCain recreated in his mind movies he'd seen. Anderson reconstructed complete novels from memory. **Yuri Nosenko, a K.G.B. defector whom the C.I.A. wrongly accused of being a double agent and held for three years in total isolation (no reading material, no news, no human contact except with interrogators) in a closet-size concrete cell near Williamsburg, Virginia, made chess sets from threads and a calendar from lint (only to have them discovered and swept away).**

EXERCISE 3

The following paragraph from *Biographical Notice of Ellis and Acton Bell* by Charlotte Brontë consists of four sentences: two simple declarative sentences, a cumulative sentence, and finally a periodic sentence. Keep the simple sentences as they are; then rewrite the periodic sentence as cumulative and the cumulative as periodic. Compare the two paragraphs. Discuss the relationship among the sentences in each paragraph and the rhetorical effect of syntax on meaning and tone.

> The bringing out of our little book was hard work. As was to be expected, neither we nor our poems were at all wanted; but for this we had been prepared at the outset; though inexperienced ourselves, we had read the experience of others. The great puzzle lay in the difficulty of getting answers of any kind from the publishers to whom we applied. Being greatly harassed by this obstacle, I ventured to apply to the Messrs. Chambers, of Edinburgh, for a word of advice; *they* may have forgotten the circumstance, but *I* have not, for from them I received a brief and business-like, but civil and sensible reply, on which we acted, and at last made a way.

EXERCISE 4

Identify each of the following sentences as periodic, cumulative, or inverted, and discuss the impact of using that pattern. (Each sentence is a direct quotation from essays in this book, so you might want to check the context of the sentence to appreciate its impact more fully. Note that some sentences use more than one unusual pattern.)

1. Similarly, chemicals sprayed on croplands or forests or gardens lie long in soil, entering into living organisms, passing from one to another in a chain of poisoning and death.
   — Rachel Carson (p. 399, para 12)

2. Among them are many that are used in man's war against nature.
   — Rachel Carson (p. 400, para. 16)

3. I see the spectacle of morning from the hill-top over against my house, from day-break to sun-rise, with emotions which an angel might share.
   — Ralph Waldo Emerson (p. 410, para. 16)

4. Not less excellent, except for our less susceptibility in the afternoon, was the charm, last evening, of a January sunset.
   — Ralph Waldo Emerson (p. 411, para. 17)

5. When a noble act is done, — perchance in a scene of great natural beauty; when Leonidas and his three hundred martyrs consume one day in dying, and the sun and moon come each and look at them once in the steep defile of Thermopylæ; when Arnold Winkelried, in the high Alps, under the shadow of the avalanche, gathers in his side a sheaf of Austrian spears to break the line for his comrades, are not these heroes entitled to add the beauty of the scene to the beauty of the deed?
   — Ralph Waldo Emerson (p. 412, para. 20)

6. Because just as important to me as her victories is her willingness to be an emotionally complete person while also being black.
   — Claudia Rankine, (p. 709, para. 17)

7. The oldest, easiest to swallow idea was that the earth was man's personal property, a combination of garden, zoo, bank vault and energy source, placed at our disposal to be consumed, ornamented or pulled apart as we wished.

— Lewis Thomas (p. 425, para. 4)

8. The impact on the rest of the biosphere is everywhere negative, the environment becoming unstable and less pleasant, our long-term future less certain.

— E. O. Wilson (p. 464, para. 2)

9. We, like all other species, are a product of a highly successful and potentially important line that goes back all the way to the birth of humanity and beyond that for billions of years, to the time when life began.

— E. O. Wilson (p. 468, para. 22)

10. This might turn out to be a special phase in the morphogenesis of the earth when it is necessary to have something like us, for a time anyway, to fetch and carry energy, look after new symbiotic arrangements, store up information for some future season, do a certain amount of ornamenting, maybe even carry seeds around the solar system.

— Lewis Thomas (p. 427, para. 14)

11. But those of us who are lucky enough to choose where we live would do well to ask ourselves, as part of that calculation, whether the choices we make for ourselves are necessarily the best for our home communities — and for the country.

— J. D. Vance (p. 602, para. 14)

12. And perhaps in Africa over two hundred years ago, there was just such a mother; perhaps she painted vivid and daring decorations in oranges and yellows and greens on the walls of her hut; perhaps she sang — in a voice like Roberta Flack's — *sweetly* over the compounds of her village; perhaps she wove the most stunning mats or told the most ingenious stories of all the village storytellers.

— Alice Walker (p. 880, para. 49)

13. My favorite memory is of a sunny Sunday morning, standing in front of her dressing table, my mother clasping her necklace around my neck, a delicate gold wisp with a fish-shape pendant, the mouth of the fish open as though in delighted surprise.

— Chimamanda Adichie (p. 920, para. 1)

14. Never mentioned or even implied is the shamefulness of a job that doesn't permit a worker to afford his own commute.

Jia Tolentino (p. 826, para. 8)

EXERCISE 5

The following selection is paragraph 14 of "Politics and the English Language" by George Orwell (p. 1033). Read the paragraph carefully, and identify whether the underlined sentences are cumulative or periodic. Discuss the effect of the syntax in each case. Then, imitating the structure of each, write a sentence of your own on a political issue.

In our time, political speech and writing are largely the defence of the indefensible. Things like the continuance of British rule in India, the Russian purges and deportations, the dropping of the atom bombs on Japan, can indeed be defended, but only by arguments which are too brutal for most people to face, and which do not square with the professed aims of the political parties. Thus political language has to consist largely of euphemism, question-begging and sheer cloudy vagueness. Defenceless villages are bombarded from the air, the inhabitants driven out into the countryside, the cattle machine-gunned, the huts set on fire with incendiary bullets: this is called *pacification*. Millions of peasants are robbed of their farms and sent trudging along the roads with no more than they can carry: this is called *transfer of population* or *rectification of frontiers*. People are imprisoned for years without trial, or shot in the back of the neck or sent to die of scurvy in Arctic lumber camps: this is called *elimination of unreliable elements.* Such phraseology is needed if one wants to name things without calling up mental pictures of them. Consider for instance some comfortable English professor defending Russian totalitarianism. He cannot say outright, "I believe in killing off your opponents when you can get good results by doing so." Probably, therefore, he will say something like this:

> While freely conceding that the Soviet regime exhibits certain features which the humanitarian may be inclined to deplore, we must, I think, agree that a certain curtailment of the right to political opposition is an unavoidable concomitant of transitional periods, and that the rigors which the Russian people have been called upon to undergo have been amply justified in the sphere of concrete achievement.

EXERCISE 6

Following are five examples of unusual sentence patterns. Choose two or three; then write your own sentences, using each example as a model.

1. Neither in its clearness, its colour, its fantasy of motion, its calmness of space, depth, and reflection or its wrath, can water be conceived by a low-lander, out of sight of sea.

   — John Ruskin, *Modern Painters*

2. There are hills, rounded, blunt, burned, squeezed up out of chaos, chrome and vermilion painted, aspiring to the snow-line.

   — Mary Austin, "The Land of Little Rain"

3. The yucca bristles with bayonet-pointed leaves, dull green, growing shaggy with age, tipped with panicles of fetid, greenish bloom.

   — Mary Austin, "The Land of Little Rain"

4. Scores of millions of years before man had risen from the shores of the ocean to perceive its grandeur and to venture forth upon its turbulent waves, this eternal sea existed, larger than any other of the earth's features, vaster than the sister oceans combined, wild, terrifying in its immensity and imperative in its universal role.

   — James Michener, *Hawaii*

5. Something will have gone out of us as a people if we ever let the remaining wilderness be destroyed; if we permit the last virgin forests to be turned into comic books and plastic cigarette cases; if we drive the few remaining members of the wild species into zoos or to extinction; if we pollute the last clear air and dirty the last clean streams and push our paved roads

through the last of the silence, so that never again will Americans be free in their own country from the noise, the exhausts, the stinks of human and automotive waste. And so that never again can we have the chance to see ourselves single, separate, vertical and individual in the world, part of the environment of trees and rocks and soil, brother to the other animals, part of the natural world and competent to belong in it.

— Wallace Stegner, "Wilderness Letter"

9. Subordination in Complex Sentences

One way that writers build longer sentences that are logical and clear is through subordination. **Subordination** is the use of a subordinating conjunction to make the meaning of one clause dependent on another clause. Although there are different types of subordination, involving both clauses and phrases, we are focusing here on the **complex sentence** — that is, a sentence formed by an **independent clause** and a **dependent clause** that begins with a subordinating conjunction.

Just because a clause is subordinate does not mean that what it says is unimportant. The ideas in both clauses contribute to the meaning of the sentence. It is the job of subordination to tell us how those ideas are related. This ability to connect ideas is the reason subordination is so effective; by using *because*, you tell your reader that one thing causes another; by using *when*, you indicate that two things are related chronologically. Thus, you can show the logical relationships in a rather lengthy sentence so that the length in no way impedes clarity.

Note the relationship between the dependent and independent clauses in the following sentence:

It is only when he acquires education, property, popularity and influence; only when he attempts to rise above his ancient level, where he was numbered with the beasts of the field, and aspires to be a man and a man among men, that he invites repression.

— Frederick Douglass (p. 205)

In this example, Douglass uses the subordinate clause to establish the chronology of events that lead to the main point of the sentence — that is, how human beings can be oppressed.

Subordinating conjunctions can be classified by the relationships they indicate:

Contrast or **Concession**: *although, even though, though, while, whereas*

While many Americans assume that most poor families live in subsidized housing, the opposite is true; nationwide, only one in four households that qualifies for rental assistance receives it.

— Matthew Desmond (p. 828)

Cause and Effect, or **Reason**: *because, since, so that*

But since I am a woman it is necessary in the twentieth century to explain why women have adopted revolutionary methods in order to win the rights of citizenship.

— Emmeline Pankhurst (p. 1018)

Condition: *if, once, unless, should*

> For instance, as college presidents begin to feel the heat about divestment, I've heard from several who say, privately, "I'd be more inclined to listen to kids **if they didn't show up at college with cars.**"
>
> — Bill McKibben (p. 443)

Time: *when, whenever, after, before, as, once, since, while, until*

> About five years ago, my two sisters and myself, **after a somewhat prolonged period of separation**, found ourselves reunited, and at home.
>
> — Charlotte Brontë (p. 895)

> **Since the great and terrible battle with which its name is associated and which has now passed into history as the birth of many battles,** no event has occurred here so important in its character and influence and so every way significant, as the event which we have this day met to inaugurate and celebrate.
>
> — Frederick Douglass (p. 194)

Punctuation

Correct punctuation adds clarity to longer sentences. The rule of thumb is: use a comma to set off a subordinate clause that opens a sentence unless that sentence is very short. Notice that each of the opening clauses in the preceding examples from Desmond, Brontë, and Douglass is set off with a comma. Note that the comma comes not after the subordinating conjunction but after the entire clause. If you read the examples aloud, you'll probably find yourself naturally pausing at the end of the subordinate clause. Of course, these rules are not rigid; they are matters of style. Notice that Bill McKibben, sharing his recollection of what several college presidents have said to him, decided not to interrupt the rhythm of the sentence with the pause of a comma before "if."

When the subordinate clause follows the independent clause, it gets a little trickier. Most of the time there is no comma at all because the dependent clause is necessary to the meaning of the sentence; this is called a *restrictive clause*. In some cases, however, the dependent clause adds information but is not necessary to the meaning of the sentence. For example:

> Well, there is only one answer to that alternative; there is only one way out of it, unless you are prepared to put back civilization two or three generations: you must give those women the vote.
>
> — Emmeline Pankhurst (p. 1024)

Here the subordinate clause is not essential to the meaning of the sentence, so it is set off with a comma; this is called a *nonrestrictive clause*. This all may sound a bit familiar to you. You may remember that in the discussion of appositives (p. 1145) we also talked about using commas with essential and nonessential elements. Here the rule is the same: essential information must be included and thus should not be set off with a comma; nonessential information that can be excluded should be set off with a comma.

Keep in mind that a dependent clause cannot stand alone. When you're using a dependent clause, be careful not to end up with a *sentence fragment* — that is, a dependent clause followed by a period. To correct a sentence fragment, simply attach it to the independent clause.

Rhetorical and Stylistic Strategy

One strategy is to use subordination to blend short sentences into more graceful, longer sentences. Consider the following two sentences:

> I must have seen a great number of old friends there. I cannot recall precisely who.

Both are complete sentences. As readers, we understand them easily. The relationship between the two is temporal. But consider the difference with the addition of a subordinating conjunction:

> I must have seen a great number of old friends there, though I cannot recall precisely who.
>
> — Ta-Nehisi Coates (p. 983)

Here the conjunction *though* indicates a contrast between the many old friends and difficulty of recognizing them in that specific context. Combining the two short sentences does not make the resulting sentence more difficult to understand; on the contrary, the longer sentence is easier to understand because it highlights the problem of the speaker's inability to remember who was there and hints at his disoriented emotional state.

A writer has to determine which clause should be dependent and which should be independent in a complex sentence. Although one clause is just as important as the other, the independent clause usually carries the most force, so you should put the idea you want to emphasize in an independent clause. Sometimes, the choice is obvious because the relationship is chronological or cause and effect, but other times either clause could be independent. Consider the following example:

> Most hostages survived their ordeal, Fletcher said, although relationships, marriages, and careers were often lost.
>
> — Atul Gawande (p. 1068)

What would the difference in effect have been if Gawande had written the following?

> Although relationships, marriages and careers were often lost, many hostages survived their ordeal.

Both examples indicate that the relationship between the two clauses is one of contrast. But the second example puts the emphasis on relationships, careers, and marriages when, in fact, the ordeal is the main event in the sentence and deserves more emphasis; the ordeal affected the hostages, not vice versa.

Where to place the subordinate clause is another choice a writer must make. For instance, examine once again the dependent clause in the following example:

> As long as she remains healthy, she will most likely tie and eventually pass Graf's 22 majors, regardless of what happens at the U.S. Open this year.
>
> — Claudia Rankine (p. 711)

The dependent clause ("As long as she remains healthy") could have been put at the end of the sentence or even in the middle. Why do you think Rankine placed it at the beginning? Perhaps placing the dependent clause in the middle of all those descriptive phrases would have muddled the sentence, making it difficult to decipher. As for putting it at the end, consider this example:

> She will most likely tie and eventually pass Graf's 22 majors, regardless of what happens at the U.S. Open this year, as long as she remains healthy.

The effect is different. In the original sentence, Rankine signals at the outset the high stakes of Serena's health: "As long as she remains healthy." However, if this clause appears at the end of the sentence, it gets buried. By the time we've read about the possibility of Serena's record breaking, her health — most important — seems beside the point.

Exercises

EXERCISE 1

Combine each of the following pairs of sentences into one sentence, using subordination. You might shift the order of the sentences, and in some cases you may have to change the wording slightly. Be sure to punctuate correctly.

1. The investigators have gathered and analyzed all the evidence. We may expect a full report.
2. Tom had listened to the music of Bruce Springsteen for years. He had no idea a live performance could be so exciting.
3. The team has suffered its share of injuries this year. It could have improved its performance by giving Flynn more time on the field.
4. We will not be able to resolve this situation amicably. We must be willing to leave our prejudices at the door.
5. The crime rate has escalated near the mall. Many people have stopped shopping at the mall.
6. Rose Henderson has the qualifications to become a first-rate senator. Most of us knew she did not have a good chance to be elected. We worked hard on her campaign.
7. Lan Cao is a law professor at the College of William and Mary. She is also the author of the novel *Monkey Bridge*.
8. I'm not feeling well today. I plan to leave the office early.
9. Apple offered a free iPod with every MacBook. Sales of the MacBook improved dramatically.
10. The affluent population of Dallas, Texas, is increasing steadily. Housing prices are rising beyond what someone with a middle-class salary can afford.
11. We all realize the necessity for increased security. We need to protect our civil liberties.
12. Thousands of vacationers travel to our national parks in search of solitude and fresh air. Other people prefer the excitement of casinos and amusement parks.

EXERCISE 2

Identify each subordinate clause in the following sentences and explain its effect.

1. I can never forget it. It was deeply impressed upon me. By my mother. Not upon my memory, but elsewhere.

   — Mark Twain (p. 313)

2. Mohammedans are Mohammedans because they are born and reared among that sect, not because they have thought it out and can furnish sound reasons for being Mohammedans; we know why Catholics are Catholics; why Presbyterians are Presbyterians; why Baptists are Baptists; why Mormons are Mormons; why thieves are thieves; why monarchists are monarchists; why Republicans are Republicans and Democrats, Democrats.

   — Mark Twain (p. 315)

3. This notice has been written because I felt it a sacred duty to wipe the dust off their gravestones, and leave their dear names free from soil.

   — Charlotte Brontë (p. 900)

4. It is the kiss that you do not have time to share, before she walks out of your life.

   — Ta-Nehisi Coates (p. 990)

5. If my life ended today, I would tell you it was a happy life — that I drew great joy from the study, from the struggle toward which I now urge you.

   — Ta-Nahesi Coates (p. 993)

6. If you spoke of fashion, it had to be either with apology or with the slightest of sneers.

   — Chimamanda Adichie (p. 921)

7. And because of men and women like John Lewis, Joseph Lowery, Hosea Williams, Amelia Boynton, Diane Nash, Ralph Abernathy, C.T. Vivian, Andrew Young, Fred Shuttlesworth, Dr. Martin Luther King Jr., and so many others, the idea of a just America and a fair America, an inclusive America, and a generous America — that idea ultimately triumphed.

   — Barack Obama (p. 1079)

8. And if we make such an effort, no matter how hard it may sometimes seem, laws can be passed, and consciences can be stirred, and consensus can be built.

   — Barack Obama (p. 1083)

9. If I have unjustly wrestled a plank from a drowning man, I must restore it to him though I drown myself.

   — Henry David Thoreau (p. 1002)

10. There will never be a really free and enlightened State, until the State comes to recognize the individual as a higher and independent power, from which all its own power and authority are derived, and treats him accordingly.

    — Henry David Thoreau (p. 1014)

EXERCISE 3

Analyze the use of subordinate clauses in the following passages. Pay particular attention to how the writer varies sentence patterns.

1. The man was a uniformed police officer. As a criminal defense attorney, I knew that my survival required careful, strategic thinking. I had to stay calm. I'd just returned home from my law office in a car filled with legal papers, but I knew the officer holding the gun had not

stopped me because he thought I was a young professional. Since I was a young, bearded black man dressed casually in jeans, most people would not assume I was a lawyer with a Harvard Law School degree. To the officer threatening to shoot me I looked like someone dangerous and guilty.

— Bryan Stevenson (p. 1102)

2. If my life ended today, I would tell you it was a happy life — that I drew great joy from the study, from the struggle toward which I now urge you. You have seen in this conversation that the struggle has ruptured and remade me several times over — in Baltimore, at The Mecca, in fatherhood, in New York. The changes have awarded me a rapture that comes only when you can no longer be lied to, when you have rejected the Dream. But even more, the changes have taught me how to best exploit that singular gift of study, to question what I see, then to question what I see after that, because the questions matter as much, perhaps more than, the answers.

— Ta-Nehisi Coates (p. 993)

3. As I have tried to show, modern writing at its worst does not consist in picking out words for the sake of their meaning and inventing images in order to make the meaning clearer. It consists in gumming together long strips of words which have already been set in order by someone else, and making the results presentable by sheer humbug. The attraction of this way of writing is that it is easy. It is easier — even quicker, once you have the habit — to say *In my opinion it is not an unjustifiable assumption that* than to say *I think*. If you use ready-made phrases, you not only don't have to hunt about for the words; you also don't have to bother with the rhythms of your sentences, since these phrases are generally so arranged as to be more or less euphonious. When you are composing in a hurry — when you are dictating to a stenographer, for instance, or making a public speech — it is natural to fall into a pretentious, Latinized style. Tags like *a consideration which we should do well to bear in mind* or *a conclusion to which all of us would readily assent* will save many a sentence from coming down with a bump. By using stale metaphors, similes, and idioms, you save much mental effort, at the cost of leaving your meaning vague, not only for your reader but for yourself.

— George Orwell (p. 1031)

4. A minority is powerless while it conforms to the majority; it is not even a minority then; but it is irresistible when it clogs by its whole weight. If the alternative is to keep all just men in prison, or give up war and slavery, the State will not hesitate which to choose. If a thousand men were not to pay their tax-bills this year, that would not be a violent and bloody measure, as it would be to pay them, and enable the State to commit violence and shed innocent blood. This is, in fact, the definition of a peaceable revolution, if any such is possible. If the tax-gatherer, or any other public officer, asks me, as one has done, "But what shall I do?" my answer is, "If you really wish to do anything, resign your office." When the subject has refused allegiance and the officer has resigned his office, then the revolution is accomplished.

— Henry David Thoreau (p. 1006)

EXERCISE 4

In a national magazine that features writing on cultural and political subjects, find a passage that is effective in its use of subordination. Discuss how each subordinate clause works to support the speaker's rhetorical purpose.

ARGUMENT STRATEGIES

Rogerian Argument

In Chapter 3 we looked at how Amy Domini used features of the Rogerian approach to argument in her article, "Why Investing in Fast Food May Be a Good Thing" (p. 75). In this appendix, we'll walk you through another. Following is an excerpt from "Letter to a South-ern Baptist Pastor: Salutation" in which biologist Edward O. Wilson appeals to common values as well as reason in order to establish common ground with his audience. As you read, be sure to keep in mind that Rogerian argument is based on the assumption that fully understanding an opposing position is essential to responding to it persuasively. The goal is to refute this opposing position in a way that accommodates rather than alienates.

from **Letter to a Southern Baptist Pastor**

E. O. WILSON

Dear Pastor:

We have not met, yet I feel I know you well enough to call you friend. First of all, we grew up in the same faith. As a boy I too answered the altar call; I went under the water. Although I no longer belong to that faith, I am confident that if we met and spoke privately of our deepest beliefs, it would be in a spirit of mutual respect and good will. I know we share many precepts of moral behavior. Perhaps it also matters that we are both Americans and, insofar as it might still affect civility and good manners, we are both Southerners.

I write to you now for your counsel and help. Of course, in doing so, I see no way to avoid the fun-damental differences in our respective worldviews. You are a literalist interpreter of Christian Holy Scripture. You reject the conclusion of science that mankind evolved from lower forms. You believe that each person's soul is immortal, making this planet a way station to a second, eternal life. Salva-tion is assured those who are redeemed in Christ.

I am a secular humanist. I think existence is what we make of it as individuals. There is no guarantee of life after death, and heaven and hell are what we create for ourselves, on this planet. There is no other home. Humanity originated here by evolution from lower forms over millions of years. And yes, I will speak plain, our ancestors were apelike animals. The human species has adapted physically and mentally to life on Earth and no place else. Ethics is the code of behavior we share on the basis of reason, law, honor, and an inborn sense of decency, even as some ascribe it to God's will.

For you, the glory of an unseen divinity; for me, the glory of the universe revealed at last. For you, the belief in God made flesh to save mankind; for me, the belief in Promethean fire seized to set men free. You have found your final truth; I am still searching. I may be wrong, you may be wrong. We may both be partly right.

Does this difference in worldview separate us in all things? It does not. You and I and every other human being strive for the same imperatives of security, freedom of choice, personal dignity, and a cause to believe in that is larger than ourselves. 5

Let us see, then, if we can, and you are willing, to meet on the near side of metaphysics in order to deal with the real world we share. I put it this way because you have the power to help solve a great problem about which I care deeply. I hope you have the same concern. I suggest that we set aside our differences in order to save the Creation. The defense of living Nature is a universal value. It doesn't rise from, nor does it promote, any religious or ideological dogma. Rather, it serves without discrimination the interests of all humanity.

Pastor, we need your help. The Creation — living Nature — is in deep trouble. Scientists estimate that if habitat conversion and other destructive human activities continue at their present rates, half the species of plants and animals on Earth could be either gone or at least fated for early extinction by the end of the century. A full quarter will drop to this level during the next half century as a result of climate change alone. The ongoing extinction rate is calculated in the most conservative estimates to be about a hundred times above that prevailing before humans appeared on Earth, and it is expected to rise to at least a thousand times greater or more in the next few decades. If this rise continues unabated, the cost to humanity, in wealth, environmental security, and quality of life, will be catastrophic.

Surely we can agree that each species, however inconspicuous and humble it may seem to us at this moment, is a masterpiece of biology, and well worth saving. Each species possesses a unique combination of genetic traits that fits it more or less precisely to a particular part of the environment. Prudence alone dictates that we act quickly to prevent the extinction of species and, with it, the pauperization of Earth's ecosystems — hence of the Creation.

You may well ask at this point, Why me? Because religion and science are the two most powerful forces in the world today, including especially the United States. If religion and science could be united on the common ground of biological conservation, the problem would soon be solved. If there is any moral precept shared by people of all beliefs, it is that we owe ourselves and future generations a beautiful, rich, and healthful environment.

I am puzzled that so many religious leaders, who spiritually represent a large majority of people around the world, have hesitated to make protection of the Creation an important part of their magisterium. Do they believe that human-centered ethics and preparation for the afterlife are the only things that matter? Even more perplexing is the widespread conviction among Christians that the Second Coming is imminent, and that therefore the condition of the planet is of little consequence. Sixty percent of Americans, according to a 2004 poll, believe that the prophecies of the book of Revelation are accurate. Many of these, numbering in the millions, think the End of Time will occur within the life span of those now living. Jesus will return to Earth, and those redeemed by Christian faith will be transported bodily to heaven, while those left behind will struggle through severe hard times and, when they die, suffer eternal damnation. The condemned will remain in hell, like those already consigned in the generations before them, for a trillion trillion years, enough for the universe to expand to its own, entropic death, time enough for countless universes like it afterward to be born, expand, and likewise die away. And that is just the beginning of how long condemned souls will suffer in hell — all for a mistake they made in choice of religion during the infinitesimally small time they inhabited Earth.

For those who believe this form of Christianity, the fate of ten million other life forms indeed does not matter. This and other similar doctrines are not gospels of hope and compassion. They are gospels of cruelty and despair. They were not born of the heart of Christianity. Pastor, tell me I am wrong!

However you will respond, let me here venture an alternative ethic. The great challenge of the twenty-first century is to raise people everywhere to a decent standard of living while preserving as much of the rest of life as possible. Science has

10

provided this part of the argument for the ethic: the more we learn about the biosphere, the more complex and beautiful it turns out to be. Knowledge of it is a magic well: the more you draw from it, the more there is to draw. Earth, and especially the razor-thin film of life enveloping it, is our home, our wellspring, our physical and much of our spiritual sustenance.

I know that science and environmentalism are linked in the minds of many with evolution, Darwin, and secularism. Let me postpone disentangling all this (I will come back to it later) and stress again: to protect the beauty of Earth and of its prodigious variety of life forms should be a common goal, regardless of differences in our metaphysical beliefs. . . .

You are well prepared to present the theological and moral arguments for saving the Creation. I am heartened by the movement growing within Christian denominations to support global conservation. The stream of thought has arisen from many sources, from evangelical to unitarian. Today it is but a rivulet. Tomorrow it will be a flood.

I already know much of the religious argument 15 on behalf of the Creation, and would like to learn more. I will now lay before you and others who may wish to hear it the scientific argument. You will not agree with all that I say about the origins of life — science and religion do not easily mix in such matters — but I like to think that in this one life-and-death issue we have a common purpose.

[2006]

E. O. Wilson begins by establishing common ground with his audience; he talks about the traditions and values that he and his reader share. He acknowledges their differing "world-views," yet he is confident that they might meet "in a spirit of mutual respect and good will" and that they "share many precepts of moral behavior" (para. 1). Wilson focuses on commonality while acknowledging differences, which he does with respect — and perhaps more importantly, without judgment. Throughout, he signals to his reader that he is trying to understand his reader's views. As he differentiates their positions he doesn't claim that his is superior: "I may be wrong, you may be wrong. We both may be partly right" (para. 4). He also mentions that he and his reader both strive for the "same imperatives" as they each serve "a cause to believe in that is larger than ourselves" (para. 5). Before he makes his case — that is, before he addresses his subject directly — he appeals to the good sense and ethical principles of his reader by acknowledging his or her power and authority directly: "I put it this way because you have the power to help solve a great problem about which I care deeply" (para. 6). Wilson knows that he will not convince his reader to share his exact thoughts and beliefs, but he does consider convincing that reader to join with him in pursuit of a common goal within reach: "I suggest that we set aside our differences," Wilson says, "in order to save the Creation" (para. 6). As he develops his argument, when he says, "Surely we can agree . . ." (para. 8), he's not saying that the reader will agree with his position or worldview but with his purpose, which is to save the natural world — what he knows his reader views as God's creation. This strategy is an important aspect of the Rogerian approach, which often demonstrates that the subject is an immediate and urgent one not only to the speaker and his or her audience, but to everyone.

As he continues his letter, Wilson identifies himself as a "secular humanist" and addresses fundamentalist views opposed to his own — views with which he thinks his reader might sympathize — but he casts them as too extreme to be reasonable in paragraphs 10 and 11. This strategy moves his reader's views closer to his own. Wilson then returns to what he calls "a common goal," that is, "protecting the beauty of Earth" (para. 14), or "the Creation," and its prodigious variety of life forms. He address the self-interest of his audience to suggest that everyone can gain if they address the issue of conservation and environmentalism from a common ground (para. 13). In his final paragraphs, Wilson acknowledges positive signs from the religious community regarding conservation as a movement toward common ground, and concludes with humility, understanding, and sympathy toward his audience as they share "a common purpose" (para. 15).

From start to finish, Wilson's piece is a model of Rogerian argument. His approach suggests that only by finding and recognizing common ground can the two sides work together — not to win the argument, but to work on a problem together and find a solution that is acceptable to both sides.

ACTIVITY

Following is an excerpt from "Truth: Remarks on the Removal of Confederate Monuments in New Orleans," a speech given by Mayor Mitch Landrieu in 2017. Analyze how Landrieu uses Rogerian tactics to make his argument. What common ground does he establish with his audience? How does he show that he fully understands the opposing position? How does his refutation of this position avoid alienating his audience?

---

from Truth
Remarks on the Removal of Confederate Monuments in New Orleans

---

MITCH LANDRIEU

Thank you for coming.

The soul of our beloved City is deeply rooted in a history that has evolved over thousands of years; rooted in a diverse people who have been here together every step of the way — for both good and for ill.

It is a history that holds in its heart the stories of Native Americans: the Choctaw, Houma Nation, the Chitimacha. Of Hernando de Soto, Robert Cavelier, Sieur de La Salle, the Acadians, the Islenos, the enslaved people from Senegambia, Free People of Color, the Haitians, the Germans, both the empires of France and Spain. The Italians, the Irish, the Cubans, the south and central Americans, the Vietnamese and so many more.

You see: New Orleans is truly a city of many nations, a melting pot, a bubbling cauldron of many cultures.

There is no other place quite like it in the world that so eloquently exemplifies the uniquely American motto: *e pluribus unum* — out of many we are one.

But there are also other truths about our city that we must confront. New Orleans was America's largest slave market: a port where hundreds of thousands of souls were brought, sold and shipped up the Mississippi River to lives of forced labor, of misery, of rape, of torture.

America was the place where nearly 4,000 of our fellow citizens were lynched, 540 alone in Louisiana; where the courts enshrined "separate but equal"; where Freedom riders coming to New Orleans were beaten to a bloody pulp.

So when people say to me that the monuments in question are history, well what I just described is real history as well, and it is the searing truth.

And it immediately begs the questions: why there are no slave ship monuments, no prominent markers on public land to remember the lynchings or the slave blocks; nothing to remember this long chapter of our lives; the pain, the sacrifice, the shame — all of it happening on the soil of New Orleans.

5

1195

So for those self-appointed defenders of his- 10
tory and the monuments, they are eerily silent
on what amounts to this historical malfeasance,
a lie by omission.

There is a difference between remembrance
of history and reverence of it. For America and
New Orleans, it has been a long, winding road,
marked by great tragedy and great triumph. But
we cannot be afraid of our truth.

As President George W. Bush said at the
dedication ceremony for the National Museum
of African American History & Culture, "A great
nation does not hide its history. It faces its flaws
and corrects them."

So today I want to speak about why we
chose to remove these four monuments to the
Lost Cause of the Confederacy, but also how
and why this process can move us towards healing and understanding of each other.

So, let's start with the facts.

The historic record is clear: the Robert E. 15
Lee, Jefferson Davis, and P.G.T. Beauregard statues were not erected just to honor these men,
but as part of the movement which became
known as The Cult of the Lost Cause. This
"cult" had one goal — through monuments and
through other means — to rewrite history to
hide the truth, which is that the Confederacy
was on the wrong side of humanity.

First erected over 166 years after the founding of our city and 19 years after the end of the
Civil War, the monuments that we took down
were meant to rebrand the history of our city
and the ideals of a defeated Confederacy.

It is self-evident that these men did not fight
for the United States of America. They fought
against it. They may have been warriors, but in
this cause they were not patriots.

These statues are not just stone and metal.
They are not just innocent remembrances of a
benign history. These monuments purposefully
celebrate a fictional, sanitized Confederacy;
ignoring the death, ignoring the enslavement,
and the terror that it actually stood for.

After the Civil War, these statues were a part
of that terrorism as much as a burning cross on
someone's lawn; they were erected purposefully to
send a strong message to all who walked in their
shadows about who was still in charge in this city.

Should you have further doubt about the 20
true goals of the Confederacy, in the very weeks
before the war broke out, the Vice President of
the Confederacy, Alexander Stephens, made
it clear that the Confederate cause was about
maintaining slavery and white supremacy.

He said in his now famous "Cornerstone
speech" that the Confederacy's "cornerstone rests
upon the great truth, that the negro is not equal
to the white man; that slavery — subordination
to the superior race — is his natural and normal
condition. This, our new government, is the first,
in the history of the world, based upon this great
physical, philosophical, and moral truth."

Now, with these shocking words still ringing in your ears, I want to try to gently peel
from your hands the grip on a false narrative of
our history that I think weakens us and make
straight a wrong turn we made many years ago
so we can more closely connect with integrity to
the founding principles of our nation and forge
a clearer and straighter path toward a better city
and more perfect union. . . .

As clear as it is for me today — for a long time,
even though I grew up in one of New Orleans'
most diverse neighborhoods, even with my family's long proud history of fighting for civil rights — I
must have passed by those monuments a million
times without giving them a second thought.

So I am not judging anybody, I am not
judging people. We all take our own journey on
race. I just hope people listen like I did when
my dear friend Wynton Marsalis helped me see
the truth. He asked me to think about all the
people who have left New Orleans because of
our exclusionary attitudes.

Another friend asked me to consider these 25
four monuments from the perspective of an
African American mother or father trying to

explain to their fifth grade daughter who Robert E. Lee is and why he stands atop of our beautiful city. Can you do it?

Can you look into that young girl's eyes and convince her that Robert E. Lee is there to encourage her? Do you think she will feel inspired and hopeful by that story? Do these monuments help her see a future with limitless potential? Have you ever thought that if her potential is limited, yours and mine are too?

We all know the answer to these very simple questions.

When you look into this child's eyes is the moment when the searing truth comes into focus for us. This is the moment when we know what is right and what we must do. We can't walk away from this truth.

And I knew that taking down the monuments was going to be tough, but you elected me to do the right thing, not the easy thing and this is what that looks like. So relocating these Confederate monuments is not about taking something away from someone else. This is not about politics, this is not about blame or retaliation. This is not a naïve quest to solve all our problems at once.

This is, however, about showing the whole world that we as a city and as a people are able to acknowledge, understand, reconcile and, most importantly, choose a better future for ourselves, making straight what has been crooked and making right what was wrong. 30

Otherwise, we will continue to pay a price with discord, with division, and yes, with violence.

To literally put the Confederacy on a pedestal in our most prominent places of honor is an inaccurate recitation of our full past, it is an affront to our present, and it is a bad prescription for our future.

History cannot be changed. It cannot be moved like a statue. What is done is done. The Civil War is over, and the Confederacy lost and we are better for it. Surely we are far enough removed from this dark time to acknowledge that the cause of the Confederacy was wrong.

And in the second decade of the 21st century, asking African Americans — or anyone else — to drive by property that they own; occupied by reverential statues of men who fought to destroy the country and deny that person's humanity seems perverse and absurd.

Centuries-old wounds are still raw because they never healed right in the first place. 35

Here is the essential truth: we are better together than we are apart. Indivisibility is our essence. Isn't this the gift that the people of New Orleans have given to the world? . . .

We have not erased history; we are becoming part of the city's history by righting the wrong image these monuments represent and crafting a better, more complete future for all our children and for future generations.

And unlike when these Confederate monuments were first erected as symbols of white supremacy, we now have a chance to create not only new symbols, but to do it together, as one people.

In our blessed land we all come to the table of democracy as equals.

We have to reaffirm our commitment to a future where each citizen is guaranteed the uniquely American gifts of life, liberty and the pursuit of happiness. 40

That is what really makes America great and today it is more important than ever to hold fast to these values and together say a self-evident truth that out of many we are one. That is why today we reclaim these spaces for the United States of America.

Because we are one nation, not two; indivisible with liberty and justice for all, not some. We all are part of one nation, all pledging allegiance to one flag, the flag of the United States of America. And New Orleanians are in, all of the way.

It is in this union and in this truth that real patriotism is rooted and flourishes.

Instead of revering a 4-year brief historical aberration that was called the Confederacy we can celebrate all 300 years of our rich, diverse history as a place named New Orleans and set the tone for the next 300 years.

After decades of public debate, of anger, of anxiety, of anticipation, of humiliation and of frustration. After public hearings and approvals from three separate community led commissions. After two robust public hearings and a 6–1 vote by the duly elected New Orleans City Council. After review by 13 different federal and state judges. The full weight of the legislative, executive, and judicial branches of government has been brought to bear and the monuments in accordance with the law have been removed. 45

So now is the time to come together and heal and focus on our larger task. Not only building new symbols, but making this city a beautiful manifestation of what is possible and what we as a people can become.

Let us remember the once exiled, imprisoned and now universally loved Nelson Mandela and what he said after the fall of apartheid. "If the pain has often been unbearable and the revelations shocking to all of us, it is because they indeed bring us the beginnings of a common understanding of what happened and a steady restoration of the nation's humanity."

So before we part let us again state the truth clearly.

The Confederacy was on the wrong side of history and humanity. It sought to tear apart our nation and subjugate our fellow Americans to slavery. This is the history we should never forget and one that we should never again put on a pedestal to be revered.

As a community, we must recognize the significance of removing New Orleans' Confederate monuments. It is our acknowledgment that now is the time to take stock of, and then move past, a painful part of our history. Anything less would render generations of courageous struggle and soul-searching a truly lost cause. 50

Anything less would fall short of the immortal words of our greatest President Abraham Lincoln, who with an open heart and clarity of purpose calls on us today to unite as one people when he said:

"With malice toward none, with charity for all, with firmness in the right as God gives us to see the right, let us strive on to finish the work we are in, to bind up the nation's wounds, to do all which may achieve and cherish: a just and lasting peace among ourselves and with all nations."

Thank you.

The Toulmin Model

In Chapter 3, we discussed the Toulmin model as a way to analyze and understand how argument works — particularly how looking at an author's assumptions can help us see the logical progression of his or her argument.

Remember, the Toulmin model has six elements: claim, support, warrant, backing, qualifier, and reservation:

- **Claim:** an arguable assertion
- **Support (or evidence):** evidence for the validity of the claim
- **Warrant (or assumption):** an assumption linking the claim to the evidence
- **Backing:** evidence that adds to the authority of the warrant
- **Qualifier:** a reminder that the claim is arguable rather than absolute (for example, *usually, probably, maybe, in most cases, most likely*)
- **Reservation:** an explanation of the terms and conditions necessitated by the qualifier

The Toulmin model is particularly helpful for analyzing older works with archaic diction and complex syntax. Following is an excerpt from an eighteenth-century text entitled *Rights of Man*, a book by Thomas Paine that was published in 1791. In it, Paine refers to the newly established United States of America as an example to illustrate his support for revolution as a means of overthrowing tyranny.

from Rights of Man

THOMAS PAINE

If we look back to the riots and tumults, which at various times have happened in England, we shall find, that they did not proceed from the want of a government, but that government was itself the generating cause; instead of consolidating society, it divided it; it deprived it of its natural cohesion, and engendered discontents and disorders, which otherwise would not have existed. In those associations which men promiscuously form for the purpose of trade, or of any concern, in which government is totally out of the question, and in which they act merely on the principles of society, we see how naturally the various parties unite; and this shows, by comparison, that governments, so far from being always the cause or means of order, are often the destruction of it. The riots of 1780 had no other source than the remains of those prejudices, which the government itself had encouraged. But with respect to England there are also other causes.

Excess and inequality of taxation, however disguised in the means, never fail to appear in their effects. As a great mass of the community are thrown thereby into poverty and discontent, they are constantly on the brink of commotion; and deprived, as they unfortunately are, of the means of information, are easily heated to outrage. Whatever the apparent cause of any riots may be, the real one is always want of happiness. It shows that something is wrong in the system of government, that injures the felicity by which society is to be preserved.

But as fact is superior to reasoning, the instance of America presents itself to confirm these observations. If there is a country in the world, where concord, according to common calculation, would be least expected, it is America. Made up, as it is, of people from different nations, accustomed to different forms and habits of government, speaking different languages, and more different in their modes of worship, it would appear that the union of such a people was impracticable; but by the simple operation of constructing government on the principles of society and the rights of man, every difficulty retires, and all the parts are brought into cordial unison. There the poor are not oppressed, the rich are not privileged. Industry is not mortified by the splendid extravagance of a court rioting at its expense. Their taxes are few, because their government is just; and as there is nothing to render them wretched, there is nothing to engender riots and tumults. . . .

One of the great advantages of the American revolution has been, that it led to a discovery of the principles, and laid open the imposition, of governments. All the revolutions till then had been worked within the atmosphere of a court, and never on the great floor of a nation. The parties were always of the class of courtiers; and whatever was their rage for reformation, they carefully preserved that fraud of the profession.

In all cases they took care to represent government as a thing made up of mysteries, which only themselves understood; and they hid from the understanding of the nation, the only thing that was beneficial to know, namely, *That government is nothing more than a national association acting on the principles of society.*

5

Annotation

To respond thoughtfully to Paine's ideas, you must analyze his argument to determine his claims and stated position. Applying the Toulmin model can help you to recognize assumptions that underlie Paine's position, help you express abstract ideas, and also clearly identify his main point.

Paine begins with an idea that might seem ironic to us now.

If there is a country in the world, where concord, according to common calculation, would be least expected, it is America.

Sentence 2 has two arguments. Using the Toulmin method, the first is: "Because America is made up of diverse people from different backgrounds, values, and customs, therefore unity among them would not work in practice, since people of different ethnicities, languages, and cultures aren't expected to get along."

Made up, as it is, of people from different nations, accustomed to different forms and habits of government, speaking different languages, and more different in their modes of worship, it would appear that the union of such a people was impracticable; but by the simple operation of constructing government on the principles of society and the rights of man, every difficulty retires, and all the parts are brought into cordial unison. There, the poor are not oppressed, the rich are not privileged. Industry is not mortified by the splendid extravagance of a court rioting at its expense. Their taxes are few, because their government is just; and as there is nothing to render them wretched, there is nothing to engender riots and tumults. . . .

The next argument in that sentence may be paraphrased: "Because in America government is based on the principles of society and the rights of man, people of diverse values and culture may be brought into cordial unison, since fairness promotes cooperation and justice trumps prejudice and conflict."

At the end of the paragraph the argument runs as follows: "Because equality obviates wretchedness, therefore it also engenders peace, since unrest results from inequity. "

Sentences 3 and 4 present the results of the second assumption and claim: equality, restraint, and moderation.

One of the great advantages of the American revolution has been, that it led to a discovery of the principles, and laid open the imposition, of governments. All the revolutions till then had been worked within the atmosphere of a court, and never on the grand floor of a nation. The parties were always of the class of courtiers; and whatever was their rage for reformation, they carefully preserved the fraud of the profession.

In all cases they took care to represent government as a thing made up of mysteries, which only themselves understood; and they hid from the understanding of the nation the only thing that was beneficial to know, namely, That government is nothing more than a national association adding on the principles of society.

Here Paine discusses the influence that the American Revolution had on the nature of government as perceived by the governed. Applying the Toulmin method, we would make this paraphrase: "Because the rulers of nations had traditionally kept the nature of government hidden from the governed, it took the American Revolution to expose the deceits of the rulers and to reveal the true nature of government, since it was effected not from within the ruling class but from the people they ruled."

The following op-ed, by David Brooks, appeared in a 2017 issue of the *New York Times*. Using the Toulmin model, annotate the essay, being sure to identify the claim, support, warrant, backing, qualifier, and reservation.

How Covenants Make Us

DAVID BROOKS

When you think about it, there are four big forces coursing through modern societies. Global migration is leading to demographic diversity. Economic globalization is creating wider opportunity but also inequality. The Internet is giving people more choices over what to buy and pay attention to. A culture of autonomy valorizes individual choice and self-determination.

All of these forces have liberated the individual, or at least well-educated individuals, but they have been bad for national cohesion and the social fabric. Income inequality challenges economic cohesion as the classes divide. Demographic diversity challenges cultural cohesion as different ethnic groups rub against one another. The emphasis on individual choice challenges community cohesion and settled social bonds.

The weakening of the social fabric has created a range of problems. Alienated young men join ISIS so they can have a sense of belonging. Isolated teenagers shoot up schools. Many people grow up in fragmented, disorganized neighborhoods. Political polarization grows because people often don't interact with those on the other side. Racial animosity stubbornly persists.

Odder still, people are often plagued by a sense of powerlessness, a loss of efficacy. The liberation of the individual was supposed to lead to mass empowerment. But it turns out that people can effectively pursue their goals only when they know who they are — when they have firm identities.

Strong identities can come only when peo- 5 ple are embedded in a rich social fabric. They can come only when we have defined social roles — father, plumber, Little League coach. They can come only when we are seen and admired by our neighbors and loved ones in a certain way. As Ralph Waldo Emerson put it, "Other men are lenses through which we read our own minds."

You take away a rich social fabric and what you are left with is people who are uncertain about who they really are. It's hard to live daringly when your very foundation is fluid and at risk.

We're not going to roll back the four big forces coursing through modern societies, so the question is how to reweave the social fabric in the face of them. In a globalizing, diversifying world, how do we preserve individual freedom while strengthening social solidarity?

In her new book "Commonwealth and Covenant," Marcia Pally of N.Y.U. and Fordham offers a clarifying concept. What we want, she suggests, is "separability amid situatedness." We want to go off and create and explore and experiment with new ways of thinking and living. But we also want to be situated — embedded in loving families and enveloping communities, thriving within a healthy cultural infrastructure that provides us with values and goals.

Creating situatedness requires a different way of thinking. When we go out and do a deal, we make a contract. When we are situated within something it is because we have made a covenant. A contract protects interests, Pally notes, but a covenant protects relationships. A covenant exists between people who understand they are part of one another. It involves a vow to serve the relationship that is sealed by love: Where you go, I will go. Where you stay, I will stay. Your people shall be my people.

People in a contract provide one another services, but people in a covenant delight in offering gifts. Out of love of country, soldiers offer the gift of their service. Out of love of their craft, teachers offer students the gift of their attention.

The social fabric is thus rewoven in a romantic frame of mind. During another period of national fragmentation, Abraham Lincoln aroused a refreshed love of country. He played upon the mystic chords of memory and used the Declaration of Independence as a unifying scripture and guide.

These days the social fabric will be repaired by hundreds of millions of people making local covenants — widening their circles of

attachment across income, social and racial divides. But it will probably also require leaders drawing upon American history to revive patriotism. They'll tell a story that includes the old themes. That we're a universal nation, the guarantor of stability and world order. But it will transcend the old narrative and offer an updated love of America.

In an interview with Bill Maher last month, Senator Cory Booker nicely defined patriotism by contrasting it with mere tolerance. Tolerance, he said, means, "I'm going to stomach your right to be different, but if you disappear off the face of the earth I'm no worse off." Patriotism, on the other hand, means "love of country, which necessitates love of each other, that we have to be a nation that aspires for love, which recognizes that you have worth and dignity and I need you. You are part of my whole, part of the promise of this country."

That emotion is what it means to be situated in a shared national life.

10

PRACTICE AP® ENGLISH LANGUAGE AND COMPOSITION EXAM

MULTIPLE-CHOICE QUESTIONS

Questions 1–15. Read the following passage carefully before you choose your answers.

The following passage is excerpted from "Education" by Ralph Waldo Emerson (1878).

The two points in a boy's training are, to keep his *naturel* and train off all but that — to keep his *naturel*, but stop off his uproar, fooling, and horseplay — keep his nature and arm it with knowledge in the very direction to which it points. Here are the two capital facts, Genius and Drill. This first is the inspiration in the well-born healthy child, the new perception he has of nature. Somewhat he sees in forms or hears in music or apprehends in mathematics, or believes practicable in mechanics or possible in political society, which no one else sees or hears or believes. This is the perpetual romance of new life, the invasion of God into the old dead world, when he sends into quiet houses a young soul with a thought which is not met, looking for something which is not there, but which ought to be there: the thought is dim but it is sure, and he casts about restless for means and masters to verify it; he makes wild attempts to explain himself and invoke the aid and con-sent of the by-standers. Baffled for want of lan-guage and methods to convey his meaning, not yet clear to himself, he conceives that thought not in this house or town, yet in some other house or town is the wise master who can put him in possession of the rules and instruments to execute his will. Happy this child with a bias, with a thought which entrances him, leads him, now into deserts now into cities, the fool of an idea. Let him follow it in good and in evil report, in good or bad company; it will justify itself; it will lead him at last into the illustrious society of the lovers of truth.

In London, in a private company, I became acquainted with a gentleman, Sir Charles Fellowes, who, being at Xanthos, in the Aegean Sea, had seen a Turk point with his staff to some carved work on the corner of a stone almost buried in the soil. Fellowes scraped away the dirt, was struck with the beauty of the sculptured ornaments, and, looking about him, observed more blocks and fragments like this. He returned to the spot, procured laborers and uncovered many blocks. He went back to England, bought a Greek grammar and learned the language; he read history and studied ancient art to explain his stones; he interested Gibson the sculptor; he invoked the assistance of the English Government; he called in the succor of Sir Humphry Davy to analyze the pigments; of experts in coins, of scholars and connoisseurs; and at last in his third visit brought home to England such statues and marble reliefs and such careful plans that he was able to reconstruct, in the British Museum where it now stands, the perfect model of the Ionic trophy-monument, fifty years older than the Parthenon of Athens, and which had been destroyed by earthquakes, then by iconoclast Christians, then by savage Turks. But mark that in the task he had achieved an excellent education, and become associated with distinguished scholars whom he had interested in his pursuit; in short, had formed a college for himself; the enthusiast had found the master, the masters, whom he sought. Always genius seeks genius, desires nothing so much as to be a pupil and to find those who can lend it aid to perfect itself.

Nor are the two elements, enthusiasm and drill, incompatible. Accuracy is essential to beauty. The very definition of the intellect is Aristotle's: "that by which we know terms or boundaries." Give a boy accurate perceptions. Teach him the difference between the similar and the same. Make him call things by their right names. Pardon in him no blunder. Then he will give you solid satisfaction as long as he lives. It is better to teach the child arithmetic and Latin grammar than rhetoric or moral philosophy, because they require exactitude of performance; it is made certain that the lesson is mastered, and that power of performance is worth more than the knowledge. He can learn anything which is important to him now that the power to learn is secured: as mechanics say, when one has learned the use of tools, it is easy to work at a new craft.

---

1. What does paragraph 1 imply about the speaker's beliefs regarding nature?

   a. Nature is a force that may lead humans into folly.

   b. Nature is an expression of God in humans and will lead one to educate oneself if it is nurtured.

   c. Nature provides resources that humans can harvest to improve society and civilization as a whole.

   d. Nature is a frightening wilderness against which humans must protect themselves.

   e. Genius and Drill will drive nature out of the young student.

2. Based on the passage, the speaker views horseplay as

   a. a natural part of growing up, which should be tolerated by adults

   b. a distraction from a young boy's more essential nature as a learner

   c. a dangerous pastime, which can lead to injury and, more importantly, lack of discipline

   d. an important part of Genius and Drill

   e. something that should be included in the plan for each school day

3. In the context of the passage, the word "fool" (toward the end of para. 1) refers to

   a. a person of low intelligence

   b. a jester

   c. a genius

   d. a madman

   e. a subservient follower

4. The sentence structure of the last two sentences of paragraph 1

   a. reflects the wandering exploration a student will willingly do if allowed to think

   b. forcefully directs the reader through the steps of teaching young people

   c. gives equal and solid weight to the examples of the principles the speaker argues

   d. mocks, through the use of rhythm, the foolishness of the student

   e. provides a vivid portrait of a lover of truth

5. The mode of organization of paragraph 2 is mostly

   a. narration

   b. cause and effect

   c. comparison and contrast

   d. definition

   e. analogy

6. The purpose of paragraph 2 is to

   a. argue the essential elements of human nature

   b. show the inherent godliness of human nature

   c. provide an example of a person's natural desire to learn

   d. build the speaker's ethos by dropping the names of well-known acquaintances

   e. clearly present the speaker's teaching methods for the audience

7. By mentioning that Fellowes's discovery was "fifty years older than the Parthenon of Athens" (middle of para. 2), the speaker

   a. discredits Fellowes

   b. shows that his own discovery was superior to Fellowes's

   c. shows how much a naturally motivated person can learn

   d. demonstrates how impressive Fellowes's discovery was

   e. gives context for the beginning of his contemporary college system

8. The style of the first half of paragraph 3 is best described as

   a. casual

   b. argued by example

   c. didactic and directive

   d. critical and ironic

   e. imagistic and associative

9. In the first sentence of paragraph 2, the speaker uses "enthusiasm" as a rough synonym for

   a. drill

   b. genius

   c. nature

   d. education

   e. beauty

10. Who is most likely the primary audience for this passage?

    a. students

    b. psychologists

    c. parents

    d. writers

    e. geniuses

11. What is the function of paragraph 3?

    a. It explores the second of the two "capital facts."

    b. It explains Emerson's conception of "Genius."

    c. It provides a contrast to the example of Sir Charles Fellowes.

d. It elaborates Greek education practiced at the Parthenon of Athens.

    e. It offers an alternative conception to that of "Genius."

12. The sentence "Somewhat he sees in forms or hears in music or apprehends in mathematics, or believes practicable in mechanics or possible in political society, which no one else sees or hears or believes" (para. 1), is best identified as

    a. an inverted sentence that restates and emphasizes an idea stated earlier

    b. a cumulative sentence that expands Emerson's conception of "Genius"

    c. a sentence fragment that further explains the meaning of the previous sentence

    d. a declarative sentence that states what inspires the "well-born healthy child"

    e. a periodic sentence that prepares the reader for the following sentence

13. Which of the following words in paragraph 1 would be most idiosyncratic according to today's usage?

    a. want

    b. capital

    c. horseplay

    d. bias

    e. romance

14. The passage contains each of the following EXCEPT

    a. sarcasm

    b. metaphor

    c. analogy

    d. allusion

    e. personification

15. Each of the following pairs are nearly synonymous EXCEPT

    a. "inspiration" and "perception" (para. 1)

    b. "bias" and "thought" (para. 1)

    c. "fooling" and "horseplay" (para. 1)

    d. "accuracy" and "exactitude" (para. 4)

    e. "similar" and "same" (para. 4)

Questions 16–28. Read the following passage carefully before you choose your answers.

The following passage is excerpted from "The Atlanta Exposition Address" by Booker T. Washington (1895).

Mr. President and Gentlemen of the Board of Directors and Citizens.

One-third of the population of the South is of the Negro race. No enterprise seeking the material, civil, or moral welfare of this section can disregard this element of our population and reach the highest success. I but convey to you, Mr. President and Directors, the sentiment of the masses of my race when I say that in no way have the value and manhood of the American Negro been more fittingly and generously recognized than by the managers of this magnificent Exposition at every stage of its progress. It is a recognition that will do more to cement the friendship of the two races than any occurrence since the dawn of our freedom.

Not only this, but the opportunity here afforded will awaken among us a new era of industrial progress. Ignorant and inexperienced, it is not strange that in the first years of our new life we began at the top instead of at the bottom; that a seat in Congress or the state legislature was more sought than real estate or industrial skill; that the political convention of stump speaking had more attractions than starting a dairy farm or truck garden.

A ship lost at sea for many days suddenly sighted a friendly vessel. From the mast of the unfortunate vessel was seen a signal, "Water, water; we die of thirst!" The answer from the friendly vessel at once came back, "Cast down your bucket where you are." A second time the signal, "Water, water; send us water!" ran up from the distressed vessel, and was answered, "Cast down your bucket where you are." And a third and fourth signal for water was answered, "Cast down your bucket where you are."

The captain of the distressed vessel, at last heeding the injunction, cast down his bucket, and it came up full of fresh, sparkling water from the mouth of the Amazon River. To those of my race who depend on bettering their condition in a foreign land or who underestimate the importance of cultivating friendly relations with the Southern white man, who is their next-door neighbour, I would say: "Cast down your bucket where you are" — cast it down in making friends in every manly way of the people of all races by whom we are surrounded.

Cast it down in agriculture, mechanics, in commerce, in domestic service, and in the professions. And in this connection it is well to bear in mind that whatever other sins the South may be called to bear, when it comes to business pure and simple, it is in the South that the Negro is given a man's chance in the commercial world, and in nothing is this Exposition more eloquent than in emphasizing this chance. Our greatest danger is that in the great leap from slavery to freedom we may overlook the fact that the masses of us are to live by the productions of our hands, and fail to keep in mind that we shall prosper in proportion as we learn to dignify and glorify common labour and put brains and skill into the common occupations of life; shall prosper in proportion as we learn to draw the line between the superficial and the substantial, the ornamental gewgaws of life and the useful. No race can prosper till it learns that there is as much dignity in tilling a field as in writing a poem. It is at the bottom of life we must begin, and not at the top. Nor should we permit our grievances to overshadow our opportunities.

16. The rhetorical function of the first two sentences of the selection is to

    a. establish authority

    b. appeal to logos and ethos

    c. appeal to pathos and logos

    d. make abstract generalizations

    e. present factual information

17. The speaker's primary audience can best be described as

    a. political leaders and government officials

    b. former slaves and low-income workers

    c. business owners and entrepreneurs

    d. women and gender minorities

    e. activists and social workers

18. In paragraph 2, "Ignorant and inexperienced" modifies which of the following?

    a. "it"

    b. "our" and "we"

    c. "first years"

    d. "a seat" and "stump speaking"

    e. "we"

19. In paragraph 3, the author uses an extended analogy between

    a. a leaking vessel and social conventions

    b. a body of water and a lack of resources

    c. a ship's captain and effective leadership

    d. the search for water and the search for labor

    e. the Amazon River and environmental exploitation

20. The sentence that begins "To those of my race" (para. 3) contains which of the following?

    a. gerund

    b. relative clause

    c. past participle

    d. inverted adverbial phrase

    e. compound subject

21. Which of the following abilities of Southern Negroes is emphasized in paragraph 4?

    a. physical labor

    b. creativity

    c. elocution

    d. athleticism

    e. intellect

22. In this selection (paras. 1–4), the speaker claims his suggestion will improve all of the following EXCEPT

    a. race relations

    b. economic development

    c. industrial progress

    d. free enterprise

    e. racial equality

23. In the sentence that begins "Our greatest danger" (middle of para. 4), the word "superficial" is parallel in meaning and function to

    a. "substantial"

    b. "ornamental"

    c. "gewgaws"

    d. "of life"

    e. "the useful"

24. The predominant ideologies advocated in the overall selection are

    a. collectivism and social responsibility

    b. humanism and intellectual freedom

    c. Christianity and moral obligation

    d. conformity and a strong work ethic

    e. individualism and creative freedom

25. In the first paragraph, "this section" refers to

    a. "the Negro race"

    b. "the South"

    c. "The Atlanta Exposition"

    d. "One-third of the population"

    e. "The Board of Directors"

26. In the opening sentence of the paragraph 2, "this" refers to which of the following phrases in paragraph 1

    a. "to cement the friendship of the two races"

    b. "at every stage of its progress"

    c. "disregard this element of our population"

    d. "reach the highest success"

    e. "than any occurrence since the dawn of our freedom"

27. One purpose of paragraph 4 is to deliver a message of

a. didactic instruction

b. cautious optimism

c. fierce ambivalence

d. concerned admonition

e. cautious optimism

28. In the speech, Washington makes cogent use of each of the following juxtapositions EXCEPT

a. "superficial" and "substantial" (para. 4)

b. "tilling a field" and "writing a poem" (para. 4)

c. "the bottom of life" and "the top" (para. 4)

d. "seat in Congress" and "real estate" (para. 2)

e. "domestic service" and "the professions" (para. 4)

Questions 29–42. Read the following passage carefully before you choose your answers.

The following passage is excerpted from "Women's Brains" by Stephen Jay Gould (1980).

In the Prelude to *Middlemarch*, George Eliot lamented the unfulfilled lives of talented women:

> Some have felt that these blundering lives are due to the inconvenient indefiniteness with which the Supreme Power has fashioned the natures of women: if there were one level of feminine incompetence as strict as the ability to count three and no more, the social lot of women might be treated with scientific certitude.

Eliot goes on to discount the idea of innate limitation, but while she wrote in 1872, the leaders of European anthropometry were trying to measure "with scientific certitude" the inferiority of women. Anthropometry, or measurement of the human body, is not so fashionable a field these days, but it dominated the human sciences for much of the nineteenth century and remained popular until intelligence testing replaced skull measurement as a favored device for making invidious comparisons among races, classes, and sexes. Craniometry, or measurement of the skull, commanded the most attention and respect. Its unquestioned leader, Paul Broca (1824–80), professor of clinical surgery at the Faculty of Medicine in Paris, gathered a school of disciples and imitators around himself. Their work, so meticulous and apparently irrefutable, exerted great influence and won high esteem as a jewel of nineteenth-century science.

Broca's work seemed particularly invulnerable to refutation. Had he not measured with the most scrupulous care and accuracy? (Indeed, he had. I have the greatest respect for Broca's meticulous procedure. His numbers are sound. But science is an inferential exercise, not a catalog of facts. Numbers, by themselves, specify nothing. All depends upon what you do with them.) Broca depicted himself as an apostle of objectivity, a man who bowed before facts and cast aside superstition and sentimentality. He declared that "there is no faith, however respectable, no interest, however legitimate, which must not accommodate itself to the progress of human knowledge and bend before truth." Women, like it or not, had smaller brains than men and, therefore, could not equal them in intelligence. This fact, Broca argued, may reinforce a common prejudice in male society, but it is also a scientific truth. L. Manouvrier, a black sheep in Broca's fold, rejected the inferiority of women and wrote with feeling about the burden imposed upon them by Broca's numbers:

> Women displayed their talents and their diplomas. They also invoked philosophical authorities. But they were opposed by *numbers* unknown to Condorcet or to John Stuart Mill. These numbers fell upon poor women like a sledge hammer, and they were accompanied by commentaries and sarcasms more ferocious than the most misogynist

imprecations of certain church fathers. The theologians had asked if women had a soul. Several centuries later, some scientists were ready to refuse them a human intelligence.

Broca's argument rested upon two sets of data: the larger brains of men in modern societies, and a supposed increase in male superiority through time. His most extensive data came from autopsies performed personally in four Parisian hospitals. For 292 male brains, he calculated an average weight of 1,325 grams; 140 female brains averaged 1,144 grams for a difference of 181 grams, or 14 percent of the male weight. Broca understood, of course, that part of this difference could be attributed to the greater height of males. Yet he made no attempt to measure the effect of size alone and actually stated that it cannot account for the entire difference because we know, a priori, that women are not as intelligent as men (a premise that the data were supposed to test, not rest upon):

> We might ask if the small size of the female brain depends exclusively upon the small size of her body. Tiedemann has proposed this explanation. But we must not forget that women are, on

the average, a little less intelligent than men, a difference which we should not exaggerate but which is, nonetheless, real. We are therefore permitted to suppose that the relatively small size of the female brain depends in part upon her physical inferiority and in part upon her intellectual inferiority.

In 1873, the year after Eliot published *Middlemarch*, Broca measured the cranial capacities of prehistoric skulls from L'Homme Mort cave. Here he found a difference of only 99.5 cubic centimeters between males and females, while modern populations range from 129.5 to 220.7. Topinard, Broca's chief disciple, explained the increasing discrepancy through time as a result of differing evolutionary pressures upon dominant men and passive women:

> The man who fights for two or more in the struggle for existence, who has all the responsibility and the cares of tomorrow, who is constantly active in combating the environment and human rivals, needs more brain than the woman whom he must protect and nourish, the sedentary woman, lacking any interior occupations, whose role is to raise children, love, and be passive.

---

29. It can reasonably be inferred that the primary purpose of this selection is to

a. question the accuracy of Broca's data

b. show that women have inferior intelligence to men

c. trace the history of brain science, especially its use to demonstrate the inferiority of women's brains

d. criticize scientific work that interpreted data to support common social prejudices

e. show the relationship between literature and brain science

30. Which of the following does Stephen Jay Gould NOT assume about his readers?

a. They are at least passingly familiar with George Eliot.

b. They are primarily women.

c. They may not be familiar with anthropometry.

d. They value accurate data.

e. They are not misogynists.

31. What is the rhetorical purpose of the parenthetical passages in this excerpt?

a. to insert tangential comments that are not central to Gould's thesis

b. to poke fun at his own assumptions about the superiority of men over women

c. to emphasize key points about scientific reasoning

d. to define key terms in the history of brain science for the reader

e. none of the above

32. What is the likely reason Gould chose to use such terms as "apostle" (para. 3) and "disciple(s)" (paras. 2 and 5) in the passage?

   a. The terms have connotations regarding religious faith.

   b. The terms create irony.

   c. The terms emphasize the power of ideology over scientific progress.

   d. The terms reflect the zeal of Broca and his contemporaries.

   e. all of the above

33. Which of the following excerpts from the passage best expresses its purpose?

   a. "Broca's work seemed particularly invulnerable to refutation." (para. 3)

   b. "But science is an inferential exercise, not a catalog of facts. Numbers, by themselves, specify nothing. All depends upon what you do with them." (para. 3)

   c. "Women, like it or not, had smaller brains than men and, therefore, could not equal them in intelligence." (para. 3)

   d. " 'Women displayed their talents and their diplomas. They also invoked philosophical authorities. But they were opposed by *numbers* unknown to Condorcet or to John Stuart Mill.' " (para. 3)

   e. "Topinard, Broca's chief disciple, explained the increasing discrepancy through time as a result of differing evolutionary pressures upon dominant men and passive women." (para. 5)

34. Gould's use of the quotation from Broca stating that " 'there is no faith, however respectable, no interest, however legitimate, which must not accommodate itself to the progress of human knowledge and bend before the truth' " (para. 3) is primarily an example of

   a. irony

   b. allusion

   c. anaphora

   d. appeal to logos

   e. formal diction

35. Why does Gould go out of his way to defend the accuracy of Broca's data?

   a. to emphasize Broca's own scientific integrity

   b. to create pathos surrounding Broca and his contemporaries for the purpose of defending their limited philosophical and historical perspective

   c. to honor the legacy of a well-respected scientist

   d. to emphasize to the reader that "science is an inferential exercise" (para. 3)

   e. to underscore the great strides science has made since Broca's time

36. In the excerpt from Topinard's work (para. 5), which of the following is NOT an assumption Topinard makes?

   a. Raising children is a sedentary activity.

   b. Loving is not an interior occupation.

   c. Raising children is not a direct part of fighting for existence.

   d. Loving is a carefree activity that does not involve the "cares of tomorrow."

   e. Hunting requires large brains, because humanity must outsmart its prey to survive.

37. The language is figurative in each of the following phrases EXCEPT

   a. "won high esteem as a jewel of nineteenth-century science" (para. 2)

   b. "a man who bowed before facts and cast aside superstition" (para. 3)

   c. "Broca's argument rested upon two sets of data" (para. 4)

   d. "science is an inferential exercise, not a catalog of facts" (para. 3)

   e. "a black sheep in Broca's fold" (para. 3)

38. Overall, Gould's tone might be best described as

   a. laudatory

   b. frustrated

   c. admonitory

   d. objective

   e. sardonic

39. Gould offers the quotation from Broca, "there is no faith, however respectable, no interest, however legitimate, which must not accommodate itself to the progress of human knowledge and bend before truth," as

   a. a counterargument that he will later refute

   b. a challenge to the ideas of Maneuverer

   c. an appeal to authority to support his thesis

   d. evidence to establish Broca's credibility

   e. an ironic commentary on Broca's authority

40. Each of the following is viewed negatively by Gould EXCEPT

   a. "innate limitation" (para. 2)

   b. "scrupulous care and accuracy" (para. 3)

   c. "superstition and sentimentality" (para. 3)

   d. "differing evolutionary pressures" (para. 5)

   e. "invidious comparisons" (para. 2)

41. Gould writes: "Women, like it or not, had smaller brains than men and, therefore, could not equal them in intelligence" (para. 3). The purpose of this sentence is

   a. to offer a counterargument that he will later disprove with empirical scientific evidence

   b. to present a counterintuitive position that he will later address and qualify

   c. to anticipate his later claim that "we know, a priori, that women are not as intelligent as men"

   d. to present a position counter to that given in the opening quotation from George Eliot

   e. to present by paraphrase the position that Broca holds before refuting it

42. Which of the following presents a contrast that best supports Gould's position?

   a. "inferential exercise" and "catalog of facts" (para. 3)

   b. "anthropometry" and "craniometry" (para. 2)

   c. "feminine incompetence" and "innate limitation" (paras. 1 and 2)

   d. "intelligence testing" and "skull measurement" (para. 2)

   e. "commentaries and sarcasms" and "misogynist imprecations" (para. 3)

Questions 43–52. Read the following passage carefully before you choose your answers.

The following passage is excerpted from "High-School Confidential: Notes on Teen Movies" by David Denby (1999).

The most hated young woman in America is a blonde — well, sometimes a redhead or a brunette, but usually a blonde. She has big hair flipped into a swirl of gold at one side of her face or arrayed in a sultry mane, like the magnificent pile of a forties movie star. She's tall and slender, with a waist as supple as a willow, but she's dressed in awful, spangled taste: her outfits could have been put together by warring catalogues. And she has a mouth on her, a low, slatternly tongue that devastates other kids with such insults as "You're vapor, you're Spam!" and "Do I look like Mother Teresa? If I did, I probably wouldn't mind talking to the geek squad." She has two or three friends exactly like her, and together they dominate their realm — the American high school as it appears in recent teen movies. They are like wicked princesses, who enjoy the misery of their subjects. Her coronation, of course, is the senior prom, when she expects to be voted "most popular" by her class. But, though she may be popular, she is certainly not liked, so her power is something of a mystery. She is beautiful and rich, yet in the end she is preeminent because . . . she is preeminent, a position she works to maintain with Joan Crawford–like tenacity. Everyone is afraid of her; that's why she's popular.

She has a male counterpart. He's usually a football player, muscular but dumb, with a face like a beer mug and only two ways of speaking — in a conspiratorial whisper, to a friend; or in a drill sergeant's sudden bellow. If her weapon is the snub, his is the lame but infuriating prank — the can of Sprite emptied into a knapsack, or something sticky, creamy, or adhesive deposited in a locker. Sprawling and dull in class, he comes alive in the halls and in the cafeteria. He hurls people against lockers; he spits, pours, and sprays; he has a projectile relationship with food. As the crown prince, he claims the best-looking girl for himself, though in a perverse display of power he may invite an outsider or an awkward girl — a "dog" — to the prom, setting her up for some special humiliation. When we first see him, he is riding high, and virtually the entire school colludes in his tyranny. No authority figure — no teacher or administrator — dares correct him.

Thus the villains of the recent high-school movies. Not every American teen movie has these two characters, and not every social queen or jock shares all the attributes I've mentioned. (Occasionally, a handsome, dark-haired athlete can be converted to sweetness and light.) But as genre figures these two types are hugely familiar; that is, they are a common memory, a collective trauma, or at least a social and erotic fantasy. Such movies . . . as *Disturbing Behavior, She's All That, Ten Things I Hate about You*, and *Never Been Kissed* depend on them as stock figures. And they may have been figures in the minds of the Littleton shooters, Eric Harris and Dylan Klebold, who imagined they were living in a school like the one in so many of these movies — a poisonous system of status, snobbery, and exclusion.

◆ ◆ ◆

Do genre films reflect reality? Or are they merely a set of conventions that refer to other films? Obviously, they wouldn't survive if they didn't provide emotional satisfaction to the people who make them and to the audiences who watch

them. A half century ago, we didn't need to see ten Westerns a year in order to learn that the West got settled. We needed to see it settled ten times a year in order to provide ourselves with the emotional gratifications of righteous violence. By drawing his gun only when he was provoked, and in the service of the good, the classic Western hero transformed the gross tangibles of the expansionist drive (land, cattle, gold) into a principle of moral order. The gangster, by contrast, is a figure of chaos, a modern, urban person, and in the critic Robert Warshow's formulation he functions as a discordant element in an American society devoted to a compulsively "positive" outlook. When the gangster dies, he cleanses viewers of their own negative feelings.

High-school movies are also full of unease and odd, mixed-up emotions. They may be flimsy in conception; they may be shot in lollipop colors, garlanded with mediocre pop scores, and cast with goofy young actors trying to make an impression. Yet this most commercial and frivolous of genres harbors a grievance against the world. It's a very specific grievance, quite different from the restless anger of such fifties adolescent-rebellion movies as *The Wild One*, in which someone asks Marlon Brando's biker "What are you rebelling against?" and the biker replies "What have you got?" The fifties teen outlaw was against anything that adults considered sacred. But no movie teenager now revolts against adult authority, for the simple reason that adults have no authority. Teachers are rarely more than a minimal, exasperated presence, administrators get turned into a joke, and parents are either absent or distantly benevolent. It's a teen world bounded by school, mall, and car, with occasional moments set in the fast-food outlets where the kids work, or in the kids' upstairs bedrooms, with their pinups and rack stereo systems. The enemy is not authority; the enemy is other teens and the social system that they impose on one another.

5

43. Which of the following best summarizes David Denby's argument in this excerpt?

  a. Recent high school movies most often represent a rebellion against adult authority.

  b. Recent high school movies most often represent a culture reflected within other films rather than reality.

  c. Recent high school movies most often represent the ultimate victory of the social queen and the jock.

  d. Recent high school movies often provide a fantasy outlet for the poor, unpopular, nonathletic, and average-looking teens to envision becoming the social queen or the jock.

  e. Recent high school movies can become cautionary tales, jarring the unpopular teen into realizing that there is a heavy price paid for being the enemy: a social queen or a jock.

44. The first two paragraphs of the piece present portraits of high school villains drawn in broad strokes. Which of the following quotations represents an appeal to logos by qualifying Denby's argument?

  a. "The most hated young woman in America is a blonde — well, sometimes a redhead or a brunette, but usually a blonde." (para. 1)

  b. "Her coronation, of course, is the senior prom." (para. 1)

  c. "He hurls people against lockers." (para. 2)

  d. "We needed to see it settled ten times a year in order to provide ourselves with the emotional gratifications of righteous violence." (para. 4)

  e. "The fifties teen outlaw was against anything that adults considered sacred." (para. 5)

45. In which of the following examples does Denby directly call on the audience's prior experiences and perceptions?

  a. "She's tall and slender, with a waist as supple as a willow, but she's dressed in awful, spangled taste." (para. 1)

  b. "But as genre figures these two types are hugely familiar; that is, they are a common memory, a collective trauma, or at least a social and erotic fantasy." (para. 3)

  c. "Such movies . . . as *Disturbing Behavior*, *She's All That*, *Ten Things I Hate about You*, and *Never Been Kissed* depend on them as stock figures." (para. 3)

  d. "Do genre films reflect reality? Or are they merely a set of conventions that refer to other films?" (para. 4)

  e. "A half century ago, we didn't need to see ten Westerns a year in order to learn that the West got settled." (para. 4)

46. The following sentence appears at the end of paragraph 3: "And they may have been figures in the minds of the Littleton shooters, Eric Harris and Dylan Klebold, who imagined they were living in a school like the one in so many of these movies — a poisonous system of status, snobbery, and exclusion." From Denby's perspective, which word in the sentence implies false thinking on the part of the shooters?

  a. poisonous

  b. exclusion

  c. shooters

  d. figures

  e. imagined

47. Which of the following best describes the shift in tone from the beginning to the end of the fifth paragraph?

  a. from a tone of light humor and borderline dismissal to one of closer examination and concern

  b. from a tone of urgent concern to one of general absurdity and ironic flippancy

  c. from a tone of suspiciousness to one of focused anger and activism

  d. from a tone of hilarity and absurdity to one of condemnation

  e. from a tone of balanced objectivity and rationality to one of saddened realization

48. Which of the following does Denby NOT assume about his audience?

  a. They have a general knowledge about the Littleton shootings.

  b. They will recognize the lines quoted in the first paragraph.

1213

c. They are Americans.

d. They have a general awareness of the history of film.

e. all of the above

49. In context, what does the word "benevolent" mean in the second half of paragraph 5?

a. generous with money and other provisions

b. morally virtuous

c. generally pleasant, supportive, and harmless

d. restrictive, authoritarian

e. clingy, needy, and self-serving

50. Each of the following sentences is ironic EXCEPT

a. "No authority figure — no teacher or administrator — dares correct him." (para. 2)

b. "But, though she may be popular, she is certainly not liked." (para. 1)

c. "Everyone is afraid of her; that's why she's popular." (para. 1)

d. "But no movie teenager now revolts against adult authority, for the simple reason that adults have no authority." (para. 5)

e. "He's usually a football player, muscular but dumb, with a face like a beer mug and only two ways of speaking . . ." (para. 2)

51. In the passage, Denby equates popularity in the world of high school movies with

a. power

b. stupidity

c. merit

d. meanness

e. humiliation

52. Each of the following supports an answer of "yes" to the second rhetorical question at the beginning of the fourth paragraph EXCEPT

a. It is implied by information about films provided in the preceding paragraph.

b. In order, it follows the first rhetorical question, which opened the paragraph.

c. The contents of the first two paragraphs suggest a negative answer to the first rhetorical question.

d. It is lengthier than the first question, giving it greater credibility.

e. It is suggested by the opening conjunction, "or."

Questions 53–61. Read the following passage carefully before you choose your answers.

The following passage is excerpted from "Mother Tongue" by Amy Tan (2003).

Lately, I've been giving more thought to the kind of English my mother speaks. Like others, I have described it to people as "broken" or "fractured" English. But I wince when I say that. It has always bothered me that I can think of no other way to describe it other than "broken," as if it were damaged and needed to be fixed, as if it lacked a certain wholeness and soundness. I've heard other terms used, "limited English," for example. But they seem just as bad, as if everything is limited, including people's perceptions of the limited English speaker.

I know this for a fact, because when I was growing up, my mother's "limited" English limited *my* perception of her. I was ashamed of her English. I believed that her English reflected the quality of what she had to say. That is, because she expressed them imperfectly her thoughts were imperfect. And I had plenty of empirical evidence to support me: the fact that people in department stores, at banks, and at restaurants did not take her seriously, did not give her good service, pretended not to understand her, or even acted as if they did not hear her.

My mother has long realized the limitations of her English as well. When I was fifteen, she used to have me call people on the phone to pretend I was she. In this guise, I was forced to ask for information or even to complain and yell at people who had been rude to her. One time it was a call to her stockbroker in New York. She had cashed out her small portfolio and it just so happened we were going to go to New York the next week, our very first trip outside California. I had to get on the phone and say in an adolescent voice that was not very convincing, "This is Mrs. Tan."

And my mother was standing in the back whispering loudly, "Why he don't send me check, already two weeks late. So mad he lie to me, losing me money."

And then I said in perfect English, "Yes, I'm getting rather concerned. You had agreed to send the check two weeks ago, but it hasn't arrived."

Then she began to talk more loudly. "What he want, I come to New York tell him front of his boss, you cheating me." And I was trying to calm her down, make her be quiet, while telling the stockbroker, "I can't tolerate any more excuses. If I don't receive the check immediately, I am going to have to speak to your manager when I'm in New York next week." And sure enough, the following week there we were in front of this astonished stockbroker, and I was sitting there red-faced and quiet, and my mother, the

real Mrs. Tan, was shouting at his boss in her impeccable broken English.

We used a similar routine just five days ago, for a situation that was far less humorous. My mother had gone to the hospital for an appointment, to find out about a benign brain tumor a CAT scan had revealed a month ago. She said she had spoken very good English, her best English, no mistakes. Still, she said, the hospital did not apologize when they said they had lost the CAT scan and she had come for nothing. She said they did not seem to have any sympathy when she told them she was anxious to know the exact diagnosis, since her husband and son had both died of brain tumors. She said they would not give her any more information until the next time and she would have to make another appointment for that. So she said she would not leave until the doctor called her daughter. She wouldn't budge. And when the doctor finally called her daughter, me, who spoke in perfect English — lo and behold — we had assurances the CAT scan would be found, promises that a conference call on Monday would be held, and apologies for any suffering my mother had gone through for a most regrettable mistake.

(line marker: 5)

---

53. Which of the following best describes Amy Tan's purpose in including the following sentence: "It has always bothered me that I can think of no other way to describe it other than 'broken,' as if it were damaged and needed to be fixed, as if it lacked a certain wholeness and soundness" (para. 1)?

 a. to criticize the limited terminology used to describe her mother's speech

 b. to persuade readers that her mother's speech is poor

 c. to educate readers about the correct terms to use in reference to immigrant English speakers

 d. to mock her mother's speech

 e. to concede that terms like "broken" are the best way to describe her mother's English

54. In context, the word "empirical" (last sentence of para. 2) is best interpreted to mean

 a. experimental

 b. practical

 c. preliminary

 d. feasible

 e. tentative

55. What is the author's primary purpose in paragraphs 3–6?

 a. to highlight the similarities between how she and her mother each use the English language

 b. to criticize the treatment of her mother due to her use of nonstandard English

 c. to exemplify her complicated relationship to her mother's use of the English language

d. to prove specific details about the quality of her mother's English

e. to document a misunderstanding about the way her mother speaks English

56. Which of the following best characterizes the tone in this passage?

a. objective and informal

b. personal and reflective

c. ironic and candid

d. subjective and argumentative

e. formal and analytical

57. Paragraph 7 relies primarily on which of the following rhetorical devices?

a. analogy

b. hyperbole

c. generalization

d. figurative language

e. anecdote

58. Tan's attitude toward her mother's use of English is one of

a. extreme shame

b. justifiable disappointment

c. condescending admiration

d. conflicted respect

e. none of the above

59. The phrase "impeccable broken English" at the end of paragraph 6 is an example of

a. consonance

b. figurative language

c. oxymoron

d. irony

e. symbol

60. Which of the following best describes the rhetorical effect achieved by juxtaposing the lighthearted stockbroker anecdote (paras. 3–6) and the serious hospital anecdote (para. 7)?

a. It makes an appeal to authority.

b. It presents a range of examples to support the author's thesis.

c. It criticizes the health-care system in the United States.

d. It emphasizes the injustices faced by limited English speakers.

e. It appeals to the reader's sense of humor.

61. Regarding her mother's "limited" English, Tan writes, "… because she expressed them imperfectly her thoughts were imperfect." With this statement, she presents

a. a serious problem to be solved

b. a false impression to be corrected

c. a spurious claim to be qualified

d. a counterargument to be addressed

e. a challenging assertion to be defended

SYNTHESIS QUESTION: VIOLENT IMAGES

Suggested reading time: 15 minutes

Suggested writing time: 40 minutes

INTRODUCTION

Susan Sontag writes in *Regarding the Pain of Others:* "Perhaps the only people with the right to look at [graphic war] images of suffering of this extreme order are those who could do something to alleviate it . . . or those who could learn from it. The rest of us are voyeurs, whether or not we mean to be" (42). What purpose do violent images serve? When is it appropriate to show shocking or horrific events that happen to others?

ASSIGNMENT

Read the following sources and accompanying information carefully. Then, in an essay that synthesizes at least three sources for support, take a position that defends, challenges, or qualifies Sontag's claim that we should view images of violence only when viewing leads to action or knowledge.

Use the sources to support your position; avoid mere paraphrasing or summary. Your argument should be central; the sources should support this argument. Remember to attribute both direct and indirect citations.

You may refer to the sources as Source A, Source B, and so on, or by the description in the parentheses. Authors, titles, and publication data are included for your convenience.

Source A (Lester)

Source B (Woolf)

Source C (Sontag)

Source D (Barnet and Bedau)

Source E (Tomorrow)

Source F (Kennedy and Patrick)

Source G (Moore)

The following is excerpted from a book on ethics in photojournalism.

Nora Ephron (1978) in her book, *Scribble Scribble Notes on the Media*, devoted a chapter to a description and reaction to Stan Forman's fire escape tragedy. Ephron concluded that "I recognize that printing pictures of corpses raises all sorts of problems about taste and titillation and sensationalism; the fact is, however, that people die. Death happens to be one of life's main events. And it is irresponsible and more than that, inaccurate — for newspapers to fail to show it . . ." (p. 61).

One photograph that was delayed for several weeks by censors concerned for the public's reaction was published in *Life*. Captioned, "Here lie three Americans . . . ," George Strock's shocking picture of the maggot covered bodies of U.S. servicemen face down in the sand of a distant island's beach was the first picture of killed American soldiers published in a U.S. magazine. Many readers were stunned by the visually graphic image. But Susan Moeller (1989) in her chronicle of war photography, *Shooting War*, noted that many soldiers praised the photograph and the accompanying editorial. A lieutenant wrote, "Your Picture of the Week is a terrible thing, but I'm glad that there is one American magazine which had the courage to print it." A private wrote, "This editorial is the first thing I have read that gives real meaning to our struggle" (p. 207).

SOURCE B

Woolf, Virginia. *Three Guineas*. Harcourt, Brace, 1938.

The following is an excerpt from a book-length essay by Virginia Woolf on how to prevent war.

[B]esides these pictures of other people's lives and minds — these biographies and histories — there are also other pictures — pictures of actual facts; photographs. Photographs, of course, are not arguments addressed to the reason; they are simply statements of fact addressed to the eye. But in that very simplicity there may be some help. Let us see then whether when we look at the same photographs we feel the same things. . . .

Those photographs are not an argument; they are simply a crude statement of fact addressed to the eye. But the eye is connected with the brain; the brain with the nervous system. That system sends its messages in a flash through every past memory and present feeling. When we look at those photographs some fusion takes place within us; however different the education, the traditions behind us, our sensations are the same; and they are violent. You, Sir,[1] call them "horror and disgust." We also call them horror and disgust. And the same words rise to our lips. War, you say, is an abomination; a barbarity; war must be stopped at whatever cost. And we echo your words. War is an abomination; a barbarity; war must be stopped. For now at last we are looking at the same picture; we are seeing with you the same dead bodies, the same ruined houses.

---

[1]"You, Sir" refers to the man Woolf is writing to.

SOURCE C

Sontag, Susan. *Regarding the Pain of Others*. Farrar, Straus and Giroux, 2003.

The following is an excerpt from a book about the history and impact of depictions of violence.

There now exists a vast repository of images that make it harder to maintain this kind of moral defectiveness.[1] Let the atrocious images haunt us. Even if they are only tokens, and cannot possibly encompass most of the reality to which they refer, they still perform a vital function. The images say: This is what human beings are capable of doing — may volunteer to do, enthusiastically, self-righteously. Don't forget.

This is not quite the same as asking people to remember a particularly monstrous bout of evil. ("Never forget.") Perhaps too much value is assigned to memory, not enough to thinking. Remembering is an ethical act, has ethical value in and of itself. Memory is, achingly, the only relation we can have with the dead. So the belief that remembering is an ethical act is deep in our natures as humans, who know we are going to die, and who mourn those who in the normal course of things die before us — grandparents, parents, teachers, and older friends. Heartlessness and amnesia seem to go together. But history gives contradictory signals about the value of remembering in the much longer span of a collective history. There is simply too much injustice in the world. And too much remembering (of ancient grievances: Serbs, Irish) embitters. To make peace is to forget. To reconcile, it is necessary that memory be faulty and limited.

---

[1]The moral defectiveness that Sontag describes earlier is possessed by one who is "perennially surprised that depravity exists."

SOURCE D

Barnet, Sylvan, and Hugo Bedau. "Photography and Truth." *Critical Thinking, Reading, and Writing.* Bedford/St. Martin's, 2002.

The following is an excerpt from a college writing textbook introducing the subject of photography.

Photographs have historically been considered especially powerful as tools of persuasion, in part because a photo, unlike, say, a drawing or a graph, is generally believed to show real people and events rather than an artist's or statistician's conception of the truth. "The camera doesn't lie." Of course, this common saying is at best an oversimplification. We will leave aside for the moment the fact that photographs can be tampered with (and with increasing ease using new digital technologies). Even an unretouched photograph is far from a pure or unmediated look at the truth. A skilled photographer, like any other artist, makes many significant choices that affect the final image we see. Decisions about what to include within the frame — and what to exclude — as the precise moment to take the picture, are most obvious. Additionally, though, such elements as depths of field, color balance, length of exposure, light and shadow, and dozens of other considerations make a huge difference in the impact of the photograph on the viewer. A gritty, grainy black-and-white photo of a bombed building is likely to be more effective than a color photograph of the same building because the color itself may help to make the photo attractive, sensuous, appealing.

SOURCE E

Tomorrow, Tom. "This Modern World." 2003, www.thismodernworld.com. Cartoon.

The following is a political cartoon by the popular online cartoonist Tom Tomorrow.

ITS TIME FOR THE *11:00 NEWS*...

GOOD EVENING! IN THE NEWS TONIGHT-- 100,000 DEMON-STRATORS GATHERED IN THE STREETS OF SAN FRANCISCO TODAY TO PROTEST AGAINST THE WAR IN THE GULF...

100,000 PEOPLE? GOSH, BIFF-- THAT'S COMPLETELY AT ODDS WITH THE CURRENT MEDIA PERCEPTION OF A NATION ***STRONGLY UNITED*** BEHIND THE ***PRESIDENT!***

THAT'S ***TRUE***, BETTY! THAT'S WHY WE'LL DOWNPLAY THE MAGNITUDE OF THE EVENT BY RUNNING ONLY A FEW BRIEF SECONDS OF FOOTAGE FROM THE DEMONSTRATION...

...FOLLOWED IMMEDIATELY BY COVERAGE OF FIFTEEN ***PRO-WAR*** DEMONSTRATORS IN WALNUT CREEK-- SUBTLY INDICATING THAT THE TWO EVENTS ARE OF ***EQUAL IMPORTANCE!***

FINALLY, WE'LL CONCLUDE THE SEGMENT WITH THE LATEST ***NETWORK NEWS POLL*** SHOWING THAT A SOLID 97% OF THE AMER-ICAN PEOPLE BELIEVE THE ANTI-WAR PROTESTERS ARE ***TRAITOROUS DOGS*** FOR WHOM ***HANGING*** IS ***TOO GOOD!***

COMING UP NEXT: REALLY COOL FOOTAGE OF JET FIGHTERS AND EXPLOSIONS.

FIRST THESE MESSAGES...

© Tom Tomorrow

SOURCE F

Kennedy, Liam, and Caitlin Patrick. *The Violence of the Image: Photography and International Conflict.* I.B. Tauris, 2014.

The following is excerpted from a book on the relationship between war and photography.

Photography and warfare have long existed in a symbiotic relationship — they share technologies and "ways of seeing" — and the emergence of new forms of warfare and of visual technology and representation underline this. In recent years, virtual battlefields of images and information have taken on an important role in the production of foreign policy and international relations. And so, management of the field of vision becomes a key component in the geopolitical stratagems of twenty-first-century conflicts. For photographers there are new challenges to make visible the realities of warfare and conflict under such conditions. There are also new challenges to make violence and its conditions and results meaningful, for new forms of warfare have conditioned new forms of violence, much of it "untethered" from the grand political narratives of the twentieth century. A key concern of this book is to examine the shifting relations between visuality and the violence of conflict, which now often involves protracted, "managed" catastrophes for particular groups, often non-combatants, as well as high-tech or set-piece battles.

The proliferation and convergence of new media technologies — satellite, the internet, digital image production — has greatly expanded the media sphere in which imagery of contemporary conflict circulates, and also expanded the global capacities for visually documenting abuses and violations. With citizen journalists playing an increasingly significant part in such visual documentation, there are now many initiatives to capture and use this capacity. This has become especially important in the visual documentation and communication of human rights abuses. Photography has taken on a fresh valence in this context as an accessible mode of documentary evidence, yet it is bedevilled by issues of authenticity and verifiability that underline the ideological conditions of the relationship between seeing and believing.

Moore, Suzanne. "Sharing Pictures of Corpses on Social Media Isn't the Way to Bring a Ceasefire." *The Guardian*, 21 July 2014.

The following is from a newspaper article on violent images shared via social media.

How many pictures of dead children do you need to see before you understand that killing children is wrong? I ask because social media is awash with the blood of innocents. Twitter is full of photos of the murdered children of Gaza. Sometimes carried by screaming fathers, sometimes by blood-soaked women. Some bodies are torn to pieces. One no longer has a head.

Such images of war, of obscenity, of the "reality" of what sophisticated weapons do are everywhere. There is no more privacy. At one time the media would have thought carefully about which images could be made public. Lines are drawn and then crossed but all notions about respect for the dead have been ripped apart by the advent of social media.

Perhaps they already were.... We see shrouds and horrors all the time and television news warns us in the aftermath of every bomb that we may be disturbed.

But now on Twitter especially there are endless pictures of dead toddlers. These are tweeted and retweeted to convey horror at what is going on in Gaza. This is obscene. Yet the moveable feast of semi-aroused outrage that is Twitter alights on one injustice after another. A while ago my feed was full of butchered elephants bleeding where their tusks had been removed. Before that were lions accompanied by the grinning idiots who had killed them. None of these images persuaded me to think any differently than I already did. This stuff is disgusting. Of course....

Does this competitive outrage matter? After all, 270 children were killed in Syria last month. But that is not trending.

Seasoned journalists were quite rightly disgusted that the bodies of those who died on flight MH17 were lying naked where it crashed. They were given no dignity. Where is our basic decency? We are told that to understand war we need to see the slaughter of civilians. The awful reality is that all wars look much the same. We need not just to see but to imagine. Those who cannot imagine the suffering of others are those who continue to justify it.

I don't need to see any more images of dead children to want a ceasefire, a political settlement. I don't need you to tweet them to show me you care. A small corpse is not a symbol for public consumption. It is for some parent somewhere the loss of a precious person. To make these images common devalues the currency of shared humanity. We do not respect those living in awful conflict by disrespecting their dead. Stop.

ANALYSIS PROMPT

Suggested Time — 40 minutes

Read Abraham Lincoln's "The Gettysburg Address" carefully, and in a well-organized essay, analyze the rhetorical strategies that Lincoln uses to achieve his purpose.

Four score and seven years ago our fathers brought forth on this continent a new nation, conceived in liberty, and dedicated to the proposition that all men are created equal.

Now we are engaged in a great civil war, testing whether that nation, or any nation, so conceived and so dedicated, can long endure. We are met on a great battle-field of that war. We have come to dedicate a portion of that field, as a final resting place for those who here gave their lives that that nation might live. It is altogether fitting and proper that we should do this.

But, in a larger sense, we can not dedicate, we can not consecrate, we can not hallow this ground. The brave men, living and dead, who struggled here, have consecrated it, far above our poor power to add or detract. The world will little note, nor long remember what we say here, but it can never forget what they did here. It is for us the living, rather, to be dedicated here to the unfinished work which they who fought here have thus far so nobly advanced. It is rather for us to be here dedicated to the great task remaining before us — that from these honored dead we take increased devotion to that cause for which they gave the last full measure of devotion — that we here highly resolve that these dead shall not have died in vain — that this nation, under God, shall have a new birth of freedom — and that government of the people, by the people, for the people, shall not perish from the earth.

ARGUMENT PROMPT

Suggested Time — 40 minutes

Yesterday, the medical journal *Neurology* published a study suggesting that professional football players are four times more likely to die from the Alzheimer's disease and ALS (Lou Gehrig's disease) than the general population. This is just the most recent addition to a growing body of evidence linking football to neurodegenerative disease. . . .

. . . [I]n local youth football leagues, . . . children as young as eight years old practice up to six hours a week in full pads.

— Kendra Gagnon,
Pediatric Physical Therapist

Football in America is part of the everyday lives of millions of fans; in the NFL alone, football is a $9 billion industry. More and more evidence supports the fact that football simply cannot be made safer with better helmets or different rules. Some have suggested that football be regulated more firmly by government agencies; still others have suggested that we begin the process of dismantling professional football since the game is just too dangerous.

Take a position on football in American family life, and discuss the pros and cons that parents might consider when deciding whether or not to involve their children in the sport. In a fully developed essay, weigh the various sides of the issue and draw conclusions.

Print Resources

1. A Book with One Author

A book with one author serves as a general model for most MLA citations. Include author, title, publisher, and date of publication.

Beavan, Colin. *No Impact Man*. Farrar, Straus and Giroux, 2009.

2. A Book with Multiple Authors

Kasarda, John D., and Greg Lindsay. *Aerotropolis: The Way We'll Live Next*. Farrar, Straus and Giroux, 2011.

3. Two or More Works by the Same Author

Multiple entries should be arranged alphabetically by title. The author's name appears at the beginning of the first entry, but is replaced by three hyphens and a period in all subsequent entries.

Gladwell, Malcolm. *What the Dog Saw, and Other Adventures*. Little, Brown and Company, 2009.

—. *David and Goliath: Underdogs, Misfits, and the Art of Battling Giants*. Little, Brown and Company, 2013.

4. Author and Editor Both Named

Vidal, Gore. *The Selected Essays of Gore Vidal*. Edited by Jay Parini, Vintage Books, 2009.

Alternately, to cite the editor's contribution, start with the editor's name.

Parini, Jay, editor. *The Selected Essays of Gore Vidal*. By Gore Vidal, Vintage Books, 2009.

5. Anthology

Oates, Joyce Carol, editor. *Telling Stories: An Anthology for Writers*. W. W. Norton, 1997.

Selection from an anthology:

Irving, Washington. "Rip Van Winkle." *Conversations in American Literature: Language, Rhetoric, Culture*, edited by Robin Aufses, et al., Bedford/St. Martin's, 2015, pp. 435–48.

6. Translation

Wiesel, Elie. *Night*. Translated by Marion Wiesel, Hill and Wang, 2006.

7. Entry in a Reference Work

Because most reference works are alphabetized, you should omit page numbers.

Lounsberry, Barbara. "Joan Didion." *Encyclopedia of the Essay*, edited by Tracy Chevalier, Fitzroy, 1997.

For a well-known encyclopedia, use only the edition and year of publication. When an article is not attributed to an author, start the entry with article's title.

"Gilgamesh." *The Columbia Encyclopedia*. 5th ed., 1993.

8. Sacred Text

Unless a specific published edition is being cited, sacred texts should be omitted from the Works Cited list.

The New Testament. Translated by Richmond Lattimore, North Point Press, 1997.

9. Article in a Journal

The title of the journal should be followed by the volume, issue, and year of the journal's publication, as well as the page range of the article.

> Marshall, Sarah. "Remote Control: Tonya Harding, Nancy Kerrigan, and the Spectacles of Female Power and Pain." *The Believer*, vol. 12 no. 1, 2014, pp. 1–10.

10. Article in a Magazine

In a weekly:

> Heller, Nathan. "The Big Uneasy: What's Roiling the Liberal-Arts Campus?" *The New Yorker* 30 May 2016, pp. 48–57.

In a monthly:

> Shulevitz, Judith. "The Brontës' Secret." *The Atlantic*, June 2016, pp. 38–41.

11. Article in a Newspaper

If you are citing a local paper that does not contain the city name in its title, add the city name in brackets after the newspaper title. When citing an article that does not appear on consecutive pages, list the first page followed by a plus sign. The edition only needs to be included if it is listed on the paper's masthead.

> Edge, John T. "Fast Food Even Before Fast Food." *The New York Times,* 30 Sept. 2009, late ed., pp. D1+.

12. Review

In a weekly:

> Miller, Laura. "Descendants." Review of *Homegoing*, by Yaa Gyasi, *The New Yorker,* 30 May 2016, pp. 75–77.

In a monthly:

> Simpson, Mona. "Imperfect Union." Review of *Mrs. Woolf and the Servants*, by Alison Light, *The Atlantic*, Jan./Feb. 2009, pp. 93–101.

Electronic Resources

13. Article from a Database Accessed through a Subscription Service

Apply the normal rules for citing a journal article, but include the name of the subscription service in italics and the Digital Object Identifier, if available.

> Morano, Michele. "Boy Eats World." *Fourth Genre: Explorations in Nonfiction*, vol. 13, no. 2, 2011, pp. 31–35. *Project MUSE*, doi:10.1353/fge.2011.0029.

14. Article in an Online Magazine

Follow the author name and article title with the name of the magazine in italics, the date published, and the URL of the article.

> Schuman, Rebecca. "This Giant Sculpture of Kafka's Head Perfectly Encapsulates His Strange Relationship to Prague." *Slate*, 24 May 2016, www.slate.com/blogs/ browbeat/2016/05/24/this_giant_moving_ sculpture_of_kafka_s_head_is_the_ perfect_tribute_to_kafka.html.

15. Article in an Online Newspaper

> Alter, Alexandra. "This Summer, Girls in Titles and Girls in Peril." *The New York Times*, 26 May 2016, www.nytimes.com/2016/05/27/ books/hot-days-cool-books.html.

16. Online Review

> Stevens, Dana. "The New *It* Has Too Much Insane Clown, Not Enough Posse." Review of *It*, directed by Andrés Muschietti. *Slate*, 16 Oct. 2017, www.slate.com/arts/2017/09/ the-new-adaptation-of-stephen-kings-it- reviewed.html.

17. Entry in an Online Reference Work

> "Eschatology." *Merriam-Webster*, 7 Apr. 2016, www.merriam-webster.com/dictionary/ eschatology.

18. Work from a Website

"Wallace Stevens (1879–1955)." *Poetry Foundation*, 2015, www.poetryfoundation .org/bio/wallace-stevens.

19. Entire Website

Website with editor:

Dutton, Dennis, editor. *Arts and Letters Daily*. Chronicle of Higher Education, www .aldaily.com.

Website without editor:

Academy of American Poets. *poets.org*. 2016, www.poets.org/.

Personal website:

Mendelson, Edward. Home page. Columbia U, 2013, english.columbia.edu/people/ profile/394.

20. Entire Web Log (Blog)

Holbo, John, editor. *The Valve*, www.thevalve .org/go.

21. Entry in a Wiki

"Pre-Raphaelite Brotherhood." *Wikipedia*, 25 Nov. 2013, wikipedia.org/wiki/ Pre-Raphaelite_Brotherhood.

Other Sources

22. Film and Video

Follow the film title with the director, notable performers, the distribution company, and the date of release. For films viewed on the web, follow this with the URL of the website used to view the film. If citing a particular individual's work on the film, you may begin the entry with his or her name before the title.

The Hurt Locker. Directed by Kathryn Bigelow, performances by Jeremy Renner, Anthony Mackie, Guy Pearce, and Ralph Fiennes, Summit, 2009.

Viewed on the web (use original distributor and release date):

Nayar, Vineet. "Employees First, Customers Second." *YouTube*, 9 June 2015, www .youtube.com/watch?v=cCdu67s_C5E.

23. Interview

Include the name of the interviewer if it is someone of note.
Personal interview:

Tripp, Lawrence. Personal interview, 14 Apr. 2014.

In print:

Dylan, Bob. "Who Is This Bob Dylan?" Interview by Tom Junod. *Esquire*, 23 Jan. 2014, pp. 124+.

On the radio:

Thompson, Ahmir "Questlove." Interview with Terry Gross. *Fresh Air*, NPR, 27 Apr. 2016.

On the web:

Thompson, Ahmir "Questlove." Interview with Terry Gross. *Fresh Air*. NPR, 27 Apr. 2016, www.npr.org/2016/04/27/475721555/ questlove-on-prince-doo-wop-and-the- food-equivalent-of-the-mona-lisa.

24. Lecture or Speech

Viewed in person:

Smith, Anna Deavere. "On the Road: A Search for American Character." Jefferson Lecture in the Humanities, John F. Kennedy Center for the Performing Arts, Washington, 6 Apr. 2015. 44th Jefferson Lecture.

Viewed on the web:

Batuman, Elif. Lowell Humanities Series. Boston College. 13 Oct. 2010. frontrow .bc.edu/program/batuman. Lecture.

25. Podcast

Carlin, Dan. "King of Kings." *Hardcore History Podcast*, 28 Oct. 2015, www.dancarlin .com/hardcore-history-56-kings-of-kings.

26. Work of Art or Photograph

In a museum:

> Hopper, Edward. *Nighthawks*. 1942, Art
> Institute, Chicago. Oil on canvas.

On the web:

> Thiebaud, Wayne. *Three Machines*. 1963, De Young
> Museum, San Francisco, art.famsf.org/
> wayne-thiebaud/three-machines-199318.

In print:

> Clark, Edward. *Navy CPO Graham Jackson Plays
> "Goin' Home."* 1945, *The Great LIFE
> Photographers*, Bulfinch, 2004, pp. 78–79.

27. Map or Chart

In print:

> "U.S. Personal Savings Rate, 1929–1999." *Credit
> Card Nation: The Consequences of America's
> Addiction to Credit*, by Robert D. Manning,
> Basic, 2000, p. 100.

On the web:

> "1914 New Balkan States and Central Europe
> Map." *National Geographic*, maps.national
> geographic.com/maps/print-collection/
> balkan-states-map.html.

28. Cartoon or Comic Strip

In print:

> Finck, Liana. Cartoon. *The New Yorker*, 30 May
> 2016, p. 30.

On the web:

> Zyglis, Adam. "City of Light." *Buffalo News*,
> 8 Nov. 2015, adamzyglis.buffalonews
> .com/2015/11/08/city-of-light/.
> Cartoon.

29. Advertisement

In print:

> Rosetta Stone. *Harper's*, Aug. 2008, p. 21.
> Advertisement.

On the web:

> Seamless. *The Washington Post*, 4 Apr. 2016,
> www.washingtonpost.com.
> Advertisement.

GLOSSARY

ad hominem Latin for "to the man," this fallacy refers to the specific diversionary tactic of switching the argument from the issue at hand to the character of the other speaker. If you argue that a park in your community should not be renovated because the person supporting it was arrested during a domestic dispute, then you are guilty of *ad hominem*.

ad populum *fallacy (bandwagon appeal)* This fallacy occurs when evidence boils down to "everybody's doing it, so it must be a good thing to do."

> You should vote to elect Rachel Johnson— she has a strong lead in the polls.

Polling higher does not necessarily make Senator Johnson the "best" candidate, only the most popular.

alliteration Repetition of the same sound beginning several words or syllables in sequence.

> [L]et us go forth to lead the land we love . . .
>
> — John F. Kennedy

allusion Brief reference to a person, event, or place (real or fictitious) or to a work of art.

> Let both sides unite to heed in all corners of the earth the command of Isaiah . . .
>
> — John F. Kennedy

analogy A comparison between two seemingly dissimilar things. Often, an analogy uses something simple or familiar to explain something unfamiliar or complex.

> I was imagining winning as a free space, one where the unconscious racist shenanigans of umpires, or the narratives about her body, her "unnatural" power, her perceived crassness no longer mattered.
>
> — Claudia Rankine

If I have unjustly wrested a plank from a drowning man, I must restore it to him though I drown myself. . . . But he that would save his life, in such a case, shall lose it. This people must cease to hold slaves and to make war on Mexico, though it cost them their existence as a people.

> — Henry David Thoreau

anaphora Repetition of a word or phrase at the beginning of successive phrases, clauses, or lines.

> . . . not as a call to bear arms, though arms we need—not as a call to battle, though embattled we are . . .
>
> — John F. Kennedy

anecdote A brief story used to illustrate a point or claim.

annotation The taking of notes directly on a text.

antimetabole Repetition of words in reverse order.

> [A]sk not what your country can do for you—ask what you can do for your country.
>
> — John F. Kennedy

antithesis Opposition, or contrast, of ideas or words in a parallel construction.

> [W]e shall . . . support any friend, oppose any foe . . .
>
> — John F. Kennedy

appeal to false authority This fallacy occurs when someone who has no expertise to speak on an issue is cited as an authority. A TV star, for instance, is not a medical expert, though pharmaceutical advertisements often use celebrity endorsements.

> According to former congressional leader Ari Miller, the Himalayas have an estimated Yeti population of between 300 and 500 individuals.

archaic diction   Old-fashioned or outdated choice of words.

> . . . beliefs for which our forebears fought . . .
>
> — John F. Kennedy

argument   A process of reasoned inquiry. A persuasive discourse resulting in a coherent and considered movement from a claim to a conclusion.

Aristotelian triangle   See **rhetorical triangle**.

assertion   A statement that presents a claim or thesis.

assumption   See **warrant**.

asyndeton   Omission of conjunctions between coordinate phrases, clauses, or words.

> [W]e shall pay any price, bear any burden, meet any hardship, support any friend, oppose any foe to assure the survival and the success of liberty.
>
> — John F. Kennedy

audience   The listener, viewer, or reader of a text. Most texts are likely to have multiple audiences.

> Gehrig's audience was his teammates and fans in the stadium that day, but it was also the teams he played against, the fans listening on the radio, and posterity—us.

background   The part of an image that is behind the objects depicted in the foreground. See also **foreground**.

backing   In the Toulmin model, backing consists of further assurances or data without which the assumption lacks authority. For an example, see **Toulmin model**.

bandwagon appeal   See **ad populum fallacy**.

begging the question   A fallacy in which a claim is based on evidence or support that is in doubt. It "begs" a question whether the support itself is sound.

Giving students easy access to a wealth of facts and resources online allows them to develop critical thinking skills.

bias   A prejudice or preconceived notion that prevents a person from approaching a topic in a neutral or an objective way.

circular reasoning   A fallacy in which the argument repeats the claim as a way to provide evidence.

> You can't give me a C; I'm an A student!

claim   Also called an assertion or proposition, a claim states the argument's main idea or position. A claim differs from a topic or subject in that a claim has to be arguable.

claim of fact   A claim of fact asserts that something is true or not true.

> The number of suicides and homicides committed by teenagers, most often young men, has exploded in the last three decades . . .
>
> — Anna Quindlen

claim of policy   A claim of policy proposes a change.

> Yet one solution continues to elude us, and that is ending the ignorance about mental health, and moving it from the margins of care and into the mainstream where it belongs.
>
> — Anna Quindlen

claim of value   A claim of value argues that something is good or bad, right or wrong.

> There's a plague on all our houses, and since it doesn't announce itself with lumps or spots or protest marches, it has gone unremarked in the quiet suburbs and busy cities where it has been laying waste.
>
> — Anna Quindlen

classical oration   Five-part argument structure used by classical rhetoricians. The five parts are:

introduction (**exordium**)   Introduces the reader to the subject under discussion.

narration (**narratio**)   Provides factual information and background material on the subject at hand or establishes why the subject is a problem that needs addressing.

confirmation (**confirmatio**)   Usually the major part of the text, the confirmation includes the proof needed to make the writer's case.

refutation (**refutatio**)   Addresses the counterargument. It is a bridge between the writer's proof and conclusion.

conclusion (**peroratio**)   Brings the essay to a satisfying close.

closed thesis   A closed thesis is a statement of the main idea of the argument that also previews the major points the writer intends to make.

> The three-dimensional characters, exciting plot, and complex themes of the Harry Potter series make them not only legendary children's books but enduring literary classics.

complex sentence   A sentence that includes one independent clause and at least one dependent clause.

> If a free society cannot help the many who are poor, it cannot save the few who are rich.
>
> — John F. Kennedy

composition   The physical arrangement of visual elements within the frame of an image.

compound sentence   A sentence that includes at least two independent clauses.

> The energy, the faith, the devotion which we bring to this endeavor will light our country and all who serve it and the glow from that fire can truly light the world.
>
> — John F. Kennedy

concession   An acknowledgment that an opposing argument may be true or reasonable.

In a strong argument, a concession is usually accompanied by a refutation challenging the validity of the opposing argument.

> Lou Gehrig concedes what some of his listeners may think—that his bad break is a cause for discouragement or despair.

confirmation   In classical oration, this major part of an argument comes between the narration and refutation; it provides the development of proof through evidence that supports the claims made by the speaker.

connotation   Meanings or associations that readers have with a word beyond its dictionary definition, or denotation. Connotations are often positive or negative, and they often greatly affect the author's tone. Consider the connotations of the words in the following example, all of which mean "overweight."

> That cat is *plump*. That cat is *fat*. That cat is *obese*.

context   The circumstances, atmosphere, attitudes, and events surrounding a **text**.

> The context for Lou Gehrig's speech is the recent announcement of his illness and his subsequent retirement, but also the poignant contrast between his potent career and his debilitating disease.

counterargument   An opposing argument to the one a writer is putting forward. Rather than ignoring a counterargument, a strong writer will usually address it through the process of concession and refutation.

> Some of Lou Gehrig's listeners might have argued that his bad break was a cause for discouragement or despair.

counterargument thesis   A type of thesis statement that includes a brief counterargument, usually qualified with *although* or *but*.

> Although the Harry Potter series may have some literary merit, its popularity has less to do with storytelling than with merchandising.

1233

cumulative sentence   Sentence that completes the main idea at the beginning of the sentence and then builds and adds on.

> But neither can two great and powerful groups of nations take comfort from our present course—both sides overburdened by the cost of modern weapons, both rightly alarmed by the steady spread of the deadly atom, yet both racing to alter that uncertain balance of terror that stays the hand of mankind's final war.
>
> — John F. Kennedy

deduction   Deduction is a logical process wherein you reach a conclusion by starting with a general principle or universal truth (a major premise) and applying it to a specific case (a minor premise). The process of deduction is usually demonstrated in the form of a syllogism:

MAJOR PREMISE:	Exercise contributes to better health.
MINOR PREMISE:	Yoga is a type of exercise.
CONCLUSION:	Yoga contributes to better health.

diction   A speaker's choice of words. Analysis of diction looks at these choices and what they add to the speaker's message.

either/or (false dilemma)   In this fallacy, the speaker presents two extreme options as the only possible choices.

> Either we agree to higher taxes, or our grandchildren will be mired in debt.

enthymeme   Essentially a syllogism with one of the premises implied, and taken for granted as understood.

> You should take her class because I learned so much from her last year.
>
> *(Implied premise: If you take her class, you will learn a lot too.)*

equivocation   A fallacy that uses a term with two or more meanings in an attempt to misrepresent or deceive.

> We will bring our enemies to justice, or we will bring justice to them.

ethos   Greek for "character." Speakers appeal to ethos to demonstrate that they are credible and trustworthy to speak on a given topic. Ethos is established by both who you are and what you say.

> Lou Gehrig brings the ethos of being a legendary athlete to his speech, yet in it he establishes a different kind of ethos—that of a regular guy and a good sport who shares the audience's love of baseball and family. And like them, he has known good luck and bad breaks.

exordium   In classical oration, the introduction to an argument, in which the speaker announces the subject and purpose, and appeals to ethos in order to establish credibility.

fallacy   See **logical fallacy**.

false dilemma   See **either/or**.

faulty analogy   A fallacy that occurs when an analogy compares two things that are not comparable. For instance, to argue that because we put animals who are in irreversible pain out of their misery, so we should do the same for people, asks the reader to ignore significant and profound differences between animals and people.

figurative language (figure of speech)
Nonliteral language, sometimes referred to as tropes or metaphorical language, often evoking strong imagery and/or figures of speech to compare one thing to another either explicitly (simile) or implicitly (metaphor). Other forms of figurative language include personification, paradox, overstatement (hyperbole), understatement, metonymy, synecdoche, and irony.

first-hand evidence   Evidence based on something the writer *knows*, whether it's from personal experience, observations, or general knowledge of events.

focus   The point in an image to which the viewer's eye is immediately drawn. This can also refer to the level of clarity in an image — elements in high focus are clear and distinct, while elements in low focus are blurred and indefinite.

foreground   The part of an image that is nearest to the viewer.

framing   The presentation of visual elements in an image, especially the placement of the focal point of an image in relation to other visual aspects of that image.

hasty generalization   A fallacy in which a faulty conclusion is reached because of inadequate evidence.

> Smoking isn't bad for you; my great aunt smoked a pack a day and lived to be 90.

hortative sentence   Sentence that exhorts, urges, entreats, implores, or calls to action.

> Let both sides explore what problems unite us instead of belaboring those problems which divide us.
>
> — John F. Kennedy

hyperbole   Deliberate exaggeration used for emphasis or to produce a comic or ironic effect; an overstatement to make a point.

> I mumble thanks for the advice, feeling like I've just been stripped naked by the crazed enforcer of some ancient sumptuary law: No chatting for you, girl. No fancy service ethic allowed for the serfs.
>
> — Barbara Ehrenreich

imagery   A description of how something looks, feels, tastes, smells, or sounds. Imagery may use literal or figurative language to appeal to the senses.

> Currer Bell's book found acceptance nowhere, nor any acknowledgement of merit, so that something like the chill of despair began to invade her heart.
>
> — Charlotte Brontë

imperative sentence   Sentence used to command or enjoin.

> My fellow citizens of the world: ask not what America will do for you, but what together we can do for the freedom of man.
>
> — John F. Kennedy

induction   From the Latin *inducere*, "to lead into," induction is a logical process wherein you reason from particulars to universals, using specific cases in order to draw a conclusion, which is also called a generalization.

> Regular exercise promotes weight loss.
> Exercise lowers stress levels.
> Exercise improves mood and outlook.

> GENERALIZATION: Exercise contributes to better health.

inversion   Inverted order of words in a sentence (variation of the subject-verb-object order).

> United there is little we cannot do in a host of cooperative ventures. Divided there is little we can do.
>
> — John F. Kennedy

irony   A figure of speech that occurs when a speaker or character says one thing but means something else, or when what is said is the opposite of what is expected, creating a noticeable incongruity.

> I grant that this food [babies] will be somewhat dear, and therefore very proper for landlords, who, as they have already devoured most of the parents, seem to have the best title to the children.
>
> — Jonathan Swift

juxtaposition   Placement of two things closely together to emphasize similarities or differences.

> The nations of Asia and Africa are moving at jet-like speed toward gaining political independence, but we still creep at horse-and-buggy pace toward gaining a cup of coffee at a lunch counter.
>
> — Martin Luther King Jr.

logical fallacies   Logical fallacies are potential vulnerabilities or weaknesses in an argument. They often arise from a failure to make a logical connection between the claim and the evidence used to support it.

line   A path traced by a moving point in an image, either real or implied. Lines convey a sense of borders, direction, and motion to the viewer.

logos   Greek for "embodied thought." Speakers appeal to logos, or reason, by offering clear, rational ideas and using specific details, examples, facts, statistics, or expert testimony to back them up.

> Gehrig starts with the thesis that he is "the luckiest man on the face of the earth" and supports it with two points: (1) the love and kindness he's received in his seventeen years of playing baseball and (2) a list of great people who have been his friends, family, and teammates.

metaphor   Figure of speech that compares two things without using *like* or *as*.

> And if a beachhead of cooperation may push back the jungle of suspicion . . .
>
> — John F. Kennedy

metonymy   Figure of speech in which something is represented by another thing that is related to it or emblematic of it.

> The pen is mightier than the sword.

modifier   An adjective, adverb, phrase, or clause that modifies a noun, pronoun, or verb. The purpose of a modifier is usually to describe, focus, or qualify.

> Sprawling and dull in class, he comes alive in the halls and in the cafeteria.
>
> — David Denby

mood   The feeling or atmosphere created by a text.

narration   In classical oration, the factual and background information, establishing why a subject or problem needs addressing; it precedes the confirmation, or laying out of evidence to support claims made in the argument.

nominalization   The process of changing a verb into a noun.

> *Discuss* becomes *discussion*. *Depend* becomes *dependence*.

occasion   The time and place a speech is given or a piece is written.

> In the case of Gehrig's speech, the occasion is Lou Gehrig Appreciation Day. More specifically, his moment came at home plate between games of a doubleheader.

open thesis   An open thesis is one that does not list all of the points the writer intends to cover in an essay.

> The popularity of the Harry Potter series demonstrates that simplicity trumps complexity when it comes to the taste of readers, both young and old.

oxymoron   A paradox made up of two seemingly contradictory words.

> But this peaceful revolution . . .
>
> — John F. Kennedy

paradox   A statement or situation that is seemingly contradictory on the surface, but delivers an ironic truth.

> There is that scattereth, yet increaseth.
>
> —The Bible
>
> To live outside the law you must be honest.
>
> — Bob Dylan

parallelism   Similarity of structure in a pair or series of related words, phrases, or clauses.

> Let both sides explore. . . . Let both sides, for the first time, formulate serious and precise proposals. . . . Let both sides seek to invoke. . . . Let both sides unite to heed . . .
>
> — John F. Kennedy

pathos   Greek for "suffering" or "experience." Speakers appeal to pathos to emotionally motivate their audience. More specific appeals to pathos might play on the audience's values, desires, and hopes, on the one hand, or fears and prejudices, on the other.

> The most striking appeal to pathos is the poignant contrast between Gehrig's horrible diagnosis and his public display of courage.

periodic sentence   Sentence whose main clause is withheld until the end.

> To that world assembly of sovereign states, the United Nations, our last best hope in an age where the instruments of war have far outpaced the instruments of peace, we renew our pledge of support . . .
>
> — John F. Kennedy

peroration   In classical oration, the final part of an argument. It follows the refutation and typically appeals to pathos as it moves the audience toward the conclusion.

persona   Greek for "mask." The face or character that a speaker shows to his or her audience.

> Lou Gehrig is a famous baseball hero, but in his speech he presents himself as a common man who is modest and thankful for the opportunities he's had.

personification   Attribution of a lifelike quality to an inanimate object or an idea.

> . . . with history the final judge of our deeds . . .
>
> — John F. Kennedy

polemic   Greek for "hostile." An aggressive argument that tries to establish the superiority of one opinion over all others. Polemics generally do not concede that opposing opinions have any merit.

polysyndeton   The deliberate use of multiple conjunctions between coordinate phrases, clauses, or words.

> I paid for my plane ticket, and the taxes, and the fees, and the charge for the checked bag, and five dollars for a bottle of water.

post hoc ergo propter hoc   This fallacy is Latin for "after which therefore because of which," meaning that it is incorrect to always claim that something is a cause just because it happened earlier. One may loosely summarize this fallacy by saying that correlation does not imply causation.

> We elected Johnson as president and look where it got us: hurricanes, floods, stock market crashes.

propaganda   The spread of ideas and information to further a cause. In its negative sense, propaganda is the use of rumors, lies, disinformation, and scare tactics in order to damage or promote a cause.

purpose   The goal the speaker wants to achieve.

> One of Gehrig's chief purposes in delivering his Farewell Address is to thank his fans and his teammates, but he also wants to demonstrate that he remains positive: he emphasizes his past luck and present optimism and downplays his illness.

qualified argument   An argument that is not absolute. It acknowledges the merits of an opposing view, but develops a stronger case for its own position.

qualifier   In the Toulmin model, the qualifier uses words like *usually*, *probably*, *maybe*, *in most cases*, and *most likely* to temper the claim a bit, making it less absolute. For an example, see **Toulmin model**.

qualitative evidence   Evidence supported by reason, tradition, or precedent.

quantitative evidence   Quantitative evidence includes things that can be measured, cited, counted, or otherwise represented in numbers — for instance, statistics, surveys, polls, census information.

rebuttal In the Toulmin model, a rebuttal gives voice to possible objections. For an example, see **Toulmin model**.

red herring A type of logical fallacy wherein the speaker relies on distraction to derail an argument, usually by skipping to a new or irrelevant topic. The term derives from the dried fish that trainers used to distract dogs when teaching them to hunt foxes.

> We can debate these regulations until the cows come home, but what the American people want to know is, when are we going to end this partisan bickering?

refutation A denial of the validity of an opposing argument. In order to sound reasonable, a refutation often follows a concession that acknowledges that an opposing argument may be true or reasonable. One of the stages in classical oration, usually following the confirmation, or proof, and preceding the conclusion, or peroration.

> Lou Gehrig refutes that his bad break is a cause for discouragement by saying that he has "an awful lot to live for!"

reservation In the Toulmin model, a reservation explains the terms and conditions necessitated by the qualifier. For an example, see **Toulmin model**.

rhetoric Aristotle defined rhetoric as "the faculty of observing in any given case the available means of persuasion." In other words, it is the art of finding ways of persuading an audience.

rhetorical appeals Rhetorical techniques used to persuade an audience by emphasizing what they find most important or compelling. The three major appeals are to ethos (character), logos (reason), and pathos (emotion).

rhetorical question Figure of speech in the form of a question posed for rhetorical effect rather than for the purpose of getting an answer.

> Will you join in that historic effort?
>
> — John F. Kennedy

rhetorical triangle (Aristotelian triangle) A diagram that illustrates the interrelationship among the speaker, audience, and subject in determining a text. See page 7.

Rogerian argument Developed by psychiatrist Carl Rogers, Rogerian arguments are based on the assumption that fully understanding an opposing position is essential to responding to it persuasively and refuting it in a way that is accommodating rather than alienating.

satire The use of irony or sarcasm to critique society or an individual.

scheme Artful syntax; a deviation from the normal order of words. Common schemes include parallelism, juxtaposition, antithesis, and antimetabole.

second-hand evidence Evidence that is accessed through research, reading, and investigation. It includes factual and historical information, expert opinion, and quantitative data.

shape A two-dimensional form that occupies an area with identifiable boundaries. It can be created by a line (such as a square outlined in pencil on white paper), a shift in texture (such as a square of unmown lawn in the middle of a mown lawn), or a shift in color (such as a blue polka dots on a red shirt).

simile A figure of speech used to explain or clarify an idea by comparing it explicitly to something else, using the words *like*, *as*, or *as though*.

> When people asked her how she felt about the peace talks that were happening right before she died, she puffed up like a proud little bird and said, in Arabic, "I never lost my peace inside."
>
> — Naomi Shihab Nye

SOAPS   A mnemonic device that stands for Subject, Occasion, Audience, Purpose, and Speaker. It is a handy way to remember the various elements that make up the rhetorical situation.

speaker   The person or group who creates a text. This might be a politician who delivers a speech, a commentator who writes an article, an artist who draws a political cartoon, or even a company that commissions an advertisement.

> In his Farewell Address, the speaker is not just Lou Gehrig, but baseball hero and ALS victim Lou Gehrig, a common man who is modest and thankful for the opportunities he's had.

stance   A speaker's attitude toward the audience (differing from tone, the speaker's attitude toward the subject).

straw man   A fallacy that occurs when a speaker chooses a deliberately poor or oversimplified example in order to ridicule and refute an idea.

> Politician X proposes that we put astronauts on Mars in the next four years. Politician Y ridicules this proposal by saying that his opponent is looking for "little green men in outer space."

subject   The topic of a text. What the text is *about*.

> Lou Gehrig's subject in his speech is his illness, but it is also an expression of his gratitude for all of the lucky breaks that preceded his diagnosis.

syllogism   A logical structure that uses the major premise and minor premise to reach a necessary conclusion.

MAJOR PREMISE:	Exercise contributes to better health.
MINOR PREMISE:	Yoga is a type of exercise.
CONCLUSION:	Yoga contributes to better health.

synecdoche   Figure of speech that uses a part to represent the whole.

> In your hands, my fellow citizens, more than mine, will rest the final success or failure of our course.
>
> — John F. Kennedy

syntax   The arrangement of words into phrases, clauses, and sentences. This includes word order (subject-verb-object, for instance, or an inverted structure); the length and structure of sentences (simple, compound, complex, or compound-complex); and such schemes as parallelism, juxtaposition, antithesis, and antimetabole.

synthesize   To combine two or more ideas in order to create something more complex in support of a new idea.

text   While this term generally means the written word, in the humanities it has come to mean any cultural product that can be "read" — meaning not just consumed and comprehended, but investigated. This includes fiction, nonfiction, poetry, political cartoons, fine art, photography, performances, fashion, cultural trends, and much more.

thesis statement   The chief claim that a writer makes in any argumentative piece of writing, usually stated in one sentence.

tone   A speaker's attitude toward the subject conveyed by the speaker's stylistic and rhetorical choices.

Toulmin model   An approach to analyzing and constructing arguments created by British philosopher Stephen Toulmin in his book *The Uses of Argument* (1958). The Toulmin model can be stated as a template:

> *Because (evidence as support), therefore (claim), since (warrant or assumption), on account of (backing), unless (reservation).*

> Because it is raining, therefore I should probably take my umbrella, since it will keep me dry on account of its waterproof material, unless, of course, there is a hole in it.

trope Artful diction; from the Greek word for "turning," a figure of speech such as metaphor, simile, hyperbole, metonymy, or synecdoche.

understatement A figure of speech in which something is presented as less important, dire, urgent, good, and so on, than it actually is, often for satiric or comical effect. Also called *litotes*, it is the opposite of hyperbole.

> You might want to write clearly and cogently in your English class.
>
> The night in prison was novel and interesting enough.
>
> — Henry David Thoreau

warrant In the Toulmin model, the warrant expresses the assumption necessarily shared by the speaker and the audience.

wit In rhetoric, the use of laughter, humor, irony, and satire in the confirmation or refutation of an argument.

zeugma Use of two different words in a grammatically similar way that produces different, often incongruous, meanings.

> When you open a book, you open your mind.
>
> Now the trumpet summons us again—not as a call to bear arms, though arms we need—not as a call to battle, though embattled we are—but a call to bear the burden . . .
>
> — John F. Kennedy

ACKNOWLEDGMENTS

Kareem Abdul-Jabbar, "College Athletes of the World, Unite," *Jacobin,* Nov. 12, 2014. Copyright © 2014 by Jacobin Foundation. Used with permission.

Joel Achenbach, "Why Science Is So Hard to Believe," *The Washington Post,* Feb. 12, 2015. Copyright © 2015 The Washington Post. All rights reserved. Used by permission and protected by the Copyright Laws of the United States. The printing, copying, redistribution, or retransmission of this Content without express written permission is prohibited.

Chimamanda Ngozi Adichie, "Why Can't a Smart Woman Love Fashion?" originally published in *ELLE.* Copyright © 2014 Chimamanda Ngozi Adichie, used by permission of The Wylie Agency LLC.

Danielle Allen, "What Is Education For?" originally appearing in the *Boston Review,* May 9th, 2016. Used with permission.

Will Allen, "A Good Food Manifesto for America." Copyright © 2008 Growing Power, Inc. Reprinted with permission of the author.

Lori Arviso Alvord, M.D. and Elizabeth Cohen Van Pelt, "Walking the Path Between Worlds" from *The Scapel and the Silver Bear.* Copyright © 1999 by Lori Arviso Alvord and Elizabeth Cohen Van Pelt. Used by permission of Bantam Books, an imprint of Random House, a division of Penguin Random House LLC. All rights reserved.

Emily Anthes, "Lovely grub: are insects the future of food?" *Mosaic Science,* October 14, 2014. https://mosaicscience.com/story/eating-insects

Anne Applebaum, "If the Japanese Can't Build a Safe Reactor, Who Can?" *The Washington Post.com/ Opinions,* March 14, 2011. Copyright © 2011 The Washington Post. All rights reserved. Used by permission and protected by the Copyright Laws of the United States. The printing, copying, redistribution, or retransmission of this Content without express written permission is prohibited.

James Baldwin, "A Talk to Teachers." Originally published in *The Saturday Review.* Collected in James Baldwin, *Collected Essays* published by Library of America. Copyright © 1963 by James Baldwin. Used by arrangement with the James Baldwin Estate.

Angelica Jade Bastién, "Have Superheroes Killed the Movie Star?" *Village Voice,* Sept. 15, 2016. Copyright © 2016 by Angelia Jade Bastien. Used with permission.

Shane Battier, "Let Athletes Be Students," *The Players' Tribune,* Oct. 24, 2016. Copyright © 2016 by The Players' Tribune. Used with permission.

Mark Bauerlein, excerpt(s) from *The Dumbest Generation: How the Digital Age Stupefies Young Americans and Jeopardizes Our Future (or, Don't Trust Anyone Under 30).* Copyright © 2008 by Mark Bauerlein. Used by permission of Tarcher, an imprint of Penguin Publishing Group, a division of Penguin Random House LLC. All rights reserved.

Sven Birkerts, excerpt from "On or About" from *Changing the Subject: Art and Attention in the Internet Age,* pp. 9–13. Copyright © 2015 by Sven Birkerts. Reprinted with the permission of The Permissions Company, Inc., on behalf of Graywolf Press, Minneapolis, Minnesota, www.graywolfpress.org

Michael R. Bloomberg, August 3, 2010 Speech of Mayor Michael R. Bloomberg of the City of New York is used with permission of the City of New York.

Emily Bobrow, from "The Man Trap," *1843 Magazine,* June/July 2017. Copyright © 2017 by The Economist. Republished with permission; permission conveyed through Copyright Clearance Center, Inc.

Leon Botstein, "Let Teenagers Try Adulthood," *The New York Times,* May 17, 1999. Copyright © 1999. Reprinted by permission of the author.

Ray Bradbury, "The Affluence of Despair," *The Wall Street Journal,* April 3, 1998. Copyright © 1998 by Dow Jones. Republished with permission; permission conveyed through Copyright Clearance Center, Inc.

Judy Brady, "I Want a Wife," *Ms. Magazine,* 1972. Copyright © 1970 by Judy Brady. Reprinted by permission of the author.

David Brooks, "Individual pursuits tear at nation's social fabric," *The Columbus Dispatch,* Apr. 6, 2016. Copyright © 2016 by David Brooks. Used with permission.

Matt Bruenig, "The Case Against Free College," *Dissent,* Fall 2015. Copyright © 2015 by University of Pennsylvania Press. Reprinted with permission of the University of Pennsylvania Press.

Frank Bruni, "To Get to Harvard, Go to Haiti?" *The New York Times,* August 13, 2016. Copyright © 2016 The New York Times. All rights reserved. Used by permission and protected by the Copyright Laws of the United States. The printing, copying, redistribution, or retransmission of this Content without express written permission is prohibited.

Charles Camosy, "Trump Won Because College-Educated Americans Are Out of Touch," *The Washington Post,* November 8, 2016. Copyright © 2016 by Charles Camosy. Used with permission.

Nicholas Carr, "The Illusion of Knowledge." From *Utopia is Creepy: And Other Provocations.* Copyright © 2016 by Nicholas Carr. Used by permission of W. W. Norton & Company, Inc.

Rachel Carson, "A Fable for Tomorrow" and "The Obligation to Endure" from *Silent Spring* by Rachel Carson. Copyright © 1962 by Rachel L. Carson. Renewed 1990 by Roger Christie. Reprinted by permission of Houghton Mifflin Harcourt Company and the Frances Collin Literary Agency. All rights reserved.

Jimmy Carter, "Losing my religion for equality," *The Age,* 2009. Copyright © 2009 The Age. Used with permission.

Winston Churchill, "Blood, Toil, Tears, and Sweat," May 13, 1940. © The Estate of Winston S. Churchill. Reproduced with permission of Curtis Brown, London on behalf of The Estate of Winston S. Churchill.

Ted Closson, "A GoFundMe Campaign Is Not Health Insurance," *The Nib,* May 25th, 2017. Copyright © 2017 by Ted Closson. Used with permission.

Ta-Nehisi Coates, excerpt(s) from *Between the World and Me.* Copyright © 2015 by Ta-Nehisi Coates. Used by permission of Spiegel & Grau, an imprint of Random House, a division of Penguin Random House LLC. All rights reserved.

Georgia Cole, Ben Radley and Jean-Benoît Falisse, "Who Really Benefits from Celebrity Activism?" *The Conversation,* July 10, 2015.

Stephanie Coontz, from "The Myth of Male Decline," *The New York Times,* Sept. 29, 2012. Copyright © 2012 The New York Times. All rights reserved. Used by permission and protected by the Copyright Laws of the United States. The printing, copying, redistribution, or retransmission of this Content without express written permission is prohibited.

Jessa Crispin, excerpt from *Why I Am Not a Feminist: A Feminist Manifesto.* Copyright © 2017 Melville House Publishing. Used with permission.

Emerson Csorba, "The Constant Sharing Is Making Us Competitive and Depressed," *The New York Times,* Nov. 28, 2016. Copyright © 2016 The New York Times. All rights reserved. Used by permission and protected by the Copyright Laws of the United States. The printing, copying, redistribution, or retransmission of this Content without express written permission is prohibited.

David Denby, "High-School Confidential: Notes on Teen Movies" originally published in *The New Yorker,* May 31, 1999. Copyright © 1999 Reprinted by permission of the author.

Matthew Desmond, from "How Homeownership Became the Engine of American Inequality," *New York Times Magazine,* May 9, 2017. Copyright © 2017 The New York Times. All rights reserved. Used by permission and protected by the Copyright Laws of the United States. The printing, copying, redistribution, or retransmission of this Content without express written permission is prohibited.

Amy Domini, "Why Investing in Fast Food May Be a Good Thing." First published in *Ode magazine,* March 2009. Used with permission.

Nobel Prize Banquet Speech by Bob Dylan. Published by The Nobel Foundation. Used with permission.

Gerald L. Early, *A Level Playing Field: African American Athletes and the Republic of Sports* by Gerald L. Early, Cambridge, Mass.: Harvard University Press. Copyright © 2011 by the President and Fellows of Harvard College.

Roger Ebert, review of *Star Wars*, from *The Chicago Sun-Times,* January 1, 1977. Reprinted with permission of the author.

Barbara Ehrenreich, "Serving in Florida" from *Nickel and Dimed* by Barbara Ehrenreich. Copyright © 2001 by Barbara Ehrenreich. Used by permission of Henry Holt and Company, LLC. All rights reserved.

Lars Eighner, "On Dumpster Diving." From *Travels with Lizbeth: Three Years on the Road and on the Streets.* Copyright © 1993 Lars Eighner. Reprinted by permission of St. Martin's Press. All rights reserved.

Keith Ellison, "The Argument for Tuition-Free College," *American Prospect,* April 14, 2016. Copyright © 2016 by The American Prospect. Used with permission.

William Faulkner, "An Innocent at Rinkside," *Sports Illustrated,* January 24, 1955. Copyright © 1955 by Estelle Faulkner and Jill Faulkner Summers. Renewed 1965, 2004 by Penguin Random House LLC; from *Essays, Speeches, and Public Letters* by William Faulkner, edited by James B. Meriwether. Used by permission of Random House, an imprint and division of Penguin Random House LLC. and W. W. Norton & Company, Inc. All rights reserved.

Roberto A. Ferdman, "The perils of being manly," *The Washington Post,* March 28, 2016. Copyright © 2016 The Washington Post. All rights reserved. Used by permission and protected by the Copyright Laws of the United States. The printing, copying, redistribution, or retransmission of this Content without express written permission is prohibited.

Jonathan Safran Foer, "Let Them Eat Dog," *The Wall Street Journal,* Oct. 31, 2009. Copyright © 1998 by Dow Jones. Republished with permission; permission conveyed through Copyright Clearance Center, Inc.

Henry Louis Gates, Jr., "Restoring Black History," *The New York Times,* September 24, 2016. Copyright © 2016 The New York Times. All rights reserved. Used by permission and protected by the Copyright Laws of the United States. The printing, copying, redistribution, or retransmission of this Content without express written permission is prohibited.

Atul Gawande, "Hellhole," originally published in *The New Yorker,* March 30, 2009. Used with permission from the author.

Lou Gehrig, "The Luckiest Man on the Face of the Earth." Speech given on July 4, 1939. Lou Gehrig™ is a trademark of Rip van Winkle Foundation. Licensed by CMG Worldwide, Inc. All rights reserved. Used with permission. www.LouGehrig.com

Bahar Gholipour, "Lab-Grown Meat May Save a Lot More than Farm Animals' Lives," published by *NBC News,* April 6, 2017. Used with permission from the author.

Malcolm Gladwell, "Man and Superman," Sept. 9, 2013. Copyright © 2013 by Malcolm Gladwell. Used with permission.

Malcolm Gladwell, from *Outliers.* Copyright © 2008 by Malcolm Gladwell. Used by permission of Little, Brown and Company.

Malcolm Gladwell, "Small Change," *The New Yorker,* October 4, 2010, and "Offensive Play," *The New Yorker,* October 19, 2009. Copyright © Malcolm Gladwell. Used with permission of the author.

Sara Goldrick-Rab and Nancy Kendall, "Make the First Two Years of College Free," Scholars Strategy Network.

Alison Gopnik, "Is Screen Time Dangerous for Children?" *The New Yorker,* November 28, 2016. © Conde Nast. Used with permission.

Stephen Jay Gould, "Women's Brains." Copyright © 1980 by Stephen Jay Gould. Reprinted with permission.

Greif, Mark, "Get Off the Treadmill: the art of living well in the age of plenty," *Guardian,* Sept. 23, 2016. Copyright © 2017 by Guardian News & Media Ltd. Used with permission.

Broti Gupta, "The Rules of the United Airlines Fight or Flight Club," *The New Yorker,* April 11, 2017. Copyright © 2017 by The New Yorker. Used with permission.

Rahawa Haile, "How Black Books Lit My Way Along The Appalachian Trail," *BuzzFeed News,* Feb. 2, 2017. Used with permission.

Nikole Hannah-Jones, "Have We Lost Sight of the Promise of Public Schools?" *The New York Times Magazine,* June 29, 2016. Copyright © 2016 The New York Times. All rights reserved. Used by permission and protected by the Copyright Laws of the United States. The printing, copying, redistribution, or retransmission of this Content without express written permission is prohibited.

Cristina Henríquez, "Doubly Denied" in *Double Bind: Women on Ambition* edited by Robin Romm. Copyright © 2017 by Cristina Henriquez. Used with permission.

Kali Holloway, from "Toxic Masculinity is Killing Men: The Roots of Men and Trauma," *Alternet,* June 6, 2015. Copyright © 2015 by Alernet. Used with permission.

1243

INDEX